Power and Authority, A Trial of Two Swords

Power and Authority,
A Trial of Two Swords

**A History of the Union of the Holy Roman Empire
and the Kingdom of Sicily (1186-1250)**

Willem J. Zwalve

eleven

Published, sold and distributed by Eleven
P.O. Box 85576
2508 CG The Hague
The Netherlands
Tel.: +31 70 33 070 33
Fax: +31 70 33 070 30
e-mail: sales@elevenpub.nl
www.elevenpub.com

Sold and distributed in USA and Canada
Independent Publishers Group
814 N. Franklin Street
Chicago, IL 60610, USA
Order Placement: +1 800 888 4741
Fax: +1 312 337 5985
orders@ipgbook.com
www.ipgbook.com

Eleven is an imprint of Boom uitgevers Den Haag.

ISBN 978-94-6236-341-0
ISBN 978-94-0011-221-6 (E-book)

dedicated to the memory of
Jan Lokin
(1945-2022)

The Roman Emperor Frederick II
(*De arte venandi cum avibus*, Biblioteca Apostolica Vaticana, ms. Pal. lat. 1071, *f.* 1, *v°*)

Introduction

For the best part of my academic career, I have been conversing with medieval jurists about the intricacies of Roman property law and medieval feudal law. There are few spectacular statements about contemporary political events in their writings, which is not to be wondered at since there are very few, if any, references to current political events in the writings of modern property lawyers as well. Yet, my medieval interlocutors were living in tumultuous times. Most of them were living in the thirteenth century, when six jurists – Accursius, Sinibaldo Fieschi (Pope Innocent IV) and Guillaume Durant in Italy, Philippe de Beaumanoir in France, Henry Bracton in England and Eike of Repgow in Germany – laid the solid foundations of contemporary European legal culture: the continental 'civil law'-tradition based on Roman and canon law (Accursius, Innocent IV, and Guillaume Durant), the English 'common law'-tradition (Bracton), and the tradition of continental French and German customary law (Beaumanoir and Eike of Repgow). While they were writing their authoritative treatises, influencing the law for centuries to come, war was raging all around them since their era was dominated by the bitter conflict between the Sicilian king and Roman Emperor Frederick II of Hohenstaufen and the Roman papacy. Having finally deserted the camp of the lawyers after almost fifty years of service, I decided to write the biographies of these lawyers to place them in their historical context. In preparing their biographies, I found myself constantly referring to and commenting on political events prior to the thirteenth century to clarify the origins of the political problems of the time and slowly but surely something very different grew out of my hands, a history of the origins and progress of the major geopolitical conflict of that era caused by the union of the German empire and the kingdom of Sicily, culminating in the trial of Frederick II at the Council of Lyon I in 1245.

A great Dutch lawyer (and an eminent medievalist as well), Eduard Maurits Meijers, once justly observed that in writing (legal) history one is always confronted with the awkward question of how far to go back in time to explain the function of a particular (legal) institution. Is it really necessary to go back to classical Roman law to do so all the time? My answer to that question has always been: 'No, it is not, but sometimes it is'. And so it is in this story. The thirteenth century was a very formalistic legal age and historical precedent was central to the political debate of the time. Pope Innocent III (1198-1216) based his territorial claims in Italy on documents from the 8th and 9th century, calling for a short history of the origins of the medieval Roman empire to which these documents are closely related. On the other hand, the origins of the Kingdom of Sicily can indeed be explained without going back that far in time since it was, as we shall see, a relatively 'modern' feudal construct.

I have composed this book for slow and fast reading. Ever since I was a young student, I have enjoyed reading and rereading the pages of Gibbon's *Decline and Fall* as published in Everyman's Library and Grote's *History of Greece*, fast-reading the pages and slow-reading the footnotes containing the sources from which these authors took their information and the comments and anecdotes added there so as not to interrupt the flow of the story they were telling in the text above. No wonder, therefore, that I deplore the present custom of publishing a history book with endnotes, all the more so since most of the time not even a ribbon marker is added in order to easily access the endnotes. It makes awkward reading, at least *if* one is interested in the sources on which a story is based. More often than not the endnotes do not even contain these sources at all, but rather a bare reference or just a reference to secondary literature where the sources for a particular statement are to be found, making for an even more awkward reading experience since most of the time one has to consult a library to find that literature, frequently to find out that the book in question refers to yet another, older, study that does indeed contain and discuss the contemporary source on which a particular historical assessment is based.

I am convinced that direct contact with these sources is of great interest to an educated reader since it directly connects him with the medieval world. He becomes acquainted with the momentous importance of the Ghibelline chronicles of Piacenza and the chronicles of Genoa for the history of the medieval kingdom of Italy; he learns about the learned lawyer from Lodi, Otto Morena, who wrote an excellent contemporary account of Barbarossa's exploits in Lombardy; he reads that an uncle of that emperor wrote his biography; he reads a first-hand account of the submission of Frederick I Barbarossa to Pope Alexander III in Venice; he learns that the Emperor Frederick II had a special voice of his own, his grandiloquent letters full of irony composed by his learned chancellor Piero della Vigna, and much more. All these sources should not be relegated to endnotes and certainly not as bare references but should be highlighted *and* translated on behalf of a reader unfamiliar with the learned language in which they have been composed. Therefore, I have introduced the primary sources this story is based on, practically all of them written in Latin, in footnotes, adding a translation of my own and thereby enabling the (slow) reader to appreciate (and criticize) my interpretation of a text. Whenever a translation has not been added, a translation or a close paraphrasis of the primary source is to be found in the text itself. As a matter of course, not all sources relating to a specific person or event could be included and a selection had to be made, for which I am solely responsible, as I am for the translations. I have also inserted additional information in the footnotes about persons and events related to in the text I deemed of interest to a (slow) reader but would have interrupted the flow of the story when inserted in the text itself[1].

There is another reason to account for my modus operandi. As a renowned German medievalist, Peter Classen, once remarked, a present writer on medieval history is forced to concentrate on his own interpretation of the primary sources of his story now that the scholarly literature about them has become almost infinite. Naturally, I am highly indebted to the work of many scholars who have written in great detail about many of the persons and subjects discussed in these pages but adding a comprehensive and exhaustive bibliography would, if feasible at all, have amounted to the publication of at least one additional volume. Instead, I have added a select bibliography of the secondary literature consulted at the end of the book.

I wish to thank my editor, Gary Vos, for watching over my use of the English language, my editor Ingrid Knotters at Boom, my publisher Wirt Soetenhorst for his enthusiasm in publishing this book, and my dear wife Titia, my σύζυγος for more than fifty years, who acquiesced in yet another project frustrating our *otium cum dignitate*. I have dedicated the book to the memory of Jan Lokin, professor of Roman law in the University of Groningen, as a gesture of gratitude for our long-time friendship and collaboration.

Willem Zwalve   Leiden
9 June 2022

---

1   The rendering of proper names has been a challenge. It is usual in English literature to 'anglicize' foreign proper names, but absolute consistency is impossible, even undesirable. As a rule, common Latin, French, Italian, and German names such as *Jean de* Grailly, *Giovanni di* Procida, and *Gullielmo di* Monferrato are rendered as John of Grailly, John of Procida, and William of Montferrat, while the names of literary personages are retained in the form in which they are commonly known: Johannes Teutonicus, Piero della Vigna, and Guillaume Durant. But I have allowed myself many exceptions to this rule of thumb, especially whenever an English rendering of foreign proper names would make them practically unrecognizable. Accordingly, I have retained the proper names of Corrado Capece, Giacomo da Pecorara, Giovanni Gaetano Orsini, and many others.

Contents

The Emperor Henry VI
(Univ. Heidelberg, Cod. Pal. germ. 848 (Cod. Manesse), f. 6 ro (Wikimedia Commons))

Prologue

Innocent IV

In the morning of the feast day of St John the Apostle (27 December), in the year after the incarnation of Christ 1244, Pope Innocent IV celebrated Mass in the Cathedral of St John in the city of Lyon. Pope Innocent announced in his sermon that it was his wish to call a general council of all Christendom at Lyon to be opened on the feast day of St John the Baptist, 24 June 1245[1]. The Christian world was beset with all kinds of imminent threats and greatly perturbed by 'the affair of the church and the prince' (*negotium inter ecclesiam et principem*) and so Innocent summoned 'the kings of the earth, the prelates of the churches and the other princes of the world' to help him find a solution to all of these predicaments. At the end of his summons the Pope informed the addressees that he had sent for 'said prince' (*dictus princeps*) to appear in that general council in person or by his proxies in order to answer to the grievances brought against him by the pope and others[2]. The prince concerned was not mentioned by name, but the whole Christian world knew who he was. It was Frederick of Hohenstaufen, emperor of the Holy Roman Empire, second of that name, king of the Germans, king of Jerusalem and king of Sicily. The pope had issued a summons against the most illustrious, if not the most powerful, prince in the Christian world. It was an unprecedented incident, but it was issued by the most eminent lawyer ever to have occupied Saint Peter's throne.

Innocent IV was born in Genoa in 1195. He was a son of Ugo, count of Lavagna, first in his family to take the surname of Fieschi persisting in Ugo's branch of the extended family of the counts of Lavagna ever since. Ugo's son was christened Sinibaldo, so Innocent was known to the world as Sinibaldo Fieschi before he became pope in 1243. At the

---

1 Nicolaus de Carbio, *Vita Innocentii IV* cap. 18, ed. Pagnotti 93: '*Festo autem nativitatis Domini celebrato, dum in festo beati Ioannis evangeliste missam mane in Lugdunensi ecclesia celebraret ac predicaret populo verbum Dei, ibi publice nunciavit concilium generale in festo beati Ioannis Baptiste venturo proximo celebrandum*'.

2 The papal summons has come down to us *in extenso* in *Annales Placentini Gibellini* ad ann. 1244, MGH *SS* 18, 488-489. It has this declaration at the end: '*Sciturus quod nos dictum principem in citatione nostra citavimus, ut per se vel suos nuncios in concilio celebrando compareat, responsurus nobis et aliis qui aliquid contra ipsum proponendum duxerint satisfactionem ydoneam prestiturus*'.

time of his birth the skyline of Genoa was not dominated by the spires of churches but, as with all Italian cities of the time, by high fortified towers, *torri*, out of which the city-clans fought each other. There were about eighty of them in Genoa in the thirteenth century. Some of them are still standing and one conspicuously so. It is the tower of the Palazzo Ducale in the old city centre. It was originally part of the mansion of the Fieschi family, built by Sinibaldo's great-grandfather Alberto. Later, the tower was sold to the city (in 1311) and incorporated into the town hall so that it has been preserved until now. It is the only surviving medieval building in the city directly related to Sinibaldo who must have lived there in his youth. He was a younger son, since he was destined for a career in the church. At a very early age he was sent to his father's brother Opizo, who was bishop of Parma[3]. As he tells us himself, Sinibaldo was an 'alumnus of the church of Parma'[4]. After his training in the *artes* in that city, he went to Bologna to study canon and Roman law. He heard the greatest masters of both law faculties there: a very old Azo, the great compilator Accursius, and Jacobus Balduinus in Roman law, and Laurentius Hispanus, Vincentius, Johannes Teutonicus (another great compilator), and Johannes de Albenga in canon law[5]. We do not know for certain whether Sinibaldo graduated in both faculties, as was not unusual in his days, but he certainly did so in canon law, to which he dedicated his whole life as a scholar. After his graduation, *magister* Sinibaldo, as he was now, obtained a canonry in Parma from his uncle there and may have read canon law in Bologna for a time. If he ever did, he did not do so for long, since he entered the bureaucracy of the papal *curia* in Rome soon after[6]. In 1226 he is first attested as an *auditor contradictarum litterarum*, one of the learned lawyers to whom the pope delegated trial hearings in cases pending before the papal court[7]. By 1227 he was vice-chancellor of the Holy Roman Church and cardinal-priest of the San Lorenzo in Lucina[8].

---

3 Salimbene de Adam, *Cronica* ad ann. 1233, MGH *SS* 32, 69: '*Ante istum episcopum fuit domnus Opiço de Lavania Ianuensi, qui fuit pulcher homo et honesta persona, ut dicunt, et barbanus fuit domni Innocentii pape quarti*'.

4 Letter of Innocent IV to the abbot of the monastery of St John the Evangelist in Parma (1243) in Ireneo Affò, *Storia della città di Parma* III, Parma 1793, no 67, 375: '<*Parmensis ecclesia>, cuius nos alumpnum fuisse recolimus*'.

5 Diplovatatius (Tomasso Diplovatacio, 1468-1541), *De claris iuris consultis, Pars posterior*, ed. Kantorowicz/Schulz, Bologna 1968, *s.n.* 'Innocent IV', 128: '*audivit Bononiae in legibus Azonem iam senem, Accursium Florentinum et Iacobum Balduinum. In iure canonico Laurentium Hispanum, Vincentium, Ioannem Theutonicum et Iacobum de Albasio*'.

6 For most of the great canon lawyers of the thirteenth century, such as Henry of Susa ('Hostiensis'), Guillaume Durant and many others, a chair in canon law was just a stepping-stone to a bureaucratic career.

7 Potthast, *Regesta* I, 679.

8 Potthast, *Regesta* I, 939.

The cardinal-priest of the San Lorenzo in Lucina was promoted by his sponsor Pope Gregory IX (1227-1241), an outstanding canon lawyer as well. When he was still known to the world as Hugo dei Conti di Segni (named Ugolino, *c.* 1150-1241), Ugolino, cardinal-bishop of Ostia, had been one of the chief diplomats of the mighty Pope Innocent III (1198-1216), to whom he was closely related, and of his successor Honorius III (1216-1227), a scholarly bureaucrat rather than an autocrat. Cardinal Ugolino was outraged by the accommodating policy of Pope Honorius in what was the key European geopolitical issue of the twelfth and thirteenth century, the union of the kingdom of Sicily and the Holy Roman Empire, the *unio regni ad imperium*, definitively brought about in 1186 by the marriage of Henry VI, son and heir of the Roman Emperor Frederick I 'Barbarossa', and Constance of Hauteville, heir to the throne of Sicily. The 'union' created an empire stretching from the beaches of the North Sea to the shores of Africa. Never before in European history, not even in the days of Charlemagne, had a European monarch been as close to realizing the restoration of Constantine's universal Christian Roman Empire as Henry VI was. The prospect was a nightmare to Innocent III, Gregory IX and to Sinibaldo Fieschi who made the disengaging of that union his sole mission after he was elected to the throne of St Peter on 25 June 1243 as Innocent IV. The new pope was the leading canon lawyer of his time and consequently the rule of law (*ordo iuris*) had to be observed in this as a matter of course, calling for a formal trial to depose the incumbent Roman Emperor and King of Sicily, Frederick II. Whatever the merits or demerits of the papal indictment against the Emperor Frederick II personally, it was clear to all contemporaries that the real issue was about the breaking up of the *unio regni ad imperium*. Therefore, I shall deal with the origins, the vicissitudes, and the consequences of that political union for all the parties concerned first. It is the subject of the first part of this book. In the course of the history of the *unio* the person of the defendant, Frederick II, and his past experiences with the Church of Rome will be introduced to better understand the charges brought against him. The second part deals with the trial itself, the court and its competence, the law involved and, lastly, the execution and aftermath of the sentence of the court.

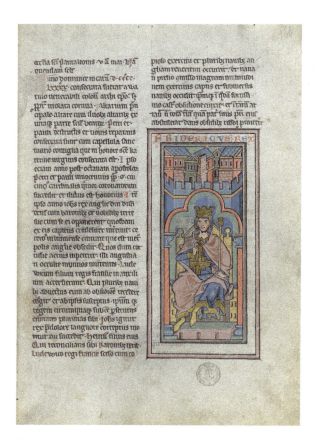

The Emperor Frederick II
(*Chronica regia coloniensis*, Royal Library of Belgium, Ms 467, f. 144 *r*)

Part I

Unio regni ad imperium

King Roger II of Sicily crowned by Christ
(Martorana, Palermo (Wikimedia Commons, curtesy of Matthias Süßen))

1

The Kingdom of Sicily

The Kingdom of Sicily was a papal creation. It originated in a scheme by one of the greatest medieval revolutionaries, Pope Gregory VII (1073-1085), when he was still a cardinal, born as Hildebrand. The object of that plan was to secure military support for a recent 'coup' by Hildebrand and his fellow cardinals. In 1057 they had elected one of them, Frederick of Lotharingen, recently consecrated as cardinal-priest of S. Chrisogono, to succeed Pope Victor II as Pope Stephen IX (1057-1058) *without* the approval of the King of the Germans[1]. Victor II was the last pope to be appointed by a German emperor of the medieval Roman Empire. During his reign as Roman emperor, the German King Henry III (1017-1039-1046-1056) had deposed no fewer than three popes and nominated four, Germans all of them, Clement II (1046-1047), Damasus II (1048), Leo IX (1049-1054), and Victor II (1055-1057). In those days the Roman emperor was still regarded as vicar of Christ (*Christi vicarius*)[2] and God's anointed (*christus Dei*), supreme over all contemporary European kings and princes who merely looked on as the German king and emperor disposed of the succession to the Roman episcopal See as he saw fit, as if it was just another of the episcopates in his empire of which he could also dispose as it pleased him. Hildebrand, while still a monk, had witnessed the councils of Sutri and Rome in 1046, where Henry III had deposed the infamous Pope Benedict IX and his successors Silvester III and Gregory VI[3] and

Freedom of the Church

---

1   *Annales Altahenses maiores* ad ann. 1057, MGH *SS rer. Germ.* 4, 54: '*Ipsa aestate papa Victor moritur, et in eius locum frater Gotefridi ducis Fridericus, cognomine Stephen, a Romanis subrogatus,* ignorante rege' (emphasis added).
2   Wipo, *Gesta Chuonradi II imperatoris* cap. 3, MGH *SS rer. Germ.* 61, 22-23 on the Emperor Conrad II: 'You have been raised to the highest dignity. You are the vicar of Christ' (*Ad summam dignitatem pervenisti. Vicarius es Christi*)'. See also cap. 5 (26).
3   Benedict IX was beyond contempt. See the verdict of Pope Victor III (1086-1087), *Dialogi* 3, 53-54 (Migne *PL* 149, col. 1003-1004): 'I recoil with horror from the scandalous and foul life of Benedictus after his ascent to the priesthood and how abominable it was' (*Benedictus ... cuius quidem post adoptum sacerdotium vita quam turpis, quam foeda, quamque exsecranda exstiterit, horresco referre*). Benedict was driven from Rome by the people in 1045 and replaced

appointed a new pope, Clement II, who crowned Henry as Roman emperor. After his coronation, the newly anointed emperor Henry III administered a solemn oath to the Roman people never to consecrate a pope before the pope's election was confirmed by the emperor[4]. These were the crucial events shaping Hildebrand's politics. He saw it as his mission in life to free the Church of all interference by secular powers, not only by the old and well-established enfranchisee, the people of Rome, in his eyes (and not far from the truth) a rampant mob manipulated by the Roman nobility, but first and foremost of the interference by the Roman emperor and German king, necessarily defying imperial authority.

The new ecclesiastical challengers of imperial authority were not the usual local Roman perverts and intellectual lightweights on the throne of St Peter of the previous century[5], but ascetic and well-educated

by Johannes, bishop of Sabina, who took the name Silvester III, a popular election never confirmed by the emperor. Silvester was deposed by Benedict when he reconquered Rome in the same year. After that, Benedict continued, as Pope Victor III testifies, 'to persevere in the same wicked and perverse deeds as before' (*in eisdem pravis et et perversis operibus ut ante perseverabat*). In the very same year of his return, Benedict sold his pontificate to his godfather John Gratian, the archpriest of the St John ad Portam Latinam, for the price of 2000 pound (*Liber pontificalis*, ed. Duchesne 2, 270): '<*Benedictus*> *ipse eum* <*scl. episcopatum suum*> *dedit Iohanni archicanonico sancti Johannis ad Portam Latinam, suo patrino*' and the addition from ms. Vat. Lat. 1340 there. See also Victor III, *Dialogi* 3, 54 (Migne *PL* 149, col. 1004): '<*Benedictus*> *Joanni archipresbytero ... non parva ab eo accepta pecunia, summum sacerdotium relinquens tradidit*'. Silvester and Gregory VI were deposed in Sutri (*Annales Corbeienses* ad ann. 1046, MGH *SS* 3, 6): '*Synodus ... Sutriae, in qua in praesentia regis secundum instituta canonum depositi sunt papae duo, medius et ultimus*'. Benedict was deposed in Rome and succeeded by bishop Suidger of Bamberg, who took the name Clement II (*Annales Corbeienses* ad ann. 1046, MGH *SS* 3, 6): '*depositus est papa Benedictus, et unanimi cleri ac populi electione in locum eius substitutus est Suidgerus Bavenbergensis episcopus, et postera die nomine Clementis papa consecratus, domnum Heinricum voto ac favore maximo populi Romani coronavit imperatorem*'.
4   *Annales Romani* ad ann. 1046, MGH *SS* 5, 469: '*ut a nemine consecretur nisi prius a rege investiatur almus pontifex*'. This is a confirmation of the procedure as prescribed in Lothair's *Constitutio romana* of 824: all Romans were to swear that 'the one chosen with my approval shall only be consecrated after he has sworn an oath in the presence of an imperial emissary and the people' (MGH *Capit.* 1, no 161, 324: '*et ille qui electus fuerit me consentiente consecratus pontifex non fiat, priusquam tale sacramentum faciat in praesentia missi domini imperatoris et populi*'). The oath the pope himself had to swear was an oath of loyalty. See for the formula MGH *Capit.* 1, no 161, 324: '*Promitto ego ille per Deum omnipotentem et per ista sacra quattuor evangelia et per hanc crucem domini nostri Iesu Christi et per corpus Petri principis apostolorum, quod ab hac die in futurum fidelis ero dominis nostris imperatoribus Hludowico et Hlotario diebus vitae meae, iuxta vires et intellectum meum, sine fraude atque malo ingenio*'. The procedure was renewed by the German king Otto I, shortly after his coronation as emperor in 962 (see *infra* p. 68). Election by the people and the clergy of Rome, confirmation by the emperor, and subsequent consecration of a new patriarch had been the standard procedure under the Roman Empire itself after Christianity had become state religion.
5   By the end of the 10th century the prestige of the Roman papacy had reached an all-time low as is testified by bishop Arnulf of Orléans (*c.* 940-1003), chief advisor to King Hugo Capet (*Acta concilii Remensis* § 28, MGH *SS* 3, 672): 'Why then is such an abominable man

monks dedicated to imposing their austere lifestyle not on the Church alone but on the world at large, grim and bitter men, convinced of their moral and intellectual superiority over the secular princes of the world *and* over the secular clergy as well, forming a *fourth* estate, superior to the other three, the (secular) clergy, the warriors, and the farmers[6]. The only guarantor of their independence from the secular princes *and* the secular clergy, especially the bishops of the dioceses in which their monasteries and abbeys were situated, was the pope and accordingly it was from one of those rare abbeys directly subject to the pope and to no other secular or ecclesiastical authority, the abbey of Cluny, that their reform movement gained momentum. Consequently, the policy of this monastical lobby was aimed at strengthening the position *and* the prestige of the Roman patriarch, preferably by raising one of them as successor to St Peter. They had their chance in 1057, after the demise of Pope Victor II, and it was one of Hildebrand's greatest triumphs during his long tenure as archdeacon of the Holy Roman Church, the most powerful official in the Church after the pope, when the very irregularly elected and consecrated Pope Nicholas II (1059-1061) issued a bull, confirmed by a council gathered in the Lateran palace, making the cardinals of the church the sole electors of a new pope. The people of Rome were disenfranchised, for good as it turned out, and so was the emperor[7]. It was, of course, a colossal affront to the dignity of the emperor and the empire. But the German King Henry IV (1050-1053-1084-1106) was still a minor and not yet crowned as emperor.

---

placed on the highest see, a man not even worthy of a place among the lower clergy? What, dear fathers, do you think of a man like that sitting on the highest see, all dressed up in purple and gold? What, I say, do you think about such a man?' (*Cur ergo in summa sede sic infimus constituitur, ut etiam in clero nullum habere locum dignus inveniatur? Quid hunc reverendi patres in sublimi solio residentem veste purpurea et aurea radiantem, quid hunc, inquam, censetis?*).

6   For the regular clergy as a fourth estate see Abbo of Fleury (*c.* 945-1004), *Apologeticus ad Hugonem et Rodbertum reges Francorum*, Migne, *PL* 139, col. 464.

7   This famous bull has been printed in many places. As a matter of course, I use the version of Gratian's *Decretum* (Dist. 23, cap. 1): 'We decide and ordain that, when a pope of this universal Roman Church dies, the cardinal-bishops shall first deliberate together very diligently on the matter of the election and after that they shall bring in the other cardinals. Then the clerics and the people may demonstrate their adhesion to the new election ... All this with due respect to our son Henry, who is now king and aspires to become emperor with the consent of God in the near future ... and all his successors who will have obtained that dignity in person from the Apostolic See' (*decernimus et statuimus, ut obeunte huius Romanae ecclesiae universalis pontifice, imprimis cardinales episcopi diligentissime simul de electione tractantes, mox sibi clericos cardinales adhibeant: sicque clerus et populus ad consensum novae electionis accedant ... salvo debito honore et reverentia dilectissimi filii nostri Heinrici, qui in presentiarum rex habetur, et futurus imperator Deo concedente speratur ... et successorum illius, qui ab hac apostolica sede personaliter hoc ius impetraverint'*).

The Treaty
of Melfi

It was to secure the future of 'the freedom of the Church' (*libertas ecclesiae*), meaning the free election of a pope by the *collegium* of cardinals, that Pope Nicholas and his cardinals decided to enter into negotiations with two Norman rulers in South Italy, Richard of Capua and Robert of Hauteville, named 'Guiscard' ('the Smart'), count of Apulia. The two potentates were successors to the ruthless Norman mercenaries who had been able to establish themselves in South Italy since the first decades of the 11th century. Richard and Robert, on their part, wanted to secure an unassailable legal title to their conquests – past, present and future – in South Italy[8]. Parts of South Italy belonged to the Roman Empire of the German kings, other parts (Apulia and Calabria) to the Byzantine Empire[9] and Sicily to an Arab emir. The pope felt he was able to provide that incontestable legal title.

The 'Donation of Constantine' (*Constitutum Constantini*) is the most famous forgery in legal history, but it was regarded as genuine and authentic during the best part of the Middle Ages[10]. It was certainly considered so by the cardinals Hildebrand and Humbert, cardinal-bishop of Santa Rufina, assisting Pope Nicholas II in his negotiations with the Norman potentates. The cardinals had already made extensive use of it

---

8   The first Norman mercenary to gain a foothold within the South-Italian establishment, still (but not for long) dominated by Lombard princes, was a certain Rainulf. At a diet in Capua in 1038 Rainulf was granted the county of Aversa, at the suggestion of the Lombard prince of Salerno, by the Emperor Conrad II in person to hold as an imperial fief. See Amatus of Monte Cassino (11th century), *Ystoire de li Normant* 2,6 (ed. Delarc 57): '*li emperor fust en bone volonté vers Raynulfe et lo impereor s'enclina a la volonté de lo prince et o um lance publica et o un gofanon dont estoit l'arme impérial conferma à Raynolfe lo conté d'Averse et de son territoire*'. There were three Hauteville brothers from Normandy present at this occasion, all of them still in the service of the prince of Salerno. They learned an important lesson: there was more to be gained in South Italy than just fame and money. One of them, Drogo, was elevated as count of Apulia by Emperor Henry III in 1047 (*Chronica monasterii Casinensis* (Leo Marsicanus) 2,78, ad ann. 1047, MGH *SS* 7, 683). Drogo was succeeded as count of Apulia by his half-brother Robert Guiscard.
9   The claim of the Byzantine Empire to Apulia and Calabria had always been contested by the German emperors. The son of the first German Roman Emperor Otto I, Otto II (955-961-973-983), led an expedition to conquer all of South Italy in 980, but was thoroughly defeated by the Arab emir of Sicily Abd-al-Qasim near Cotrone (modern-day Crotone) in Calabria in 982: see *infra* p. 85.
10   The 'Donation of Constantine' was known later in the Middle Ages from Gratian's *Decretum* (Dist. 96, cap. 14), to which it was added by Gratian's successor Paucapalea. The *Decretum* was only published around 1150, but the text of Constantine's 'Donation' was widely known before that time from the Pseudo-Isidorian Decretals (ed. Hinschius, Leipzig 1863, 249-254), composed before 857. The 'Donation' was not a product of the compilers of this collection though; it was copied by them from an older source. The best modern edition of the 'Donation' is by H. Fuhrmann, MGH, *Fontes iuris* 10, 92 *ff.* The date and purpose of this forgery are still a matter of controversy and will probably remain so. It is my impression that it is related to the coronation of Pepin the Short and his sons by Pope Stephen II in Paris in 754 and the simultaneous grant of the Roman patriciate to Pepin and his sons: see *infra* p. 45-47.

shortly before in their dealings with the Byzantine Empire resulting in the great schism of 1054[11] and it was crucial in their later negotiations with Robert Guiscard and Richard of Capua at Melfi in August 1059, if only to convince the Normans of the superior title of the pope to what once had been the western part of the old Roman Empire. According to one of the provisions in the 'Donation of Constantine', the Roman emperor Constantine had abandoned the western part of his empire to the Roman Patriarch Silvester I to dispose of it as it pleased him and voluntarily retreated to Constantinople, content to rule over just the eastern part of the empire[12]. Consequently, it was in the pope's power to dispose of any part of the western Roman Empire, notwithstanding any claim to the contrary, such as, for example, by the German emperor. Accordingly, Robert Guiscard and Richard transferred all the land they controlled and were to control in the future[13] to the pope and swore a solemn oath of fealty to Nicholas II after which the pope invested them with all the land they had surrendered to him, now to have and to hold from him as his vassals[14]. It was a feudal construct the Normans were familiar with, since it was quite common in northern France at the time, where it was known as a 'fief de reprise'. It was mostly employed to win the protection of the new lord. In this case it was done to protect the title of the two Normans against any claim of, especially, the German emperor, since they now held all their land from the highest

---

11   See a letter of Pope Leo IX to the Byzantine Patriarch Michael Kerrularios in Mansi 19, col. 635-658 (col. 643-645), also in Migne *PL* 143, col. 744-769 (col. 753-755) and in C. Will, *Acta et scripta quae de controversiis ecclesiae graecae et latinae saeculo undecimo composita sunt*, Leipzig 1861, 65-85 (72-74), containing a large portion of the *Donatio*, a document that Pope Leo claims to have seen and touched himself (*ipso visu et tactu*).

12   Dist. 96, cap. 14 (post alia): 'In order to prevent that the papal crown falls into hard times, but is even more distinguished by glory and power than earthly authorities, we transfer and assign to our aforementioned most holy and universal Pope Silvester our aforementioned palace, the city of Rome, and all the provinces of Italy and the western regions, together with the villages and cities, and we pronounce by this our divine and pragmatic sanction that he and his successors may dispose thereof and we concede that they will stay subject to the authority of the Holy Roman Church' (*Unde ut pontificalis apex non uilescat, sed magis quam terreni inperii dignitas gloria et potentia decoretur, ecce tam palatium nostrum, ut predictum est, quam Romanam urbem, et omnes Italiae seu occidentalium regionum prouincias, loca et ciuitates prefato beatissimo Pontifici nostro Siluestro uniuersali Papae contradimus atque relinquimus, et ab eo et a successoribus eius per hanc diualem nostram et pragmaticum constitutum decernimus disponenda, atque iuri sanctae Romanae ecclesiae concedimus permansura*).

13   It was explicitly provided that Sicily, as yet to be conquered from the Arabs, was included in the transaction as well. The island was conquered by Robert Guiscard's younger brother Roger between 1061 and 1091. Roger was invested by his brother as 'count of Sicily'. His son Roger II was the first king of Sicily as we shall see presently.

14   We have only the transaction between the pope and Robert Guiscard in two separate charters, printed in I.M. Watterich, *Pontificum Romanorum qui fuerunt inde ab exeunte saeculo IX usque ad finem saeculi XIII vitae* Tom. I, Leipzig 1862, 233-234. The charters investing Richard must have been similar.

authority conceivable. In return, they had sworn to defend the pope and all possessions of the Holy See against all its enemies[15]. That oath was put to the test by Hildebrand when he finally had become pope in 1073 as Gregory VII, unleashing a relentless war against all the enemies of the 'freedom of the church', first and foremost against the German king Henry IV[16]. It brought him initial triumphs, as in Canossa in 1077[17], but in the end just bitterness and despair. When he finally died on 25 May 1085, he was an exile in Salerno and a large part of the city of Rome was burnt down, not by Henry IV and his German troops, but by Robert Guiscard's Normans called in by the pope to 'liberate' the city[18].

Roger II becomes king of Sicily

Robert Guiscard, 'the terror of the world' (*terror mundi*), did not survive Gregory VII for long. He died on 17 July 1085. His position as the leading Norman force in South Italy was taken over by his nephew Roger II of Hauteville (1095-1154), the son of his brother Roger I, count of Sicily. Roger II was able to secure a position on the Italian mainland as well. In 1128 he was invested by Pope Honorius II as duke of Apulia[19]. He annexed the principality of Tarento two years later, making him the most powerful Norman vassal of the pope in South

---

15   From Robert's oath to Pope Nicholas II (Watterich 234): '*Sanctae Romanae ecclesiae ubique adiutor ero ad tenendum et ad acquirendum regalia sancti Petri eiusque possessiones pro meo posse, contra omnes homines. Et adiuvabo te, ut secure et honorifice teneas Papatum Romanum terramque sancti Petri et principatum*'.
16   Gregory's favorite Bible-quotation was from Jeremiah (48:10): 'Cursed be he that keepeth backe his sword from blood'. See for this quote *Das Register Gregors VII.*, 1,15 (1 July 1073) (MGH *Epp. sel.* 2,1, p. 23); 1,17 (8 July 1073) (MGH *Epp. sel.* 2,1, p. 28); 2,5 (10 Sept. 1074) (MGH *Epp. sel.* 2,1, p. 131); 2,66 (29 March 1075) (MGH *Epp. sel.* 2,1, p. 221); 3,4 (3 Sept. 1075) (MGH *Epp. sel.* 2,1, p. 249); 4,1 (25 July 1076) (MGH *Epp. sel.* 2,1, p. 291) en 4,2 (25 Aug. 1076) (MGH *Epp. sel.* 2,1, p. 296).
17   On the Canossa incident see *infra* p. 333, fnt. 23.
18   In 1083 Henry IV and his German troops, accompanied by Henry's anti-Pope Clement III, had conquered the 'Città Leonina', the fortified right bank of the Tiber inclosing St Peter and the Vatican, leaving Gregory VII besieged in his last place of refuge, Castel Sant'Angelo. Gregory called in the Normans to relieve him. When they finally arrived, Henry IV, after being crowned emperor by Clement III in St Peter's (right under the nose of Gregory VII in Castel Sant'Angelo), had already left, but the Norman 'liberators' started to plunder and set fire to part of the city. The results were disastrous. The descendants of Rollo's Norman Vikings completed the work begun by the Goths and Vandals. It was only after the great fire of Rome of 1084 that a large part of the city did indeed become 'disabitato'. See on these events at Rome in 1084: Gaufredus Malaterra (a contemporary chronicler in the service of count Roger of Sicily, Robert Guiscard's brother), *De rebus gestis Rogerii, Calabriae et Siciliae comitis et Roberti Guiscardi ducis fratris eius* 3, 37, RIS² 5.1, 79-80 and the *Vita Gregorii VII* in the *Liber pontificalis*, ed. Duchesne 2, 290.
19   Falco Beneventanus (*c.* 1070-*c.* 1144), *Chronicon Beneventanum* ad ann. 1128, ed. D'Angelo, 44. Pope Honorius had tried to stop the progress of Roger II on the South Italian mainland by leading a military expedition against him. It ended, as most papal military ven-

Italy. This was the reason why Pope Anacletus II (1130-1138) invoked Roger's support in his conflict with a rival pope, Innocent II (1130-1143)[20], who – thanks to the intervention of Bernard of Clairvaux – was supported by the kings of England and France and by the newly elected king of the Germans, Lothair III[21]. Anacletus was prepared to pay a very high price for Roger's support: Roger wanted to be king of Sicily and Anacletus complied, at the same time investing him as duke of Apulia, Calabria and Naples, and as prince of Capua[22].

---

tures into southern Italy invariably did, in a miserable failure and important concessions to the Normans.

20   The succession of Pope Honorius II (1124-1130) was a disaster, a direct consequence of the absence of a majority rule in the bull of Nicholas II on the election of a new pope. The affair was badly managed by the strong man in the papal curia, the arch-chancellor cardinal Aymeric de la Châtre. A committee of eight cardinals, selected by Aymeric, elected Gregorio Papareschi, a Roman, who took the name Innocent II, but one of the members of that committee, Pietro Leoni, another Roman, was dissatisfied and had himself elected by no fewer than 27 cardinals. He chose the name Anacletus II. Only 16 cardinals sided with Innocent II. The whole bungled affair can be reconstructed from two contemporary letters, one by bishop Uberto of Lucca to the German bishop Norbert of Magdeburg (St. Norbert) (*Codex Udalrici*, ed. Jaffé, *Bibliotheca rerum germanicarum* V, Berlin 1869, no 246, 425-427) and another emanating from the cardinals siding with Anacletus to the German king Lothair III (*Ann. eccl.* Tom. 18, Paris 1869, ad ann. 1130 §§ 16-22, 420-422). It was only under Alexander III that it was finally settled that a two-third majority was required for the election of a new pope. The rule was codified in the *Liber extra* (1234), X. 1,6,6, and remains in force to the present day.

21   Innocent II was unable to hold his own in Rome, where Anacletus had strong support, thanks to the financial means of his extremely rich family, the Pierleoni's of Trastevere. Since most Italian bishops sided with Anacletus, Innocent II was forced to seek refuge in France, as Pope Urban II had done before him. There he gained the valuable support of Bernard of Clairvaux, a good friend (*specialis amicus*) of cardinal Aymeric who supported Innocent II. It was thanks to St Bernard's recommendation that Innocent II was recognized by the French Church and King Louis VI as the true pope in a council held at Étampes. See abbot Arnaud (Ernaldus) of Bonneval († 1157, St Bernard's friend and biographer) *Vita sancti Bernardi* 2,1,3 (Migne *PL* 185, col. 270). The English king followed suit at Chartres (Ernaldus, *Vita sancti Bernardi* 2,1,4, Migne *PL* 185, col. 271). The German king Lothair III sided with Innocent II at the recommendation of another saint, archbishop Norbert of Magdeburg. At a synod held at Liège in 1131 and presided over by Innocent II and king Lothair the 'anti-Pope' Anacletus II was excommunicated: *Annalista Saxo*, ad ann. 1131, MGH *SS* 6, 767.

22   Falco Beneventanus, ad ann. 1130, ed. D'Angelo, 46: '*Eodem anno, predictus Anacletus venit Beneventum; deinde Abellinum civitatem ivit et cum predicto duce Rogerio stabilivit, ut eum regem coronaret Siciliae*'. See also *Chronica monasterii Casinensis* (Petrus Diaconus) 4,97, ad ann. 1130 (MGH *SS* 7, 811)): '*Petrus praeterea cardinalis Roggerio duci Apuliae coronam tribuens, et per privilegium Capuanum principatum, et ducatum Neapolitanum cum Apulia, Calabria et Sicilia illi confirmans, regemque constituens, ad suam partem attraxit*'. The original grant of Anacletus to Roger is printed in *Ann. eccl.* Tom. 18, Paris 1869, ad ann. 1130 §52, 432-433: '*concedimus igitur et donamus et auctorizamus tibi et filio tuo Rogerio … coronam regni Siciliae et Calabriae et Apuliae … Haec omnia supradicta, has nostras concessiones, sic concedimus, tradimus et auctorizamus tibi et tuis filiis habenda et possidenda iure perpetuo, dum nobis nostrisque successoribus homagium et fidelitatem, competenti nobis … facies*'.

Anacletus II was able to hold out in Rome until his demise in 1138 in spite of broad support for Innocent II on the far side of the Alps and notwithstanding an intensive publicity campaign (tainted with antisemitism) directed against him by St Bernard[23] and even despite an impressive military campaign of the German Emperor Lothair III directed against his vassal, 'the Sicilian usurper' (St Bernard), 'King' Roger II in 1137. It was only after Anacletus's demise that Innocent II was able to read Mass in St Peter's for the first time[24]. The pope's attention was drawn to Sicilian affairs immediately after his return to Rome since Roger II had quickly reconquered all territory he had lost on the South Italian mainland in 1137 during the campaign of Lothair III. Lothair, already ageing, had been forced by his own troops to break off his campaign. It was simply too hot for ironclad German knights in Apulia in mid-summer. The men were tired, homesick, and irritated because they were under the impression they were fighting for the pope rather than for their king and empire[25]. After the retreat of the German army from South Italy and the demise of the Emperor Lothair III on his way back to Germany in 1137[26], the supporters of Lothair and Innocent in South Italy were fair game for Roger II[27]. Innocent II decided to stop Roger's progress by sending an army into Campania. It was a fatal decision. Military campaigns commanded by popes usually

---

23 See the letter of St Bernard to the German king Lothair III (*Epistolae*, ep. 189, Migne, *PL* 182, col. 294) where he urges that king to chase 'the Jewish race' (*Judaica soboles*) from the throne of St Peter's. The Pierleoni's of Trastevere were converted Jews.

24 Innocent II has not been absent from Rome all the time. He had returned to Rome for a short spell in 1133, accompanied by the German king Lothair III. The king had come to Italy for his coronation as Roman emperor and, to the great disappointment of Innocent, with a retinue much too small to be a serious threat to Anacletus and his adherents. It was only thanks to the local support of the Roman Frangipani family (always stout champions of the German kings) that the pope was able to crown Lothair in St John's, much to the chagrin of Lothair who preferred St Peter's, but that church and the surrounding 'Città Leonina' were firmly in the hands of Anacletus. After Lothair left for Germany, Innocent's position in Rome was unsustainable (as it had been in 1130) and he was forced to flee to Pisa.

25 See for the revolt of the German soldiers *Annalista Saxo* ad ann. 1137, MGH *SS* 6, 773. This chronicle relates that the troops even threatened to kill Pope Innocent who accompanied the German emperor.

26 *Ottonis episc. freisingensis Chronica* 7,20, MGH *SS Rer. germ.* 45, 339: 'And so Lothair fell seriously ill on his way back from Italy and that mighty emperor has died in a shoddy lodging in the mountains near Trento' (*Igitur Lothair ex Italia rediens apud Tridentinum morbo correptus in ipsis montibus, in vilissima casa imperator potentissimus ... plenus dierum obiit*). *Annalista Saxo* ad ann. 1137 (MGH *SS* 6 p. 775) has the same details.

27 Romoald of Salerno (*c.* 1115-1181), *Chronicon* ad. ann. 1137-1138, MGH *SS* 19, 422-423: 'As soon as he had heard that the pope and the emperor had retreated, King Roger came to Campania over sea and land with a mighty army' (*Rex Rogerius audiens apostolicum et imperatorem recessisce ... per mare et terram cum magno exercitu in Terram Laboris venit*).

ended in disaster[28] and so it did on this occasion. On 22 July 1139 the papal army was caught in an ambush at Gallucio and the pope, his cardinals, his army, and the papal treasure fell into the hands of Roger II[29].

After three days of negotiations, Innocent II was forced to enfeoff Roger II with the kingdom of Sicily and to invest Roger's sons Roger and Alfonso with the duchy of Apulia and the principality of Capua respectively[30]. It seems a crushing defeat for Innocent II and it still is usually represented as such by most historians, but the pope and his archdeacon Aymeric may not have been dissatisfied with the result at all. They had secured the suzerainty of the Holy See over the South Italian kingdom and in doing so had effectually counteracted the claim of the empire to that territory. Only two years previously the Roman emperor, Lothair III, had painfully confronted the pope with that claim. Lothair had practically conquered all of Apulia at the time and wanted to invest one of the local rebels against Roger II, Count Ranulf of Alife, with the duchy of Apulia. Innocent II objected, contending that it was not the emperor, but the pope who was entitled to invest

His title confirmed by Innocent II

---

28   Pope Leo IX had waged war against the South Italian Normans in 1053 and was thoroughly beaten by the Normans near Civitate. The pope, a broken man after this experience, died soon after. On this episode see *Annales romani* ad ann. 1054, MGH *SS* 5, 470. For another failed attempt at subduing the Norman military by Pope Honorius II in 1128 see *supra* p. 32, fnt. 19.

29   Romoald of Salerno, *Chronicon* ad. ann. 1138, MGH *SS* 19, 423: 'But Pope Innocent gathered a large army of Romans and Campanians and invaded the land of the king. He laid siege to the castle of Gallucio. As soon as the king heard of this, he sent his son Roger, duke of Apulia, against him with a huge army. When he arrived, he relieved Gallucio, defeated the Romans, and made the pope and many nobles that were with him his captives' (*Papa vero Innocent ... magnum exercitum de Romanis et Campaninis congregavit, et terram regis ingressus ... Gallucium castrum obsedit. Quod audiens rex Rogerius Rogerium filium suum ducem Apulie contra eum cum magno exercitu misit. Qui veniens castrum obsidione liberavit, Romanos devicit, domnum papam et multos cum eo nobiles Romanos cepit*). For further details see Falco Beneventanus, ad ann. 1139 (ed. D'Angelo, 96).

30   Falco Beneventanus, ad ann. 1139, ed. D'Angelo, 96: 'After the deeds and charters were completed by both parties, the king himself and his sons, the duke and the prince, appeared before the pope on July 25. and begged him forgiveness, clutching his feet, and subjected to the authority of the pope completely. They swore on the holy scriptures to serve St Peter, Pope Innocent and his canonically elected successors loyally and to all the other things that were written down. Immediately thereupon, he invested King Roger with the kingdom of Sicily by way of a banner, and the duke, his son, with the duchy of Apulia and the prince, his other son, with the principality of Capua' (*Et capitularibus et privilegiis ab utraque parte firmatis, rex ipse et dux, filius eius, et princeps, septimo die stante mensis Iulii, ante ipsius Apostolici presentiam veniunt, et pedibus eius advoluti misericordiam petunt et ad pontificis imperium usquequaque flectuntur. Continuo per Evangelia firmaverunt beato Petro, et Innocentio papae eiusque successoribus canonice intrantibus fidelitatem deferre et cetera, quae conscripta sunt. Regi vero Rogerio statim Siciliae regnum per vexillum donavit, duci, filio suo, ducatum Apuliae, principi, altero filio eius, principatum Capuanum largitus est*). The original deed of enfeoffment is printed in Mansi 21, col. 396-397.

Ranulf with that duchy[31]. Animosities ran high because neither part was inclined to give in and in the end Ranulf was invested with the duchy of Apulia by the pope *and* the emperor combined, the pope holding the upper part of the banner handed over to Ranulf as symbol of his investiture and the emperor the lower part[32]. The German knights witnessing the event must have been disgusted and it was surely the main reason why they refused to carry on the 1137 campaign against Roger II. As it happened, Ranulf of Apulia had just died in 1139[33], shortly before Innocent II had invested Roger II with the kingdom of Sicily. When investing Roger's son with the duchy of Apulia, Innocent II knew that he disposed of a duchy to which the emperor had a rival claim. Innocent II did not mind, since he had managed to install a new German king in the place of Lothair III whom he supposed to be more accommodating than that old Saxon warrior. It was Conrad III (1093-1138-1152), the first member of the Hohenstaufen dynasty to sit on Charlemagne's throne in Aachen as 'king of the Germans' (*Theutonicorum rex*) and elected Roman emperor (*rex Romanorum*).

---

31 Romoald of Salerno, *Chronicon* ad. ann. 1137, MGH *SS* 19, 422: 'The pope and the emperor had a serious difference of opinion. The pope contended that the investiture with the duchy of Apulia belonged to the Roman pontiff as of right and that this had been observed for a long time by his predecessors. The emperor however asserted that this was the right of the empire and that the duchy of Apulia ought to be granted on imperial authority' (*inter Apostolicum et imperatorem magna contentio est oborta. Apostolicus enim ascerebat investituram ducatus Apulie ad ius Romani pontificis pertinere et hoc a suis predecessoribus fuisse iam longo tempore firmiter observatum. Imperator e contrario affirmabat, hoc ad ius pertinere imperii, et ducatum Apulie debere auctoritate imperatoria ordinari*).

32 Romoald of Salerno, *Chronicon* l.c.: 'since at the time neither party was able to produce documents, the main issue could not be decided and they settled on a compromise: that the pope and the emperor should invest count Ranulf with the banner of the duchy of Apulia, which has indeed happened, because the pope, holding the upper part of the banner, and the emperor, holding the lower part, have invested count Ranulf with the duchy of Apulia' (*deficientibus ad presens utriusque partis instrumentis et rationibus, controversia hec ad plenum diffiniri non poterat, communi consensu ad hunc finem concordie devenerunt: ut apostolicus et imperator per vexillum comitem Raidulfum de ducatu Apulie investirent ... Quod est factum est, nam apostolicus accepto vexillo a superiori parte, imperator ab inferiori, comitem Raidulfum de ducatu Apulie investierunt*).

33 Falco Beneventanus, ad ann. 1139, ed. D'Angelo, 93: '*Hoc anno Rainulphus dux ... ardentissimo febris sinochae calore correptus, ultimo die stante mensis Aprilis, ex hoc mundo decessit apud civitatem Troianam*'.

King Conrad III
(*Chronica regia coloniensis*, Royal Library of Belgium, Ms 467, *f. 63 v°*)

2

The Holy Roman Empire

The Rise of a New Roman Empire in the West

After the removal of the last emperor of the Roman empire in the West in 476, Italy was temporarily ruled by a succession of 'German' war lords, Odoacer from 476 to 493 and the Ostrogoth king Theodoric from 493 until his demise in Ravenna, the last capital of the Roman Empire in the West, in 526. The emperor of the Eastern, 'Byzantine', Roman Empire Justinian (482/483-527-565) seized the opportunity of Theodoric's contested succession to invade Italy and to restore Roman control over the Italian peninsula. But the Roman 'Reconquista' was not to last for long[1]. In 568, shortly after the demise of the great Justinian, the Lombards, a new tribe of fierce warriors from the middle of the European continent, invaded the Italian peninsula with great slaughter and mayhem[2], driving the Roman armies from the best part of that peninsula but for a narrow strip of land in the middle, linking the port of Ravenna with the city of Rome, and the faraway southern extremities of Apulia and Calabria. After this (almost) complete collapse of Roman, or rather Byzantine, authority in Italy, succeeding popes, beginning with Pelagius II (579-590) and Gregory the Great (590-

The Lombard problem

---

1 The short-lived Byzantine reconquest of the Italian peninsula had enormously important long-lasting consequences, since Justinian ordered that his recent law codes, the *Institutes*, the *Digest*, and the *Codex Justinianus*, were to be introduced in the Italian peninsula and copies of these codes to be sent to Italy: *Constitutio pragmatica* of 13 August 554, App. VII in the edition of the Justinian *Novels* by Schoell and Kroll § 11. Consequently, Roman law was to survive in the West in the form of Justinian's *Corpus Iuris Civilis*.

2 Pope Gregory the Great (590-604) draws a bleak picture of circumstances in Italy after the Lombard invasion (*Homiliae in Ezechiel*, Lib. ii, Hom. vi, § 22, Migne, *PL 76*, col. 1009D-1010A): 'What joy is there still left in the world? We see sorrow everywhere; we hear lamentations all around. The cities have been destroyed, castles ruined, the countryside depopulated and turned into a desert. No one lives in the country and almost no one has remained in the cities' (*Quid est jam, rogo, quod in hoc mundo libeat? Ubique luctus aspicimus, undique gemitus audimus. Destructae urbes, eversa sunt castra, depopulati agri, in solitudinem terra redacta est. Nullus in agris incola, pene nullus in urbibus habitator remansit*).

604), unsuccessfully urged succeeding emperors in Constantinople to come to the rescue of all true 'Catholic' Christians in Italy.

Most of the Lombards were not pagans but schismatic (Arian) Christians, as were most other German tribes settling in the west after the collapse of the Western Roman Empire. Consequently, Nicene 'Catholicism' was the religion of the indigenous Roman population of the new 'Germanic' kingdoms in what had once been the Western Roman Empire: Franks and Burgundians in Gaul, Visigoths in Gaul and Spain, and Ostrogoths and Lombards in Italy. Hence, the privilege of being called a 'true' (meaning 'orthodox' Nicene) Christian came to be reserved for indigenous 'Romans' exclusively, turning all 'true' Christians into 'Romans' in the process and making the pope in Rome the sole spiritual leader of all 'Romans' (Catholics) in the West[3]. There was only one possible ally in the West to provide the support which the emperor in Constantinople failed to deliver. Clovis (*c.* 466-481-511), the king of the pagan Frankish tribe, had converted to Catholic Christianity in 497 and was hailed as a new Constantine by his (Roman) Christian subjects in Gaul, a clear reference to the legendary conversion of the Emperor Constantine I by Pope Silvester I[4]. The Frank was also highly decorated by the Roman Emperor Anastasius I (*c.* 439-491-518) who raised Clovis to an honorary consulate and rewarded him with the highest honour a Roman emperor could bestow on his officials, the patriciate[5], a title held by only one other 'German' king at the time, the

---

3 There were five patriarchs in the Christian Roman Empire, the patriarchs of Antioch, Alexandria, Jerusalem, Constantinople, and Rome. Four of the patriarchs were subjects of the Eastern Roman Emperor. The patriarch of Rome was the supreme ecclesiastical authority in the Western Roman Empire. His position was confirmed by a statute of the Western Roman Emperor Valentinian III of 8 July 445: Nov. Valent. III, 17. Ambrose (339-397), bishop of Milan, was first to name the only 'true' Christian church 'the *Roman* church' (*ecclesia Romana*): *Epistolae*, ep. 11, nr 4 (Migne, *PL* 16, col. 986). In doing so he stressed the primacy of the Roman patriarch over the other patriarchs and the position of the city of Rome as the spiritual capital of the world (*caput mundi*).

4 Gregory of Tours, *Historiarum* 2,31, MGH *SS rer. Merov.* 1.1, 77: 'the new Constantine proceeded to the baptismal basin to erase the disease of the old leprosy' (*procedit novos Constantinus ad lavacrum deleturus leprae veteris morbum*). Thanks to the intervention of St Peter and Paul, Constantine was miraculously cured of leprosy (paganism) by pope Silvester. It was part of the Silvester-legend: see *supra* p. 31.

5 Gregory of Tours, *Historiarum* 2,38, MGH *SS rer. Merov.* 1.1, 88: '*Igitur ab Anastasio imperatore codecillos de consulatu accepit*'. For the elevation to the patriciate see the ancient table of contents to chapter 38 of the second book of the *Historiae* of Gregory of Tours: '*De patriciato Chlodovechi regis*' (MGH *SS rer. Merov.* 1.1, 35) (emphasis added). For the title '*patricius*' as a reward for the highest Roman functionaries, ex-consuls, praetorian prefects, city prefects, and the highest military commanders (*magistri militum*) see C. 12,3,3 pr. (Zeno). Later, the Exarch of Ravenna was also styled as a *patricius*.

legendary Theodoric, king of the Ostrogoths in Italy[6]. This imperial policy of involving the Frankish royalty into the framework of Roman institutions was adopted by the Roman papacy. Pope Gregory III (731-741) sent several requests to the Frankish strongman Charles Martel († 741), Charlemagne's grandfather, to rescue Rome from the Lombard threat, offering to abandon the emperor in Constantinople and to raise Charles to the Roman consulate[7]. Charles Martel died in 741 and it was with his son, Pepin 'the Short' (714-747-768), that the Popes Zachary (741-752) and Stephen II (752-757) succeeded to arrange an alliance against the Lombards that was to change the course of European history.

In 749 two Frankish envoys, Bishop Burchard of Würzburg, a disciple of Boniface, and Fulrad, abbot of St Denys, arrived in Rome on a special mission to pope Zachary. The pope was to advise the Franks on a curious constitutional problem in their kingdom. Pepin might be 'Leader of the Franks' (*Dux Francorum*), but he was not the king of that mighty tribe now ruling over the main part of continental Western Europe. King of the Franks was the Merovingian Childeric, third of that name, a descendant of the mighty Clovis, but he was king in name only, like all his immediate predecessors. True power rested with the 'mayor of the palace' (*maior domus*), an office held by Pepin and his ancestors. The envoys were to put the question to the pope whether this anomaly was to last or should be undone by assigning the royal title to the man exercising real power. The pope conveniently suggested '*that it was better that the man wielding real power should be called king rather than the man without royal power*'[8]. Fortified by this legal opinion, the

A new king of the Franks

---

6   For the grant of the patriciate to Theodoric see Anonymus Valesianus (*c.* 527), *pars posterior* 11,49, MGH *Auct. Ant.* 9, 316: '*Zeno itaque recompensans beneficiis Theodericum, quem fecit patricium et consulem*'.

7   For this episode see 'Fredegar', Continuatio III (8th century), cap. 110, in Bouquet 2, 457: 'In those days (739-741) the Holy Father Gregory (III) twice sent an ambassy from the Roman See of the holy Apostle Peter to the aforementioned prince (Charles Martel) carrying the keys of the venerable grave and the chains of Saint Peter and great and magnificent gifts, something that formerly would have been unheard of, offering a treaty that he would abandon the party of the emperor and that he would grant the Roman consulate to the said prince Charles' (*Eo etenim tempore bis a Roma sede sancti Petri apostoli beatus papa Gregorius claves venerandi sepulchri cum vincula sancti Petri et muneribus magnis et infinitis legationem, quod antea nullis auditis aut visis temporibus fuit, memorato principi destinavit, eo pacto patrato, ut a partibus imperatoris recederet et <Romanum consulatum> praefato principi Carolo sanciret*). The edition of Krusch (MGH *SS rer. Merov.* 2, 179) reads '*Romano consulto*' rather than '*Romanum consulatum*'. Krusch's reading makes no sense and the reading of the *Recueil* is indirectly confirmed by the chronicle of Moissiac (818-830) ad ann. 734, MGH *SS* 1, 291-292.

8   *Annales regni Francorum* (787-829) ad ann. 749, MGH, SS rer. Germ. 6, 8: 'Bishop Burchard of Würzburg and the Chaplain Foldradus were sent to Pope Zachary to ask for his opinion on the kings of France, who did not have effective power at the time, whether that was

envoys returned to Gaul informing the Frankish nobles that the pope in Rome had ruled that the prevailing constitutional *status quo* was contrary to 'Christian order' (*ordo christianitatis*) and that they had the authority (*mandatum*) of the pope to depose Childeric and raise Pepin to the throne[9]. Consequently, Pepin was enthroned as king of the Franks at Soissons in 751. Childeric was deposed, his long hair was cut, and he was to spend the rest of his living days in a monastery[10].

Something unusual transpired at Pepin's inauguration. Contrary to the custom of the tribe, the new king was anointed by Boniface, the special legate sent by the pope to the Frankish court to bring Christianity to the pagan tribes in Germany, like the Saxons and the Frisians[11]. It was not a complete novelty, since the consecration of a king by the process of anointment, inspired by the Old Testament (1 Samuel 10:1), was already practiced in Visigothic Spain a century before and also in Britain, from where Boniface, who was a native of Saxon Britain, must have taken the ritual[12]. It added a special Christian dimension to the elevation of a king, who was raised to the dignity of 'God's anointed' (*christus Dei*), ruling by 'the grace of God' (*Dei gratia*). It marked the definitive break with the pagan past of the Franks, but it also meant that the intervention of a representative of the church was an indispensable part of the inauguration of a Frankish king[13].

---

a good thing or not. And Pope Zachary sent word to Pepin that it was better to call that man king who had real power, rather than the man who had no royal power and so, in order not to disturb the natural order of things, he allowed Pepin to be made king on apostolic authority' (*Burghardus Wirzeburgensis episcopus et Foldradus capellanus missi fuerunt ad Zachariam papam, interrogando de regibus in Francia, qui illis temporibus non habentes regalem potestatem, si bene fuisset an non. Et Zachary papa mandavit Pepino, ut melius esset illum regem vocari, qui potestatem haberet quam illum, qui sine regali potestate manebat; ut non conturbaretur ordo, per auctoritatem apostolicam iussit Pepinum regem fieri*).

9   *Annales Laurissenses minores* (last entry 817) ad ann. 750, MGH, *SS* 1, 116: '*Mandavit itaque praefatus pontifex regi et populo Francorum, ut Pepinus qui potestate regia utebatur, rex appelaretur, et in sede regali constitueretur*'.

10   *Annales regni Francorum* ad ann. 752, MGH *SS rer. Germ.* 6, 10: '*Hildericus vero, qui false rex vocabatur, tonsoratus est et in monasterium missus*'.

11   *Annales regni Francorum* ad ann. 750, MGH *SS rer. Germ.* 6, 8-9: '*Pepinus … unctus per manum sanctae memoriae Bonifacii archiepiscopi et elevatus a Francis in regno in Suessonis civitate*'.

12   For Visigothic Spain see the contemporary report of the consecration of King Wamba in 672 in Julianus Toletanus (*c*. 642-690), *Historia Wambae regis* 3, MGH, *SS rer. Mer.* 5, 503. Julianus himself was the bishop performing the anointment. The Celtic kings of Britain were anointed according to Gildas (6th century), *De excidio Britanniae* c. 19, ed. Giles, 239 ('*ungebantur reges*'), as were the Irish kings around 700: see the collection of rules of canon law compiled around 700 in Ireland, known as the *Collectio Hibernensis* Lib. 25 (*De regno*), cap. 1 (*De ordinatione regis*) (ed. H. Wasserschleben, Giessen 1874, 90) containing a quote from 1 Samuel 10:1. The Saxons in Britain may have borrowed this ritual from the Celts.

13   Anointment was completely alien to the inauguration of a Roman and Byzantine emperor. The Byzantines did not understand it and believed that a Frankish king was lubricated

In 751, the same year Pepin was consecrated king of the Franks, the Lombard King Aistulf (c. 700-756) conquered the last Byzantine stronghold north of Rome, the city of Ravenna, seat of the Byzantine military governor (ἔξαρχος) of the strip of land in the middle of the Italian peninsula still under Byzantine control, the so-called 'Exarchate' of Ravenna. There was no doubt that Rome, the last major city still nominally under Byzantine rule, was to be Aistulf's next objective. Pope Stephen II, who succeeded Pope Zachary in 752, was desperate since no help from Constantinople was forthcoming[14]. Instead, the Byzantine Emperor Constantine V (718-741-775) begged the pope to persuade the Lombard king to restore the 'Exarchate' to its lawful sovereign rather than send an army to support his Italian subjects[15]. Pope Stephen, a native Roman, finally had enough. He concluded that a monarch incapable of defending his subjects had forfeited his rights and should be replaced by someone who could. The new king of the Franks was the obvious candidate and Stephen II took the unprecedented step of travelling to Gaul himself to see to it that Pepin did.

Pope Stephen II
goes to Gaul

After very delicate diplomatic preparations[16], Pope Stephen left Rome in October 753 and after a long journey through Lombard territory and crossing the Alps via the Great St Bernard Pass in the middle of winter he arrived in the neighbourhood of Ponthion, where King Pepin resided, on 6 January 754. On the last stage of his journey, the pope had been accompanied by the young Frankish Prince Charles, who must have been much impressed by all 'the pomp and circumstance' the pope displayed during his progress through Gaul[17]. At Ponthion the pope and the new king of the Franks met for the first time[18]. There was much to talk about.

---

from head to toe at his inauguration: Theophanes Confessor († 817/818), *Chronographia* ad A.M. 6289/ A.D. 789, ed. Classen, 733. The last king to be anointed on the European continent was Charles X of France in 1842. There is now but one anointed European monarch left: the King of England.

14   *Liber pontificalis, Stephen II* 15, ed. Duchesne 444: 'ab imperiale potentia nullum subveniendi auxilium'.

15   *Liber pontificalis, Stephen II* 17, ed. Duchesne, 444-445.

16   The pope had to travel through hostile Lombard territory to reach Gaul. The solution to the problem was that he had himself officially invited by king Pepin and was accompanied by Frankish envoys through the Lombard kingdom, even visiting the Lombard capital Pavia. King Aistulf could and would not risk a war with Pepin since there were good relations between Franks and Lombards at the time.

17   For the details of Stephen's voyage to Gaul see *Liber pontificalis, Stephen II* 19-24, ed. Duchesne, 445-447. For the instruction to prince Charles to accompany the pope through Gaul see Fredegar (Continuatio) cap. 119 (36), MGH *SS rer. Merov.* 2, 183.

18   The meeting of Pope Stephen and King Pepin is legendary. The papal source (the *Liber pontificalis, Stephen* II, ed. Duschesne 1, 447), composed not long after the demise of the pope, emphasizes that the king rendered 'squire service' to the pope at this occasion, meaning that he escorted the pope on foot, holding the pope's horse by the bridle and holding the stirrup

The Donation
of Pepin

It was not an easy choice Pepin had to make. He had recently been elected as king of the Franks by his nobles, but he could not be sure of the loyalty of all of them[19]. To complicate matters, there were friendly relations between Franks and Lombards ever since the great Lombard king Liutprand (*c.* 680-712-744) had assisted Pepin's father in his famous victory over the invading Arabs at Poitiers in 732. Pepin had even been adopted by king Liutprand[20]. It took the pope, who stayed at the abbey of St Denys, months to persuade Pepin to wage war on the Lombards. In the end, he prevailed because he knew about Pepin's weakness: Pepin's desire to consolidate the legitimacy of his royal title *and* his wish to secure that position for his sons, Charles and Karloman. The pope convinced Pepin that it was in his power to satisfy both aspirations.

Pepin and the pope celebrated Easter in the royal villa at Quierzy. Shortly before, on 1 March 754, the king had held a diet at Braisne-sur-Vesle where his reluctant nobles finally conceded to an expedition against the Lombards for the next year[21]. During Easter the pope and

---

as that holy man dismounted. The contemporary Frankish sources, the chronicle of Moissiac (ad ann. 741, MGH *SS* 1, 292-293) and Fredegar (Continuatio) cap. 119 (36), MGH *SS rer. Merov.* 2, 183), do *not* report this incident but emphasize instead that the pope prostrated himself before the king 'covered in dust and ashes' (*aspersus cinere et indutus cilicio in terram prostratus*), humbly begging for help against the Lombards. The incident of 'squire service' is mentioned here for the first time. Since it also occurs in the 'Donation of Constantine' (*Const. Const.* § 16, ed. H. Furhrmann, MGH, *Fontes iuris* 10, 92), this is a good indication that this document (on which *supra* p. 30, fnt. 10) was composed around the same time, most probably even on this occasion, on which more shortly.

19   After the demise of his father, Pepin had shared the office of 'mayor of the palace' with his brother Karloman, dividing the Frankish kingdom between them: Pepin in the west (Neustria) and Karloman in the east (Austrasia). Karloman resigned and retired to a monastery in Italy in 745, leaving Pepin in sole control of the entire kingdom but entrusting his son Drogo to the custody of his brother: Fredegar, Cont. ad ann. 747, MGH *SS rer. Mer.* 2, 181. Karloman and Drogo still must have had supporters among the Frankish nobility. The situation became extremely complicated by the completely unexpected return of Karloman to Gaul in 754 (shortly after the arrival of the pope), clearly to support the interests of his son. Pepin now acted decisively, obviously with the consent of the pope. Karloman and his son were arrested and confined to a monastery. See for the whole episode: *Annales Laureshamenses* ad ann. 753, MGH *SS* 1, 26.

20   For Pepin's adoption by King Liutprand see Paul the Deacon (†796/799), *Historia Lombardorum* 6,53, MGH *SS rer. Germ.* 48, 237.

21   *Annales Mettenses priores* (804-830) ad ann. 754, MGH *SS rer. Germ.* 10, 46: 'In the same year king Pepin held a diet according to the custom on 1 March near his villa at Braisne. After consulting his nobles, he announced that he would depart for Italy with his whole army' (*Eodem anno Pepinus rex placitum habuit secundum consuetudinem Kal. Martii Brennaco villa publica. Accepto inde consilio obtimatum suorum, partibus Italiae se cum omni apparatu suo profecturum esse indixit*). See on this diet also Fredegar (Continuatio) cap. 119 (36), MGH *SS rer. Merov.* 2, 183. For the initial reluctance of the nobles see Einhard, *Vita Karoli magni* 6, MGH, *SS* 2, 446: 'Some of the leading nobles he used to consult were so disinclined to yield to his will that they loudly proclaimed they would desert him and go home' (*quidam e primoribus*

his royal host were considering the possible territorial consequences of a successful expedition against Aistulf. What transpired between the king of the Franks and his guest had far-reaching consequences and we must therefore dwell on this at some length since they were still very relevant in the thirteenth century.

The decision of the pope to visit the king of the Franks had been prompted by the conquest of the Exarchate by Aistulf in 751 and it was the future of that territory that was discussed at Quierzy. As we shall see shortly, Pepin had no design of conquering the Lombard kingdom and deposing Aistulf. He was merely accommodating the pope in his designs. As we have just seen[22], the Byzantine emperor, the legitimate sovereign of that territory, had requested the pope to urge the Lombard king to restore the Exarchate to the emperor but Pepin and Pope Stephen decided that this was not to be. Clearly, given the reluctance of his nobles, Pepin was not going to fight a war against a befriended nation on behalf of a distant Byzantine prince who was incapable of looking after his own affairs. It was therefore resolved that the territory conquered by Aistulf in 751 should be handed over to the pope rather than the emperor. It was not without precedent. Not long before, in 727 or 728, Pope Stephen's predecessor, Pope Gregory II (715-731), had concluded a treaty with the Lombard king Liutprand, who had conquered the town of Sutri in Tuscany, on imperial territory, to restore that town *not* to the empire but to the pope as a gift by the Lombard king to Peter and Paul[23]. The agreement between Pepin and Stephen was put down in writing and the deed (*donationis pagina*) was consigned to the papal archive[24]. After having reached this arrangement with the king of the Franks, it was the turn of Pope Stephen to provide a consideration for the concessions of King Pepin.

On 28 July 754 Pepin *and* his two sons, Charles and Karloman, were anointed by Pope Stephen II as kings of the Franks in the abbey of St Denys near Paris. The ceremony was the apex of papal diplomacy since it was meant to achieve two goals at the same time: the confirma- Pope Stephen II grants the Roman patriciate to Pepin

---

Francorum cum quibus consultare solebat, adeo voluntati eius renisi sunt, ut, se regem deserturos domumque redituros, libera voce proclamarent).
22   P. 43.
23   For this incident see *Liber pontificalis, Gregorius II* 21, ed. Duchesne 1, 407.
24   The details of the agreement of Quierzy ('<*promissio> quae Francia in loco qui vocatur Carisiaco facta est*) have only come down to us in the *Liber pontificalis* in the biographies of Stephen II (46-47, ed. Duchesne 1, 453-454) and Hadrian I (41-42, ed. Duchesne 1, 498), but the authenticity cannot be doubted: see the letters of Stephen II to Pepin and his sons from 755 in *Codex Carolinus* no 6 (MGH *Epp.* 3, 488-490) and 7 (MGH *Epp.* 3, 490-493), referring to 'your gift' (*donatio vestra*).

tion of Pepin's royal title *and* the establishment of a *hereditary* monarchy since the pope compelled the Frankish primates present at the occasion 'never to elect a king sprung from the limbs of another'[25]. Having thus secured Pepin's claim to the throne *and* the title of his descendants, the pope added another dignity to boot, a title unrelated to Pepin's kingship over the Franks: he conferred on Pepin *and* his sons the high honour of the patriciate[26], a *Roman* title formerly bestowed on Clovis, the founding father of the Frankish Merovingian dynasty[27]. The problem was that this purely *secular* title had been bestowed on Clovis by the proper authority, the Roman emperor[28], but Pope Stephen was about to renounce the authority of the Roman Empire. It is explicitly stated in the almost contemporary 'Note on the anointment of king Pepin' (*clausula de unctione Pippini regis*)[29] that the earlier election and subsequent anointment of Pepin at Soissons in 751 had happened 'on the authority *and* the power' (*per auctoritatem* et *imperium*) of the late Pope Zachary[30]. It was customary to use this opposition of 'authority' and 'power' to refer to the difference between the (ecclesiastical) authority of the pope on the one hand and the (secular) power of the emperor on the other[31]. Ordinary, the Latin word for 'power' used in this context is *potestas*, but here an even stronger term is employed: *imperium*, invariably referring to *secular* power at the time[32]. In Roman times that word had always referred to the power of the Roman emperor himself. Here it is used to emphasize that the pope *combined* ecclesiastical authority

---

25   *Clausula de unctione Pepini regis* (767), MGH, *SS* 15.1, 1: '*ut numquam de alterius lumbis regem in aevo presumant eligere*'.

26   *Clausula de unctione Pepini regis* (767), MGH, *SS* 15.1, 1: '*in regem* et patricium *una cum predictis filiis Carolo et Carlomanno in nomine sanctae trinitatis unctus et benedictus est*' (emphasis added).

27   See *supra* p. 40.

28   See *supra* p. 40 and fnt 5.

29   As this famous document states, it was inserted into a copy of a book on miracles by Gregory of Tours in 767. Several scholarly attempts to assign a later date to this document have been disproved.

30   *Clausula de unctione Pepini regis* (754), MGH, *SS* 15,1, 1: '*Ipse praedictus domnus florentissimus Pepinus rex pius per auctoritatem et imperium sanctae recordationis domni Zachariae papae et unctionem sancti chrismatis per manus beatorum sacerdotum Galliarum et electionem omnium Francorum tribus annis antea in regni solio sublimatus est.*

31   Most famously so in the letter of pope Gelasius to the Roman Emperor Anastasius (Gelasius, *Epistola VIII ad Anastasium imperatorem*, ed. Thiel, *Epistulae Romanorum Pontificum Genuinae* 1, Brunsberg 1868, 350-351): 'There are two institutions governing this world: the holy authority of the popes and the royal power' (*Duo quippe sunt, imperator Auguste, quibus principaliter mundus hic regitur: auctoritas sacra pontificum, et regalis potestas*). On this letter see *infra* p. 77-81.

32   Niermeyer's *Lexicon* refers to Willibald's contemporary biography of St Boniface (chap. 7, MGH *SS rer. Germ.* 57, 40). The word is used once more by Willibald (chap. 6, (32)), also referring to the reign of secular rulers.

and secular power, more precisely the power of the Roman emperor. Consequently, the pope was entitled to bestow the Roman patriciate on Pepin and his sons. There can be little doubt that this strange phrase was inspired by the Donation of Constantine and its contention that the Emperor Constantine had transferred the Western Empire to Pope Silvester before retiring to Constantinople[33]. It may well be that this famous forgery was even composed for this special occasion to corroborate the *imperium* of the pope. In conferring the Roman patriciate on Pepin Pope Stephen had crossed a line. Only twenty years before his predecessor pope Gregory II (715-731) had explicitly written to the Byzantine Emperor Leo III that he, Gregory, had *'no authority to concede imperial dignities'*[34]. Now the pope did precisely that. It marked the definitive break of the Roman patriarch, once an imperial official[35], with the Roman emperor in Constantinople.

King Pepin led an expedition to Italy twice, in 754 and 756, to meet his commitment to the pope. Aistulf was no match for Pepin and when he was finally forced to surrender and asked for the terms of a cessation of hostilities, he was given to understand that he had to do 'justice' (*iustitia*) to the pope, meaning that he had to hand over Ravenna, the Pentapolis, Narni, and Ceccano[36], his recent conquests in the Byzantine Exarchate, to the pope. It is clear from this that Pepin and his Frankish nobles were not bent on the deposition of Aistulf or even the conquest of the Lombard kingdom[37]. After settling the Lombard matter, King Pepin

Charlemagne conquers the Lombard kingdom

---

33   See *supra* p. 31.

34   From the second letter (in Greek) of Gregory II to Leo III, Mansi 12, col. 975-982 (978): 'οὐκ ἔχει ἐξουσίαν ὁ ἀρχιερεύς … προβαλέσθαι ἀξίας βασιλικάς'.

35   According to Roman public law, the election of a pope by the people and clerics of Rome ought to be confirmed by the emperor in Constantinople before the new pope could be consecrated. There still was a model for the letter requesting imperial confirmation of the papal election in the *Liber diurnus*, completed in the pontificate of Pope Hadrian I (772-795): cap. 58 (*De electione pontificis ad principem*), ed. De Rozière, Paris 1869, 103-107. The last time the Byzantine emperor was officially petitioned to confirm a papal election was probably at the occasion of the election of Pope Gregory II (715). The elimination of imperial control over papal nominations caused a rapid decline in the moral standards of the papacy since it fell prey to the Roman nobility. On this see *infra* p. 49, fnt. 48.

36   The 'Pentapolis' included five cities south of Ravenna: Rimini (*Ariminium*), Pesaro (*Pisaurum*), Fano (*Fanum Fortunae*), Senigallia (*Sena Gallica*), and Ancona. Narni is in Umbria and Ceccano in Lazio.

37   For the peace terms see the chronicle of Moissiac ad ann. 752-768, MGH *SS* 1, p. 293. The terms were similar to the terms agreed upon after the first expedition. Aistulf had failed to comply with these terms, forcing Pepin to return to Lombardy in 756. The Frankish nobles seem to have been crucial in preserving the Lombard kingdom and maintaining Aistulf on the throne. See Fredegar (Continuatio) cap. 121 (38), MGH *SS rer. Merov.* 2, 185: '*Aistulfus ... iterum per subplicationem sacerdotes* et obtimates *Francorum veniam et pacem praedicto rege subplicans*' and a little further '*Pepinus ... ad petitionem obtimatibus suis vitam et regnum*

returned to Gaul without visiting Pope Stephen, who had returned to Rome at the end of 754 where the news will have reached him that the 'apostle of the Germans', Boniface, had recently been granted the grace of martyrdom by the pagan Frisians[38]. Shortly before King Pepin left Italy, he had met with two ambassadors from the Byzantine Emperor Constantine V. They had been dispatched to Italy after news of Pepin's first Lombard expedition had reached Constantinople. The imperial ambassadors were still in Rome in 756 and went to meet Pepin near Pavia *'demanding that he should hand over the city of Ravenna and the rest of the cities of the Exarchate to imperial control'*[39]. Pepin flatly refused: *'he would for no reason whatsoever allow these cities to be taken away from the power and the right of the Roman church and the pope'*[40]. After the departure of King Pepin to Gaul, Abbot Fulrad of St Denys was left behind in Italy to complete the formal conveyance to the pope of all territory comprised in the 'Donation of Pepin'[41].

---

iterato concessit' (emphasis added). He now had to pay an additional heavy tribute to the Franks though.

38 *Annales regni Francorum* ad ann. 754, MGH *SS rer. Germ.* 6, 12: 'Archbishop Boniface, preaching and bringing the word of the Lord in Frisia, was made a martyr' (*Et domnus Bonefacius archiepiscopus in Frisia nuntians verbum Domini et praedicando martyr Christi effectus est*). It seems that Boniface's influence at the Frankish court was closely linked to Pepin's brother Karloman and that his role was over after Karloman resigned.

39 *Liber pontificalis, Vita Stephani II* 44, ed. Duchesne 1, 453: '*deprecans … ut Ravennantium urbem vel cetera eiusdem exarcatus civitates imperiali tribuens concederet ditioni*'.

40 *Liber pontificalis, Vita Stephani II* 44, ed. Duchesne 1, 453: '*nulla penitus ratione easdem civitates a potestate beati Petri et iure ecclesiae Romanae vel pontifici apostolicae sedis quoquo modo alienari*'.

41 It is usual among historians to represent the treaty between Pepin and Pope Stephen as a 'gift' (*donatio*) by Pepin to the pope. None of the original parties to it can have conceived of it in this way. It suggests that the cities and territories comprised in it belonged to King Pepin at law, which they clearly did not, as everyone, including the pope and King Pepin, knew at the time. What really happened is that a territory once belonging to the Roman emperor in Constantinople was now assigned to the pope. It had been illegally occupied by the Lombards and was passed on *by the Lombards* (*not* by Pepin) to the pope rather than to the Roman emperor in Constantinople. Medieval canonists were well aware of this: these territories already belonged to the church on account of the 'Donation of Constantine' and consequently there was no gift at all, but merely the confirmation of a gift, meaning the 'Donation of Constantine': Gl. *'Atque viculis'* ad *Decretum* Dist. 63, cap. 30: 'He does not donate here, but merely confirms a donation since all this and much more already belonged to the Church before', referring to the 'Donation of Constantine' in *Decretum* Dist. 96, cap. 14 (*Non concedit hic, sed concessa confirmat, nam omnia haec et alia plura iam prius fuerant ecclesiae: infra 96. dist. 'Constantinus'*). All this suggests that the forgery of the 'Donation of Constantine' was an essential part of the policy of Pope Stephen II, convincing Pepin (*and* his reluctant Frankish nobles) of the legal title of the pope to the territory that was to be 'restored' to him rather than to the emperor in Constantinople.

King Pepin died on 24 September 768 and in accordance with Salian law[42] his realm was divided among his two sons, Charles and Karloman. The arrangement was not to last for long. Karloman died on 4 December 771 and Charles was consecrated as king of all Franks at Corbeny only a few weeks later[43]. Karloman's widow – fearing (probably rightly) that Charles would fare with her children as his father Pepin had once done with the children of his own brother also called Karloman[44] – fled to Italy where she and her children were kindly received by king Desiderius[45], who had succeeded to the Lombard throne after the demise of King Aistulf in 756[46]. It was a declaration of war.

Desiderius's rise to the Lombard throne had been sponsored by Pope Stephen II and King Pepin, primarily because he was supposed to be 'a very peaceful man' (vir mitissimus)[47]. The Lombard was to thoroughly disappoint his sponsors: he conspired with the Byzantines, harassed the territories of the Exarchate recently transferred to the pope, and even violently interfered in the papal succession after the demise of Pope Paul I (757-767)[48]. Despite all of this, the Lombard king still

---

42 *Lex Salica* 34, § 6, MGH, *LL nat. Germ.* 4,2, 214. The fine distinction, drawn by Roman law, between the succession to the private estate of a deceased monarch and the succession to the throne of his realm, the former ruled by private law and the latter dictated by the provisions of public law, was unknown to Frankish law: the kingdom was regarded as the personal estate of the monarch, to be dealt with according to the provisions of *private* rather than public law.

43 *Annales Mettenses priores* ad ann. 771, MGH *SS rer. Germ.* 10, 57-58: 'But King Charles arrived at the royal palace of Corbeny. Archbishop Wilehard and Fulrad, head of the royal chapel, and other bishops and clerics came to meet him there, as did the counts Warinus and Adhalard and other princes coming from the territories of Karloman and they consecrated the most illustrious Charles as their lord and thus he obtained the monarchy of the whole kingdom of the Franks' (*Rex vero Carolus ad Corbiniacam villam publicam pervenit. Ibi venientes ad eum Wileharius archiepiscopus et Fulradus capellanus cum aliis episcopis ac sacerdotibus, Warinus quoque et Adhalardus comites cum aliis principibus, qui fuerant ex partibus Carolomanni, et unxerunt super se dominum suum Carolum gloriossissimum regem, et obtinuit feliciter monarchiam totius regni Francorum*).

44 See *supra* p. 44, fnt. 19.

45 Einhard, *Vita Karoli magni* 3, MGH, *SS* 2, 445: 'After the demise of Karloman, his wife and sons and some of the most distinguished among his nobles, fled to Italy, placing herself and her children without any reason under the protection of Desiderius, the king of the Lombards, renouncing the brother of her husband' (*defuncto Karlomanno, uxor eius et filii cum quibusdam, qui ex optimatum eius numero primores erant, Italiam fuga petiit, et nullis existentibus causis, spreto mariti fratre, sub Desiderii, regis Langobardorum, patrocinium se cum liberis suis contulit*).

46 For the succession to the Lombard throne after the death of Aistulf see *Liber pontificalis*, *vita Stephani II* 48 and 49, ed. Duchesne 1, 454-455.

47 Letter of Pope Stephen II to King Pepin in *Codex Carolinus* no 11, ed. Grundlach, MGH *Epp.* 3, 504-507(506)): '*Desiderius, vir mitissimus*'.

48 After the death of Pope Paul I, brother to Pope Stephen II, in 767 the Roman papacy fell victim to the greed of the local Roman nobility, due to the absence of imperial supervision

had the support of part of the Frankish nobility and of the Queen Dowager Bertrada, Charlemagne's mother, who even arranged a marriage between her son Charles and one of Desiderius's daughters in 770. But Desiderius's decision to give asylum to Karloman's widow and her sons proved fatal to his cause. Charlemagne repudiated his Lombard wife, exercised his army by organizing an expedition into Saxony in 772, and entered Lombardy with a huge and battle-hardened army in 773 to solve the Lombard problem once and for all. He was quick to lay his hands on Karloman's widow and her sons. They were arrested in Verona and disappeared from history without leaving a trace[49]. Having eliminated Karloman's issue, Charles decided to visit the graves of the Apostles Peter and Paul and to meet the new pope, Hadrian I (772-795), in Rome, leaving the bulk of his army besieging Desiderius in his last stronghold, his capital Pavia.

The Donation of Charlemagne

King Charles and Pope Hadrian celebrated Easter in Rome. On Wednesday after Easter, 6 April 774, Charles solemnly confirmed the promise of his father, adding substantial territories to it 'spontaneously and from the kindness of his heart' (*propria voluntate, bono ac libenti animo*)[50]. A copy of Charles' promise, 'confirmed by his own signa-

---

(see *supra* p. 28). A local potentate, the lord of Nepi, invaded Rome and had his brother consecrated as pope (Constantine II, 767-768), only to be deposed by a Lombard agent of Desiderius, who advanced a candidate of his own, Philip (768), who was, on his turn, deposed and replaced by Pope Stephen III (768-772). There had been blood on the streets of Rome on occasion of a papal succession before, but this was the first time it was shed because of the political and economic benefits involved. It was not to be the last time. The papal succession of 767 marked the beginning of the 'dark ages' of the Roman papacy. Our most important source of the events following the demise of Pope Stephen II is the *Liber pontificalis, Stephen III*, 1-16, *ed.* Duchesne 1, 468-473.

49 *Liber pontificalis, Hadrianus* I, 34, ed. Duchesne 1, 496.

50 *Liber pontificalis, Hadrianus* I, 42, ed. Duchesne 1, 498: 'The pope strongly insisted that Charles kept the promise his late father Pepin and he himself had made. He complied with everything. And when he asked that the promise which was made in France in a place called Querzy was read to him, he and his courtiers agreed with everything that was contained in it. And he ordered spontaneously and from the kindness of his heart that another promise of a donation was to be composed in place of the old one in which he promised to assign the same cities and territories to Saint Peter and the pope, indicating the borders as they were specified in the same donation, meaning from Luni, with the island of Corsica, to Suriano, next to the Monte Bardano, that is near Verceto, then to Parma and Reggio and from there to Mantua and Mount Silicis, together with the entire Exarchate of Ravenna, as it originally was, and the provinces of Venice and Istria, and the duchies of Spoleto and Benevento' (*pontifex ... constanter eum deprecatus est ... ut promissionem illam, quam eius sanctae memoriae genitor Pepinus quondam rex et ipse ... fecerant ... adimpleret in omnibus. Cumque ipsam promissionem, quae Francia in loco quo vocatur Carisiaco facta est, sibi relegi fecisset, complacuerunt illi et eius iudicibus omnia quae ibidem erant adnexa. Et propria voluntate, bono ac libenti animo, aliam donationis promissionem ad instar anterioris ipse ... adscribi iussit ... ubi concessit easdem civitates et territoria beato Petro easque praefato pontifici contradi spopondit per designatum confinium,*

ture' (*propria sua manu corroberans*) and that of all the abbots, bishops, dukes, and counts present, was solemnly deposited by Charles himself on the grave of Saint Peter and some copies were handed over to Charles personally[51]. None of these copies has survived and the contemporary Frankish sources do not mention Charles' 'donation' at all. We only know the extent of it from the *Liber pontificalis*. Nevertheless, the 'donations' of Charles and his father cannot be discarded as papal fiction, since their authenticity is confirmed by later correspondence between Pope Hadrian and Charlemagne, especially so in a letter sent by Hadrian to Charlemagne in 778, four years after the 'donation', complaining that the king had still not discharged his promise[52]. Pepin never surrendered actual control over the territories 'assigned' to the pope and neither did Charlemagne, nor any of his successors for that

---

sicut in eadem donatione continere monstratur, id est: a Lunis cum insula Corsica, deinde in Suriano, deinde in monte Bardone, id est in Verceto, deinde in Parma, deinde in Regio; et exinde in Mantua atque Monte Silicis, simulque et universum exarchatum Ravennantium, sicut antiquitus erat, atque provincias Venetiarum et Istria; necnon et cunctum ducatum Spolitinum seu Beneventanum).

51   *Liber pontificalis*, Hadrianus I,43, ed. Duchesne 1, 498: 'Aliaque eiusdem donationis exempla per scrinium huius sanctae nostrae Romanae ecclesiae adscriptam eius excellentia secum deportavit'.

52   *Codex carolinus* no 60, MGH *Epistolae* 3, 585-587 (587)): 'We beg of you, our beloved son and illustrious king, for the love of God and the bearer of the keys to the kingdom of heaven who condescended to grant the throne of the kingdom of your father to you, to order the implementation within our lifetime of everything you have promised to the same for the sake of your soul and the stability of your kingdom, so that the Church of the almighty God may remain exalted and that all you have promised may be fulfilled, just as the Holy Catholic and Apostolic Church of Rome has been elevated and exalted in the days of the holy Pope Silvester by the grant of the power over these territories in the West by the mighty and most pious Emperor Constantine of blessed memory. May she remain exalted like this in your blessed lifetime, so that all nations who hear of this may say: 'Lo and behold, a new and most Christian Constantine has arisen in our days by whose intervention God has condescended to assign all to his Holy Church of Peter, the holy prince of Apostles". (*hoc deprecamur vestram excellentiam, amantissime fili et praeclare rex, pro Dei amore et ipsius clavigeri regni caelorum, qui solium regni patris vestri vobis largiri dignatus est: ut secundum promissionem, quam polliciti estis eidem Dei apostolo pro animae vestrae mercaede et stabilitate regni vestri, omnia nostris temporibus adimplere iubeatis, ut ecclesia Dei omnipotentis ... exaltata permaneat et omnia secundum vestram pollicationem adinpleantur ... sicut temporibus beati Silvestri Romani pontificis a sanctae recordationis piissimo Constantino magno imperatore per eius largitatem sancta Dei catholica et apostolica Romana ecclesia elevata atque exaltata est, et potestatem in his Hesperiae partibus largiri dignatus, ita et in his vestris felicissimis temporibus ... exaltata permaneat, ut omnes gentes, quae hoc audierint, edicere valeant ... ecce novus christianissimus Dei Constantinus imperator his temporibus surrexit, per quem omnia Deus sanctae suae ecclesiae beati apostolorum principis Petri largiri dignatus est*). This letter is extremely important since it proves beyond any doubt that the forgery of the 'Donation of Constantine' was already current *before* 778 and was, even more importantly, directly related to the 'Donation of Pepin'.

matter. If the pope was to have any 'power' (*potestas*) over the territories and cities 'conveyed' to him, it was to be purely symbolical[53].

After Charles had returned from Rome to his army before the walls of Pavia, 'the wrath of God descended on the Lombards'[54]. The city was taken, Desiderius was captured and dispatched to a monastery, and the Lombard princes submitted to the king of the Franks[55]. Henceforward, the Lombard kingdom was to be a constituent part of the Frankish empire but as a separate vassal kingdom, the 'kingdom of Italy' (*regnum italicum*), to be ruled by a Frankish king from its ancient capital Pavia[56]. The first Frankish 'king of Italy' was Charles' third son Pepin (777-810), duly consecrated by Pope Hadrian in Rome as 'king of Italy' in 781[57].

Charlemagne
crowned as
Roman Emperor

Pope Hadrian I died on Christmas Day 795 after a pontificate of 23 years, an extraordinary long period for a Roman pope. During all these years he had been on excellent terms with Charlemagne, who deeply mourned the demise of the man he regarded as his 'father'[58]. Hadrian's successor Leo III was elected the next day and consecrated

---

53 It is unclear what the Frankish kings (Pepin and Charlemagne) really intended with their territorial grants to the pope, given the fact that they were never to be seriously completed by a genuine transfer of possession. The pope had no troops of his own to enforce the establishment of actual control over these territories and depended on Frankish forces to help him do so, which they never did. Consequently, the 'Papal State' remained confined in this period to the borders of the old Byzantine 'duchy' (*ducatus*) of Rome, a province of the ancient Byzantine Exarchat.

54 *Liber pontificalis*, Hadrianus 44, ed. Duchesne 1, 499: '*ira Dei super omnes Langobardos qui in eadem civitate erant crassaretur atque seviret*'.

55 *Annales regni Francorum* ad ann. 774, MGH *SS rer. Germ.* 6, 3): '*Et revertente domno Carolo rege a Roma, et iterum ad Papiam pervenit, ipsam civitatem coepit et Desiderium regem cum uxore et filia vel cum omni thesauro eius palatii. Ibique venientes omnes Langobardi de cunctis civitatibus Italiae, subdiderunt se in dominio domni gloriosi Caroli regis et Francorum*'. See also *Chronica monasterii Casinensis* (Leo) 1,12, ad ann. 773, MGH *SS* 7, 589.

56 The Lombard kingdom covered an area much bigger than the present Italian province of Lombardy. It consisted of North Italy, the margraveship of Tuscany, the duchy of Spoleto and, nominally, the duchy of Benevento in the south. Charlemagne had not conquered that duchy and the Lombard duke of Benevento Arechi II reacted to Charles' conquest by declaring himself independent of the Lombard kingdom, assuming the lofty title of 'prince (*princeps*)'.

57 *Annales Laureshamenses*, ad ann. 781 (MGH *SS* 1, p. 31-32): '*Perrexit rex Carlus Romam, et baptizatus est ibi filius eius, qui vocabatur Carlomannus; quem Adrianus papa mutato nomine vocavit Pepinum, et unxit in regem super Italiam*'. Pepin was initially christened as Karloman but renamed by Hadrian as Pepin at the instigation of Charles. This was the first time Charles returned to Italy after his 773-774 expedition.

58 Charlemagne organized a poetry contest for an epitaph on the deceased pontiff. It was won by Alcuin. The epitaph was inscribed on marble and installed in Saint Peter, where it still is. This is how it ends (*Epitaphium Hadriani papae*, MGH *Poetae* 1, 113, r. 23-24): 'I join our names with their titles, Hadrian-Charles, I the king and you the father' (*Nomina iungo simul titulis, clarissime, nostra/'Hadrianus Carolus', rex ego tuque pater*).

the day after[59]. Not so long ago, the election of a Roman patriarch had to be confirmed by the emperor in Constantinople before he could be consecrated[60]. Now the Roman *patricius* in the West, Charlemagne, was immediately notified of the election *and* consecration of Leo[61]. The emperor in Constantinople, Constantine VI, was simply ignored.

The pontificate of Leo III (795-816) was not a happy one. His predecessor had reigned for a very long time and members of Hadrian's family must have been granted lucrative leases of papal real estate[62]. It seems that Hadrian's relatives were uneasy about the future of their vested interests, causing them to attack the pope in 799[63]. Leo was severely wounded but survived the assassination attempt and fled to the *patricius Romanorum*, Charlemagne, who was in Saxony at the time. It was there, at Paderborn, that Charlemagne met Leo, now miraculously healed from all the wounds inflicted on him[64]. Charles had heard serious complaints about the administration of Leo and decided to come to Rome himself to restore order there, sending Leo ahead accompanied by some royal envoys to secure his safety[65]. Leo returned

---

59   *Liber pontificalis, Leo III* 2, ed. Duchesne 2, 1: '*a cunctis sacerdotibus seu proceribus et omni clero, necnon et obtimatibus vel cuncto populo Romano, Dei nutu, in natale beati primi martyris Stephani electus est, et sequenti die, in natale sancti Johannis apostoli et evangelistae, ad laudem et gloriam omnipotenti Deo, pontificis in sedem apostolicam ordinatus est*'.

60   See *supra* p. 47, fnt. 35.

61   *Annales regni Francorum* ad ann. 796, MGH *SS rer. Germ.* 6, 98: 'Pope Hadrian died and as soon as he had succeeded him, Leo sent envoys with gifts to the king, the keys to the grave of Saint Peter and the banner of the city of Rome' (*Adrianus papa obiit, et Leo, mox ut in locum eius successit, misit legatos cum muneribus ad regem; claves etiam confessionis sancti Petri et vexillum Romanae urbis eidem direxit*).

62   The pope was not entitled to dispose of real estate belonging to the Church at will, since it was inalienable (for this see C. 1,2,14 pr. (Leo and Anthemius, 470)). He could, however, grant a lease of papal real estate for a term of years, creating the problem whether the leases would be renewed after the term had expired on the same (favourable) conditions as before. Since Hadrian's papacy had lasted for a very long time, some of these terms may have been about to expire, which accounts for the unrest among his relatives after his demise.

63   The contemporary Byzantine chronicler Theophanes Confessor (*c.* 760-817/818), *Chronographia* ad ann. 789, ed. Classen I, Bonn 1839, 732, indicates that the insurrection against Leo III was initiated by relatives of Hadrian I.

64   According to the *Liber pontificalis* (*Leo III* 12, ed. Duchesne 2, 4-5), Leo had been blinded and his tongue had been cut out, details confirmed by Charles' biographer Einhard, *Vita Karoli magni* 28, MGH, *SS* 2, 458: '*erutis oculis, linguaque amputata*'. Thanks to the help of the Lord at the intervention of St Peter, his eyesight was miraculously restored, as was his tongue: *Liber pontificalis, Leo III* 13 (ed. Duchesne 2, 5): '*Domino annuente atque beato Petro clavigero regni caelorum suffragante, et visum recepit et lingua ad loquendum illi restituta est*'. For the meeting at Paderborn see *Annales Lauresbamenses* ad ann. 799, MGH *SS* 1, 37): '*domnus rex ... resedit ad Padresbrunna, et ibi venit ad eum domnus Leo apostolicus, quem antea volebant Romani interficere, et suscepit eum domnus rex honorifice*'.

65   *Annales Lauresbamenses* ad ann. 799, MGH *SS* 1, 37: '*domnus rex ... resedit ad Padresbrunna, et ibi venit ad eum domnus Leo apostolicus, quem ... postea cum pace et honore magno eum remisit ad propriam sedem; et missi domni regis deducebant eum honorifice*'. The

to Rome on 29 November 799 and was reinstalled in his Lateran palace, anxiously awaiting the arrival of the mighty king of the Franks and Roman *patricius*[66]. Charles announced an expedition to Italy at a diet held at Mainz in August 800 and by the end of November of that year he was before the walls of Rome. It was there, on 1 December 800, that he finally disclosed the real purpose of his visit to his vassals: his coronation as Emperor of the Romans[67]. The issue had been the subject of secret negotiations between Charles and the pope on the one hand and the imperial court in Constantinople on the other since there was to be no restoration of the Roman Empire in the West without the approval of the Roman emperor in the East[68]. It seems that the incumbent ruler in Constantinople, Irene (797-802), had agreed and Charles now felt free to announce his coming coronation publicly. There was, however, a delicate issue to be decided before that ceremony could be performed since the participation of the pope, as patriarch of Rome, was considered indispensable[69]. But Pope Leo III was a seriously compromised pontiff, who stood accused of misgovernment.

---

possibility to put the pope on trial was discussed at the time in the court of Charlemagne. See on this issue a letter by Alcuin to Archbishop Arno of Salzburg, written in 799, in MGH, *Epistolae* 4, no 179, 296-297 and *infra* p. 55, fnt. 71. Archbishop Arno was among the royal envoys accompanying the pope on his way back to Rome.

66   For Leo's return to Rome see *Liber pontificalis, Leo III* 19-20, ed. Duchesne 2, 6.

67   As a matter of course, Charles had disclosed the objectives of his Italian expedition on the Mainz diet in August: the reinstatement of Leo III in Rome and the punishment of the rebellious 'prince' of Benevento (see *supra* p. 52, fnt. 56). He had split his army in Ravenna, ordering his son Pepin, the king of Italy, to proceed to Benevento while he went to Rome with the rest of the army. For all this see *Annales Laureshamenses,* ad ann. 800, MGH *SS* 1, 38 and *Annales regni Francorum* ad ann. 800, MGH *SS rer. Germ.* 6, 110. Consequently, when it is reported that Charles 'convened an assembly where he disclosed to all why he had come to Rome' (*rex contione vocata, cur Romam venisset, omnibus patefecit* (*Annales regni Francorum* ad ann. 800, MGH *SS rer. Germ.* 6, 111)) on 1 December, he must have disclosed something new, *i.e.* his impending imperial coronation.

68   Theophanes Confessor, *Chronographia* ad ann. 794, ed. Classen I, 736-737, reports an ambassy of representatives of Pope Leo and Charles to Constantinople. He believed it was about a possible marriage between the incumbent Byzantine emperor, Irene, and Charles, thus uniting East and West. He was close, since the real subject seems to have been the restoration of the union between the Eastern and the Western Roman Empire by the resuscitation of the Western Empire. Frankish sources (*Annales regni Francorum* ad ann. 798, MGH *SS rer. Germ.* 6, 104) mention Byzantine envoys at the court of Charlemagne in Aachen in 798. Charles was indeed a widower since the demise of his wife Luitgard in 800 but he will certainly not have considered a marriage with Irene, a very dangerous woman. She had deposed and murdered her own son, the Emperor Constantine VI, in 797.

69   Ever since the consecration of Pepin I (see *supra* p. 42), the participation of a cleric was a crucial element in the inauguration ceremony of a Frankish king. He had to perform the unction and the laying on of hands on the head of the king to bestow the spiritual blessing. It was to be a part of the installation of the new Roman emperor in the West as well. In this, it differed from the inauguration of a Byzantine emperor. See *supra* p. 42, fnt. 13 and *infra* p. 56, fnt. 75.

Even before his inauguration as Roman emperor, Charlemagne was confronted with a conundrum that was to trouble all his successors, including Frederick II[70]: could a pope be put on trial? The issue had been discussed in Charlemagne's court before his departure to Rome and his learned advisor Alcuin had observed that '*he remembered to have read once that the Apostolic See may judge but is not to be judged*'[71]. Alcuin was well informed, since there was, indeed, a rule of canon law that the pope was immune from persecution by any authority but for God[72]. As a matter of course, the Roman clergy supporting Leo III referred to this rule: '*We dare not judge the Apostolic See which is the head of all the churches of God*'[73]. Nevertheless, Charles seems to have put pressure on the pope since Leo was ready to exculpate himself by publicly swearing an oath of purgation[74]. It was only after this ceremony that the king agreed to be crowned and consecrated as Roman emperor by that pontiff on 25 December 800 in the old basilica Constantine had built for Saint Peter. It was the first time a Roman patriarch officially participated in the inauguration of a Roman emperor.

According to the reports of Charles' coronation, Charles was instated according to the ritual for the inauguration of a contemporary

---

70   See *infra* p. 340.

71   MGH, *Epistolae* 4, no 179, 297: '*Memini me legisse quondam, si rite recordor … apostolicam sedem iudiciariam esse, non iudicandam*'.

72   *Decretum* C. 9, q. 3, cap. 13: 'No one shall judge the First See. The judge <of all> will not be judged by the emperor and not by the clergy, neither by kings, nor by the people' (*Nemo enim iudicabit primam sedem iustitiam temperare desiderantem. Neque enim ab Augusto, neque ab omni clero, neque a regibus, neque a populo iudex iudicabitur*). Gratian copied this rule from the 'Decretals of Pseudo-Isidor' (ed. Hinschius, 449), "the Pantheon of papal prerogatives" (Ullmann), compiled sometime in the middle of the ninth century and containing many forged documents, sometimes much older, such as the Donation of Constantine (see supra p. 30, fnt. 10) and this one as well. It was concocted as long ago as the early sixth century when Pope Symmachus (498-514) was put on trial on charges of embezzlement and indecent conduct before a council convened in Rome at the behest of King Theodoric. Symmachus's lawyers rewrote a genuine decretal of Pope Gelasius I (C. 9, q. 3, cap. 16), containing the rule that the pope is the highest court of appeal of the Church, in the sense that the pope himself cannot be judged by anyone but God, attributing it to a fictitious council held in Rome during the pontificate of Silvester I (c. 20, Mansi 2, col. 632), hence the name '*Constitutum Silvestri*'. The charges against Symmachus were dropped accordingly (*Acta synhodorum habitarum Romae* 498, 501, 502, *Quarta synodus* (501), ed. Mommsen, MGH *Auct. Ant.* 12, 431): '*Symmachus papa sedis apostolicae praesul … sit immunis*'.

73   *Liber pontificalis, Leo III* 21, ed. Duchesne 2, 7: 'We dare not judge the Apostolic See which is the head of all the churches of God. For all of us are judged by him and his vicar but he himself is to be judged by no one, as has been the custom of old' (*Nos sedem apostolicam, quae est caput omnium Dei ecclesiarum, iudicare non audemus. Nam ab ipsa nos omnes et vicario suo iudicamur: ipsa autem a nemine iudicatur, quemadmodum et antiquitus mos fuit*).

74   *Liber pontificalis, Leo III* 21, ed. Duchesne 2, 7: 'I am ready to purify myself of these false charges that have been unjustly brought against me' (*de talibus falsis criminationibus quae super me nequiter exarserunt, me purificare paratus sum*).

Byzantine emperor, consisting of the coronation and the public assent of the people present at the occasion (*acclamatio*), cheering three times 'Life and victory to Charles, the most pious *Augustus*, the great peace bringing emperor crowned by God!' (*Karolo piissimo augusto a deo coronato, magno et pacifico imperatore vita et victoria!*)[75]. A new Constantine had arisen in the West, endowed with all the authority of the Roman emperors of old, as Charlemagne himself made abundantly clear immediately after his coronation. He discarded the Roman title of *patricius* and styled himself as 'Charles, the most sublime *Augustus* crowned with the consent of God, ruling the Roman Empire' (*Karolus, divino nutu coronatus, Romanum regens imperium, serenissimus augustus*)[76]. The elevation of Charlemagne as Roman emperor in the West created new challenges for the Roman papacy. True as it might be that it had now definitively dissociated itself from the authority of (and the submission to) the emperor in Constantinople, it had established a new power much closer to Rome, a monarch surpassing all other kings and princes in the West. As king of the Franks and Lombards, Charlemagne ruled over many nations in the West, but as Roman emperor he ruled over all. Even the kings not subject to his immediate power (*potestas*), like the petty Saxon kings in Britain or the king of Denmark, were sub-

---

75 The '*acclamatio*' was the key element in the inauguration of an emperor of the ancient Roman Empire. The '*acclamatio*' of Charlemagne is reported by two contemporary sources independent of each other: in the *Liber pontificalis*, Leo III 23, ed. Duchesne 2, 7 and the *Annales regni Francorum* ad ann. 801, MGH *SS rer. Germ.* 6, 112. Both sources also mention the coronation of Charles by the pope. Charles' anointment is mentioned by the *Liber pontificalis* but is missing in the *Annales regni Francorum*. The *Liber pontificalis*, however, significantly leaves out an essential element stressed by the *Annales regni Francorum*: 'the pope prostrated himself before him according to the ancient tradition of the emperors' (*ab apostolico more antiquorum principum adoratus est*). It was the *adoratio* (προσκύνησις) owed by a subject to the imperial majesty in contemporary Byzantine court ceremonial. The ancient Roman emperors in the West were never coronated, let alone anointed, by the pope in Rome since the ancient Roman imperial inauguration was a purely secular affair. Coronations were sometimes part of it, but not necessarily by a cleric. Justinian I was coronated by his predecessor, his uncle Justin (*Chronicon Paschale* ad ann. 527, ed. Dindorf, 616): 'the most pious Justinian was coronated by the most Godfearing Justin, his uncle' (ὁ εὐσεβέστατος Ἰουστινιανὸς ... ἐστέφθη ὑπὸ τοῦ θειοτάτου Ἰουστίνου τοῦ αὐτοῦ θείου). It was only later that the patriarch of Constantinople did, indeed, crown the emperor, but always after the '*acclamatio*'. The anointment of a monarch is a custom typical of the West: see *supra* p. 42, fnt. 13.
76 For this style see Charles' *Capitulare italicum*, issued in 801, MGH, *Capit.* 1, no 98, 204. The imperial statute is dated as follows: 'in the 23rd year of our reign in Francia, in the 28th year of our reign in Italy, *in the first year of our consulate*' (*anno vero regni nostri in Frantia xxxiii, in Italia xxviii, consulatus autem nostri primo*) (emphasis added). To the medieval mind, the Roman Empire had not fallen long ago, but was still a reality: the Roman Empire of the East, the Byzantine Empire, was very much alive and a force to be reckoned with, especially on the Italian peninsula. The Roman Empire was generally identified with the legendary 'Fourth World-Empire', the 'Last Empire', revealed to Nebuchadnezzar by the prophet Daniel (Daniel 2:36-40).

ject to his imperial authority (*auctoritas*) since the Roman emperor was *totius orbis imperator*, the Lord of the World, to whom all kings and princes owed obedience[77]. The pope had been instrumental in the rise of the Carolingian dynasty, first by securing the royal title for Pepin and his descendants and later by raising Charles to the august dignity of Roman emperor. It was a potential threat to the supreme authority of the papacy though, certainly so when the emperor publicly demonstrated his own authority as emphatically as Charlemagne did in 813 by crowning his son Louis as co-emperor at Aachen himself[78]. Shortly after, on 28 January 814, the Great Charles (*Carolus Magnus*, Charlemagne) died, leaving his son Louis in sole command[79]. He simply styled himself as 'Louis, emperor by divine providence' (*Hludowicus, divina ordinante providentia imperator augustus*)[80], indicating that he derived his title from God directly and at the same time demonstrating that a clerical imperial consecration was dispensable. The aging Pope Leo III did not

---

77   Pope John VIII (872-882) styled the Roman emperors as 'lords of the whole world' (*totius orbis domini, Epistolae*, Ep. 104, Migne *PL* 126, col. 753) and reminded the son of the emperor Charles the Bald (875-877) that, once he had succeeded to the empire, 'all kingdoms shall be subject to you' (*omnia vobis regna subjecta existent*, Ep. 242, Migne *PL* 126, col. 853).

78   The best record of this important event is in the contemporary chronicle of Moissiac ad ann. 813, MGH *SS* 1, 310-311: 'Charles held a diet with the bishops, abbots, counts and magnates of the realm to establish his son Louis as king and emperor. All of them agreed, saying that it was good, and it pleased all of the people and with the consent and acclamation of everyone he elevated his son Louis as emperor and he granted the imperial power to him with a crown of gold, while all the people applauded and cried out 'Long live the emperor Louis'. And there was great joy among the people that day because the emperor praised the Lord, saying 'Praise to you, oh Lord, who made me see the son born of my seed sitting on my throne today with my own eyes' (*Karolus ... habuit consilium cum praefatis episcopis et abbatibus et comitibus et maioribus natu Francorum, ut constituerent filium suum Ludovicum regem et imperatorem. Qui omnes pariter consenserunt, dicentes hoc dignum esse: omnique populo placuit, et cum consensu et acclamatione omnium populorum Ludovicum filium suum constituit imperatorem secum, ac per coronam auream tradidit ei imperium, populis acclamantibus et dicentibus:* Vivat imperator Ludovicus. *Et facta est laetitia magna in populo in illa die. Nam et ipse imperator benedixit Dominum dicens:* Benedictus es domine Deus, qui dedisti hodie sedentem in solio meo ex semine meo filium, videntibus oculis meis). See also *Annales regni Francorum* ad ann. 813, MGH *SS rer. Germ.* 6, 138: 'having summoned his son Louis, the king of Aquitane, to his presence at Aachen, he crowned him and made him consort to the imperial title' (*evocatum ad se apud Aquisgrani filium suum Hludowicum Aquitaniae regem, coronam illi inposuit et imperialis nominis sibi consortem fecit; Bernhardumque nepotem suum, filium Pepini filii sui, Italiae praefecit et regem appellari iussit*). Louis was king of Aquitane since the *Divisio regnorum* of 806 (see *infra* p. 62). Louis' biographer Thegan (*fl.* 800-850), a cleric from Trier (*Gesta Hludowici imperatoris* 6, MGH *SS rer. Germ.* 64, 184), reports that Charles did not crown his son, but that Louis crowned himself at the order of his father.

79   *Annales regni Francorum* ad ann. 814, MGH *SS rer. Germ.* 6, 140: '*Domnus Karolus imperator, dum Aquisgrani hiemaret, anno aetatis circiter septuagesimo primo ... V. Kal. Febr. rebus humanis excessit*'.

80   See the 815 and 816 statutes of Louis in MGH *Capit.* 1, no 132 and 133, 261 and 263. Note that Louis left out all the tribal royal titles Charlemagne had still added to his own style.

react, but his successor, Pope Stephen IV (816-817), did. He realized the authority of the Roman pontiff had to be reasserted at all cost.

The
Hludowicianum

The pontifical transition of 816 was crucial since Pope Stephen IV was the first pope to be elected after the restoration of the Roman Empire in the West. It accounts for the urgency of his mission to visit the Emperor Louis. According to the time-honoured Byzantine tradition, a papal election ought to be confirmed by the emperor before the pope could be consecrated[81], but Pope Stephen had been elected *and* consecrated without imperial confirmation[82]. He had administered an oath of loyalty to the emperor to the people of Rome immediately on his accession[83], but he realized his precipitous ordination might cause offence to the emperor, which is why he had sent two ambassadors ahead to announce his imminent arrival in Gaul 'to account for his ordination'[84]. The emperor and the pope met at Reims on or about 2 October 816[85]. The pope, a scion of a Roman noble family and educated in the

---

81 See *supra* p. 47, fnt. 35.

82 *Liber pontificalis*, Stephen IV 1, ed. Duchesne 2, 49: '*dum de hac vita migraret antefatus domnus Leo papa ... illico ... Stephen ad sacrum pontificates culmen est electus. Qui uno omnes affectu parique amore eum ad ecclesiam beati Petri apostoli perducentes, Dei ordinante providentia, papa Urbis consecratus est*'.

83 Thegan, *Gesta Hludowici imperatoris* 16, MGH *SS rer. Germ.* 64, 196: '*statim, postquam pontificatum suscepit, iussit omnem populum Romanum fidelitatem cum iuramento promittere Ludovico*'.

84 Louis' anonymous biographer, usually called 'The Astronomer' (*Astronomus*) because of his attention to astronomic events, *Vita Hludowici imperatoris* (840-845) 26, MGH *SS rer. Germ.* 64, 364: 'he did not hesitate to go to the emperor after his consecration and hurried to him with great haste. He sent an ambassy ahead to account for his ordination' (*post sui consecrationem ad domnum imperatorem venire non distulit ... summa cum festinatione ei occurrere festinavit. Premisit tamen legationem, que super ordinatione eius imperatori satisfaceret*). See also *Annales regni Francorum* ad ann. 816, MGH *SS rer. Germ.* 6,144: 'Stephen hastened to come to the emperor travelling as fast as he could, while he sent two envoys ahead to explain his consecration to the emperor' (*Stephen ... quam maximis poterat itineribus ad imperatorem venire contendit, missis interim duobus legatis, qui quasi pro sua consecratione imperatori suggererent*). The urgency of Stephen's mission is also stressed by the *Liber pontificalis*, Stephen IV 2, ed. Duchesne 2, 49: 'As soon as that most holy man was ordained as pontiff, he went on a journey to Gaul, to the most pious and illustrious lord, the Emperor Louis, to reinforce the peace and unity of the Holy Church of God' (*Hic sanctissimus vir, in pontificatu iam positus, pro confirmanda pace et unitate sanctae Dei ecclesiae, Franciae arreptus est iter, apud piissimum et serenissimum domnum Ludowicum imperatorem*).

85 It is reported by one of Louis' biographers, Thegan, that Louis prostrated himself three times before the pope at this occasion (*Gesta Hludowici imperatoris* 16, MGH *SS rer. Germ.* 64, 196): '*princeps prosternens se cum omni corpore in terra tribus vicibus ante pedes sancti pontificis ... salutavit pontificem*'. The 'Astronomer' does not mention this (*Vita Hludowici imperatoris* 26, MGH *SS rer.Germ.* 64, 366), nor do the *Annales regni Francorum* ad ann. 816, MGH *SS rer. Germ.* 6,144. The incident as reported by Thegan is highly unlikely, if only because there were people present who still remembered that pope Leo III had prostrated himself before Charlemagne as the Byzantine ritual prescribed (see *supra* p. 56, fnt. 75).

court of Hadrian I and Leo III, seems to have employed a risky diplomatic tactic to distract the attention of his counterpart, the emperor,
from the weakness of his position by maximizing his demands. The
tactic worked (as it sometimes does): Stephen seems to have advanced
an acceptable excuse for his precipitate ordination; he persuaded the
emperor to have himself be crowned and consecrated by him *and* he
achieved the confirmation of all the privileges granted (but not executed) by Louis' predecessors, Pepin and Charles, at the same time[86].
It was a stunning accomplishment, most likely due to the gullibility of
the Emperor Louis[87].

Pope Stephen IV died soon after he had returned to Rome. He was
succeeded by Paschal I (817-824), elected *and* consecrated only two
days after the demise of his predecessor. Accordingly, he sent a 'letter of apology' (*excusatoria epistola*) to Louis expressing his regret of
having been forced to unwillingly accept his ordination[88]. Paschal also
requested the confirmation of the special privileges Louis, his father,
and grandfather had granted to his predecessors and Louis conveniently complied (yet again), sending Paschalis's ambassador Theodorus
back to Rome with a copy of his grant (*pactum*)[89]. The 'donations' of
Pepin and Charlemagne are now lost, but Louis' grant, the so-called

---

86 *Annales regni Francorum* ad ann. 816, MGH *SS rer. Germ.* 6,144: 'Having explained the
cause of his arrival and after a solemn mass had been celebrated in the usual way, he crowned
him by placing a crown on his head. After many gifts were exchanged and many sumptuous
banquets held and having establshed a solid mutual friendship established and other benefits
granted to the advantage of the Holy Church of God, the pope went to Rome and the emperor
to his palace in Compiègne' (*Qui statim imperatori adventus sui causam insinuans celebratis ex
more missarum sollemniis eum diadematis inpositione coronavit. Multis deinde inter eos muneribus et datis et acceptis conviviis opipare celebratis et amicitia vicissim firmissimo robore constituta
aliisque utilitatibus sanctae Dei ecclesiae pro temporis opportunitate dispositis pontifex Romam,
imperator Compendium palatium petiit*).
87 This is how the *Liber pontificalis*, Stephen IV 2, ed. Duchesne 2, 49, describes his achievement: 'There are hardly words to describe the honour and exultation with which he was received by the aforementioned most pious prince and the people of the Franks. And the Lord
granted him such favour that he succeeded to be granted everything of all he had come to ask
for' (*cum Franciam pervenisset, tanto honore atque exultatione a praedicto piissimo principe atque
Francorum populo susceptus est quanto vix lingua narrare potest; et tantam illi Dominus gratiam
largire dignatus est ut omnia quaecumque ab eo poposcisse dinoscitur, in omnibus impetravit*).
88 *Annales regni Francorum* ad ann. 817, MGH *SS rer. Germ.* 6,145: '*Stephen papa …obiit.
Cui Paschalis successor electus post completam sollenniter ordinationem suam et munera et excu-
satoriam imperatori misit epistolam, in qua sibi non solum nolenti, sed etiam plurimum renitenti
pontificatus honorem veluti impactum adseverat*'. For the vacancy of two days see *Liber pontificalis*, Stephen IV 2, ed. Duchesne 2, 50: '*Et cessavit episcopatus dies II*'.
89 *Annales regni Francorum* ad ann. 817, MGH *SS rer. Germ.* 6,145: '*Missa tamen alia legatione pactum quod cum praecessoribus suis factum erat etiam secum fieri et firmari rogavit. Hanc
legationem Theodorus et detulit et ea, quae petierat, impetravit*'.

Hludowicianum, has survived (more or less)[90] and was widely known in the Middle Ages, if only because fragments of it were inserted into Gratian's *Decretum* (Dist. 63, cap. 30), the authoritative textbook of canon law throughout the Middle Ages. It is an astonishing document, meticulously specifying all cities, villages, islands, and territories granted to the pope on and near the Italian peninsula, including, of course, the Exarchate of Ravenna and the Marche, but also territories in Tuscany, Umbria, Campania, and other regions of the peninsula, explicitly stipulating that they were all to be held 'in his own right, sovereignty, and dominion' (*in iure suo, principatu atque ditione*) by Paschal and his successors. It is one of the key documents of European medieval history since all medieval Roman emperors to be crowned by the pope were to confirm the *Hludowicianum*[91]. However, due to the medieval clergy's notorious propensity for forgery, the original content of the *Hludowicianum* is, to put it mildly, a matter of dispute. The original is lost, and we do not have a contemporary copy: the modern editions are largely dependent on copies from the 11th and 12th century[92]. This makes one of the most important aspects of the *Hludowicianum* rather dubious. It concerns the grant to the Roman people of the right to elect *and* consecrate the pope without previous confirmation by the emperor, contrary to the well-documented procedure in the ancient Christian Roman Empire[93]. If this particular provision ever was in the

---

90 The latest edition of the *Hludowicianum* is by Kölzer (2016), MGH *DD LdF* 1, no 125, 312-320.

91 See the Bolognese civilian Odofredus († 1265) in his *Lectura super Digesto veteri* ad D. 1,12,1 (ed. Lyon 1550, *f.* 27 vo): 'the popes are shrewd enough never to grant a crown to him before he has confirmed all their privileges to them' (*domini papae sunt ita sagaces, quod non dant ei coronam nisi primo confirmet ei omnia sua privilegia*).

92 From the collection of canon law compiled by Cardinal Deusdedit (†1098/1099): Lib. 3, cap. 280, ed. V.W. of Glanvell, Paderborn 1905, 385-389 and the *Liber censuum* compiled by Cardinal Cencio Savelli (later Pope Honorius III) in 1192, ed. Fabre-Duchesne 1, no 77, 363-365.

93 See supra p. 47, fnt. 35. The relevant provision in the *Hludowicianum* is as follows (MGH *DD LdF* 1, no 125, 319): 'When a pope of this most holy see has left the world on divine invitation, no man from our kingdom, be he a Frank or a Lombard or a man from whatever tribe subject to our power, shall have the right to do wrong to the Romans, publicly or privately, and to hold an election, and no man may dare to do something bad on that account in the cities and territories belonging to the church of the holy Apostle Peter. But the Romans shall be free to honourably bury their pontiff with all due respect and without any obstruction and to consecrate without any ambiguity or contradiction the one all Romans have unanimously elected according to the custom of the Church by divine inspiration and by the intercession of St Peter to the rank of pontiff, and as soon as he has been consecrated ambassadors shall be sent to us or our successors as kings of the Franks, to establish friendship, love, and peace between us and him' (*Quando diuina uocatione huius sacratissimae sedis Pontifex de hoc mundo migrauerit, nullus ex regno nostro aut Francus, aut Longobardus, aut de qualibet gente homo sub nostra potestate constitutus, licentiam habeat contra Romanos aut publice, aut priuatim uenien-di, uel electionem faciendi, nullusque in ciuitatibus aut territoriis ad ecclesiae B. Petri apostoli*

original *Hludowicianum*, it did not survive for long, since it was already repealed in 824 by a statute of Lothair I issued in Rome.

In 823 news had reached the Emperor Louis I that two papal officials loyal to the empire had been murdered in Rome and that Pope Paschal I was most likely involved in that crime[94]. Consequently, the emperor sent some agents to Rome to look into the affair. Paschal I swore an oath of purgation to them that he had nothing to do with that crime (most probably committing perjury in doing so), but he died soon after. When the emperor heard in 824 that the succession to Paschal I was contested and that two competing popes had been elected, he sent his son to Rome again[95] to investigate the matter of the murder of the papal officials; to have a careful look at the administration of justice in Rome and to finally settle the problem of the papal election and consecration. Lothair I did as he was told and issued a statute in Rome, providing that no pope was to be consecrated without imperial approval and that after being elected and consecrated with the assent of the emperor, the pope had to swear an oath of allegiance to the emperor in the presence of imperial representatives[96]. The election of Pope Eugenius II as successor to Paschal I was confirmed by Lothair and after the demise of Eugenius in 827, his successor Gregory IV (827-844) was only consecrated after a previous examination by an imperial envoy sent to Rome for that purpose[97]. The *Constitutio romana* of 824 makes one wonder whether the original *Hludowicianum* did really contain a provision allowing the pope to be consecrated *without* previous authorization by the emperor. It certainly was *not* in the confirmation of the *Hludowicianum* by the Emperor Otto I on his elevation as Roman emperor in 962. Otto I

Constitutio romana

---

potestatem pertinentibus aliquod malum propterea facere presumat; sed liceat Romanis cum omni *ueneratione et sine qualibet perturbatione honorificam suo Pontifici exhibere sepulturam, et eum, quem diuina inspiratione et B. Petri intercessione omnes Romani uno consilio atque concordia sine aliqua promissione ad Pontificatus ordinem elegerint, sine qualibet ambiguitate uel contradictione more canonico consecrare, et, dum consecratus fuerit, legati ad nos, uel ad successores nostros reges Francorum dirigantur, qui inter nos et illum amicitiam et caritatem ac pacem societ*). Significantly, it is *this* part of the *Hludowicianum*, rather than the territorial concessions it contained, that was excerpted by Gratian in his *Decretum* (Dist. 63, cap. 30).

94 For this episode see *Annales regni Francorum* ad ann. 823 and 824, MGH *SS rer. Germ.* 6, 161-166.

95 Lothair had just returned from a visit to Rome in 823, *infra* p. 62, fnt. 100.

96 *Constitutio romana*, MGH *Capit.* 1, no 161, 324): '*et ille qui electus fuerit* me consentiente *consecratus pontifex non fiat, priusquam tale sacramentum faciat in praesentia missi domini imperatoris et populi*' (emphasis added).

97 *Annales regni Francorum* ad ann. 827 (MGH *SS rer. Germ.* 6, 173-174): '*Gregorius presbyter tituli sancti Marci electus, sed non prius ordinatus est, quam legatus imperatoris Romam venit et electionem populi, qualis esset, examinavit*'.

(912-936-962-973) was the first in the long line of German kings to be crowned and consecrated Roman emperor by the pope in Rome[98].

The Tribal Kingdom

Rapid
decline of
Charlemagne's
empire

The memory of Charlemagne looms large over medieval European history, but his empire did not survive the unfortunate rule of his son Louis the Pious (813-840). Charles had made his testament in 806, dividing his enormous realm in accordance with Salian tribal law over his three sons, Charles (the eldest), Pepin, and Louis[99]. There was *no* provision on the succession to the empire, but after Charles and Pepin had died, in 811 and 810 respectively, his only surviving son Louis was the sole successor, which is why Charlemagne appointed him as co-emperor in 813. Unlike his father, Louis I did indeed provide for the 'unity of the empire' (*unitas imperii*) in his political testament, the *Ordinatio imperii* of 817. Louis crowned his eldest son Lothair as co-emperor at Aachen in 817, just like his father had crowned him in 813, but he assigned two separate kingdoms to his two younger sons, Pepin (Aquitane) and Louis (Bavaria), to be held from their older brother as their overlord (*maior potestas*)[100]. Louis' *Ordinatio* provided, furthermore, that the two kingdoms subject to the Emperor Lothair were to be indivisible as well, specifying that the nobles of the kingdom should elect one

---

98 Otto I was not the first 'German' king to be crowned emperor in Rome. That was Arnulf of Carinthia, who was crowned by Pope Formosus in 896 (Regino of Prüm, *Chronicon* ad ann. 896, MGH *SS rer. Germ.* 50, 144): '*Arnulfus … a Formoso apostolicae sedis presule cum magno honore susceptus est et ante confessionem sancti Petri coronatus imperator creatur*'. He was, however, the first in the line of German kings to succeed to the crown of the empire until the end of the Holy Roman Empire in 1806.

99 *Divisio Regnorum*, MGH *Capit.* 1, no 45, 126-130.

100 *Ordinatio imperii* §§ 1 and 2, MGH, *Capit.* 1, no 136, 271. See also *Annales regni Francorum* ad ann. 817, MGH *SS rer. Germ.* 6, 146: 'he held a diet at Aachen according to the custom, where he crowned his first-born Lothair and made him his consort to the title of emperor and the empire; the others were called kings, one of Aquitane and the other of Bavaria' (*conventum Aquisgrani more solito habuit, in quo filium suum primogenitum Hlotarium coronavit et nominis atque imperii sui socium sibi constituit, caeteros reges appellatos unum Aquitaniae, alterum Baioriae praefecit*). Like his father before him, Lothair was later (in 823) consecrated as emperor on a visit to Rome at the insistence of Pope Paschalis I: *Annales regni Francorum* ad ann. 823, MGH *SS rer. Germ.* 6, 160-161: 'But Lothair, when he was dispensing justice in Italy as his father had ordered him and was already about to leave Italy, came to Rome at the request of the pope and was honourably received by him and he received the crown of the kingdom and the title of emperor and Augustus on the holy day of Easter in St Peter' (*Hlotarius vero, cum secundum patris iussionem in Italia iustitias faceret et iam se ad revertendum de Italia praepararet, rogante Paschale papa Romam venit et honorifice ab illo susceptus in sancto paschali die apud sanctum Petrum et regni coronam et imperatoris et augusti nomen accepit*). The 'crown of the kingdom' was the crown of the Lombard kingdom.

of the sons of a king who had died leaving more than one son[101]. It was the origin of the 'French' and 'German' states, 'West Francia' and 'East Francia'. Louis' misfortune was that, after having disposed of his empire in 817, he remarried after the demise of his first wife Irmengard in 818 and unfortunately sired a fourth son, Charles, with his second spouse Judith who was left out of the 817 arrangement (*ordinatio*)[102], much to the chagrin of Judith. The result was civil war between both the three eldest sons and their father and the brothers among themselves, initiating the rapid collapse of the Carolingian Empire and leaving it practically defenceless against the onslaught of the Vikings.

This is not the place to recount the sad story of the mindless civil wars ravaging the Carolingian Empire during and after the reign of Louis the Pious. Suffice it to say that Louis, 'the German' (806-876), and his half-brother Charles, 'the Bald' (823-840-875-877)[103], succeeded in decisively beating their brother Lothair near Fontenoy in 841 and divided Charlemagne's empire in the subsequent treaty of Verdun (843), probably the most consequential treaty in European history leaving its indelible mark on the map of Western Europe even in our own time[104]. Louis was assigned the Eastern, 'German', part of the Empire, Charles the Western, 'French', part, while Lothair, Louis' first born and still titular emperor, held on to an extended strip of land in the

---

101 *Ordinatio imperii* § 14, MGH, *Capit.* 1, no 136, 272: '*Si vero aliquis illorum decedens legitimos filios reliquerit, non inter eos potestas ipsa dividatur; sed potius populus pariter conveniens unum ex eis, quem Dominus voluerit, eligat*'.

102 *Annales regni Francorum* ad ann. 819, MGH *SS rer. Germ.* 6, 150: '*imperator inspectis plerisque nobilium filiabus Huelphi comitis filiam nomine Judith duxit uxorem*' and *Annales Mettenses priores* ad ann. 830, MGH *SS rer. Germ.* 10, 96: '*ipsa* <scl. Judith> *dicto imperatori filium valde eligantem nomine Carolum pepererat*'.

103 Pepin, king of Aquitane, had died in 838, after which Louis I assigned Aquitane to his youngest son Charles, disowning Pepin's minor son Pepin II, causing civil war in Aquitane with most of the nobles taking the side of Pepin against their new king Charles. Pepin II died childless sometime after 864, after he had been imprisoned by Charles the Bald. He was a foolish and reckless man, responsible for inviting the Vikings to join him in his civil war with Charles.

104 The most important source of the civil wars between the sons of Louis the Pious is the *Historiae*, written by Nithard († 845), a grandson of Charlemagne (he was the son of one of Charlemagne's daughters). On the battle of Fontenoy see Nithard, *Historiarum* II, 10-III, 1, MGH *SS rem. Germ.* 44, p. 24-29 and *Annales Bertiniani* (Prudentius of Troyes) (835-861) ad ann. 841, MGH *SS rem. Germ.* 5, 25. The treaty of Verdun was prepared by the triumphant brothers Louis the German and Charles the Bald in a conference at Strasbourg in 842, famous in German and French national history because it turned out the Franks had ceased to share the same language: Louis spoke to his men in the *lingua theodisca* (Lit.: 'the vulgar tongue', 'Deutsch'), whereas Charles addressed his men in the *lingua romana* ('the Romance tongue'). The so-called oaths of Strasbourg are the oldest monuments of the German and French language. They have survived in the report of the conference in Nithard, *Historiarum* III, 5 in MGH *SS rem. Germ.* 44, p. 35-37. For a short summary of the Verdun treaty see the contemporary *Annales Fuldenses* ad ann. 843, MGH *SS rem. Germ.* 7, 34.

middle ranging from the North Sea to the borders of the ancient duchy of Rome in Italy. Lothair I (795-813-855) cared little for the unity of what was left to him of Charlemagne's empire: shortly before he died in 855, he divided his realm over his three sons. His first-born, Louis II (*c.* 825-875), had already been crowned king of Lombardy and Roman emperor before[105] and was to be confined to Italy. Louis' younger brother Lothair II (835-855-869), named after his father, was granted the main part of his father's transalpine possessions soon to be called after him, Lotharingia. The youngest of the three brothers, Charles, was left with the kingdom of Provence[106] and after he died childless in 863 his kingdom was split between his surviving brothers Lothair II and Louis II. When Lothair II expired in 869 without leaving a legitimate offspring, his uncles Louis the German and Charles the Bald split Lotharingia between them in the treaty of Meersen (870)[107], creating two independent kingdoms north of the Alps and a third in Italy, all of them soon to be bereaved of a representative of the Carolingian race as their royal master.

The German
succession

Ever since the demise of King Louis the Child (893-900-911), the last representative of the Carolingian dynasty in the eastern half of

---

105   For the coronation of Louis II as 'king of the Lombards' (*rex Langobardorum*) in 844 by Pope Sergius II (844-847) see *Liber pontificalis*, Sergius II 13, ed. Duchesne 2, 89 and *Annales Bertiniani* (Prudentius of Troyes) (835-861) ad ann. 844, MGH *SS rem. Germ.* 5, 30. For his coronation as Roman emperor by Pope Leo IV (847-855) in 850 see *Annales Bertiniani* (Prudentius of Troyes) ad ann. 850, MGH *SS rem. Germ.* 5, 38.

106   For the treaty of Prüm see Regino of Prüm († 915), *Chronicon* ad ann. 855, MGH *SS rer. Germ.* 50, 77: '*Anno dominicae incarnationis dccclv. Lothair convocatis primoribus regni imperium filiis suis divisit; Ludovico Italiam tradidit eumque imperatorem appellari fecit, equivoco vero, id est Lothario, regnum, quod ex suo nomine vocatur, concessit, Carolo autem, qui iunior natu erat, Provintiae regnum largitus est.*

107   The division of Lotharingia in the treaty of Meersen is reported in great detail in *Annales Bertiniani* (Hincmar of Reims) ad ann. 870, MGH *SS rem. Germ.* 5, 109-113. It was later (in 880) corrected in the treaty of Ribémont, much to the disadvantage of the king of West-Francia since all of Lotharingia was thereby assigned to the king of East-Francia in return for his promise to renounce his claim to the throne of West-Francia. For the treaty of Ribémont between the 'German' King Louis the Younger (835-876-882) and the two sons of King Louis II of West-Francia ('the Stammerer', 846-877-879), who shared the kingdom between them, see Regino of Prüm, *Chronicon* ad ann. 879(880), MGH *SS rer. Germ.* 50, 115: 'they conceded the whole part of the kingdom of Lothair that was held by their grandfather and father to him' (*portionem regni Lotharii, quam avus paterque tenuerat, ex integro illi concesserunt*). I must apologize to the reader for the many Pepins, Louises, Lothairs and Charleses on these few pages, but he may rest assured: the Carolingian race will soon have vanished 'because the royal race became extinct by premature deaths or the sterility of the spouses' (*ipsa regia stirpe partim immatura aetate pereunte partim sterilitate coniugum marcescente*) (Regino of Prüm, *Chronicon* ad ann. 881, MGH *SS rer. Germ.* 50, 117).

Charlemagne's empire we now know as 'Germany'[108], the choice of a successor fell on the chieftains of the various German tribes living in that kingdom, Saxons, Bavarians, Swabians, Franks, and Thuringians. They were assisted by three representatives of the clergy, a 'tribe' of its own[109], the incumbents of the three oldest episcopates in the kingdom, dating back to Roman times, the archbishops of Mainz, Cologne, and Trier. In practice, however, the king was succeeded by the son he had presented to his tribal chieftains as his successor during his lifetime. It was not a typically German procedure, since it was also the standard procedure in the kingdom of France after the demise, in 987, of Louis V, the last Carolingian king of the western half of Charlemagne's empire we now know as 'France'. The only difference is that the house of Hugo Capet (939-987-996) was able to produce a continuous chain of succession until 1328[110], whereas the German line of succession was at times interrupted. It was on these occasions that a true election was called for but, even then, consanguinity was of importance.

The German tribal leaders elected the chieftain (*dux*) of the Frankish tribe as their new king in 911, primarily because he was a Frank and because it was felt that a member of the Frankish tribe ought to rule over East-Francia[111]. It was Conrad I (911-918)[112]. His short reign was trou-

---

108 The Carolingian monarchy was hereditary see *supra* p. 46. As a matter of course, the same held for the three monarchies carved out of Charlemagne's empire by the treaty of Verdun (843). In West-Francia the direct Carolingian line expired after the demise of King Louis V (987). The magnates of West-Francia elected Hugo Capet (939-996) as his successor, the first of 'the kings of the third race' ('les roys de la troisième race'), as the saying is in France.
109 In the early Middle Ages, the clergy was legally considered as a distinct tribe, living under Roman law rather than the law under which a member of the clergy was originally born. See *Lex ribuaria* 61,1, MGH, *LL nat. Germ.* 3,2, p. 109: '*secundum legem romanam, quam ecclesia vivit*' and the Lombard *Leges Liutprandi* art. 153, MGH, *LL* 4 (*Leges Langobardorum*) 175: 'Whenever a married Lombard has fathered sons or daughters and subsequently has become a cleric due to the inspiration of God, then the sons and daughters who were born before he converted to the clergy live according to the same law as he himself had lived when he fathered them and they have to bring their legal proceedings under that same law' (*Si quis Langobardus uxorem habens filios aut filias procreavit, et postea inspirationem Dei compulsus clericus effectus fuerit, tunc filii aut filiae qui ante eius conversionem nati fuerunt, ipsam legem vivant, quam ille vivebat, quando eos genuit, et causam suam per ipsam legem finire debeant*).
110 The last French king to be presented as co-regent during the lifetime of his predecessor in order to secure an uncontested succession was King Philip II 'Auguste' (1065-1079-1223). As from then the French monarchy was hereditary by custom.
111 Whenever a member of another German tribe than the Frankish tribe was elected king of the Germans, he changed tribal 'nationality' by operation of law and became a Frank (Eike of Repgow (c. 1180-c. 1233), *Sachsenspiegel, Landrecht* III, 54 § 4, ed. Eckhard, MGH *Fontes iuris N.S.* 1,1, 240): 'As soon as he is elected, the king shall live according to Frankish law, whatever his origin may be' (*De koning scal hebben vrenkisch recht swen he gekoren is, of welker bord <dat> he si*).
112 *Annales Alamannici*, ad ann. 912, MGH SS 1, p. 55: '*Hludowicus rex mortuus. Chonradus filius Chonradi comitis a Francis et Saxonibus seu Alamannis ac Bauguariis rex electus.*

bled by attempts at secession in Lotharingia and Bavaria and devastating incursions of his realm by Vikings from the north and Hungarians from the south. The first Conrad realized his lineage lacked the good fortune (*fortuna*) and fortitude (*fortitudo*) required to keep the kingdom together and personally endorsed the election of a more powerful and fortunate warlord from the tribe of the Saxons after his demise[113]. And so it came to pass that the tribal chieftains elected the Saxon Henry the Fowler (*c.* 876-919-936) as their new king after the demise of the 'unfortunate' Conrad I. Henry must have been a remarkable man since he refused to be crowned and consecrated after his election: '*it is sufficient for me to be called king. I leave the unction and the crown to better men*', he is reported to have said[114]. With Henry begins the Saxon dynasty[115], ruling the German kingdom for more than a century. His son and successor Otto I (912-936-962-973) was the first of his lineage to be crowned Roman emperor by Pope John XII in 962, a privilege of the king of the Germans ever since.

Otto I in Italy

The King of Italy and Roman Emperor Louis II had died on 12 August 875 without a male heir and without having appointed a successor during his lifetime. Consequently, the kingdom of Italy and the imperial title were claimed by the kings of East and West Francia, Louis the German and his half-brother Charles the Bald. Even before the demise of Louis II of Italy, Pope Hadrian II (867-872) had reassured Charles the Bald that he would allow no one but him to be raised to the imperial dignity[116] and his successor John VIII (872-882) remained true to that promise. Accordingly, Charles the Bald was crowned and consecrated as emperor of the Romans in St Peter's by John VIII on Christmas Day 876[117], much to the chagrin of his 'German' half-brother Louis and his sons. It was one of the 'German' Louis' sons though who was the last direct descendant of Charlemagne to be crowned Roman emperor in Rome, another Charles (839-876-881-888)[118], known to posterity by

---

113   For this see Widukind of Corvey († after 973), *Rerum Gestarum Saxonicarum* 1,25, MGH, *SS rer. Germ.* 60, 37-38.

114   Widukind, *Rerum Gestarum Saxonicarum* 1,26, MGH, *SS rer. Germ.* 60, 40. '*Satis michi est, ut ... rex dicar ... penes meliores vero nobis unctio et diadema sit*'.

115   The dynasty is known in German national history as the race of Liudolf ('Liudolfinger'), after the Saxon Duke Liudolf, grandfather to Henry the Fowler.

116   From a letter of Hadrian II to Charles the Bald sent in 872 (Migne *PL* 122, col. 1320): '*numquam acquiescemus, exposcemus, aut sponte sucipiemus alium in regnum et imperium Romanum, nisi teipsum*'.

117   *Annales Bertiniani* (Hincmar of Reims) ad ann. 879, MGH *SS rem. Germ.* 5, 127: '*in diem nativitatis Domini beato Petro multa et pretiosa munera offerens, in imperatorem unctus et coronatus atque imperator Romanorum appellatus est.*

118   Regino of Prüm, *Chronicon* ad ann. 881, MGH *SS rer. Germ.* 50, 117: '*Anno dominicae incarnationis dccclxxxi Carolus ... Romam perveniens a presule apostolicae sedis Iohanne et senatu Romanorum favorabiliter exceptus cum magna gloria imperator creatus est*'.

his rather unflattering sobriquet 'the Fat' to distinguish him from all the other Charleses his dynasty produced. He was the last Carolingian to 'rule' over the entire undivided Carolingian Empire as well. His 'rule' also marks the nadir of his lineage since he was deposed as king of West-Francia in 887 and a year later as king of East Francia. When that miserable man died on 12 January 888, 'stripped of all his dignities and belongings', the Carolingian Empire expired with him, never to be restored[119].

After the demise of Charles the Fat, the kingdom of Italy and the imperial crown fell victim to the shenanigans of a number of Italian magnates on the one hand *and* the pope in Rome on the other who passed on the imperial title from one ephemeral pretender to another[120]. The last in this sorry line of petty Italian imperial aspirants was the nominal Lombard King Lothair of Arles (*c.* 927-950), married to Adelaide of Burgundy (*c.* 931-999). After her husband expired, Adelaide was taken captive by the Italian strongman (and successor of her husband) Berengar II of Ivrea, but she was able to escape with the help of a Tuscan knight, Azzo of Canossa († 988)[121]. It must have been from his impregnable castle that she entreated Otto I to come to her rescue. Otto, a widower since 946, obliged, conquered the Lombard kingdom and married Adelaide in Pavia in 952. Otto had planned to proceed from Lombardy to Rome straight away but was prevented from doing so by a rebellion of his son Liudolf (who disapproved of his marriage to Adelaide) and, even more importantly, by the imminent threat of a Hungarian invasion into his German kingdom. Otto succeeded in quenching the rebellion of his son and in rallying all the tribes of the German nation to face the Hungarian onslaught in a decisive battle on the Lechfeld near Augsburg (August 955). Otto was victorious and was hailed on the battlefield by his German troops as 'father of the father-

---

119 Regino of Prüm, *Chronicon* ad ann. 888, MGH *SS rer. Germ.* 50, 128 – 129: '*Anno dominicae incarnationis dccclxxxviii. Carolus imperator, tertius huius nominis et dignitatis, obiit pridie Idus Ianuar. ... circa finem vitae dignitatibus nudatus bonisque omnibus spoliatus*'.

120 There have been no fewer than five 'Roman emperors' crowned and consecrated by successive popes between the demise of Charles the Fat (888) and the inauguration of Otto I (962), all of them corroborating their claim to that lofty title with their pretended title as 'king of Italy': Guido and Lambert of Spoleto, Arnulf of Carinthia, Louis the Blind (a grandson of the Emperor Louis II through his mother Ermengard), and Berengar I of Ivrea.

121 On this episode see *Chronicon Novaliciense* (11th century) V,10, ed Bethmann, MGH *SS rer. Germ.* 21, 68. Azzo was highly rewarded by Otto I for his services to Adelaide. When he died in 988, Azzo was count of Reggio, Modena, and Mantua. His grandson Boniface († 1052) was also count of Brescia, Cremona, and Ferrara as well as margrave of Tuscany. Boniface's only surviving child, his daughter Matilda (1045-1115), was the richest heiress in the Italian kingdom. About her and her estate see *infra* p. 83, fnt. 31.

land' (*pater patriae*) and even, Roman style, as 'emperor' (*imperator*)[122]. Consequently, it was a very different man who entered Italy once again in 962 proceeding to Rome to be consecrated there as emperor of the Romans by Pope John XII.

The Ottonianum and the Roman synod of 963

Pope John XII (955-964) was a pervert and a disgrace to the throne of St Peter, a perfect example of the shocking moral decline of the Roman papacy in this era[123]. As a matter of course, Otto I was well-informed about this, as he was about the fact that the pope needed his military support against Berengar II of Ivrea, yet another Lombard threatening the Papal State[124]. Otto was crowned and consecrated as Roman emperor by a compliant Pope John on Sunday 2 February 962[125]. Eleven days later, Otto subscribed to a document containing his confirmation of the *Hludowicianum*, the *Ottonianum*[126]. Significantly, it did

---

122 Widukind, *Rerum Gestarum Saxonicarum* 3,49, MGH, *SS rer. Germ.* 60, 128): '*triumpho celebri rex factus gloriosus ab exercitu pater patriae imperatorque appellatus est*'.
123 John XII was born Octavian (!) and was a grandson of the notorious Marozia (890-937), a daughter of Theophylact, count of Tusculum, who had his nephew installed as pope (Sergius III, 904-911) to guard over the interests of the counts of Tusculum. Marozia had an affair with Pope Sergius who fathered a child with her who was to be pope as well, John XI (931-935), a fact not even passed over in silence by the *Liber pontificalis* (*Johannis XI*, ed. Duchesne 2, 243): '*natione Romanus, ex patre Sergio papa*'. During the pontificate of her son, Marozia ruled over Rome unchallenged. She was married to Duke Alberic of Spoleto, with whom she had another son also called Alberic. It was this Alberic, styling himself as *princeps Romanorum*, who succeeded his mother as ruler over Rome after having Marozia imprisoned. His son Octavian was raised to the throne of St Peter at his father's insistence. According to his contemporary, the diplomat Liudprand of Cremona (920-972) (*Historia Ottonis* 10, MGH, *SS rer. Germ.* 41,167), Pope John turned the Lateran Palace into a whore house: '*sanctum palatium lupanar et prostibulum fecisse*'. The *Liber pontificalis* (*Johannis XII*, Duchesne 2, 246) concurs: 'he spent his whole life in adultery and vanity' (*totam vitam suam in adulterio et vanitate duxit*).
124 Berengar II of Ivrea (c. 900-966) had subjected in Germany to the suzerainty of Otto I as king of Italy in 952: Adalbert, *Continuatio Reginonis* (967) ad ann. 952, MGH *SS rer. Germ.* 50, 165; Widukind, *Rerum Gestarum Saxonicarum* 3,11, MGH, *SS rer. Germ.* 60, 110. He was (unwisely) allowed to return to Lombardy with his son Guido after that, where they soon conquered the duchy of Spoleto and threatened the papal territories, contravening the authority of Otto I. It was John XII himself who called for German support in 960: Liudprand of Cremona (920-972), *Historia Ottonis* 1, MGH, *SS rer. Germ.* 41, 159. Berengar II is not to be mistaken for his maternal grandfather, Berengar I (c. 850-924), king of Italy and Roman emperor from 915 until his demise.
125 Adalbert, *Continuatio Reginonis* (967) ad ann. 962, MGH *SS rer. Germ.* 50, 171: '*Rex natale Domini Papiae celebravit; indeque progrediens Romae favorabiliter susceptus acclamatione totius Romani populi et cleri ab apostolico Johanne, filio Alberici, imperator et augustus vocatur et ordinatur*'. See also *Annales Sangallenses maiores* (1056) ad ann. 961 and 962, MGH *SS* 1, 79: '(961) *Otto rex secundam profectionem in Italiam fecerat cum magno exercitu in mense Augusto.* (962) *Ipse a papa Octaviano benedicitur in purificatione sanctae Mariae, die dominico*'. Remarkably, the contemporary German historian Widukind of Corvey does not mention Otto's imperial coronation.
126 The so-called '*Ottonianum*' has been edited by Th. Sickel in MGH *DD* 1 (Konr. I; Heinr. I; Otto I) Otto I, nr 235, 322-327. Unlike with the *Hludowicianum*, there is a con-

not confirm Louis' alleged grant to the Romans of the privilege to elect and consecrate a pope without the previous consent of the emperor, but the confirmation of the *Constitutio romana* of 824 instead, thus securing the right of the emperor to intervene in papal elections[127]. It was not to be long before the newly crowned emperor was to exercise that privilege.

Pope John was not only a degenerate, but he was also completely unreliable. He had sworn an oath of allegiance to the emperor, as the *Constitutio romana* prescribed, but soon after Otto had left Rome the pope decided to change sides and to conspire against the emperor with the son of Berengar II of Ivrea, Adalbert, who was warmly received in Rome by the pope while his father was besieged by the emperor. The Lombards seemed less dangerous enemies, now that the pope had experienced the might of his German imperial friend. As soon as the emperor was informed of this, he returned to Rome immediately. He met with no resistance from the Romans since the pope and Adalbert had already fled the city and now Otto decided to tighten his grip on the papal elections even more by imposing a solemn oath on the Romans 'never to elect and ordain a pope without the consent and the election of the emperor'[128]. Having done that, he convened a synod at Rome to depose Pope John XII and to preside over the election of a successor. One of the bishops present was Bishop Liudprand of Cremona (*c.* 920-970/972) to whom we owe the proceedings of the synod[129]. This time, there were no objections by the many prelates attending that 'the first See is not to be judged by anyone' (*prima sedes non iudicatur a quoquam*)[130]. To the contrary: John XII was deposed and replaced by a Roman nobleman who chose to be called Leo, eighth of that name. After a short and tumultuous pontificate[131], Leo VIII died in 965. He

---

temporary copy of the *Ottonianum* still in the Vatican Archive (*ASV*, A.A., Arm. I-XVIII 18). It is an extraordinary document, written in golden letters on purpled parchment, one of the showpieces of the *Archivio Segreto*.

127 For the *Constitutio romana* see supra p. 61 and for its confirmation in the *Ottonianum* see MGH *DD* 1 (Konr. I; Heinr. I; Otto I) Otto I, nr 235, 326: 'Subject in everything to the power of us, our sons, and our successors as contained in the agreement, the constitution and the firm promise of Pope Eugenius and his successors' (*Salva in omnibus potestate nostra et filii nostri posterorumque nostrorum, secundum quod in pacto et constitutione ac promissionis firmitate Eugenii pontificis successorumque illius continetur*).

128 Liudprand of Cremona, *Historia Ottonis* 8, MGH, *SS rer. Germ.* 41, 164: '*numquam se papam electuros aut ordinaturos praeter consensum et electionem domni imperatoris Ottonis caesaris augusti filiique ipsius regis Ottonis*'.

129 *Historia Ottonis* 9-16, MGH, *SS rer. Germ.* 41, 164-172, also in Mansi 18, col. 465-469.

130 On this maxim see *supra* p. 55.

131 Otto I learned a hard lesson about local Roman politics in 963. His pope, Leo VIII, was not accepted by all Romans and as soon as the emperor had left Rome, Johannes XII was able to return to the city. He called a synod repealing the decisions of the previous synod convened

was succeeded by another representative of the Roman nobility, John XIII (965-972), elected and consecrated with the permission of the emperor. It was John XIII who crowned and consecrated Otto's son, Otto II (955-961-967-983), as co-emperor on Christmas Day 967 in St Peter[132], securing the rule of the Saxon house in the German kingdom and the Roman empire.

The Salian emperors

After the death of the king and emperor Henry II in 1024, the line of the Saxon Liudolfingers became extinct in the direct line, but the German chieftains chose a Frankish nobleman, Conrad of Worms, as his successor, most probably because he could claim to be a descendant of Otto I[133]. Conrad II (*c.* 990-1024-1027-1039), the first of the Salian line of German kings, was duly crowned as emperor in Rome on 26 March 1027 by Pope John XIX. The direct Salian line ended in 1125 with the death of Henry V (1081-1098-1111-1125).

The Salian emperors had been at loggerheads with the popes ever since Gregory VII had initiated the investiture struggle in 1073, culminating in the excommunication of Henry IV in 1076. From the perspective of the pope the absolute nadir of that conflict had been reached when Henry V had Pope Paschalis II (1099-1118) and his cardinals arrested in Rome in 1111 and forced them to agree to a solution to the investiture problem that was very much in his favour, after which Henry was duly crowned as emperor by that humiliated and intimidated pope[134]. It was an episode the Roman *curia* never forgot[135] and after Henry V died without issue, a heavenly judgment on him no doubt, two of the leading German clerics, the archbishops of Cologne

---

by Otto I and deposing Leo VIII (for the *Acta* of this synod see MGH *Const.* 1 no 380, 532-536). John XII died soon after, allegedly mortally wounded by the husband of the woman he had raped (Liudprand of Cremona, *Historia Ottonis* 20, MGH, *SS rer. Germ.* 41, 173-174). The Romans subsequently elected a new pope without the consent of the emperor, Benedict V (964). He was deposed by the emperor and abducted to Germany, where he died in 966.

132 Widukind, *Rerum Gestarum Saxonicarum* 3,70, MGH, *SS rer. Germ.* 60, 147 (from a letter by Otto I): '*Filius noster in nativitate Domini coronam a beato apostolico in imperii dignitatem suscepit*'. Otto II had already been crowned and consecrated in 961as co-regent in Germany by his uncle bishop Bruno of Cologne, a brother of his father. Bishop Bruno was a very powerful (and a very learned) man: he was appointed duke of Lotharingia by his brother and was the mainstay of his brother's reign in Germany.

133 Conrad's grandmother from his father's side, Liudgarda, was a daughter of Otto I from his first marriage with Edgith, an English princess. Conrad's uncle Bruno was a pope, Gregory V (996-999).

134 On the events in Rome in 1111 see *Relatio Registri Paschalis II*, MGH *Constitutiones* 1, Henr. V, no 99 (147-150), containing the excuse (duress) of Paschalis II for his concessions to Henry V.

135 The Norman vassals of the pope in South Italy could not come to his rescue since there was a power vacuum in the region at the time. The sons of Robert Guiscard had both died in 1111 and their sons and heirs were both still minors, as was Roger II of Sicily.

and Mainz, were determined to end his line once and for all. From a dynastic perspective, there was an obvious successor in the person of Frederick of Hohenstaufen, duke of Swabia and a grandson of king Henry IV through his mother Agnes. In order to emphasize that the German kingdom was not a hereditary monarchy, but an electoral monarchy, archbishop Adalbert of Mainz, in his quality as 'warden of the kingdom' (*custos regni*) during an interregnum, organized an election to be held on 25 August at a diet in Mainz. Legend has it that the diet was attended by tens of thousands of people from all parts of the kingdom and even from beyond since the election of a German king and future emperor was an occasion of great international importance. From France, for example, no less a person than Abbot Suger of St Denys himself, the *de facto* ruler of that kingdom at the time, was present as an observer. The whole event was supervised by archbishop Adalbert and two special personal representatives (*legati*) sent to Germany by Pope Honorius II. By their combined effort they were able to outmanoeuvre Frederick of Hohenstaufen and to facilitate the election of Lothair of Supplinburg, duke of Saxony and an unwavering enemy of the last two Salian kings and emperors[136]. Lothair III had no male heir, but his daughter Gertrud was married to the Bavarian duke Henry the Proud (1108-1139), whom king Lothair had invested with the duchy of Saxony as well[137], thus making his son in law the most powerful prince in the German kingdom and the obvious successor to the German throne and the imperial crown.

---

136 On the election of 1125 see *Narratio de electione Lotharii Saxoniae ducis in regem Romanorum* (ed. Wattenbach, MGH *SS* 12, 509-512), written shortly after the event. On the presence of the papal representatives see the chronicle of Anselm of Gembloux († 1136) ad ann. 1125, MGH *SS* 6, 375. The presence of Abbot Suger is attested for by a deed of compromise between the abbot and count Maynard of Morspeck completed 'on that famous assembly held at Mainz for the election of an emperor' (*in illo celebri colloquio quod de electione Imperatoris apud Maguntiam habitum est* (printed in the 'Recueil de pièces justificatives' in Felibien, *Histoire de l'Abbaye royale de Saint-Denys*, Paris 1706, xciv, no 125).
137 *Annales S' Disibodi* ad ann. 1126, MGH *SS* 17, 23: *Filius ducis Baioariae ducatu Saxoniae a rege donatur.* At the time of Henry's investiture with Saxony, his father Henry 'The Black' was still alive; the old duke died later in 1126 leaving the duchy of Bavaria to Henry as well.

The Emperor Lothair III
(*Chronica regia coloniensis*, Royal Library
of Belgium, Ms 467, *f. 62 r°*)

The 'election'
of Conrad III

Pope Innocent II and his cardinals mistrusted Henry the Proud. He
was too powerful to their liking, since Henry was not only duke of
Saxony and Bavaria, but margrave of Tuscany as well[138], making him
the neighbour of the pope in Italy. Duke Henry and Innocent II were
on bad terms since the last campaign of Lothair III in Italy (1136-1137).
The duke had displayed more interest in the conquest of South Italy
than in the 'liberation' of Rome, where the 'anti-pope' Anacletus II still
held sway at the time. Here was a candidate for the German throne who
was more than likely to press the claim of the empire to South Italy and
Sicily once he became king of the Germans[139]. Innocent II was therefore determined to stop him. As soon as the news of Lothair's demise
had reached the pope, Innocent II sent a German prelate, Dietwin,
cardinal-bishop of Porto/Santa Rufina, to Germany as his personal
representative (*legatus*) with that mission[140]. He was to join there with

---

138   Henry is styled as '*dux Baioariae et marchio Tusciae*' in a charter of Lothair III dated
on 22 September 1137 (MGH *DD* 8, no 119, 193). Lothair had sent his son in law to Tuscany
with an army of 3000 German knights in order to restore the imperial order there. Henry was
quite successful in that mission. See *Annalista Saxo* ad ann. 1137, MGH *SS* 6, 773 and Falco
Beneventanus, ad ann. 1137, ed. D'Angelo, 76.
139   Henry the Proud was the richest prince of Europe at the time. He boasted that his power extended from Denmark to Sicily (*Ottonis episc. freisingensis Chronica* 7,23, MGH *SS Rer.
germ.* 45, 345): '*princeps ... cuius auctoritate, ut ipse gloriabatur, a mari usque ad mare, id est a
Dania usque in Siciliam, extendebatur*'. Especially the claim that his domain extended to South
Italy as well must have raised eyebrows in the papal *curia*.
140   For Cardinal Dietwin's mission see his obituary in *Annales Palidenses* (ending in 1182,
with later additions until 1340) ad ann. 1151, MGH SS 16, 85: '*missus a domno papa*' and
Ottonis episc. freisingensis Chronica 7,22, MGH *SS Rer. germ.* 45, 343. See further below in
fnt. 141.

72

Archbishop Adalbero of Trier, who had already been appointed as the pope's other personal representative in Germany[141]. Innocent II had his own candidate as successor to Lothair III. He had met him during Lothair's campaign in South Italy. It was Conrad of Hohenstaufen, a younger brother of Frederick of Hohenstaufen who had been thwarted in the 1125 election[142]. Conrad had also established friendly relations with Archbishop Adalbero of Trier and Cardinal Dietwin during that campaign[143].

Circumstances in Germany were favourable for the timely interference by the papal agents, since the election of a successor to Lothair had been delayed until Whitsuntide 1138, due to a vacancy in the archiepiscopate of Mainz. The papal legates knew that a repetition of the 1125 procedure was out of the question. They simply could not risk a diet where Henry the Proud was present: he was too powerful for that. Their solution was an outright 'coup d'état', arguing that a fair and open election for a new German king was impossible under the prevailing circumstances, that is in view of the likely undue influence of Henry the Proud[144]. At a secret meeting in Coblenz on 7 March 1138,

The election of Frederick I

---

141   On the appointment of Adalbero as papal *legatus* in Germany see Innocent's letter to the German episcopate in *Innocentii II papae epistolae et privilegia*, ep. 284, Migne *PL* 179, col. 333-334: 'We therefore command you and order you on the authority of the present letter to observe obedience and reverence to our brother' (*Mandamus itaque vobis, et praesentium auctoritate praecipimus ut eidem fratri nostro oboedientiam et reverentiam deferre*).

142   Conrad and his older brother Frederick had rebelled against Lothair III after 1125 and were excommunicated by Innocent II. Frederick had his younger brother even elected as rival king of the Germans by other rebelling princes. The Hohenstaufen brothers had, however, come to a reconciliation with Lothair in 1135 with the help of St Bernard. See *Ottonis episc. freisingensis Chronica* 7,19, MGH *SS Rer. germ.* 45, 333-334. Bishop Otto of Freising was a half-brother of Frederick of Hohenstaufen. His information on the involvement of St Bernard in the reconciliation of the Hohenstaufen brothers with Lothair III must therefore have rested on first-hand information. One of the conditions of the compromise was that the brothers promised to participate in a new Italian campaign to support Pope Innocent II. As a matter of course, the brothers were thereupon readmitted to the bosom of the Church.

143   For Adalbero of Trier see Balderic († 1157/1158), *Gesta Alberonis archiepiscopi Trevirensis* cap. 15, MGH *SS* 8, 252: 'Conrad, at one time a rival king, was reconciled with king Lothair during that campaign and entered into very friendly relations with archbishop Adalbero, because he <the archbishop> recognized his royal vigour and intellect' (*Conradus, tunc superpositus rex, in predicta expeditione Lothario regi reconciliatus est, et domino Alberoni archiepiscopo, quia penes eum regni videbat robur et mentem existere, sese familiaritate magna et servitio adiunxit*). For Dietwin see *Annales Palidenses* ad ann. 1151, MGH *SS* 16, 85: 'Hic <Thiedwinus> familiarissimus regi Conrado'.

144   See for his argument *Ottonis episc. freisingensis Chronica* 7,22, MGH *SS Rer. germ.* 45, 343: 'Some of the princes feared that duke Henry, who was superior by name and dignity in the kingdom at the time, would prevail due to his influence' (*Quidam autem ex principibus timentes ne forte in generali curia Heinricus dux, qui tunc precipui et nominis et dignitatis in regno fuit, per potentiam praevaleret*) and especially a letter of archbishop Adalbero of Trier (Jaffé, *Bibliotheca rerum germanicarum* V, *Monumenta Bambergensia*, Berlin 1869, 530), one of the papal legates present at the election, to archbishop Conrad of Salzburg, who had not

Conrad of Hohenstaufen was 'elected' king by a few prelates (the arch-bishops of Trier and Cologne, the bishop of Worms and, of course, car-dinal Dietwin) and only one secular prince of the kingdom, Conrad's brother Frederick[145]. It was highly irregular, but it was 'according to the will and the command of pope Innocent' (*volente et iubente domno papa Innocentio*)[146]. Conrad was crowned as king by cardinal Dietwin at Aachen only a week later and styled himself, as his predecessor had already done, 'king of the Romans' (*rex Romanorum*)[147]. As must have been anticipated by the conspirators at Coblenz, most German secular princes complied with the choice of Conrad III, since they did indeed fear the might of Henry the Proud, who threatened to overshadow them all. Most of them, except of course Henry the Proud himself, swore fealty to their new lord at a diet convened in Bamberg. The result was civil war with Henry the Proud and his brother Welf, the sixth of that name in the family.

Conrad III has never been crowned emperor in Rome. After par-ticipating in the disastrous Second Crusade (1147-1150), he died on 15 February 1152 at Bamberg during the preparations of his Italian coronation campaign. His succession was the result of a deliberate effort of the leading secular German princes (*summi principum*) to minimize, if not neutralize, the influence of the pope on the election of a German king and future emperor as had happened with the election of Lothair III and Conrad III. Time was therefore of the essence to be ahead of the pope and his legates. The election of a new king was

---

been involved in their plans, arguing that Henry the Proud 'has suffocated our holy mother the Roman Church by his power' (*<mater> nostra sancta Romana ecclesia ... sua potentia suf-focavit*).

145 Conrad's older brother Frederick, duke of Swabia, had been a candidate for the succes-sion of Henry V in 1125 (see *supra* p. 71). Why did the duke now support his younger brother rather than stand for election again this time? Duke Frederick had already promoted his brother as German king once before, in 1127, when Conrad was elected by the nobles rejecting the election of Lothair III (see *supra* fnt. 142). Later sources suggest that duke Frederick was disqualified because he was one-eyed (*monoculus*), but none of the contemporary sources men-tions this and he was certainly not physically disqualified in 1125. My guess is that his health was failing after 1125, since he did not, unlike his brother Conrad, accompany Lothair III on his 1137 campaign in South Italy as he should have done (see *supra* in fnt. 142). The fact that there were no reprisals for this failure to follow king Lothair suggests that duke Frederick had a good excuse. He may already have been suffering for some time of the 'serious ailment' (*gravis infirmitas*) that finally killed him in 1147: see *infra* p. 88, fnt. 13.

146 *Annales minores S^i Jacobi monasterii Leodiensis*, ad ann 1137, MGH *SS* 16, 640.

147 *Ottonis episc. freisingensis Chronica* 7,22, MGH *SS Rer. germ.* 45, 343-344: '*ad palatium Aquis a predicto cardinale .... cooperantibus Coloniense, Treverense archiepiscopis cum ceteris episcopis in regem ungitur*'. The *Annalista Saxo* ad ann. 1138, MGH *SS* 6, 776 adds that Conrad III was the 84th emperor since Augustus and that he was crowned in the 1890th year after the foundation of the city, *i.e.* Rome. The identification of the medieval 'German' empire with the ancient Roman Empire cannot be made clearer than this.

settled within two weeks after Conrad III had died. Conrad's nephew Frederick of Hohenstaufen, the eldest son of his brother Frederick, was elected at Frankfurt on 5 March, and duly crowned at Aachen only four days later[148]. By the time the pope, Eugenius III (1145-1153), was informed of the demise of Conrad, the German succession was already an accomplished fact[149].

---

148   There are three important contemporary sources for the election of Frederick I. One is a letter of Abbot Wibald of Corvey, an influential diplomat and advisor to Conrad III, to the incumbent pope, Eugenius III, printed in Jaffé, *Bibliotheca rerum Germanicarum* I, Berlin 1864, *Wibaldi epistolae* no. 375, 503-505 (also in MGH *Const.* 1, no 138, 192-193), informing the pope on the affair. It emerges from this letter that soon after (if not even before) the demise of Conrad 'the leading princes sent each other frequent messengers and letters to convene in order to consider the future of the realm' (*ceperunt deinde summi principum sese per nuncios et literas de habendo inter se colloquio pro regni ordinatione sollicitare* (504 (193)). The other source is Frederick I himself, in his letter to Pope Eugenius, printed in Jaffé, *Bibliotheca rerum Germanicarum* I, Berlin 1864, *Wibaldi epistolae* no. 372, 499-501 (also in MGH *Const.* 1, no 137, 191-192), on which more shortly. Another source is the report of Barbarossa's uncle Bishop Otto of Freising, a half-brother of his father, in his *Gesta Friderici* 2,1-2, MGH *SS rer. Germ.* 46, 102-104.

149   The extraordinary speed of Frederick's election and coronation may be explained when these events were already planned before the demise of King Conrad, not for the election and coronation of Frederick, but for the planned election and coronation of Frederick's nephew, the minor son of Conrad III, also called Frederick (1145/46-1167). Conrad III had had another son, Henry (1136-1150), who had been elected king of the Romans in 1147, but Henry had died in 1150. It is more than likely that Conrad wanted his surviving younger son elected as the new king of the Romans before he departed for Italy. This may explain why, as Otto of Freising (an eyewitness) reports, so many princes, even from Italy, were present at the election ceremony in Frankfurt. It was the first time in German history that the son of a reigning king was passed over as his successor. We know from a charter (*Monumenta Boica* 68, no 97, 68-70, with the additions from the original in Simonsfeld's *Jahrbücher des deutschen Reiches unter Friedrich I.*, Leipzig 1908, 21, fnt. 9), dated on 20 February 1152, *i.e.* only five days after king Conrad's demise, that Frederick held a conference (*colloquium*) with several nobles and prelates 'on the reorganization and composition of the state of the realm' (*de reformando et componendo regni statu*). We also know about other '*colloquia*' on the same issue among the leading nobles and prelates during these few days from the letters of the ubiquitous Abbot Wibald (Jaffé, *Bibliotheca rerum Germanicarum* I, Berlin 1864, *Wibaldi epistolae* no 364-367, 492-496). It seems that Barbarossa seized the opportunity of the unexpected demise of King Conrad to convince a large part of the electorate to elect him, rather than the minor son of Conrad, at the date already fixed for the election ceremony of the latter.

3

Frederick I 'Barbarossa'

Frederick I (1122-1152-1155-1190), whom the Italians named 'Redbeard' (Barbarossa), was the first emperor after Otto III with a true grand strategy[1]. He brought it to the fore in a programmatic letter to Pope Eugenius III, informing the latter of his election and coronation. It was the 'regeneration of the Roman Empire' (*reformatio Romani imperii*)[2]. Many eventful years later, the English diplomat and philosopher John of Salisbury (*c.* 1120-1180), who was in Rome when Frederick's ambassadors bringing the letter arrived there, still remembered their mission very well. Frederick's emissaries had revealed the true plans of their monarch 'by a slip of the tong' (*lingua incauta*), says John: '*he would change the supreme power over the whole world and subject the world to the city <of Rome>*'[3]. The 'restored' Roman Empire Frederick had in mind was not the classical Roman Empire of Augustus and Constantine, but a more recent Roman empire, that of his Saxon and Salian predecessors, such as Otto I and Henry III, before it had been humiliated by Gregory VII and his successors[4]. This was the message conveyed to Eugenius III in diplomatic language, using phrases from the most famous letter ever sent by a pope to a Roman emperor, the letter of Pope Gelasius I (492-496) to the Emperor Anastasius I (430-491-518).

Ever since the days of Constantine's conversion to Christianity and the final introduction of Christianity as an exclusive state religion in

Frederick I defines 'Gelasian' doctrine

---

1   On the policy of Otto III see *infra* p. 85-86.
2   From Frederick's letter, drafted by Abbot Wibald of Corbey (printed in Jaffé, *Bibliotheca rerum Germanicarum* I, Berlin 1864, *Wibaldi epistolae* no. 372, 500): 'May the greatness of the Roman Empire be restored to its ancient power and glory with the help of God' (*Romani imperii celsitudo in pristinum suae excellentiae robur Deo adiuvante reformetur*).
3   John of Salisbury, *Epistolae*, Ep. 59, in *Joannis Saresberiensis Opera omnia* 1, ed. J.A. Giles, 65: '*se totius orbis reformaturum imperium, et urbi subiiciendum orbem*'
4   Frederick I later clarified this position in a speech (a genuine lecture) to ambassadors of the city of Rome (and, indirectly, to the pope as well) as reported by Bishop Otto of Freising: *Ottonis episc. freisingensis Gesta Friderici* 2,30, MGH *SS rer. Germ.* 46, 136-139, on which more later (p. 97).

380 by the Roman Emperor Theodosius I[5], Christian doctrine was a matter of political importance since the answer to the question who was to be regarded as a 'true' Christian had important legal consequences. Since the early Christian theologians were mostly unable to provide a satisfactory definition themselves, the emperors, beginning with Constantine, usually called a general synod to do so and when even a synod could not, the emperor regarded it his duty to define Christian doctrine himself for the sake of the preservation of peace in the realm[6]. In 482 the Emperor Zeno (*c.* 425-474-491) did so with his so-called 'Act of Union' (*Henotikon*)[7]. It caused a schism in the Church, since the Patriarch of Rome, Simplicius, refused to comply[8]. The schism survived the Emperor Zeno and Pope Simplicius, as well as his successor Felix III, who was succeeded by Pope Gelasius I in 492. In his famous letter to Zeno's successor Anastasius I (430-491-518), Pope Gelasius articulated a principle denying the emperor the right to define Christian doctrine. That was a matter for the clergy exclusively: '*There are two institutions governing this world: the holy authority of the popes and the royal power*'[9]. According to Gelasius, Christ had ordained in his infinite wisdom '*that each of these institutions has its own distinct competence and dignity*'[10]. The exercise of secular power was the domain of the emperor. It was the domain of the pope to exercise his spiritual power for the preservation of the unity of the Church by defining Christian doctrine. It leaves the impression of two clearly distinct and autonomous domains, the secular and the spiritual, but unfortunately Pope Gelasius had ven-

---

5   The imperial constitution to that effect, the famous *lex 'Cunctos populos'*, is in Justinian's *Codex*: C. 1,1,1.

6   In the later, Christian, Roman Empire, theology had replaced politics. Consequently, theological controversies caused serious riots in the streets of Constantinople, Antioch, and Alexandria.

7   The emperor of the later, Byzantine, Roman Empire was regarded as 'equal to an apostle' (ἰσαπόστολος) and as God's representative on earth, *vicarius dei*, even by the Roman patriarchs, for example by Pope Anastasius II (496-498), Gelasius' successor: see his letter to his namesake, the Emperor Anastasius in Thiel, *Epistulae Romanorum Pontificum Genuinae* 1, Brunsberg 1868, 620: '*per instantiam vestram, quam velut vicarium Deus praesidere iussit in terris*'. See also the so-called 'Ambrosiaster', composed during the pontificate of Damasus I (336-384), *Liber quaestionum* 91,8 ed. Souter, *CSEL* 50, 157: 'the prince is venerated as God's representative on earth' (*rex adoratur in terris quasi vicarius Dei*). Consequently, the emperor was entitled to watch over Christian doctrine.

8   The Roman patriarch felt safe to do so, since Italy was ruled by the Ostrogoth King Theodoric (454-493-526) at the time, an Arian heretic himself, who did not care about catholic orthodoxy nor about the emperor in faraway Constantinople.

9   Gelasius, *Epistola VIII ad Anastasium imperatorem*, ed. Thiel, *ERPG* 1, 350-351): '*Duo quippe sunt, imperator Auguste, quibus principaliter mundus hic regitur: auctoritas sacra pontificum, et regalis potestas*'.

10   Gelasius, *De anathematis vinculo* § 1, ed. Thiel, *ERPG* 1, Gelasius, *Tractatus* IV, 567): '*Christus ... sic actionibus propriis dignitatibusque distinctis officia potestatis utriusque discrevit*'.

tured to add an observation in his letter to the emperor on the relation between the two domains, emphasizing that '*the authority of the popes is higher since they have to account to God for the conduct of kings on Judgment Day*'[11], leaving the impression that the pope is *superior* to the emperor. This text from Gelasius' letter to Anastasius had been inserted into the *Decretum*[12], the authoritative textbook on canon law composed by the monk Gratian in or around 1140, more than ten years before Barbarossa's election. It was the textbook that served as the basis of the contemporary canon law courses in the university of Bologna. Gratian, however, did not cite Gelasius directly, but indirectly, from a quote of this line in a letter of Pope Gregory VII to Bishop Hermann of Metz defending his excommunication of the German King Henry IV[13]. After quoting Gelasius, Gregory VII (*not* Gelasius) immediately added that '*supported by this authority many pontiffs have excommunicated kings and emperors*'[14], a line Gratian also copied from Gregory VII (while attributing it to Gelasius), as he did with the historic precedents mentioned by Gregory VII to support his bold assertion that the pope had the right to excommunicate and even depose an emperor[15]. In short, Gregory VII and Gratian were using the quotation from Gelasius' letter to Anastatius to support the doctrine of papal supremacy as fully developed by Gregory VII in his *Dictatus papae*[16]. It was a very biased interpretation of the Gelasian doctrine, originally merely emphasizing the papal privilege to define Christian doctrine, and Frederick I wanted to make it clear from the start that he did not agree with it.

---

11   Gelasius, *Epistola VIII ad Anastasium imperatorem*, ed. Thiel, *ERPG* 1, 351): '*In quibus tanto gravius est pondus sacerdotum, quanto etiam pro ipsis regibus Domino in divino reddituri sunt examine rationem.*'.

12   *Decretum* Dist. 96, cap. 10.

13   The famous letter is printed in *Das Register Gregors VII.*, VIII, 21, MGH *Epp. sel.* 2.2, 546-562. The quotation from Gelasius' letter is on 553.

14   *Das Register Gregors VII.*, VIII, 21, MGH *Epp. sel.* 2.2, 153: '*Talibus ergo institutis talibusque fulti auctoritatibus plerique pontificum alii reges alii imperatores excommunicaverunt*'. Compare *Decr.* Dist. 96, cap. 10.

15   See on this issue *infra* p. 333-343.

16   For this famous document see *Das Register Gregors VII.*, MGH *Epp. sel.* 2.1, 202-206.

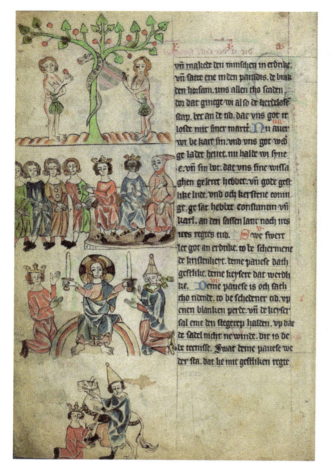

The doctrine of the two swords and the emperor performing squire service to the pope (*Sachsenspiegel*, Landesbibliothek Oldenburg CIM I 410, *f.* 6 v°)

Two Swords   There is a clear reference to Gelasius' letter (or rather Gratian's version of it) in Barbarossa's letter to Pope Eugenius III, informing the pope of his election: '*since there are two institutions governing the world, the holy authority of the popes and the royal power, we are prepared to bow our head in pious devotion to all priests of Christ*'[17]. By these lines Frederick I indicated that he adhered to a strict dualist interpretation of what has come to be known as the 'doctrine of the two swords'. Each

---

17 Jaffé, *Bibliotheca rerum Germanicarum* I, Berlijn 1864, *Wibaldi epistolae* no. 372, p. 500 (also in MGH *Const.* 1, no 137, 191-192 (192)): '*Cum enim duo sunt, quibus principaliter hic mundus regitur, videlicet auctoritas sacra pontificum et regalis potestas, omnium Christi sacerdotum oboedientiae devoti colla submittere parati sumus*'.

power, the emperor and the pope, held its own sword directly from God. The exclusive sovereignty of secular power in all secular affairs was emphasized in the opening lines of Frederick's letter: '*It behoves the father of the fatherland to vigilantly observe the institutions of the ancient kings and to tenaciously adhere to their venerable instructions, so that he demonstrates that the kingdom God has assigned to him is preserved by law and custom as well as by arms and war*'[18]. There is a lot of doctrinal learning compressed in these few lines. Not only that the power of the king came from God directly, without, that is, the mediation of the pope, but also that the king was supreme legislator in secular affairs and that Barbarossa strictly adhered to the traditional constitution and customs of his country, implying that the pope had no authority to interfere in the election of a German king. The last part of the sentence contains a clear reference to Roman law, the opening lines of Justinian's famous *Const. 'Imperatoriam'*[19], reasserting the position of the king and emperor as sole legislator.

This was a message the like of which the papal *curia* had not received in a very long time, if ever at all, and it must certainly have raised some eyebrows, if only because the addressee, Pope Eugenius III, had just recently been informed by no less an authority than St Bernard himself that he, the pope, held *both* swords, the spiritual as well as the secular[20]. Barbarossa's message was delivered to the pope around December 1152 by three German envoys, accompanied by two Italian noblemen, who had also been authorized to conclude a treaty with the pope in view of Frederick's intention to come to Rome as soon as possible to be crowned there by the pope. The cardinals negotiating with Barbarossa's envoys advanced two conditions. The first related to the pope's conflict with the people of Rome, on which more later[21], but the second directly concerned South Italy and the kingdom of Sicily.

The Treaty of Konstanz

---

18 Jaffé, *Bibl.* I, *Wibaldi epistolae* no. 372, 499: '*Patrem patriae decet, veneranda priscorum instituta regum vigilanter observare et sacris eorum disciplinis tenaci studio inherere, ut noverit regnum sibi a Deo collatum legibus ac moribus non minus adornare quam armis ac bello defensare*'.
19 *Const. Imperatoriam* pr.: '*Imperatoriam maiestatem non solum armis decoratam, sed etiam legibus oportet esse armatam, ut utrumque tempus et bellorum et pacis recte possit gubernari*'.
20 Bernard of Clairveaux, *De consideratione* 4,3 (Migne *PL* 182, col. 776): 'That <meaning the secular sword> is also yours, which may on occasion be drawn on your command, but not by your hand. If it were not so, if that did in no way belong to you as well, the Lord would not have responded to the words of the Apostles 'See, here are two swords', saying 'It is enough', but 'It is one too much'. (*Tuus ergo et ipse, tuo forsitan nutu, etsi non tua manu evaginandus. Alioquin si nullo modo ad te pertineret et is, dicentibus Apostolis,* Ecce gladii duo hic; *non respondisset Dominus* Satis est, *sed* Nimis est). See also St Bernard *Ep.* 256 (Migne *PL* 182, col. 464), addressed to Eugenius III as well: '*Petri uterque est*'.
21 P. 95.

It was more than ten years ago now that Pope Innocent II had suffered a terrible humiliation at the hands of Roger II and had been forced to invest Roger with the kingdom of Sicily, but that outrage was still not forgotten, let alone forgiven. The pope and most of the cardinals wanted from Barbarossa what they had wanted from Lothair III and from Conrad III in the past: no less than the conquest of South Italy on behalf of the Church[22]. Since it had come to the attention of the pope that Barbarossa's predecessor Conrad III had entered into negotiations with the Byzantine emperor on a possible partition of South Italy between the western and the eastern empire[23], the pope demanded that Barbarossa guaranteed that he would never concede any part of Italy to the schismatic Byzantine emperor. The German envoys, who knew that Barbarossa disapproved of the Byzantine policy of his uncle, had no objection to this clause[24]. In addition, the cardinals demanded an assurance from Barbarossa that he would not negotiate with Roger II of Sicily and his successors without the permission of the pope. Evil though he might be in the eyes of the pope, the king of Sicily was the pope's vassal and consequently could not enter into territorial negoti-

---

22   St Bernard had time and again urged Lothair III and Conrad III to come to the rescue of the pope in Rome and to wage war on the Sicilian 'usurper'. See his letter to Lothair III in Bernard of Clairvaux, *Epistolae*, ep. 189 (Migne, *PL* 182, col. 294): 'It is the duty of Caesar to defend his own crown against the Sicilian usurper, since it is beyond doubt that anyone who makes himself king in Sicily, is in revolt against Caesar'(*est Caesaris propriam vindicare coronam ab usurpatore Siculo ... sit procul dubio omnis qui in Sicilia regem se facit, contradicit Caesari*). And a letter to Conrad III in *S. Bernardi Epistolae*, Ep. 244 (Migne *PL* 182, col. 440-442(442)): 'gird your sword on your thigh, oh almighty man, and may Caesar restore to himself what has belonged to Caesar, and to God what belongs to God' (*accingere gladio tuo super femur tuum, potentissime, et restituat sibi Caesar quae Caesaris sunt, et quae sunt Dei Deo*). Unfortunately, however, Conrad gave in to another harangue of Bernard: a call to take the cross against the infidel, thus preventing his intervention in Rome and in South Italy.
23   The papal *curia* was very upset by these initiatives of Conrad. See a letter written in 1149 by the then archdeacon, Cardinal Guido, to Abbot Wibald, urging Wibald to convince Conrad otherwise (Jaffé, *Bibliotheca rerum Germanicarum* I, no 198, 316-317): 'as has been reported to the pope and to us and as rumour has it, King Conrad is inclined to reward good with evil, God forbid, and has decided to seriously damage and harm the holy Roman Church in conjunction with the emperor in Constantinople' (*sicut domno papae ac nobis significatum est et rumores etiam increverunt ... rex C(onradus) mala pro bonis, quod Deus avertat, reddere nititur, et cum Constantinopolitano imperatore sanctam Romanam ecclesiam ... graviter si poterit affligere et infestare disponit*). There were very good diplomatic relations with Constantinople during the reign of Conrad III. The Emperor Manuel Komnenus (1118-1143-1180) was married to a sister-in-law of Conrad III, Bertha of Sulzbach.
24   Art. 3 of the draft agreement as concluded at Rome, between eight cardinals on the part of the pope and the five envoys of Barbarossa (MGH *Constt.* 1, no 144, 201): '*Graecorum quoque regi nullam terram ex ista parte maris concedet*'. There was an additional clause, compelling Barbarossa to militarily intervene whenever the Byzantine emperor invaded parts of Italy. Since Barbarossa had no intention to concede any part of Italy to the Byzantine emperor, his envoys did not object to this either.

ations with a third party without the permission of his lord, the pope. Barbarossa's envoys did not object to this clause either, since they knew that it was not their master's intention to negotiate with Roger, but rather to destroy that Sicilian usurper[25]. In return for these concessions on the part of Barbarossa, the pope promised that he would crown Barbarossa 'without difficulty or objection' (*sine difficultate et contradictione*)[26]. The Roman draft agreement was ratified by Barbarossa at Konstanz on 3 March 1153[27], within a year, that is, after his succession to the throne, revealing his intention that Italy was the land where 'the regeneration of the empire' (*reformatio imperii*) was to be accomplished by adding South Italy and Sicily to the empire.

Barbarossa had paid a very high price for a peaceful and uncontested succession to the German throne. First and foremost, he had to satisfy and appease the powerful Guelphs, Henry the Lion, the son of Henry the Proud, and his uncle Welf VI. The former was gratified by a promise to restore to him the duchy of Bavaria which his father Henry the Proud had lost due to his rebellion against Conrad III[28]. It was a delicate business since that duchy had been assigned by Conrad III to his half-brother margrave Henry of Austria in 1142. Consequently, Barbarossa had to compensate his Austrian uncle properly in order to convince the Austrian to renounce his Bavarian duchy. He did so by elevating Austria to a duchy and making it a practically independent territory within the German kingdom[29]. The duchy of Saxony, also forfeited by Henry the Proud, had already been restored to Henry the Lion in 1142[30]. In doing so, Barbarossa had reinstated a very powerful and possibly rival dynast in Germany. Welf VI, Henry the Lion's uncle, was gratified with substantial Italian territories: the margraveship of Tuscany, the duchy of Spoleto, the principality of Sardinia and all the land of the famously rich countess Matilda of Tuscany[31]. Last

The Italian policy of Frederick I

---

25   Art. 1 of the draft agreement (MGH *Constt.* 1, no 144, 201): '*Domnus siquidem rex iurare faciet … quod ipse nec trevam nec pacem faciet … cum rege Rogerio Siciliae sine libero consensu et voluntate Romanae ecclesiae et domni Papae Eugenii vel successorum eius*'.
26   Art. 4 of the draft agreement (MGH *Constt.* 1, no 144, 201).
27   *Pactum constantiense*, MGH *Constt.* 1, no 145, 202-203.
28   See *supra* p. 74.
29   *Constitutio ducatus Austriae* (1156), MGH *Const.* 1, no 159, 221-223.
30   *Annales Sⁱ Disibodi*, ad ann. 1142, MGH *SS* 17, 26.
31   *Historia Welforum* cap. 28 ad ann. 1152, MGH *SS* 21, 468. The estate of Matilda of Tuscany is the great legal conundrum of the Italian Middle Ages. Matilda (1045-1115) had been margrave of Tuscany, countess of Reggio in Emilia, of Mantua, Modena, Ferrara, Brescia, and Cremona. She had been the most important secular supporter of Pope Gregory VII. It was at her Canossa castle that Henry IV made his submission to Gregory VII. She died without issue but had transferred the title to all her enormous allodial possessions to Gregory VII and the Holy Church and confirmed that donation on 17 November 1102: E. en W. Goez,

but not least, the duchy of Swabia, his own duchy, was assigned to king Conrad's minor son Frederick, Barbarossa's nephew[32]. The result of all these settlements was that Barbarossa was not a major territorial force in Germany in his own right, which explains his desire to create a solid power base of his own in Italy instead. This was the rationale of Barbarossa's Italian policy, but the frustrated 1136-1137 campaign of Lothair III into South Italy had demonstrated that it could not be achieved with German knights alone. Barbarossa had to secure a firm foothold and support in Italy itself as well. Consequently, the kingdom of Italy had to be reformed.

Die Urkunden und Briefen der Markgräfin Mathilde of Tuszien, in MGH *DD MT* Dep. no 37, 415 and 73, 213. As from then she held her former allodial possessions in fief from the church. All her imperial fiefs (except Ferrara, which she held from the pope) reverted as of right to the Emperor Henry V in his quality as king of Italy at Matilda's death. The problem was that, shortly before her demise, she seems to have transferred the fiefs she held from the pope since 1102 to the Emperor Henry V, with whom she had been reconciled. The papacy never recognized this transaction, and the matter of Matilda's estate became a serious 'apple of discord' between successive popes and emperors. See *infra* p. 87.

32   King Conrad's son Frederick is already mentioned as 'duke of Swabia' (*Suevorum dux*) in a charter of Frederick I from 27 January 1153, MGH *DD FI* no 45, 75.

4

The Italian Kingdom

The first three Saxon emperors were deeply involved in Italian affairs. Otto I incorporated the Italian kingdom in his empire. His son Otto II (955-961-973-983) even led an expedition to conquer South Italy in 980 but was thoroughly defeated by the Arab emir of Sicily Abd-al-Qasim near Cotrone in Calabria in 982. Otto II (narrowly) survived that battle but fell victim to a secret weapon Italy had in store for all foreign invaders from the north: malaria. He died in Rome on 7 December 983 and was buried in St Peter's, the only German emperor to be interred there. His son and heir, Otto III (980-983-996-1002) dedicated his whole short reign as Roman emperor to what he called 'the restoration of the empire' (*renovatio imperii*)[1], even making Rome itself the new capital of his 'restored' Roman Empire. The imperial dream of the young emperor may have been inspired by his mother Theophanu (*c.* 955-991), a Byzantine princess, and his teacher Johannes Philagathos, a Greek from Rossano in southern Italy. But he was also strongly supported in his venture by Gerbert of Aurillac (*c.* 946-1003), the most learned man of his age. Gerbert was present in Rome when Otto III was crowned there in 996 by Pope Gregory V, the first in a line of German popes nominated by a German emperor[2]. Otto III and Gerbert were attracted to each other in mutual admiration and Otto nominated Gerbert as pope to succeed Gregory V in 999. Gerbert chose to be called Silvester, the second of that name after Silvester I who legendarily baptized Constantine I. The new Silvester and the new Constantine were to share the government of Christendom between them, Otto III in his palace on the Roman Aventine and Silvester in his Lateran Palace close by. It was a short-lived dream of happy co-operation between the secular and the spiritual leader of the world, but the

---

1   Reading of the inscription on a seal of Otto III attached to a charter of 999: Landesarchiv Baden-Württemberg, Signature: HStAS H 51 U 4.
2   See supra p. 27. Gregory V (996-999), born Bruno of Worms, was a great-grandson of Otto I and accordingly a close relative of Otto III. He was an uncle of the later Roman Emperor Conrad II.

Romans did not appreciate the German presence among them[3]: they rebelled against Otto, forcing him to leave Rome in 1001 and to die, deeply disappointed with his Roman subjects, in a castle in Tuscany on 23 January 1002. He was just 21 years of age[4].

Later German kings did not share the Italian enthusiasm of the last of the Ottos. During hundred and fifty years (from the demise of Otto III in 1002 to the election of Frederick I in 1152) all but one of the German kings visited their Italian domain only occasionally, mostly for no other reason than to be crowned in Rome as Roman emperor and to return to Germany as quickly as possible. The only exception was the last emperor of the Salian line, Henry V (*c.* 1081-1099-1111-1125). In 1116 Henry V fled to Italy, when his position in the German kingdom itself had become almost untenable after his excommunication in 1113, leaving Barbarossa's father, a son of his sister Agnes, behind to defend the Salian interests in the German territories against the mighty Saxon Duke Lothair of Supplinburg[5]. Henry V stayed in

---

3   Benedict, a monk in the monastery of St Andrew on Mount Soracte near Rome and a contemporary of Otto III, wrote in his *Chronicon* (MGH *SS* 3, 719): 'Woe Rome! Oppressed and abused by so many nations and now raped by a Saxon king. Suppressed by the sword, the strength of your people has been brought to naught. They carry your gold and silver away in their pouches' (*Vé Roma! quia tantis gentis oppressa et conculcata; qui etiam a Saxone rege appreensa fuistis, et gladiati populi tui, et robor tua ad nichilum redacta est! Aurum et argentum tuum in illorum marsuppiis deportant*).

4   The policy of Otto III to create a new, restored, Roman Empire with the city of Rome as its ecclesiastical *and* secular capital is often regarded as completely unrealistic but that is an unhistorical assessment. It overlooks the reality the Roman Empire was to Otto III, a son of a Byzantine princess. On Pentecost 1000 he repeated an act of reverence once performed by his predecessor Augustus. Augustus had the tomb of Alexander the Great opened on a visit to Alexandria and Otto III had the tomb of Charlemagne opened in Aachen to stand face to face with the great Charles (see respectively Suetonius, *Divus Augustus* 18 and Thietmar of Merseburg, *Chronicon* 4,47, MGH *SS rer. Germ. N.S.* 9, 185-186). Earlier that year, Otto III had completed a diplomatic mission to Poland, where he met the Polish Duke Boleslav I ('Chrobry') in Gnesen (Gniezno), crowning him with one of his own crowns and naming him 'co-operator of the empire' (*cooperator imperii*) and 'friend and ally of the Roman people' (*populi Romani amicus et socius*) (Anonymus Gallus, *Gesta ducum sive principum Polonorum* (the oldest Polish chronicle, written about 1115 by a French priest), MGH *SS* 9, 428-429). By turning Gnesen into an archiepiscopate independent of the German archiepiscopate of Magdeburg at the same time, Otto III practically created the Polish kingdom by incorporating that policy within the framework of his contemporary 'Roman Empire'. Shortly after his return to Rome in 1001, Otto III and Silvester II repeated the same strategy with Hungary, creating the archiepiscopate of Gran (Esztergom), also independent of the German archiepiscopates, and sending a royal crown to the recently converted Hungarian chieftain Waik, who took the Christian name of Stephen. These are momentous diplomatic achievements of lasting importance.

5   *Casus monasterii Petrishusensis* (the oldest part of this chronicle ends in 1164) 3,43 (1115), MGH *SS* 20, 659): 'he could not make a stand in the German kingdom anymore and committed it to the care of Duke Frederick of Swabia, a son of his sister, and absconded to Italy himself' (*in Theutonico regno non posset subsistere, set Frederico duci Suevorum, filio sororis suae,*

Italy for two years, far longer than any of his Salian predecessors, rul-ing the Lombard kingdom and the vast estates of Matilda of Tuscany, which she had transferred to him[6], with the support of lawyers like Irnerius, the first of the famous Bolognese teachers of Roman law[7]. On his return to Germany in 1118, Henry V must have shared his Italian experiences with his Hohenstaufen relatives, Barbarossa's father and his uncle Conrad, and when the Hohenstaufen brothers, Frederick and Conrad, revolted against Lothair III in 1127, it was Conrad of Hohenstaufen who tried to set up a rival kingdom in Italy in 1128[8]. Conrad was even crowned and consecrated as king of Italy at Monza by Bishop Anselm of Milan in that year[9], but he was forced to return to Germany soon, primarily because the former vassals of Countess Matilda of Tuscany declined to recognize him[10]. After he had returned

---

summam rerum commendavit et ipse in Italiam secessit). See also Ekkehard of Aura, ad ann. 1115, MGH *SS* 6, 249.

6   See *supra* p. 83, fnt. 31.

7   Irnerius' presence at the court of Henry V in Italy is well attested: see the charters of Henry V published in *Die Urkunden Heinrichs V. und der Königin Mathilde*, MGH *DD H5* (digital prepublication, http:// https://data.mgh.de/databases/ddhv/toc.htm) no 173 (6 May 1116); 177 (12 May 1116); 178 (13 May 1116) and 179 (15 May 1116), all from Governolo. See also no 163 (Padua, 20 March 1116); 164 (Padua, 22 March 1116); 168 (8 April 1116, Reggio) and no 195 (19 October 1116, Castel Quarneto: 'Guarnerio giudice del sacro pala-zzo'). Irnerius was also instrumental in the Roman election of Cardinal Mauricius of Braga as anti-pope ('Gregory VIII') in 1118 (Landulphus de sancto Paulo (*fl.* 1077-1137), *Historia Mediolanensis* 45 ad ann. 1118, MGH *SS* 20, 40): 'Master Guarnerius and many legal experts convened the Roman people to elect a pope and some smart schoolmaster lectured from the pulpit of St Peter in a long oration on the decrees of the popes on papal succession. After that had been thoroughly discussed and explained, the people elected some bishop from Spain as pope' (*magister Guarnerius de Bononia et plures legis periti populum Romanum ad eligendum papam convenit; et quidam expeditus lector in pulpito Sancti Petri per prolixam lectionem decreta pontificum de substituendo papa explicavit. Quibus perlectis et explicatis, tantus populus elegit in papam quendam episcopum Yspaniae*). As a matter of course, Irnerius was excommunicat-ed for this by the Council of Reims, presided over by Pope Calixtus II (January 1119). The contemporary list of people excommunicated there has been published by W. Holtzmann, 'Zur Geschichte des Investiturstreites', in *Neues Archiv* 50 (1935) 318-319(319): '*Gwarnerius Bononiensis legis peritus*'.

8   At the instigation of his older brother Frederick, Conrad of Hohenstaufen had been elect-ed by some Swabian and Frankish magnates in 1127 as king of the Germans in opposition to King Lothair III (*Ottonis episc. freisingensis Gesta Friderici*, MGH *SS rer. Germ.* 46 1,19): '*Conradus a fratre ac quibusdam aliis rex creatus*'.

9   *Ottonis episc. freisingensis Chronica* 7,17, MGH *SS Rer. germ.* 45, 333-334: '*Conradus ... a Mediolaneensibus ... honorifice suscipitur, ac ab eorum archiepiscopo Anselmo Modoyci, sede Italici regni, in regem ungitur. Pro his aliisque prefatus archiepiscopus a summo pontifice deponi-tur*'. Conrad (and his brother Frederick) had been excommunicated by Pope Honorius II pre-viously in 1128: *Annalista Saxo* ad ann. 1128, MGH *SS* 6, 765) and *Ottonis episc. freisingensis Chronica* 7,17, MGH *SS Rer. germ.* 45, 333-334. Archbishop Anselm was excommunicated for having consecrated an excommunicate.

10   *Ottonis episc. freisingensis Chronica* 7,18, MGH *SS Rer. germ.* 45, 335: '*Conradus, qui a Mediolanensibus rex constitutus fuerat, pene omnibus suis amissis, periculose ad patriam*

to Germany, Conrad and his brother Frederick finally made their peace with Lothair III in 1135, thanks to the intervention of Bernard of Clairvaux[11]. In 1137 Conrad even participated in Lothair's campaign in South Italy, where he attracted the attention of Pope Innocent II[12]. Conrad and his nephew Frederick of Swabia, his brother's son, must have been close since Frederick joined his uncle in the ill-fated Second Crusade (1147-1150), much to the chagrin of his father[13]. During the long time they spent together on that campaign, the Redbeard will have learned a lot from his uncle about his experiences in Lombardy and Tuscany in 1128 and in South Italy 1137.

Barbarossa comes to the Italian kingdom

In October 1154 Barbarossa crossed the Alps over the Brenner Pass on his way to Rome, as so many German kings had done before him in order to be crowned by the pope as Roman emperor. On 24 April 1155 he was at Pavia to receive another crown in advance in the local church of S. Michele. It was the famous iron crown of the Lombard kings of Italy[14], the very same crown his uncle Conrad had worn on his inauguration as king of Italy in 1128. The *regnum italicum* consisted of a large cluster of cities, a legacy of its Roman past, and consequently was mainly ruled on behalf of the German king by the bishops of the

---

repedaverat'. It seems that the pope (Honorius II) took possession of the inheritance of Mathilda of Tuscany after the demise of Henry V. There is a charter from 1128 of a man called Albert of Verona, acting as 'duke and margrave' in Tuscany and explicitly stating that he had been nominated by Pope Honorius (published in J. Ficker, *Forschungen zur Reichs- und Rechtsgeschichte Italiens* IV(*Urkunden*), Insbruck 1874, nr. 102, 147): '*Albertus Dei gratia dux, marchio et comes, divina cooperante gracia et beati Petri et domni pape Ho.<norii> eius vicarii munere ad huius honoris provectus fastigia'*. Albert, rather than Conrad, was recognized by the vassals of Mathilda in 1128 as they wrote to Lothair III around this time (in a letter published by Wattenbach, *Iter Austriacum 1853*, in *Archiv für Kunde österreichischer Geschichtsquellen* 14 (1855) 85-86): 'we have made him (Albert) our lord because we believed he was a vigorous man' (*Nos eum putantes esse strenuum virum, nostrum dominum fecimus*). I should add that no vassal could pay homage to an excommunicate lord, excluding the excommunicate Conrad as a possible successor to Henry V.

11 *Ottonis episc. freisingensis Chronica* 7,19, MGH *SS Rer. germ.* 45, 333-334 ('*interventu Clarevallensis abbatis Bernhardi'*).

12 See *supra* p. 73.

13 Duke Frederick was mortally ill at the time and had made his son Frederick (the 'Redbeard') his heir which is why he was very angry with his brother, King Conrad, that he had allowed his son to join him on his crusade. Bernard of Clairvaux tried to set his mind at ease before he died shortly after. See for this episode *Ottonis episc. freisingensis Gesta Friderici* 1,41, MGH *SS rer. Germ.* 46, 59-60.

14 Otto of Freising, *Gesta Friderici* 2,27, MGH *SS rer. Germ.* 46, 132: '*rex a Papiensibus ad ipsorum civitatem ... invitatur, ibique ... in ecclesia sancti Michaelis ... coronatur'*. The crown of Lombardy is made of gold and studded with precious jewellery, but it contains an iron band on the inside, said to have been forged from a nail from the cross of Christ. It is a priceless reliquary, now in the cathedral of Monza.

cities as his personal representatives (*missi*) or even as counts (*comites*)[15]. Before the Investiture Controversy, they had all been royal appointees as a matter of course, more often than not of German origin. After that, they were mainly recruited from the local urban nobility[16], but by then the bishops had lost most of their secular power to representatives of the urban citizenry, predominantly nobles, who presented themselves, Roman style, as *consules*. This phenomenon changed the political perspective of the rulers of the Lombard cities. When the bishops were still predominant and still incorporated in the imperial administration, they were the mainstay of the power of the German king in his Lombard kingdom[17]. After their fall from secular power, the political point of view of the new, local, rulers of the cities did not extend further than the direct sphere of influence of their cities, recognizing no other interests than the direct interests of their cities. The result was anarchy, as was rightly perceived by Barbarossa's uncle, Bishop Otto of Freising, in his sharp analysis of the political situation in the Lombard kingdom

---

15 Archbishops, bishops, and abbots formed the top of the Lombard feudal pyramid, as the *Libri feudorum* (*LF*) 1,1 confirms. Margraves and counts were of equal rank as *capitanei regis* (*LF* 1,1), but quantitatively of secondary importance in Lombardy. On the *Libri feudorum* see below in fnt. 20.

16 The Investiture Controversy destroyed the traditional administrative structure of the German kings in their Italian kingdom. Henry IV was supported by most of his Lombard bishops in his controversy with Gregory VII. As a matter of course, all of them were excommunicated by Gregory VII and replaced by Gregory's appointees. This left the question who was to be recognized as the *de facto* incumbent of an episcopal see to the citizenry and so it came about that the populace of the Lombard cities discovered their own 'liberty' in the process of the struggle for the liberty of the Church. A very good example is the situation in Milan in 1075, when there were no less than three nominal archbishops of that city. One of them, Azzo, was supported by Gregory VII and the rebellious city *plebs*; another, Gothefredus, allegedly a simoniac rumoured to have bought his episcopate from his predecessor Guido da Velate, appointed by Emperor Henry III in 1045, but (temporarily) supported by the German king. None of them was acceptable to the aristocrats of the city who were able to defeat the rebellious *plebs* in 1075. They advised the German king to send them another bishop. Henry IV complied and sent a cleric form Milan working in the king's chancery, Theodald, to the city as the new archbishop. Theodald was accepted by the victorious urban nobility. It was the *casus belli* allowing Gregory VII to excommunicate Henry IV (and Theodald) in 1076. Despite his excommunication, Archbishop Theodald held the Milanese arch-episcopate until his demise in 1085. On the events of 1075 in Milan see Arnulf, *Gesta archiepiscoporum Mediolanensium* 5,5 (MGH *SS* 8, 29-30) and Bonizo, *Liber ad amicum* 6 and 7, MGH *Ldl* 1, 598 and 605-606.

17 A very good example are the actions of Bishop Leo of Vercelli († 1026) after the demise of Emperor Otto III in 1002. The Italian nobles had seized the opportunity to elect one of their own, Margrave Arduin of Ivrea, as the new king of the Lombards, but Leo urged Otto's successor, King Henry II (973-1002-1014-1024), to come to Lombardy as soon as possible. Leo had Henry crowned as king of the Lombards in Pavia in 1004: *Thietmar of Merseburg* 6,6(5), MGH *SS rer. Germ. N.S.* 9, 280/281. The German king failed to secure the tenuous position of his bishops in Lombardy, however, since he left Italy in the same year and waited no less than ten years before returning to his Lombard kingdom.

at the advent of Barbarossa in 1154[18]. There had been no German king in Lombardy for fifteen years and due to the regular absence of the German kings, the Lombard cities had been able to establish themselves as practically independent policies, gaining control over the surrounding countryside (the *contado*) at the expense of the rural nobility, some of them immediate vassals of the king (*capitanei regis*), such as the powerful counts of Biandrate and Montferrat, and fighting each other in endless feuds[19]. Barbarossa had to put his Lombard kingdom to order first, before entering into the conclusive phase of the *reformatio imperii*, the conquest of South Italy and Sicily.

The constitutional problems ahead

Barbarossa convened all his Italian vassals at a diet held at Roncaglia lasting from 30 November till 6 December 1154. Practically all secular and clerical lords of the kingdom were present and so were the Lombard cities, represented by their *consules*. It was at this diet that one of the Lombard *consules*, the Milanese Oberto dell Orto (†1175), one of the greatest lawyers of his time[20], must have realized the full scope of

---

18   *Ottonis episc. freisingensis Chronica* 7,29, MGH *SS Rer. germ.* 45, 356): 'Because the cities of Italy became insolent due to the absence of the king, the Venetians fought cruel wars with the men from Ravenna, the Veronese and the men from Vicenza with Padua and Treviso, the Pisans and Florentines with the men from Lucca and Sienna. They disrupted practically all of Italy in those days by their bloodshed, plunder, and arson' (*His diebus propter absentiam regis Italiae urbibus in insolentiam decidentibus Veneti cum Ravennatensibus, Veronenses et Vicentini cum Paduanis et Tarvisiensibus, Pisani, Florentini cum Lucensibus et Senensibus atrociter debellantes totam pene Italiam cruore, predis et incendiis permiscuere*).

19   *Ottonis episc. freisingensis Gesta Friderici* 2,13, MGH *SS rer. Germ.* 46, 116): 'Due to their commanding power, the cities started to refer to the surrounding territory as their 'counties'. And in order not to be short of personnel to suppress their neighbours, they did not hesitate to call people of low standing, even craftsmen, to military service and public office, people other nations keep away like the plague from noble positions becoming freeborn men. And thus, it has come about that they have far surpassed other cities in the world in wealth and power. They were empowered not only by their characteristic industry, but also by the traditional absence of the emperors preferring to remain on the far side of the Alps' (*Consueverunt autem singuli singula territoria ex hac comminandi potestate comitatus suos appellare. Ut etiam ad comprimendos vicinos materia non careant, inferioris conditionis iuvenes vel quoslibet contemptibilium etiam mechanicarum artium opifices, quos ceterae gentes ab honestioribus et liberioribus studiis tamquam pestem propellunt, ad miliciae cingulum vel dignitatum gradus assumere non dedignantur. Ex quo factum est, ut caeteris orbis civitatibus divitiis et potentia longe premineant. Iuvantur ad hoc non solum, ut dictum est, morum suorum industria, sed et principum in Transalpinis manere assuetorum absentia*).

20   On the presence of Oberto at the 1154 diet at Roncaglia see Otto of Freising, *Gesta Friderici* 2,16, MGH *SS rer. Germ.* 46, 119: '*presentibus duobus consulibus eiusdem civitatis <Mediolanensium>, Oberto de Orto et Girardo Nigro*'. Oberto was not an academic, but a practicing lawyer, a judge and administrator, many times *consul* of his native city. His letters addressed to his son, instructing him on the principles of customary Lombard feudal law, are at the core of the *Libri feudorum*, a private collection of letters, treatises, decisions of feudal courts, and legal *consilia*, most of them concentrating on the construction of statutes on Lombard feudal law issued by Conrad II, Lothair III, and Frederick I. The collection, an ever-expanding text over time, gained its definitive form around 1250. It obtained an authori-

the constitutional problems ahead. There were two competing ideolo-
gies on a collision course, an 'imperial' ideology, based on late-Roman
public law, and 'republican' principles derived from customary feudal
law[21]. Barbarossa's predilection for Roman law was displayed for all the
world to see shortly later when he, 'en route' to Rome, came to Bologna,
where he granted his famous privilege to the students and professors of
civil (*i.e.* Roman) law in that city, the *Authentica 'Habita'*, and ordered
that privilege to be inserted into the *Codex Justinianus*[22]. Barbarossa
was, as he states himself, very pleased with the work of the professors
teaching Roman law, since they '*illuminate the world and teach our subjects to obey God and us, His servant*'[23]. Not a word about obedience to
the pope.

tative status after it was added to the 'Volumen' part of the medieval manuscripts of Justinian's
Corpus Iuris and provided with an extensive gloss, probably composed by Accursius. The seminal edition is by K. Lehmann, *Das langobardische Lehnrecht*, Göttingen 1896 (repr. Aalen
1971, with Lehmann's *Consuetudines feudorum*, Göttingen 1892). I should stress that the *Libri
feudorum* should not be confused with the *Lombarda*, an older systematic compilation of
Lombard law composed in the last decades of the 11th century on the basis of the *Liber legis
Langobardorum*, a chronological compilation, composed some decades before the *Lombarda*,
of all the statutes of the Lombard kings and their Carolingian and German successors, closing
with a statute of Henry III. It is important to emphasize that these Lombard collections were
compiled by the same kind of practicing lawyers as Oberto was. They were first and foremost
concerned with customary law, but on the other hand not just superficially acquainted with,
but veritably steeped in Roman law as well, as is exemplified by the extensive *Expositio* to the
Liber legis Langobardorum, also composed before the end of the 11th century.
21   Oberto dell Orto secured the primacy of customary law over Roman law for centuries to
come by a phrase in the *Libri feudorum* (*LF* 2,1) that was to dominate the doctrine of sources
of law all over the European continent until the end of the eighteenth century: 'The authority
of Roman law is not worthless, but not to the extent that it prevails over custom and usages'
(*Legum autem Romanarum non est vilis authoritas, sed non adeo vim suam extendunt, ut usum
vincant aut mores*). It was a deliberate reversal of a statute of Constantine (C. 8,52,2), providing that 'The authority of customary law is not worthless, but not to the extent that it prevails
over reason and statutory law' (*Consuetudinis ususque longaevi non vilis auctoritas est, verum
non usque adeo sui valitura momento, ut aut rationem vincat aut legem*).
22   The famous Authentica 'Habita' was added to C. 4,13,5 and is printed in most modern editions of the Justinian *Codex*. The date is not 1158, but 1155: see W. Stelzer, 'Zum
Scholarenprivileg Friedrich Barbarossas (Authentica 'Habita')', in: *Deutsches Archiv für
Erforschung des Mittelalters* 34 (1978) 123 *ff* (146-153).
23   In the Authentica 'Habita': *quorum scientia totus illuminatur mundus, et ad obediendum
Deo et nobis, eius ministris, vita subiectorum informatur*.

REGIBVS
CORONAM FERREAM
SOLLEMNI RITV ACCEPTVRIS
HEIC
SOLITVM POSITVM FVISSE
VETVS OPINIO
TESTATVR

'Ancient tradition holds that here stood the throne for the kings about to solemnly receive the iron crown'
(Floor tile in the Basilica of S. Michele Maggiore in Pavia, author's photograph)

5

Pope Hadrian IV and Frederick I

The last emperor to be crowned at Rome before Barbarossa was Lothair III in 1133. Something had happened during that ceremony in 1133 that seems to have bothered some German princes, accounting for Barbarossa's rather doctrinal letter to Pope Eugenius III announcing his election[1]. Before his coronation, Lothair III had publicly sworn an oath to the pope that resembled an oath of fealty, suggesting that Lothair submitted to the pope as a vassal of the Church[2]. It was certainly interpreted so by Innocent II, who had the scene painted on the walls of his Lateran Palace with a legend leaving no doubt about it[3]. It was also common knowledge that Lothair III, even before his coronation at Rome, had publicly rendered 'squire service' to Pope Innocent II, meaning that he had escorted the pope on foot, holding

An awkward meeting at Sutri

---

1 See *supra* p. 77-81.

2 The oath of Lothair III was important to the pope, since the papal camerlengo Cencio Savelli (later Pope Honorius III) included it in his famous *Liber censuum* (1, no 141, 414): 'I, Lothair, promise and swear to you, Pope Innocent, and your successors to guarantee your personal safety regarding life and limb and captivity, and to defend the papacy and its honour, and to conserve the demesne of St Peter you have, and to recover what you do not have at the best of my possibilities' (*Ego Lothair rex promitto et iuro tibi domino pape Innocentio tuisque successoribus securitatem vite et membri et male captionis, et defendere papatum et honorem tuum, et regalia sancti Petri que habes manu tenere, et que non habes iuxta meum posse recuperare*). For an even more explicit oath of fealty by the emperor see a second imperial coronation ceremony (*ordo coronationis*) in the *Liber censuum* (1, 1*-6* (1*)): '*In nomine domini nostri Ihesu Christi ego N. rex et futurus imperator Romanorum promitto, spondeo, polliceor atque per haec evangelia juro coram Domino et beato Petro apostolo tibi N. beati Petri apostoli vicario* fidelitatem, *tuisque successoribus canonice intrantibus, meque amodo protectorem ac defensorem fore huius sancta Romane ecclesie et vestre persone vestrorum successorum in omnibus utilitatibus in quantum divino fultus fuero adiutorio, secundum scire meum ac posse, sine fraude et malo ingenio. Sic me Deus adiuvet et hec sancta evangelia*' (emphasis added). It is unclear for which coronation this oath was meant and if it was in fact ever sworn in this way at all.

3 According to Bishop Otto of Freising (*Gesta Friderici* 3,10, MGH *SS rer. Germ.* 46, 177), the legend read as follows: 'The king comes before the gates, first swearing to uphold the privileges of the city, after that he becomes a vassal of the pope, from whom he receives the crown' (*Rex venit ante fores, iurans prius Urbis honores/Post homo fit papae, sumit quo dante coronam*). On this painting in the Lateran Palace see also *Annales Sancti Panthaleonis Coloniensis maximi* ad ann. 1157, MGH *SS* 17, 766.

the pope's horse by the bridle and holding the stirrup as that holy man dismounted[4]. It was a demeaning service, reeking of submission as well, and it was deeply disturbing to Barbarossa, since an important clause in the Treaty of Konstanz seemed to directly relate to this. It obliged Barbarossa 'to protect and defend the honour and the rights of the pope as was befitting a dedicated and special 'advocate' (*advocatus*) of the Holy Roman Church'[5]. The obligation did not necessarily imply feudal submission to the pope[6], but given the close connection between this clause in the Treaty of Konstanz and the oath of Lothair III sworn in 1133, which was interpreted by some as an oath of fealty, it made Barbarossa wary. He wanted to avoid any kind of behaviour towards the pope from which it might be concluded that he accepted that pontiff as his superior, let alone as his feudal suzerain, as 'the Sicilian usurper', Roger II, was indeed required to do. As far as Barbarossa was concerned, he expected the same kind of service from the Bishop of Rome as he had been expecting from the Bishop of Cologne at his coronation in Aachen in 1152: to perform the religious ceremony customarily attendant on the elevation of a German king to Roman emperor, no more and no

---

4   The incident occurred at the synod of Lièges in 1131 and is reported by Abbot Suger of S. Denys, who was probably present at the occasion: *Vita Ludovici Grossi regis* xxxi, *Oeuvres complètes de Suger*, ed. A. Lecoy de la Marche, Paris 1867, 136. Squire service by an emperor to the pope is mentioned in the Donation of Constantine (*Const. Const.* § 16, ed. H. Furhrmann, MGH, *Fontes iuris* 10, 92): 'holding the bridle of his horse, we have rendered squire service to him out of respect for St Peter' (*tenentes frenum equi ipsius pro reverentia beati Petri stratoris officium illi exhibuimus*). It is reported in the *Liber pontificalis* that Pepin I rendered squire service to Pope Stephen II (*Vita Stephani II*, ed. Duchesne I, 447), but the contemporary Frankish sources make no mention of it. The ceremony probably originated in Italy with the courtesy rendered by the Lombard kings to the Roman pontiff after the conversion of the Lombards from Arianism to Catholicism. As a matter of course, no classical Roman or Byzantine emperor ever rendered squire service to a Roman pope, nor did any of the Saxon and Salian German emperors.

5   Treaty of Konstanz §2 (MGH *Const.* 1, no 145, 203): '*Honorem papatus et regalia beati Petri sicut devotus et specialis advocatus sancta Romane ecclesie contra omnes homines pro posse suo conservabit et defendet, que nunc habet. Que vero nunc non habet, recuperare pro posse iuvabit, et recuperare defendet*'.

6   An *advocatus* (Germ. 'Vogt') was a person appointed by a bishop or an abbot to take care of the secular administration of the property of an episcopate or a monastery, especially the criminal jurisdiction as well as the military protection involved, since a cleric could not wield the secular sword. An *advocatus* could hold his office as a fief, but this was not necessarily so. In any way, the use of the term may still have been offensive, since it made the emperor into a papal appointee, which he was not since he was 'elected by God and appointed by the princes' as an old German source emphasized (Widukind of Corvey (10th century), *Rerum Gestarum Saxonicarum* 2,1, MGH, *SS rer. Germ.* 60, 65): '*a Deo electum ... a cunctis principibus regem factum*'. One of the cardinals negotiating the Treaty of Konstanz was the canonist Rolando Bandinelli, cardinal-priest of S. Marc, later Pope Alexander III. On him see *infra* p. 101-103.

less[7]. All this explains the awkwardness displayed by Barbarossa at his first personal meeting with Pope Hadrian IV at Sutri on 9 June 1155[8]. It was about the squire service the pope expected of him at the occasion. Barbarossa refused, but Hadrian insisted[9], causing a major diplomatic incident because the pope refused to give Barbarossa the kiss of peace since the king had offended his dignity. In the end, it was decided that Barbarossa could render squire service as a special courtesy towards the pope without offending the honour of the empire, which he did at a carefully orchestrated 'casual' meeting with the pope on the next day.

After tempers had cooled, the pope and the Redbeard departed for Rome together. While still on their way, Barbarossa was offered an excellent opportunity to impress Hadrian IV with his independence from papal power. Barbarossa was met by a delegation of the rebellious Roman citizenry, eager to liberate themselves from the political power of their bishop as the Lombard cities had done some time before. The Romans had decided that one of the ways to achieve that was to offer the imperial crown to Barbarossa. The manner in which they proceeded to that end showed that the citizens of Rome had completely lost sight on the political realities of their day and age. They lived in a Roman, if not romantic, fantasy world of their own creation, stimulated by the rebellious anticlerical speeches of the political philosopher Arnold of Brescia († 1155)[10], who had been preaching and teaching in

Barbarossa meets ambassadors from Rome

---

7   On this issue see Barbarossa himself in 1157 (Otto of Freising, *Gesta Friderici* 3,11, MGH *SS rer. Germ.* 46, 188): 'We are gladly prepared to pay due respect to our father <the pope>, but we owe the free crown of our empire to divine favour alone. We recognize that in the election the first vote belongs to the archbishop of Mainz, and after him the other lords, according to their rank; the royal anointment falls to the bishop of Cologne, but the highest one, which is the imperial, belongs to the pope. All the rest is superfluous and wicked' (*Debitam patri nostro reverentiam libenter exhibemus, liberam imperii nostri coronam divino tantum beneficio adscribimus, electionis primam vocem Maguntino archiepiscopo, deinde quod superest caeteris secundum ordinem principibus recognoscimus; regalem unctionem Coloniensi, supremam vero, quae imperialis est, summo pontifici; quidquid praeter haec est, ex habundanti est, a malo est*).

8   The principal account of this famous event is written by an eyewitness, Pope Hadrian's nephew Cardinal Boso, recently promoted to the position of camerlengo and author of some important biographies of his uncle and subsequent popes: *Gesta pontificum romanorum, vita Adriani IV*, in *Liber pontificalis.* ed. Duchesne 2, 390-392. There is a shorter version, probably also written by Boso, in the *Liber censuum* (1, 414). Another account, not by an eyewitness but relying on the testimony of another eyewitness, Bishop Gerold of Oldenburg, is in Helmhold of Bosau (*c.* 1120-†after 1177), *Cronica slavorum* 1,81, MGH *SS rer. Germ.* 32, 152-154.

9   Helmhold of Bosau has a slightly different rendering of the facts, since according to him the pope complained that Barbarossa had performed his squire service incorrectly by holding the left stirrup of the pope's horse and not the right one, as he should have done.

10   Arnold was driven from France, where he had been teaching alongside Abélard, by Bernard of Clairvaux who despised Arnold (as that saintly man despised Abélard as well). He sought refuge in Konstanz, but was also driven from there, since St Bernard warned all of Europe for that dangerous 'enemy of the cross of Christ, that schismatic, that disturber

Rome until recently, on the one hand, and the fatal illusion that the classical Roman Empire still existed, and that Rome still was the capital of that empire, on the other. Accordingly, they were convinced that it was up to them, rather than the pope, to offer the imperial crown to the German king. They insisted the pope had nothing to do with that. Did not Justinian's *Digest* explicitly state that the Roman emperor derived his sovereignty (*imperium*) from a decree of the people of Rome transferring their sovereignty to the emperor[11]? There was no mention of a special role for the pope anywhere in Justinian's code.

When the emissaries of the Roman citizenry met the emperor and the pope on their way to Rome, they were received by Barbarossa who was disposed to hear them. The Roman envoys brought Barbarossa important news: the ancient Roman senate and the ancient Roman equestrian order (*ordo equester*) had arisen from the ashes of the past in order to enable Barbarossa to restore the 'ancient glory' (*antiqua magnificentia*) of the Roman Empire with the help and advice of the Roman senate and the arms of the Roman equestrian order. What followed was even more absurd. Barbarossa might be 'an immigrant from the far side of the Alps' (*advena ex Transalpinis partibus*), but he could be naturalized as a Roman citizen nevertheless and be endowed with the imperial crown by the people of Rome, provided he complied with three conditions: he had to swear that he would confirm all the privileges of the city of Rome, that he would not use force against his Roman subjects, and, last but not least, that he would pay 5000 pounds in return for the privilege of being elevated to the dignity of the Roman imperial crown

---

of the peace, that sower of discord' (*S. Bernardi Epistolae*, *Ep.* 195, Migne *PL* 182, col. 361-363(363)). In the end, the Cardinal-deacon of SS. Cosmas and Damian Guido, papal legate in Bohemia, offered him asylum. As a matter of course, St Bernard also warned Cardinal Guido for that monster 'whom Brescia has puked out, whom Rome has turned away from with disgust, who has been banned from France, who is despised by Germany and whom Italy will not welcome' (*l.c.*). Guido did not heed that saintly warning and took Arnold with him back to Italy, where he was received by Pope Eugenius III, who ordered him to go and preach in Rome by way of penance. It was a serious mistake that must have outraged St Bernard, for what Arnold preached in Rome with great success was rebellion against the secular power of the Church. In the end Pope Hadrian IV had had enough of it and laid the city of Rome under interdict for as long as Arnold stayed in the city. He was indeed banned from the city and stayed for a while near S. Quirico in Tuscany, where he was arrested by Barbarossa on request of the pope. He was handed over to papal officials and transferred to Rome, where Arnold was hung on order of the city-prefect, a papal functionary. His body was burnt, and the ashes were scattered into the Tiber, so that his grave could not become a place of worship for his admirers (Otto of Freising, *Gesta Friderici* 2,28, MGH *SS rer. Germ.* 46, 134).

11   D. 1,4,1 (Ulpian): 'What pleases the emperor, has force of law, since the people transfer on and to him all its power and authority by way of the royal law which is passed concerning his sovereignty' (*Quod principi placuit, legis habet vigorem: utpote cum lege regia, quae de imperio eius lata est, populus ei et in eum omne suum imperium et potestatem conferat*). See the same fragment from Ulpian in Justinian's *Institutes* 1,2,6.

by the people of Rome[12]. It was a preposterous affront and Barbarossa was outraged. He taught the Romans *and* the pope a history lesson he hoped they would not forget. Rome had ceased to be the capital of the empire long ago, ever since the capital was transferred 'to the imperial city in the east' (*ad Orientis urbem regiam*), meaning Constantinople. It was a clear reference to the old Silvestrian legend[13], but what followed was *not* the papal version of that legend, the Donation of Constantine, but a very different and certainly more realistic story: the Roman Empire belonged to the Germans by right of conquest. 'It belongs to me as of right' (*legittimus possessor sum*) and 'not on account of anyone's favour' (*nullius beneficio*) Barbarossa asserted. As far as their conditions were concerned, he reacted in a way that was addressed to all Italian cities: 'it is incumbent on a prince to administer the law to his people, not the other way around' (*principem populo, non populum principi leges prescribere oporteat*)[14]. After that, the Romans envoys were summarily dismissed.

Frederick I was crowned shortly after, on 18 June, as Roman emperor in St Peter's. After a serious riot in the narrow streets of Trastevere, instigated by the Roman rebels on the very same day[15], Barbarossa and the pope left the city for the safer (and cooler) Alban hills south of Rome. It was there, in Frascati, that they discussed the situation in South Italy. King Roger II had died in February 1154 and was succeeded by his son, William I (*c.* 1120-1154-1166). The new Sicilian king was facing the usual revolt of his Norman barons, always frustrated by the fact that the Sicilian kingdom was not governed on feudal principles involving the nobility as a matter of course, but was administrated, Roman (or rather Byzantine) style, by a professional civil service, recruited from the civilized urban elite. It was common knowledge at the time that the revolt of the barons was incited by the pope[16], who now wanted

Barbarossa refuses to invade Sicily

---

12   See for the message of the Roman envoys Otto of Freising, *Gesta Friderici* 2,29, MGH *SS rer. Germ.* 46, 135-136.

13   See *supra* p. 31.

14   For Barbarossa's reply see Otto of Freising, *Gesta Friderici* 2,30, MGH *SS rer. Germ.* 46, 136-139. As a matter of course, we do not know if these words actually were spoken by Barbarossa, since Bishop Otto was not present at the occasion. We do, however, have a supporting letter by Barbarossa himself to his uncle and biographer informing him of the event (*Gesta Friderici*, MGH *SS rer. Germ.* 46, 3), to which the emperor may have added further specific details verbally later, on his return to Germany in 1155.

15   Reportedly, a thousand Romans died that day and countless citizens were either wounded or captured by the German soldiers who had been expecting them. See for the details Otto of Freising, *Gesta Friderici* 2,33, MGH *SS rer. Germ.* 46, 141-142.

16   William of Tyre, *Historia etc.* 18,2 (Migne *PL* 201, col. 709-710): 'The pope tried to call his own nobles to arms against him <William I>, and he was not disappointed, because the pope persuaded the mightiest baron of his kingdom, Robert de Bassavilla, a son of an aunt

Barbarossa and his army to side with them and so do away with the Hautevilles once and for all. The pope was supported by some of the German clerics in Barbarossa's own court[17], and the Byzantine Emperor Manuel even offered a large amount of money to Barbarossa in order to persuade him to fight William[18], clearly hoping for a partition agreement with Barbarossa later, as he had arranged with Barbarossa's uncle, Conrad III[19]. But the newly crowned emperor of the Romans declined to proceed against the Sicilian Normans. He must have been reminded of the failed 1136-1137 campaign of Lothair III and the revolt of the German knights, who did not want to fight on behalf of the pope[20]. Barbarossa decided to go home[21], much to the chagrin of Hadrian IV, who felt that Barbarossa deserted him at this critical juncture.

---

of the king, and many other nobles to rise against him' (*Dominus papa … principes proprios contra eum nititur armare; nec in ea parte fraudatus est a desiderio suo. Nam potentissimum regni sui comitem, eiusdem regis amitae filium, Robertum videlicet de Bassavilla, cum multis aliis viris nobilibus … contra eum insurgere persuasit*).

17   From the chronicle of Otto of St Blasius (1200-1210), MGH *SS Rer. germ.* 47, 7-8: 'On the urging of the archbishop of Cologne, Bishop Hermann of Konstanz, and some other princes, he was inclined to proceed further against William, the son of Roger, who held Apulia, usurping the title of king' (*suadentibus Coloniensi archiepiscopo et Hermanno Constantiensi episcopo et quibusdam aliis principibus, ad ulteriora contra Wilhelmum filium Rogeri, qui Apuliam usurpato regio nomine tenebat, progredi disposuit*).

18   Barbarossa himself in a letter to Otto of Freising, *Gesta Friderici*, MGH *SS rer. Germ.* 46, 4.

19   See *supra* p. 82.

20   See *supra* p. 34.

21   Barbarossa in the letter to Otto of Freising just mentioned, *Gesta Friderici*, MGH *SS rer. Germ.* 46, 4: 'But because our army was rather exhausted by all the exertion and fighting, the princes preferred to go home rather than proceed to Apulia' (*Quia vero milicia nostra propter multos labores et bella nimis attrita fuit, placuit magis principibus redire quam in Apuliam descendere*). See also Otto of St Blasius, MGH *SS Rer. germ.* 47, 8: 'dissuaded by others, he returned to the far side of the Alps, postponing it <*i.e.* the conquest of Sicily> for a later occasion' (*ab aliis dissuasus hoc in posterum differens ad Cisalpina revertitur*).

The Emperor Frederick I 'Barbarossa'
(*Chronica regia coloniensis*, Royal Library
of Belgium, Ms 467, *f.* 103 *v*)

The year 1155 was a decisive year for King William I of Sicily since the revolt of the barons of Apulia caused a revolt in Sicily itself as well[22]. His situation seemed almost hopeless after a substantial Byzantine army had landed in Brindisi. It was William's Prime Minister (*ammiratus ammiratorum*) Maio of Bari (†1160), son of a justice in the Supreme Court of the kingdom, who saved the king. Maio roused the Hauteville spirit in the mighty though reluctant warrior that was William. Once prompted into action, the king crushed the revolting Sicilian barons, smashed the Byzantine army and routed the rebellious barons in South Italy one after the other, all within two months' time (1156)[23]. The

King William I
asserts his
authority

---

22   Romoald of Salerno, *Chronicon* ad. ann. 1155, MGH *SS* 19, 428: 'Many of the revolting barons of Apulia stirred up a serious war in Apulia. When they heard of this, the barons of Sicily raised a war against the king on Sicily as well' (*Multi etiam de baronibus Apulie rebelles effecti guerram maximam in Apulia excitaverunt. Quo audito barones Sicilie et ipsi similiter guerram contra regem in Sicilia commoverunt*).

23   See the short resumé of events in South Italy in 1156 in *Annales Pisani*, composed by the lawyer Bernardus Marango (†1182/1188) ad ann. 1156, *RIS*² 6.2, 15: 'In the month of May King William came to Apulia with a mighty army and unleashed a great war against the barons of Apulia and the emperor of Constantinople and defeated them, capturing all the Greeks, and he seized thirty galleys of the emperor, with all their men; destroyed Bari and made Prince Robert his prisoner. He regained control over all of Apulia within two months and held it. The emperor of the Greeks was much depressed by this' (*Rex igitur Guillelmusin mense Madio de Cicilia venit in Apuliam cum magno exercitu, et fecit bellum magnum cum baronibus Apulie et exercitu imperatoris Constantinopolitani, et divicit eos et omnes Grecos retinuit, et triginta galeas imperatoris cum totis hominibus habuit, et Bari destruxit, et principem Robertum cepit, et totam Apuliam in duobus mensibus recuperavit et retinuit. Unde Grecorum imperator magnam tristitiam habuit*).

rebels who had managed to escape William's sword, fled to the pope, who had led an army into Apulia as well and resided in Benevento, a papal enclave in South Italy. Hadrian should not have done so, for once again a pope faced the wrath of an Hauteville. The pope, now besieged by William, felt deserted and deceived by all and everyone who had sworn to stand by him[24]. Hadrian saw no other way out of his predicament than to pass under the same yoke as that other wanting warrior-pope, Innocent II, had been forced to do in 1139[25]: he made his peace with William and enfeoffed the Sicilian with the kingdom of Sicily, the duchy of Apulia, and the principality of Capua, the three papal fiefs constituting the 'Sicilian' kingdom[26].

---

24   Boso (*Gesta pontificum romanorum, vita Adriani IV*, in *Liber pontificalis,* ed. Duchesne, 2, 395): '*pontifex deceptum se fore cognovit et ab omnibus qui secum firmiter stare iuraverant penitus derelictum*'.
25   See *supra* p. 35.
26   Romoald of Salerno (one of the diplomats negotiating the treaty of Benevento on the part of King William), *Chronicon* ad. ann. 1156, MGH *SS* 19, 429: 'He <William> came to an agreement with the pope. Pope Hadrian benevolently received King William, who humbly kissed his feet. After having sworn an oath of fealty, as is customary, he became the vassal of the pope and the pope enfeoffed him with one banner for the kingdom of Sicily and with another for the duchy of Apulia and with a third banner for the principality of Capua' (*Ipse ... cum papa concordatus est. Nam Adrianus papa ... regem Wilhelmum ad pedes suos humiliter accedentem benigne recepit. Qui facto iuramento, ut moris erat, liggius homo pape devenit, et papa ipsum per unum vexillum de regno Sicilie, per aliud de ducatu Apulie, per tercium de principatu Capue investivit*). The treaty is in MGH *Const.* 1, no 413 and 414, 588-591.

6

Cardinal Bandinelli

The Treaty of Benevento (June 1156) between Hadrian IV and William I spectacularly confirmed the title of the Hautevilles to South Italy and Sicily and consequently infuriated Barbarossa. The emperor was even more enraged when he learnt that the pope had granted extraordinary ecclesiastical prerogatives to the Sicilian king he himself did not have, *dominus mundi* though he was. Two examples: there was to be no appeal by clerics to the papal court from Sicily without permission of the king and episcopal elections in Sicily needed the approval (*assensus*) of the king before the nominees could be consecrated[1]. Most important of all were the legatine powers granted by the pope to the king of Sicily alone of all European princes, making the king of Sicily, as personal representative (*legatus*) of the pope, practically the head of the Church on Sicily[2]. These were prerogatives no other European king had after the Investiture Controversy. The emperor had been left out completely and felt betrayed by the pope. Barbarossa regarded Hadrian's dealings with

---

1 *Pactum Beneventanum, Privilegium Wilh. regis* art. 10, MGH *Const.* 1, no 413, 589-590.
2 *Pactum Beneventanum, Privilegium Wilh. regis* art. 9, MGH *Const.* 1, no 413, 589. The legatine powers were first granted to William's grandfather, Roger I, the 'Great Count', in the treaty of Salerno (5 July 1098) with Pope Urban II, See Gaufredus Malaterra († after 1099), *De rebus gestis Rogerii comitis* 4,29 (ad ann. 1098), *RIS²* 5.1, 108: 'We have promised and confirm by the authority of the present deed that we will not appoint a legate of the Roman Church in the land under your rule without your wish or consent; and even more than this, we want all that is to be done by a legate to be resolved by your diligence in the place of a legate' (*promissimus, litterarum ita auctoritate firmamus: qutod ... nullum in terra potestatis vestrae, praeter voluntatem aut consilium vestrum, legatum Romanae Ecclesiae statuemus; quinimmo, quae per legatum acturi sumus, per vestram industriam legati vice cohiberi volumus*). These traditional Sicilian ecclesiastical privileges of the king of Sicily were to be central to the conflict between Frederick II and the papacy: see *infra* p. 188 and 227. To understand this special position of the island of Sicily, it is important to remember that the island had only been recently reconquered after almost 200 years of Arab rule. Catholicism had virtually disappeared from the island, if it had ever been dominant, since all Christians still living on the island under Arab rule adhered to Greek orthodoxy. Consequently, a new Catholic ecclesiastical infrastructure had to be rebuilt on the island from scratch by Roger I, exercising quasi-legatine powers in the process. By indeed granting legatine powers to the king of Sicily in 1098, the pope was merely confirming the ecclesiastical *status quo* on the island.

the Sicilian usurper as a clear breach of the Treaty of Konstanz of 1153 between himself and Pope Eugenius III[3]. He had sworn that he would not negotiate with Roger II of Sicily and his successors without the permission of the pope and so he believed that his counterpart, the pope, was under a similar obligation[4]. After the Treaty of Benevento good relations between Barbarossa and the pope were never fully restored. As of then, the emperor fundamentally distrusted the pope and his cardinals, especially Cardinal Bandinelli, who was chiefly responsible for the Treaty of Benevento[5].

Cardinal
Bandinelli

Rolando Bandinelli, the future Pope Alexander III, is one of the ablest politicians ever to have served the Church of Rome. He has long been identified with the canonist Rolandus, author of one of the first commentaries on Gratian's *Decretum*. That identification is now rightly contested, but it can hardly be denied that Bandinelli had indeed read canon law in Bologna before 1150, when he entered the papal *curia*, that is about the same time when Gratian finished his *Decretum*. There is reliable evidence that Gratian finished his *Decretum* 'when Jacob read Roman law and Alexander, who was later Pope Alexander III, read theology'[6]. Before the days of Gratian, the teaching of canon law was still a part of theology. The canonist Rolandus, for example, still considered himself a theologian, even announcing a theological treatise in his commentary on Gratian's *Decretum*[7]. There was as yet no clear distinction between canon lawyers and theologians in the days of Bandinelli, but his entire career betrays a legal approach to the problems with which he was confronted. The Treaty of Benevento is just such an example. He must have been very content with that Treaty, since it permanently blocked the claim of the emperor to South Italy. The cardinal realized, as Gregory VII had done before him[8], that the Normans in South Italy were not to be treated as enemies, but as the only possible guarantors

---

3   See *supra* p. 81-83.
4   The reciprocity of contractual promises was a commonly accepted principle of civil law at the time. See Cynus of Pistoia (1270-1336/1337), *Lectura Codicis* ad C. 8,41,1 (ed. Venice 1493, *f.* 358 *r*, l. col.): 'It cannot be accepted that one party to a contract is allowed to do something the other party may not' (*nec debet ex contractu uni partium licere quod alteri non licet*). Naturally, the same holds for the reverse.
5   For the involvement of Cardinal Bandinelli, cardinal-priest of S. Marco and papal chancellor, in the treaty of Benevento see MGH *Const.* 1, no 413, 589 and Boso, *Gesta pontificum romanorum, vita Adriani* IV, in *Liber pontificalis*, ed. Duchesne 2, 395. Cardinal Bandinelli had also been co-responsible for the Treaty of Konstanz: see *supra* p. 94, fnt. 6.
6   See the Gl. 'mcxli' on C. 2, q. 6, cap. 31.
7   *Die Summa magistri Rolandi*, ed. Thaner, Innsbruck 1874, 193 (on C. 33, q. 3). Bandinelli was posthumously praised as a great teacher of theology (read: canon law) by the learned Abbot of Mont St Michel Robert of Torigni († 1186) in his chronicle ad ann. 1181, MGH *SS* 6, 531: '*obiit Alexander papa tertius ... in divina pagina preceptor maximus*'.
8   See *supra* p. 30.

of the 'liberty of the Church' (*libertas ecclesiae*), the only force in Italy that could credibly withstand and oppose the might of the German emperors. Cardinal Bandinelli was, in short, the leading representative of a 'Sicilian' faction within the papal *curia*.

In 1157 Bandinelli was charged by the pope to head a diplomatic mission to Barbarossa. The cardinal met the emperor at Besançon, the capital of Burgundy and part of the empire. What transpired there has become legendary in German national history. Bandinelli, as chancellor head of the papal mission, publicly read a letter by the pope to Barbarossa, reminding the emperor of the many 'favours' (*beneficia*) the emperor had recently received from the Holy Father in Rome, most prominently of course the crown of the empire. Since the letter was written in Latin, it had to be translated simultaneously into German on behalf of the court's illiterate members. The German chancellor, Rainer of Dassel, acted as interpreter and translated the word 'favour' (*beneficium*) as 'fief', implying that the emperor had received the empire as a papal fief, thus placing Barbarossa at the same level with the contemptible Sicilian usurpers who had indeed received their kingdom as a papal fief. This was an intolerable insult, causing great turmoil among the courtiers. In the ensuing heated debate one of the papal ambassadors (Bandinelli?) cried out aloud "If he does not have it from the pope, from whom then does he have it"[9]? This clearly suggests that the papal ambassador had, indeed, intended that fatal word '*beneficium*' to mean exactly what Rainer thought it meant: a fee. At this point, the count palatine at the Rhine, Otto of Wittelsbach, drew his sword threatening to smash the head of the offender. Barbarossa, however, intervened and avoided bloodshed, but he immediately dismissed the papal ambassadors, ordering them to leave the German kingdom straight away. The German bishops were as shocked as the emperor and his nobles were and sent a letter to the pope in support of Barbarossa. Their letter contained an attachment, a memorandum composed by the emperor

The Besançon incident

---

9   *Gesta Friderici* 3,10, MGH *SS rer. Germ.* 46, p. 177: '*A quo ergo habet, si a domno papa non habet imperium?*'. The main source for the Besançon incident is Rahewin's continuation of Otto of Freising's *Gesta Friderici* (Bishop Otto died in 1158) 3,8-10, MGH *SS rer. Germ.* 46, p. 172-177), who has the entire letter of the pope, but leaves out, as too offensive to report, the crucial word '*beneficium*'. However, as is evident from a letter by Pope Hadrian, written later in 1157 (Mansi, 21, col. 790-791 (791)), it had been part of the original wording. In another, later, letter (inserted in full in *Gesta Friderici* 3,23, MGH *SS rer. Germ.* 46, p. 195-197 (196)) Hadrian IV gives another construction to that word, *i.e.* 'a good deed' (*bonum factum*). It sounds rather lame. The person most probably responsible for the draft of the original letter read at Besançon, Cardinal Bandinelli, was a lawyer and lawyers at the time had but one construction of that word (*beneficium*) within a legal context, to wit a fee (*feudum*): see the contemporary *Libri Feudorum* 2,23,1 (Oberto del'Orto).

himself. It comprised a completely secularized version of Barbarossa's earlier restatement of the 'Gelasian' doctrine of the two powers[10], now leaving the pope out of the equation: '*There are two things by which our empire must be ruled, the sacred decrees of the emperors and the good customs of our predecessors and forefathers. We cannot and do not want to exceed these limits; whatever disagrees with this, we do not accept*'[11]. The Besançon incident and the imperial reaction to it must have confirmed Cardinal Bandinelli in his conviction that the Sicilian alliance was vital to the interests of the Church.

---

10 See *supra* p. 77-81.

11 *Gesta Friderici* 3,11, MGH *SS rer. Germ.* 46, 188, with the corrections of Weiland, MGH *Const.* 1 no 167, 233: '*Duo sunt, quibus nostrum regi oportet imperium, leges sanctae imperatorum et usus bonus predecessorum et patrum nostrorum. Istos limites excedere nec volumus nec possumus; quidquid ab his discordat non recipimus*'.

7

The Parliament of Roncaglia

After the Treaty of Benevento Barbarossa was confronted with a situation in South Italy very different from what it had been when he left the Italian peninsula in the previous year. Instead of a weakened, if not collapsing, kingdom of Sicily, he was now confronted with a new king of Sicily invigorated by his recent successes, William I, who had shown to the world that he was a force to be reckoned with. Conquering that kingdom would not be easy and required the active assistance of his Italian subjects in the Lombard kingdom. Barbarossa had learned, however, during his short visit in 1154-1156 that anarchy prevailed in his Italian kingdom and that there was one city in particular standing in the way of the establishment of a strong central government in the kingdom: Milan. If he succeeded in bringing down that city, he believed to be able to bring the rest in line soon enough[1]. So, it was with a huge army this time that Barbarossa descended from the Brenner Pass into the Lombard plain once again in 1158. The army was accompanied by an impressive array of 'wise men, very learned in the law' (*multitudo prudentium et in lege doctissimorum*)[2]. They advised the emperor to summon the Milanese in court before advancing against them militarily[3]. Barbarossa complied. The Milanese were summoned, tried, and convicted for rebellion and declared enemies of the state.

Barbarossa
takes on Milan

---

1   Barbarossa in a letter to his biographer Otto of Freising (*Gesta Friderici* 2,50, MGH *SS rer. Germ.* 46, 158): 'Since the pride of the Milanese has already long ago risen against the Roman Empire and even threatens to undermine the whole of Italy by its force and to subject it to its control, we have decided to raise the whole might of the empire to their destruction, so that the vulgar mob may not dare to trample on our glory' (*quia Mediolanensium superbia iam diu caput contra Romanum erexit imperium et modo sua fortitudine totam Italiam subvertere vel suo nititur subiugare dominio, ne ... gloriam nostram plebs improba conculcare valeat ... ad destructionem eorum omne robur imperii excitare intendimus*).
2   *Gesta Friderici* 3,29, MGH *SS rer. Germ.* 46, 202.
3   Rahewin (*Gesta Friderici* 3,30, MGH *SS rer. Germ.* 46, p. 204) writes that the emperor issued a 'peremptory summons' (*edictum peremptorium*) against the Milanese and explains this procedure in a way that makes it clear that it derived from Roman law. There is even a striking resemblance between Rahewin's description of the procedure and a passage from Justinian's *Digest* (D. 5,1,68-72).

On 25 July Barbarossa's army laid siege to Milan and the city was forced to surrender after no more than a month. The terms of surrender were humiliating: the citizens were to swear an oath of obedience and fealty to the emperor, the city was under an obligation to restore to the emperor all exclusive privileges of the Lombard kings (*regalia*) they had usurped in the past, they had to pay a fine of no less than 9000 pounds of silver, and, finally, had to surrender 300 hostages from all levels of the citizenry[4]. Peace was to be restored, moreover, by a solemn act of submission, performed on 7 September 1158 by twelve Milanese consuls. Bare footed, each one holding a sword over his head, they approached the imperial presence. Oberto dell'Orto, 'a wise man proficient in Lombard and Latin' (*vir sapiens et lingue tam Lombardice quam Latine eruditus*), acted as their spokesman and begged for clemency for himself and his citizens[5]. Barbarossa demonstrated mercy, as was befitting a true emperor, and accepted their penance. He seems to have genuinely believed that, after a public humiliation like this, the Milanese would never rise again. As we now know, the emperor was wrong, but he felt free at the time to release the king of Bohemia and the duke of Bavaria from his service and called for a great parliament[6] of all his Lombard vassals to be held at Roncaglia from St Martin's day (11 November) next, where the Italian kingdom was to be reformed on the basis of Roman public law. The emperor was advised on this by four famous professors of Roman law from Bologna, who were invited to attend especially for that purpose[7].

---

4   See for the terms of the peace treaty Rahewin, *Gesta Friderici* 3,47, MGH *SS rer. Germ.* 46, 221-224, also printed in MGH *Constt. F.1* no 174 (241-243).

5   The solemn act of submission is reported by an eyewitness, Vincent of Prague († after 1178), *Annales* ad ann. 1158, MGH *SS* 17, 675. Vincent was a notary in the service of Duke Wladislaw of Bohemia, who was only recently (in 1158) elevated to the high rank of king of Bohemia by Barbarossa as a reward for his many services (*ob fidele servicium*) to the empire (MGH *SS* 17, 667-668). In return, Wladislaw supplied most of the troops for Barbarossa's campaign.

6   The use of the term 'parliament' for the diet of Roncaglia is not anachronistic, since it was already called thus by the Genovese Consul Caffaro di Caschifellone (c. 1080-1166) in his city chronicle ad ann. 1158 (MGH *SS* 18, 26): '*in Runcalliam parlamentum fecit*'.

7   The best source for the parliament of Roncaglia is the eyewitness account of Otto Morena, a judge and consul from Lodi who wrote a history of his city and the exploits of Frederick I in Lombardy. Otto Morena, *Historia* ad ann. 1158 (Nov. 11), MGH *SS rer. Germ. N.S.* 7, 58: '*Interea domnus imperator colloquium in Roncalia in sancto Martino proximo veniente maximum se constituit habiturum, precepitque omnibus fere Ytalie principibus atque civitatum consulibus, ut ipsi colloquio interessent. Ad quod etiam quattuor principales legis doctores, videlicet domnos Bulgarum et Martinum Gosiam seu Iacobum atque Ugonem de Porta Ravegnana, Bononie magistros, interesse fecit*'.

The old *regnum italicum* was reformed on the basis of three statutory provisions, issued by Barbarossa at the parliament[8]. The most important law is the *lex 'Omnis iuridictio'*, providing that *'All public authority and all executive power rests with the emperor and all officials must receive their offices from the emperor and have to swear an oath as is prescribed by the law'*[9]. The oath to be sworn by all Lombard officials, like the city consuls, was to be the oath administered to all Roman officials as prescribed by Justinian[10], *not* the feudal oath of fealty sworn by vassals to their lord. There was only one realm in Europe at the time, where public officials, civil servants (*officiales*), were appointed on the same basis and that was the Sicilian kingdom, which may have served as another model for Barbarossa's 'reformation' of the Lombard kingdom. The consuls from Milan present at Roncaglia must have realized

The *lex 'Omnis iurisdictio'*

---

8   The three basic constitutional laws of Barbarossa's 'reformed' Italian kingdom have long been lost, since the Lombard feudal lawyers, such as Oberto dell'Orto, deliberately expunged them from their commentaries on Barbarossa's other laws issued at Roncaglia. Until fairly recently, there was only a passing reference to one of them in the Gl. 'Criminalibus' on the *Pax Constantiae* and in a legal advice (*consilium*) by the 14th-century civilian Baldus de Ubaldis (*Consiia* V, cons. 300, ed. Venice 1580, *f.* 75). We owe our knowledge of all three basic laws to the Italian scholar Vittore Colorni, *Die drei verschollenen Gesetze des Reichstages bei Roncaglia*, Aalen 1969 (Germ. transl. of the Italian original (1967)), who found them in a Parisian manuscript of the *Libri feudorum* (*BNF*, Ms. Lat. 4677, *f.* 55 ro).

9   MGH, *DD. F* 1,2, no 238 (p. 29-30): *'Omnis iurisdictio et omnis districtus apud principem est et omnes iudices a principe administrationem accipere debent et iusiurandum praestare, quale a lege constitutum est'*. For the translation of *'iurisdictio'* as 'public authority', or even 'absolute power' (*imperium merum*) see the Gl. 'Criminalibus' on the *Pax Constantiae* art. 1: *'nemo sani capitis dubitat merum imperium iurisdictionem esse'*, commenting on Barbarossa's *lex 'Omnis iuridictio'*. See also Azo (*c.* 1150-1220), *Summa Codicis* ad C. 3,17 (*De iurisdictione omnium iudicum*), ed. Lyon 1596, 235: *'Iurisdictio* is derived from the word *ditio* (meaning power) and *ius*, making it equivalent to legitimate power. *Iurisdictio* is to be distinguished, since one kind is absolute and is with the emperor exclusively, the other is less absolute and belongs to the other magistracies' (*Dicitur autem iurisdictio a ditione (quod est potestas) et iure: quasi dicat, legitima potestas. Dividitur autem iurisdictio: quia alia est plenissima et ea est in solo principe; alia est minus plena et ea est in caeteris magistratis*). The translation 'jurisdiction' (Germ.: 'Gerichtsbarkeit') is simply wrong, as is the translation of the word *'iudex'* as 'judge'. In the Middle Ages this word means 'public official' or 'magistrate', including a judge. The four professors from Bologna were, in as far as the *lex 'Omnis iuridictio'* is concerned, inspired by D. 48,14,1 pr., a passage from a treatise by the 3rd-century Roman lawyer Modestinus on Augustus' law against electoral fraud (*ambitus*): 'This law has now ceased to apply in the town <Rome>, since the appointment of magistrates falls to the oversight of the emperor, rather than the favour of the people' (*Haec lex in urbe hodie cessat, quia ad curam principis magistratuum creatio pertinet, non ad populi favorem*). This is why there was no need to insert the *lex 'Omnis iuridictio'* into Justinian's *Codex*, as had happened with the *authentica 'Habita'*: it was a well-established rule of Roman law.

10   Nov. 8, cap. 7, 12 and 14 (535) = Coll. 2, tit. 3. The Latin translation of the Greek original was taken from the so-called *Authenticum*, a Latin translation of a collection of novels made in Justinian's own time on behalf of students who could not read Greek. Ever since Irnerius recognized this translation as the 'original' (*authenticum*), it was widely known in the Middle Ages. The text was later split up in nine 'collations' (*Collationes*).

this. Henceforward they were to be mere copies of Sicilian *officiales*, bureaucratic appointees and servants of the emperor rather than the elected servants of their urban compatriots. It was intolerable, but they submitted to the will of the emperor, for now at least, as their bishop had done[11]. Barbarossa issued a series of other laws at Roncaglia[12] and closed the diet on 26 November. '*After achieving all of this*', a contemporary wrote, '*the emperor left Roncaglia, believing that he had brought everything to a good conclusion and had established peace in his realm*'[13]. The emperor was to be bitterly disappointed.

The Lombard conundrum

The 'peace' dictated by Barbarossa at Roncaglia in 1158 did not even last a year. By July 1159 the city of Crema was in open rebellion and was besieged by the emperor. The town was supported by three other Lombard cities, Brescia, Piacenza, and Milan. As so many of his predecessors, Barbarossa was confronted with a political problem none of the medieval German kings and emperors has been able to solve. The cause was the competition between the practically independent Lombard cities, a consequence of the many years of absence of German kings in Lombardy. Once a German king had arrived in his Italian kingdom, every decision he made in favour of one of the Lombard cities, was immediately experienced as an insult, if not as a declaration of war, by one or two of the others. And whenever the king compromised with a hostile city, it was regarded as treason by his allies, causing the latter to defect and make war on the king. In the end there was but one sentiment joining the cities together, their common distrust of their German king. Then as now, there are only two possible solutions to a situation like this. A complete retreat from the territory or a complete military subjection of it by eliminating all local areas of insurrection and installing an effective central government, supported by a permanent standing army, able to maintain a sustainable peace. The first alterna-

---

11 Archbishop Oberto da Pirovano of Milan (1146-1166) had appropriately opened the Roncaglia parliament with an oration on a famous passage from Justinian's *Digest*, D. 1,4,1 (Ulpian): 'What pleases the emperor, has force of law, since the people transfers on and to him all its power and authority by way of the royal law which is passed concerning his sovereignty' (*Quod principi placuit, legis habet vigorem: utpote cum lege regia, quae de imperio eius lata est, populus ei et in eum omne suum imperium et potestatem conferat*). The speech is reported by Rahewin, *Gesta Friderici* 4,5, MGH *SS rer. Germ.* 46, 237-239.
12 Some of the laws issued by Barbarossa at the Roncaglia parliament were not contested by the Lombard lawyers and treated as part and parcel of Lombard law, such as Barbarossa's famous statute on peace in Lombardy (*Constitutio pacis*) and an important statute limiting the right of feudal tenants to freely dispose of their tenure. They found their way in the *Libri feudorum* in *LF* 2,53(54) and 2,55 respectively.
13 Otto Morena, *Historia* ad ann. 1158, MGH *SS rer. Germ. N.S.* 7, 62): '*Hiis itaque sic peractis, cum imperator omnia se bene peregisse et imperium suum, sicut se decebat, in pace quieta optineret putaret ... de Roncalia tandem discessit*'.

tive was unthinkable at the time: medieval German kings regarded the Lombard kingdom as an integral part of their empire and consequently were unable to give it up. It was simply incompatible with the 'honour of the empire' (*honor imperii*)[14]. The second alternative was unfeasible at the time: medieval German kings lacked the financial and military means, as well as the secular administrative expertise and personnel[15], to successfully implement a policy like that. The result was an endless and hopeless involvement in a political and military quagmire, exacerbated by constant interference of outside powers, such as the Byzantine emperors, the kings of Sicily and, last but not least, the Roman pontiff.

---

14   For this, see a letter written (but not sent) by a desperate Barbarossa many years later (in 1167) to Bishop Albert of Freising (MGH *DD F1,2*, no 538, 485-486): 'Let the heavens be struck dumb on taking notice of the unspeakable treason some Lombard cities have committed against our majesty and the honour of the empire without any cause or preceding fault of our own. The rebellion is not only directed against us personally, because, by throwing off the yoke of our government, they try to reject and eliminate the empire of the Germans that has been bought and upheld up till now with great cost and effort, by the blood of many princes and illustrious people, saying "We do not want this man to rule over us" <Luke 19:14>' (*Cum celi stupeant ... ab auditu nefandissime traditionis, quam quedam civitates Longobardiae ... contra nostram maiestatem, contra imperii honorem sine causa sine aliqua precedenti culpa commiserunt ... Non enim in nostram solummodo redundat rebellio personam, quia iugo dominationis nostre proiecto Teutonicorum imperium, quod multo labore multisque dispendiis ac plurimorum principum et illustrium virorum sanguine emptum et hactenus conservatum refutare et exterminare conantur, dicentes: "Nolumus hunc regnare super nos"*).

15   Paradoxically, an administrative elite was indeed trained at the law school of Bologna (and soon in other Lombard cities as well) at the time, but it was not to serve the needs of the imperial court, but of the Lombard municipalities themselves and the papal and episcopal bureaucracies of Italy and beyond.

8

Pope Alexander III

When Barbarossa was laying siege to Crema, he accidentally[1] received
intelligence of a secret treaty between the insurgent Lombard cities and
Pope Hadrian not to conclude a peace treaty with the emperor without
mutual approval[2]. Relations between the papal court and Barbarossa
had already been steadily worsening over the course of 1159, but this
piece of information outraged the emperor and confirmed all his suspicions of the papal *curia*. It was high treason. Practically coinciding
with the receipt of this intelligence, the emperor was informed that
Pope Hadrian IV had died in Anagni on 1 September 1159. The pope
was already ailing for some time, and Barbarossa had sent two of
his most trusted courtiers to Rome to interfere with the election of
Hadrian's successor, more precisely to frustrate the possible election of
that detestable head of the 'Sicilian' faction in the papal *curia*, Cardinal
Bandinelli[3]. Barbarossa knew, of course, that it was Bandinelli who was
behind the treaty between the pope and the rebelling Lombard cities.
He now learned that Bandinelli was elected pope and had chosen the

A contested
papal election

---

1   Abbot Fastré of Clairvaux and some of his Cistercian monks had tried to broker a peace
between Milan and the emperor in 1159. During the negotiations they learned that Milan
felt bound by its promise to Pope Hadrian not to conclude a peace treaty or a truce with
Barbarossa without the pope's approval. This information was shared with Barbarossa. See on
this incident Rahewin, *Gesta Friderici* 4,79, MGH *SS rer. Germ.* 46, 330.
2   *Gesta Federici I imperatoris in Lombardia* (1162-1177, by an anonymous Milanese author)
ad ann. 1159, MGH *SS rer. Germ.* 27, 38-39): 'Meanwhile, when Crema was being besieged,
the Milanese conspired with the men from Brescia and Piacenza and sent envoys to Pope
Hadrian, who was in Anagni, and these three cities concluded a treaty with him that they
would not make peace or come to an agreement with the Emperor Frederic without the permission of Pope Hadrian or his successors, and the men from Crema joined in this treaty. The
pope promised the same to them' (*Sed interim, dum obsideretur Crema, Mediolanenses iuraverunt cum Brixiensibus et Placentinis et miserunt legatos ad Adrianum papam, qui erat in Anagni,
et concordiam fecerunt iste tres civitates cum eo, quod exinde non pascicerentur vel aliquam concordiam facerent cum Federico imperatore absque licentia Adriani pape vel eius catholici successoris;
et ita iuraverunt Cremenses. Papa quoque e converso idem convenit cum eis*).
3   Barbarossa's observers in Rome at the time were Otto of Wittelsbach and Count Guido de
Biandrate. See Rahewin, *Gesta Friderici* 4,62, MGH *SS rer. Germ.* 46, 289 and Romoald of
Salerno, *Chronicon* ad. ann. 1159, MGH *SS* 19, 430.

name Alexander III, but also that the election had not been uncontested, since there was a rival nominee, Cardinal Ottaviano Monticelli, a Roman noble, who had taken the name Victor IV[4]. The election of Cardinal Ottaviano was by a clear minority, but since there was as yet no rule on how to decide a contested election, each of the two contenders might regard himself as properly elected, as had happened with the contested election of Innocent II and Anacletus II after the demise of Pope Honorius II[5]. As far as Barbarossa was concerned, Alexander III was completely unacceptable and consequently he opted for Victor IV, initiating a schism dividing the Church for almost twenty years.

The Pavia
Council

Barbarossa decided to solve the problem of a dual pontificate as his distant ancestor Henry III had done more than hundred years before[6]. He called for a great council, to be presided over by himself and held in 1160 at Pavia, the old Lombard capital, where the matter was to be decided. But times had changed since the days of the mighty Salian emperors. The kings of France and England, 'kinglets' (*reguli*) though they might have been in the eyes of Barbarossa[7], were no longer inclined to let a German emperor dispose of the throne of St Peter as he saw fit. 'Who appointed the Germans as judges over the nations?' (*quis Teutonicos constituit judices nationum?*), wrote John of Salisbury[8], a compatriot and friend of Hadrian IV. He spoke for all: French and English clerics were absent at the council of Pavia, a publicity disaster with a predictable outcome, the recognition of Victor IV. But Victor was rejected by all nations outside the sphere of influence of the German Empire. Alexander III had refused to answer the summons of Barbarossa to appear in Pavia. He claimed immunity: no one but God had the right to stand in judgment over a pope[9]. As a matter of course, he was excommunicated at Pavia by the compliant council[10]. Alexander III responded in kind: he had already excommu-

---

4   On the papal election of 1159 see the well-informed and detailed report of Gerhoch of Reichersberg (*c.* 1092-1169), *De investigatione Antichristi* L. 1, cap. 53, MGH *Ldl* 3, 360-361), who refused to take sides for Victor IV. See also Boso's report in his biography of Alexander III (*Liber pontificalis*, ed. Duchesne 2, 397-400).

5   See *supra* p. 33.

6   See *supra* p. 27.

7   For this derogatory title of the other European kings, current in Germany at the time, see John of Salisbury, *Epistolae*, Ep. 189 (ed. Giles, Oxford 1848, 332) and *Chronica regia coloniensis* ad ann 1161, MGH *SS rer. Germ.* 18, 107.

8   John of Salisbury, *Epistolae*, Ep. 59, in *Joannis Saresberiensis Opera omnia* I (*Epistolae*), ed. J.A. Giles, 64.

9   See Alexander's letter to Barbarossa inserted in Boso's biography, *Gesta pontificum romanorum, Alexander III*, ed. Duchesne, *Le Liber pontificalis* II, 401, also printed in MGH *Constt.* 1 F.1 no 185, 256-257. See on the doctrine of papal immunity *infra* p. 339-340.

10   The *Acta* of the 1160 council of Pavia are to be found in Rahewin, *Gesta Friderici* 4,77 and 80, MGH *SS rer. Germ.* 46, 324-328 and 331-336.

nicated Cardinal Ottaviano, 'calling himself Victor IV', in 1159 and on 24 March 1160 he excommunicated Barbarossa as well, releasing all subjects of this oppressor of the Church from their oath of fealty[11]. It was a declaration of war.

Alexander III managed to escape the troops sent by Barbarossa to arrest him and sought refuge in France, as had Innocent II in 1130[12], and as had happened with Innocent II, he was recognized as the legitimate pope by the kings of France and England at Beauvais in July 1160[13]. It was a major diplomatic setback for Barbarossa, but the emperor surprised and impressed all of Europe in 1162 by punishing the citizens of Milan in an exemplary way. The city had submitted in 1158[14] but revolted again and was now made an example of for all the world to be shocked an awed by. Frederick had already been able, after a prolonged siege, finally to destroy the rebellious city of Crema in 1160 and proceeded from there to Milan, the centre of Lombard resistance. On 1 March 1162 the city was forced to surrender. This time, there was no mercy. On 19 March the Milanese consuls were ordered to evacuate the city within a week[15], after which the emperor surrendered the

The destruction of Milan

---

11   Boso, *Gesta pontificum romanorum, Alexander III* (*Liber pontificalis* ed. Duchesne 2, 403): '*ipsum <imperatorem> tamquam principalem Ecclesie Dei persecutorem, excommunicationis vinculo sollempniter innodavit, et omnes qui ei iuramento fidelitatis tenebantur astricti, secundum antiquam predecessorum patrum consuetudinem ab ipso iuramento absolvit*'.

12   See *supra* p. 33, fnt. 21.

13   *Annales Cameracenses* (1152-1170, written by Lambertus Waterlos (1108-*c*. 1170)) ad ann. 1160, MGH SS 16, 534: 'Around the feast of the holy Mary Magdalene, the said kings decided to convene the Church of both kingdoms at Beauvais in order to discuss the conflict about the Apostolic See. Envoys of the Emperor Frederic also arrived there with letters. As the kings were discussing the delegation of the emperor and the discord on the Apostolic See, some spoke out in favour of Victor, siding with the emperor, but others fiercely resisted and would rather obey Pope Alexander. It was for this reason that, after the envoys of the emperor were dismissed expecting a favourable outcome, on the third day after they had been dismissed in peace by the kings, Pope Alexander was, at the insistence of the party of the king of England, recognized by all in France and so he was foisted upon England by their king (*Prope ergo festum Beatae Mariae Magdalenae a memoratis regibus utrorumque regnorum ecclesiam placuit congregari Belnaro, quatinus illic discuteretur de dissidio sedis apostolicae. Illic siquidem nuntii Frederici imperatoris regibus cum epistolis occurerunt. Regibus sane tractantibus de imperatoris legatione atque ac de dissidio sedis apostolicae, quidam cum imperatore Victori assentiebant; quidam vero acriter resistebant, sed potius Alexandro papae obediendum malebant. Ob hanc causam nunciis amotis imperatoris in spe concordiae, tertia die illis dimissis a regibus cum pace, mox regis Angliae factione Alexander papa in Gallica ab omnibus recipitur; et sic per regem in Anglia intruditur*).

14   See *supra* p. 105.

15   Acerbus Morena, *Historia* ad ann. 1162, MGH SS rer, Germ. NS 7, 156: '*Sequenti deinde die Lune postea precepit imperator consulibus Mediolani, ut usque ad octo dies facerent omnes personas tam masculos quam feminas exire civitatem Mediolani*'. Acerbus continued the history of his father Otto. He was present at Milan in 1162.

great city of Milan for complete demolition to its archenemies from Cremona, Pavia, and Lodi, loyal supporters of the imperial cause. Only the immense city-walls, largely still of Roman origin, were able to withstand the destructive energy of Barbarossa's vengeful Lombard allies[16]. It was at this juncture that Barbarossa made a serious strategic mistake. He should have used the momentum gained at Milan to proceed with his plan to invade the Sicilian kingdom later in 1162[17]. Preparations were already well advanced, and the emperor had even succeeded in joining two traditionally and relentlessly rival maritime powers, Genoa and Pisa, to his force[18]. If ever there was a good chance to conquer South Italy and Sicily it was now[19], but Barbarossa decided differently.

A failed summit

As soon as he had heard that Alexander III had taken refuge in France, Barbarossa sent a letter to the French Chancellor Hugues de Champfleury, bishop of Soissons, warning him not to receive that schismatic and onetime chancellor (*quondam cancellarius*) at court and making it very clear that he would regard a friendly reception of Alexander at the French court as a *casus belli*[20]. Barbarossa's chancellor, Rainald of Dassel, took the initiative to defuse the situation by suggesting a conference between the two monarchs to his French counterpart[21]. Barbarossa realized he could not risk a confrontation with the French king and possibly even with the king of England as well, a vassal of the king of France. It would have frustrated his Italian priorities. This is

---

16 On the destruction of Milan in 1162 see Acerbus Morena, *Historia* ad ann. 1162 (MGH *SS rer, Germ. NS* 7, 157) and *Gesta Federici I imperatoris in Lombardia* ad ann. 1162, MGH *SS rer. Germ.* 27, 54.

17 Vincent of Prague, *Annales* ad ann. 1162, MGH *SS* 17, 680: 'After the destruction of Milan, the emperor exercised his imperial power throughout Italy, for all of Italy trembled in his presence and after he had consigned his own governors to the cities of Italy, he decided to direct his armies in the direction of Sicily to take action against the Sicilian over the duchy of Apulia' (*Imperator autem Mediolano destructo, in tota Italia imperialem exercebat potestatem, tota enim in conspectu eius tremebat Italia, et in urbibus Italie suis positis potestatibus, versus Siciliam cum Siculo de ducatu Apulie rem acturus suos disponit exercitus*).

18 For the alliance with Pisa see *Annales Pisani* ad ann. 1162, *RIS²* 6.2, 23 and the charter of Frederick I in MGH *Const.* 1, no 205, 282-287.

19 There had been a serious rebellion in the Sicilian kingdom between 1159 and 1161, due to excessive fiscal pressure. The great Prime Minister Maio, the mainstay of the realm, was murdered (1160) and the king had even been taken prisoner by rebels in 1161. Thanks to the support of the Sicilian clergy (Romoald of Salerno), William I was released but he had lost his eldest son in the disorder and was a broken man after that. It was highly unlikely that Sicily could withstand an attack by a foreign force at the time. The Sicilian troubles were the reason why Alexander III sought refuge in France rather than in Sicily.

20 The letter is printed in *Recueil* 16, Paris 1878, 202. The closing line reads as follows: 'It could cause a hatred between our kingdom and his which we could not easily constrain or control' (*Tantum enim ac tale odium inter nostrum imperium et suum regnum exinde posset oriri, quod non de facili compescere possemus aut sedare*).

21 Letter of Rainald of Dassel to Hugues de Champfleury in *Recueil* 16, Paris 1878, 202-203.

why he did not immediately press on to South Italy in 1162 but decided
to meet King Louis VII of France at St Jean de Losne, near Dyon, at the
border of the empire and the kingdom of France, instead. Barbarossa
ordered all the princes of the empire and its satellites, such as the kings
of Bohemia, Hungary, and Denmark, to join him there on 29 August
1162[22]. He had decided to settle the problem of the schism once and for
all[23], for each king was to bring 'his' pope with him[24]. The conference
of St Jean de Losne was, if possible, an even greater publicity disaster
than the council of Pavia had been, for when Barbarossa finally arrived,
late in the evening, Louis had already left[25]. He had not been inclined
to wait for the emperor. Barbarossa was furious and also left, leaving his
Chancellor Rainald of Dassel to clean up the mess[26]. The archbishop-
elect of Cologne arranged another meeting with Louis VII and lectured
the French king and his prelates on the constitutional position. It was
the position of Henry III that had, indeed, been taken for granted by
all European princes for a long time[27]: *'Our Lord Frederic, emperor of*

---

22 The invitation is printed in MGH *Const.* 1 *F.1* no 208 (290) (to the clerical princes)
and 209 (291) (to the secular princes). On the negotiations leading up to the conference see
Hugues de Poitiers's history of the monastery of Vézelay between 1140 and 1167, *Recueil* 12,
329-330 (also in MGH *SS* 26, 146-147).

23 It is not unlikely that Barbarossa believed he could bully Louis VII into submission,
since the French king was widely regarded as a simpleton. For this see Walter Map (*c.* 1130-
1209/1210), *De nugis curialium*, cap. 5, dist. 5, ed. Montague Rhodes, Oxford 1914, 221:
'*posset ydiota videri*'. Another contemporary, cardinal Boso (*Gesta pontificum romanorum,
Alexander III, Liber pontificalis*, ed. Duchesne 2, 405), characterizes Louis as a man of a 'col-
umbine simplicity' (*columbina simplicitas*). This may have been one of the reasons why his wife,
Eleanor of Aquitane, a very intelligent woman, had divorced Louis in 1152 and married his
Plantagenet rival, Henry II of England, in the same year.

24 Naturally, Alexander III had informed the king of France that he refused to participate
in the conference. It was beneath his dignity to stand trial in any court (Boso, *Gesta pontificum
romanorum, Alexander III, Liber pontificalis,* ed. Duchesne 2, 406): '*videbatur indignum et
sanctorum Patrum statutis contrarium ut summus pontifex et prima sedes aliquod deberet huma-
num subire iudicium*'.

25 This incident is reported in Helmhold of Bosau (*c.* 1120-†after 1177), *Cronica slavorum*
1,91, MGH *SS rer. Germ.* 32, 178). It is not in two other reports of the St Jean de Losnes conference, Cardinal Boso's biography of Alexander III (*Gesta pontificum romanorum, Alexander
III, Liber pontificalis* ed. Duchesne 2, 406-407) and Hugues de Poitiers, *Recueil* 12, 330 (also
in MGH *SS* 26, 147), nor in the (later) report of the great Danish historian Saxo Grammaticus
(*c.* 1150-1220), *Gesta Danorum*, Book 14 ad ann. 1162, ed. Holder, Strassburg 1886, 539 (also
in MGH *SS* 29, 114).

26 For Barbarossa's departure from St Jean de Losne see Helmhold of Bosau, *Cronica
slavorum* 1,91, MGH *SS rer. Germ.* 32, p. 178: '*Tunc cesar vehementer iratus secessit a curia*'
and Boso, *Alexander III, Liber pontificalis*, ed. Duchesne 2, 407: 'the emperor was looking for
a more honourable excuse than he could find to leave the place, because he was unable to stay
there and commit the evil he had in mind' (*imperator nec moram ibidem facere nec malum
quod in corde gestabat poterat exercere, occasionem recedendi de loco ipso honestiorem quam potuit
studuit invenire celeriter*).

27 See *supra* p. 27.

the Romans and special protector of the Roman Church, hereby informs you that no other bishops than those who are subjects of the Roman Empire are allowed to participate in the election of a Roman pope. You are therefore well advised to approach him with your bishops and clergy as a friend and an ally and you must heed their decision'[28]. It was clear that Barbarossa and his advisors regarded the pope as an imperial cleric and since, according to the Worms Concordat of 1122, the emperor had the right to decide a contested succession to an episcopate within the empire by selecting the nominee of 'the wiser part' (*sanior pars*)[29], he had the right to decide a contested papal election as well by supporting the choice of the *sanior pars* of the electors. Other kings, princes, and prelates had no right to interfere with this. This was completely unacceptable to the French prelates and their king. Louis VII was now firmly committed to the cause of Alexander III and Barbarossa had wasted precious time.

Barbarossa
marches on Rome

Fortunately, we do not need to go into all the details of Barbarossa's Italian campaigns. He was back in Italy in 1163, only to find a new nucleus of open anti-imperial resistance in Lombardy consisting of the cities of Verona, Padua, and Vicenza[30] and, even worse, general discontent in other cities, even in the traditionally loyal towns, about the administration of the local governors (*rectores*) he had appointed there, mostly German nobles, military men, some of them very young and all of them with little or no administrative experience. There was an enormous culture gap between these men and the former experienced Lombard urban administrators, more often than not lawyers, such as Oberto dell'Orto from Milan and Otto Morena from Lodi. Barbarossa realized his forces in Lombardy were inadequate to deal swiftly with the situation there and returned to Germany in order to raise an army that would enable him to accomplish all his Italian ambitions. In 1166 the emperor was in Lombardy again, this time with a huge army consisting of his German subjects and reinforced by a large number of mer-

---

28   Cardinal Boso, *Gesta pontificum romanorum, Alexander III, Liber pontificalis,* ed. Duchesne 2, 407: '*Mandat vobis dominus noster Fredericus imperator Romanorum et specialis advocatus Romanae ecclesiae quod ad nullos ecclesiarum prelatos de causa electionis Romani pontificis pertinet iudicium ferre, nisi ad eos tantum qui sub imperio Romano existunt; ideoque bonum videtur et iustum ut cum episcopis et clero vestro ad eum tamquam amicum et socium accedere et illorum sententiam debeatis audire'.* See also the résumé of Rainald's speech in Saxo Grammaticus, *Gesta Danorum,* Book 14 ad ann. 1162, ed. Holder, Strassburg 1886, 539; also in MGH *SS* 29, 114.
29   *Pax Wormatiensis, Privilegium pontificis,* MGH *Const.* 1, no 108, art. 1 (161).
30   Acerbus Morena, *Historia* ad ann. 1164, MGH *SS rer, Germ. NS* 7, 174: '*Et hisdem temporibus Veronenses et Paduani ac Vicentini ... contra imperatorem rebelles extiterunt partim propter pecuniam Venetorum'.* The Venetians were worried about the increasing power of Barbarossa in the Lombard kingdom and feared his possible subsequent conquest of South Italy and Sicily. It would seriously jeopardize their economic interests in the Levant.

cenaries, mainly from the duchy of Brabant (*Branbanzones*). He was joined in Lombardy by forces from the Italian cities still loyal to him and held a conference in Lodi to set the military priorities straight. It was decided to march on Rome directly, since it was there that the main enemy of Barbarossa's Italian policy resided, Alexander III[31].

Pope Alexander III had returned to Italy in 1165. The people of Rome, always erratic in their politics, had recalled the pope[32]. They wanted to have nothing to do with the new anti-pope, Paschalis III, nominated by the emperor after the demise of his Pope Victor IV[33]. Since Genoa and Pisa were now in an alliance with the emperor, Alexander had been transported to Sicily first by seamen from the Provence. The pope was warmly welcomed by his loyal vassal king William I, who provided a fleet to transport the pope and his retinue to Ostia[34]. On 23 November 1165 Alexander was back in Rome and took possession of the Lateran Palace. It was there that he learned that King William had died on 7 May 1166. This was a very serious setback for Alexander since he had counted on Sicilian military support in the now inevitable confrontation with Barbarossa. William's successor, his son William II (1155-1166-1189), was still a minor under the custody of his mother Margaret of Navarre, who was, as the pope soon learned, unable to control the ever-unreliable Norman nobility because of her unwelcome and, as it turned out, unlucky choice of foreign advisors. It seemed that the opportunity Barbarossa had lost in 1162 was made good by the fortunate demise of William I, but the wheel of fortune turned against the emperor.

On 29 May 1167 two imperial armies, led by Rainald of Dassel and Christian of Buch, the archbishop of Mainz, crushed a Roman army

Alexander III back in Rome

The Roman disaster

---

31   Acerbus Morena (Anon. continuatio), *Historia* ad ann. 1166 (MGH *SS rer, Germ. NS 7*, 180-181): 'It was there <at Lodi> that he held a great conference of Lombards and Germans and on that conference there he decided to march on Rome with his whole army' (*Ibique <Laude> maximum colloquium Longobardorum Alamanorumque fecit et ibi in ipso colloquio cum toto suo exercitu Romam ire disposuit*).

32   Boso, *Gesta pontificum romanorum, Alexander III, Liber pontificalis*, ed. Duchesne 2, 412.

33   Cardinal Ottaviano, 'Victor IV', unexpectedly died at Lucca, where he resided, on 20 April 1165. Rainer of Dassel, who was in Tuscany at the time as imperial legate, was responsible for the election by the cardinals loyal to Ottaviano of Cardinal Guido of Crema, the cardinal-priest of S. Calisto, who took the name Paschalis III (Maragone, *Annales Pisani* ad ann. 1165, *RIS*² 6.2, 31): '*Octavianus, qui vocabatur papa Victor, Lucane civitati XII. kal. Maii mortuus est. Hoc audiente cancellario, Lucam ivit festinanter et cum cardinalibus ipsius Victoris secundo die elegit Guidonem Cremonensem in papam, qui postea vocatus est Pasqualis papa*'. The election of Paschalis III was later confirmed by Barbarossa and Paschalis was recognized as the only legitimate pope by most of the German clergy and nobles at the diet in Würzburg of 1165: Rahewin, *Gesta Friderici*, Appendix ad ann. 1166, MGH *SS rer. Germ. 46*, 348.

34   Boso, *Gesta pontificum romanorum, Alexander III, Liber pontificalis*, ed. Duchesne 2, 412-413.

117

before the ancient walls of Tusculum. Never after Cannae had a Roman army ever suffered a defeat like this, wrote Cardinal Boso[35]. Thousands of lives were lost, and Rome was practically defenceless. As soon as he heard of this, Barbarossa hastened to join his armies there and in the month of July, the hottest month of the year, the whole imperial army was concentrated before Rome for the final assault and the capture of Alexander III. It was then that disaster struck. It was, to the contemporaries, a divine judgement. Barbarossa's army was annihilated by a terrible pestilence, malaria most probably[36]. The men died by the thousands within a week and those who survived[37], such as Barbarossa himself, were hardly fit for active military service. Rome, indeed, had fallen to the emperor but at enormous cost, whereas the ultimate price to be gained there, Alexander III, had eluded Barbarossa once again: the pope had been able to escape, disguised as a pilgrim, and fled to Gaeta, on Sicilian territory[38].

The Lombard
League

Frederick I is reported as having said that he did not care whether the Italian cities liked him or not, as long as they feared him[39]. He now had to fear the cities that did not like him. Barbarossa's army had hardly left Lombardy on its way to Rome in 1167, when the Lombard city of

---

35   Boso, *Gesta pontificum romanorum, Alexander III, Liber pontificalis,* ed. Duchesne 2, 415-416: '*ab eo tempore quo Annibal Romanos aput Cannas devicit, tantam Romanorum stragem nullus recolit extitisse*'.

36   Acerbus Morena (Anon. continuatio), *Historia* ad ann. 1167, MGH *SS rer, Germ. NS* 7, 206-207: 'And, lo and behold, while these things were happening at Rome, some terrible, strange, and deadly disease struck the emperor and his entire army as if by divine judgement' (*dum haec Rome agitabantur, ecce quaedam maxima et mirabilis atque mortalis pestilentia super imperatorem eiusque totum exercitum divino miraculo accidit*). Acerbus Morena himself also died at this occasion. His death is described by the anonymous continuator of his *Historia*. See on the great pestilence before Rome also Boso, *Gesta pontificum romanorum, Alexander III, Liber pontificalis,* ed. Duchesne 2, 417-418. Another victim of this deadly plague was young Duke Frederick of Swabia, King Conrad's son and Barbarossa's nephew. He died childless and consequently the duchy reverted to Barbarossa, who granted it to one of his sons, also called Frederick. On the succession in the duchy of Swabia see *infra* p. 150, fnt. 7.

37   One of the most prominent victims of the plague was the archbishop of Cologne, Barbarossa's chancellor and closest advisor, Rainald of Dassel. It was Rainald who had been responsible for the addition of the adjective 'holy' to the designation of the Roman Empire. It was to emphasize that, next to and independent of the Holy Roman Church (*sacra Romana ecclesia*), there was a 'Holy Roman Empire' (*sacrum Romanum imperium*) as well. The first imperial charter to have this designation is from March 1157 (MGH *DD F.1,1* no. 163, 280). To further underline the independency of the empire, Rainald had orchestrated the sanctification of Charlemagne at Aachen on 29 December 1165, promoting the founder of the holy empire to the honour of the altars. It was for this occasion that the archbishop-elect of Cologne was finally consecrated as a priest and archbishop.

38   Romoald of Salerno, *Chronicon* ad. ann. 1167, MGH *SS* 19, 436: '*Alexander papa ... in habitu peregrini cum paucis Urbem exiit, et Gaietam usque pervenit*'.

39   Boso, *Gesta pontificum romanorum, Alexander III, Liber pontificalis,* ed. Duchesne 2, 411: '*Ytalie civitates ... a quibus potius timeri voluit, quam amari*'.

Cremona, traditionally most loyal to the imperial cause, revolted against the administration of its German governor (*rector*), the young Count Henry of Diez, a favourite of Barbarossa[40]. The men from Cremona concluded an anti-imperial alliance with the cities of Brescia, Mantua, and Bergamo (March/May 1167), later on in the year to be joined by the cities of the earlier Veronese alliance, Verona, Padua, and Vicenza. This was the nucleus of the famous Lombard League. The Lombard cities had finally realized that they could only successfully resist the power of the emperor by joining forces. Consequently, they created something new in European politics, a treaty organization (*societas*) based on a common oath (*coniuratio*), with its own board of governors (*rectores*), consisting of representatives of the participating cities and appointed on an annual basis. The *rectores* of the League had to swear a solemn oath on their inauguration to act 'for the common benefit' (*ad communem utilitatem*) of all participating cities[41] and even appropriated typical imperial prerogatives, such as jurisdiction in appeal and taking cognizance of disputes between the participating cities. The commonality the emperor had been unable to dictate with his Roncaglia legislation had finally come about by the common hostility of the Italian cities to that very legislation. The new spirit of Lombard solidarity was exemplified by the reconstruction of Milan in April 1167 with the help of the citizens of Cremona, who had enthusiastically participated in the destruction of that city only five years before[42]. The imperial governors were powerless to interfere and forced to leave one after the other, together with the schismatic bishops appointed by Barbarossa's anti-popes[43], even from an up-till-then staunchly loyal town as Lodi[44]. The emperor was unable to do anything about it and fled from Italy like a

---

40 See *infra* p. 131.
41 Vignati, 147.
42 *Gesta Federici I imperatoris in Lombardia* ad ann. 1167, MGH *SS rer. Germ.* 27, 61: 'On April 27, 1167 the men from Bergamo, Brescia, and Cremona before others accompanied them <the people from Milan> back to their town. After that, on the fifth of September, came Archbishop Gandinus, who belonged to the party of Pope Alexander'. (*venerunt Pergamenses primum et Brixienses et Cremonenses mclxvii. quinta feria, quinta Kal. Madii et introduxerunt eos <scl. Mediolanenses> in civitatem. Post haec vero Galdinus archiepiscopus, qui erat cum papa Alexandro, venit quinto die Septembris*). The Milanese have immortalized the event and the support of the citizens of Cremona, Brescia, and Bergamo with a relief of the fierce warriors of these cities immured in the newly restored 'Porta Romana'. The accompanying inscription has Oberto dell'Orto mentioned as one of the consuls of Milan dedicating that monument. It is now to be seen and admired in the museum of the Castello Sforzesco.
43 Barbarossa's popes did not enjoy divine blessing. Victor IV died in 1164 and Paschalis III in 1168. He was replaced by Cardinal John of Struma, cardinal-bishop of Albano, who took the name of Calixtus III. Rahewin, *Gesta Friderici*, Appendix ad ann. 1168, MGH *SS rer. Germ.* 46, 350. He resigned in 1178.
44 On the defection of Lodi see Acerbus Morena (Anon. continuatio), *Historia* ad ann. 1167, MGH *SS rer, Germ. NS* 7, 186-195 and 193-194.

thief in the night, narrowly escaping capture in the little town of Susa in Piemonte[45].

Alessandria

For seven years Barbarossa licked the wounds of his disastrous fourth Italian campaign. In those years of imperial absence, the Lombard League gained control in most Lombard cities, with only very few exceptions, such as the Lombard capital Pavia and the city of Como. Even some of the emperor's previously loyal vassals in chief (*capitanei regis*), such as the count of Biandrate[46], joined the League. In May 1168 the League defeated one of the last allies of Barbarossa in Lombardy, the marquess of Montferrat, near Rovereto, where he was building a new town. The League took over and renamed it 'Alessandria', paying tribute to the man who had become the symbol of Italian resistance against imperial domination, Pope Alexander III[47], who resided in Benevento at the time under the protection of King William II of Sicily. The foundation of Alessandria was an outrageous insult to Barbarossa in person and to the 'honour of the empire' in general, but it was only in 1172 that the emperor was able to convince a German diet at Worms to support a new Italian expedition[48]. The position of Pavia and the mar-

---

45 See for the Susa incident (9 March 1168) John of Salisbury *Epistolae*, Ep. 244, in *Joannis Saresberiensis Opera omnia* II (Epistolae), ed. J.A. Giles, Oxford 1848, 132-133.

46 The utterly loyal Count Guido de Biandrate (on him *supra* p. 111, fnt. 3) died around 1170. In that year his son, also called Guido, contracted a peace treaty (*concordia*) with the city of Vercelli, a member of the League, thus becoming an associate member of the League. See the deed to that end in Vignati, 212-213.

47 Boso, *Gesta pontificum romanorum, Alexander III, Liber pontificalis*, ed. Duchesne 2, 418-419: 'In the year of the incarnation of the Lord 1168, in the first indiction, and in the eighth year of the pontificate of Pope Alexander III, Cremona, Milan, and Piacenza together raised a powerful army against the rebellion of the men from Pavia and the marquess of Montferrat at a place called Rovereto and there they designated an area for the construction of a city to the glory of God and St Peter and the whole of Lombardy, and enclosed the place with a spacious ditch. They gathered all the people living in the surrounding villages, such as Marengo, Gamundi, Bergulio, Huvilla, and Soleria, to live there with their families and belongings and soon the city became large and strong. To make it even more glorious and famous, it was decided by all that the city forever should be called Alessandria, to the reverence of St Peter and Pope Alexander' (*Anno igitur dominice incarnationis mclxviii, indictione i, anno autem pontificatus domni Alexandri pape iii, Cremona cum Mediolano et Placentia in manu valida pariter convenerunt contra rebellionem Papiensium et marchionis Montisferrati ad villam que vocatur Rovoretum, ibique ad honorem Dei et beati Petri et totius Lombardie construende civitatis ambitum designarunt, et locum ipsum spatiato fossato clauserunt. Convenerunt ergo illic ad habitandum cum familiis et omnibus suis universi habitatores qui morabantur in circumpositis villis, videlicet in Marengo, Gamundi foro, Bergulio, Huvilla et Soleria; et repente facta est civitas magna et fortis. Ut autem gloriosior ubique haberetur atque famosior, placuit omnibus ut ipsa civitas pro reverentia beati Petri et pape Alexandri imperpetuum nominaretur Alexandria*).

48 *Chronica regia coloniensis* ad ann 1172, MGH *SS rer. Germ.* 18, 121: 'The emperor held a famous diet at Worms, where he, having complained about the behaviour of the Italians and the supporters of Roland <Alexander III>, announced another campaign to Italy with

quess of Montferrat had become untenable and they urgently requested help from the emperor. There was, however, little enthusiasm among the German princes to participate in yet another military expedition to Italy. They still remembered the disastrous outcome of the previous campaign and the most powerful German prince, Henry the Lion, flatly refused to take part. So, it was with a much-reduced contingent from the empire, mainly consisting of Bohemian knights, increased by a large number of mercenaries from Flanders and elsewhere[49], that Barbarossa appeared in Lombardy once again in September 1174[50]. This time, his strategy was not as clear as before.

Barbarossa had sent his new chancellor, Christian of Buch (1130-1183), the archbishop of Mainz, ahead to secure the southern flank of Lombardy by keeping the members of the Lombard League in the Romagna, such as Bologna, occupied, and as a defence force against possible attempts of the king of Sicily to come to the relief of the Lombards and Pope Alexander, who now resided in Anagni, south of Rome, since 1173[51]. The main incentive of Barbarossa's expedition therefore seems to have been purely personal. The emperor wanted to take revenge and punish the Lombards[52]. The campaign was doomed from the start. It was late in the year and the rainy season in Lombardy had started. Yet Barbarossa decided to besiege Alessandria to set an

The siege of Alessandria

---

the approval of all the princes, to be undertaken after the course of two years' (*Imperator apud Wormatiam curiam celebrem habuit; ubi conquestus de Italicis et illis qui partibus favebant Ruolandi ... iudicio cunctorum principum expeditionem in Italiam iterum indixit, post circulum duorum annorum determinatam*).

49 Boso, *Gesta pontificum romanorum, Alexander III, Liber pontificalis*, ed. Duchesne 2, p. 427: 'The emperor had a great mass of barbarous people with him, men familiar with the art of war. Very evil people, rapacious and desperate, he had collected from Flanders and the surrounding areas, people who nobody cares for since they care for nobody' (*Habebat enim circa se multitudinem copiosam barbaricae gentis, homines assuetos in bellicis artibus, viros nequissimos, rapaces et desperatos, quos de Flandria et circumpositis locis collegerat, et quod neminem amantes nemo amat*).

50 *Annales Placentini Gibellini* ad ann. 1174 (MGH *SS* 18, 462): 'In September he went to Italy again with a great army consisting of Bohemians, mercenaries and others, at the insistence of Pavia and the marquess of Montferrat, who had sent messengers to Germany because of Alessandria, a city the called 'Palea'' (*mense Septembris ad instantiam et peticionem Papiensium et marchionis Montisferati, qui nuncios in Alamaniam ante conspectum suum direxerant, propter Alexandriam quam civitatem Palee appellabant, iterum repetit Lombardiam cum magno exercitu Biemorum, Brienzorum et aliorum*). Alessandria was called 'Palea' ('Strawtown'), because it was still under construction at the time and the citizens therefore lived in temporary accommodations.

51 *Chronica regia coloniensis* ad ann 1171, MGH *SS rer. Germ.* 18, 121: '*Imperator Christianum Mogontium archiepiscopum in Italiam misit*'.

52 Many years later, in 1185, Barbarossa admitted that the primary motive of his expedition had been to punish the Lombards for the foundation of Alessandria (MGH *DD F1,4* no 895, 145-147).

example, as he had done with Milan in 1162. For months on end, from October 1174 until April 1175, the imperial army was stuck in the mud before Alessandria without making any progress at all, while sustaining substantial losses in countless fruitless assaults. When he was finally forced to raise the siege of Alessandria, Barbarossa's army was hungry, exhausted, diminished, and demoralized and, to make matters even worse, confronted by a considerable relief force of the Lombard League. The emperor knew that he could not risk a battle with that army, certainly not with the victorious Alessandrians at his back, and decided to negotiate a truce. It was a crucial moment in the history of Lombardy, since by negotiating a truce with the Lombard League at Montebello (16 and 17 April 1175), the emperor implicitly recognized that League as a legal entity, as a subject of international law[53].

The Battle of Legnano

It was the declared objective of the truce of Montebello to bring about a peace treaty between the League and the emperor[54], but that was not Barbarossa's intention: he wanted to buy time until reinforcements had arrived from Germany. Pending the subsequent negotiations, there was a *drôle de guerre* allowing Barbarossa to retreat behind the safe walls of Pavia and wait for the reinforcements from Germany he had urgently called for[55]. They finally arrived in May 1176, some 2000 knights headed by the new archbishop of Cologne, Philip of Heinsberg. It was not enough, as the emperor was to find out only a few weeks after the arrival of the fresh German troops. On 29 May 1176 his army was

---

53   See the opening line of the truce of Montebello (MGH *DD F.1.3* no 638, 136): 'This treaty is concluded between Frederick, by the grace of God emperor of the Romans, and the men from Lombardy, the Marche, Venice, and the Romagna as well as their entire League of places and persons' (*Talis concordia facta est inter dominum Fredericum die gratia Romanorum imperatorem et Lonbardos et Marchianos et Venetos atque Romaniam et omnem eorum societatem tam locorum quam personarum*). Note that the individual cities and persons, nobles belonging to the League, are not mentioned by name here.

54   The treaty contained a plan to refer the conflict between the League and the emperor to a committee of six, three representatives of the League and three of the emperor, that was to negotiate a compromise. If the committee was unable to reach a compromise, the matter was to be referred to the consuls of Cremona. As was to be expected, the committee could not reach an agreement and so the consuls of Cremona prepared a compromise (see for this '*arbitrium consulum Cremonensium*', MGH *Const. 1, F.1* no 245, 344-346). It was rejected by most Lombard cities and was unacceptable to Barbarossa as well, since it contained a complete reversal of his basic legislation issued at Roncaglia.

55   Barbarossa had hoped to convince his powerful nephew Henry the Lion to come to his aid in Italy. He even arranged a meeting with Henry at Chiavenna, famous in German national history, where Henry refused to come to the rescue. On this conference see the chronicle of Otto of St Blasius, MGH *SS Rer. germ.* 47, 33-34. Barbarossa did not forget and forgive this insult. He later (in 1181) stripped Henry of all his imperial fiefs (Saxony and Bavaria) and banished him from the empire. Henry found refuge in England, where he and his family lived at the court of his father-in-law, King Henry II. Barbarossa assigned the Bavarian duchy to Otto of Wittelsbach, the first in the long line of Wittelsbachs ruling Bavaria until 1918.

thoroughly beaten at Legnano by a Lombard force consisting of troops from Milan, Piacenza, Verona, Brescia, Novara, and Vercelli[56]. It was the end of all Barbarossa's Italian ambitions. He had completely and utterly failed in his effort to 'reform' the Italian kingdom. There was no other way out of his predicament now than to come to terms with the pope and the Lombard League[57].

---

56 The victorious Lombards were triumphant. Directly after the battle of Legnano they sent a letter to all the other members of the League informing them of their triumph (Vignati, 281-282(281): 'Let it be known to you that we have to report a glorious victory over the enemies. There is no count of the number of the slain, drowned, or captured. We have the shield, the banner, the cross, and the lance of the emperor. We found a treasure of gold and silver in his baggage train and we have made so much booty that we believe there is no one who can make a true estimate of it. We do not credit this victory to us alone, but we want to share it with the pope and all of Italy' (*Notum sit vobis nos ab hostibus gloriosum reportasse triumphum. Interfectorum vero submersorum captivorum non est numerus. Scutum imperatoris vexillum crucem et lanceam habemus. Aurum et argentum multum in clitellis eius repperimus et spolia hostium accepimus quorum estimationem non credimus a quoquam posse definiri. Que quidem nostra non reputamus sed ea domini Pape et Ytalicorum communia esse desideramus*).

57 Barbarossa had narrowly escaped the slaughter at Legnano. At Pavia, where the Empress Beatrix resided, he was presumed dead and the empress was already wearing a mourning garb when after some days Barbarossa turned up in the middle of the night in the company of only a few knights. Boso, *Gesta pontificum romanorum, Alexander III, Liber pontificalis*, ed. Duchesne 2, 433: '*De imperatoris vero persona ... diu apud omnes dubitatio maxima fuit, in tantum quod eius uxor, in luctu et mestitia posita, etiam lugubrem vestem induerit*' and Romoald of Salerno, *Chronicon* ad. ann. 1176, MGH *SS* 19, 442: '*et cum aliquantis diebus fuisset absconditus et quo divertisset esset ignotum, nocte cum paucis Papiam intravit*'.

9

Peace in Venice

Barbarossa's fatal misfortune at Legnano also put an end to his grand design of uniting South Italy and Sicily to the empire by force of arms. Ironically, that objective had seemed, once more, within reach only a few weeks before the disaster at Legnano. The army of Christian of Buch which Barbarossa had sent ahead in 1171 to protect his southern flank had done an extremely good job there. By 1175 the archbishop of Mainz was in firm control of Tuscany, the Marche of Ancona and the duchy of Spoleto[1]. He had decisively beaten the strongest member of the League in the Romagna, Bologna, in that year as well[2] and was on friendly terms with the city of Rome[3]. He was now a serious threat to Alexander III, who resided in Anagni at the time, only some 40 miles south of Rome. It must have been for this reason that King William II of Sicily sent a strong army northward to the relief of the pope in March 1176. It was thoroughly beaten by Christian, who chased the remnants of the Sicilian relief force to the borders of the Sicilian kingdom[4]. At this time, news of Barbarossa's debacle at Legnano reached him with instructions to contact the pope in Anagni and to open negotiations as soon as possible. The emperor had sent three other emissaries to Christian with full powers of attorney to assist him in his negotiations

Negotiations in Anagni

---

1   For the successes of Christian of Buch at the time see Romoald of Salerno, *Chronicon* ad. ann. 1172-1173, MGH *SS* 19, 441.
2   *Corpus Chronicorum Bononiensium* ad ann 1175, *RIS²* 18.2, 41 (Cr.Villola): '*Eo anno Bononienses fuerunt sconfiti a dicto chancellario*'.
3   For the pro-imperial sentiment of the Romans at the time see their letter to the imperial chancellor for Italian affairs, the archbishop of Cologne, Philip of Heinsberg, in *Chronica regia coloniensis* ad ann. 1172, MGH *SS rer. Germ.* 18, 121.
4   *Annales Ceccanenses* (also known as *Annales Fossae novae*, stopping in 1218) ad ann. 1176, MGH *SS* 19, 286: 'The chancellor of the emperor of the Germans came to Cellae <now Carsoli> and laid siege to that town. The counts of the king of Sicily went up in arms against him with a huge army. The German people defeated them and took many prisoners and they fled on March 10' (*Comites vero regis Siciliae cum ingenti exercitu insurrexerunt in eum; et gens quidem Alemannorum fuit super eos, et plerosque cepit, atque in fugam verterunt 6 Idus Martii*). See also *Annales Cassinenses* ad ann 1176, MGH *SS* 19, 312.

with Alexander III[5]. The imperial embassy was friendly received by the Roman pontiff at Anagni on 21 October 1176. It was then, at Anagni, that Alexander III demonstrated all his diplomatic skills, emerging as the greatest of all medieval popes.

The papal
peace strategy

Alexander immediately perceived the strategy of the imperial embassy. The emperor was out for a separate peace agreement with the pope to drive a wedge between the pope and his Lombard allies to be in a better position to deal with the Lombards later. The pope wanted to have nothing of the kind. He was out for a comprehensive peace agreement of all the parties concerned, the Lombards, the emperor *and* the king of Sicily, settling Italian affairs once and for all. He reminded the imperial envoys that he was still bound by the agreement with his Lombard allies not to conclude peace with the emperor without the involvement of the Lombards[6]. The problem was, however, that the pope had no powers of attorney to act on behalf of his Lombard allies and the king of Sicily. All papal concessions to the emperor, especially the lifting of his excommunication, were therefore made dependent on the condition precedent that Barbarossa made his peace with the Lombards and the king of Sicily first and, of course, that the emperor also recognized Alexander as the legitimate Roman pontiff. The latter issue, 'the most important matter' (*quod primum et principale*)[7], was quickly settled. Barbarossa had no qualms to dismiss his anti-pope Calixtus III (whom he had never met) and to grudgingly recognize Alexander as the legitimate pope. Alexander showed his magnanimity by not punishing his errant brother, 'the man who is called Calixtus' (*is qui dicitur Calixtus*), but to guarantee that he would find an abbey for him somewhere, where John of Struma could honourably take residence as abbot for the rest of his living days[8]. Barbarossa's envoys conceded that their lord would agree to make peace with the Lombards[9], as well as with the

---

5   Boso, *Gesta pontificum romanorum, Alexander III, Liber pontificalis*, ed. Duchesne 2, 433: '*Misit ergo imperator Fredericus ad presentiam domni Alexandri pape W(ichmann) Magdeburgensem archiepiscopum, Christianum Maguntinum et P(= Conradum) Varmatiensem electos, atque Ar.(duinum) protonotarium regni, maiores imperii principes, cum plenaria potestate complende pacis inter Ecclesiam et imperium*'. See also Romoald of Salerno, *Chronicon* ad. ann. 1176, MGH *SS* 19, 442.

6   See *supra* p. 111.

7   Art. 1 of the treaty of Anagni (*Pactum Anagninum*), MGH *Const. F. 1*, no 249, 350.

8   Art. 13 of the treaty of Anagni (*Pactum Anagninum*), MGH *Const. F. 1*, no 249, 351: '*Ei autem qui dicitur Calixtus una abatia dabitur*'.

9   Art. 9 of the treaty of Anagni (*Pactum Anagninum*), MGH *Const. F. 1*, no 249, 351: 'The emperor shall make true peace with the Lombards in accordance with what has been agreed by intermediaries appointed for that purpose by the pope, the emperor, and the Lombards' (*Pacem etiam veram dominus imperator faciet cum Lombardis secundum quod tractabitur per mediatores quos dominus papa et dominus imperator et Lombardi ad perficiendum interposuerunt*).

king of Sicily[10]. Both concessions amounted to a complete reversal of Barbarossa's Italian grand strategy. Not only was he to make his peace with the rebels in Lombardy, his disloyal subjects, and to recognize their organization, the League, as a legitimate contracting party on top of that, but he also had to make his peace with the Sicilian usurper, the 'king' of Sicily, thus making that despicable upstart a legitimate member of European royalty. In doing so, he practically renounced his claim on South Italy and Sicily as parts of the empire. The only (secret) concession the imperial ambassadors were able to obtain from the pope was his acknowledgment that, if the mediators of the emperor and the Lombards were unable to reach a compromise, peace would be imposed on conditions set forth by a joint committee consisting of an equal number of mediators appointed by the pope and the emperor[11].

The agreement reached at Anagni was *not* a peace treaty between the emperor and the pope, as Alexander III hastened to inform the Lombards who had got wind of the negotiations there and were afraid that the pope would make a separate peace with the emperor. He reassured the Lombards that he would only make peace with the emperor after peace was concluded between the emperor, the Lombards, and the king of Sicily, and that he would come to Lombardy himself, despite his old age, to bring that about[12]. Alexander also sent letters to the king of Sicily to inform that monarch of the agreement reached at Anagni and to invite him to send his ambassadors to the peace conference which the pope had planned in either Ravenna or Venice. Initially the pope had suggested Bologna as venue, a convenient place for all the legal expertise that was at hand there, but Barbarossa's chief negotiator, Christian of Buch, did not feel secure in that city, which he had

The pope goes to Venice

---

10   Art. 10 of the treaty of Anagni (*Pactum Anagninum*), MGH *Const. F. 1*, no 249, 351: '*pacem veram reddet dominus imperator regi Sicilie*'.
11   Art. 9 of the treaty of Anagni (*Pactum Anagninum*), MGH *Const. F. 1*, no 249, 351: 'And if, after peace was concluded appropriately between the pope, the Church and the emperor, something were to emerge in the peace negotiations between the emperor and the Lombards that could not be dealt with by the mediators, that what had been decided by the majority of the mediators appointed by the pope and the emperor shall stand' (*Et si, postquam de pace inter dominum papam, ecclesiam et imperatorem dispositum fuerit sufficienter, aliquid in tractatu pacis domini imperatoris et Lombardorum emerserit quod per mediatores componi non possit, arbitrio maioris partis mediatorum, qui ex parte domini pape et domini imperatoris ad id constituti sunt, stabitur*'). The imperial negotiators were hoping they had opened an opportunity to still override the Lombards by this clause. They were counting on the fact that pope and emperor had promised mutual support whenever the 'honour of the empire' or the rights of the Church were at stake: art. 7 of the treaty of Anagni (*Pactum Anagninum*), MGH *Const. F. 1*, no 249, 350-351.
12   Letter of Alexander III to the Lombards in MGH, *Epp., Briefe d. dt. Kaiserzeit* 8 (*Die Tegernseeer Briefsammlung des 12. Jahrhunderts*) no 188, 220-221.

only recently fought[13]. In the end, it was decided that Venice was to be the location of the conference. Something very unusual was about to happen, something Europe had never seen before, an international peace conference where all the main parties involved were to gather to conclude a treaty that was to end the schism in the Church and finally bring peace to Italy.

The Ferrara conference

King William II of Sicily sent two of his most trusted counsellors, the lawyer Roger of Andria, Chief Justice of South Italy, and Archbishop Romoald of Salerno (*c.* 1115-1181), to Lombardy with full powers of attorney to represent him in the negotiations with the emperor[14]. He also supplied a fleet of eleven galleys to bring his envoys and the pope and his retinue safely to Venice. Archbishop Romoald and the pope knew each other well. They had been the chief architects of the Treaty of Benevento[15] and must have had much to talk about in view of their past cooperation and the imminent conference in Venice. Alexander III and Romoald arrived at Venice on 24 March 1177 and were warmly welcomed by Doge Sebastiano Ziani and the people of Venice. Two weeks later the pope was already on his way again, this time to meet the Lombards at Ferrara. It was there, in the recently consecrated cathedral of S. Georgio, that Alexander held an important speech reported by Archbishop Romoald. The pope reminded the Lombards of all tribulations of the past decades and of their shared sufferings at the hand of the emperor. He praised the Lombards for the courage with which they had fought 'for the dignity of the Church and the freedom of Italy' (*pro statu ecclesie et libertate Italie*)[16]. But now, he said, the emperor had finally shown repentance, and as the Lombards had shared their victory at Legnano with him, so he wanted to share the peace that was about to be agreed with them. There was to be no peace agreement without the Lombards' consent. He touched a raw nerve here, since the Lombards made it very clear to the pope at the occasion that, as far as they were concerned, there could be no peace that would disgrace the 'honour of

---

13 See *supra* p. 125.
14 Romoald of Salerno, *Chronicon* ad. ann. 1177, MGH *SS* 19, 443: '*Rex autem Wilhelmus Romoaldo secundo Salernitano archiepiscopo et Rogerio comiti Andrie magno comestabulo et magistro iusticiario tocius Apulie et Terre Laboris per litteras suas dedit in mandatis, ut honorifice preparati simul cum papa in Lombardiam pergerent, et pro parte regia componende pacis cum imperatore tractatui interessent*'. Archbishop Romoald's report in his *Chronicon* is the best source for the events at Venice. He was not only an eyewitness, but an insider to all major developments.
15 See *supra* p. 100.
16 Romoald of Salerno, *Chronicon* ad. ann. 1177, MGH *SS* 19, 445.

Italy' (*honor Italie*) and jeopardize their liberty[17]. They would rather die a glorious death in liberty than live a miserable life in slavery[18]. Having said that, they agreed to the presence of the king of Sicily's representatives at the negotiating table and appointed seven delegates of their own who would represent the League at the conference, four bishops and three lawyers from Milan, Verona, and Brescia. Alexander left Ferrara on 9 May, taking the representatives of the League with him in his Sicilian galleys. The next day he was back in Venice[19].

By now, the eyes of all of Europe were on Venice. The kings of England and France sent official observers. Thousands of prelates from the German Empire and the Lombard kingdom with their servants thronged into the town, together with a crowd of city consuls and nobles from Lombardy and beyond, all of them with their retinue too and all of them looking for accommodation. The Rialto was crawling with other interested foreigners as well, people from as far away as Spain and Hungary, not wanting to miss a moment of the great event. A contemporary Venetian source mentions more than 8000 guests[20], all

---

17 The members of the League were alarmed by the negotiations between the emperor and the pope in Anagni. On their distrust of these proceedings, see *Annales Mediolanenses maiores* (1162-1177) ad ann. 1177, MGH *SS* 18, 378: 'But in the same year the emperor sent envoys to Pope Alexander and secretly made a treaty with him, and they convened a conference in Venice, publicly feigning to bring about a peace treaty between the Lombards and the emperor. Pope Alexander accepted Frederick again as the most Christian emperor, thereby breaking the promise he had made to the Lombards. But as soon as he arrived in Venice, he sent a letter to the Lombards saying that he would cut himself up rather than make peace without the Lombards. But he abandoned the Lombards' (*Eodem vero anno imperator direxit nuntios ad Alexandrum papam, et clam pactus est cum eo; et statuerunt colloquium apud Venecias, publice simulantes velle componere pacem inter Lonbardos et imperatorem ... Alexander papa recepit Federicum in christianissimum imperatorem ... deserendo fidem quam Longobardis promiserat. Nam ex quo fuit Venetiae, direxit litteras Mediolanensibus, quibus dixit, quod prius dimitteret se sectari, quam pacem absque Mediolanensibus faceret. Sed Longobardos deseruit*).

18 Romoald of Salerno, *Chronicon* ad. ann. 1177, MGH *SS* 19, 445: 'Your Holiness must know, and the Imperial Majesty must surely acknowledge, that we gladly accept the peace of the emperor, with the honour of Italy preserved, and that we wish for his favour, as long as our freedom remains intact. We gladly grant him what Italy owes him as of old and we do not deny his ancient rights, but our freedom, which we have acquired as a legacy from our fathers, grandfathers, and great-grandfathers and which we fear to lose with our lives, we will never surrender. For we prefer a glorious death in freedom over a miserable life in slavery' (*Sciat autem vestra sanctitas et imperialis potentia evidenter agnoscat, quod nos gratanter imperatoris pacem, salvo Italie honore, recipimus et eius gratiam, libertate nostra integra remanente, preoptamus. Quod ei de antiquo debet Italia, libenter exsolvimus, et veteres illi iustitias non negamus; libertatem autem nostram, quam a patribus nostris avis et proavis hereditario iure contraximus, nequaquam relinquimus, quam amittere nisi cum vita timemus; magis enim volumus gloriosam mortem cum libertate incurrere, quam vitam miseram cum servitute servare*).

19 Romoald of Salerno, *Chronicon* ad. ann. 1177, MGH *SS* 19, 446.

20 *Historia ducum veneticorum* 12 (*Qui interfuerunt predicte paci*), ad ann. 1177, MGH *SS* 14, 89.

of them anxiously awaiting the arrival of the last person missing from the event.

Barbarossa's reservations

Barbarossa was not welcome in Venice as long as he was excommunicated but for the time being he resided in the neighbourhood, in Pomposa, halfway between Ravenna and Venice. His delegation, headed by Christian of Buch, arrived in Venice practically unnoticed. The mood of the imperial ambassadors cannot have been optimal. Barbarossa had been dragging his feet ever since the Anagni agreement, even trying to convene another general council to be held at Pavia, but his own episcopate talked him out of that hopeless plan[21]. Archbishop Christian and the other imperial envoys at Anagni had sworn a solemn oath that their lord would ratify the agreement reached there[22], but they were well aware of the fact that Barbarossa was not happy. What vexed the emperor most was the 'due reverence' (*debita reverentia*) he was to perform to the pope[23]. That ceremony had already given rise to serious trouble when Barbarossa had met Hadrian IV at Sutri in 1155[24] and it was even more painful now that Barbarossa was to meet with Alexander III, a man who had openly defied him for decades and whom he must have held personally responsible for all vicissitudes befalling the Empire and himself. It was a prospect almost too embarrassing to contemplate, but there was no way around it.

Barbarossa confronted with an ultimatum

Meanwhile, Barbarossa's ambassadors were negotiating on his behalf in Venice. Alexander III had suggested to decide the issue of peace with the Lombards first, before entering into negotiations about peace with the Church and the king of Sicily[25]. It soon turned out that the Lombards were unwilling to negotiate on the basis of the infamous imperial legislation issued at Roncaglia in 1158[26]. Instead, they suggested to negotiate on the basis of a peace treaty drafted by the consuls of Cremona after the truce of Montebello[27]. It took the imperial negotiators by surprise and resulted in unproductive quibbling about the details of that draft treaty. Alexander III, always the diplomat, realized

---

21   For this see *Annales S. Georgii in Silva Nigra* ad ann. 1176, MGH *SS* 17, 296; *Annales Palidenses* ad ann. 1176, MGH *SS* 16, 94) and especially a letter of Patriarch Udalrich of Aquilea from November 1176, MGH, *Epp., Briefe d. dt. Kaiserzeit* 8 (*Die Tegernseeer Briefsammlung des 12. Jahrhunderts*) no 40, 59-61.

22   See the '*Promissio legatorum imperialium*' in MGH *Const. F. 1*, no 250, 353-354. The Roman law of agency did not recognize direct representation and consequently all contracts entered into by agents on behalf of their principal had to be ratified by that principal in order to become binding upon him.

23   Art. 1 of the treaty of Anagni (*Pactum Anagninum*), MGH *Const. F. 1*, no 249, 350.

24   See *supra* p. 93-95.

25   Romoald of Salerno, *Chronicon* ad. ann. 1177, MGH *SS* 19, 446-447.

26   See *supra* p. 107-108.

27   See *supra* p. 122.

that a peace agreement was not within reach and suggested a truce of six years with the Lombards during which a definitive peace agreement was to be negotiated between the parties concerned[28]. This, however, was beyond the powers of Barbarossa's negotiators who had to consult the emperor on the matter. Barbarossa was furious when he learned of the developments at the conference and started to prevaricate again, even opening secret negotiations with the pope behind the back of his own diplomats[29]. As soon as Archbishop Christian heard of this, he and his fellow negotiators took an unprecedented step: they set an ultimatum to their lord. If Barbarossa continued to prevaricate, they would publicly recognize Pope Alexander III as their spiritual leader[30]. As far as they were concerned, the imperial game was over, and the emperor ought to acknowledge that fact. Barbarossa finally conceded. He agreed to a truce of six years with the Lombards and of fifteen years with the king of Sicily, all as suggested by Alexander, and ordered the young Count Henry of Dietz to swear a solemn oath to that effect on his behalf (*in anima sua*) in the presence of the pope. The count did as he was instructed as soon as he arrived in Venice in the company of the imperial negotiators[31], thereby meeting the condition precedent to the

---

28 Romoald of Salerno, *Chronicon* ad. ann. 1177, MGH *SS* 19, 447.

29 Romoald of Salerno, *Chronicon* ad. ann. 1177, MGH *SS* 19, 448.

30 Romoald of Salerno, *Chronicon* ad. ann. 1177, MGH *SS* 19, 451: 'Your imperial Majesty should know that some of us have been commissioned by you to go to Anagni and negotiate with Pope Alexander for peace with the Church, with the king of Sicily, and with the Lombards. He <the pope> himself, as the holy man and a great friend of peace that he is, has left the Campagna at our insistence and has gone to Venice, willing to carry out all he had promised and also to vigorously promote peace. You, however, want to distance yourself from our advice and to shirk from the proposed treaty, as we believe at the instigation of the wrong people. However, on the basis of our obligations to the Empire, we are willing to obey you in secular affairs and to provide the customary services for the rights we exercise. But since you are the lord of our bodies, but not of our souls, we do not want to lose our souls on your behalf by giving priority to secular affairs over heavenly ones. Therefore, Your imperial Majesty should know that from now on we recognize Alexander as our Catholic pope and obey him as our father in spiritual matters. Under no circumstance will we worship the idol <Calixtus> whom you have set up in Tuscany' (*Bene debet imperialis maiestas recolere, quod quidam e nostris ex mandato vestro Anagniam accedentes, cum Alexandro papa de pace ecclesie et imperii, de pace regis Sicilie et Lombardorum tractatum habuimus. Et ipse, utpote vir sanctus, pacis cupidus et amator, nostro consilio et hortatu Campaniam deserens, Venetias iam intravit, paratus ea, que de bono pacis promiserat, firmiter consumari. Vos autem, ut credimus, suggestione pravorum hominum a consilio nostro vultis recedere, et a pacis proposito declinare. Nos vero ex iure debiti, quo imperio tenemur adstricti, parati sumus vobis, ut domino, in temporalibus obedire et pro regalibus, que tenemus, consuetum vobis servitium facere. Set quia nostrorum estis corporum, non animarum dominus, nolumus pro vobis animas nostras perdere et terrena celestibus anteferre. Quare noscat imperialis discretio, quod nos de cetero Alexandrum in catholicum papam recipimus, et ei ut patri in spiritualibus obedimus. Idolum vero, quod erexistis in Tuscia, nullatenus adoremus*).

31 Boso, *Gesta pontificum romanorum, Alexander III, Liber pontificalis*, ed. Duchesne 2, 439: 'I, Count of Dietz, swear that the emperor has instructed me to take the oath on his behalf

conclusion of peace between the emperor and the Church. The emperor could now proceed to Venice to be reconciled with the Church and have his excommunication lifted. Barbarossa arrived at the Lido on 23 July 1177. He was to meet the pope at the Rialto on the next day.

Barbarossa
in Venice

24 July 1177 was a Sunday, and it must have been, in this season, a beautiful day. Early in the morning, Alexander III had sent some of his cardinals to the Lido to receive Barbarossa back into the bosom of the Church[32]. Doge Ziani was also present, providing his own gondola to escort the emperor from the Lido to the Rialto, where the pope, his cardinals, the high clergy from the *regnum italicum* and Germany, Archbishop Romoald and thousands of curious people from Italy and abroad expected the arrival of Barbarossa. A deep silence must have fallen over St Marc's square as the emperor of the Holy Roman Empire approached the throne of Alexander III. What would Barbarossa do?

According to our eyewitness, Archbishop Romoald, the emperor was inspired by the Holy Spirit. Standing before Alexander's throne, he stripped himself of all the trappings of his imperial dignity and fell prostrate to the feet of the pope. Tears came to the eyes of Alexander, a very old man by now. He let the emperor rise, gave him the kiss of peace and blessed him, whereupon the crowd in the square intoned a spontaneous *Te Deum*[33]. It was a short ceremony but of great symbolical significance, explaining the emotion of Alexander. He had fought as

---

that I will now take and that after he has given me that order, he has not withdrawn that order. And I swear by order of the emperor on his behalf that once he has arrived in Venice, now that all problems and disputes have been resolved, he will let an oath be sworn on his behalf that he will establish peace with the Church as negotiated by the negotiators and put into writing, and peace with the king of Sicily for fifteen years, as documented, and that he will keep the truce with the Lombards, as established by negotiators on both sides, and as written in the document under the same negotiators, in good faith' (*Ego comes Dedo iuro quod domnus imperator mandavit mihi ut in anima sua iurarem iuramentum quod nunc facturus sum, et postquam mandavit non revocavit mandatum. Et ego ex mandato imperatoris iuro in anima sua quod ex quo venerit Venetias, omni questione et contradictione amota, faciet iurari in anima sua quod pacem Ecclesie, sicut disposita est per mediatores et scripta, et pacem regis Sicilie usque ad XV annos, sicut scripta est, et treuguam Lombardorum, sicut est per mediatores utriusque partis dispositum, et in scripto quod est apud eosdem mediatores continetur, bona fide servabit*).

32 Romoald of Salerno, *Chronicon* ad. ann. 1177, MGH *SS* 19, 452: '*papa ... Hubaldum Hostiensem et Wilhelmum Portuensem et Malfridum Penestrinum episcopos et quosdam de cardinalibus ad imperatorem transmisit. Qui venientes, ipsum et suos ab excommunicationis vincilo absolverunt*'.

33 Romoald of Salerno, *Chronicon* ad. ann. 1177, MGH *SS* 19, p. 452: '*Cumque ad papam appropriasset, tactus divino spiritu, Deum in Alexandro venerans, imperiali dignitate postposita, reiecto pallio, ad pedes pape totum se extenso corpore inclinavit. Quem Alexander papa cum lacrymis benigne elevans, recipit in osculo et benedixit, moxque a Teotonicos* Te Deum laudamus est excelsa voce cantatum'. See for the same details Boso, *Gesta pontificum romanorum, Alexander III, Liber pontificalis*, ed. Duchesne 2, 439-440.

pope for the liberty of the Church and, by implication, for the liberty of Italy for almost twenty years and even longer than that as member of the papal *curia*. He must have been aware that he had gained a triumph outshining the ephemeral victory of Gregory VII at Canossa by far. Unlike Gregory, he had not humiliated the emperor, but he had shown the man who considered himself *dominus mundi* his proper place, not at the gate of a secluded castle in the wintery Tuscan mountains, but for all the world to see on a sunlit square in Venice. Gregory's policy had resulted in years of civil war, whereas Alexander's diplomacy stood in the sign of peace. The next day, the feast day of St James, the emperor attended mass in S. Marco and afterwards performed due reverence (*debita reverentia*) to the pope by holding the stirrup as that venerable pontiff mounted his snow-white horse, and escorting Alexander several meters on foot through the crowd, holding the pope's horse by the bridle[34].

---

34   Romoald of Salerno, *Chronicon* ad. ann. 1177, MGH *SS* 19, p. 453: '*Finita autem missa, cum papa ad suum palatium vellet redire, imperator dexteram eius accipiens, eum usque ad portas ecclesie satis honeste deduxit. Cumque equum suum album de more vellet ascendere, imperator ex alia parte eccedens, strevam eius tenuit, et postquam equum ascendit, ipsum aliquantulum stratoris more per freni lora deduxit, quem papa benedicens, ad hospitium redire permisit*'. See for the same details Boso, *Gesta pontificum romanorum, Alexander III, Liber pontificalis*, ed. Duchesne 2, 440.

10

The Second Storm from Swabia

The *Pax Veneta* was concluded on 1 August 1177 in the chapel of the patriarch of Grado's palace, where the negotiators on behalf of the treaty parties had held their conferences. It was a long session since three treaties were to be sworn to on that day by all parties. The six-year truce with the Lombards took most of the time since all the parties concerned, city-consuls and nobles from both sides[1], had to swear to it[2]. The peace with the Church and the king of Sicily was more quickly concluded, since they were, according to Archbishop Romoald, 'more or less the same' (*quasi una*)[3]. The peace treaty with the Church still contained an explicit clause, partly a reiteration of the agreement reached at Anagni, that the emperor was to conclude a peace for the duration of fifteen years with the king of Sicily[4]. The separate peace with the king of Sicily[5] amounted to no less than the recognition by Barbarossa of the political *status quo* in South Italy. Alexander III had operated very diligently here, since he had brokered a peace treaty between the emperor and his vassal, the king of Sicily, thereby not only firmly establishing his own position as liege lord of that king, but also securing the feudal title of his Sicilian vassal. A long-term peace agreement with the Lombards was only concluded at Konstanz on 25 June 1183 (*Pax Constantiae*)[6]. Long-term relations between the empire and Sicily were to be settled in a very different way.

The Peace of Konstanz

---

1 The text of the truce with the Lombards is printed in MGH *Const.* 1, *Const. F1* no 259, 360-362. It has more than twenty cities still belonging to the 'party of the emperor' (*pars imperatoris*).
2 Romoald of Salerno, *Chronicon* ad. ann. 1177, MGH *SS* 19, 454 and Boso, *Gesta pontificum romanorum, Alexander III, Liber pontificalis*, ed. Duchesne 2, 440.
3 Romoald of Salerno, *Chronicon* ad. ann. 1177, MGH *SS* 19, 447.
4 The text of the peace treaty with the Church is printed in MGH *Const.* 1, *Const. F1* no 260, 362-365. See art. 9 (363) for the reference to the peace treaty with the king of Sicily.
5 The text of the peace treaty with the king of Sicily is printed in MGH *Const.* 1, *Const. F1* no 268, 370-371.
6 The text of the peace of Konstanz is printed in MGH *Const. F.1*, no 293, 411-418. The treaty is based on an agreement between negotiators of the Lombard League and the emperor reached at Piacenza on 30 April 1183. The agreement would have been very much to Oberto

Barbarossa
returns to
Lombardy

In the first days of September 1184, Frederick I 'Barbarossa', now in his sixties, arrived in his Italian kingdom for the sixth and, as it turned out, last time. At this occasion he came 'without an army' (*sine armis*)[7], since the emperor was at peace now with all his Lombard subjects. Barbarossa was even warmly received at Milan[8] and triumphantly toured the Lombard kingdom to meet with the pope at Verona. This was Lucius III (1181-1185), a very stubborn old man, who had succeeded Alexander III in 1181[9]. Lucius was an exile, since the Roman citizenry had, once again, risen against the temporal power of the pope[10]. He had, in fact, only been able to maintain his position around Rome thanks to the military support of Archbishop Christian of Mainz, who had been ordered by Barbarossa to come to the aid of the pope as the emperor was bound to do, due to a specific clause in the peace treaty with the pope[11]. Papal relations with the Lombard League had, moreover, steadily deteriorated since the demise of Alexander III, mainly because the pope interfered in local Lombard politics by forbidding the city consuls

---

dell'Orto's liking. The imperial legislation of Roncaglia was implicitly repealed and the cities obtained their sovereign rights (*regalia*) by imperial concession. In form, the *pax Constantiae* is an imperial privilege confirming the legal status of the *Societas Lombarda* in conformity with Roman law (D. 3,4,1 pr. (Gaius)), in substance it is a feudal contract containing the conditions of submission of a vassal to his lord. These conditions were very carefully framed and amended to the very last, especially in as far as the practical autonomy of the cities was concerned. An important example is art. 29 of the first Piacenza draft agreement (MGH *Const. F. 1*, no 288, 399), stipulating that feudal disputes between the emperor and a citizen of a member city of the League were to be decided in the city where the dispute originated 'according to the customary law of Lombardy' (*secundum consuetudinem Lombardie*). This was amended in art. 32 of the final draft (MGH *Const. F. 1*, no 289, 402) as reading 'according to the customary law *of that city*' (*secundum consuetudinem* illius civitatis), emphasizing the autonomy of the Lombard cities. The *Pax Constantiae* became the basis of medieval Lombard public law and was even integrated in the *Volumen* part of the medieval manuscripts of Justinian's *Corpus Iuris*, as an appendix to the *Libri feudorum* (see *supra* p. 90, fnt. 20).

7   *Annales Weingartenses Welfici*, ad ann. 1184, MGH *SS* 17, 309: '*Eodem anno in Augusto imperator sine armis Italiam ingressus est*'.

8   *Annales Placentini Gibellini* ad ann. 1184, MGH *SS* 18, 465: '*Mense septembris imperator Fredericus venit Lombardiam, et primo intravit Mediolanum pacifice*'.

9   *Annales Casinenses* (till 1182) ad ann. 1181, MGH *SS* 19, 312: '*Alexander papa obiit apud civitatem Castelli, et Hubaldus Ostiensis episcopus ordinatur in papam Lucium apud Velletrum*'.

10   Roger of Hoveden († 1201), *Chronica* ad ann. 1183, ed. Stubbs, II, London 1869, 282: 'In the same year, a serious conflict arose between the Romans and Pope Lucius over certain rights that his predecessors used to grant the Romans, but which the aforementioned pope had vowed never to grant. Hence, the Romans rebelled and regularly looted and set fire to the territory of the pope. But the pope went to his fortified castles and cities, fleeing from one place to another' (*Eodem anno ortum est grave discidium inter Romanos et papam Lucium, super consuetudinibus quibusdam quas praedecessores sui Romanis facere solebant, quas praedictus papa juravit se numquam facturum. Unde Romani indignati sunt, et frequenter rapinas et iniquas combustiones fecerunt in terra domini papae. Dominus vero papa de loco in locum fugiens, castella suas et civitates munitas adiit*).

11   Art. 6 of the peace treaty with the church, MGH *Const.* 1, *Const. FI* no 260, 363.

to raise taxes from the local clergy on pain of excommunication[12]. No wonder, therefore, that Barbarossa expected to find a compliant pope at Verona to negotiate with on a delicate topic that had become dear to his heart, the coronation of his son and heir Henry VI (1165-1169-1191-1197) as co-emperor.

The Emperor Henry VI
(*Chronica regia coloniensis*, Royal Library
of Belgium, Ms 467, f. 118 *v*)

Henry VI had already been elected king of the Germans in 1169, only four years old at the time, and Barbarossa wanted to secure the succession to the imperial crown as well, now that his son had become of age. But he had underestimated the obstinacy of Pope Lucius: 'there cannot be two emperors at the same time' (*non posse simul duos imperatores regnare*), the pope is reported to have said[13]. The argument of Pope Lucius was rather weak, as he (and Barbarossa) must have known, since there had been at least three medieval Roman emperors crowned in the lifetime of their predecessors, Louis I (813), Lothair I (817), and Otto II (967). However, the papal stance became unnegotiable once stunning news from Germany had reached Verona: the annunciation of the betrothal of King Henry VI and the Sicilian heiress Constance,

---

12   Art. 19 of the Lateran Council of 1179, in Mansi 22, col. 228-229.
13   Arnold of Lübeck († 1211/1214), *Chronica slavorum* 3,11, MGH *SS* 21, 156. See also *Chronica regia coloniensis* ad ann. 1185, MGH *SS rer. Germ.* 18, 134: '*fertur papa respondisse … non esse conveniens duos imperatores preesse Romano imperio*'.

a (posthumously born) daughter of King Roger II and the aunt of King William II[14].

Henry VI
marries
Constance
of Sicily

Barbarossa had tried to establish friendly relations with the Sicilian kingdom in 1176 by suggesting a marriage between King William II and the imperial daughter Beatrix. William had declined the offer though, allegedly not wanting to offend the pope by marrying into the family of an excommunicate[15]. After the *Pax Veneta* things were different. King William had been married to Joan, a daughter of King Henry II of England, in the meantime, but his aunt Constance was still available to seal a permanent peace between the empire and the Sicilian kingdom replacing the temporary truce agreed at Venice. The news of the impending marriage between Constance of Sicily and the German king and heir must have utterly shocked the papal *curia*. A union of the Sicilian kingdom and the German Empire, the nightmare of papal policymakers for at least a century, was within reach since the marriage of King William and his English bride had been childless for almost seven years now[16] and Princess Constance was the only surviving heir of Roger II next to her nephew William[17]. What was even more disturbing, was the fact that King William, on announcing the impending marriage of his aunt to the German heir in 1184, had imposed a solemn oath on his Sicilian barons to accept his aunt and her future German husband as their sovereigns in case he died childless[18].

---

14   King Henry VI announced his betrothal to Constance on 29 October 1184 at a diet held in Augsburg. *Annales Marbacenses* ad ann. 1184, MGH *SS rer. Germ.* 9, 55: '*Interea rex Heinricus curiam apud Augustam civitatem Recie habuit; ubi desponsavit Constantiam filiam regis Apulie Rogerii*'.

15   Romoald of Salerno, *Chronicon* ad. ann. 1176, MGH *SS* 19, 441. The marriage proposal to King William is a sure sign that Barbarossa's primary aim of his fifth expedition into Italy was primarily to punish the Lombards (see *supra* p. 121, fnt. 52). Consequently, he needed to secure the southern sector of the Italian war zone, if need be by a marriage of his daughter with the Sicilian king. In the end, Archbishop Christian and his army sufficed (see *supra* p. 125).

16   Legend has it that King William II had the beautiful cathedral at Cephalu built as a gift to God in order 'to make her bear fruit whom He had rendered sterile' (*ut fecundam redderet quam sterilem fecerat*, Ryccardus de S. Germano (*c.* 1165-1244), *Chronica* ante ann. 1189, *RIS²* 7.2, 4.

17   It is reported that King William II had his aunt Constance locked away in a monastery for this reason.

18   Ryccardus de S. Germano, *Chronica* ante ann. 1189, *RIS²* .2, 6: 'There was an aunt of the king in the palace of Palermo, whom the king gave in marriage to the German King Henry, the son of the Roman Emperor Frederick. It happened on this occasion that all the counts of the kingdom were ordered by the king himself to swear an oath that if the king died childless, they would serve his aunt and the aforementioned king of Germany as loyal vassals' (*Erat ipsi regi amita quaedam in palatio Panormitano, quam idem rex ... Henryco Alamannorum regi filio Frederici Romanorum imperatoris in coniugem tradidit, quo etiam procurante factum est, ut ad regis ipsius mandatum omnes regni comites sacramentum prestiterint, quod si regem ipsum absque liberis mori contigeret, ammodo de facto regni tamquam fideles ipsi sue amite tenerentur*

The pope and his cardinals at Verona were now suddenly confronted with the fact that they were about to lose the two mainstays of papal policy in the past century: the Sicilian king *and* the Lombard cities. Barbarossa had finally learned that diplomacy paid off and even succeeded in bringing the city of Milan over to his side by granting extensive territorial privileges to that city[19], now the undisputed de facto capital of Lombardy. Even worse, from the papal perspective, was that Barbarossa was firmly in control of Tuscany, thanks to the operations there of his trusted chancellor, Archbishop Christian of Mainz, in the previous years[20]. It was there, in Tuscany, probably in Montefiascone, that a definitive peace treaty with the king of Sicily was concluded[21]. By 28 August 1185 Princess Constance had already reached Rieti, some 100 kilometres north of Rome, where she was warmly received 'by a great crowd of princes and barons' (*maxima multitudo principum et baronum*)[22] representing her future husband who was still in Germany where he acted as regent for his father at the time. On the day his future wife arrived at Rieti, Henry buried his mother, the old Empress Beatrix, the consort of his father for so many years, in the imperial tomb in the cathedral of Speyer. After performing that sad filial obligation, he left for Italy for a more joyous occasion.

On 25 November 1185 Pope Lucius III died in Verona. He was succeeded by Cardinal Umberto Crivelli from Milan, who took the name Urban III[23]. If Barbarossa cherished the illusion that he would find a more flexible pope in Urban, he was soon disappointed. The new pope turned out as intractable as his predecessor, if not more so. The Crivelli family had suffered considerably in 1162, when Barbarossa had ordered

The Roman 'Kaiser'

---

et dicto regi Alamannie viro eius). See also Benedictus of Peterborough († 1193), *Gesta regis Henryci secundi* ad ann. 1189, ed. Stubbs II, London 1867, 102: '*Et fecit <scl. Wilhelmus, rex Siciliae> principes regni, tam clericos quam laicos, jurare fidelitates praedictae Constantiae contra omnes homines, salva fidelitate sua. Deinde dedit eam in uxorem Henryco regi Alemannorum, filio Frederici imperatoris Romanorum*'. The word '*deinde*' (thereafter) is emphasized here to stress that the Sicilian barons had committed themselves to the succession of Constance and her husband even before their marriage.

19   MGH *Const.* 1 no 303 (11 February 1185), 429: '*Concedimus itaque Mediolanensibus omnia regalia, quae imperium habet in archiepiscopatu Mediolanensi*'. Naturally, the men from Cremona were not pleased by this change of policy.

20   See *supra* p. 125. Archbishop Christian had died in Tusculum in 1183, while defending Pope Lucius III against the citizens of Rome (see *supra* p. 136).

21   *Annales Casinenses* ad. ann. 1185, MGH *SS* 19, 313: '*Pax firma inter imperatorem Fredericum et regem Guillelmum facta est … Praefatus rex Constantiam amitam suam transmisit in coniugem ad illustrem regem Heinricum filium Frederici imperatoris*'.

22   See the inscription in the episcopal palace of Rieti commemorating the event, reported in P. Galletti, *Memorie di tre antiche chiese di Rieti*, Rome 1765, 149.

23   Radulph de Diceto († 1199), *Imagines historiarum* ad ann. 1185, ed. Stubbs II, London 1876, 38-39: '*Lucius Papa, vii. Kal. decembris, Veronae sepultus est. Humbertus Mediolanensis archiepiscopus ipsi die, cardinalium omnium consensu, Papa creatus, et vocatus est Urbanus*'.

the destruction of Milan, and the pope, already a grown man at that time, had witnessed that event himself and had not forgotten nor forgiven. He must have been disgusted by the change of Milanese policy in siding with the emperor. Urban III demonstrated his irritation by his conspicuous absence from the wedding of Constance and Henry VI on 27 January 1186. It was an event too humiliating for the old pope to witness. The wedding ceremony was celebrated in Milan, at the special request of the Milanese themselves as a sign of the favour of the emperor they had recently regained[24]. From that day on, Henry VI styled himself as *Caesar* ('Kaiser'), the old Roman title of a designated successor to the imperial title[25]. The new German Caesar turned out to be a man of action as soon as he had arrived on the Italian scene. Shortly after his marriage, he led an army to Tuscany to punish the city of Siena for having dared to resist an imperial ban to extend its influence over the adjacent *contado* at the cost of the local feudal lords[26]. From there, he entered the papal territories to establish imperial order there as well, in close cooperation with the citizens of Rome and at the expense of the authority of the pope[27]. It seems that, due to Henry's invasion of papal territory and the quickly deteriorating relation between Urban III and Barbarossa, the pope decided to excommunicate the emperor and his son, but his sudden demise on 20 October 1187 prevented that from happening[28]. His successor, Alberto de Morra, a former professor of canon law in Bologna who took the name Gregory VIII, quickly abandoned the idea, since he needed Barbarossa more than ever to lead a new crusade against the sultan of Egypt and Syria, Saladin (Salah-ad-Din, 'the Compassion of the Faith', 1137-1174-1193), who had con-

---

24   Otto of St Blasius (1200-1209) 28, ad ann. 1184, MGH *SS rer. Germ.* 47, 39: '*rogantibus Mediolanensibus, ut in signum adepte imperialis gratie nuptias filii apud Mediolanum celebraret*'.
25   Radulph de Diceto, *Imagines historiarum* ad ann. 1186, ed. Stubbs II, London 1876, 39.
26   For Barbarossa's ban on extending the *contado* of the Tuscan cities (except for Pisa and Pistoia) see *Gesta Florentinorum* ad ann. 1085, MGH *SS rer. Germ. N.S.* 8, 248: 'In questo anno Di I. anzi Aghosto venne lo'nperadore Federigho in Firenze e a tutte le citta tolse il contado infino alle mura, trattone a Pisa e a Pistoia'. For Henry's suppression of Siena see *Annales Senenses* ad ann. 1186, MGH *SS* 19, 226: '*3. Kal. Iunii anno Domini 1186 obsedit rex Henrycus, qui post fuit imperator, civitatem Senensem*'.
27   *Annales Placentini Guelfi* ad ann. 1186, MGH *SS* 18, 416: 'Thereafter, the aforementioned King Henry went with a large army to Rome and the Campagna and took many places there and destroyed them because of the conflict he had with Pope Urban' (*Deinde predictus rex Anricus semotus, magno exercitu habito versus Romam in Campaniam pro discordia quam habebat cum domno Urbano papa ivit, et multa loca cepit et destruxit*).
28   *Annales Marbacenses* ad ann. 1187, MGH *SS rer. Germ.* 9, 57: 'In the same year, there were peace negotiations between the pope and the emperor, but they were unsuccessful, because he <the pope> wanted to excommunicate the emperor and the King. But God prevented that evil plan, since he died in that year' (*Ipso anno inter apostolicum et imperatorem de pace agebatur, sed nichil profuit, quia de excommunicatione imperatoris et regis agebat. Deus autem malignum ipsius consilium dissipavit. Nam eodem anno mortuus est*).

quered Jerusalem on 2 October 1187 after annihilating the army of the Kingdom of Jerusalem at the Horns of Hattin. The fall of Jerusalem shocked the Christian world. Three great kings took the cross to retake the city where Christ had lived and suffered: King Henry II of England, King William II of Sicily and Emperor Frederick I. None of them was to reach the Holy Land. The English king died in his great castle Chinon on 6 July 1189, King William II of Sicily expired, childless, on 18 November of the same year, and Barbarossa drowned on 10 June 1190 in the river Saleph (now Göksu), in southeast Anatolia[29].

The unexpected demise of King William II in 1189 created a power vacuum in the Sicilian kingdom. The designated successors to the late king, his aunt Constance and her consort Henry VI, were far away in the German territories where Henry acted as regent during the absence of his father on his ill-fated crusade. Pope Clement III (1187-1191), who had succeeded the short-lived Pope Gregory VIII, took advantage of the occasion for a final effort to prevent a union of the empire and the Sicilian kingdom. Despite their solemn oath of 1184[30], the always unreliable Sicilian barons had chosen one of them, Tancred of Lecce (1138-1194), a bastard of a son of King Roger II, as successor to King William[31] and the pope, the feudal overlord of the Sicilian kingdom, assented to that election[32]. Tancred was firmly in control when two European kings landed in Sicily, where they had agreed to join forces with William II and proceed to the Holy Land, King Philip II of France (1165-1179-1223) and Richard I of England (1157-1189-1199).

Richard I was a cruel and impossible man, a fool with the self-destructive propensity to make the wrong enemies and the wrong friends at the wrong time, as he did on Sicily. As a matter of principle, he quarrelled with his French rival, King Philip of France. But after some initial bickering with Tancred of Lecce as well, he concluded a

Tancred of Lecce and Richard of England

---

29   On the death of Barbarossa see *Gesta Federici I. imp. in expeditione sacra* ad ann. 1190, MGH *SS rer. Germ.* 27, 96). What was left of Barbarossa after the usual dissection of his body was buried in Antioch. His grave has never been located.
30   See *supra* p. 138.
31   Ryccardus de S. Germano, *Chronica* ad ann. 1190, ed. *RIS²* 7.2, 8: 'This Tancredus was an illegitimate son of Duke Roger, whose father Roger was first to acquire the title of king of the Sicilian kingdom, which is why, because he derived a claim from his descent from the royal family, he was elected king above the other barons of the kingdom' (*Tancredus iste ducis Roggerii filius fuerat naturalis, cuius pater Roggerius primus in regno Sicilie regis sortitus est nomen, et hac de re quia hunc habebat titulum quod de stirpe regia descendisset, inter alios regni comites est electus in regem*).
32   Ryccardus de S. Germano, *Chronica* ad ann. 1189, *RIS²* 7.2, 8: '*Romana in hoc curia dante assensum*'.

friendly alliance with the Sicilian rebel[33]. It was to cost him very dearly later[34], since Henry VI was not a man to forgive or forget an insult like that.

The coronation
of Henry VI

By January 1191 Henry VI was back on Italian soil. In February he was in Bologna, granting that city the privilege to coin its own currency[35] and by April he was in Rome where he was expected by yet another Roman pontiff, Celestine III, who had succeeded Clement III after the demise of the latter on 27 March 1191[36]. The pope, who was co-responsible for the Sicilian coup by Tancred of Lecce, was not overenthusiastic to crown Tancred's rival as Roman emperor, but Henry was willing and able to pay a price the pope could not refuse. Clement III had been allowed to return to Rome by the Roman citizenry in 1188 on condition that he would surrender the little city of Tusculum to the Romans 'for destruction' (*ad diruendum*)[37]. As a matter of course, Clement III and Celestine III were incapable of convincing the citizens of Tusculum, up till then their loyal subjects, to leave their city and surrender it to the Romans. Consequently, the pope asked Henry VI for assistance and so the ancient city of Tusculum paid the price for a residence permit of the pope in Rome and a quick and uncontested coronation of Henry

---

33   As soon as he was elected, Tancred had the widow of King William II, Joan, a sister of Richard I, imprisoned and all her property confiscated. Tancred realized he needed an ally like King Richard and paid a substantial compensation to the English king in order to cool his wrath at that affront to the dignity of the Plantagenets. See for the treaty between Richard and Tancred Benedictus of Peterborough, *Gesta regis Ricardi* ad ann. 1190, ed. Stubbs II, London 1867, 133-138. As far as Richard was concerned, there was a personal and dynastic motive for his treaty with Tancred. His sister Margaret was married to the Saxon Duke Henry the Lion, who had lived as an exile at the court of the English king since 1181 (see *supra* p. 122, fnt. 55). Richard had befriended the Saxon duke, who furtively returned to Germany in 1189 as soon as Barbarossa had decided to join the third crusade, in order to regain some of the possessions he had lost there on his conviction in 1181. See for further details Arnold of Lübeck, *Chronica slavorum* 4,7, MGH *SS* 21, 170. The friendly connections between the Plantagenets and the Saxon Guelphs, the enemies of the house of Hohenstaufen, was a decisive factor in the election of Otto IV, a son of Henry the Lion, as German king in 1198: see *infra* p. 153.
34   See *infra* p. 145-147.
35   L. Savioli, *Annali Bolognesi* II,2, Bassano 1789, no 298, 167-168.
36   In spite of a rapid succession of popes – Lucius III († 1185, Verona), Urban III († 1187, Ferrara), Gregory VIII († 1187, Pisa), Clement III († 1191, Rome) all dead within a timeframe of less than ten years – continuity in papal policy was guaranteed by the college of cardinals. Celestine III (Giachinto Bobone, a scion of the old Roman noble Orsini family), for example, had been cardinal-deacon of S. Maria in Cosmedin ever since 1144, meaning that he had been co-responsible for papal policy since the days of Hadrian IV and Alexander III before he became pope at an advanced age. Consequently, the composition of the college of cardinals is as important for the understanding of medieval papal policy as are the personal qualities and predilections of an individual and mostly ephemeral pope.
37   See the treaty between Clement III and the Roman senate in *Liber censuum* 1, no 84, 373-374 (374).

VI by the pope (15 April 1191)[38]. The city, where Cicero once lived, was conquered by Henry VI, surrendered to the pope, and subsequently completely destroyed by the Romans. It was never rebuilt; its ruins can still be seen on a hilltop overlooking the present town of Frascati[39].

After their coronation, Henry and Constance proceeded to the Sicilian kingdom to confront the usurper Tancred. The imperial advance into South Italy, however, was stopped before the gates of Naples. The city refused to recognize Henry and had to be besieged during the month of June. It was then that, once again, a great and seemingly invincible German army was destroyed by the secret weapon medieval Italy had in store for foreign invaders from the north: malaria. Henry lost almost his entire army and barely escaped from that disease himself[40]. It was an almost complete reprise of Barbarossa's doomed siege of Rome in 1167[41] and, like his father before him, Henry had no choice but to depart from Italy as quickly as possible. To make matters even worse, his wife Constance, who was residing at Salerno for health reasons, was taken captive by the citizens of Salerno and surrendered to Tancred[42]. The union of the *regnum Siciliae* with the Empire now seemed further away than ever. Pope Celestine III thought so too and sent two of his cardinals to Tancred in 1192 to receive the oath of fealty of his new Sicilian vassal, after which Tancred was duly invested with the kingdom of Sicily, the duchy of Apulia, and the principality of Capua[43]. Pope Celestine III must have known that in doing so he was playing a very dangerous game, since his formal recognition of Tancred of Lecce as king of Sicily amounted to an act of war against Henry VI and his wife. Consequently, Celestine needed a valuable hostage as collateral in his dealings with Henry and persuaded Tancred to sur-

His failed Sicilian campaign

---

38   Arnold of Lübeck, *Chronica slavorum* 5,4, MGH *SS* 21, 181: '*rex Urbem ingreditur ... et domnus imperator una cum imperatrice benedicitur et coronatur*'.
39   For the Tusculum affair see Roger of Hoveden, *Chronica* ad ann. 1191, ed. Stubbs, III, London 1870, 102-105 and *Chronica regia coloniensis* ad ann. 1191, MGH *SS rer. Germ.* 18, 152.
40   Magnus of Reichersberg, *Chronica* (ending in 1195) ad ann. 1191, MGH 17, 518: '*exercitum suum paene totum pestilentia et aliis infortuniis perdidit*'. Roger of Hoveden, *Chronica* ad ann. 1191, ed. Stubbs, III, London 1870, 164): '*amisit fere totum exercitum suum ex corruptione aeris et ipse aegrotabat usque ad mortem*' and *Annales Stadenses* (1232-1264) ad ann. 1192, MGH *SS* 16, 352: '*Invaluit autem maxima pestilentia in exercitu ... Imperator quoque est graviter infirmatus*'.
41   See *supra* p. 117-118.
42   Geoffrey of Viterbo (c. 1120-c.1196), *Gesta Heinrici VI*. v. 85-88, MGH *SS* 22, 336): '*Imperatrix patitur, cepit medicinam/ Salernitani stulti capiunt reginam/ coacta velle nolle mittunt in carinam/ ad Panormum ducitur; preparant ruinam*'.
43   See the letter of Tancred to Celestine III and his oath of fealty printed in Huillard-Bréholles, *Examen des chartes de l'église Romaine contenues dans les rouleaux dits rouleaux de Cluny*, Paris 1865, 64-66. The deed of investment is printed *ibidem* at 66-68.

render the Empress Constance to him under the unlikely pretext that she would be able and willing to bring about peace between Henry VI and Tancred, with himself, the pope, acting as mediator[44]. Tancred, imprudently, agreed and in doing so abandoned the only surety he possessed in his own dealings with Henry VI. By June 1192, Constance was on her way to Rome, accompanied, or rather guarded, by the cardinal-priest of S. Nicola in Carcere Tulliano, Egidio di Anagni[45]. To the pope's dismay, Egidio's company was intercepted near Ceprano, already in the Papal State, by a German army under the command of Abbot Roffredo dell'Isola of Montecassino, who had sided with Henry VI. The abbot brought Constance in safety to the duchy of Spoleto, from where she returned to Germany later in that year[46]. Now that the empress was safe, Henry VI had his hands free to settle his score with Tancred of Lecce.

The capture of Richard of England

Henry VI missed his father's charisma and talent to keep the centrifugal forces in the German kingdom at bay by compromising with the princes of the realm. As soon as he had returned to Germany, late in

---

44 Peter of Eboli (*fl.* 1196-1220), *Liber ad honorem Augusti* v. 1010-1046, ed. G.B. Siragusa, Rome 1906, 72-73: '*a Coelestino littera missa fuit … hiis igitur lectis, tibi mitto, remitte maritam/ ipsa suum poterit pacificare virum*'. See on the release of Constance at the instance of Celestine also *Continuatio Aquicinctina Sigeberti* (1200-1250) ad ann. 1192, MGH *SS* 6, 429: '*Tancredus Apulie tyrannus, a Celestino papa conpulsus, imperatricem de custodia relaxans, imperatori remittit*'. The suggestion here that the empress was handed over to the emperor directly is incorrect, however, as will be explained shortly.

45 *Annales Ceccanenses* (a.k.a. *Annales Fossae Novae*, ending in 1218) ad ann. 1193 (1192), MGH *SS* 19, 292: 'In this year Pope Celestine sent Cardinal-deacon Aegidius from Anagni to Palermo. He brought the Empress Constance back, whom the men from Salerno had given to King Tancred, and escorted her honourably to Rome' (*Hoc anno dominus Coelestinus papa misit domnum Aegidium diaconum cardinalem Anagniae Panormum; retulit imperatricem Constantiam, quam Salernitani dederant regi Tancredo, et honorifice duxit eam Romam*). The text adds, incorrectly, that it was the pope who subsequently sent the empress back to Germany.

46 *Annales Casinenses* ad ann. 1192, MGH *SS* 19, 316: 'The emperor sent Count Berthold to Italy with an army and sent the abbot just mentioned with him, but while Berthold stayed in Tuscany, he entrusted the troops to the abbot. While he <the abbot> was thus returning, he encountered the aforementioned empress near Ceprano. She had already been released by the king and was escorted by cardinals sent for that purpose by the pope, who believed he could negotiate with her about peace in Rome. But the empress declined to visit the City and, passing through Tivoli, was welcomed in the territory of Spoleto' (*Imperator Bertoldum comitem cum exercitu mittit in Italiam, et cum eo remittit supradictum abbatem; sed Bertoldus in Tuscia demorans, milites abbati concedit, cum quibus rediens Ceperani adloquitur supradictam imperatricem iam a rege remissam, ducentibus eam cardinalibus ad hoc missis a papa, qui putabat Romae cum ea de concordia tractare. Sed eadem augusta Urbis declinat ingressum, et per Tiburim in partes Spoleti recipitur*). Count Berthold of Künßberg was sent to Italy from Germany, where the abbot of Montecassino was staying with the emperor at the time. The abbot returned to South Italy with Berthold to prepare for the imminent war with Tancred of Lecce. For the return of Constance to Germany see *Chronica regia coloniensis* ad ann. 1193, MGH *SS rer. Germ.* 18, 156.

but to accept indeed, since during his absence his brother John threatened to take over his English throne and his enemy King Philip II of France threatened Richard's substantial continental domains in France. He was to make good use of his new status as a prince of the empire later, though[56]. With the empress safe and sound in Germany, his treasury filled with English silver, and the political situation in Germany stabilized, Henry VI was now ready to take on Tancred of Lecce. In this instance too, fortune favoured him.

On 20 February 1194, around the time when Richard I embarked in Antwerp to finally return to his English kingdom, Tancred of Lecce died in Palermo[57]. His only surviving son[58] and heir, William, was still a child. Under these circumstances the future of the house of Hauteville was doomed. When Henry VI appeared in Italy with a huge army in May 1194, no Sicilian baron was inclined to risk his life and property for a mere child and consequently Henry VI was able to take control of South Italy and Sicily virtually without any resistance[59]. The emperor and his younger brother Philip triumphantly entered Palermo on 30 November 1194[60]. On 25 December Henry was crowned king of Sicily[61]. It was a day of enormous geopolitical significance with

Henry VI is crowned king of Sicily

---

praedictum, tenendum de ipso pro quinque milibus librarum sterlingorum singulis annis de tributo solvendis; et investivit eum inde imperator per duplicem crucem de auro'.

56 See *infra* p. 153.

57 *Annales Siculi* ad ann. 1194, MGH *SS* 19, 496: '*vigesimo die Februarii obiit dictus rex Tankredus*'.

58 Tancred had his eldest son and heir Roger crowned as king in 1192, but Roger died in 1194. Roger was married to a daughter of the Byzantine Emperor Isaac II Angelos, Irene Angelina. On her see *infra* fnt. 60.

59 *Annales Marbacenses* ad ann. 1195, MGH *SS rer. Germ.* 9, 65: '*tota Apulia et Sycilia nec non Calabria cum summa prosperitate et sine aliquo damno in suam iurisdictionem redacta*'. See also *Gesta Innocentii PP. III* 18, Migne *PL* 214, col. xxx: '*Hic <scl. Henrycus imperator> ergo regnum ingressus, sine pugna illud obtinuit, nemine resistente*'. The *Gesta Innocentii* were written not long after the demise of Pope Innocent, probably by the canonist Petrus Beneventanus († 1219/1220),

60 *Annales Marbacenses* ad ann. 1195, MGH *SS rer. Germ.* 9, p. 65: '*imperator ... Palermum sedem regni Sycilie dominica qua cantatur* Dicit Dominus ego cogito *cum magna gloria intravit*'. Henry VI arrested Tancred's widow Sybilla and her children and had them deported to Germany. According to Roger of Hoveden, *Chronica* ad ann. 1194, ed. Stubbs, III, London 1870, 270, Tancred's son William was blinded and even castrated at the occasion. Sybilla and her daughter were later able to escape from their German prison and fled to France, where Tancred's daughter Elvira was married to Count Walter of Brienne – a couple that was to play a role in South Italy later: see *infra* p. 160. The widow of the eldest son of Tancred of Lecce, Irene Angelina (see on her *supra* fnt. 58), was betrothed to Philip of Swabia, the youngest brother of Henry VI. The couple married in 1197.

61 *Annales Aquenses* (1169-1196), ad ann. 1193(1194), MGH *SS* 24, 39: '*Heinricus imperator ... in die natalis Domini apud Panormum in regem Siclum gloriose coronatus est*'. See also Roger of Hoveden, *Chronica* ad ann. 1194, ed. Stubbs, III, Londen 1870, 276.

far-reaching consequences: the 'union of the kingdom and the empire' (*unio regni ad imperium*), the spectre of the papal *curia* for more than a century, had finally come to pass. As far as the German 'imperialists' of the time were concerned, South Italy and Sicily were finally 'restored' to the empire to which these territories had always belonged, the 'kingdom of Sicily' being an aberration, an anomaly extorted by Roger II from Pope Innocent II[62]. Barbarossa's dream had finally become a reality, the restoration of the Roman Empire 'to its ancient power and glory' (*in pristinum suae excellentiae robur*)[63]. Never before in European history since the days of Charlemagne had a monarch ruled over so large a territory. Henry VI reigned from the beaches of the North Sea till the shores of North Africa. No wonder, then, that the emperor now envisaged an even grander design, the conquest of the Byzantine Empire[64], the great ambition of the Normans of South Italy ever since the days of Robert Guiscard. If successful, he would, indeed, have become 'the master of the world' (*dominus mundi*), but fortune decided differently. The emperor, aspiring to become a new Constantine, unexpectedly expired in Messina on 27 September 1197 in the middle of the preparations for that expedition. He was just 32 years of age. The 'Second Storm from Swabia'[65] had blown over prematurely.

---

62   Otto of St Blasius, *Chronica* 28, MGH *SS Rer. germ.* 47,39 on the consequences of the marriage of Henry VI and Constance: 'by receiving the kingdom of Sicily, the duchy of Apulia and the principality of Capua by way of dowry from his in-law after the death of the latter, he restored to the Roman Empire what was taken away from it by Roger after the demise of Emperor Lothair, when he had captured Pope Innocent and extorted the royal title from him' (*per hoc regnum Sicilie cum ducatu Apulie principatuque Capue Hainrico regi dotis nomine post mortem suam a socero delegatum recipiens Romano imperio restituit, quod post mortem Lotharii quondam imperatoris a Rogerio, capto papa Innocencio regioque nomine ab eo extorto, imperio ablatum fuerat*). Otto of St Blasius mistakenly took Constance for a sister of King William II. See for this traditional 'imperialist' view of the Sicilian kingdom as an anomaly already *Ottonis episc. freisingensis Chronica* 7,34, MGH *SS Rer. germ.* 45, 348-349: 'Roger captured Pope Innocent in an ambush and extorted the authority of the royal title from him' (*Rogerius Innocentium papam … ex insidiis cepit et regii nominis in Sicilia ab eo auctoritatem … extorsit*).
63   See *supra* p. 77.
64   Otto of St Blasius 43, ad ann. 1196, MGH *SS rer. Germ.* 47, 69: '*His diebus Heinricus imperator … ad optinendam Greciam imperiumque Constantinopolitanum intendit animum*'.
65   Dante, *Paradiso* 3,119.

11

Innocent III and the Kingdom of Sicily

Good fortune smiled on Henry VI one last time when a son and heir was born to him at Jesi in the Marche of Ancona on 26 December 1194. The child was named after his famous grandfathers, Frederick I and Roger II: Fridericus Rogerius[1]. His mother Constance called him Constantinus[2]. Henry VI had tried to take advantage of the occasion for a failed attempt to convert the German electoral monarchy into a hereditary monarchy[3], but his son was duly elected according to the ancient tradition as 'king of the Romans' in the last months of 1196[4]. There were very good reasons for the German princes, clerical as well as secular, to resist the dynastic policy of Henry VI. The *unio regni ad imperium* resulted in a situation where one of them, the heir to the Sicilian kingdom, outranked them all, thus disturbing the delicate balance of power within the German kingdom. In making the Sicilian king the hereditary king of Germany as well, they would practically have abolished that German kingdom, since it would have merged into

Birth of Frederick II

---

1 *Annales Casinenses* ad. ann. 1195, MGH *SS* 19, 318: '*Constancia imperatrix filium parit in marchia Anconitana, quem in auspicium cumulandae probitatis inculcatis avorum nominibus Fredericum Roggerium, seu Roggerium Fredericum vocat*'.

2 *Annales Stadenses* ad ann. 119, MGH 16, 353: '*Vocabatur autem a matre alio nomine Constantinus*'.

3 *Annales Marbacenses* ad ann. 1196, MGH *SS rer. Germ.* 9, 68: 'The emperor wanted the princes to confirm a new and unheard-of law for the Roman kingdom, that the kings would follow each other according to hereditary succession, as in France and other kingdoms' (*imperator novum et inauditum decretum Romano regno voluit cum principibus confirmare, ut in Romanorum regnum, sicut in Francie vel ceteris regnis, iure hereditario reges sibi succederent*). The appeal to the French constitution was incorrect at the time, since French kings were presented during the lifetime of their predecessor as well (see *supra* p. 65, fnt. 110). The incumbent king of France, Philip II, was crowned in 1179, fourteen years old, during the lifetime of his father, King Louis VII.

4 *Annales Marbacenses* ad ann. 1196, ed. Bloch, MGH *SS rer. Germ.* 9, 69: '*Interea in Theutonicis partibus, mediantibus Cunrado Maguntino archiepiscopo et duce Suevie Philippo, omnes fere principes prestito iuramento filium imperatoris in regem eligerunt*'.

a new and enormous hereditary empire, a new *imperium Romanum* that would have ceased to belong to the *natio Germanica*, but to the family of the emperor ruling over it. By insisting on the electoral character of the German monarchy the German princes succeeded in driving a constitutional wedge between the hereditary Sicilian kingdom and the electoral German empire.

The unexpected demise of Henry VI caused utter confusion in Germany and Italy[5]. The elected 'king of the Romans', Frederick II, was a minor, only two years old, and incapable at law as well as in fact to act for himself. The child was, moreover, not in Germany, but in Foligno, in the duchy of Spoleto, where his mother Constance had left her son in the custody of Duke Conrad of Urslingen and his wife[6]. Shortly before the emperor expired, Henry VI had ordered his brother, Duke Philip of Swabia, who was in Germany at the time[7], to bring the child to Germany in order to have it anointed as king[8], but Philip arrived too late. The dowager Empress Constance had been ahead of him.

He is raised in Sicily

Soon after the sudden demise of Henry VI rumours circulated that his death had been due to poisoning and that his wife was the perpetrator of that crime[9]. Unfounded as this allegation most certainly is, it nevertheless reflects a widespread impression at the time that relations between the imperial couple were strained during the last years of their marriage. Not only was the empress at least ten years older than her husband, but she was also a proud Sicilian lady and consequently not pleased with the way her husband had dealt with Sicilian nobles, sev-

---

5 *Annales Marbacenses* ad ann. 1197, MGH *SS rer. Germ.* 9, 70: '*totus orbis in morte ipsius conturbatus fuit*'.

6 *Breve chronicon de rebus siculis*, MGH *SS rer. Germ.* 77, 62: '*Puer autem parvus Fredericus, qui erat sub tutela et nutritura uxoris Conradi ducis Spoletani in civitate Fuligni*'. Constance knew the Urslingen couple. She had been received by Duke Conrad and his wife after her escape from papal custody in 1192 (see *supra* p. 144). Count Conrad of Urslingen had been appointed Duke of Spoleto and Count of Assisi by Barbarossa. He was close to Henry VI and it may have been on Henry's insistence that his son and heir was left with the German couple.

7 Philip, the youngest son of Barbarossa and initially destined for an ecclesiastical career, made a remarkable career in the last years of the reign of his oldest brother Henry VI. In 1194 Henry had granted him the duchy of Tuscany (Burchard of Ursberg, *Chronicon* ad ann. 1195, MGH *SS rer. Germ.* 16, 73) and, after the demise of his other elder brother Conrad in 1196, Philip was raised as duke of Swabia, compelling Philip and his wife to leave Italy for Germany to take over the duchy (Burchard of Ursberg, *Chronicon* ad ann. 1196, MGH *SS rer. Germ.* 16, 74). Philip was excommunicated by Pope Celestine III in 1197 for invading papal territory when he was in Tuscany.

8 Otto of St Blasius 45, ad ann. 1197, MGH *SS rer. Germ.* 47, 71: '*Phylippus dux Swevie … ab imperatore prius citatus erat hac de causa, ut filium ipsius ex Apulia perduceret in Germaniam, ubi a principibus in regem electus a Coloniensi episcopo inungeretur, ut moris est*'.

9 Burchard of Ursberg († after 1231), *Chronicon* ad ann. 1197, MGH *SS rer. Germ.* 16, 75): '*Multi asserebant eum <scl. Heinricum> interisse veneno procurante uxore sua*'.

eral relatives of her among them. After the discovery of a conspiracy of some Sicilian barons after 1194, Henry, a vengeful and merciless man, took the opportunity to punish some of the barons who had sided with Tancred of Lecce in 1189 at the same time. The (true or alleged) conspirators were executed in unspeakably cruel ways that reportedly distressed Constance[10]. The dowager empress was also discontented with the Germans in the company of her husband, most notably with Henry's sinister henchman Markward of Annweiler. As soon as Henry had died, Constance ordered all Germans to leave the Sicilian kingdom at once[11]. Here was a lady clearly *not* pleased with the union of the Sicilian kingdom and the empire. It must have been for this reason as well, that she sent for her son to be brought over to Palermo as soon as possible to prevent the boy being taken away to Germany as her husband had ordered[12]. She obviously wanted to distance herself (and her son) from the German interests of her husband and his family as far as possible. The young Frederick Roger, her Constantine, was to be raised as a Sicilian prince at the court in Palermo. It was there that Frederick, not yet four years old, was anointed king of Sicily at the day of Pentecost 1198. His mother died in the same year, leaving the little royal orphan in the immediate care of Walter of Pagliara, the chancellor of the Sicilian kingdom, and appointing Pope Innocent III (1198-1216) as his guardian[13].

Pope Celestine III had died soon after Henry VI, on 8 January 1198. At this occasion, the cardinals for once elected a younger candidate.

Innocent III

---

10   Burchard of Ursberg, *Chronicon* ad ann. 1197, MGH *SS rer. Germ.* 16, 75: '*Multi asserebant eum <scl. Heinricum> interisse veneno procurante uxore sua*, pro eo quod nepotes ipsius suppliciis interfecerat' (emphasis added). See also Roger of Hoveden, *Chronica* ad ann. 1196, ed. Stubbs IV, London 1871, 27: '*Constancia imperatrix videns mala quae imperator gesserat, cum gente sua foedus iniit contra imperatorem maritum suum*'.

11   Ryccardus de S. Germano, *Chronica* ad ann. 1197, *RIS²* 7.2, 19: 'The empress who stayed in Palermo in mourning garb for the death of her husband, the emperor, worrying about the peace and tranquillity in the kingdom, banished Markward, the empire's first servant, together with all Germans from the kingdom' (*Imperatrix Panormi remanens in veste lugubri de nece imperatoris viri sui, regnique paci consulens et quieti, Marcialdum imperii senescalcum cum Teutonicis omnibus de regno exclusit*).

12   Ryccardus de S. Germano, *Chronica* ad ann. 1197, *RIS²* 7.2, 19: '*Imperatrix filium suum ... ad se duci iubet in regnum*'.

13   *Breve chronicon de rebus siculis*, MGH *SS rer. Germ.* 77, 62-63: '*Fredericus ... qui veniens in festo Pentecostes in ecclesia Panormitana ... unctus fuerit in regem ... Et in sequenti festivitate sancti Andree ipsa domina Constantia ibidem mortua fuit, relinquens eundem puerum sub tutela supradicti domini Innocentii summi pontificis et ecclesie Romane, et custodes ipsius dimisit dominum Bartholomeum supradictum archiepiscopum Panormitanum, dominum Matheum archiepiscopum Capuanum et dominum Gualtherium episcopum Troyanum et regni Sicilie cancellarium. Et infra spatium modici temporis ipsi domini Panormitanus et Capuanus ibidem in Panormo defuncti sunt, et remansit solus dominus Gualterius, qui curam ipsius pueri prudenter et fideliter egit*'.

This was Lothario dei Conti di Segni, cardinal-deacon of SS Sergius and Bacchus, who took the name Innocent III, clearly a reference to his predecessor Innocent II. The new pope was a learned man. He had studied theology in Paris and canon and Roman law in Bologna[14], making him a representative of the new generation of canon lawyers in the *curia*, like Pope Gregory VIII, who had consecrated him as sub-deacon[15]. At 29 he was promoted a cardinal by Pope Clement III in 1190[16]. He was just thirty-seven years of age at the time of his elevation to the chair of St Peter. At the end of his pontificate, in 1216, he ruled over Europe as once the ancient Roman emperors had done.

Contemporary Portrait of Innocent III from the apse of Old St Peter's (Museo di Roma, Palazzo Braschi, Rome, author's photograph)

Contested elections

Innocent III was in a unique position in 1198. The German Empire was in a state of total confusion since the succession to the throne was contested. Some German princes, mainly from the north-western parts of the Empire, were not inclined to recognize the duly elected 'king of the Romans', Frederick II. Instead, they opted for a Guelph, a son of the old firebrand Henry the Lion who had died in 1195. Henry's eldest son, also called Henry, was unavailable at the time since he had not yet returned from a pilgrimage and time was of the essence.

---

14   *Gesta Innocentii PP. III* 2, Migne *PL* 214, col. xvii: '*Hic primum in urbe, deinde Parisiis, tandem Bononiae, scholasticis studiis insudavit … fuerit tam in humano quam in divino jure peritus*'.
15   *Gesta Innocentii PP. III* 2, Migne *PL* 214, col. xviii: '*Hunc sanctae memoriae Gregorius octavus papa in subdiaconem ordinavit*'.
16   *Gesta Innocentii PP. III* (*c.* 1208) 3, Migne *PL* 214, col. xviii: '*Hunc … Clemens III papa promovit in diaconum cardinalem, vicesimum nonum aetatis annum agentem, assignans ei ecclesiam Sanctorum Sergii et Bacchi*'.

Consequently, a younger son of the Saxon Lion was approached, Otto of Poitou (*c* 1175-1218). Otto had been raised in England, at the court of his grandfather King Henry II, where his father and his family lived in exile since 1182[17]. He befriended King Richard I; who granted his German nephew the county of Poitou in 1196[18]. In these years, Otto figured prominently in France as one of Richard's war lords in his incessant struggles there with King Philip II of France. It was now that Richard's elevation as a prince of the German realm, a consequence of his submission to Henry VI in 1194[19], proved convenient. Richard was invited by the German princes in the north-west to join them in a conference held at Cologne to elect a new king. Of course, Richard did not contemplate a return to that kingdom, but he sent his personal representatives to promote the cause of his nephew (and vassal)[20]. Otto of Poitou was elected 'king of the Romans' (Otto IV) on 9 June 1198 in Cologne and crowned in Aachen[21]. The traditional crown and the other regal paraphernalia, however, could not be used at the occasion, since they were in the possession of another German king, Philip of Swabia[22].

Immediately after his return from his failed mission to Italy to bring the young Frederick to Germany, Philip of Swabia held a conference at Hagenau Castle with all the officials and ministerials (*officiales et ministeriales*) of the house Hohenstaufen, joined by some local princes and barons, on how best to protect the interests of Frederick II[23]. It seems to have been his idea to act as 'protector of the realm' (*defensor imperii*) during Frederick's minority and absence. Philip was supported by a large gathering of German princes, secular and clerical, from the eastern part of the German kingdom, including the powerful dukes of Bavaria and Saxonia[24], convening at Arnstadt in Thuringia on 6 March 1198.

The election of Philip of Swabia

---

17 See *supra* p. 122, fnt. 55.

18 Roger of Hoveden, *Chronica* ad ann. 1196, ed. Stubbs IV, London 1871, 7: '*Eodem anno Ricardus rex Angliae dedit Othoni nepoti suo comitatum Pictavis*'.

19 See *supra* p. 146.

20 For this episode see Roger of Hoveden, *Chronica* ad ann. 1198, ed. Stubbs IV, London 1871, 37-38.

21 *Annales S' Gereonis Coloniensis* (1191-1202) ad ann. 1198, MGH *SS* 16, 734: '*quinto Idus Iunii electus est Colonie Otto in regem, et eodem anno Aquisgrani consecratus 4. Idus Iulii*'.

22 Burchard of Ursberg, *Chronicon* ad ann. 1197, MGH *SS rer. Germ.* 16, 76: '*in potestate sua haberet <scl. Philippus> insignia imperialia, utpote coronam et crucem et alia, quae attinebant*'.

23 Burchard of Ursberg, *Chronicon* ad ann. 1197, MGH *SS rer. Germ.* 16, 76: '*Philippus ad partes Reni se contulit in continenti et nativitatem Domini in castro Haginou celebravit, ubi venerunt ad eum et officiales et ministeriales et quidam de principibus et baronibus terre, cum quibus habuit mysterium consilii sui*'.

24 The presence of duke Bernard of Saxonia is mentioned in *Chronicon Sampetrinum* (*Cronica S. Petri Erfordensis moderna, c.* 1335) ad ann. 1198, MGH *SS rer. Germ.* 42, 199. I

The princes considered various possibilities to save the position of their young king and to protect the immediate interests of his house and the realm until Frederick's arrival in Germany. A possibility was, indeed, to appoint Frederick's uncle Philip as 'protector of the realm', or even as temporary king, during the minority of his nephew. In the end, however, they decided to elect Philip of Swabia in the place of his nephew as 'king of the Romans' (Mühlhausen, 8 March 1198)[25], probably because there were serious doubts that Frederick II would ever be available as king, given the conduct of his mother Constance who was still alive at the time. The German Empire now had three elected kings: Otto IV, Philip I, and, of course, Frederick II. The result was a civil war lasting twelve years[26].

Innocent III and the German election

It was customary for a newly elected German king to inform the pope of his election. Accordingly, Pope Innocent received two letters from Germany, one from the German princes siding with Philip of Swabia[27] and another from Otto IV[28]. In addition to these, the pope received yet another letter from Sicily, sent by the Empress Constance, with the request to invest her and her son with the kingdom of Sicily, the duchy of Apulia, and the principality of Capua[29]. Thus, it came about that a Roman pontiff had to sit in judgement over three German kings. It was a complete reversal of the events at Sutri and Rome one-hundred and fifty years earlier, when a German king sat in judgement over three popes[30]. The letter from the German princes siding with Philip contained a caution to the pope not to interfere in the affairs of the Empire[31]. It was a reprimand the pope could not let go by without a

---

should add that the Guelphs had lost the duchy of Saxony in 1181, due to the conviction of Henry the Lion (*supra* p. 122, fnt. 55). Barbarossa used the occasion to split the enormous duchy into three parts, assigning the eastern part to count Bernard of Anhalt as the new and considerably reduced duchy of Saxony.

25 There are conflicting reports on the 1198 electoral conferences in Thuringia. I have based my reconstruction on the report of Otto of St Blasius 46, ad ann. 1198, MGH *SS rer. Germ.* 47, 72-73 and the famous *Deliberatio* (on which more later) of pope Innocent III, who was very well informed on the events there.

26 Otto of St Blasius 46, ad ann. 1198, MGH *SS rer. Germ.* 47, 74: '*Itaque uterque regum pro principatu suo satis agens bellum hoc civile pene per xii annos pertinaciter protelarunt*'.

27 *Registrum Innocentii III papae super negotio Romani imperii* 14, ed. Kempf, 33-38.

28 *Registrum super negotio Romani imperii* 3, ed. Kempf 10-13.

29 *Gesta Innocentii PP. III* 21, Migne *PL* 214, col. xxxi-xxxii: '*Direxit* <scl. imperatrix Constancia> *autem incontinenti nuntios cum muneribus ad Innocentium, devotissime postulans ut regnum Sicilie, ducatum Apulie, et principatum Capuae … sibi et filio suo concedere dignaretur*'. Innocent III complied with her request; the deed of investment is printed in HB 1.1, 17. For further details on Constance's investiture by Innocent III see *infra* p. 187-188.

30 See *supra* p. 27.

31 *Registrum super negotio Romani imperii* 14, ed. Kempf 36: 'we urgently request the benevolence of the Apostolic dignity not to extend his hand illegally on the rights of the Empire

stern rebuke from his own side. In a letter addressed to Duke Berthold of Zähringen, himself at one time mentioned as a possible candidate for the succession of Henry VI but now siding with Philip of Swabia[32], Innocent III lectured the German princes on his position in the election of a German king. It was, of course, the privilege of the German princes to hold a free election of a king. Innocent III would and could not interfere with that, but it was his responsibility as pope to examine whether the person elected by the princes was *qualified* to be anointed by him as emperor, thus making the pope the final arbiter in the coronation process[33] on account of the *plenitudo potestatis*, 'absolute sovereignty', he claimed as representative of Christ (*vicarius Christi*)[34].

In 1200, the pope presented a memorandum (*deliberatio*) to his cardinals on the question how to proceed 'in the matter of the Roman Empire' (*super negotio imperii Romani*). It is a carefully composed document dealing with the problem at hand on the basis of three tests: 'what is lawful, what is right, and what is expedient' (*quod liceat, quod deceat, quod expediat*)[35]. After thoroughly scrutinizing all three contenders, Innocent decided in favour of Otto IV[36]. His own ward, Frederick II,

---

in any way' (*dignitatis apostolicae clementiam omni studio et attentione rogamus ut ... ad jura imperii manum cum iniuria nullatenus extendatis*).

32   See Otto of St Blasius 46, ad ann. 1198, MGH *SS rer. Germ.* 47, 73.

33   This is the famous decretal 'Venerabilem'. Innocent III had it inserted into the compilation of his own decretals compiled in 1210, the so-called *Compilatio tertia* (1,6,13, E. Friedberg (ed.), *Quinque compilationes antiquae*, Leipzig 1882, 107). It was later inserted into the codification of canon law compiled at the order of Innocent's nephew Pope Gregory IX in 1234, the so-called *Liber extra* (X): X. 1,6,34. It remained in force until 1917 when the *Liber extra* was finally repealed and replaced by a new *Codex iuris canonici*. By then, there were no more Roman emperors. For X. 1,6,34 ('Venerabilem') see *infra* p. 334-336.

34   Innocent III to all German princes, ecclesiastical and secular (*Registrum super negotio Romani imperii* 33, ed. Kempf 106): 'the Apostolic See, where absolute sovereignty resides on account of divine institution' (*sedes apostolica ... apud quam ex institutione divina plenitudo residet potestatis*', repeated in the letter to the duke of Zähringen. See on the doctrine of *plenitudo potestatis* more extensively *infra* p. 331-334.

35   *Registrum super negotio Romani imperii* 29, ed. Kempf 77: '*tria sunt circa singulos attendenda, quid liceat, quid deceat, quid expediat*'. Innocent used these three criteria frequently, see, for example, his decretal 'Magnae devotionis' (X. 3,34,7): '*tria praecipue duximus in hoc negotio attendenda: quid liceat secundum aequitatem, quid deceat secundum honestatem et quid expediat secundum utilitatem*'.

36   The case of Philip of Swabia was a hard nut to crack for Innocent III. Philip had been excommunicated by Pope Celestine III for his invasion of papal territory (see *supra* p. 150, fnt. 7) and, consequently, was ineligible, but his excommunication had been lifted by a papal legate sent by Innocent to Germany to negotiate with Philip over the terms of his reconciliation with the Church. Innocent III considered the act of his legate unauthorized, but the pope had been able to assess that it had happened *after* the election, so that Philip was still an excommunicate *at* the election, making it null and void anyway. He proceeded by explaining why it was morally unjustified to confirm the election of Philip. He came 'from a family of persecutors of

'the child' (*puer*)[37], was ineligible. The pope, correctly, contended that Frederick II had not even been baptized at his election and was therefore disqualified from election, making his election null and void. Innocent then proceeded to argue that it was wrong to elect a king and future emperor who was an infant and therefore subject to the custody of a guardian[38] and that it was inexpedient as well, since by confirming the election of Frederick II the union of the kingdom of Sicily and the German Empire would be restored, to the great detriment of the interests of the Church[39]. Naturally, this last argument was decisive.

Innocent realized that his public rejection of Frederick II as king of the Germans might cause a scandal, since he was the guardian of Frederick and, consequently, under the obligation to act in the interest of his ward. This is why he emphasized that Frederick II '*has not been entrusted to our care to acquire the Empire for him, but so that we may secure the kingdom of Sicily*'[40]. This was a very important issue for Innocent. His guardianship of Fredrick II was *not* a consequence of the testamentary disposition of the Empress Constance, who had named Innocent as guardian of her son in her testament[41], which would have made him responsible indeed for *all* the interests of his ward; rather, it was a feudal guardianship (*Lehnsvormundschaft*; 'wardship'), to which

---

the Church' (*de genere persecutorum*), summing up all offenses against the Church by the late Salian and Hohenstaufen emperors, starting with the arrest of Pope Paschalis II by Henry V (*supra* p. 70) and ending with the murder of the bishop of Liège and the involvement of Henry VI (*supra* p. 145, fnt. 48), all crimes for which their descendants had to pay 'unto the third and fourth generation' (*Deuteronomy* 5:9). He concluded by contending that a confirmation of the election of Philip was inexpedient as well, since, by allowing a brother to succeed his brother, the suggestion might arise that the German monarchy was hereditary rather than electoral, 'thus making hereditary what should be a spontaneous gift' (*sic efficeretur hereditarium quod debet esse gratuitum*). All of these arguments applied to Frederick II as well.

37   *Registrum super negotio Romani imperii* 29, ed. Kempf 76-77: '*tres sunt in reges electi, puer, Philippus et Otto*'.

38   *Registrum super negotio Romani imperii* 29, ed. Kempf 78: '*Numquid enim regeret alios qui regimine indiget aliorum*'. This was part of the '*quod deceat*' arguments, since there was no objection at law to the election of a minor as king of the Germans. Many minors had been elected king of the Germans (Henry VI among them), and of France, by the way. Nevertheless, Innocent III considered it wrong. How can a man be the guardian of his subjects when he himself stands in need of a guardian? Innocent added interesting observations here on the possibility of temporary rule 'by a deputy' (*per procuratorem*) during the minority of the king, or even of the election of a temporary king during the minority of Frederick II, clearly because he knew that the German princes in Thuringia had been considering these possibilities. Innocent rejected them.

39   *Registrum super negotio Romani imperii* 29, ed. Kempf 79: '*Quod non expediat ipsum imperium obtinere patet ex eo quod per hoc regnum Siciliae uniretur imperio, et ex ipsa unione confunderetur Ecclesia*.

40   *Registrum super negotio Romani imperii* 29, ed. Kempf 79: '*non sit nobis commissus ut ei obtineamus imperium, sed regnum Siciliae potius defendamus*'.

41   See *supra* p. 151.

the pope was entitled at law since the heir of his vassal (Constance of Sicily) was a minor[42]. The relation between the pope and the minor king of Sicily should, therefore, be considered from the perspective of feudal law alone, leaving out all other interests of his ward, which did not concern his feudal lord, the pope. Consequently, as far as the succession in the Empire was concerned, Innocent owed no obligations to his ward and was free to act as he saw fit. Everyone at the time (1200) knew, moreover, that Innocent III took his duties as guardian of his Sicilian ward very seriously, since he was waging war, at great cost to the papal treasury, in South Italy on behalf of Frederick II.

In their long and bitter controversy with Frederick II, three succeeding popes, Honorius III, Gregory IX, and Innocent IV, all emphasized time and again how grateful that prince ought to be for all the support the Apostolic See had provided him with during his minority. Frederick II always answered these papal laments with irony, emphasizing that he did, indeed, owe all he had to the Holy Church. Privately, however, he was full of bitterness over the conduct of Innocent III as his guardian. He never forgave the papacy for it, as becomes clear at the (very rare) occasions when Frederick loses his usual composure and reveals his anger after receiving yet another reproachful papal letter. He blamed Innocent III for all the misfortunes befalling the Sicilian kingdom after the demise of his mother. It was his mother who had banned all the German soldiers of fortune in the service of Henry VI from the Sicilian kingdom[43], but it was the policy of Innocent III that brought them back, wreaking havoc on the kingdom[44].

Papal involvement in Sicilian affairs

One of the Germans banned from Sicily by Frederick's mother was Markward of Annweiler. He was originally a man of unfree status, serving Henry VI as a 'ministerial', making a career in Italy, as many other imperial 'ministerials' had done. In 1194 Henry VI manumitted his trusted servant and henchman and invested him with the duchies of

---

42 Innocent III emphasized this point later (in 1207) in a letter to Fredrick II (HB 1,1, 124-126 (125)): '*ballii rationem quod non tam ex dispositione materna quam jure regni suscepimus*'.
43 See *supra* p. 151.
44 It is a view of events almost certainly imparted to Frederick by the crafty politician closest to him during his minority, Walter of Pagliara, the bishop of Troia. See for this view a fragment from a letter sent by Frederick to Honorius III in or about April 1226 (HB 2.2, 932-933), the full contents of which (a long list of complaints on the conduct of Innocent III 'when I was still in diapers' (*dum in cunis ego agerem*)) can be reconstructed from the responding letter by Honorius (MGH *Epp. saec. xiii* 1, no 296, 216-222). In his answer to this papal letter, Frederick regained his usual self-control (Winkelmann, *Acta imperii inedita seculi xiii*, Insbruck 1880, no 286, 261-262).

Ravenna, the Romagna and the Marche of Ancona[45], making him a neighbour of the duke of Spoleto, Conrad of Urslingen. All these provinces, Ravenna, the Romagna, the Marche, and the duchy of Spoleto, until then firmly controlled by Henry VI and his German appointees, were claimed by Innocent III as belonging to the 'patrimony of St Peter' (*Patrimonium Petri*). The pope made it very clear, right from the beginning of his papacy, that he wanted to create a sovereign Papal State in the middle of Italy, since '*the liberty of the Church is nowhere better served than where the Roman Church exercises complete sovereignty in ecclesiastical as well as in temporal affairs*'[46]. He based his title to these regions on an ancient imperial grant, the *Hludowicianum*, by the Emperor Louis I to Pope Paschalis I (817) and inserted in the basic textbook of medieval canon law, Gratian's *Decretum* (Dist. 63, cap. 30)[47]. All these territories had been lost to the Church in the past, but Innocent III made it an absolute priority of his policy to restore them to the control of the pope. Now that the German Empire was in confusion, Innocent III saw an excellent opportunity in the resulting power vacuum in Italy to realize the 'restoration' of the Papal State. He was especially successful in the provinces assigned to Markward of Annweiler and Conrad of Urslingen. When they returned to their duchies in 1197 after being expelled from Sicily by the Empress Constance[48], they found the cities there in open rebellion. Conrad of Urslingen quickly concluded that his position in the duchy of Spoleto was untenable and left for Germany, where he sided with Philip of Swabia, leaving his entire duchy to Innocent III[49]. Markward of Annweiler, however, desperately held on as long as he could in the Romagna and the Marche until news of the demise of Constance reached him and he left as well, in his case back to South Italy and Sicily[50], causing a major disruption of the civil administration of the Sicilian monarchy since he claimed to have been appointed by Henry

---

45   Burchard of Ursberg, *Chronicon* ad ann. 1195, MGH *SS rer. Germ.* 16, 72-73: '*Eo tempore imperator Marquardum de Anninwilir, dapiferum et ministerialem suum, libertate donavit et ducatum Ravenne cum Romania, marchiam quoque Ancone sibi concessit*'.

46   *Innocentii III PP Regestorum*, lib. 1, no 27 (Migne *PL* 214, col. 21): '*Nusquam melius ecclesiasticae consulitur libertati quam ubi Ecclesia Romana tam in temporalibus quam spiritualibus plenam obtinet potestatem*'.

47   On the *Pactum Hludowicianum* see *supra* p. 58-61.

48   The fact that Conrad of Urslingen was banned from Sicily as well, reveals that there was no love lost between that gentleman and the Empress Constance. It allows for the conclusion that Constance was forced by her husband to part with her child, leaving it in the custody of the Urslingen couple against her will. See *supra* p. 150, fnt. 6.

49   *Gesta Innocentii* 9 (Migne *PL* 214, col. xxiv-xxv): '*Recuperavit ergo Romana Ecclesia ducatum Spoleti et comitatum Assisii, videlicet Reatem, Spoletum, Asisium, Fulgineum et Nuceram, cum omnibus diocesis suis. … <Conradus> de mandato domini papae rediit in Theotoniam*'.

50   *Gesta Innocentii* 9 (Migne *PL* 214, col. xxiv): '*<Marcualdus> reliquit Marchiam, et regnum intravit. Reducta est igitur tota Marchia, praeter Ascolum, ad dominium et fidelitatem Ecclesiae,*

VI as executor of his will and as guardian of the young king and his kingdom[51]. Of course, a confrontation with the council of dignitaries (*familiares*) appointed by the empress Constance in her will was inevitable, since the Council, Walter of Pagliara most prominently among its members, acted as executor of the will of the queen rather than of the (suspect) testament of the late king and emperor which, even if genuine, was overruled by the will of the queen anyway[52]. The result was armed conflict, because Markward could count on considerable support, not only of his own troops[53], but also of many German warlords, former captains in the army of Henry VI. Some of them had returned to the Sicilian kingdom after the demise of Queen Constance, as Markward himself had done, others had simply not complied with Constance's order to leave the kingdom and had persisted in the strongholds assigned to them by Henry VI. Among the latter was the notorious Diepold of Schweinspeunt, a terrible man with a background similar to Markward and, due to his military prowess, raised by Henry VI as count of Acerra and invested with the strong castle of Rocca D'Arce, close to the border with the Papal State[54]. Men like Markward, Diepold, and others were soldiers of fortune[55], owing no loyalty at all to the minor orphan who

---

videlicet Ancona, Firmum, Auximum, Camerinum, Fanum, Esim, Senegalia, et Pensaunium cum omnibus diocesis suis'.

51   Ryccardus de S. Germano, *Chronica* ad ann. 1198, *RIS*² 7.2, 19: 'But as soon as the aforementioned Markward heard of the empress' demise, he came to the kingdom, not without help and guidance by people from the kingdom, after having gathered an army of villains he bought or hired' (*Dictus vero Marcualdus cognito de morte imperatricis, congregato malignorum exercitu quos prece pretiove conduxerat, regnum non sine illorum qui erant de regno auxilio et ducatu intravit*). For Markward's claim as executor of the will of Henry VI see *Gesta Innocentii* 9 (Migne *PL* 214, col. xxiii): *'et eum <Marcualdum> executorem sui fecerat <Henrycus> testamenti'*. See also *Gesta Innocentii* 23 (Migne *PL* 214, col. xxxix): *'Marcualdus ... praetendens, quod, ex testamento imperatoris, ipse debebat esse balius regis et regni'*. The 'will' of Henry VI (printed in MGH *Const.* 1, no 379, 530-531) is a clear forgery (see the convincing arguments of J. Ficker, *Forschungen zur Reichs- und Rechtsgeschichte Italiens* 2, Insbruck 1869, 324). The text is only (partly) known from the *Gesta Innocentii* 27 (Migne *PL* 214, col. lii), where it is said to have been discovered among the possessions of Markward seized after the battle of Monreale (1201), a temporary setback for Markward in his ongoing struggle with the papal forces supporting the council appointed by Constance.

52   . The alleged 'will' of Henry VI had become legally irrelevant, since Constance and her son were invested by Innocent III with the kingdom of Sicily after the demise of Henry VI (*supra* p. 154, fnt. 29), making the pope the guardian of his minor vassal Frederick after the demise of Constance by operation of law.

53   Markward also mobilized the Muslims of Sicily for his interest (*Gesta Innocentii III Papae* 26, Migne *PL* 214, col. xlix): *'Marcualdus, attractis sibi Saracenis Siciliae'*.

54   Burchard of Ursberg, *Chronicon* ad ann. 1195, MGH *SS rer. Germ.* 16, 73: *'Prefato etiam Diepoldo quasdam provincias Apulie commisit <scl. Henrycus VI>, ponens eum in quodam castro, quod vocatur Rocca de Arce'*.

55   Among the German knights present in South Italy was also a cutthroat called Odo, one of the men who had assassinated Albert of Brabant (on the murder of Albert see *supra* p. 145,

was king of Sicily in name only, nor to the pope, who sent troops to wage war on them in Sicily and on the South Italian mainland. They thrived like fish in the water of the anarchy prevailing in South Italy, like the Norman mercenaries before them[56] and just like these Norman mercenaries they were only after their own private interests.

Walter of Brienne

To make matters even worse, Innocent III decided to bring in an outsider, Walter of Brienne, to fight Markward, Diepold, and the likes of them as his *condottière*. Count Walter III of Brienne (*c.* 1166-1205) had particular interests of his own in South Italy since he was married to Elvira, a daughter of the usurper Tancred of Lecce[57]. It was another 'service' Frederick II was never to forgive nor forget[58], not only because Innocent III invested the count of Brienne with the county of Lecce without his consent (1200)[59], but even more so because he brought a possible pretender onto the Sicilian scene, Tancred's widow Sybilla and her offspring[60]. The event was to have devastating consequences for young Fredrick. He had been in the relatively safe custody of the council and Bishop Walter of Pagliara up till then, but the bishop now changed his policy. He, correctly as I believe, perceived the presence of

---

fnt. 48). Odo, who had been made count of Laviano by Henry VI, was slain in Apulia in the fights there with Walter of Brienne: *Gesta Innocentii III Papae* 34, Migne *PL* 214, col. lxii.

56   See *supra* p. 30.

57   On Elvira of Lecce see *supra* p. 147, fnt. 60.

58   Frederick's complaints about the mission of Walter of Brienne are obvious from the answer of Honorius III (see *supra* p. 157, fnt. 44), defending the decision of Innocent III to appoint Walter (HB 2.1, 592). Frederick II was still angry about it many years later (HB 6.1, 389 (1246)): 'Under the pretext of our defence, he <Innocent III> sent Walter of Brienne to the kingdom, who, being the son in law of the usurper Tancred, thirsted for our blood and our death' (*G. de Brenna, qui velut gener Tancredi regis intrusi mortem nostrum et sanguinem sitiebat, sub defensionis nostre specie misit in regnum*).

59   The letter of Innocent III informing the Sicilian council of the investiture of Walter of Brienne with the county of Lecce is in the *Gesta Innocentii III Papae* 25, Migne *PL* 214, col. xlvii-xlix. The enfeoffment of Walter of Brienne with Lecce was highly irregular if not illegal. A feudal guardian was not entitled to dispose of the tenures of his ward, certainly not when there was a sub-tenant in possession, as happened to be the case with the county of Lecce. There is a letter from Innocent III to another count of Lecce, only known by his initial (R), shortly before Walter's investiture placing his fief under papal protection (*Innocentii III PP Regesta* II (1199), 182, Migne *PL* 214, col. 733).

60   Innocent III stresses in his letter to the Sicilian royal council informing it on the investiture of Walter of Brienne that he had procured a solemn oath of Walter 'that he would not himself, or by means of another, conspire against the person and the honour of the king and the Sicilian kingdom' (*quod nec per se, nec per alium machinabatur quidquam contra personam regis, honorem ipsius, et regnum Siciliae*): *Gesta Innocentii III Papae*, Migne *PL* 214, col. xlviii. It will not have impressed Walter of Pagliara. He had supported Henry VI and Constance against Tancred of Lecce from the start and knew that Tancred's widow Sybilla, Walter's mother-in-law, who accompanied her daughter and son in law, was a very dangerous woman. She is said to have advised her husband not to release Constance (see *supra* p. 144), but to have her killed instead (Petrus of Eboli (*fl.* 1196-1220) *Liber ad honorem Augusti* v. 895-912, ed. G.B. Siragusa, Rome 1906, 66).

Walter of Brienne as a far more serious threat to Frederick (and his own safety) than Markward of Annweiler and consequently he made an alliance with that German warlord. He surrendered Sicily to Markward and went to the South Italian mainland himself to fight the count of Brienne, in close alliance with that other German war lord, Diepold of Acerra, leaving the young king in the personal custody of his brother, who treacherously surrendered the child to Markward[61]. Frederick's life was now in danger, but since Markward's precarious title to power rested on his position as the alleged guardian of Frederick, he spared the child[62]. Markward did not survive his 'coup' for long though. He died, from natural causes, in September 1202[63]. There was no way the papal guardian could prevent that his ward was captured and held hostage by yet another German captain, this time a man called William Capparone, who styled himself 'guardian of the king and captain-in-chief of Sicily' (*custos regis et magister capitaneus Siciliae*)[64]. Bishop Walter now had lost all control of Sicilian affairs and was doing badly on the mainland as well against the forces of Walter of Brienne. Consequently, he turned sides once again by submitting to the pope, who had excommunicated him for turning against the count of Brienne. He promised obedience to Innocent III and was absolved as quickly as he had been excommunicated[65]. Innocent's blatant opportunism is even more shocking in the case of Diepold of Schweinspeunt, who had also fought Walter of Brienne and was excommunicated as well. Diepold, after suffering many defeats at the hands of Walter of Brienne, was besieged by Walter in one of his strongholds, but was able to surprise Walter and his soldiers sleeping in their unguarded tents. The count of Brienne did not survive the ensuing slaughter (11 June 1205).

---

61 For these events see *Gesta Innocentii III Papae* 32-35, Migne *PL* 214, col. lvi-lxii.

62 The author of the *Gesta Innocentii III Papae* 35, Migne *PL* 214, col. lxii, suggests Markward spared Frederick because Markward believed that the Sicilian throne would then fall, as of right, to Walter of Brienne, 'on account of his wife' (*ratione conjugis*). This suggestion by an author close to Innocent III illustrates how threatening the introduction of Walter of Brienne really was to all who had stood by Henry VI, his wife Constance, and their child Frederick.

63 *Gesta Innocentii III Papae* 35, Migne *PL* 214, col. lxii; Ryccardus de S. Germano, *Chronica* ad ann. 1202,
*RIS*² 7.2, 23: '*Marcualdus, superveniente dissinteria, miserabiliter expiravit*'.

64 *Gesta Innocentii III Papae* 36, Migne *PL* 214, col. lxii-lxiii. Innocent III sent a legate to Sicily to negotiate with Capparone but, as was to be expected, the mission was unsuccessful. The cardinal was, however, allowed to visit Frederick, who is reported to have been very pleased with the consolation that prelate was able to afford him (*de sua consolatione gaudebat* (Migne *PL* 214, col. lxv)).

65 *Gesta Innocentii III Papae* 36, Migne *PL* 214, col. lxiii-lxiv: '*Cancellarius autem, opportunum sibi tempus aestimans advenisse, iterato exhibens juratoriam cautionem, quod mandatis apostolicis per omnia obediret, absolutionis beneficium impetravit*'.

It was the end of the papal expeditionary force in South Italy. Diepold, the slayer of Innocent's *condottière*, soon thereafter also submitted to the pope[66] and was likewise absolved because Innocent 'believed he could be of use to the Church' (*credens eum ecclesiae profuturum*)[67].

The King
comes of age

Diepold and Bishop Walter of Pagliara, now nominally acting as agents of Innocent III, hastened from the mainland to Sicily to deal with William Capparone, still in possession of the king at Palermo. Cardinal Gerardo, the papal legate in Sicily, joined them on their way to Palermo. What exactly transpired there subsequently is rather confusing[68], but the outcome is not. Diepold was able to lay his hand on the young king, by whatever means is unclear, but was arrested by Walter of Pagliara and forced to surrender Frederick. Diepold was subsequently imprisoned by Bishop Walter but managed to escape to the mainland, where he resumed the mischief that was his favourite pastime – murder, arson, and plunder. As we shall see later[69], he was responsible for even more serious trouble in the near future. William Capparone disappeared in the obscurity from whence he came. The young Sicilian king was now, once again, in the custody of Walter of Pagliara, who remained in charge of affairs until the advent of the king's majority in 1209. It was in that year that Innocent III presented his Sicilian ward with his only positive contribution to his reign: a wife[70]. Constance of Aragon (1179-1222) was fifteen years older than her husband and already an experienced woman in many ways. She had been married before to King Emeric of Hungary (1174-1196-1204), with whom she had a son, but Constance outlived both her husband and her son and returned to her native Aragon, where her brother Peter was king, the second of that name. The king of Aragon was a vasal of the pope, as was the king of Sicily[71]. Consequently, King Peter was crowned as king of Aragon by

---

66   For Diepold's motives see *infra* p. 168, fnt. 5.

67   *Annales Casinenses* ad. ann. 1205, MGH *SS* 19, 319: '*Diopuldus et se ipsum humilians, domnus papa missis nuntiis suis fecit ipsum Diopuldum et suos ab excommunicatione absolvi, credens eum ecclesiae profuturum*'. The monk from Montecassino writing this chronicle adds that Diepold was 'well received' (*bene receptus*) by the pope and the people of Rome on his visit to the city in 1206. On Diepold's murder of Walter of Brienne and his subsequent absolution see also *Gesta Innocentii III Papae* 38, Migne *PL* 214, col. lxvii-lxviii.

68   See the conflicting stories in *Gesta Innocentii III Papae* 38, Migne *PL* 214, col. lviii-lxix and in Ryccardus de S. Germano, *Chronica* ad ann. 1207, *RIS*² 7.2, 24-25.

69   *Infra* p. 180-181.

70   The right to choose a wife for a minor vassal was an important incident of feudal wardship.

71   The idea to create a feudal relationship between the Holy See and secular princes seems to have originated with Gregory VII. The first instance was the enfeoffment of Robert Guiscard with Apulia and Sicily in 1059 (see *supra* p. 32). In 1068 king Sancho Ramirez of Aragon turned his kingdom over to the pope, from whom he received it back as his vassal. The advan-

the pope, Innocent III, in Rome in 1205[72]. During his stay in Rome, Peter and Innocent discussed the plan to marry the pope's Sicilian ward to a princess from the house of Aragon[73]. In the end, the choice fell on the elder of Peter's two sisters, Constance. She was married to Frederick II in August 1209[74]. The marriage was a success. For the first time since the premature death of his mother, Frederick had someone beside him whom he could completely trust. In later years he even must have believed he owed his Sicilian crown to her, since he gave it to Constance in her grave when she died in 1222, a very unusual gift.

The involvement of Innocent III in Sicilian affairs during the minority of Frederick II has been thus far related in some detail since it reveals the background of Frederick's later attitude towards the Roman papacy. Frederick must have felt very lonely and forlorn in the period when Innocent III was his guardian, living as he did in Palermo 'like a lamb among the wolves' (*quasi agnus inter lupos*)[75]. There is a moving letter by Frederick II, sent to all the kings and princes of the world calling for help[76]. The letter was written in 1201, when Frederick was still only seven years old. It is therefore supposed to have been written by others on his behalf, but it contains a unique idea Frederick II was to repeat time and again later in his life: an appeal to the solidarity of all kings and other secular princes. Due to the circumstances of his youth, the extraordinary intelligent child had become a man before his time[77],

Lessons learned

---

tage to be gained from this by a prince was that his kingdom stood under the special protection of the Church, threatening all intruders with immediate excommunication.

72 *Innocentii III PP. Regestorum* VII, no 229 (Migne *PL* 215, col. 550-551).

73 In a letter to king Peter 'on the issue of the marriage between your sister and our dear son in Christ Frederic' (*super negotio matrimonii inter tuam sororem et charissimum in Christo filium nostrum Fredericum* (*Innocentii III PP. Regestorum* XI, no 4 (Migne *PL* 215, col. 1312)), Pope Innocent relates that Peter and he 'have talked about it at one time' (*aliquando tecum fuerimus viva voce locuti*) and had exchanged many letters on the issue. The only time Innocent and king Peter met face to face was in Rome in 1205.

74 *Annales Siculi* ad ann. 1209, MGH *SS* 19, 496: '*decimo quinto mensis Augusti duodecimae indictionis domna Constancia de Aragonia applicuit Panormum; et domnus rex Fridericus in eodem mense desponsavit eam*'.

75 'Nicolaus de Jamsilla', *Historia de rebus gestis Friderici II imperatoris eiusque filiorum Conradi et Manfredi*, in Muratori, *Rerum Italicarum Scriptores* VIII, Milan 1726, col. 493. The attribution of the authorship of this history to a certain Nicolaus de Jamsilla is based on an error but has stuck with modern scholarship. It was written by an anonymous author close to the court of Manfred: see *infra* p. 424, fnt. 39.

76 HB 1.1, 78-79 (June 1201).

77 Fredrick's precociousness was already noticed by his contemporaries, such as Innocent III, who was well informed by his legates. In his letter to King Peter of Aragon (*supra* fnt. 73) he praises Frederick in the following words 'he has reached the years of discernment, having passed the threshold of puberty rather swiftly' (*de janua pubertatis passu velociori annos discretionis ingreditur* (Migne *PL* 215, col. 1313)).

decisively influenced by the exceptional experiences of his childhood, especially in as far as his attitude towards the papacy was concerned. Thanks to the example of the policy and perhaps even the lessons of Bishop Walter of Pagliara, Frederick II perceived the pope primarily as a devious political agent, playing power games on the Italian peninsula and elsewhere, primarily aimed at consolidating and enhancing his own secular power and authority at the expense of the Empire and other secular powers. He had also learned that the pope did not shrink from deceit or duplicity, as Innocent III had clearly done with the introduction of Walter of Brienne on the Sicilian scene[78]. Duplicity, opportunism, equivocation, and even deceit were the instruments of political survival, as he had learned during his minority, and Frederick II was to make use of these instruments for the rest of his life. With everything he said or wrote, especially when addressing a pope, one should always be aware of the persistent tone of irony, ambiguity, and dishonesty, refined by the arts of his brilliant ghost-writer, Piero della Vigna (Petrus de Vinea, *c.* 1190-1249), the man 'who held both keys to Frederick's heart'[79].

The ruined kingdom

At his accession to majority in 1209, the young king was confronted with a ruined kingdom. The Chancellor Walter of Pagliara, Markward of Annweiler, and William Capparone had fatally diminished the royal demesne by granting away large parts of it to keep the Sicilian and South Italian barons as well as their own men satisfied; extremely favourable fiscal privileges had been granted, especially to the Genoese, and the royal civil service, once the paradigm of effective governance for all of Europe, was corrupted by the sale of offices[80]. The worst of all wrongs, however, were the soldiers of fortune like Diepold and his compatriots

---

78   To Innocent III the use of deceit (*dolus*) was a completely acceptable instrument of diplomacy, as he once instructed some of his bishops (*Innocentii III PP. Regestorum* XI, no 232 (Migne *PL* 215, col. 1546): 'such deceit should rather be called prudence' (*talis dolus prudentia potius sit dicendus*), referring to the Apostle Paul in 2 Corinthians 12:16: 'Being crafty, I caught you with guile'.
79   Piètro della Vigna was a South Italian poet, lawyer, and courtier, serving Fredrick II first as a notary, later as a judge in the High Court (*magna curia*) of the realm and as an important diplomat. He was, until his arrest (on charges of corruption) in 1249, in fact the first minister of the Sicilian kingdom. His literary legacy consists of a huge collection of letters, written in the service of Fredrick II, and his poetry (in the vernacular, one of the first Italian poets to do so). Dante honoured his memory in a moving scene in *Inferno* 13, 55-78. Huillard-Bréholles published most of Piètro's letters in his monumental *Historia Diplomatica Friderici Secundi*, Paris 1852-1861.
80   For the mismanagement of Walter of Pagliara during the king's minority see *Gesta Innocentii III Papae* 31, Migne *PL* 214, col. liv-lv: '*Gualterius autem, Troianus episcopus, et regni Siciliae cancellarius ... conferebat et auferebat comitatus et baronias; instituebat justitiarios et Camerarios, secretaries et stratigotos; vendebat et expendebat et impignorabat dohanas et bajulatio accipiebat, et expendebat redditus et proventus*'. Innocent III tried to do something about it, but his warnings and injunctions were not heeded in Sicily.

terrorizing the countryside on the mainland from their strongholds all over Apulia. They were a permanent threat to the peace of the realm and consequently their expulsion, if not extermination, was a priority of the new government. The South Italian German warlords realized this and decided to bring a prince to their side whom the young Sicilian king could not possibly hope to overcome: Otto IV, recently crowned by Innocent III as Roman emperor.

12

Otto IV and the Kingdom of Sicily

Pope Innocent III suffered one disaster after another in 1204, the seventh year of his reign. One way or another, they were all related to his fatal choice, in 1200, in favour of Otto of Poitou, rather than Philip of Swabia, as successor to Henry VI. Otto IV had been elected in 1198 by only a minority of the German princes, all of them from the northwest of the German kingdom, whereas Philip was supported by a clear majority[1]. In order to strengthen the case of his German protagonist, Innocent had sent a legate to Germany in 1201 who excommunicated all who resisted Otto[2], but it proved remarkably ineffective. In 1204 all German bishops and many of the secular princes who had hitherto still supported Otto went over to Philip, even Otto's own brother, the Count Palatine Henry, deserted him[3]. Otto's cause seemed lost beyond any hope. Philip of Swabia, on the other hand, felt strong enough to send a powerful army under the command of Bishop Lupold of Worms, a stout-hearted warrior, to Italy in 1204 in order to regain control of the territories Innocent III had only recently 'restored' to the

Papal
adversities

---

1   The rule that a majority decision is binding has never been part of canon law. A qualified majority, such as for example in the election of a new pope, was sometimes binding, but a simple majority never was. One always had to take account of the individual authority (*auctoritas*) of the members of a group of voters. A minority consisting of authoritative voters (*sanior pars*) might be preferable over a majority of less authoritative individuals, as Innocent III explicitly states in his 'decretal' 'Dudum' (X. 1,6,22). A majority decision was only binding *per se* on the condition that the *maior pars* included the *sanior pars*. To hold differently would have amounted to the recognition of mob rule. Innocent III also stressed the point in his *Deliberatio*: 'in elections the zeal, dignity, and the number of the electors must be taken into account' (*in electionibus circa electores zelus, dignitas et numerus attendatur*) and, further on in his discourse, 'not just the majority in numbers, but the soundness of their judgement is required of electors' (*nec tantum pluralitas quoad numerum, sed salubritas quoad consilium in elegentibus requiratur*) (*Registrum super negotio Romani imperii* 29, ed. Kempf 88-89).
2   See the letter of legate Guido, cardinal-bishop of Praeneste, to Innocent III (*Registrum super negotio Romani imperii* 51, ed. Kempf 138): '*excommunicatis omnibus qui se ei ducerent opponendos*'. The cardinal sketches a rather bleak picture of Otto's chances of success in his letter.
3   On the massive desertion of former adherents of Otto IV, including his brother, see *Chronica regia coloniensis* ad ann 1204, MGH *SS rer. Germ.* 18, 218-219.

papal domain[4]. Lupold met with little resistance in the *regnum itali-cum*. By March 1205 he was in control of the duchy of Spoleto, restoring it to Henry of Urslingen, a son of Conrad who had died in 1202[5]. Innocent's 'restored' Papal State was crumbling fast. Meanwhile, in Rome the citizenry had risen, once again, against the papal regime in the city, forcing the pope to run off to Anagni. According to Innocent, the revolt originated with citizens dissatisfied with his choice in favour of Otto IV: 'we have suffered a lot of adversity because of you' (*propter te multa passi sumus adversa*), the pope later wrote to Otto[6]. The greatest disaster befalling Innocent III in 1204 was, of course, the misguided Fourth Crusade (1202-1204) and the brutal capture and sack of Constantinople (24 November 1204). Pope Innocent III was furious with his legate in the crusading army: '*We have not instructed you to conquer the Byzantine Empire, but to defend the remnants of the Holy Land*'[7]. The pope was an intelligent man and he immediately perceived that after this catastrophe a reconciliation between the Latin 'Catholic' Church and the Greek 'Orthodox' Church was impossible[8]. In this matter too, there was a connection with Philip of Swabia, since Philip

---

4 *Chronica regia coloniensis* ad ann 1203, MGH *SS rer. Germ.* 18, 172: 'Bishop Lupold entered Italy again with a huge army and started to lay waste to everything that belonged to the pope' (*Lupoldus episcopus cum magno belli apparatu Italia denuo ingressus est, cuncta que ditioni apostolice attinebant ferro et igni hostiliter devastare cepit*).
5 See a charter of Bishop Lupold in his capacity as imperial legate in Italy, published in J. Ficker, *Forschungen zur Reichs- und Rechtsgeschichte Italiens* IV (Urkunden), Insbruck 1874, no 210, 262-263, dated 12 March 1205 and completed in the county of Urbino, mentioning Henry as *dux Spoletanus*. Ficker (no 211, 263-264) also has a charter of Philip of Swabia in favour of the citizens of Assisi for the services rendered to Lupold. The charter is dated 29 July 1205, the services rendered to Lupold must have considerably predated it. Lupold's invasion of Spoleto, right on the border of the Sicilian kingdom, may have been the reason why Diepold of Schweinspeunt sided with the pope around the same time (*supra* p. 162). Lupold was a man of Philip of Swabia, Frederick's uncle, and Diepold may have been afraid to be crushed by the Hohenstaufens making common cause against him and his ilk causing mischief in South Italy.
6 *Registrum Innocentii III papae super negotio Romani imperii* 153, ed. Kempf, 350. It was at this occasion that the huge 'torre' of Innocent's family, the Conti, was stormed and considerably reduced in height. See a letter from Innocent to his brother Riccardo (*Innocentii III PP Regestorum* VII, ep. 133, Migne *PL* 215, col. 422-425 (424)). The remains of the 'Torre dei Conti' can still be seen in Rome at the corner of Via Cavour and Via dei Fori Imperiali.
7 *Innocentii III PP. Regestorum* VIII, ep. 126, Migne *PL* 215, col. 699-702 (700): '*non ad capiendum Constantinopolitanum imperium, sed defendendas reliquias terrae sanctae ... vos duxerimus delegandos*'.
8 *Innocentii III PP. Regestorum* VIII, ep. 126, Migne *PL* 215, col. 699-702 (701): 'How can the Greek Church, so afflicted with adversity and persecution, be brought back to ecclesiastical unity and worship with the Holy See, seeing in the Latins nothing but the instrument of its doom and the product of the devil, rightly despising them even more than dogs?' (*Quomodo enim Graecorum Ecclesia, quantumcumque afflictionibus et persecutionibus affligatur, ad unitatem ecclesiasticam et devotionem sedis apostolicae revertetur, quae in Latinis non nisi perditionis exemplum et opera tenebrarum aspexit, ut iam merito illos abhorreat plus quam canes?*)'.

had supplied the Venetian Doge Enrico Dandolo (*c.* 1107-1205), the *de facto* leader of the Fourth Crusade, with the perfect excuse to attack Constantinople[9].

On 6 January 1205 Philip of Swabia was newly elected and finally crowned at Aachen by the archbishop of Cologne. It was an act of mutual reconciliation between Philip and the princes from the north-west of the realm, nicely orchestrated by Philip to emphasize that by now all German princes, clerical and secular, supported him[10]. Innocent III finally realized that he had bet on the wrong German horse and opened serious negotiations with Philip of Swabia. The negotiations were very delicate, if only because practically all interlocutors of the papal envoys had been excommunicated for serving Philip, exposing pontifical duplicity and stark opportunism at the same time by now treating Otto IV as a 'quantité négligable'. It was for all these reasons that Innocent III sent his best man to Germany, someone he could absolutely trust. It was his nephew Ugolino dei Conti di Segni, cardinal-bishop of Ostia and first among the cardinals of the Holy Roman Church in that capacity, who absolved Philip from his excommunication[11]. The object of Ugolino's mission was

Philip of Swabia prevails

---

9   Philip was married to a daughter of the Byzantine Emperor Isaac II Angelos, Irene Angelina (see *supra* p. 147, fnt. 60), who took the name Maria after her conversion to Catholicism. The Emperor Isaac had been deposed in 1195 and his son and heir Alexios had found asylum at the court of his sister Irene ('Maria') in Germany. Philip, Alexios's brother-in-law, decided to support his cause and sent him to the crusaders in Croatia, where they were besieging the city of Zara, a city belonging to the kingdom of Hungary, at the behest of the Doge of Venice, Enrico Dandolo, who had supplied the crusading army with ships on condition that the crusaders would render some services to Venice on their way to the Holy Land. The arrival of a Byzantine pretender supplied the Doge was the excuse he needed to attack Constantinople rather than Jerusalem.

10   *Chronica regia coloniensis* ad ann 1205, MGH *SS rer. Germ.* 18, 219-220: 'King Philip, as he had announced, came with almost all the princes of the kingdom to Aachen, where he was met by the bishop of Cologne with a great retinue. There the king, after consultation with his own, renounced the royal title and the crown, so that the princes would not lose the right to a free election which was theirs according to the ancient tradition, and he asked to be harmoniously chosen by all. And so it happened. He was elected by all, and anointed and consecrated there, together with his wife Maria, in the Church of Holy Mary by the archbishop of Cologne' (*Philippus igitur rex, ut proposuerat, cum universis pene principibus regni Aquisgrani venit, ubi cum maximo apparatu et obsequio Coloniensis ei occurit. Ibi rex, consilio cum suis habito, ut principes suam liberam electionem secundum antiquitatis institutum non perdant, regium nomen et coronam deponit et ut concorditer ab omnibus eligatur precatur. Quod et factum est ibidem in ecclesia beatae Mariae; ab omnibus eligitur et a Coloniensi archiepiscopo cum Maria, uxore sua, ungitur et consecratur*).

11   Arnold of Lübeck, *Chronica slavorum* 7,6 (ad ann. 1207), MGH *SS* 21, 234: '*domnus apostolicus duos cardinals delegavit – nomen unius Hugo episcopus, et alterius Leo – ut Philippum ab excommunicatione solverent*'. Papal legates as a rule acted in duo. Leo was cardinal-priest of S. Croce and was outranked by Ugolino. Ugolino was the first cardinal created by his uncle. He became cardinal-deacon of S. Eustacio in 1198, having served as an *auditor* before that,

to secure from Philip the same promises Otto IV had made to the pope at his accession in 1198 and later confirmed at Neuß in 1201[12]. Otto's promises were very important to the pope, since they amounted to the recognition of his main Italian political objective, the 'restoration' of the Papal State, indicating clear boundaries and including Ravenna, the Marche of Ancona, and the duchy of Spoleto, as well as the recognition of the feudal primacy of the pope over the kingdom of Sicily. Barbarossa and Henry VI would never have consented to concessions like these, if only because a territorial wedge would have been driven between the Italian kingdom and the kingdom of Sicily by abandoning the Marche of Ancona and the duchy of Spoleto to the pope. Philip was not inclined to abandon any imperial territory to the pope either, causing the negotiations to drag on for years. In the end, it was not Philip, but Innocent who gave in.

King Philip of Swabia
(*Chronica regia coloniensis*, Royal Library of Belgium, Ms 467, f. 137 r°)

---

and was promoted cardinal-bishop of Ostia in 1204. While still a cardinal-deacon, he had been sent on a mission to Sicily to negotiate with Markward of Annweiler. Innocent III promoted two other members of his family to the cardinalate: Giovanni (1200) and Ottaviano (1205).

12   Otto's promises to the Church are in MGH *Const.* 2, no 16, 20-21 and no 23, 27-28. But for one clause (on which more later, p. 176) they are identical. We do not know who is responsible for the text of these promises, but they are clearly dictated by papal officials and may have been communicated to Otto, as the price to be paid for papal recognition, by a Milanese intermediary present at Aachen in 1198 and mentioned in Innocent's *Registrum super negotio imperii* twice (*Epp.* 3 and 6, ed. Kempf 13 and 18).

In or about January 1208 King Philip sent an ambassy to the pope, headed by the patriarch of Aquileia, Wolfger, a trusted counsellor of the king and his legate in the Italian kingdom[13]. The ambassadors were 'to bring about peace and unity between the church and the empire and between you and me'[14]. As late as May 1208 a final agreement was concluded in Rome. In the matter of the kingdom of Sicily Philip's plenipotentiaries agreed to the status quo. King Frederick, Philip's nephew, was about to reach majority soon anyway and his marriage to an Aragonese princess was already subject to negotiations between the pope and the king of Aragon[15]. Consequently, a possible reunion of the Sicilian kingdom with the German Empire was averted. This was a success for the papal party, of course, but there was a high price to pay for it. Innocent III was forced to abandon his hopes of restoring the Papal State at the expense of the Empire. Instead of that, Philip's agents in Rome made Innocent III an offer he could not possibly refuse. They suggested a marriage between one of Innocent's nephews, a son of his brother Riccardo, and a daughter of king Philip, a possibility already raised at an earlier occasion to bring about peace between the pope and Philip[16], but this time made even more attractive since Philip added the duchy of Tuscany as a gift to his future son in law, raising the house of the Conti di Segni to staggering heights, since the Tuscan duchy was the richest in Italy. Innocent III accepted[17]. Now Otto IV had to be

Philip comes to terms with Innocent III

---

13 Wolfger had been bishop of Passsau before he was promoted to the ancient chair of Aquileia in 1204. He was, when still bishop of Passau, an opponent of papal interference in the succession of Henry VI and Innocent's choice of Otto IV as German king. Wolfger's opposition to his German policy irritated Innocent III, who wanted him censured (*Inn. III PP Registrum de negotio Romani imperii* 70 ed. Kempf 194-196 (2 October 1202). When Wolfger was promoted to the patriarchate of Aquileia, Innocent sent him a letter ordering Wolfger to send a document to the pope 'within a month' (*infra mensem*) promising absolute obedience to the pope 'in the matter of the Roman Empire as well as in others' (*tam super imperii Romani negotio, quam etiam super aliis*) (*Inn. III PP Registrum de negotio Romani imperii* no 114 ed. Kempf 283-284. Wolfger remained true to the Empire.

14 From Philip's letter to the pope (*Registrum Innocentii III papae super negotio Romani imperii* 140, ed. Kempf 332: '*quibus dedimus plenitudinem potestatis et auctoritatem omnimodam inter Ecclesiam et imperium et inter vos et nos pacem et concordiam reformare*'.

15 See *supra* p. 162.

16 For this promise see MGH *Const.* 2, no 8 (May 1203), 9: '*filiam meam nepoti eius in coniugium dabo*'. Innocent declined the offer, since he still adhered to the cause of Otto IV at the time.

17 For the 1208 agreement between Philip and Innocent III see Burchard of Ursberg, *Chronicon* ad ann. 1208, MGH *SS rer. Germ.* 16, 88-89. 'As trustworthy people have told us, a promise was made to the pope that a daughter of the king was to be given in marriage to a son of his brother Riccardo, who had already been made a count at the suggestion of the pope. The pope did not achieve to recover the land in Tuscany, Spoleto, and the Marche that his predecessors had tried to recover from the emperors so many times, hoping that they would fall to his nephew on account of his marriage' (*propter hoc, ut retulerunt nobis viri veredici, promittitur pape, quod filia regis daretur in uxorem filio fratris sui Richardi, qui iam comes fuerat*

informed of what had transpired at Rome: someone had to tell him that his rival Philip was to be crowned emperor in Rome. It was a difficult assignment and therefore entrusted to Innocent's nephew, Cardinal Ugolino. The cardinal was in Verona, on his way to Germany, when terrible news reached him by a special courier from Bamberg: King Philip had been murdered there on 21 June 1208 by Count Otto of Wittelsbach[18]. What was the pope to do now?

Innocent III
and Otto IV

Otto IV must have been a very angry and embittered man in the summer of 1208, when news of the murder of his rival reached him. All but a few of his original supporters in Germany had deserted him; his main foreign financial supporter, the king of England, was in trouble himself[19] and knew that Pope Innocent III had written him off[20]. He must have been enraged even more when he received a letter from the pope, written soon after Innocent had learned about the murder of Philip of Swabia, urging Otto to ignore the previous notice of an agreement with Philip, assuring him of his continued support, advising him not to bear

---

effectus pape suffragio; nec statuit papa repetere terras, quas multotiens ab imperatoribus repetere consueverunt ante cessores sui in Tuscia et Spoleto et marchia Ancone, sperans, quod in potestatem nepotis sui propter predictas nuptias possent devenire). The duchy of Spoleto was already granted to Henry of Urslingen (see *supra* p. 168, fnt. 5), whereas the Marche of Ancona had belonged to Markward of Annweiler (see *supra* p. 157-158), who had died in 1202, but there may have been heirs having a claim to it (a daughter of Markward was married to the powerful Tuscan count of Guerra). The only region Philip was entitled to dispose of was Tuscany, since it was his own duchy, as he had been created duke of Tuscany by Henry VI (see *supra* p. 150, fnt. 7). That Tuscany was indeed promised to Innocent's nephew may be inferred from the letter of Frederick complaining about the behaviour of Innocent III during his minority, referred to earlier (*supra* p. 157, fnt. 44). Frederick writes that 'he <Innocent III> deluded my uncle Philip to take Tuscany from me by a marriage while I was an adolescent' (HB 2.2, 933: *Hetruriam mihi adolescenti sublaturus per nuptias Philippum patruum delusit*). Frederick refers to himself as being an 'adolescent' at the time, which must mean that he refers to an event happening shortly before he became an adult on 26 December 1208.
18   The courier was sent to Wolfger of Aquileia, Philip's legate, who was with Cardinal Ugolino at the time. Ugolino's letter to Pope Innocent, written shortly after the event, is the best source of what actually transpired in Bamberg. It is to be found in *Registrum Innocentii III papae super negotio Romani imperii* 152, ed. Kempf 348-349(349). Ugolino is very succinct on the motive of the murderer. He writes that 'Philip had given him a daughter and had taken her away' (*cui dominus Philippus filiam dederat et abstulerat*). It is very tempting to assume that the daughter Philip had promised his murderer was the very same daughter he later promised to the nephew of the pope.
19   See *infra* p. 195-197.
20   Innocent III had informed Otto IV that 'his rival' (*adversarius tuus*) had sent envoys to Rome (*Registrum Innocentii III papae super negotio Romani imperii* 150, ed. Kempf 346) and as soon as he had reached an agreement with Philip's representatives in Rome, Innocent III sent a letter to Otto IV, informing him that he would let him know soon what the outcome of the negotiations had been (*Registrum Innocentii III papae super negotio Romani imperii* 151, ed. Kempf 347). Innocent left it to his nephew Ugolino to present the bitter pill to Otto IV in person.

grudges and to conduct himself as tactfully as possible, and, last but not least, subtly reminding him of the fact that there still was another pretender to the German crown, Frederick II[21]. The pope also wrote an urgent letter to another king, Philip II of France, explaining his continued support of Otto IV after the demise of Philip of Swabia. There were very important reasons for doing so.

Philip II of France has gained the sobriquet 'Auguste' in French national history for having extended the borders of his royal domain far beyond the rather confined territory of his ancestors[22]. He did so at the expense of King John of England, the only surviving son of the mighty King Henry II after the demise of his brother Richard in 1199. The kings of England were French magnates ever since the conquest of England by Duke William of Normandy (1066). The language of the English court was French and consequently the language of English law was also French and has even remained so long after the Middle Ages ('law French'). It is important to emphasize this, since it helps to understand the importance that English kings attached to their possessions in France. Since his marriage with Eleanor of Aquitaine in 1152, Henry II was beyond doubt the mightiest prince of France, far more powerful even than the king of France himself, to whom he owed allegiance for all his extended French fiefs, Normandy, Anjou, Maine, Touraine, Poitou, and Aquitaine. Together with England, Henry's domain was a genuine 'Plantagenet Empire'. And it was a constant threat to the king of France. Ever since the (failed) invasion of France by King Henry I of England in alliance with his German son-in-law, the Emperor Henry V, in 1124[23], an Anglo-German alliance was the nightmare of every French king, as it was to Philip II. This is why Philip II supported the cause of Philip of Swabia against Otto IV from the start[24], since under Otto IV, arguably the first 'anglomaniac' on the European continent, an Anglo-German alliance was more than just likely. Philip had only recently, by the end of 1205, conquered practically all continental

Innocent III and Philip 'Auguste'

---

21 *Registrum Innocentii III papae super negotio Romani imperii* 153, ed. Kempf 351.

22 The Latin noun *Augustus* is derived from the verb *augeo, i.e.* 'to add to'. Ever since official documents of the emperors of the Holy Roman Empire were written in German rather than Latin, the imperial title *semper Augustus* was always translated as 'immer Mehrerer des Reiches'.

23 French national sentiment originated in this invasion. It was then, in 1124, that Abbot Suger of S. Denys, the first French patriot, raised the Oriflamme, handing it to King Louis VI to lead the 'ost' of France against the invaders.

24 See the letter of Philip II to Innocent III in *Registrum super negotio Romani imperii* 13, ed. Kempf 31-32. As a matter of course, King Richard I sent a letter to the pope promoting the cause of his nephew and vassal Otto of Poitou: *Registrum super negotio Romani imperii* 5, ed. Kempf 15-17.

territories of King John[25], leaving that luckless king with England and a very small territory in southwestern France, Gascogny. The king of France, in the eyes of Barbarossa still just another kinglet (*regulus*)[26], had become a major player on the European political scene and Philip II was not amused when he heard that the cause of Otto IV was still supported by the pope after the assassination of his natural ally in Germany, Philip of Swabia. It was for this reason that Innocent III sent another[27] reassuring letter to Philip II. The pope assured King Philip that there was nothing to be feared from Otto IV, since he had the guarantee of Otto that he would obey the wish of the pope and would make peace with the king of France[28]. Innocent III was sincere in this, since he did, indeed, have a commitment to that effect, sealed and sworn to, by Otto IV. There was a special clause to that effect in the promises made to Innocent III by Otto IV at Neuß in 1201[29]. Philip II was a shrewd politician and will have had his doubts about the value of that guarantee.

---

25   Philip II had used feudal law to his great advantage. He had summoned his vassal John to appear in a court of his peers presided over by his lord, Philip II, in 1202 to answer to the serious charges brought against him by John's own vassal, Hugh of Lusignan, who held a county in Aquitaine from John. Hugues, correctly, claimed that John had kidnapped and married Isabella of Angoulême, who was already betrothed to Hugues, thus violating the bond of mutual reliance and trust between a vassal and his lord. John refused to appear in court, contending that a duke of Normandy had immunity. Philip ruled that it would be unjust to suppose that he could not summon the duke of Aquitaine because that duke happened to be duke of Normandy as well. John was sentenced for contumacy, forfeiting all his fiefs to the crown and allowing Philip II to call in the 'ost' to conquer all remaining territories of John in France. See for this incident Ralph of Coggeshall (abbot of Coggeshall 1207-1218), *Chronicon anglicanum*, ad ann. 1202, ed. Stevenson, London 1875, 135-136.
26   See *supra* p. 112.
27   The pope had also sent reassuring letters to the king of France at the occasion of his original choice of Otto IV as German king in 1200. See his letters to Philip II of 1 March and 9 June 1201 (*Registrum Innocentii III papae super negotio Romani imperii* 47 and 50, ed. Kempf 129-132 and 135-136) and 26 March 1202 (*Registrum Innocentii III papae super negotio Romani imperii* 64, ed. Kempf 177-185).
28   *Registrum Innocentii III papae super negotio Romani imperii* 165, ed. Kempf 370: 'We have, moreover, taken care to guard over the safety of you and your kingdom, since we have received a secure promise from Otto himself, in writing and with a golden bull attached and confirmed under oath, that he will under all circumstances obey our will and demand to agree to and observe peace with you' (*indemnitati tuae ac regni tui super hoc curavimus praecavere, certa promissione ab eodem Ottone recepta sub aurea bulla scripto pariter et juramento firmata quod de pace vel concordia tecum componenda et observanda nostro per omnia parebit arbitrio et mandato*).
29   See MGH *Const.* 2, no 23(1201), 28: 'I will obey your advice and demand that peace is to be made between me and Philip, the king of the French' (*consilio tuo et mandato parebo de pace vel concordia facienda inter me et Philippum regem Francorum*). This is the only additional clause to Otto's promises to the pope made immediately after his election in 1198 (see *supra* p. 170, fnt. 12).

Innocent III wrote letters to all leading German princes who had supported Philip before his assassination – the king of Bohemia, the dukes of Zähringen, Saxony, Bavaria, and Austria, the margrave of Brandenburg, and others – to side with Otto IV for the sake of peace in the realm[30]. This time he was successful. The German princes, not recognizing Otto's earlier 1198 election, unanimously elected him on 11 November 1208 at a well-attended diet in Frankfurt. Otto was not subsequently crowned at Aachen though, as was the custom. He must have thought himself already crowned and consecrated at Aachen before[31]. Now that the German civil war had finally come to an end, the king ought to be crowned and consecrated as emperor by the pope in Rome as quickly as possible, but papal assent to the election was indispensable according to Innocent's decretal 'Venerabilem'[32] and so the pope sent his two by now familiar legates for German affairs, the cardinals Ugolino and Leo, to Germany again, this time to see whether Otto IV still stood by the promises he had made to the pope at Neuß in 1201[33]. As it turned out, Otto did not. It was a first sign that things might go terribly wrong.

Otto IV is re-elected

We do not know what exactly transpired in the discussions between the papal legates and Otto IV. It is unlikely that Otto was not informed on the precise contents of the agreement reached at Rome between the representatives of Philip of Swabia and Innocent III. Otto had met the chief negotiator on Philip's part, Wolfger of Aquileia, before at a diet held at Augsburg on 6 January 1209, where he had appointed that patriarch as his legate in the Italian kingdom, a confirmation of Wolfger's previous appointment by Philip of Swabia[34], and had even granted Wolfger the duchy of Carniola (Krain) and the marquisate of Istria[35]. Yet, Otto IV confirmed all but one of the concessions he had made to the pope at Neuß in 1201. He conceded to the creation of the Papal State Innocent so badly wanted, including Ravenna, the Marche, and the duchy of Spoleto – territorial aspirations the pope had aban-

He refuses to make peace with France

---

30 *Registrum Innocentii III papae super negotio Romani imperii* 155-158, ed. Kempf 354-358.
31 *Chronica regia coloniensis* ad ann 1208, MGH *SS rer. Germ.* 18, 227. As a gesture of reconciliation, the king was betrothed to Beatrix of Hohenstaufen, the eldest daughter of Philip of Swabia. She had already been suggested to Otto IV before by her father in an attempt at peace with Otto, but the Guelph had declined.
32 See *supra* p. 155.
33 See the letter of Innocent III to Otto IV from January 1209 in *Registrum Innocentii III papae super negotio Romani imperii* 179, ed. Kempf 385-387.
34 See *supra* p. 171.
35 On Wolfger's appointment as Otto's legate in Italy, more shortly. On the grant of the duchy of Krain and the marquisate of Istria to Wolfger see C. Buttazzoni, *Del Patriarca Volchero e delle agitazioni politiche a'suoi tempi*, Triest 1871, 45. If the transcript there is correct, the grant is dated 1208 (47), rather than 1209. This must be an error, as the editor acknowledges (48).

doned in his 1208 negotiations with Philip. He also conceded to the suzerainty of the pope over the Sicilian kingdom. In addition, he even abandoned the important privilege of the German king to interfere in contested episcopal elections within his kingdom[36]. There was, however, *one* clause among all the concessions he had made to the pope in 1201 which Otto now absolutely refused to repeat. It was his promise to make peace with Philip II of France[37]. Cardinal Ugolino, however, did not make it a breaking-point, since he had gained important additional ecclesiastical concessions from Otto IV. Peace with France was left out of the charter completed on 22 March 1209 in Speyer[38], and, as far as Otto IV was concerned, it was out of the question as well.

Otto IV
comes to Italy

On 6 January 1209 Otto IV sent an instruction to his Italian subjects, informing them on the nomination of Wolfger of Aquileia as his personal representative in the *regnum italicum*[39]. The letter was not only sent to his subjects in Lombardy proper, but also 'all over Tuscany, the duchy of Spoleto, the Marche of Ancona, and the Romagna' (*per universam Tusciam necnon in ducatu Spoleti et marchia Anconitana et Romaniola*), territories coveted by Innocent III[40] and granted to the pope by Otto IV at Neuß in 1201. Wolfger was aware of this, but

---

36   Why did Otto IV not simply insist on the agreement that Philip had made with the pope in Rome? The answer is, to a lawyer like Cardinal Ugolino, quite simple: the contract with Philip was not Otto's contract, it was, as the saying is in the civil law, a *res inter alios acta*. Otto was already bound by another promise, *i.e.* the promise he had made at Neuß in 1201. The papal negotiators held a trump card to play in their game with Otto, namely Frederick II, already held out as a possible alternative candidate by Innocent III (see *supra* p. 173). If they did indeed play that card, as I am convinced they did, it must have made Otto IV extremely nervous, explaining his subsequent policy.

37   See *supra* p. 174.

38   Otto's final *Promissio Romanae ecclesiae facta* is in MGH *Const.* 2 no 31, 36-37.

39   MGH *Const.* 2 no 28, 33.

40   Innocent III had claims on Tuscany as well: 'The duchy of Tuscany belongs at law to the Roman Church in full property, as we have seen with our own eyes in the privileges granted to the Roman Church' (*ducatus Tusciae ad jus et dominium Ecclesiae Romanae pertineat, sicut in privilegiis Ecclesiae Romanae oculata fide perspeximus contineri*) (*Innocentii III PP Regestorum*, lib. 1, no 15, Migne *PL* 214, col. 14). When he was trying to 'restore' the territory of the Papal State in 1198, Innocent III tried to bring large parts of Tuscany under his control as well. But he had been less successful there than in the duchy of Spoleto and the Marche of Ancona (*supra* p. 158). In 1197 the Tuscan cities had finally formed their own league after the demise of Henry VI and the Tuscan League was not prepared to exchange one oppressor (the emperor) for another (the pope). This assessment makes it even more likely that Philip of Swabia, who was of course aware of the papal claims to Tuscany, did indeed offer the duchy of Tuscany to Innocent III in 1208 (*supra* p. 171). I should add that the 'privileges' Innocent claims to have seen with his own eyes were primarily the *Hludowicianum* (*supra* p. 58-61), where certain 'cities, castles, strongholds, and villages in the land of Tuscany' (*in Tusciae partibus*) are indeed mentioned (A. Hahn, 'Das Hludowicianum, Die Urkunde Ludwigs d. Fr. für die römische Kirche', in *Archiv für Diplomatik* 21 (1975) 130-131). The *Hludowicianum* is explicitly referred

he ignored it completely. After accepting the homage of the Lombard cities, including Milan, in the name of his master[41], he took control of the Romagna as if it was an imperial fief. Innocent III was appalled and sent a furious letter to Wolfger, adding a copy of Otto's recent promises in Speyer to boot[42]. Wolfger ignored the papal letter as well. He served the Empire, not the pope, and for the sake of the Empire he had been prepared to serve the new king, Otto IV, in spite of his personal misgivings[43]. It was now clear for all to see what the policy of the new regime in Italy was about: the complete restoration of the status quo in Italy as it had been under Henry VI. In July 1209 Otto IV himself led a huge army over the Brenner Pass into the Lombard plain and 'all of Italy trembled with fear'[44]. What was the German king to do 'with the unusually large army' (*cum magno et inusitato exercitu*)[45] he had brought with him? By 1 September 1209 Otto was in the vicinity of Bologna and the citizens held their breath. Like all cities in the Romagna, they had occupied imperial territory after the demise of Henry VI and now expected retribution by the 'terrible army' (*terribilis exercitus*) facing their city. They surrendered without any resistance and restored the territories they had illegally occupied to the Empire[46]. From Bologna Otto followed the old Roman road across the Apennines into Tuscany

---

to in the promises made by Otto IV in 1198, 1201 and 1209 (MGH *Const.* 2, nos 16, 21, ln.1; nos 23, 28, ln. 3 and nos 31, 37, ln. 23).

41   *Annales Placentini Guelfi* ad ann. 1209, MGH *SS* 18, 424: '*patriarcha Aquilegiensis, domni Ottonis regis Romanorum legatus, mense Aprilis in Lombardiam venit pro sacramentis fidelitatis recipiendis; que Mediolanenses primo fecere, postea Papienses et Placentini et Cremonenses*'.

42   *Inn. III PP Registrum de negotio Romani imperii* 186, ed. Kempf 395-396.

43   There are signs that Wolfger had his misgivings about Otto IV. He was, as one of the very few ecclesiastical princes, not present at Otto's election in Frankfurt. He was urged by the pope himself to appear at the diet of Augsburg (*supra* p. 175): see Innocent's letter to Wolfger in *Registrum Innocentii III papae super negotio Romani imperii* 167, ed. Kempf 373.

44   *Annales S. Justinae Patavinae* ad ann. 1209, MGH *SS* 19, 150: '*Circa haec tempora Otto dux Sansoniae in regem Alemanie electus descendit de Alemania et venit in Lunbardiam cum exercitu copioso. In cuius adventu terribili tremuit Italia nimio pavore concussa*'. See also *Chronicon Estense* ad ann 1209, *RIS²* 15.3, 7): '*tremuit Italia*'.

45   *Annales Ceccanenses* ad ann. 1209, MGH *SS* 19, 298: '*advenit Oddo rex cum magno et inusitato exercitu*'.

46   Tolosanus, *Chronicon Faventinum* cap. 134 (ad. ann. 1209), *RIS²* 28.1, 123. The city of Bologna had already surrendered the imperial territory it had illegally occupied to Wolfger of Aquileia. Title to these territories must have been a subject of discussion in the law school there. Two of the representatives of Bologna assigning these territories to Wolfger were law professors, Hugolinus and Bandinus (see the deed of transfer in Savioli, *Annali Bolognesi* 2,2, Bassano 1789, no 382, 297). Hugolinus de Presbyteris († after 1233) was famous at the time, not only for his learning in Roman law, but also for his thorough knowledge of feudal law. On him see *infra* p. 562-563.

and arrived at Viterbo late in September 1209, where he was expected by Innocent III[47].

His conference
with
Innocent III
in Viterbo

As we know from Innocent's correspondence with the king of France, hard words were spoken in Viterbo between the pope and the German king who expected to be crowned by Innocent as emperor of the Romans. Otto was euphoric over the ease with which his legate Wolfger had been able to achieve the subjection of the Italian kingdom and when Innocent confronted the king with the charter containing the territorial promises he had made at Speyer earlier in the year, Otto advised the pope 'to throw it in a wastepaper basket' (*quod cartam servaremus in archa*)[48]. That really shocked Innocent. He must have realized that he now faced the consequences of his own *volte face* of 1208, when he had deserted Otto IV and had sided with Philip. Otto IV knew as good as anyone concerned that it had only been due to the hand of an accidental assassin, Otto of Wittelsbach, that had prevented Innocent III of placing the crown of the empire on the head of his sworn enemy, Philip of Swabia. He had been deceived and deserted by the pope before, so why should he keep to his own word? Innocent III was now in a very delicate, if not impossible, position. Could he refuse to crown Otto IV? Was this man, a self-confessed oath-breaker, really fit for the imperial crown? For years, starting in 1201, Innocent III had publicly proclaimed to the world that Otto was and after the assassination of Philip of Swabia he had, once again, initiated a publicity campaign in support of Otto. He could not now withdraw from that, not without great damage to his own reputation as a professional judge of character and certainly not with 'the terrible army' on his doorstep. Innocent tried as best as he could to save peace in Europe by reminding Otto IV of his previous promise of 1201 to make and preserve peace with the king of France. But Otto would have nothing of it. '*I cannot for shame lift up my face without spot as long as Philip occupies the land of my uncle*', he is reported to have responded to Innocent's appeals to peace[49].

---

47 *Annales Ceccanenses* ad ann. 1209, MGH *SS* 19, 298: '*tempore aestatis post ascensionem Domini papa Innocent ivit Viterbium ... et tamdiu ibi stetit, quousque advenit Oddo rex cum magno et inusitato exercitu*'.
48 From the report of the meeting with Otto IV in Viterbo, sent by Innocent III to Philip II of France, dated on 1 February 1211, published in J.F. Böhmer, *Acta imperii selecta*, Innsbruck 1870, no 920, 629-630 (630).
49 Innocent III to King Philip II (Böhmer, *Acta imperii selecta*, Innsbruck 1870, no 920, 629-630 (630)): 'when we talked with him about peace between you and him, he pompously answered that he could not, for shame, lift up his face without spot as long as you occupy the land of his uncle' (*cum viva voce super pace inter te et ipsum reformanda eum convenimus, sic inflate nobis respondit, quod quamdiu detineres terram avunculi sui, prae nimia confusione non posset faciem levare*). The expression 'to lift up one's face without spot' is from Job 11:15. Since Otto's categoric refusal to make peace with France is only reported by Pope Innocent, Otto's

Some of the cardinals present seem to have advised Innocent III not to proceed with the coronation of Otto after all these insults and dishonesties[50], but the pope still hoped he could save one last concession that Otto had explicitly made: the recognition of the suzerainty of the Church over the kingdom of Sicily. Henry VI had never acknowledged the suzerainty of the pope over South Italy, but Otto IV had explicitly recognized the title of the Church to Sicily and South Italy, not once, not twice, but three times. Even Philip of Swabia had recognized the title of the Church in 1208[51] and Otto IV seems not to have spoken out against it either. It was for that price, whatever it was worth, that Innocent III reluctantly decided to crown Otto as Roman emperor, fourth of that name.

The coronation of a medieval Roman emperor was rarely an occasion of great joy to the citizens of Rome, since it usually resulted in a bloodbath[52]. The coronation of Otto IV on 4 October 1209 was no exception. Even while that ceremony was still in progress within Saint Peter's, the slaughter had already started outside that venerable basilica. For three days on end there was fighting in the streets of Rome between Romans and imperial troops, many among them from Lombardy and the Romagna[53]. Some days after, Otto IV wrote a letter to the pope, thanking Innocent III for his coronation and inviting him for a personal conference to talk about *'things concerning the honour of God, the profit of the Holy Roman Church, and the necessary peace of the entire*

His coronation by Innocent III

---

compelling argument for war is suppressed. Philip II had occupied Poitou, Otto's own fief that he held from the king of England (see *supra* p. 153). He was, as a vassal of the English king, honour-bound to support his English lord against all his foes. He would have broken his oath of fealty to the English king by making peace with the king of France. It should be noted that Otto's original promise to make peace with the king of France was made in 1201, that is *before* king John forfeited his French fiefs and *after* John had made peace with the king of France himself in 1200 at Le Goulet and did homage for all his French fiefs, including Otto's fief Poitou(Matthew Paris, *Chronica maiora* ad ann. 1200, ed. H.R. Luard 2, London 1874, 461-462).

50   See the anonymous continuation (stopping in 1229) of the chronicle of the learned Abbot Robert of Mont S. Michel (Robertus de Monte) in *Recueil* 18, 343: *'Otto Rex Alemannorum Romae consecratus est Imperator Romanorum, quamvis cardinales pauci ... contradicerent'.*

51   See *supra* p. 171.

52   For just one of many examples see *supra* p. 97 on the coronation of Barbarossa.

53   On these riots see the continuation of the chronicle of Robert of Mont S. Michel in Bouquet, 18, Paris 1822, 343: *'in urbe Roma fuit bellum tribus diebus inter partes'.* See also Tolosanus, *Chronicon Faventinum* cap. 134 (ad. ann. 1209), *RIS²* 28.1, 123: *'Coronatus est itaque dominus Otto in Romanorum imperatorem mense octobri die vi* <read: *iv*> *in ecclesia Sancti Petri, et in urbe Teutonici cum Romanis maximum commiserunt certamen, in quo quidem bello milites Faventini, more maiorum preliantes, a principe et ab exercitu tot gloriam acquisiverunt non modicam'.*

Church'[54]. Since the recent riots in the city prevented him from entering Rome again, he asked the pope to select a place where they could safely meet to talk about these important matters. Innocent III answered on 11 October, politely excusing himself for his inability to leave Rome on short notice 'considering all the circumstances' (*pensatis omnibus circumstantiis*)[55]. Innocent III and Otto IV never met again.

The Emperor Otto IV
(*Chronica regia coloniensis*, Royal Library of Belgium, Ms 467, *f. 127 v*)

Otto IV meets
with Sicilian
malcontents

In February 1210 Otto IV was in Tuscany. On 6 February he granted an important privilege to the city of Siena. Among the persons witnessing to the charter was the notorious Diepold of Schweinspeunt, count of Acerra[56]. Only four days later Diepold appears as a witness again in another charter of Otto IV, but now styling himself as duke of Spoleto[57], the very duchy Otto IV had conceded to the pope just a

---

54 *Inn. III PP Registrum de negotio Romani imperii* 193, ed. Kempf 406-407: '*quae honorem Dei et salutem sacrosanctae Romanae Ecclesiae et quietem necessariam totius Ecclesiae respicere viderentur*'.
55 *Inn. III PP Registrum de negotio Romani imperii* 194, ed. Kempf 408.
56 The charter is published in J.-M. Fioravanti, *Memorie storiche dell città di Pistoia*, Lucca 1758, 203-204, now available in the pre-publication ('Vorab-Edition') of the MGH edition of the *Diplomata* of Otto IV (A. Rzihacek and R. Spreitzer, 2020), BFW 350, accessible on the MGH website.
57 The charter is published in Giovanni Lami, *Deliciae eruditorum* 4, Florence 1737, 212-214, now also available in the pre-publication ('Vorab-Edition') of the MGH edition of the

year before. It is a sure sign that Otto IV never intended to keep his word and it also bears witness to the fact that Diepold had succeeded in securing the favour of the new emperor within a very short time. The last time Diepold was mentioned in these pages, he had just escaped from the Sicilian prison to which Walter of Pagliara had consigned him, joining the other German warlords on the South Italian mainland and making trouble there[58]. Diepold and his sort realized that their time was over, now that young King Frederick of Sicily had finally come of age in 1209 and had initiated his policy of restoring order in his kingdom. The concerns of the German warlords were shared by some of the South Italian Norman barons, such as Count Peter of Celano, a master in the fine art of high treason[59]. During the minority of King Frederick, many of them had been granted fiefs and other privileges at the expense of the royal domain they now, correctly, feared King Frederick was about to withdraw. All of these men were in need of a powerful ally and they were sure to find one in Otto IV. Otto was, by now, the uncontested king of the Germans, just crowned as Roman emperor, *and* he had a huge army with him, eager for war and plunder and led by captains, 'ministerials' most of them, looking for the same opportunities Henry VI had offered to his own 'ministerial' captains, men like Markward of Annweiler, Diepold, and his two brothers Otto and Siegfried, William Capparone, and many others.

Diepold and Peter of Celano successfully presented their own interests as truly being the interests of the Empire. They contended that 'no one ought to reign over Apulia who had not received his kingdom and crown from the Roman emperor'[60], implying that the kingdom of Sicily belonged to the empire and that it was about time the proper authority, Otto IV, asserted his rights there as well. The decision to invade the Sicilian kingdom therefore seems to have been made within just a few months after Otto's coronation, as late as February 1210[61]. Past experiences had taught, however, that conquering that kingdom was not a

He decides to invade Sicily

Diplomata of Otto IV (A. Rzihacek and R. Spreitzer, 2020), BFW 351. The duchy of Spoleto must have been vacant after the demise of Duke Henry of Urslingen (see *supra* p. 171, fnt. 17). On the grant of the duchy of Spoleto by Otto IV to Diepold see also *Annales Cassinenses* ad ann 1209, MGH *SS* 19, 329 and Ryccardus de S. Germano, *Chronica* ad ann. 1210, *RIS²* 7.2, 32.

58 See *supra* p. 162.

59 Diepold and Peter of Celano were related, since one of Peter's daughters was married to a son of Diepold.

60 *Chronica regia coloniensis continuatio 2*, ad ann. 1210, MGH *SS rer. Germ.* 18, 186: '*in Apulia nullum debere regnare, nisi regnum et coronam ab Romano imperatore suscepisset*'. The anonymous chronicler ironically adds that 'whether they did so in bad faith or not, must be left undecided' (*utrum haec in dolo facerent necne, incertum habetur*).

61 *Annales Ceccanenses* ad ann. 1210, MGH *SS* 19, 300: '*Oddo dictus imperator ... consilio domni Petri comitis de Celano et consilio Diopuldi ingressus est regnum Apuliae*'. See also *Annales Casinenses* ad ann. 1209, MGH *SS* 19, 319.

matter to be taken lightly. Otto had learned that lesson and made the necessary preparations. In the months directly following his decision he made a tour through his Italian domain, Tuscany, the Romagna, and Lombardy, regions now completely 'under the imperial yoke' (*sub jugo imperii*)[62] as they had been under the reign of Henry VI. Everywhere he went, Otto demanded and obtained military assistance for his impending Sicilian campaign[63]. In August 1210 the emperor was ready.

Otto IV is
excommunicated

Otto's first attack was not yet directed at the Sicilian kingdom, but at papal possessions in Tuscany, Aquapendente, Radicofani, and Montefiascone-Tuscan cities Innocent III had been able to bring under his control in his otherwise frustrated attempt of 1198 to add the duchy of Tuscany to the Papal State[64]. Philip of Swabia had been excommunicated for a similar attack[65], but now the pope hesitated. He tried to negotiate and still only threatened with the possibility of excommunication[66], but to no avail. Instead of apologies, Innocent received a letter from Otto instructing the pope on the position of the Roman pontiff in the real world. It is a kind of letter Frederick II would never have written, since it is rather blunt and straightforward, but it contains much Frederick would have agreed to in private: '*as you know very well, we have absolute sovereignty* (plenitudo potestatis) *in secular affairs, over which you are not suited to offer an opinion, since those who administer the sacraments may not inflict corporal punishment*[67]. *You have to be content with absolute power in religious affairs, always bearing in mind that in secular affairs we want to rule over the entire empire in our capacity as*

---

62   *Annales Placentini gibellini* (*c.* 1285) ad ann. 1197 (describing events of 1209 and 1210), MGH *SS* 18, 468: '*omnes Lombardos et Tuscos sub iugo imperii habuit*'.

63   Zie *Annales Placentini guelfi* (*c.* 1235) ad ann. 1210, MGH *SS* 18, 425: 'In the same year and in the same indiction, the aforementioned lord Otto, having been crowned, required troops from all governors of all the cities of Lombardy to go with him to Apulia' (*Eodem anno et supradicta indictione dictus domnus Otto habita corona per civitates Lombardie petiit a rectoribus uniuscuiusque civitatis auxilium militum, qui in Apulie exercitu secum proficisci deberent*).

64   See *supra* p. 176, fnt. 40.

65   See *supra* p. 150, fnt. 7.

66   From an undated letter of Innocent III to Otto IV (published by F. Mone in *Anzeiger für Kunde der deutschen Vorzeit* 7 (1838), col. 346-347): 'since we are bound to protect the property of the Church with the spiritual sword, we advise and urge you and moreover instruct you not to go on trespassing on the rights of the Holy See by yourself or through the intervention of others on pain of excommunication and that you must comply without fraud with what you have sworn to us' (*Cum igitur gladio spirituali bona ecclesiastica defendere teneamur, te monemus et hortamur, atque sub poena excommunicationis damus firmiter in mandatis, quatenus apostolicae sedis jura per te vel per alium nullatenus inquietes et quae nobis jurasti, studeas sine fraude observare*).

67   A direct quotation from Gratian's *Decretum* C. 23, Q. 8, cap. 30.

emperor'[68]. It was a clear refutation of all interference of the pope in secular affairs and an unambiguous denial of all aspirations of secular power Pope Innocent III might have had over any territory within the empire, such as for example the duchy of Spoleto. Otto IV wanted to rule 'over the entire empire' (*per totum imperium*), including the Sicilian kingdom, just as Henry VI had done. When Otto IV crossed the border of Frederick's kingdom in the first weeks of November 1210, Innocent III had enough. On 18 November he decided to excommunicate Otto IV for breaking his oath to protect the Sicilian kingdom[69]. All his subjects were to be relieved of their oath of loyalty and everyone aiding and abetting him in his attempt to conquer the Sicilian kingdom was to be excommunicated by operation of law.

The news of Otto's excommunication reached the German territories in 1211[70]. By that time, it had also come to the attention of Philip II of France, who immediately opened a diplomatic offensive to undermine the position of his declared enemy Otto IV by suggesting to the German princes that there was an obvious alternative for their discredited monarch: Frederick of Sicily[71]. His diplomacy was successful. Support for Otto IV had never been wholehearted among the German grandees anyway and by September 1211 they elected Frederick of Sicily at Nuremberg as their new king and sent two ambassadors to Italy to inform the pope and to invite Frederick of Sicily to Germany[72].

---

68   From a letter of Otto IV to Innocent III, probably containing a reply to the papal letter cited previously in fnt. 66 (published in S.F. Hahn, *Collectio monumentorum* etc. I, Brunswick 1724, 209): '*In temporalibus vero plenam, ut scitis, habemus potestatem, de quibus vobis non convenit iudicare, quoniam his, a quibus ecclesiae sacramenta tractantur, iudicium sanguinis agitare non licet. Habeatis igitur in spiritualibus libere plenitudinem potestatis, firmiter attendentes, quod temporalia tamquam imperator per totum imperium intendimus iudicare*'.
69   *Annales Casinenses* ad. ann. 1210, MGH *SS* 19, 320: '*Dictus imperator contra iuramentum quod fecerat domno papae Innocentio, regnum intravit et Capuam; propter quod domnus papa ipsum in octava sancti Martini excommunicavit*'.
70   See Innocent's letter to all German princes from April 1211, printed in J.F. Böhmer, *Acta imperii selecta*, Innsbruck 1870, no 921, 630-631. Innocent's letter is very interesting because he anticipates the bitter feelings which the excommunication of Otto must have provoked among the German princes who had supported Philip of Swabia from the start and had only reluctantly accepted Otto IV. He excuses himself for what, with hindsight, had been a mistake (causing ten years of civil strife in Germany). 'But', he writes, 'God, who knows everything before it happens, promoted Saul as king, but later substituted him with a younger and pious man' (*deus, qui omnia noverat antequam fierent, promoveri fecit Saulem ... in regem ... et ei pium substituit iuniorem*) (631). There is a clear reference here to Frederick II (David). See on the reason for the delay of the publication of Otto's excommunication *infra* p. 185.
71   Guillelmus Armoricus (Guillaume le Breton, *c.* 1165-*c.* 1225), *De gestis Philippi Augusti* ad ann. 1211 (*Recueil* 17, 85): '*barones Alemanniae*, mediante consilio Philippi Regis Franciae, *elegerunt Fredericum filium Henryci imperatoris*' (emphasis added).
72   Burchard of Ursberg, ad ann. 1211, MGH *SS rer. Germ.* 16, 99: 'The princes of Germany gathered there, the king of Bohemia, the dukes of Austria and Bavaria and the landgrave of Thuringia and others have elected King Frederick of Sicily to be crowned as emperor, to whom

How was the pope to react to this news, and, even more important, what would Otto IV do now that the German princes had, once again, deserted him?

Otto IV
leaves Italy

The news of the desertion of the German princes and the election of Frederick of Sicily most probably reached Otto IV by Lombard messengers sent to South Italy to warn the king and emperor. The news from Germany had already caused unrest in Lombardy and in the Marche of Ancona. Some cities, Cremona most prominently among them, and nobles[73] had already sided with the rebellious German princes, whereas others, Milan and Piacenza, remained loyal to the Guelph Otto[74]. It may have been the news of the insurgence in the Italian kingdom that unsettled Otto IV most, causing him to make what probably was a strategic mistake. When the news reached him, in October or November 1211, he was in complete control of South Italy and about to invade Sicily itself. The days of Frederick of Sicily seemed numbered and the young

---

they had already in the past, when he was still in diapers, sworn their allegiance. They appointed two envoys to promote his election in the city of Rome and with the said King Frederick of Sicily and to bring the same to Germany' (*Tunc principes Alamanniae, rex videlicet Boemie, dux Astrie, dux Bawarie et langravius Turingie et alii quam plures convenientes Fridericum regem Sicilie elegerunt in imperatorem coronandum, cui etiam olim, cum adhuc in cunis esset, iuraverant fidelitatem. Nuntios itaque acquirunt, qui hanc suam electionem tam in civitate Romana quam apud prefatum Fridericum regem Sicilie promoveant et ipsum in Alamanniam perducant*). For Nuremberg see *Chronicon Sampetrinum* ad ann. 1211, MGH *SS rer. Germ.* 46, 209.

73 The most prominent representative of the North Italian nobles to desert Otto IV was Azzo VI d'Este (1170-1212), a distant relative of Otto IV. Azzo (or Azzolino, as he is also known) was a precursor of the later Italian Renaissance princes. He was a highly cultured man, entertaining troubadours from the Provence and all over Italy at his famous court in Este, but he was also a 'condottière', hiring his sword to cities in need of a famous warrior commanding their armies. In 1210 Otto IV had named him margrave of the Marche, 'like margrave Markward has had it' (*sicut Marchio Marquardus habuit*): see the charter published in L.A. Muratori, *Delle antichtà Estensi ed Italiane* I, Modena 1717, 392-393. Azzo had had his eyes on the city of Ferrara for a long time, but it was assigned by Otto IV to a German, Hugo of Worms. Hugo is another example of German 'ministerials', men of very low stature in German society, to rise to high positions in Italy at the time. He had arrived there, like so many others of his ilk, in the company of Henry VI, who had made him 'count of Siena' in 1195 (on Hugo see Ficker 2, 231). Now that Azzo was relieved of his oath of loyalty, he was free to attack Hugo and drive him from Ferrara (*Annales Cremonenses* ad ann. 1211, MGH 18, 805). On 7 June 1211 Innocent III allowed 'his beloved son' (*dilectus filius*) Azzo to build a strong castle in the city of Ferrara 'so that he may better defend (*read*: dominate) the city and preserve its loyalty to the Roman Church' (*Innocentii III PP Regestorum* XIV no 80, Migne *PL* 216, col. 440: '*castrum, per quod ipsam <civitatem> melius defendere valeat et ad fidelitatem Romanae Ecclesiae conservare*'). The castle, a beautiful example of Italian medieval military architecture, still dominates the city centre of Ferrara.

74 The party names 'Guelfs' and 'Ghibellines' originated in this period: the 'Guelfs' siding with Otto IV and the 'Ghibellines' with Frederick II.

king was already about to take flight to North Africa[75], but Otto IV decided to postpone the Sicilian invasion and hasten northwards[76]. He was never to return.

Innocent III had decided to excommunicate Otto IV on 18 November 1210 but he waited until 31 March 1211 to publicize his sentence[77]. It shows that the pope continued to have his doubts. We know from a very reliable source, present in Rome at the time, that Innocent was still negotiating with Otto IV even after 18 November 1210, when Otto IV was already deep in Sicilian territory[78]. *'The pope struggled with the deposition of the Emperor Otto. It was a delicate affair'*, our contemporary source writes[79]. The problem of Innocent III was that he was out of options now. Philip of Swabia was dead, and Otto IV compromised beyond any hope, leaving him with but one card left in his deck[80], Frederick of Sicily, a possibility he had absolutely rejected

---

75   As reported in a letter by an anonymous adversary of Frederick II, inserted in the *Epistolae* of the German cleric Albert Behaim (*c.* 1180-1260) (MGH *Briefe d. spät. MA* 1, no 54, 216-217): 'when he wanted to take flight to the Arabs, having a galley ready near his palace for that purpose, because the Emperor Otto had decided to cross the Strait of Messina and sail over to Sicily after occupying Apulia' (*dum ad Saracenos fugere aspirabat, habens galeam ad hoc iuxta suum palatium preparatam, eo quod Otto cesar regno Apulie occupato disponebat Fari amne transmisso in Syciliam transfretare*).

76   *Annales Placentini Guelfi* ad ann. 1211, MGH. *SS* 18, 425: 'When the emperor was about to depart for Sicily, messengers and servants of his brothers and friends from Germany arrived and ambassadors from Milan and Piacenza came to the imperial hall, informing him that the pope and some German princes, as well as the marquis of Este and the men from Cremona and all belonging to their party had elected Roger Frederick as their emperor and lord and had given and promised the crown to him. They instantly advised and urgently begged the emperor that he should abandon everything and leave for home immediately. After hearing their advice and requests, the emperor returned to his own country' (*Cumque domnus imperator in Siciliam proficisci pararet, legati atque canzellarii fratrum et amicorum eius de Alamania ac Mediolani et Placentie ambaxatores ad domnum imperatorem perexere, ei denuntiantes, domnum papam et quosdam Alamanie principes, marchionem de Heste, et Cremonenses, et eos omnes de eorum parte, Rogerium Federicum pro imperatore et domino elegisse, et coronam ei dedisse et promisisse; domnum imperatorem instanter admonendo et supliciter rogando, ut ad propria omnibus dimissis redire deberet. Quo audito domnus imperator eorum precibus et admonitione repatriavit*).

77   Ryccardus de S. Germano, *Chronica* ad ann. 1211, *RIS²* 7.2, 33-34: '*Innocent papa in die sancto Iovis excommunicationem latam in Ottonem ac eius sequaces confirmat*'.

78   Burchard of Ursberg, *Chronicon* ad ann. 1211, MGH *SS rer. Germ.* 16, 100, reports that he was in Rome at the time and that he had heard from one of the papal negotiators that he had been sent no less than five times by Innocent on a mission to bring about peace with Otto, residing at Capua at the time, until Lent 1211. It was only after Otto IV proved absolutely uncompromising that negotiations were finally broken off.

79   Burchard of Ursberg, *Chronicon* ad ann. 1212, MGH *SS rer. Germ.* 16, 101: '*Laboravit papa super depositione Ottonis imperatoris, quod fuit arduum negotium*'.

80   From a modern perspective, the pope seems to have had another possibility, *i.e.* a choice in favour of one of the other princes of the empire, such as, for example, the duke of Bavaria or the duke of Austria, the king of Bohemia being ineligible because he was not a German. This was not an option at the time, since the Hohenstaufen name still carried so much weight

ten years before[81], not only because Frederick came 'from a race of per-secutors of the Church' (*de genere persecutorum*), but primarily because in Frederick's case a union of the kingdom of Sicily and the empire seemed inevitable. The pope had excommunicated Otto IV for trying to bring about just that, so how was he to prevent that union to happen and still support the king of Sicily as future emperor? It seemed an insoluble conundrum, but there is no such thing to a shrewd lawyer like Innocent III.

Frederick II accepts his election and submits to the papal conditions

In January or February 1212, Anshelm of Iustingen, one of the envoys sent to Italy by the German princes after the election of Frederick, arrived in Sicily from Rome, where he had spoken with the pope. The pope had confirmed Frederick's election, but will have made it very clear that, if Frederick was inclined to accept the German invitation, he should resign his Sicilian crown. There was to be no union of the empire with the Sicilian kingdom on Innocent's watch. The German envoy must have convinced the pope that he could persuade Frederick to agree to this condition since Innocent III organized a public ceremony where Frederick was acclaimed emperor by the people of Rome[82]. Not everyone in Palermo was enthusiastic about the German offer though. Especially Queen Constance strongly advised her husband against it. Like her namesake, Frederick's mother, she mistrusted Germans, an antipathy shared from experience by many of the Sicilian courtiers also

---

that it was almost irresistible. The incidental election of a Guelph opponent (Otto IV) and the ensuing resistance to his elevation had taught that lesson to the pope and his cardinals.
81 See *supra* p. 155-156.
82 Burchard of Ursberg, *Chronicon* ad ann. 1210, MGH *SS rer. Germ.* 16, 99: 'After much trouble and many dangerous adventures, Anshelm finally arrived in Rome and arranged there that Frederick was acclaimed emperor by the citizens and the people of Rome on the advice and the intervention of Pope Innocent. And the pope confirmed his election' (*Anshalmus magno labore et periculis plurimis Romam usque pervenit ibique consilio et interventu domni Innocentii pape obtinuit ut a civibus et populo Romano Fridericus imperator collaudaretur, et de ipso factam electionem papa confirmavit*). Much has been made of this text (the only source about what transpired in Rome between the pope and the German ambassador), due to the obviously irresistible temptation to bring it in connection with the famous Roman doctrine that the emperor derived his *imperium* from the *lex regia* passed by the people of Rome (Inst. 1,2,6 and D. 1,4,1 (Ulpian)), on which see *supra* p. 96. There is no such connection, since the election confirmed by Pope Innocent here is the election of Frederick by the German princes at Nuremberg, rather than an 'election' by the people of Rome. The *acclamatio* of a new em-peror by the people of Rome, however, was not unusual, even customary, as was (and is) the acclamation of a new pope after his election.

advising Frederick against it[83]. Frederick decided otherwise; he accepted the offer[84].

It is from this moment on that Frederick's great struggle with the papacy commences. A teenager, a boy of seventeen, takes on the most powerful institution of his time, trying to outdo it at its own game of duplicity, deception and equivocation. It is because of this that our story now becomes more complex, since from this time on some important details of Frederick's policy are directly related to his trial at Lyon. This applies, for example, to the question of what exactly transpired in Sicily after Frederick had accepted the German offer. Innocent III had sent Cardinal Gregorio Crescenzi as his legate to Sicily and it is to him that Frederick swore the traditional oath of fealty to the pope for the kingdom of Sicily, the duchy of Apulia, and the principality of Capua in Messina someday in February 1212[85]. In addition to that, he issued two charters on the same day. The first[86] is to testify to the fact that he had just sworn fealty to the pope in the hands of Cardinal Gregorio and for the rest pertains to the conditions under which he received Sicily, Apulia, and Capua in fee from the pope. The second charter contains an elaboration on the first charter, relating to the clause on the procedure to be followed in the elections of bishops in the kingdom[87]. Both charters were of enormous importance to the pope, since they confirmed the contents of Innocent's previous feudal contract with the Empress Constance from 1198[88]. Innocent III had driven a very hard bargain with Frederick's mother at that time. Constance had taken it for granted that she would be invested by the pope with Sicily, Apulia, and Capua on the same conditions as her immediate predecessors[89],

---

83   Burchard of Ursberg, *Chronicon* ad ann. 1211, MGH *SS rer. Germ.* 16, 99-100: 'His wife, a daughter of the king of Aragon who had previously been married to the king of Hungary, tried to persuade him urgently not to go, just like many Sicilian nobles who feared it would bring him into great danger because of the treachery of Germans' (*Uxor namque ipsius, filia regis Aragonensis, quam prius uxorem habuerat rex Ungarie, plurimum studuit eum revocare, ne iret, similiter et multi potentes Sicilie, timentes evenire sibi periculum propter fraudem Alamannorum*).

84   Burchard of Ursberg, *Chronicon* ad ann. 1211, MGH *SS rer. Germ.* 16, 100: 'But he himself ... courageously went on his way to take over the empire, leaving his wife, his son and his country behind' (*Ast ipse ... relictis uxore et filio et terra viriliter iter arripuit ad accipiendum imperium*).

85   HB 1.1, 200-201 has the formula of the oath, also in MGH *DD F II*, 1 no 149, 289-291.

86   HB 1.1, 201-203.

87   HB 1.1, 203-204.

88   HB 1.1, 17-20. See *supra* p. 154.

89   *Gesta Innocentii PP. III* 21, Migne *PL* 214, col. xxxi-xxxii: 'She <the Empress Constance> immediately sent messengers with gifts to Pope Innocent, devotedly requiring whether he would condescend to grant the kingdom of Sicily, the duchy of Apulia, and the principality of Capua, with their accessories, to her and her son, according to the example on which his predecessors had granted them to her predecessors' (*Direxit autem incontinenti nuntios cum*

William I and William II, that is on the basis of the treaties of Salerno and Benevento and the important ecclesiastical privileges these treaties conferred to the Sicilian king[90]. Innocent III wanted to repeal all of these special privileges of the Sicilian king[91] since he considered them contrary to the dignity of the pope (*dignitas apostolica*) and the freedom of the Church (*libertas ecclesiae*). After some bitter bargaining[92], Constance could only save one out of the four great clerical privileges of the Sicilian king and even that only in a watered-down version. She retained the right of assent in episcopal elections[93], meaning that no newly elected bishop in Sicily could be consecrated without having first obtained royal assent to his election. It was an important victory for the pope[94], but Frederick always considered the concessions forced on his mother as legally objectionable[95] and had already ignored one of her concessions to Innocent III when he was still a minor[96]. He was now

---

muneribus ad dominum Innocentium, devotissime postulans ut regnum Siciliae, ducatum Apuliae et principatum Capuae, cum <ceteris> et adjiacentibus, sibi et filio suo concedere dignaretur, secundum formam qua praedecessores eius concesserunt illa praedecessoribus suis).

90   On the treaty of Benevento and the special privileges it conferred to the king of Sicily see *supra* p. 101, fnt. 2.

91   There was a precedent for this, namely the concordat between Tancred of Lecce and Pope Celestine III of 1192 (see *supra* p. 143). Tancred had made important concessions to the pope in return for his investment. Of course, Tancred's concessions were not binding on his aunt (Frederick's mother): Constance was not Tancred's heir.

92   See *Innocentii III PP Regestorum*, lib. 1, *Epp.* 410-412 (Migne *PL* 214, col. 387-390).

93   HB 1.1, 20: '*Electionem factam et publicatam denuntiabunt vobis et vestrum requirent assensum. Sed antequam assensus regius requiratur, non inthronizetur electus*'. In the treaty of Benevento, the king of Sicily had been granted a right of veto in episcopal elections: MGH *Const.* 1, no 414, 589-590 (art. 11).

94   *Gesta Innocentii PP. III* 21, Migne *PL* 214, col. xxxii: 'But that very clever pope, considering that the privilege of investment, granted first by Hadrian and later renewed by Clement, on the four chapters, that is about elections, legates, appeals and councils, not only undermined the apostolic dignity, but also ecclesiastical freedom, ordered the empress to renounce them completely' (*Ipse vero sagacissimus pontifex, diligenter attendens quod privilegium concessionis, indultum primo ab Adriano et renovatum postmodum a Clemente, super quattuor capitulis, videlicet electionibus, legationibus, appellationibus et conciliis, derogabat non solum apostolicae Dignitatis, verum etiam ecclesiasticae libertati, mandavit imperatrici ut illis capitulis renuntiaret omnino*).

95   The privileges of the treaty of Benevento were granted to William I and his heirs, and consequently not to be repealed unilaterally by the pope. The assent to their repeal by Constance was obtained under duress and therefore voidable. As we shall see later (p. 221-222), Frederick considered all royal concessions after the demise of 'good King William' (William II, †1189) as suspect *a priori*.

96   Frederick's first open conflict with a pope was in 1208 and concerned the right of Sicilian clerics to appeal to the pope. The treaty of Benevento provided that there was no appeal on the pope by Sicilian clerics, unless the king permitted the appeal (MGH *Const.* 1, no 414, 589 (art. 9)), but this provision was repealed in the concordat between Constance and Innocent of 1198. Frederick, angry about some clerics who had appealed to the pope in connection with a dispute within the clergy of Palermo over the succession to the archiepiscopal see of that city, had punished the appellants with exile. He was reprimanded by Innocent III, who reminded

forced to accept them, as his mother had been, since he needed the goodwill of Pope Innocent to support him in his German adventure, but there was a mental reservation to his submission. Frederick's second excommunication was immediately connected with this issue[97].

Cardinal Gregorio Crescenzi, the papal legate in Sicily, presented yet another condition for Innocent's support of Frederik's German ambitions. Frederick was instructed to crown his son as king of Sicily before he departed for Germany[98]. Frederick may have been just seventeen years old at the time, but he was a very precocious young man, having already sired a son, Henry, by Constance of Aragon in 1211[99]. Frederick did as he was told and had his son crowned as king of Sicily, another Sicilian king 'in diapers' (in cuneis), as he himself once had been. In doing so, he literally submitted to the papal policy preventing a union of the crown of Sicily with the crown of the German Empire, but there was a *reservatio mentalis* here as well, since Frederick did not renounce his *own* title as king of Sicily. Kings all over Europe had their infant sons crowned as nominal co-regent during their lifetime to secure an undisputed succession at their demise[100], so the coronation of his son Henry as king of Sicily was an empty gesture if it was not combined with his simultaneous abdication. As we shall see, Innocent III realized this[101]. Sometime in March 1212 Frederick of Sicily sailed from Messina to Gaeta, leaving his infant son and kingdom in the care of his wife Constance of Aragon who was to reign the kingdom for the next four years[102].

He leaves Sicily

---

the young king that his own mother had renounced this privilege. See Innocent's letter to Frederick in *Innocentii III PP Regestorum*, lib. 11, Ep. 208 (Migne *PL* 214, col. 1523-1525).

97 See *infra* p. 378.

98 In an important letter to Innocent III (see *infra* p. 211), written in Strasbourg in 1216, Frederick explicitly states that he had his son crowned at the insistence of Innocent (*Promissio Argentinensis*, MGH *Const. F1* no 58, 72): '*filium nostrum Heinricum, quem* ad mandatum vestrum *in regem fecimus coronari*' (emphasis added).

99 Burchard of Ursberg, *Chronicon* ad ann. 1211, MGH *SS rer. Germ.* 16, 100: 'But he himself, since he already had a very young son by his wife, Henry, shortly to be made king, courageously went on his way to take over the Empire, leaving his wife, his son, and his country behind' (*Ast ipse, cum parvulum iam ex coniuge haberet filium, Hainricum videlicet postmodum regem factum, relictis uxore et filio et terra viriliter iter arripuit ad accipiendum imperium*).

100 See *supra* p. 65.

101 See *infra* p. 190.

102 Queen Constance was not only fifteen years older than her spouse, but she had her own experience with courtly intrigues and civil war during her previous marriage with King Emeric of Hungary (1174-1196-1204), who had to deal with his rebellious younger brother Andreas during his entire short reign. Emeric died in 1204, leaving his four-year old son and heir Ladislaus and his widow Constance in the care of that very same deceitful brother. Constance and her son, virtually prisoners of Andreas, succeeded in escaping Hungary and found refuge with Duke Leopold VI of Austria. Ladislaus died in 1205 and Duke Leopold

He meets
Innocent III

After a stay of some weeks in Gaeta, Frederick arrived at Rome in April 1212. He was most honourably welcomed there by the pope, the cardinals, and the senate and people of Rome[103]. It was the first time Innocent III laid eyes on his past ward, who now did homage to him personally for the Sicilian kingdom, a fact later emphasized in Frederick's trial[104]. Innocent had invited some nobles from the Italian *regno* loyal to him, most notably Marques Azzo d'Este[105], to come to Rome and discuss the details of Frederick's further progress through the Italian kingdom to the German border, a very perilous journey since many Lombard cities, Milan most importantly among them, were still loyal to Otto IV. It was decided that it was safest for Frederick first to proceed by sea to Genoa and from there, right through hostile Milanese territory, to Pavia, the ancient Lombard capital that had already sided with Frederick. Even according to medieval standards, it was a reckless, if not desperate, venture with a very uncertain outcome, as Innocent III must have realized. Since Frederick was financially in dire straits as well, the pope was prepared to help him, of course not with a gift of money, but with a loan, secured by mortgages on substantial real property in South Italy[106]. We do not know for certain what was further discussed between Frederick and Innocent III in Rome, but it is unlikely that two subjects were not mentioned: the restoration of all the territory Innocent claimed as belonging to the Papal State and occupied by Otto IV, contrary to his promises of 1198, 1201, and 1209[107], on the one hand, and the union of the Sicilian kingdom with the Empire on the other. As far as the restoration of 'papal' territory is concerned, Innocent III must have obtained assurances from Frederick similar, if not identical, to the promises of Otto IV[108]. Concerning the union of

---

sent Constance back to Aragon. She was of no more use to him after the demise of her son, but Constance had learnt a lot. It was at her initiative that Frederick had parted company with his guardian Walter of Pagliara in 1210 (*Breve chronicon de rebus siculis*, MGH *SS rer. Germ.* 77, 66): '*Que <Constantia> ... una cum viro suo eundem cancellarium ... a curia eorum excluserunt*'.
103   Ryccardus de S. Germano, *Chronica* ad ann. 1211, *RIS*² 7.2, 34: '*rex ... per mare ad Urbem vadit, ubi a papa Innocentio et a ceteris cardinalibus senatu populoque Romano ingenti cum honore receptus est*'.
104   See *infra* p. 354.
105   On Azzo d'Este see *supra* p. 184, fnt. 73. On the presence of Azzo and other Lombard nobles in Rome at the time see *Annales Placentini Guelfi* ad ann. 1212, MGH. *SS* 18, 426: '*Ipso <Federico> ibidem existente, marchio de Heste et Petrus Traversarius et alii quam plures nobiles ipsum visitaverunt, ibidem cum eo et summo pontifice locuti fuerunt*'.
106   See the mortgage granted by Frederick to Innocent III at Rome in April 1212 in MGH *DD FII*, 1 no 158, 305-306. Innocent III and his successors time and again complained about the enormous expenditures they had made on behalf of Frederick II as if it concerned gifts, but the money was lent rather than donated to Frederick. See the previous mortgages granted in 1210 by Frederick to Innocent III in MGH *DD FII*, 1 no 124, 241 and no 138, 266.
107   See *supra* p. 170, 175 and 176.
108   See *infra* p. 194.

the Sicilian *regno* and the Empire, Innocent III must have realized by now that the coronation of Frederick's son as king of Sicily was a rather empty gesture, but he did not insist on an immediate abdication of Frederick as king of Sicily as long as Frederick was not yet crowned in Germany. For the time being, Frederick might style himself as 'king of Sicily *and* Roman emperor elect' (*rex Sicilie* et *in Romanorum imperatorem electus*), but that was, to the pope, a provisional, though unfortunate, state of affairs. It was Frederick's first diplomatic success in his long struggle with the papacy, since the pope had conceded to a temporary union of the Sicilian kingdom with the Empire. Innocent III used to refer to Frederick of Sicily as 'the boy' (*puer*). He made the same mistake as Cicero had once made, who likewise spoke of Octavian, Caesar's heir, as 'the boy'. Both men were incapable of contemplating the possibility of an adolescent being as clever and devious as they considered themselves to be.

Frederick's passage to Germany was already legendary during his own lifetime and has justly remained so ever since. It is, indeed, a testimony to his great personal courage and exuberance. The first part was, relatively[109], easy. It took him by ship from Ostia to Genoa, where he arrived on the first day of May 1212[110]. The Genovese had already been granted many important trade privileges on Sicily in the recent past and were prepared to help Frederick in return for even more. He stayed in Genoa for more than a month, allowing the news of his departure for Germany to reach the city of Milan, still loyal to Otto IV, where preparations were made to intercept him. Frederick left Genoa on 14 July en route to Pavia, the first friendly city willing to receive him. He was protected on this part of his journey by an important Italian vassal, the marquess of Montferrat, who accompanied him to Pavia, where he arrived on 22 July. From here, the next stage to Cremona was extremely dangerous, since Milan controlled most of the territory and the Milanese were out to hunt him down. On 28 July, a Saturday, a Pavian war party left the city in the middle of the night to escort Frederick to the river Lambro, where Azzo d'Este was to meet Frederick and escort him to Cremona. The Milanese hunting party picked up the scent and went after Frederick and his Pavian horsemen racing to the Lambro. They were intercepted at the river crossing, where a fierce battle ensued. The Milanese were victorious but missed their

His passage to Germany

---

109   It was not without danger, since Pisa was still loyal to Otto IV and Pisan galleys patrolled the Tyrrhenian Sea to intercept him. It was one of the reasons Frederick had been forced to stay at Gaeta for almost a month before being able to sail to Rome.

110   The best account of Frederick's journey through hostile Italian territory is in *Annales Placentini Guelfi* ad ann. 1212, MGH. *SS* 18, 426.

quarry who had been able to cross the river in the melee of the battle. From there he was escorted safely to Cremona by Azzo d'Este and his Cremonese troops, arriving there on Sunday morning. He had covered more than 50 miles (80 km.) in the middle of the night through hostile territory, fought a battle, swam the Lambro, escaped the Milanese and still his tribulations were not over, since the easy way over the Alps was closed to him by Duke Louis I of Bavaria, who had sided with Otto IV again after Otto's return to Germany in March 1212. There was no other way through the Alps now than a very perilous road northwards through the almost inaccessible mountains of what is now the east of Switzerland[111]. Via Chur and the abbey of St Gallen, he reached the German city of Konstanz just as it was about to receive Otto IV within its walls[112].

After returning to his German kingdom in March 1212, Otto IV had spent most of his time in the north of Germany, fighting the landgrave of Thuringia, one of the leading German princes siding with Frederick. Sometime in August news must have reached him there that Frederick had succeeded in escaping the Milanese and was now about to enter Germany. Otto hastened south and by the first days of September he had reached the city of Überlingen on the banks of Lake Konstanz, just about 12 kilometres from the city of Konstanz, sending messengers to the bishop of Konstanz announcing that he planned to visit that city presently. As legend has it, he had already sent his cooks ahead to prepare his meal in Konstanz when Frederick of Sicily suddenly appeared at the gates of the city, accompanied by no more than sixty knights. Bishop Conrad of Konstanz opened the gates of his city to Frederick, closing them to the excommunicate Otto IV who arrived just three hours later[113]. The young Sicilian king, still not eighteen years old, had managed to stage a spectacular coup. He had

---

111   Burchard of Ursberg, *Chronicon* ad ann. 1212, MGH *SS rer. Germ.* 16, 109: '*cum non posset directo itinere venire in Alamanniam, de valle Tridentina per asperrima loca Alpium et invia et iuga montium eminentissima obliquando iter suum venit in Retiam Curiensem*'.
112   Guillaume le Breton, *De gestis Philippi Augusti* ad ann. 1210, *Recueil* 17, 85: '*Fredericus ... venit Constanciam ... Eodem die venturus erat Otho in eandem civitatem*'.
113   Guillaume le Breton, *De gestis Philippi Augusti* ad ann. 1210 (*Recueil* 17, 85): 'Otto had already sent his servants and cooks ahead to prepare his meal. He was no more than three miles away from that city when Frederick entered with sixty knights, followed by Otto, who knew he was about to come, with two hundred knights. But after Frederick had entered, the gate was closed to Otto and he and his men were bravely driven away. People say that if Frederick had been three hours later, he would never have entered Germany' (*Otho ... iam praemiserat famulos suos et coquos, qui iam cibos paraverant, nec distabant a civitate per tres leugas, quando Fredericus cum sexaginta militibus intravit, quem Otho cum ducentis militibus, eius adventum sciens, sequebatur. Sed, Frederico recepto, clausa est Othoni ianua, et ipse cum suis viliter est repulsus; et dicunt quod, si Fredericus moram fecisset per tres horas, numquam intrasset Alemanniam*).

gained control of a major German city and was in the middle of traditional Hohenstaufen territory, the duchy of Swabia, Alamannia proper.
What followed was a triumphal progress with an ever-increasing army
of supporting German princes, secular and clerical, through the Rhine
valley, from Konstanz to Basel and by October taking the great royal
castle of Hagenau (now Haguenau in France) in the Alsace (October
1212). The power of Otto IV in his German kingdom disintegrated
with lightning speed, forcing him to fall back on his powerbase in the
Saxon north[114]. On 2 December 1212, within three months after his
arrival in Germany, 'the boy Frederick' (*Fridericus puer*) was elected
king by a great assembly of princes in Frankfurt and crowned a week
later in Mainz, Aachen still being on Otto's side[115]. Even to medieval
standards, when miracles still happened frequently, Frederick's accomplishment was an uncommon miracle. It must have strengthened his
conviction that he was born with a special mission.

Shortly before his election at Frankfurt, on 18 November 1212,   He pays
Frederick had met the French 'dauphin', later King Louis VIII (1187-   his debts
1223-1226), at Vaucouleurs (*Vallis Coloris*), on the French border, where
the two princes concluded a treaty of friendship and mutual assistance,
stipulating '*that we will never make peace with Otto, once calling himself
emperor, and John of England, and their manifest supporters*'[116]. It was the
cornerstone of Frederick's policy during his entire reign, a close alliance
with France. In doing so, he also paid a debt he owed to the king of
France for the support Philip II 'Auguste' had always given to his house

---

114   *Annales Marbacenses* ad ann. 1212, MGH *SS rer. Germ.* 9, 84: 'Otto withdrew from
there and returned to Saxony … Frederick, however, having besieged and taken Hagenau
Castle, until then held by Otto's supporters, went from city to city, all welcoming him, and in
a short time gained control over the land' (*Qui <Otto> secedens inde reversus est in Saxoniam
… Fridericus autem obsesso et dedito sibi castro Hagenowe, quod adhuc tenebant fideles Ottonis,
veniebat de civitate in civitatem, et receperunt eum; et in brevi tempore obtinuit terram*).
115   *Annales S. Iacobi* (*Reineri Annales*) (1200-1230) ad ann. 1212, MGH *SS* 16, 665: 'The
boy Frederic returned to Frankfurt, to be chosen as emperor on the first Sunday of the Advent
… On the first Sunday of the Advent, there was a great meeting of princes electing the boy
Frederic as emperor: among them were ambassadors from the pope and the king of France,
and we have been told that there were 5000 knights there' (*Fredericus puer Fenchenfor revertitur, dominica prima adventus Domini eligendus in imperatorem … Dominica prima adventus
Domini maximus conventus principum convenit, et Fredericum puerum in imperatorem elegit,
inter quos fuerunt nuntii domni pape et nuntii regis Francie; et sicut nobis relatum est, fuerunt ibi
5 milia militum*). *Annales Ianuenses* (Ogerii Panis) ad ann. 1212, MGH *SS* 18, 132: 'On the
next Sunday, to wit on 9 December, he honourably received the crown at Mainz' (*Die vero
dominica veniente, nona die videlicet Decembris, in civitate Magantie honorifice coronam recepit*).
116   *Foedus cum Philippo II. Rege Franciae*, MGH *Const.* 2, no 44, 55: '*quod nos cum Otthone
quondam dicto imperatore et Iohanne rege Angliae et eorum auxiliatoribus manifestis nullam
pacem faciemus*'. See on this important conference also Guillaume le Breton, *De gestis Philippi
Augusti* ad ann. 1211 (*Recueil* 17, 85).

since the demise of his father, Henry VI. A year later, in December 1213, Frederick paid another debt, this time to his uncle Philip of Swabia. He held a diet at Speyer on Christmas day, where he announced that the body of his uncle should be transferred from Bamberg, where he was assassinated and buried[117], to Speyer to be buried in the imperial vault in the cathedral, joining the great Salian kings and emperors interred there[118]. In doing so, Fredrick honoured the memory of his uncle and his important role in defending the Hohenstaufen interests in Germany at a time when he was unable to do so himself. It is also a clear indication that Frederick believed that his uncle had never been a threat to his own position during his minority in Sicily, as is confirmed by Philip's acquiescence to the Sicilian status quo in his 1208 agreement with Innocent III[119]. There was yet another debt to be discharged by Frederick. It was the political debt he owed to Pope Innocent III. He did so by simply repeating the promises made by Otto IV in 1198, as the pope must have insisted on in his meeting with Frederick in Rome[120]. The charter containing the confirmation of all the territorial gifts to the Apostolic See 'since the time of Louis' (*a tempore Ludowici*), a reference to the *Hludowicianum* again, was signed, sealed, and delivered by the king at Eger on 12 July 1213[121]. It was testified to by many of the great clerical and secular princes of the realm, such as the archbishop of Mainz and other prelates, the king of Bohemia, the dukes of Bavaria and Austria, and the landgrave of Thuringia, making the document an important act of state, signing away, as it did, important parts of what was traditional imperial territory in Italy to the pope[122]. The German

---

117 See *supra* p. 172.
118 *Annales S. Iacobi* (*Reineri Annales*) ad ann. 1214, MGH *SS* 16, 670: '*Fredericus rex Apulie et Allemanniae curiam celebrem habet Spire in natale, qui de consilio amicorum suorum corpus patrui sui Philippi regis, de Bavenberg, ubi ab impio comite fuit interfectus et sepultus, fecit deferri Spire, et ibi sepelliri in ecclesia honorifice, ubi imperatorum et regum corpora plurima sunt tumulata*'. Philip's tomb can still be seen in the crypt of Speyer Cathedral, built by the Emperor Conrad II as a burial place for the Salian line of kings and emperors. Philip of Swabia is the only Hohenstaufen king to be interred there. Conrad III was buried in Bamberg; Barbarossa's grave has never been located (supra p. 141, fnt. 29) and Henry VI was buried in Palermo.
119 See *supra* p. 171. It is sometimes contended that the South Italian German war lords, Markward of Annweiler in particular, acted in close contact with Philip of Swabia. It is highly unlikely they were Philip's men, since they were guided by their own interests exclusively.
120 See *supra* p. 190.
121 *Promissio Egregensis Romanae ecclesiae facta*, art. 6, MGH *Constt.* 2, no 46-51, 57-63. The Eger charter included the release of 'the land of Countess Matilda' (*terra comitissae Mathildis*): art. 6 (no 47, 59; 48, 60; 49, 62). On this issue see *supra* p. 83, fnt. 31.
122 By contrast: the 1198 promise of Otto IV has no witnesses to it; his 1201 promise is contained in a deed passed in the presence of the notary Philip and two minor papal officials; the 1209 promise bears Otto's seal and is passed by the bishop of Speyer acting as deputy for archchancellor Siegfried of Mainz. The special character of Frederick's Eger charter is highlighted by the fact that some of the grandees of the Empire not personally testifying to that

princes clearly had lost all personal interest in Italian imperial affairs, considering them primarily a private Hohenstaufen concern. The Eger charter was one of the central documents produced in the case against Frederick II at Lyon[123].

The final battle for the German crown was not fought on German soil, but in France, at Bouvines, on 27 July 1214. Otto IV was one of the commanders on the battlefield that fateful day. His presence there originated in his unstinting loyalty to the king of England, his uncle John. In April 1212, at the time when Frederick of Sicily and Pope Innocent were already planning his downfall in Rome, Otto sent a letter to King John, assuring him that he would assist John 'with all his might' (*totis viribus suis*) to recover the continental territory John had lost to Philip II of France[124]. There was another reason for Otto to console and support his uncle since King John had been excommunicated by Pope Innocent in 1208[125] and sentenced by the pope in 1212 with forfeiture of his throne. Innocent III had ordered the king of France, John's arch-enemy Philip II, to execute that sentence by assigning the English kingdom,

The battle of Bouvines

---

charter later explicitly confirmed it. There is a charter, dated on 6 October 1214, of the Count Palatine at the Rhine, Louis of Wittelsbach, one of the chief princes of the realm, doing so (MGH *Constt.* 2, no 51, 63).

123 See *infra* p. 354. The Eger charter misses a clause on which Innocent III had insisted in his dealings with Otto IV: a peace treaty with France (see *supra* p. 174 and 176). The pope must have known he did not have to insist on this issue with Frederick of Sicily, since the king of France was the natural ally of Frederick. It is an indication that Innocent III must have intensively discussed European politics, the relations of the German Empire with France and England, with Frederick at Rome in 1212.

124 See *supra* p. 173-174. Otto's letter is referred to in a letter by King John to his continental French vassal the count of Thouars, dated on 4 March 1212 (Rymer, 50): 'You must know that the emperor, our cousin, has sent us a letter, declaring that he is prepared to assist us with all his might when we want and how we want. He also indicates in this letter that he instructed everyone who loves him and who owes him fealty to assist us, we being his dear uncle, to regain what is ours and that he will regard anything done against us as done to him personally' (*Sciatis quod Dominus Imperator, Nepos noster, misit ... litteras suas de credentia, mandans quod totis viribus suis, quando et sicut voluerimus, nos paratus esset adiuvare ... Mandavit etiam per litteras suas omnibus, qui ei in fide et in amore tenentur, quod, sicut nos diligunt, nobis tamquam caro avunculo suo sint auxiliantes ad jus nostrum conquirendum, et quicquid nobis fecerint, sibi factum reputabit*).

125 The conflict between Innocent III and King John originated in a dispute over the succession to the see of the archbishop of Canterbury. Archbishop Hubert Walter, a common lawyer and chancellor of England, had died in 1205 and his succession was contested. The chapter requested the king to decide the contest and John chose John de Gray, another common lawyer, as successor to Hubert Walter. But Innocent III would not have him and opted for Stephen Langton, with whom the pope was acquainted. King John refused to comply, resulting in his excommunication.

now being a *res nullius*, an ownerless asset, to Philip[126]. Frederick II knew about all of this, since the French 'dauphin' surely must have informed him about it at the conference in Vaucouleurs. Frederick, who had first-hand knowledge about Innocent's intentions[127], must have realized the French were being played by the pope, who never really intended to surrender England to the king of France since that would have disturbed the European balance of power. Innocent used the French threat as a means to force King John to bow to his will and he was successful. On 15 May 1213 John surrendered his English kingdom to the pope[128], receiving it back as a papal fee[129]. Innocent III accepted the kingdom of England on 4 June 1213[130]; lifted all the clerical sanctions against King John and instructed the English barons to loyally serve their king again as if nothing had happened[131]. Cardinal Nicola de Romanis, bishop of Tusculum, was sent to England to act as papal legate there. On the previous day, Innocent had sent a letter to King Philip of France informing him of the mission of Cardinal Nicola and expressing his hope that the cardinal could bring about a peaceful settlement between the kings of England and France[132]. By then, the pope cannot seriously have believed peace was still an option. Hostilities had already started in Flanders and developed their own dynamism. War was inevitable.

King John had managed to bring about an apparently impressive alliance for the war to reconquer his French domain. It consisted of his

---

126   Roger of Wendover (†1236), *Flores Historiarum* ad ann. 1212, ed. Coxe III, Londen 1841, 241-242: 'Then the pope passed sentence. King John was deposed from the English throne and was to be replaced by another, to be provided by the pope, who was considered more worthy. For the execution of this sentence the pope wrote to the almighty King Philip of the French to assume this task in remission of all his sins and that he and his successors should rightly possess the kingdom of England forever, after the king of the English was re-moved from the throne of the kingdom' (*Tunc papa ... sententialiter diffinivit, ut rex Anglorum Johannes a solio regni deponeretur, et alius, Papa procurante, succederet qui dignior haberetur. Ad huius quoque sententiae executionem, scripsit domnus Papa potentissimo regi Francorum Philippo; quatenus in remissionem omnium suorum peccaminum hunc laborem assumeret, et, rege Anglorum a solio regni expulso, ipse et successores sui regnum Angliae jure perpetuo possiderent*). Philip's 'sins' related to his failed (second) marriage with the Danish Princess Ingeborg. Philip wanted a divorce, but Innocent III would have nothing of it. See on this incident *infra* p. 338, fnt. 49.
127   See *supra* p. 195, in fnt. 123.
128   Both parties, King John and Pope Innocent, ignored that England had already been granted by Richard I to the German emperor: see *supra* p. 146.
129   See the charter of surrender and enfeoffment in *Innocentii III PP Regesta* 16, no 77, Migne *PL* 216, col. 878-879. John's oath of fealty to the pope is on col. 880 (*Ego Joannes ab hac hora inantea fidelis ero Deo et beato Petro et Ecclesiae Romanae ac domino meo papae Innocentio* etc.).
130   *Innocentii III PP Regesta* 16, no 79, Migne *PL* 216, col. 881-882.
131   *Innocentii III PP Regesta* 16, no 80-82, Migne *PL* 216, col. 882-884.
132   *Innocentii III PP Regesta* 16, no 83, Migne *PL* 216, col. 884-885.

nephew Otto IV and three of Otto's northern vassals, the mighty Duke Henry of Brabant, father-in-law to Otto[133], Duke Henry of Limburg and Count William I of Holland. The alliance was completed by Count Ferrand of Flanders, a rebel vassal of the king of France. In the summer of 1214, the Anglo-German alliance attacked. The plan was that John's allies would invade France from the north, whilst John himself would attack from the south. From the perspective of Otto IV, it seems an extremely foolish enterprise. His own position in Germany was in great peril at the time: in 1212 Frederick of Sicily had been crowned in Mainz and began to threaten his northern possessions by invading Saxony proper in the next year. To begin a war against the king of France under these circumstances was sheer folly, but Otto IV was determined to stand by his uncle. The plan of attack of the allies failed spectacularly, because the advance of King John from the south was frustrated by Crown Prince Louis. On 27 July 1214 Otto IV faced the French 'ost' at Bouvines and was decisively beaten by Philip of France and his army. Otto IV ignominiously fled the battlefield, just barely escaping a French royal prison[134]. After this crushing defeat at Bouvines, the Guelph Otto was a spent force to the world at large and to Germany in particular. Frederick II was now in a position to be crowned and consecrated once again as king of the Germans and emperor elect, this time at the proper place, on Charlemagne's throne in Aachen.

---

133 Otto IV had married Beatrix of Hohenstaufen, a daughter of Philip of Swabia, in 1212 (see *supra* p. 175, fnt. 31), but Beatrix had died in the same year. He now was able to marry Maria of Brabant, to whom he had already been betrothed before.

134 The most trustworthy account of the battle of Bouvines is the *Relatio Marchiensis de pugna Bovinensi*, written not long after the battle in the monastery of Marchiennes, in the vicinity of Bouvines (MGH *SS* 26, 391): 'But Otto, whom the authority of the pope forbids us to call emperor, left without all relief and help and having been thrown of his horse, or rather horses, since, as some people recall, he was thrown off his horse three times, quickly took flight, with only one companion. And having been beaten in battle, he evaded the hands of the king of France by thus furtively escaping' (*Otto autem, quem auctoritate domini pape imperatorem nominare prohibemur, ab omnium solatio et auxilio destitutus et ab equo sive ab equis, prout quidam recolunt, ter ad terram depulsus, quasi solus, solo quidem comite contentus, fugam celerem arripere festinavit; sicque regis Francie manus latenter fugiendo et in conflictu bellico superatus evasit*). Count Ferrand of Flanders was captured on the battlefield and spent years in a prison in France. Henry of Brabant, Henry of Limburg, and William of Holland managed to escape the wrath of the king of France and sided with Frederik II soon after. The battle of Bouvines plunged King John into a political abyss, forcing him to grant the Magna Charta to his rebellious barons on 15 June 1215. Otto IV retired to his allodial possessions near Brunswick in Saxony, a political 'quantité négligable' until death delivered him from his miserable existence in 1218, his uncle John having already preceded him in the grave in 1216. It is worth noting here that descendants of the Brunswick Guelphs are kings and queens of England since 1714. Anglomania was still rampant among the German Guelphs in the 20th century as is testified by the famous English case *Attorney-General v. Prince Ernest August of Hannover* [1957] AC 436.

13

Crusade

Frederick of Sicily was crowned and consecrated king of the Germans in Aachen on 25 July 1215 by the papal legate Archbishop Siegfried II of Mainz. Something transpired on this occasion that was to haunt Frederick for the rest of his life. After the coronation ceremony, a priest from Xanten preached the crusade, whereupon Frederick took the cross[1], committing himself to participate in the new crusade planned by Innocent III to make amends for the disgrace of the Fourth Crusade (1202-1204)[2]. It is often contended, even now, that Frederick's decision was spontaneous, an act of youthful enthusiasm. It is highly unlikely. Frederick was too smart and calculating for that. He seems to have been motivated by the great council which Innocent III had announced on 18 April 1213, to convene at Rome on 1 November 1215[3]. Frederick knew that a new crusade was the ultimate aspiration of Innocent III. It was the principal objective of the great Lateran Council to remove all obstacles standing in the way of the liberation of the Holy Land. The pope had emphasized in his invitation that one of the main obstacles was political discord in occidental Europe, making the council a very political conference. It was the reason why invitations to attend the council were not only sent to clerics, but to secular princes as well[4]. One

Frederick II takes the cross

---

1 *Chronica regia coloniensis* ad ann 1215, MGH *SS rer. Germ.* 18, 236: '*Fridericus ... Aquisgrani veniens ... in festo sancti Jacobi a Syfrido legato apostolicae sedis, Coloniensi episcopo non existente, in regem ungitur et in regali sede collocatur. Quo mox consecrato, Iohanne Xantensi scolastico ibidem crucem predicante, ad subventionem Sanctae Terrae cruce signatur*'. The chronicler notes the presence at Aachen of Duke Henry of Brabant and Duke Henry of Limburg, two allies of Otto IV at Bouvines (see *supra* p. 197), but already siding with Frederick II just a month later. After Bouvines, Otto IV had only one supporter left in the German kingdom, the margrave of Brandenburg (*Reineri annales*, ad ann. 1216, MGH *SS* 16, 675): 'While Otto remained in Saxony, destitute of all support, but for the margrave of Brandenburg' (*Ottone in Saxonia manente omni auxilio destituto, exept de Brandebrois marchione*).

2 On the Fourth Crusade see *supra* p. 168.

3 See Innocent's invitation *Vineam Domini Sabaoth* of 19 April 1213 in Migne *PL* 216, col. 823-827.

4 See the list of secular addressees in Innocent's invitation in Migne *PL* 216, col. 826. Of course, the list is not Innocent's, but inserted by the editors of his *Regesta* as an introduction

of the theatres of discord was the Roman Empire, where the excommunicate Otto IV still held out against his rival Frederick II. Consequently, 'the matter of the Roman Empire' (*negotium super Romano imperio*) had to be finally settled by a general council of all Catholic Christianity, presided over by the pope exercising his *plenitudo potestatis*. Frederick may have been informed that the Guelph Lombard cities, Milan and Piacenza, were planning to plead the cause of Otto IV at the council[5]. He hoped that by taking the cross he could conciliate the council and the pope beforehand. But whatever may have motivated him, stark calculation or youthful enthusiasm, his decision to take the cross had fateful consequences.

The Fourth
Lateran
Council

The Fourth Lateran Council, opening on 11 November 1215 in Rome, was the greatest council ever held in that city. There were more than 400 patriarchs, archbishops, and bishops from all over the Christian world present, more than 800 abbots and other prelates, while practically all European kings and princes and many Italian cities sent their ambassadors[6]. It was a conference the size of which Europe had not seen since the days of the great congress of Venice in 1177[7], but whereas the Venice congress of Alexander III had been about peace, the Lateran Council of Innocent III was all about discipline and, ultimately, war, the crusade against heretics at home and infidels abroad. Some aspects of the Lateran Council as well as the failed Fifth Crusade (1217-1221) are crucial for the appreciation of Frederick's trial at Lyon. In fact, they are interrelated. As was just indicated the Fifth Crusade ended in disaster and one of the (many) reasons for that debacle was the fact that there was a concurrent crusade going on, also initiated by Innocent III, competing with the Fifth Crusade. This was the Albigensian Crusade

---

to Innocent's invitation to the secular princes, which has a slightly different redaction than his invitation to the clergy of Europe. The secular princes were invited, it says, 'because in this general council much must be discussed pertaining to the state of your class of persons' (*cum in hoc generali consilio sint multa tractanda quae ad statum vestri ordinis pertinebunt*).

5   *Annales Placentini Guelfi* ad ann. 1215, MGH *SS* 18, 431: 'The men from Milan and Piacenza and all of their party, as well as the men from Cremona and Pavia and all of their party, have sent ambassadors at the invitation of the pope, hoping and believing that the discord between the Emperor Otto and Frederick, the king of Sicily, should be resolved and settled peacefully' (*Mediolanenses et Placentini et totius eorum partis legati, et Cremonenses et Papienses et totius eorum partis ambaxatores, de mandato domini pape perexere, sperantes et credentes, discordiam que est inter domnum Ottonem imperatorem et Federicum Scicilie regem acordari debere pariter et pacisci*).

6   Ryccardus de S. Germano, *Chronica* ad ann. 1215, *RIS²* 7.2, 61: '*interfuerunt autem regum et principum totius orbis nuntii*'. Burchard van Ursberg, *Chronicon* ad ann. 1212, MGH *SS rer. Germ.* 16, 111, mentions ambassadors sent by the kings of England, France, Hungary, Jerusalem, Cyprus, Aragon, and many others. He also mentions the numbers of the participants just mentioned in the text. They are corroborated by other sources.

7   See *supra* p. 129.

(1209-1229), which was still in full progress when the Fourth Lateran Council opened in 1215 and many of the canons enacted at the Lateran Council are directly or indirectly related to that crusade, rather than the upcoming Fifth Crusade. Therefore, something must be said about that terrible crusade.

Heresy was a constant source of concern to the medieval papacy. It was traditionally proliferating in the Lombard cities, but the proverbial heretics were the 'Cathars' (*Cathari*) of southern France[8]. The Third Lateran Council, convened by Alexander III in 1179, had already enacted a canon directed against this heresy. All Cathars were excommunicated, as well as anyone communicating with them in any way. The local authorities were instructed to prosecute them[9]. It did not prevent the sect from prospering, especially in and around the domain of Count Raymond VI of Toulouse (1156-1222). Raymond was too lax in prosecuting the sect in the eyes of Innocent III, who sent legates to oversee the proper persecution of Cathar heretics in the Languedoc. In 1209 one of these papal legates, Pierre Castelneau, was murdered. Innocent III blamed Raymond of Toulouse for the crime since Raymond had recently been censured by Pierre and Pierre had been killed by one of Raymond's servants[10]. The pope instantly sent an instruction to the bishops in the Languedoc on how to deal with the count of Toulouse. The bishops were to confirm Raymond's excommunication and to publicly announce that all Raymond's vassals were relieved of their oath of fealty, 'since a man who is disloyal to the Lord must not be served loyally' (*cum ei qui Deo fidem non servat fides servanda non sit*)[11]. In addition, Innocent directed his bishops in the Languedoc to make it known that all Raymond's land forfeited to any good Catholic who occupied it[12]. This was a novelty, since Pope Lucius III had decreed in

The Albigensian Crusade

---

8   The modern Dutch and German word for 'heretic' – 'ketter', 'Ketzer' – is derived from *Cathari*, from the Greek καθαροί, meaning 'the purified'. I must refrain from an introduction to their belief. Practically all we know about it comes from the contemporary introduction of the Cistercian monk Peter of Vaux-de-Cernay (*c.* 1182- *c.* 1218), an important source for the Albigensian Crusade, *Historia Albigensis* cap. 10-19, ed. Guébin and Lyon, vol. 1, 9-20. Peter was an eyewitness.
9   Can. 27 of the Third Lateran Council, Mansi 22, col. 231-233.
10 For the murder of Pierre Castelneau and Innocent's reaction see Innocent's letter to the bishops in the Languedoc in *Innocentii III PP. Regestorum* 11, 26, Migne *PL* 215, col. 1354-1358.
11 *Innocentii III PP. Regestorum* 11, 26, Migne *PL* 215, col. 1357.
12 *Innocentii III PP. Regestorum* 11, 26, Migne *PL* 215, col. 1357: 'you must announce that everyone bound by fealty, friendship, or contract to said count are released from him on apostolic authority as of now and that any catholic man may not only persecute him personally, but may also appropriate and keep his land, saving the right of his lord' (*omnes qui dicto comiti fidelitatis seu societatis aut foederis huiusmodi juramento tenentur astricti, auctoritate apostolica*

1185[13] that the land of an excommunicated lay prince was to be placed under interdict, a religious sanction implying a cessation of all divine activities (*cessatio a divinis*) within his territory, except the administration of extreme unction and the baptism of infants. Innocent III added a secular sanction: expropriation[14]. Since Raymond of Toulouse was, nominally, a vassal of the king of France, the implication was that all his land reverted to the king of France. Consequently, Innocent sent a letter to Philip II imploring him to lead a crusade against the Cathars and chase their sponsor Raymond of Toulouse and the vassals still loyal to him from their land, replacing them by good Catholics[15]. Philip II, however, declined. He told the papal ambassadors that he was himself threatened by 'two lions', Otto IV and John of England, at the same time. It was therefore impossible for him to leave 'Francia' and open a third front in the south[16]. Philip Auguste indicated in a separate letter to Innocent III that he had his reservations about the secular sanctions

---

denuntietis ab eo interim absolutos et cuilibet catholico viro licere, salvo iure domini principalis, non solum persequi personam eiusdem, verum etiam occupare ac detinere terram ipsius).

13   The decretal of Lucius III has been inserted in the *Liber Extra* of Gregory IX: X. 5,7,9.

14   The sanction of expropriation for heresy was first introduced by Innocent III in 1199 in his decretal 'Vergentis', also inserted later (1234) into Pope Gregory's codification of canon law, the *Liber Extra* (X. 5,7,10). It was inspired, as the pope himself states, by the *crimen laesae maiestatis* of Roman law (C. 9,8,5). This accounts for the curious emphasis on the fact that the children of a convicted heretic, even if good Catholics themselves, were deprived of their inheritance by the confiscation of the property of their father, which is also to be found in C. 9,8,5,1. See on this issue also *infra* p. 205, fnt. 27.

15   *Innocentii III PP. Regestorum* 11, 27, Migne *PL* 215, col. 1358-1359(1359): 'You must not hesitate to persecute him \<the count of Toulouse\> with the might of imminent royal oppression, by removing him and chasing his supporters from the castles of their lord, and by taking away their land, where you must install Catholic tenants, after the heretics have been evicted, who shall serve in sanctity and righteousness in the presence of God the teachings of the orthodox faith under your blessed guidance' (*pondere non desinas inductae super eum \<comitem Tolosanum\> regalis oppressionis urgere, ipsum et fautores eiusdem de castris domini depellendo, et auferendo terras eorum; in quibus, relegatis haereticis, catholicos habitatores instituas, qui secundum orthodoxae tuae fidei disciplinam in sanctitate et justitia sub tuo felici regimine serviant coram Deo*).

16   For this argument of the king see Peter of Vaux-de-Cernay, *Historia Albigensis* par. 72, ed. Guébin and Lyon, vol. 1, Paris 1926, 73-74: 'he did not want to leave France on any account' (*nec ipse a Francia ullo modo exire vellet*). The expression illustrates that to contemporaries 'France' proper was the northern part of the kingdom. The southern part of the French monarchy was, to the king of France, a foreign country, ruled by practically independent princes, such as the counts of Toulouse, who were his vassals only in name, where people spoke a different language (the 'langue d'oc'), were ruled by different laws (Roman law, rather than the northern 'coutumes') and enjoyed a courtly culture very different from the austere northern cultural climate. The cultural focus of the south of France was on Italy, rather than the north. A good example is the career of one of the greatest medieval lawyers, Guillaume Durant (1237-1296), who was from Puymisson, not far from Béziers in the Languedoc. He studied law in Bologna, not in Paris (for canon law) or Orléans (for Roman law), and never served the king of France.

the pope had imposed: expropriation and occupation. Philip wrote that he had been informed by 'learned and enlightened men' (*viri litterati et illustrati*), theologians and canonists from the university of Paris no doubt, that the pope could not do this without a previous sentence of excommunication for heresy and that Raymond's land, even if he was indeed excommunicated as a heretic after due process, was not to be disposed of by the pope, since it reverted to him, the king of France, as of right and accordingly it was his to dispose of[17]. Innocent III had realized this, since in his letter to the bishops in the Languedoc announcing his sanctions, he had indicated that expropriation and occupation should always proceed 'subject to the title of the suzerain lord' (*salvo iure domini principalis*), but Philip had made it very clear that the pope had no right to dispose of territory within his kingdom without his consent. The irritation is obvious[18], but Innocent III was not particularly impressed.

King Philip may not have wanted to participate personally in Innocent's campaign against the Cathars and Raymond of Toulouse, but he did not discourage his northern vassals to join the Albigensian Crusade. Pope Innocent III had appointed the Cistercian Abbot Arnaud Amaury to lead the crusade as his legate and it was at Arnaud's insistence that the French nobles joining the crusade chose one of them, Simon of Montfort (*c.* 1160-1218)[19], as their commander[20]. Simon wielded 'the sword of blood' (*gladius sanguinis*), handed to him on papal authority,

The third canon of the Fourth Lateran Council

---

17 King Philip's original answer to Innocent's request has survived. It can be found in L. Delisle, *Catalogue des actes de Philippe-Auguste*, Paris 1856, no 1085, printed in the Appendice 512-513(513): 'Concerning the fact that you have released the land of the aforesaid count for occupation, you should know that we have been informed by learned and enlightened men, that you cannot do this legally before he has been condemned for his wicked heresy. When he has indeed been condemned, this does merely mean that you also must apply to us that we may make that land available, since it belongs to us' (*De eo autem quod vos predicti comitis terram exponitis occupantibus, sciatis quod a viris litteratis et illustratis didicimus quod id de iure facere non potestis, quousque idem de heretica pravitate fuerit condempnatus. Cum autem condempnatus fuerit, tantum demum id significare debetis et mandare ut terram illam exponamus tamquam ad foedum nostrum pertinentem*). There is another letter on the matter of Philip's possible intervention in the Albigensian affair in Delisle, no 1069, also published in the Appendice 512. This last letter must have been available to Peter of Vaux-de-Cernay since he gives a good résumé of it (see fnt. 16).
18 Pope Innocent had interfered some years before in what King Philip also regarded as a purely feudal affair: see on this affair *infra* p. 337.
19 Simon, Lord of Montfort-l'Amaury, had inherited the title of Earl of Leicester from his mother's side. His youngest son and namesake Simon of Montfort (*c.* 1208-1265) was to rise to fame in England, where he led the rebellion of the barons against King Henry III and became the father of English parliamentary government.
20 Peter of Vaux-de-Cernay, *Historia Albigensis* par. 101, ed. Guébin and Lyon, vol. 1, Paris 1926, 101-102.

with great enthusiasm. The Albigensian Crusade stands out even in medieval history for its extreme brutality and cruelty. The genocidal slaughter in the Languedoc was still going on with undiminished fury when the Lateran Council opened in 1215 and Innocent III decided to convert his incidental disciplinary measures against Raymond of Toulouse into general legislation[21]. They were inserted into the notorious third canon of the Fourth Lateran Council, institutionalizing the Inquisition. As far as princes unwilling to properly prosecute heretics within their principalities were concerned, it reproduced almost verbatim the procedure followed in the case of Raymond of Toulouse, including the salvatory clause about the rights of the *dominus principalis*, the feudal suzerain of such a prince. It did, however, add one important proviso: *'providing he does not himself cause an obstacle in this matter, or opposes another impediment'*[22]. This leaves the question what was to be done with such a lord, a king or an emperor. The answer was in the closing line of this provision: *'the same applies to those who have no suzerains'*[23], meaning that kings and emperors[24] could expect to be treated like Raymond of Toulouse if they were excommunicated for disobeying the pope. It was not an empty threat, as all the participants to the council knew from recent experience. The pope had applied his ruling in the case of Raymond of Toulouse also in the case against the obstinate king of England: King John had been excommunicated *and* deposed by Innocent, assigning John's kingdom to the king of France[25].

The third canon of the Fourth Lateran Council compelled all bishops to inspect their dioceses at least twice a year to hunt for heretics. All inhabitants were required to report heretics to the ecclesiastical authorities on pain of excommunication. After the persons thus brought to the attention of the bishop had been subjected to an inquiry (*inquisitio*) and found guilty, they were to be handed over to the local secular authorities for punishment since the hands of clerics should not be besmirched by

---

21 Innocent III is the first of the great medieval papal legislators. In 1210 he published a collection of his own decretals, composed by his secretary Peter of Benevento (later papal legate in the Languedoc), by sending it to the law school of Bologna with the instruction to use it 'in the courts and in the classes' (*tam in iudiciis quam in scholis*). Modern scholarship has dubbed it *Compilatio tertia*, for reasons too complex to explain here. The seminal edition is in E. Friedberg, *Quinque compilationes antiquae*, Leipzig 1882 (see for the quote from the arenga p. 105).

22 The third canon of the Fourth Lateran Council was inserted in the codification of Innocent's nephew Pope Gregory IX, the *Liber Extra* (1234), containing most decretals from Innocent's *Compilatio tertia* (X 5,7,13): *'dummodo super hoc ipse nullum praestet obstaculum, nec aliud impedimentum opponat'*.

23 X 5,7,13: *'eadem nihilo minus lege servata circa eos qui non habent dominos principales'*.

24 Since 1204, there were two Catholic emperors, one in the west and the other residing in Constantinople, the 'Latin' emperor of the Byzantine Empire.

25 See *supra* p. 195-196.

blood[26]. Immediately linked to all this was the introduction, in canon 21, of the duty of every Catholic, man and woman, to go to confession at least once a year. Non-compliance resulted in excommunication. In this way the clergy acquired an iron grip on the lives and minds of all believers, meaning every living man and woman, since non-believers and heretics were to be exterminated. No contemporary secular ruler held a power to match the totalitarian power which the Church wielded over a ruler's subjects.

The Council dealt in separate sessions with secular affairs obstructing the war on heretics and infidels. Innocent III rightly perceived the Albigensian war as an impediment and distraction to the great crusade destined to 'liberate' the Holy Land, if only because it offered potential 'crusaders' an excuse to join the war against the heretics rather than the infidels. The Languedoc was closer to home and offered more prospects of personal gain than Palestine or Egypt. The pope therefore placed the matter on the agenda of the Council, inviting the principal parties concerned, Raymond VI of Toulouse and Simon of Montfort, to settle the matter once and for all. Raymond VI appeared in person, accompanied by his son and namesake Raymond VII (1197-1249)[27]. Simon was represented by his brother Guy. The Toulousan affair was dealt with in a plenary session of the Council and destroyed all hope Raymond VI might have had of ever regaining his domain. He was convicted[28] of having failed his duty to persecute heretics, deposed as count of Toulouse, and exiled from that county to do penance abroad. All the land occupied by the crusaders, including the city of Toulouse,

The matter of Raymond VI of Toulouse

---

26   This is the reason why canon 18 of the Council banned all clerics from practicing the beneficial craft of surgery. The canon was inserted in the *Liber Extra* (X. 3,50,9). Clement III (1187-1191) had even condemned all medical occupation as incompatible with the office of a priest (X. 1,14,7). This provision was still in the 1918 Codex Iuris Canonici. The new CIC of 1983 has repealed the ban.

27   The presence of Raymond's son confronted the pope with the legal dilemma involved in the affair of the Languedoc. If Raymond VI was indeed to be deposed, his son was the logical successor to his titles, since the county of Toulouse was a hereditary fee held from the king of France. The pope had, however, decided earlier, in his decretal 'Vergentis' (see *supra* p. 202, fnt. 14), that expropriation of a heretic involved the expropriation of his children as well, even if they were good Catholics themselves. It was all in accordance with Scripture, since the iniquities of the fathers had to be visited on their children (*Deuteronomy* 5:9).

28   The full text of the sentence of the Fourth Lateran Council in the case of Raymond VI of Toulouse was discovered in the 17th century by the Benedictine scholar Luc. d'Achery (1609-1685), who first published it in his *Spicilegium veterum aliquot scriptorum* etc. Tom. 7, Paris 1666, 210-211. This text is reprinted in Mansi 22, col. 1070, with due reference to D'Achery. De Vic and Vaisette in their *Histoire générale de Languedoc* Tom. 3, Paris 1737, 251 merely refer to D'Achery's *Spicilegium*, without printing the sentence, which is corrected in the new edition of that book by A. Molinier, *Hist. Gén.* etc. Tom. 8, Toulouse 1879, 681, without due reference to D'Achery.

was assigned to Simon of Montfort *'to hold from the persons from whom it must at law be held'*[29]. This was an unheard-of decision, since according to feudal law a vassal could only forfeit his fee after due process in the court of his lord, in this case the king of France, as had happened in the case of King John[30], whereas the appointment of a new vassal in his stead was the right of the lord, rather than the pope or a council, as King Philip had made abundantly clear in his correspondence with Innocent III[31]. The pope and his council were arrogating jurisdiction over secular matters they simply did not have, *except* when a superior jurisdiction of the pope over all matters spiritual *and* secular on account of his 'absolute sovereignty' (*plenitudo potestatis*) was accepted, as Innocent III certainly did[32]. Be this as it may, Simon of Montfort was received by Philip II of France at a diet held in Melun in April 1216, where Simon did homage to the king and was enfeoffed with all fiefs previously held from the French crown by Raymond VI, the duchy of Narbonne, the county of Toulouse, and the viscounties of Béziers and Carcassonne[33]. King Philip was a realist and did not want to risk open

---

29   From the sentence of the Council as published in Mansi 22, col. 1070: *'ut eam <terram> teneat ab ipsis a quibus de jure tenenda est'*. See on the sentence also Peter of Vaux-de-Cernay, *Historia Albigensis* par. 570-572, ed. Guébin and Lyon, vol. 2, Paris 1930, 259-265. The use of the plural here (*a* quibus *de jure tenenda est*) is deliberate since the southern part of the domain of the counts of Toulouse (the counties of Foyx and Commynges) were held from the king of Aragon. It was further decided that Raymond's land Simon had not (yet) occupied, the Marquisat de Provence, the western part of the county of the Provence, was assigned to Raymond's son Raymond VII, leaving him with only a small part of the once great Toulousan domain. The marquisate (and the county of Provence) did not belong to the kingdom of France, but (nominally) to the Empire, making Raymond VII a vassal of Frederick II. This may have been the main reason why the Council did not deprive Raymond VII of his imperial tenures.
30   See *supra* p. 174 and in fnt. 25.
31   See *supra* p. 203.
32   See on this issue *infra* p. 336-339.
33   Delisle, *Catalogue des actes de Philip-Auguste*, Paris 1856, no 1659-1661; see also Peter of Vaux-de-Cernay, *Historia Albigensis* par. 573, ed. Guébin and Lyon, vol. 2, Paris 1930, 264-265. There was to be no Montfort dynasty in the Languedoc though. Simon was killed shortly after his enfeoffment, in 1218, when he besieged the city of Toulouse, which had risen against him, siding with its old lord, Raymond VI and his son. Simon's son Amaury, who succeeded him, was not the great warrior his father had been, whereas Raymond VII turned out to be the warrior his father had not been. By 1224 Raymond VII had recovered practically all the land his father had lost. Amaury fled to the king of France, offering him all the land and titles his father had only recently obtained. King Louis VIII (Philip II had died in 1223) accepted and now headed the crusade against the 'heretic' Raymond VII, but died in the Languedoc in 1226. His widow, Blanche of Castile, guardian to her minor son Louis IX and a very capable regent, finally oversaw the end of the whole messy affair of the Albigensian Crusade by concluding a treaty with Raymond VII in 1229, granting him a very much reduced county of Toulouse. His daughter and heir Joanne was to marry Blanche's younger son Alphonse de Poitiers. When Raymond VII died in 1249, the county came into the hands of Alphonse and when the latter died childless in 1271, the county escheated to the French crown, the only

conflict with the pope at the time, so he accepted the vassal whom Innocent III imposed upon him. It was now clear for all kings and princes what it meant to stand up against the will of the pope. Innocent III had completely humiliated one of the principal nobles of the French kingdom, disinheriting his son in the process, by unleashing a terrible war of extinction against fellow Christians under the sign of the cross[34].

Frederick of Sicily was not himself present at the great Council in Rome, but his bishops and representatives were and will have informed him on everything that had transpired there. He must have been particularly interested in the affair of the counts of Toulouse, since Raymond VI and his son Raymond VII were his brothers in law[35]. The decision of the Council shocked him[36]. His main interest was, however, 'the matter of the Roman Empire' (*negotium super Romano imperio*) that was also on the agenda of the Council. It was to be dealt with on its session of 20 November[37]. After the usual opening ceremony, the pope gave the floor to Archbishop Berardo of Palermo, Frederick's closest adviser since his coming of age, replacing Walter of Pagliara as the leading

The matter of the Empire

---

beneficiary of more than twenty years of bloodshed and misery the Albigensian Crusade had brought the people of the Languedoc.

34   The Cathars were not living in isolation, but among the Catholic Christians in the cities, castles, and villages of the Languedoc. The killing, when it came, was indiscriminate, as happened on 22 July 1209 at Béziers. 'Kill them all, God will know who are His' (*Caedite eos. Novit enim Dominus qui sunt eius*) was the command of the papal legate Arnaud Amaury (Caesarius of Heisterbach (*c.* 1180-after 1240), *Dialogus miraculorum*, Dist. Quinta (De daemonibus), cap. 21, ed. J. Strange I, Cologne 1851, 302), a reference to 2 Timothy 2:19: 'The Lord knoweth them that are his'. Of course, we do not know for certain whether the papal legate did indeed give this outrageous order, but it is a fact that practically all citizens of Béziers were slaughtered under his responsibility and under his own eyes. According to the triumphant letter sent by the legate to inform Pope Innocent III about the glorious capture of Béziers, 'almost 20,000 people' (*fere viginta milia hominum*) were massacred on that day (*Innocentii III PP. Regestorum* 12, 108, Migne, *PL* 216, col. 137-141(139)). See also Peter of Vaux-de-Cernay, another eyewitness, *Historia Albigensis* par. 90, ed. Guébin and Lyon, vol. 1, Paris 1926, 91-92.

35   Raymond VI was married to Elenore of Aragon, a sister of Frederick's wife Constance, whereas another sister of Constance, Sancha, was married to Raymond VII, making Sancha the daughter-in-law of her own sister. The king of Aragon, Peter II (1178-1196-1213), another brother-in-law of Frederick, had come to the rescue of Raymond VI, but was defeated and (accidentally) killed in the battle of Muret (1213).

36   See *infra* p. 235.

37   Ryccardus de S. Germano, *Chronica* ad ann. 1215, *RIS²* 7.2, 71-72. Before 1964 Ryccardus de S. Germano was the only source for the proceedings of the Council on the affair of the Empire, but from that point onwards we have a second anonymous eyewitness account by a German cleric: S. Kuttner and Ant. García y García, 'A New Eyewitness Account of the Fourth Lateran Council', *Traditio* 20 (1964) 123-129, edited with an extensive commentary (129-167). There are some discrepancies between the two accounts. Since the new account is more detailed than Ryccardus', it has been followed in the text. The new account also has a report on the conviction of Raymond VI (*l.c.* 124-125).

member of the royal *curia*. The archbishop read a letter addressed to the Council by Frederick II and afterwards addressed the Council on the case of Frederick and his election as emperor of the Roman Empire by the German princes. It must have been an impressive oration, since it is reported that 'all were hanging on his lips'[38]. After Berardo's speech, the ambassadors of Milan asked for permission to address the Council, causing an uproar among the attendants. Marquess William VI of Montferrat, an Italian vassal and traditional ally of Frederick[39], argued that the Milanese should not be allowed to address the Council. It is at this point that the pope intervened and addressed the marquess in Italian rather than Latin. Innocent made a joke and said that he would hear anyone, guilty or not guilty, rich or poor, even the Devil himself, if he was capable of repentance[40]. After this aside, he returned to Latin and allowed the Milanese to proceed. They continued to produce and read a letter addressed to the Council by Otto IV, requesting absolution and the reversal of his excommunication, a first step, of course, to his political rehabilitation as Roman Emperor. They were rebutted by the marquess of Montferrat naming six reasons why Otto's excommunication should not be reversed. Without going into these arguments, it is interesting to note that the pope allowed the Milanese a rejoinder on all these points, going through them one by one and even commenting on their remarks in defence of Otto IV. After the Milanese rejoinder, the session of the Council for that day was closed, postponing sentencing to the last session of the Council, ten days later[41].

The pope opened the third and final session of his Council with a solemn declaration of faith directed against the Cathars and a similar declaration, condemning some aspects of the teachings of the famous mystic Joachim of Fiore on the nature of the Trinity. After this, the pope turned the attention of the Council to secular affairs, primarily, of course, to the matter of the Empire[42]. The pope delivered a short

---

38 Ryccardus de S. Germano, *Chronica* ad ann. 1215, *RIS²* 7.2, 71: '*ab ore ipsius pendentibus universis*'.
39 He had been of great assistance to Frederick in his dangerous adventure in Lombardy in 1212: see *supra* p. 191.
40 *Traditio* 20 (1964) 126, r. 107-110: '*dicens quod ob hoc sanctum Concilium sit institutum, ut culpabilis et inculpabilis, simul in unum dives et pauper, ibidem audiantur, adhiciens etiam quod si diabolus posset penitere, certe recipiendus esset*'.
41 The report published by Kuttner and García y García and the report of Ryccardus de S. Germano differ considerably at this point. The latter recalls that the session got completely out of hand after the rejoinder of the Milanese and ended in uproar. The former merely states that the session was closed after the rejoinder of the Milanese. I prefer this version of events, since I believe the tumult Ryccardus refers to was at the beginning of the session, when the margrave of Montferrat (and others) denied an audience to the Milanese.
42 The case of Raymond VI of Toulouse and the affair of the Empire were not the only secular matters the pope and his Council were to decide. King John, always in trouble, had

sentence: '*Let there be no doubt about it that we confirm what the princes of Germany and the Empire have decided concerning King Frederick of Sicily, we do indeed want to favour and promote him in everything and we shall put that into effect*'[43]. This was the end of the 'matter of the Roman Empire'. Otto IV was now officially a 'former emperor' (*quondam imperator*) and Frederick, the king of Sicily, as Innocent III still styled him, was the properly elected and now universally recognized emperor of the Roman Empire, to be crowned soon, as the pope indicated. It was an important declaration, but it merely confirmed the decision of the German princes to depose Otto IV and replace him with Frederick II: it was not the Fourth Lateran Council that deposed Otto IV since he had already been deposed by the German princes.

Having decided the fate of the empire, Innocent III proceeded to the ratification of the 70 canons of the Fourth Lateran Council. He did so in the style of a Roman emperor. Once upon a time the acts of a church council were the decisions of that council, composed after careful deliberation in the council, as had been the case with the *senatus consulta*, the decisions of the Senate, in the early Roman Empire. Now the canons of the Lateran Council were presented as 'enactments of the pope' (*constitutiones domini papae*)[44] confirmed by the Council, just as in the later Roman Empire the *oratio principis* (the address of the emperor) was confirmed by the unanimous adhesion of the Senate. After all seventy canons of the Council had been read and confirmed the *Te Deum laudamus* was sung by all, concluding the Fourth Lateran Council. Fourteen days later, the pope issued an order that all crusaders were to gather at Brindisi or Messina in the kingdom of Sicily on 1 June 1217 to depart for their glorious expedition to liberate the Holy Land, announcing that he himself would be there to join them[45]. He expected

The crusading army is to depart on 1 June 1217

---

appealed to the pope, now his suzerain, about his conflict with the English barons. The barons were excommunicated. Magna Charta had already been quashed by the pope before the Council.

43   *Traditio* 20 (1964) 128, r. 181-183: '*Nulli debet esse dubium: Quod principes Alimannie et imperii circa Fridericum Cecilie regem fecerunt, ratum habemus, immo ipsum fovere et promovere in omnibus volumus et complebimus*'. See also Ryccardus de S. Germano, *Chronica* ad ann. 1215, *RIS²* 7.2, 73, l. col. (62, r. col.).

44   A. García y García (ed.), *Constitutiones concilii quarti Lateranensis*, Rome 1981, 6-7. The editor rightly stresses that the decisions of the council were composed by Pope Innocent himself.

45   *Ad liberandam terram sanctam* (14 December 1215), Migne *PL* 217, col. 269: '*diffinimus, ut ita crucesignati se praeparent, quod in Kalendas Junii sequentis post proximum, omnes qui disposuerunt transire per mare, conveniant in regnum Siciliae; alii, sicut oportuerit, et decuerit, apud Brundisium, et alii apud Messanam, et partes utrobique vicinas, ubi et nos personaliter, Domino annuente, disposuimus tunc adesse*'.

Frederick II to be there as well so that the two swords of Christendom, the pope and the emperor, were drawn in a joined effort to regain the Holy Land.

Pope Innocent III, fresco mid-13th century, Santuario di Sacro Speco di San Benedetto, Subiaco (Lazio) (author's photograph)

14

Procrastination and Deception

Frederick II never seriously intended to sever the ties between the Empire and the Sicilian kingdom. He said so in his letters to the pope, but his acts betrayed a different purpose. On 1 July 1216 he sent a document to Pope Innocent III from Strasbourg, where he resided at the time. It is a masterpiece of diplomacy. Frederick solemnly promised that he would emancipate his son Henry, whom he had crowned as king of Sicily at the pope's demand, leaving his South Italian kingdom to his son, to have and to hold as a vassal of the pope, as soon as he had received the crown of the empire, thus making his coronation at Rome the condition precedent to the severance of the ties between the Empire and the Sicilian kingdom[1]. As he was making these promises, his wife and son had already been summoned to join him in Germany, where they arrived late in 1216[2]. As soon as his son, by now five years old, had arrived, Frederick made him duke of Swabia[3]. The young 'king

---

1 *Promissio Argentinensis*, MGH *Const.* 1, *F1* no 58, 72: 'Desiring to provide for the Roman Church and the kingdom of Sicily, we do promise and concede that we will, after receiving the crown of the Empire, immediately emancipate our son Henry, whom we have had crowned as king at your bidding, from parental power and that we will leave him the entire Sicilian kingdom on both sides of the Faro <the Strait of Messina>, to have and to hold from the Roman Church, as we hold it only from her, and also that *from that moment onward we shall not have it and not call ourselves king of Sicily* ... So that, after we have been called to the imperial dignity by divine favour, there may not be any impression left at any time that there still is any trace of a union between the kingdom and the Empire' (*Cupientes tam ecclesie Romane quam regno Sicilie providere, promittimus et concedimus, statuentes ut, postquam fuerimus imperii coronam adepti, protinus filium nostrum Heinricum, quem ad mandatum vestrum in regem fecimus coronari, emancipemus a patria potestate ipsumque regnum Sicilie, tam ultra Farum quam citra, penitus relinquamus ab ecclesia Romana tenendum, sicut nos illud ab ipsa sola tenemus; ita quod ex tunc nec habebimus nec nominabimus nos regem Sicilie ... ne forte pro eo, quod nos dignatione divina sumus ad imperii fastigium evocati, aliquid unionis regnum ad imperium quovis tempore putaretur habere*) (emphasis added).
2 *Breve chronicon de rebus Siculis* ad ann. 1214, MGH *SS rer. Germ.* 77, 70; *Reineri annales* ad ann. 1216, MGH *SS* 16, 675: '*Uxor Frederici regis ... intravit Allemaniam cum Heinrico filio suo*'.
3 Frederick's son is mentioned as duke of Swabia in a charter of Frederick from 13 February 1217, MGH *DD F.2, 2* no 398, 450-451.

of Sicily' thus joined the exclusive 'club of princes' ruling the German Empire and electing its king from among the members. Clearly, it was the intention of Frederick to have his son crowned as king of the Germans as well.

Innocent III probably never read Frederick's letter and the promises it contained. He died in Perugia on 16 July 1216. Two days later Cencio Savelli, cardinal-priest of the S. Giovanni e Paulo, was chosen as his successor, taking the name Honorius III (1216-1227). He was sixty-six at his election, an old man by the standards of the time. Unlike his immediate predecessor, Honorius III was primarily a scholar. He had been a cardinal since 1193 and before that a canon, acting as *camerarius*, treasurer, of the Church since 1188. In this capacity he edited the famous *Liber censuum*, containing an exhaustive survey of the revenues of all the land belonging to the Holy Roman Church and as such one of the most important monuments of medieval history[4]. He also wrote a biography of his famous predecessor Gregory VII[5], but unlike the latter Honorius III was not a fanatic, always ready to draw his spiritual sword (*gladius spiritualis*) whenever it was called for[6]. He was certainly not a warrior. Pope Innocent III had planned to lead his crusade himself, but his successor excused himself on account of his old age and weakness and appointed a Spanish canonist, Cardinal Pelayo Gaytán, as his legate, a very unfortunate choice as subsequent events were to demonstrate.

The Fifth Crusade

Frederick II should have been ready to leave for Palestine by 1 June 1217 at the latest, but he was not. He had to settle the matter of the election of his son first. It was a most delicate affair, since he knew very well that the pope was against that plan. Many, if not all, German clerical princes also knew. As far as the secular princes were concerned, the election of Frederick's son was not a foregone conclusion following their election of Frederick II himself. The election of a duke of Swabia who

---

4 In addition to 'the book of rents' proper, the *Liber censuum* contains a collection of formularies of contracts and promises pertaining to the Holy Roman Church, for example the promise of Robert Guiscard to pay rent for his Sicilian fee (1, 421-422); a description of the city of Rome (*Mirabilia*); a description of ceremonies, for example the election procedure of a new pope (1, 311-313) and the ceremony for the coronation and anointing of a Roman emperor (*Ordo ad coronandum imperatorem*) (two versions) (2, 1*-6* and 420-421); a list of privileges of the Roman Church, such as the famous *Hludowicianum* (1, 363-365) as well as the infamous 'Donation of Constantine' (copied from Gratian's *Decretum*); and a chronicle of popes. It was supplemented by later papal officials, for example with an important biography of Pope Gregory IX (2, 18-36).

5 Honorius' *Sancti Gregorii VII vita* is published in *Medii Aevi Bibliotheca Patristica* I, *Honorii III Romani Pontificis Opera Omnia* I, Paris 1879, 571-608.

6 A quotation from Scripture favoured by Gregory VII was Jeremiah 48:10: 'Cursed be he that keepeth back his sword from blood'. See *supra* p. 32, fnt. 16.

also happened to be the *hereditary* king of Sicily would seriously disrupt the delicate balance of power among the members of the German 'club of princes' (*Fürstenverein*)[7]. They had accepted Frederick, but only at the insistence of the king of France *and* the pope as the only acceptable alternative to Otto IV. The fact that it took Frederick more than three years to finally settle this affair to his advantage suggests that there must have been considerable resistance to his plan.

Meanwhile, in the summer of 1217, it turned out that Innocent's call for a new crusade to liberate the Holy Land had met with little enthusiasm among the European princes and the populace at large. France still had its own crusade in the Languedoc, while the king, Philip II, was not sympathetic to the whole idea of crusading anyway, which that shrewd prince must have considered as a distraction of more pressing concerns at home and abroad. The king of England, Henry III (1207-1216-1272), was a minor and incapable of leading a crusade, even if the young king had not had a civil war at his hands, which he did[8]. What was to decide the fate of the Fifth Crusade was the departure, in May 1217, of an armada of some 300 Dutch ships carrying a considerable crusading army to the Holy Land[9]. It was commanded by Count William I of Holland, who was doing penance for the fact that he had fought with the excommunicate Otto IV at Bouvines[10]. When the Dutch fleet joined the crusaders already in Palestine in the last days of April 1218, it was decided to make use of this armada and attack Egypt rather than Jerusalem. The invasion was directed at 'the key to Egypt' (*clavis totius Aegypti*)[11], the port of Damietta, the principal port of the Egyptian sultanate at the time. The fleet reached Damietta at the end of May 1218. Most of the Dutch crusaders left for home in September after securing entrance to Damietta by capturing the strong fortress

---

7   See *supra* p. 212.

8   King John had a full-blown civil war at his hands when he died in 1216. His rebellious barons had invited the French crown-prince, Louis, to join them in the fight against their king, even offering the crown of England to Philip's ambitious son.

9   There is a Frisian eyewitness account of the Dutch expedition, *De itinere Frisonum* (ed. Röhricht, *Quinti belli sacri scriptores minores*, Geneva 1879, 57-70), taken from Abbot Emo's chronicle (1214-1234) of the monastery of 'Bloemhof' (*Floridus Hortus*) in the Dutch province of Groningen (*Cronica Floridi Horti*, ed. Jansen and Janse, Hilversum 1991, 60-82), ending with the arrival of the fleet at Acre. The fleet left in the last days of May 1217 from the estuaries of the Meuse (Vlaardingen) and the Lauwers (Dokkum), arriving in Acre in the last days of April 1218. For the number of ships see Oliver of Cologne (an eyewitness), *Historia Damiatina*, ed. Hoogeweg, Tübingen 1894, 172 (*fere trecentas naves*) and *Gesta crucigerorum Rhenanorum*, ed. Röhricht, *Quinti belli sacri scriptores minores*, Geneva 1879, 29 (*cum trecentis fere navibus*). See also *Chronica regia coloniensis* ad ann 1217, MGH *SS rer. Germ.* 18, 239.

10   See *supra* p. 197.

11   Matthew Paris, *Chronica maiora* ad ann. 1219, ed. H.R. Luard 3, London 1876, 53.

213

blocking the tributary of the Nile giving access to the city[12]. Their departure was cancelled out by the arrival of the papal legate Gaytán and a group of Italian, French, and English crusaders. The advent of the papal legate and a considerable number of prelates unsettled the leadership of the campaign. Until then, it had been under the joint command of secular princes, John of Brienne (c. 1170-1237), a brother of Walter of Brienne[13], most prominent among them since he had been married to Queen Mary of Jerusalem († 1212), the heiress of the kingdom of Jerusalem, and consequently styling himself king of Jerusalem[14]. The papal legate and his clerical retinue now intervened in the strategy of the campaign, causing discord and indecision. A remarkable incident occurred when the new sultan of Egypt, Al-Kamil (c. 1177-1218-1238), offered peace terms to the initial successful crusaders in 1219 which the sultan supposed they could impossibly refuse: he offered to restore the entire territory of the kingdom of Jerusalem, including the city itself, safe for two castles. In addition, he offered to surrender all his captives and a truce for a term of thirty years, as well as a tribute to be paid by him during that period. It was, indeed, an offer the crusaders could hardly refuse, since it realized all the objectives of the crusade 'to liberate the Holy Land' (*ad liberandam Terram Sanctam*) without further bloodshed. King John of Jerusalem, the leading nobles of that kingdom, as well as the French and German crusaders were in favour of accepting it, but the papal legate Gaytán and the other clerics, as well as the leaders of the military orders, the Templars and the Knights of St John, were against and so this golden opportunity to recover a substantial part of the kingdom and the city of Jerusalem was lost due to the stubborn insistence of the clerics on holy war rather than peace[15]. It was a fatal decision. The crusaders were able to capture Damietta on 5 November 1219, but the quarrels over the strategy and the war aims of the crusade continued to intensify, certainly so after Al-Kamil offered

---

12   On the early departure of the Dutch see Oliver of Cologne, *Historia Damiatina*, ed. Hoogeweg, Tübingen 1894, 186 and the chronicle of Alberic of Trois Fontaines († after 1252), MGH *SS* 23, 907. According to the latter they were duly punished for their premature departure by a great flood in their country. This was the terrible St Marcellus flood of 1219 that inundated large parts of the Netherlands only to be regained from the sea in the 20th century.
13   On Walter of Brienne see *supra* p. 160-161. The Brienne family was relatively minor French nobility, rising to distinction in the 13th century by royal protection and marriage, the medieval equivalent to the rise of the German house of Saxen-Coburg in the 19th century.
14   John of Brienne was acting as guardian for his daughter with Mary of Jerusalem, Queen Isabella II of Jerusalem (1212-1228). On her and her father see *infra* p. 214.
15   See on this remarkable episode Oliver of Cologne, *Historia Damiatina* 30, ed. Hoogeweg, Tübingen 1894, 222-223; *Gesta crucigerorum rhenanorum* ad ann. 1219, ed. Röhricht, *Quinti belli sacri scriptores minores*, Geneva 1879, 54; Matthew Paris, *Chronica maiora* ad ann. 1219, ed. H.R. Luard 3, London 1876, 53 and *Estoire d'Eracles* 32,9 (*Recueil des Historiens des Croisades, Historiens Occidentaux* 2, Paris 1859, 339).

peace terms yet again, this time on even more favourable conditions than before. The offer was rejected once more at the instance of the legate after a heated debate in the war council[16]. By now, in February 1220, the king of Jerusalem was so disgusted with the intransigence and the conduct of the legate, that he left for Acre, leaving behind a fatally stationary army, divided against itself, anxiously awaiting the long-expected arrival of Frederick II.

Frederick II was still in Germany in February 1220 and there were no signs in any of the designated ports, Brindisi and Messina, indicating an imminent departure of Frederick to the Holy Land, as a concerned Honorius III wrote to Frederick[17]. The king was playing a dangerous game of procrastination. He needed time to secure the position of his son as king of the Germans before leaving Germany. Frederick had written a letter to Honorius in January 1219, excusing himself for his delay to depart for the Holy Land in time, due to pressing business in Germany, especially the settlement of a regency there during his absence[18]. The pope granted Frederick dispensation and fixed a deadline for his departure on 24 June 1219[19]. Frederick was now under pressure from the pope, but also from his secular and ecclesiastical princes who were still reluctant to concede to Frederick's wishes. In the summer of 1219 news of Frederick's plans for his son had reached the Roman *curia* from the papal observer at Frederick's court, the lawyer Alatrinus, a sub-deacon, who was to play a very important diplomatic role in the years to come. Frederick was informed of the rumours circulating in the *curia* and responded by sending a reassuring letter to the pope. He was, he said, merely trying to secure the inheritance of his son in case something should befall him during his absence from Germany in service of the Church[20]. He must also have requested another postponement of his departure, since Honorius III granted yet another deadline, ending on 29 September 1219, this time even threatening with excommunication if the king did not meet it[21]. The pressure on Frederick mounted, since he knew he needed more time than that. Consequently, he decided to placate the pope by sending a confirmation to Honorius III of all the

Mounting pressure on Frederick II and Honorius III

---

16 On this second offer see *Estoire d'Eracles* 32,11 (*Recueil des Historiens des Croisades, Historiens Occidentaux* 2, Paris 1859, 341-342).
17 Honorius to Frederick (1 October 1219, MGH *Epp. saec. xiii*, 1 no 106, 75-76(75): 'Where are the ships, where are the galleys your royal attention has equipped for transport? Where are the freighters fit for carriage?' (*Quas naves, quas galeas ad transfretandum regia fecit sollicitudo parari? Que vasa usui transfretationis accomoda?*).
18 HB 1.2, 584-586.
19 MGH *Epp. saec. xiii*, 1 no 95, 68-69.
20 MGH *Epp. saec. xiii*, 1 no 96, 69.
21 HB 1.2, 630-631; MGH *Epp. saec. xiii*, 1 no 97, 70 (18 May 1219).

promises he had already made to Pope Innocent III at Eger in 1213[22]. The charters containing this confirmation are from September 1219, when the second deadline transpired. It was an empty gesture, since Frederick II conceded to nothing he had not already granted before, but it served its purpose. Honorius III wrote to Frederick II expressing his gratitude for Frederick's magnanimity, but also his deep concerns about Frederick's sincerity. He reminded the king that two earlier deadlines for his departure had already been missed and that missing the third, now ending on 21 March 1220, might have serious consequences. Frederick was advised to make haste[23]. Honorius III must also have been under mounting pressure by now, since if he did not realize himself that he was being played by Frederick II, his cardinals, and especially Cardinal Ugolino, must have reminded him that he was. Less than a few weeks before the expiration of the last and third deadline, another solemn charter issued by Frederick II arrived at Rome. It contained a reiteration of Frederick's 1216 promise to Innocent III[24], now expressing to Honorius III his earnest intention to keep the Empire and the kingdom of Sicily separate. This time, however, there was a novelty, since Frederick added that he would succeed to the kingdom of Sicily if his son Henry might expire without issue or brothers, not on account of his title as emperor, but as heir to his son, to have and to hold that kingdom from the Church of Rome[25]. Only nine days later Frederick wrote yet another letter to Honorius, full of the usual (and completely disingenuous) expressions of extreme gratitude for all services past and present rendered to him by the Church, but now requesting to be invested by the pope with the kingdom of Sicily for life[26]. It was a bold recantation of his promise, made only nine days earlier, to completely severe the ties between the Empire and the Sicilian kingdom. He also indicated that, though he was ready to depart for the Holy Land him-

---

22   HB 1.2, 675-676; MGH *Const.* 2, *F.2*, no 65-66, 77-80. For the Eger concessions see *supra* p. 194.

23   HB 1.2, 691-693; MGH *Epp. saec. xiii*, 1 no 106, 75-76.

24   See *supra* p. 211.

25   MGH *Const.* 2, *F1* no 70, 82. The text is identical to MGH *Const.* 1, *F1* no 58, 72 (see *supra* fnt. 1), but has this addition at the end: 'But if, God forbid, our just mentioned son should die without a son or brother, we do reserve for ourselves that we can succeed him in the kingdom in that case, *not on account of a prerogative of the empire, but according to the law of succession*, like any father would to his son, and that we shall receive, hold, and resume possession of it from the Roman Church and we shall swear an oath on behalf of it' (*Ceterum quia forte quod absit posset contingere, memoratum filium nostrum decedere nullo filio vel germane relicto, reservamus nobis, ut in hoc casu* non iure imperii sed ratione successionis legitime, *tamquam quivis pater filio, ei succedere possimus in regnum, it aquod illud a Romana recipiemus, tenebimus et recognoscemus ecclesia et iuramentum prestabimus pro eodem*) (emphasis added).

26   HB 1.2, 741-744. It should be noted that in all these charters and letters Frederick styled himself as king of Sicily.

self, his German nobles were not, and he might therefore miss the deadline which the pope had fixed on 21 March 1220[27]. Cardinal Ugolino must have been furious, but Honorius complied once more and granted yet another postponement, this time until 1 May 1220[28]. By the time this deadline expired, Frederick was still in Germany.

Frederick's son Henry, king of Sicily, was finally elected 'king of the Romans' at a diet held in Frankfurt in April 1220[29]. The support of the ecclesiastical princes of the empire had been decisive and they were rewarded shortly after, on 26 April, by the grant of extensive class privileges, securing their property rights and, above all, their position as territorial lords[30]. Frederick realized that the election of his son would create an outrage in Rome, and he hastened to write a letter to Honorius, claiming that he had had nothing to do with it since his son had been elected king of the Romans by the German princes 'without our knowledge and in our absence' (*nobis insciis et absentibus*) and completely 'by surprise' (*ex insperato*)[31]. He would have refused to accept the election, if he had known of it in time, '*because it has happened without your knowledge and approval*'[32]. There was, moreover, no intention of a possible union of the kingdom of Sicily with the Empire[33]. In diplomacy, disingenuity must be exercised with prudence and this was a reckless letter, containing at least one blatant lie. Frederick II was treating the pope and his cardinals like the fools they certainly were not. Of course, they knew that Frederick had been planning this move for years, postponing his departure for the Holy Land time and again. The papal observer Alatrinus kept the Roman *curia* well informed about everything that transpired at Frederick's court, and he may well have seen Frederick's great privilege to the German ecclesiastical princes

Henry (VII) elected King of the Romans

---

27 HB 1.2, 743: '*sed timemus ... aliqui dies possint ultra prefixum nobis terminum preterire*'.
28 HB 1.2, 746-747 (extract); MGH *Epp. saec. xiii*, 1 no 112, 79-80.
29 *Reineri annales* ad ann. 1220, MGH *SS* 16, 677: 'Frederick held a famous diet at Frankfurt, unlike the prior ones: all the princes did homage there to his son Henry. A journey was announced there as well in view of the imperial consecration at Rome and an expedition in order to liberate the church in the east from the yoke of the Saracenes' (*Fredericus rex curiam habet celebrem prioribus dissimilem in Frankefort; ibi omnes principes filio suo Heinrico fidelitatem fecerunt. Ibi ordinata est via de consecratione imperii Rome suscipienda, de transitu ad orientalem ecclesiam liberandam de postestate Agarenorum*).
30 *Privilegium in favorem principum ecclesiasticorum*, MGH *Const. F2*, no. 73, 86-91.
31 Frederick to Honorius III, 13 July 1220 (HB 1.2, 803): '*ex insperato presentes principes et maxime illi qui prius promotioni dicti nostril filii obviarant, nobis insciis et absentibus, elegerunt eundem*'.
32 Frederick to Honorius III, 13 July 1220 (HB 1.2, 803): '*Cuius electio cum nobis patefieret, sicut fuerat celebrata absque vestra notitia seu mandato ... ipsi electioni contradiximus consentire*'.
33 Frederick to Honorius III, 13 July 1220 (HB 1.2, 804): '*Absit enim quod imperium commune aliquid habere debeat cum regno*'.

with his own eyes, including Frederick's words of gratitude for their assistance in the recent election of his son[34]. There was one cardinal in the *curia* certainly not deceived by Frederick's mellifluous letters on this or any other occasion and that was the bishop of Ostia, Ugolino: what else could the election of Frederick's son have been about but the confirmation of the union of the Sicilian *regno* with the German Empire? There were now no fewer than *two* kings of Sicily, father and son, both of them king of the Romans as well. It was preposterous and completely at odds with the policy of his uncle, the great Innocent III. Nonetheless, Honorius III set all these objections and warnings aside. He regarded the presence of the secular leader of Christianity, the king of the Romans, indispensable for the success of the crusade and was even prepared to fulfil Frederick's condition for the definitive severance of the Empire and the Sicilian kingdom, his coronation as Roman emperor[35].

Frederick II returns to Italy

On 19 February 1220 Frederick announced to Pope Honorius III his imminent departure for Italy and informed him that he had sent Abbot Kuno of the abbey of Fulda ahead to ensure the pope and the people of Rome of his enduring loyalty and devotion to the Church and the people of Rome[36]. As soon as the matter of the election of his son was settled, he sent a message to all prelates, princes, and cities of his Italian kingdom announcing his imminent arrival there and the appointment of Bishop Conrad of Metz as his viceroy in the *regnum italicum*[37]. By September 1220 Frederick was back in Italy, leaving his son Henry (VII)[38] behind in Germany under the custody of Archbishop Engelbert of Cologne, *totius regni Romani per Alemanniam provisor*[39]. In November 1220 he was in the neighbourhood of Rome, pitching his

---

34 See the preamble to Frederick's privilege for the ecclesiastical princes of 26 April 1220 (MGH *Const. F2*, no. 73, p. 89): '*Digna recolentes animadversione, quanta efficatia et fide dilecti fideles nostri principes ecclesiastici nobis hactenus astiterint, ad culmen imperii nos promovendo, promotos in ipso firmando et* demum filium nostrum Heinricum in regem sibi et dominum benivole atque concorditer eligendo, *censuimus eos* etc. (emphasis added).

35 See *supra* p. 211.

36 HB 1.2, 743-744: '<*Fuldensis abbas*> *quem ecce mittimus ad vos et populum Romanum ut vestre paternitati devotionem nostrum et principum voluntatem exponat, expositurus nihilominus tam per litteras nostras quam viva voce senatori et populo Romano devotionem quam gerimus ad Ecclesiam et personam vestram*'.

37 MGH *Const. F. II* no. 71, p. 83-84.

38 Frederick's son Henry was the seventh of that name to be elected king of the Germans. His number is always placed in parentheses. For the reason see *infra* p. 276. Henry VII (without parentheses) is Henry of Luxemburg (1278/79-1308-1312-1313), German king and Roman emperor, Dante's *alto Arrigo*.

39 Caesarius of Heisterbach, *Vita Engelberti* 1,5, ed. Böhmer, *Fontes rerum germanicarum* 2, Stuttgart 1845, 299.

camp near the Monte Mario after the tradition of all German kings coming to Rome to be crowned by the pope. It was there that the last negotiations were to be concluded before Frederick could be crowned and consecrated as Roman emperor. The cardinal bishop of Tusculum, Nicòlo Chiaramonti, a Sicilian and papal legate in Germany, and the ubiquitous papal Chaplain Alatrinus were instructed to close the covenant with Frederick II. Their instruction has survived, and it shows that Honorius III was still not convinced of Frederick's sincerity in severing the ties between the kingdom of Sicily and the German Empire, despite all assurances. It had been brought to the attention of the pope that Frederick had summoned his Sicilian barons to come to his coronation in Rome in order to renew their oath of fealty to him. Why should Sicilian barons do homage to a Roman emperor in Rome[40]? It was all very suspect. The pope also had little faith in Frederick's intention to come to the rescue of the crusaders in Egypt on short notice. The papal negotiators were instructed to convince Frederick of the fact that he was to be crowned for that purpose exclusively[41]. Frederick accepted all the terms of his coronation, including a solemn declaration that the kingdom of Sicily did not belong to the Empire and that the Empire would never lay claim to it (as his father had done)[42].

Frederick II was crowned and consecrated emperor of the Romans on 22 November 1220, a Sunday, in St Peter's. The pope later wrote to his legate Cardinal Gaytàn in Egypt that he had crowned Frederick among great rejoicing and peace among the citizens of Rome, since the riots usually eclipsing an imperial coronation did not, for once, occur on this special occasion[43]. Honorius also informed his legate that he had the personal guarantee of the emperor that Frederick would send

His imperial coronation

---

40 From the instruction of Pope Honorius for Cardinal Chiaramonti and Alatrinus (MGH *Const. F II* no 83, 105): 'he has called all the prelates and the magnates of the kingdom <of Sicily> to the imperial coronation and he demanded a renewal of their oath of fealty from them, by which the aforementioned union seems to be brought about, to the disadvantage of the Apostolic See and posterity. That is why many people have been rightly surprised' (*prelatos et magnates regni ad coronam vocarit imperii et ab eis de novo fidelitatis exegerit et exigat iuramenta, per que in sedis apostolice necnon posteritatis sue dispendium videtur prefata unio procurari; unde multi non immerito admirantur*).
41 MGH *Const. F2*, no 83, 105: '*ipsum ita instanter ad coronam vocavimus specialiter hac de causa*'.
42 *Declaratio regis de regno Siciliae*, MGH *Const. F2*, no 84, 105: '*nos per hoc scriptum authenticum profitemur, imperium nichil prorsus iuris habere in regno Sicilie nec nos racione imperii obtinere aliquid iuris in ipso*'.
43 Honorius III to Cardinal Gaytàn (15 December 1220), HB 2.1, 82: '*tue fraternitati exponimus nos dominica ante adventum Domini proxima charissimum in Christo filium nostrum Fredericum Romanorum imperatorem, semper augustum et regem Sicilie et illustrem imperatricem consortem eius in principis Apostolorum basilica cum inestimabili alacritate ac pace civium Romanorum solemnissime coronasse*'.

an army to Egypt by March 1221 and that the emperor himself would follow in August of that year[44]. In order to corroborate that guarantee, Frederick II had taken the cross once again, immediately after his coronation as Roman emperor in St Peter's, just as he had done after his coronation as king of the Germans at Aachen in 1215[45]. He received the cross out of the hands of Cardinal Ugolino[46], who had also administered the unction at his imperial consecration, the privilege of the cardinal-bishop of Ostia[47]. Frederick II had, once again, made promises he only intended to keep when it suited him.

---

44 HB 2.1, 82: '*prestita nobis securitate quod tibi et christiano exercitui in proximo martio succursum magnifice destinabit et in sequenti augusto personaliter transfretabit*'.
45 See *supra* p. 199.
46 For this detail see Frederick II himself in 1227 (HB 3, 40: '*Post susceptionem vero imperialis corone, per manus reverendi Patris Domini Gregorii nunc apostolici, tunc episcopi Ostiensis, iterum crucis signaculum reverenter accepimus*'.
47 Burchard of Ursberg, *Chronicon* ad ann. 1220, MGH *SS rer. Germ.* 16, 114): '*F(ridericus) Rome coronatur in imperatorem in basilica sancti Petri de mandato Honorii pape per ministerium domini Hugolini, tunc Hostiensis episcopi, postmodum apostolici*'. See for the ceremonial role of the bishop of Ostia in the coronation ritual *Liber Censuum* 1, 4*, l. col.): '*Episcopus Hostiensis ungat brachium dextrum de oleo exorcizato et inter scapilias* etc.'.

15

Excommunication I

In December 1220 Frederick II returned to his Sicilian kingdom after an absence of eight years. When he had recklessly left Sicily as an impetuous adolescent in 1212, he had hardly begun to initiate the reforms that were necessary after so many years of mismanagement during his minority[1]. Now that he was finally back as an experienced adult, he set in motion a programme of reforms which he must have conceived during his prolonged stay in Germany. Only a few days after his return, Frederick convened a diet at Capua where he issued twenty statutes, the 'Assizes[2] of Capua', containing that programme[3]. It justifies the reputation which Frederick already had gained during his lifetime as 'the wonder of the world' (*stupor mundi*)[4]. The restoration of good, meaning effective, government was central to that programme. To begin with, Frederick turned the legal clock back to 1189, the year 'good King William' (William II) had died[5], meaning that all later legislation was

Frederick II returns to the Sicilian kingdom

---

1 See *supra* p. 164-165.

2 The word 'assize' (*assisa*) comes from the French verb *s'asseoir*, 'to take a seat', and denotes the decision of a royal court or parliament reached at its 'session'.

3 The text of the Assizes of Capua has long been lost, though some of the statutes issued there have been inserted into the *Liber augustalis*, Frederick's codification of 1231 (see *infra* p. 251-260). The complete text of the Assizes is only known since the end of the 19th century, after the Italian scholar A. Gaudenzi discovered an old manuscript of the important chronicle of Ryccardo of San Germano (*c.* 1165-1244), an official at the court of Frederick II, containing all the Assizes *in extenso*. They are included in C.A. Garufi's edition of that chronicle: *Ryccardi de Sancto Germano notarii Chronica*, *RIS²* 7.2, ad ann. 1220, 88-93, l. col. With the Assizes of Capua Frederick followed the example of his maternal grandfather, the great Roger II, who had also issued a code of 'Assizes', the 'Assizes of Ariano', in 1140, after being invested with the kingdom of Sicily by Innocent II (see *supra* p. 35). See *infra* p. 252 for a further account of Roger's and Frederick's 'Assizes'.

4 Matthew Paris, *Chronica maiora* ad ann. 1250, ed. H.R. Luard V, 190: '*principum mundi maximus Frethericus, stupor quoque mundi et immutator mirabilis*'. See also ad ann. 1250 (196): '*stupor mundi Frethericus*'.

5 *Ryccardi de Sancto Germano notarii Chronica* ad ann. 1220, *RIS²* 7.2, Bologna 1936-1938, 88): 'To begin with, we command all our vassals, ecclesiastical prelates, counts, barons, citizens, and villagers, and everyone residing in our kingdom strictly to observe the good conventions and customs they used to live by at the time of King William' (*Inprimis precipimus*

repealed as of right. Above all else, it meant that all later royal grants of fees and privileges were nullified. Everyone in the kingdom claiming a royal fee or privilege from a later date than the year of the demise of King Henry, Frederick's father, was ordered to produce and deliver all relating documents for approval (or rejection) by the royal court by the end of the following year[6]. All later grants by Frederick were done under the express condition subsequent of retraction (*salvo mandato et ordinatione nostra*), guaranteeing the loyalty of the grantees[7]. It is significant that the loudest objections voiced against Frederick's enactment came from Pope Honorius III on behalf of the Church of Sicily, accusing Frederick of illegal expropriation of church property[8]. Another prominent dupe of Frederick's decision to annul all privileges granted after the demise of King William II were the Genovese. When Frederick returned to Italy in 1220, he received an embassy from Genoa in the neighbourhood of Bologna. The Genovese ambassadors requested a renewal of their important trade privileges in Sicily granted to them by Markward of Annweiler in 1200[9]. They expected a positive

---

omnibus fidelibus, videlicet prelatis ecclesiarum, comitibus, baronibus, civibusque, terris et omnibus de regno nostro omnes bonos usus et consuetudines, quibus consueverunt vivere tempore regis Guillelmi, firmiter observari).

6   Assizes of Capua 15 (Garufi, 91, l. col.). Why Frederick in this case decided to turn the clock back to the year of his father's demise, rather than the death of King William II, is not entirely clear. The usurper Tancred of Lecce had also granted fees and privileges to the prejudice of the royal demesne in order to gain the support of the Sicilian nobility. Probably, Frederick still needed their support as well, for the moment.

7   The retraction-clause was rarely omitted. If it was, it was a sign of great confidence in the person of the grantee. When the Cistercian monastery of Holy Mary at Casanova asked for confirmation of a privilege granted after the demise of King Henry VI, the king confirmed it adding that 'although we have decided that in some of our privileges a clause is to be added saying "save for etc.:", we have decided to leave it out in the present grant as a special favour' (Winkelmann, *Acta imperii inedita seculi XIII*, Innsbruck 1880, no 239, 221-222: *licet in quibusdam privilegiis nostris illam clausulam iussimus apponi, qua dicitur:* salvo mandato etcetera, *a praesenti tamen privilegio eam de gratia nostra decrevimus amovendam*). Frederick favoured the Cistercian order throughout his life. He died in the robe of Cistercian monk: see *infra* p. 416.

8   The protest of Honorius has not survived, but we do have Frederick's response to it (HB 2.1, 139-140, 3 March 1221), stating that 'the aforementioned emperor, our father, has granted away much that belonged to the kingdom under an implied condition of retraction which he had better not done, and after the demise of the emperor many forged privileges have been found bearing his seal by which the major part of our demesne had been given away' (*quod predictus imperator pater noster multa de regno sub spe revocationis concesserat que debuerat retinere, et post obitum imperatoris de sigillo suo privilegia multa falsa inventa sunt quibus major pars nostri demanii fuerat occupata*).

9   The privileges granted by Markward to the Genovese are printed in *Liber iurium reipublicae Genuensis* I, Turin 1854, no 437, col. 462-464. Many Italian cities kept a public record of all treaties, privileges, and covenants a city had contracted or granted, a so-called *Liber iurium*. The Genovese *Liber iurium* was composed in 1229 at the order of the famous Bolognese pro-

answer, having supported Frederick in 1212[10], but the king was evasive: he said that the matter would have to wait until his return in his Sicilian kingdom[11]. The Genovese trading privileges in Sicily were not renewed, causing a break between Frederick and Genoa, the hometown of master Sinibaldo Fieschi, then in the service of Cardinal Ugolino.

The main objective of the Assizes of Capua was the restoration of the royal bureaucracy and the centralized administration of the kingdom. One way of ensuring this was to eliminate all traces of urban autonomy within the kingdom. All locally elected consuls and interim administrators (*podesti*)[12] in the kingdom were brushed aside and replaced by royal functionaries, 'bailiffs' (*balivi*), with a special appointed royal justice (*justiciarius*) at their side to adjudge civil cases 'without delay, trickery, or deceit'[13], *not* on the basis of local customary law or local by-laws, but on the basis of the customary law of the kingdom approved of by the king and, of course, royal legislation[14] – all as it had been in the good old days of King William II and very much like the 'reformation' Frederick 'Barbarossa' had had in mind for his Lombard kingdom with his infamous *Lex 'Omnis iurisdictio'*[15]. The Lombards had successfully prevented that 'reformation' in the Italian kingdom (Lombardy) from taking place, but there was hardly any resistance in South Italy and Sicily. Some cities in the Sicilian *regno*, Naples and Capua most prominently, had indeed resisted royal autocracy in the recent past, but there was no tradition of urban self-government in the *regno* as there was in Lombardy, the Romagna, and Tuscany. The Sicilian monarchy was firmly rooted in Roman/Byzantine traditions of autocratic centralized government. Even the members of the nobility played a part in government only as functionaries within the state apparatus, as *officiales*

The Assizes of Capua

---

fessor of civil law Jacobus Balduinus, who was *podestà* of Genova in that year. See also *infra* p. 361-362.

10   See *supra* p. 191.

11   See the contemporary continuation of the *Annales Ianuenses* by the Genovese notary Marchisio Scriba ad ann. 1220, ed. L.T. Belgrano, *Annali genovesi di Caffaro e di suoi continuatori* II, Genova 1901, 168: '*vix partem de eo quod ad imperium pertinebat voluit confirmare, suas excusationes preponens, quod quicquid ad regnum Sicilie attinebat, nisi prius esset in regno, non poterat aliquatenus confirmare*'.

12   On the important institution of 'interim city administrator' (*podestà*) in contemporary Italy see *infra* p. 229.

13   Assizes of Capua 6 (Garufi, 89, l. col.): '*Item ordinamus ut Magistri iustitiarii et iustitiarii, qui a nobis fuerint ordinati, iurent ad sancta Dei evangelis, ut unicuique conquerenti iustitiam faciant sine fraude, et quam citius poterunt sine fraude conquerentes expediant*'.

14   Assizes of Capua 14 (Garufi, 91, l. col.): '*Item precipimus ne in aliqua civitate ordinetur potestas, consulem aut rectorem non habeant, set balivus per ordinatos camerarios curie statuatur, et iustitia per iustitiarios et ordinatos curie regatur iuris ordine et approbatis Regni consuetudinibus observetur*'.

15   See *supra* p. 107-108.

serving the king, without any prerogative to a position within the royal bureaucracy since anyone having the necessary (legal) skills was welcome. Frederick even established a law school in Naples in 1224 to educate the elite of his civil service locally, rather than in Bologna[16]. It was the first state-sponsored university in Europe.

Sicilian affairs

Frederick II had left his Sicilian kingdom in 1212 headlong for Germany. In 1220, he did not even consider leaving that kingdom for Egypt, as the pope expected him to do. He wanted to implement the programme of the Assizes of Capua first. One of the priorities expressed in the Assizes was the demilitarization, pacification, and disarmament of Sicilian society. As once was the case in the classical Roman Empire, the carrying of arms was forbidden, as was any attempt to take the law into one's own hand[17]. The Emperor Augustus had qualified the private possession of offensive weapons as 'private violence' (*vis privata*) and had consequently proscribed it, much to the wonder and disbelief of medieval legal commentators for whom 'private violence' was a fact of life[18]. The dismantling of all privately-owned castles and other strongholds proliferating within the kingdom after the good old days of King William II was the logical prerequisite of this policy. Many of them were still held by German war lords, such as the abominable Diepold of Schweinspeunt. Frederick had him arrested, stripped of his county of Acerra[19], and released him only after Diepold's brother Siegfried had surrendered all strongholds still in possession of the brothers[20]. After that, the Schweinspeunt brothers disappeared from history, as did the other German war lords of Apulia. Their castles were either demolished

---

16   Pope Honorius III had placed the University of Bologna under ecclesiastical supervision in 1219. Only persons licensed by the archdeacon of the bishop of Bologna were allowed to teach: see Honorius' bull in Sarti 2, no xvii, 260. The clerical influence over the Bolognese university was enhanced by the dominating presence of St Dominic and his Orators, who chose Bologna, rather than Rome, as their headquarters.
17   Assizes of Capua 3 and 4 (Garufi, 89, l. col).
18   See D. 48,6,1 (Marcianus) and the Accursian gloss (Gl. 'Lege Julia' to D. 48,6,1): 'Note how remarkable it is that just the possession of arms at home, or carrying them, is considered violence' (*Nota mirabile quod reputatur vis, solum habere arma domi, vel portare*).
19   After the removal of Diepold, the county of Acerra was granted to Thomas of Aquino, one of the closest collaborators of Frederick: *Ryccardi de Sancto Germano notarii Chronica* ad ann. 1221, *RIS²* 7.2, Bologna 1936-1938, 94, r. col. Thomas had a brother, Landulf, who was a royal justice in Campania. Landulf had a son, also called Thomas (1225-1274), who was to rise to great scholarly fame and even sanctity, the *doctor angelicus*.
20   *Ryccardi de Sancto Germano notarii Chronica* ad ann. 1221, *RIS²* 7.2, Bologna 1936-1938, 93-94.

or occupied by regular troops in the service of the king, now serving as army barracks rather than private strongholds[21].

The Sicilian Muslims were another concern, most of them living in the island's interior mountain districts. They had been in rebellion on and off, siding with Markward of Annweiler in the recent past[22], and Frederick had to engage in several campaigns to subdue them. When he had finally done so, in 1223, he decided to deport the entire rural Muslim population of Sicily, some 20,000 men with their extended families, to the South Italian mainland, to be settled there in the city of Lucera. The Muslims of Lucera were free to practice their religion and to live according to Islamic law, applied by their own Islamic judges. From that time onwards, the Lucera Muslims supplied Frederick with an extremely loyal military force over which the pope did not have any control whatsoever. Frederick even built a palace for himself in this city living under Islamic law. The pope and his cardinals never forgave Frederick for this outrageous act, happening at a time when heretics in the French Languedoc were duly exterminated rather than deported.

Meanwhile, in Egypt, the Fifth Crusade had reached its critical stage. Frederick had sent Duke Louis of Bavaria ahead to Egypt with a considerable army shortly after his coronation, as he had promised to Honorius[23]. Duke Louis arrived at Damietta in May 1221. It was the occasion enticing the papal legate Gaytàn to retake the offensive by attacking Cairo, the capital of the Egyptian sultanate, itself. King John of Jerusalem, just returned from Acre, advised against this reckless plan, but was overruled by the legate. About halfway between Damietta and Cairo, near Al Mansurah, the advance of the crusaders came to a halt. They were stuck in the mud of the rising floodwater of the Nile, aggravated by the Egyptians who had pierced the dikes, and surrounded and outnumbered by the army of Al-Kamil. The morale of the crusading army resembled the spirit of the crew of a sinking ship: most of the regular troops were blind drunk when the army attempted a desperate escape[24]. It failed and there was no other way out of the predicament

The Fifth
Crusade ends
in disaster

---

21 Assizes of Capua 19 (Garufi, 92, l. col.): 'We command that all castles, strongholds, walls, and moats built since the demise of King William until now and not in our own power, are to be handed over to our representatives to be destroyed completely' (*Precipimus etiam ut omnia castra, munitiones, muri et fossata, que ab obitu regis Guillelmi usque ad hec tempora de novo sunt facta in illis terris et locis, que non sunt in manus nostras, assignentur nuntiis nostris, ut ea funditus diruantur*).

22 See *supra* p. 159, fnt. 53.

23 See *supra* p. 219-220.

24 For this detail see Oliver of Cologne, *Historia Damiatina* 74, ed. Hoogeweg, Tübingen 1894, 270-271: 'what aggravated our disasters was that the people, blind drunk that day from the wine that could not be carried off but was freely available to be guzzled down the throats

now than to surrender to the mercy of the sultan. Al-Kamil was merciful. He accepted the surrender of the army on condition of the surrender of Damietta, a truce of eight years and the exchange of all prisoners of war. All the leaders of the army, including the papal legate, the duke of Bavaria and King John, were to be kept as hostages until Damietta had been restored to the sultan[25]. On 8 September 1221 Al-Kamil entered Damietta and *'thus the noble city of Damietta was lost, due to the sins, the folly, the jealousy, and the malice of the clergy and the religious orders, a city which had been conquered at great cost and with great struggle'*[26]. The Fifth Crusade had ended in complete disaster, largely due to the incompetence of the papal legate, as many contemporary observers believed[27]. Yet Pope Honorius III laid all the blame with Frederick II and his constant prevarication, as did Cardinal Ugolino. Ugolino's personal protégé, Francis of Assisi (1181/1182-1226)[28], had returned from Egypt physically broken and almost blind, whereas Frederick enjoyed life in Apulia, surrendering to all kinds of 'worldly pleasures' (*voluptatibus terrenis*)[29], while steadily consolidating his authority in the Sicilian kingdom at the same time. Pope Honorius III instructed Frederick II that it was his duty as emperor to reverse the disgrace of the Fifth Crusade by personally heading a new crusade to the Holy Land, even implicating excommunication if the emperor failed to do so[30].

---

of the reckless, remained in stupor in the camp or lay prostrate along the way, incapable to be moved along' (*Accessit cladibus nostris, quod populus eo die plurimum inebriatus vino, cuius habundantia deferri non poterat, sed gratis expositum incautos ingurgitaverat, soporatus in castris remansit aut per viam prostratus excitari noluit*).

25 For the conditions of the treaty see Oliver of Cologne, *Historia Damiatina* 79, ed. Hoogeweg, Tübingen 1894, 275-276.

26 *Estoire d'Eracles* 32,17 (*Recueil des Historiens des Croisades, Historiens Occidentaux* 2, Paris 1859, 352): 'Ensi fu perdue la noble cité de Damiate par peché et par folie et par orgueil et la malice dou clergé et des religions, la quell avoit esté conquise a grant cost et a grant travail'.

27 King John of Jerusalem is reported to have laid all the blame on the legate (*Estoire d'Eracles* 32,16 (*Recueil des Historiens des Croisades, Historiens Occidentaux* 2, Paris 1859, 351): 'Sire legaz, sire legaz, mau fussiez vos onques issu d'Espaigne, car vos avez les Crestiens destruis et mis a tout perdre'.

28 Francis came to Damietta in 1219. He intended to end the fighting by converting Al-Kamil to Christianity. Francis was received by the sultan, who sent him on his way again after kindly hearing the futile exhortations of that saintly man. Innocent III had given Francis permission to preach, thus protecting him against the suspicion of heresy his sermons provoked. Since Francis was a charismatic orator, but certainly not an efficient administrator, Pope Honorius III appointed Cardinal Ugolino as patron (*protector*) of Francis and his followers, who obtained the status of officially recognized religious order on 29 November 1223 as *fratres minores*, the Order of Friars Minor (OM).

29 See on the condemnation of Frederick's personal lifestyle by Pope Gregory IX (Ugolino) and his successor Innocent IV *infra* p. 355 and 378.

30 Letter of Honorius III to Frederick II from 19 November 1221, MGH *Epp. saec. xiii* 1, no 183, 128-130.

On 23 June 1222 the Empress Constance died at Catania, while her husband Frederick was away rounding up the Muslims of Sicily. The empress' demise opened new opportunities for Pope Honorius to commit Frederick II to a new crusade. It so happened that John of Brienne, the titular king of Jerusalem, was in Rome at the time, seeking support for the beleaguered kingdom of Jerusalem and a husband for his daughter, Queen Isabella (1212-1225-1228), who was willing and able to restore Jerusalem to her crown. The pope called a conference for March 1223 to be held at Ferentino, on papal territory, to plan a new crusade for the liberation of Jerusalem. John of Brienne was invited, as was Frederick. The pope suggested a marriage of the Jerusalem heiress to Frederick and Frederick accepted. He promised to marry Isabella and swore to leave for the Holy Land on 24 June, the feast day of St John the Baptist, 1225[31]. Yet again, Frederick had committed himself to a crusade and a date of departure, and yet again he would fail to keep his promise.

The increasing hostility within the papal *curia* against Frederick II was not only caused by his constant procrastination, but also by his religious policy within the kingdom of Sicily. Frederick II never accepted the loss of the special ecclesiastical privileges of the kings of Sicily his mother had relinquished in her concordat with Innocent III[32]. There was, however, one of these privileges still available to him and that was the right of approval (*assensus*) of all episcopal elections in Sicily. The king could not appoint bishops, but he could block the consecration and consequently the entry into office of a bishop by withholding his approval to the election, thus indirectly forcing the chapter of an episcopate to elect a bishop acceptable to Frederick. Frederick exercised this privilege liberally and as a matter of course, causing the rejected bishops to appeal to the pope in Rome, who was not amused. Honorius

The Ferentino conference

Rising animosity in the *curia* against Frederick II

---

31   MGH *Epp. saec. xiii* 1, no 225, p. 153 (Honorius III): 'at our suggestion and the advice of the persons just mentioned, the emperor voluntarily accepted a term for his departure on the feast day of St John the Baptist two years from now, while spontaneously swearing a solemn oath to that ... At the instance of the aforementioned patriarch (of Jerusalem) and other people from the Orient and in the presence of us, our fellow-friars, and a crowd of people attending the conference, he also confirmed under oath that he would marry the legitimate daughter of the king' (*imperator ad nostrum bene placitum et consilium predictorum transfretandi terminum in festo beati Iohannis baptiste post biennium proximo secuturo prompta voluntate suscepit, corporale super hoc exhibens spontaneus iuramentum ... ad instantiam patriarche predicti et aliorum orientalium in nostra et fratrum nostrorum presentia et multitudinis hominum, qui ad colloquium venerant, se ducturum in uxorem legitimam filiam regis eiusdem iurisiurandi religione firmavit*'. See also *Ryccardi de Sancto Germano notarii Chronica* ad ann. 1223, *RIS²* 7.2, Bologna 1936-1938, 107, r. col.: '*promisit publice usque ad biennium in terre sancte subsidium transfretare, et filiam dicti regis ducere in uxorem iuravit*'.
32   See *supra* p. 188.

III protested vigorously against Frederick's indiscriminate use of his right of approval[33]. It was clearly contrary to the precious 'freedom of the Church' (*libertas ecclesiae*). As the years advanced and Frederick II progressively tightened his grip on his South Italian kingdom, a steadily increasing number of frustrated clerics and dissatisfied South Italian barons, banished from the kingdom for obstructing royal policy, arrived at Rome adding to the curial antipathy to Frederick there. The discontent with Frederick (and the ever-indulgent policy of Honorius III) within the *curia* must have reached a boiling point when the emperor, once again, asked for a postponement of his crusade in 1225[34]. There was, however, no alternative to Frederick II since the only other monarch with sufficient prestige to lead a crusade, the king of France, was occupied in the Languedoc in a crusade of his own[35]. Honorius III therefore sent the Cardinals Gualo and Gaytàn, of Damietta fame, to Frederick in order to negotiate a new date of departure. They reached an agreement at S. Germano on 22 July 1225. The detailed terms of the treaty were put in writing to be divulged for all the world to take notice of in *litterae patentes*[36]. The key condition of the treaty was that the emperor would be excommunicated automatically if he failed to depart for the Holy Land by August 1227[37].

It was after this treaty was concluded that Frederick II made a fatal strategic decision. Until then, his career had been a succession of impressive achievements brought about by his diplomatic skills, extraordinary

---

33   Honorius III to Frederick II, 27 June 1223, MGH *Epp. saec. xiii* no 232, 160-162(161)): 'What is happening here? Does it mean that we do not have the same right and power in the kingdom of Sicily as we do have, as is common knowledge, in France, England, Spain, and the other Christian kingdoms and even in the Empire? Or shall we have less authority and power in the kingdom of Sicily because we have more right and sovereignty there, which belongs, so to speak, to the Apostolic See?' (*Quid enim? Non obtinebimus eam iurisdictionem vel potestatem in regno Sicilie, quam in Francie, Anglie, Hispanie ac ceteris Christianorum regnis et in ipso imperio noscimur obtinere? Numquid in regno Sicilie minus auctoritatis vel potestatis habebimus, quia in eo tanquam in sedis apostolice patrimonio plus iuris et iurisdictionis habemus?*).

34   Ryccardus de S. Germano, *Chronica* ad ann. 1225, *RIS²* 7.2, 120, r. col: '*Honorius papa Urbe exiens propter seditiones et bella que in ea fiunt sub Parentio senatore, apud Tybur se contulit, ad quem pro dilatione passagii optinenda imperator mittit regem predictum et patriarcham*'. In 1225 Honorius III was forced to leave Rome for Tivoli due to a revolt against papal government in the city. Frederick had sent King John of Jerusalem and the patriarch of Jerusalem to the pope with his request.

35   Ryccardus de S. Germano, *Chronica* ad ann. 1225, *RIS²* 7.2, 123, r. col: '*Hoc anno rex Francie monitus per domnum Romanum apostolice sedis legatum, contra Albigenses cum copioso Francorum exercitu in Provinciam vadit*'. See on this expedition of Louis VIII *supra* p. 206, fnt. 33.

36   The treaty of S. Germano is printed in MGH *Const. 2 F2*, no 102, 129-131. See also the report of the negotiations by Frederick II himself in MGH *Const. 2 F2*, no 116, 151-152.

37   For this see clause 8 of the treaty of S. Germano (*Const. 2 F2*, no 102, 130): '*predicta omnia observabimus bona fide, lata ex nunc excommunicationis sententia, in quam incidemus, si non transiverimus in passagio suprascripto*'.

good fortune, personal bravery, and sheer insolence: he had outmanoeuvred Otto IV; he had outwitted the pope by maintaining the
union of the Empire with the Sicilian kingdom against all odds; he
had succeeded in securing the succession to the Empire and the Sicilian
kingdom by the election of his son as German king; and he was beginning to restore order and good governance within his Sicilian kingdom
– all within a few years. He now faced a final challenge: to secure the
link between the Sicilian kingdom and the German Empire by bringing the Italian kingdom under his control. Frederick believed he could
bring this about within the time frame of the treaty of S. Germano. The
plan did not seem unrealistic at first sight: his father had succeeded in
achieving this, as had Otto IV, who even had been surprised by the ease
with which his legate Wolfger of Aquileia had been able to subject that
traditionally unruly kingdom[38].

Frederick's first move was to call for a general diet of German and
Lombard princes, nobles, prelates, and representatives of the cities to be
convened at Cremona on Easter 1226[39]. The invitation to the diet disclosed only in very general terms what was to be discussed and decided
there: '*we hold a solemn diet about the support for and the expedition to the
Holy Land and about the honour and the reform of the state of the Empire*'
was all it said[40]. The references to the 'honour of the Empire' (*honor
imperii*) and the 'reform of the Empire' (*reformatio imperii*) sounded
very suspicious in many Lombard cities. The last emperor to have raised
these topics was Frederick's grandfather, Frederick I 'Barbarossa', and
the Lombard cities had fought long and hard to prevent Barbarossa's
'reform' from materializing, as their governors were to remind them.
Practically all 13th-century Lombard cities had ceased to be governed
by annually elected local *consules*, but were managed by a professional
administrator, a *podestà*, more often than not a lawyer, from outside
the city who contracted with the city to administer justice and oversee city politics for a year at a high salary. They brought their own
staff of professionally trained lawyers with them and usually travelled

*Frederick II
turns his
attention to
Lombardy*

---

38 See *supra* p. 171 and 175.
39 Ryccardus de S. Germano, *Chronica* ad ann. 1225, *RIS*² 7.2, 121, r. col: '*Tunc imperator ipse principibus Alamanniae, ducibus, comitibus et potestatibus Lombardie per suas mandat
litteras, ut in futuro pascha resurrectionis Domini apud Cremonam ad eum convenire deberent*'.
The text of the letter of invitation is in the extended version of Ryccardus's *Chronica*, *RIS*² 7.2,
Bologna 1936-1938, 125-126, l. col.
40 Ryccardus's *Chronica*, *RIS*² 7.2, 126, l. col.: '*pro succursu et itinere terre <sancte>, pro
honore quoque et reformatione status imperii solempnem curiam celebramus*'. See also *Chronica
regia coloniensis* ad ann. 1226, MGH *SS rer. Germ.* 18, 258: '*pro statu imperii reformando et
negotiis terre sancte*'.

to another city after their term of office[41]. These were men who knew what was going on in the world and they will certainly have taken good notice of how Frederick II had just 'reformed' his Sicilian kingdom in the 'Assizes of Capua': there were no autonomous cities left in that kingdom[42]. No wonder, therefore, that the Lombard cities requested a confirmation of their special status under the Peace of Konstanz[43]. Frederick reacted in his typical oblique way by making his confirmation of the Lombard privileges subject to a condition precedent: *'if you have satisfied fully the grace of the emperor and have given hostages'*[44]. This was very disconcerting: Milan especially was concerned. The Milanese had hunted Frederick II like a wild animal in 1212[45], supported Otto IV until the last on the Fourth Lateran Council[46], and consequently expected little sympathy from Frederick II. The Lombard apprehension was intensified as soon as news reached the cities there that the emperor had raised a Sicilian army to accompany him to Cremona[47] and that Frederick expected a considerable military force from Germany to arrive at Cremona as well, commanded by his son Henry (VII). What were the plans of the emperor with this combined force of German and Sicilian troops in Lombardy[48]? The Milanese decided to act before it

---

41   A good example is Rambertino Guido Buvalelli from Bologna (†1221). He had studied law in his native city and travelled around Lombardy for some time as a wandering poet and troubadour, for example at the court of Azzo VI d'Este (see *supra* p. 184, fnt. 73). After he had hung his harp upon the willows, Rambertino started an impressive career as a professional city administrator. He was *podestà* in Milan, Parma, Modena, Mantua, Genova and Verona. He is highly praised for his governance of Genova in the chronicle of Genova by the Genovese notary Marchisio (*fl.* 1220-1224) *Annales Ianuenses* ad ann. 1220, MGH *SS* 18, 142. The proliferation of city-government by a 'podestà' is one of the main causes, if not the main cause, of the reception of Roman law in the secular law courts of Lombardy, the Romagna and Tuscany. When the 'podestà' was not an experienced civilian himself, he had trained civilians in his personal staff, assisting him in his administration of justice.
42   See *supra* p. 223.
43   See *supra* p. 135
44   *Chronicon Faventinum* ad ann. 1226, ed. Rossini, *RIS* 28.1, Bologna 1936-39, 156: 'The governors of Lombardy, remembering all the bad things that had happened in the past and wanting to prevent worse to happen in the future, called on the emperor at once to renew the privileges that had been granted at Konstanz, to which he replied: "I will renew them, if you have fully satisfied the grace of the emperor and have given hostages"' (*Ilico rectores Lombardie mala recolentes preterita volentes futura vitare deteriora, una ad imperatorem privilegia, que aput Constanciam facta fuerant, reformare clamaverunt; quibus protulit: "Cum plenarie imperialem habebitis gratiam, nobis datis obsidibus, reformabo"*).
45   See *supra* p. 191.
46   See *supra* p. 208.
47   Ryccardus de S. Germano, *Chronica* ad ann. 1226, *RIS²* 7.2, 135, r. col: '*Imperator ipse baronibus et militibus infeudatis ceteris mandat, ut omnes se preparent ad eundum secum in Lombardiam*'.
48   A separate, second invitation to attend the diet at Cremona addressed to the *podestà* and citizens of Viterbo was sent by Frederick while he was already on his way to Lombardy,

was too late. They renewed the old Lombard League (5 March 1226)[49] and at once blocked the northern access to the Lombard plain, the 'Chiusa di Verona', a narrow passage through the mountains in the valley of the Adige at the end of the Brenner Pass. When Henry (VII) arrived there with his German army, he was unable to advance and forced to retreat[50]. Frederick was furious. He had not met with adversities like this before and opted for the nuclear option immediately, the very same option Pope Honorius had been so hesitant to choose in his own case: Frederick had the Lombard League excommunicated by his German and Sicilian prelates for obstructing the crusade he was planning[51] and withdrew all the privileges they had been granted in the Peace of Konstanz[52]. It was a declaration of war.

The decision of Frederick II to concentrate a great combined German-Sicilian army in Lombardy also worried the Roman *curia*, even more so since Frederick led his Sicilian army right across papal territory, the duchy of Spoleto which he had recently 'restored' to the pope[53]. When Honorius III heard that Frederick was raising troops there as well, the old man flew into a rage. It was the incident referred to earlier[54], when all the pent-up rage, frustration, and rancour from

His failure to reform the Italian kingdom

---

probably from Spoleto. It does not mention the crusade at all, but focusses on the deplorable state of the Italian kingdom and concludes as follows (HB 2.1, 548-549(549)): 'Consequently, desiring to reform the rights of the Empire to the best condition, and sympathizing with the oppression of the subjects, we have on the advice of the princes of our court convened a solemn diet to be held on Easter next at Cremona' (*Volentes igitur jura imperii in statum optimum reformare, subditorumque oppressionem condolentes, apud Cremonam, proximo die festivitatis Resurrectionis dominice nunc instantis, de consilio principum palatinorum solemnem indiximus curiam celebrandam*). It justifies the assessment that Frederick's primary concern was political 'reform' in the Italian kingdom rather than his upcoming crusade.

49 The new Lombard League consisted of the cities Milan, Verona, Piacenza, Vercelli, Lodi, Alessandria, Treviso, Padua, Vicenza, Torino, Novara, Mantua, Brescia, Bologna, and Faenza (Ryccardus de S. Germano, *Chronica* ad ann. 1226, *RIS²* 7.2, 137, r. col).

50 Ryccardus de S. Germano, *Chronica* ad ann. 1226, *RIS²* 7.2, 137 and 138, r. col: '*Tunc Henricus rex Alamannie cum copioso exercitu suo venit usque Veronam, set Lombardis impedientibus, ultra procedere non est permissus ... Tunc predictus Alamannie rex ... in Alamanniam redit cum suis*'.

51 For the excommunication of the Lombard League see MGH *Const*. 2, no 105, 132-134, mentioning (132-133) Milan, Brescia, Mantua, Verona, Treviso, Padua, Vercelli, Bologna, Faenza, Piacenza, and Alexandria.

52 MGH, *Const*. 2, no 107, 139: 'We have deprived all aforementioned cities and their citizens of everything they might resort to, collectively and individually, on account of the Peace of Konstanz ... and also that they are not allowed to make by-laws and the ones they have made we declare null and void and that, if they are to make them in the future, they shall be deemed void and of no effect' (*Privavimus sententialiter civitates predictas et cives earum omnibus, que possent eis ex pace Constantie universis et singulis provenire ... Item quod statuta non fatiant et facta cassavimus, et quod, si de cetero fecerint, ipso iure inania et irrita censeantur*).

53 See *supra* p. 194.

54 P. 157, fnt. 44.

the recent and distant past exploded from both sides in a unprecedently bitter exchange of letters between Honorius III and Frederick II. In the end, Frederick succeeded in appeasing the pope, who wanted to avoid war in Lombardy at all costs since it would stand in the way of the crusade. Honorius convened a conference in Rome to broker a peace between the Lombard League and Frederick II. The Lega sent ambassadors and Frederick sent Hermann of Salza, the grandmaster of the Teutonic Order, one of his closest collaborators and advisors[55]. In November 1226 they reached an agreement: the emperor lifted all sanctions against the Lega and the Lega promised to keep the peace in Lombardy and the Romagna and to put 400 knights at the disposal of the emperor for the duration of two years, to be put into service in the coming crusade[56]. By the time this agreement was concluded, Frederick was already back in his Sicilian kingdom. His first attempt at 'reforming' the Italian kingdom had completely failed, and his opponents had not only been forewarned by this failure, but also discovered his ultimate objective and the fundamental weakness in his strategy. The union of the Sicilian kingdom and the German Empire had been the grand strategy of Frederick's grandfather Barbarossa. He had failed to achieve that goal by war but had succeeded by diplomacy. Frederick's grand strategy was to unite the two great kingdoms on the Italian peninsula, the Italian kingdom and the kingdom of Sicily, by force of arms, since without control over the Italian kingdom, the union of the German Empire and the Sicilian kingdom was insecure. His failed campaign in Lombardy had revealed that weakness, since it had established that the union of two great armies from Germany and Sicily could be literally blocked by the Lombard League at the 'Chiusa di Verona', making the Lombard League the natural ally of the pope if he came into conflict with Frederick II, as it had been in the days of Alexander III. There are clear signs that members of the *curia* were already preparing for that

---

55 Hermann of Salza (*c.* 1175-1239) was grandmaster of the Teutonic Order (*Ordo Theutonicorum* (OT)) since 1209. The 'Friars of the House of Holy Mary of the Germans' (*Fratres Domus S. Mariae Theutonicorum*), as they were officially called, were recognized as a distinct military order by Innocent III in 1199. The members were mostly of 'ministerial' status, as was Hermann himself. He was part of Frederick's close entourage since 1216. He was consulted on all important occasions and sent on the most important diplomatic missions.
56 Ryccardus de S. Germano, *Chronica* ad ann. 1226, *RIS²* 7.2, 139, r. col.: *'Mense Novembris Reginus et Tyrensis archiepiscopi cum magistro domus Alamannorum a cesare mittuntur ad papam pro compositione inter ipsum et Lombardos facienda. Inter quos, mediante papa, facta est in hunc modum: quod imperator generaliter remittit omnibus predictis civitatibus, legatis presentibus ibidem, et ipsi pro parte civitatum iuraverunt pacem inter se invicem observare, et denuo committere cum domno imperatore milites 400 ad subsidium terre sancte in transfretatione sua'.*

contingency, since we know that it was the ubiquitous papal agent, master Alatrinus, who reactivated the Lombard League in 1226[57].

Honorius III died on 18 March 1227. He was succeeded by Cardinal Ugolino, who took the name Gregory IX[58], a reference no doubt to Gregory VII, to whom Honorius III had dedicated a biography. Gregory IX (1227-1241), like his uncle Innocent III, had studied theology in Paris and was educated in Roman and canon law (*utrumque ius*) in Bologna[59], but unlike his immediate predecessor he was not primarily a scholar, but a diplomat, administrator, and lawyer. He was a very old man by the standards of the time, in his seventies, but still invigorated with the energy and determination of Innocent III, a man who would not, like Honorius III, 'keep back his sword from blood' if it was called for. The indulgent policy of his predecessor must have frustrated the pope. His patience with Frederick II had already run out long before he ascended the throne of St Peter. Within a month after his consecration, he sent an urgent letter to Frederick II to make haste with his departure for the Holy Land[60]. Landgrave Ludwig of Thuringia, who had taken the cross, and the grandmaster of the Teutonic Order, Hermann of Salza, received similar orders[61]. Gregory made it very clear that the ultimate deadline fixed for Frederick's departure was August 1227 and that there were to be no more excuses, since failing to meet that deadline resulted in the excommunication of Frederick II by operation of law.

By the end of July, a great expeditionary force had gathered near Brindisi, where Frederick had mustered a large fleet to transport the crusaders to the Holy Land. It was an unfavourable season to amass so many people there and, as was to be expected, before long a contagious disease began to spread in the camp *'because of the bad air, which is dangerous for pilgrims and with which divine providence, the depth of which cannot be fathomed by man, by mysterious judgement has afflicted*

Gregory IX excommunicates Frederick II

---

57 Pope Honorius had sent Alatrinus to Lombardy in 1226 'at whose suggestion Milan and many connected cities conspired against the emperor, making an alliance, which has been called the Lombard League for a long time' (*Chronica regia coloniensis* ad ann. 1226, MGH *SS rer. Germ.* 18, 258, 'cuius suggestione Mediolanum et multe civitates complices contra imperatorem coniuraverunt, facientes collegium, quod Longobardorum societas per multa tempora est vocatum').
58 Ryccardus de S. Germano, *Chronica* ad ann. 1227, *RIS*² 7.2, 146: '*Mense Martii dictus Honorius papa obit xv. Kalendas aprilis et Hugolinus Ostiensis episcopus in papam Gregorium substitutus est illi*'.
59 Nicolaus Rosell (1314-1362), named 'the cardinal of Aragon' (*cardinal Aragonius*), in his biography of Gregory IX (*vita Greg.*) cap. 2, in *Liber censuum* 2, 18, r. col.: '*utriusque iuris peritia eminenter instructus*'.
60 MGH *Epp. saec. xiii* 1, no 351, 267-268.
61 MGH *Epp. saec. xiii* 1, no 353 and 354, 269.

various territories of the earth and especially our kingdom'[62]. The emperor and landgrave of Thuringia fell ill, but nevertheless decided to board ship. When the fleet reached the port of Otranto, at the extreme south of Apulia, hardly two days sailing after leaving Brindisi, the situation of the landgrave and the emperor had critically deteriorated. A war council was held, and it was decided that the emperor could not continue the voyage on account of his ill health and should not do so in the Sicilian national interest. The decision came too late for the landgrave. He died in Otranto. The ailing emperor stayed behind in Apulia, while the duke of Limburg and grandmaster Hermann took over command of the expedition. It was agreed that the emperor should follow later, in May next year[63]. Once again, Frederick II had missed a deadline for his departure for Palestine, but this time it was a fatal deadline. Unlike Honorius III, Gregory IX was not inclined to accept excuses. The emperor was declared an excommunicate on 29 September 1227 and on 10 October Gregory IX published a circular letter, an encyclical, explaining his reasons for doing so. He was convinced that the emperor had abused his crusading vows for years on end to put pressure on the *curia* to satisfy his own secular interests[64]. Frederick II immediately sent ambassadors to the pope to explain his reasons for postponing his departure, but Gregory refused to receive them[65].

---

62 Frederick II in MGH *Const.* 2, no 116, 152: '*De corruptela vero aeris, que nocuit peregrinis, per quam divina providentia, que previderi non potest ab homine, diversas mundi partes et regni nostri specialiter occulto iudicio flagellavit*'.
63 Events at Brindisi and Otranto have been taken from the report of Frederick II in MGH *Const.* 2, no 116, 152-153. Whether the emperor was really ill, or was just procrastinating again, is still a matter of debate. True as it may be that one cannot always (if ever) take Frederick II at his word, I see no reason to doubt his report. Serious outbreaks of life-threatening contagious diseases (such as cholera) were not infrequent in Apulia even as late as the 20th century, as the present author witnessed himself.
64 MGH *Epp. saec. xiii* 1, no 368, 282: 'He has, under the sign of the cross, fully and perfectly achieved all his own interests up till now' (*sub crucis vexillo usque ad hec tempora negotia propria plenius et perfectius consummavit*).
65 Ryccardus de S. Germano, *Chronica* ad ann. 1227, *RIS*² 7.2, 148: '*ad suam excusationem suos dirigit nuntios imperator, Reginum scilicet et Barensem archiepiscopos, Raynaldum dictum ducem Spoleti et comitem Henricum de Malta*' and Frederik II in MGH *Const.* 2, no 116, 153: '*dominus eosdem nuntios nostros recipere noluit nec audire*'.

16

Atonement

Frederick II immediately reacted to the encyclical letter of Gregory IX
informing the European public of the excommunication of the Roman
emperor. He issued a long encyclical letter himself[1], informing the
same audience how badly he had been treated by Gregory and his predecessors, now for the first time openly, albeit reluctantly[2], revealing
how much damage the misguided policy of Innocent III had caused to
his interests, culminating in the coronation of Otto IV, thus depriving
him of his rightful German throne[3]. The longest section of the letter
contains an extensive defence of his decision, or rather the resolution
of his council, to personally stay behind in Apulia rather than continue
his voyage to the Holy Land. At the same time, Frederick sent a letter
to the king of England, not only complaining about his excommunication, but principally warning that king for the highhanded policy
of the Roman pontiff and his officials, bishops and, especially, papal
legates. It was a wake-up call for the solidarity of European princes
against the encroachments on their secular powers by the Roman pontiff and his *curia*. He reminded King Henry III of the tribulations of
Count Raymond VI of Toulouse and of the misfortunes of his father,
King John, both excommunicated, humiliated, and deprived of their
principalities by a power-hungry Roman pontiff[4]. He also censured the
scandalous and notorious greed of the pope and his clerics: '*behold the
practices of the Romans, behold the snares of the prelates trying to entrap
each and every man, hunting for money and trying to subject free men and
to unsettle the peaceful, dressed up as sheep, while being rapacious wolves,
sending legates back and forth with powers to excommunicate, to suspend*

---

1   HB 3, 36-48; also in MGH *Const.* 2, no 116, 148-156.
2   HB 3, 37 (MGH *Const.* 2, no 116, 148): 'We speak reluctantly, but we cannot be silent'
(*Inviti loquimur, sed tacere nequivimus*).
3   See for Frederick's criticism of Innocent's guardianship during his minority *supra* p. 157.
4   See *supra* p. 201 and 195-196. The letter of Frederick to King Henry III is in HB 3, 48-50.
The text is from Matthew Paris, *Chronica maiora* ad ann. 1228, ed. Luard III, 151-153; Roger
of Wendover, *Flores Historiarum* ad ann. 1228, ed. Coxe IV, Londen 1842, 165-166, has an
excerpt.

and to punish, not in order to sow fruit-bearing seed, being the word of God, but to wheedle and scrape money, harvesting what they have never sown[5]. Frederick II touches upon an issue here that he was to repeat many times later on in his struggle with the papacy[6]: his insistence on church reform based on the ideal of the early Church, the *ecclesia primitiva*, when saintly apostles living in poverty and humility spread the word of the gospel rather than anathemas, earning him the sobriquet 'Hammer of the Church' (*malleus ecclesiae*)[7]. He concluded his letter with a reference to the Roman poet Horace: 'your own interest is at stake, when the house of your neighbour is on fire'[8].

Gregory reacted to Frederick's propaganda by having the emperor solemnly excommunicated once more at a synod held at Rome on 23 March 1228[9]. But Frederick did not shy away from intimidation either. Three days after the pope had once more publicly excommunicated the emperor, Gregory wanted to celebrate Easter in St Peter's but was accosted by a mob, incited by Frederick's Frangipani allies in Rome, and forced to leave the city. The pope did not return to Rome until two years later, residing in Perugia in the meantime[10]. In order to keep the Romans on his side, Frederick sent one of his top lawyers, Roffredo of Benevento, professor in his Naples law school, to Rome where Roffredo read Frederick's apology against Gregory's sentence of excommunication from the stairs of the Capitol with the approval of the Senate and the people of Rome[11].

Preparations of Frederick II for a new crusade

When Pope Gregory IX was leaving Rome, Archbishop Berardo of Palermo, Frederick's most trusted advisor, returned to Sicily from an important diplomatic mission to Egypt. He was accompanied by Emir Fakhr ad-Din ('the Glory of the Faith') Yusuf, advisor to Sultan

---

5   HB 3, 49-50: '*Ecce mores Romanorum, ecce laquei prelatorum, quibus universos ac singulos quaerunt illaqueare, nummos emungere, liberos subjugare, pacificos inquietare, in vestibus ovium, cum sint intrinsecus lupi rapaces, legatos huc et illuc mittentes, excommunicare, suspendere, punire potestatem habentes, non ut semen, id est verbum Dei, seminent fructificandum, sed ut pecuniam extorqueant, colligant, et metant quae numquam seminarunt*'. Comp. Matthew 25:24.
6   See also *infra* p. 357.
7   Matthew Paris, *Chronica maiora* ad ann. 1246, ed. H.R. Luard IV, 559.
8   Horace, *Epistulae* 1,18,84: *Tunc sua res agitur, paries cum proximus ardet.*
9   Gregory IX in a letter to the prelates of Apulia in HB 3, 52-55 (also in MGH *Epp. saec. xiii* 1, no 371, 288-289). See on this second excommunication also *infra* at p. 246-247.
10   On this incident see Burchard of Ursberg, *Chronicon* ad ann. 1227, MGH *SS rer. Germ.* 16, 124: '*cum papa rursus excommunicaret imperatorem, fecerunt <scl. Frangentes-panem>, ut a populo pelleretur turpiter extra civitatem, unde apud Perusium eo anno et sequenti ibi permansit*' and the *Vita Greg.* cap. 6, in *Liber censuum* 2, 20.
11   Ryccardus de S. Germano, *Chronica* ad ann. 1227, *RIS²* 7.2, 149: '*Tunc prudentem virum magistrum Roffridum de Benevento mittit ad Urbem cum excusatoriis suis, quas idem magister publice legi fecit in Capitolio, de voluntate senatus populique Romani*'.

Al-Kamil, bringing precious gifts for Frederick, an elephant among them[12]. It had been the object of Berardo's mission to open negotiations with the sultan about Frederick's coming crusade to the Holy Land. Never before in the history of the crusades had an expedition to the Holy Land been planned and coordinated in advance with a Muslim sultan. It confirms not only that Frederick wanted to go ahead with the crusade to which he had committed himself, but also that his objectives were not primarily military, but chiefly political. They were threefold: firstly, he wanted to publicly invalidate Gregory's reproaches by personally leading an army to the Holy Land; secondly, he intended to take possession of the prestigious kingdom of Jerusalem on behalf of his son Conrad, who had inherited the title of his recently deceased mother Isabella;[13] and thirdly, he wished to reopen the way to Jerusalem and other holy places in Palestine, such as Bethlehem and Nazareth, to Christian pilgrims. Frederick knew that the Egyptian sultan had twice offered to restore Jerusalem to the crusaders in Damietta, an offer unwisely rejected by the papal legate, Cardinal Gaytàn[14]. The emperor was curious to know whether that offer was still negotiable, and it turned out that it was. Al-Kamil had a good reason of his own to be compliant once again, because he happened to be engaged in civil war with his brother Al-Mu'azzam, emir of Syria. Since Jerusalem belonged to the domain of Al-Mu'azzam, Al-Kamil hoped that he could join his forces with Frederick's crusading army and thus conquer Syria. Frederick was more than ready to assist the sultan, with Jerusalem, Bethlehem, and Nazareth as his price. It seems a rather cynical plan to use a crusade as a means to settle an internal Arab conflict on the one hand and to restore the reputation of a Christian emperor on the other, but it was sound politics. When Frederick finally embarked on his 'crusade', the sixth, in June 1228, he was fairly certain he would achieve a result that would, once again, confirm his reputation as 'the wonder of the world' (*stupor mundi*). Before his departure, he arranged for his succession in

---

12 Ryccardus de S. Germano, *Chronica* ad ann. 1228, *RIS²* 7.2, 149: *'Archiepiscopus Panormitanus nuntius a Soldano ad Cesarem rediens, elephantem unum, mulos et pretiosa quedam alia munera ipsi imperatori detulit ex parte Soldani'*. For the presence of Fakhr ad-Din see the contemporary chronicle of Ibn Wasil (1208-1298) in F. Gabrieli, *Die Kreuzzüge aus arabischer Sicht*, Zürich 1973, 326 and the extract from the Arab historian Al-Maqrizi (1364-1442) ad ann. 624 (1227), in M. Amari, *Biblioteca Arabo-Sicula* II, Turin and Rome 1881, 260 (Italian translation) and the French summary in Michaud-Reinaud, *Bibiliothèque des Croisades* IV, Paris 1829, 427.
13 Queen Isabella of Jerusalem, Frederick's second wife, had died in childbirth on 25 April 1228; she was buried in Andria: *Breve chronicon de rebus siculis*, MGH *SS rer. Germ.* 77, 80. Of all Frederick's wives, only Constance of Aragon has been buried among the kings and queens of Sicily in the Cathedral of Palermo. It confirms the special relationship between Frederick and his first wife (see *supra* p. 163).
14 See *supra* p. 214-215.

the Empire and the Sicilian *regno*. The settlement confirms the assessment that he has never seriously contemplated to sever all ties between the Empire and the Sicilian kingdom. Despite all the solemn promises he had made to that end, he decided to appoint his oldest son Henry (VII) as his heir in the Empire *and* the Sicilian kingdom (*in imperio et regno*) and provided that his son Conrad would succeed if Henry (VII) might die childless[15]. In addition, Frederick appointed Rainald of Urslingen, the duke of Spoleto, as his representative (*legatus*) in the Marche of Ancona, thereby undoing all territorial concessions he had made to Innocent III and Honorius III[16]. According to Roman law, gifts were always granted under the implied condition subsequent that the grantee would not act ungratefully to the grantor[17] and Frederick contended that condition had occurred, allowing him to dispose at his pleasure of Spoleto, the Marche, and the other territories previously granted to the pope.

Frederick II in
the Holy Land

When Frederick II arrived in Acre, on 7 September 1228, the political situation in Palestine had changed considerably. The Emir Al-Mu'azzam had died unexpectedly, and Sultan Al-Kamil was now confident he could conquer Syria without the aid of Frederick's crusaders. He was in Palestine, near Nablus, with a considerable army, but negotiations continued nevertheless, not in the least because of the excellent personal relations between the negotiators, Archbishop Berardo, the Emir Fakhr ad-Din, and Frederick himself[18]. The relations between the crusading emperor and the other crusaders and clerics in Palestine, on the other hand, deteriorated rapidly, due to the intervention of Gregory IX. News of Frederick's excommunication had not yet reached Palestine at his arrival but was spread soon thereafter by two Franciscan monks carrying letters of Gregory addressed to Patriarch Gerold of Jerusalem. The pope instructed the patriarch to immediately publicize Frederick's

---

15   Ryccardus de S. Germano, *Chronica* ad ann. 1228, *RIS*² 7.2, 151: '*Imperator regni prelatis et magnatibus coram se apud Barolum congregatis, … proponi fecit et legi subscripta capitula in modum testamenti: ut … si deficere imperatorem contingeret, sibi in imperio et regno succederet Henricus filius eius maior: quod si illum absque liberis mori contingeret, Chunradus filius eius minor succederet illi*'.

16   See the charter in HB 3, 65, also in MGH, *Const* 2, no 117, 156.

17   C. 8,55(56),10.

18   There were no linguistic problems, since Frederick was fluent in Arabic, one of the many languages spoken in Sicily. The emperor was a polyglot, fluent in Italian, Greek, and Latin as well. He wrote poetry in the Sicilian Italian dialect and his scientific treatise *De arte venandi cum avibus*, a genuine ornithological study, in Latin. He may even have had a grasp of Hebrew too. In addition, he must also have spoken German, a language he may have learned during his stay in Germany between 1212 and 1220. There were very few Germans among his Sicilian entourage though; Grandmaster Hermann of Salza and Count Raynald of Urslingen were among the exceptions.

excommunication and to forbid all military orders, the Templars, the Knights of St John, and the Teutonic Order, to support or otherwise get involved with the excommunicate Frederick[19]. The result was a disastrous division in the army since the German and Sicilian knights, as well as the Knights of the Teutonic Order, remained loyal to Frederick and continued to accept his overall command, despite his excommunication. The estrangement between the emperor and the other two military orders rapidly turned into outright hostility. The Templars and the Knights of St John were shocked to see the leader of a crusading army openly and friendly receiving the Arab envoys of Sultan Al-Kamil without letting them join the ongoing negotiations[20]. The patriarch of Jerusalem, for his part, missed no opportunity to frustrate Frederick II in all his endeavours. At the same time, news began to reach Frederick that Gregory IX planned an invasion of his Sicilian kingdom[21]. It is, therefore, a miracle that Frederick achieved to conclude a treaty with Al-Kamil, who was well informed of the discord among the crusaders, despite all this. On 18 February 1229 a treaty was sworn to between Frederick II and Al-Kamil, agreeing to a ten-year truce and the transfer of Jerusalem, Nazareth, and Bethlehem to the emperor, including a corridor from the Christian coastal cities to Jerusalem[22]. It is a unique treaty designed to promote peace at considerable personal cost to both princes concerned, since not everyone, Muslim and Christian, agreed with it[23].

---

19 *Estoire d'Eracles* 33,5 (*Recueil des Historiens des Croisades, Historiens Occidentaux* 2, Paris 1859, 370): '*Et tant come li empereres estoit herbergé a Ricordane, dui frere Menor vindrent a Acre de par l'Apostoile, qui apporterent letres au patriarche de Jerusalem. En quoi il manda qui il feist denoncier l'empereor Fedric por escomenié et parjur, et que il deffendist au Temple et a l'Ospital de Saint Johan et a celui des Alemans que il ne fussent en son commandement ne riens ne feissent por lui*'.

20 Michaud-Reinaud, *Bibiliothèque des Croisades* IV, 429; *Estoire d'Eracles* 33,4 (*Recueil des Historiens des Croisades, Historiens Occidentaux* 2, 369); *Breve chronicon de rebus siculis*, MGH SS rer. Germ. 77, 88. The Templars and the Knights of St John even went as far as to secretly inform Al-Kamil of a good opportunity to capture or even kill Frederick II. The sultan was shocked by this and conveyed their message to Frederick, who now knew, if he did not already know before, what he was up against. See for this incident Matthew Paris, *Chronica maiora* ad ann. 1229, ed. H.R. Luard III, 177-179). It is confirmed by independent Arab sources: Michaud-Reinaud, *Bibiliothèque des Croisades* IV, 429.

21 See *infra* p. 241-242.

22 The text of Frederick's famous treaty with Al-Kamil has come down to us only fragmentarily from a letter of Patriarch Gerold to Gregory IX in a French version, with additional comments by Gerold in Latin. It is printed without Gerold's comments in MGH *Const.* 2, no 120, 160-161 and with his comments in MGH *Epp. saec. xiii* 1, no 380, 296-298. Frederick himself gives a short summary in an encyclical letter of 18 March 1229, MGH *Const.* 2 no 122, 162-167 (165).

23 The status of Jerusalem was as problematic as it is now, since 'Al-Quds' ('the Holy Place') is sacred to Muslims as well as to Christians and Jews. On the Temple Mount are the Dome of the Rock and the Al-Aqsa mosque, sacred buildings in the Muslim tradition. Consequently,

Frederick II
in Jerusalem

After securing free entrance for all Christian pilgrims to Jerusalem, Frederick entered the Holy City on 17 March 1229, where he visited the Church of the Holy Sepulchre but was also shown around the Temple Mount by the imam of the Al-Aqsa mosque and the Emir Schems ed-Din, the qadi of Nablus[24]. On the next day, a Sunday, mass was to be celebrated in the Church of the Holy Sepulchre. Grandmaster Hermann of Salza had advised the emperor not to participate, since he was still an excommunicate, but Frederick did appear in church after mass. He advanced to the altar, took a crown deposited there for him to take, put it on his head, and took his seat on a throne[25]. From there, he delivered an oration in Italian, which was translated in Latin and German by Grandmaster Hermann of Salza immediately afterwards. Now that his crusade had come to a close with the surrender of Jerusalem and other holy places to Christianity, Frederick took the opportunity to justify his

---

they were excluded from the transfer of Jerusalem to Frederick in Art. 2 of the treaty: Christians had no access. This was completely unacceptable to the Christian clerics and especially to the Templars. It was outrageous to Patriarch Gerold since the the muezzin was still to be heard in the place where Christ had suffered. See his comment on Art. 2 (MGH *Epp. saec. xiii* 1, no 380, 297): 'this is manifestly outrageous and does not need further comment. It is a covenant between Christ and the devil' (*Haec est abusio manifesta que expositione non indiget, hec est conventio Christi ad Belial*), referring to 2 Corinthians 6:15 ('what concord has Christ with Belial?'). Conversely, the release of Jerusalem was equally unacceptable to many contemporary Muslims. See the Arab criticism of the treaty in Michaud-Reinaud, *Bibiliothèque des Croisades* IV, 433-435 and F. Gabrieli, *Die Kreuzzüge aus arabischer Sicht*, 329 and 332.

24   The imam left a famous eyewitness-account of Frederick's visit to these holy places, with a very unfavourable description of Frederick's appearance. He mentions that, when the time for midday-prayer had come, the emperor allowed the Muslims among his attendants to participate, including his old teacher in mathematics. See Michaud-Reinaud, *Bibiliothèque des Croisades* IV, 430-432 and F. Gabrieli, *Die Kreuzzüge aus arabischer Sicht*, 333-334.

25   Frederick's conduct on this occasion is the subject of an unending debate among historians. Frederick is supposed to have boldly crowned himself king of Jerusalem without the interference of the clergy (*sine consecratione*). True as it may be that Frederick always styled himself 'king of Jerusalem' (*Iherusalem rex*) after his marriage to Isabella of Jerusalem, as John of Brienne had done after his marriage to Isabella's mother, Frederick was not king of Jerusalem at the time. After the death of Queen Isabella, her son with Frederick, Conrad, was king of Jerusalem. Frederick acknowledged this, since he had *not* made arrangements for the succession to the kingdom of Jerusalem at his departure from Sicily in 1228 (see *supra* p. 238) as he had indeed done for the Empire and the Sicilian kingdom. It was not necessary, since his son Conrad was already king of Jerusalem. It is striking, moreover, that Patriarch Gerold was shocked by Frederick's appearance in church, but only because Frederick was an excommunicate, *not* because he crowned himself 'king of Jerusalem' without consecration. See his account of the occasion as reported by Matthew Paris, *Chronica maiora* ad ann. 1229, ed. H.R. Luard III, 180. Even Pope Gregory IX did not take offence, since he does *not* mention the 'coronation' among the many offences he accused Frederick of having committed during his stay in the Holy Land: see his letter to the princes of Europe of 18 July 1228 (MGH *Epp. saec. xiii* 1, no 397, 315-317). Gerold and the pope knew that European kings usually appeared 'under a crown' (*sub corona*) on solemn occasions. There was nothing unusual in this. The matter was, significantly, passed over in silence in the sentence of deposition of Frederick II.

conduct from the first day he took the cross in Aachen, back in 1215, until now. The reaction of the patriarch of Jerusalem was as predictable as it was perplexing to the pilgrims in Palestine: the city of Jerusalem and all holy places were placed under interdict[26], making the city and its holy places, inaccessible to Christians for so long, a prohibited area to all Christians again but this time on the authority of the Church itself. Frederick was disgusted and did not stay in Palestine for long after that. His presence in the Sicilian kingdom was urgently called for, since it had been invaded by an army raised by Pope Gregory IX. He took to the sea on 1 May, never to return to the Holy Land again[27].

Gregory IX invades the Sicilian kingdom

Naturally, Gregory IX did not acknowledge Frederick's treaty with Al-Kamil and declared it null and void. The emperor had misused the sword handed to him by the representative of Christ by not carrying it into battle, but shamefully surrendering it to the infidel, the enemy of Jesus Christ[28]. Now that sword had to be handed over to someone else, not to wield it in the Holy Land, but to wage war against the excommunicate emperor in his Sicilian kingdom. Ironically, it was John of Brienne, Frederick's onetime father-in-law, who was charged with the command of the army that was supposed to take possession of the Sicilian kingdom[29]. Frederick had forfeited his Sicilian fees due to

26 Hermann of Salza, MGH *Const.* 2, no 123, 168: '*Hiis ita peractis, venit die lune sequenti archiepiscopus Cesariensis missus a domino patriarcha et ecclesiam sancti Sepulchri et omnia loca sancta posuit sub interdicto*'. Crusading armies were always accompanied by large numbers of non-combatant pilgrims taking advantage of the army's protection. The presence of these crowds of militarily (and otherwise) useless people was a heavy burden on the combatant crusaders and greatly reduced their efficiency.

27 *Breve chronicon de rebus siculis*, MGH *SS rer. Germ.* 77, 92: 'the Emperor Frederick returned to Acre in April, where he heard that a papal army had invaded the Sicilian kingdom and occupied it all the way to Capua ... he took to the sea on the first day of May' (*imperator Fredericus mense aprilis supradicte indictionis reversus est in Acconensem civitatem, ubi audivit, quod papalis exercitus intraverat regnum Sicilie et usque Capuam totam terram occupaverat ... primo madii supradicte indictionis ... mare intravit*).

28 Gregorius IX to the European princes (18 juli 1228) in MGH *Epp. saec. xiii* 1, no 397, 315-317 (315): '*arma Christiane militie, gladii potestatem de altari beati Petri sumpti, ad vindictam malefactorum laudemque bonorum sibi a Christo per suum vicarium assignati, quo pacem Christi, fidem ecclesie defenderet et muniret, soldano Babilonie, inimico fidei, adversario Iesu Christi, cultori perditi Machometi, impudentissime resignavit*'.

29 Ryccardus de S. Germano, *Chronica* ad ann. 1228, *RIS*[2] 7.2, 152: '*tunc Iohannem quondam Iherosolimitanum regem, et Iohannem de Columpna cardinalem, cum copioso militari et pedestri exercitu dirigit contra eum*', meaning Frederick's *legatus*, Duke Raynald of Spoleto. See also Burchard of Ursberg, *Chronicon* ad ann. 1228, MGH *SS rer. Germ.* 16, 125: '*Papa vero captata occasione de absentia imperatoris copiosum exercitum destinavit in Apuliam*'. John of Brienne had been made commander in chief of the papal army in 1227: see the letter of Gregory IX to John in MGH *Epp. saec. xiii* 1, no 339, 257-258. Frederick and John of Brienne never had been on good terms ever since Frederick's marriage with John's stepdaughter Isabella. John accused Frederick of imprisoning his stepdaughter in a harem. He was probably right.

his excommunication and the pope was now free to repossess it in order to grant it to a worthier person.

History had taught that conquering South Italy was never an easy enterprise even for the best of commanders such as the old Saxon warrior Lothar III[30] and it was certainly not so for a pope. All military expeditions of Roman pontiffs into South Italy in the past invariably had ended in disaster[31]. The situation of Gregory IX was even more difficult than that of most of his predecessors entering upon a similar campaign since he could not rely on troops from Rome itself. The Romans had risen against their pope once more and had sent Gregory in exile to Perugia[32]. Even worse, the Romans were waging war on the cities in the neighbourhood that remained loyal to the pope, such as Viterbo. Consequently, the pope was dependent on help from outside the Papal State and gambled on the Lombard League to support him in his war against Frederick II. Unfortunately for Gregory, the League was unable to come to his aid since the Lombard cities happened to be fighting among themselves once again in 1229[33]. The pope had no choice but to raise an army mainly consisting of mercenaries, despite a canon of the Third Lateran Council explicitly forbidding the employment of mercenaries on pain of excommunication[34]. The money for these mercenaries had to be raised by the faithful all over Europe, clergy and laity alike, and whoever did not pay the taxes levied by Gregory for this special purpose was excommunicated[35]. It made Gregory IX extremely unpopular throughout Europe, all the more so since the money thus extorted from Christendom was employed for quite different purposes than a crusade, for not even Gregory IX could qualify the expedition into South Italy as such. The troops fighting for the pope there did not wear the cross but were under a banner bearing the sign of the papal keys.

---

30 See *supra* p. 34 and 35.
31 See *supra* p. 32, fnt. 19 and 35 and fnt. 28.
32 See *supra* p. 236.
33 In the Romagna, Bologna, a member of the League, and Modena were at war. Modena was assisted by Cremona and Parma, Bologna by a number of other cities in the Romagna and Lombardy, Milan and Piacenza among them. Bologna and its allies were heavily defeated on 5 September 1229 in the battle of S. Cesaro. Gregory IX had to broker peace between these cities first before he could hope for some support for his own war. In the end, he received some military assistance of but a few cities. On all this see Giovanni of Bazano (*c.* 1285-1363/1364), *Chronicon Mutinense* ad ann. 1229, *RIS²* 15.4 18-19.
34 Burchard of Ursberg, *Chronicon* ad ann. 1228, MGH *SS rer. Germ.* 16, 124: '*magnamque pecuniam erogavit militibus in soldum*'. For the general prohibition of the employment of mercenaries see can. 17 of the Third Lateran Council, Mansi 22, col. 232.
35 Roger of Wendover, *Flores Historiarum* ad ann. 1229, ed. Coxe IV, London 1842, 200-204.

It is unnecessary to go into the details of Gregory's expedition against the kingdom of Sicily[36], if only because it turned out as disastrous as all previous papal campaigns into South Italy. The turning point was the sudden arrival of Frederick II in Brindisi (10 June 1229). Frederick was able to recover all territory lost to the 'key troopers' in the previous months in no time. The cardinals with Gregory in Perugia must have held their breath since nothing prevented Frederick of joining his victorious forces with the rebellious Romans and turn against the papal territories or even the pope himself. There were already envoys from Rome with Frederick, congratulating him on his successes in his war against the papal army[37]. In the end, Gregory IX had no choice but to react positively to the attempts at mediation initiated by the grandmaster of the Teutonic Order, Hermann of Salza. It was at this juncture that Gregory and his cardinals decided to fundamentally rearrange the papal strategy in Italy.

Ever since the days of Alexander III the papal policy in Italy had rested on two pillars: an alliance with the Norman kings of Sicily and with the Lombard League. The purpose of the alliance was focused on a common enemy, the German Empire. The *unio regni ad imperium* had changed all that and Gregory IX was even more aware of this than all his cardinals. He had been the specialist in German *and* Lombard affairs during the reign of Innocent III and Honorius III and he realized the German Empire was no longer the enemy since the German princes had lost all interest in Italian affairs, leaving that to the Hohenstaufens as their private preserve[38]. Consequently, the danger to the Papal State had ceased to come from the north, but now came from the south, from the kingdom of Sicily. The union of the Italian and Sicilian kingdom threatened to turn the Italian peninsula into an autocratic state, potentially crushing all papal aspirations of secular power in Italy. Consequently, Gregory and the *curia* concentrated on strengthening their ties with the only ally left in Italy, the Lombard League. The problem was that this ally was, formally at least, a subject of the king of Italy who happened to be king of Sicily as well. Consequently, the new papal policy amounted to a deliberate and sustained interference with the internal affairs of the kingdom of Italy. The excuse the pope advanced for his constant meddling in Lombard politics was his desire to promote peace in Lombardy for the sake of the

Rearrangement of papal policy

---

36 See the report of the war in Ryccardus de S. Germano, *Chronica* ad ann. 1228 and 1229, *RIS² 7.2, 152-163*. The army was commanded by John of Brienne and the papal legate Cardinal Gaytàn, the same miserable twosome that had 'led' the fifth crusade.

37 Ryccardus de S. Germano, *Chronica* ad ann. 1228 and 1229, *RIS² 7.2, 163*: '*Tunc nobiles quidam Romani ad imperatorem aput Aquinum veniunt ex parte senatus Populique Romani; cum quo moram per triduum facientes, ad Urbem reversi sunt*'.

38 See *supra* p. 195.

crusade, since all crusaders (and pilgrims) heading for the Holy Land had to pass through Lombardy to reach one of the seaports on the Italian peninsula, Genoa, Pisa, Venice, Messina, or, preferably, Brindisi. The peace between the Lega and Frederick II mediated by Honorius III in 1226 is an example of this[39], and so is the peace between Bologna and Modena mediated by Gregory IX in 1229[40]. Unrest in Lombardy and the Romagna was not only caused by the constant petty wars between the cities but was also aggravated by serious social conflicts within the cities between the 'knights' (*milites*), the urban nobility and rich merchants who could afford to serve their city on horseback, and the 'foot-soldiers' (*pedites*) from the lower ranks of the urban population. The *pedites* were hit harder economically by the constant state of war the cities were in than the *milites*. They had to abandon their shops and trade, while receiving a smaller share in the spoils than the knights, whereas in battle their lives rather than those of the knights were at stake[41]. Consequently, the *pedites* started to organize themselves in 'societies of arms' (*societates armorum*) demanding more participation in city politics, until then dominated by the urban nobility and the local societies of merchants and bankers. This social conflict spread all over Lombardy between the end of the 12th and the middle of the 13th century and regularly involved extreme violence, as for example at Piacenza in 1219[42]. Gregory IX was familiar with these conflicts. He had mediated an internal peace between the warring parties in Bologna himself in 1221, while acting as papal legate in the Italian kingdom[43]. At the same time, an *imperial* legate was active in Lombardy as well, also trying to mediate peace between the warring parties in the cities. This was Bishop Conrad of Metz, who brokered a (provisional) peace

---

39   See *supra* p. 232.

40   See *supra* p. 242 in fnt. 33.

41   In medieval warfare knights were rarely killed in battle. If it happened, it was an unfortunate occupational hazard since knights used to be captured rather than killed to be ransomed later. Foot soldiers could not raise a ransom and were consequently killed in battle or beaten to death afterwards. After a battle it was usual for the victorious party to make up a list of all captured knights and assign them to the knights in the army who were thus rewarded for their service by the ransom which they received for the prisoners assigned to them. We still have the list made up after the battle of Bouvines. It is printed in MGH *SS* 26, 391-393. There is a similar list made up after the battle of Cortenuova (on which *infra* p. 286-287).

42   See *Annales Placentini Guelfi* ad ann. 1219 and 1220, MGH *SS* 18, 437-438.

43   *Annales Placentini Guelfi* ad ann. 1221, MGH *SS* 18, 438: 'Peace was made in the city of Bologna between the common people and the knights of the city by Ugolino, bishop of Ostia, cardinal of the Roman *curia* and legate for all of Italy' (*in civitate Bononie facta est concordia inter populum et eiusdem civitatis milites per domnum Ugolinum episcopum Ostensem Romane curie cardinalem et totius Italie legatum*). Comp. *Corpus Chronicorum Bononiensium* ad ann 1221, *RIS*² 18.2, 71 (Cron. Vill.)): 'In the same year Ugolino, the bishop of Ostia and legate of the pope, entered Bologna with the patriarch of Aquileia' (*eodem anno dominus Ugolinus Hostiense episcopus et legatus domini pape intravit Bononiam cum patriarcha Aquilee*).

between the *milites* and *pedites* of Piacenza in 1220[44]. Here we have a *papal* functionary, a legate, involved in the internal affairs of the kingdom of Italy alongside an *imperial* functionary charged with the very same mission. The king of Italy (Frederick II), or any other king, could not prevent a papal legate from entering his kingdom[45] and so had to accept the presence of a papal functionary constantly interfering with any conflict within his kingdom, including any conflict the emperor himself might have with the Lombard League or one of its members, thinly veiled as the promotion of peace on behalf of the crusade. It was unacceptable for Frederick II as a matter of principle, since it meant that he had to accept an arbitrator presumably partial to the League, as became abundantly clear during the negotiations leading up to the restoration of peace between Frederick and Pope Gregory.

To gain the confidence of the League, Gregory involved the Lombards in his negotiations with Frederick from the start. He gave his guarantee to the League that he would not make his peace with Frederick without consulting the League first[46], just as Alexander III had done in his conflict with Frederick 'Barbarossa'[47]. In doing so, Gregory had in

The Peace of
S. Germano

---

44   For Bishop Conrad's peace settlement in Piacenza of 29 October 1220 see Böhmer, *Acta imperii selecta*, Innsbruck 1870, no 945, 655-656. It did not end the conflicts in Piacenza conclusively though: see *infra* p. 284. As was to be expected, the feuding parties within the cities identified with one of the parties in the greater conflict on the Italian peninsula, the pope or the emperor, 'Guelphs' and 'Ghibellines'. There is no clear rule that the nobility chose the part of the emperor and the common people the part of the pope. In Piacenza they did, but only because Bishop Conrad made a settlement favouring the nobility, thus forcing the 'people's party' in the Guelph camp. In another city it could be the other way around.
45   There was, originally, only one European king who could: the king of Sicily. It had been provided in the Treaty of Benevento that the pope could only send a legate to Sicily with the permission of the king (see *supra* p. 101). That privilege had been revoked by Innocent III in his concordate with Constance of Sicily (see *supra* p. 188).
46   See a letter of Gregory IX to the governors of the League from 10 November 1229, sending a first peace proposal to the governors for their comments and advice (MGH *Epp. sel.* 4, no 3, 27): 'Since we have full confidence in your loyalty and devotion, we want to honour you as our special sons and have deemed it necessary that this document should be sent to you, so that we may proceed as we shall see fit in this matter according to the honour of God and the Church and their peace after taking your advice. This is why we ask your opinion by this papal letter and request that you, having taken due notice of it, do communicate your advice to us, being reassured that your mother the Church will never desert you, but will under all circumstances look after your peace and quiet, as she will for her own' (*Et quia de fide ac devotione vestra indubitatam fiduciam obtinentes vos intendimus tamquam speciales filios honorare, scriptum ipsum ad vos duximus transmittendum, ut vestro intellecto consilio secundum honorem Dei et ecclesie pacemque suorum procedamus in facto, sicut viderimus expedire. Ideoque dis(cretionem) v(estram) ro(gamus) et mo(nemus) at(tente), per a(postolica) s(cripta) mandantes, quatinus eo perspicaciter intellecto nobis vestrum consilium intimetis, scituri pro certo, quod ecclesia mater vestra numquam vos deseret, sed in omni statu quieti et paci vestre sicut sue studebit utiliter providere*).
47   See *supra* p. 111 and 128-129.

fact made the Lombard League a party to the negotiations about the lifting of its monarch's excommunication. Frederick was furious about this[48], but the negotiations continued, nevertheless. In July 1230 an agreement was reached, thanks to the intervention of some German ecclesiastical and secular princes[49]. The peace treaty is known as the 'Peace of S. Germano'[50], after the place where Frederick solemnly swore to meet the conditions for his absolution[51]. The terms of the Peace of S. Germano must be considered more closely, since they played an important role in Frederick's trial in Lyon[52].

Frederick had not only been excommunicated because he had passed the deadline set for his departure for the Holy Land, but for some additional reasons as well. He had also promised[53] to provide thousand knights and 150 ships and had agreed to deposit 100,000 ounces of gold as a security for his undertaking, to be spent for the use and benefit of the Holy Land if he failed to meet his primary obligation. According to the pope, the emperor had failed to meet these obligations also. But failing to meet the conditions of Frederick's covenant with the Cardinals Gualo and Gaytàn at S. Germano on 22 July 1225, was not the only sin for which Frederick had been excommunicated. In his solemn confirmation of Frederick's excommunication on March 23, 1228[54] the pope had added additional reasons, completely unrelated to Frederick's 1225 agreement with the cardinals at S. Germano[55]: Frederick had refused to allow the bishop of Tarento to take possession of his see; he had confiscated land and personal property belonging to the Templars and the Knights of St John in Sicily; he had divested Count Roger of Aquila of

---

48   See a letter of one of the mediators, Bishop Thomas of Capua, to Gregory IX from February 1230 (MGH *Epp. sel.* 4, no 10, 12-14 (13)): 'Furthermore, even before I returned to the kingdom, he <*i.e.* Frederick II> has found out that waiting for an answer from the Lombards has delayed the reconciliation. He has taken that very badly and considered it a mockery and an insult' (*Porro presenserat, antequam Regnum intrarem, quod responsi expectatio Lonbardorum reconciliationem suspendebat ipsius; hoc procul dubio grave tulit, hoc ad illusionem retulit et contemptum*).
49   See *infra* p. 247-248.
50   All documents relating to the Peace of S. Germano have been collected and edited by K. Hampe in MGH *Epp. Sel.* 4, 'Die Aktenstücke zum Frieden von S. Germano 1230'.
51   As a matter of course, Frederick II did not swear himself: a prince cannot swear that he will act in good faith, since he is always supposed to act in good faith. The oath was taken, on Frederick's behalf (*in anima sua*), by Thomas of Aquino, the count of Acerra, one of Frederick's closest confidants.
52   See *infra* p. 378.
53   For this agreement see *supra* p. 227.
54   See *supra* p. 236.
55   For the additional reasons for Frederick's excommunication see the letter of Gregory IX to the prelates of Apulia from March 1228 in HB 3, 52-55, also in MGH *Epp. saec. xiii* 1, no 371, 288-289 and Gregory's letter to the excommunicate Frederick, written late in 1227, in HB 3, 32-34, also in MGH *Epp. saec. xiii* 1, no 370, 286-287.

his fee, although Roger had taken the cross and consequently was under the special protection of the Apostolic See; he had imprisoned Roger's son and failed to release him, in spite of frequent requests by the pope to do so; he had failed to keep his compromise with two Sicilian nobles, Count Thomas of Celano and Count Rainald of Aversa, on behalf of whom the pope himself had interceded[56]. Frederick had also unsuccessfully been summoned by the pope to desist from his (unspecified) oppression of Sicilian monasteries and churches. It was a long list of sins, for all of which Frederick had to atone before receiving absolution. But there were other conditions as well, political conditions[57], first and foremost a general amnesty for all subjects of Frederick in Germany, Lombardy, and the Sicilian kingdom having sided with the pope during Frederick's excommunication; Frederick had to promise not to raise taxes from the clergy in the Sicilian kingdom, and, furthermore, that no Sicilian cleric was to be summoned before a Sicilian secular court. On top of all this, he was to restore all territory occupied by his forces in the Marche of Ancona and the duchy of Spoleto and had to abandon the last of all the old ecclesiastical privileges of the kings of Sicily granted in the Treaty of Benevento, the right of approval (*assensus*) of episcopal elections within the kingdom.

When viewed from a distance of almost eight hundred years, it seems as if the papal demands were completely unrealistic. The pope had been thoroughly defeated in his Sicilian campaign, but dictated the peace terms as if he had been victorious. Out of touch with reality as he may seem to a modern observer, the pope was not so according to the standards of his time. The fact is that at this time and age the Roman pontiff had become practically *sacrosanctus*, 'untouchable', meaning that Frederick II did not have the option his grandfather still had, or rather believed he still had, *i.e.* to simply arrest the pope and to substitute another in his place. Frederick II never even considered the possibility of replacing Gregory IX (or Innocent IV) by another, more compliant, pope[58]. He did not do so, even though he must have known that the pope was trying to sow unrest in his German kingdom at the time by sounding if Otto of Brunswick (1204-1252), a nephew of Otto IV

The decisive role of the German princes

---

56 Needless to say, the three counts just mentioned belonged to the nobility resisting Frederick's reforms in the Sicilian kingdom.
57 For all of these conditions see *infra* p. 248, fnt. 63.
58 Frederick must also have realized that by arresting the pope he would have disrupted his important diplomatic ties with the king of France and other European monarchs. He would have completely isolated himself diplomatically and consequently the option was out of the question.

and the only male representative of the house of Guelph still alive[59], was willing to rise against the despicable house of Hohenstaufen[60]. The attempt was unsuccessful, but the prospect of a possible civil war in Germany because of Frederick's excommunication must have stirred the German princes into action. In March 1230 a delegation of German princes, secular and ecclesiastical, arrived in Italy 'to conclude peace' (*pro tractanda pace*)[61]. It was largely thanks to their intervention that a peace agreement finally was reached consisting of Frederick's complete submission to all demands of Gregory IX, including the additional political concessions on which the pope had insisted. The German princes personally guaranteed that Frederick would observe all conditions imposed on him. And so it happened that the count of Acerra, Thomas of Aquino, swore on behalf of the emperor on 23 July that his lord would submit to the pope 'for everything for which we have been excommunicated' (*pro omnibus pro quibus excommunicati sumus*)[62]. The additional political concessions were documented separately, some of them later in the week[63]. For a naïve observer it seems as if Frederick II had won the war and lost the peace, but for a true appreciation of

---

59   Otto of Brunswick was the only son and heir of another son of Henry the Lion, William of Winchester (1184-1213). William was married to Helena, a sister of King Canute VI of Denmark.

60   In 1228 Pope Gregory IX sent Cardinal Odo of Montferrat as his legate to Germany and Denmark in order to initiate a rising against Frederick II in Germany and to try to win Otto of Brunswick over to his side. Otto flatly refused and thus prevented a civil war in Germany (*Chronica regia coloniensis continuatio 4*, ad ann. 1228, MGH *SS rer. Germ.* 18, 260-261): '*Otto cardinalis de Carcere Tulliano, legatione accepta, Theutoniam et Daciam mittitur; cuius intentio erat imperatoris gravamen procurare et super hoc consilium expetere Ottonis dicti ducis de Lunimburg. Sed idem Otto contra imperatorem rennuit aliquid attemptare*'. Otto of Brunswick was royally rewarded for this by Frederick II later: see *infra* p. 278-279. On Cardinal Odo's mission in Germany, see also Conrad de Fabaria, *Casus s. Galli* (1203-1240) 16, MGH *SS* 2, 181: '*Romanus pontifex cardinalem misit ad machinationem discordie ac perturbacionis in regem et principes*'.

61   *Breve chronicon de rebus siculis*, MGH *SS rer. Germ.* 77, 94/96: '*Superveniente vero mense Martii patriarcha Aquilenus et archiepiscopus Salceburgensis cum episcopo Ratisponensi, qui postea factus est fuit imperii cancellarius, et dux Austriae cum duce Maraniae et duce Caruntiae pro tractanda pace inter apostolicam ecclesdiam et imperatorem venerunt*'. According to the chronicle of Burchard of Ursberg (*Chronicon* ad ann. 1230, MGH *SS rer. Germ.* 16, 127), who also mentions the six German princes just named, there were also more mediators from Italy, Germany, and even from the papal *curia* itself (*multis aliis quoque mediantibus, tam de curia Romana, quam etiam Italia et Alemannia*).

62   MGH *Const.* 2, no 127, 171 = MGH *Epp. Sel.* 4, III.1, 57.

63   MGH *Epp. Sel.* 4, III.2, 58. (general amnesty); MGH *Epp. Sel.* 4, III.10 and 11 (restitution of all territory occupied in the Marche and the duchy of Spoleto); MGH *Epp. Sel.* 4, III.12 (freedom of episcopal elections and concessions in the matter of Count Thomas of Celano and Count Rainald of Aversa; compensation and restitution of confiscated property to the Templars and the Knights of St John); MGH *Epp. Sel.* 4, III.15, 74 (fiscal immunity of the Sicilian clergy and no summons of the Sicilian clergy in a secular court).

the full extent of Frederick's diplomatic achievement in his difficult negotiations with the headstrong pope attention should be drawn to what is *not* in the Peace of S. Germano: the severance of all ties between the German Empire and the Sicilian kingdom as a condition to peace with the pope. Innocent III and Honorius III had been insisting on this time and again for years, but Gregory IX did not touch the issue at this occasion, distracted as he was by what were in fact minor problems compared to that great geopolitical challenge facing the papacy. After S. Germano, Frederick was formally recognized by the pope as Roman emperor *and* king of Sicily and he was, finally, released from his crusading vows.

On 28 August 1230 Frederick II and his court were solemnly readmitted to the community of the faithful in the chapel of Sª Giusta in the village of Ceprano[64]. Gregory decided to celebrate the event by inviting Frederick to his native town Anagni, where he resided at the time. The emperor and the pope had a private dinner and a long conversation together, with only Grandmaster Hermann of Salza present at the occasion[65]. It must have been a fascinating diner party since neither of the two participants will have entertained the vain illusion that a lasting peace had been established at S. Germano.

---

64 Ryccardus de S. Germano, *Chronica* ad ann. 1230, *RIS²* 7.2, 171: '*tunc imperator ipse in castris ante Ceperanum, in cappella sancte Iuste, die Mercurii in festo beati Augustini, per Sabinensem est episcopum ab excommunicationis vinculo absolutus. Similiter et omnes sui*'.
65 Ryccardus de S. Germano, *Chronica* ad ann. 1230, *RIS²* 7.2, 171: '*Mense Septembris, prima die mensis eiusdem, qui fuit dies dominicus, cesar invitatus a papa, cum esset in castris in pede Anagnie ... et eo die cum papa sedit in mensa, et solus cum solo, magistro tamen Teutonicorum presente, in papali camera, consilio longo se tenuere diu; et die lune sequenti cum gratia pape et cardinalium ad castra reversus est*'.

17

Competing Legislators

The Emperor

Only a few days after he left the pope in Anagni, Frederick II issued an order to the administrators of all provinces of the Sicilian kingdom instructing each one of them to select four wise men from his province, *'men who know the Assizes of our grandfather King Roger and the customs and habits, general as well as local, obtaining in the days of Roger and William II, our nephew of blessed memory, and send them to us without delay'*[1]. This is the first sign that Frederick wanted to implement a plan he must have had in mind ever since the Assizes of Capua, if not even earlier: the comprehensive codification of Sicilian royal law. His example were the Assizes of Ariano of his grandfather Roger II[2], but the size, the quality, and the ambition of Frederick's codification surpass that model by far. It is a project comparable only to Justinian's *Codex*. Frederick, now 35 years of age, had come at a point in his personal development where he wanted to rival one of his greatest predecessors as Roman emperor, the great Justinian, who had insisted that an emperor should not only excel in war (*armis*), but also by his legislation (*legi-*

Frederick II decides to codify Sicilian royal legislation

---

1 Winkelmann, *Acta imperii inedita seculi XIII*, vol. 1, Innsbruck 1880, no 761, 605: *'Mandamus et precipimus fidelitati vestre, quatenus quattuor de antiquioribus viris per unamquamque iurisdictionem vestram, qui tempore sint et scientia potiores, qui sciant assisas regis Rogeri avi nostri, usus quoque et consuetudines tempore Rogeri (et) Guillelmi secondi, consobrini nostri memorie recolende, generaliter in partibus ipsis obtentas, eligatis et ad nostrum presenciam sine dilacione qualibet destinetis'*. The text is an extract from the correspondence of Frederick II compiled in the imperial chancery. It has come down to us in a manuscript situated in Marseilles (hence the name *Excerpta Massiliniensia*). The extracts of the letters are not dated but the context of this fragment allows the conclusion that the original letter cannot have been written long after 1 September 1230. The original 'register' of Frederick's correspondence is lost. The archive of the medieval kings of Sicily was burned deliberately in 1943 by the German army as a reprisal. The Germans were not aware of the fact that in doing so they were destroying the correspondence of the man many Nazis (Himmler among them) regarded as the greatest German king and emperor.
2 See *supra* p. 221, fnt. 3.

bus)³. Frederick's code is important in the context of the charges that were brought against him at his trial in Lyon. Gregory IX and Innocent IV accused the emperor of being a heretic, if not an atheist⁴. He was neither and his codification testifies to that, not because it contains harsh legislation against all kinds of heresy⁵, but primarily because it stands out as a monument to his Christianity and as a token of his deep personal relation with God. It was a sentiment he shared with his grandfather Roger II. Roger's code was also inspired by Justinian's legislation and consequently he had added an introduction to his code as well, as Justinian had done with every part of his legislative projects, the *Codex*, the *Digest*, and the *Institutes*. Roger's introduction is unique in the history of European legislation since it offers one of the very first examples, if not the first example, of a medieval king presenting his kingship not as a private patrimonial *right*, but as a public *office*, comparable to the priestly office⁶, an office entrusted to the king directly by God, since 'By me kings reign and princes decree justice' (Proverbs 8:15)⁷. Frederick repeated this theme by also presenting his new code, as Roger had done, as a sacrifice '*to the living God, repaying the doubled talents he has credited to us, to the glory of Jesus Christ from whom we have received everything we have*'⁸.

---

3 Const. *Imperatoriam* pr.: '*Imperatoriam maiestatem non solum armis decoratam, sed etiam legibus oportet esse armatam, ut utrumque tempus et bellorum et pacis recte possit gubernari*'.

4 See *infra* p. 295 and 378.

5 For this see *LA* (*Liber augustalis*) 1,1-3. The best edition of Frederick's code is by W. Stürner, *Die Konstitutionen Friedrichs II. für das königreich Sizilien*, Hannover 1996 (MGH *Const.* 2, Suppl.); the best modern commentary is H. Dilcher, *Die sizilische Gesetzgebung Kaiser Friedrichs II.*, Cologne/Vienna 1975. There is an English translation of Frederick's code, edited by James M. Powell, Syracuse 1971.

6 I used the edition of Joh. Merkel, *Commentatio qua iuris Siculi sive assisarum regum regni Siciliae fragmenta ex codicibus manu scriptis proponuntur*, Halle 1856, 15-40 (15, Prologue): 'We believe that nothing is more agreeable to the Lord than that we present to him as a sacrifice that what we know him to be, to wit mercy and justice; by which sacrifice the kingly office aspires to the privilege of the priestly office, hence a wise man and a lawyer has called the lawyers priests' (*Nichil enim gratius Deo esse putamus, quam si id simpliciter offerimus, quod eum esse cognovimus, misericordiam scilicet atque justitiam: in qua oblatione regni officium quoddam sibi sacerdotii vendicat privilegium, unde quidam sapiens legisque peritus juris interpretes juris sacerdotes appellat*). Comp. D. 1,1,1,1 (Ulpian): '*merito quis nos sacerdotes appellet: iustitiam namque colimus et boni et aequi notitiam profitemur*'.

7 Assizes of Ariano, Prologue (ed. Merkel 15): '*Hoc enim ipsum, quod ait inspiramentum de munere ipsius largitoris accepimus, dicente ipso "Per me reges regnant et conditores legum decernunt iustitiam"*.'

8 *LA, Prooemium*, MGH *Const.* 2, Suppl., 147: '*volentes duplicata talenta nobis credita reddere Deo vivo in reverentiam Iesu Christi, a quo cuncta suscepimus, que habemus*'. Comp. Matthew 25:14-30.

The Introduction (*Prooemium*) to the code of royal law for the kingdom of Sicily issued by Frederick in 1231 is one of the most impressive legal documents of the Middle Ages. It is more theoretical in nature than any of Justinian's introductions since it contains Frederick's personal philosophy of law, or rather, to be more precise, his justification of legislation. That justification was based on a theological premise. Frederick relates how God had created the world and had shaped man in His image, how He had given him a companion in life and had endowed them with immortality. But He had done so 'by subjecting both to a certain law' (*ambo sub quadam lege precepti*) which they had disobeyed. As punishment for man's sin, God had withdrawn the gift of immortality, leaving descendants as heirs to the original sin of their predecessors. Because of their sinful nature, the descendants of the first man and woman fell into discord and hatred among themselves, dividing up the common ownership of property by natural law and creating disputes among men. '*Therefore, by this compelling necessity of things and no less by the inspiration of Divine Providence, princes of nations were created through whom the license of crimes might be corrected. And these judges of life and death for mankind might decide, as executors in some way of Divine Providence, how each man should have fortune, estate, and status. The king of kings and the prince of princes demands above all from their hands that they have the strength to render account perfectly of the stewardship committed to them*'[9]. This fragment from the *Prooemium*, written in the 'grand style' (*stilus supremus*) current in the Sicilian royal chancery and cultivated by Piero della Vigna, contains the core of Frederick's political philosophy. Kingship is not only a product of Divine Providence (*divina provisio*), but also of 'the necessity of things' (*rerum necessitas*). Kings are created by necessity to bring peace and justice (*pax et justitia*), two concepts 'embracing each other like two sisters', to mankind[10]. Kingship is therefore presented as an autonomous divine institution, independent of other institutions also inspired by Divine Providence, such as the Church: there had been emperors long before there were popes[11]. As with his grandfather, kingship was not

The king sole guarantor of peace and justice

---

9   *LA, Prooemium*, MGH *Const.* 2, Suppl., 147: '*Sicque ipsarum rerum necessitate cogente nec minus divine provisionis instinctu principes gentium sunt creati, per quos posset licentia scelerum coherceri; qui vite necisque arbitri gentibus, qualem quisque fortunam, sortem statumque haberet, velut executores quodammodo divine sententie stabilirent; de quorum manibus, ut villicationis sibi commisse perfecte valeant reddere rationem, a rege regum et principe principum … requiruntur*'. (English transl. James M. Powell).

10   *LA, Prooemium*, MGH *Const.* 2, Suppl., 147: '*principes gentium sunt creati … ut … pacem populis eisdemque pacificatis iustitiam, que velut due sorores se invicem amplexantur, pro posse conservent*'.

11   This argument had already been put forward by the famous canonist Huguccio († 1210), cited in the Gl. 'Ad regem' on X. 4,17,7: '*ante fuit imperium quam Apostolatus*'.

presented by Frederick as a private patrimonial right, but as an office, a stewardship (*villicatio*), entrusted by God to an individual accountable to God alone[12].

Legislation
his exclusive
domain

The essential part of the king's office is to pass laws to promote peace. It is emphasized in Frederick's code in a remarkable way, in one of the provisions partly copied from Justinian's codes: '*It is not without great foresight and wise deliberation that the Romans have conferred the right to issue laws and the sovereignty to the Roman emperor by the royal law*'[13]. The 'royal law' referred to here is the *lex regia* mentioned by the Roman lawyer Ulpian in Justinian's *Digest* as the constitutional basis of the sovereignty (*imperium*) of the emperor[14]. There is no contradiction between Frederick's theory on the divine origin of kingship and Ulpian's theory of the popular vote bestowing sovereignty on the emperor, since according to Frederick the *institution* of kingship is divine, but the way the functionary exercising kingship is called to that office may differ. It may be by election (as in the classical Roman and in the contemporary Romano-German Empire) or by hereditary succession (as in France and the Sicilian kingdom). Although this section in Frederick's code is of Justinian origin, it contains a significant extension of Justinian's quotation from Ulpian's *Institutes*. Whereas Ulpian (Justinian) merely states that the emperor derives only his *imperium*, his sovereignty, from the vote of the people, Frederick II makes it a twofold grant: the right to legislate *and* sovereignty (*condende legis ius* et *imperium*). He does so in order to emphasize that legislation is the exclusive prerogative of the

---

12 Gregory IX did not share Frederick's exalted theory of royal authority. He followed the cynical opinion of his great predecessor, papal namesake, and inspiration, Gregory VII, who had no regard for the ruling emperors, kings, and princes of the world at all: '*who does not know that kings and princes are the descendants of those who, ignoring God, by pride and malice, by plunder and murder, and by almost all heinous acts of the world, have been made so bold by blind greed and intolerable presumption as to rule over their equals, that is mankind, at the inspiration of the devil?*'(*Das Register Gregors VII.*, 8,21, MGH *Epp. sel.* 2,2, 552: '*Quis nesciat reges et duces ab iis habuisse principium, qui Deum ignorantes superbia rapinis perfidia homicidiis postremo universis pene sceleribus mundi principe diabolo videlicet agitante super pares, scilicet homines, dominari caeca cupidine et intollerabili presumptione affectaverunt?*'). Comp. Augustinus, *De civitate dei* 4,4: '*Remota itaque iustitia quid sint regna nisi magna latrocinia?*'.

13 *LA* 1,31, MGH *Const.* 2, Suppl.,185: '*Non sine grandi consilio et deliberatione perpensa condende legis ius et imperium in Romanum principem lege regia transtulere Quirites*'.

14 D. 1,4,1 (Ulpian, *libro primo Institutionum*): 'Everything that pleases the emperor has force of law, since the people have conferred to him and on him their entire sovereignty and power by the royal law that has been passed on his sovereignty' (*Quod principi placuit, legis habet vigorem: utpote cum lege regia, quae de imperio eius lata est, populus ei et in eum omne suum imperium et potestatem conferat*). Justinian was very pleased with this *dictum* of Ulpian: he repeated it twice, so that it appears in *every* part of his codification project. In the *Institutes* at Inst. 1,2,6 and in the *Codex* at C. 1,17,7.

emperor, as his grandfather Frederick I had done before him[15], thereby clarifying that the emperor was not just the *executive* branch of papal government over mankind, as he was according to the prevailing doctrine within the Roman *curia* at the time, but an autonomous and independent monarch exclusively commissioned by God to judge, legislate, and enforce his will parallel to the pope. It is a special insistence only comprehensible when put into the perspective of a remarkable incident occurring at Frederick's coronation as emperor in 1220[16].

The Emperor Frederick II receives a copy of his code of law
(*Liber augustalis*, Biblioteca Apostolica Vaticana, ms Reg.lat. 1948, *f. 4 r°*)

Pope Honorius III had instructed his agents negotiating with Frederick II in his camp near Monte Mario on the final conditions for his impending coronation to hand a document to Frederick containing a set of statutes composed in the papal chancery which he was to issue

The incident of the coronation statutes

---

15   See *supra* p. 77-81.
16   See *supra* p. 219.

immediately after his coronation as emperor[17]. Frederick complied and promulgated these statutes as imperial legislation on the day of his coronation[18]. The imperial statutes were sent to the law professors in Bologna with the instruction to insert them into their manuscripts of Justinian's *Codex*, just as had happened in the past with Barbarossa's *Authentica 'Habita'*[19], thus making them a part of European common law[20]. Frederick's letter to the Bolognese professors was accompanied by a separate letter of Honorius III, containing a recommendation *and* a confirmation of the statutes sent by Frederick: '*We, Bishop Honorius, servant of the servants of God, praise, approve, and confirm these statutes enacted by Frederick the emperor of the Romans for the benefit of all Christians*'[21]. Some of the statutes issued by Frederick II at his corona-

---

17 From the papal instruction to the negotiators (MGH *Const.* 2, no 83, 104): 'By the common advice of our brethren we do instruct you to strongly insist that the statutes we send you herewith enclosed shall be published, in the proper words and retaining their purport, as general legislation in the name of the king, and that they shall be sent to us, corroborated by the royal seal, to be published solemnly under the name of the emperor at the day of his coronation in the basilica of the prince of apostles' (*De communi fratrum nostrorum consilio vobis auctoritate mandamus, quatenus efficaciter studeatis, ut capitularia, que vobis mittimus presentibus inclusa, sub competentibus verbis, servata sententia, sub nomine regio in leges publicas redigantur nobisque mittantur regie bulle roborata munimine, in die coronationis sub imperiali nomine in basilica principis apostolorum solemniter publicanda*).
18 A substantial part of the coronation statutes consists of the confirmation of the third canon of the Fourth Lateran Council ('*Excommunicamus*', see *supra* p. 204) by secular legislation. Art. 7 of Frederick's coronation statutes largely copies '*Excommunicamus*', as is properly indicated in the edition in MGH *Const.* 2 no 85, 108-109. The numbering in this edition differs slightly (but rather confusingly) from the one in HB, since Art. 4 of the HB edition (HB 2.1, 2-6) is edited as Art. 4 and 5 in the MGH edition.
19 See *supra* p. 91.
20 From Frederick's letter to the professors accompanying a copy of the statutes sent to them (MGH *Const. F II* no 86, 110): 'On the day we received the imperial crown from the hands of our most Holy Father the pope, we have issued a number of statutes to the honour of God and his Holy Church that we have directed to be attached to the present letter, ordering you by this imperial letter to have them inserted into your copies of the *Codex* and that you have to read them henceforward as laws that will obtain for all time' (*Ad honorem Dei omnipotentis et ecclesie sancte sue in die, qua de manu sacratissimi patris nostri summi pontificis suscepimus imperii diadema, edidimus quasdam leges, quas presenti pagina fecimus adnotari, per imperialia vobis scripta mandantes, quatinus eas faciatis in vestris scribi codicibus et de cetero legatis solenpniter tamquam perpetuis temporibus valituras*).
21 Besides being inserted into the manuscripts of the Justinian *Codex* at the proper places separately as so-called '*authenticae*', Frederick's entire legislation issued at the day of his coronation was also inserted comprehensively into a separate part of the medieval manuscripts of Justinian's *Corpus Iuris Civilis*, the so-called *Volumen*, containing the last three books of the *Codex*, Justinian's *Institutes*, and some medieval sources of law, the *Libri Feudorum* and the *Pax Constantiae* among them. It is there that Honorius' confirmation is to be found as a closing section of Frederick's legislation of 20 November 1220: '*Nos vero Honorius episcopus servus servorum dei has leges a Friderico Romanorum imperatore filio nostro carissimo pro utilitate omnium Christianorum editas laudamus approbamus et confirmamus*'. It can also be found in P. Krüger's *editio minor* of Justinian's *Codex* (11th ed., Berlin 1954, 513).

tion were *also* inserted into the official collection of all decretals issued by Pope Honorius III in 1226, the so-called *Compilatio quinta*. The pope refers to them explicitly in his introduction to that collection. It contained, he wrote, decretals decided 'by us and our brethren (*per nos vel fratres nostros*) as well as decretals 'which we have ordered others to decide' (*quae aliis commissimus decidenda*)[22]. The whole incident must have been extremely offensive to Frederick, since it conveyed the impression that imperial legislation was to be regarded as subordinate legislation delegated by the pope to the executive branch of the papal monarchy, the emperor, and thus seemed to confirm the papal prerogative on general legislation as was once claimed by Gregory VII[23]. In forcing Frederick to issue legislation dictated by the papal chancery in his own name, Honorius III violated the intimacy of Frederick's highly personal relationship with God entitling him to bring his sacrifice to God, the law, at his own initiative and in his own right. The act of legislation was to him, as it had been to his grandfather Roger II, equivalent to the administering of a sacrament by a priest, or to an Old Testament priestly sacrifice[24]. Further on in his code he even works out a doctrine amounting to a true 'theology of legislation'.

According to Frederick II, the emperor, ordained by God, '*is the father as well as the son of justice, the master and the servant; father and master by issuing the law on the one hand and by maintaining it on the other; son and servant by reverencing the law on the one hand and by administering access to it on the other*'[25]. It has proved impossible to connect this quotation to any previous similar reflection on the mission of the prince as legislator. It is genuine Frederician doctrine, cast in the words and style of his ghost-writer Piero della Vigna, expressing a legal 'Holy Trinity' consisting of the father, the son, and the law emanating from the father and the son. Accordingly, Frederick ascribed a sacred meaning to the administration of justice by his judges, amounting to a genuine 'cult of

The Cult of Justice

---

22 From the introduction to the *Compilatio quinta*, E. Friedberg, *Quinque compilationes antiquae*, Leipzig 1882, 151.

23 The contention that only the pope was entitled to issue legislation was part of the famous *Dictatus Papae* of Gregory VII, a document drafted by Gregory VII in or around March 1075, before his conflict with Henry IV (*Das Register Gregors VII.*, MGH *Epp. sel.* 2,1, 203): '*Quod illi soli licet pro temporis necessitate novas leges condere*'.

24 As he does in the *Prooemium* by presenting his code as the sacrifice of 'the calf of our lips' (*vitulus labiorum*, a reference to Hosea 14:2(3)): 'by promoting justice and legislating we have decided to sacrifice the calf of our lips' (*colendo iustitiam et iura condendo mactare disponimus vitulum labiorum*).

25 LA 1,31: '*Oportet igitur Cesarem fore iustitie patrem et filium, dominum et ministrum, patrem et dominum in edendo iustitiam et editam conservando; sic et iusitiam venerando sit filius et ipsius copiam ministrando minister*'.

justice' (*cultus justitiae*)[26], since it is the judge who administers the grace of the father, the son, and the law to litigants. Consequently, being involved in litigation in court amounts to participating in a sacred ceremony and therefore requires silence[27]: all persons present in court must observe silence out of respect for the judge administering the sacrament of the 'peace of justice' (*quies iustitiae*)[28] and who, in doing so, serves God by serving the law emanating from God's anointed appointee. These are not the ideas of a heathen, an atheist, or an agnostic, as Voltaire and Nietzsche have represented Frederick II. The emperor was certainly not the first European 'enlightened monarch', a title arguably belonging to his 18th-century Prussian namesake, but he certainly was the first European 'absolute monarch', styling himself after the absolute monarchs of the classical Roman Empire, such as Augustus, another 'boy' (*puer*) who had also outwitted powerful opponents much older than himself[29]. In the very same year his code was issued, Frederick introduced a new monetary unit for the kingdom of Sicily, his famous golden *augustalis*, showing himself in profile, dressed up as a classical Roman emperor with a laurel wreath rather than a crown on the obverse and on the reverse a Roman eagle[30], revealing a striking resemblance with a golden coin (*aureus*) issued by Augustus in 27 BCE. It even has the same inscription: *Caesar Augustus*. It was a symbol of absolute monarchy, as was his code. It was published in August 1231 at Melfi in Apulia[31] and remained in force in the Sicilian kingdom until the end of that kingdom in the nineteenth century.

The nature of
Frederick's code

In his new code, Frederick also provided for some of the topics which he had already provided for in some of his coronation statutes. For exam-

---

26 The headnote to *LA* 1,32, on discipline in the courts, reads '*De cultu iustitiae*'.
27 *LA* 1,32: 'Silence is required in the cult of justice' (*Cultus iustitiae silentium reputatur*). Comp. Isaiah 32:17: 'And the work of righteousness shall be peace; and the effect of righteousness quietness and assurance forever' (*Et erit opus justitiae pax, et cultus justitiae silentium, et securitas usque in sempiternum*).
28 *LA* 1,32: '*statuimus in posterum litigantes et quoslibet alios in iudicio existentes cum reverentia magistratus iura reddentis quietem iustitie observare*'.
29 See *supra* p. 191.
30 Ryccardus de S. Germano, *Chronica* ad ann. 1231, *RIS²* 7.2, 176: '*Nummi aurei, qui Augustales vocantur, de mandato imperatoris in utraque sycla Brundusii et Messene cuduntur*'. See also idem ad ann. 1232, *RIS²* 7.2, 182: '*Figura Augustalis erat habens ab uno latere caput hominis cum media facie, et ab alio aquilam*'.
31 Ryccardus de S. Germano, *Chronica* ad ann. 1231, *RIS²* 7.2, 176: '*Constitutiones imperiales Melfie publicantur*'. Frederick wanted his code to be called after himself, *Codex Fredericianus*, as Justinian had done with his own code (*Prooemium*: '*nostri nominis sanctiones*'), but that did not sink in, because it was unacceptable to the Angevin successors of the Hohenstaufens. The common designation in the Middle Ages was *Liber augustalis*, 'the imperial book', and later, quite neutral, as *Constitutiones Regni Siciliae*.

ple, two of his statutes directed against heretics (*LA* 1,1-2) are obviously inspired by two provisions from his coronation statutes (Art. 6 and 7)[32]. This is not an unwarranted repetition of legislation, since the *Liber augustalis* was meant to be an exhaustive and comprehensive codification of all Sicilian royal legislation, including his own, such as, for example, provisions from the Assizes of Capua. Consequently, all royal legislation *'not inserted into our present code of statutes cannot obtain any force or authority in or out of court'*[33]. The constitutional aspects are complex though, since Frederick did *not* publish his code in his quality as king of Sicily, but as Roman emperor since only a Roman emperor had the authority to legislate, as Justinian had specifically emphasized[34]. This may even have been Frederick's prime incentive to codify all Sicilian royal legislation. Ever since his imperial coronation, he had risen above the level of all territorial rulers, kings and princes, attaining the status of universal monarch, *dominus mundi*[35]. When observed from this exalted perspective, all legislation by inferior princes, even by his own royal Sicilian ancestors, was presumptuous and lacking confirmation by the proper authority, the emperor, certainly so after the Sicilian kingdom was now definitively reunited with the Empire[36]. It

---

32 MGH *Const.* 2 no 85, 108-109. The considerable differences in wording and style are due to the fact that Frederick's coronation statutes had been drafted by the papal chancery (see *supra* p. 255), not by his own. The new statutes were drafted by Piero della Vigna in his own exuberant Sicilian style.

33 *Liber augustalis, Prooemium i.f.*, MGH *Const.* 2, Suppl., 148: '*ut ex eis, que in presenti constitutionum nostrarum corpore minime continentur, robur aliquod nec auctoritas aliqua in iudiciis vel extra iudicia possint assumi*'. It should be stressed that Frederick's code was only exclusive as far as royal legislation was concerned. The rest of the sources of law obtaining in the kingdom remained in force as before, provided they were not conflicting with the *Liber augustalis*. The hierarchy of sources of law obtaining in the Sicilian kingdom is provided for as follows (*LA* 1,62.1): royal legislation, customary law, and common law, being either Roman law or Lombard law, dependent on the origin of the litigants (note the absence of city by-laws in this inventory of Sicilian sources of law). Roman law was by far the most important secondary source of law in the kingdom and even in the *Liber augustalis* itself 25% of its contents can be traced back to Roman law, as the German scholar Hermann Dilcher, *Die sizilianische Gesetzgebung Kaiser Friedrichs II.*, Cologne 1975, has been able to assess: see his summary on 793-794. In Sicilian litigation Roman law was employed extensively in the construction of the provisions of Frederick's code.

34 Const. 'Tanta' § 21: '*imperiale culmen … cui solum concessum est leges condere*'.

35 See Frederick II in a charter of 1235 (MGH *Const.* 2, no 197, 263): '*Dominus, qui regna constituit et firmavit imperium … nos supra reges et regna preposuit et in imperiali solo sublimavit*'. Even outside the Empire Frederick was considered *dominus mundi*. See the Englishman Roger of Wendover, *Flores Historiarum* ad ann. 1235, ed. Coxe IV, Londen 1842, 338: '*quasi dominus et moderator totius orbis*'.

36 Marinus de Caramanico († *c.* 1285), a justice in the Sicilian High Court, wrote an extensive commentary on the *Liber augustalis* and its *Prooemium*, included in *Constitutiones Regni Siciliae*, Naples 1771. On p. xxxiii-xl, he elaborates on the right of the *king* of Sicily to issue statutes and emphasizes that this right does not belong to the *emperor* exclusively, but

was, moreover, only in his quality as emperor that he could modify or even repeal imperial legislation in Sicily based on the old maxim of Roman law that 'posterior imperial constitutions derogate prior constitutions'[37]. In this way – that is, on his imperial authority – he exempted himself and his Sicilian functionaries from the statutory *duty*, as laid down in his coronation legislation for all local authorities and territorial princes, to prosecute heretics (and infidels) and from the penalties (expropriation) for failing to do so: '*Excommunicamus*'[38] did not and could not apply fully in the Sicilian kingdom[39], since it was not comprehensively copied as secular legislation in Frederick's code. It was precisely for failing to comply with that part of the papal constitution that he was summoned and charged with heresy by Innocent IV in 1245[40].

The Pope

Gregory IX disapproves of the Sicilian codification project

As soon as news had reached him that Frederick II was planning the introduction of a comprehensive law code, Pope Gregory IX reacted as though bitten by a snake. He immediately sent word to Frederick to instantly desist from his project, since by persisting with that disastrous initiative he would imperil the 'public freedom' (*publica libertas*) of his subjects[41]. On the very same day he sent an angry letter to Bishop Jacob of Capua, a member of the committee working on Frederick's code, ordering him to end his cooperation in that wicked project at once[42].

---

also to the king of Sicily, stating that the king of Sicily is emperor in his kingdom: (xxxix, l. col) *Rex Siciliae est princeps in regno*. It has been contended by some scholars that this is the first time this famous maxim was used. I will not express an opinion on this, but it must be noted that Caramanico's commentary was written during the reign of Charles of Anjou (*c* 1226-1266-1285), who expelled and even exterminated the Hohenstaufens (see *infra* p. 457 ff) and, consequently, had to stress his position as a king completely independent of the Empire.

37 D. 1,4,4 (Modestinus).
38 For this see *supra* p. 256, fnt. 18.
39 It could not fully apply in the Sicilian kingdom since it would have obliged the king to prosecute, expel, and possibly even execute all his many Muslim and Jewish subjects as well as all his Greek subjects adhering to the orthodoxy of the Byzantine Empire, heretics according to the Church of Rome.
40 See *infra* p. 295 and 378.
41 HB 3, 289 (5 July 1231) (also in MGH *Epp. saec. xiii* 1, no 443, 357): 'We have received information that you intend to issue new statutes, either at your own initiative or enticed by the ill-conceived counsel of misguided people. The inevitable consequence of this will be that you will be called a persecutor of the Church and an overthrower of public freedom' (*Intelleximus siquidem, quod vel proprio motu vel seductus inconsultis consiliis perversorum, novas edere constitutiones intendis, ex quibus necessario sequitur, ut dicaris ecclesie persecutor et obrutor publice libertatis*). See for the pope as defender of 'public freedom' *infra* p. 561.
42 HB 3, 290: 'You must realize what you will have to expect and fear if you continue to voluntarily assist, as we have been informed for certain, our beloved son Frederick, the emper-

Two weeks later the pope sent a reassuring letter to Frederick that he had changed his mind and that his suspicion of the project had been taken away[43]. He does not write what had changed his mind, but the most probable reason is that he had been informed in the meantime, either by Frederick himself or by Bishop Jacob, that Frederick's project was not competing with his own codification project.

In 1230 Pope Gregory IX had instructed the Catalan canonist Raymon de Peñaforte (*c.*1175-1275) to compose a comprehensive codification of *all* papal legislation, including canons of general councils, such as the Third and Fourth Lateran Council, issued after the publication of Gratian's *Decretum* (*c.* 1150). Gregory's code was therefore commonly known (and cited) as the 'Additional Book' (*Liber Extra* (X))[44]. As with Frederick II's codification, the model for Gregory's codification was Justinian's *Codex*, containing all imperial legislation from the times of the Emperor Hadrian to Justinian himself. Of course, the pope wrote an introduction (*Prooemium*) to his code as well, closely following Justinian's constitutions announcing the codification of all imperial legislation in his *Codex*[45]. This is the bull *Rex pacificus*, far less philosophical and stylistically overblown than Frederick's *Prooemium*, since it follows the practical and relatively unassuming style of Justinian's introductory constitutions much more closely. It refers to the five older collections of papal decretals[46], the inconsistencies and overlap between

Gregory's code of canon law

---

or of the Romans, in composing statutes as unconducive to salvation as they are conducive to enormous scandals, statutes of which you ought to be the most obvious opponent' (*videto quid te sperare valeat vel timere dum, sicut nobis est pro certo relatum, carissimo filio nostro Friderico Romanorum imperatori constitutiones destitutivas salutis et institutivas enormium scandalorum edenti voluntarius obsequens eas dictas ... quibus deberes esse patentissimus contradictor*).

43   MGH *Epp. saec. xiii* 1, no 447, 360 (27 July 1231): '*omnino suspicione deposita*'.

44   The assignment of Raymon was, relatively, simple. There were five collections of canon law current at the time covering the period, the five so-called *Compilationes antiquae*. The *Compilatio prima*, composed by the Bolognese canonist Bernardus Balbi from Pavia (Bernardus Papiensis, †1213) covers the period from Gratian until the end of the pontificate of Clement III (1191). It set the model of all later four collections *and* Gregory's code, consisting, as it did, of five books (*Iudex, Iudicium, Clerus, Connubia, Crimen*), each book subdivided in several titles. The *Compilatio secunda* covers the period from Clement III until Innocent III. It was composed by a Welshman, John of Wales (Johannes Galensis, †1285). The *Compilatio tertia*, compiled in 1210 at the instruction of Innocent III by his notary Petrus Beneventanus Collivacinus, contains all decretals of Innocent III until 1210. The *Compilatio quarta*, containing decretals of Innocent III omitted in the official collection, the *Compilatio tertia*, and decretals issued by Innocent III after 1210, including all canons of the Fourth Lateran Council, was privately compiled by the great German canonist Johannes Teutonicus (†1245), who also composed the great gloss on Gratian's *Decretum*. The *Compilatio quinta* is the official collection of decretals of Honorius III, issued in 1226.

45   Constt. 'Haec quae necessario', 13 February 528, and 'Cordi', 16 November 534. Comp. the Gl. 'Similitudinem' on *Rex pacificus*: '*Idem dicit Imperator et eandem causam assumit*', referring to Justinian's Constt. 'Haec quae necessario' and 'Cordi'.

46   See *supra* fnt. 44.

them, and the unnecessary prolixity of some. Consequently, he ordered master Raymond to bring all decretals from the five previous collections still obtaining together in one volume, leaving out all that was superfluous and adding decretals of his own[47]. Gregory's *Liber Extra* was promulgated on 5 September 1234 and remained in force until 1917.[48]

Nature and effectiveness of Gregory's code

Frederick's code did not compete with Gregory's code, since Frederick's *Liber augustalis* only obtained within the kingdom of Sicily and *not*

---

47 X. *Prooemium* ('Rex pacificus'): 'We have ordered that the constitutions and decretals of our predecessors, at present dispersed over various books, shall be brought together in one volume by our beloved son brother Raymon on behalf of the common good, and especially on behalf of students, weeding out what is superfluous and adding our own decretals, by which operation some things that were not entirely clear in the older collections, are now clarified. Because it is our wish that only this collection is used in the courts and the schools, we strictly forbid to make another without special permission of the Holy See' (*Sane diversas constitutiones et decretales epistolas praedecessorum nostrorum, in diversa dispersas voluminal … ad communem, et maxime studentium, utilitatem per dilectum filium fratrem Raymundum (…) illas in unum volumen resecatis superfluis providimus redigendas, adiicientes constitutiones nostras et decretales epistolas, per quas nonnulla, quae in prioribus erant dubia, declarantur. Volentes igitur, ut hac tantum compilatione universi utantur in iudiciis et in scholis, districtius prohibemus, ne quis praesumat aliam facere absque auctoritate sedis apostolicae speciali*).

48 The code of Gregory IX was only exclusive as far as papal legislation issued after Gratian's *Decretum* was concerned. Like Frederick's code, it did not affect other sources of law: see *supra* p. 259, fnt. 33. Consequently, Roman law continued to be applied in ecclesiastical courts whenever a subject *not* covered by positive canon law was at hand, as was already provided in Gratian's *Decretum* (Dist. 10, cap.12) and emphasized by the Gl. 'In negotiis'. Customary law might also be applied whenever positive law – canon law (Gratian's *Decretum* and Gregory's code) and Roman law (Justinian's *Corpus Iuris*) – failed to provide an answer: (Gl. 'Cum deficit lex' on Dist. 1, cap. 5) 'when all positive law is lacking, the judge must have recourse to a general custom or even a local custom if there is no general custom' (*deficiente omni iure procedat <iudex> ad generalem consuetudinem, vel etiam particularem, cum defuerit generalis*). Ever since the days of Gregory VII (see his famous *dictum* in *Decretum* Dist. 8, cap. 5), canon law, like Roman law, tended to suppress customary law, making its application in a court of law subject to three conditions: it should be rational, well established, and, even more importantly, it should be approved of by the legislator: (X. 1,4,11, Gregory IX) 'The authority of a long-standing custom is not worthless, but not to the extent that it prevails over positive <meaning Roman> law, unless it is rational and lawfully established' (*Licet etiam longaevae consuetudinis non sit vilis auctoritas: non tamen est usque adeo valitura, ut vel iuri positivo debeat praeiudicium generare, nisi fuerit rationalis et legitime sit praescripta*). According to the Gl. 'Legitime' on X. 1,4,11 a 'lawfully established custom' (*consuetudo legitime praescripta*), was a custom 'approved by the legislative authority' (*sciente illo qui potest ius condere*). This is compliant with Roman doctrine as established by Constantine I in C. 8,52(53),2, explicitly approved by Gratian in Dist. 11, cap. 4. Frederick II also stressed that only customs approved of by the legislator (the king) were to be applied in Sicilian courts: Assizes of Capua 14 (see *supra* p. 223). It is characteristic of autocratic (late imperial Roman, papal and Sicilian) rule to restrict recourse to customary law as much as possible. Contemporary Lombard jurists did not agree with that policy since it impaired the autonomy of the cities: see *supra* p. 91, fnt. 21 and *infra* p. 561 ff.

within the Empire as a whole[49], which is probably the reason why Gregory withdrew his initial criticism of Frederick's codification plan. If Frederick had really intended to make a code of law for the entire empire instead, it would have been a very different matter. Legislating for the entire empire, in theory, amounted to legislating for Catholic Christianity as a whole and this, *universal* legislation, was something Gregory regarded as his preserve and if it was to be done by an emperor, it was best done at the initiative *and* on the authority of the pope, as had indeed happened with Frederick's 1220 coronation statutes[50]. Gregory's code did have universal force of law as a matter of course, binding as it was on all ecclesiastical courts all over Catholic Christendom[51]. The actual effectiveness of Gregory's code, otherwise always a problem with medieval legislation, was impressive, not in the least because the contents of the code were made known to the legal community at large within a very short period after its publication through a number of excellent and very practically minded commentaries, first and foremost the great commentary of Pope Innocent IV[52] and, a good second, the commentary (*Lectura*) and abridgement (*Summa*) of Henry of Susa (†1271), cardinal-bishop of Ostia and therefore commonly known as 'Hostiensis'[53], whom we shall meet later in the trial of Frederick II[54]. Another important factor promoting the wide recognition of Gregory's code was, of course, the administration of justice of the papal court, the *Rota romana*, the most important court of appeal in western

---

49   On this see Frederick's *Prooemium*: 'We desire that these laws bearing our name shall only obtain in the kingdom of Sicily' (*Presentes igitur nostri nominis sanctiones in regno tantum Sicilie volumus obtinere*). On the title of Frederick's code see *supra* p. 258, fnt. 31.

50   See *supra* p. 257.

51   X. 1,2,1: '*Canonum statuta ab omnibus custodiantur*'.

52   *Commentaria in quinque libros decretalium*. See on Innocent's commentary further *infra* p. 329, fnt. 3.

53   *Lectura in Decretales Gregorii IX* and *Summa super titulis Decretalium*. Hostiensis' *Summa* was soon recognized as a masterpiece and widely cited as the *Summa aurea*. Since much of the *Liber Extra*, especially in the second book, is about the law of procedure, Gregory's code and the commentaries of Innocent IV and Hostiensis are quoted extensively in the *Speculum iuris* of Guillaume Durant († 1296), at one time in his career *auditor* in the papal court. His treatise on the law of procedure in ecclesiastical courts is one of the most influential legal treatises ever written. It is mainly due to Durant's treatise and its wide circulation that the canon law of procedure as codified in Gregory's code came to dominate the law of procedure of secular courts on the European continent as well, especially in Italy and France. Durant wrote (*Speculum* Lib. II, Part. III, Tit. *De appellationibus* § 10, no 14) that 'the 'style' of the court of Rome, being the master of all, must be followed by inferior courts' (*stylus Romanae curiae, quae, tamquam magistra omnium, ab inferioribus est sequenda*). This came to pass during his lifetime, mainly because even the secular courts (such as the Parlement de Paris) were packed with canonists.

54   See *infra* p. 363.

Christendom, guaranteeing the uniform application of the code all over Europe.

The publication of Gregory's code greatly enhanced the influence of canon law in Europe, even in the secular courts. It was generally accepted that canon law prevailed over secular law, for example Roman law, whenever the application of secular law would sanction a sin, a condition so broadly formulated that canon law practically always prevailed over secular law[55]. Consequently, knowledge of canon law was indispensable for secular lawyers and many of them graduated in both Roman and canon law as 'master in both legal disciplines' (*doctor utriusque iuris*)[56]. Conversely, knowledge of Roman law was indispensable for canonists since Gregory's code (and Gratian's *Decretum*) was applied in ecclesiastical courts and explained in the law schools with Roman law as a constant frame of reference. One look at the enormous gloss on Gregory's code composed by the Bolognese professor Bernardus de Botone from Parma (†1263) suffices to be convinced of this. Roman law was to canon law what philosophy was to theology.

Gregory IX at war with the Romans

Gregory's code was not promulgated in Rome, but in Spoleto, since Gregory IX had been forced to leave Rome in May 1234. The pope suffered the humiliation of being expelled from Rome by the people of the city yet again[57]. It is another confirmation of one of the most curious phenomena of the Middle Ages. Popes like Innocent III and Gregory IX ruled over Europe as once the emperors of the classical Roman Empire had done, but the closer one came to Rome, the less sway papal authority held, least of all in Rome itself, where the position of the pope was always precarious. The doctrines of Arnold of Brescia[58] had never been forgotten in the city. His teachings had even inspired a heretic sect, the 'Arnoldists', still present in the city even after Gregory IX had presided over an intensive persecution of heretics in the city

---

55 Usury is a simple example. Roman law allowed the stipulation for interest on a loan of money, normally at a maximum of 6% annually (C. 4,32,26,2). Canon law did not, interest being contrary to Scripture (Luke 6:35). Gregory's code (X. 5,19,3) branded creditors stipulating for interest on their loans as usurers and threatened them with excommunication. Consequently, interest paid over a loan could be recovered in an ecclesiastical court (X. 5,19,9 and 13). The question was whether canon law prevailed over Roman law in a secular court. The answer was affirmative: Bartolus de Sassoferrato (1314-1357), *Commentaria in secundam Digesti Veteris partem*, ad D. 12,6,26 pr. (ed. Turin 1574, no 8, *f.* 53 *r*, l. col.): '*Hodie vero de iure canonico, immo potius de iure divino, obligationi usurarum lex resistit in totum*'.
56 The first lawyer to have graduated in both disciplines seems to have been Lanfrancus da Crema (†1229), who read and wrote authoritatively on both Roman and canon law.
57 For Gregory's first expulsion from Rome see *supra* p. 236.
58 See *supra* p. 95.

and a subsequent awe-inspiring *auto-da-fé* in 1231[59]. In 1234 Arnold's anti-clerical doctrines incited the Romans to, once again[60], reduce the pope to a state of truly apostolic poverty by confiscating all papal territory on behalf of the city and turning it into a Roman *contado*[61]. Gregory and his cardinals fled to Rieti and sent letters to the German bishops for military support to subdue the rebellious Romans[62], at the same time requesting the Lombard League to grant free passage to all German troops coming to the rescue of the pope[63]. Much to Gregory's surprise (and to the misgiving of his cardinals), Frederick II visited the pope at Rieti offering his support[64]. It was an unexpected initiative on the part of Frederick, who had previously supported the Romans in their conflicts with Gregory[65], but the emperor wanted to ensure the pope's support in a sudden crisis emerging in his German kingdom. News had reached him that his son, the king of the Romans Henry (VII), had revolted against his imperial authority[66].

---

59 *Vita Greg. IX*, cap. 14, in *Liber censuum* 2, 23: 'Because, due to the absence of the pastor, that contagious disease of wicked heresy had spread, he <Gregory> condemned many priests, many clerics, and many lay people of either sex who were infected by that leprosy, some of them on account of the testimony of witnesses, others on account of their own confession, before the doors of the church of S. Maria Maggiore, after he had held a thorough investigation in the presence of the senator and the people of Rome' (*Quia in urbe propter pastoris absentiam ille contagiosus morbus heretice pravitatis irrepserat ... inquisitione prehabita diligenti, ante hostium majoris basilice Virginis gloriose, senatoreac populo Romano presentibus, multos presbyteros, clericos multos, et utriusque sexus laicos huiusmodi lepra conspersos, tum testibus, tum propria confessione damnavit*). See also Ryccardus de S. Germano, *Chronica* ad ann. 1231, *RIS²* 7.2, 173: 'In February several heretics were detected in the city, some of whom were burned at the stake because they could not be converted' (*Mense Februario ... nonnuli Patarenorum in Urbe inventi sunt, quorum alii sunt igne cremati, cum inconvertibiles essent*).

60 They had done so before in 1145, during the pontificate of Eugenius III. On this episode see *Ottonis episc. freisingensis Chronica* 7,31, MGH *SS Rer. germ.* 45, 359-360.

61 *Vita Greg. IX*, cap. 19, in *Liber censuum* 2, 25: '*Urbis senator inter statuta que in ecclesiastice libertatis exitium et enormem sedis apostolice lesionem temerarius edidit ... in Petri patrimonio quereret novi comitatus abusum*'. For the 1234 conflict between the pope and the Romans see especially Roger of Wendover, *Flores Historiarum* ad ann. 1234, ed. Coxe IV, London 1842, 322-324.

62 *Annales Erphordenses* ad ann. 1235, MGH *SS* 16, 30: '*domnus papa directis in Alemanniam nunciis, ab omnibus episcopis atque regalibus abbatiis milites ac subsidium ad Romanos impugnandos postulavit*'.

63 The letter is printed in Savioli, *Annali Bolognesi* 3,2, Bassano 1795, no 510, 140-141.

64 Ryccardus de S. Germano, *Chronica* ad ann. 1234, *RIS²* 7.2, 188: '*Mense Madii Imperator ... aput Reate ad papam vadit ... se ad servitium ecclesie exponens contra Romanos*'. For the misgivings of the pope and his cardinals see *Vita Greg. IX*, cap. 20, in *Liber censuum* 2, 25: '*domino papa et fratribus de eius fide dubitantibus*'.

65 See *supra* p. 236.

66 Ryccardus de S. Germano, *Chronica* ad ann. 1234, *RIS²* 7.2, 189: '*Hoc anno, quod Henricus rex contra Imperatorem patrem suum seditionem in Alemannia fecerit, fama fuit*'. Comp. *Vita Greg. IX*, cap. 25, in *Liber censuum* 2, 27: 'the emperor asked for the support of the Holy See against his son Henry' (*imperator contra Henricum ipsius filium ... sedis apostolice subsidium imploravit*).

18

Excommunication II

Gregory IX had been trying to stir unrest in the German kingdom during his war with Frederick II[1], causing the German princes to send a delegation to Italy to broker a peace between the emperor and the pope to prevent civil war. It was largely due to this initiative that peace was finally made at S. Germano in 1230[2]. Among the German princes present were Duke Leopold VI of Austria, father-in-law to Frederick's son Henry (VII) and a firm and lifelong supporter of the cause of the Hohenstaufens, and Bishop Siegfried of Regensburg, also a loyal supporter of Frederick. They must have informed Frederick personally of the serious conflicts between his son and the leading German princes[3], primarily Duke Louis of Bavaria, whom Frederick had appointed as guardian of his son after the unfortunate murder of Archbishop Engelbert of Cologne in 1225[4]. As soon as he had reached majority in 1228, Henry ruled without the advice of the princes and tried, mainly on the advice of his 'ministerials', to establish a hold in the territories

Henry (VII) and the German princes

---

1   Conrad de Fabaria, *Casus s. Galli continuatio III* (1203-1240) 16, MGH *SS* 2, 180: 'While Emperor Frederick was doing his best overseas for the recovery of the holy sepulchre, Bishop Gregory of Rome, ninth of that name, was doing his very best to take the empire away from him and his son King Henry' (*Domino imperatore Friderico semper augusto interim in ultramarinis pro recuperacione sepulcri Domini labore maximo dante operam, Gregorius nonus Romane Urbis pontifex, modis quibus poterat, elaborabat, ipsum ab imperio perturbare, filiumque suum Heinricum regem*). See also *supra* p. 247.
2   See *supra* p. 245-247.
3   Duke Leopold had a private grudge against Frederick's son, since it was common knowledge that King Henry (VII) wanted to divorce his wife, a daughter of Leopold. See *Annales Wormatienses* ad ann. 1233, MGH *SS* 17, 43: '*nobilissimam matronam Margaretham coniugem suam, illustris ducis Austrie filiam, deserere voluit*'. Duke Leopold died in S. Germano shortly after, leaving his duchy to his son Frederick.
4   Burchard of Ursberg, *Chronicon* ad ann. 1225, MGH *SS rer. Germ.* 16, 121: '*Ludoicus dux Bavariorum curator regis Hainrici in rebus tam propriis quam imperialibus in Alamannia efficitur*'. Henry (VII) had even waged war against Louis in 1229 since Louis was suspected of having sided with Gregory IX (Conrad de Fabaria, *Casus s. Galli* 16, MGH *SS* 2, 180): 'the duke of Bavaria offered his support and counsel by the covert treason against the king of which he was suspected at the time' (*dux Bavariae prebuit assensum et consilium palliacione fallacie, quam ergo regem tunc temporis habuisse visus est*).

of the German princes by building castles and especially by granting franchises to some of the cities within their territories[5]. It was a policy bound to provoke the resistance of the princes. Consequently, it was a policy of which his father strongly disapproved. Frederick was, first and foremost, a Sicilian king with an Italian grand strategy. German politics were, to him, a sideshow he was glad to leave to the German princes who had just been instrumental in bringing about his reconciliation with the pope. The German princes, most notably among them Bishop Siegfried of Regensburg who had been appointed arch-chancellor of the Empire by Frederick II in 1230, were aware of the opinion of the emperor and consequently felt emboldened to make a stand against his son. After their return, they were in a position to force upon Henry a charter at a diet held at Worms in May 1231 that rightly may be considered the 'Magna Charta' of all German 'territorial lords' (*domini terrae*, 'Landesfürsten'), the 'Charter in Favour of the Princes' (*Constitutio in favorem principum*), secular and ecclesiastical[6]. It begins with a provision forbidding the king to build castles or enfranchise cities to the disadvantage of the princes[7], but the core of the charter is Art. 6, securing jurisdictional sovereignty of the princes in their territories: '*every prince shall freely enjoy his liberties, jurisdictions, county courts and hundreds for himself, his freemen and vassals according to the approved custom of his land*'[8]. In addition to this, it was provided in a separate charter, also testified to at Worms on the same day, that the princes had legislative powers within their territories as well, on condition that legislation was approved of, *not* by the emperor, but 'by the better and major men of the land', thus laying the foundation of territorial parliaments[9].

Assassination of Duke Louis of Bavaria

As we shall see shortly, Frederick II did not disapprove of these privileges in principle, but he did disapprove of the fact that they had been

---

5   He did so, for example, with the city of Nijmegen in 1230 (HB 3, 425), thus creating an urban community independent of the counts of Gelre and Kleve and the dukes of Brabant. The charter contains the clause that the rights granted to the citizens were extended 'to everyone they have received as co-citizens among the people who have migrated to their city' (*ut quoscunque in concives recipiant qui ad ipsorum civitatem se duxerint transferendos*), causing many serfs and villeins of the surrounding lords to seek the refuge of the 'freedom of the city'. See on this issue *infra* p. 270, fnt. 21.

6   Printed in MGH *Const.* 2 no 304, 418-420.

7   MGH *Const.* 2 no 304, 419: '*Statuentes in primis, quod nullum novum castrum vel civitatem in preiudicium principum construere debeamus*'. The charter contains a whole set of dispositions directed against the German cities and its citizens, especially against free immigration into the cities of serfs, criminals, and vassals from princely territories.

8   MGH *Const.* 2 no 304, 419: *Item unusquisque principum libertatibus, iurisdictionibus, comitatibus, centis sibi liberis vel infeodatis utetur quite secundum terre sue consuetudinem approbatam*'.

9   MGH *Const.* 2 no 305, 420: '*ut neque principes neque alii quilibet constituciones vel nova iura facere possint, nisi meliorum vel maiorum terre consensus primitus habeatur*'.

brought about and confirmed by solemn royal charters as a result of a power struggle between his son and the German princes. He summoned the nobles and cities of the Italian kingdom, as well as Henry (VII) and the German princes to meet him at a diet to be convened in Ravenna in November 1231 to consult them 'on the well-being of the Empire and the Lombards' (*de bono imperii et Lombardorum*)[10]. The invitations for the Ravenna diet were sent mid-September 1231[11]. Late in September 1231 news reached Frederick of a disastrous development in Germany: Duke Louis of Bavaria had been murdered on 16 September by an unknown assassin at Kehlheim in Bavaria. The assassination of Louis of Bavaria caused considerable commotion among the German princes and Frederick was widely suspected of having been involved[12]. Frederick was indeed charged for this murder by Innocent IV at the council of Lyon[13], but his involvement is not very likely. Frederick's German policy was based on good relations with the German princes and the assassination of one of them was not something the princes took lightly, as Frederick's father had experienced after the assassination of the son of the duke of Brabant in 1192 that was generally blamed on Henry VI[14]. It had almost cost his father his throne. It just was not sound politics, at least not as far as Frederick was concerned.

The Ravenna diet had to be postponed to late December 1231. The Lombard League suspected Frederick of planning another strike against Lombardy as he had been plotting in 1226[15] and consequently the League blocked the 'Chiusa di Verona' once again to prevent the German princes from entering Lombardy[16], at the same time gathering

Frederick II and the German princes

---

10   *Annales Placentini Gibellini* ad ann. 1231, MGH *SS* 18, 470: '*Imperator autem Fridericus missit per litteras et nuncios civitatibus societatis Lombardorum, ut coram eo ambaxatores destinarent, ut cum eis de bono imperii et Lombardorum pertractaret*'.
11   For this see *Annales Ianuenses* (Bartolomeo scriba) ad ann. 1231, MGH *SS* 18, 177: '*Eodem quippe anno circa medium mensem Septembris dominus imperator Fredericus ordinavit celebrare generalem curiam apud Ravennam*'.
12   *Annales Scheftlarienses maiores* (1162-1248) ad ann. 1231, MGH *SS* 17, 340: '*De nece igitur tanti principis non modica disturbatio inter principes fuit*' and on the suspected involvement of Frederick II *Chronica regia coloniensis* ad ann 1231, MGH *SS rer. Germ.* 18, 263: '*Hoc autem conscientia imperatoris creditur gestum esse*'. For similar insinuations see Conrad de Fabaria, *Casus s. Galli* 18, MGH *SS* 2, 181; *Annales Stadenses* ad ann. 1231, MGH 16, 361 and *Hermanni Altahensis Annales* (1250-1305) ad ann. 1231, MGH 17, 391 (with the date). See on the assassination of Louis of Bavaria and Hohenstaufen involvement also *infra* p. 276, fnt. 54 and p. 402.
13   See *infra* p. 377.
14   See *supra* p. 145.
15   See *supra* p. 229-230.
16   *Annales Ianuenses* (Bartolomeo scriba) ad ann. 1231, MGH *SS* 18, 178: '*Sed quia Lombardi domno imperatori erant contrarii et inobedientes, non permiserunt principes Alemanniae pertransire nec ad ipsam curiam accedere, et suspensa est curia usque prope natale Domini*'.

a huge army to defend the freedom of the League[17]. Nevertheless, some German ecclesiastical and secular princes did arrive in Ravenna in December, but Henry (VII) was not among them. Frederick II celebrated Christmas in Ravenna with his German princes, appearing at Mass 'under the imperial crown' (*imperiali diademate insignitus*)[18] to honour his guests. He granted an imperial charter to the princes, confirming their policy to restrain the independence of the cities in Germany and emphasizing in exalted terms the important share (*pars sollicitudinis*) of the princes in the administration of the empire[19], clearly trying to conciliate them. From Ravenna the emperor proceeded to Friuli, where he had summoned his son to appear before him in order to account for his behaviour. This time, Henry (VII) had no alternative but to obey[20]. Father and son, who had not seen each other for more than ten years, met near Aquileia in April 1232. It was not a happy reunion. Henry (VII) had seriously imperilled the cornerstone of his father's German policy, the cooperation with the German princes, secular and ecclesiastical[21], and had even waged war against one of the most influential

---

17   At a conference in Bologna on 26 October 1231, the League decided to raise an army of 3000 knights, 10,000 foot-soldiers and 1500 archers: *Annales Placentini Guelfi* ad ann. 1231, MGH *SS* 18, 453.

18   *Chronica regia coloniensis* ad ann 1231, MGH *SS rer. Germ.* 18, 263.

19   From the preamble of the charter (MGH *Const.* 2, No 156, 192): 'Since we possess the dignity of the Roman monarchy and are invested with absolute sovereignty (*plenitudo potestatis*) chiefly on the authority of Him by whom kings reign and princes receive their principalities, placing our throne above all nations and kingdoms, it is proper that the imperial majesty not only protects but also fosters the ancient rights of those by whom he has received it and in whom the highness of our glory consists since they are called to their share in power (*pars sollicitudinis*) together with us, having received their dignity and distinction from Our Highness' (*Cum Romane monarchiam dignitatis, ipso auctore per quem reges regnant et principes optinent principatus, qui super gentes et regna constituit sedem nostram, principaliter teneamus et simus in potestatis plenitudine constituti, imperatoriam condecet maiestatem, eos per quos cepit et in quibus consistit nostre glorie celsitudo, qui et vocati sunt nobiscum in partem sollicitudinis, cum a nostra celsitudine decus recipient et decorem, non solum in suis antiquis iuribus tueri pariter et fovere*). Note that Frederick's chancery (Piero della Vigna) uses exactly the same terms, *plenitudo potestatis* and *pars sollicitudinis*, that were used in the papal chancery to describe the share of power (*pars sollicitudinis*) which the emperor had in ruling Christianity under the absolute sovereignty (*plenitudo potestatis*) of the pope. See *infra* p. 380.

20   Frederick had sent the imperial chancellor, Bishop Siegfried of Regensburg, who had been with him in Ravenna, to Germany to put extra pressure on Henry (VII) to answer the summons of the emperor and meet him in Friuli.

21   Shortly after receiving the summons of Chancellor Siegfried of Regensburg, Henry (VII) granted a charter to the city of Worms, to the detriment of that city's bishop and directly counteracting Frederick's imperial charter issued in Ravenna restraining the grant of 'liberties' to the cities. Henry's charter is in HB 4.2, 564. It contains the ominous sentence 'because His Majesty the emperor, our father, has completely assigned and committed the land of Germany to our authority' (*quia serenissimus dominus imperator pater noster nostre ditioni deputavit terram Alemannie plenius et commisit*). Bishop Siegfried must have been aware of Henry's grant and must have informed the emperor as soon as he rejoined Frederick, in the company

German princes, the duke of Bavaria[22], while alienating another, the duke of Austria, by discrediting his wife, a sister of the duke[23]. What exactly was said during their interview, we do not know, but we do know that Frederick insisted that his son swore to adhere to the instructions he had received from his father. The German princes present at the occasion guaranteed that Henry (VII) would keep his promise and solemnly declared that they considered themselves to be released from their oath of loyalty to Henry (VII) if he did not[24]. After this humiliating experience, Henry (VII) was sent back to Germany. A few weeks later, in May, Frederick extolled his German princes even more than he had already done at Ravenna by confirming the 'Charter in Favour of the Princes' (*Constitutio in favorem principum*) which his son had granted the previous year[25]. In doing so, he accepted the fragmentation of legislation and the administration of justice in the German territories as a *fait accompli*[26]. In June 1232 Frederick II was back in Apulia[27], dissatisfied with the political situation in Lombardy and disappointed by his son Henry (VII). There was, however, a redeeming feature: in Friuli, Frederick had made an alliance with Ezzelino III da Romano (1194-1259), a formidable north-Italian warlord, who captured Verona in the same year and garrisoned the city with German troops from Tirol, thus securing the 'Chiusa di Verona'[28]. The main road over the Alps from and to Germany was now open to Frederick.

---

of Henry (VII) and a number of German princes, in Friuli. Henry's grant to the citizens of Worms was nullified by his father in May 1232 at the request of the bishop of Worms (HB 4.1, 335-336).

22   It has just been contended that Frederick's involvement in the assassination of Duke Louis of Bavaria is unlikely. Yet many contemporary sources (see *supra* p. 269, fnt. 12) do insist on Frederick's connivance. They may, however, have heard rumours connecting 'the king' with that heinous crime, meaning Henry, rather than his father. As we shall see shortly (infra p. 272), Duke Otto of Bavaria held Henry (VII) personally responsible for the murder of his father. The involvement of Henry (VII) in the murder of the duke of Bavaria may explain why Frederick was outraged by the conduct of his son in Germany. If the rumour of Henry's involvement was true, it threatened the monarchy.

23   The new duke of Bavaria, Otto II, was not present in Ravenna and Friuli. Duke Frederick of Austria was at Friuli, as is confirmed by *Annales Rudberti Salisburgenses* (1200-1286) ad ann. 1232, MGH *SS* 9, 785.

24   For the declaration of the princes see MGH *Const.* 2, no 170, 210. Sadly, the document does not contain the instructions Frederick gave his son, since it was recorded in a separate document, now lost.

25   MGH *Const.* 2, no 171, 211-213. There are only minor and insubstantial differences between Frederick's grant and the previous grant of his son.

26   On this issue see *infra* p. 277-278.

27   *Chronica regia coloniensis* ad ann 1231, MGH *SS rer. Germ.* 18: '*Circa Ascensionem imperator in Apuliam regreditur navali itinere*'.

28   *Annales Sanctae Justinae Patavinae* ad ann. 1232, MGH 19, 154: 'The Emperor Frederick went to Friuli in the month of March and there a treaty was concluded between him and Ezzelino directed against the Marquess D'Este, the count of S. Bonifacio, and the whole of

The emperor, the
pope, and the
Lombard League

Henry (VII) could and would not accept his submission in Friuli and
by August 1233 he was waging war, once again, against Duke Otto
of Bavaria, who blamed Henry personally for the assassination of
his father[29]. Even worse than this disturbance of the delicate balance
of power in Germany was Henry's open rebellion against his father
by entering into negotiations with the Lombard League in 1234[30].
Frederick had summoned the members of the League to appear before
him at the diet of Ravenna in December 1231 to account for their hostile closure of the 'Chiusa di Verona'[31]. As a matter of course, the members of the League refused to appear and were consequently banned[32].
Subsequent attempts by Grandmaster Hermann of Salza on the part of
the emperor[33] and by two papal legates on the part of the pope to broker a compromise between the emperor and the League dragged on for
years. Neither party was really interested in a compromise, nor were the

---

the Marche and Lombardy as later events were to reveal' (*Federicus imperator in mense Martii
... in Forum Iulii transmeavit; ibique facta est compositio inter ipsum et Ecelinum in detrimentum
marchionis Estensis et comitis Sancti Bonifacii et totius marchie et etiam Lumbardie, sicut postea
patuit per effectum*). The count of S. Bonifacio was the leader of the Guelf party in Verona; the
Montecchi were the leaders of the Ghibellines. For Ezzelino's capture of Verona see *Annales
Veronenses* ad ann. 1232, MGH *SS* 19, 8. In coming years, Ezzelino was to be Frederick's most
important ally in Lombardy.

29 *Annales Marbacenses* ad ann. 1233, MGH *SS rer. Germ.* 9, 95: '*Heinricus ... movit expeditionem adversus ducem Bawarie, qui propter mortem patris sui non bene sentiebat cum rege*'.

30 *Annales Marbacenses* ad ann. 1235, MGH *SS rer. Germ.* 9, 96: 'He <Henry> sent the
Marshal of Iustingen to Lombardy to conclude a treaty between him and Milan. The marshal
brought some of the Milanese nobles and other people of their party with him to these borders to ratify the treaty between them and the king' (*Misit quoque marscalcum de Iustingen in
Lombardiam, ut Mediolanenses sibi confederaret; qui etiam adduxit secum quosdam de melioribus
Mediolanensium et partis eorum ad fines istos, ut inter regem et ipsos pactum federis confirmarent*).
The treaty between Henry (VII) and the Lombard League is well documented: see Henry's
letters in MGH *Const.* 2 no 325-326, 435-436; his safeguard on behalf of the Lombard envoys (13 November 1234) (no 327, 436) and the treaty itself (17 December 1234) (no 328,
436-438). Dating contacts between Henry (VII) and the Lombard League to late in 1234 is
missing the fact that Henry's letter of 12 November 1234 must have been preceded by earlier
negotiations. Diplomatic letters like these mark the end, rather than the beginning, of a negotiating process.

31 See *supra* p. 269.

32 *Annales Ianuenses* (Bartolomeo scriba) ad ann. 1231, MGH *SS* 18, 178-179. The banning
order included an injunction to all cities in Lombardy not to elect a *podestà* from one of the
cities of the League on pain of being banned as well. The Genoese, who had sent ambassadors
to Ravenna, were stupefied (*stupefacti*) by this, having elected a *podestà* from Milan shortly
before. They refused to disavow him and were consequently banned by the emperor as well.
This was the reason why Frederick, on his way from Ravenna to Friuli, made a visit to Venice,
Genoa's long-time rival. See on this visit *Annales Placentini Gibellini* ad ann. 1231, MGH *SS*
18, 470.

33 See the documents of the negotiations between Grandmaster Hermann and the Lombard
League between March and May 1232 in MGH *Conct.* 2, no 161-168, 199-209.

papal legates[34]. The Lombard League insisted on the autonomy granted to the Lombard cities by the Peace of Konstanz and resisted any attempt by the king of Sicily to establish effective control over the Italian kingdom with the support of German armies[35], whereas Frederick II was only conditionally inclined to accept the Peace of Konstanz[36] and completely disinclined to accept 'the luxury of an elusive liberty' (*libertatis cuiusdam vagae luxuria*)[37] the Lombards claimed on the basis of that Peace. The pope, for his part, resisted a fusion between the Sicilian and Italian kingdom as strongly as he had resisted a fusion between the Empire and the Sicilian kingdom in the past. Any attempt from his part to act as a neutral mediator was therefore questionable, since he was necessarily biased in favour of the Lombards, as Frederick emphasized time and again[38]. A comprehensive peace agreement between the emperor and the Lombards was certainly not in the interest of the pope since it was by the ongoing disagreement between the Lombards and the emperor that he continued to be able to intervene in the internal affairs of the Italian kingdom[39]. This is why the 'compromise' he finally facilitated between the emperor and the Lombards merely addressed the offense to the 'honour of the empire' consisting of the closure of the 'Chiusa di Verona' by the Lombards and the ensuing frustration of the diet of Ravenna, without dealing directly with the main constitutional issue at hand, being the actual status of the Peace of Konstanz. Frederick II made this abundantly clear in his acceptance of the papal compromise (14 August 1233) by not mentioning the League as such, but merely referring to 'some communities in Lombardy' (*aliquae de universitatibus Lombardie*)[40]. He forgave those cities their sin of having impeded the diet of Ravenna and lifted the ban they had been under

---

34 Gregory's choice of legates for this mediating mission testifies to his disingenuity. One of them was Cardinal Odo of Montferrat, the very same man who had been trying to incite civil war in Germany in 1228 (see *supra* p. 248, fnt. 60), and the other was Cardinal Jacopo da Pecorara, bishop of Palestrina, a native of Piacenza of strong anti-Ghibelline convictions, as his later conduct (see *infra* p. 284 and 291) was to prove beyond any doubt.

35 The League wanted to limit the number of German knights that were allowed to enter Lombardy to one hundred and without arms (MGH *Const.* 2, no 176, 218): '*De numero militum, qui venturi erunt, petunt, quod non veniant ultra centum et sine armis*'. They must have understood that the emperor would never accept a clause like this.

36 For Frederick's condition see *supra* p. 230.

37 Frederick II in a letter to the kings of France and England justifying his Lombard policy (HB 4.2, 873, June 1236).

38 For example, in a confidential letter (HB 4.1, 442-444, also in MGH *Const.* 2, no 180, 222-223) addressed to Cardinal Rinaldo dei Conti di Segni, the later Pope Alexander IV, on the 'compromise' that was finally reached between the emperor and the Lombards.

39 See *supra* p. 243-245.

40 MGH *Const.* 2, no 182, 224-225 (shortened version in HB 4.1, 451-452).

since then, without having received a 'fair compensation' (*equa satisfactio*) himself for all the inconveniences he had suffered at their hands[41].

Frederick's decision to oblige the pope by accepting this 'compromise' with the Lombards was caused by the fact that he had a serious insurgency in Sicily at his hands at the time that had to be dealt with before he could turn his attention to Lombard and German matters again[42]. He suppressed the rebellion in the summer of 1233 with extreme cruelty, burning the rebels as heretics, since according to Frederick's code (*LA* 1,1) and his own absolutist logic[43], treason amounted to heresy. By February 1234 Frederick was back in Apulia and from there he went to Campania, where news reached him that Gregory IX had fled to Rieti and was at war with the citizens of Rome[44]. He was informed of the ongoing negotiations between his son Henry (VII) and the Lombard League at about the same time. In May Frederick was with the pope in Rieti, offering his support in Gregory's struggle with the Romans. Gregory's cardinals had no illusions about Frederick's motive for doing so. They supposed Frederick was seeking the support of the pope for his coming intervention in Germany and the deposition of his son Henry (VII), to be replaced by his younger son Conrad, the king of Jerusalem, now six years old, who accompanied his father to be introduced to the pope at Rieti as the new king of the Romans[45]. It is fair to surmise that Frederick II had by now indeed decided to depose Henry (VII) and to substitute his other son Conrad in Henry's place. It would help him if the pope would facilitate that royal rearrangement by excommunicating Henry (VII)[46]. This is precisely what transpired at Rieti[47]. Gregory

---

41 Frederick to Cardinal Rinaldo di Segni (HB 4.1, 443, MGH *Const.* 2, no 180, 223).

42 On this rebellion, concentrated in Messina and some other cities in eastern Sicily, see Ryccardus de S. Germano, *Chronica* ad ann. 1233, *RIS*² 7.2, 185 and *Breve chronicon de rebus siculis*, MGH *SS rer. Germ.* 77, 98-100.

43 See *supra* p. 253-254.

44 See *supra* p. 265.

45 Ryccardus de S. Germano, *Chronica* ad ann. 1234, *RIS*² 7.2, 188: '*Mense Madii Imperator … aput Reate ad papam vadit, ducens secum Conradum filium suum, et se ad servitium ecclesie exponens contra Romanos*'. *Vita Greg. IX*, cap. 25, in *Liber censuum* 2, 27: 'the emperor asked for the support of the Holy See against his son Henry' (*imperator contra Henricum ipsius filium … sedis apostolice subsidium imploravit*). See also *supra* p. 265.

46 Shortly after his submission to his father at Friuli, Henry (VII) had written a letter to Pope Gregory (10 April 1233, MGH *Const.* 2, no 316, 426-427), informing the pope of his oath of obedience sworn to his father, subjecting himself voluntarily to ecclesiastical censure and indicating that he was to be excommunicated by the pope forthwith if he was ever to act against his promise. According to Frederick, who must have pressed his son to write such a letter, that condition had now been met.

47 Frederick was still residing with the pope at Rieti when Gregory sent a letter to Archbishop Theodoric of Trier on 5 July 1234 (HB 4.1, 473-476), informing the bishop that he had taken notice of Henry's letter of 10 April 1233 and authorizing Bishop Theodoric to excommunicate Henry (VII) forthwith if Henry did not keep his promises. Four days earlier, Frederick had

IX was happy to oblige Frederick II by dispensing with one king of the Romans and king of Sicily, Henry (VII), leaving but one other person representing the union of the Empire and the Sicilian kingdom, Frederick II, to be dealt with in due time[48].

Gregory IX had not expected Frederick's offer of support in his struggle with the Romans. The pope had called for help from the bishops in Germany instead, asking them to send troops to Italy and at the same time urging the Lombards, always suspicious of German knights entering Italy, to let them pass unhindered, since they were contributing to the good work of the Church[49]. It was with their support and Frederick's Sicilian forces that Cardinal Raniero Capocci, a formidable soldier, waged war against the rebellious Romans. Frederick, who held no personal grudge against the Romans, as he wrote to the pope[50], preferred hunting with his falcons in the Tuscan mountains rather than lead the papal army himself. In September 1234 he left for his Sicilian kingdom, feigning illness once again[51]. Frederick had other priorities.

Frederick II and his son Conrad depart for Germany

also written a letter to Bishop Theodoric, a very loyal supporter of the house of Hohenstaufen, expressing his regrets for not having been able to visit Germany for so long, but announcing that he would come to Germany in the coming year to convene a diet at Frankfurt. Frederick's letter is in Eltester/Goerz (edd.), *Urkundenbuch zur Geschichte der ... mittelrheinischen Territorien* III (1212-1260), Coblenz 1874, no 506, 393-393. With letters like these, one should always take into account that they were delivered by special couriers with an additional oral message containing further information too sensitive to be put into writing since letters could (and sometimes did) fall into the wrong hands. For an example see *infra* p. 448.

48 There is an indication that Gregory was playing a very devious double game at the time by inciting Henry (VII) against his father and even instigating contacts between the Lombard League and Henry. For this supposition see *Annales Placentini Gibellini* ad ann. 1234, MGH *SS* 18, 470: 'King Henry, the son of the emperor, entered into a conspiracy with the Lombard League on the advice of some German princes and without permission or authority of his father, so that the men from Milan, Brescia, and Bologna sent envoys to King Henry. *This happened at the instigation of Pope Gregory*' (*Rex Henricus filius imperatoris consilio quorundam principum Alamannie absque consensu et voluntate patris conspirationem cum societate Lombardorum pertractavit, ita quod Mediolanenses, Brixienses, Bononienses miserunt in Alamanniam ambaxatores coram rege Henrico; et* haec de mandato pape Gregorii tractabantur) (emphasis added). Setting up a son and heir against his father, the reigning monarch, had a precedent in papal politics. It was done by Pope Paschalis II, who incited the successful rebellion of King Henry V against his father, Henry IV, in 1104. Cardinal Odo of Montferrat had not considered this as a possibility in 1228 (*supra* p. 248, fnt. 60), but after the public estrangement between Frederick and his son in Friuli, it became an obvious option.

49 See *supra* p. 265.

50 Frederick to Gregory (27 March 1235, HB 4.2, 945): 'Though we ourselves had no reason for any disagreement with the Romans, yet we have been persuaded by the requests of you and your fellow-friars for the honour of our mother, the Church of Rome' (*Nos autem licet materiam non habuimus Romanorum dissidium prosequendi, ob honorem tamen Romane ecclesie matris nostre, ad vestra et fratrum vestrorum monita inducti fuimus*).

51 See Frederick's letter to Gregory in Winkelmann, *Acta imperii inedita seculi xiii*, 1, Innsbruck 1880, no 334, 296. Gregory's cardinals were disgusted by Fredrick's lack of enthusiasm for the war and his hunting parties. See *Vita Greg. IX*, cap. 20, in *Liber censuum* 2, 26.

In April 1235 the emperor and his son Conrad sailed from Rimini to Aquileia and by June 1235 they were on German soil. The epiphany of the emperor of the Romans, surrounded by an impressive and eccentric Saracen bodyguard, followed by an even more exotic host of 'Ethiopians' with camels, dromedaries, panthers, and even an elephant[52], was enough to suppress any possible resistance. From all over the German realm, the princes flocked to the imperial presence[53].

The deposition of Henry (VII)

One of the first things Frederick arranged in Germany, was a meeting with Duke Otto of Bavaria. The duke and the emperor met in Regensburg and were reconciled, which can only have succeeded if Frederick was able to convince the duke that he had had no part in the assassination of his father[54]. Henry (VII) had no choice now but to surrender at the mercy of his father. Frederick was merciless. He had caught his son in the act of high treason since the ambassadors of the Lombard League were still in Germany. They were arrested and interrogated about their mission[55]. Henry (VII) was imprisoned and sent off to a castle in distant Calabria, where he died miserably in 1242, probably from the consequences of a failed suicide attempt[56].

The Diet of Mainz

Frederick's short stay in Germany, from June 1235 until August 1236, is famous in German legal history. In 1231 Frederick had issued a codification for his Sicilian kingdom, the *Liber augustalis*[57]. He now decided to act for the promotion of peace and justice (*pax et iustitia*)

---

52 For these details see *Gotifredi Viterb. Gesta Henrici VI, Continuatio* ad ann. 1235, MGH *SS* 22, 348. For Frederick's elephant see *Annales Placentini Gibellini* ad ann. 1235, MGH *SS* 18, 470. For Frederick's departure and arrival in Aquileia see Ryccardus de S. Germano, *Chronica* ad ann. 1235, *RIS²* 7.2, 190.

53 Frederick to the Lombard cities loyal to him in *Annales Placentini Gibellini* ad ann. 1235, MGH *SS* 18, 471 (HB 4.2, 945-947 (946)): '*occurentibus nobis undique principibus nostris*'.

54 *Annales Scheftlarienses maiores* ad ann. 1235, MGH *SS* 17, 340: 'The Emperor Frederick came to the land of the Germans from Italy. Travelling through Bavaria, he had a conference with the princes at Regensburg. He was reconciled with Duke Otto of Bavaria in the matter of the assassination of his father, for which he was rumoured to be responsible' (*Imperator Fridericus de Italia ad terras Teutonicorum venit, per Bavariam transiens, Ratispone cum principibus colloquium habuit; Ottoni duci Bawarie pro mortis patris, de qua suspectus habebatur, reconciliatur*). Duke Otto later gave his daughter Elisabeth in marriage to Frederick's son Conrad for which he even was excommunicated (see *infra* p. 402). He would hardly have done so, if he still held Frederick responsible for the murder of his father.

55 Tolosanus, *Chronicon Faventinum* cap. 156, ed. Rossini, *RIS²* 28. 1, Bologna 1936-1939, 135.

56 For the surrender of Henry (VII) see *Gotifredi Viterb. cont.* ad ann. 1235, MGH *SS* 22, 348. For his demise Ryccardus de S. Germano, *Chronica* ad ann. 1242, *RIS²* 7.2, 213 and *Breve chronicon de rebus siculis*, MGH *SS rer. Germ.* 77, 102. As we now know, Henry (VII) suffered from a severe form of facial leprosy: Gino Fornaciari, Francesco Mallegni, Pietro De Leo, 'The Leprosy of Henry (VII)', *The Lancet* 353 (1999) 758. The signs of this illness may already have been obvious in 1235, explaining why Frederick II moved his son out of sight.

57 See *supra* p. 251-260.

in his German kingdom as well. However, he did not do so in the same manner as he had done in Sicily. The legal culture of the German kingdom was too different for that. In Sicily, Lombard and Roman *statutory* law (the *Lombarda* and Justinian's *Corpus Iuris*) provided the common law basis on which Frederick's *Liber augustalis* elaborated in more detail[58]. There was no such basis in Germany: *'In all of Germany in matters concerning private law the people live according to customs and unwritten law passed down from antiquity, part of which, if it ever comes to a judicial decision, is decided on the basis of a vague opinion, rather than on the basis of statutory law or on the basis of a custom confirmed by a judicial decision in a defended action'*[59]. Thus, the sorry state of contemporary German law is rendered by one of Frederick's Sicilian lawyers who drafted the Latin preamble to his famous *Constitutio pacis*[60], the first German imperial statute to be published in German as well as in Latin[61], issued at a great diet in Mainz on 15 August 1235. This state of affairs did not allow for a codification like Frederick's Sicilian code, or even something resembling the Assizes of Ariano of his grandfather, the less so since Frederick's position was seriously impaired by the great privilege, the *Constitutio in favorem principum*, which he had granted to all German territorial princes in 1232[62]. Nevertheless, Frederick endeavoured to promote the rule of law in Germany by strictly forbidding his subjects to take the law into their own hands as they were accustomed to do, resulting in the endless destructive feuds character-

---

58 For this assessment see *supra* p. 259, fnt. 33.

59 *Const. pacis*, Prooemium, MGH *Const.* 2, no 196, 241: *'per totam Germaniam constituti vivant in causis et negotiis privatorum consuetudinibus antiquitus traditis et iure non scripto ... quorum partem aliquam, si quando casus trahebat in causam, ficta magis opinio quam statuti iuris aut optente contradictorio iudicio consuetudinis sentencia terminabat'.*

60 The *Prooemium* to Frederick's *Constitutio pacis* was written by an Italian lawyer familiar with the intricacies of contemporary (Roman) law. The proof is in the sentence 'a custom confirmed by a judicial decision in a defended action' (*optente contradictorio iudicio consuetudinis*). It contains a reference to D. 1,3,34 and it does so by implicitly taking sides in a contemporary scholarly dispute on the interpretation and even the constitution of the text of D. 1,3,34: see the Accursian Gl. 'Contradicto iudicio' on D. 1,3,34.

61 *Const. pacis*, MGH *Const.* 2, no 196, 241-247 (Latin version) and 250-263 (German version).

62 See *supra* p. 271. It is tempting to make a connection with Frederick's Assizes of Capua (*supra* p. 223), although there are substantial differences. The Assizes of Capua was a highly political document, containing a blueprint for the reform of the administration of the Sicilian kingdom. The *Constitutio pacis* contains nothing of the kind. The *Constitutio in favorem principum* stood in the way of any attempt at creating a centralized monarchy in Germany as was taken for granted in the Assizes of Capua. Frederick II has never shown any interest in integrating his German kingdom into an administrative union with his Italian territories. His political priorities were not in Germany, but in Italy, where he did, indeed, strive for an administrative union of the Italian and Sicilian kingdoms: see *infra* p. 297-298.

istic of German society at the time[63]. He also established a central court of appeal, modelled after the example of the Sicilian supreme imperial court of justice (*magna curia imperialis*), by appointing a new court official, the Court Justiciary ('Hofrichter') and a special notary who was to keep a record of all the decisions of the court[64].

Reconciliation with the Guelphs

Frederick II had returned to Germany with two objectives in mind: to restore order by deposing his son Henry (VII) and substituting his other son Conrad and to gain the support of the German princes for a definitive military solution to the Lombard problem. The *Constitutio pacis* was a major symbol of the restoration of order in Germany. Another was the final reconciliation with the house of the Guelphs at the same diet in Mainz. The Guelph Otto of Brunswick (1204-1252), the last surviving male heir of the mighty Henry the Lion, had frustrated the attempts of Gregory IX and his legate Cardinal Odo of Montferrat to initiate a rising against the house of Hohenstaufen in Germany in 1228[65]. Now he was to be rewarded. The Guelph was readmitted to the exclusive club of German princes by raising his extensive allodial possessions in the Lüneburg area to a duchy, the duchy of Brunswick-Lüneburg[66]. The new German duke swore fealty to Frederick and pub-

---

63 *Const. pacis*, Art. 5 (243): 'We ordain that no one, whenever damage or personal injury has been inflicted on him, is allowed to exact vengeance, unless his complaint has been brought before a judge resulting in a definitive decision according to the law' (*Statuimus igitur, ut nullus, in quacumque re dampnum ei vel gravamen fuerit illatum, se ipsum vindicet, nisi prius querelam suam coram suo iudice propositam secundum ius usque ad diffinitivam sententiam prosequatur*). Some of the phrasing has been borrowed from *LA* 1,8.

64 *Const. pacis*, Art. 28 and 29 (246-247). Frederick's establishment of a central imperial court for his German kingdom might have given the initial impetus to the development of a German 'common law', as did the Parlement de Paris for France and the great courts of common law, such as the Court of Common Pleas, for England. It was not to materialize, due to the *Constitutio in favorem principum* and especially because of the discontinuities in the German Empire after the demise of Frederick. Even after the restoration of (more or less) 'normal' circumstances in Germany with the election of Rudolf of Habsburg (1218-1273-1291) the Reichshofgericht never attained to a position even remotely resembling the importance of the Parlement de Paris in France or the royal courts of justice in Westminster. The Reichshofgericht was a stillborn institution. There has never been anything in medieval Germany like the extensive records of the Parlement de Paris or the records of the courts of law in Westminster. It was only in 1495 that a more or less effective central court of appeal for the German kingdom was established (the Reichskammergericht), by then promoting Roman law, rather than 'German' law, as the common law of the Empire. Far more important for the future of German law than Frederick's *Constitutio pacis* was the publication, shortly before 1235, of a comprehensive treatise on Saxon law (the *Sachsenspiegel*) composed (in German) by Eike of Repgow, a vassal of the archbishop of Magdeburg.

65 See *supra* p. 248.

66 See the imperial charter of 21 August 1235, MGH *Const.* 2 no 197, 263-265. See also *Annales Marbacenses* ad ann. 1235, MGH *SS rer. Germ.* 9, 97: '*in eadem curia nobilem virum dictum de Luneburch et de Bruneswich ex regali prosapia oriundum, nepotem Ottonis quondam imperatoris, de consilio principum fecit ducem*'. Naturally, Otto's allodial possessions had to

licly renounced all ambition for the German crown, thus finally ending the long feud between Guelphs and Hohenstaufens[67]. At the same time, Frederick II, a widower now for more than six years, adopted a typical Guelph tradition by marrying an English princess, Isabella of England, a sister of King Henry III. The couple married in Worms on 15 July 1235[68]. Of course, Frederick had reassured the king of France, Louis IX (1214-1226-1270), beforehand that the imminent marriage of a German king to an English princess, always a matter of concern to the kings of France[69], would not stand in the way of the continuation of their good relations[70].

The great diet of Mainz was concluded with a magnificent dinner, where the emperor appeared *sub corona* to give emphasis to the splendour of the occasion[71]. It was an impressive conclusion to an historic diet, but it could hardly make up for the fact that the emperor, who had called the diet 'in order to reform the state of the land' (*pro reformatione totius terrae status*)[72], had failed to reach his primary objective: the election of his son Conrad as successor to Henry (VII). It proved even harder to win the approval of the German princes, ecclesiastical and secular, for the election of Conrad than it already had been for the election of Henry (VII)[73], the more so since Frederick II was out of

Frederick's son Conrad not elected king of the Romans

---

be converted into imperial tenures by transferring his land to the emperor and receiving it back as a 'fief de reprise'. See MGH *Const.* 2 no 197, 264. In addition, Frederick bought and enfeoffed Otto of Lüneburg with the remaining parts of the Guelph inheritance, such as the city of Brunswick, that had fallen to the two daughters of Henry, a brother of Otto IV and an uncle of Otto of Lüneburg, Agnes and Irmengard, married to Duke Otto of Bavaria and Count Hermann of Baden respectively.

67   MGH *Const.* 2 no 197, 264: '*Otto de Luneburch flexis genibus coram nobis, omni odio et rancore postpositis que inter proavos nostros existere potuerunt, se totum in manibus nostris exposuit, nostris stare beneplacitis et mandatis*'.

68   See *Annales Wormatienses* ad ann. 1235, MGH SS 17, 44: '*Supervenit itaque breviter domna Elisabeth imperatrix, soror domni regis Anglie, cum qua domnus imperator celebravit nuptias in Wormatia sollempniter in divisione apostolorum*'. Contemporary rumour had it that Isabella was sent to Frederick's harem forthwith: Matthew Paris, *Chronica maiora* ad ann. 1235, ed. H.R. Luard 3, London 1876, 325.

69   See *supra* p. 173.

70   Frederick II to Louis IX, 25 April 1235, HB 4.1, 539-540. There were rumours at the time that Frederick II did indeed consider adopting the policy of Otto IV to enter into an offensive Anglo-German alliance against France. See Matthew Paris, *Chronica maiora* ad ann. 1235, ed. H.R. Luard 3, London 1876, 340. Since it would seriously have frustrated Frederick's Italian policy, it is highly unlikely that he ever seriously contemplated the idea. Frederick always insisted on good relations with France.

71   *Chronica regia coloniensis continuatio* 4, ad ann. 1235, MGH *SS rer. Germ.* 18, 267): '*imperator diademate imperiali insignitus*'.

72   Frederick in the charter granted to Otto of Lüneburg, MGH *Const.* 2 no 197, 264: '*pro reformatione tocius terre status indicta Maguncie curia generali*'.

73   See *supra* p. 213.

great privileges to grant to the German princes in exchange for their consent. There were no more constitutional favours to be granted to the princes without completely dismantling the German kingdom. The situation was complicated even further by the fact that Pope Gregory had sent an observer to the diet, the lawyer master Peter, who seems to have been secretly engaged in preventing the election of Conrad as well as in frustrating the attempts of Frederick to secure the support of the German princes for an expedition against the rebellious Lombard cities[74]. It must therefore have given Frederick at least some satisfaction that he was able to inform the pope that the German princes had decided unanimously to support his Lombard expedition. In order to prevent the pope from endlessly prolonging his attempts at 'mediation' in Lombardy, Frederick set a term to the papal efforts: he gave Gregory until Christmas 1235 to negotiate a peace with the rebellious Lombard cities that would bear out the honour of the Empire[75]. To demonstrate his personal goodwill, Frederick sent his chief diplomats, Grandmaster Hermann of Salza and Piero della Vigna, to assist in these negotiations. It was a diplomatic gesture since Frederick did not seriously contemplate peace with the Lombards but for their complete submission to his authority.

Frederick II realized that his Lombard policy would inevitably entail an open conflict with Gregory IX and he therefore decided to advertise his reasons for a military intervention in Lombardy beforehand in an open letter to the kings of France and England[76]. His father and grandfather would never have contemplated an initiative like this. The Lombard affair was, to them, an internal matter of the Empire for which they were not accountable to anyone except to God. The premature demise of Frederick's father and the imperial papacy which Innocent III had been able to establish in the ensuing power vacuum had changed all that. Now a Roman emperor had to justify his Lombard policy to his European colleagues by emphasizing that it was not, as the pope alleged, a war, but the legitimate 'judicial prosecution' (*exsecutio iuris*) of his rebellious subjects[77]. But there is more to this letter. Ever

Frederick
justifies his
Lombard policy

---

74 There is a letter from Gregory to the German princes invited to the diet, dissuading them to support Frederick's Lombard policy: MGH *Const.* 2, no 194, 239. For the activities of 'magister Petrus' in preventing the election of Conrad, or even anyone else from the house of Hohenstaufen, as king of the Germans see Frederick II in an encyclical letter issued after his second excommunication: MGH *Const.* 2, no 224, 308-312(309).

75 MGH *Const.* 2, no 195, 239-240.

76 HB 4.2, 872-880. The first line reads 'We speak reluctantly, but we cannot stay silent' (*Inviti loquimur, sed tacere non possumus*), as in earlier apology: see *supra* p. 235.

77 HB 4.2, 879: '*non guerre nomine debuit tam salubre propositum denotari, sed iuris executio potius, a qua omnis abest iniuria*'.

since his youth[78], Frederick II had perceived the pope primarily as a political actor hungry for secular power at the expense of the Empire. Innocent III's attempts at 'restoring' papal secular authority in Italy[79] was, to him, sufficient proof. He had witnessed the dismal fate of the counts of Toulouse, his brothers-in-law, and the terrible humiliation of his father-in-law King John, demonstrating the boast of canon law that *'the necks of kings and princes are under the knees of priests'*[80]. He himself had to suffer constant interference by the pope in the internal affairs of his Italian kingdom, forcing him to make a dishonourable peace with rebellious subjects. By extensively relating what caused him to disregard the papal call for peace, he made it clear to the kings of France and England that what happened to him, might happen to them as well[81]. It was another call for the solidarity of the kings of France and England if it came to a conflict with the pope on account of his actions in Lombardy. It was left to Piero della Vigna to find the proper words for this message[82].

By August 1236 Frederick was back in Lombardy and welcomed in Verona by his warlord Ezzelino, thanks to whom he had been able to cross the Brenner Pass unhindered[83]. The emperor had brought an army of 1000 fully armoured German knights with him[84], a force

Frederick in Lombardy and in Austria

---

78 See *supra* p. 164.

79 See *supra* p. 158.

80 *Decretum* Dist. 96, cap. 10: *'videas regum colla et principum submitti genibus sacerdotum'.* The quotation is from the famous letter of Gregory VII to Bishop Hermann of Metz (*Das Register Gregors VII.*, 8,21, MGH *Epp. sel.* 2,2, 544-563 (555). On this letter see also *infra* p. 330.

81 For this see the admonition at the end of the letter (HB 4.2, 880): 'Look sharply if it is in your interest that, when you yourselves at one time may decide to suppress a bold audacity of your subjects, someone from outside interferes with your affairs by advancing some reason or pretext by which he frustrates or holds up your plans' (*oculo cernite perspicaci si vobis expediat quod, cum ad edomandam interdum protervam audaciam subditorum intenditis, vestris negotiis extrinsecus aliquis se interponat, causamque aliquam aut occasionem afferat per quam vestra precidat proposita vel retardet*).

82 See the heading of the letter in one of the manuscripts in which it (partly) survives (BNF, Cod. Latinus no 8567, *f.* 27 vo): *'Fred. Imperator per Petrum de Vineis'.*

83 See *supra* p. 271.

84 *Annales Veronenses* ad ann. 1236, MGH *SS* 19, 10: *'Eodem anno 16. Augusti domnus Fredericus imperator cum tribus milibus militibus Theutonicis venit Veronam, et in monasterio sancti Zenonis benigne receptus est per dictum domnum Icerinum de Romano'.* A German source, the *Chronica regia coloniensis, Cont. 4* ad ann 1236, MGH *SS rer. Germ.* 18, 269, has 1000 knights, rather than the 3000 of the Veronese chronicle. The discrepancy can be explained by the fact that a fully armoured knight usually was accompanied by two mounted squires. In addition, there were 500 German knights present in Verona, sent ahead by Frederick in May 1236 under the command of his legate Gebhard of Arnstein: *Chronica regia coloniensis, Cont. 4* ad ann 1236, MGH *SS rer. Germ.* 18, 268. It is said (see *supra* p. 270, fnt. 17) that the Lombard League could raise an army of 3000 knights at the time. This is a

much smaller than his father and grandfather had with them in their Italian campaigns. In addition to his German troops, the emperor had to rely on military support from the Lombard cities loyal to him, such as Pavia, Cremona, Parma, Modena, and Reggio; troops from the Sicilian kingdom, such as the formidable Saracen warriors from Lucera; troops commanded by war lords like Ezzelino and the redoubtable Salinguerra Torelli (*c.* 1170-1245)[85]; and, last but not least, mercenaries, to be paid for by his subservient Sicilian taxpayers. The German contribution to Frederick's Lombard army was relatively small because the duke of Bavaria and the king of Bohemia were on a punitive expedition with a considerable army against the outlawed Duke Frederick II of Austria[86]. This is why the emperor, after quickly consolidating his position in the north-eastern part of Lombardy with the help of Ezzelino, went to Austria with his son Conrad to 'reform' that duchy after Duke Frederick had been ousted out of most (but not all) of it. It was there, in the Austrian capital of Vienna, that Frederick finally was able to achieve the election of his son Conrad as king of the Germans in February 1237.

Frederick's son Conrad nominated as 'king elect'

The election of Conrad IV (1228-1237-1254) in Vienna is a curiosity in medieval German constitutional history. According to the charter documenting his election[87], he was elected by an electoral college consisting of the archbishops of Trier, Mainz, and Salzburg, four bishops (of Bamberg, Regensburg, Freising, and Passau) and four secular princes, Duke Otto of Bavaria, who was also count palatine at the Rhine, King Venceslas of Bohemia, Landgrave Henry of Thuringia, and Duke Bernhard of Carinthia. The electoral college presented itself at this occasion as representing the ancient Roman senate[88]. This

---

number from a Lombard source, making the Lombard force, according to the German way of counting, smaller than Frederick's German army.

85 Salinguerra sided with Frederick II mainly because of his feud with Azzo d'Este (see on Azzo *supra* p. 184), who had sided with the pope. Their feud was about the possession of the city of Ferrara.

86 It sometimes, though rarely (as in the case of Henry the Lion (*supra* p. 122)), happened that a German prince misbehaved in such a way that he was outlawed by his peers. Ever since the demise of his father Duke Leopold in S. Germano in 1233 (see *supra* p. 267, fnt. 3), Duke Frederick of Austria had been waging war on his neighbours, the duke of Bavaria and the kings of Bohemia and Hungary. In 1235 Duke Frederick finally was outlawed for disturbing the peace of the realm and the duke of Bavaria and the king of Bohemia were commissioned to occupy the duchy and to arrest the duke. Frederick II and the duke of Austria were later reconciled: see *infra* p. 369.

87 MGH *Const.* 2, no 329, 439-441.

88 MGH *Const.* 2, no 329, 439-441(440): '*nos Sifridum Maguntinum, Theodericum Treverensem, Eberhardum Saltzburgensem archiepiscopos, Ecbertum Bambergensem, Sifridum Ratisponensem, imperialis aule cancellarium, Frisingensem et Pataviensem episcopos, Ottonem palatinum comitem Rheni ducem Bawarie, Venceslaum regem Bohemie, Henricum lantgravium*

unique assessment was inspired by the doctrine of 'transfer of empire' (*translatio imperii*), but *not* as it was reported in the famous decretal '*Venerabilem*' of Innocent III[89], but as it was expounded by Frederick's grandfather Barbarossa in Otto of Freising's biography of Frederick I[90], a book Frederick II must have read. There is no reference to a 'transfer of empire' to the Germans *by the pope*, as in *Venerabilem*, but the Roman Empire had come to reside with the German nation 'on account of reasons no less credible than necessary' (*non minus probabili quam necessaria ratione*), that is, by means of conquest. After the Roman Empire had thus been transferred to the Germans, the privilege to elect the emperor, once residing in the senators of ancient Rome, now belonged to the princes of the German Empire[91]. Exercising that privilege, the electoral college chose Conrad as their *electus rex* ('king elect'), a curious title Conrad carried for the rest of his (short) life, since he never was crowned king of the Germans in Aachen as tradition prescribed and as all German kings had been before him, including his half-brother Henry (VII)[92]. In addition, the electors solemnly declared that they designated Conrad as 'emperor to be' (*futurus imperator*), to whom the imperial title would spring as of right after the demise of his father[93].

Thuringie et B. ducem Carinthie, principes, qui circa hoc Romani senatus locum accepimus, *qui patres et imperii lumina reputamur*' (emphasis added).

89   See *infra* p. 334-336.

90   See *supra* p. 97.

91   MGH *Const.* 2, no 329, p. 439-441(440): 'True as it may be that from the origin of the city *<i.e.* Rome> supreme power over the realm and the right to elect an emperor resided with the senators, yet, due to the subsequent and continuous expansion of the empire and its ever-increasing power, the dignity of a fortune like that could not be limited to but one city, however royal above all. After it has wandered, as if on a meandrous journey, to the ultimate boundaries *<i.e.* Constantinople>, it has finally come to reside with the German princes on account of reasons no less credible than necessary, so that the origin of imperial power emanates from the same persons by whom its welfare and defence are secured' (*Nam quamquam in Urbis initiis ... apud ... patres summa regni potestas et imperialis creationis suffragium resideret, ex successivis tamen et continuis incrementis imperii, postmodum calescente virtute tante fortune fastigium apud unicam civitatem, licet pre ceteris regiam, non potuit contineri. Sed postquam etiam remotissimos terminos quadam girovaga peregrinatione lustravit, tandem apud Germanie principes non minus probabili quam necessaria ratione permansit, ut ab illis origo prodiret imperii, per quos eiusdem utilitas et defensio procurantur*). Comp. the remarks of Frederick I 'Barbarossa' in *Ottonis episc. freisingensis Gesta Friderici* 2,30, MGH *SS rer. Germ.* 46, 137: '*Penes nos sunt consules tui. Penes nos est senatus tuus*'.

92   See *supra* p. 217.

93   MGH *Const.* 2, no 329, p. 439-441(441): '*nos ... unanimiter vota nostra contulimus in Conradum antedicti imperatoris filium ... eligentes ipsum ... in Romanorum regem et in futurum imperatorem nostrum post obitum patris habendum*' and '*domino imperatori sacramento firmavimus, quod prefatum Conradum a nobis in regem electum post mortem prenominati patris sui dominum et imperatorem nostrum habebimus*'.

Frederick
attempts to rally
the European
princes into an
anti-clerical
alliance

It is clear from the document attesting to the election of Conrad IV that Frederick II was now in open defiance of the pope. In 1220, after the election of Henry (VII), he had still sent his excuses to Pope Honorius for not asking his consent for the election of his son[94]. Now he intentionally brushed aside a papal decretal, '*Venerabilem*' (X. 1,6,34), not only by refusing to request the the pope's approval of Conrad's election, but also by publicly contesting, if not mocking, the papal version of the doctrine of '*translatio imperii*', that most important expression of papal sovereignty (*plenitudo potestatis*) in Gregory's code. He was clearly treading in the fateful footsteps of his grandfather, who had also defied papal aspirations and also tried to subject Lombardy to his imperial will. Frederick must have believed that he had a far better chance to achieve that goal than Barbarossa, since, unlike his grandfather, he had all the resources of the Sicilian kingdom at his disposal.

Frederick II has always believed that European kings and princes ought to unite in a common effort to resist the active interference of the Roman pontiff in secular affairs and that it was in their common interest to relegate the pope's activities to purely spiritual affairs. It was to this end that he took a very unusual initiative in 1236: a conference of European princes to settle the problem before his military campaign in Lombardy. The emperor had a recent example at hand to demonstrate the intolerable interference of the pope in the affairs of his Italian kingdom to his European colleagues. Gregory IX had appointed Giacomo da Pecorara, the cardinal-bishop of Palestrina, as his legate in Lombardy in 1236, purportedly to promote 'peace' in Lombardy[95]. Cardinal Giacomo da Pecorara, a native of Piacenza, took the opportunity to change the political situation in his native city. Piacenza was under the authority of a local strongman, Guillelmo de Andito, at the time, who had handed over the city to the emperor in the previous year, but the papal legate succeeded in driving Guillelmo and his sons from Piacenza and installing a Venetian *podestà*, thus bringing the city over to the Lombard League, all 'under the pretext of peace' (*sub specie pacis*). Piacenza was in rebellion against the emperor ever since[96]. This was not mediation, but party politics, and it outraged Frederick. No European king could tolerate papal legates to incite rebellion in his realm and the emperor wanted the European princes to make a united front against this presumptuous papal policy. The conference was to

---

94 See *supra* p. 217.
95 See the letter of Gregory IX to Frederick II announcing the appointment of Cardinal-Bishop Giacomo da Pecorara of Palestrina as papal legate in Lombardy '*ad promovendum pacis et concordiae*' in HB 4.2, 870-871. It appears from this letter that the pope had deliberately sent another legate than the one for which Frederick II had been asking.
96 For the Piacenza incident see *Annales Placentini Gibellini* ad ann. 1236, MGH *SS* 18, p. 470-474 (474): '*exinde Placentini rebelles imperatori fuerunt*'.

convene at Vaucouleur, the usual venue for meetings of French and German monarchs, on 24 June 1237. Frederick's initiative alarmed the pope, who decided to put a stop to it. We do not know by what means Gregory IX succeeded in convincing King Louis IX of France that the conference was a trap, but it may have been the suspicion of a collusion between the king of England, now closely related to Frederick II by his marriage to a sister of Henry III, and the German emperor, always a cause of concern to French monarchs. Louis decided to be prepared and gathered an impressive army to accompany him to the conference. Frederick II was startled by this and cancelled the meeting, to be post-poned to 24 June 1238[97]. Nothing is heard of it later since the emperor was too far ahead of his time. The idea of limiting the *plenitudo potes-tatis* of the pope to spiritual affairs and of subjecting papal authority to the control of a general council of the Church belongs to a later time and age.

Frederick II wrote an angry letter to Gregory IX complaining about the hostile intervention of Cardinal Giacomo da Pecorara in Piacenza. The emperor was tired of papal interference in his Italian kingdom under the pretext of peace and he refused to accept further mediation by par-tial 'brokers' (*proxenetae*) between his Lombard subjects and himself. At the time he wrote the letter, he must still have hoped that his confer-ence with the other European monarchs at Vaucouleur would take place and therefore he wrote to the pope that he much preferred the inter-vention of his royal friends rather than a manifest enemy like Cardinal Giacomo da Pecorara of Palestrina[98]. Gregory IX answered with a bitter letter of his own, rejecting all Frederick's complaints about that faith-ful servant of the Church and bringer of peace, Cardinal Giacomo da Pecorara, and heaping countless reproaches on the emperor. At the end of his letter, Gregory brought up the heavy artillery of papal dogma to impress on the recipient that '*the priests of Christ are the fathers and*

Gregory IX
asserts his
plenitudo potestatis

---

97   For the projected Vaucouleur conference see Matthew Paris, *Chronica maiora* ad ann. 1237, ed. H.R. Luard III, 393; Matthew Paris, *Historia Anglorum* (*Historia minor*) ad ann. 1237, ed. Madden II, London 1866, 397 and Guillaume de Nangis (†1300), *Chronicon* ad ann. 1238, in *Recueil* 20, 548.

98   Hahn, *Collectio Monumentorum* etc. 1, Brunswick 1724, 218-223(220): 'You must, fur-thermore, not accept it as a sign of anger, but rather as a warning that we do not want our cause to be smothered at the bosom of the bishop of Palestrina, a very different person than the one you have written about <in the letter referred to *supra* in fnt. 95, a man whom we have come to know as an enemy rather than as an arbiter of peace. We do not accept any other interme-diaries between ourselves and our subjects than our princes and friends' (*Non indignationi preterea debetis ascribere sed cautelae, quod causam nostram in sinu Prenestini Episcopi suffocare noluimus, quem alium prorsus invenimus, quam scripsistis, quem adversarium evidentem potius, quam federis arbitrum sumus experti ... inter nos et imperio nostro subiectos nullos recipimus prox-enetas, sed principes et collaterales nostros solummodo*).

the masters of the kings and princes of all the faithful'[99]: the Donation of Constantine, his own version of the doctrine of 'transfer of empire' (*translatio imperii*), and his *plenitudo potestatis*, emphasizing that in granting the crown of the empire to Frederick II, the pope had done so 'without in any way diminishing the substance of his own authority'[100]. The emperor had to bow to the will of the pope, Gregory wrote, quoting his great inspirer Gregory VII: '*You must see that the necks of kings and princes are under the knees of priests. Christian emperors not only have to put their administration of affairs under the control of the Roman pontiff, but also must not give preference to other advisors*'[101]. Frederick II must have regarded the references in Gregory's letter to the Donation of Constantine and the papal doctrine of 'transfer of empire' as an insult to his intelligence and the quotation from Gregory VII as an outright affront to the dignity of the Empire.

The battle of
Cortenuova

In September 1237 Frederick II was back in Lombardy, where he gathered a much stronger force than in the previous year. He had brought extra forces from Germany with him, while substantial reinforcements were arriving from Tuscany and Apulia, Muslim Lucera alone sending an army of 7000 mounted archers[102]. He was now ready to take on the Lombard League. His punitive campaign started with the city of Mantua, surrendering to Frederick's overwhelming force on 1 October 1237[103]. By taking Mantua, Frederick had driven a wedge between the members of the League in Lombardy proper and Bologna, the most important member of the League in the Romagna, since Modena to the north of Bologna sided with the emperor. Consequently, there were no troops from Bologna involved in the great battle which Frederick was able to force upon the Lombard League at Cortenuova, some twenty kilometres south of Bergamo. The League suffered a terrible defeat there on 27 November 1237. It lost no fewer than 10,000 men: from Milan alone 800 knights, among them the *podestà*, Pietro Tiepolo, a son of

---

99 HB 4.2, 914-923 (922) (also in MGH *Epp. saec. xiii* 1, no 703, 599-607(605)): '*sacerdotes Christi regum et principum omnium fidelium patres et magistri censentur*'.
100 HB 4.2, 922 (also in MGH *Epp. saec. xiii* 1, no 703, 604): '*nichil de substantia suae iurisdictionis imminuens*'.
101 HB 4.2, 919 (also in MGH *Epp. saec. xiii* 1, no 703, 602): '*regum colla et principum submitti videas genibus sacerdotum, et Christiani imperatores subdere debeant executiones suas non solum Romano pontifici, quin etiam aliis presulibus non preferre*'. The last sentence no doubt refers to Frederick's planned conference with the other European kings and princes in Vaucouleur. For the quotation of Gregory VII (in *Decr.* Dist. 96, cap. 10) see *supra* p. 281, fnt. 80.
102 Parisius de Cereta († after 1277), *Annales Veronenses* ad ann. 1237: '*14. Septembris applicuerunt in districtu Mantuano septem milia Saraceni sagittarii missi de Apulia in adiutorium domni imperatoris*'.
103 Rolandinus Patavinus, *Chronica* ad ann. 1237, MGH *SS* 19, 66-67.

the Doge of Venice, while 3000 foot-soldiers were taken captive[104]. The knights were made prisoners to be transferred to Apulia and released (or executed[105]) later but were first paraded through the streets of Cremona in Frederick's great triumphal procession[106]. The Milanese *carrocio*, the symbol of urban autonomy, was a prominent part of that pageant, worthy of the triumphal procession of a Roman emperor. Frederick had it sent to Rome as a gift to the people of Rome. Partisans of the emperor put it on display on top of the Capitol, as was done in antiquity with the prominent spoils of war of the Roman emperors of old. The pope was 'deeply saddened' (*ad mortem doluit*) by this gesture, especially because some of his own cardinals participated in the event[107].

Great battles are sometimes qualified as 'decisive', meaning that they have produced significant political results. They seldom do, since mostly it is diplomacy which decides whether a great battle is indeed 'decisive'. The battle of Legnano was 'decisive' because Barbarossa opened serious peace negotiations with Pope Alexander III after his defeat by the Lombard League. The battle of Cortenuova was not 'decisive'. It was a great military victory for Frederick II, in fact the greatest he ever achieved, but it had no 'decisive' diplomatic outcome. The Lombards tried hard but failed because of the intransigence of Frederick II. They offered to dissolve the Lombard League and even to renounce all benefits of the Peace of Konstanz, but Frederick II insisted on unconditional surrender and complete submission to his sovereignty[108]. This the mem-

---

104   For these numbers see *Annales Placentini Gibellini* ad ann. 1237, MGH *SS* 18, 477. The number of 10,000 Lombard casualties is confirmed by Ryccardus de S. Germano, *Chronica* ad ann. 1237, *RIS*² 7.2, 196. The enormous number of prisoners from Milan and other cities of the League is confirmed by the extensive list of prisoners taken at Cortenuova compiled soon after the battle by Frederick's chancery. It is printed in HB 5.1, p. 610-623.

105   The son of Doge Tiepolo was later executed as a reprisal for the raids of Venetian galleys on the coast of Apulia: *Annales Placentini Gibellini* ad ann. 1240, MGH *SS* 18, 484.

106   Frederick's great victory at Cortenuova was made known to the citizens of the Empire in an encyclical letter composed by Piero della Vigna. It contains a detailed description of the triumphal procession in Cremona: HB 5.1, 137-139.

107   *Annales Placentini Gibellini* ad ann. 1238, MGH *SS* 18, 478: '*Eodem namque mense mandavit imperator Romam carocium Mediolani super mullos qui illud portaverunt, cum multis signis et vexillis et tubis per partes Pontremulli. Quod carocium cum apud Romam duxissent, domnus papa usque ad mortem doluit, et illud in urbem introducere prohibere voluit; quod utique sentiens pars imperatoris que erat in ipsa urbe, illud carocium intus civitatem honorabiliter conduxerunt; quod positum fuit in Capitolio per cardinales*'.

108   See on this episode *Annales Placentini Gibellini* ad ann. 1237, MGH *SS* 18, 478 and Matthew Paris, *Chronica maiora* ad ann. 1238, ed. H.R. Luard III, 495-496) and especially Fredrick II himself in a famous encyclical letter from 1244 (see *infra* p. 313, fnt. 41): HB 6.1 p. 204-221(215) (August 1244, also in MGH *LL* 2, p. 346-352(349)): 'They have offered to submit publicly to us for the honour of ourselves and the Empire and to lay their banners at our feet; they have also offered to dissolve the League and to renounce from the Peace of Konstanz' (*obtulerunt nobis pro honore nostro et imperii publice ponere se in mercede nostra et proicere vexilla eorum ad pedes nostros, obtulerunt etiam societates dissolvere et renunciare paci a*

bers of the League, especially Milan, categorically refused. They were not prepared to agree to a *reformatio imperii* Barbarossa-style, meaning the *de facto* restauration of the infamous *Lex 'Omnis iurisdictio'* Frederick's grandfather had forced upon them at Roncaglia in 1158[109]. Like their grandfathers before them[110], they were determined to die as free men for the 'honour of Italy' (*honor Italiae*) rather than live the miserable lives of the slaves of an oriental despot.

Frederick
excommunicated
a second time

The emperor had learned nothing from his grandfather's failed Italian expeditions nor from the vicissitudes of earlier German emperors trying in vain to subdue the Lombard cities. Just as his grandfather had suffered a serious and humiliating setback before the walls of the city of Crema shortly after the submission of the Milanese in 1158[111], Frederick II suffered an even more serious debacle before the walls of Brescia within a year after Cortenuova. The citizens of Brescia had the audacity to brave the victor of Cortenuova and inflicted a terrible blow to the military prestige of the emperor. A last and devastating sortie by the men of Brescia forced Frederick to withdraw after a siege of no less than four months (July-October 1238). It was an enormous boost to Lombard resolve and decided their future strategy. They avoided pitched battles, forcing the emperor to arduous and (mostly) unsuccessful sieges of the strongly defended Lombard cities, slowly but surely exhausting his resources. By this Lombard strategy, Frederick's Italian war was drawn into a military quagmire with no end in sight.

By 1239 Gregory IX realized that the momentum of the Lombard war had turned against the emperor and decided to isolate his opponent politically. On 20 March 1239 he excommunicated Frederick II for a second time: '*On the authority of the Father, the Son, and the Holy Ghost and of the holy Apostles Peter and Paul and Ourselves, we excommunicate and anathematize Frederick, the man who is called emperor*'[112]. He produced a long list of complaints against Frederick II, primarily about Frederick's alleged misconduct in his Sicilian kingdom, where churches

---

Constancie). It was the submission to his absolute sovereignty (*iurisdiccionem et merum imperium*) that was the breaking-point, as Frederick II himself clarifies (HB 6.1 p. 204-221(216 and 217)): '*super jurisdictionibus autem contentio erat*' and '*de iurisdictione ... similiter contentio fuit*' and especially (217) '*De iurisdiccione autem, quam nos simpliciter sicut quilibet rex in terra sua habere volebamus, similiter contemptio fuit*'. On the meaning of the word '*iurisdictio*' in this context see *supra* p. 107, fnt. 9.

109   See *supra* p. 107-108.
110   See *supra* p. 129.
111   See *supra* p. 106.
112   HB 5.1, 286-289(286): '*Excommunicamus et anathematizamus auctoritate Patris et Filii et Spiritus Sancti et beatorum apostolorum Petri et Pauli et nostra Fredericum dictum imperatorem*'.

and monasteries were expropriated, illegally taxed, and even sacked at the behest of the king; where many episcopal sees were left vacant far too long, to the great detriment of the faith; where clerics were illegally arrested, incarcerated, and even murdered at the command of the king, and much more, but there was one matter passed over in silence: 'the Lombard affair' (*negotium Lombardorum*). Gregory had to avoid the impression that by excommunicating Frederick he was actively taking sides in a political conflict, but the real motive of Frederick's second excommunication was purely political: the pope wanted to dispense with Frederick II, and he believed that he had a good candidate to replace the Hohenstaufen prince as emperor.

19

Frustrated councils

In 1239 Pope Gregory IX sent Cardinal Giacomo da Pecorara of Palestrina, that master of the subtle art of intrigue, as his legate to France with a very delicate mission. Cardinal Giacomo had been sent as a legate to the Provence in the previous year but had been unable to reach his destination because Frederick II had stopped him from causing mischief there as the cardinal had done before in Piacenza[1]. This time, however, Cardinal Giacomo travelled in disguise. He safely arrived at the court of Louis IX carrying a letter from the pope, profusely praising the many services the kings of France had rendered the church in the past, shortly explaining why he had excommunicated that enemy of the Church, Frederick II, and warmly recommending the bearer, Cardinal Giacomo[2]. The letter does not say what precisely the mission of the cardinal was, other than requesting the support of the king for Gregory's policy. Letters like these were not meant to reveal confidential information, since the true message of the pope to the king of France was to be delivered by the bearer orally. We know from other sources what that message was: Gregory IX suggested another 'transfer of empire' (*translatio imperii*), this time from the Germans to the

Cardinal Pecorara's secret mission to France

---

1 See *supra* p. 284. The obstruction of Cardinal Giacomo da Pecorara's mission to the Provence was one of the charges brought against Frederick in Gregory's sentence of excommunication: HB 5.1, 286-289(286): '*Item excommunicamus et anathematizamus eumdem, pro eo quod venerabilem fratrem nostrum Prenestinum episcopum, Apostolice sedis legatum, ne in sua legatione procederet quam in Albigensium partibus pro corroboratione catholice fidei sibi commisimus, per quosdam fideles suos impediri mandavit*'. As we know from the instruction of Cardinal Giacomo da Pecorara (MGH *Epp. saec. xiii* 1, no 731, 630-631), it was his mission to absolve Count Raymond VII of Toulouse (on him see *supra* p. 205-207), who had been excommunicated (once again). Raymond was a vassal of Frederick II for his fief in the Provence and also Frederick's brother-in-law (see *supra* p. 207). It clearly was Cardinal Giacomo da Pecorara's mission to drive a wedge between Frederick II and his vassal in the Provence. In September 1239 Frederick II received a letter from Raymond promising to assist him 'against all our ecclesiastical and secular enemies and especially against the pope and his supporters' (*contra omnes inimicos nostros ecclesiaticos et mundanos et specialiter contra papam et fautores eius*): HB 5.1, 403-404 (404).
2 Gregory's letter to Louis IX is in HB 5.1, 457-461.

French[3] by substituting Count Robert of Artois, the king's brother, for Frederick II as Roman emperor[4]. King Louis, or rather his wise mother, the Queen Dowager Blanche of Castile, was not inclined to play that dangerous game and forbade Robert to accept the offer of the imperial crown[5]. The king also had the good sense to inform Frederick II about the papal démarche forthwith. Frederick's efforts to appeal to the solidarity of the European princes seemed to have paid off, but there was an important proviso to Louis's attitude in the whole affair of the Empire. He had made it very clear to Gregory IX that he refused to partake in any hostile act against his 'good neighbour' (*bonus vicinus*) Frederick, *unless* the emperor was convicted by a general council of Christendom[6].

---

3   *Chronica regia coloniensis continuatio 5*, ad ann. 1239, MGH *SS rer. Germ.* 18, 273-274: 'The pope sent letters of excommunication to all the provinces of the Church. He also sent the bishop of Palestrina to France. After he had reached France, travelling in disguise for fear of the emperor, he proposed on the authority of the pope to transfer the empire, that was said to be vacant, from the Germans to the French, urgently requesting the king of France to accept it' (*Itaque papa litteras ex communicationis ad omnes mittit provincias. Mittit etiam in Galliam legatum Prenestinum episcopum, qui, metu imperatoris mutato habitu, regnum Francie ingressus, proponit ad mandatum pape Romanum imperium, quod dicebatur vacare, a Germanis transferre in Gallos, ad hoc recipiendum sollicitando regem Francorum*).
4   Matthew Paris, *Chronica maiora* ad ann. 1239, ed. H.R. Luard III, 624, has a summary of the substance (*summa et tenor*) of Gregory's message to Louis IX: 'Let it be known to the beloved son of the Church, the illustrious king, and all of the French nobility, that after due consideration and consultation with all of our brethren, we have condemned Frederick, who calls himself emperor, and have deprived him of the imperial office, and that we have replaced him by Count Robert, brother to the king of the French, who, in all his efforts, has proved to be a strong supporter and champion, not only of the Roman church, but of the Church at large. Consequently, you must not hesitate to accept this spontaneously presented dignity with open arms, for the realization of which we shall amply provide money, labour, and influence' (*Noverit dilectus filius ecclesie spiritualis, illustris rex, et totum Francorum baronagium, nos deliberacione et tractatu diligenti omnium fratrum nostrorum condempnasse et a culmine imperiali abiudicasse Frethericum dictum imperatorem et Robertum comitem, fratrem regis Francorum, loco ipsius elegisse substituendum, quem etiam omnibus nisibus ecclesia non tantum Romana, sed universalis, duxit non segniter adiuvandum et efficaciter promovendum. Nullo igitur modo tantam sponte oblatam <dignitatem> apertis brachiis suscipere pigritemini, ad quam opes et operam et opem habundanter effundemus consequendam*).
5   Alberich of Troisfontaines († after 1250), *Chronica* ad ann. 1241, MGH *SS* 23, 949: '*res ista de mandato pape delata fuerat ad domnum Robertum fratrem regis Francie, sed de consilio et providentia matris opus intactum remansit*'. In 1240 Frederick wrote a letter to Robert of Artois, thanking him for this gesture of friendship and solidarity: HB 5.2, 1086-1087. Alberich reports that similar offers had been made to a son of the king of Denmark and to Otto of Brunswick previously, all of them in vain. Otto of Brunswick is reported as having said 'that he did not want to suffer a demise like his uncle, the Emperor Otto <IV>' (*quod nollet mori simili morte, qua patruus suus imperator Otto fuit mortuus*). This was the second time Otto of Brunswick refused to accept the crown of the Empire from the hands of the pope (see *supra* p. 247).
6   Matthew Paris, *Chronica maiora* ad ann. 1239 (ed. H.R. Luard III, p. 625): '*Qui si meritis suis exigentibus deponendus esset, non nisi per generale concilium cassandus iudicaretur*'. Louis' response as reported by Matthew Paris is presented by Matthew as an answer of the French

It is hardly a coincidence that Frederick II was contemplating the possibility to call for a general council of Christendom at the very same time. It may even have been the very idea which he had wanted to propose to his fellow princes at the aborted Vaucouleur conference.

The news of his excommunication did not come as a surprise to Frederick II. He was informed beforehand that it was forthcoming and had sent a message to the college of cardinals to prevent it from happening. It is one of his diplomatic masterpieces since he consigned a shared responsibility (*equa participatio*) to that college for the decisions of the pope[7]. At the same time, Frederick had sent his best lawyers, Thaddaeus of Suessa and Walter of Ocra, to Rome to plead his case with the cardinals. The lawyers carried a letter from Frederick II to the cardinals, urging them to convene a general council, to be attended by the cardinals and the other high clergy of Europe, the German princes, and all the kings and princes of Europe, where the emperor could appeal against the actions of a manifestly unjust and biased pope[8]. Gregory IX, however, excommunicated the emperor before the cardinals could act (20 March 1239)[9]. The pope widely distributed his sentence of excommunication

Frederick II urges the cardinals to call a general council

---

nobility to the papal initiative, rather than of Louis himself. This was not the only occasion the king used his nobility as an excuse to reject a papal request. For another important instance, see *infra* p. 323. Note that Louis's grandfather, Philip Auguste, had also refused to support the papal war against Count Raymond VI of Toulouse *unless* Raymond had been duly tried and convicted for heresy (which he was not at the time): see *supra* p. 203.

7   Letter from 10 March 1239, HB 5.1 282-283: '*cum ad singula que presidens Sedi Petri proponuit statuere, vel denuncianda decreverit, equa participatio vos admittat*'.

8   MGH *Const.* 2, no 214 (March 1239), 289-290(290): 'They have been given full powers of attorney by our majesty to appeal on our behalf before the venerable assembly of fathers against the charges and the unfair prosecution by the same father <the pope>, first of all to the living God, to whom we owe all we are, and after that to a future pope, to a general council, to the princes of Germany, and generally to all kings and princes of the world and all other Christians' (*concessa eis ab excellencia nostra potestate plenaria, ut a gravamine et iniquo processu patris eiusdem coram tam venerabili cetu patrum primo ad Deum vivum, cuius nutibus attribuimus quicquid sumus, et deinde ad futurum summum pontificem, ad generalem synodum, ad principes Alamanie et generaliter ad universos reges et principes orbis terre ac ceteros christianos pro parte nostra libere valeant appellare*). Also in HB 6,1 p. 275-277, but incorrectly dated later.

9   There is a remarkable letter from Cardinal Giovanni Colonna to his colleague Odo of Monferrat, the cardinal-deacon of the S. Nicola in Carcere, who was papal legate in England at the time (1237). Colonna complains about the erratic behaviour of Gregory IX, his impulsive actions and the lack of opposition within the college of cardinals (Matthew Paris, *Chronica maiora* ad ann. 1237, ed. H.R. Luard III, 445-446): 'I have wanted to change the situation, as I have often tried. But then there is a shameful lack of support. Advice is ignored; every time a compulsion is not checked by the restraint of prudence there is an impulsively agitated run to the abyss not allowing for any restraint' (*Voluimus reformare statum, ut saepe temptavimus; et ecce deformis destitutio subintravit. Incassum traduntur consilia, ubi voluntas non sistitur fraeno prudentiae, sed impetu agitata prosilit ad proclivia, nec patitur retardari*). Colonna was not yet a partisan of Frederick II at the time but wanted to avoid an all-out confrontation with the emperor. It was to him and other independently minded cardinals like him that

all over Christendom and unleashed his shock troops, Dominicans and Franciscans, into the world to preach against Frederick, the enemy of Christ. Frederick II reacted promptly by also publishing an encyclical letter, addressed to the German princes and all other European princes and kings, calling for a general council[10], accusing the pope of personal bias and complaining of the presumptuous papal interference in the affairs of his Italian kingdom, once again warning European kings and princes that it was in their own interest to support him and to stand up against the papal claim of political supremacy[11]. Frederick's letter to the European princes contained an extensive and very personal attack on Gregory IX who had drawn, as Frederick put it, the spiritual sword against him in a purely secular affair, the Lombard question[12]. Gregory reacted furiously in an outrageously vehement diatribe against

---

Frederick addressed his letters calling for a general council. Cardinal Colonna later fell out with Gregory IX: see *infra* p. 300.

10   HB 5.1, 295-307(304) (also in MGH *Const.* 2, no 215, p. 290-299(297)): 'That is why, through our envoys and letters, we have called upon the cardinals of the Holy Roman Church to convene a general council of prelates and other faithful Christians, to which your ambassadors and those of the other princes must also be invited, in the presence of all of whom we are prepared to reveal personally and prove all that we have said and even worse things than that' (*ecce quod sacrosancte Romane ecclesie cardinales ... per nuncios nostros et litteras attestamur, ut generale concilium prelatorum et aliorum Christi fidelium debeant evocare; nunciis etiam vestris et reliquorum principum accersitis, in quorum presencia nos ipsi presentes cuncta que diximus sumus hostendere et probare parati, et his etiam duriora*).

11   HB 5.1, 295-307(305) (also in MGH *Const.* 2, no 215, p. 290-299 (298)): 'Be aware that similar perils also threaten your own affairs, since the humiliation of all other kings and princes seems easy once the power of the Roman emperor, whose shield takes the first blows, is broken' (*Similia vobis in vestris imminere pericula timeatis. Facilis etenim aliorum omnium regum et principum humiliatio creditur, si cesaris Romani potencia, cuius clipeus prima iacula sustinet, conteratur*).

12   Frederick to the cardinals (HB 6.1, 275-277(277), also in MGH *Const.* 2, no 214, 289-290(290)): 'since he believes he can do anything he likes he draws the spiritual sword against us in a secular affair' (*dum credat sibi licere quod libeat, spiritualem contra nos gladium temporaliter exerat*). See also Frederick in his earlier letter to the cardinals (HB 5,1 282-284 (283)): 'Who does not wonder and is not surprised that the one who occupies the throne of the catholic church (I wish he were a righteous judge) and is surrounded by a congregation of so many venerable fathers prefers to proceed unadvised and draws the spiritual sword in favour of Lombard rebels' (*Quis enim non miretur et stupeat, quod tot venerabilium patrum congregatione munitus Ecclesie generalis sedens in solio (utinam justus iudex) inconsulte velit procedere ... et ob favorem Lombardorum rebellium exercere spiritualem gladium*).

the emperor[13], accusing him (among many other sins) of blasphemy, if not outright atheism[14].

In April 1239 Gregory IX sent a new legate to Lombardy, Gregorio de Montelongo. The legate turned the Lombard rebellion against Frederick II into a crusade against the excommunicate who called himself emperor. The soldiers of the League took the cross and the banners of the League were now displaying the keys of Saint Peter and the Cross[15]. This must have been a disturbing development for some of the cardinals still hoping for a peaceful settlement, such as Cardinal Giovanni Colonna, since the pope acted in breach of secular as well as canon law by initiating executory measures against an excommunicate within a year after his excommunication[16]. It did not disturb the conscience of a very learned lawyer, Cardinal Sinibaldo Fieschi, who was dispatched to the Marche of Ancona in 1239[17]. Sinibaldo was actively involved in a 'coup' to bring Ravenna, until then staunchly loyal to the emperor, over to the papal party and the Lombard League

Gregory IX launches a crusade against Frederick II

---

13   From the opening lines of Gregory's invective (MGH *Epp. saec. xiii* 1, no 750 (1 July 1239), 645-654(646)): 'A monster has risen from the sea with its mouth full of blasphemy, with the claws of a bear and the maw of a lion, and the rest of his limbs belonging to a leopard, ravingly opening his beak blaspheming the name of the Lord. Look closely at the head, the body, and the backside of that beast. It is Frederick who calls himself emperor' (*Ascendit de mari bestia blasphemie plena nominibus, que pedibus ursi et leonis ore deseviens ac membris formata ceteris sicut pardus, os suum in blasphemias divini nominis aperit ... caput, medium et finem huius bestie Fr. dicti imperatoris diligenter inspicite*).

14   MGH *Epp. saec. xiii* 1, no 750, 645-654(653): 'there is proof that this king of pestilence has said that the whole world has been deceived by three impostors, to use his own words, Jesus Christ, Moses, and Mohammed' (*probationes ... sunt parate, quod iste rex pestilentie a tribus barattatoribus, ut eius verbis utamur, scilicet Christo Iesu, Moyse et Machometo, totum mundum fuisse deceptum*). Even worse than this, if possible, was the charge (*l.c.*) that Frederick was supposed to have said that 'a man must believe nothing else than what can be proved by reason and the observation of nature' (*homo nichil debet aliud credere, nisi quod potest vi et ratione nature probare*).

15   *Annales Placentini Gibellini* ad ann. 1239, MGH *SS* 18, 481: 'In the month of April the pope sent Gregorio de Montelongo, his notary and legate, to the city of Milan. As soon as he had arrived there, he went to Old Lodi, after the citizens had taken the cross at his initiative and two banners were made, one with the cross and another with the keys on it' (*de mense Aprilis domnus papa direxit Gregorium de Montelongo eius notarium et legatum in civitatem Mediolani; qui statim ut ibi accessit, sumptis civibus de mandato eius signo crucis et paratis duobus vexillis cum crucibus et clavibus intus, venit ad Laudum vegium*). De Montelongo never attained the cardinalate. He was made bishop of Tripoli in 1249 and elevated as patriarch of Aquileia in 1251.

16   Art. 7 of Frederick's coronation statutes, an adaption of X 5,7,13 ('*Excommunicamus*'): see *supra* p. 256, fnt. 18.

17   There are two letters in the correspondence of Gregory IX (MGH *Epp. saec. xiii* 1, no 767 and 779, 666 and 677) styling Sinibaldo as *rector Marchie Anconitane* at the time.

in that year[18]. It was a painful experience for Frederick II, who favoured Ravenna as an imperial city[19], and it may have been one of the reasons why he formally reversed the donation of the Marche of Ancona and the duchy of Spoleto which he had conferred on the pope and the Church at Eger in 1213[20]. The loss of Ravenna was one of the many drawbacks Frederick had to suffer in 1239: the brother of Ezzelino da Romano, Alberico, went over to the papal party, as did Azzo d'Este and the count of Sambonifacio, all of them powerful war-lords, while his attempts at subduing Milan, Piacenza, and Bologna had resulted in as many costly failures[21]. But his greatest misfortune was the loss of his trusted advisor and chief negotiator, Grandmaster Hermann of Salza, who died on the very same day Frederick was excommunicated. It was an irreparable loss since the grandmaster was an undisputed authority in Frederick's court as well as in the Roman curia and consequently an important asset in the diplomatic relations between the emperor and the pope. None of the successors of Hermann of Salza succeeded in rising to his level of authority. Meanwhile Gregory IX was closing the diplomatic net around Frederick II. To begin with, Gregory IX made a covenant with Venice to support him in the conquest of the Sicilian kingdom, granting important privileges to that city in the Sicilian kingdom once the pope had gained effective control there[22]. At the same time, he had joined a treaty between Milan, Piacenza, and Genoa, promising that he would not make peace with the emperor without the consent of the other parties[23].

---

18   *Chronica regia coloniensis continuatio 5*, ad ann. 1239, MGH *SS rer. Germ.* 18, 274: '*Item papa, misso Suenebaldo, avertit Ravennam ab imperatore*'. See the letter to the citizens of Ravenna from Gregory IX (MGH *Epp. saec. xiii* 1, no 767, 666). According to the contemporary *Chronicon* of Pietro Cantinelli from Bologna ad ann. 1239, ed. Fr. Torraca, *RIS²* 28.2, 3, the city of Bologna, the strongest representative of the Lombard League in the region, supplied the necessary military support. See on the involvement of Bologna also *Corpus Chronicorum Bononiensium* ad ann 1239, ed. A. Sorbelli, *RIS²* 18.1, part 2, 112 (Cron. A) and *Spicilegium Ravennatis Historiae* ad ann. 1238, ed. Muratori, *Rerum Italicarum Scriptores* 1.2, Milan 1725, col. 578 E. On the fall of Ravenna in 1239 see also *Annales Placentini Gibellini* ad ann. 1239, MGH *SS* 18, 481. Frederick was able to reconquer Ravenna in the next year but lost it again sometime later. After that the city definitively came over to the Guelph side.
19   He wrote a bitter letter to the citizens of Ravenna, expressing his disappointment with their conduct: HB 5.1, 371-373.
20   See *supra* p. 194 and 216. For the recall of the donations see MGH *Const.* 2, no 218, 302-303. According to Roman law a donation could be made undone due to the ingratitude of the donee: C. 8,55,10.
21   On all this *Annales Placentini Gibellini* ad ann. 1239, MGH *SS* 18, 481-482.
22   For the detailed treaty between Venice and the pope (23 September 1239) see MGH *Epp. saec. xiii* 1, no 833), 733-736.
23   *Annales Placentini Gibellini* ad ann. 1239, MGH *SS* 18, 481: 'At the same time, the men of Milan and Piacenza made a treaty with Genoa, sending ambassadors over sea to the pope who was in the city, and made a covenant with him that henceforward they would not make

Gregory's treaty with the leading members of the Lombard League made him officially a party to the conflict between Frederick II and his Lombard subjects. He was at war now with Frederick on issues not directly related to Frederick's excommunication. Frederick II was excommunicated for many reasons, but not because of his conflict with his rebellious Lombard subjects. Undoing his excommunication had now become a complicated matter, since the pope could not make his peace with the emperor without breaking his agreement with the Lombards not to make peace with Frederick without their consent. Alexander III had been in a similar position in his negotiations with the representatives of Frederick I at Anagni in 1176[24]. Pope Alexander had solved the conundrum by organizing a peace conference at Venice, but there were significant differences between the position Alexander III had been in at that time and the position of Gregory IX in 1239, the most important being that Gregory IX was confronted with the political consequences of the *unio regni ad imperium*, even more serious than before, now that Frederick II was regaining control over the Marche of Ancona and the duchy of Spoleto, thereby securing the corridor between Apulia and the Italian kingdom. There was, from the perspective of Gregory, only one way to prevent the looming subjection of the entire Italian peninsula to the absolute power of the king of Sicily: the deposition of Frederick II and the undoing of the *unio*. This could not be achieved without a war and so, like his namesake Gregory VII before him, Gregory IX decided that he should not 'keep back his sword from blood' (Jeremiah 48:10). Consequently, he opposed all peace initiatives of his cardinals.

Gregory's worst nightmare materialized in the early months of 1240, when Frederick II appeared before Rome with a strong army after subduing Tuscany and taking the important city of Viterbo. The emperor was reorganizing his Italian domain at the time, restructuring the administrative organization of the Italian kingdom and the kingdom of Sicily into a new unified state, a true *reformatio imperii*. His favourite son Enzio was appointed viceroy (*vicarius generalis*) in the Italian kingdom which was divided into new provinces that were governed *not*, as his predecessors had done, by imperial representatives bearing *feudal* titles such as dukes, counts, or margraves *of* a certain territory, but by 'representatives of the Holy Empire' (*sacri imperii vicarii*) *in* a

Frederick II before the walls of Rome

---

peace or a treaty with the Emperor Frederick without the consent of the pope or his successor. And the pope made the same promise to them' (*Eodem tempore Mediolanenses et Placentini cum Ianuensibus iuraverunt, mittentes per mare ambaxatores ad domnum Gregorium papam qui erat in Urbe, et concordium cum eo facientes, quod exinde non pasciscerentur vel concordium aliquod facerent cum imperatore Frederico absque voluntate domni pape vel eius successorum. Et ipse domnus papa illud idem eis convenit*).

24   See *supra* p. 126.

certain province. It was the final implementation of Barbarossa's *lex 'Omnis iuridictio'*. The administration of justice and local government was in the hands of imperial appointees: *vicarii* in the provinces, *capitanei* on the lower, regional, level, and in the cities *podesti* appointed by the emperor (but paid for by the cities), many of them of Sicilian origin and all of them with a staff of professional civil servants, *officiales*, Sicilian style. The fusion of the two Italian kingdoms was at hand and it seemed only logical to promote the city of Rome, the capital of the world (*caput mundi*), as the administrative centre of this newly reorganized 'Pan-Italian' state and there were, indeed, people at the time who believed that this was what Frederick had in mind[25]. He had certainly given that impression to the people of Rome, who received a letter from the emperor expressing his wish to 'restore the city of Rome to its ancient glory' and promising to elevate its citizens to high office in the administration of the Empire[26]. The Romans were ready to open the gates of the city to the emperor and Frederick was about to enter Rome triumphantly[27], when, in a last desperate attempt to win over the Romans, Pope Gregory organized an impressive religious pageant. Now that the citizens themselves were unwilling, the pope entrusted the defence of the city to the Holy Apostles Peter and Paul themselves. Their relics were solemnly carried through the streets of Rome from the Cathedral of St John to the great Basilica of St Peter. The people of Rome, always emotionally incontinent, succumbed to this pathetic gesture and now rallied to the support of Gregory by taking the cross in defence of the pope[28]. Frederick realized that a siege of Rome was out

---

25   The Dominican brother Bartholomew to the bishop of Brixen (HB 5.2, 1146-1147(1147)): 'He <the emperor> has taken the road to Rome with a large force of Germans, Lombards, and men from the Sicilian kingdom, wanting to raise the signs of his power and clemency in the capital of the world in order to spread virtue from the head to the limbs' (*ipse cum magna milicia Germanorum, Lombardorum et regni versus Romam iter suum direxit, intendens in mundi capite potentie et etiam clementie sue signa relinquere ut virtus a capite in membra diffundatur*).
26   HB 5.2, 760-762(760), February 1240: 'Ever since our earliest youth our heart has always been on fire to restore Rome, the initiator and originator of the Roman Empire, to its ancient glory and, ever since the burden of the Empire has been entrusted to us, to honourably implicate its nobles and citizens in the administration of the realm, by appointing some of them at our side in public offices at the imperial court and others as presidents of regions and governors and commanders of provinces' (*Ardens semper fuit cor nostrum ab etatis nostre principio ... ut autorem pariter et auctricem imperii Romani reformaremus Romam in statu dignitatis antique, ac procerers ac cives suos ... ex commisso nobis imperii honoris onere, non indigne ad partes solicitudinis vocaremus; quosdam preficientes circa latus nostrum publiciis officiis aule Caesaree; quosdam ad presidiatus regionum pariter ac provinciarum administrationes et regimina statuentes*).
27   At this time, Frederick sent a letter to an anonymous addressee informing the recipient of his recent successes in Tuscany and his imminent admission to the city of Rome (HB 5.2, 762-763(763)): '*urbem feliciter ingredi disponamus*'.
28   *Annales Placentini Gibellini* ad ann. 1239, MGH *SS* 18, 483: '*Interea domnus papa erat in Urbe; ad quem imperator multos ambaxatores mandavit, et omnes Romani clamabant: Veniat, ve-*

of the question since it would only add fuel to the fire of papal propaganda against him. He garrisoned the cities he controlled in the vicinity of Rome, such as Viterbo, and returned to Apulia in the early days of March 1240[29], leaving his son Enzio in command of the war scene in Lombardy, the Marche, and the Romagna.

There must have been considerable panic in the papal *curia* during the days Frederick II was before the walls of Rome. Some of the cardinals had enough of Pope Gregory's aggressively anti-imperial policy and contacted Frederick II, who responded by sending his ambassadors to the city[30]. The cardinals revitalized Frederick's earlier initiative to convene a general council[31] and even succeeded in coming to an agreement with Frederick. The council was to convene on Easter next year (1241) and until that day a truce (*treuga*) was to be observed[32]. The agreement still stood even after subsequent events at Rome and Frederick's ensuing departure for Apulia. Not all cardinals agreed with this course, however. When news of the truce reached Cardinal Giacomo da Pecorara in France, where he was raising money to finance Gregory's war against Frederick, he sent an angry letter to Gregory IX, informing him that he had raised enough money in France to wage war against Frederick for a whole year, urging the pope not to give

A temporary truce

---

niat imperator, et accipiat Urbem! Unde papa audiens vociferationem eorum timuit valde, et congregatis Romanis extrasit foras reliquias beatorum Petri et Pauli dicens: Ecce reliquie pro quibus civitas vestra veneratur; ego autem non possum facere magis alter homine! et alia verba consimilia, extrahens coronam de capite suo et imposuit super reliquias, dicens: Vos sancti defendite Romam, si homines Romani nollunt defendere. Quapropter maior pars Romanorum ibidem incontinenti levaverunt signum crucis in defensionem ecclesie'.

29 Annales Placentini Gibellini ad ann. 1239, MGH SS 18, 483: 'videns imperator nichil ibi posse facere, motus exinde equitavit in Apuliam, dimittens comitem Simonem cum 400 militibus in custodia Viterbii'.

30 Annales Placentini Gibellini ad ann. 1239, MGH SS 18, 483: 'Interea domnus papa erat in Urbe; ad quem imperator multos ambaxatores mandavit' (emphasis added) and Matthew Paris, Chronica maiora ad ann. 1240, ed. H.R. Luard 4, London 1877, 30: 'ex tunc congregate sunt cardinales, dicentes quod noluerunt Papales impetus in periculum totius Christianitatis amplius tolerare'.

31 See *supra* p. 294.

32 Matthew Paris, Chronica maiora ad ann. 1240, ed. H.R. Luard IV, 30: 'Thus the cardinals, after careful consideration and with the consent and at the initiative of the emperor, notified that they agreed to his initiative to convene a general council as quickly as possible, to be assembled in the traditional way. The day of Easter of the coming year was fixed as the day for the council to begin, so that the Church might be revitalized from the day of the resurrection of the Lord' (*Igitur significaverunt cardinales, inito prolixiori concilio, domino etiam imperatore consentiente et petente, quod iuxta petitionem suam bene volebant, ut convocaretur Concilium generale, sub quanta posset competenter celeritate, et rite celebrandum. Praefixus est igitur dies concilii proximo adveniente dies Paschae, ut a die, cum resurgente Domino resurgens ecclesia valeat feliciter respirare*). For the truce see Matthew Paris, Chronica maiora ad ann. 1240, ed. H.R. Luard IV, 58: 'Papam cum imperatore treugas usque ad Concilium in proximo Pascha celebrandum accepisse' and *infra* in fnt. 35.

in and to cancel the truce[33]. That truce must have bothered Gregory IX since it was a clear breach of his promise to the Lombards not to enter into negotiations with the emperor without their participation[34]. He therefore demanded that the Lombards were to be included in the truce already agreed upon between Frederick and the cardinals. His chief negotiators, Cardinal Colonna and Cardinal Rinaldo dei Conti di Segni, a relative of the pope, were ordered to relay this message to the emperor. Cardinal Colonna was furious, since he was expected to withdraw from the agreement that he had negotiated by introducing additional conditions not previously discussed. He therefore refused to comply with Gregory's request, but the new papal condition reached Frederick nevertheless. As a matter of course, the emperor refused to accept this added condition and so the truce was cancelled[35]. The decision to convene a general council, however, was not.

Gregory IX calls a general council

• After the cancellation of the truce, negotiations between Frederick II and the pope came to a halt[36], despite an attempt by Frederick's brother-in-law, Richard of Cornwall (1209-1272), to reopen negotiations. Richard visited the emperor and his wife, Richard's sister, in Sicily, on his way back from his tour of crusading duty in the Holy Land[37] and he offered his assistance in the plight of his brother-in-law. As Richard later wrote, he made a 'little detour' (*diverticulum*) to Rome in 1241 to persuade the pope to come to terms with the emperor[38]. It was a complete failure. Richard found Gregory 'inflexible and rebellious' (*inexorabilis et rebellis*) and returned to Sicily, having seen enough of Rome and the papal *curia* to displease him thoroughly. '*It pleases me, that you*

---

33   For Cardinal Giacomo da Pecorara's reaction see Matthew Paris, *Chronica maiora* ad ann. 1240, ed. H.R. Luard IV, 58-59.

34   See *supra* p. 296.

35   For this incident see Matthew Paris, *Chronica maiora* ad ann. 1240, ed. H.R. Luard IV, 59 and a letter from Frederick II to an unknown prince or king, written on 18 July 1240, explaining why the truce between him and the pope was cancelled (HB 5.2, 1014-1017(1015)): 'Pope Gregory demanded that the Lombards, rebels against us and outlawed in the Empire, should be included in the truce and that he could not accept the truce if they were excluded, which was unacceptable to us' (*Gregorius dictus papa petebat Lombardos rebelles nostros et nostri bannitos imperii treugis ipsis debere muniri. Quibus exclusis treugas ipsas non poterat acceptare ... Quod intolerabile visum est nobis*).

36   The German princes tried to mediate in 1239, sending the new Grand Master of the Teutonic Order, Conrad of Thuringia, to Italy. See their letters to the pope compiled in MGH *Const.* 2, no 225-232, 313-317. This time, their initiative was to no avail. See *infra* p. 308

37   For Richard's achievements in Palestine see below p. 356, fnt. 21.

38   See Richard's letter about his travels and his experiences in the Holy Land in Matthew Paris, *Chronica maiora* ad ann. 1241, ed. H.R. Luard IV, 141: '*diverticulum fecimus, curiam Romanam adeundo*'.

have learned by experience what we have told you before', was Frederick's reaction to Richard's account of his Roman experiences[39].

All negotiations for peace might have failed, but Gregory adopted the initiative of his cardinals to convene a general council, albeit with a very different purpose. On 9 August 1240 Gregory sent invitations to the clergy of Europe to congregate at Rome on the date already fixed by the cardinals for the general council they had had in mind, Easter 1241. Similar invitations were sent to the kings of France, England, Scotland, Hungary, Denmark, Castile, Aragon, Portugal, and Bohemia, to the German princes, the count of Flanders, the English high nobility, and to the Doge of Venice. Invitations were also sent to the cities of the Lombard League and the nobles in alliance with it, such as Azzo d'Este, the count of Sambonifacio, and Alberico da Romano, all of them sworn enemies of Frederick II. The pope called a European summit, but without a proper agenda, since it was unclear for what specific reason all these ecclesiastical and secular dignitaries were to convene, except that the pope indicated that he needed their counsel 'on grave events and matters concerning the Apostolic See' (*grandes apostolice sedis eventus et causas*)[40]. Frederick II, who was not invited (he was excommunicated), noticed that the word 'peace' (*pax*) was missing in the papal invitation[41].

Frederick II saw through the game Pope Gregory IX was playing. He repeatedly emphasized that his conflict was not with the Church, but with the person of Gregory IX[42]. The priest Gregory was a 'public enemy of the Empire' (*publicus hostis imperii*) bent on the extermination of Frederick II in person and the house of Hohenstaufen in gen-

---

39   Matthew Paris, *Chronica maiora* ad ann. 1241, ed. H.R. Luard IV, 148: '*Placet mihi, quod quae dictis praelibavimus, experimento didicistis*'. Richard staid for two more months at the court of Frederick II, having a perfectly good time there: see *infra* p. 356, fnt. 21.

40   HB 5.2, 1020-, also in MGH *Epp. saec. xiii* 1, no 781, 679 (to the archbishop of Soissons). See for the impressive list of other invitees (MGH 680-683).

41   Frederick II in his encyclical letter to the European princes, on which more shortly (HB 5.2, 1037-1041(1039), also in MGH *Const.* 2 no 233, 318-321(319)): 'look at the content of this invitation, where nothing at all is written about a future peace treaty' (*formam huius convocacionis attende, in qua nil omnino de future pacis tractatu describitur*).

42   HB 5.2, 1037-1041(1040), also in MGH *Const.* 2 no 233, 318-321(320)): 'For the reverence due to the highest King, we think that the aforementioned bishop must be given to understand that we have no quarrel whatsoever with our mother the Holy Roman Church, but that we defend the justice of the Empire against the attacks of a priest of this kind and that we ward off injustice' (*ob reverentiam summi Regis sic nominato episcopo duximus respondendum quod nos cum sacrosancta Romana Ecclesia matre nostra discordiam non habemus aliquam, sed ab huiusmodi Romani pontificis impetus justitiam imperii nostri defendimus et injuriam propulsamus*).

eral, as Frederick wrote to the king of France[43]. Frederick had proposed a general council of Christianity in 1239 to have it sit in trial over 'a corrupt judge' (*iudex corruptus*) and to demonstrate his own innocence and the justice of the cause of the Empire in the process[44]. Gregory was now playing that very same game: he wanted a general council of Christendom to sit in judgement over Frederick II. The emperor was not going to allow that to happen, *'especially since we deem it highly improper for us, our empire, and all princes of the world to subject the cause of our honour to a prejudiced or a synodal court'*[45], as he wrote to the European kings and princes and all his subjects in the empire, warning them that he denied a free passage through his territory to anyone who wanted to attend the council Gregory had convened[46]. Since Frederick valued his good relations with the king of France above all, he sent a separate letter to Louis IX, also warning him that he would stop anyone who wished to come by land or over sea to a council that was convened to threaten his life[47].

The battle of
Monte Christo

Despite all imperial threats, the city of Genoa was willing to transport the papal legates Giacomo da Pecorara and Odo of Montferrat and a considerable number of French and Lombard bishops and other prelates to Rome. It was a perilous adventure under the circumstances[48],

---

43   HB 5.2, 1075-1077(1076): '*nos perdere cogitaret <scl. Papa> et eo impetu nostrum et nostri generis nomen perpetuo crederet abolere'*.
44   Frederick II in an encyclical letter from 16 March 1240 (HB 5.2, 841-846(843), also in MGH *Const.* 2 no 224, 308-312(310)): 'We have sent letters and envoys to his fellow-friars, asking them to convene a general council, in which we promised to demonstrate with crystal-clear arguments the wickedness of a corrupt judge and the justice of our Empire as well as our own innocence' (*Nos autem ... ad fratres suos literas et legatos transmissimus generale petentes concilium convocari, in quo iudicis corrupti nequitiam ac imperii nostri justitiam et innocentiam nostram argumentis arguere luce clarioribus spondebamus*).
45   Frederick in his encyclical letter to the European kings and princes on the general council the pope had announced, warning them that he would not allow free passage to their subjects if they might decide to participate in that council (HB 5.2, 1037-1041(1040), also in MGH *Const.* 2 no 233, 318-321(320)): '*presertim cum nobis, imperio et omnibus terre principibus inde-centissimum iudicemus, causam honoris nostri suspecto foro subicere vel iudicio synodali*'. HB 5.2, 1040 has the reading '*ecclesiasticum forum*', rather than '*suspectum forum*'. I prefer the latter reading: see the editor of MGH *Const.* 2, Lud. Weiland, in his comments on MGH *Const.* 2 no 233, 317-318 and 320(e).
46   HB 5.2, 1037-1041(1040), also in MGH *Const.* 2 no 233, 318-321(320): '*omnibus ad concilium evocatis per terram nostre dicioni subiectam in personis et rebus securitatem quamlibet denegamus*'.
47   HB 5,2 1075-1077(1076): '*Serenitas igitur regia non miretur si nos vocatis ad vocationem eiusmodi transitum terra marique paratis obstaculis prohibemus, cum pro certo sciamus quod ... ad salutis nostre dispendia convocantur*'.
48   For what follows see the chronicle of the Genoese city notary Bartolomeo scriba ad ann. 1241, ed. Pertz *SS* 18, 194-197, the short report in *Annales Placentini Gibellini* ad ann. 1241, MGH *SS* 18, 484, and Nicolaus de Carbio, *Vita Innocentii IV* cap. 3, ed. Pagnotti 77-78.

since ambassadors from Pisa had visited Genoa shortly before to warn the city that the Pisans would not hesitate to capture Genoese ships carrying passengers destined for the council. Consequently, there were many in Genoa opposed to the adventure, even more so since there was also an imperial fleet out at sea commanded by a Genoese admiral, Ansaldo de Mari, in the service of the Sicilian king. The acting *podestà* of Genoa, a nobleman from Piacenza and consequently sympathetic to the cause of the Lombard League, had some trouble convincing the citizens to agree to his decision but in the end it was decided to prepare a fleet of 27 armed galleys for the purpose. On 3 May 1241 the Genoese fleet encountered a combined Pisan-Sicilian fleet near the little island of Monte Christo. The ensuing naval battle was a disaster for the Genoese: only five of their galleys escaped, all other ships were either sunk or captured. The papal legates and all bishops and prelates on the Genoese galleys were taken prisoner and transported to Pisa, where they were handed over to imperial officials who moved them to Apulia to be incarcerated there. Gregory's Roman council was effectively frustrated.

Shortly after the battle of Monte Christo, Frederick wrote a triumphant letter to the German princes, informing them of that victorious battle and of his own victory over Faenza, a city that had finally fallen after a prolonged siege, whilst his allies of Pavia had inflicted a terrible defeat on the Milanese[49]. He also informed them that he was planning to enter the Papal State with his army to finally conquer Rome itself. In August 1241 Frederick was before the walls of Rome once again and it was there that he was among the first to learn that Gregory IX had expired, almost hundred years old, on 22 August 1241. Frederick II immediately informed his brother-in-law, King Henry III of England: '*he has finally died, the one by whom peace was denied to the world, who stirred up discord and imperilled the lives of countless people*'[50].

---

49   HB 5.2, 1126-1128.
50   HB 5.2, 1165-1167(1166): '*Revera mortuus est, per quem pax terre deerat, et vigebat dissidium, et quamplures in mortis periculum incidebant*'.

20

Diversions

As far as Frederick was concerned, the war in the papal territories was over after the demise of Gregory IX. He had always emphasized that his quarrel was not with the Church, but with the iniquitous priest Gregory. Now that Gregory had finally died, there was no cause for him to prolong the siege of Rome and he left for his Sicilian kingdom, leaving behind garrisons in Tivoli and Viterbo. Meanwhile, the cardinals gathered in Rome to elect a new pope. Many of them, like Cardinal Colonna[1], had left the city during the last months of Gregory's pontificate, either because they feared the wrath of the emperor or the rage of the pope[2]. At their return in Rome, the local strongman Matteo Orsini, a Guelf appointed by Gregory IX as senator of Rome, immediately incarcerated the college of cardinals in the 'Septizonium', a monumental ruin at the foot of the Palatine, where they were to remain until they had elected a new pope[3]. It was the first 'conclave' in the history of the papacy[4]. The college interned in these uncomfortable ruins consisted of only ten cardinals[5] and was hopelessly divided. It proved almost impos-

---

1 Ryccardus de S. Germano, *Chronica* ad ann. 1241, *RIS²* 7.2, 210: '*Johannes de Columpna cardinale discors a papa discedit, seque confert in Prenestino*'.
2 The dispersion of the college of cardinals during the last months of Gregory's pontificate is noted by many contemporaries and most of them agree that it was mainly due to the discord regarding Gregory's policy among them: see Matthew Paris, *Chronica maiora* ad ann. 1242, ed. H.R. Luard 4, London 1877, 194: '*animis dissipati, extincto caritatis inter eos igniculo*'; Nicolaus de Carbio, *Vita Innocentii IV* cap. 6 (ed. Pagnotti p. 79-80): '*cardinales, qui per Frederici imperatoris persecutiones et dissensiones fuerant per diversa loca, tanquam oves non habentes pastorem, dispersi*'; Salimbene de Adam (1221-1288/89), *Cronica* ad ann. 1241, MGH SS 32, 174: '*cardinales discordes erant et dispersi*'.
3 For what follows see Matthew Paris, *Chronica maiora* ad ann. 1241, ed. H.R. Luard IV, 164-165; 168; 170 and 172)
4 The word 'conclave' is derived from the Italian expression 'con chiave', meaning 'behind locked doors' (litt.: 'with the key').
5 The cardinals present (Matthew Paris, *l.c.* 164-165) were the Englishman Robert Somercotes, cardinal-deacon of S. Chrisogono; the Spaniard Gill Torres, cardinal-deacon of SS Cosmas and Damian; Goffredo Castiglione, cardinal-priest of S. Marco; the bishop of Ostia Rinaldo dei Conti (a relative of Gregory IX, by whom he was promoted, later Pope Alexander IV); Riccardo Annibaldi, cardinal-deacon of S. Angelo in Pescheria; Romano

sible to find a two-third majority for one of them, as was required by the bull of Alexander III[6], until the cardinals, exhausted after weeks of seclusion, in the end agreed upon Cardinal Castiglione, who took the name of Celestine IV. Matthew Paris writes that Celestine was already in his dotage and physically very weak[7]. Celestine's pontificate lasted no longer than a few weeks. He died on 10 November 1241. By that time, most cardinals had already left Rome since none of them wished to be enclosed in the ruins of the 'Septizonium' once again and thus began a period of *sedis vacantia* lasting more than a year.

It was rumoured at the time that Frederick II had favoured the election of cardinal Castiglione, Celestine IV[8]. The emperor must have hoped for a milder man to succeed the inflexible Gregory IX, someone like Honorius III had been. He may even have held hopes that he could close a favourable deal with that dotard, although his experience with Gregory IX must have taught him the lesson that old age is certainly not a guarantee for wisdom, flexibility, or leniency. Whatever Frederick's expectations might have been, Celestine's demise postponed his reconciliation with the Church indefinitely, certainly so since the cardinals, most of whom were staying in Anagni now[9], refused to elect a new pope as long as Frederick held the Cardinals Giacomo da Pecorara and Odo of Montferrat imprisoned, thus putting the blame for the prolonged *sedis vacantia* on Frederick. Similar criticism was voiced elsewhere[10] and with serious consequences. In the last months of 1241 two of the most important German ecclesiastical princes, the archbishops of Cologne

---

Bonaventura, cardinal-bishop of Porto (Santa Rufina); Cardinal Stefano dei Conti (another nephew of Innocent III, by whom he was promoted); Cardinal Raniero Capocci, deacon of S. Maria in Cosmedin; Cardinal Colonna; and Sinibaldo Fieschi. The English cardinal succumbed during the conclave. Matthew Paris reports a rumour that he had been poisoned by his colleagues Cardinal Giacomo da Pecorara of Palestrina and Odo of Montferrat were not participating, since they were still incarcerated by Frederick II. Note that there was no cardinal from the German Empire at the time.

6   See *supra* p. 33, fnt. 20.

7   Matthew Paris, *Chronica maiora* ad ann. 1241, ed. H.R. Luard IV, 172: '*in aetatem senilem declinantem et debilitatum*'. See also Martin of Troppau († 1278), *Chronicon* (Celestinus IV), MGH *SS* 22, 439: '*senex et infirmus electus, cito moritur*'.

8   Matthew Paris, *Chronica maiora* ad ann. 1241, ed. H.R. Luard IV, 164: '*huic electioni favit imperator*'.

9   Except for Cardinal Colonna, who was incarcerated by Matteo Orsini after the election of Celestine IV (Matthew Paris, *l.c.* 168). Colonna was by now a partisan of Frederick II and consequently persecuted by Orsini, who had Colonna's urban stronghold, the mausoleum of Augustus ('Lagusta'), besieged (Ryccardus de S. Germano, *Chronica* ad ann. 1241, *RIS*² 7.2, 210). The traditional rivalry between the two great Roman noble houses of Orsini and Colonna begins with this episode.

10   Matthew Paris, *Chronica maiora* ad ann. 1243, ed. H.R. Luard IV, 239: '*Credebatur enim et dicebatur … quod ipse <imperator> principaliter ecclesiae Romanae promotionem impediret, et vacationem sedis Apostolicae procuraret*'.

and Mainz, Conrad of Hochstaden and Siegfried (III) of Eppstein[11], turned against the emperor, claiming that Frederick frustrated the election of a new pope[12]. The defection of the archbishop of Mainz was extremely frustrating and embarrassing to Frederick since he had appointed the archbishop as 'caretaker of the realm' (*procurator imperii*) in 1237. Because his son Conrad IV was still a minor in 1241, Frederick appointed not one, but two leading German princes as 'caretakers of the realm' to replace the archbishop: Landgrave Henry of Thuringia and King Venceslas of Bohemia[13]. It was Frederick's way of honouring two secular princes who had been crucial to keep Germany on his side after his second excommunication in 1239. To properly appreciate this move, we have to make a step back in time.

Not long after Frederick's second excommunication, a diet of the German princes was called by his son, King Conrad IV, no doubt on the advice of Archbishop Siegfried of Mainz, then still the loyal 'caretaker' of the emperor in Germany. The diet convened at Eger (now Cheb, in the Czech Republic) on 1 June 1239. It was to decide a reaction of the German princes to Frederick's excommunication. There were at least two papal agents active in Germany at the time, inciting the princes to elect a new king. Cardinal Giacomo da Pecorara was trying to find interested parties elsewhere after his failure in France[14], whereas another exceptionally venomous (and very learned) papal agent was

German reactions to Frederick's second excommunication

---

11   Archbishop Siegfried was the third of his name and successor to his uncle, Archbishop Siegfried II, who had crowned Frederick as king of the Germans in 1215 (see *supra* p. 199).
12   *Chronica regia coloniensis continuatio 5*, ad ann. 1241, MGH *SS rer. Germ.* 18, 282. Archbishop Siegfried of Mainz promised by deed, dated on 10 September 1241, to join Archbishop Conrad of Cologne in his struggle for the cause of Pope Gregory IX (then already dead for a few weeks): T.S Lacomblet, *Urkundenbuch für die Geschichte des Niederrheins* etc. II, Düsseldorf 1846, no 257, 131. Consequently, Archbishop Conrad must already have turned against the emperor at an earlier date.
13   HB 6.2, 831-832 (a charter of Conrad IV from 1242): 'On the advice of Landgrave Henry of Thuringia, whom the emperor our father has appointed as guardian over ourselves and the empire in Germany' (*de consilio ... Henrici lantgravii Thuringie ... quem augustus pater noster procuratorem nobis et imperio deputavit per Germaniam*). For King Venceslas as *procurator imperii* see a charter from June 1242 in *Regesta diplomatica nec non epistolaria Bohemiae et Moraviae* I, Prague 1855, 503. That the two princes have exercised their function jointly and not successively is proven by a letter, sent by Frederick to both 'caretakers' of his son to keep a closer look at the education of the young king (HB 6.1, 243-245). Frederick sent a letter to his son at the same time, urging him to improve his manners and not so subtly reminding him of the dismal fate of his half-brother, Henry (VII) (HB 6.1, 245-246). Huillard-Bréholles dates these (undated) letters at 1244 ('*circiter*'), but they may well have been written at an earlier date.
14   *Chronica regia coloniensis continuatio 5*, ad ann. 1239, MGH *SS rer. Germ.* 18, 274: '*Rege autem Francorum hoc recusante, legatus similiter sollicitavit quosdam alios reges et principes*'. For Cardinal Giacomo da Pecorara's proposals to the king of France see *supra* p. 291-292.

active in Germany as well, especially in his native Bavaria. His name was Albert Behaim, an archdeacon who had been working as an advocate in the papal court and who had been sent to Germany by Gregory IX to spread the news of Frederick's excommunication and to sow the seed of discord there. Albert succeeded in bringing Duke Otto of Bavaria over to the papal side and it was through him that he attempted to persuade the German princes to elect a new king in the place of Frederick and his son Conrad. The motion was supported by the king of Bohemia but failed since the powerful 'landgraves' of Thuringia and Meissen resolved to side with the ecclesiastical princes still supporting Frederick and his son at the time[15]. Instead of sending a delegation of princes to the pope, as had been so successfully done in 1230[16], the diet decided to send Conrad of Thuringia, a brother of the landgrave and successor of Hermann of Salza as grandmaster of the Teutonic Order, to Italy to reconcile pope and emperor. The ecclesiastical and secular princes supporting this mission all sent individual letters to the pope to endorse it[17], but Grandmaster Conrad died in Rome on 27 July 1240 without accomplishing anything[18]. Meanwhile, Albert Behaim was still trying to find support for the election of a rival king, but this second attempt failed too, since the king of Bohemia, 'or rather the king of Blasphemy', had made his peace with Frederick II, leaving Duke Otto of Bavaria (and Albert Behaim) completely isolated[19]. It was for this reason that Frederick promoted the two German secular princes chiefly responsible for the consolidation of the Hohenstaufen position in the German kingdom in 1239 to the dignity of 'caretakers of the realm' after the defection of the archbishops of Mainz and Cologne, the two leading ecclesiastical princes of the German kingdom, in 1241, since it was obvious that his second excommunication and the prolonged *sedis vacantia* was now seriously compromising Hohenstaufen authority

---

15 See the excerpt of Albert's letter to Gregory IX in C. Höfler, *Albert von Beham*, Stuttgart 1847, 5: '*per mediatores Chunradus in suam sententiam traxit Thuringum Misniumque*' (also in HB 5.1, 345). See also *Annales Stadenses* ad ann. 1240, MGH 16, 367: 'Pope Gregory tried to persuade the princes to elect another, but he achieved nothing, because some of the princes wrote to him "that it was not his right to replace an emperor, but merely to crown the one that was elected by the princes"' (*Papa Gregorius ... principes super electione alterius sollicitavit, sed nichil profecit, quia quidam principum ei rescripserunt: "Non esse sui iuris, imperatorem substituere, sed tantum electum a principibus coronare"*). The letter referred to here has survived: Böhmer, *Acta imperii selecta*, Innsbruck 1870, no 965, 671-672 (also in HB 5.1, 398-400).

16 See *supra* p. 248.

17 See the letters by several German bishops, including Archbishop Siegfried of Mainz, the landgrave of Thuringia, the dukes of Brabant, Brunswick, Saxonia, and the margrave of Brandenburg in HB 5.2, 985 – 991; MGH *Const.* 2 no 225-232, 313-317.

18 *Annales Erphordenses* ad ann. 1238 and 1240, MGH *SS rer. Germ.* 42, 96 and 98.

19 See Albert's disillusioned report to Gregory IX in Höfler, *Albert von Beham*, Stuttgart 1847, 14-16(14) (also in HB 5.2, 1024-1027(1024)): '*rex Bohemiae vel potius Blasphemiae*'.

in the German territories. There was another incident, also occurring in 1241, that must have seriously disturbed the minds of all German princes, casting serious doubts on the efficacy of Hohenstaufen rule in Germany.

In the early months of 1241 two great Mongol armies, led by two grandsons of Genghis Khan, Batu and Orta, invaded western Europe. The king of Hungary, Bela, was thoroughly beaten by the southern Mongol army in the battle of Mohi (11 April 1241), while the northern Mongol force had completely routed a hastily raised army of German knights in the vicinity of Liegnitz in the duchy of Silezia (9 April 1241). The emperor had been informed in advance of the impending danger, but he excused himself to king Bela and his German subjects. He could not leave Italy to come to the rescue, since his Italian enemy (the pope) could not be trusted to leave his Sicilian kingdom unharmed if he did. He reminded the addressees that the pope, 'that dearest father of us all' (*iste carissimus pater noster*)[20], had once before invaded his Sicilian kingdom when he, the emperor, was abroad on a crusade. Thus, it transpired that as the Empire was threatened by a formidable enemy, the emperor was on the march indeed, but not to the endangered borders of the Empire, but to lay siege to Rome[21]. At the time when European civilization was endangered as never before, pope and emperor were entangled in a disastrous conflict, each blaming the other for his inability to lead Christendom in this hour of need. As we now know, European civilization was saved by sheer luck[22], but the contemporaries of Frederick and the pope were unaware of that. To them, the Mongol threat was all but over, and the events of 1241 had demonstrated that the German Empire had not only been totally unprepared, but also leaderless at the time, primarily due to the Italian priorities of the emperor. The elected German King Conrad IV was a twelve-year old minor, only capable of a symbolic gesture: he took the cross against the 'Tartars', as the Mongols were called, at a diet held, late in 1241, at Esslingen near Stuttgart[23], but he was incapable of organizing a unified German front against the Mongol aggression. The German princes were left on their

The Mongol invasion

20 Frederick in his letter from 20 June 1241 to his German subjects on the Tartar threat (HB 5.2, 1139-1143(1141), also in MGH *Const.* 2 no 235, 322-325(325)). In the same vein to king Bela of Hungary, in HB 5.2, 1143-1146.
21 See *supra* p. 297.
22 Ögedei Khan, son and successor of Genghis Khan, had suddenly died in 1241. The ensuing succession struggle forced Batu and Orta to call off the further invasion of Europe.
23 HB 5.2, 1214-1215; MGH *Const.* 2, no 336, 445-446. See also *Chronica regia coloniensis continuatio 5*, ad ann. 1241, MGH *SS rer. Germ.* 18, 281.

own[24] and some of them may have concluded that the absence of the emperor, due to his preoccupation with Italian affairs, now seriously jeopardized the safety of the German kingdom.

Frederick II realized the prolongation of the papal *sedis vacantia* was not to his advantage and released Cardinal Odo of Montferrat in August 1241[25], but he retained Cardinal Giacomo da Pecorara, a man he thoroughly detested, in custody. It was only in May 1243 that he finally sent him off to Anagni as well, to join his fellow-cardinals there[26], at the same time urging them to elect a new pope as soon as possible[27]. On 25 June 1243 the cardinals finally and unanimously agreed upon the choice of a new pontiff. It was Sinibaldo Fieschi, the cardinal-priest of S. Lorenzo in Lucina, who chose to be called Innocent, fourth of that name[28].

---

24   Matthew Paris (ad ann. 1241, ed. Luard IV, 109-111) has an alarming letter, sent by the landgrave of Thuringia to Duke Henry II of Brabant, married to his niece Sophia, on the impending danger of the Mongols and calling for immediate military support. The letter is dated on 10 March 1241, just weeks before the disastrous battle of Liegnitz. A similar letter was sent to the king of England by the Archbishop of Cologne (Matthew Paris, ad ann. 1241, ed. Luard IV, 111). It is a clear sign that young King Conrad IV and his ministerial advisors failed to organize a national defence.
25   Ryccardus de S. Germano, *Chronica* ad ann. 1242, *RIS²* 7.2, 215: '*Eo mense <Augusti> Oddo cardinalis liberatur*'.
26   Ryccardus de S. Germano, *Chronica* ad ann. 1243, *RIS²* 7.2, 216: '*Item mense Madii Prenestinus episcopus imperatore mandante liberatus est, et aput Anagniam ad cardinales cum honore remissus*'. See also Matthew Paris, *Chronica maiora* ad ann. 1243, ed. H.R. Luard IV, 240. The French clerics captured in the battle of Monte Christo had been released much earlier under strong diplomatic pressure by King Louis IX. Louis made it abundantly clear to Frederick that he would regard a refusal to immediately release the French prisoners as a *casus belli* and he reminded the emperor that he had done Frederick a great favour in the recent past (HB 6.1, 19): 'if you want to draw your attention to the past: we have publicly rejected the bishop of Palestrina and other envoys of the Church, who wanted to ask for our support much to your disadvantage, and they have not been able to achieve anything in our kingdom against Your Majesty' (*si ad preterita mentis vestre oculos vultis reflectere, Penestrinum episcopum et alios legatos Ecclesie, in prejudicium vestrum volentes subsidium nostrum implorare, manifeste repulimus, nec in regno nostro contra majestatem vestram potuerunt aliquid obtinere*). Frederick realized he was not in a position to refuse Louis's demand and released the prisoners (Guillaume de Nangis, *Chronicon* ad ann. 1241 (*Recueil* 20, 332)): '*Cuius verba et rationes imperator intelligens omnes, licet invitus, pariter liberavit, regem Ludovicum offendere pertimescens*'.
27   For Frederick's insistence on a speedy election of a new pope see his letters to the college of cardinals from March, May, and July 1242: HB 6.1, 35-36; 44 and 59-61, also in MGH *Const.* 2, no 236-238, 326-328,
28   Nicolaus de Carbio, *Vita Innocentii IV* cap. 6, ed. Pagnotti, 80: '*Mentibus in Deum directis, devotissime missa cantata et invocata sancti Spiritus gratia, in pace ac multa tranquilitate omnes unanimiter et concorditer vota sua direxerunt in dominum Sinibaldum tituli sancti Laurentii in Lucina presbyterum cardinalem; qui alto Dei consilio ad summum sacerdotii apicem anno Domini millesimo ccxliii. vi. die exeunte iunio, extitit sublimatus et, sicut moris est, proprio arrogato nomine, fuit Innocentius nuncupatus*'.

It is often contended that Frederick II and Cardinal Fieschi had been on good terms, even friends, before Sinibaldo was raised to the throne of St Peter[29]. It is highly unlikely. Frederick had a supporter in the 'conclave' that had elected Celestine IV, Cardinal Colonna, who must have informed the emperor of the attitude of Cardinal Fieschi. Fieschi had not supported the favourite of Frederick II (Celestine IV) at that occasion, but had rather opted for Cardinal Romano Bonaventura, a renowned lawyer like Sinibaldo himself and a strong supporter of Gregory's anti-imperial policy[30]. Nothing that Fieschi ever did before or after his election betrays any friendly attitude towards the emperor. To the contrary: Cardinal Fieschi had been personally responsible for the defection of Ravenna in 1239[31], a slight Frederick II did not forget, nor forgive[32]. Whatever his personal feeling about the new pope might have been, the emperor had to publicly welcome his election, if only to advertise his good will to the Church and his commitment to make a fresh start with the new pontiff. That is why he warmly congratulated Innocent with his election[33] and why he ordered the usual praises (*Laudes*) to be sung in churches throughout the Sicilian kingdom to celebrate the election of the new pope[34]. He needed to come to terms with Innocent IV to have his excommunication lifted. The insight that absolution was never to be had did not (yet) enter his mind.

In his congratulatory letter to Innocent IV Frederick II announced that he hoped for a peace 'subject to the right and honour of the Holy

Frederick II and Innocent IV

29 The purported friendship between Frederick II and Cardinal Fieschi before the latter's election is mainly based on a famous dictum of Frederick II reported in a fourteenth-century chronicle (Galvano Flamma (†1344), *Historia Mediolanensis*, cap. 276, ad ann. 1242, Muratori 11, col. 680): 'I have lost a good friend, since no pope can be a Ghibelline' (*Perdidi bonum amicum, quia nullus papa potest esse Gibellinus*). It is too good a *bon mot* to be left out of a story, but it is too bad a source to be taken very seriously. For a further dubious reference to an alleged '*amicitia*' between Frederick and Sinibaldo Fieschi see *infra* fnt. 33.
30 For this see Matthew Paris, *Chronica maiora* ad ann. 1241, ed. H.R. Luard IV, 164-165.
31 See *supra* p. 295.
32 See Frederick's encyclical letter from 16 March 1240, complaining of the mischief Gregory IX had caused in his Lombard kingdom (HB 5.2, 841-846(844), also MGH *Const.* 2 no 224, 308-312(311)): 'By the manipulations of Cardinal master S(inibaldo), who was appointed legate in the Marche at the time, he succeeded in taking the city of Ravenna from us and the Empire and to swear an oath of loyalty to the Church' (*Civitatem etiam Ravene ... tractante magistro S. cardinali et legato tunc in Marchia constituto, nobis et imperio subtrahens fecit sibi et ecclesie fidelitatis sacramenta prestare*).
33 HB 6.1, 104-105, also in MGH *Const.* 2 no 239, 328-329. Frederick calls Innocent 'an old friend' (*vetus amicus*) because he wants to remind him of the fact that the members of his family, the counts of Lavagna, were vassals of the Empire (*e nobilibus imperii*), so that he hopes and trusts that the new pope will respect the honour of the Empire and its just call for peace (*vetus amicus ... per quem confidat imperium vota pacis et sue justicie inviolata servari*).
34 Ryccardus de S. Germano, *Chronica* ad ann. 1243, *RIS²* 7.2, 217: '*quo audito domnus imperator, qui tunc erat Melfie, ubique per regnum laudes iussit Domino debitas decantari*'.

Roman Empire' (*salvis iure et honore sacri Romani imperii*). Negotiations did indeed resume. In August 1243 the pope sent ambassadors to Frederik's court to find out if and, if so, on what conditions peace negotiations could be effectively initiated. Their instruction, probably written by the pope himself, has survived[35]. It is couched in the astute style of the calculating lawyer that Innocent was. The negotiators were to find out if the emperor, as a gesture of his good will, was prepared to release all prisoners he had made in the battle of Monte Christo. If he was, the papal negotiators were empowered to open peace negotiations and to find out what satisfaction the emperor was prepared to offer for all the offenses he was excommunicated for by Gregory IX. This was a crucial point to Frederick and his lawyers. They wanted to concentrate the negotiations on the justice of the charges brought against Frederick in Gregory's sentence of excommunication and the possible means of giving satisfaction for the charges shown to be legitimate, but the Lombard question was to be kept out of the agenda, since it was *not* related to Frederick's excommunication[36]. It was the one issue on which Frederick could make no concessions, since 'the right and honour of the Empire' (*ius et honor imperii*) did not allow it.

Negotiations to
restore peace

Innocent had included a potentially poisonous option in the instruction to his envoys: '*if the prince says that he has in no way unlawfully caused damage to the Church, or if he says that we have unlawfully caused damage to him, we are prepared to convene the kings, prelates, and princes, secular and ecclesiastical, at a safe place to gather there themselves, or by their official representatives, and the Church is willing to offer satisfaction to the prince on the advice of that council if she has caused damage to him in any way, and to revoke her sentence if she has unjustly passed it over him*'[37]. The pope did not abandon the idea of a general council, but he phrased his proposal in such a way that it would sit in judgement over the Church rather than the emperor, thus coming very close to the purpose of the council on which Frederick himself had insisted at an earlier stage[38]. Frederick assured the papal envoys that peace with the pope and the Church was his priority, but he rejected the proposal for a general council, realizing that it would in fact come down to a trial of himself rather than the Church. He preferred, as he wrote later, 'a shortcut to

---

35   MGH *Epp. saec. xiii* 2, no 7, 7, also in MGH *Const.* 2, no 240, 329-330.
36   See *supra* p. 288-289.
37   MGH *Epp. saec. xiii* 2, no 7, 7: '*si princeps dicat, quod in nullo lesit ecclesiam contra iustitiam, vel si dicat, quod nos lesimus eum contra iustitiam, parati sumus vocare reges, prelatos et principes, tam seculares quam ecclesiasticos, ad aliquem tutum locum, ut per se vel solempnes nuntios illuc veniant, et de consilio concilii parata est satisfacere principi, si in aliquo eum lesit, et revocare sententiam, si quam iniuste contra eum tulit*'.
38   See *supra* p. 294.

peace' (*viam pacis breviorem*)[39] and sent his closest advisors, Piero della Vigna, Thadaeus of Suessa, and Archbishop Berardo of Palermo, to the pope with his proposals. That, however, was a step too far. The pope refused to see them, since all three of them had been excommunicated, as Innocent wrote to his envoys at Frederick's court[40]. After this obstacle was removed by means of *ad hoc* absolutions, negotiations could begin in earnest. It is not necessary to enter into these negotiations in great detail, since they are mere diplomatic diversions[41]. There was a fundamental and irreconcilable difference of opinion between emperor and pope on the character of the peace, excluding the possibility of a compromise acceptable to both parties.

The diplomatic situation in August 1243 resembles the preliminaries to the Peace of S. Germano, now more than ten years ago[42]. The negotiations between Frederick II and Gregory IX had come to a deadlock, due to the same underlying difference of opinion that frustrated the negotiations between Frederick II and Innocent IV now. It was 'the affair of the Lombards' (*negotium Lombardorum*). Then as now, the pope was allied with the Lombard League, having promised not to enter into negotiations with the emperor without the involvement of the Lombards, thus turning what was, formally, a matter of ecclesiastical discipline into an issue of secular politics. Peace had been finally agreed at S. Germano in 1230, but only thanks to the mediation (and the pressure) of a number of important German secular and ecclesiastical princes who had travelled to Italy 'to conclude peace' (*pro tractanda pace*). This time, however, there was no impressive delegation from Germany to force pope and emperor out of their diplomatic stalemate[43].

---

39   HB 6.1, 206, also in MGH *Const.* 2 no 252, 342 (encyclical letter of August 1244).

40   HB 6.1, 115-116, also in MGH *Const.* 2 no. 241, 331 (26 August 1243): 'The prince should not be surprised that we have not received the envoys he has sent to our presence, since the Roman pontiff never receives persons he knows to have been excommunicated before they have received absolution according to the precept of the Church' (*princeps ipse mirari non debet, si suos non admisimus nuntios ad nostram presentiam destinatos, cum nunquam Romanus pontifex excommunicatos scienter recipiat, antequam absolutionis beneficium iuxta formam ecclesie consequantur*).

41   The best summary of these negotiations is Frederick's extensive report in his encyclical letter of August 1244 in HB 6.1, 205-221, also in MGH *Const.* 2 no 252, 341-351.

42   See *supra* p. 245-246.

43   Grandmaster Conrad of Thuringia, the mediator dispatched to the pope by the German princes in 1239, had died in Rome in 1240 (see *supra* p. 308). His successor, Gerhard of Malberg, not only missed the prestige of Hermann of Salza, but also the powers to act in the name of the German princes. He is only mentioned in Frederick's congratulatory letter to Innocent IV (HB 6.1, 105) as one of the messengers bearing that letter. Frederick made no further use of him. Gerhard of Malberg was forced to resign as the order's grandmaster in 1244 and replaced by Henry of Hohenlohe. On him see *infra* p. 346.

Cardinal
Capocci takes
the initiative

The negotiations dragged on and on, much to the chagrin of Cardinal Raniero Capocci, who wanted no peace at all but was out for the destruction of Frederick II. Cardinal Raniero, now the strong man in the *curia*, was to Innocent IV what Ezzelino was to Frederick II, a completely ruthless war-lord. Raniero, cardinal-deacon of S. Maria in Cosmedin, was from Viterbo, a city occupied by imperial forces at the time[44]. He was appointed bishop of his native city by Innocent IV in 1243 and the cardinal decided to bring it back under papal control and to put an end to all peace negotiations at the same time. In September 1243 he succeeded in taking control of the walls and gates of the city, completely isolating and besieging the imperial garrison in the castle within the city. The local imperial commander, Simon of Theate, clearly the wrong man at the wrong place, sent desperate letters to Frederick II to come to his rescue[45], forcing the emperor into immediate action. By the end of September Frederick was before the walls of Viterbo. The siege lasted for more than two months and had to be raised in November without achieving any result[46]. Even the safe conduct of the hard-pressed imperial garrison Frederick had agreed with Cardinal Capocci turned into a disaster: the men were robbed, physically abused, and some of them were even murdered under the eyes of the cardinal[47].

A preliminary
peace
agreement

Frederick's misfortune before Viterbo seriously damaged his reputation, as had his similar debacle before Brescia in 1238[48], but it did not interrupt the ongoing peace negotiations. The matter of the Lombards continued to be the main obstacle. As a precondition to peace with the Church, Innocent IV wanted the emperor to make peace with the Lombards and release all his remaining prisoners, including the persons arrested before his excommunication in 1239[49], especially the hundreds

---

44   See *supra* p. 97 and 299.
45   See the letters in HB 6.1, 125-130.
46   On the siege of Viterbo see Ryccardus de S. Germano, *Chronica* ad ann. 1243, *RIS²* 7.2, 217-218). It is the last report in this important chronic. See also Nicolaus de Carbio, *Vita Innocentii IV* cap. 8, ed. Pagnotti 83-84 and the detailed, but much later, information in Niccola della Tuccia (1400-1473/1474), *Cronache e Statuti della Città di Viterbo* ad ann. 1243, ed. Ciampi, *Documenti di Storia Italiana* V, Florence 1872, 21-24.
47   See Frederick's letter to the king of France on the Viterbo affair in HB 6.1, 142-145.
48   See *supra* p. 288.
49   HB MGH *Const.* 2 no 252, 346 (Frederick II): 'Since the Church had committed itself to the Lombards, he claimed that he could not make peace with us in any other way unless he could bring peace to them and that we should offer peace to the Lombards, rebels of the Empire whom he called supporters of the Church, and set free the Lombard captives' (*petiit ut, quia ecclesia se ad hoc obligaverat Lombardis, quod non aliter nobiscum pacem faceret nisi poneret ipsos in pace, ut Lombardis, quos ecclesie adherentes vocabat, rebelles imperii, pacem daremus et liberaremus captivos ipsorum*).

of Lombards taken captive after the battle of Cortenuova[50]. Of course, the imperial negotiators[51] objected to this, since these Lombards were to be regarded as rebels and punished accordingly by their lawful monarch. It is reported that Innocent IV rebutted by questioning the right of Frederick II to sit in judgement over his Lombard subjects. It was an outrageous contention to the envoys of the emperor since it put in question Frederick's title to the crown of Italy[52]. As the imperial ambassadors must have known, that is precisely what the pope did. His predecessor, Gregory IX, had made an unsuccessful attempt at another 'transfer of empire' (*translatio imperii*), this time from the Germans to the French, directly after Frederick's second excommunication in 1239[53], but he had not stopped there: his agents had been active in Germany to find a substitute for Frederick II and his son Conrad IV[54]. After the defection of the two leading ecclesiastical princes of Germany, the archbishops of Cologne and Mainz, renewed attempts to replace the Hohenstaufens in Germany were to be expected. By the early months of 1244 Frederick's negotiators even may have been informed of ongoing consultations to that end between representatives of the pope and another German prince, the landgrave of Thuringia[55]. Hence the urgency of the imperial negotiators to come to an agreement with their papal counterparts[56]. On Maundy Thursday, 31 March 1244, they swore to a preliminary agreement in the name of the emperor. Innocent IV had orchestrated

---

50 See *supra* p. 286-288.
51 The imperial negotiators were Piero della Vigna, master Thaddaeus of Suessa, and Count Raymond VII of Toulouse. The addition of the latter, a vassal of Frederick II for his Provencal fiefs (see *supra* p. 291, fnt. 1), is remarkable since he was excommunicated many times.
52 MGH *Const.* 2 no 252, p. 346 (Frederik II): 'The pope firstly questioned whether the Lombards could be summoned in the court of the Empire, something not even the Lombards themselves had ever questioned before, since it is a fact that they belong to the Empire and are vassals of the Empire. The envoys further contended that it would be a very bad precedent if the pope questioned or put in doubt the jurisdiction of the Empire or of any king over their vassals, since nothing could then be done against a manifest wrongful act committed against the Empire or all other kings. Nevertheless, he <the pope> insisted, to our obvious prejudice and more so to our shame, that these captives were to be released without even an oath of fealty to be sworn by the Lombards' (*dominus papa primo de Lombardis conveniendis in curia imperii retulit questionem, quam Lombardi ipsi nullo tempore ante retulerant, cum ipsos de imperio et vassallos imperii fore constaret. Perniciosissimum exemplo preterea sepedicti nuncii fore dicebant, si de iurisdictione vassallorum imperii seu quorumlibet regum per dominum papam questio seu dubietas aliqua referetur. Nichil exinde in manifestam imperii et omnium fere principum iniuriam potuit optineri; immo in evidencius nostrum preiudicium et manifestiorem nostram iniuriam, nullis eciam sacramentis fidelitatis prestitis per Lombardos, ipsos captivos restitui postulabat*).
53 See *supra* p. 291-292.
54 See *supra* p. 292, fnt. 5.
55 See *infra* p. 317.
56 The negotiations on the part of the pope were conducted by the Cardinals Rinaldo, Stefano dei Conti, Cardinal Gil Torres, and Cardinal Odo of Montferrat: HB 6.1, 208-209, also in MGH *Const.* 2 no 252, 343 (encyclical letter of August 1244).

a proper ceremony for the occasion, attended by a host of pilgrims and many celebrities, the emperor of the Eastern Roman Empire among them[57].

The agreement finally concluded between the imperial and papal negotiators contained enormous concessions by the emperor, including a confession of guilt for everything for which he originally had been excommunicated by Gregory IX in 1239 and, of course, the return of all papal territories occupied by the emperor[58]. The oath sworn to by Frederick's representatives at Rome was unlike the oath sworn to by the representatives of his grandfather Frederick I at Anagni in 1176. After reaching a preliminary agreement with Pope Alexander III and his cardinals, the imperial representatives at Anagni had sworn a solemn oath that their lord would *ratify* the agreement reached there[59]. The representatives of Frederick II at Rome in 1244, however, had sworn in the name of Frederick II (*in anima sua*) and on the express authority of the emperor[60] that he would implement the agreement. In a case like this, the emperor was directly bound by his own oath as sworn to by his representatives without the need of further ratification[61]. What happened subsequently is a perfect example of the futility of any agreement between parties missing all confidence in the sincerity and the good faith of each other. It is likely that Innocent IV regarded the concessions of Frederick II as a one-sided submission by the emperor to his demands, whereas it is certain that Frederick II regarded his concessions as a *quid pro quo*, being the revocation of his excommunication. Therefore, the imperial representatives with the pope insisted on a timetable for the absolution of the emperor, whereas the pope insisted on the immediate performance of the imperial concessions, especially the restoration of papal territories, without any indication

---

57 It was the unfortunate Emperor Baldwin II (*c.* 1217-1228-1273), whose Latin Eastern Roman Empire, the miscarriage of the Fourth Crusade (*supra* p. 168), had by now been reduced to the city of Constantinople. The 'Greek' Emperor John III Vatatzes (*c.* 1193-1222-1254) was in the process of recovering the Byzantine Empire and Baldwin was in Rome to ask for the pope's support. On the good relations between the Byzantine Emperor John Vatatzes and Frederick II see *infra* p. 350.
58 The agreement is inserted in Frederick's encyclical letter of August 1244, HB 6.1, 207-210, also in MGH *Const.* 2 no 252, 343-344.
59 See *supra* p. 130.
60 See the powers of attorney granted by Frederick II to his Roman representatives on 28 March 1244 (MGH *Const.* 2 no 248, 338): '*Per presens scriptum ... specialem et plenam concedimus potestatem iurandi in anima et pro parte nostra*'.
61 This was an exception to the rule of Roman law not recognizing direct representation: see *supra* p. 130, fnt. 22. See on this issue the Gl. 'Et iurare' on *Decretum* Dist. 63 cap. 33 (*Tibi domino*).

of an imminent absolution of the emperor[62]. Consequently, the agreement resulted in a stalemate, neither party being inclined to make a move without the other doing so first. The situation was complicated by political considerations. Innocent IV was uneasy about the absence of a clause in the agreement committing the emperor to make peace with the Lombards, but he was unable to force that clause upon the emperor, as his predecessor Alexander III had been able to do in 1176[63]. He knew that the second excommunication of Frederick II by Gregory IX was perceived by many, even within the clergy, as primarily motivated by Gregory's anti-imperial Lombard policy[64]. He also knew that Frederick II was actively engaged in a diplomatic offensive to stress that argument, culminating in Frederick's 1236 initiative to call a summit of European princes to put a halt to papal interference in the internal political affairs of their realms[65]. Consequently, he could not openly make the Lombard affair a breaking-point in the negotiations with the emperor, but he practically suspended the absolution of the emperor by making it dependent on the precedent condition of Frederick making peace with the rebellious Lombard cities, something he knew the emperor would never do. Frederick was not prepared to give in to that demand and desisted from the agreement shortly after[66]. There was no commitment whatsoever on the part of the emperor to make peace with rebels and there was no sincere commitment to peace on the part of Innocent IV, not as long as the threat of a unified Sicilian and Italian kingdom loomed over the Papal State.

Meanwhile, in Germany, the Archbishops Siegfried of Mainz and Conrad of Cologne continued attacking Hohenstaufen domains, harassing and excommunicating cities and territories loyal to the emperor and trying to bring over other German princes to the papal side. Landgrave Henry of Thuringia, Heinrich 'Raspe' as he was called[67], was the most powerful secular prince in the diocese of the archbishop

Heinrich 'Raspe' is approached

---

62   On this issue see Frederick's encyclical letter of August 1244, HB 6.1, 205, also in MGH *Const.* 2 no 252, 345.

63   See *supra* p. 126.

64   The German ecclesiastical princes had explicitly protested against the purely political reasons for Frederick's excommunication in their 1239 letter to Gregory IX (*supra* p. 308, fnt 15): 'you have proceeded against him <Frederick II> in this way because of your bias in favour of the Milanese and their supporters' (*in favorem Mediolanensium et suorum sequacium processeritis taliter contra eum*) (Böhmer, *Acta imperii selecta*, no 965, 672).

65   See *supra* p. 284.

66   HB 6.1, 190, also in MGH *Epp. saec. xiii* 2, no 63, 46 (Innocent IV to the landgrave of Thuringia, 30 April 1244): '*non post multos dies elegit resilire quam parere*'.

67   *Annales Stadenses* ad ann. 1245, MGH SS 16, 369: '*Heinricus lantgravius, cognomento Raspe*'.

of Mainz[68] and the prime target of the archbishop to bring over to his side. The principality of Heinrich Raspe consisted of a large, consolidated territory in the German heartland, roughly comprising the present 'Länder' of Hessen and Thuringia. In 1241, he had married Beatrix, a daughter of Duke Henry II of Brabant, who was married at the time to his niece, Sophie of Thuringia[69]. Heinrich Raspe's new father-in-law was a partisan of the Hohenstaufens, as Heinrich himself still was at the time since he was appointed 'caretaker of the realm' by Frederick II in that very same year[70]. By 1243, however, he seems to have been wavering, since he dropped the proud style of 'caretaker of the realm' from his charters from then onwards. It was in that year that he must also have realized that his third marriage was to be as barren as the preceding two had been. In June 1243 Frederick II issued a charter, at the request of Heinrich Raspe himself, granting Thuringia to a nephew of Heinrich Raspe, Margrave Henry of Meißen, in case Heinrich Raspe might die childless[71]. In doing so, Heinrich Raspe had practically made his last will to the benefit of a staunch supporter of Frederick II[72]. Sometime in 1244, however, he had established contacts with Frederick's principal opponent in the German territories, Archbishop Siegfried of Mainz, who was his guest in Wartburg Castle, the impressive fortress at Eisenach, the capital of his Thuringia principality, in late July 1244[73]. He was in correspondence with the pope at

---

68   Landgrave Heinrich of Thuringia was a younger brother of Landgrave Ludwig of Thuringia, who had died in Otranto in 1227 (see *supra* p. 234). Landgrave Ludwig had a son with his wife Elizabeth (canonized in 1235, just four years after her demise), Hermann, who was only five years old at his father's demise. During Hermann's minority, his uncle Heinrich 'Raspe' acted as his guardian. When the young landgrave died childless in 1241, his uncle succeeded him.

69   Beatrix was a daughter of Duke Henry II of Brabant with his first wife, Maria, a daughter of Philip of Swabia. Maria had died in 1235. Before his marriage to Beatrix of Brabant, Heinrich Raspe had been married to a daughter of the margrave of Brandenburg and, after her demise in 1231, to a daughter of the duke of Austria who had died in 1241. All these marriages were childless.

70   See *supra* p. 307.

71   HB 6.1, 100-101. Margrave Henry of Meißen was a son of Heinrich Raspe's sister Jutta. By this arrangement, Heinrich Raspe had disinherited the offspring of his niece Sophie of Thuringia, the only other heir to the old dynasty of the Ludowingers. Sophie was a daughter of a saint, Elizabeth of Thuringia (see *supra*, fnt. 68), and there are serious indications that Heinrich Raspe detested her saintly mother. After the demise of Heinrich Raspe in 1247, his niece Sophie claimed her part in the inheritance, initiating a war of succession lasting 17 years and ending with a settlement creating a new principality out of the Thuringia inheritance, the principality of Hessen. Sophie's son Henry ('the child from Brabant') was the first prince of Hessen.

72   Margrave Henry of Meißen and his uncle from Thuringia had been instrumental in securing the Hohenstaufen position at the Eger diet of 1239: see *supra* p. 307.

73   *Nassauisches Urkundenbuch* I, Wiesbaden 1886, no 512, 332 has a charter, issued by Siegfried of Mainz at Eisenach on 18 July 1244. It is unlikely that the archbishop was not staying with Heinrich Raspe in Wartburg Castle during his visit of Eisenach.

the same time, since Pope Innocent IV had sent him a letter in April 1244, informing him that the emperor had failed to implement the peace agreement reached at Rome on 31 March[74]. The pope incited Heinrich Raspe to proceed with 'the matter of the faith you have so commendably initiated' (*negotium fidei per te laudabiliter inchoatum*), assuring him of his enduring support[75]. It was a clear incitement to open rebellion.

Frederick II must have been aware of the contacts between the pope and Heinrich Raspe, but was able, for the time being, to prevent his 'caretaker' in Germany to defect openly from the imperial cause[76]. Possibly, Innocent IV knew or surmised that Frederick was informed about his conspiratorial contacts with Heinrich Raspe. It explains why the pope began to panic. Frederick had not hesitated to arrest and imprison a considerable number of cardinals and high clerics in the recent past. Why would he not arrest a pope as well, as his predecessor Henry V had once done and, indeed, as his grandfather had tried to do with Alexander III[77]? The emperor might have suffered a setback before the walls of Viterbo recently, but he was certainly not defeated and still occupied a large part of the Papal State around Rome. The Romans recently might have sided with the pope, but they were never to be relied on, certainly not since Frederick was actively conspiring

The pope panics

---

74 See *supra* p. 315.
75 MGH *Epp. saec. xiii* 2, no 63, 46: 'If the feelings of devotion you say you have towards the Roman Church are laudably put into effect, it is important indeed that you proceed without delay with the affair of the faith you have so commendably initiated, thus enhancing the number of your merits and engaging the Apostolic See even stronger to promote your name and honour, since we are determined that we will never forsake you in that affair' (*Sane, ut devotionis affectum, quem erga Romanam ecclesiam habere diceris, exhibeas laudabiliter in effectu, expedit, ut negotium fidei per te laudabiliter inchoatum promptius exequaris, ut exinde uberior tibi crescat cumulus meritorum et apostolicam sedem ad incrementum tui nominis et honoris fortius habeas obligatam; nos enim in proposito gerimus, quod te in dicto negotio minime deseramus*).
76 This is how I have interpreted the confusing reports in Matthew Paris, *Chronica maiora* ad ann. 1243, ed. H.R. Luard IV, 268-269 and ad ann. 1244, ed. H.R. Luard IV, 356-357. It seems clear to me that Heinrich Raspe still backed down from open rebellion against the emperor in 1244. This is why the events reported in Matthew Paris, *Chronica maiora* ad ann. 1245, ed. H.R. Luard IV, 495 are likely to be assigned to the year 1244: 'The landgrave refused to consent and to get mixed up in a foolhardy affair like this, since he preferred peace with security, content as he was with his duchy, rather than the uncertain outcome of a war, certainly so of a war against Frederick, a man who had distinguished himself in war many times and was as sly as a fox. The Milanese qualified the prudence of the landgrave as cowardice' (*idem Andegravius malens pacem cum securitate, suo contentus ducatu, quam ancipitis belli certamina et fata guerrae fortunalis experiri, maxime contra Frethericum, bellicis negotiis multotiens expertum et vulpinis fallaciis argumentosum, renuit adquiescere vel tantae temeritati consentire ... Mediolanenses ... prudentiam memorati Andegravii pusilanimitatem vocantes*). If the Lombards got wind of these developments in Germany at the time, the emperor himself surely will have been informed as well.
77 See *supra* p. 70 and 118.

against papal rule in the city at the time with the connivance of his traditional Frangipani allies[78]. Consequently, Innocent reacted with suspicion to Frederick's invitation for a personal meeting[79]. What did Frederick expect from a conference with the pope? Was he going to beg for absolution, as his predecessor Henry IV once had done at Canossa? It was hardly conceivable. Nevertheless, Innocent indicated that he was prepared to meet the emperor in Narni, in the north of the Papal State. The meeting never took place, since the pope never seriously intended to meet with Frederick personally: *'the Roman pontiff never receives persons he knows to have been excommunicated'*[80]. Innocent IV had different plans.

He leaves Italy
and seeks
asylum in France

Pope Innocent IV had been elected at Anagni by a very small college of nine cardinals, one of whom died shortly after his consecration: Cardinal Colonna, a supporter of the emperor, expired on 9 February, 1244[81], leaving the pope with only seven cardinals. This is one of the reasons he promoted no fewer than twelve new cardinals on 28 May 1244[82]. Five of these new cardinals were French prelates[83]. Innocent had a special reason for the promotion of these French cardinals. He

---

78   An anonymous cardinal complains in 1244 of Frederick's subversive activities in the city (HB 6.1, 184-186). At the same time (before 1 May 1244), the Frangipani's had transferred their share in half of the Colosseum and a neighbouring stronghold to Frederick II. The contract was declared null and void by Innocent IV, since his Frangipani vassals (as he claimed they were) were not entitled to dispose of their fiefs without the consent of their lord (the pope): HB 6.1, 187-188.

79   For these attempts by Frederick see his encyclical letter of 1244: HB 6.1, 214, MGH *Const.* 2 no 252, 347.

80   HB 6.1, 115 (MGH *Const.* 2, no 241, 331) (Innocent IV, 26 August 1243): *'nunquam Romanus pontifex excommunicatos scienter recipiat'*.

81   Matthew Paris, *Chronica maiora* ad ann. 1244, ed. H.R. Luard IV, 287: *'Sub eodem eiusdem anni tempore, videlicet in octavis Purificationis beatae Virginis, obiit ... Johannes de Columpna cardinalis Romae'*.

82   Nicolaus de Carbio, *Vita Innocentii IV* cap. 12, ed. Pagnotti 85: *'cum non essent tunc nisi septem in Ecclesia cardinales, primo anno pontificatus sui ... duodecim cardinales ... ordinatione decentissima Ecclesiam adornavit'*.

83   Pierre de Colmieu, the archbishop of Rouen, was appointed cardinal-bishop of Albano. He had been taken prisoner at Monte Christo and was involved in the peace negotiations with Frederick II in 1243; Eudes de Châteauroux, a Franciscan and chancellor of the university of Paris, was appointed cardinal-bishop of Sabina; Pierre de Bar, was a professor at the university of Paris and became cardinal-priest of S Marcello; Guillaume de Talliante, a Benedictine monk, was appointed cardinal-priest of SS XII Apostoli. He had been involved in the peace negotiations with Frederick II in 1243 as well; Hugh of Saint-Cher was a prominent Dominican lawyer and theologian. He was appointed cardinal-priest of S. Sabina. Six of the other seven new cardinals were Italians, among them William Fieschi, a nephew of the pope. There were now twelve Italian cardinals, five from France, one from Spain, and one from England (John Tollet), but none from Germany. It is a clear sign of the rising prominence of the French kingdom and the decline of the German Empire.

knew that the success of his plans was largely dependent on the neutrality, if not the support, of the only European prince capable of frustrating them and that was king Louis IX of France. Louis might be a very pious Catholic, but he (or rather his mother) was shrewd enough not to let himself be used as a pawn in the purely political power struggle between pope and emperor. He wanted to stay out of that, even making it very clear to the pope that Frederick's excommunication would in no way influence his good relations with the emperor[84]. Innocent, for his part, knew that the king of France traditionally had played a crucial part in that power struggle nevertheless: Urban II, Gelasius II, Innocent II, and Alexander III all had found refuge in France in their continuing conflict with succeeding German emperors. Innocent IV wanted to flee to France as well, where he planned to convene the general council that was to sit in judgement over Frederick II[85]. The escape route over land to France was closed to Innocent, since the emperor controlled all of it and consequently the pope sent some of his Fieschi relatives present in his court in Rome back to their native city to ask for help[86]. At Genoa, the other members of the Fieschi clan actively supported the request of their relative and thus it happened that the *podestà* of that year, Philippo Vicedomino from Piacenza, decided to put a fleet of no fewer than 22 well-armed galleys at the disposal of the pope and his cardinals. The fleet left Genoa on 21 June 1244. It was a risky affair since the imperial admiral Ansaldo de Mari was known to be at sea with a fleet as well, threatening a reprise of the Monte Christo debacle.

Innocent IV left the city of Rome in the first week of June 1244 and went to Civita Castellana, on his way, as he let it be known, to meet the emperor at Narni. The pope stayed at Civita Castellana for two weeks, waiting for news from Genoa. On 26 or 27 June he left, not, however, heading east in the direction of Narni, but west to nearby Sutri, where he arrived on 27 June. The Genoese fleet had safely reached the port of Civitavecchia the day before. Meanwhile, Frederick II, who was in Terni, just 6 miles (10 km.) east of Narni, at the time, must have been informed of the arrival of the Genoese fleet since at his arrival in Sutri the pope received news that 300 knights had been dispatched by the

---

84   See *supra* p. 292.
85   Nicolas of Carbio, *Vita Innocentii IV* cap. 13 and 14, ed. Pagnotti 86-89, is an eye-witness account of Innocent's flight from Rome. See also the Genovese chronicle of Bartolomeo scriba ad ann. 1244, MGH *SS* 18, 213-215 and Matthew Paris, *Chronica maiora* ad ann. 1244, ed. H.R. Luard IV, 354-356.
86   Innocent IV has looked after his relatives very well during his pontificate. Two of his nephews, WIlliam and Ottobono Fieschi (promoted to the cardinalate in 1251, later Pope Hadrian V) became cardinals of the Holy Roman Church and other relatives were massively enriched as well. It was generally regarded as rather scandalous at the time: see *Annales Placentini Gibellini* ad ann. 1245, MGH *SS* 18, 489.

emperor to arrest him, as the pope was convinced. Innocent therefore rushed out of Sutri immediately and fled in disguise on horseback in the middle of the night, accompanied by just a few of his closest servants, through the mountains and forests west of Sutri to Civitavecchia, where he arrived in the evening of 29 June. He had covered about 37 miles (60 km.) through difficult terrain in a night and a day, no mean feat for a frail scholar of fifty years of age, already an old man according to the standards of the time. He embarked the very next day for Genoa, leaving behind a few ships at Civitavecchia to transport his cardinals to Genoa later. Innocent had ordered only four cardinals to stay behind in Italy. Cardinal Raniero Capocci was to continue the war against Frederick II; Cardinal Stefano dei Conti was left behind as papal vicar in Rome; Cardinal Riccardo Annibaldi was appointed *rector* of the papal Campagna province and Cardinal Rinaldo dei Conti stayed behind without a special commission[87]. Frederick II had missed his last opportunity to lay his hands on the pope, just as his grandfather had in 1167, when Alexander III narrowly had escaped from Rome[88].

Despite the season, the passage to Genoa was no smooth voyage since a heavy summer storm rose soon after Innocent IV sailed from Civitavecchia. After two terrifying days at sea, the galley carrying the pope reached the little island of Capraria (now Capraia) and a day later Porto Venere, where the ships sheltered for three days, allowing the pope, clearly a landlubber despite his Genoese origins, to recover from his recent maritime experiences. The bad weather was good fortune, though, since the imperial fleet missed the Genoese ships because of it. On 7 July Innocent IV safely arrived in his native city and was given a warm welcome by his compatriots. The pope, however, was so weakened by his recent tribulations that he immediately retreated to a Cistercian monastery, where he stayed no less than three months to recover, as his biographer and travelling companion Nicholas of Calvi reports[89]. This prolonged stay in the Cistercian monastery of St Andrew near Genoa did, however, have other reasons as well. Innocent IV just did not know where to convene the general council he planned to call. Genoa itself was out of the question. The city could not be reached over land, due to the ongoing war in Lombardy, and not by sea either, because of the continuing threat of the imperial fleet cruising in the Tyrrhenian

---

87   For these four cardinals see Nicolas of Carbio, *Vita Innocentii IV* cap. 13, ed. Pagnotti 87-88.
88   See *supra* p. 118.
89   Nicolas of Carbio, *Vita Innocentii IV* cap. 15, ed. Pagnotti 89: '*Propter quod eum oportuit trium mensium spacio modo in monasterio Sancti Andree prope civitatem ipsam cisterciensis ordinis commorari*'.

Sea. Innocent IV wanted to go to France and the Cistercians were to persuade the king of France to grant the pope asylum in his kingdom.

Every year in September, the Cistercian order held a general chapter in Cîteaux. It was always an impressive occasion, since all abbots of all monasteries belonging to the order had to attend, but the 1244 general chapter was to be even more so, since the king of France himself had announced his attendance. Louis IX was gravely ill in 1244 and wanted the monks at Cîteaux to pray for his recovery[90]. The ailing king was accompanied by his two brothers Robert and Alphonse, and, as always, by his mother, Queen Blanche, who had the special permission of the pope to enter the great abbey of Cîteaux with her ladies in waiting. The abbot of the Genoese Cistercian monastery of St Andrew, where Innocent was still 'recovering', carried a letter from the pope, requesting the chapter to urge the king of France to grant asylum to Innocent IV, reminding the king of '*the ancient and well established custom and freedom of France to protect the pope against the insults of the emperor and to receive him in his kingdom, as the king had granted support and asylum to Pope Alexander, when he had to flee from the aggression of the persecutor of the Church Frederick*'[91]. The Cistercians did as they were asked and begged the king to grant asylum to the pope, but Louis was evasive. Naturally, he was prepared to offer asylum to the pope, but he had to hear and consider the advice of his nobles, thus delaying a decision on the matter[92]. Louis knew or surmised what the pope was up to, and he had no intention of hosting a general council that was to sit in judgement over his 'good neighbour' Frederick II, who had sent envoys to the general chapter to prevent just that[93]. In the end, Innocent IV was *not* granted asylum in France[94]. It must have been a terrible disappointment

---

90   Matthew Paris, *Chronica maiora* ad ann. 1244, ed. H.R. Luard IV, 397: '*Eodem anno rex Francorum L(odovicus) ex reliquiis corruptelae, quam in Pictavia, cum negotiis bellicis indulsisset, contraxerat, graviter infirmatus*'.

91   Matthew Paris, *Chronica maiora* ad ann. 1244, ed. H.R. Luard IV, 392: '*ut secundum antiquam et consuetam Franciae consuetudinem et libertatem, patrem suum et pastorem summum et praecipuum ecclesiae rectorem, videlicet Romanum pontificem, contra insultus imperatoris ... potenter tueri dignaretur. Et si necessitatis articulus expostularet ... eum in regno suo benigne receptaret, sicut quondam bonae memoriae Alexandro Papae exulanti et a facie Fretherici imperatoris persequentis fugienti ... consolationem et refugium noscitur praestitisse*'.

92   Matthew Paris, *Chronica maiora* ad ann. 1244, ed. H.R. Luard IV, 393: '*ipsum Papam, si hoc esset consilium optimatum suorum ... exulantem liberaliter receptaret*'.

93   Matthew Paris, *Chronica maiora* ad ann. 1244, ed. H.R. Luard IV, 393: '*Habuit autem imperator ibidem nuntios suos solempnes, ut quod ab ipsis postularetur effectum non sortiretur*'.

94   A later English chronicle (closing in 1326), containing an adaptation of and a complement to the *Flores Historiarum* of Matthew Paris has some more information on this episode. According to this source, the pope had indicated that he wanted to go to Reims, but the French nobles strongly advised the king against this, and Louis wrote a letter to the pope to that effect (*Flores Historiarum* ad ann. 1244, ed. Luard II, 282-283): '*Rescripsit ergo dominus rex Franciae domino Papae moderate proceres suos nullatenus velle consentire ut in Franciam*

for Innocent, but he gained one important concession from Louis IX: the king had emphatically and unconditionally guaranteed the personal safety of the pope[95].

Innocent IV
goes to Lyon
and calls a
general council

In the first week of October 1244, Innocent IV left Genoa. After the refusal of the king of France to grant him asylum, he had asked for asylum in England and Aragon, but his requests were rejected there as well[96]. In the end, he decided to seek refuge in a city as close to the French border as he could find, mindful of the guarantee of his personal safety by the king of France. He went to the town of Lyon on the Saône. The part of the town on the west bank of the river belonged to the kingdom of France, the *part du royaume*, and the part on the east bank belonged to the Empire, the *part de l'empire*, making the city practically independent of both monarchies. After a very arduous journey[97], Innocent finally arrived at Lyon on 2 December 1244. The pope and his retinue settled in the local monastery of St Just, situated at the west bank of the river. Innocent IV obviously was in for a long stay, since he established a university there, where Roman and canon law were to be taught as well as theology[98]. It was to provide the legal elite supporting the *curia* and the papal supreme court of justice, the *Rota romana*, now also residing at Lyon[99]. Within a month after his arrival,

---

veniret'. A letter like his must indeed have been sent by Louis IX to the pope since at Cîteaux the king had postponed the matter for later decision.
95 Matthew Paris, *Chronica maiora* ad ann. 1244, ed. H.R. Luard IV, 392: '*favorem praestitit, affirmando, quod quantum honestas permitteret, ipsius imperatoris injurias ab ecclesia propulsaret'*.
96 Innocent may have considered to settle in Bordeaux, in the continental possessions of the king of England, close to the kingdom of his vassal, the king of Aragon. According to Matthew Paris, *Chronica maiora* ad ann. 1245, ed. H.R. Luard IV, 409-410, Innocent's requests were rejected because of the papal court's infamous reputation, 'the stench of which sends a very malodorous smell into the air' (*cuius foetor usque ad nubes fumum teterrimum exhalabat*). On the requests of asylum in England and Aragon see also Matthew Paris, *Chronica maiora* ad ann. 1245, ed. H.R. Luard IV, 422-423. See for another attempt of Innocent to settle in Bordeaux *infra* p. 411.
97 For the details see Nicolas of Carbio, *Vita Innocentii IV* cap. 15, ed. Pagnotti 89-90.
98 Nicolas of Carbio, *Vita Innocentii IV* cap. 16, ed. Pagnotti 91: '*secundo anno sui pontificatus apud Lugdunum in sua curia generale studium ordinavit, tam de theologia, quam de decretis, decretalibus pariter et legibus'*.
99 In the days of Innocent IV all decisions of the 'auditors' of the 'Rota' still had to be ratified by the pope personally: Durant, *Speculum*, Lib. I, Part. I, Tit. *De auditore* no 3 (ed. Bassel 1574, 100, l. col). Since there had been a *sedis vacantia* of almost two years, there were many cases pending in court at the time still to be decided by the pope. See Nicolas of Carbio, *Vita Innocentii IV* cap. 16, ed. Pagnotti 91: 'By his industrious wisdom, he concluded within a very short time not only the cases brought during the time of the *sedis vacantia*, but also the ones that had been left undecided for a very long time by his predecessors' (*Causas enim non solum tempore vacationis exortas, verum etiam a longis retro temporibus a suis predecessoribus indecisas, sub brevissimo temporis spacio sua industri sapientia terminabat*). Innocent must have been very

on 27 December 1244, the pope announced that a general council of the Church was to convene at Lyon on the next feast day of St John the Baptist, 24 June 1245[100]. In the following days, the pope sent invitations to all kings, princes, prelates, and other important clerics of Europe to appear at the council in person or by their representatives. Unlike his predecessor Gregory IX, Innocent IV left no doubt about the subjects to be discussed at that general council:

> 'We have decided to convene the kings on earth, the ecclesiastical prelates, and other princes of the world so that our Church may obtain the splendour of its rightful legal position through the healthy advice and advantageous help of the faithful and to quickly be able to remedy the deplorable danger of the Holy Land and the troubled empire of Romania and to find a remedy against the Tartars and other contemptors of the faith and persecutors of Christian people, as well as the matter that is pending between the Church and the emperor.'[101]

---

busy and yet he found the time to begin writing his famous commentary on the decretals of Gregory IX.

100   Nicolas of Carbio, *Vita Innocentii IV* cap. 18, ed. Pagnotti 93: '*Festo autem nativitatis Domini celebrato, dum in festo beati Ioannis evangeliste missam mane in Lugdunensi ecclesia celebraret ac predicaret populo verbum Dei, ibi publice nunciavit concilium generale in festo beati Ioannis Baptiste venturo proximo celebrandum*'.

101   HB 6.1, 247; MGH *Epp. saec. xiii* 2, no 78 (3 January 1245, to the archbishop of Soissons) 56: '*nos, ut ipsa ecclesia per fidelium salubre consilium et auxilium fructuosum status debiti possit habere decorem, et deplorando Terre Sancte discrimini et afflicto Romanie imperio propere valeat subveniri ac inveniri remedium contra Tartaros et alios contemptores fidei ac persecutores populi Christiani, necnon pro negotio, quod inter ecclesiam et principem vertitur, reges terre, prelatos ecclesiarum et alios mundi principes duximus advocandos*'.

Part II

Dies Irae

The Council of Lyon
(Matthew Paris, *Chronica maiora*, Cambridge, Corpus Christi College, ms. 016, *f.* 187 v°)

1

The Summons

'*Let it be known that we have sent for the said prince by our summons to appear, either in person or by his representatives, in the council that is to be held to answer to us and to others who have put forward something against him and to give proper satisfaction*'[1]. It is clear from this section of Innocent's invitation to attend the general Council of the Church at Lyon that Frederick II was to formally stand trial there. It was to be a show trial, a formality (*ad solemnitatem*), since the pope was convinced he could depose a Roman emperor in his own right, without the assistance of a general council: '*the presence of a council is but for show, since the sentence of the pope alone, without a council, suffices for the condemnation of an emperor; he <the pope> alone has full sovereignty*'[2]. As is the way of the lawyer, this assessment of Sinibaldo Fieschi[3], writing in his capacity as a legal expert and not as pope, is corroborated by some authorities taken from Gratian's *Decretum*, first and foremost

An emperor on trial

---

1 *Annales Placentini Gibellini* ad ann. 1244, MGH *SS* 18, 488-489: '*Sciturus quod nos dictum principem in citacione nostra citavimus, ut per se vel suos nuncios in concilio celebrando compareat, responsurus nobis et aliis qui aliquid contra ipsum proponendum duxerint satisfactionem ydoneam prestiturus*'.
2 Innocentii IIII. PM *Commentaria in V. libros Decretalium* App. post X 2,27(*De re iudicata*),25, cap. ii (ed. Venice 1570, 380, r. col.): '*praesentia concilii est ad solemnitatem, quia etiam sine concilio solius papae sententia sufficeret ad damnationem imperatoris; ipse solus habet plenitudinem potestatis*'.
3 Innocent's commentary on the *Liber extra* of Gregory IX is unique, since he does not only comment on the decretals in Gregory's code, but also on some of his own decretals, including the sentence against Frederick II, which he added (and commented on: see *infra* p. 379-380) as an appendix to X 2,27,25. The sentence of deposition of Frederick II was later inserted into the codification of Bonifacius VIII (1298), known as 'the sixth book' (*Liber Sextus* (VI)), since it is a supplement to the five books of Gregory's *Liber Extra*: VI° 2,14,2. Innocent IV emphasized that his comments should be interpreted as his own opinions as a legal scholar, *not* as papal pronouncements (Innocentii IIII. PM *Commentaria* ad X. 5,2,35 (600, l. col.): 'but here the pope did not make a rule of law, though it is believed so, but merely states his opinion, which does not prejudice the opinion of others' (*sed hic papa non faciebat de hoc canonem, licet sic arbitraretur; et talis esset opinio sua, quae non praeiudicaret aliorum opinionibus*). See also his casual remark in his comments on X. 1,6,20 (61, l. col.) 'therefore I believe, though it may be that this it is not accepted, *etc.*' (*Et ideo crederem, licet in hoc forsitan non credatur*, etc.).

C. 15, q. 6, cap. 3 (*Alius*)[4]: '*Another Roman pope has deposed a king of the Franks, not because of his crimes, but because he was unqualified for office and substituted Pepin, Charlemagne's father, for him and released all Franks from the oath of fealty they had sworn to him*'[5]. This is a fragment excerpted by Gratian from the famous letter of Pope Gregory VII addressed in 1081 to Bishop Hermann of Metz, who had his doubts about the legality of the excommunication of the German King Henry IV by Gregory VII in 1076[6].

Historical precedents Ever since the excommunication of Henry IV, the 'deposition' of the Merovingian King Childeric III by Pope Zachary in 751 was the precedent invariably cited in favour of the right of the pope to depose a secular ruler. The deposition of King Childeric III, the last of the *rois fainéants*, and his substitution by Pepin the Short, Charlemagne's father, is a historical fact, but the role of the pope in his deposition is less clear, as was already asserted by the protagonists of Henry IV in the times of Gregory VII himself[7]. Even now, when looking at the historical evidence, it seems that Pope Zachary did not depose that unlucky king himself, but that the pope was merely asked for his opinion by Pepin and the Frankish nobles whether *they* could do so[8]. Another famous 'precedent', also advanced by Pope Gregory VII in 1081, concerns the excommunication of Emperor Theodosius I by Bishop Ambrose of Milan in 390[9]. The excommunication of Theodosius I by Saint Ambrose is also

---

4   The other authorities cited here by Innocent are C. 9, q. 3 cap. 10 (*Patet*) and 11 (*Fuit*). The former text states that a judgement of the Apostolic See is beyond all criticism (*apostolicae sedis iudicium a nemine est retractandum*); the latter notes that the Apostolic See can quash any judgement by an inferior authority (*ab aliis damnatos vel excommunicatos Apostolica solvit auctoritas*). The references are hardly appropriate.

5   C. 15, q. 6, cap. 3 (*Alius*): '*Alius item Romanus pontifex regem Francorum non tam pro suis iniquitatibus quam pro eo, quod tantae potestati non erat utilis, a regno deposuit et Pipinum Caroli Magni imperatoris patrem in eius loco substituit omnesque Francigenas a iuramento fidelitatis, quam illi fecerant, absolvit*'.

6   *Das Register Gregors VII.*, 8,21, MGH *Epp. sel.* 2,2, 544-563(554). Another fragment from the letter of Gregory VII to Bishop Hermann of Metz is in Dist. 96, cap. 10 '*Duo sunt*'. See *infra* p. 365, fnt. 61 and *supra* p. 79-80, fnt. 13.

7   See the anonymous *Liber de unitate ecclesiae conservanda*, written by a German monk in or about 1092, MGH *Ldl* 2, 186: 'When Pope Zachary had decided that what they were asking for was fair and expedient, he consented to their request, a consent that has later been confirmed by Pope Stephen, and *Pepin has been made king by the election of the nobles*' (*Quorum postulationem cum aequam atque utilem Zacharias papa iudicasset, ad ea quae postulabant consensit, atque eiusdem consensus sententiam postea Stephanus papa confirmavit, et Pippinus factus est rex communi suffragio principum*) (emphasis added). There is now a new edition of this remarkable book, with a German translation, by I. Schmale-Ott, *Quellen zum Investiturstreit* 2, Darmstadt 1984 (the quotation is on 276).

8   See *supra* p. 41-42.

9   *Das Register Gregors VII.*, 8,21, MGH *Epp. sel.* 2,2, 554: 'And St Ambrose, a saint, but not a universal bishop, excluded Theodosius the Great from the Church by excommunicating him for a crime that did not seem so serious to other priests' (*Et beatus Ambrosius, licet sanctus non*

an undisputed historical fact, but it could hardly be advanced as an argument that a bishop could *depose* an emperor. To the contrary, since Saint Ambrose himself had emphasized that he still owed due respect to the emperor but just could not admit him to the Eucharist[10]. The bishop of Milan clearly distinguished between two entities, Theodosius the emperor and Theodosius the member of the Christian community. Saint Ambrose bowed his head to the secular *potestas* of his emperor, but the emperor had to submit to the spiritual *auctoritas* of his bishop. The spiritual sanction (excommunication) did not imply a secular sanction (deposition) as of right. It was a point already raised against Gregory's use of this 'precedent' by his own contemporaries[11]. By the time of Innocent III, the canonists realized that historical precedent alone was of little use to settle the question whether the pope could depose a ruling king or emperor[12]. It had to be answered on the basis of positive canon law exclusively and it was Innocent III who delivered the legal instruments to answer that question in the affirmative.

When Lothario dei Conti di Segni, as he was then, was studying canon law in Bologna, there was a curious text in Gratian's *Decretum* that was never read by the professors there. It was the Donation of Constantine (Dist. 96, cap. 14), the legendary 'gift' of the western part of the Roman Empire to Pope Silvester I by Constantine I[13]. In the enormous *apparatus* of glosses composed around the text of Gratian's *Decretum* by

The doctrine of plenitudo potestatis

---

tamen universalis ecclesiae episcopus, pro culpa, quae ab aliis sacerdotibus non adeo gravis videbatur, Theodosium Magnum imperatorem excommunicans ab ecclesia exclusit).

10   *Ambrosius*, Ep. 51,13 (Ambrose to Theodosius in 390), Migne *PL* 16, col. 1163: 'I do, I say, have no cause whatsoever to be disobedient to you, but I have my reservations, I dare not offer the sacrament to you, if you would choose to attend' (*ego, inquam, causam in te comtumaciae nullam habeo, sed habeo timoris: offerre non audeo sacrificium, si volueris assistere*).

11   *Liber de unitate*, MGH *Ldl* 2, 194 (Schmale-Ott, 304): 'St Ambrose did not divide the Church, but merely taught that unto Caesar must be rendered what is Caesar's and unto God what is God's' (*Sed ipse quoque sanctus Ambrosius ecclesiam non divisit, sed ea quae Caesaris sunt Caesari et quae Dei Deo reddenda esse docuit*). The proposition that a bishop or patriarch could *depose* a ruling Roman emperor was completely preposterous according to Roman public law. St Ambrose, who was trained as a lawyer, was aware of this.

12   Gregory VII had mentioned three historical precedents for the deposition of an emperor or a king by the pope in his famous letter to Bishop Hermann of Metz (*supra* p. 78-79): the deposition of Childeric III, the excommunication of Theodosius I, *and* the alleged excommunication of the Emperor Arcadius by Pope Innocent I for deposing Johan Chrysostom, the patriarch of Constantinople. The last precedent still figures in the fragment from Gregory's letter excerpted by Gratian in Dist. 96, cap. 110, but there is no historical trace of an excommunication of Arcadius by Pope Innocent I. The contemporaries of Gregory VII had already drawn attention to this (*Liber de unitate*, MGH *Ldl* 2, 196 (Schmale-Ott, 310)): 'we do not know where this comes from' (*unde hoc assumptum sit, nos quidem adhuc incertum tenemus*). The canonists were practical lawyers preferring positive law (papal decretals) over the outcome of a contested scholarly historical debate.

13   See *supra* p. 31.

Innocent's teacher, the canonist Johannes Teutonicus, there is but one short gloss on Dist. 96, cap. 14: *'this later addition is not read in classes'*[14]. There were many reasons not to read that forgery in class. It was *not* because it was already recognized as a forgery at the time, although some people had suspicions[15], but primarily because it suggested the secular power (*potestas*) of the Roman pontiff was based on an *imperial* privilege. It was against this error that Innocent III held one of his most important sermons. He did so, significantly, on the feast day of St Silvester (31 December) in the first year of his papacy. Of course, he did (and could) not deny the authenticity of the Donation of Constantine[16]. To the contrary: *'the good Emperor Constantine assigned and conceded the city <of Rome> and the Senate with all its people and dignities and the royal authority over the West to him'*[17], but Innocent III stressed that Constantine's gift did not bestow upon Pope Silvester any power Silvester did not already have before. Pope Silvester was the successor of St Peter and the vicar of Christ on earth (*vicarius Christi*)[18]. In this capacity the pope was not just a great priest, but the greatest of all priests, because he was sublime in priestly authority *and* royal power. *'the representative of the King of Kings and the Lord of Lords (Rev. 19:16), forever priest after the order of Melchizedek (Psalms 110:4)'*, the legendary priest-king of Salem (Genesis 14:18)[19]. It was because of this that

---

14   Gl. 'Constantinus' ad Dist. 96, cap. 14: *'Palea ista non legitur in scholis'*.

15   It is generally taken for granted that the humanist Lorenzo Valla first exposed the Donation of Constantine as a fraud. He was not. In 1001 the Emperor Otto III had already established that the document containing the 'Donation of Constantine' was a hoax (*imaginarium scriptum*): MGH *DD* Otto III, no 389, 820. More than a century later, in 1152, a Roman citizen close to Arnold of Brescia (if not Arnold himself) wrote a letter to Frederick I Barbarossa informing the emperor that the Donation was 'a lie and a heretical falsehood' (*mendacium et fabula heretica*): Jaffé, *Bibliotheca rerum Germanicarum* I, Berlin 1864, *Wibaldi epistolae* no. 404, 542. Barbarossa may also have known from another source, since his uncle, the historian Bishop Otto of Freising, made some devastating remarks about it in his *Chronica*: *Ottonis episc. freisingensis Chronica* 4,3, MGH *SS Rer. germ.* 45, 187-188. Bishop Otto ironically points out that Theodosius would hardly have divided the Roman Empire over his two sons, the western part to Honorius and the eastern part to Arcadius, if Constantine had already assigned the western part of the Empire to the pope.

16   The most famous depiction of the Silvester legend and the Donation of Constantine is on the walls of the Silvester chapel in the monastery of SS Quattro Coronati in Rome. It is supposed to have been painted during the papacy of Innocent III.

17   *Innocentii III papae sermones in sanctis*, Sermo VII, In festo S. Silvestri (Migne *PL* 217, col. 481): *'Constantinus egregius imperator ... urbem pariter et senatum cum hominibus et dignitatibus suis, et omne regnum Occidentis ei <scl. Silvestro papae> tradidit et dimisit'*.

18   *Innocentii III papae sermones in sanctis*, Sermo VII, In festo S. Silvestri (Migne *PL* 217, col. 482): *'Fuit ergo beatus Sylvester successor Petri, vicarius Jesu Christi'*.

19   *Innocentii III papae sermones in sanctis*, Sermo VII, In festo S. Silvestri (Migne *PL* 217, col. 481): *'Fuit ergo B. Silvester sacerdos, non solum magnus, sed maximus, pontificali et regali potestate sublimis. Illius quidem vicarius, qui est "Rex regum et Dominus dominantium" (Apoc. 19), "Sacerdos in aeternum, secundum ordinem Melchisedech" (Psal. cix)'*.

the pope was endowed as of right with 'absolute sovereignty' (*plenitudo potestatis*), a 'divine institution' (*divina institutio*)[20], *not* on account of the Donation of Constantine, since it was the Lord, not Constantine, who had granted it to the Apostolic See as a special privilege[21]. The sermon of Innocent III is the climax of a development resulting in a major change of paradigm in papal representation. Once upon a time, the powerful Saxon and Salian emperors of the Roman Empire, Henry II, Conrad II and Henry III, had styled themselves as 'vicar of Christ' (*vicarius Christi*)[22], the pope being the representative of St Peter, rather than Christ. In Innocent's time the emperor had lost this special charisma, now attaching to a priest, the Roman pontiff, making him, rather than the emperor, 'King of Kings and Lord of Lords'[23]. It followed from this, that the 'dualist' interpretation of Pope Gelasius' letter to the Emperor Anastasius[24], resulting in the image of the two swords, one for the emperor and another for the pope, based on Luke 22:38, was now completely out of date. Innocent's nephew, Pope Gregory IX, agreed: '*Both swords have been given to the Church, but only one of them is drawn by the Church, the other has to be raised on account of the Church by a secular prince; one by a priest, the other by a soldier on the instruction of a priest*'[25]. This is not a harmless game of metaphors, but a very powerful expression of papal supremacy culminating in the claim to 'absolute sovereignty' (*plenitudo potestatis*) by the pope, the ecclesiastical equivalent of Barbarossa's secular *Lex 'Omnis iurisdictio*'[26]. The practical legal consequences were laid down by Innocent III in a number of important decretals codified by himself in his *Compilatio Tertia* and later inserted

---

20 *Registrum super negotio Romani imperii* 33, ed. Kempf 106: '*sedes apostolica … apud quam ex institutione divina plenitudo residet potestatis*'.

21 For the qualification of papal '*plenitudo potestatis*' as an '*apostolicae sedis privilegium*' see *Innocentii III PP. Regestorum* 2, 220 (Migne *PL* 214, col. 779).

22 See *supra* p. 27.

23 It was a change in paradigm caused by the embarrassing conduct of Henry IV at Canossa in the winter of 1077, begging for absolution during three days at the gate of the castle of Matilda of Tuscany where Gregory VII was staying at the time. The incident was widely publicized by the pope himself: *Das Register Gregors VII.*, 4,12, MGH *Epp. sel.* 2,1, 311-314. Even his own advisors, like Bishop Eberhard of Naumburg († 1079), were convinced that Henry 'had acted inappropriately and that he had done irreparable damage to the glory of his office and had betrayed the dignity of the state by that utterly revolting submission' (*Lamberti Annales* ad ann. 1077, MGH *SS* 5, 260, '*regem secus ac deceat egisse, crimenque gloriae suae intulisse numquam abolendum … is foedissima subiectione … dignitatem rei publicae prodiderit*'). The damage to the imperial charisma was, indeed, irreparable.

24 See *supra* p. 80.

25 From a letter by Gregory IX from 1234 in Mansi 23, col. 60: '*Uterque igitur gladius ecclesiae traditur: sed ab ecclesia exercetur unus; alius pro ecclesia, manu saecularis principis est eximendus, unus a sacerdote, alius ad nutum sacerdotis administrandus a milite*'. The pope is clearly citing St Bernard: see *supra* p. 81, fnt. 20.

26 On Barbarossa's *Lex 'Omnis iurisdictio*' see *supra* p. 107-108.

into the *Liber Extra* of his nephew Gregory IX, the legal armoury from which Innocent IV drew his arguments in his case against Frederick II.

Legal authorities:
the decretal
'*Venerabilem*'

The most important expression of *plenitudo potestatis* is Innocent's decretal '*Venerabilem*'[27], issued as a response to the caution of the German princes in 1198 that the pope should abstain from actively interfering with the election of a German king and future emperor. Innocent III responded that he could and should, lecturing the clearly ignorant German princes on their and his position respectively[28]. He conceded the right to elect a new king to the German princes, especially so since, as he emphasized, that privilege originally had been granted to the German princes by the Apostolic See[29]. In order to support this rather bold, if not outrageous, assertion, Innocent did *not* directly refer to the Donation of Constantine, but to the doctrine of *translatio imperii*, the transfer of title to the Roman Empire from the Byzantines ('the Greeks') to the West. It concerns the coronation of Charlemagne as Roman emperor by Pope Leo III in 800. According to a story already current at the time of Charlemagne himself, the throne of the Roman Empire had become vacant ever since it was occupied by a woman, the Empress Irene (797-802), and consequently Pope Leo had decided to bestow the crown of the Empire on Charlemagne[30]. Innocent III used stories like this and, of course, the prominence of the pope in the coronation ceremony of Charlemagne as presented in the 'book of papal biographies' (*Liber pontificalis*)[31], to emphasize the *plenitudo potestatis* of the pope. He reasoned as follows: whenever the throne of the Empire is vacant, it reverts as of right to the 'King of Kings', the pope as vicar of Christ[32], to dispose of as he sees fit, and

---

27   *Compilatio tertia* 1,6,19 = X. 1,6,34, giving an abridged version of the letter to the duke of Zähringen and other German princes in *Registrum super negotio Romani imperii* 33, ed. Kempf 102-110.

28   See *supra* p. 154-155.

29   X. 1,6,34: (post alia) '*illis principibus ius et potestatem elegendi regem … recognoscimus (ut debemus) … praesertim cum ad eos ius et potestas huiusmodi ab Apostolica sede pervenerit*'.

30   *Annales Laureshamenses* (before 820), ad ann. 801, MGH *SS* 1, 38. See *supra* p. 55.

31   *Liber pontificalis*, Leo III 23 (Duchesne 2, 7). The account in the *Liber pontificalis* ought to be compared with the report of Charlemagne's coronation in the *Annales regni Francorum* ad ann. 801, MGH *SS rer. Germ.* 6, 112, emphasizing that the pope prostrated himself before the emperor after the coronation (*Post laudes ab apostolico more antiquorum principum adoratus est*), a detail significantly missing in the *Liber pontificalis*. This was the *adoratio* (προσκύνησις) owed by a subject to the imperial majesty in the contemporary Byzantine coronation ceremony.

32   See also Innocent IV on X. 2,2,10 ('*Licet*'): 'There is a special relationship between the pope and the emperor, since the pope consecrates and examines him and the emperor is his protector, swears to him, and holds the empire from him <reff. to X. 1,6,34, 'Venerabilem' and *Decr.* Dist. 63, cap. 30> and this is why he is succeeded by the pope at law in what he holds from the Church of Rome whenever there is a vacancy in the Empire' (*specialis coniunctio est*

having found the king of the Franks worthy of the imperial title, Pope Leo III bestowed it upon Charlemagne[33]. Since, according to Roman law, a Roman emperor was chosen by the people represented by the Senate[34], that rule prevailed in the new German 'Roman' Empire as well, the German princes representing the people as the 'Senate' of the Roman Empire[35]. Consequently, in electing a king of the Germans and future emperor, the princes exercised a privilege granted to them by the pope (Leo III), since it was by his *translatio* that they had become senators of the new Roman Empire of the Germans. Another consequence was the contention that, whenever the German electors did not elect a new emperor, the pope, exercising his *plenitudo potestatis*, could do so instead, and that, when the electors had chosen more than one emperor, it fell to the pope to make a choice among the contenders[36].

---

inter Papam et Imperatorem, quia Papa eum consecrat et examinat, et est imperator eius advocatus et iurat ei et ab eo imperium tenet <supra, *De elect.*, 'Venerabilem', 63. Dist. 'Ego etc. tibi domino') *et inde est, quod in iure quae ab ecclesia Romana tenet succedit Papa, imperio vacante). There is more than just an implicit reference here to feudal law and its institution of 'escheat', *i.e.* the right of the lord to immediate possession of the land of a tenant dying without issue. See for a contemporary opinion that the emperor was, indeed, the vassal of the pope the famous canonist Hostiensis, *Lectura* ad X 1,6,34 ('Venerabilem'), ed. Strassburg 1512, *f.* 62 vo, r. col.): '<the emperor> who has received so many benefices of the Roman Church and is its vassal' (<*imperator*> *qui tot beneficia recepit a romana ecclesia et ipsius existit feudatarius*).

33 Innocent's *Compilatio tertia* has been glossed by the canonists Tancred († *c.* 1235) and Vincentius Hispanus († 1235-1239) shortly after the demise of Innocent III. Their glosses were incorporated in the famous *apparatus* on the *Liber Extra* composed by Bernardus Parmensis (†1263). It has an interesting gloss by either Vincentius or Tancred on 'Venerabilem', Gl. 'Transtulit' ad X. 1,6,34, according to which the actual 'transfer' of the Empire happened in 776 (*translatio illa facta est anno Domini septingentesimo septuagesimo sexto*), adding that Charlemagne was crowned by Leo III after a lapse of fifteen years (*Carolus coronatus est a Leone Papa iii elapsis post hoc quindecim annis*). The obvious emphasis on a lapse of time between the actual *translatio* and the coronation of Charlemagne serves to draw attention to the fact that the pope was emperor in the interim. Unfortunately, the glossator does not indicate what exactly occurred in 776 to have caused a *translatio* in that year. It was the year Constantine VI was appointed as co-emperor by his father Leo IV, who died in 780, leaving his wife Irene as regent over her son. Constantine VI was deposed (and murdered) by his mother in 797.

34 For this assessment (the *lex regia*) see Inst. 1,2,6; C. 1,17,1,7 and D. 1,4,1 pr.

35 See for the allusions to Roman constitutional law in this context the comment on 'Venerabilem' by Hostiensis (Henry of Susa, cardinal-bishop of Ostia, †1271) in his *Lectura* ad X. 1,6,34 (ed. Strassburg 1512, vol. 1, *f.* 61, r. col. ro – l. col. vo), referring to D. 1,2,2,7– 9 and 11; Inst. 1,2,6 and C. 1,17,1,7, and adding: '*Haec iura probant quod imperator a populo eligitur et habet iurisdictionem*'. The Senate as representative of the people is to be deduced from Hostiensis's reference to D. 1,2,2,11. For the electors of the German king as the 'Senate' of the Roman Empire of the German nation see also the charter confirming the election of Frederick's son Conrad as 'king elect'of the Germans (1237, MGH *Const.* 2, no 329, 440), where the electors explicitly state that they acted in this matter 'in the place of the Roman Senate' (*Romani senatus locum* <*accipientes*>). See *supra* p. 282.

36 X. 1,6,34: 'when the votes of the princes in an election are divided, we can, after admonition and due examination, favour one of them' (*cum in electione vota principum dividuntur, post admonitionem et expectationem alteri partium favere possimus*). See also Hostiensis, *Lectura* ad

Imperial authority therefore originally and ultimately rested with the pope and whenever he conferred that authority on an elected king of the Germans he did so 'without in any way diminishing the substance of his own authority' (*nichil de substantia suae iurisdictionis imminuens*)[37], thereby degrading the emperor to the status of a mere agent of papal authority and since, according to the Roman law of agency, the powers of an agent could be revoked unilaterally by the principal[38], so could the pope unilaterally annul the power of an emperor, as he had once taken it from the Greeks. Ever since '*Venerabilem*' the doctrine of *translatio imperii* served as conclusive proof that the pope was entitled to depose an emperor[39]. Naturally, it was a power to be used most sparingly, in exceptional circumstances only[40]. Therefore, Innocent III gave some examples when he was entitled to exercise his discretion: a person publicly excommunicated was unfit for office and consequently was to be deposed, as was a notorious oath-breaker, a heathen, or a heretic, all of them charges brought against Frederick II at Lyon.

The decretal '*Excommunicamus*'

Another strong argument for the right of the pope to depose secular princes was, of course, X 5,7,13 ('*Excommunicamus*'). It contained the codification of the extraordinary measures Innocent III had employed against Count Raymond VI of Toulouse at the onset of the Albigensian crusade[41], later ratified by the third canon of the Fourth Lateran Council as a general rule of law: the pope had the right to expropriate any prince excommunicated for failing to properly prosecute heretics within his domain. If that prince had no superior liege lord, the pope could depose

---

X. 1,6,34 (ed. Strassburg 1512, vol. 1, *f.* 62, r. col. ro): '*Electoribus igitur negligentibus imperatorem eligere, papa eliget et si plures electi sunt, de iure utriusque cognoscet et diffiniet*'.

37   Gregory IX in an important letter to Frederick II (23 Oct. 1236), MGH *Epp. saec. xiii* 1, no 703, 604. See on this letter also *supra* p. 285.

38   Inst. 3,26,9.

39   See the Gl. 'Deposuit' ad C. 15, q. 6, cap. 3 (*Alius*): '*Ergo Papa deponit imperatorem nam et transferre potest imperium, ut Extra de elect. Venerabilem*'. After the promulgation of the Decretals of Gregory IX, the *Liber extra*, in 1234, the *apparatus* of Johannes Teutonicus to Gratian's *Decretum* was updated by the canonist Bartholomaeus Brixiensis (†1258) with references to the *Liber extra*.

40   See Innocentii IIII. PM *Commentaria in V. libros Decretalium* App. post X 2,27 (*De re iudicata*), 25, cap. ii (ed. Venice 1570, 380, r. col.): 'The pope does well to base a sentence of deposition of an emperor not only on many crimes, but also on many different kinds of sin, since there must be a compelling cause for the deposition of an emperor. It is not similar to the deposition of a cleric, who may be deposed on account of a single sin, because emperors and other princes cannot be deposed without many major harmful incidents' (*bene facit Papa, quod non solum multa crimina, sed etiam multa genera peccatorum subiecit sententiae depositoriae imperatoris, magna enim causa subesse debet depositioni imperatoris. Non est simile eius ad depositionem clericorum, qui pro quolibet peccato deponi possunt ... quia imperatores et alii principes deponi non possunt absque magnis et multis periculis*).

41   See *supra* p. 201.

him and appoint another in his place[42]. In the case of Raymond VI of Toulouse, a vassal of the king of France, Philip 'Auguste', had expressed some objections to the action of Innocent III, since the pope arrogated jurisdiction over secular matters of feudal law – the deposition of a vassal of the king and disposing of his tenures – he did not have, at least not according to the king of France[43]. The king had done so before, when the pope had interfered in a feudal conflict between Philip and his vassal, King John of England.

Philip and John had concluded a peace treaty in 1200 (the treaty of Le Goulet)[44], but in 1202 Philip had invaded John's continental territories nevertheless under the pretext that John had failed to obey a summons to appear in the court of his lord, the king of France, to answer to serious charges brought against him[45]. John appealed to the pope, accusing Philip of a breach of the treaty of Le Goulet. Innocent III decided to take cognizance of the matter, but King Philip objected, arguing that it was a matter of feudal law over which the pope had no jurisdiction. As a matter of course, Innocent III overruled that objection. He did so in a very important decretal: X. 2,1,13 ('*Novit ille*'). The pope stressed that he did not intend to intrude upon the feudal jurisdiction of the king of France, but that he merely proceeded against the king 'on account of a sin' (*ratione peccati*) the king was said to have committed, making it a matter of ecclesiastical censure rather than secular jurisdiction[46]. The pope was authorized, of course, to take cognizance of a matter like this: '*everyone who is in his right mind knows that it is our duty to correct any Christian for any mortal sin and to punish him with ecclesiastical censure if he has defied correction*'[47]. The argument conveys the impression of

The decretal '*Novit ille*'

---

42 See *supra* p. 201.

43 See *supra* p. 203.

44 For the treaty of Le Goulet see Matthew Paris, *Chronica maiora* ad ann. 1200, ed. Luard II, 474.

45 For this episode see *supra* p. 174, fnt. 25.

46 X. 2,1,13: '*Non enim intendimus iudicare de feudo, cuius ad ipsum spectat iudicium … sed decernere de peccato, cuius ad nos pertinet sine dubitatione censura, quam in quemlibet exercere possumus et debemus*'. For this the pope cited Matthew 18:15-17 *in extenso*: 'Moreover if thy brother shall trespass against thee, go and tell him his fault between thee and him alone: if he shall hear thee, thou hast gained thy brother. But if he will not hear thee, then take with thee one or two more, that in the mouth of two or three witnesses every word may be established. And if he shall neglect to hear them, tell it unto the Church: but if he neglect to hear the Church, let him be unto thee as an heathen man and a publican' (*si peccaverit in te frater tuus, vade et corripe eum inter te et ipsum solum. Si te audierit, lucratus eris fratrem tuum; si te autem non audierit, adhibe tecum adhuc unum vel duos, ut in ore duorum vel trium testium stet omne verbum. Quod si non audierit eos, dic ecclesiae; si autem ecclesiam non audierit, sit tibi sicut ethnicus et publicanus*).

47 X. 2,1,13: '*nullus, qui sit sanae mentis, ignorat, quin ad officium nostrum spectet de quocunque mortali peccato corripere quemlibet Christianum, et, si correctionem contempserit, ipsum per districtionem ecclesiasticam coercere*'.

neatly separated jurisdictions with clearly distinct methods of coercion, the secular and the spiritual sword, but the Gloss warns against this misconstruction[48]. The pope holds both swords rather than just one and consequently he may wield the temporal sword as well and take cognizance of a purely secular matter if need be, such as, for example, when a secular authority has denied access to justice, or whenever there is a vacancy in the empire.

The decretal
'*Per venerabilem*'

For this assessment, the Gloss refers to X. 4,17,13 ('*Per venerabilem*'), another famous, if not the most renowned, decretal of Innocent III. In this case, the pope had been requested to legitimize the bastards of Count William of Montpellier. Count William had underpinned his request by a reference to the legitimation by the pope of the illegitimate children of King Philip of France with Agnès de Méranie[49]. His request was denied, since, unlike the king of France[50], the count of Montpellier had a superior secular lord, the king of France, to whom he could (and should) have addressed his request. The pope refused to exercise temporal jurisdiction in this particular case but added an important *obiter dictum* explaining that he could, if it was called for: '*We do not only exercise secular jurisdiction in the Papal State, where we have full sovereignty in secular affairs, but sometimes also in other regions, not because we want to prejudice the right of another, but because it says so in Deuteronomy*'[51]. The pope then cites Deut. 17:8-12, giving supreme jurisdiction in difficult cases to the Levites who serve the Lord. This quote from the Old Testament is supported by some references to the New Testament, beginning, of course, with Matthew 16:18-19, the grant of the power to bind and loosen to St Peter, 'the representative of Him who is forever priest according to the order of Melchisedech and appointed by God as judge over the living and the dead'[52] and

---

48 Gl. '*Iurisdictionem nostram*' ad X. 2,1,13.
49 Philip 'Auguste' had been married to Princess Ingeborg of Denmark in 1193, after the demise of his first wife Isabella of Hainault (1190). For reasons unknown, Philip divorced Ingeborg in that very same year with the compliance of the archbishop of Reims. Ingeborg appealed to the pope, who refused to recognize the annulment of her marriage to Philip. In spite of this, Philip married Agnès de Méranie in 1196, causing Innocent III to lay the whole kingdom of France under interdict in 1200. The matter was resolved by the demise of Agnès in 1201. She had two children with Philip, Marie, and Philip. The whole unsavoury affair did not jeopardize the legitimacy of the royal succession in France, since Philip had a son with his first wife Isabella of Hainault, who succeeded him as Louis VIII in 1223.
50 X. 4,17,13: '*quum rex Franciae superiorem in temporalibus minime recognoscat*'.
51 X. 4,17,13: '*non solum in ecclesiae patrimonio (super quo plenam in temporalibus gerimus potestatem) verum etiam in aliis regionibus, certis causis inspectis, temporalem iurisdictionem casualiter exercemus; non quod alieno iuri praeiudicare velimus, sed quia sicut in Deuteronomio continentur*'.
52 X. 4,17,13: '*Eius vicarius, qui est sacerdos in aeternum secundum ordinem Melchisedech, constitutus a Deo iudex vivorum et mortuorum*'.

concluding with a famous quotation from Paul (1 Corint. 6:3): 'Know ye not that we shall judge angels? How much more things that pertain to this life?'. The Apostle Paul is writing in this way, says Innocent III, 'to explain his absolute sovereignty' (*ut plenitudinem potestatis exponeret*). Consequently, whenever a difficult or ambiguous case occurs in a secular court, there is recourse to the Apostolic See and the decision of the Apostolic See is to be obeyed on pain of excommunication[53]. The conclusion to be drawn from all this was that historical precedent had become completely irrelevant[54] now that it was settled law that the pope was the supreme judge of all Christendom, including kings and emperors, on the strength of the *plenitudo potestatis* granted to him by God as the representative on earth of the King of Kings and the Lord of Lords. Legal doctrine had completely superseded historical precedent. Nevertheless, Innocent IV refrained from deposing Frederick II on his own authority, but convened a general council for the purpose, due to the reservations of the king of France. The question now was whether Frederick II would answer the papal summons.

Frederick II refused to personally appear at his trial in Lyon. '*It is not appropriate for the Holy Empire to stand trial in a synodal court*', he is reported as having said[55]. The emperor certainly thought so, since we know from his own letters that he did indeed regard it as '*highly improper for us, our empire and all princes of the world to subject the cause of our honour to a synodal court*'[56]. This claim of immunity stands in striking contrast to Frederick's contention that the pope was *not* immune from prosecution in a synodal court. In 1240 he had even tried to bring Gregory IX before a general council of the Church to stand trial as a corrupt judge[57]. There were, to be sure, historical precedents for this. Popes had been deposed under the old Roman Empire: Justinian had deposed Pope Silverius I for high treason in 537[58] and the Emperor Constans II had deposed and banished Pope Martin I in 653[59]. Otto I had deposed two popes, John XII and Benedict V, and

Frederick II refuses to stand trial

---

53   X. 4,17,13: '*cum aliquid fuerit difficile vel ambiguum, ad iudicium est Sedis Apostolicae recurrendum: cuius sententiam, qui superbiens contempserit observare, mori praecipitur, id est, per excommunicationis sententiam velut mortuus a communione fidelium separari*'.
54   The assessment is emphasized by the Gl. 'Deposuit' ad C. 15, q. 6, cap. 3 (*Alius*), *supra* fnt. 5.
55   Matthew Paris, *Chronica maiora* ad ann. 1245, ed. H.R. Luard IV, 437: '*nec sacrum decet imperium ... judicio sisti sinodali*'.
56   See *supra* p. 302.
57   See *supra* p. 293 ff.
58   Procopius, *Gethica* 5,25,13 and Liberatus Diaconus, *Breviarium* (*c.* 560) cap. 22 (ed. Migne, *PL* 68, col. 1040)
59   *Liber pontificalis*, Martinus 8, ed. Duchesne I, Paris 1886, 338.

the Emperor Henry III had organized and presided over two synods at
Sutri and Rome in 1046 to have no fewer than three popes deposed[60].
The last emperor to have presided over a council of the Church convened to depose a pope had been Frederick's grandfather Barbarossa in
1160. The failed council of Pavia[61] marked the end of an era, since the
excommunication of Alexander III and the confirmation of the election
of Victor IV were not recognized by the rest of Christianity. Alexander
III had refused to appear at Pavia appealing to his alleged immunity[62]:
no one but God had the right to stand in judgement over a pope. In the
time of Alexander III this contention was supported by what we now
know is a forgery, the *constitutum Silvestri*. It had found its way into
Gratian's *Decretum*[63] and became one of the central tenets of the papal
monarchy. It was Gregory VII, a witness of the councils of Sutri and
Rome, who canonized that doctrine in his famous *Dictatus*: 'He may
himself not be judged by anyone' (*a nemine ipse iudicari debeat*)[64]. The
pope was immune from the jurisdiction of any power on earth, secular
or ecclesiastical, as was repeatedly confirmed by Gratian's *Decretum*[65].
It was Innocent III who settled the doctrine in a sermon to celebrate the
day of his consecration: *'But only Peter has received absolute sovereignty.
Now you see who that servant is who has been appointed to rule over his
flock, truly the vicar of Christ, the successor to Peter, the anointed of the
Lord, God to Pharaoh, constituted in the middle between God and man,
close to God, but above man, smaller than God, but greater than man,
who judges over all, but is judged by no one'*[66]. It seems clear from this
that Frederick's plan to call a general council to sit in judgement over
Gregory IX never had any chance of success since it would have been
contrary to established canon law[67]. The pope, however, could call a

---

60 See *supra* p. 27 and 154.
61 See *supra* p. 112.
62 See *supra* p. 112.
63 See *supra* p. 55.
64 *Das Register Gregors VII.*, 2, MGH *Epp. sel.* 2,1, no 55a ('*Dictatus papae*, § 19), 206.
65 C. 9, q. 3, cap. 13 (cited *supra*, p. 55 fnt. 72) is the *locus classicus*, but see also Dist. 40, c.
6 and the Gl. 'A nemine' and C. 9, q. 3, cap. 14-17. Some traces of the old state of affairs did,
however, survive in Gratian's *Decretum*: see C. 2, q. 7, c. 41, where Pope Leo IV voluntarily
submits to the jurisdiction of the Emperor Louis II. The apparent contradiction was overcome
by the assessment that the pope could indeed voluntarily submit to the jurisdiction of the
emperor, since the pope could also depose himself: see the Gl. 'Aliena' on C. 2, q. 7, c. 41,
referring to Dist. 21, c. 7.
66 *Innocentii III papae sermones de diversis, Sermo 2 (In consecratione pontificis maximi)*,
Migne *PL* 217, col. 653-660(658): '*Solus autem Petrus assumptus est in plenitudinem potestatis.
Iam videtis quis iste servus, qui super familiam constituitur, profecto vicarius Jesu Christi, successor
Petri, Christus Domini, Deus Pharaonis: inter Deum et hominem medius constitutus, citra Deum,
sed ultra hominem: minor Deo, sed major homine: qui de omnibus judicat, et a nemine judicatur*'.
67 A case against Gregory IX was not entirely out of the question though, since a pope *could*
be deposed on account of heresy: *Decretum*, Dist. 40, c. 6. Because the concept of 'heresy' was

general council to assist him in sitting in judgment over the emperor. Frederick's appeal to immunity was inadmissible according to canon law, since no one was exempt from a summons by the vicar of Christ. Imperial immunity was not even pleaded by Frederick's counsel at his trial in Lyon. The only objection to the summons raised there was that it had never been properly presented to the defendant since Innocent had issued his summons 'in a public sermon' (*in predicatione publica*) without serving a writ of summons (*citatio*) to the emperor in person[68].

---

open to extensive construction, it might even include notorious and incorrigible misdemeanours (such as simony and adultery) scandalizing the reputation of the Church and amounting to conduct in contempt of office (see the Gl. 'A fide devius' to Dist. 40, c. 6). On this issue see also *infra* p. 575-576.

68   Nicolaus de Carbio, *Vita Innocentii IV* cap. 18, ed. Pagnotti 93. See on this issue *infra* p. 366-367 and 385.

The Donation of Constantine, fresco mid-13th century, Basilica dei Santi Quattro Coronati, Oratorio di San Silvestro, Rome (Wikimedia Commons)

2

The Venue

During his entire prolonged stay at Lyon, from 1244 to 1251, Innocent IV resided in the monastery of St Just on the west bank of the Saône. His residence there indicates that the pope was convinced Frederick II threatened his life. The monastery was a genuine fortress with moated walls guarded by no less than twenty-two towers and only accessible through two massive gateways. It was a heavily fortified area within a heavily fortified city. Around Easter 1245 two prominent German prelates visited the pope in his stronghold, the archbishops of Cologne and Mainz. They came to reassure the pope that, once he had deposed Frederick II, the imperial succession in Germany was safe in their hands. Of course, Conrad IV was not an option. Conrad was sixteen by now, but his election had not been confirmed by the pope and he had not been crowned and consecrated as king of the Germans at Aachen, as he should have been, and consequently the young king was politically a *quantité négligable*. The archbishops were sure they could finally persuade the still reluctant landgrave of Thüringia, Heinrich Raspe, to accept a nomination if only the pope would excommunicate Frederick II once again in order to help the landgrave to overcome his obvious scruples. Innocent IV complied and excommunicated Frederick II once again on Maundy Thursday 1245, exactly a year after the emperor had sworn to make his peace with the Church[1]. The pope ordered that the

---

1 *Annales Wormatienses* ad ann 1245, MGH *SS* 17, 49: 'The archbishops of Mainz and Cologne have visited the pope before Easter and have talked a lot with him there against the emperor, promising the pope that, if he deposed the emperor, they would doubtless and without delay present a mighty king in his place for him and the Church, which pleased the curia much. The pope was so encouraged by their promises and suggestions that he has solemnly and publicly denounced the emperor in the presence of the people as a person not only excommunicated by his predecessor Gregory, but also by himself, which terrified and astounded many people. Having achieved this, the archbishops immediately returned to their native land and tried to inflict as much mischief as they could to the emperor all over Germany, looking everywhere to find a king they could put in his place' (*Accesserunt itaque ad summum pontificem ante pascha Maguntinus et Coloniensis archiepiscopi, et multa apud eum contra domnum imperatorem ibidem tractaverunt; promittentes etiam domno pape, quod si imperatorem deponeret, regem potentem in loco suo sibi et ecclesie absque mora et indubitanter presentarent.*

renewed excommunication of Frederick II should be read in all churches within the French kingdom[2]. The emperor had many supporters there, especially among the French barons, who were very frustrated by the continuous encroachments of ecclesiastical courts on their seignorial jurisdiction and consequently recognized Frederick's anti-clerical cause as their own. It must have been one of the reasons why they had dissuaded their king to grant asylum to the pope[3]. Louis IX himself also must have been very displeased by the aggressive and uncompromising policy of Gregory IX and Innocent IV. He had been critically ill in 1244[4] and had taken the cross on his sickbed, miraculously recovering after that[5]. Since then, Louis had but one aspiration: the fulfilment of his crusading vow. The ongoing conflict between the emperor and the pope frustrated the implementation of that oath. This is why Louis decided to decline the invitation of the pope to personally attend the council[6]. The king of France refused to partake as a figurant in a charade organized by the pope to depose a befriended monarch. It was a part below the dignity of a king. Moreover, pious though he was, Louis disliked the excessive use of the sentence of excommunication by his own clerics. His biographer Joinville devotes an entire section to this: he recounts that the king had once been criticized by his bishops for not having ordered secular punishment (forfeiture of the estate) of a person excommunicated by the Church. Louis simply replied that it was not his policy to execute a sentence of excommunication whenever he felt it was wrong (*contre Dieu et contre raison*) to do so[7]. He may well have

---

Super quo curia multum congratulabatur. Hiis enim promissionibus et suggestionibus domnus papa a dictis archiepiscopis ad hoc inductus est, quod statim in cena Domini cum divina in Lugduno celebraret, domnum imperatorem sollempniter et coram omni populo excommunicatum tam a predecessore suo domno Gregorio quam ab ipso publice denuntiavit. Super quo perterriti et admirati sunt universi. Hiis vero peractis, statim ad sua reversi sunt archiepiscopi memorati, et per totam Theutuniam quecunque poterant mala imperatori tractare modis omnibus conabantur, temptantes etiam ubique, ubi regem super eum possent invenire). According to the *Annales Placentini Gibellini* ad ann. 1245, MGH *SS* 18, 489, the emperor's son Enzio and Margrave Lancia, a relative of Frederick's mistress Bianca Lancia and one of Frederick's chief war-lords, were also excommunicated on this occasion.

2 Matthew Paris, *Chronica maiora* ad ann. 1245, ed. H.R. Luard IV, 406-407.
3 See *supra* p. 323.
4 See *supra* p. 323.
5 Jean de Joinville (1224-1317), *Histoire de Saint Louis*, cap. 24, 107, ed. Wailly, 47 and Guillaume de Nangis, *Chronicon* ad ann. 1245 (*Recueil* 20, 550-551). Joinville's biography of Louis IX is a masterpiece and a very reliable source, since he knew the king well and often had confidential conversations with Louis. Few medieval princes, if any, have had a similar biographer.
6 For Innocent's invitation to Louis IX see MGH *Epp. saec. xiii* 2, no 78 (III) (3 January 1245), 57-58.
7 Joinville, *Histoire de Saint Louis*, cap. 13, 61-64, ed. Wailly, 28: 'Et le roy dist que il ne le feroit autrement; car ce feroit contre Dieu et contre raison, se il contreignoit la gent à eulz absoudre, quant les clercs leur feroient tort'.

believed that what the pope was up to in Lyon was '*contre Dieu et contre raison*' as well.

Recent developments in the Holy Land instigated a last desperate attempt to reconcile the pope and the emperor. In July 1244 Jerusalem had been stormed and taken by a horde of Turkish nomads, having fled from Asia before the armies of the Mongols and now fighting for the new Egyptian sultan, As-Salih Ayub (1205-1240-1249), a son of Al-Kamil. All Christians in the city were massacred, the churches, including the Church of the Holy Sepulchre, were desecrated and burnt, leaving the holy city practically inhabitable. Catastrophe was soon to succeed disaster. On 17 October 1244 the combined Christian force in Palestine suffered a devastating defeat near Gaza by an Egyptian army led by the redoubtable Emir Baibars. The loss of life was horrendous, only rivalled by the losses suffered at Hattin in 1187[8], the Grandmasters of the Temple and the Hospital of St John were both slain along with thousands of knights. Only a few survivors had been able to escape to Jaffa. Jerusalem was lost (now definitively, as it turned out) and what was left of the kingdom of Jerusalem seemed all but lost. Frederick II, who still styled himself king of Jerusalem, acting as the guardian of his son Conrad, was informed about the loss of Jerusalem soon after the event by a messenger from Patriarch Albert of Antioch[9]. The emperor was not only shocked, but also furious about the stupidity of the Grandmasters of the Temple and the Hospital of St John to enter into an offensive alliance with the sultan of Damascus against the Ayubite sultan of Egypt, despite a truce with that Egyptian prince concluded only shortly before by Richard of Cornwall[10], Frederick's brother-in-law, thus forcing the Egyptian sultan to unleash his Turkish horde on Jerusalem. Good relations with the Egyptian sultan were essential according to Frederick and the breach of the truce with As-Salih was therefore a fatal mistake, surely to entail even worse disasters, all the more so since he, the emperor, was unable to come to the rescue himself due to the ongoing conflict with the pope. Frederick wrote this letter even before he was informed of the catastrophe near Gaza[11]. After that debacle,

An unsuccessful attempt at reconciliation

---

8   See *supra* p. 141.
9   For this and what follows see Frederick's letter to the European kings and princes in HB 6.1, 236-240.
10   On the truce with the sultan of Egypt see the detailed account by Richard of Cornwall himself in his letter about his adventures in Palestine in Matthew Paris, *Chronica maiora* ad ann. 1241, ed. H.R. Luard IV, 141-145.
11   The news of the destruction of the army of the kingdom of Jerusalem near Gaza only reached Frederick in February 1245. He immediately informed Richard of Cornwall about this disastrous consequence of the breach of the truce which Richard had concluded with the Egyptian sultan. See Frederick's letter of 27 February 1245 to Richard of Cornwall in HB 6.1,

Patriarch Albert of Antioch, an Italian, left Palestine on a mission to Europe to end the conflict between pope and emperor as quickly as possible for the sake of the Holy Land[12]. He met with the emperor first, urging him to a reconciliation with the pope, and subsequently with the pope in Lyon, begging him to come to terms with the emperor. It was all in vain. Once again, as in the Mongol crisis of 1241[13], the two heads of European Christendom, the pope and the emperor, were locked in lethal conflict, critically jeopardizing the safety of Europe and European interests abroad.

Patriarch Albert of Antioch did all he could to bring about peace and even contacted Cardinal Raniero of Viterbo, a declared enemy of the emperor[14], for the purpose. He beseeched the cardinal not to renew hostilities against the emperor that would impede the cause of peace[15]. Open warfare had been resumed recently by imperial troops laying waste to the environments of Cardinal Raniero's native Viterbo, calling for an immediate response by the cardinal. But Cardinal Raniero refrained from immediate action, reassuring the citizens of Viterbo that 'peace was at hand and that their freedom from exertion was closer than they believed'[16]. The efforts of the patriarch of Antioch resulted in a mission to the pope by Henry of Hohenlohe, the new grandmaster of the Teutonic Order[17]. It is, however, unclear what exactly the grand-

---

254-259. About the fall of Jerusalem and the battle near Gaza see also a letter by Guillaume de Châteauneuf, master of the Order of the Hospital of St John, in Matthew Paris, *Chronica maiora* ad ann. 1244, ed. H.R. Luard IV, 307-311.

12   The Patriarch of Jerusalem, Robert of Nantes, was appointed by Gregory IX in 1241, but only arrived in Palestine in 1244, just in time to witness the sack of Jerusalem and the debacle near Gaza. He clearly was the wrong person to achieve a reconciliation between the pope and Frederick II, since he had been a bishop in Apulia, probably of Aquino, but was expelled from the Sicilian kingdom by Frederick II. Gregory IX appointed him bishop of Nantes in 1236 and promoted him to the patriarchate of Jerusalem in 1241: Alberic de Troisfontaines, *Chronica* ad ann. 1236 and 1241, MGH *SS* 23, 940 (with fnt. 4) and 949.

13   See *supra* p. 309.

14   See *supra* p. 314. We have two letters from Albert to Cardinal Raniero: MGH *Const.* 2, no 255 and 257, 354 and 355-356.

15   Patriarch Albert to Cardinal Raniero (April 1245) (MGH *Const.* 2, no 257, 355-356): '*Igitur paternitatem vestram humiliter deprecamur, quatenus per vos vel per vestros homines nichil injurie aut molestie innovetur, quod valeat bonum propositum impedire*'.

16   Cardinal Raniero to the citizens of Viterbo (Winkelmann, *Acta imperii inedita seculi XIII*, Innsbruck 1880, no 722, 568): '*pax est in portis et quies vestra proximior quam credatis*'. See also an earlier letter by the cardinal to the men of Viterbo (Winkelmann no 720, 566-567) warning them for traitors within their midst since the emperor was bent on recapturing Viterbo. He reports (567) that the emperor was said to have stated 'that if he had one foot in paradise, he would retract it in order to have his revenge on Viterbo' (*si unum pedem teneret in paradiso, illum inde extraheret, dummodo se posset de Viterbiensibus vindicare*). At the same time Cardinal Raniero opened a diplomatic offensive directed against the peace initiative of the patriarch of Antioch: see *infra* p. 349.

17   See *supra* p. 313, fnt. 43.

master had to offer on behalf of the emperor to satisfy the demands of the pope[18]. On 30 April 1245 Innocent IV sent a letter to the patriarch of Antioch, who was with the emperor again at the time, with his last offer of reconciliation[19]. It was not a serious offer, since the pope had already made up his mind to depose Frederick II. He had held a conference shortly before with the two leading German archbishops and electors on the succession of Frederick II in Germany and they had assured him that a substitute was at hand[20]. He was not going to disavow his two German prelates and his Lombard allies by making peace with the emperor at this late juncture. Moreover, the deadline to come to terms with the pope had already expired: the invitations for the general council had been sent in December 1244, and the council was to convene for its opening session on 24 June next, only a few weeks away now. Yet, it seems still not to have dawned on Frederick II that absolution was just not to be had from Innocent IV, not now, nor ever. He even made another 'last' effort to come to terms with the pope only two days before the opening of the Council.

According to Innocent's summons, the council[21] was to open on the feast day of St John the Baptist, 24 June 1245, but the opening session was postponed for a few days, to be held on 28 June, a Wednesday, in the Cathedral of St John. Two days before, however, an important preliminary meeting of all participants then present was convened in

A last attempt at reconciliation

---

18   Frederick's letter of credential to the pope on behalf of the grandmaster (HB 6.1, 266-267; MGH *Const.* 2, no 256, 354-355) does not contain specific details, except a vague reference to the matter of the Holy Land. It is surmised that Frederick's offer at this occasion may not have been unlike the offer made later on his behalf by master Thaddaeus of Suessa in Lyon: see *infra* p. 348.
19   Since the pope's offer was not serious, the details may be relegated to the footnotes. Innocent demanded that the emperor immediately released all his prisoners and that he should restore all the land of the Church he had occupied, adding that 'the release of the prisoners and the restitution of the land must have come to our notice before the council that is to be held with the support of God and that we cannot postpone and where we shall proceed with these and other things as the law requires' (HB 6.1, 271-272; MGH *Const.* 2, no 258, 356: '*ita quod huiusmodi tam captivorum quam terre restitutio posset ad nostram pervenire notitiam ante Concilium a nobis, annuente Domino, celebrandum, in quo postponere non poterimus quin super iis et aliis prout de jure fuerit procedamus*').
20   See *supra* p. 343.
21   There are two main sources for the First Council of Lyon (Lyon I). Most important is the extensive report of Matthew Paris, *Chronica maiora* ad ann. 1245, ed. H.R. Luard IV, 430-473 (for the discussion of the trial henceforth referred to as 'MP'). Matthew has not attended the council himself, but his account is based on both oral reports of English clerics who had and on documents supplied to him, such as an accurate transcript of the sentence of the pope. The other source is much more compact, but just as important. It probably was written by an eyewitness working in the papal chancery. It is printed in MGH *Const.* 2 no 401, 513-516 under the (modern) rubric *Relatio de concilio Lugdunensi* (as from now '*Relatio*').

the refectory of the monastery of St Just[22]. According to our only source for this meeting, Matthew Paris, 140 archbishops and bishops were present at the occasion, as were most of the cardinals, the patriarchs of Constantinople and Aquileia, the Latin emperor of Constantinople, Count Raymond VII of Toulouse, the envoys of the king of England, and the representative of Frederick II, his trusted lawyer master Thaddaeus of Suessa. It seems to have been the purpose of the meeting to establish an agenda for the business of the general council. The patriarch of Constantinople was first to address the attendants on the pathetic state of the Latin empire, now reduced to the city of Constantinople itself, 'at which the pope kept silent'[23]. After this painful silence, the English clerics present asked for the sanctification of Archbishop Edmund of Canterbury by the council. The pope, however, decided that there was more urgent business: '*Too many difficult affairs of the Church that cannot be delayed call for our attention*'[24]. It turned out there was but one urgent affair to be decided by the council, the affair of the Church and the emperor (*negotium inter ecclesiam et principem*). It was now that master Thaddaeus addressed the meeting[25]. He conveyed a last offer of peace from the emperor to the pope: Frederick declared that he was prepared to restore the unity of the entire Eastern Latin Empire with the Roman Church and to go to war against the Greeks, the Mongols, the Saracenes, and all other enemies of the Church, doing so 'at his own expenditure' (*sumptibus propriis*). In addition, the emperor promised to restore all possessions of the Church which he had occupied and to pay compensation, all on return for the restoration of his peace and former friendship with the Church[26]. A similar offer may have been made to the pope on behalf of the emperor shortly before by Henry of Hohenlohe, the grandmaster of the Teutonic Order, as a result of the peace initiative of Patriarch Albert of Antioch[27]. That initiative had been discredited by a diplomatic counteroffensive by a major oppo-

---

22 MP 431: '*die Lunae proxima post festum nativitatis Sancti Johannis Baptistae ... in refectorium religiosorum Sancti Justi apud Lugdunum*'.
23 MP 432: '*Ad quod Papa tacuit*'.
24 MP 432: '*Urgent nos dilationem non capientia ecclesiae nimis ardua negotia*'.
25 MP 432: '*Affuit etiam praesens ibidem magister Thaddaeus de Suessa, domini imperatoris procurator, vir prudens et eloquentiae singularis, miles, et legum doctor, et sacri palatii judex imperialis, pro domino suo imperatore tam constanter quam diligenter responsurus*'.
26 MP 432-433: '*Pro cuius pace et pristinae amicitiae reformatione optulit pro domino suo confidenter ad unitatem Romanae ecclesiae totum Romaniae, id est, Graeciae imperium, revocare; et quod sese Tartaris et Chorosminis, Sarracenis, et aliis ecclesiae hostibus et contemptoribus, Christo fideliter militando, potenter opponet; et quod statum Terrae Sanctae discrimini magno jam patentis, sumptibus propriis personaliter pro posse suo reformabit; et ablata Romanae ecclesiae restituendo, de injuriis satisfacere*'. The 'Chorosminians' were the Turks who had stormed and sacked Jerusalem in 1244 (*supra* p. 345).
27 See *supra* p. 345-347.

348

nent of Frederick II, Cardinal Raniero of Viterbo, who had sent a letter to some anonymous attendants of the council, assuring them that the 'tyrant and butcher of the priests of the Lord' (*sacerdotum Domini laniator et tyrannus*) continued to harass the papal dominions in spite of his promise to the patriarch of Antioch not to do so and urging them to depose the emperor[28]. We do not know for certain whether Innocent IV actually saw Cardinal Raniero's letter, but we do know that the pope was not impressed by Frederick's latest offer for peace: '*Oh, how many, how many, promises have been made, yet never and nowhere kept. But it is clear that these promises too are only made now to prevent the axe from striking at the root, making a mockery of the council and trying to disband it*'[29]. Frederick should keep the oath sworn on his behalf at Rome on Maundy Thursday, 31 March 1244[30]. Period. Even if he would accept the offer made to him and the emperor should happen to withdraw from it later, as the pope was sure he would, whom was he to approach as a guarantor[31]? At this, master Thaddaeus surprised the pope by mentioning that the kings of France and England were prepared to stand as sureties for the emperor. This was unacceptable to the pope, outwitting Frederick's counsellor: suppose, he said, that the emperor was not to keep his word, as again the pope was sure he would not, then the Church was left with not just one, but no fewer than three adversaries, the three most powerful princes of the world[32]. Thus ended the last attempt by the emperor to come to terms with

---

28 Winkelmann, *Acta imperii inedita* I, Innsbruck 1880, 568-570(569): 'You have to know for certain that, if the Church now remains silent and does not strike at the enemy with a sentence of deposition, she will lose all supporters she now has in Germany, Italy, and elsewhere and all will submit to the rule of the tyrant. The patriarch of Antioch is not to be believed in this matter, since after his meeting with the impious one, the tyrant and butcher of the priests of the Lord has perpetrated even more cruel acts, despite the promise he made to him not to attack the papal patrimony, and he has kept none of his other promises' (*scituri pro certo, quod si nunc ecclesia tacuerit, ut non ferat deiectionis sententiam contra hostem, omnes adiutores amittet, quos in Germania, Liguria et alibi habere videtur, omnesque se tyrampni subicient ditioni ... Antiochenus ... patriarcha non creditur in hoc facto ... quia post suum adventum ad impium licentius crudeliora commisit sacerdotum domini laniator et tyrampnus de non violando patrimonio, ut sibi promiserat ... et de aliis nil servavit*). The letter is by an anonymous author but must be attributed to Cardinal Raniero of Viterbo. The letter also contains an attempt at discrediting another patriarch involved in the peace initiative of Albert of Antioch, the patriarch of Aquileia. On him see *infra* p. 350, fnt 36 and p. 375.

29 MP 433: '*O quam multa, quam multa, sunt promissa! Numquam vel nusquam tamen adimpleta. Sed et haec nunc constat sunt promissa, ut secures jam ad radicem posita, illuso concilio et soluto, per dilationem avertatur*'.

30 MP 433: '*Pacem nuper in anima sua juratam secundum formam praestiti sacramenti teneat et adquiesco*'. On this oath see *supra* p. 315.

31 MP 433: '*quis nunc pro eo cavens, fidejuberet ut cogeret resilientem?*'.

32 MP 433: '*Nolumus, quia si pacta commutasset vel penitus infirmasset, nec aliud credimus propter frequentiam, aliquo tempore inposterum, oporteret nos animadvertere in eosdem; et tunc haberet ecclesia tres, quibus non sunt in saeculari potentia majores, immo nec pares, inimicos*'.

the Church before the council convened. When viewed from the perspective of the pope, the rejection of Frederick's offer stands to reason. Frederick had failed to comply with his promises to the pope time and again in the past and even now, at this crucial occasion, his insincerity was obvious. How could Frederick seriously maintain that he would fight the enemies of the Latin emperor of Constantinople, given the fact that he had just betrothed his daughter Constance to the Byzantine Emperor Joannes III Vatatzes of Nicaea, the sworn enemy of the Latin emperor of Constantinople, Baldwin II[33]? No wonder, therefore, that Pope Innocent made short work of it. At this point, master Thaddaeus realized that any arrangement with the pope was out of the question and that the trial and possible deposition of Frederick II was imminent. The preliminary session was concluded with an address by the bishop of Beirut informing the meeting on the state of the Holy Land and a letter was read from the nobles residing in Palestine on the disastrous recent events there. '*The depressing contents of it moved the audience to tears*'[34]. After this emotional address, the meeting ended. The agenda of the council was fixed, and the trial of Frederick II was about to proceed as planned.

Setting
the stage

The plenary sessions of the general council opened on 28 June 1245, a Wednesday, in the Cathedral of St John. Innocent IV had taken care to arrange an impressive staging of the event[35]. The pope himself was enthroned high in the cathedral's choir, to his right was a throne reserved for the emperor of Constantinople and to his left were seats for the other secular princes present and for the clerks of the council. Below these seats were places for the patriarchs of Constantinople, Antioch, and Aquileia[36] and below these was a bench for the cardi-

---

33 For the marriage of Frederick's daughter with the Byzantine emperor see Matthew Paris, *Chronica maiora* ad ann. 1244, ed. H.R. Luard IV, 299 and 357. It was deemed a disgrace all over Catholic Europe, since the girl had to convert to orthodoxy and take a new name, Anna. She is known in Byzantine sources as Anna Alamanna.

34 MP 433: '*Quorum tenor lugubris omnes audientes ad lacrimarum, nec immerito, movit effusionem*'.

35 For this see *Relatio*, 513.

36 There was an unfortunate incident (*scandalum*) before the opening of the session concerning the seat of the patriarch of Aquileia, since the other two patriarchs present did not consider him worthy of the honour to be seated next to them. He was, in fact, an archbishop, but was allowed to style himself a patriarch for historical reasons. In the end, the patriarch of Aquileia was allowed a seat next to the other two patriarchs on the order of the pope himself. It may all have been orchestrated in advance by Innocent in order to embarrass the patriarch of Aquileia, Berthold of Andechs, a German aristocrat who was known to be sympathetic to Frederick II (see *infra* p. 375). He had even been excommunicated for a time because of his imperial sympathies and had been actively involved in the recent efforts of the patriarch of Antioch to arrange peace between the emperor and the pope.

nal-deacons present, all cardinals wearing the broad-rimmed red hat recently rewarded to them by Innocent IV as a token of their dignity. Two tribunes facing the middle of the nave had been erected to the left and the right of the papal tribune. The cardinal-priests and the cardinal-bishops on the superior benches to the right and to the left and the archbishops and bishops on the inferior benches. In the middle of the nave were benches for the other bishops present, for the abbots and other clerics, for the representatives of the secular princes and cities invited, and, of course, for the representatives of Frederick II.

The cathedral cannot have been filled completely on the occasion. There is some uncertainty about the number of attendants, but it is certain that there were considerably fewer participants than had taken part in the Fourth Lateran Council of 1215. Matthew Paris has 140 archbishops and bishops in the preparatory meeting of 26 June and a contemporary German source mentions a total of 250 bishops on the council itself[37]. There were very few clerics from Germany or the Sicilian kingdom present[38] and no secular prince from there at all. Many English clerics had excused themselves and consequently the council seems to have mainly consisted of clerics, nobles and representatives of the cities from the Italian kingdom, as well as French and, especially, Spanish clerics[39]. It is a matter of record that only 'approximately' (circa) 150 prelates attached their seal to the final sentence of the council[40], casting considerable doubt on the assertion that the council represented catholic Christendom as a whole.

---

37 *Annales Erphordenses*, ad ann. 1254, MGH *SS rer. Germ.* 42, 100.

38 MP 430-431: '*De Alemannia, guerra imperiali perturbata, pauci prelati ad concilium minime convenire potuerunt*'. See also *Annales Stadenses* ad ann. 1245, MGH *SS* 16, 369: '*Plures episcopi Teutoniae ad concilium non iverunt*'. We know that, apart from the bishop of Freising (on him see *infra* p. 371), two bishops from the Empire were present at Lyon, Bishop Robert of Lièges and Bishop Nicholas of Prague. From the Sicilian kingdom, Archbishop Marino Filangieri of Bari was present at the council. He had been very active as a diplomat in the early years of Frederick's reign, but fell into disgrace in the early forties, living in exile in Rome in 1243 and 1244, as did the other Sicilian prelate present at the council, Peter of Calenum, on whom more later on (*infra* p. 357). According to Innocent's biographer Nicolaus de Carbio (*Vita Innocentii IV* cap. 19, ed. Pagnotti 94) Archbishop Berardo of Palermo, Frederick's trusted advisor, was also present, but in his capacity as an ambassador of the emperor.

39 The overrepresentation of Spanish clerics is stressed by the '*Relatio*' (515): '*prelati Yspanie, qui multum magnifice ac generaliter melius quam alia natio ad concilium venerant*'.

40 *Relatio* 516 *i.f.*

3

The Trial

The First Session

After mass was celebrated, the pope opened the first session of the council with a sermon on Psalms 94:19: 'In the multitude of sorrows within me thy comforts delight my soul' (*Secundum multitudinem dolorum meorum in corde meo consolationes tuae laetificaverunt animam meam*). There were five sorrows troubling his heart, the pope lectured, referring of course to the five wounds of Christ: the first wound was the depravity (*deformitas*) of the prelates and their servants; the second concerned the insolence of the Saracenes; the third was the state of the Latin Empire, where Ioannes Vatatzes, the emperor of the schismatic Greeks, had regained control but for the beleaguered city of Constantinople itself; the fourth wound was the terror of the Mongols; and the fifth and deepest wound was Frederick II, the enemy and persecutor of the Church of Christ and all of his servants[1]. The pope had a lot to say on all of these issues, but coming to the last and most grievous one, his voice broke and tears came to his eyes, moving his audience to compassion[2]. As every orator knows, this is the moment to change the tone from grief to indignation and Innocent did not hesitate to do so. From the role of a grieving spiritual leader, he now stepped into the role of a public prosecutor. According to his own instructions on the prosecution of an emperor[3], a pope did well to charge the defendant

(margin: Innocent IV brings his charges*)*

---

1 MP 434 and the '*Relatio*' 514 agree but for the '*deformitas*' of the prelates, where Matthew Paris has the pope complain about the continuing plague of heresy, especially in Lombardy. There may be no contradiction here, since it is quite possible that the pope attributed the spread of heresies to the bad example of the prelates.
2 MP 435: 'And when the pope proceeded on this issue as seemed the proper way to do, he moved all who listened to him with a deep feeling of compassion. Tears came rolling from his eyes and his speech was interrupted by sobs' (*Et prosecutus dominus Papa materiam hanc quantum videbatur expedire, cunctos audientes dolore compassionis salubriter sauciavit. Exitus enim aquarium deduxerunt oculi eius, et singultus sermonem proruperunt*).
3 See *supra* p. 336, fnt. 40.

with as many crimes and sins as possible and Innocent read out a long indictment against Frederick II.

The first charge brought against the emperor was perjury, breach of oath. The pope produced two charters of Frederick II, each one with a golden bull attached, issued on behalf of Pope Honorius III. One of them contained, as Innocent alleged, an oath of fealty (*iuramentum fidelitatis*) to the pope by Frederick II 'like a vassal swears to his lord' (*tamquam vasallus suo domino*) and the other held Frederick's assurance to Honorius III that the kingdom of Sicily belonged to the Roman Church from which he held it in fee. A third charter was produced to corroborate the territorial concessions made to the Church by Frederick. There can be little doubt that the pope was referring to the charters issued by Frederick II in 1219, confirming his earlier concessions to Innocent III at Eger in 1213 and Haguenau in 1216[4]. The pope contended that the emperor had not complied with all these promises and consequently had forsworn himself[5]. Master Thaddaeus was allowed to rebut the accusations of the pope and he did so with fervour[6]. He produced papal documents seemingly contradicting the allegations of the pope and also referred to the many wrongs (*multa mala*) committed against the emperor by the Church, corroborating this contention with documents as well. His rebuttal impressed the audience[7], but the pope, as clever a lawyer as Thaddaeus was, succeeded in refuting his arguments by pointing out that all papal concessions referred to by master Thaddaeus were conditional (on the conduct of the emperor, no doubt), whereas all the emperor's concessions were unconditional[8]. Master Thaddaeus, in reply, produced promises made by the pope to the emperor on which the pope was in default, contending that since the pope was in default of his obligations, the emperor was entitled not to keep his own promises[9], a rather weak defence since it implies that

---

4   See *supra* p. 215-216.

5   '*Relatio*' 514. MP is less precise here (435): 'He accused him of multiple perjury, and that he never kept his contracts and nowhere his promises, rejecting to hold on to the truth. In order to better convince the audience about these things, he showed the community letters with golden imperial seals attached' (*Imponebatque ei multiplex periurium, et quod, spreto veritatis tenore, numquam pacta, nusquam promissa conservabat. Super quibus ut magis haec audientes certificaret, signorum imperialium de auro appensione communitas ostendit epistolas, quibus evidenter arguit et redarguit ipsum super perjurio*).

6   The rebuttal of master Thaddaeus: '*Relatio*' 515; MP 435-436.

7   '*Relatio*' 515: '*multis eius responsio fuit grata*'.

8   MP 435: '*non sibi ad invicem contradictoriae adversabantur, cum Papales epistolae conditionales fuissent, imperatoriae vero absolutae; et apparuit laesio fidei manifeste ex parte imperatoris, qui, cum omnia absolute promiserat, nec inde aliquid secundum promissa compleverat*'.

9   MP 435-436: '*Ad quod Thadaeus ... literas alias ex adverso Papales ostendens, et asserens, quod in eis continebatur non fuisse observatum; unde dominum suum suis promissis parere non debuisse*'.

the emperor was, indeed, not keeping his promises, or at least not all of them. It was generally felt that the pope had the best of the argument on perjury[10], but that was not the only charge brought against Frederick II[11].

Pope Innocent also brought charges of sacrilege and heresy against Frederick II. The charge of sacrilege (*sacrilegium*) was serious and very hard to deny, since it was notorious. Everyone present at the council knew, some of them from personal experience, that Frederick had attacked, captured, and imprisoned many prelates and other clerics on their way to the failed council called by Gregory IX in 1241[12]. Attacking and maltreating a cleric was a crime and a special kind of sacrilege, 'sacrilege on account of the person' (*sacrilegium ratione personae*)[13], to be punished by excommunication. The even more serious charge of heresy was less obvious but was based on a number of facts that were considered to be notorious at the time. Frederick had built a town (Lucera) for the Muslims of his kingdom to live in[14]; he was alleged to have taken part in their religious ceremonies, scorning Christian religion in doing so. The emperor had also established friendly relations with the sultan of Egypt and other Muslim princes. Even worse than that, the emperor was accused of having sinfully and shamelessly defiled himself by having had obscene intercourse with 'Saracene girls, or rather prostitutes' (*mulierculae et potius meretriculae Sarracenicae*)[15].

It is not reported how master Thaddaeus responded to the charge of sacrilege on this day[16], but Matthew Paris has his reaction to the charge of heresy. Thaddaeus stated that he could not answer to that charge

The charge of heresy

---

10 '*Relatio*' 515: 'But the pope replied well to each of these arguments, as if he had foreseen them, justifying himself and the Church' (*Sed dominus papa respondit ad singula bene, ac si providisset, se et ecclesiam excusando*).
11 The '*Relatio*' 515 says that the first session ended at this point (*Et sic illius diei fuit sessio terminata*). This cannot be true, since the sentence of the pope convicted Frederick on more charges, all of them to be found in the report of the first session in MP 435.
12 See *supra* p. 302-303.
13 See Innocentii IIII. PM *Commentaria in V. libros Decretalium* on X 5,39,27 (ed. Venice 1570, 655, l. col.): 'There is also such a thing as sacrilege on account of the person, when a cleric is harmed' (*Item est sacrilegium ratione personae, cum persona ecclesiastica laeditur*). See on this issue also *infra* p. 365.
14 See *supra* p. 225.
15 For all this see MP 435: '*In fine autem praedicationis suae proposuit enormitates imperatoris, scilicet heresin, sacrilegium, et inter alia mala, quod civitatem quondam in Christianitate construxerat novam, fortem et magnam, quam Sarracenis populaverat communitatem; ipsorum utens sed potius abutens ritibus et superstitione, spreto Christianorum consilio et religione; familiaritatemque specialem contraxerat, ut asserebat, cum Soldano Babiloniae, et quibusdam aliis Sarracenorum primatibus; distractusque et obscoenis illectus illecebris, concubitu muliercularum, et potius meretricularum Sarracenicarum, indifferenter et impudenter polluebatur*'.
16 But see *infra* p. 358-359.

by which he must have been surprised since Frederick II had not been excommunicated for heresy. He contended that in order to investigate whether the emperor was a heretic or not, the presence of the accused himself was required[17]. He did, however, make some preliminary remarks on that charge and why it was *prima facie* unfounded: the emperor did *not* allow usurers to reside in any of his lands. Matthew Paris adds that this was a deliberate slight to the Roman *curia*, since it was common knowledge that the city of Rome was full of usurious bankers[18] and, maybe, even a slur on the pope himself as well, since the lawyer pope Innocent IV was leading in finding ingenuous ways around the ban on charging interest on money loans (Luke 6:35)[19]. On the charges that Frederick entertained friendly relations with Muslim princes abroad and with Muslims in his own kingdom, master Thaddaeus argued that the emperor had acted prudently in doing so and had spared his Christian Sicilian subjects from shedding their blood unnecessarily by preferably employing Muslims in his military expeditions[20]. As far as Frederick's alleged intercourse with Muslim '*meretriculae*' was concerned, Thaddaeus responded that this was something no one could prove, and, moreover, the Muslim girls in Frederick's Sicilian court were not prostitutes, but artists, dancers, and jugglers, who had been removed from the court anyway since the emperor had learnt their presence had caused offence[21]. At this point, the first session of the council was closed. It was to reconvene a week later[22].

---

17 MP 436: '*Domini mei, super isto articulo, qui est gravissimus, non possit quis certificari, nisi esset dominus meus praesens, ut ex oris sui assertione elici possit, quod in cordis sui latet secretario*'.

18 MP 436: '"*Sed quod non sit haereticus, probabile potest haberi argumentum. Non enim in imperio vel regnis suis aliquem usurarium habitare permittit*", in hoc curiam Romanam redarguens, quam constat hoc vitio maxime laborantem*'.

19 Innocent's commentary on X 5,19 (*De usuris*),6 and the use of rent charges as an alternative to a money loan on interest has been authoritative throughout the Middle Ages.

20 MP 436: '"*Hoc ultro factum et prudenter esse ad rebellionem scilicet quorundam et insolentiam reprimendam sibi jure subditorum et seditionem expurgandam. Utitur enim ipsis in expeditionibus, quarum non aestimat casum alicui Christiano deplorandum; et sic parcit Christiano sanguini, ne frustra effundatur*'".

21 MP 436: '«*Muliercularum itaque Sarracenarum non utitur concubitu, et quis hoc posset probare? Sed joculatione et quibusdam artificiis muliebribus, quas jam, quia suspectas, amovit irredituras*»'. The girls had certainly not offended Richard of Cornwall, who had seen them perform during his stay at Frederick's court in Sicily (*supra* p. 300-301) and wrote an enthusiastic account of it: Matthew Paris, *Chronica maiora* ad ann. 1241, ed. H.R. Luard IV, 147.

22 There is a discrepancy between our two main sources (Matthew Paris and the '*Relatio*'), probably due to a misunderstanding by Matthew Paris, who does not clearly separate his report of events during the council's first and second session. According to Matthew, master Thaddaeus requested to suspend the council for a period at the end of the first session to enable Frederick to attend the council to answer to the charge of heresy personally. Matthew has a story here, probably invented by himself, that the pope strenuously refused the suspension and that he would not allow the emperor to appear at the council in person (MP 437), a most unlikely proposition since the pope had summoned Frederick to appear before his

The Second Session

A witness to the character of Frederick II

The council convened for its second session on Wednesday 5 July at the same venue, the Cathedral of St John. After the usual opening ceremony, mass, and prayer, the pope called a witness to testify to the character of the accused. It was a Sicilian prelate, Bishop Peter of Calinum[23]. Bishop Peter had been living in exile in Rome after he had been expelled from the Sicilian kingdom by Frederick II. The bishop sketched a biography of Frederick steeped in vitriol 'from his childhood on' (*a pueritia sua*)[24]. The episcopal philippic culminated in the exposure of the abject purpose of Frederick's ecclesiastical policy. It was argued that it was Frederick's obvious intention to reduce all prelates and clergy to that pristine state of poverty they had been living in during the days of the early Church, the *ecclesia primitiva*[25], when, to quote Frederick himself, saintly men still spread the words of the gospel, rather than anathemas[26]. This was what Frederick wanted indeed, but it was hardly a reason to excommunicate and depose him, if only because Saint Francis had held similar convictions. Master Thaddaeus did not go into this, however, in his response to the testimony of Bishop Peter, but preferred to expose the bishop's bias: '*Your testimony is not to be trusted, but neither should your words be passed over in silence. You are the son of a traitor, convicted and hanged after due process in the court of my lord, whose example you are following by acting like your father did*'[27]. This put an end to the invective of Bishop Peter[28], but not to the

---

court. According to Matthew, the pope did grant a suspension 'of almost two weeks' (*indutiae fere duarum hebdomadarum*) only 'on the next day' (*sequenti die*). Matthew may have heard from his informants that the pope had granted a suspension of almost two weeks 'in the next session' (*sequenti sessione*), when, as we know from the '*Relatio*', Innocent did indeed grant a suspension of twelve days: see *infra* p. 360. I have, therefore, followed the chronology of the '*Relatio*'.

23 Now Carinola, a little town in the north of the Campagna, not far from the border with the Papal State. The Episcopal See was abolished in 1818.

24 '*Relatio*' 515: '*Calinensis Cisterciensis ordinis de regno Apulie, qui exul erat, surrexit et mirabiliter descripsit vitam malam et ignominiosum progressum dicti imperatoris*'. This is the '*unus archiepiscopus*' mentioned in MP 437-438.

25 '*Relatio*' 515: '*ad hoc intendebat precipue, ut prelati et clerus ad illam reverterentur paupertatem, in qua fuerant tempore ecclesie primitive, quod maxime patebat per litteras, quas per mundum contra clerum et ecclesiam transmittebat*'.

26 See *supra* p. 236.

27 MP 437-438: '*Non tibi fides adhibenda est, sed nec verbis tuis silentium accomodandum; filius enim es proditoris, judiciaiter in curia domini mei convicti et suspensi, cuius tu sequens vestigia niteris patrissare*'.

28 MP 438: '*Siluit igitur ille accusator, amplius mutire nec ausus nec permissus*'. The report of Matthew Paris is confirmed by the '*Relatio*' (515): 'It was then that the lawyer Thaddaeus arose and put forward many serious accusations against the said bishop of Calinum, saying that it was not from his zeal for justice that he had dared to bring these charges against the emperor,

indignation of the other prelates present, especially the many Spanish clerics. Master Thaddaeus had not responded thus far to the charge of sacrilege and the arrest and incarceration of so many distinguished clerics after the battle of Monte Christo and he was now hard pressed to answer to it.

The capture of the prelates and other clerics at Monte Christo was, indeed, an unfortunate incident, master Thaddaeus admitted, but it should be borne in mind that it happened in the mêlée of a fierce and confusing naval battle during which it had been impossible to keep the combatants and non-combatants among the enemy apart. If his master had been present at the occasion, which he was not, he most certainly would have tried to do that and to have seen to their deliverance[29]. At this, the pope himself intervened, asking the obvious question why the emperor had not released the captured clerics immediately after the battle[30]. As invariably happens in a situation like this, the response to an awkward question calls for a protracted argument from an embarrassed counsellor for the defence and so it did in this case. Master Thaddaeus expounded at length on the background of the failed council convened by Gregory IX in 1241; how that pope had changed the original purpose of the council that was planned by his cardinals[31] and called a council to be attended by 'public enemies of the Empire' rather than by the people the pope should have invited[32]. It was for this reason that the emperor had sent letters to the other European princes to dissuade their

The charge of sacrilege

---

but out of malice and because he <the emperor> had punished him and his relatives for manifest crimes' (*Tunc surrexit iudex Thaddaeus et multa gravia proposuit contra dictum episcopum Calinensem, quod non zelo iusititiae, sed malevolentia et eo quod ipsum et suos pro manifestis excessibus punierat, talia contra imperatorem proponere procurarat*). According to Ryccardus de S. Germano, *Chronica* ad ann. 1239, *RIS2* 7.2, 200, Bishop Peter had been banished from the Sicilian kingdom, together with the bishops of Teano, Calvi, Venafro, and Aquino. His exile is also mentioned in the *Vita Greg.* cap. 30, in *Liber censuum* 2, 30, adding that his brother had been executed, most probably for high treason. This is confirmed by Frederick II himself in his letter of July 31, 1245 (HB 6.1, 333). The report in the '*Relatio*' (515) does not have the following dialogue between master Thaddaeus and the pope on the 'sacrilege' of Monte Christo, but merely observes that 'nothing else was done in the second session' (*et sic in secunda sessione nichil aliud factum fuit*), which is unlikely. It should be emphasized that the '*Relatio*' is a very compact *résumé* of the Council of Lyon I, leaving very little room for a detailed account of the proceedings.

29 MP 438: '"*Verum doluit super hoc dominus meus; et hoc praeter intentionem suam et occasionaliter contigit. Sed non potuit ipsos praelatos ab inimicis suis in illo repentino et vehementi assultu et navali, ut bene scire potest, sequestrare, quin indifferenter cum hostibus involverentur. Et si praesens dominus meus ibidem exstitisset, utique diligenter liberationi eorum insudasset*"'.

30 MP 438: '*Ad hoc Papa: "Post eorum captionem, quare insontes, aliis retentis, liberos abire non permisit?"*'.

31 See *supra* p. 293-294.

32 MP 438: '*idem Papa cum vocandos tantum vocare debuisset, publicos imperii convocavit inimicos*'.

clergy to attend that 'utterly dishonest council' (*subdolum concilium*) and why he had denied free passage through his territory to all who did want to attend, warning anyone who did so of the dire consequences[33]. That was why *'the Lord had justly delivered them into the hands of the man they had so arrogantly despised'*[34]. Nevertheless, the emperor had released most of the captured prelates forthwith[35], retaining only the bishop of Praeneste and some other insolent clerics who had dared, even when still in irons, to threaten him to his face with excommunication. Predictably, the dialogue between the pope and master Thaddaeus now took an unpleasant turn. The pope interrupted Frederick's counsellor, remarking that his master must have been desperate about the outcome 'of such a gathering of excellent men' (*tam bonorum et tanta congregatio virorum*) that would surely have absolved him, if he did indeed deserve to be absolved. Master Thaddaeus did not share that conviction: *'How could my master have any confidence in a council where well-disposed persons were joined by his opponents and presided over by the chief enemy of my master, Pope Gregory?'*[36]. The Spanish prelates were outraged by this response and one of them rose to encourage the pope to punish the emperor for all his offences against the church, assuring Innocent that he and his brothers from Spain would stand by him, no matter what he would decide[37].

It was at this point that master Thaddaeus requested a suspension of the council. The charge of heresy, not yet argued at the trial, had taken him by surprise and he had no authority of his master to answer for him on this charge. He needed time to inform his master and to try to convince the emperor to either appear at the council in person to answer to that charge, or to extend the authority of his counsellor to answer to it on his behalf[38]. The alternative presented here by Matthew Paris is important, since it confirms that Thaddaeus did not (and could

Master Thaddaeus requests a suspension

---

33 MP 438-439. See for Frederick's warning *supra* p. 302.
34 MP 439: *'Unde non immerito tradidit eos Dominus in manum eius, quem superbe contempserunt'*.
35 MP 439, a reference no doubt to the early release of the French prelates, many of whom were present at the council. See *supra* p. 310, fnt. 26.
36 MP 439: *'Quomodo confidere posset dominus meus, ut conjunctos hostibus haberet propitios in concilio, ubi praesidere habuit domini mei inimicus capitalis, scilicet papa Gregorius?'*.
37 'Relatio' 515: *'Postmodum surrexit archiepiscopus de Yspanis, qui multum dominim papam animavit ad procedendum contra imperatorem, referendo plurima que contra ecclesiam fecerat, et quomodo tota sua fuerat intentio, ut deprimeret ecclesiam iuxta posse, promittens quod ipse et alii prelati Yspanie ... domno pape assisterent in personis et rebus iuxta sue beneplacitum voluntatis'*.
38 MP 436: *'Thadaeus ... supplicavit humiliter sibi concedi modicam saltem dilationem inducialem, ut domino suo nuntiare posset, et tam affectuose quam efficaciter consulendo persuadere, ut personaliter ad concilium, quod eum expectavit, venire properaret, aut ulteriorem concederet eidem potestatem'* (emphasis added). Master Thaddaeus's assertion is confirmed by Nicolas of Carbio, *Vita Innocentii IV* cap. 19, ed. Pagnotti 94, who complains about the fact that the imperial

not) guarantee his master's presence at the council, but merely mentions it as a possibility, as an alternative to an extension of his powers of attorney. The impression (and the prospect) of an appearance at the council by the emperor himself was, however, created, all the more so since there was a rumour that the emperor was already on his way to attend the council[39]. It seems that Pope Innocent initially was not inclined to grant a suspension but changed his mind at the insistence of the representatives of the kings of England and France[40]. Convinced as he might have been of his *plenitudo potestatis*, Innocent IV was not in a position to snub the king of England and certainly not the king of France, the guarantor of his personal safety. The representatives of the kings of France and England must have been under the impression that peace between the emperor and the pope was still a viable option, since the pope made a disingenuous demonstration of his desire for peace by granting a suspension of the council for a period of twelve days. The council was to reconvene on 17 July[41]. According to the '*Relatio*' (and Matthew Paris) the suspension of the council for a period 'of almost two weeks' (*fere duarum hebdomadarum*) caused discontent (*tedium*) among the prelates and especially among the Templars and Hospitallers responsible for the personal safety of the pope and the council. The military orders had hired a considerable number of soldiers to guard the walls of the fortress of St Just and the Lyon city walls, practically placing the city under a state of siege. The sudden suspension of the council implied a prolongation of that state of siege at great cost to the Templars and Hospitallers[42].

---

representatives at the council argued that they had no authority to represent the emperor 'on these matters' (*super his negociis auctoritatem plenariam non habentes*).

39 '*Relatio*' 515: '*dictus iudex Thaddaeus supplicabat instanter, quod prorogaretur tercia sessio, pro eo quod imperator, prout ipse per certos habebat nuntios … iter arripuerat ad concilium veniendi*'. It is often contended that Thaddaeus believed his master was in Turin at the time (July 5). That contention is based exclusively on the text of the '*Relatio*' passed over in the snippet just cited. It reads as follows in Weiland's edition in the MGH: '*ac ipse qui in civitate Thaurinensi fuerat, ad eum plures alios miserat*'. One has to presuppose a change of subject in the subordinate clause to support that contention, but this is not all: this obscure phrase in the '*Relatio*' has been emended by the editor (Weiland) to let it make sense (if any), since all manuscripts of the '*Relatio*' have a different order of the text which the editor could not explain. The phrase should read as follows: '*ac ipse ad eum plures alios qui in civitate Thaurinensi fuerant miserat*', meaning 'and he himself had sent him many others, who were in the city of Turin'.

40 MP 437: '*ad instantiam procuratorum regum Angliae et Franciae*'.

41 '*Relatio*' 515: '*Et quia dominus papa hoc quam plurimum affectabat, ut possent inter eos pacis federa reformari, usque ad diem Lune post octabas secunde sessionis, que fuerat in die Mercurii … prorogavit terciam sessionem*'.

42 MP 437: 'not without inconvenience to many staying in Lyon' (*non sine multorum gravamina Lugduni expectantium*). '*Relatio*' 515: 'It did not happen without irritation from the side of many prelates and others, such as the Templars and Hospitallers, who had been busy procuring many armed men for the defence of the pope and the council, because of the

The Adjournment

The pope, his cardinals, and many other prelates were very busy during the recess of the council preparing for its third and final session. A genuine council was primarily supposed to be a legislative assembly and consequently a substantial number of statutes ought to be prepared in order to be submitted for confirmation on the last session of the council, just as had happened on the Fourth Lateran Council[43]. But there was more to be done. Before leaving Rome, Innocent and his clerical staff must have ransacked the papal archives for documents supporting the case against Frederick II. The pope had produced many of them during the first session of the council[44]. In preparing his case against the emperor, Innocent IV realized it depended not only on grants and privileges issued by Frederick II himself, but also on charters issued in favour of the Church by the predecessors of the emperor. He therefore ordered the composition of a comprehensive collection of copies (*transumpta*) of all these grants and to add similar grants issued by other kings and princes as well[45], amounting to a genuine general constitutional charter of the Church within the European *secular* political structure to be confirmed by the council. It was explicitly ordained that the collection was to have the same force of law as the original grants and charters contained therein[46]. The model for a collection of copies of privileges like this was, for once, not Justinian's *Codex*, but a contemporaneous phenomenon. Many cities in the Italian kingdom at the time had a so-called *Liber iurium*, containing a collection of copies of all privileges of the cities, all important treaties with other cities and foreign rulers and even important contracts, such as land

Codification of the secular privileges of the Church

---

burden <of the cost> of the men and because of the uncertain state of affairs prevailing in the town that had to be heavily guarded day and night by many armed men' (*Quod non fuit sine multorum tedio prelatorum et aliorum, Templariorum et Hospitalariorum, qui multos armatos ad custodiam domini pape et concilii iussi studuerant destinare, et propter pressuram hominum et dubietatem, que in ipsa civitate, que custodiebatur per armatos plurimos die ac nocte fortiter, assistebat*).

43 See *supra* p. 209.

44 See *supra* p. 354.

45 '*Relatio*' 516: '*omnia privilegia Romane ecclesie, que a principibus mundi tam ab imperatoribus quam regibus concessa fuerant*'.

46 '*Relatio*' 516: '*volebat quod vires haberent sicut ipsa originalia, que inibi lecta erant*'. The meaning of this ambiguous phrase is clarified by the sanction added to the composition itself (HB 6.1, 317): 'Let no man dare to infringe the document of this decree or to be so bold as to act against it. If someone has dared to do so, he must know that he will incur the wrath of the almighty God and the Holy Apostles Peter and Paul' (*Nulli ergo omnino hominum liceat huius decreti paginam infringere vel ei ausu temerario contraire. Si quis autem hoc attemptare presumpserit, indignationem omnipotentis Dei et beatorum Petri et Pauli apostolorum eius se noverit incursurum*).

leases and the like. The *Liber iurium* of Innocent's native Genoa, for example, was compiled at the order of one of his Bolognese teachers in civil law, Jacobus Balduinus, when Jacobus was *podestà* of Genoa in 1229[47]. The crucial difference between these private collections and the *Liber iurium* of the Church as compiled at the behest of Innocent IV was that his collection was meant to be an authoritative restatement of the secular privileges of the Church in a court of law and, as such, it is unique[48]. Most importantly of all, it was to finally settle the papal title to the duchy of Spoleto and the Marche of Ancona.

Preparing
a definitive
judgment

The principal matter to be dealt with during the recess was, of course, the resumption of the case against Frederick II. In the course of the first and second session of the council the trial had proceeded from the initial indictment by the pope; a (partial) rebuttal by Frederick's acting counsellor; the testimony of a witness to the (depraved) character of Frederick II; and accusations against Frederick II by Spanish prelates. But the trial was all but over. Master Thaddaeus had not answered to the charge of heresy brought against Frederick II, since he had no powers of attorney to answer to it. Nevertheless, Innocent IV decided to proceed with the matter 'in private' (*in secretis*), as he later admitted[49]. This is not contrary to the *ordo iuris*, the rule of due process, at least *not* in an ecclesiastical court. The medieval ecclesiastical courts followed the law of procedure of post-classical Roman law, where the judge decided over the law as well as over the facts of a case without a jury. A trial hearing is necessary to get the facts of a case straight, but when the facts are evidenced by notoriety (*facta notoria*) and consequently undeniable, a trial hearing is unnecessary: '*in notoriis iuris ordo non requiritur*'[50]. In such a case, a judge may decide the case without further hearing the prosecutor or the accused, as Innocent III had done in 1200, when he ruled without a trial that Philip of Swabia was not

47 *Liber iurium reipublicae Genuensis* I, Turin 1854, no 681, col. 871-872. See *supra* p. 222, fnt. 9
48 See for a reconstruction of the so-called '*Transumpta*' of Lyon G. Battelli, 'I Transunti di Lione' in *MIÖG* 62 (1954) 348-364.
49 Innocent IV in a letter to the general chapter of the Cistercians (September 1245) in Matthew Paris, *Chronica maiora* ad ann. 1245, ed. H.R. Luard IV, 480, also in HB 6.1, 347.
50 Gl. 'Evidentia' ad X. 5,1,9. See also a *dictum* by Gratian after *Decretum* C. 2, q. 1, c. 16 (*In manifestis ... iudiciarius ordo non requiritur*). See also the Gl. 'Notorium' on X. 3,2,7, distinguishing *fama*, *manifestum*, and *notorium* and defining 'notorium' as '*quid ita exhibet se conspectui hominum quod nulla potest tergiversatione celari*', a definition originating in X. 3,2,8 (*Tua*): 'when their crime is so exposed that it may justly be called public knowledge, in such a case there is no need for a witness or an accuser since a crime like that cannot be concealed by any subterfuge' (*si crimen eorum ita publicum est, ut merito debeat appellari notorium, in eo casu nec testis nec accusator est necessarius, cum huiusmodi crimen nulla possit tergiversatione celari*). It is an important definition, as we shall see shortly (p. 377).

qualified for office, although elected by a majority of German princes[51]: *'sunt enim notoria impedimenta ducis'*[52]. The question to be answered now was whether the charges brought against Frederick II were, indeed, 'evidenced by notoriety' (*notoria*), pre-empting further trial hearings accordingly. Innocent had been an *auditor contradictarum litterarum* in the papal court in his earlier career[53], hearing cases to be decided by the pope later, and it was common practice for an *auditor* at the time to hear the advice of his learned brothers 'in private' (*in secretis*) whenever a moot point of law was raised during a trial[54]. Accordingly, the pope consulted his cardinals and some of the bishops present at the council.

Among the bishops present at Lyon was a famous canon lawyer, later in life rivalling even the authority of Innocent IV as a legal scholar. He was an Italian, just recently (in 1244) consecrated as bishop of Sisteron in the Provence. His name was Henry of Susa (Lat. *Segusia*)[55], a small town in the Savoyard Alps[56]. Henry had studied in Bologna, where he had graduated in both legal disciplines, Roman law and canon law, and had read canon law in Paris before he came to England, most probably among the Savoyards in the retinue of Eleanor of Provence, who married King Henry III in 1236[57]. Henry of Susa must have had close

An important legal brief

---

51 See *supra* p. 155.
52 X. 1,6,34 (*Venerabilem*). See the commentary on X. 1,6,34 by Henry of Susa (ed. Strrassburg 1512 f. 62 vo): 'And here is a question to be answered directly: Why have you rejected Philip, who had not been convicted, nor had confessed? To which he <the pope> answers: the duke's impediments are common knowledge and consequently there is no need for an inquest' (*Et hic est antipophora. Posset enim quis dicere: quare reprobasti Philippum non convictum, non confessum ... Et ipse respondet: sunt enim notoria* etc. ... *ideo non requiritur examinatio*).
53 See *supra* p. 22.
54 The great contemporary authority on the law of procedure, Guillaume Durant (also an *auditor* in the papal court), favourably contrasts this practice of the Roman court with the standard practice in secular courts in Italy at the time, where it was usual to ask for the advice of *external* legal experts, preferably law professors, whose income largely depended on the opinions (*consilia*) they wrote on behalf of the courts and the parties concerned: Durant, *Speculum, Lib. II, Part. II, Tit. De Requisitione consilii* (ed. Basel 1574, 762-766). An auditor of the *Rota* did not have to ask for external advice, since he could rely on the in-house expertise of the other auditors. This practice of the medieval papal court is the origin of the famous (and still secret) 'deliberation in chamber' of modern continental European courts.
55 The presence of Henry of Susa at the Lyon council is not corroborated by direct evidence. His name is not mentioned in any of the reports of the council, nor mentioned among the witnesses to the documents passed at the council, such as the *transumpta* of Lyon. However, it is very unlikely that the Provençal bishop of Sisteron, a recently appointed papal chaplain to boot, was *not* present at the Lyon council.
56 It is not likely that Henry of Susa held imperial sympathies. It was at Susa that Frederick I 'Barbarossa' was held up on his flight from Italy in 1167 (see *supra* p. 120) and barely escaped imprisonment. The little town was severely punished for this act of *laesio maiestatis* in 1174.
57 Matthew Paris hated the Savoyard attendants of the queen and especially Henry of Susa, whom he accuses of defrauding the king and using his money to buy himself 'some episcopate

links with the Provence, since he was dean of Antibes before he became bishop of Sisteron. He knew Innocent IV, since he had visited the pope on a diplomatic mission on behalf of Henry III when Innocent was still staying in Genoa. The pope made Henry a papal chaplain, no doubt in recognition of his impressive legal expertise[58]. Henry was not involved in the composition of Innocent's *Liber iurium*, but he most likely was in the preparation of the case against Frederick II. In his extensive commentary on X. 1,6,34 (*Venerabilem*) in his *Lectura* on the code of Gregory IX, Henry inserted a *consilium*, a legal brief, composed, as he says, by 'some bishop' (*quidam episcopus*) present at the council, most probably meaning himself. The brief concentrated on four issues: firstly 'on the power to depose' (*super potentia deponendi*); secondly 'on contempt of the keys' (*super contemptu clavium*), meaning contempt of papal authority, especially by ignoring a sentence of excommunication; thirdly 'on the capture, robbery, and killing of prelates' (*super captione, depredatione, interfectione prelatorum*); and fourthly 'on the breaking of the peace concluded with the Church' (*super fractione pacis per ecclesiam firmate*)[59].

On the first issue, Henry stated that all the authorities agreed that an emperor could be deposed by the pope on account of a mortal sin if the emperor proved to be incorrigible, especially when the universal Church had been scandalized and shocked by it[60]. The brief continues by contending that if Pope Zachary had had the power to depose the king of the Francs (Childeric), who had not even received his crown from the pope and who had not been examined and approved of by the pope, then Pope Innocent 'most certainly' (*multo fortius*) had the power to depose Frederick II for his iniquities since the emperor

---

in his own country' (*quendam in suis partibus episcopatum*): *Chronica maiora* ad ann. 1244, ed. H.R. Luard IV, 353.

58   See on this mission of Henry of Susa a letter by Innocent IV to King Henry III from July 22, 1244 in Rymer, I.1, 150.

59   Henry of Susa, *Lectura sive apparatus super quinque libris Decretalium* ad X. 1,6,34 (*Venerabilem*), ed. Strassburg 1512, *f.* 62 vo, l. col.: 'in all of which Frederic had sinned, as the *curia* was convinced of' (*in quibus omnibus, sicut pro constanti habebat curia, peccaverat Fredericus*).

60   Ed. Strassburg 1512, *f.* 62 vo, l. col.: '*Secundum opinionem maiorum meorum imperatorem pro quolibet mortali peccato deponi potest. Quod intelligo de gravibus et si incorrigibilis sit; maxime quando universalis ecclesia inde scandalizatur et concutitur*. Henry refers to the Gl. 'A fide devius' by Johannes Teutonicus to *Decretum*, Dist. 40, cap. 6, which is remarkable since it concerns the question if *a pope* could be deposed. He could not, but for one reason: heresy (see *supra* p. 340, fnt. 67). At the end of the gloss, however, there is this question: 'But for which sin can an emperor be deposed? (*sed pro quo peccato potest Imperator deponi?*) The answer is: 'for any sin, if he is incorrigible' (*pro quolibet; si est incorrigibilis*). The other, unspecific, reference is to the famous *Summa* of the Bolognese professor in canon law Hugucio.

was inferior to him (*qui subest ei*)[61]. The brief expands in more detail on the second issue[62], the sin of '*contemptus clavium*'. It was based in Scripture on Matthew 18:17 ('*But if he neglects to hear the Church, let him be unto thee as an heathen man and a publican*')[63] and codified as a legal doctrine by Honorius III in his decretal '*Gravem*', inserted in X. 5,37,13 and amended by Innocent III in X 5,7,13 (*Excommunicamus, § Moneamus*)[64]: anyone failing to give satisfaction and seeking absolution within a year after his excommunication, became a heretic by operation of law, since '*a man who lives in disobedience and refuses to learn and to do what is good is ostensibly an adherent of Satan rather than Christ*' and '*such a sin amounts to paganism and idolatry*'[65]. On account of all this, the brief concludes that in the case of the emperor '*it is obvious that the doctrine applies, since a man who mocks the privilege of the Roman Church, doubtlessly falls into heresy*'[66]. He was even more affirmative in the matter of the killing, capture, robbery, and incarceration of prelates during and after the battle of Monte Christo.

It is the duty of an emperor to see that justice is done, to protect the oppressed, strangers, orphans, and widows. It is also his duty to restore dilapidated churches, to build new ones[67], and to honour and protect the clergy at all times, and not to persecute the members of the clergy[68]. The 45th canon of the Fourth Lateran Council, inserted in Gregory's code (X. 5,37,12 (*In quibusdam, § sacri*)), provided that any feudal vassal (*feudatarius*) who dared to kill or mutilate a cleric, either 'by himself or by his proxies' (*per se vel per alios*), forfeited his fief by operation of law. The conclusion to be drawn from this was obvious: '*No one is more*

---

61 Ed. Strassburg 1512, *f.* 62 vo, l. col. The references here are to Gratian's *Decretum*: C. 15, q. 6, cap. 3 (*Alius*) and Dist. 96, cap. 10 (*Duo sunt*) and 11 (*Si imperator*).

62 He does so by citing extensively from Gratian's *Decretum*: Dist. 22, cap. 1 (*Omnes*); C. 24, q. 1, cap. 14 (*Haec est fides*), cap. 15 (*Rogamus*), cap. 19 (*Alienus*) and cap. 20 (*Omnibus consideratis*) '*et quasi per totum*' <scl. huius causae>. He also refers to Justinian's codification: C. 1,5,7 et C. 1,1,8 and Col. 9,14 (*De ecclesiasticis titulis* (= Nov. 131)).

63 On Matthew 18:17 see also *supra* p. 337, fnt. 46.

64 Cited by Henry on *f.* 62 vo, l. col – r. col, also referring to *Decretum* C. 11, q. 3, cap. 36 (*Rursus*) and 37 (*Quicumque*).

65 Ed. Strassburg 1512, *f.* 62 vo, r. col: '*qui enim rebelliter vivit et discere atque agere bona recusat, magis diaboli quam Christi membrum esse ostenditur*', citing *Decretum* Dist. 38, cap. 16 (*Nullus episcopus*) and '*talem enim peccatum paganitatis incurrit et scelus idolatriae*', citing Dist. 81, cap. 15 (*Si qui sunt presbyteri*).

66 *F.* 62 vo, l. col: '*Planum est quod sufficit, quia qui romane ecclesie privilegio detrahit hic procul dubio in heresim labitur*'.

67 A constantly recurring reproach of Frederick at the time was that he was not known to have ever built a new church in his kingdom, whereas he had allowed new mosques to be built there (in Lucera). See on this issue also *infra* p. 378.

68 The brief refers to *Decretum* Dist. 96, cap. 16 (*Boni principis*); C. 23, q. 5, cap. 20 (*Principes*); cap. 23 (*Regum officium*) and cap. 26 (*Administratores*). There is a constant reference implied in these texts to Jeremiah 22:1-30.

deserving of this penalty than the emperor, who has received so may favours from the Roman Church and is its vassal and, moreover, the titles mentioned earlier are only appropriate to him as long as he rules well[69]. On the last issue, breaking the peace with the Church, the brief is rather succinct: anyone acting against the peace of the Church forfeits his office and dignities by operation of law and loses all his privileges[70]. '*Taking all of this into consideration*', the brief concludes, '*and even more that could be cited if time and the availability of books allowed for it, there can be no doubt on the power to depose*'[71]. Whether it was expedient to do so was, of course, another matter. Henry refrained from giving an opinion on this[72], but he added some general considerations to take into account. What advantage was the Church to gain by it in the long run (*ex expectatione diuturna*)? How many kings and princes would support the Church and how many would still support the emperor? He left it to the circumspection of the pope to make a decision but nevertheless finished his advice with a last caution. A proper summons (*citatio*) was required, even when a sentence was to be passed on the basis of facts evidenced by notoriety and accordingly due process (*ordo iuris*) was not required[73]. Clearly, there were doubts whether the emperor had been duly summoned, since the issue is mentioned two times in the brief and another time shortly before Henry inserted that document in his commentary on '*Venerabilem*', maybe even inciting him to add the brief. Existing concerns about a proper summons are also obvious in the biography of Innocent IV by his secretary Nicolas of Carbio, who

---

69 *F.* 62 vo, r. col.: *Nulli convenit magis haec poena quam imperatori, qui tot beneficia recepit a romana ecclesia et ipsius existit feudatarius, necnon et ei competunt quamdiu bene regit nomina supradicta*). The last phrase refers to the contemporary proverb 'when you have lost the substance, you do not deserve to carry the title' ('*si re priveris, nec nomen habere mereris*' (Gl. 'Nomen non habent' ad *Decretum* Dist. 68, cap. 5 (*Chorepiscopi*)), as do the earlier references in the brief to C. 3,12,3(4) *i.f*; Inst. 2,7,3 and X. 5,40,3. It allows for the conclusion *a contrario* that whoever forfeits the title of emperor, is also stripped of the power: (earlier on in the brief) 'it takes the title of a good and religious prince from him and consequently, having lost the title, he misses the effect of it' (*aufert enim nomen boni principis et religiosi, unde si caret nomine per consequens et effectu*).

70 The brief refers to C. 24, q. 1, cap. 32 (*Qui contra ecclesiae pacem*); X. 1,5,1 (*Ad haec*) and 2 (*Gratum gerimus*); C. 11, q. 3, cap. 63 (*Privilegium*) and X. 2,24,10 (*Querelam*).

71 *F.* 62 vo, r. col: '*Unde his omnibus consideratis et aliis quae allegari possent si temporis spatium suffragaretur et librorum copia: liquet satis de potestate depositionis*'.

72 *F.* 62 vo, r. col: '*Utrum autem expediat ... nolo ponere os in celum*'.

73 *F.* 62 vo, r. col: *Eligat igitur et determinet sanctitatis vestrae circumspectio quod magis debeat expedire. Illud autem notandum: quod ad hoc ut sententia etiam in notoriis rite feratur citatio sive monitio praecedere debet*', referring to X. 2,24,21 (*Ad nostram iii*) and X. 2,28,5 (*Cum sit Romana*) § *Praeterea*. See on this issue also Henry's commentary on X. 2,28,5 (*Cum sit Romana*) § *Praeterea*, ed. Strassburg 1512, *f.* 402 vo, r. col.: 'no one is to be condemned without a summons or a warning even if he is said to be a notorious sinner' (*non est aliquis sine citatione vel admonitione quantumcumque dicatur notorius condemnandus*).

emphasizes that Frederick II had been summoned by the pope 'in a public sermon' (*predicatione publica*) since 'due to his malice' (*eiusdem malitia faciente*) another, more proper, way of summoning the emperor had been impossible[74].

At the insistence of the pope, the private council of prelates and legal experts advising him on the question whether Frederick II could be sentenced without a further trial debated the case against the emperor *pro* and *contra*, 'just as it is done in the universities' (*ut solet in scholis*) in classes where a moot point of law was debated[75]. The delicate matter of the summons cannot have been passed over in these deliberations. It was decided that Frederick could be sentenced without a further trial on four charges based on undeniable facts (*notoria*): breach of oath, breach of peace, sacrilege, and heresy. Since these charges 'could not be concealed by any equivocation' (*quae nulla possunt celari tergiversatione*) due process (*ordo iuris*) did not apply and possible defects in the summons could be ignored[76]. It was at this point in the proceedings that

The papal *decisio*

---

74 Nicolas of Carbio, *Vita Innocentii IV* cap. 16, ed. Pagnotti 91: '*Et tunc in predicatione publica per se ipsum citavit memoratum imperatorem Fredericum … cum, eiusdem militia faciente, non posset ad ipsum alia citatio pervenire*'. Some decades after the council of Lyon I the question whether someone could be legally summoned by way of a 'solemn and public summons' (*citatio sollemnis et publica*) was still undecided. Durant (†1296), *Speculum Lib. II, Part. I, Tit. De Citatione § Sequitur* (ed. Basel 1574, 438, r. col.) ruled that he could, based on X. 1,5,1 (*Ad haec*) and 3,4,11 (*Ex tuae*). Of course, Innocent IV also discussed the issue in his commentary on X. 1,5,1 (ed. Venice 1570, 45, l. col.), revealing his preference for a positive answer to the question, as he should since the most famous summons by way of a public sermon in legal history was issued by himself. Pope Urban IV shared that conviction: see *infra* p. 446, fnt. 133.
75 Innocent IV in a letter to the general chapter of the Cistercians (September 1245) in Matthew Paris, *Chronica maiora* ad ann. 1245, ed. H.R. Luard IV, 480: '*in secretis aliqui fratrum induerunt personam advocati pro ipso, aliqui autem econtra personam adversantis, ut ex objectionibus et responsionibus inquirentium et disputantium, ut solet in scholis, causae veritatis radicitus hinc indeque discuteretur*' (also in HB 6.1, 347). See also '*Relatio*' 516: 'But attention should be drawn to the fact that the pope sought the advice of individual prelates in those days whether he could and should proceed against him on the basis of the facts that were manifest and how many of them all agreed on his deposition' (*Sed est diligenter attendendum, quod papa in illis diebus consilium petierat singulariter a prelatis, utrum posset vel deberet procedere per ea, que manifesta fuerant contra eum, et quantum ad depositionem eius omnes concordarunt*).
76 From the sentence of the pope (HB 6.1, 321): '*quattuor gravissima <scelera> que nulla possunt cellari tergiversatione, commisit*'. The phrase '*que nulla possunt cellari tergiversatione*' is a direct quotation from X. 3,2,8 (*Tua*) (see *supra* p. 362, fnt. 50). According to Henry of Susa (*Lectura* on X. 2,28,5 (*Cum sit Romana*) § *Praeterea*, ed. Strassburg 1512, f. 402 vo, r. col) many scholars argued that a proper summons was unnecessary in a case like this on account of *Decretum* C. 2, q. 1, cap. 15 and especially cap. 17, to which X. 2,28,5 (*Cum sit Romana*) § *Praeterea* may be added. Both of these texts deal indirectly with the conundrum of 1 Corinthians 5:3, where the Apostle Paul 'absent in body, but present in spirit' had sentenced a Corinthian Christian as a notorious fornicator without a trial and even a summons. It was an authority used by the author of the legal brief dealt with in the text above as an argument for the contention that a proper summons was not required in the case of a notorious sinner like

the contemporary practice of the papal court required that the party (or parties) involved in a procedure was (or were) to be notified of the decision (*decisio*) reached 'in chamber' by the papal auditors before the definitive sentence (*sententia diffinitiva*) was to be passed, at this time still by the pope himself[77]. Consequently, master Thaddaeus must have been informed about the decision of the pope, his cardinals, and legal advisors before the definitive sentence was to be passed in the third and final session of the council.

The Third and Final Session

Frederick II
in Verona

Frederick's counsellor, master Thaddaeus, had been granted a stay of 'almost two weeks' (*fere duarum hebdomadarum*) after the second session of the council. It was the impression among some of the attendants of the council that the adjournment was granted to allow the emperor some time to come to the council himself to answer to the charge of heresy personally[78]. That was a misapprehension since Frederick never intended to stand trial in person at Lyon to be humiliated publicly by the pope. Master Thaddaeus must have known this and consequently he cannot have expected his lord to appear at the council in person. The

---

Frederick II (Henry of Susa, *Lectura*, ed. Strassburg 1512, *f.* 62 vo, r. col): 'He was summoned, so much is certain, but let us suppose he was not, then, I ask, why was it that he <Paul> has condemned an absent and unsummoned Corinthian? <references to C. 2, q. 1, cap. 17 and X. 2,28,5 (*Cum sit Romana*) § *Praeterea*>. Certainly, because a crime evidenced by notoriety does not require an examination' (*citatus fuerit, hoc est certum. Sed esto quod non fuerit: quero quare amplius Corinthium absentem et irrequisitum condemnavit? Certe quia excessus notorius examinatione non indiget*).

77   In the 13th century, lawyers hearing cases as *auditores contradictarum litterarum* still had no authority to pass sentence but had to refer a case to the pope himself for the passing of the definitive sentence. That is why they were called '*auditores*' (*Speculum, Lib. II, Part. II, Tit. De Relationibus* (ed. Basel 1574, 769, r. col.). Consequently, *every* procedure in the papal court involved a 'report' (*relatio*) to the pope, as only incidentally happened in a civil procedure during the later Roman Empire, when a lower judge asked the emperor for advice on an ambiguous point of law (*relatio ad principem*). If he did so, he was under the statutory duty (C. 7,61,1,2) to provide the litigants with a copy of his report (*consultationis exemplum*). The papal court emulated this procedure (see the Gl. 'De inquisitionis processu' on X. 2,28,68), now applying to every case hanging in the papal court itself as a matter of principle. The procedure is described by Durant, *Speculum l.c.* It implied that the parties were necessarily informed of the provisional decision (*decisio*) of the '*auditor*' and his advisory council before the definitive sentence (*sententia definitiva*) was passed by the pope. The procedure is of enormous importance in the history of continental European law since the history of law reporting on the continent begins with the publication of these *Decisiones sacrae rotae Romanae*.

78   See on this issue *supra* p. 356. See also Nicolaus de Carbio, *Vita Innocentii IV* cap. 19, ed. Pagnotti 94: 'they <master Thaddaeus and the other representatives of the emperor at Lyon> promised that he would come to the council personally if only he were waited for momentarily' (*qui, si expectaretur modicum, promictebant ipsum personaliter adventurum*).

question, therefore, is, what was he hoping to achieve by a postponement of almost two weeks?

Thaddaeus had parted company with his master at Parma after 26 May 1245[79], well knowing that Frederick was on his way to an important diet held at Verona. There were significant matters of state to be discussed there to which master Thaddaeus must have been privy. Frederick was to meet in Verona with the duke of Austria, once declared a rebel[80], but now an important ally of the emperor. The marriage of the Austrian duke had been childless for some years and his only heirs were his sister Margaret and his niece Gertrud, a daughter of his brother Henry (†1228). The emperor, now fifty years of age, was a widower ever since the demise of his third wife Isabella of England in 1241 and now contemplated a marriage with one of the Austrian heiresses, Gertrud, since a marriage with the other, Margaret, was out of the question, because she had been married to his own son, the unlucky King Henry (VII)[81]. Frederick had promised the duke to raise his duchy to the status of a kingdom as a price for Gertrud's hand[82]. This was why a diet of German princes was convened at Verona only a few weeks before the pope had called his council to convene at Lyon. The emperor arrived at Verona on 2 June 1245[83]. When his ambassadors to the Lyon council left him at Parma, they cannot have known how long the Verona diet was to last and they certainly will not have foreseen the complication frustrating Frederick's marriage with Gertrud. By 5 July, when master Thaddaeus asked for a suspension of the council 'for almost two weeks', the emperor was still in Verona. Frederick must have been in a very bad mood by that time, since the marriage project with Gertrud had failed. Matthew Paris has a rumour, that the girl – she was at least thirty years younger than Frederick – declined to marry an excommunicate[84], but the real reason seems to have been that the pope interfered, since Gertrud was already engaged to a son of the king of Bohemia

---

79   According to *Annales Placentini Gibellini* ad ann. 1245, MGH *SS* 18, 489, Frederick arrived at Parma on 26 May and it was from there that he sent master Thaddaeus 'to the council that the pope had called' (*misit iudicem Thaddaeum Lugdinum ad concilium quod domnus papa convocaverat*).

80   See *supra* p. 282.

81   See *supra* p. 271.

82   The charter testifying to the elevation of the Austrian duchy to the status of a kingdom had already been prepared: MGH *Const.* 2, no 261, 358-360. It was never implemented.

83   According to an inscription in the Church of S. Stefano in Verona, printed in G.-B. Biancolini, *Notizie delle chiese di Verona* I, Verona 1749, 17: '*Die veneris secundo intrante iunio m.cc.xlv. indictione tertia venit imperator F. in Verona et duxit secum elefantem*'. Frederick had convened a diet there which lasted a few weeks (Rolandus Patavinus, *Chronica* 5,13, MGH *SS* 19, 82): '*Duravit hoc colloquium pluribus septimanis*'.

84   Matthew Paris, *Chronica maiora* ad ann. 1245, ed. H.R. Luard IV, 474: 'when the girl heard about this, she resolutely refused the embraces and the marriage with Frederick until he

From Lyon to
Verona and
back again

at the time and, more importantly, because the emperor was, indeed, an excommunicate[85]. It was a very embarrassing incident and it made Frederick quite angry[86]. His temper will not have improved when his trusted servant Walter of Ocra arrived in Verona with news from Lyon.

Master Walter must have been dispatched to the emperor by master Thaddaeus of Suessa directly after he had learned that the pope rejected Frederick's last offer of peace at the preparatory session of 26 June[87]. The pope had granted Walter a term of twenty days to return to Lyon[88], a reasonable term for a journey from Lyon to Verona and back, since we know it took the Latin Emperor Baldwin II less than a week to reach Lyon from Verona, travelling at an average of 62 miles (100 km.) a day, not unusual at the time[89]. Travelling at the pace of Baldwin II, master Walter may have reached Verona on or about 3 July. Frederick left Verona as late as 8 July, suggesting that he was going to meet the

---

was absolved' (*cum ad notitiam puellae pervenisset, amplexus et nuptias ipsius F(retherici), donec absolveretur, constanter refutavit*).

85   *Annales Ianuenses* (Bartolomeo scriba) ad ann. 1245, MGH *SS* 18, 216-217: 'The Emperor Frederick went to Verona, where he held a diet in the middle of May and awaited the niece of the duke of Austria to marry her and make her his consort. But when the duke of Austria received a papal order that as long as the lord Frederick remained in contumacy with the Church, he could in no way give away his niece in marriage to him, the duke desisted and did not want to give her' (*Dominus Fredericus imperator ... ivit ... Veronam, ut in medio mense Maio curiam teneret ibi, expectando neptem ducis Austriae ut eam desponsaret et transduceret in consortem. Cum autem domnus dux Austrie mandatum apostolicum recepisset, ut quam diu domnus Fredericus in contumacia perseveraret cum ecclesia, nullo modo suam neptem in coniugem ei daret, distulit ipse domnus dux et noluit eam dare*). On the Austrian heiresses, Margaret and Gertrud, see also *infra* p. 469, fnt. 234.

86   *Annales Ianuenses* (Bartolomeo scriba) ad ann. 1245, MGH *SS* 18, 217: '*commotus ad iram*'.

87   See *supra* p. 349.

88   Frederick II in his reaction (see *infra* p. 381) in HB 6.1, 331-337(335), also in MGH *Const.* 2, no 262, 360-366(364): '<*magister Gualterius de Ocra capellanus, notarius et fidelis noster> qui de conveniencia summi pontificis et quorundam ex fratribus ad nos missus per viginti dies expectari debuit*'. There is a discrepancy between the edition by HB and the edition in the MGH, since the latter mentions a term of twenty days and the former a term of twelve. The manuscript tradition allows for both terms, but the former is more likely, as will be shown shortly. The emperor suggests that the council should have been postponed until the return of master Walter, but that the pope opened the council on 28 June, two days after Walter's departure. See *supra* p. 350.

89   The Emperor Baldwin II of Constantinople was with Frederick II at his diet in Verona on 17 June 1245 (*Fragmenta memorialis potestatum Mutinae* ad ann. 1245, *RIS*² 15.4, 189): '*Imperator Constantinopolitanus qui dicebatur Balduinus venit Mutinae die veneris xvi. Mensis iunii et sequenti die ivit Veronam ad imperatorem Fridericum, qui erat ibi*'. Baldwin covered a distance of about 62 miles (100 km.), from Modena to Verona, in one day. We also know that Baldwin was at the preliminary meeting of the council in Lyon on 26 June (see *supra* p. 350). Consequently, he can only have stayed in Verona for a very short time, possibly just a day or two. If he left Verona on 19 June, it would have taken him less than a week to reach Lyon, also travelling at an average of 62 miles (100 km.) a day. A well-trained endurance horse may cover even greater distances in a day, even on difficult terrain.

pope at Lyon[90]. If he really wanted to reach Lyon before the expiration of the term set by the pope to master Walter[91], he could still have done so even at this late date, but the emperor preferred not to travel at the pace of Baldwin of Constantinople. After leaving Verona, he went to Cremona first (9 July)[92] and from there to Pavia (10 July), Tortona (11 July), Alessandria (12 July), Asti (13 July), and Turin (15 July)[93], still about halfway between Verona and Lyon. The itinerary makes it clear that Frederick had no intention to be at Lyon on 17 July. He held on to his conviction that it was inappropriate for a Roman emperor to stand trial in a synodal court[94] and so '*he stayed there <in Turin>, waiting for an answer from the messengers he had sent to the pope*'[95]. It is therefore probably only at Turin that Frederick finally decided to send yet another delegation to the council consisting of the bishop of Freising, Conrad of Tölz, Henry of Hohenlohe, the grandmaster of the Teutonic Order, and Piero della Vigna[96], all of whom had still been with Frederick on the diet in Verona and were travelling in his retinue. Even after hearing the news of the rejection of his peace initiative by the pope on 26 June, Frederick had still not given up hope that peace with the Church could

---

90 Rolandus Patavinus, *Chronica* 5,13, MGH *SS* 19, 82: '*Exivit igitur dominus imperator de civitate Verone die octavo intrante iulio eodem anno, et dicebat se velle ad dominum papam accedere*'. The Genoese chronist Bartolomeo scriba did not believe the suggestion (*Annales Ianuenses*, ad ann. 1245, MGH *SS* 18, 217): '*pretending* that he, Frederick, wanted to make haste to go to the council, he left Verona' (Fingens *autem se domnus Fredericus velle ad Concilium properare, secessit de Verona*) (emphasis added).

91 Master Walter must have left Lyon after the preparatory meeting of 26 June as soon as possible, probably already on 27 June. If he did, he had to back in Lyon by July 15.

92 *Annales Placentini Gibellini* ad ann. 1245, MGH *SS* 18, 489: '*Imperator die dominico viiii. mensis iulii venit Cremonam*'.

93 *Annales Placentini Gibellini* ad ann. 1245, MGH *SS* 18, 489: '*Et inde semotus cum rege Conrado filio suo et magna militum comitiva Papiam equitavit*'; *Ann. Ian.* ad ann. 1245, MGH *SS* 18, 217: '*venit Papiam, deinde Alexandriam ... Deinde venit Terdonam ... et iacuit domnus Fredericus in Terdona nocte una, et ivit in Ast, deinde Taurinum*'. The assessment that the emperor first went to Alessandria and after that to Tortona is certainly wrong: it must have been the other way round. It should be noticed that the emperor was travelling rapidly only during the first two stages of his journey: from Verona to Cremona, a distance of about 62 miles (100 km.) and from Cremona to Pavia (some 50 miles (80 km.)). After this, he travelled at a much slower pace: from Pavia to Tortona (some 27 miles (45 km.)); from Tortona to Alessandria (some 12 miles (20 km.)); from Alessandria to Asti (some 21 miles (35 km.)) and from there to Turin (some 30 miles (50 km.)).

94 Matthew Paris, *Chronica maiora* ad ann. 1245, ed. H.R. Luard IV, 437: '*nec sacrum decet imperium ... judicio sisti sinodali*'. See on this *supra* p. 302 and 339.

95 *Annales Ianuenses* (Bartolomeo scriba) ad ann. 1245, MGH *SS* 18, 217: '*ibique moram faciens, expectans responsionem suorum nuntiorum quos mandaverat ad papam*'.

96 Frederick II in his reaction (see *infra* p. 381) in HB 6.1, 331-337(335), also in MGH *Const.* 2, no 262, 360-366(364): '*venerabilem Frisingensem episcopum, dilectum principem, fratrem H. magistrum domus Hospitalis sancta Marie Teutonicorum et magistrum Petrum de Vinea magne curie nostre iudicem, dilectos fideles nostros, quos ultimo pro omnimoda consummacione tractate pacis ad concilium miseramus*'.

be achieved, since he wrote a letter to the clergy and citizens of Worms on 8 July, the day he left Verona, that he was about to come to terms with the pope and that peace with the Church was imminent[97].

The delegation sent by Frederick carried a last peace initiative from the emperor. It must have been the initiative master Thaddaeus was awaiting when he requested a postponement of the last session of the council on 5 July. The '*Relatio*' confirms this supposition, since it explicitly states that the pope granted a suspension 'so that peace between them <meaning the pope and the emperor> might be restored' (*ut possent inter eos pacis federa reformari*)[98]. Frederick's new proposal must have been very similar, if not equal, to the offer he made later, after his deposition: he promised to spend the rest of his life in the Holy Land, fighting for the cause of Christ and 'never to return' (*irrediturus*), provided his son Conrad was also to be absolved and recognized as Frederick's successor in the Empire[99]. It was a desperate proposal the pope could hardly reject, coming, as it did, close to a voluntary abdication, casting serious doubts, as always with Frederick, on its sincerity, but, more importantly, it came too late: there was no way the imperial ambassadors could have reached Lyon from Turin in time for the last session of the council on 17 July and the pope was disinclined to prolong the recess, even for just a few more days[100]. One wonders why Frederick waited so long to send a delegation with a new peace proposal to Lyon. It may be that he finally realized that absolution was never to be had from Innocent IV, no matter what he offered by way of satisfaction. '*I see crystal clear now that the pope aspires to my confusion with all his might*', he is reported as having said on hearing the news of the rejection of his earlier peace initiative[101]. When the final session of the council convened on 17 July, Frederick's ambassadors from Turin

---

97 Frederick II to the clergy and citizens of Worms on July 8, 1245 (HB 6.1, 315-316(315)): 'We promise that we will loyally include the clergy and the citizens of Worms in our settlement we are about to make with the Roman Church' (*promittimus quod tam clericos quam laicos Wormatiae civitatis ... compositioni nostre quam facturi sumus cum ecclesia Romana ... fideliter assumemus*).

98 '*Relatio*' 515.

99 See *infra* p. 396.

100 Frederick II in his reaction in HB 6.1, 331-337(335), also in MGH *Const.* 2, no 262, 360-366(364): 'the pope did not even want to wait three days' (*saltem per triduum summus pontifex noluit prestolari*). If the imperial ambassadors were really still three days away from Lyon on July 17, they cannot have left Turin long before that, since the distance between Turin and Lyon (about 185 miles (310 km.)) could be covered in about four days, even taking into account the crossing of the Alps. Master Walter of Ocra, however, did reach Lyon in time to hear the sentence of the pope: Matthew Paris, *Chronica maiora* ad ann. 1245, ed. H.R. Luard IV, 456.

101 Matthew Paris, *Chronica maiora* ad ann. 1245, ed. H.R. Luard IV, 437: '*Video luce clarius, quod ad confusionem meam toto conamine aspirat Papa*'.

had not yet arrived and he had failed to appear himself, causing indignation among many of the attendants of the council who accused him of contempt of court (*contumacia*)[102]. Master Thaddaeus, who already knew by now what was coming, must have been consulting with the representatives of the kings of France and England and other secular princes on how to prevent a disaster from happening while anxiously working on a speech to object publicly to the coming papal sentence at the same time.

The third and final session of the first council of Lyon had a busy agenda. After the usual religious ceremonies, mass, and prayer, Innocent IV announced, with the approval of the council, that the feast of the Nativity of Mary was to be celebrated with an octave. The pope then read out some provisions relating to the three other main issues of the council, the recovery of the Holy Land, the support of the emperor of Constantinople, and the defence against the Mongols[103]. In addition, a considerable number of 'papal constitutions' (*constitutiones papae*) were promulgated, most of them relating to the law of procedure, a subject very dear to the legal scholar Innocent IV[104]. The pope then submitted his *Liber iurium*, his collection of copies of all privileges granted to the church of Rome by emperors, kings, and princes[105], for confirmation by the council, adding that the collection was to be as authentic as the original privileges copied therein[106]. The representa-

Master Thaddaeus objects

---

102   Matthew Paris, *Chronica maiora* ad ann. 1245, ed. H.R. Luard IV, 437: '*Constanter igitur et acerrime in pleno et iam plenissimo concilio imperator Frethericus quasi toti ecclesie contumax et rebellis, a quattuor mundi partes inhabitantibus accusatur*'.
103   '*Relatio*' 516: '*Et peractis officiis, ut in prima, post multa dicta et hinc inde audita, antequam ad sententie prolationem accederet, nativitati beate Virginis gloriose ordinavit octavam, sacro concilio approbante. Deinde dominus papa quasdam constitutiones, que pro recuperatione Terre Sancte ac alias, que pro subsidio Romani imperii, et etiam alias, que contra Tartaros facte fuerunt, fecit legi*'.
104   According to Matthew Paris (*Chronica maiora* ad ann. 1245, ed. H.R. Luard IV, 473) some of these papal constitutions had been promulgated before the council, some of them during the council and some even after the council (*quaedam ante concilium, quaedam durante concilio, quaedam vero post concilium sunt statuta*). He is clearly referring to a collection of constitutions composed shortly after the council. Innocent IV has sent a collection of constitutions promulgated in the council of Lyon I to the university of Paris, with the usual instruction to employ them 'in classes and in the courts' (*in judiciis quam in scolis*) and to insert them at the proper places in the code of Gregory IX. The cover letter is printed in H. Denifle, *Chartularium universitatis parisiensis* I, Paris 1889, no 153, 188. Most of Innocent's constitutions promulgated at the council of Lyon were later inserted in the code of Pope Boniface VIII, the *Liber sextus*. Innocent the legal scholar acted as he had instructed the professors in Paris (and doubtlessly Bologna as well) by commenting on his own constitutions at the proper places in his commentary on the decretals of Gregory IX.
105   On this collection see *supra* p. 361.
106   '*Relatio*' 516: '*Item postmodum dominus papa dixit, quod omnia privilegia Romane ecclesie, que a principibus mundi tam ab imperatoribus quam regibus concessa fuerant, eadem exemplari*

tives of the king of England present at the council objected to some of the privileges in the collection granted by King John, especially his surrender of the kingdom of England to the pope, claiming that it was null and void since the king had acted without the approval of his barons. They announced that they would appeal against this and some other controversial privileges 'to a future pope' (*ad futurum pontificem*)[107], thus preventing a possible recourse to the doctrine of prescription in as far as these contested privileges were concerned. It was after this that master Thaddaeus rose to publicly protest against the condemnation of Frederick II on which he had already been informed[108]. The text of his objection has survived[109]:

'Because the emperor has not been summoned before the council, since a summons issued in a sermon is null and void according to canon as well as civil law, and because it is also obscure since it does not indicate why the emperor has been summoned to appear or send a personal representative to answer on his behalf in the council, and since the pope is at war with him and is his enemy and has assumed the role of judge and prosecutor against all law and intends to pass a definitive sentence before the trial has even started and before the charges have been substantiated, since all the charges brought against the emperor by the pope and others are utterly denied, I, Thaddaeus of Suessa, justice of the imperial supreme court, having been appointed as special representative by my lord the emperor, declare that the sentence to be passed against my lord the emperor by the pope in the present council is null and void. If, however, it does have any substance, which I utterly deny since the rule of due process has not been observed, I appeal against it on behalf of my lord the emperor to a future

---

fecerat et in eis apponi fecit sigilla omnium qui aderant prelatorum, et volebat quod vires haberent sicut ipsa originalia, que inibi lecta erant'.

107 *'Relatio'* 516: *'Tunc surrexerunt nuntii regis Anglie et pro autenticatione quorundam privilegiorum concessorum a rege Anglie ipsi ecclesie, que asserebant facta preter consilium principum terre, licet in privilegiis illis contrarium diceretur, ad futurum pontificem et pro quibusdam constitutionibus, que pro subsidio faciendo ecclesie facte fuerant, appellarunt'.* On this see also MP 444-445.

108 See *supra* p. 368.

109 *'Relatio'* 516: 'Then justice Thaddaeus rose, perceiving that the axe had already been laid at the root, considering the confirmation of so many privileges, and he appealed to a future pope and a general council if he <the pope> wanted to proceed against the aforementioned emperor' (*Tunc surrexit iudex Thaddaeus percipiens, quod iam securis erat posita ad radicem, pro multorum privilegiorum autenticatione, et si contra predictum imperatorem vellet procedere, appellabat ad futurum pontificem et concilium generale*). A copy of master Thaddaeus's letter of protest is in Bibliothèque nationale de France (BnF), MS Latin 2954, *f.* 2 vo.

pope and to a universal council of kings, princes and prelates, because the present council is not universal'[110].

The pope reacted only to the last of master Thaddaeus' objections by emphasizing that the council was truly to be regarded as a proper general council to which many secular and ecclesiastical princes had been invited and that the invitees from the Empire were only absent due to Frederick's prohibition to attend the council. He therefore refused to allow the appeal[111]. It was at this moment that the patriarch of Aquileia and the ambassadors of the kings of England, France, and other European princes intervened, beseeching the pope not to pass sentence on the emperor, but Innocent was adamant. He even threatened the patriarch, a known supporter of Frederick II[112], to depose him if he would not keep quiet[113]. The pope was supported by the Spanish, the Lombard, and many of the French prelates present and so, brushing aside all objections raised by the representatives of the secular princes, he proceeded by ordering the sentence of deposition passed against Frederick II to be read publicly[114]. After the reading of the sentence, master Thaddaeus loudly quoted, for all to hear, the prophet

Innocent IV rejects all objections

---

110 HB 6.1, 318; MGH *Const. 2* no 399, 508: '*Cum dominus imperator citatus non fuit ad concilium, cum citatio in predicatione facta nulla fuerit ipso iure canonico et civili, et etiam incerta fuerit, non continens super quo dominus imperator citaretur ut veniret vel procuratorem mitteret in concilio responsurum, sit etiam dominus papa in guerra cum eo et sit inimicus ipsius, et contra omne jus assumat partes judicis et actoris, et ante ceptum iudicium, antequam de propositis constet, cum contra dominum imperatorem proposita per summum pontificem et alios omnino negentur, intendat diffinitivam sententiam promulgare; ego Thadaeus de Suessa, magne imperialis curie judex, a domino meo imperatore procurator ad hoc specialiter constitutus, dico nullam fore sententiam contra dominum meum imperatorem per summum pontificem in presenti concilio promulgandam. Si tamen aliqua sit, quod omnino diffiteor, cum nullus sit in ea juris ordo servatus, ab ipsa ad futurum romanum pontificem et ad universale concilium regum, principum et prelatorum, cum presens concilium universale non sit, pro parte domini imperatoris appello*'.
111 '*Relatio*' 516: '*Ad que dominus papa respondit humiliter et benigne, quod illud erat concilium generale, quia tam principes seculares quam ecclesiastici ad illud fuerant invitati; sed omnes, qui in iurisdictione imperatoris fuerant, ad illud eos accedere non permisit; propter quod appellationem non admittebat eandem*'. On this incident see also MP 440.
112 See *supra* p. 350, fnt. 36.
113 *Annales Placentini Gibellini* ad ann. 1245, MGH *SS* 18, 489: '*Preterea nuncii et procuratores regis Francorum, regis Anglorum aliorumque regum occidentalium insistentes supplicabant domno pape ut ipsam differet sentenciam. Similiter patriarcha Aquilegiensis dixit domno pape quod due columpne erant que mundum substinebant, scilicet ecclesia una et imperium alia. Unde domnus papa dixit patriarche, ut taceret, alioquin aufferet ei anulum*'. Matthew Paris (*Chronica maiora* ad ann. 1245, ed. H.R. Luard IV, 439) adds that the king of England's ambassadors also intervened on behalf Frederick II's children.
114 *Annales Placentini Gibellini* ad ann. 1245, MGH *SS* 18, 489-490: '*Et ita domnus papa voluntate illius concilii clericorum et maxime instigantium et instigatu archiepiscopi Galicie et clericorum Yspanie, Lombardorum aliarumque partium sentenciam depositionis contra imperatorem protulit*'.

Zephania (1:15): 'This is a day of wrath, a day of calamity and misery' (*Dies ista dies irae, calamitatis et miseriae*)[115], but the pope rose and broke into the *Te deum laudamus*. 'After that hymn had been chanted by all, the council was dissolved'[116].

'Thadaeus de Suessa, the advocate of Frederick, withdraws perplexed' (*Thadeus de Suessa procurator Fretherici recedit confusus*)
(Matthew Paris, *Chronica maiora*. Cambridge, Corpus Christi College, ms. 016, f. 187 vº)

The Sentence

The sentence passed by Innocent IV against Frederick II at the council of Lyon was intended as an impressive demonstration of papal secular power 'to be remembered forever' (*ad memoriam sempiternam*)[117]. It did not contain any ecclesiastical censure, since Frederick II had already been excommunicated before, but it amounted to a purely political act by the pope, exercising his *plenitudo potestatis* by administering *secular* justice as was, according to canon law, his right in extraordinary cases, such as this one[118]. Innocent IV himself stated that 'there must be a

---

115 Matthaeus Parisiensis, *Chronica maiora* ad ann. 1245, ed. H.R. Luard IV, 456.
116 '*Relatio*' 516: '*qua lecta dominus papa surrexit et incepit 'Te deum laudamus', quo ympno decantato per omnes fuit concilium dissolutum*'.
117 MGH *Const.* 2, no 400, 508 and HB 6.1, 319 (Rubr.): '*Innocentius episcopus servus servorum Dei sacro presente concilio ad rei memoriam sempiternam*. See the Gl. 'Ad apostolicae dignitatis' on VIº 2,14,2, explaining why the sentence was headed as being intended '*ad memoriam sempiternam*': 'so that thereby is revealed how great the authority and the power of the Church is and so that the Church may be feared even more' (*ut per hoc appareat quanta sit auctoritas et potestas ecclesiae et ut magis timeatur ecclesia*). The code of Boniface VIII was glossed by the famous Bolognese canonist Iohannes Andreae (†1348).
118 See *supra* p. 338-339.

compelling cause for the deposition of an emperor'[119] and so the pope presented a carefully composed judgment to the council[120].

The judgment opens with an introduction, recalling the events lead- | The emperor ing up to the peace sworn to by the imperial representatives at Rome on 31 March 1244[121]: 'he swore an oath, but yet afterwards he did not comply with what he had sworn to' (*prestiterit iuramentum, postmodum tamen quod iuraverat non implevit*)[122]. Because more than a year had now elapsed since then and the emperor still refrained from complying with his promises, the pope was in conscience bound to take legal action against him[123]. The emperor was charged with four 'very serious crimes' (*gravissima scelera*): perjury, breaking of the peace, sacrilege, and heresy, all four of them 'evidenced by notoriety' (*que nulla possunt cellari tergiversatione*)[124]. The pope then proceeded by illustrating all four of these offences separately and by adding some others in the process, like the serious sin of 'contempt of the keys' (*contemptus clavium*)[125] and the assassination of Duke Louis of Bavaria in 1231. Frederick's notorious perjury was supported by a reference to three oaths he had forsworn: his oath of fealty for the kingdom of Sicily, sworn to Pope Innocent III in Sicily in February 1212, renewed in Rome in April of that year[126], and the promises he had made to Innocent III and Honorius III at Eger in 1213 and at Hagenau in 1219 respectively[127]. He had kept none of these promises, occupying all the territories he had granted to the Church and committing the sin of 'contempt of the keys' (*contemptus clavium*) in the process by not only mocking the privilege of the Church by ignoring the sentence of excommunication passed against him but also by forcing his clerics, officials, and subjects to ignore that

(marginal note:) The emperor declared guilty of four serious crimes

---

119   Innocentii IIII. PM *Commentaria in V. libros Decretalium* App. post X 2,27(*De re iudicata*), 25, cap. ii (ed. Venice 1570, 380, r. col.): '*magna enim causa subesse debet depositioni imperatoris*'.

120   The sentence was not inserted in the '*Relatio*', but is preserved in Matthew Paris' report of events at the council of Lyon I (*Chronica maiora* ad ann. 1245, ed. H.R. Luard IV, 445-455), taken from a copy sent to the king of England. It corresponds with the text of another source reporting the sentence *in extenso*, *Annales Placentini Gibellini* ad ann. 1245, MGH *SS* 18, 490. There is also a contemporary copy of the sentence in the Vatican archive (ASV A.A. Arm. I-XVIII, 171). The sentence is edited by Rodenberg in MGH *Epist. Saec. XII* 2, no 124, 88-94; Weiland in MGH *Const.* 2, no 400, 508-512 and in HB 6.1, 319-327. An excerpt of the sentence has been inserted in the code of Boniface VIII, the *Liber sextus* (VI° 2,14,2).

121   See *supra* p. 314-316.

122   MGH *Const.* 2, no 400, 509; HB 6.1, 321.

123   MGH *Const.* 2, no 400, 509; HB 6.1, 321: '*cogimur urgente nos conscientia juste animadvertere in eundem*'.

124   See for the meaning of this quote *supra* p. 362, fnt. 50.

125   On *contemptus clavium* see *supra* p. 365.

126   For this see *supra* p. 190.

127   For these grants see *supra* p. 195, 216 and 354 (Innocent IV using them in his indictment).

sentence. That Frederick was a breaker of the peace was illustrated by the notorious fact that the emperor had not complied with the conditions of the peace of S. Germano of 1230[128]. The pope expands on some of these conditions, most extensively on Frederick's intolerable interference with the episcopal elections within his Sicilian kingdom in spite of his promise at S. Germano not to do so. That the emperor had committed sacrilege was evident from the fact that he had attacked, arrested, and imprisoned a large number of prelates and other clerics on their way to the failed council called by Gregory IX in 1241[129]. The pope then proceeded to the charge of heresy, the most serious of all. The crime of 'contempt of the keys' amounted to heresy in itself, but that was not enough. Frederick II had fraternized with Muslim princes, honourably receiving their envoys at his Sicilian court. He had copied Muslim customs – keeping a harem, for example, and leaving honourable Christian princesses, his spouses, in the sequestered custody of castrated servants. Even more disgusting (*execrabilius*) was the fact that he had, when in Jerusalem in 1229, allowed the name of Mohammed to be proclaimed publicly from the Temple Mount 'by day and by night' (*diebus et noctibus*)[130]. He had, moreover, given his daughter away to be married to an enemy of God and the Church, a man excommunicated together with all his supporters, counsellors, and adherents, the Greek usurper Joannes Vatatzes. Last but not least, Frederick II had ostensibly neglected one of the most important obligations of a Christian prince: building and restoring churches, monasteries, and hospitals. The pope concluded this part of the sentence with a rhetorical question: '*Are these not serious and convincing arguments for a suspicion of heresy against him?*'[131]. Since the kingdom of Sicily itself had not been considered in the arguments, the pope added a last argument supporting Frederick's forfeiture of that kingdom: he had reduced his subjects, clerics as well as laymen, to 'a quasi-servile condition' (*sub servili quasi conditione*) and, a rather mundane argument, had neglected to pay the rent which

---

128 On the peace of S. Germano see *supra* p. 245-247.

129 On this incident see *supra* p. 302-303.

130 See on the status of the Temple Mount in Frederick's treaty with sultan Al-Kamil *supra* p. 239, fnt. 23.

131 MGH *Const.* 2, no 400, 512; HB 6.1, 326: '*Nonne igitur hec non levia, set efficacia sunt argumenta de suspitione heresis contra eum?*'. All in all, the pope presented a rather weak case of heresy against Frederick II. Later canonists must have thought so too: the arguments supporting the charge of heresy were omitted in the excerpt of the sentence inserted in the *Liber sextus*. The pope, obviously, did not seriously believe Frederick had ever really said that that the world was deceived by three impostors, Moses, Jezus and Mohammed (see *supra* p. 295, fnt. 14). Repeating that outrageous accusation was simply counterproductive since it would only have weakened his case even more.

he owed the pope for that kingdom for nine years and more[132]. After presenting his arguments, the pope proceeded to pass sentence on the emperor:

'Having diligently considered the above-mentioned and many other abominable crimes with our brethren and the holy council in advance and because we, though unworthy, are acting as vicar of Christ on earth and since it has been said about us in the person of the Holy Apostle Peter that "whatsoever thou shalt bind on earth shall be bound in heaven", we solemnly declare, notify, and rule by way of sentence that the said prince, who has shown himself unworthy of the imperial title, the royal title, or any other title or office and who has been deposed by God not to rule or reign anymore because of his iniquities and crimes, caught up as he is in his own sins, has been deposed by God and has forfeited all honour and office. We herewith release all who are beholden to him by an oath of fealty from that oath forever and we do, on apostolic authority, strictly forbid anyone to obey or serve him as emperor or king from now on and we decree that anyone who does assist him with aid and counsel or renders him a service from now shall be excommunicated as of right on account of that. Those who are entitled to elect an emperor of the Empire shall be at liberty to elect another as his successor. As far as the kingdom of Sicily is concerned, we shall provide for that, in consultation with our brother cardinals, in a manner that we shall have deemed appropriate'[133].

Innocent IV has written a learned commentary on the sentence of deposition which he himself had passed, a very rare phenomenon. It should be read together with that sentence:

---

132 MGH *Const.* 2, no 400, 512; HB 6.1, 326: '*Posset etiam merito reprehendi, quod mille squifatorum annuam pensionem, in qua pro eodem regno ipsi ecclesiae Romane tenetur, per novem annos et amplius solvere pretermisit*'. According to X. 3,18,4, an ecclesiastical fee was forfeited as of right after two successive instalments of the rent had been missed.

133 MGH *Const.* 2, no 400, 512; HB 6.1, 326-327: '*Nos itaque super premissis et quam pluribus aliis nephandis excessibus cum fratribus nostris et sacro concilio deliberatione prehabita diligenti, cum Jhesu Christi vices licet immeriti teneamus in terris, nobisque in beati Petri apostoli persona sit dictum "Quodcumque ligaveris super terra erit ligatum et in celis" memoratum principem qui se imperio et regnis omnique honore ac dignitate reddidit tam indignum, quique propter suas iniquitates atque scelera a Deo ne regnet vel imperet est abjectus, suis ligatum peccatis et abjectum omnique honore ac dignitate privatum a Domino ostendimus, denunciamus ac nichilominus sentenciando privamus; omnes qui ei juramento fidelitatis tenentur astricti, a juramento huiusmodi perpetuo absolventes; auctoritate apostolica firmiter inhibendo ne quisquam de cetero sibi tamquam imperatori ac regi pareat vel intendat et decernendo quoslibet qui deinceps ei velut imperatori aut regi consilium vel auxilium prestiterint vel favorem, ipso facto vinculo excommunicationis subjacere. Illi autem ad quos in eodem imperio imperatoris spectat electio, eligant libere alium in eius locum successorem. De prefato vero Sicilie regno providere curabimus cum eorundem fratrum nostrorum cardinalium consilio, sicut viderimus expedire*'.

'The pope deposes the emperor and that is legitimate, since Christ, the son of God, when he was still among us, was even then forever the natural lord and could according to natural law pass a sentence of deposition, damnation, or whatever else on emperors or whomever else, being persons he had created and upon whom he had bestowed natural and spontaneous gifts and kept them alive, and so can his representative, because he would not have been a good shepherd, if I may venture to say so with all due respect to him, if he had not left behind one representative to succeed him who was able to do all that. Peter was that representative and the same must be said about the successors of Peter because it would have been likewise absurd if he left humankind created by him without the rule of one man after the demise of Peter'[134].

There is nothing new in these astonishing, if not outrageous[135], papal postulates, concurring as they do with the doctrine as developed by Innocent III in his sermon of 31 December 1198[136]: the pope, as the vicar of Christ on earth, is endowed with the divine privilege of *plenitudo potestatis*. He is the Lord of Lords, priest-king in the order of Melchisedech, who is judge over all but cannot himself be judged by any man. Emperors and kings are only assigned a *pars sollicitudinis*, a share in government, entrusted to them by the pope subject to the condition subsequent that they do not act against the will of Christ as interpreted by his living representative on earth, the pope[137]. The argument was corroborated, on the same council, by the *de facto* deposition of King Sancho II of Portugal on account of his manifest incompetence,

---

134 Innocentii IIII. PM *Commentaria in V. libros Decretalium* App. post X 2,26,25, cap. ii (ed. Venice 1570, 381, 1. col.): '*Papa deponit imperatorem et hoc est iure, nam cum Christus filius Dei dum fuit in hoc seculo et etiam ab aeterno dominus naturalis fuit, et de iure naturali in imperatores et quoscumque alios sententias depositionis ferre potuisset et damnationis et quascunque alias, utpote in personas quas creaverat et donis naturalibus et gratuitis donaverat et in esse conservaverat et eadem ratione et vicarius eius potest hoc, nam non videretur discretus dominus fuisse, ut cum reverentia eius loquar nisi unicum post se talem vicarium reliquisset qui haec omnia posset; fuit autem iste vicarius eius Petrus et idem dicendum est de successoribus Petri, cum eadem absurditas sequeretur, si post mortem Petri humanam naturam a se creatam sine regimine unius personae reliquisset*'.
135 Christ himself had emphasized that 'my kingdom is *not* of this world' (Joh. 18:36).
136 See *supra* p. 331-334.
137 There is neither in the sentence of deposition itself, nor in Innocent's commentary on the sentence a reference to historical precedent, just casually touched upon in Innocent's commentary as an introduction to the sentence (see *supra* p. 329). Only a minor papal functionary, Nicolaus de Carbio, not a lawyer, still refers to historical precedents: *Vita Innocentii IV* cap. 19, ed. Pagnotti 95. Neither Nicolaus nor any canonist ever refers to the 'deposition' of the Emperor Henry IV as a precedent, by the way, since Henry was excommunicated by Pope Gregory VII, but deposed by the German princes who elected Rudolph of Rheinfelden in his place in 1077: Bruno, *De bello Saxonico* (c. 1080) 91, MGH *SS* 5, 365.

replacing him with his brother Alphonso as 'caretaker' (*coadiutor*) of the realm by the grace of the pope[138].

Frederick's Reaction

The news of his deposition reached Frederick II in Turin, where he and his son Conrad IV were still residing[139]. Matthew Paris reports that the emperor, on hearing the news, called for his treasure chest, took a crown from it and declared *sub corona*, emphasizing the solemnity of the occasion, that from now on he was free from any obligation to keep peace with the pope[140]. As master Thaddaeus had realized, Innocent's sentence of deposition amounted to a declaration of war, bringing 'misery and disaster' (*miseria et calamitas*) rather than peace. Heeding the motto of Gregory VII 'not to keep back his sword from blood' (Jeremiah 48:10)[141], the pope had drawn a secular sword against the emperor, leaving Frederick no choice but to draw his own. At the same time, he ordered his lawyers to compose a document publicly refuting the papal sentence as null and void. It was an extended version of master Thaddaeus' letter of protest against that sentence and was edited as an encyclical letter to be publicized all over the Christian world, but primarily addressed to all the princes of Europe[142].

---

138   On the deposition of King Sancho at the council of Lyon I see Nicolaus de Carbio, *Vita Innocentii IV* cap. 20, ed. Pagnotti 96 ('*in ipso concilio*'). The papal decree '*Grandi non immerito*' was later partly inserted in the *Liber sextus*: VI° 1,8,2. The complete text is printed in *Ann. eccl.* Tom. 21, Paris 1870, ad ann. 1245 §§ 68-71, 309-311.
139   The news may have been brought to him by his representatives returning from Lyon, since they left soon after the closing of the council. Late in July 1245, Frederick issued a charter in Turin (HB 6.1, 327) on behalf of Countess Margaret of Flanders, witnessed by most of his original representatives at the Lyon council, master Thaddaeus and the archbishop of Palermo, as well as the later ambassadors, master Piero della Vigna and the bishop of Freising. The latter had met with Pope Innocent at Lyon before, as we know from Innocent's decree from 3 August 1245, absolving the bishop from his excommunication (HB 6.1, 337), suggesting that these ambassadors had indeed arrived at Lyon, but too late as they learned at their arrival.
140   *Chronica maiora* ad ann. 1245, ed. H.R. Luard IV, 474: '*Nunc autem ab amore et veneratione necnon et ab omnimodo pacis absolvor adversus Papam obligatione*'.
141   See *supra* p. 32, fnt. 16.
142   Frederick's public reaction is printed in HB 6.1, 331-337 and in MGH *Const.* 2, no 262, 360-366. It survived in Matthew Paris, *Chronica maiora* ad ann. 1246, ed. H.R. Luard IV, 538-544, wrongly attributing the letter to 1246 rather than 1245; in the 13th-century Scottish Chronicle of Melrose ad ann. 1245 (*Chronica de Mailros*, ed. J. Stevenson, Edinburgh 1835, 171-176); in the collection of letters by Piero della Vigna (*Petri de Vineis Friderici II. Imp. Epistolarum Libri VI*, ed. J.R. Iselin, Basle 1740, Tom. 1, Lib. 1, cap. 3 (84-92)); in the letters of Albert Behaim (Höfler, *Albert von Beham*, Stuttgart 1847, 81-85) and in a number of manuscripts, including a Prague manuscript, containing the letter as addressed to the king of Bohemia. See Weiland's introduction to his edition in MGH *Const.* 2, no 262, 360-361.

Frederick's reaction begins by denying the legitimacy of the sentence, since it had been passed by a judge unqualified to take cognizance of the matter[143]. The pope did, indeed, have *plenitudo potestatis*, but only and exclusively in spiritual matters, *not* in secular affairs: *'it is not written in any divine or secular law that he has been granted the power to transfer the imperial title at will or to pass judgment that the kings and princes of the world are to be punished secularly by taking away their kingdoms'*[144]. As a matter of fact, there *was* a provision of secular law granting that power to the pope, as Frederick's lawyers surely must have realized: the decretal *'Venerabilem'* of Innocent III. Since explicitly denying force of law to this decretal would have drawn them into a constitutional quagmire, they avoided this course and concentrated on the purely procedural aspects of the Lyon judgment instead: *'suppose, without prejudice to us, that he does have that power, is this then a part of his absolute sovereignty that he may take legal action against anyone he asserts to be under his jurisdiction without due process?'*[145].

Due process | 'Due process' at the time meant the rules of Roman criminal procedure, as applied in two different kinds of Roman criminal litigation: either a criminal procedure was initiated *and* prosecuted by a private citizen in the court of the Roman *praetor* or another official by way of a formal charge (*accusatio*), or the procedure was initiated *and* prosecuted by a Roman imperial official on the basis of the denunciation (*delatio*) of a crime by a private citizen. The former was the classical *iudicium publicum legitimum* of Republican origin; the latter was the *cognitio extra ordinem* of Roman imperial times. There is, however, no historical development wherein the younger procedure gradually superseded the older form of criminal procedure: they continued to exist side by side, at the choice of the citizen, in Justinian's *Codex* with a discretion of the imperial officials not to take on a case brought to their attention by denunciation, leaving the denunciator but one way of filing criminal charges: prosecuting the perpetrator himself. Both forms of Roman criminal procedure were still in use in secular courts on the Italian peninsula in the Middle Ages and certainly in ecclesiastical courts. Innocent III had added a third procedure, the *inquisitio*, not based on a formal *accusatio*, or a denunciation, but on rumour

---

143   HB 6.1, 332; MGH *Const.* 2, no 262, 362: *'si dici sententia debeat, quam iudex incompetens promulgavit'*.

144   HB 6.1, 332; MGH *Const.* 2, no 262, 362: *'nusquam verumtamen legitur divina vel humana lege sibi concessum, quod transferre pro libito possit imperia, aut de puniendis temporaliter in privatione regnorum regibus aut terre principibus judicare'*.

145   HB 6.1, 332; MGH *Const.* 2, no 262, 362: *'esto sine prejudicio nostro, quod habeat hujusmodi potestatem, est ne istud de plenitudine potestatis ipsius, quod nullo prorsus ordine juris servato, animadvertere possit in quoslibet quos asserit sue jurisdictioni subjectos?'*

(*fama*)[146], for example of heresy, compelling an ecclesiastical official (a bishop, the pope) to appoint an investigator (*inquisitor*) to inquire whether a rumour was false or based on fact and to proceed against the person or persons uncovered during the investigation as suspect of a crime. Since all of the three modes of procedure just mentioned were employed by ecclesiastical courts[147] and because they all had different rules of procedure[148], it was crucial to establish which one of them was brought against Frederick II at the council of Lyon. Frederick's lawyers considered the possibilities. Was the trial against their master based on a formal charge (*accusatio*)? If so, then where was the formal entry of the charge into the records of the court (*inscriptio*), containing the precise name of the *accusator*, the precise rules of law presumed to have been infringed by the defendant, and a factual description of the criminal act presumably perpetrated by the defendant, all of them required in a procedure *per accusationem*[149]? Who, furthermore, was the person actually acting as *accusator*? If the trial was to be regarded as based on denunciation, then who was the denunciator? And if the trial was an inquisition, where were the 'frequent complaints of infamy' (*clamosa insinuatio*) that had to precede an inquisition according to canon law[150] and who were the officially appointed investigators (*inquisitores*)? Whichever

---

146   The first papal instruction on the new *modus procedendi* is in X. 5,3,31 (2 December 1199), '*Licet Heli*'. The scriptural basis of the new procedure was in Gen. 18:21: 'I will go down now, and see whether they have done altogether according to the cry (*clamor*) of it, which is come unto me; and if not, I will know'.

147   See X 5,1,24 (can. 8 of the Fourth Lateran Council): '*tribus modis possit procedi, per accusationem videlicet, denuntiationem et inquisitionem*'.

148   The main difference between the new procedure *per inquisitionem* and the two older forms of criminal procedure were in the rules of evidence. In the two older procedures, the judge was not *ex officio* authorized to investigate the truth but had to rely on the evidence produced in court by means of wager of law (*compurgatio*). In the procedure *per inquisitionem* a judge could actively engage in establishing the truth of the rumour that was brought to his attention. The objection that an inquisitor was in fact acting as prosecutor and judge at the same time was raised from the start: see the 'casus' on X. 5,3,31: '*not* as if he is himself prosecutor and judge' (*non tamquam ipse sit accusator et judex*) (emphasis added).

149   For these details see D. 48,2,3 pr. (Paul), containing a model *inscriptio* for a charge of adultery. See also C. 9,1,1 and 3. The procedure was later inserted by Frederick II into his *Liber augustalis*, in a Novel of 1246: *LA* 1,53.4, mentioning that it was in conformity with 'ancient law' (*prout veteribus legibus est inductum*), meaning Roman law. Since in this case criminal proceedings were initiated and prosecuted by a citizen, rather than a public official, the private prosecutor had to swear an oath against malicious accusation (*iusiurandum calumniae*): see C. 2,58,1 pr. and *LA* 2,14 (Fred. II).

150   X 5,1,24: '*sicut accusationem legitima debet praecedere inscriptio, sic et denunciationem caritativa monitio, et inquisitionem clamosa insinuatio praevenire*'. See also X. 5,3,31: 'A clamour reaches a prelate, whenever scandals are reported to him by way of public rumour, or by way of the frequent complaints of subjects and it is then that he must descend and view, *i.e.* to send someone and inquire whether there is any truth to the clamour that has reached him' (*Tunc enim clamor pervenit ad praelatum, quum per publicam famam aut insinuationem*

procedure applied, none of the rules of due process involved were followed in the trial of Frederick II[151]. Naturally, the emperor's lawyers were aware of the canon law doctrine that due process, the *ordo iuris*, was not required whenever the facts of a crime were evidenced by notoriety (*notoria*)[152]. It was a preposterous doctrine according to Frederick's lawyers: '*in this way any judge could convict anyone at will, without due process, just by declaring the crime notorious*'[153]. Anyway, they strongly denied the notoriety of the crimes brought against their emperor. Yet, despite the dubious 'doctrine of notoriety', witnesses had still been produced at the council, such as the bishop of Calinum, a manifest enemy of the emperor[154], whose testimony should have been rejected, since canon law itself provided that the testimony by enemies of a defendant was inadmissible as evidence[155]. As far as the other 'witnesses' were concerned, the Spanish prelates, they simply did not know what they were talking about, since they lived far from Italy and were not familiar with events occurring there: '*their appearance with its malicious bias made them hostile to the cause of our justice*'[156]. Frederick's reaction then continues with another hypothesis. Suppose the prosecutor and the judge were indeed legitimate, then there was a third party missing at the trial: the defendant[157]. The lawyers now turned their attention to what was, even to some of the canon lawyers participating in the deliberations *in camera* during the adjournment of the trial[158], the weakest point in the case against Frederick II from a strictly legal perspective: the fact that Frederick had not been properly summoned.

---

frequentem subditorum sibi referuntur excessus, et tunc debet descendere et videre, id est, mittere et inquirere, utrum clamorem, qui venit, veritas comitetur).
151 HB 6.1, 332; MGH *Const.* 2, no 262, 362: '*Processit enim contra nos nuper, ut dicitur, non per accusationis ordinem, cum nec accusator apparuisset idoneus nec inscriptio praecessisset, nec per denunciationem, legitimo denunciatore cessante, nec per inquisitionis modum, quam clamosa insinuatio non precessit, cum etiam nullorum inquisitorum facta nobis exstiterit copia*'.
152 See *supra* p. 362.
153 HB 6.1, 333; MGH *Const.* 2, no 262, 362: '*Asserit omnia fore notoria, que nos esse notoria manifeste negamus, et esse notoria per legitimorum testium nomina non probantur. Sic enim quilibet iudex posset per se solum crimen asserendo notorium spreto iuris ordine quemlibet condempnare*'.
154 See *supra* p. 357.
155 HB 6.1, 333; MGH *Const.* 2, no 262, 362-363: '*Insurrexerunt in nos in concilio, sicut dicitur, aliqui testes iniqui, sed valde pauci, quorum unum velut Calinensem episcopum ... nobis odiosum et iure propterea repellendum*'. For the canon law ban on the admission of witnesses hostile to the defendant see X 5,1,19 (Innocent III).
156 HB 6.1, 333; MGH *Const.* 2, no 262, 363: '*eosdem venenose subordinationis inductio nostre iusticie fecit infestos*'.
157 HB 6.1, 333; MGH *Const.* 2, no 262, 363: '*Sed esto praeterea quod legitimi fuerint ... actor et iudex, defuit tertius, reus*'.
158 See *supra* p. 366.

The emperor was summoned 'without due formality' (*informiter*), since he had only been informed by hearsay that he had been summoned in a public sermon by the pope to appear in Lyon to do justice to the pope and other persons, without mentioning their names, nor the specific complaints which they had filed against him[159]. Consequently, the absence of Frederick II could not possibly be construed as contempt of court (*contumacia*), because 'the summons was null and void' (*nulla fuerit citatio*), even more so since it did not even contain a proper peremptory term (*terminus peremptorius*) for the defendant to appear in court, as was required by law. Frederick's lawyers then came up with an additional argument, supporting their contention that the emperor had not been in contempt of court by not personally appearing at the trial in Lyon. It constituted contempt of court when a defendant did not appear in person to answer to the charges brought against him in one of the two traditional Roman *criminal* procedures (*per accusationem* and *per delationem*), but it had been effectively established that Frederick's trial at Lyon could not possibly be construed as falling under the rules of any of these two criminal procedures. Consequently, Frederick's trial could only be qualified as a trial *per inquisitionem*, which was subject to the rules of Roman *civil* procedure, as Innocent III, the *auctor intellectualis* of that procedure, had indicated explicitly himself[160]. This contention was corroborated by the papal summons itself, instructing the emperor to appear at the council 'either in person *or* by his representatives' (*per se* vel *suos nuncios*). A summons like this, even supposing it was valid, *quod non*, could only have been issued in a *civil* procedure, rather than in criminal proceedings, since representation was not allowed in criminal proceedings according to Roman law: a defendant in a *criminal* trial always had to appear in person and if he did not, he was indeed in contempt of court[161]. The pope, however, had allowed Frederick to

The summons contested

---

159 HB 6.1, 333-334; MGH *Const.* 2, no 262, 363: '*Citati namque in predicatione sua Lugdunum, sicut audivimus, licet prorsus informiter, videlicet quod ipsi citanti et aliis, nullis aliorum omnino personis aut causis expressis, facturi iusticiam deberemus per nos vel per responsales ydoneos comparere*' (emphasis added).

160 X. 5,3,32 (*Per tuas*): '*non criminaliter, sed civiliter*'.

161 D. 48,1,13,1 (Papinian): '*Ad crimen iudicii publici persequendum frustra procurator intervenit, multoque magis ad defendendum*'. For the explanation of the exclusion of legal representation in criminal trials see the Gl. 'Multo magis' on D. 48,1,13,1: '*quia cum per procuratorem litigatur procurator ipse damnatur vel absolvitur, quod non posset in criminalibus fieri*'. Due to the absence of a doctrine of direct representation in Roman law (see *supra* p. 130, fnt. 22), the legal representative of a defendant in private litigation was convicted himself if he failed to prove the cause of his principal. Condemnations in private lawsuits always resulted in a sentence to pay damages to the plaintiff, which the representative could later recover from his principal. This by definition was impossible in criminal proceedings, where convictions resulted in exile, corporal punishment, or even the death penalty. Of course, the rule did not exclude the availability of legal assistance by advocates in criminal trials, but an advocate did

send representatives. Consequently, the emperor was not in contempt of court (*contumax*), since his representative, master Thaddaeus, was present in court with full powers of attorney[162] and ready to explain why his principal could not attend personally, but unfortunately he had not been allowed to do so[163]. By these and other arguments Frederick's lawyers supported their contention that the sentence passed against their master was null and void and that the pope and his advisors had acted injudiciously and precipitately due to their long-held resentment and prejudice against the emperor, emphasizing the precipitancy of the pope by his unwillingness to wait a few days for the imminent arrival of the imperial ambassadors, the bishop of Freising, Henry of Hohenlohe, the grandmaster of the Teutonic Order, and Piero della Vigna[164].

Frederick warns the European monarchs

After dealing with the procedural aspects of the trial[165], Frederick's lawyers turned their attention to the sentence itself. It was clearly 'full of animosity and pretention' (*animosa nimis et ampullosa non minus*): the emperor of the Holy Roman Empire, 'the master and lord of imperial majesty' (*imperialis rector et dominus maiestatis*), was convicted for injuring his own majesty[166], ridiculously subjecting the one man who was 'above the laws' (*legibus solutus*, D. 1,3,31), the emperor, to the law[167]. Frederick emphasizes that he is, of course, subject to spiritual

---

not represent his client. In ancient Athens even that was not allowed: Demosthenes never personally held the forensic speeches he wrote for his clients, as Cicero did in Rome.

162   For the whole argument see HB 6.1, 334; MGH *Const.* 2, no 262, 363: '*Contumaciam nostram praeterea magistri Tadei de Suessa ... procuratoris plenum mandatum excusat, cuius auctoritas ex eo, quod contra nos non ex civilibus sed ex criminalibus sit processum atque frustra procurator intervenerit, nullatenus enervatur, cum ipsius citationis tenor, qua nos aut procurators nostros exigit, manifeste contrarium dedisset intelligi, videlicet quod contra nos non criminaliter set civiliter fuisset agendum*'.

163   HB 6.1, 334; MGH *Const.* 2, no 262, 363: '*presentes pro certo non fuimus, sed ex iustis caussis absentes, ad quarum allegationem admissi nostri legitimi responsales non fuerunt*'.

164   HB 6.1, 335; MGH *Const.* 2, no 262, 364: '*Manifestum namque precipitium et ex preconcepto jam dudum animi fervore fuisse dinoscitur in predictis, dum venerabilem Frisingensem episcopum ... fratrem H., magistrum domus sanctae Marie Theutonicorum, et magistrum Petrum de Vinea ... saltem per triduum summus pontifex noluit prestolari*'. On their embassy see *supra* p. 371.

165   Having established that the whole procedure was null and void, the lawyers abstained from entering into a detailed rebuttal of the four specific charges brought against their master. There is, however, one exception: the papal contention that Frederick had forfeited his Sicilian fief by not paying the *census* for more than nine years (see *supra* p. 378-379). It was alleged that the instalments had been properly paid to the papal treasury until Frederick's second excommunication and the instalments due after that were consigned to the custody of some Sicilian prelates and deposited in their churches (HB 6.1, 335; MGH *Const.* 2, no 262, 364-365).

166   The crime of heresy was, to Frederick II (see *LA* 1,1), a case of *laesio maiestatis*.

167   HB 6.1, 335; MGH *Const.* 2, no 262, 365: '*Apparet nichilominus animosa nimis et ampullosa non minus ex ipsius inflicte pene severitate sententia, per quam imperator Romanus, imperialis rector et dominus maiestatis, lese maiestatis dicitur crimine condempnatus, per quam ridiculose subicitur legi qui legibus omnibus imperialiter est solutus*'. According to Frederick's

censure, as are all good Catholics, but an emperor cannot be subjected to *secular* punishment (deposition) since he has no secular superior and is only answerable to God[168]. At the end of his reaction, the emperor directly addresses the princes of Europe. They were to consider the consequences of recognizing the legitimacy of the papal sentence and the procedure it was based on, how that would not only result in the ruin of himself, but of all kings and princes[169]: '*It is with us that it begins, but you must know that it will end with you, since they do not expect any resistance once our might is crushed*'[170]. It is yet another call for the solidarity and the support of all European princes in a cause that concerned them all.

Frederick's official reaction to his deposition was a devastating account of all that had gone wrong in his 'trial' at Lyon from a strictly legal point of view and it made a profound impression on many European princes who were beginning to fear the arrogance (*superbia*) of the Roman *curia* and consequently distanced themselves from the cause of the pope[171]. It must have deeply troubled Innocent IV. He was an outstanding lawyer and the scathing public criticism of his personal management of that trial must not only have offended him, but it really must have stung him to be publicly exposed as a juristic blunderer by Frederick's legal counsellors. This is why he wrote to the general chapter of the Cistercian

Innocent IV rejects all criticism

---

own 'theology of the law' (*supra* p. 257-258) the papal sentence amounted to the theological enormity of subjecting the Father and the Son to the Holy Spirit.

168   HB 6.1, 335; MGH *Const.* 2, no 262, 365: '<*imperator*> *de quo temporales pene sumende, cum temporalem hominem superiorem non habeat, non sunt in homine, sed in Deo. Spirituales autem penas per sacerdotales nobis penitentias indicendas … reverenter accipimus et devote servamus*'.

169   HB 6.1, 336; MGH *Const.* 2, no 262, 365: '*Advertat igitur prudentia tua, si predicta sententia, nulla ipso iure, nullus ipso iure processus, non magis in nostrum quam in omnium regum et principum ac quarumlibet dignitatum temporalium perniciem debeat observari*'. The emperor adds that the papal sentence and the trial at Lyon were not favoured by the presence or the consent of the German princes, the only persons entitled to raise and depose him (<*sententia*> *quam nulla nostrorum Germanie principum, a quibus assumptio status et depressio nostra dependent, presentia vel consilia firmaverunt*).

170   MGH *Const.* 2, no 262, 365-366: '*A nobis incipitur, sed noveritis, quod finietur in vobis, quia, nostra potentia primitus conculcata, resistentiam aliquam non expectant*'.

171   Matthew Paris, *Chronica maiora* ad ann. 1246, ed. H.R. Luard IV, 544: '*Haec autem epistola cum ad notitiam multorum principum pervenisset, corda a domino Papa protinus averterunt, superbiam Romanae curiae, si contingeret Frethericum succumbere, merito formidantes*'. There was a rumour at the time that Innocent IV had agreed to compromise with the king of England on a particular issue much against his will, fuming that 'We must make a compromise with your prince in order to wear down these recalcitrant princelings, since once the dragon <Frederick II> has been brought down or pacified, the little serpents will soon be crushed' (Matthew Paris, *Chronica maiora* ad ann. 1245, ed. H.R. Luard IV, 423: '*Expedit ut componamus cum principe vestro, ut hos regulos conteramus recalcitrantes; contrito enim vel pacificato dracone, cito serpentuli conculcabuntur*').

order not to heed 'the criticism of inexperienced and ignorant people' (*imperitorum et veritatis ignarorum obloquia*) who contended that he and his brothers had proceeded precipitately and injudiciously against the emperor. To the contrary: '*we cannot remember another case ever to have been decided with such scrutiny and more diligent consideration*'[172]. Privately, Innocent IV must have been very frustrated that, due to the reservations of the king of France, he had been forced to concede to the charade of a public trial of Frederick II before a general council since he was convinced to be entitled to dispose of the emperor without due process in his own right.

Shortly after his public reaction, Frederick sent an open letter[173] addressed to all the subjects of the king of France, but primarily directed at the French nobility, among which, as we have seen[174], the emperor could count on considerable support. The great French barons sympathized with his cause, because they realized the emperor's conflict with the pope was not dissimilar to their own frustrating experiences. The ecclesiastical courts were intruding on the administration of secular law within their jurisdiction as well. A case could be taken out of their own courts and transferred to an ecclesiastical court at the request of one of the parties concerned, just because that party alleged a sin was involved, calling for ecclesiastical censure rather than secular condemnation[175]. Frederick cleverly played into these frustrations by emphasizing in his letter that his conflict with the present pope and his predecessors was precisely about this issue. The clerics had unlawfully appropriated secular powers by transferring purely secular private lawsuits from the baronial courts, where they belonged, into the ecclesiastical courts at the request of clerics or laymen, thus depriving

Frederick II
appeals to the
French nobility

---

172 Matthew Paris, *Chronica maiora* ad ann. 1245, ed. H.R. Luard IV, 480 (HB 6.1, 347): '*Non vos moveant imperitorum et veritatis ignarorum, precamur, obloquia, ut a nobis quasi praecipitanter et absque deliberato fratrum et multorum peritorum moroso consilio contra ipsum Frethericum fuerit sententiatum. Non enim meminimus umquam causam cum tanta deliberatione et diligenti examinatione fuisse excussam*'. The author of the '*Relatio*', or his superior in the papal chancery, must also have been expecting criticism of the way the trial of Frederick II had been handled at Lyon, since it concludes with the following lines 'But it should be emphasized that the pope in those days asked for the advice of the prelates individually whether he could and should proceed against him on the basis of the things that were manifest and that as many as all concurred in his deposition, so that he had the seal of all of them attached to the sentence as soon as it had been put down in writing, so that about 150 seals were attached to the sentence when it was made public' (*Sed est diligenter attendendum, quod papa in illis diebus consilium petierat singulariter a prelatis, utrum posset vel deberet procedere per ea, que manifesta fuerant contra eum, et quantum ad depositionem eius omnes concordarunt: ut statim ipsi sentente, que scripta erat, sigillum cuiuslibet faciebat apponi, ita quod in prolatione sentetie circa C et L sigilla ipsi sentetie fuerant appensa*).
173 HB 6.1, 349-352; MGH *Const.* 2, no 264, 369-371.
174 See *supra* p. 344.
175 See *supra* p. 337.

the barons of their revenues[176]. In this way, the emperor cultivated the support of the French barons hoping they would encourage the king of France to act as an arbiter in the conflict between him and the pope[177]. Despite his deposition, Frederick II had still not given up hope that a final arrangement could be found to prevent the execution of the Lyon sentence.

---

176   HB 6.1, 350; MGH *Const.* 2, no 264, 370: 'whenever a dispute or a lawsuit is brought in the ordinary way between lords and vassals or between two neighbouring lords, the popes interfere at the request of only one of the parties involved by exercising secular powers. They take cognizance of and preside over litigation in secular affairs, on feudal tenures or affairs ruled by urban law, to be tried in an ecclesiastical court at the request of clerics or laymen to the prejudice of the jurisdiction and the honour of kings and princes' (*questione sive discensione inter dominos et vasallos seu inter duos nobiles et vicinos invicem contendentes prout assolet emergente, predicti summi pontifices ad petitionem unius partis tantummodo partes suas temporaliter interponunt ... in prejudicium jurisdictionis et honoris regum et principum predictorum, ad petitionem clericorum seu laycorum, cognitiones causarum de rebus temporalibus, possessionibus pheodalibus seu burgesaticis in ecclesiastico foro tractandas recipiunt et committunt*).
177   See *infra* p. 395. Frederick's letters had a considerable impact in France. When the French barons rallied to object against the avarice and presumptuousness of the clergy in 1247 in a number of manifestos, one of them contained phrases borrowed from Frederick's letters: see Matthew Paris, *Chronica maiora* ad ann. 1247, ed. H.R. Luard IV, 593-594.

4

Execution

With his sentence of 17 July 1245, Innocent IV had legally broken the union of the Empire with the kingdom of Sicily. He was at liberty to find a successor for the kingdom of Sicily himself, while the decretal 'Venerabilem' entitled him to watch over the choice of the imperial electors for a succession to the imperial crown, since the pope had never recognized the election of Conrad IV. Never again was a German king to rule over the Sicilian kingdom[1]. The pope now had to see to the execution of his sentence in the Empire and the Sicilian kingdom. According to an imperial statute, promulgated by Frederick II himself among his 1220 coronation statutes, an excommunicate who had not repented within a year after his excommunication became an outlaw by operation of law[2], and according to canon law an unrepentant excommunicate might even be killed with impunity, provided the killing was inspired by religious zeal rather than just lust for murder[3]. After Frederick's deposition, not even the crime of *laesio maiestatis* applied to a murderer of the emperor since he had been divested of his majesty by order of the pope. It is more than just likely that Innocent IV himself planned at least two (if not more) attempts on the life of Frederick II after the latter's deposition. There were sound political reasons for the pope to have Frederick assassinated, or rather executed, since that would have solved the practical problem of the succession to the imperial and Sicilian crown by one lethal stroke. That problem was particularly pressing as far as the imperial succession was concerned.

Execution
by way of
assassination

---

1 The only exception to this central tenet of papal politics is, of course, Charles V, king of Aragon and Sicily since 1516, king of the Germans since 1519, and Roman emperor since 1530, but Charles was exceptional in many ways, a human and constitutional mutant, accumulating lofty titles as though they were small change.

2 S. 3 of Frederick's coronation statutes, MGH *Const.* 2, no 85, 108. On the coronation statutes see *supra* p. 255-257.

3 For this see *Decretum* C. 23, q. 5. cap. 47: 'We do not consider those to be murderers who out of zeal for their Catholic mother have slaughtered some excommunicates' (*Non enim eos homicidas arbitramur, quos adversus excommunicatos zelo catholicae matris ardentes, aliquos eorum trucidasse contigit*).

By 17 July 1245 there was still no openly declared alternative to Frederick II in the German kingdom. The pope and the archbishops of Mainz and Cologne were in contact with Heinrich Raspe of Thuringia on the issue, but the landgrave was hesitating[4]. He had sworn an oath of fealty to the emperor and that may still have meant something to him. He may also have known that most, if not all, of the other secular German princes looked unfavourably on the conspicuous interference of the pope with the government of their kingdom. The convenient demise of Frederick II would have removed the qualms of his reluctant successor, Heinrich Raspe.

The Parma conspiracy

Innocent IV and his Fieschi family had strong ties with the city of Parma. Innocent's uncle Opizo, the brother of his father, had been bishop of Parma from 1194 to 1225. Young Sinibaldo Fieschi had lived and studied there and, not surprisingly, had many friends and relatives among the citizens of Parma[5]. One of them was Bernardino, a son of Rolando Rubeo. Bernardino was married to a sister of Innocent[6] and was the linchpin of a conspiracy to assassinate the emperor and his son Enzio. Frederick II left Turin after 5 August 1245[7] and went to Cremona, having sent his son Conrad IV back to Germany with a substantial army and a lot of money to help him defend the Hohenstaufen interests in Germany[8]. In Cremona the emperor learnt that the news of his deposition had incited seditious sentiments in Parma, a city then under imperial control and administered by a Sicilian *podestà*, Tebaldo Francesco. Frederick therefore decided to leave Cremona for Parma as soon as possible[9]. On his way to Parma, the emperor visited the abbey of Fontevivo, halfway between Fidenza and Parma. It was there that he found documentary evidence in the abbey's sacristy incriminating

---

4 See *supra* p. 317-319.
5 Nicolaus de Carbio, *Vita Innocentii IV* cap. 25, ed. Pagnotti 99: '*cives Parmenses potentiores et nobiliores, nepotes et consanguinei domini pape*'. See also *supra* p. 22.
6 *Annales Placentini Gibellini* ad ann. 1246, MGH *SS* 18, 493: '*ipse Bernardinus Rolandi Rubei erat cugnatus domni pape*'. A *cognato* is a brother-in-law in Italian. See also Salimbene de Adam (1221-1288/89), *Cronica* ad ann. 1247, MGH *SS* 32 199: '*domnus Bernardus Rolandi Rubei de Parma, qui fuit cognatus domni pape Innocentii quarti – habuit enim sororem pape uxorem*'.
7 Frederick's public reaction to his deposition is dated on Aug. 5, 1245, at Turin.
8 *Annales Placentini Gibellini* ad ann. 1245, MGH *SS* 18, 491-492: '*imperator, qui erat apud Taurinum … Conradum filium suum cum honorabili militum comitiva et maximo thesauro … in Alamaniam destinavit*'.
9 *Annales Ianuenses* (Bartolomeo scriba) ad ann. 1245, MGH *SS* 18, 217: '*Separavit se de Taurino et ivit Cremonam; et cum intellexisset ibi, quod homines civitatis Parme contra ipsum rebelles fiebant, festinanter ivit illuc*'.

Bernardino and others of planning his assassination[10]. On his arrival in Parma, the conspirators had already escaped and found refuge in Piacenza, where they were welcomed as heroes and continued their conspiratorial activities[11]. What the emperor had not learned from the documents he had found at Fontevivo, was that Bernardino and his accomplices had succeeded in bringing the local Sicilian *podestà*, Tebaldo Francesco, over to their side, promising him an important position in the future Sicilian administration after the removal of the emperor and the installation of a new papal government in that kingdom, something only Bernardino, brother-in-law to the pope, can have presented as a plausible prospect for the Sicilian nobleman, a prominent member of Frederick's court[12]. Frederick was unaware of the mortal danger lurking among his own immediate Sicilian acquaintance.

Whereas there is only an indication of involvement of the pope in the Parma conspiracy against Frederick's life (the close family connection between the pope and the leading conspirator), there is more evidence of the pope's involvement in the Sicilian conspiracy. As was observed earlier, the pope had left four cardinals behind in Italy, one of them, Cardinal Riccardo Annibaldi, was charged with keeping an eye on the Sicilian kingdom as *rector* of the Campagna province, directly bordering on that kingdom[13]. By the end of 1245 Cardinal Annibaldi was planning an invasion of the Sicilian kingdom 'for the liberation of the dismal people of that kingdom' (*pro liberatione miserorum de Regno*) on the pope's instruction[14]. There was no prospect of an

The Sicilian conspiracy

---

10   *Annales Placentini Gibellini* ad ann. 1246, MGH *SS* 18, 492: '*equitavit <imperator> cum militibus suis Fontanam-vivam, invenitque in secretario illius monasterii scripturas de proditione et morte sua et regis Hencii*'.

11   *Annales Placentini Gibellini* ad ann. 1245, MGH *SS* 18, 492: '*Quapropter statim Bernardus Rolandi Rubei, Bernardus de Cornazano, Mons et Guido et Rolandus fratres Lupi, et Girardus de Corrigio milites eiusdem civitatis absentantes, venerunt Placentiam, ubi recepti fuerunt cum magno honore*'.

12   *Annales Placentini Gibellini* ad ann. 1246, MGH *SS* 18, 493: '*Bernardus Rolandi Rubei et alii tractaverant cum Tebaldo Francisco, qui in eodem anno in Parma extiterat per potestatem, mortem imperatoris et regis Encii, pollicentes ipsi Tebaldo se regnum Scicilie per domnum papam concessuros, sperantes habere magnam virtutem et potestatem a domno papa, quoniam ipse Bernardinus Rolandi Rubei erat cugnatus domni pape*'. See also *Annales Ianuenses* (Bartolomeo scriba) ad ann. 1246, MGH *SS* 18, 220.

13   See *supra* p. 322. For what follows see the letter sent by an anonymous cardinal to Innocent IV discovered and edited by K. Hampe, 'Papst Innozenz IV und die sizilische Verschwörung von 1246' in *Sitzungsberichte der Heidelberger Akademie der Wissenschaften*, Ph.-hist. Klasse 8 (1923), 4-6 ('Hampe'). I have followed Hampe's contention that the writer of the letter must have been none other than Cardinal Annibaldi.

14   Hampe 6: 'I am busy as best as I can to humbly execute your wish and command as I have received them about help for the Holy Land and about the things contained in your apostolic letter concerning the former emperor F<rederick>, to lend support at the given time and place to the liberation of the dismal people of the kingdom and the invasion of the kingdom by the

impending 'liberation' of the people of the Sicilian kingdom from the oppressive rule of Frederick II without the elimination of that tyrant himself and the prospect of support from within the kingdom itself. Cardinal Annibaldi assured the pope in February 1246 that the voice of Frederick would be silenced 'soon without a doubt' (*velociter sine dubio*)[15]. The plan did not succeed. In March 1246 Frederick's son in law Riccardo Sanseverino, count of Caserta, married to Violante, Frederick's daughter by his mistress Bianca Lancia, disclosed the conspiracy of Tebaldo Francesco and other Sicilian barons to assassinate Frederick II. It was just in time, since the attempt on Frederick's life was planned for the next day[16]. However, the Sicilian conspirators who were with Frederick in Tuscany were able to escape to Rome. Tebaldo Francesco and another conspirator, William of Sanseverino, were in the Sicilian *regno* at the time, obviously in contact with Cardinal Annibaldi and anxiously awaiting impending events. On hearing that their conspiracy had been exposed, they took refuge in two strongholds. Frederick, who realized he had just barely escaped a lethal attack, was furious and left for the Sicilian *regno* at once. As soon as he arrived there, he settled the score with the conspirators, dealing with them as mercilessly and cruelly as his father once had done with other Sicilian conspirators[17]: they had committed the unspeakable crime of *laesio maiestatis* and were executed accordingly after being interrogated first, revealing the involvement of the pope[18]. Innocent's plan to execute the

---

Romans' (*quod in mandatis recepi de terre orientalis auxilio et de hiis, que circa F. quondam principem in rescripto habentur apostolico de dando loco et tempore suo adiumentum pro liberatione miserorum de Regno et ad ingressum Romanorum in Regnum, studeo secundum meum posse modicum vestrum inplere humiliter beneplacitum et mandatum*).

15   Hampe 5: 'As far as this matter is concerned, I beg Your Holiness not to worry and not to be disturbed by these tribulations, since his <Frederick's> roarings of power will be silenced soon without a doubt, the Lord shall strike dumb disturbances like these on our behalf, the storm shall abate to a soft breeze and soon his surge shall be suppressed in accordance with the will of God' (*Ad hec, licet ex superhabundanti, vestre supplico reverentissime sanctitati, quatinus non turbemini nec istis tribulacionibus moveamini, quia procul dubio contereretur velociter eius fremitus potestatis, tranquilabit nobis Omnipotens turbaciones huiusmodi, procella mitescet in auram et precipiente Domino silebunt in proximo fluctus eius*).

16   *Annales Ianuenses* (Bartolomeo scriba) ad ann. 1246, MGH *SS* 18, 220: '*Comes vero de Casertis fecit hec scire domno Frederico*'. Frederick addressed an extensive memorandum on the conspiracy and its aftermath to the king of England: Matthew Paris, *Chronica maiora* ad ann. 1246, ed. H.R. Luard IV, 570-575 (HB 6.1, 403-406). See on this conspiracy also a letter by a certain master Terrisius to Count Raymond of Toulouse, printed in Winkelmann, *Acta imperii inedita*, Innsbruck 1880, no 725, 570-571(571): '*inter diem mortis et vite unus solus dies medius*'.

17   See *supra* p. 151.

18   See Frederick in his letter to the king of England (HB 6.1, 405): 'The just mentioned perpetrators of that heinous crime, the ones who had taken flight and the ones who had been besieged, have declared that they openly adhered to the cause of the Holy Roman Mother-Church, pressed by the society of the friars minor, from whom they have received the sign of

emperor and solve the problem of Frederick's succession in the Empire and the Sicilian kingdom by one decisive move had failed, for the time being. The pope now had to face an attempt by the king of France, the one prince he could not afford to turn down, to make him retract his condemnation of the emperor.

Frederick II had written a letter to Louis IX of France, as he had done to the other European princes, emphasizing the iniquity and the political bias of the pope's sentence[19]. Frederick and Louis were always on good, even friendly, terms, despite the emperor's excommunication, since Louis was critical of an indiscriminate use of the instrument of excommunication and certainly of the inequitable execution of ecclesiastical censure by way of secular punishment[20]. On the other hand, Louis IX was a devout Catholic and had taken the cross to serve the Church in the Holy Land. Consequently, the king of France was the ideal mediator to arrange a compromise between the pope and the emperor. Innocent IV had rudely rebuffed the objections to his sentence expressed by Louis' representatives at the Lyon council, but whether he would dare to do so when faced by Louis himself was by no means certain. The king of France had always been the mainstay of papal government and Innocent IV especially depended on the king's protection. Without Louis' guarantee of his personal safety, the pope was practically at the emperor's mercy. Frederick now inquired with Louis whether he was willing to intervene and mediate on his behalf, promising the king in return to assist and accompany him in his coming crusade[21]. Louis agreed and called a conference with the pope, to

Louis IX tries to mediate

---

the cross against us, pretending to have been authorized by the pope on account of apostolic letters, and they assert that the pope is the instigator of our assassination and expropriation' (*Prefati namque facinoris patratores, tam fugitivi videlicet quam obsessi, fratrum Minorum stipati consortio, crucis ab eis contra nos signo recepto, authoritatem summi pontificis per Apostolicas literas pretendentes, negocium aperte se gerere sacrosancte Romane matris ecclesiae predicant et predicte mortis et exhereditationis nostre summum pontificem asserunt incentorem*).

19   See *supra* p. 388.
20   See *supra* p. 344-345.
21   See Frederick's open letter to the French from 22 September 1245 (HB 6.1, 349-352(351); MGH *Const.* 2, no 264, 369-371()): 'we place the dispute that exists between us and the aforementioned pope in the hands of the king, since it also concerns him, and we are ready to correct and completely restore to its lawful state everything the king has decided that should be restored to the Church by us, after hearing the advice of his peers and nobles and having carefully considered our rights and the rights of the Empire. And after peace between the Church and us has been restored in this way, we offer ourselves ready and willing to sail to the lands oversea under this hopeful omen' (*nos ... causam que inter nos et summum pontificem vertitur supradictum, quatenus contingit eumdem, in manibus ponimus regis eiusdem, parati omnia quecumque per nos idem rex de consilio parium nobiliumque suorum, visis et diligenter auditis nostris et imperii juribus, Ecclesie viderit emendanda, corrigere et in statum debitum integre reformare; ac deinde pace per hoc inter nos et Ecclesiam procedente ... promptos nos offerimus et*

be held in Cluny, late in November 1245, where he was to communicate and support Frederick's last and desperate offer for peace with the
Church: in return for his absolution, the emperor promised to spend
the rest of his life in the Holy Land, fighting for the cause of Christ and
'never to return' (*irrediturus*), provided his son Conrad was also to be
absolved and recognized as Frederick's successor in the Empire[22].

Unfortunately for Frederick, the effort of the king of France on his
behalf was compromised from the start. Louis met the pope at Cluny
not only to intervene on behalf of Frederick II but also to ask the pope
a special favour on his own behalf, giving Innocent IV the welcome
opportunity of a trade-off. Louis was concerned about the winding up
of the estate of his father-in-law, Count Raymond-Berengar of Provence,
who had died in August 1245. The count had no male heir, but he had
four daughters. One of them, Margaret, was married to Louis; another,
Eleanor, was married to King Henry III of England; another, Sancha,
was married to King Henry's brother, Richard of Cornwall. The count's
youngest daughter, Beatrice, was still unattached, but it was to her that
the count had bequeathed the Provence in his will, stipulating that as
long as his heir was still unmarried, the county was to be under the
special protection of the Church, meaning the pope[23]. The problem was
that Louis' wife, Margaret of Provence, was the eldest of the daughters
and consequently contested her father's will. The problem was complicated even further by the fact that the count of Provence had met
Count Raymond VII of Toulouse shortly before his demise during the
Lyon council and had promised his daughter Beatrice in marriage to
the latter[24]. This was something Louis could never allow to happen:

---

paratos ... ad transmarinas partes ... omine prospero transfretare). On the purpose of this letter
see also *supra* p. 388. On Louis' role as mediator see also Matthew Paris, *Chronica maiora* ad
ann. 1246, ed. H.R. Luard IV, 523: '*Super quo negotio constituit procuratorem et mediatorem
dominum regem Francorum*'.

22 Matthew Paris, *Chronica maiora* ad ann. 1246, ed. H.R. Luard IV, 523: '*Optulit autem
dictus Frethericus ut in Sanctam Terram irrediturus abiret, quoad viveret Christo ibidem militat-
urus, et totum regnum integraliter pro posse restiturus cultui Christiano, ita scilicet ut, filio suo loco
ipsius in imperiali dignitate substituto, pie dispensetur cum eodem Fretherico*'.

23 *Annales Ianuenses* (Bartolomeo scriba) ad ann. 1245, MGH *SS* 18, 218: '*Item ipso anno
mense Augusti, sicut Deo placuit, domnus Raymundus Berengarius comes et marchio Provincie
et comes Fulcalcherii diem clausit extremum, et heredem sibi instituit filiam suam domnam
Beatricem et terram suam totam subditam, et sub protectione Romane ecclesie esse debere precepit
domnum Romeum de Villanova baiulum totius terre sue et filie dimisit quousque maritaretur*'. The
regent appointed by the count, Romeo de Villanova († 1250), is exalted by Dante in *Paradiso*
VI, 127-142.

24 For this significant detail see the chronicle of Guillaume de Puylaurens (Guillelmus de
Podio Laurentii) (*c.* 1200-† after 1274), cap. 45, ed. Duvernoy, Paris 1976, p. 176-178: 'The
pope held his council, which the counts of Toulouse and the Provence were attending, negotiating with the pope on the marriage between the count of Toulouse and the last daughter
of the count of Provence for which the pope had to give dispensation because of the impedi-

Count Raymond VII of Toulouse was supposed to be the last of his house, not to remarry and possibly father another heir[25], let alone to substantially extend his demesne in the Languedoc with the county of Provence. Louis needed the assistance of the pope to prevent this from happening and to find an arrangement for the Provence favourable to the interests of France and the house of the king. Under these circumstances, King Louis' efforts to reconcile the emperor with the pope were jeopardized since the king was not in a position to put serious pressure on the pope. Louis tried nevertheless, but to no avail. Innocent was never to recognize another Hohenstaufen as emperor since in doing so he would have perpetuated the disastrous *unio regni ad imperium*. He rejected Frederick's proposal, referring, as he had done at the preparatory meeting at Lyon, to the countless promises Frederick had not kept in the past. When the king reminded Innocent that it was the duty of a priest not to deny a repentant sinner the grace of salvation and that it was in the interest of his own impending crusade to bring about peace between the emperor and the pope, Innocent reacted irritatedly: he threw his head back and refused to listen to any more of it. Louis was disgusted and angered by the pope's intransigence: '*he had found no humility whatsoever with the servant of the servants of God*', he is reported as saying after this futile interview with the pope[26]. Nevertheless, the interests of France had to prevail over all other considerations and Louis IX ceased to insist on a retraction of the papal sentence against Frederick II in return for Innocent's endorsement of the Provence settlement: Beatrice of Provence was not to marry Raymond VII of Toulouse, but Louis' youngest brother Charles, the count of Anjou[27], who became the nemesis of the house of Hohenstaufen.

---

ment of affinity' (*dominus papa suum concilium celebravit ... cui interfuerunt ... Tholosanus et Provincie comites, qui ibi coram papa tractaverunt de coniugio inter ipsum comitem Tholosanum et ultimam eiusdem comitis Provincie contrahendo, papa dispensaturo super eo propter affinitatis impedimentum*)

25 The only child and heir of Raymond VII, his daughter Joanne, was married to Louis' brother Alphonse, who was understood to succeed Raymond after his demise: see *supra* p. 206, fnt. 33.

26 Matthew Paris, *Chronica maiora* ad ann. 1246, ed. H.R. Luard IV, 524: '*Quod cum dominus Papa erecta et rejecta cervice refutasset, dominus rex Francorum recessit iratus et indignans, eo quod humilitatem quam speraverat in servo servorum Dei minime reperisset*'.

27 Matthew Paris, *Chronica maiora* ad ann. 1246, ed. H.R. Luard IV, 546: '*Disponente igitur et sic volente rege Francorum cum suo consilio, collatus est comitatus Provinciae Karolo fratri regis Francorum natu minori*'.

Heinrich Raspe
'elected' king of
the Romans

Meanwhile, in Germany, a special papal legate, the Bishop-Elect Philip of Ferrara, dispatched to Germany by the pope soon after the council[28], tried to convince the still reluctant Heinrich Raspe to revolt against Frederick openly. Finally, probably only as late as March 1246, the legate and the archbishop of Cologne succeeded to persuade the landgrave by offering him a large amount of money[29]. The king of the Romans, however, was not a papal appointee: the princes of the realm had to decide on the succession of Frederick II, if it was called for, and many of them were not inclined to accept the pope's sentence. Innocent IV had overplayed his hand by exercising a privilege to which only they were entitled: '*it does not pertain to the pope to install or depose an emperor, but to crown the one who is elected by the princes*'[30]. The annoyance of the German princes must have turned into genuine outrage when Innocent ventured to send them a letter in April 1246, instructing them to elect the landgrave of Thuringia as their new king 'unanimously and without any delay' (*unanimiter absque dilationis dispendio*)[31]. The following day, he ordered his legate in Germany, the bishop-elect of Ferrara, to coerce all German princes to comply on pain of excommunication[32]. Even Innocent III had still recognized the privilege of the German princes to freely elect their king in his decretal '*Venerabilem*', subject, that is, to his right of approval[33]. Now they received a papal instruction in advance, ordering them to unanimously elect a papal nominee. No wonder, therefore, that none of the German secular princes attended the diet

---

28 *Chronica regia coloniensis, Cont. 5* ad ann. 1245, MGH *SS rer. Germ.* 18, 287-288: '*modico tempore post concilium celebratum idem papa misit Philippum Ferrariensem electum in Teuthoniam, incitans et exhortans principes ad eligendum novum regem*'. See also Nicolaus de Carbio, *Vita Innocentii IV* cap. 21, ed. Pagnotti 96: '*Consequenter dictus summus pontifex dominum Philippum tunc Ferrariensem electum ad novi regis electionem, qui Frederico succederet, faciendam, in Alamaniam destinavit*'.

29 *Chronica regia coloniensis, Cont. 5* ad ann. 1245, MGH *SS rer. Germ.* 18, 288: '*Qui <scl. electus Ferrariensis> transitum faciens iuxta Coloniam, conductu domni episcopi Coloniensis ad lantgravium Thuringie pervenit; qui eum benigne recipit aspirans ad regnum*'. For the financial contribution by the pope see Matthew Paris, *Chronica maiora* ad ann. 1246, ed. H.R. Luard IV, 544-545: '*Promisit <Papa> igitur eidem pecuniare subsidium copiosum*'; Nicolaus de Carbio, *Vita Innocentii IV* cap. 21, ed. Pagnotti 96 and 97: '*non sine magnis sumptibus et expensis ecclesie*' and '*papa ... xv milia marcharum argenti dicto regi transmisit*' and *Chronica regia coloniensis, Cont. 5* ad ann. 1246, MGH *SS rer. Germ.* 18, 289. Frederick himself believed the legate and the archbishop of Cologne had told the landgrave that he was dead: HB 6.1, 516.

30 *Annales Stadenses* ad ann. 1245, MGH *SS* 16, 369: '*Qua sententia per mundum volante, quidam principum cum multis aliis reclamabant, dicentes: "Ad papam non pertinere, imperatorem eis vel instituere vel destituere, sed electum a principibus coronare"*'.

31 Letter of Innocent IV 'to the archbishops and all other noble princes of Germany entitled to elect the king of the Romans' (*Archiepiscopis et nobilibus viris aliis principibus Theutonie habentibus potestatem eligendi Romanorum regem*): MGH *Epp. saec. xiii* 2, no 159, 120-121(120).

32 MGH *Epp. saec. xiii* 2, no 161, 122.

33 See *supra* p. 155 and 334-336.

convened by the archbishop of Mainz, Siegfried III of Eppstein, for the 'election' of Heinrich Raspe. The diet was to be held on 22 May at Würzburg, but the electors[34] were not welcome there and had to move to nearby Höchheim (now Veitshöchheim). It was there that Heinrich Raspe was 'elected' by two archbishops, the by now well-known conspirators from Mainz and Cologne, under the watchful eye of the papal legate Philip of Ferrara[35]. It was an outright *coup d'état*, similar to the election of Conrad III in 1138[36], and consequently Heinrich Raspe was dubbed a 'Papist King' (*Pfaffenkönig*) even during his lifetime[37]. Innocent's letter 'to the princes of Germany entitled to elect the king of the Romans' (*principibus Theutonie habentibus potestatem eligendi Romanorum regem*) raises the question who were qualified to elect a German king at the time.

Innocent had addressed his instruction to seven German secular princes separately, the king of Bohemia, the dukes of Bavaria, Brabant, Saxony, and Brunswick, and the margraves of Meißen and Brandenburg[38]. The

The German electoral college

---

34   According to the chronicle of Ellenhard (1257-1304) (*Chronicon* ad ann. 1246, MGH *SS* 17, 121), the archbishops of Mainz, Cologne, and Trier and the bishops of Strasbourg, Speier, and Metz 'and others' (*et alii*), meaning other bishops, attended the conference.

35   *Chronica regia coloniensis, Cont. 5* ad ann. 1246, MGH *SS rer. Germ.* 18, 289: '*Eodem tempore domnus archiepiscopus Coloniensis et Moguntinensis iuxta Herbipolim conveniunt et lantgravium Thuringie ibidem presentem eligunt in regem*'. See also *Annales Stadenses* ad ann. 1246, MGH *SS* 16, 369: '*Heinricus lantgravius Thuringiae iuxta Herbipolin in ascensione Dominia Moguntino et Coloniense et quibusdam principibus in regem eligitur*'. The last text mentions the presence of 'some princes' (*quidam principes*), but they cannot have been secular princes of the realm entitled to elect the king. Through coincidence we happen to know precisely who were present at the election of Heinrich Raspe. A charter issued by the new king the day after his election (MGH *DD* HR/W no 3, 6-7(7)) is witnessed by the archbishops of Cologne and Mainz, the papal legate, and a few nobles belonging to the retinue of Heinrich Raspe, who were most certainly not princes of the realm entitled to elect the king. The Saxon world chronicle, long attributed to Eike of Repgow, explicitly states that there was only one prince of the realm present at Heinrich Raspe's election: Heinrich himself (*Sächsische Weltchronik*, ad ann. 1246, MGH *SS* Dt. Chron. 2, 256): 'Then they elected Landgrave Heinrich of Thuringia as king near Würzburg; there was no secular prince present, but for him' (*Do koren se den lantgreven Heinrike van Duringen to koninge bi Wirceburch; dar ne was nen leien vorste, wane he alene*).

36   See *supra* p. 74.

37   *Annales Stadenses* ad ann. 1246, MGH *SS* 16, 370: '*Coeperunt interea illi, qui plenum favorem non habebant ad talia, eundem lantgravium* regem *dicere* clericorum'. Due to his irregular election, Heinrich Raspe is not styled as Henry VII in German historiography. He is always known by his name and sobriquet (Raspe). Henry VII of Germany was count Henry of Luxembourg, who was elected king of the Romans in 1308. For the identity of Henry (VII) see *supra* p. 218, fnt. 38.

38   MGH *Epp. saec. xiii* 2, no 160, 121. This letter was addressed to only one prelate, the bishop of Würzburg, because the pope must have been informed already that the election was to be held in that city. There is, apart from the general instruction to *all* princes of Germany entitled to elect the king of the Romans, no separate instruction from the pope to individual

Saxon lawyer Eike of Repgow, who died shortly before 1246, mentions only three of them in his famous *Sachsenspiegel* as entitled to elect the king: the Count Palatine at the Rhine, who at the time happened to be duke of Bavaria as well, the duke of Saxony, and the margrave of Brandenburg, adding that the king of Bohemia was not qualified 'since he is not a German'[39]. This must be an *indicativus pro imperativo*, since the classic quartet of four German secular princes qualified to elect the king of the Romans is complete when the king of Bohemia is added to this trio. Eike adds three ecclesiastical princes to the electoral board: the archbishops of Mainz, Cologne, and Trier[40]. This electoral college of seven princes of the realm, consisting of the four secular and three ecclesiastical princes just mentioned, was also recognized by the canon lawyers at the time[41]. The number of seven electors seems to have been inspired by Saint Augustine, since that number represents the Holy Spirit[42] inspiring the choice of the electors. Though definitively confirmed by imperial statute only as late as 1356[43], an electoral college consisting of seven princes of the realm may be considered as already

---

German *ecclesiastical* princes, probably because the pope knew the archbishops of Mainz and Cologne were on his side anyway, as was the archbishop of Trier.

39 Eike of Repgow, *Sachsenspiegel*, Lehnrecht 4,2 (MGH *Fontes iuris NS* 1,2, 23): '*Swenne aver de Dudeschen enen koning kesen, unde he to Rome varet to der wiunge , so sint plichtich ... de palenzgreve van dem Rine (des rikes druzte), de hertoge van Sassen (des rikes marscalk) unde de markgreve van Brandeborch (des rikes kemerere), dorch dat deme pavese wetelik si des koninges redeleke kore. De koning van Behemen, des rikes scenke, ne hevet nenen kore, dur dat he nicht dudisch n'is*'. The so-called *Schwabenspiegel*, composed not long after Eike's *Sachsenpiegel*, adds the king of Bohemia, provided his father or mother is German (*Schwabenspiegel*, Lehnrecht 12 (8b), MGH *Fontes iuris N.S.* 4.1, 405): '*der chünig von pehaim ob er ein tewtscher man ist von vater oder von der müter*'.

40 Eike of Repgow, *Sachsenspiegel*, Lehnrecht 4,2, MGH *Fontes iuris NS* 1,2, 23: '*Swenne aver de Dudeschen enen koning kesen, unde he to Rome varet to der wiunge , so sint plichtich ... de biscop van Trire unde van Megenze unde van Kolne*'. See also *Schwabenspiegel* Lehnrecht 12 (8b), MGH *Fontes iuris N.S.* 4.1, 405: '*der pischof von maintze vnd der pischof von trier vnd der von koln*'.

41 Henry of Susa, *Lectura sive apparatus super quinque libris Decretalium* ad X. 1,6,34 (*Venerabilem*), ed. Strassburg 1512, *f.* 61 ro, r. col.: '*Moguntino, Coloniensi, Treverensi episcopis, comiti Rheni, duci Saxonie, marchioni Brandenburgensis, et septimus est dux Bohemie, qui modo est rex. Sed iste secundum quosdam non est necessarius, nisi quando alii discordant, nec habuit istud ius ab antiquo, sed de facto hoc hodie tenet*'.

42 Saint Augustine, *In Joannis evangelium* 21,8, Migne *PL* 35, col. 1963: '*septenario numero significatur Spiritus sanctus*'. See also Isidore of Seville, *Liber numerorum qui in sanctis scripturis occurunt* 8,39 (Migne *PL* 83, col. 187): '*convenienter itaque septenario numero significatur Spiritus sanctus*', a clear citation from St Augustine.

43 In the 'Golden Bull' of the Emperor Charles IV, MGH *Const.* 11, 560-633. The origins of the electoral college are highly controversial. The most likely theory seems to me that the double election of Otto IV and Philip of Swabia in 1198 (see *supra* p. 152-154) inspired a doctrine limiting the number of princes qualified to elect the Roman emperor to seven, with an even distribution of three secular and three ecclesiastical princes, adding a seventh member (the king of Bohemia) in case of a deadlock, as is reported by Hostiensis (see *supra* fnt. 41).

well-established by 1246[44]. Consequently, the election of Heinrich
Raspe was irregular and had to be confirmed by the electors not present at Veitshöchheim on 22 May 1246, just like the irregular election
of Conrad III at Coblenz in 1138 had to be confirmed later at a diet
convened in Bamberg[45]. Accordingly, a diet was called on the day of
the 'election' of Heinrich Raspe to convene at Frankfurt on St Jacobs
day (25 July) next in order to confirm the 'election' of Veitshöchheim[46].

On his way to Frankfurt, Heinrich Raspe was confronted by an army
led by Conrad IV trying to block his progress. In the ensuing battle,
Heinrich was victorious, and Conrad was forced to retreat[47]. It was an
ominous defeat for the young Hohenstaufen prince, now 18 years of
age. His army had mainly consisted of his Swabian vassals, but on the
day of battle two of them, the counts of Würtemberg and Gröningen,
deserted his cause and went over to the enemy[48]. It signalled the impending fall of the house of Hohenstaufen in Germany, since even among its
own Swabian vassals loyalties began to waver[49]. The main incentive to
disloyalty was greed, as it always is. On the diet at Frankfurt, Conrad
was publicly declared an outlaw, not only forfeiting all his imperial
fiefs, most importantly of course the duchy of Swabia itself, but also
all his allodial property[50]. The loss of the latter was a consequence of

Death of
Heinrich Raspe

---

44 Another contemporary, Matthew Paris (*Chronica maiora* ad ann. 1245, ed. H.R. Luard
IV, 455), also has an electoral college of seven princes of the realm: the dukes of Austria,
Bavaria, Saxony, and Brabant and the archbishops of Cologne, Mainz, and Salzburg.
45 See *supra* p. 74.
46 Letter of Heinrich Raspe to the Milanese (HB 6.1, 430-431(431); MGH *Const.* 2, no
348, 456-457(457)): '*in solemnem principum curiam, die electionis nostre a nobis indictam*'. See
also a later letter by Heinrich Raspe to the Milanese (HB 6.1, 451-452): '*Die electionis nostre
a nobis solenni principum indicta curia, in festo beati Jacobi apostoli, Franchenfort ... movimus*'
and *Chronica regia coloniensis, Cont. 5* ad ann. 1246, MGH *SS rer. Germ.* 18, 289: '*prefigentes
curiam regiam apud Frankinvort in festo Iacobi sequente*'.
47 *Chronica regia coloniensis, Cont. 5* ad ann. 1246, MGH *SS rer. Germ.* 18, 289: '*Conradus,
filius imperatoris, victus aufugit*'.
48 See for these details a letter of master Walter of Ocra to the king of England in Matthew
Paris, *Chronica maiora* ad ann. 1246, ed. H.R. Luard IV, 576, adding that the deserters had
been bribed by the pope.
49 For the disloyalty of some Swabian nobles on the day of the battle and after, see also
Ellenhard, *Chronicon* ad ann. 1246, MGH *SS* 17, 121.
50 Innocent IV in a letter to William of Holland (MGH *Epp. saec. xiii* 3, no 186, 155-156):
'Since the nobleman Conrad, a child of the onetime emperor of the Romans Frederick, has not
only been deprived of the duchy of Swabia but also of everything else that is said to belong to
him in the German kingdom by the King of the Romans Henry, your predecessor, and later
also by Your Highness in a general diet at Frankfurt with the consent of the princes of the
realm because he was a persecutor and a manifest enemy of the Church, we do authorize and
confirm that fitting expropriation on apostolic authority' (*Cum ... nobilis vir Conradus natus
condam Fr. olim Romanorum imperatoris tam a clare memorie H. rege Romanorum predecessore
tuo quam a tua celsitudine postmodum in curia generali a te apud Frankeford ex more principum*

the crusade unleashed by the papal legate Philip of Ferrara against all the German supporters of Frederick II, who were excommunicated by operation of law on account of the Lyon sentence for continuing to support the cause of Frederick II[51]. According to canon law (X 5,7,13), they were deprived of their estates by operation of law, allowing all good Catholics to occupy their land with impunity[52]. Heinrich Raspe was determined not to leave the execution of that sentence to the exclusive initiative of private entrepreneurs, like count Ulrich of Würtemberg[53], and took the matter of expropriating the Hohenstaufens into his own hands. He invaded the duchy of Swabia, only to find that Conrad IV had found a formidable ally in Duke Otto II of Bavaria. Conrad had married the duke's daughter Elisabeth on 1 September 1246, soon after his misfortune near Frankfurt[54], causing the papal legate Philip of Ferrara to promptly excommunicate the duke and to place his duchy under interdict[55]. Nevertheless, the duke remained a loyal supporter of his son-in-law, making it hard to believe that he felt that Frederick II was involved in the assassination of his father, Duke Louis I, for which the emperor had been convicted by the pope at Lyon[56]. Once again, as so many times before, papal interference in German politics provoked civil war. In January 1247 Heinrich Raspe was besieging the Swabian city of Ulm. It was mid-winter and Heinrich fell ill there, causing

---

congregata non solum ducatu Suevie set etiam omnibus bonis suis, que ad ipsum dicebantur in regno Alamanie pertinere, eiusdem regni principum accedente consensu ex eo fuerit rite privatus, quod erat persecutor ecclesie et adversarius manifestus … nos, privationem huiusmodi ratam habentes et gratam, illam auctoritate apostolica confirmamus).

51   Shortly after the diet of Frankfurt, the papal legate Philip excommunicated all German prelates who had not attended the diet (HB 6.1, 449-451). He mentions the archbishops of Salzburg and Bremen, the bishops of Passau, Freising, Brixen, Prague, Utrecht, Worms, Konstanz, Augsburg, Paderborn, and Hildesheim and the abbots of St Gallen, Ellwangen, Reichenau, Kempten, and Weissenburg. He must indeed have been very angry about the poor attendance of the diet, putting the lie to his boast that it was attended by 'an immense crowd of prelates and princes' (*immensa turba prelatorum et principum*).

52   See *supra* p. 201 and 336.

53   Count Ulrich of Würtemberg (1226-1265) had deserted King Conrad IV in the battle near Frankfurt. It is from that day on that the star of the house of Würtemberg was steadily rising. Ulrich's descendants became dukes of Würtemberg since 1495 and kings of Würtemberg since 1806, after once more deserting the cause of their emperor (Franz II), who was so disgusted with the behaviour of his German princes that he disbanded the Holy Roman Empire.

54   *Chronica regia coloniensis, Cont. 5* ad ann. 1246, MGH *SS rer. Germ.* 18, 289: '*Conradus, filius imperatoris depositi, paulo postquam victus est, duxit in coniugem filiam ducis Bavarie*'. For the date see *Annales Wormatienses*, ad ann. 1246, MGH *SS* 17, 50.

55   The duke had been close to the papal envoy in Bavaria Albert Behaim in the past (see *supra* p. 308), who wrote the duke a letter advising him to annul the marriage of his daughter. If he did, the papal legate would surely lift his excommunication and withdraw the interdict (MGH *Briefe d. spät. MA* 1, no 133, 479): '*sentencias etiam per legatum excommunicationis et interdicti in vos et terras vestras latas similiter revocabit*'. The duke ignored Albert's advice.

56   See *supra* p. 269 and 377.

him to retire to Wartburg Castle near Eisenach in Thuringia, where he died on 16 February 1247[57]. Innocent IV now had to find another prince willing and able to continue his crusade against the house of Hohenstaufen in Germany.

When Heinrich Raspe lay dying in Wartburg Castle, Frederick II, after successfully suppressing the Sicilian conspiracy[58], decided to lead an army to Germany to come to the rescue of Conrad IV[59]. By April 1247 the emperor was already back in Lombardy, in Parma, from where he sent a letter[60] to the French barons who were sympathetic to him informing them of the recent attempts by the pope to have him assassinated[61] and how the papal legates had convinced Heinrich Raspe to rise against him, at the same time assuring the addressees that he was on his way to Germany to restore order there. A little later, Frederick was in Cremona, where he arranged the marriage of his son Manfred, a child by his mistress Bianca Lancia, to a daughter of the powerful Count Amadaeus of Savoie[62]. This reinforcement of the imperial position in Piedmont must be seen in the context of Frederick's plan to bring his army to Germany via Lyon. He wrote to one of the French barons supporting him that he wanted to go there personally to undo the shame the pope had brought upon him 'against God and the law' (*contra Deum et omnem iustitiam*)[63]. There was little doubt about the

Frederick II loses Parma

---

57 *Annales Erphordenses* ad ann. 1247, MGH *SS rer. Germ.* 42, 101: 'When king Heinrich was on his second expedition in Swabia and Bavaria, he developed internal bleedings, due to too much physical exercise, and quickly returned to Thuringia, to Wartburg Castle, where he died, weakened by his illness, on 16 February' (*Henricus rex, dum secundam in Bawariam atque Sueviam fecisset expeditionem, ex nimio motu passus emorroidas, celeriter in Thuringiam ad castrum Warberc revertebatur; ubi morbo invalescente xiii. Kal. Marcii diem clausit extremum*). See also *Chronica regia coloniensis, Cont. 5* ad ann. 1247, MGH *SS rer. Germ.* 18, 290.

58 See *supra* p. 393-395.

59 For Frederick's plans in February 1247 see the letter of master Walter of Ocra to the king of England (Matthew Paris, *Chronica maiora* ad ann. 1246, ed. H.R. Luard IV, 576): '*imperator ... ordinavit in Alemanniam se conferre*'. See also Frederick's own letter to some of his Sicilian officials (HB 6.2, 577-580(578)) that he was about to leave for Germany 'in view of the obvious expediency' (*evidentis utilitatis gratia*).

60 HB 6.1, 514-518.

61 Frederick also assured the French barons that there had been no attempt of his own to have the pope assassinated, as was contended by Innocent IV. He did not want to make a martyr of Innocent. On the alleged assassination attempt on Innocent IV see Matthew Paris, *Chronica maiora* ad ann. 1246, ed. H.R. Luard IV, 585, who reports a rumour that it was a sham, invented to counter the accusations of Frederick II about similar attempts by the pope.

62 The negotiations were conducted by master Walter of Ocra. His powers of attorney for this occasion and the conditions of the marriage contract are in HB 6.1, 526-528.

63 HB 6.1, 528-529: '*Quoniam ad offerendam purgationem super notam infamie qua in congregatione prelatorum apud Lugdunum contra Deum et omnem iustitiam iste summus pontifex nos notavit ... infallibiter Lugdunum disponimus nos transferre*'. See also a letter of Frederick II to the king of France of July 1247, HB 6.2, 554-555(554). This letter raises an intriguing

way Frederick intended to make good his disgrace[64] and Innocent must have realized he was in grave danger[65]. He was saved by his agents in Piacenza, the same men who had conspired to assassinate Frederick in the previous year[66].

The city of Parma was still in imperial hands in April 1247, but Innocent IV had many supporters there. Some of them, including his brother-in-law Bernardo Rubeo, had fled to Piacenza after the disclosure of their conspiracy to assassinate the emperor in 1246 and were plotting there to take control over their native city. In June 1247 they saw the opportunity for which they had been waiting. Frederick's son Enzio was occupied elsewhere, besieging a castle near Brescia, and the exiles from Parma now decided to make their move. A small band of exiles left Piacenza, only some 35 miles (60 km.) from Parma, to take their city by force of arms. Close to Parma, at the crossing of the Taro river, they were met by troops from Parma commanded by the imperial *podestà*, Henrico Testa, who had been warned of their imminent attack. In the ensuing struggle, the *podestà* was killed and his soldiers panicked and fled, believing that reinforcements from Milan and Piacenza were near to assist the exiles. On their arrival in Parma, the exiles met no further resistance and so it happened that the strategically important city of Parma defected from the cause of the emperor. The papal legate in Lombardy, Gregorio de Montelongo, reacted immediately, rushing to Parma with a force of 800 knights from Milan and Piacenza and the papal brother-in-law Bernardo Rubeo, thus considerably reinforcing the papal hold over the city[67]. Frederick II was in Turin, on his way to Lyon, when he heard of the defection of Parma. He instantly decided to break off his campaign to Lyon and Germany and angrily dashed to Parma, because he believed he would completely lose all of Lombardy,

---

question, since it refers to an earlier letter by Frederick, informing King Louis of his plan to go to Lyon in the same words as Frederick's letter to the French baron, Count Hugo de Chatillon, just mentioned. Did King Louis approve of Frederick's plan? It was even said at the time (*Annales Ianuenses* (Bartolomeo scriba) ad ann. 1247, MGH *SS* 18, 221) that Frederick went to Lyon 'at the instance of the king of France' (*ad instantiam domni regis Francorum*), suggesting that King Louis wanted a reconciliation between pope and emperor in view of his impending crusade.

64   Salimbene, *Cronica* ad ann. 1247, MGH *SS* 32, 189: 'he <Frederick II> went to Lyon to arrest the pope and the cardinals' (*Ibat enim Lugdunum, ut caperet cardinales et papam*).

65   For this see Nicolas of Carbio, *Vita Innocentii IV* cap. 23, ed. Pagnotti 99: 'In those days Frederick came to Turin, maliciously plotting with the count of Savoie and other barons supporting him against the pope, whom he deceitfully planned to entrap at Lyon' (*Eodem vero tempore Taurinum venerat Fredericus, ubi, cum comite Sabaudie et aliis quibusdam baronibus adherentibus, nequiter machinans contra summum pontificem, ipsum Lugduni circumvenire fraudulentissime procurabat*).

66   See *supra* p. 392-393.

67   For these events see *Annales Placentini Gibellini* ad ann. 1247, MGH *SS* 18, 494.

if he definitively lost that city[68]. The subsequent siege of Parma was the turning point of Frederick's career, ending in disaster on 18 February 1248[69].

Meanwhile, in Germany, the acting papal legate there, Philip of Ferrara, was replaced after the demise of Heinrich Raspe by Peter Capocci, the cardinal-deacon of S. Georgio in Velabro, with the instruction to find a suitable substitute for that unfortunate German prince[70]. It was not an easy commission, since none of the great German princes was inclined to dance to the tune of the pope as conveniently as the landgrave of Thuringia. Significantly, therefore, the legate first turned his attention to a complete outsider, Richard of Cornwall, with his close family ties to the Guelph party in Germany, but Richard declined the offer[71]. He had been received warmly at the court of his brother-in-law, Frederick II, even trying to broker a compromise between the pope and Frederick[72]. Richard must have regarded the offer as an insult to his honour. The next person to be approached was a representative of the lower Rhine aristocracy, Count Otto II of Gelre, who declined the offer, as did his neighbour (and uncle), the mighty Duke Henry II of Brabant, father-in-law to Heinrich Raspe. It may have been at their suggestion, that the legate and the powerful archbishop of Cologne, Conrad of Hochstaden, finally turned to Count William II of Holland (1227-1256). William was a nephew of the duke of Brabant as well as of the count of Gelre[73]. Unlike their relatives in Brabant, the counts of Holland, though of ancient lineage, were minor German magnates, not belonging to the estate of princes of the realm (*Reichsfürstenstand*): William's ancestor, Count Dirk VII, had offered 5000 marcs of silver to Frederick 'Barbarossa' in 1191 to be raised to that lofty estate, but the offer was refused[74]. The fact that a young and unexperienced count

William of
Holland
'elected' king of
the Romans

---

68 *Annales Ianuenses* (Bartolomeo scriba) ad ann. 1247, MGH *SS* 18, 221: '*Statim ipse domnus Fredericus videns et cognoscens quod si civitatem Parme amitteret, extra Lombardiam esset ex toto, et nichil proficeret cum domno papa, rediit continuo versus Parmam, veniens cum furore*'. It is yet another compelling proof that Italian affairs had priority over German affairs in Frederick's mind.
69 See *infra* p. 407-408.
70 For the appointment of Cardinal Capocci see Nicolas of Carbio, *Vita Innocentii IV* cap. 22, ed. Pagnotti 97 and the letter of Innocent IV to the Milanese in HB 6.1, 510-512(511).
71 For this and what follows see Matthew Paris, *Chronica maiora* ad ann. 1251, ed. H.R. Luard V, 201.
72 See *supra* p. 300.
73 William was the oldest son of Duke Henry's sister Machteld, whereas Count Otto of Gelre was a son of Duke Henry's other sister Margaret.
74 Gislebert of Mons, *Chronicon Hanoniense* ad ann. 1191, ed. Vanderkindere, Bruxelles 1904, 265-266: '*Comes Hollandensis ... domino imperatori quinque milia marchas puri argenti, si princeps fieret, largiri promittebat*'. Count Floris III of Holland, Dirk's father, still belonged

from the outlying districts of the Empire was now offered the august title of 'king of the Romans' and considered as the future successor to Augustus, Constantine, and Charlemagne is indicative of the rapid decline of the prestige of that title. William was 'elected' on 3 October 1247 in a conference at Wordingen, near Cologne, by the archbishops of Cologne, Mainz, and Trier and only one secular prince of the realm, his uncle, the duke of Brabant, all under the watchful eye of the papal legate, Cardinal Capocci[75]. It was a reprise of the charade at Veitshöchheim in 1246, but Pope Innocent was very pleased with 'the plant he had sown with his own hands' (*planta nostra nostrisque manibus consita*) as he later asserted[76]. The young Dutch seedling made little impact in the early years of his reign. Effectively, his sphere of influence in the Empire was limited to the dioceses of the archbishops who had promoted him and even there his authority was restricted. It was only after a siege of six months that William, supported by the archbishop of Cologne and the papal legate, was finally able to bring the city of Aachen over to his side, allowing him to be crowned there by the archbishop of Cologne on 1 November 1248[77]. It was a decisive occasion. Heinrich Raspe had not been crowned at Aachen, but – more importantly – neither had Conrad IV. Frederick II had deliberately kept his

---

to the estate of princes of the Empire. He is mentioned among the '*principes nostri*' testifying to the peace of Venice between Frederick I 'Barbarossa' and the king of Sicily in 1177: MGH *DD*, Fred. I, no 694, 218. Shortly after this event, in 1180, Frederick 'Barbarossa' reduced the number of princes of the realm to dukes, margraves, and landgraves holding their territories from the emperor directly, excluding counts, such as the count of Holland. Some of them, such as the count of Hainault for example (in 1184), were later elevated to the higher estate of prince of the realm, but very rarely.

75 *Chronica regia coloniensis, Cont. 5* ad ann. 1247, MGH *SS rer. Germ.* 18, 291: '*Ipso anno Petrus legatus et multi episcopi, videlicet Conradus Coloniensis, Syfridus Moguntinensis, Arnoldus Treverensis, Gerardus Bremensis, et multi alii episcopi et dux Brabantie cum multis comitibus in campo iuxta villam Worinch conventum faciunt et novum regem eligunt Wilhelmum comitem Hollandie*'. The contemporary *Cronica Floridi Horti* (Menco) ad ann.1247, ed. Jansen and Janse, Hilversum 1991, 366, contends that 'the other princes entitled to elect were either present themselves or had sent letters excusing their absence' (*aliis principibus, ad quos pertinet electio ... vel presentibus vel se per literam excusantibus*). This is clearly wrong, since there were no other secular princes present at Wordingen and it is very doubtful that they excused themselves. Innocent IV sent a letter of thanks (MGH *Const.* 2 no 355, 462) to the 'German princes' (*principes teutonici*) having elected William at Wordingen. It was addressed to the archbishops of Cologne, Mainz, Trier, and Bremen; to the bishops of Würzburg, Strasbourg, and Münster, and the *electus* of Speyer. The letter was sent to only three secular magnates, the duke of Brabant and the counts of Gelre and Loon. The counts were not princes of the realm.

76 Innocent IV in a letter to Archbishop Gerard of Mainz, published in Gudenus, *Codex diplomaticus exhibens anecdota Moguntiaca*, Göttingen 1743, no 271, 645): '*Wilhelmum regem Romanorum illustrem, utpote plantam nostram, nostrisque manibus consitam, per Dei gratiam et provectam, dilectionis affectu prosequimur*'.

77 On the siege of Aachen and the coronation of William of Holland see *Chronica regia coloniensis, Cont. 5* ad ann. 1248, MGH *SS rer. Germ.* 18, 292-293.

son Conrad IV in a subordinate position by not having him crowned and consecrated, most likely due to the unfortunate experiences with his other son, Henry (VII), who had indeed been crowned and consecrated as *rex Romanorum*. This deliberate omission now began, slowly but surely, to erode the position of Conrad IV in Germany. Cardinal Capocci must have realized this. His work in Germany was done and he returned to Lyon to report to Innocent IV[78].

When William of Holland was elected king of the Romans near Cologne, Frederick II was laying siege to Parma. His decision to besiege that city, rather than leaving it to his son Enzio and his other Italian captains and proceeding to Germany himself as he had originally planned, is probably the most serious strategic mistake of his life. It may be that by then he had been informed of the demise of Heinrich Raspe when he made that fatal decision in April 1247 and consequently believed that the immediate danger to the interests of his house in Germany had subsided as a result, but his decision to remain in the Italian kingdom and to lay siege to Parma, allowed his opponents in Germany to take the initiative there. The siege of a city, moreover, was always a risky adventure in this era, since the military advantage lay with the defender rather than the besieger. If it failed, the loss of military prestige was enormous, as Frederick II had experienced himself after his embarrassing fiascos before the walls of Brescia in 1238 and Viterbo in 1243[79]. The city of Parma was much bigger than the other two cities and defended by Innocent's most experienced warrior, the papal legate Gregorio de Montelongo himself.

Victoria

Frederick spared no trouble and expenses to subdue Parma. He even built an entire town in the immediate vicinity of Parma to lodge his army and his headquarters, providing it with all the luxuries and facilities to which he and his soldiers were accustomed. The new town was called Victoria. It was a fatal choice of name, since it made the siege of Parma a matter of prestige for both parties concerned, the pope and the emperor, comparable to the siege of Alessandria in 1175[80] and the siege of Stalingrad many centuries later. Frederick initially believed he could take the city easily, but he was soon disappointed. The siege dragged on for months on end, creating a dangerous routine with the besiegers that became fatal to them. On the morning of 18 February 1248 Frederick left Victoria for his favourite pastime, hunting with falcons. It was to be just another day of the siege. It was this moment of carelessness,

---

78 *Chronica regia coloniensis, Cont. 5* ad ann. 1248, MGH *SS rer. Germ.* 18, 293: '*Post hec legatus ad curiam pape revertitur*'.
79 See *supra* p. 288 and 314.
80 See *supra* p. 121.

'the mother of all disasters' (*detrimentorum mater*), that became his undoing[81]. He had left the Margrave Lancia, a relative of his mistress Bianca, in command of Victoria and Lancia fell into a trap laid by the papal legate. After Frederick and his retinue had left Victoria on their hunting party, a considerable cavalry unit was sighted leaving Parma and Lancia decided to intercept it with his cavalry. It was a diversion, luring the heavy imperial cavalry out of Victoria and leaving it almost undefended, since much of the infantry was engaged elsewhere. It was the opportunity for which the legate De Montelongo had been waiting. He led a sortie from Parma with all the troops at his disposal there. Victoria was stormed, the imperial troops still there were slaughtered, and the City of Victory itself was plundered and burned to the ground. The imperial treasure and Frederick's personal belongings, his crown and many other valuable items, such as his personal library, fell into the hands of the men of Parma[82]. The emperor helplessly watched it all happening from a distance. After this disaster all hope of conquering Parma in the near future was gone and the emperor and what was left of his army were forced to fall back on Cremona. He had been wasting precious time his enemies in Germany were using to their advantage. On the very day Victoria fell, William of Holland and the papal legate were in Utrecht, where the legate preached a crusade against the city of Aachen, raising the army that was to enable William to be crowned there later on in that year[83].

Frederick lost more than his personal prestige and his crown on that fateful day near Parma. Among the imperial staff, left behind in Victoria when Frederick went out hunting, was his personal confidant and long-time advisor master Thaddaeus of Suessa. Thaddaeus was captured while defending his master's treasure, his hands were amputated, and he died some days later[84]. The loss of Thaddaeus of Suessa was irreparable. He had been the mainstay of imperial diplomacy after

81 *Annales Placentini Gibellini* ad ann. 1248, MGH *SS* 18, 496: '*cum nichil adversi suspicaretur, securitas, que semper detrimentorum mater est, non modicum dampnum ei peperit*'.
82 For the details of the capture and sack of Victoria see *Annales Placentini Gibellini* ad ann. 1248, MGH *SS* 18, 496-497; *Chronicon Parmense* ad ann. 1248, *RIS*² 9.9, 18; *Annales Ianuenses* (Bartolomeo scriba) ad ann. 1248, MGH *SS* 18, 224-225 and Salimbene, *Cronica* ad ann. 1247, MGH *SS* 32, 203-205.
83 *Chronica regia coloniensis, Cont. 5* ad ann. 1247, MGH *SS rer. Germ.* 18, p. 292: '*novus rex cum legato descendens in inferiors partes Rheni, venerunt in Traiectum, legato exhortante et inducente homines per quos transierat ad crucis assumptionem contra civitatem Aquensem*'. The legate issued a charter at Utrecht on 18 February 1248: Van Mieris, *Groot Charterboek der Graaven van Holland* I, Leyden 1753, 247.
84 *Annales Placentini Gibellini* ad ann. 1248, MGH *SS* 18, 496: '*multos ex ipsis occiderunt et iudicem Tadaeum*'; *Chronicon Parmense* ad ann. 1248, *RIS*² 9.9, 18: '*Judex Tadeus de Suasa in captura predicta remansit semivivus com manibus amputatis*'; *Annales Ianuenses* (Bartolomeo

the demise of Grandmaster Hermann of Salza[85] and Frederick could scarcely miss his experience in the diplomatic and legal battles which were to be fought in the years to come. Another member of his staff captured at Victoria was Frederick's personal physician. He escaped the fate of master Thaddaeus and was handed over to the papal legate who had plans for him, as we shall see shortly.

It is futile to enter into the details of Frederick's further campaigns in the Italian *regno* after his fiasco near Parma. He spent a good deal of the year 1248 to take his revenge on that city by ransacking the surrounding countryside, demonstrating that the emperor missed a clear objective[86]. The Lombards, excellently commanded by Gregorio de Montelongo, now had become experts in a war of attrition, drawing their enemy ever deeper into a military quagmire at great cost to Frederick's treasury and with no end in sight. The enduring war in the Italian kingdom was a matter of increasing concern to the king of France, who was about to depart for the Holy Land to fulfil his crusading vows. Louis decided to make one last effort to reconcile pope and emperor shortly before his departure for the Orient. In July 1248, on his way to Aigues-Mortes, a new Mediterranean harbour built by the king for the sole purpose of avoiding the Italian war zone, he visited Pope Innocent in Lyon to try to convince the pope one last time that the protracted war in Italy imperilled the success of his impending crusade and that peace between the emperor and the Church had to be restored. Innocent proved as impossibly intransigent as he had been at Cluny in 1245[87], whereupon Louis warned the pope that 'if the affair of the Holy Land goes wrong, you will be held responsible' (*tibi imputetur, si negotium Terrae Sanctae impediatur*)[88]. In August 1248 Louis sailed from Aigues-Mortes for the Holy Land and disaster[89].

Louis IX warns the pope

---

scriba) ad ann. 1248, MGH *SS* 18, 225: '*Iudicem Thadeum occiderunt, qui cameram custodiebat*'.

85   See *supra* p. 296.

86   On one of these raids, imperial troops, mainly consisting of exiles from Parma loyal to the emperor, encountered a detachment from Parma, headed by none other than the papal brother-in-law Bernardo Rubeo. The imperial troops were victorious, captured Bernardo and cut him to pieces on the spot: *Annales Placentini Gibellini* ad ann. 1248, MGH *SS* 18, 497. See on the death of Bernardo Rubeo also *Chronicon Parmense* ad ann. 1248, *RIS²* 9.9, 18, reporting that the Parmese retaliated by executing four of the prisoners they had made at Victoria.

87   See *supra* p. 397.

88   For this episode see Matthew Paris, *Chronica maiora* ad ann. 1248, ed. H.R. Luard V, 22-23(23); *Annales Ianuenses* (Bartolomeo scriba) ad ann. 1248, MGH *SS* 18, 225 and a letter of Frederick II to the king of England, HB 6.2, 644-646.

89   Joinville, *Histoire de St Louis* 28,125, ed. Wailly, 54. Joinville accompanied the king on his crusade and is the most important eyewitness to the Seventh Crusade.

The Seventh
Crusade

The history of the Seventh Crusade can be told in one short sentence: it was a reprise of the disastrous Fifth Crusade[90]. Its target was Egypt and the port of Damietta, rather than Palestine itself. As in the Fifth Crusade, the crusaders succeeded in taking Damietta, but things went terribly wrong after that temporary success. The Fifth Crusade had ended in disaster at Mansurah in 1221 and the Seventh Crusade ended in catastrophe after Louis IX had lost his brother Robert of Artois in a battle at Mansurah and was surrounded by superior Egyptian forces on his way back to Damietta, forcing the king to surrender (6 April 1250). Unfortunately for the French crusaders, the grandson of Frederick's friend Al-Kamil, Turanshah, was less merciful than his grandfather had been. The main part of the crusading army was slaughtered on the spot, sparing only the king, his two surviving brothers Alphonse and Charles, the most distinguished nobles and some lucky knights[91], all of them to be ransomed for exorbitant sums of money. Thanks to the efforts of his wife, Queen Margaret, who accompanied her husband on his crusade but had been left behind in Damietta (she was heavily pregnant), Louis was able to raise the first instalment of the enormous ransom (400,000 pounds of silver) that was put on his head and was allowed to join his wife at Acre in Palestine[92]. What was left of the army stayed behind in Egypt as collateral for the rest of the ransom. After paying the last instalment, Louis was joined in Acre by most of his surviving nobles and held a conference to determine what was to be done now. The king decided not to desert the nobility of Palestine and stayed in the Holy Land for another three years[93]. He did, however, sent

---

90 See *supra* p. 225-226. There is no better summary of the history of the crusades than Gibbon's observation (*Decline and Fall* chap. 59) that 'a regular story of the crusades would exhibit the perpetual return of the same causes and effects, and the frequent attempts for the defence or recovery of the Holy Land would appear so many faint and unsuccessful copies of the original'.

91 King Louis' biographer Joinville tells (*Histoire de St Louis* 65, 326, ed. Wailly, 136) that he only escaped the slaughter because it was accidentally found out that he was a relative of Frederick II, whose prestige among the Muslims saved his life. Joinville's mother, Béatrice d'Auxonne, was a niece of the emperor.

92 For the conditions of the release of the king see Joinville, *Histoire de St Louis* 70, 359, ed. Wailly, 149. By comparison: King Richard of England was released by Henri VI at a ransom of 'just' 100,000 pounds of silver (*supra* p. 146). Queen Margaret left for Acre in Palestine after giving birth to a son at Damietta. She named the child 'Tristan', after the sad circumstances under which it was born. Tristan died in Tunisia in 1270.

93 Most of the nobles advised the king to return to France as soon as possible, but the king decided differently. His return was not immediately required, he said, 'since the queen <meaning his mother> has enough men to defend it' ('car madame la royne a bien gent pour le deffendre' (Joinville, *Histoire de St Louis* 85, 436, ed. Wailly, 182)). Louis had appointed his mother as regent during his absence. The king only decided to return to France after news of the demise of Blanche de Castile (1252) reached him. She was an extraordinary woman.

his two brothers Alphonse and Charles back to France immediately[94]. They were to personally deliver an urgent message from the king to the pope. Louis had told Innocent IV on their last meeting at Lyon, shortly before his departure for the Holy Land, that if his crusade should fail, the pope would be held accountable. The king must have been disgusted that he had fought the Saracenes in the Orient, at enormous cost to himself and the kingdom of France, while the pope was calling for a crusade against the emperor and fellow-Christians in Germany and Italy. Alphonse and Charles were to inform Innocent IV that, if he would not make his peace with Frederick II, they were to drive him out of Lyon since he was clearly blinded by his hatred of the emperor and completely indifferent to the honour of the faith. The brothers did as they were told and delivered their message to the pope at Lyon in the summer of 1250[95]. It really shocked Innocent, since Louis' guarantee of his personal safety was about to be withdrawn. He immediately sent a message to the king of England with a request for asylum in Bordeaux, in the French part of Henry's kingdom[96].

---

94   Joinville, *Histoire de St Louis* 86, 438, ed. Wailly, 182.
95   Matthew Paris, *Chronica maiora* ad ann. 1250, ed. H.R. Luard V, 175: 'The aforementioned counts, together with the duke of Burgundy, who accompanied them, went immediately to the pope, as they were instructed by the king. They were to insist with great urgency, rather than flattery, that the pope had to readmit the repentant Frederick back to peace with the Church in order to induce him <Frederick> to come quickly to the rescue of the king, who was in an almost desperate situation, and that, if he did not, the duke and the counts would remove him from his see in Lyon since he was blinded by hatred and completely indifferent to the honour of the Christian faith' (*Memorati igitur comites simul cum Duce Burgundiae, qui cum eis venerat, sicut eis per regem injunctum fuerat, Papam ilico adierunt, persuadentes efficaciter, non palpando, ut … Frethericum … ad pacem ecclesiae revocans humilatum, ipsum ad hoc induceret, ut ipsi regi jam paene desperato succursum competens conferat et festinum; alioquin, ipsi dux et comites dominum Papam, tamquam in odio obstinatum et de honore Christianae fidei minime curantem, a sede removeant Lugdunensi*).
96   Matthew Paris, *Chronica maiora* ad ann. 1250, ed. H.R. Luard V, 188: 'At the same time the pope asked the king of England by way of official ambassadors for permission to take up his residence in Bordeaux, his city in Gascony, since the brothers of the king of France had visited him with the demand of the said king <Louis> and themselves that he <the pope> was to make peace with the repentant Frederick who had humbly offered satisfaction to the Church, since he was devoted to the honour of the universal Church. The brothers of the aforementioned king, the counts of Poitiers and Provence, had, moreover, blamed him that the whole disaster was brought about by the pope's selfishness' (*Tempore quoque sub eodem, missis sollempnibus nuntiis, dominus papa postulavit dominum regem Angliae, ut liceret ei saltem apud Burdegalim, civitatem suam in Wasconia, commorari. Fratres enim domini regis Francorum eum districte convenerant, rogantes ex parte dicti regis et sua, ut pacem iniret cum Fretherico humiliato et satisfactionem ecclesiae humiliter offerenti, sicut honorem universalis ecclesiae diligebat. Imponebant etiam illi dicti regis fratres, videlicet Pictaviae et Provinciae comites, quod per papae avaritiam totum evenit infortunium memoratum*). See for an earlier request for asylum in Bordeaux *supra* p. 324, fnt. 97.

Another
assassination
attempt

While Louis of France was away in Egypt fighting the infidel, Frederick II was going through a difficult period as well, suffering personal losses which must have seriously affected his state of mind. Early in 1249 there had been yet another attempt to assassinate him. The emperor informed all the other European princes about it, exposing the disgraceful means resorted to by the pope and his minions to satisfy their presumptuous lust for power[97]. The circumstances were shocking indeed. The perpetrator was Frederick's own personal physician. The man had been captured by the Parmese at Victoria and handed over to the papal legate Gregorio de Montelongo, who succeeded in persuading his prisoner to assassinate Frederick II. The physician was subsequently exchanged for a nobleman from Parma captured by Frederick. The plan to poison the emperor was eventually detected just in time on the basis of intercepted correspondence and the physician was caught in the act of preparing the deadly draught that was to kill the emperor[98]. The physician was to suffer a gruesome execution. Even more shocking to Frederick must have been the revelations about the misconduct of one of his closest confidants, one of the people he had trusted for years, the archchancellor of his Sicilian kingdom, none other than Piero della Vigna. Piero della Vigna was arrested about the same time as Frederick's physician, in February 1249, suggesting a link with the assassination attempt[99]. There was no such link, since Piero della Vigna was charged with corruption and embezzlement of public funds (*peculatus*), as can be inferred from a letter by Frederick II to his son-in-law, the count of Caserta[100].

The death of
Piero della
Vigna

Embezzlement of public funds by civil servants was a crime punishable by death according to Frederick's code, but allowing for a certain discretion on the part of the king: he could show leniency[101]. But there was no reason to do so in the case of Piero. He had not only forsworn his oath of office but also violated the integrity (*probitas*) that was the essence of the ethos of the royal Sicilian civil service. It was his civil service that had enabled the king to withstand the blow of the Sicilian baronial conspiracy of 1246 without any serious damage to his administration.

---

97   HB 6.2, 705-707, for all the subsequent details.
98   HB 6.2, 706: '*patenter in facinore deprehensus ... etiam per litteras interceptas*'.
99   For this suggestion see Matthew Paris, *Chronica maiora* ad ann. 1249, ed. H.R. Luard V, 68.
100   HB 6.2, 699-701.
101   *Liber augustalis*, 1,36,1, MGH *Const. 2, Suppl.*, 189: 'Officials of the state or judges who have embezzled public monies during the term of their administration are guilty of the crime of embezzlement and should be punished by death, unless they are granted royal clemency' (*Officiales rei publice vel iudices, qui tempore administrationis pecunias publicas subtraxerunt, obnoxii sint crimine peculatus, capite puniantur, nisi eis regia pietas indulserit*) (Transl. Powell).

The higher officials in the civil service, men like Thaddaeus of Suessa and Walter of Ocra, were well aware of the fact that baronial resistance was not only directed against the king, but also against them, men who had risen to high office by sheer competence rather than noble birth. There was a strong *esprit de corps* among the royal officials focusing on the integrity with which they served the king. It was by virtue of their *probitas* that they excelled and formed a true nobility of merit rather than of descent[102]. This was the reason why there was to be no clemency for Piero. His crime had embarrassed the king himself by adding fuel to the rumour of corruption, always threatening the reputation of a powerful civil service. In spite of his service of more than twenty years as diplomat, legal counsellor, ghost writer, and advisor, the emperor was not inclined to show mercy. Piero's eyes were gouged, and he was transported to a tower in the little Tuscan town of San Miniato to await his execution. It was there that the great chancellor took his own life[103].

Even more painful to Frederick II than the loss of Piero della Vigna and Thaddaeus of Suessa must have been the loss of his son Enzio, later in 1249. Enzio was Frederick's favourite and also his most active warrior, on whom he began to rely more and more in recent years, having made him king of Sardinia and his viceroy in the Italian kingdom (*legatus totius Italiae*)[104]. In the early summer of 1249, Enzio proceeded with an army from Cremona to the Romagna to come to the assistance of the city of Modena against her ancient rival Bologna, traditionally belonging to the Lombard League and accordingly now siding with the papal party. The Bolognese army was commanded by the former bishop-elect of Bologna, Ottaviano Ubaldini ('il Cardinale'[105]), a Tuscan nobleman who had been raised to the cardinalate by Innocent IV in 1244 and appointed papal legate in the Romagna in 1247. In May 1249 the men from Bologna were engaged taking a bridge over the river Panaro crossing the via Emilia near a village called Fossalta. It was

Enzio imprisoned in Bologna

---

102   For the class consciousness of royal civil servants see the anonymous letter addressed to Piero della Vigna and Thaddaeus of Suessa printed in the *pièces justificatives* of A. Huillard-Bréholles, *Vie et correspondance de Pierre de la Vigne*, Paris 1865, no 20 (319).

103   *Annales Placentini Gibellini* ad ann. 1249, MGH *SS* 18, 498: '*imperator ... ad civitatem Pisis accessit, duxitque secum Petrum de Vinea cui oculos de capite eruere fecit in Sancto Miniato, ubi suam vitam finivit*'. See also Matthew Paris, *Chronica maiora* ad ann. 1249, ed. H.R. Luard V, 69: '*ad columpnam, ad quem allegatus fuerat, caput fortiter allidens, seipsum excerebravit*'. Piero's suicide has been commemorated by Dante, *Inferno* 13, 58-78.

104   Frederick II was heavily relying on Enzio and his other sons by now, a sure sign that the assassination attempts, and the conspiracies recently uncovered were beginning to affect his mind: his son Manfred was with him in Victoria, his illegitimate son Frederick of Antioch was appointed his governor in Tuscany and another of his sons born out of wedlock, Riccardo, count of Chieti, was made governor of the Romagna and the duchy of Spoleto (*Annales Placentini Gibellini* ad ann. 1247, MGH *SS* 18, 496).

105   Dante, *Inferno* 10, 120.

there that Enzio's army met Cardinal Ubaldini's main force on 26 May. Enzio was defeated, taken prisoner and transported to Bologna, where he was imprisoned in a small palazzo, adjoining the impressive palazzo of the *podestà* of Bologna[106], where he was to remain as a hostage for the rest of his living days, dying there in 1272. The battle of Fossalta had even more serious consequences than the fiasco at Parma. Frederick lost control over the Romagna because Modena was forced to change sides as a consequence[107]: all the major cities in the Romagna along the via Aemilia were now under papal control.

The demise of Frederick II

Shortly before the battle of Fossalta, Frederick II had departed for Apulia, where he suffered yet another personal loss, the death of his son Richard, count of Chieti[108]. He found solace in hunting and working on his ornithological masterpiece, 'The Art of Hunting with Birds' (*De arte venandi cum avibus*), but his health began to fail. He had been ill in 1249, suffering from lupus[109], but he recovered, writing to his former son-in-law Ezzelino da Romano[110] that *we are well and restoring the limbs of our body, weary from the toils of war, in the sweet delight of our kingdom*[111]. In Apulia he learnt about the misfortune of Louis IX in Egypt, immediately reacting by sending letters to King Louis and the Egyptian sultan offering his services as mediator[112]. At the same time, he wrote a letter to the king of Castile about that 'deplorable incident' (*miserabilis casus*), emphasizing that it would never have

---

106   For the battle of Fossalta see *Corpus Chronicorum Bononiensium* ad ann 1249, *RIS²* 18.1, 126 (Cron. Villani)); *Annales Placentini Gibellini* ad ann. 1249, MGH *SS* 18, 498 and the *Annales Ianuenses* (Bartolomeo scriba) ad ann. 1249, MGH *SS* 18, 227.

107   For the defection of Modena after Fossalta see *Annales Placentini Gibellini* ad ann. 1249, MGH *SS* 18, 499: '*Mutinenses, absque rege Encio et Cremonensibus qui capti erant eorum servitio, cum Bononiensibus pacti fuerunt*'.

108   For Frederick's departure for Apulia around March 1249 see *Annales Placentini Gibellini* ad ann. 1249, MGH *SS* 18, 498: '*in portu Pisis in galeis intravit, et navigio perrexit in regnum*'. For the demise of Richard in 1249 see Matthew Paris, *Chronica maiora* ad ann. 1249, ed. H.R. Luard V, 78: '*eodemque tempore mortuus est quidam alius Fretherici filius naturalis in Apulia*'. Nothing is heard of Richard after 1249, so he must be the son referred to by Matthew Paris. Richard, Enzio, Frederick of Antioch, and Manfred all were born out of wedlock and by different women.

109   Matthew Paris, *Chronica maiora* ad ann. 1249, ed. H.R. Luard V, 78: '*Fredericus percussus est morbo, qui dicitur lupus*'.

110   Ezzelino had been married to Frederick's (illegitimate) daughter Selvaggia, who had died in 1244.

111   The letter survives in the collection of letters by Piero della Vigna. *Petri de Vineis Friderici II. Imp. Epistolarum Libri VI*, ed. J.R. Iselin, Basle 1740, Tom. 1, Lib. 2, cap. 25 (287): '*Prospere vivimus et corporis nostri membra, bellicis hactenus fatigata laboribus, deliciosa regni nostri dulcedine restauramus*'.

112   The letters do not survive but are explicitly mentioned by Joinville, *Histoire de St Louis* 87, 443, ed. Wailly, 185. On Frederick's prestige in Egypt at the time see *supra* p. 410, fnt. 91.

occurred if he or his sons had been present there, but that had, unfortunately, been impossible, due to the continuing threat of the pope to his
Sicilian kingdom[113]. Frederick was not only referring to the attack on
his kingdom organized by Gregory IX during his absence in Palestine
in 1229[114], but also to the clear and present danger of another invasion of papal forces into his kingdom. In April 1249 Pope Innocent
IV had decided to commit the papal war effort on the Sicilian front[115]
to a central command, supervised by Cardinal Peter Capocci, the rising star in the *curia* ever since his successes in Germany. All acting
papal legates there were either summarily dismissed[116] or ignominiously demoted as mere lieutenants of the new papal generalissimo[117],
demonstrating Innocent's ruthless behaviour towards his cardinals.
Obviously, the pope believed that Frederick's position in the middle
of the Italian peninsula was weakened by his recent misfortunes at
Parma and Fossalta to such an extent that an invasion into the Sicilian
kingdom itself seemed a viable objective. He was to be disappointed.
The first sign of Frederick's recovery and military resilience was the
complete destruction of Benevento, a papal enclave within the Sicilian
kingdom, in January 1250[118], later in that year (18 August) followed by
an important victory of imperial forces from Cremona under the command of a new and promising warlord in Frederick's service, Oberto
Palavicini, over a Parmese army, precisely at the spot where Victoria
once stood[119], and yet another in September by his newly appointed
legate in the Marche, Count Walter of Manupello, over none other
than Cardinal Peter Capocci himself, who barely escaped capture[120].
None of these imperial successes was 'decisive', but they put a halt to
the papal plans to invade the Sicilian kingdom in the near future, while

113   Frederick II to King Ferdinand III of Castilia, HB 6.2, 769-771.
114   See *supra* p. 241-242.
115   The Campagna, the Romagna, The Marche of Ancona, and the duchy of Spoleto, as well
as the Papal State proper.
116   The bishop of Ostia, Cardinal Rinaldo Conti, later Pope Alexander IV, was simply given
to understand that he was replaced by Cardinal Peter Capocci, because the task assigned to
him had proved to be too much for him (MGH *Epp. saec. xiii* 2, no 681 (viii), 491): '*grave tibi
nimis tanti onus negotii*'. Even Cardinal Raniero Capocci, the bishop of Viterbo, was removed
from office: MGH *Epp. saec. xiii* 2, no 681 (viii), 492, with fnt. 3 there.
117   See Innocent's instructions and letters of April 1249 in MGH *Epp. saec. xiii* 2, no 681,
486-505
118   *Annales Cavenses* (1266-1315) ad ann. 1249, MGH *SS* 3, 194: '*In hoc anno destructa est
civitas Beneventana ... videlicet 19. Kal. Febr.* (= 14 Jan. 1250).
119   *Chronicon Parmense* ad ann. 1248, *RIS²* 9.9, 19; *Annales Placentini Gibellini* ad ann.
1250, MGH *SS* 18, 502: '*et sic facta est vindicta de eis de facto Victorie*'.
120   For all of these recent successes see Frederick's letter to Joannes Vatatzes. HB 6.2, 791-
794 (September 1250), has a (modern) Latin translation of Frederick's letter in Greek. For the
original Greek letter (and a German translation) see G. Wolff, *Vier griechische Briefe des Kaisers
Friedrichs des zweiten*, Berlin 1855, 26-38.

at the same time considerably restoring imperial prestige in the Marche and in the Romagna. Frederick was optimistic about his prospects and even wrote to one of his vassals that he was considering reassuming his personal involvement in the war '*to destroy the unbridled arrogance of our enemies with the hammer of our might*'[121].

Frederick II had resided in his palace in Foggia since October 1250. In the early days of December, he decided to move to one of his other palaces, in Muslim Lucera. On his way there, he suddenly fell ill again and had to be accommodated in Fiorentino Castle, just 7 miles from Lucera. There he expired on 13 December, the feast day of St Lucia, probably from dysentery[122]. The emperor was an excommunicate, but he had been absolved and administered the last sacraments on his deathbed, dressed in the simple habit of a Cistercian monk, by his old companion Archbishop Berardo of Palermo[123]. The remains of the *stupor mundi* were transported to Palermo where an impressive porphyry tomb worthy of a Roman emperor was waiting for him. He is still there, in Palermo Cathedral, awaiting the Final Judgment.

Tomb of the Emperor Frederick II
in Palermo Cathedral
(Wikimedia Commons)

---

121 *Petri de Vineis Friderici II. Imp. Epistolarum Libri VI*, ed. J.R. Iselin, Basle 1740, Tom. 1, Lib. 2, cap. 9, 257-258 (HB 6.2, 761-762): '*Plenam dant nobis preterita fiduciam de futuris … Inter alias siquidem cogitationes nostri propositi, stabili tenacitate firmavimus, ad partes <?> in manu forti et brachio extenso personaliter nos conferre … et effrenam superbiam nostrorum rebellium … potentie nostre malleo conteramus*'.
122 Nicolaus de Carbio, *Vita Innocentii IV* cap. 29, ed. Pagnotti, 102: '*anno Domini millesimo ccl, festo beate Lucie … in Apulia castro Florentino laborans gravibus dissenteriis*'.
123 Matthew Paris, *Chronica maiora* ad ann. 1250, ed. H.R. Luard V, 190: '*Obiit autem circa eadem tempora principum mundi maximus Frethericus, stupor quoque mundi et immutator mirabilis, absolutus a sententia qua innodabatur, assumpto, ut dicitur, habitu Cisterciensium*'. *Annales Stadenses* ad ann. 1250, MGH *SS* 16, 373: '*Fridericus imperator mortuus est, ab archiepiscopo Palormitano absolutus*'.

5

Extermination

Conrad IV

Three days before he died, Frederick II, 'frail of body, but lucid of mind' (*egri corpore, sani mente*), dictated his last will and testament to his notary Nicholas of Brindisi[1]. It contained a settlement, appointing his son Conrad IV as his successor in the Empire *and* the Sicilian kingdom, Frederick's final commitment to the *unio regni et imperii*. There were two contingent remainders in the will. If Conrad IV should die without leaving an heir of his own, he should be succeeded in the Empire and the Sicilian *regno* by his younger brother Henry, and if Henry should die without issue, he should be succeeded by his half-brother Manfred[2]. During the absence of Conrad IV, Manfred was appointed his personal representative (*balius*) 'in Italy and especially in the Sicilian kingdom' (*in Italia et specialiter in regno Sicilie*), giving him full powers 'to do all we could have done, if we were still alive' (*omnia faciendi que persona nostra facere posset, si viveremus*)[3]. In addition to this, Manfred was granted the principality of Tarento[4]. As far as the pope was concerned Frederick's will was null and void since he had forfeited the kingdom

---

1   Frederick's testament is in HB 6.2, 805-810 and in MGH *Const.* 2, no 274, 382-389. The witnesses to his last will must have been present at his demise: Archbishop Berardo; Count Berthold of Hohenburg; Frederick's son-in-law Count Ricardo of Caserta; four other Sicilian nobles; John of Procida; and two lawyers, Robert of Palermo and the Grand Justiciary Ricardo de Montenigro.
2   HB 6.2, 806; MGH *Const.* 2, no 274, 385: '*Statuimus itaque Conradum Romanorum in regem electum et regni Hierosolomitani heredem dilectum filium nostrum nobis heredem in imperio et in omnibus aliis empticiis et quoquomodo acquisitis, et specialiter in regno nostro Sicilie. Quem si decedere contingit sine liberis, succedat ei Henricus filius noster. Quo defuncto sine liberis, succedat ei Manfredus filius noster*'.
3   HB 6.2, 806; MGH *Const.* 2, no 274, 385.
4   The fact that Manfred was the only son born out of wedlock mentioned in Frederick's will is conclusive proof that he was legitimized by the subsequent marriage of Frederick II with his mistress Bianca Lancia. See Matthew Paris, *Chronica maiora* ad ann. 1256, ed. H.R. Luard V, 571-572 and about legitimation by subsequent marriage in Roman law: C. 5,27,11.

of Sicily and the Roman Empire. There was nothing left for the 'former emperor' (*quondam imperator*) to dispose of. It was the pope who was to decide over the future of the Sicilian kingdom and the Roman Empire. It was true that his choice for William of Holland as 'king of the Romans' was not supported by the overwhelming majority of the German secular princes, but the demise of Frederick II changed everything. It fatally undermined the legitimacy of the position of Conrad IV, even for the princes still supporting him. Conrad had never been crowned at Aachen, but William was, giving him an advantage over his Hohenstaufen opponent that proved to be decisive after the demise of Conrad's father. Conrad IV was not a consecrated king, but merely a 'king elect' (*electus rex*). Consequently, he was perceived by many as no more than his father's agent in Germany and since the authority of an agent expires by operation of law at the demise of his principal[5], so Conrad's authority in Germany dwindled after the demise of his father[6]. The young Hohenstaufen prince – Conrad was twenty-two by now – had to make up his mind and chose to leave Germany to claim his Sicilian heritage. In October 1251 Conrad left, never to return, after mortgaging or selling most of his German real property to finance his Italian adventure[7]. His pregnant wife was entrusted to the custody of her father, Duke Otto of Bavaria.

It was only after the departure of Conrad IV for Italy that the high German secular nobility felt free to desert the Hohenstaufen cause. The first prince of the realm to do so, thanks to the mediation of a new papal legate, the Cardinal-priest of S. Sabina, Hugh of Saint-Cher, was the Guelph Duke Otto of Brunswick. On 25 January 1252 William of Holland married Duke Otto's daughter Elizabeth[8] and thereby joined the German society of princes of the realm that had excluded him up till then. Only two months later, on 25 March 1252, William was formally elected at Brunswick as king of the Romans by the secular princes qualified to do so, the margrave of Brandenburg, the duke of Saxonia,

---

5 Inst. 3,26,10.

6 There had been an attempt to assassinate Conrad on 28 December 1250 during his stay at Regensburg, planned by Bishop Albert of Regensburg, who was in a feud with the duke of Bavaria, excommunicated since the marriage of his daughter with Conrad (see *supra* p. 402 , fnt 55). For the details of the attempt on Conrad's life see the contemporary *Annales* of Abbot Hermann of the monastery of Niederaltaich (*c.* 1200-1275) ad ann. 1251, MGH *SS* 17, 395.

7 *Annales Sancti Rudperti Salisburgenses* ad ann. 1251, MGH *SS* 9, 792: '*Chunradus rex heres Friderici, occupatis et distractis per infeodationem sive per obligationem possessionibus suis ... in Lombardiam se transtulit; inde iter in Apuliam et regnum patris sui ac hereditatem per maritima statim arripiendo*'.

8 *Annales Erphordenses fratrum praedicatorum* (1220-1253) ad ann. 1252, MGH *SS rer. Germ.* 42, 110: '*Anno Domini mcclii Willehelmus rex consilio et auxilio legati, ut creditur, filiam ducis Brunswicensis duxit uxorem*'.

and the king of Bohemia[9], thus terminating a century of Hohenstaufen rule in the German territories. It must have been a memorable occasion for the papal legate and his master, Innocent IV, since it marked the definitive end of the union of the German Empire and the Sicilian kingdom and the first step in the process of the complete extermination of the Hohenstaufen dynasty of enemies of the Church. The next target was the Sicilian kingdom.

When Conrad IV was returning to the Italian kingdom in October 1251, Innocent IV had also returned to Italy after an absence of seven years. One of the last European princes to visit him in Lyon was William of Holland[10]. In April 1251 the pope left Lyon and arrived in his native Genoa on 18 May[11]. From there, he proceeded to Milan, where he stayed for three months. Early in October the pope was in Bologna and on 5 November 1251 he arrived at Perugia, where he settled for a prolonged residence[12]. Innocent had made an impressive, even triumphant, progress through Lombardy and the Romagna for months without encountering any attempt at frustrating his journey by one of Frederick's military commanders in those regions. While Innocent was travelling unopposed from Bologna to Perugia, Frederick's captains were meeting with Conrad IV near Mantua at a parliament of the cities and nobles in Lombardy and the rest of the Italian kingdom still loyal to the Hohenstaufen cause[13]. It was decided there that Conrad should

Conrad IV dies

---

9   *Annales Erphordenses fratrum praedicatorum* ad ann. 1252, MGH *SS rer. Germ.* 42, 111: '*sequenti die rex Willehelmus a marchione Brandenburgense ac duce Saxonie ceterisque huius terre magnatibus in Romanum sollemniter electus est principem ... Rex etiam Boemie pretiosis atque regalibus muneribus in signum electionis ipsum honoravit*'. Naturally, the only other secular member of the electoral college, the Count Palatine at the Rhine, did not attend: Duke Otto of Bavaria, by now the sole protector of Hohenstaufen interests in Germany (*Annales Erphordenses fratrum praedicatorum* ad ann. 1252, MGH *SS rer. Germ.* 42, 111): '*excepto duce Bawarie, qui genero suo Conrado, filio quondam imperatoris, in sui honoris ac ditionis periculum pertinaciter adherebat*'.
10   Nicolaus de Carbio, *Vita Innocentii IV* cap. 30, ed. Pagnotti, 104.
11   *Annales Ianuenses* (Bartolomeo scriba) ad ann. 1251, MGH *SS* 18, 229: '*In ipso anno sanctissimus pater Innocent papa quartus, qui propter potencias imperatoris ad civitatem Lugdunum accesserat, volens suos Ytalicos paterno affectu consolari, cum cardinalibus et tota curia de Lugduno exivit versus Ytaliam dirigendo gressus suos ... ad civitatem Ianue sanus et incollumis cum omnibus cardinalibus pervenit*'. For Innocent's itinerary see Nicolaus de Carbio, *Vita Innocentii IV* cap. 30, ed. Pagnotti, 104.
12   Nicolaus de Carbio, *Vita Innocentii IV* cap. 30, ed. Pagnotti, 107: '*die vero sequenti dominice venit Perusiam, ubi honorifice est susceptus*'.
13   *Annales Veronenses* ad ann. 1251, MGH 19, 14: '*Eodem anno de mense Octobris Conradus rex Apuliae et domnus Icerinus de Romano cum populis Veronae Paduae et Vicentiae cum magno exercitu et multis exercitis Theutonicorum iverunt ultra Menzum ad castrum Goiti districtus Mantuae, et ibi steterunt per 15 dies ad parlamentum cum Cremonensibus Papiensibus Placentinis et aliis rectoribus civitatum Lombardiae cum complicibus imperatoris*'.

set off for his Sicilian kingdom as soon as possible, since a rebellion against royal power had erupted on the mainland of that kingdom soon after the demise of Frederick II and it was obvious that the cause of Conrad in the Italian kingdom was lost without the reserves of the Sicilian kingdom. Frederick II had ruled his Sicilian kingdom with an iron fist, making his Sicilian subjects pay heavily for the war he waged elsewhere on the peninsula to establish his power there. The efficiency of Frederick's Sicilian civil service guaranteed that the subjects of the king were under immense fiscal pressure, certainly so in the last years of Frederick's reign. No wonder, therefore, that many wanted to shake off that oppressive regime as soon as the emperor had died by siding with the pope, now at law their sovereign since Frederick's Sicilian fiefs had reverted to the pope after his deposition[14]. Especially the cities, Naples and Capua foremost among them, longed for the 'freedom' of the Lombard cities, a 'freedom' denied to them by Frederick II[15]. Conrad IV found a kingdom in open revolt against Hohenstaufen rule, when he arrived at Siponto in Apulia, in January 1252[16]. Manfred had not been able to suppress the revolt in time before the arrival of his half-brother Conrad, but together the brothers succeeded in crushing the rebellion. By the end of October 1253, the last insubordinate city, Naples, surrendered to Conrad after a protracted siege[17]. He was now in possession of his father's Sicilian inheritance, but Frederick's son and heir was never to be crowned in Palermo. He died on 21 May

---

14   Nicolas of Carbio, *Vita Innocentii IV* cap. 31, ed. Pagnotti 108: '*Corradus … invasit et occupavit regnum Apulie et Sicilie in iacturam et dispendium Ecclesie, cum esset de iure ipsum regnum ad manus Ecclesie devolutum*'.

15   See *supra* p. 564.

16   *Annales Siculi* (second half of the 13th century) ad ann. 1251, MGH *SS* 19, 498: 'In the year of our Lord 1251, in the tenth indiction, in the month of January, our lord King Conrad, the son of the emperor, came from Germany over sea with a great fleet, sent by the prince <Manfred> who was governor of the whole kingdom by the order of the emperor. And he arrived in Apulia on the eighth of January of that indiction' (*Anno domini mccli. indictione decima mense ianuarii eiusdem indictionis dominus rex Conradus, filius domini imperatoris, venit de Alemania per mare cum magno extolio, misso per dominum principem qui erat ballius totius regni de mandato domini imperatoris. Et applicuit in Apuleam octavo ianuarii dicte indictionis*). The reason why the Sicilian annals give the year 1251, rather than 1252, is that the new year 1252 started in Sicily at Easter, not in January.

17   *Annales Cavenses* (ending in 1318) ad ann. 1253, MGH *SS* 3, 194: 'In that year, all the territories revolting against King Conrad had returned to him, except Naples. Consequently, the furious king assembled the entire kingdom and laid siege to that city. On the tenth of October they surrendered to him, forced by famine and the army, and the king ordered that they had to raze the city walls to the ground, and he exiled many from the city. At Capua he had done the same' (*In hoc anno omnes terrae, quae rebellatae fuerunt Corrado regi, reversae sunt ad eum praeter Neapolim; unde iratus congregavit totum regnum, et obsedit eam … Decimo itaque die intrante mense Octubris, cogente eos fame simul et exercitu, reverse sunt ad eum, et praecepit rex, et destruxerunt <ut destruxerint> totum murum eius per circuitum usque ad solum, et multos ex eis exiliavit; similiter fecit Capuae*).

1254, probably of malaria like his grandfather Henry VI[18]. He was only 25 and disappeared from this world without leaving a trace, since a last resting-place in Palermo, next to his father and grandfather, was denied to him: his remains were irretrievably lost in a fire of the church in Messina where he was provisionally laid at rest[19]. Shortly before Conrad's demise, Frederick's other son and heir, Henry, had also died. He was just sixteen[20]. The sudden passing of two of Frederick's heirs, Conrad and Henry, left but one of Frederick's testamentary heirs alive, his son Manfred.

Manfred

At the time of Conrad's demise, Pope Innocent IV had returned to the Lateran Palace at the insistence of the people of Rome and their newly elected *podestà*, Brancaleone d'Andalò (*c.* 1220-1258). Brancaleone was a Ghibelline from Bologna and had been on friendly terms with Conrad IV[21], even trying to arrange a conciliation between the pope and Conrad IV in the last weeks of 1253. As was to be expected, the

Innocent IV in search of a new king of Sicily

18   *Annales Ianuenses* (Bartolomeo scriba) ad ann. 1254, MGH *SS* 18, 232: '*rex Cunradus mortuus est, et obiit in Apulia in nocte ascensionis Domini*'. The probable cause of death of Conrad IV is confirmed by the fact that many Germans with him also succumbed at the time (*Annales Sancti Rudperti Salisburgenses* (tot 1286) ad ann. 1252, MGH *SS* 9, 792): '*Multi Deutonici, qui cum Chunrado rege Swevie Apuliam intraverant, obierunt*'. There were rumours at the time that Conrad had died by poison: Saba Malaspina († 1298) 1,4, MGH *SS* 35, 98-100 and Matthew Paris, *Chronica maiora* ad ann. 1254, ed. H.R. Luard V, 459-460. The rumours are unlikely, as are the rumours about the murder of prince Henry by his half-brother Conrad. It was papal disinformation.
19   See the Sicilian chronicle (*Historia Sicula*) of Bartolomaeo de Neocastro († 1293) cap. 1, *RIS²* 13.3, 3: '*In civitatem Messanae corpus regale portatur, ubi flamma ignus consumitur, priusquam debitae fuisset traditum sepulturae*'.
20   Matthew Paris, *Chronica maiora* ad ann. 1254, ed. H.R. Luard V, 448, reporting, but contradicting, the rumour that Henry had been murdered by his brother Conrad. It was highly unlikely, says Matthew Paris, 'since the king loved him like a brother' (*cum idem rex ipsum Henricum affectu fraterno dilexisset*). Matthew Paris calls Henry 'the hope and glory of the English' (*spes Anglorum et gloria*), because he was a son of Frederick's wife Isabella of England, a sister of King Henry III. On this issue see *infra* p. 423-424.
21   Nicolaus de Carbio, *Vita Innocentii IV* cap. 34, ed. Pagnotti, 111-112: 'In those days, the people of Rome had elected a knight from Bologna, called Brancaleone, as 'senator' of the city for the term of three years, since in Lombardy he belonged to the party of the deposed Frederick. He had been corrupted by the money of Conrad, the son of Frederick, who had already occupied the kingdom itself, receiving his envoys and openly entertaining them in the city' (*Illo vero tempore Romani quondam militem bononiensem, Brancaleonem nomine, pro triennio in senatorem Urbis elegerant, quia in Lombardia fuerat pro parte Frederici depositi ... corruptus esset pecunia Corradi, nati sepe fati Frederici, qui iam occupaverat ipsum regnum, cuius quidem nuntios recipiebat et in Urbe secum publice retinebat*).

attempt utterly failed[22]. Innocent IV had no intention of compromising with any Hohenstaufen prince: '*because the hatred he had formerly entertained against Frederick was still not quenched, he decided to take it out on his offspring and the rest of his blood*'[23]. The pope was negotiating with other parties to succeed to the Sicilian throne at the time. His first choice had been Richard of Cornwall, to whom he had already offered the crown of Germany before, after the untimely demise of Heinrich Raspe[24]. Richard declined this offer as well[25]. After this rebuff, the pope tried his luck in France, sending one of his lawyers, master Albert of Parma, to the French court with an offer of the throne of Sicily to Charles of Anjou, brother to King Louis IX. The mood at the court of France was hostile to the pope at the time. The old dowager queen and regent of France during the absence of King Louis, Blanche of Castile, was disgusted with the policies of Innocent IV, preaching war against fellow-Christians, the sons of Frederick II, while her own son was fighting the infidel in the Holy Land. She prohibited the French nobility to participate in Innocent's anti-Hohenstaufen crusades, announcing that all who did so forfeited their land and were never to return: '*Those who fight for the pope, must be sustained by the pope and are never to return*'[26]. Blanche had died on 27 November 1252, but her views on papal politics were still shared by the majority of the French nobility, always favourable to the anti-clerical policy of Frederick II. After Blanche's demise, the regency of the French kingdom was shared by Louis' brothers Alphonse and Charles until the return of the king. Consequently, Charles of Anjou was not in a position to accept the offer of Innocent IV. He had an important assignment in France itself[27] as long as the king was

---

22   Nicolaus de Carbio, *Vita Innocentii IV* cap. 35, ed. Pagnotti, 112: '*nulla potuit inter ipsos concordia provenire*'. There had been a previous, equally futile, attempt by Conrad to gain confirmation of his Sicilian title by the pope: Nicolaus de Carbio, *Vita Innocentii IV* cap. 31, ed. Pagnotti, 108.

23   Ferretus Vicentinus (Ferreto dei Ferreti, *c.* 1297-1337), *Historia rerum in Italia gestarum*, Prooemium, ed. Cipolla, *Le opere di Ferreto de'Ferreti* I, Rome 1908, 10: '*odio nundum extincto, quod olim in Federicum exercuit, in prolem eius et sanguinis reliquias sevire disposuit*'.

24   See *supra* p. 405.

25   Nicolaus de Carbio, *Vita Innocentii IV* cap. 31, ed. Pagnotti, 108; Matthew Paris, *Chronica maiora* ad ann. 1252, ed. H.R. Luard V, 346-347.

26   Matthew Paris, *Chronica maiora* ad ann. 1251, ed. H.R. Luard V, 260: '*Blanchia ... iussit omnium terras et possessions cruce signatorum in manu sua recipi, dicens, "Qui Papae militant, de Papalibus sustineantur et eant irredituri*'.

27   Charles was deeply involved at the time in the war between the sons of Countess Margaret of Flanders and Hainault, the D'Avesnes (from her first marriage) and the Dampierre's (from her second marriage). Louis IX had brokered a compromise in 1246 by assigning Hainault to the D'Avesnes and Flanders to the Dampierre's. Margaret refused to resign Hainault to the D'Avesnes. Consequently, John of Avesnes tried to oust his mother by force, aided by his brother-in-law the king of the Romans, William of Holland. Margaret was desperate and gained the support of Charles of Anjou by assigning the county of Hainault to Charles

absent and, being a vassal of his brother, he could not make a decision on this issue without the approval of the king himself. Accordingly, Charles of Anjou also declined the offer[28]. As he was instructed by the pope, in case the offer to Charles of Anjou was rejected, master Albert subsequently went to England to offer the crown of Sicily to Edmund Crouchback, King Henry's second son and still a minor at the time (1254). Innocent IV was convinced that he could count on Henry III's gullibility (*simplicitas*) to be persuaded to accept that offer in name of his son[29]. As expected, Henry III accepted the offer on the condition, however, that he and all the English knights who had taken the cross would be released from their promise to depart for the Holy Land. This was no problem for the pope, since in doing so the king committed himself to the crusade against the Sicilian Hohenstaufen brood, a crusade much more important to Innocent IV than the cause of the Holy Land[30]. His 'Roman intrigues' (*Romanae fallaciae*) shocked all the military orders and the other crusaders in the Holy Land, King Louis IX of France still among them at the time, once the news of this arrangement became known there[31]. No less shocking was the conduct of Henry III, since by the time the grant of Sicily to Edmund was completed by master Albert (on 6 March 1254)[32] the king was not yet informed about the demise of his young nephew Henry, the son of his sister Elisabeth

---

(31 October 1253). After his return to France, King Louis restored the original compromise of 1246, thus depriving his brother of the county of Hainault (1256).

28 Nicolaus de Carbio, *Vita Innocentii IV* cap. 31, ed. Pagnotti, 109): 'But after long and arduous negotiations, the count, although much inclined, decided not to accept the magnificent gift offered to him, submitting to his family's advice and through the evil intervention of malevolent people' (*sed, malignorum interveniente nequitia, post multos et longos tractatus, licet ipse comes hoc multum in corde gestaret, collateralium tamen suorum devictus consilio, hoc donum sibi tam magnificum destinatum recipere non temptavit*).

29 Matthew Paris, *Chronica maiora* ad ann. 1254, ed. H.R. Luard V, 457: 'Once the pope realized that he had "spread the net in vain in sight of the bird" (Prov. 1:17), he sent a secret ambassy to the king of England, to deceive his gullibility, since he knew the king was credulous and always prone to do himself harm, and offered the kingdom of Sicily and Apulia to him' (*Cum igitur certificaretur Papa, quod frustra jecisset rete ante oculos pennatorum, missis secretis nuntiis ad dominum regem Angliae, ut simplicitatem eius circumveniret, quoniam sciebat semper ad dampna propria pronum et credulum, optulit et concessit ei regnum Siciliae et Apuliae*).

30 Matthew Paris, *Chronica maiora* ad ann. 1254, ed. H.R. Luard V, 457: 'He released all crusaders of their primary promise, that is to depart for the Holy Land, but all were to follow the king of England to help him in taking Sicily and Apulia' (*Retorqueret enim omnes crucesignatos a principali eorum proposito, videlicet ne transfretarent in Terram Sanctam, sed omnes communiter regem Angliae sequerentur, et juvarent Siciliam et Apuliam adepturum*).

31 Matthew Paris, *Chronica maiora* ad ann. 1254, ed. H.R. Luard V, 457-458: 'Unde haec audientes Templarii et Hospitalarii, patriarcha Jerosolimitanus, et omnes Sanctae Terrae praelati et incolae, qui hostibus Christi opponuntur, et jam pejora formidabant, usque ad mortem doluerunt, Romanas fallacias detestantes*'.

32 The concession is in Rymer, I.1, 178.

with Frederick II, news of which only reached him later[33]. As soon as he had learned about the demise of Conrad IV, the pope sent news to the king of England, urging him to make haste with his Sicilian crusade, since the Sicilian kingdom was now practically there for the taking[34].

The Sicilian kingdom after the demise of Conrad IV

Manfred had been named in the testament of his father as a substitute heir after Frederick's other sons Conrad IV and Henry, but only if they died without leaving an heir of their own[35]. Consequently, Manfred was not to succeed Conrad IV as king of Sicily, since on 25 March 1252 a son had been born to King Conrad in faraway Germany[36]. His mother had called him after his father, Conrad. History knows him by the nickname the pope gave him: 'little Conrad' (*Conradinus*). We shall call him 'Conradin'. By the time his father died, the child, a toddler still, was living with his mother at Wolfstein Castle, near Landshut in Bavaria, under the care of his uncle, Duke Louis II of Bavaria[37]. The birth of an heir to Conrad IV called for the appointment of a regent in the Sicilian kingdom during the minority (and the absence) of his son. The obvious choice was Manfred, if only because Frederick II had also appointed him as regent in the Sicilian kingdom during the absence of Conrad IV[38]. It was not what Conrad IV had decided in his last will and testament. Instead of Manfred, the German Count Berthold of Hohenburg was named as regent (*baiulus*) of the kingdom[39], a clear sign that the personal relationship between Conrad IV and his half-

---

33   See the letter of Innocent IV, dated on 15 May 1254, informing Henry III of the demise of young prince Henry and thereby taking away the scruples clearly bothering the court of England at the time: Rymer, I.1, 182. For the papal confirmation of the grant of Sicily to Edmund see Innocent's bull of 14 May 1254 in Rymer I.1, 182.

34   Rymer, I.1, 184 (9 June 1254). Conrad IV had died on 21 May 1254.

35   See *supra* p. 417.

36   Hermann of Niederaltaich, *Annales* ad ann. 1252, MGH *SS* 17, 395: '*Domina Elysabeth filia Ottonis ducis Bavarie genuit Chunrado regi filium in die annuntiationis sancte Marie, et vocatus est Chunradus*'.

37   Conradin's grandfather, Duke Otto II of Bavaria, had died in 1253. Duke Otto's sons Louis II and Henry divided the Bavarian duchy between them, but the important title of Count Palatine at the Rhine, with its membership of the royal electoral committee, remained with Louis II alone.

38   See *supra* p. 417.

39   Only the introduction to the dispositions of the will of Conrad IV has survived (MGH *Const.* 2, no 345, 452-453). Our knowledge of the actual contents is based on other sources: Nicolaus de Carbio, *Vita Innocentii IV* cap. 39, ed. Pagnotti, 115 and 'Nicolaus de Jamsilla', *Historia de rebus gestis Friderici II imperatoris eiusque filiorum Conradi et Manfredi*, in Muratori, 8, col. 507. The attribution of the authorship of the latter source to a certain Nicolaus de Jamsilla is based on an error but has stuck with modern scholarship. There is still no modern edition of this extremely important source, probably written between 1261-1265 by an author very close to Manfred. There is a 19th-century edition (a reproduction of Muratori's edition) with an Italian translation: Guis. del Re, *Cronisti e scrittori sincroni Napoletani*, II, *Svevi*, Naples 1868, 101-201. There is now an English translation by Louis Mendola, *The Chronicle*

brother Manfred had deteriorated considerably during the last months of Conrad's life[40].

After the demise of Conrad IV, a pattern begins to evolve that has precedents in the earlier history of Hohenstaufen involvement with Sicily. As had happened in 1189, after the death of King William II[41], the legitimate heir to the Sicilian crown (then Henry VI, now Conradin) was in faraway Germany when the throne became vacant and the Sicilian barons preferred one of their own (then Tancred of Lecce, now Manfred) over a distant German pretender or his German represent-ative[42]. And as in 1197, after the demise of Henry VI[43], anti-German sentiment was strong. Conrad IV, though Sicilian by birth, had been raised in Germany, where he had lived for the best part of his short life. He had come to Sicily in 1252 with an army consisting of German mer-cenaries and ministerials, as had Henry VI in 1194, fortune-hunters most of them, as many of the captains in the army of Henry VI had been. Such men were not popular in the Sicilian kingdom. They never had been[44], as Frederick II had been well aware, since he had never employed Germans in the administration of his Sicilian kingdom or as commanders of his armies on the Italian peninsula. Consequently, some Sicilian barons now began to transfer their allegiance to the pope again, as they had also done immediately after the demise of Frederick II[45]. The political tension in the Sicilian *regno* was rising, since the pope, his coffers full of English silver provided by king Henry III, was gather-ing an army at the borders of that kingdom. It was under these critical circumstances that the Sicilian *baiulus*, Count Berthold of Hohenburg, sent an ambassy to the pope to arrange some kind of peace. Innocent IV rightly perceived it as a sign of weakness and maximized his demands accordingly. He insisted that the Sicilian kingdom was to be delivered to him immediately, the only apostolic concession being that he would respect the rights of Conradin 'if he had any' (*si quod haberet*)[46]. It was

---

of *Nicholas of Jamsilla, Frederick, Conrad and Manfred of Hohenstaufen, Kings of Sicily (1210-1258)*, New York 2016. On Count Berthold see *supra* p. 417, fnt. 1.

40   'Nicolaus de Jamsilla', *Historia de rebus gestis Friderici II imperatoris eiusque filiorum Conradi et Manfredi*, in Muratori, 8, col. 505: 'But the affection of the king (Conrad IV) for the prince (Manfred) did not last long' (*Parum autem duravit haec affectio Regis ad Principem*).

41   See *supra* p. 141.

42   For this sentiment of the Sicilian barons after the demise of Conrad IV see Nicolaus de Jamsilla, *Historia de rebus gestis Friderici II imperatoris eiusque filiorum Conradi et Manfredi*, in Muratori 8, col. 508.

43   See *supra* p. 151.

44   See *supra* p. 151.

45   See *supra* p. 420. For these developments see Nicolaus de Jamsilla, *Historia de rebus gestis Friderici II imperatoris eiusque filiorum Conradi et Manfredi*, in Muratori, 8, col. 508-510.

46   For this ambassy see Nicolaus de Carbio, *Vita Innocentii IV* cap. 39, ed. Pagnotti, 115 and especially Nicolaus de Jamsilla, *Historia de rebus gestis* (Muratori 8, col. 507): 'The pope, who

a concession Innocent IV hardly can have proposed seriously, since he had already granted the Sicilian kingdom to the son of the king of England at the time[47]. As was to be expected, the ambassy did not yield any result. The Sicilian barons still loyal to the house of Hohenstaufen now began to compel Manfred to take over the regency (*baiulatus*) himself. He was the only testamentary heir of Frederick II alive and it seemed highly unlikely that the legitimate heir, Conradin, would ever be capable of taking over his Sicilian inheritance himself. Surprisingly, Count Berthold of Hohenburg, was disposed to cooperate. The count, who was not up to his task and, a rarity among politicians, was aware of it, resigned and handed over the government of the kingdom to Manfred[48]. As soon as the pope heard of it, Count Berthold, Manfred, and others were excommunicated forthwith for not complying with his wish to hand over the Sicilian kingdom to him immediately[49]. At the same time, the papal army under the command of William Fieschi, the cardinal-deacon of S. Eustachio and a nephew of the pope, was on the move, crossing the border of the Sicilian *regno*. Among the knights in Cardinal William's army were many angry Sicilian exiles, barons who had been expropriated and forced into exile in the past by Frederick II and were now bent on revenge *and* on recovering their forfeited estates.

Innocent IV takes control of the Sicilian kingdom

Manfred was in a very difficult position in September 1254. The crucial question was whether he should risk facing the papal army in battle and, if not, what was the alternative. He decided to avoid armed conflict, since he could not rely on the loyalty of his own forces under the prevailing circumstances, now that even formerly trusted partisans of

---

considered the ambassy and the appeal to apostolic leniency as a sign of weakness of the party of the king rather than as a gesture of loyalty, indicated that he wanted to be put in possession of the dominion of the kingdom, promising to the minor king that he would, when he reached majority, respect his rights *as far as he had any*' (*Summus pontifex illam legatorum missionem et Apostolicae gratiae postulationem, magis debilitati partis Regiae, quam devotioni ascribens, respondit praecise, se habere velle Regni possessionem, atque dominium, promittens Regi pupillo, cum ad pubertatem venire, de jure, si quod haberet, gratiam esse faciendam*) (emphasis added).

47 The pope's disingenuity is confirmed by his bull of 27 September 1254 (MGH *Epp. saec. xiii* 3, no 320, 290) confirming the title of Conradin to the kingdom of Jerusalem and the duchy of Swabia 'and other rights wherever he may have them, whether in the kingdom of Sicily or elsewhere' (*ac alia iura, ubicunque illa sive in regno Sicilie sive alibi habeat*) and ordering that any oath of fealty relating to Sicilian fiefs sworn to the Church of Rome should include the clause 'subject to the right of the boy Conrad' (*Conradi pueri iure salvo*). Four months earlier, on 14 May 1254, he had confirmed the grant of the Sicilian kingdom to Edmund Crouchback (see *supra* p. 424, fnt. 33).

48 Nicolaus de Jamsilla, *Historia de rebus gestis* (Muratori 8, col. 508): '*Baiulatus officium se assumpsisse poenituit et ex tunc onus quidem incaute susceptum, non sine pudore deponendum existimavit*'.

49 Innocent IV in a letter to William of Holland dated 12 September 1254, MGH *Epp. saec. xiii* 3, no 314, 283.

Frederick II, such as Manfred's own brother-in-law Count Riccardo di Caserta, one of the witnesses to the testament of Frederick II, had defected to the papal party after the demise of Conrad IV[50]. After Conrad had died and Count Berthold of Hohenburg had resigned, the loyalty of Conrad's German troops, being soldiers of fortune, was also dubious, as was the loyalty of Count Berthold himself. Under these circumstances, Manfred had no choice but to submit to the pope[51] and he did so with a diplomatic gesture, worthy of his father's reputation. He notified the pope that he was willing to receive Innocent in the *regno* and to surrender the kingdom to him, subject only to his own rights and the rights of his nephew Conradin[52]. Innocent IV reacted immediately: he lifted Manfred's excommunication, confirmed all the titles granted to Manfred by Frederick II before the latter had been excommunicated, even adding the principality of Tarento, and appointed him as his representative (*vicarius*) in Apulia[53]. When Innocent IV triumphantly entered the Sicilian kingdom on 11 October 1254 by crossing the bridge over the Garigliano, Manfred seized the opportunity to make a public display of his obedience by rendering squire service to the pope, escorting Innocent on foot while holding the pope's horse by

---

50 On 29 January 1255 Innocent's successor, Pope Alexander IV, calls Riccardo 'our beloved son' (*dilectus filius*): Bourel de la Roncière *e.a.*, *Les Registres d' Alexandre IV*, Tom. I, Paris 1902, no 94, 24-25. Riccardo of Caserta was not the only Sicilian magnate to defect at this time. So did Riccardo de Montenegro, grand justiciary of Apulia and a powerful baron as well (Nicolaus de Carbio, *Vita Innocentii IV* cap. 39, ed. Pagnotti, 116), and Peter Ruffo, the governor of Calabria and of the island of Sicily (Nicolaus de Jamsilla, *Historia de rebus gestis*, Muratori 8, col. 511).

51 For Manfred's motives see Nicolaus de Jamsilla, *Historia de rebus gestis* (Muratori 8, col. 512): 'he believed it was less dangerous when he would spontaneously allow the pope to enter the kingdom than when the pope entered by force. It was certain that, if the pope entered by force, those who conspired against him would be able to cause him harm much more effectively. But when the pope obtained the kingdom voluntarily, the risk of a conspiracy was reduced' (*cogitavit enim minus esse periculum, si Papam intrare Regnum sponte ipse permitteret, quam si Papa violenter intraret ... Certus enim erat, quod si Regnum Papa violenter intraret, hi, qui contra Principem conspiraverant, efficacius sibi nocituri erant ... Sin autem voluntarie Papam in Regno reciperet, conspirationis periculum declinaret*).

52 Nicolaus de Jamsilla, *Historia de rebus gestis* (Muratori 8, col. 512): '*paratum se obtulit idem Princeps eundem Sanctissimum Patrem in Regnum recipere sine praeiudicio Regis et suo et tam ipsius Regis quam suo in omnibus jure salvo*'.

53 Saba Malaspina 1,5,1-8, MGH *SS* 35, 102-103: '*Manfredus ... meruit a sententia excommunicationis qua tenebatur absolvi. Et ... ratificavit et confirmavit dicto principi omnem donationem sibi factam per patrem ante suam depositionem*'. For the principality of Tarento see MGH *Epp. saec. xiii* 3, no 318, 287-289 (Innocent IV, 27 September 1254). Tarento had been granted to Manfred in Frederick's testament (see *supra* p. 417). Consequently, the grant was null and void according to the pope. Tarento was now granted to Manfred by the proper authority. For Manfred as papal governor of Apulia see MGH *Epp. saec. xiii* 3, no 319, 289-290 (Innocent IV, 27 September 1254).

the bridle[54]. It was the acme of *dissimulatio* and Innocent IV may even have appreciated the gesture as such.

On 20 October 1254 Innocent IV was in Capua, one of the cities that had only recently rebelled against Conrad IV. It was there that he issued a bull directed at the Sicilian clergy, the nobility, and the people of all the towns in the Sicilian kingdom. The pope solemnly guaranteed all his Sicilian subjects his special protection, confirming all their 'liberties and privileges, and their laudable customs and usages' (*libertates et immunitates, usus et laudabiles consuetudines*), at the same time emphasizing that the Sicilian kingdom belonged to the domain of the Church of Rome forever and accordingly was always to be 'subject to the authority, the jurisdiction, and the protection' (*sub potestate, iurisdictione ac presidio*) of the Apostolic See[55]. There is no reference in this document to the position of the king, let alone to Conradin personally, but it did announce that all property seized illegally (*contra iustitiam*) by Frederick II and Conrad IV in the past was to be restored to the rightful owners, clerics and nobles[56]. Accordingly, Innocent IV started to reinvest the Sicilian exiles in his retinue with their former fiefs, without any reference to the loyalty (*fides*) the newly instated vassals owed to the king. It was clear now that Innocent IV did not intend to recognize Conradin's title. Manfred will have had no illusions about the sincerity of the honours which he had received from the pope recently and may even have been informed about the grant of Sicily to the son of the king of England at the time, since he was with the court of Innocent IV from 11 October onwards. He was surrounded there by hostile Sicilian barons, former exiles, and recent turncoats, such as Borello d'Anglona[57]. Innocent IV recently had granted the county of Lesina to Borello, despite Manfred's claim to that county. Borello was killed in a scuffle with some of Manfred's servants and Manfred was blamed for this by the papal party[58]. Fearing that his enemies would seize the opportunity to get rid of him for good, Manfred fled the papal court.

---

54 Nicolaus de Jamsilla, *Historia de rebus gestis* (Muratori 8, col. 512): '*Papa regnum intrante Princeps stratoris officium ei officium exhibens fraenum tenuit, quousque ad pontem Gariliani transiret*'.
55 MGH *Epp. saec. xiii* 3, no 325, p. 297-298 (298).
56 MGH *Epp. saec. xiii* 3, no 326, p. 298-299.
57 On the affair of Borello d'Anglona see Nicolaus de Jamsilla, *Historia de rebus gestis* (Muratori 8, col. 513-521; Saba Malaspina 1,6, MGH *SS* 35, 104-105) and Nicolaus de Carbio, *Vita Innocentii IV* cap. 41, ed. Pagnotti, 117.
58 For this assessment see Saba Malaspina 1,6, MGH *SS* 35, 104-105 and Nicolaus de Carbio, *Vita Innocentii IV* cap. 41, ed. Pagnotti, 117, both authors belonged to the papal bureaucracy and were consequently biased against Manfred.

Manfred was on his own now, threatened by enemies from all sides, since Count Berthold of Hohenburg had also made his peace with Innocent IV, even inciting the pope to deal with Manfred with all the rigour of the law[59]. There was but one place in the kingdom left where Manfred could count on unwavering support: Muslim Lucera. The Muslims there knew that the pope was bent on their extermination and opened the gates of the town to Frederick's son. From there and then, Manfred swiftly restored control over the Sicilian part of the Italian peninsula with the help of his Muslim troops, gaining a decisive victory over the papal army near Foggia on 2 December 1254[60]. News of the rout of the papal army at Foggia spread all over Europe[61] and shocked the pope. He was staying at Naples at the time when the news reached him, residing in a palace that had once belonged to Piero della Vigna. It was there that he died shortly after, on 7 December 1254[62]. He had dedicated his whole pontificate to the destruction of the *unio regni ad imperium*, the union of the Sicilian kingdom with the German Empire, using all means, fair and foul, to achieve that goal. He was successful, since, but for one very exceptional case[63], no German emperor ever ruled over the Sicilian kingdom again after Frederick II. The result of this pontifical geopolitical strategy, however, was the ruin of the medieval German Empire.

Manfred strikes back

Dissolution

Richard of Cornwall (1209-1272) is the Sunday's child of the European Middle Ages. He was not only considered to be the richest man of his time, but he was the only European prince alive who could boast to have declined two prestigious European crowns. He had turned down the German crown, offered to him by Innocent IV after the demise of Heinrich Raspe as a substitute for Frederick II, as well as the Sicilian

The German succession crisis

---

59   Nicolaus de Jamsilla, *Historia de rebus gestis*, Muratori 8, col. 520. For the defection of Berthold of Hohenburg see also Nicolaus de Carbio, *Vita Innocentii IV* cap. 41, ed. Pagnotti, 117-118.

60   Nicolaus de Carbio, *Vita Innocentii IV* cap. 42, ed. Pagnotti, 118, reports that Otto of Hohenburg, a brother of Count Berthold and commander of the German troops now in papal service, committed treason by fleeing the battlefield.

61   See Matthew Paris, *Chronica maiora* ad ann. 1254, ed. H.R. Luard V, 430 and *Annales Ianuenses* (Bartolomeo scriba) ad ann. 1254, MGH *SS* 18, 232.

62   Nicolaus de Carbio, *Vita Innocentii IV* cap. 42, ed. Pagnotti, 119): '*Defunctus est dominus Innocent papa quartus Neapoli in palatio olim domini Petri de Vineis, anno Domini millesimo. ccliiii, mensis decembris die septima intrante*'. Innocent IV was buried in Naples; his tomb is in the Church of S. Gennaro.

63   See *supra* p. 391, fnt. 1.

crown, offered to him by the pope as a substitute for Conrad IV[64]. Richard must have been a gentleman, not available to some cleric for the purpose of divesting other gentlemen from what was rightly theirs. The demise of Frederick II and Conrad IV, however, changed everything. Conrad's minor son, Conradin, might be nominally duke of Swabia, but he had *not* been elected 'king of the Romans', as his father Conrad had been. According to Richard's reasoning, there was indeed a vacancy on the German throne after King William of Holland had been killed in a brawl with his own Frisian peasantry in January 1256[65]. Consequently, Richard was not disinclined to accept a possible election as king of the Romans this time. Conradin, only five years old at the time, was indeed a possible contender, but as soon as the news of the demise of King William had reached him, Pope Alexander IV (1254-1261), who had succeeded Innocent IV, let it be known to the three German clerical electors that Conradin was to be excluded from election. His reasons were the same as those already advanced by Innocent III in his famous *Deliberatio* of 1200, excluding Frederick II from election[66]: he came from the wrong family and he was still but a minor[67]. The pope also instructed the German clerical electors that they were to let it be known to the four secular electors that they would be excommunicated forthwith when they supported, or even mentioned, the cause of Conradin[68]. Unlike his predecessor Innocent IV, however,

---

64 See *supra* p. 405 and 422.
65 Melis Stoke (*c.* 1235- *c.* 1305), *Rijmkroniek van Holland* 4370-4385, ed. J.W.J. Burgers, The Hague 2004, 159), 4370-4390 (159) en Johannes de Beke (*c.* 1350), *Croniken van den Stichte van Utrecht ende van Hollant*, ed. H. Bruch, The Hague 1982, LXVIII, 290-300 (139-140). The king rode over a frozen Frisian swamp in full armour and 'sank through the ice', since then proverbial in Dutch for utter failure. For good measure, William was clubbed to death by the rebellious Frisian peasants.
66 See *supra* p. 155-156.
67 Letter to the Archbishop of Mainz, with conformed copy to the archbishops of Cologne and Trier, in Bourel de la Roncière *e.a.*, *Les Registres d'Alexandre IV*, Tom. 1, Paris 1902, no 1434, 435-437(436): 'How Frederick, once emperor of the Romans, and his ancestors and descendants have behaved towards the Mother Church is evident and known to all the world. This is why there must be a strong warning against Conradin, the son of Conrad, Frederick's son, so that he may under no circumstances be taken into consideration, mentioned, or even nominated, especially since that child is utterly unqualified and ineligible on account of his minority and tender age' (*Qualiter autem quondam Fridericus, olim Romanorum imperator, et sui progenitores et posteri erga matrem Ecclesiam se gesserint … patens est et cognitum toti orbi … Ideo de Conradino puero nato quondam Conradi praedicti Friderici filii est praecavendum omnino, ne ullo modo intendatur ad eum, nec nominetur ad hoc, nec aliquatenus eligatur: maxime cum propter infantiam, nimiumque defectum aetatis sit ad ista prorsus inhabilis, ac inelegibilis penitus puer ipse*). The last argument also excluded King William's son, Floris V (1254-1296), who was only two years old at the time.
68 *Les Registres d'Alexandre IV*, Tom. 1, Paris 1902, no 1434, 436: 'You must on our authority categorically forbid the other electors, clerical and secular, to mention his name, nominate him or consent to his nomination by announcing on the same authority a sentence of excom-

Alexander IV did not suggest a candidate of his own, thus leaving the German electors free to make a choice of their own, subject, of course, to papal approval. The way the electoral board exercised this liberty is as shocking as it is instructive: shocking because of the almost insatiable greed of the prelates and secular princes involved and instructive because it reveals the steep decline of the prestige of the title 'king of the Romans' (*rex Romanorum*).

After the demise of William of Holland, it was well established at law that his succession was to be decided by an electoral college consisting of seven princes of the realm, three clerical electors, the archbishops of Mainz, Cologne, and Trier, and four secular electors, the king of Bohemia, the count palatine at the Rhine, the duke of Saxonia and the margrave of Brandenburg[69]. Consequently, none of the increasingly important German cities was involved in the electoral process, despite the fact that it was in their common commercial interest that peace in the realm was restored by an uncontested succession to the crown. The civil war prevailing in Germany ever since the deposition of Frederick II had to come to an end and it was because of this that a considerable number of cities along the Rhine, the main trade route of Germany, decided in 1254 to constitute a league dedicated to upholding the general peace (*Landfrieden*) dictated by Frederick II at Mainz in 1235[70]. The League of the Rhine was joined by a considerable number of territorial princes, most notably among them no fewer than *four* members of the royal electoral college, the three archbishops along the Rhine and the count palatine at the Rhine[71]. After the demise of King William, the League of the Rhine held a parliament at Mainz on 12 March 1256 to decide what was to be done in order to restore royal authority and peace in the land. The members of the League had little confidence in the electoral college, since they let it be known that they would not accept a contested election[72], which is precisely what happened when the electoral college finally convened at Frankfurt on 13 January 1257.

The League of the Rhine

---

munication when they venture to act against your prohibition, being our own' (*Aliis vero co-electoribus tuis tam Ecclesiasticis quam saecularibus auctoritate nostra firmiter inhibeas, ne ipsum ad hoc nominent, vel eligant, nec in eum consentient, promulgando eadem auctoritate in eos excommunicationis sententiam, si contra hanc tuam inhibitionem venire tentaverint, imo nostram*).

69 See *supra* p. 399-401.

70 See *supra* p. 277. For the objectives of the League of the Rhine see the deed of incorporation in MGH *Const.* 2, no 428 I, 580-581.

71 See the list of constituents of the League of the Rhine in MGH *Const.* 2, no 428 VI, 584-585.

72 MGH *Const.* 2 no 428 IX, p. 586: 'For the benefit of all the people we have decided and promised to each other under oath that, if the princes who are entitled to elect a king perchance might have elected, or might want to elect, more than one contender, we will stand by none of them in word or deed, nor will we, secretly or openly, render any service to them, nor will we lend money, or allow any of them to enter a city, nor will we swear an oath of

The electors
selling their
votes

In the months preceding the Frankfurt conference, one of the electors, Duke Louis II of Bavaria, the count palatine at the Rhine, was negotiating with Richard of Cornwall about the price for which Louis was prepared to sell his vote to Richard. The negotiations on the part of Richard were conducted by John of Avesnes, count of Hainault and a brother-in-law of William of Holland. The parties agreed on a price of 12,000 pounds sterling, 4000 to be paid in advance and the rest after the election[73]. Obviously, Duke Louis had decided not to advance the cause of his ward, Conradin, out of greed or because of the papal prohibition, or both, we do not know, but he did manage to obtain a promise from Richard that the Englishman would protect the interests of Conradin as duke of Swabia and that he would not obstruct Conradin's Sicilian aspirations[74]. The mighty archbishop of Cologne, Conrad of Hochstaden, the most powerful clerical prince in the kingdom, had also contacted Richard and assured him of his vote, at a price of course (8000 pounds sterling)[75]. There was yet another vote for sale, being the vote of the archbishop of Mainz, Gerhard of Dhaun. The prelate from Mainz was in dire straits at the time, since he had been captured and incarcerated by Duke Albert of Brunswick during

---

fealty. But if the princes have elected one man to be king, then we will directly and without any contradiction render the required services and do honour to him' (*Ad salutem etiam totius populi et terrae statuimus et promissimus ibidem sub debito iuramenti, quod si domini principes, ad quos spectat regis electio, forsitan plus quam unum eligerent vel eligant, quod nos nulli ipsorum astabimus verbo vel opere aut aliqua servicia exhibemus clam vel aperte aut mutuum dabimus, vel in aliquam civitatem intromittimus neque fidelitatem iuramenti praestabimus … Si autem principes unum dominum in regem elegerint, illi continuo sine omni contradictione servicia debita et honores exhibemus*). The proclamation was repeated at a parliament of the League, held later in the year (in August) at Würzburg: MGH *Const.* 2 no 428 XI, *sub* 7, 589.

73   From the contract between Duke Louis and Richard, MGH *Const.* 2 no 379, 480. The Bavarian was also promised an English princess, a sister or daughter of Richard, as his bride. Louis was a widower ever since he had killed his wife, whom he suspected of adultery, unjustly as it turned out. Fortunately for the English princesses, the English marriage never came about.

74   MGH *Const.* 2 no 381, 481-482: 'The same Richard shall renounce all concessions and contracts relating to the kingdom of Sicily and all that pertains to it and he shall not trouble the son of Conrad and his heirs regarding that kingdom in the future and he shall protect and maintain him in his rights regarding the duchy of Swabia as well as the other fiefs and allods that are rightly his' (*Idem R(ichardus) omnibus condicionibus et pactionibus quibuscunque super regno Sicilie et eius pertinenciis habitis renunciabit nec filium domini Chunradi vel eius heredes super dicto regno decetero molestabit et ipsum in iure suo, tam in ducatu Swevie quam in aliis terris et allodiis que debet habere, fovebit et conservabit*). Richard's promise to endorse the rights of Conradin to his German fiefs and allods was corroborated by a guarantee of his personal representatives, the earl of Gloucester and John of Avesnes: MGH *Const.* 2 no 386, 485-486.

75   See the contract between Archbishop Conrad and Richard in MGH *Const.* 2 no 383, 482-483. Archbishop Conrad seems to have sold his vote much cheaper than Duke Louis, but he had been able to negotiate additional territorial concessions by Richard which were more valuable to him than cash.

a feud. Richard agreed to pay the ransom (5000 pounds sterling) to Duke Albert and an additional 3000 to the archbishop[76]. Richard was now assured of three votes in the electoral board, but he had not been able to buy the vote of the third clerical elector, the archbishop of Trier, Arnold of Isenburg, that would have gained him the majority, according to one source because the archbishop was incorruptible, but according to another because Archbishop Arnold had already sold his vote to another contender for the price of 20,000 pounds sterling[77]. The other contender was none other than the king of Castile, Alfonso the Wise (1221-1252-1284), a son of Elisabeth of Hohenstaufen, one of the daughters of Philip of Swabia, who had married King Ferdinand III of Castile in 1219, a marriage arranged by her guardian Frederick II[78]. Alfonso's briberies are less well documented than Richard's, but he seems to have won over two other electors as well, the duke of Saxony and the margrave of Brandenburg. As was observed earlier[79], the king of Bohemia, though not a German, was added to the electoral college as a seventh member to prevent the stalemate now apparent. King Ottokar II (c. 1233-1253-1278), a very powerful monarch, was not present himself at Frankfurt on 13 January 1257, but he had sent a representative with full powers of attorney to cast his vote[80].

Archbishop Arnold of Trier and Duke Albert of Saxony arrived at Frankfurt accompanied by the plenipotentiary of King Ottokar of Bohemia. Margrave Johann of Brandenburg was not with them, but had empowered the Saxon duke to cast his vote for him. A little later on that day, the archbishop of Cologne and Duke Louis of Bavaria approached Frankfurt with an impressive military escort, alarming the other electors already there. They retreated behind the walls of Frankfurt, closed the city gates, and declined the invitation of the others to come and join them to proceed with the election of a new king. The electors *outside* the city thereupon proceeded to the election of Richard of Cornwall

A contested election

---

76   For these details see Thomas Wykes (1222-1291/93), *Chronicon* ad ann. 1256, ed. Luard, London 1869, 113 and the concordant reports in *Chronicon episcoporum Wormatiensium* (*Annales Wormatienses*) (until 1300) ad ann. 1257, MGH *SS* 17, 59 and *Annales Hamburgenses* (until 1265) ad ann. 1257, MGH *SS* 16, 383.

77   Thomas Wykes, *Chronicon* ad ann. 1256, ed. Luard, Londen 1869, 115.

78   Alfonso's bid for the German throne originated in Italy, where the city of Pisa was first to recognize the Castilian king as the true successor to the Hohenstaufen heritage: see the oath of fealty (dated on 18 March 1265) sworn by the Pisans to Alfonso as emperor of the Romans in J.C. Lünig, *Codex Italiae Diplomaticus* I, Frankfurt/Leipzig 1725, no XII, col. 1061-1064.

79   See *supra* p. 400, fnt. 43.

80   For what follows see the encyclical letter of Archbishop Conrad of Cologne and Duke Louis of Bavaria about the proceedings at Frankfurt in 1257 (MGH *Const.* 2 no 385, 484-485) and the important additional information in the correspondence on and the testimony produced in the lawsuit in Rome on these proceedings (on which see *infra* p. 435) printed in *Ann. eccl.* Tom. 22, Paris 1870, ad ann. 1263, §§ 38-63,104-113.

to which they contended to be entitled since the electors *inside* the city had refused to join them[81]. The electors inside the city did not elect Alfonso immediately, but set a date at which that would happen, the first of April next. On that day, Archbishop Arnold of Trier came to Frankfurt alone, where he made a proclamation that King Alfonso had been elected king of the Romans by himself, the duke of Saxony, the margrave of Brandenburg, and the king of Bohemia[82]. The charade was completed by the fact that the representative of the king of Bohemia had previously, some days after 13 January, also assented to the election of Richard of Cornwall[83].

The nadir of the Empire	The election of two kings in 1257 marks the nadir of the medieval German Empire. It was far worse than a similar election of two kings – Otto of Poitou and Philip of Swabia – in 1198[84], since the pope as well as the German princes had lost interest: the German royal title had become almost irrelevant. Alexander IV had lost interest after having excluded the Hohenstaufens from election and the only German prince mentioned as a possible contender, a younger brother of Margrave Johan of Brandenburg (*not* the margrave himself), lost interest after his brother had sided with Alfonso of Castile. The only issue of real interest to the German princes, secular *and* clerical, was the consolidation of their own territorial power. Consequently, it suited them very well to elect a king not supposed to be too directly involved in German affairs. Alfonso of Castile never showed himself in Germany and Richard of

---

81   MGH *Const.* 2 no 385, p. 485: 'Since accordingly the right to have an election was with us and we have elected Richard of Cornwall as king of the Romans, a brother of the most glorious King Henry of England and a man outstanding by his morals, his ancestry, and above all by his nobleness' (*cum sic penes nos ius plenum remanserit eligendi, dominum Ricardum comitem Cornubie, fratrem domini H(enrici) regis Anglie illustrissimi, tam morum quam generis precipue nobilitate pollentem, eligimus in regem Romanorum*). The archbishop of Cologne and Duke Ludwig alleged that the king of Bohemia and the margrave of Brandenburg were absent, without sending plenipotentiaries. This was untrue, since the king had sent a personal representative and the margrave had commissioned the duke of Saxony to cast his vote for him. They further alleged that they had unsuccessfully invited the archbishop of Trier and the duke of Saxony to join them, suggesting that these princes were also absent.
82   *Ann. eccl.*, Tom. 22, Paris 1870, ad ann. 1263 § 58, 111, r. col.: 'The archbishop of Trier, authorized by the king of Bohemia, the duke, and the margrave, has publicly and solemnly proclaimed the said king of Castile as king and emperor of the Romans in the name of God in the same city of Frankfurt' (*Trevirensis archiepiscopus a rege Bohemiae, duce et marchione sibi super hoc potestate commissa, dictum regem Castellae suo et illorum nomine publice et solemniter in eodem oppido de Franchenford, Dei nomine invocato, in Romanorum regem et imperatorem elegit*).
83   *Ann. eccl.*, Tom. 22, Paris 1870, ad ann. 1263 § 55, 110, l. col.: '*Cui electioni <Richardi> per charissimum in Christo filium nostrum regem Bohemiae illustrem post paucos dies consensus praestito* etc.'.
84   See *supra* p. 152-154.

Cornwall was, indeed, crowned and consecrated by Archbishop Conrad of Cologne in Aachen on 17 May 1257[85], but left for England again in 1258, returning to his German kingdom only occasionally later. Emperor he was never to be, since the final decision on that issue rested with the pope (X 1,6,34 ('*Venerabilem*')) and Alfonso of Castile had filed an appeal against Richard's coronation with the pope in Rome[86]. The advocates with the Rota squeezed money out of both litigants, Richard and Alfonso, for years to come since the procedure dragged on without an end in sight, a lawyers' dream[87].

King Manfred

The news of the death of William of Holland and the contested German election of 1257 must have caused Manfred to reconsider his position. He officially had been appointed as regent (*baiulus*) of the kingdom of Sicily by Conradin, meaning Conradin's guardian, Duke Louis of Bavaria, and his mother on 20 April 1255[88] despite his excommuni-

Manfred is crowned king of Sicily

---

85   Matthew Paris, *Chronica maiora* ad ann. 1257, ed. H.R. Luard V, 640: '*Die vero Assensionis Dominicae, scilicet [decimo] sexto kalendas Junii, coronatus est comes Cornubiae Ricardus in regem Alemanniae sive Romanorum per manum Conradi archiepiscopi Coloniensis, apud Aquisgranicum*'.

86   On the issue see a letter of Pope Urban IV to King Alfonso of Castile from 17 April 1262 in MGH *Epp. saec. xiii*, no 517, 480-481, mentioning that the contenders were not (yet) prepared to subject their dispute to papal decision. They were later: see the documents in *Ann. eccl.* mentioned earlier (fnt. 80) and the following fnt. On these Roman proceedings see also the biography (in verse) of Urban IV, written shortly after Urban's demise in 1264 by the 13th-century French poet Thierry de Vaucouleurs, printed in Muratori 3.2, Milan 1734, col. 416.

87   Thomas Wykes, *Chronicon* ad ann. 1256, ed. Luard, London 1869, 115: 'But the king of Spain, putting his faith and confidence in this worthless election, sent official representatives to the papal *curia* in this dubious matter, only to return empty-handed and confused after staying there for quite some time and having spent enormous amounts of money' (*Rex autem Hispanniae in tam frivola electione spem ponens et fiduciam, misit solemnes nuncios ad curiam domini Papae pro negotio praetextato, qui diutinam in curia sed inutilem moram facientes, et innumerabilem pecuniam consumentes, in nullo penitus profecerunt, quin etiam demum confusi et vacui recesserunt*). The procedure only came to an end after the demise of Richard of Cornwall in 1272: see *infra* p. 505.

88   Böhmer, *Acta imperii selecta*, Innsbruck 1870, n. 972, 677-678(678): 'After proper consultation and careful consideration with the dukes of Bavaria, our beloved uncles, other family members, and our mother, we have ordained to grant the regency of our kingdom until our majority to the noble lord Manfred, the prince of Tarento, our beloved uncle, in whose loyalty, prudence, and competence we fully confide. The regency will necessarily be entrusted to him, and we commit the guardianship over our person to him, if perchance we come to our kingdom before that event' (*deliberato consilio et consideratione diligenti providimus, una cum dominis ducibus Bavarie, dilectis avunculis nostris, aliisque nostris consanguineis, et domina matre nostra, nobili viro Mannfredo principi Tarentino, dilecto patruo nostro, de cuius fide, prudentia et sufficientia plene confisi, balium ipsius regni nostri usque ad nostros puberes annos committimus,*

cation by Pope Alexander IV[89]. Since then, Manfred styled himself 'general representative of King Conrad II of Sicily'[90]. This official confirmation of his position, the same as he had held after the demise of Frederick II[91], helped Manfred to conclude successfully his campaign against the papal army in South Italy and the rebellious Sicilian barons and cities. By the end of 1256 he was in complete control of the island of Sicily and South Italy[92]. Now that Pope Alexander IV had successfully excluded Conradin from the succession to the German throne, making that child a powerless 'kinglet' (*regulus*)[93] in the custody of the duke of Bavaria, incapable even of effectively taking control of his German duchy of Swabia, Manfred found himself in a position not unlike the dilemma his father's uncle Philip of Swabia had faced in 1200[94]. The legitimate heir to the German throne, Frederick II, was a child in faraway Sicily then and the immediate interests of the Hohenstaufen family in Germany had demanded that the power vacuum should be filled by raising his uncle, Philip of Swabia, to the throne. It was a choice Manfred's father not only had understood, but had even appreciated[95], as Manfred must have known. He now decided to take a similar step. It was highly unlikely that young Conradin would ever be capable, or even be allowed, to realize his claim to the crown of Sicily and when a (convenient) rumour spread that the child had died in Bavaria, Manfred was crowned king of Sicily on 10 August 1258 in Palermo 'at the insistence of the magnates of the realm'[96]. Significantly, the coro-

---

ad cuius manus balium ipsum de iure devolvitur, et eius tutele personam nostram committimus, si infra hec tempora regnum nostrum predictum nos contigerit introire).

89   See the papal bull from 25 March 1255 in Winkelmann, *Acta imperii inedita seculi XIII*, Tom. 2, Innsbruck 1885, no 1044, 726-729.

90   *Annales ianuenses* (Bartolomeo scriba) ad ann. 1254, MGH *SS* 18, 233: '*Vocabat enim se hoc modo: Manfredus Frederici divi imperatoris filius princeps Taranti, honoris sancti Angeli, domini Conradi Secundi Sicilie regis vicarius generalis*'.

91   See *supra* p. 417.

92   Matthew Paris, *Chronica maiora* ad ann. 1256, ed. H.R. Luard V, 572 and Saba Malaspina 1,7, MGH *SS* 35, 111: '*Manfredus ipse tocius regni dominus remaneret*'.

93   Conradin pathetically styled himself as '*Conradus secundus die gratia regnorum Ierusalem et Sicilie rex ac dux Svevie*': see the document cited above in fnt. 88.

94   See *supra* p. 153-154.

95   See *supra* p. 194.

96   Nicolaus de Jamsilla, *Historia de rebus gestis* (Muratori 8, col. 584): 'Meanwhile, when the prince <Manfred> went to Sicily, rumour reached the kingdom that his nephew King Conrad, son of the deceased King Conrad I, had died in Germany. As soon as they heard that rumour, the counts and other magnates of the kingdom and the prelates of the churches in Sicily went to see the prince, as did the representatives of the major cities. They all urged the prince, who had ruled the kingdom up till then on behalf of the just mentioned king and himself and had brought it to great peace, to accept the administration and the crown of that kingdom himself as king and true heir of that kingdom. When this request was made to him unanimously by all, the prince has been chosen as king with the consent of all the counts and magnates and also of the prelates of the kingdom and he solemnly accepted the crown

nation of Manfred was not only supported by the Sicilian secular magnates, but also by most of the Sicilian prelates despite the fact that the king was an excommunicate, once again demonstrating that the king of Sicily posed a real challenge to papal authority and even to the unity of the Church[97].

For a short and final spell, the arts and sciences flourished at the court of the king of Sicily in Palermo as a last Hohenstaufen king endeavoured to implement the grand strategy of Frederick II: *not* the union of the Sicilian kingdom with the German Empire, a superseded policy by then, but the union of the Sicilian kingdom with the kingdom of Italy, the *regnum italicum* of old. It was not an entirely unrealistic policy, however strong the resistance of many Lombard cities might be. The Ghibelline party still had supporters in Tuscany (Siena), Lombardy (Cremona), and the Romagna (Forli) and there were still some redoubtable war-lords actively engaged in these regions on behalf of the king of Sicily, men like the notorious Ezzelino da Romano, but also Uberto Pallavicini (*c.* 1197-1269) from Lombardy, and the Genoese condottière Percivalle Doria (*c.* 1195-1264), a warrior and a poet like Frederick

Manfred's Italian policy

---

of the kingdom according to the customs and the ceremonies of his predecessors as kings of the kingdom of Sicily on 11 August in the year of the Incarnation of the Lord 1258' (*Interim autem dum in Siciliam Princeps iret, venit rumor in Regnum, quod nepos eius rex Cònradus, filius quondam Regis Conradi Primi in Alemannia obiisset: quo rumore audito Comites et alii Magnates Regni, Praelati etiam Ecclesiarum in Sicilia ad Principem profecti sunt: singularum quoque magnarum Civitatum Nuntii ex parte Civitatum suarum ad eumdem Principem perrexerunt, unanimiter omnes petentes ab eo, ut ipse Princeps, qui usque tunc pro parte praedicti Regis Conradi et sua Regnum rexerat, et in tanta pace constituerat, ipsius Regni gubernaculum et coronam tamquam Rex et ipsius Regni verus haeres acciperet: qua petitione unanimiter sibi facta ab omnibus, idem Princeps per concordem omnium Comitum et Magnatum, ac etiam Praelatorum Regni electionem in Regem electus, Coronam Regni Siciliae in Majori Ecclesia Panormitana, iuxta consuetudinem et ritum praedecessorum suorum Regni Siciliae, solemniter accepit, Anno Domini Incarnationis 1258, die undecima mensis Augusti, primae indictionis*). See for the date of 10 Augustus: *Annales Cavenses* ad ann. 1258, MGH *SS* 3, 194 (*in festo sancti Laurentii*); *Chronicon Suessanum* ad ann. 1258, ed. Pellicia, *Raccolta di varie croniche ... appartenenti alla storia del regno di Napoli*, Tome 1, Naples 1780, 55 (*in die sancti Laurentii*) and *Annales Siculi* ad ann. 1256, MGH *SS* 19, 499 (*decimo die mensis Augusti*).

97   Matthew Paris, *Chronica maiora* ad ann. 1258, ed. H.R. Luard V, 722: 'Moreover, the king and the Sicilians created archbishops and bishops without the pope's permission, even against his will, since all of them were more obedient to the king than to the pope and rendered homage and reverence to the king despite the papal prohibition' (*Insuper creaverunt rex et Appuli archiepiscopos et episcopos sine assensu ipsius Papae, immo potius eo invito, qui omnes communiter plus ipsi regi quam Papae obediebant et, contempta Papali prohibitione, regi honorem et reverentiam exhibebant*). This is why Alexander IV reacted with an extremely vicious bull, excommunicating all Sicilian prelates participating in Manfred's coronation, printed in Bart. Capasso, *Historia diplomatica Regni Siciliae inde ab anno 1250 ad annum 1266*, Naples 1874, no 310 (10 April 1259), 167-174. Among the nobles excommunicated for their attendance of the coronation of Manfred was Riccardo di Caserta (169), who had switched sides yet again by defecting from the papal cause (see *supra* p. 427). Treason was his second nature: see *infra* p. 462.

II, Enzio, and Manfred. In October 1258 Manfred appointed Doria as has lieutenant (*vicarius*) in the Romagna, Pallavicini in Lombardy, and Giordano d'Agliano, another warlord in Hohenstaufen service, in Tuscany[98]. The latter wrote Italian national history, when he led a Ghibelline army consisting of men from Siena, Ghibelline exiles from Florence, and German mercenaries to victory over Florence in the battle of Montaperti (4 September 1260). The Florentine Guelphs were so thoroughly beaten that their city was completely at the mercy of the victorious Ghibellines. The great city on the Arno was only spared complete destruction thanks to the intervention of the leader of the Florentine Ghibelline exiles in the victorious army, Manente degli Uberti (1212-1264), nicknamed 'Flourhead' (*Farinata*)[99]. The battle of Montaperti was the turning point in Manfred's career. He now had control over Tuscany (except for Lucca), but it was a success that led to his downfall. Not because his nephew Conradin now publicly turned against him[100], but mainly because the pope finally decided that the time had come to look for a more effective candidate for the Sicilian crown than the son of the immobile king of England.

Urban IV   Pope Alexander IV died at Viterbo on 25 May 1261. He had created only two cardinals during his pontificate, none of whom was to partake in the conclave deciding on his succession[101]. Consequently, the

---

98   For all these appointments see Saba Malaspina 2,2, MGH *SS* 35, 123-124.
99   For this story see Dante, *Inferno* 10, 85-93 and Giov. Villani (*c*. 1280-1348), *Nuova Cronica* 7,81, ed. Porta I, Parma 1990, 384-387.
100   As soon as news of the coronation of Manfred had reached Bavaria, Conradin had sent envoys to the pope as the sovereign lord of the kingdom of Sicily to protest against Manfred's usurpation. As was to be expected, the ambassy achieved nothing at all. See *Chronica pontificum et imperatorum Mantuana* (13th cent.), MGH *SS* 24, 216: '*Conradinus, cognita hac malitia, misit ambaxatores cum suis et magnatum litteris sigillis pendentibus ad dominum papam … Tamen nichil penitus profuerunt eidem*'. More important than this was the fact that after Montaperti the Guelphs (!) of Tuscany, meaning the only Guelph city left, Lucca, invited Conradin to come to Tuscany as quickly as possible to assist them in their war against the usurper Manfred and his Ghibelline allies, once the trusted allies of Conradin's grandfather. For this embassy see Tholomaeus of Lucca (*c*. 1236-1327), *Annales Lucenses* ad ann. 1262, MGH *SS rer. Germ. N.S.* 8, 145. Conradin responded that he was sorry to be unable to come to the rescue, due to his age, but he promised to come once he became of age and fight with them 'against Manfred, the former prince of Tarento, and the Ghibellines' (*contra Manfredum, quondam Principem tarentinum et contra ghibellinos*). Conradin's letter is printed in G.-C. Gebauer, *Leben und denckwürdige Thaten Herrn Richards, erwählten römischen Kaysers*, Leipzig 1744, 597-598. Conradin was then nine years of age and consequently the seal of his guardian, Duke Louis of Bavaria, was also attached to the letter.
101   The fate of the two cardinals appointed by Alexander IV is interesting, since it is illustrative of the political situation at the time. Cardinal Riccardo di Montecassino was abbot of the monastery of Montecassino when he was raised to the cardinalate by Alexander IV but deposed as a cardinal by the pope shortly after because Riccardo was on friendly terms with Manfred and had even participated in his coronation. Cardinal Tesauro Beccheria was tried

conclave consisted of only seven cardinals. They deliberated for months but were unable to elect one of them, which is why they finally decided to elect an outsider, the Patriarch of Jerusalem Jacques Pantaléon (*c.* 1195-1261-1264), who happened to be at the papal court at the time, on 29 August 1261. Jacques, the son of a shoemaker from Troyes, chose the name Urban IV[102], probably in honour of his predecessor Urban II, who was also from France. Urban quickly decided to strengthen the *curia* by nominating seven new cardinals soon after his consecration, three of them from France, thus considerably reinforcing the influence of the court of France in the *curia*. One of the recently appointed cardinals, Simon de Brion, was even chancellor of France at the time[103]. The new pope might have been a Frenchman, but he shared the bias of his predecessors against the house of Hohenstaufen, as became abundantly clear soon after his consecration when voices were raised in Germany in 1262 to elect Conradin as king of the Romans out of frustration with the absentee kingship of Richard of Cornwall[104]. As soon as Urban IV was informed by the king of Bohemia of this initiative, he reacted immediately[105]. The new archbishop of Mainz, Werner of Epstein, was reminded that Alexander IV had explicitly prohibited the three clerical electors from even considering Conradin and that they had been instructed to threaten the other four secular electors with excommunication if they ventured to do so[106]. Urban repeated this instruction. Never again was a member of the house of Hohenstaufen, 'that perverse

---

and sentenced to death in Florence in September 1258 for conspiring with Manfred to bring the Ghibellines back to power in that city. For the deposition of Cardinal Riccardo see the bull of Alexander IV of 10 April 1259 in Bart. Capasso, *Historia diplomatica Regni Siciliae inde ab anno 1250 ad annum 1266*, Naples 1874, no 310, 167-174(172) and for the execution of Cardinal Beccheria see G. Villani, *Nuova cronica* 7,65, ed. Porta I, Parma 1990, 359-360.

102   For the election of Urban IV see *Annales S. Iustinae Patavini* ad ann. 1261, MGH *SS* 19, 181: '*Anno Domini 1261, cum summus pontifex Alexander sex annis cum dimidio Romanam ecclesiam gubernasset, die septimo exeunte Madio vite sue cursum in civitate Viterbio pacifice terminavit ... Post cuius obitum cardinales numero octo de summo pontifice eligendo magnam inter se discordiam tribus mensibus habuerunt. Tandem septiformis Spiritus gratia illustrati, die tercio exeunte, reverendissimum virum patriarcham Ierosolimitanum, Gallicum natione, qui tunc temporis erat in curia pro negociis terre sancte, concorditer elegerunt, qui Urbanus quartus mutato nomine est vocatus*'. The chronicle mentions eight cardinals, but one of them, Cardinal Báncsa, was in his native Hungary at the time of the Viterbo conclave. The chronicle also reports that Alexander IV had appointed no cardinals during his pontificate, which is incorrect: see *supra* fnt. 101.

103   Urban IV created no fewer than fourteen cardinals during his pontificate, six of them being from France, thus establishing a strong French party in the *curia*.

104   Richard resided in England since October 1260.

105   See the letter of Urban IV to the king of Bohemia in MGH *Epp. saec. xiii* 3, no 520, 486-488.

106   See *supra* p. 430.

breed, where evil is handed down from father to son'[107], to be elected king of the Romans[108]. That nest of vipers was to be exterminated in the Sicilian kingdom as well. When the king of England was incapable or unwilling to do so, someone else needed to be found who would be.

Charles of
Anjou

In 1262 master Albert of Parma was sent to France once again[109] to find out if Charles of Anjou was still interested[110]. He was, but since he was a vassal of the king of France, he required the permission of his brother Louis IX to accept the Sicilian crown. Louis had returned to his kingdom in 1254 and was now, in 1262, the undisputed head of European royalty, a position once held by the German kings and emperors. Louis had a well-earned reputation for fairness and the equitable administration of justice, and he (and his mother) had always objected to the relentless persecution of the house of Hohenstaufen by succeeding popes. This is why the king had strong objections to the nomination

---

107 MGH *Epp. saec. xiii* 3, no 520, 487: '*in hoc pravo genere, patrum in filios cum sanguine derivata malitia, sicut carnis propagatione, sic imitatione operum nati genitoribus successerunt*'.

108 Letter of Urban IV to the archbishop of Mainz (3 June 1262), MGH *Epp. saec. xiii* 3, no 521, 488-490: 'And therefore we strongly demand, request, and beseech your brotherhood by way of this apostolic letter to the virtue of obedience and to the due loyalty you owe us and the Roman Church on pain of excommunication we now announce in advance by emphatically instructing you never to elect the child Conrad as king, nor advance him as a possible contender, nor consent to his election, so that you will be excommunicated if you have ventured to do anything that contravenes our command by nominating that Conrad, electing him, or consenting with his election and even when you have not impeded his nomination and election' (*Ideoque fraternitatem tuam monemus, rogamus et hortamur attente, per apostolica tibi scripta in virtute obedientie et sub debito fidelitatis, quo nobis et ecclesiae Romane teneris, ac sub poena excommunicationis, quam ex nunc in te proferimus, districte precipiendo mandantes, quatinus memoratum Conradum puerum nullo umquam tempore in regem eligas nec nomines neque consentias in eundem, ita quod excommunicatus existas, si contra mandatum nostrum facere vel venire presumpseris et eundem Conradum nominaveris vel elegeris aut in ipsum consenseris … et etiam si eius nominationem et electionem non impediveris*). In the end, nothing came of this intermezzo to elect Conradin, since Richard of Cornwall quickly returned to Germany in June 1262. See Thomas Wykes, *Chronicon* ad ann. 1262, ed. Luard, Londen 1869, 131: '*Eodem anno xi. kal. Julii dominus rex Alemanniae recessit de Londonia ad transferendum tertia vice in Alemanniam*'. He returned to England in February 1263 (Wykes, *Chronicon* ad ann. 1262, ed. Luard, Londen 1869, 132) as soon as he had financially satisfied the leading German princes yet again.

109 For master Albert's prior embassy to France see *supra* p. 422. In 1256 the lawyer had made a survey of all the negotiations with the king of England in the matter of the Sicilian kingdom until then at the request of Pope Alexander IV. It has survived and is published in MGH *Epp. saec. xiii* 3, no 446, 405-411.

110 The pope later, in a letter to Queen Margaret of France (on which see *infra* p. 449, fnt. 149), stated that he had first offered the crown of Sicily to Louis IX for one his sons and that he only turned to Charles of Anjou after the king had refused to contemplate that offer (*Ann. eccl.*, Tom. 22, Paris 1870, ad ann. 1264 § 2, 123): '*regnum Siciliae … charissimo in Christo filio nostro regi Francorum illustri viro tuo, ad opus alicuius ex communibus natis vestris duximus liberaliter offerendum*'.

of his brother. According to Louis IX, the crown of Sicily belonged to Conradin as a matter of course, since he was the heir of Conrad IV. When master Albert reminded the king that this was unacceptable to the pope and had been the reason why the throne of Sicily was presented to prince Edmond instead, it was just one more reason for Louis to resist the offer made to his brother[111]. The king could not square it with 'the purity of his conscience' (*puritas conscientiae*) to get involved in this dirty affair. He felt that it would, if he did, offend many because in doing so he was unlawfully violating the rights of others[112]. For all he knew, here was yet another pope acting 'against God and reason' (*contre Dieu et contre raison*)[113]. But there was more. Louis must have regarded his brother Charles totally unsuitable for the position offered to him by the pope. Charles of Anjou and his older royal brother were two completely different characters[114]. Louis IX was a very religious and conscientious man. Charles, a frustrated younger son, was a violent and completely unscrupulous man, riding roughshod over the law whenever

---

111   From a letter of Urban IV to master Albert of Parma from 1262 (*Ann. eccl.*, Tom. 22, Paris 1870, ad ann. 1262 § 21, 83-84): 'We have recently received your letter containing, amongst other things, that our beloved son in Christ, the glorious king of France, has lent his ear to the most deceitful insinuations of some people who want to dissuade him from the affair for which we have sent you to negotiate with him and has come to the conclusion by the suggestions of the same liars that Conradin, the grandson of Frederick, who was once emperor of the Romans, is entitled to the kingdom of Sicily, or, if said Conradin has, as they say, 'forfeited his right', that then Edmond, the son of our beloved son in Christ the glorious king of England, is entitled to the kingdom of Sicily on account of the grant by the Apostolic See' (*Tuas nuper recepimus litteras inter caetera continentes, quod charissimus in Christo filius noster rex Francorum illustris, verbis proculdubio subdolis aliquorum intendentium ipsum avertere a negotio, ad quod cum ipso tractandum te missimus, aures credulitatis inclinans; et eorumdem fingentium Conradinum nepotem quondam Friderici olim Romanorum imperatoris, vel si dictus Conradinus, ut eorum verbis utamur, a suo iure cecidit, nobilem virum Edmundum natum charissimi in Christo filii nostri regis Angliae illustris per concessionem Sedis Apostolicae in regno Siciliae ius habere suggestionibus informatus*).
112   Urban IV to master Albert (*Ann. eccl.*, Tom. 22, Paris 1870, ad ann. 1262 § 21, 84): 'yet he is in doubt, as rightly he should if there were any truth in these suggestions that he would, as he says, to the indignation of many violate the right of another' (*tamen dubitat, nec immerito si veritas praemissis adesset, non sine multorum, ut asserit, scandalo jus invadere alienum*).
113   See *supra* p. 344.
114   The differences of the characters of the four sons of Louis VIII and Blanche of Castile (Louis, Alphonse, Robert, and Charles) were already obvious to their contemporaries. See Thomas Tuscus (*c.* 1212-*c.* 1282), *Gesta imperatorum et pontificum*, MGH SS 22, 519: 'Two of the brothers just mentioned, Louis and Alphonse, were very friendly and mild, physically weak, and unskilled in arms. But the other two, Robert and Charles, were extremely irascible, physically strong and robust, experienced in arms, and very aggressive' (*Itaque duo predictorum iam fratrum mansueti nimis fuerunt et plani, corpore debiles et armis imbelles, Lodovicus videlicet et Alfunsus. Alii vero duo scilicet Robertus et Karolus fuerunt viri plurimum animosi, fortes corpore et robusti, armis strenui et nimium bellicosi*). Robert's aggressiveness had cost him his life in 1250, during his brother's first crusade, when he led a reckless attack against Muslim forces at Mansurah endangering the whole army (see *supra* p. 410).

it stood in the way of his ambitions. Louis IX knew this, and it must have bothered, if not angered, him: he had sat in judgment many times in appeals brought against his brother[115]. Moreover, the king's wife, Queen Margaret, detested her brother-in-law Charles[116], so much so that she made her son, the heir to the throne Philip (1245-1285), swear a solemn oath to her never to enter into any alliance with his uncle Charles[117]. As a consequence of all this, negotiations with the pope and the king of France on the Sicilian affair went all but smoothly, until they suddenly gained momentum by an incident involving Charles of Anjou even more into the bedlam of Italian politics[118].

Charles of
Anjou senator
of Rome

In 1258 the great Roman *capitano del populo* Brancaleone[119] had died, creating a power vacuum in Rome. Brancaleone had been a Ghibelline, but after his demise the Ghibelline and Guelph parties in the city were fighting for control, neither party intending to submit to the secular power of the pope. Alexander IV had already fled the city in 1257, finding refuge in Viterbo, where he died, and Urban IV has never even set a foot in Rome. During his entire pontificate he resided in Viterbo

---

115   On this issue see *Vie de Saint Louis par Guillaume de Saint-Pathus, confesseur de la reine Marguerite* (*c.* 1303), ed. Delaborde, Paris 1899, 140-141 (also in *Recueil* 20, 115). In the first part of the *Olim*, the oldest records of the Parlement de Paris, Charles of Anjou is mentioned repeatedly (ed. Beugnot, Paris 1839, 131, XII (1260); 452, XIV (1259); 460, VI (1259); 480, XV (1260); 515, IV (1261); 524, XV; 717, VII (1268)). Most of these cases are about undue influence or even force exercised by Charles.
116   Queen Margaret never forgave Charles for depriving her of her Provence inheritance (see *supra* p. 396-397). Her animosity was aggravated by the fact that Charles of Anjou behaved like a tyrant in her native Provence. See also *infra* p. 449.
117   For this oath see a letter of Urban IV to Prince Philip from 1263, printed in E. Boutarique, 'Marguerite de Provence', in *Revue des Questions Historiques* 3 (1867) 417-458 (422-423): '*sicut accipimus, carissima in Christo filia nostra, Margareta, illustris regina Francie, mater tua ... quod ... non reciperes voluntatem, confederationem, conspirationem seu obligationem aliquam cum dilecto filio viro Karolo, patruo tuo, Provincie comite inires ... a te promissionem et juratoriam cautionem exegit*'. The letter of the pope is remarkable since he was negotiating with Louis IX on the matter of the Sicilian kingdom and the possible accession of Charles of Anjou at the time. Queen Margaret resisted that, and the pope intervened in this family quarrel by trying to bring over the heir to the throne, *qualitate qua* a member of the 'conseil du roy', to his side. Philip was eighteen at the time, and consequently already of age, but he had sworn another oath to his mother to remain under her guardianship until he was thirty, just like his father Louis had been under the practical guardianship of the Queen Dowager Blanche as long as she had lived. Consequently, Queen Margaret was a political force to be reckoned with. The queen was very worried about her future at the time since her pious husband seems to have seriously contemplated to enter a monastery. See Richer of Soissons (†1267), *Gesta Senoniensis ecclesiae,* 4,44, MGH *SS* 25, 328-329.
118   Charles had already been actively engaged in Italian politics since 1259, when he started extending his influence in Piedmonte from his power base in the Provence. See on Charles' Lombard involvement Thomas Tuscus, *Gesta imperatorum et pontificum*, MGH *SS* 22, 520.
119   On Brancaleone see *supra* p. 421.

or Orvieto. Consequently, Roman urban politics were beyond papal control. They concentrated on the election of a new *podestà*, or 'senator' as he was called in Rome. Until then, the choice fell usually, as in all free Italian cities, on a respected person, mostly a lawyer, from another Italian city[120]. Brancaleone, for example, was a citizen of Bologna. On this occasion, however, the citizens, Ghibellines *and* Guelphs, decided differently: they wanted a foreign *prince* as their new ruler, thus '*recklessly and shamelessly throwing away what was left of their freedom*'[121]. The Romans probably believed that only a prince of some standing, preferably a king, was able to ward off papal attempts at gaining effective control over the city again. Since a consensus between the parties was impossible, each elected a prince of its own, thus copying the German princes who had also elected two kings rather than one in 1257: the Guelphs preferred Richard of Cornwall and the Ghibellines chose Manfred (1261)[122]. Neither was acceptable to Urban IV, if only because the election of a new 'senator' for Rome was not intended, as was usual, for a limited period, but for life[123]. However, since neither of the nominees was available on short notice and the people of Rome insisted on their princely master[124], the 'good men' (*boni homines*) who were ruling the city in the meantime proceeded to another election in late August or early September 1263. This time the Ghibellines unfortunately hesitated between Manfred and Prince Peter of Aragon, the eldest son of

---

120   See *supra* p. 229.

121   Saba Malaspina 2,9 MGH *SS* 35, 138: '*procuraverunt ... libertatis reliquas ... prodigaliter ac impudice distrahere*'.

122   Thierry de Vaucouleurs, 'Vita metrica Urbani IV' (Muratori 3,2, Milan 1734, col. 408): 'But in the last year of that pope <Alexander IV> a great dispute arose among the Romans. One party gave the rights of a senator to Richard, the brother of the king of England. All of Rome was enraged. Hence Manfred, the prince of Tarento, was elected. In this way both parties asserted their rights. Consequently, Rome fell into discord, thievery, and plunder again, so that none felt safe in his own house' (*Extremo siquidem praefati Praesulis anno/ Inter Romanos lis gravis orta fuit/ Hi fratri Regis Anglorum jura Senatus/ Ricardo dederant. Undique Roma fremit/ Inde Tarentinus Princeps Manfredus ab illis/ Eligitur. Sic pars utraque jura probat/ Haec Romae renovat discordia furta, rapinas/ Ut nullus propria tutus in aede foret*). It was not unusual at the time to elect two *podesti*, one for each party, Guelph and Ghibelline: see for example *Chronicon Parmense*, *RIS*² 9.9, 24: '*Nicolaus de Baceleriis pro parte ecclesie, domnus Andalo Andaloy pro parte imperii, ambo de Bononia, fuerunt potestates Parme in milesimo cclxvi*'.

123   On this issue see a letter by Urban IV to master Albert, dated 11 August 1263 in Edm. Martène, *Thesaurus* 2, col. 26-27(27): 'we will never allow that someone, however devoted to us and the Church, rules over the city for life' (*nullatenus pateremur, quod aliquis, quantumcunque nobis et ecclesiae predicate devotus, dictam Urbem perpetuo vitae suae tempore gubernaret*). Further on in the letter, the pope refers to the prior election for life of Richard of Cornwall: 'we have not wanted to support him when he was formerly elected to the government of the city for life' (*qui cum olim electus esset ad praefatae Urbis regimen vita sua, nos nullatenus sustinere voluimus*).

124   Thierry de Vaucouleurs (Muratori 3,2, Milan 1734, col. 413): '*Populus Romanus ... petit Dominum*'.

King James of Aragon, who had recently married Manfred's daughter Constance[125], allowing the Guelphs to have Charles of Anjou elected as senator for life, thanks to the financial endorsement of Cardinal Ricardo Annibaldi[126].

The king's troubled conscience

The election of Charles of Anjou as Roman senator for life was far from welcome to Pope Urban. In order to avoid a Ghibelline government of the city, he was forced to accept Charles' nomination, but it seriously compromised his ongoing negotiations with Charles on the matter of the Sicilian 'take over'[127] since Charles now held a position in Rome independent of the pope. The Romans had handed a trump card to Charles which he dexterously played in his Sicilian game of cards with Urban IV. The pope was not alone in being confused by the offer of the senatorship of Rome to Charles of Anjou, because so was Charles' royal

---

125 For the divided sentiment of the Roman Ghibellines see Thierry de Vaucouleurs (Muratori 3,2, Milan 1734, col. 413): '*Praedicto Carolo pars cupit una dare/ Altera Manfredo dicto, pars altera nato/ Aragonum Regis, qui gener huius erat*'. For the marriage of Peter of Aragon with Manfred's daughter Constance see the Catalan chronicle of the life of King Peter of Aragon (*Cronica del Rey En Pere e dels seus antecessors passats* by Bernat Desclot (*c.* 1240-*c.*1288) cap. 51 (Buchon, 606-607). Pope Urban IV has desperately tried to prevent the marriage alliance between Manfred and the king of Aragon: see his letter to King James of Aragon of 26 April 1262, MGH *Epp. saec. xiii* 3, no 519, 482-486, full of accusations of all kinds of heinous crimes allegedly committed by the excommunicate Manfred. It was in vain: the marriage of the crown-prince of Aragon and Manfred's daughter Constance was celebrated in Montpellier on 13 June 1262. Their marriage is of great historical importance: see *infra* p. 533 ff.
126 Urban IV to master Albert on 11 August 1263 (Martène, *Thesaurus* 2, col. 26): 'We have learned that those good men who are said to rule the city presently and are about to reform its constitution, have elected our beloved son Charles, the count of Anjou and Provence, as senator or lord of the city. Whether they have elected him to the government of the city for a limited period, or for life, we do not know' (*Intelleximus quod illi boni homines qui Urbem ad praesens regere, ipsiusque statum reformare dicuntur, dilectum filium nostrum virum Carolum Andegaviae ac Provincie comitem in senatorem ipsius Urbis, vel Dominum elegerunt, utrum autem ipsum ad certum tempus, vel perpetuo ad vitam suam ad eiusdem Urbis elegerint regimen ignoramus*). The qualification 'good men' (*boni homines*) here is, of course, ironic. It is clear from the papal letter that Urban IV had no control over the election at all, since he heard about it by rumour and did not even know at the time whether Charles' election had been for life or only for a limited period. For the role of Cardinal Annibaldi see Saba Malaspina 2,9, MGH *SS* 35, 138, who emphasizes that Charles had been elected for life (*elegerunt in dominum et senatorem Urbis perpetuum*).
127 On this issue see the letters from Urban IV to master Albert in France from 11 August 1263 (Martène, *Thesaurus* 2, col. 26-27), 25 December 1263 (Martène, *Thesaurus* 2, col. 30-33), and from 7 and 9 January 1264 (Martène, *Thesaurus* 2, col. 33-43). The word 'take over' is used deliberately here, since the negotiations between master Albert and Charles of Anjou were no less complicated than the modern-day negotiations of lawyers in the merger and acquisition practice. Everything had to be arranged in great detail. See for these details the 34 articles of the draft agreement prepared by Urban IV in 1263 (MGH *Epp. saec. xiii* 3, no 539, 510-518) and the added possible modifications (MGH *Epp. saec. xiii* 3, no 540, 518-520). For the final real 'deal' see *infra* p. 455-456.

brother. Louis had kept his distance in the Sicilian affair so far, not only on account of Conradin and Prince Edmond (and, one might add, his wife), but also on account of Manfred. Manfred had proved himself loyal to the legitimate heir to the Sicilian throne, Conradin, until the *raison d'État* had forced him to take the crown himself. The court of France might be expected to have some understanding for this, if only because Louis' grandfather Philip Augustus had supported Philip of Swabia when that Hohenstaufen prince was raised to the German throne in similar circumstances in spite of the legitimate claim of Frederick II[128]. Louis had even proposed to mediate between the pope and Manfred in 1261[129]. The king of France was interested in maintaining good relations with the king of Sicily since his dramatic past experiences as a crusader had taught him the lesson that the active cooperation of the king of Sicily was crucial to the success of the new crusade he was considering at the time. On the other hand, that cooperation seemed assured when his brother was raised to the Sicilian throne and now, suddenly, there was the offer of the Roman senatorship to Charles, making his bid for the crown of Sicily a realistic option. In short, Louis IX, a very conscientious man, was confronted with a moral dilemma.

While master Albert was negotiating with Charles of Anjou and King Louis in France, Urban IV himself was playing a diplomatic game with Manfred in Italy. The purpose of that game was twofold. By entering into negotiations with Manfred the pope kept the Sicilian at bay as long as Charles of Anjou had not yet arrived in Italy, while at the same time convincing King Louis that he, the pope, was doing everything he could to come to terms with Manfred, but to no avail. Of course, the pope never seriously contemplated a positive outcome of his negotiations with Manfred. It was a diversion, but Manfred took the bait. Sicily was a hereditary kingdom, but also a papal fief and every new king of Sicily had to do homage to the pope for his Sicilian fief. Manfred's father had done so[130] and Conrad IV had (in vain) requested confirmation of his Sicilian title from Pope Innocent IV[131]. In January 1262 Manfred had even tried to bribe the pope and his cardinals by offering them the stupendous amount of 300,000 ounces of gold 'for the confirmation of his title' (*ad status sui reformationem*), but the offer was rejected, most likely much to the dismay of some of Urban's cardinals[132]. On

Urban IV and Manfred

---

128 See *supra* p. 173.
129 See a letter from Urban IV to Louis IX first published by K. Hampe, *Urban IV und Manfred*, Heidelberg 1905, 82-84. As was to be expected, the pope declined the offer.
130 See *supra* p. 187 and 190.
131 See *supra* p. 422, fnt. 22.
132 For this incident see the letter of an anonymous informant of the king of England at the papal court in Viterbo in Rymer, I.2, 69: 'Your Highness should also be informed that the

6 April 1262 Urban issued a public summons for Manfred to appear before the pope on 1 August next to answer to serious charges brought against him[133]. Manfred had been living 'in contempt of the keys' (*in contemptu clavium*) for more than five years now since he had not properly repented after his excommunication by Alexander IV in 1255[134], suppressed the Church in the Sicilian kingdom, employed Muslims at his court, reduced the inhabitants of his kingdom 'to a servile and dishonourable status' (*ad servilem et ignominiosum statum*), and allegedly committed multiple murder[135], all of them charges brought against his father at Lyon as well, and all of them allegedly as notorious as the crimes of Frederick II had been. Surprisingly, Manfred accepted the summons, even sending an ambassy to the pope requesting a postpone-

---

Lord Manfred, the usurper of the kingdom of Sicily, has sent official envoys to the *curia* on 25 January, authorized to obtain and request the confirmation of his title. They have offered 300,000 ounces of gold to the pope and his brethren, 30,000 to be paid to them immediately and the rest in deposit' (*Cognoscat insuper Regia Celsitudo quod Dominus Manfredus, Regni Siciliae occupator, solempnes nuncios, die Jovis in conversione beati Pauli, ad Curiam destinavit; quibus obtinendi et status sui reformationem impetrandi, potestatem et speciale mandatum concessit; qui trescenta millia unciarum auri Domino Papae et suis Fratribus obtulerunt; de cujus auri quantitate triginta millia unciarum incontinenti persolventes eisdem et ipsius auri residuum in deposito*).

133 For this summons see the encyclical letter of Pope Urban IV of 11 November 1262, MGH *Epp. saec. xiii* 3, no 527, 496-498(496): 'Some time ago, on 6 April last, a day on which a great crowd of faithful people from all over the world gathers every year near the Apostolic See, we have publicly summoned Manfred, the former prince of Tarento, on certain articles in the presence of that crowd to appear before us either in person or by his official and properly authorized representatives, on the first of August to do and accept what justice demands in relation to them' (*Olim in die cene Domini proximo preterito, quo videlicet die annis singulis apud sedem apostolicam de universis mundi partibus innumerabilis fidelium convenit multitudo, Manfredum quondam principem Tarentinum super certis articulis presente ipsa multitudine manifeste citavimus, ut in Kalendis Augusti proximo preteritis coram nobis per se vel per solempnes procuratores cum sufficiente mandato comparere curare, facturus et recepturus super illis, quod iustitia suaderet*). Pope Urban had learned from the criticism of the Lyon trial of Frederick II (see *supra* p. 385-386) by emphasizing that a 'public summons' (*citatio publica*) was as good as a private summons (on this issue see *supra* p. 367, fnt. 76). Saba Malaspina 2,7, MGH *SS* 35, 134, even contends that it had become usual for the pope to issue a public summons: '*citatione publica, ut est moris*'. Unlike Innocent IV, Urban IV also took care to set out the essential facts of Manfred's offences in his public indictment.

134 See *supra* p. 435-436.

135 MGH *Epp. saec. xiii* 3, no 527, 496-497: '*super eo etiam, quod ipse, Sarracenorum ritus amplectens illosque in suis cotidianis obsequiis notabiliter secum tenens et preferens Christianis in obproprium fidei orthodoxe, regnum ipsum Sicilie ad servilem et ignominiosum statum redegit, eius incolis et habitatoribus propter acerbas et intolerabiles exactiones vix valentibus respirare*'. For the murder charges see earlier in the summons and also in Urban's letter to the king of Aragon (see *supra* p. 444, fnt 125). Some of the charges related to people, such as Peter Ruffo, count of Catanzaro, who had been sentenced to death by Manfred for high treason (see *supra* p. 427, fnt. 50), as was Count Berthold of Hohenburg. The sentence of the latter was later converted into imprisonment for life, which is why the pope passes him over since it would draw needless attention to Manfred's clemency.

ment to enable him to personally attend his trial[136]. The reason why Manfred decided to submit to a papal inquisition against him remains obscure. The tribulations of his father must have taught him that no positive outcome was to be expected, but like his father before him he seems to have believed, or was led to believe, that a reconciliation with the pope was still a viable option. There is reliable evidence that a peace treaty between Manfred and the pope was indeed negotiated at the time[137], suggesting a papal policy to keep Manfred in check, while at the same time convincing the king of France that everything was done on the part of the Church to come to a peaceful settlement with that prince. This may also explain why Urban IV, still waiting for a positive decision by the king of France on the Sicilian question at the time, was not disinclined to grant the postponement Manfred had requested. The procedure was postponed until 18 November 1262, thus securing that Manfred abstained from aggression against papal positions in the meantime[138]. A week before that date, the pope issued a decree guaranteeing free passage for Manfred (an outlaw according to imperial and canon law[139]) and his retinue, limited to a number of 800 persons, no more than 100 being allowed to bear arms[140]. By this time, Manfred was close to the border with the Papal State, ready to meet with the pope as soon as an agreement had been reached in Orvieto, where Urban resided at the time. There was to be no agreement (and no public trial) because Manfred broke off the negotiations, probably because he finally realized that he was being duped[141]. If so, he should have pro-

---

136 MGH *Epp. saec. xiii* 3, no 527, 497.

137 Martène, *Thesaurus* 2, col. 24, from a letter sent from France by the Emperor Baldwin II to Manfred in June 1263): '*tractatus pacis, qui inter vos <scl. Manfredum> et Ecclesiam tractabatur*', referring to peace negotiations *before* 1263 (*tractabatur*, past tense). Baldwin also writes (col. 25) that he had previously been at the papal *curia* and he therefore may well have played a role in these peace negotiations, which may explain why he was furious when he later, in France in 1263, learned that it was a mere diversion: see *infra* p. 448, fnt. 143. There is also a reference to these negotiations in a public letter of Conradin to the German princes (Martène, *Thesaurus* 3, col. 20-24(21) (1267)) stating that Urban IV had even been ready to confirm Manfred's title to the Sicilian kingdom, but that the agreement had come to nothing: 'that equitable apostolic father, not having any respect but rather disrespect for our right, conceded and even confirmed our kingdom to him <Manfred> and his heirs, but that treaty came to nothing as it has pleased the Lord' (*apostolicus aequus pater, ad jus nostrum respectu non habens sed despectu, regnum nostrum sibi et suis heredibus concedebat et etiam confirmabat ... vero tractatus ipse, sicut Domino placuit, caderet incompletus*).

138 MGH *Epp. saec. xiii* 3, no 527, 497.

139 See *supra* p. 391.

140 MGH *Epp. saec. xiii* 3, no 527, 498: '*ne ultra octogintarum personarum, de quibus possint esse centum dumtaxat armate*'.

141 According to Saba Malaspina 2,7, MGH *SS* 35, 136, Manfred refused to consent to the papal demand that he should restore their estates to the exiled Sicilian nobles. It was a condition Manfred could not possibly meet, if only because he had granted these estates to his own

ceeded with his army to Rome instantly, where he was elected senator
by the Ghibellines of the city in 1261, but he left for Apulia and the
comfort of his palace in Foggia instead (December 1262). It was the
strategic mistake that enabled the Guelphs of the city to elect Charles
of Anjou in 1263[142] and in the end decided Manfred's fate.

The king's
conscience
at ease

Now that Manfred had broken off negotiations with the Apostolic
See, Urban IV had what he needed to convince the king of France
that Manfred was incorrigible. The pope excommunicated Manfred
on 29 March 1263 for good measure, making him the only prince
in history enjoying the extraodinary privilege of being excommunicated three times by three successive popes. At the same time, the
papal envoys at the court of France were insisting that Manfred was
entirely to blame for the failure of the peace negotiations. The exiled
Latin Emperor of Constantinople Baldwin II[143], who was at the court
of France at the time and had been personally involved in the 'peace
negotiations' between Manfred and the *curia*[144], was disgusted by the
cynicism of papal policy. He warned Manfred, urging him to send an
embassy to the court of France to present his side of these 'negotiations'. His letter did not reach Manfred though. It was intercepted at
Rimini and came into the hands of Urban IV, who sent it to master
Albert in France to use it to his advantage[145]. On the very same day
(28 July) that Urban IV forwarded Baldwin's letter to master Albert in
France, the pope sent a letter to the king of England informing Henry
III that he retracted the grant of the kingdom of Sicily made to Prince
Edmond. The pope had the audacity to even urge the recipient, the
king of England, to publicly support the papal policy to look elsewhere
for a possible alternative to Manfred[146]. This was, of course, a move

---

Sicilian partisans. If this condition was indeed proposed during the negotiations in November
1262, it confirms my impression that the pope intended these negotiations to fail, since he
knew Manfred would never accept it.

142   On the Roman senatorial elections of 1261 and 1263 see *supra* p. 443.

143   Constantinople had been reconquered by the Byzantine Emperor Michael Palaeologus
(1223-1261-1285) on 25 July 1261, forcing the Latin Emperor Baldwin into exile. Baldwin
first went to the court of Manfred in Sicily and from there to the pope and to the court of the
king of France. He died in Naples in 1273: see *infra* p. 532, fnt. 152.

144   See *supra* p. 447, fnt. 137.

145   The letter of Baldwin to Manfred is in Martène, *Thesaurus* 2, col. 23-26; the covering
letter of Urban IV to master Albert (28 July 1263) is at col. 23.

146   From the letter of pope Urban IV to King Henry III (28 July 1263), MGH *Epp. saec.
xiii* 3, no 553, 533-537 (536): 'considering that the said Roman Church has not been freed
by your interference, which she has been expecting for quite a while, from all calamities and
tribulations, as we must reluctantly admit, we have been compelled to make a more convenient
arrangement with respect to the kingdom of Sicily, since it is of great importance to us and to
the Church to make different plans with regard to that kingdom as we deem appropriate to the
honour and the future of the said Church. Since it is our right and the right of the Church to
dispose of the said kingdom of Sicily and make arrangements as we see fit and since the con-

to take away the qualms of Louis IX, who had not only objected to the papal plans with Sicily on account of Conradin and Manfred, but also on account of the papal grant to Prince Edmond[147]. It was only after the election of his brother Charles as Roman senator in August 1263 that Louis IX, slowly but surely, began to overcome his moral scruples. There was, however, still resistance within the royal council, since Queen Margaret was not the only one opposed to the Sicilian plan, but also the powerful Duke Hugh IV of Burgundy (1213-1272), a *pair de France* and a companion of the king in his Egyptian crusade[148]. Urban IV, wisely, concentrated his efforts on bringing the queen over to his side. In May 1264 Margaret had finally given up her resistance, as the pope assured his cardinals: '*peace between our beloved daughter in Christ Margaret, the illustrious queen of France, and the count has been restored*'[149]. Around the same time, Louis IX at last decided to support

---

ditions attached to the grant of that kingdom by our predecessor have not been met, you shall not from now trouble us and the Church in the matter of that kingdom and you shall not oppose any impediment or contradiction, but by totally abstaining from them you shall not only permit us and the Church to freely dispose of that kingdom as we deem appropriate, but you shall also let it be known by word of mouth and in writing not only that it does not displease you, but even that it pleases you when the said Church negotiates about that kingdom with other princes of the world' (*considerantes quod dicta Romana ecclesia per vos non potuit neque poterat, quod inviti referimus, a suis calamitatibus et erumpnis, quantumcumque vos diutius expectaverit, liberari, propter quod omnino expediebat tam nobis quam ipsi ecclesie de prefato regno Sycilie aliter cogitare, necessario disposuimus in animo nostro de regno ipso tractare ac ordinare utiliter, prout expedire honori et profectui predicte ecclesie videremus ... Quia ergo liberum est nobis et ipsi ecclesie de predicto regno Sicilie disponere ac iuxta nostrum beneplacitum ordinare, cum condiciones, sub quibus regnum ipsum a prefato predecessore concessum extitit, adimplete non fuerunt ... nullum deinceps nobis et ipsi ecclesie super huiusmodi dicti regni negotio ingeratis, impedimentum nullumque contradictionis obstaculum opponatis, sed ab illis penitus desistentes non solum permittatis nos et eandem ecclesiam libere de regno ipso tractare et facere, sicut videremus faciendum, verum etiam et verbis ostendatis et litteris, quod vobis non displicet, immo placet, si dicta ecclesia super ipsius regni negotio tractet cum aliquibus mundi principibus*).
147 See *supra* p. 441.
148 For Queen Margaret see *supra* p. 442 and for the duke of Bourgogne see the letter of Baldwin II to Manfred in Martène, *Thesaurus* 2, col. 25.
149 Urban to his cardinals on 25 April 1264 in Theiner, *Codex diplomaticus dominii temporalis S. Sedis* I, Rome 1861, no 299, 161: '*pax inter carissimam in Christo filiam nostram Margaritam, illustrem reginam Francorum et ipsum comitem fuerit reformata*'. There is an undated letter of Urban IV to Queen Margaret, urging her to become reconciled with her brother-in-law in Duchesne, *Historiae Francorum scriptores*, Tom. V, Paris 1649, 869-870 (also in *Ann. eccl.*, Tom. 22, Paris 1870, ad ann. 1264 § 2, 122-123). It must have been written in May 1264, since on 3 May 1264 the pope still had to write a letter to King Louis urging him 'to apply pressure on the said queen by firm and effective means of persuasion so that she shows herself more relaxed, tractable and friendly in this matter of peace' (*quatenus predictam reginam ad hoc, quod facilem, tractabilem et benignam se in huiusmodi negotio pacis exhibeat, attentis et efficacibus inductionibus exhorteris*) (MGH *Epp. saec. xiii* 3, no 596, 593). On this letter to King Louis see also *supra* p. 440, fnt. 110.

his brother's bid for the Sicilian crown, thanks to the clever diplomacy of Archbishop Bartolomeo Pignatelli of Cosenza[150].

Urban IV
restates
papal policy

On 25 April 1264, Urban IV restated the papal policy vis-à-vis the kingdom of Sicily[151] in a special memorandum (*diffinitio*) for his cardinals: '*Jeremiah says that all evil comes from the north, but we say that for us and you all evil comes not from the north, but from the kingdom of Sicily*'[152]. The danger from the north, the German Empire, had ceased to be a serious threat to the Papal State long ago. Since the days of Frederick II, the real menace was the expansion of the totalitarian regime of the Sicilian monarchy over the rest of Italy, potentially threatening the Papal State from the south, the north (Tuscany), and the east (the duchy of Spoleto). True as it might be that, unlike his predecessors Henry VI, Frederick II, and Conrad IV, Manfred could not lay a claim to the title of king of Italy, belonging as it did to the Empire, he nevertheless continued the Italian policy of Frederick II[153]. It was therefore imperative to put a halt to that policy by replacing the Sicilian tyrant with someone who was willing to renounce all Italian ambitions outside the kingdom of Sicily. This is why the election of Charles of Anjou as senator for life of Rome was so embarrassing to the papal policy. Consequently, the pope decided to upgrade his embassy to the court of France in the Sicilian matter by sending Simon de Brion, the cardinal-priest of St Caecilia, to France to finalize the treaty between

---

150 Bartolomeo Pignatelli (*c.* 1200-1272) was archbishop of Cosenza in Calabria since 1254. He had supported the rebellion of Peter Ruffo against Manfred (see *supra* p. 427, fnt. 50). Consequently, he had to flee the Sicilian *regno* and joined the Sicilian exiles in the papal court. Urban IV employed him as papal legate to England in 1263, with the delicate mission to convince Henry III to relinquish the Sicilian title of his son Edmond: see the letter of Urban IV to Pignatelli in MGH *Epp. saec. xiii* 3, no 552, 533. From there, he went to the court of France to assist master Albert in his efforts to win over the king of France. Urban IV thanked him in May 1264 for his successful contribution to that effort: MGH *Epp. saec. xiii* 3, no 600, 593. On Pignatelli see also *infra* p. 463, fnt. 213.
151 See *supra* p. 243-245 and *infra* p. 565.
152 Theiner, *Codex diplomaticus dominii temporalis S. Sedis* I, Rome 1861, no 299, 159: '*Dicit Jeremias, quod omne malum ab aquilone pandetur, nos autem dicimus, quod non iam ab aquilone, sed a Regno Sicilie nobis et vobis panditur omne malum*'. For the quotation see Jerem. 1:14: 'And the Lord said unto me, out of the north an evil shall break forth upon all the inhabitants of the land' (*et dixit dominus ad me ab aquilone pandetur malum super omnes habitatores terrae*).
153 Manfred's activities in the Italian kingdom were manifestly illegal, since they constituted acts of aggression against the German Empire to which the kingdom of Italy belonged. This was stressed by his nephew Conradin at the time (see *supra* p. 438, fnt. 100), but Conradin had no claim to the Italian kingdom either, since he had not been (and never was) elected king of the Romans. The 'acting' king of the Romans, Richard of Cornwall, did nothing about it since he was involved in his brother's war with the English barons at the time. Richard was captured by the barons after the battle of Llewes (14 May 1264) and imprisoned for more than a year.

the Church and Charles of Anjou. Cardinal Simon had been chancellor of France before his promotion to the cardinalate and was suggested as papal representative in France by King Louis himself[154]. The cardinal was to be accompanied by Archbishop Bartolomeo Pignatelli of Cosenza, who had already proven his worth in France[155]. In presenting their embassy to the college of cardinals, Urban IV set out their mission in detail. In this special case special sacrifices had to be made, according to the pope: '*we are forced to tolerate things which we would otherwise never have allowed*'[156]. He meant the election of Charles of Anjou as senator of Rome. The pope was willing to accept that election for the time being '*in order to give him a freer and easier access to the said kingdom from there*'[157], but certainly not for life. The papal legates were instructed to persuade Charles of Anjou to accept the Roman election for a few years only, five years at most, and to renounce the Roman senatorship at once if he had conquered the Sicilian kingdom before that time. If, however, the Romans insisted on a nomination for life, then Charles was to accept that, but he had to swear to the pope to renounce his senatorship immediately as soon as he had conquered the Sicilian kingdom. He was also to swear that, after laying down his Roman senatorship, he would see to it that the Romans accepted a papal nominee as their new senator, meaning that Charles had to restore papal government over Rome, something of which the pope himself was incapable. If Charles of Anjou was not prepared to accept these conditions, the cardinal was instructed to break off the negotiations with Charles and return to the Apostolic See[158]. Some days later, on 3 May, the pope sent letters to his legate Cardinal Simon, to the king of France, and to all clerics of the kingdom of France to endorse the choice of Charles of Anjou as the new king of Sicily and even raising the war against Manfred to the status of a crusade, since according to Urban the liberation of the Holy Land and the Latin kingdom of Constantinople largely depended on regime change in the Sicilian kingdom[159]. On the

---

154   Theiner, *Codex diplomaticus dominii temporalis S. Sedis* I, Rome 1861, no 299, 160: '*iuxta eiusdem Comitis, et Carissimi in Christo filii nostri Ludovici Francorum Regis illustris desiderium, dilectum filium nostrum S<imonem> tituli sancta Caecilie presbiterum Cardinalem sine more dispendio destinemus ad ipsos*'.

155   For Archbishop Pignatelli's mission see MGH *Epp. saec. xiii* 3, no 600, 593.

156   Theiner, *Codex diplomaticus dominii temporalis S. Sedis* I, Rome 1861, no 299, 159: '*aliqua cogimur tolerare, que huiusmodi causis cessantibus minime pateremur*'.

157   Theiner, *Codex diplomaticus dominii temporalis S. Sedis* I, Rome 1861, no 299, 160: '*ut liberior et facilior aditus ei ad dictum Regnum exinde pateat*'.

158   For these conditions see Theiner, *Codex diplomaticus dominii temporalis S. Sedis* I, Rome 1861, no 299, 160 and also *infra* p. 455-456 and fnt 181.

159   See the letters in MGH *Epp. saec. xiii* 3, no's 593, 594, 596, 597 and 598, 583-592. On the argument that regime change in Sicily would benefit the cause of the Holy Land see no 597 (to Cardinal Simon), 591: 'Since the promotion of the matter of the Holy Land and the Empire

same day, he also sent yet another letter to Charles of Anjou, urging him not to accept the office of senator of Rome for life but for a limited period only, not extending his conquest of Sicily[160]. Clearly, the pope was beginning to realize that Charles of Anjou as senator of Rome for life and king of Sicily at the same time might turn out to be at least as much of a nuisance as Manfred was, making him escape the deadly grip of Scylla (Manfred) by falling into the terrible abyss of Charybdis (Charles of Anjou)[161].

Provencal troops in Rome

In April 1264, Charles of Anjou had sent troops to Rome commanded by the Provencal knight Jacopo Gantelmi, who was to act as his personal representative (*vicarius*) there for the time being[162]. It was the first indication that Charles was to come to Rome soon, thus putting extra pressure on his negotiations with the papal *curia* in the Sicilian affair by stressing his vested position as Roman senator[163]. Before long, the Provencal troops under Gantelmi were engaged in intense hostilities with the Roman Ghibellines and Manfred's captains in and around Rome[164]. It was only now that Manfred decided to act and to do what he should have done a year before[165]: to march on Rome while at the same time arresting the pope and his cardinals in Orvieto, where they

---

of Constantinople is known to mainly depend on the matter of the kingdom of Sicily, we [...], considering that the liberation of that land and that Empire is much easier when the affair of that kingdom has been effectively settled with the help of God, *etc.*' (*Cum promotio negotii Terre Sancte et Constantinopolitani imperii a negotio regni Sicilie pro maiori parte dependere noscatur, nos [...], attendentes quod facilior erit eorundem terre ac imperii liberatio, si huiusmodi eiusdem regni negotium fuerit efficaciter Deo favente promotum* etc.). For the proclamation of a crusade against Manfred and his Lucera Muslims see Urban's letter to Cardinal Simon of 4 May 1264 in Martène, *Thesaurus* 2, col. 70-72.

160   MGH *Epp. saec. xiii* 3, no 595, 590.

161   Urban to master Albert (25 December 1263) in Martène, *Thesaurus* 2, col. 30: '*ne dum Syllam vitare cupimus in Carybdis voraginem incidamus*'.

162   For the presence of the Provencal troops in Rome at the time see a letter of Urban IV to 'the noble Jacobo Gantelmi, personal representative in the city of our beloved son Charles, count of Anjou and Provence, the senator of the city' (*Nobili viro Iacobo Gantelmi, vicario in Urbe dilecti filii Caroli Andegaviae ac Provincie comitis, senatoris Urbis*) (MGH *Epp. saec. xiii* 3, no 610, 604 (30 May 1264)).

163   The arrival of a personal representative of Charles of Anjou in Rome was the incentive of the *diffinitio* of Urban IV of 25 April 1264 (*supra* p. 450) outlining the papal policy in the Sicilian affair and in the matter of the Roman senatorship.

164   The Roman Ghibellines rallied around Peter of Vico (†1268), a powerful feudal lord from a family traditionally in conflict with the papacy and consequently allied to Manfred, who had appointed Peter's brother as archbishop of Cosenza (Thierry de Vaucouleurs (Muratori 3,2, Milan 1734, col. 414)), the see of Bartolomeo Pignatelli (see *supra* p. 450, fnt. 150). The Guelphs from Rome under Count Pandulf of Anguillara and the Provencals under Gantelmi were fighting him in northern Lazio. See Saba Malaspina 2,10-12, MGH *SS* 35, 139-144.

165   See *supra* p. 448.

were completely isolated and practically defenceless[166]. Urban IV certainly expected him to do so. On 17 July 1264 the pope sent a gloomy letter to his legate in France, Simon de Brion, the cardinal-priest of St Caecilia, on the developments in Italy after cardinal Simon's departure for France, expressing his conviction that the siege of Orvieto was imminent[167] and urging the cardinal to incite Charles of Anjou to come to the rescue personally as soon as possible. Shortly later, Manfred's captains conclusively defeated the Provencals and the Roman Guelphs near Vetralla, some 30 miles (50 km.) south of Orvieto[168]. Urban now panicked and fled from Orvieto to Perugia, some 40 miles (70 km.) north of Orvieto.

Manfred's 1264 offensive against Orvieto had already failed when Urban IV hastily absconded to Perugia. The pope missed the importance of the recent failure of one of Manfred's armies, commanded

Manfred's failed offensive

---

166   From Urban's letter to King Louis IX of 3 May 1264, describing the 'horrors' of Manfred's reign, in *Ann. eccl.*, Tom. 22, Paris 1870, ad ann. 1264 § 13, 126 (also in Giraud, *Les registres d'Urbain IV*, Paris 1901, no 309, 395-396): 'So many other detestable and abominable acts are committed and the Church is unable to provide a proper cure for them, now that the strength of the prenamed persecutor is growing, while the same Manfred, stretching out his gory hands to its very soul, is planning to send some Germans, always the executors of his persecution, in the Tuscan part of the Papal State where we and our whole *curia* are residing. He closes the roads and passes everywhere to such effect that no one can come to us, nor can we send someone away from our *curia*' (*Quamplura insuper alia detestabilia et abominabilia committuntur ... Nec potest ipsa ecclesia, predicti persecutoris invalescentibus viribus, opportunum super his remedium adhibere, cum nuper etiam idem Manfredus truculentas manus in viscera eius immitens, quosdam Theutonicos, sue utique persecutionis ministros, in patrimonium Petri in Tuscia, in quo nos cum tota nostra curia residemus, destinare presumpserit ... sic artet undique vias et sepiat transitus, ut nullus ad nos venire valeat vel nos aliquos extra curiam nostram destinare possumus*).

167   Martène, *Thesaurus* 2, col. 82-86(85): 'He <Manfred>, believing that he cannot have peace with the Church according to his wish without arresting us, God forbid, and our brethren, the cardinals of the Roman Church, is said to have concentrated all the attention of his evil intention to lay siege to us and our *curia* in Orvieto, where we personally reside. As we have learned, he is making arrangements to come personally to the territory of Orvieto and lay siege to us and our brethren with all his might in that city with armies from Florence, Pisa, Sienna, Pistoia, Arezzo, and his other supporters, with the thousand German knights he has in Tuscany and with other auxiliaries from his troops and cohorts' (*Ipse <Manfredus> credens se cum ecclesia pacem iuxta suum libitum habere non posse, nisi per nostram, quod absit, et fratrum nostrorum, Romanae videlicet Ecclesiae cardinalium, captionem, ad obsidendum nos et curiam nostram in civitate Urbevetana, in qua personaliter residemus, cuncta suae pravae intentionis studia dicitur convertisse. Ordinat enim, sicut accepimus, et disponit cum Florentinorum, Pisanorum, Senensium, Pistoriensium, Aretinorum et aliorum suorum fautorum exercitibus et cum mille militibus Theotonicis quos habet in Tuscia, ceterisque suorum agminum et cohortum praesidiis, et cum toto etiam posse suo personaliter ad territorium praedictae Urbevetanae civitatis accedere, ac nos et fratres nostros in ipsa civitate hostiliter obsidere*).

168   On the battle near Vetralta (end of July or beginning of August 1264) see Saba Malaspina 2,12, MGH *SS* 35, 143-144.

by the redoutable condottière Percivalle Doria[169], to march on Orvieto from the duchy of Spoleto. The unfortunate demise of its commander (Doria drowned after falling from his horse while crossing a river) had caused the army to halt its progress (July 1264), preventing a concentrated assault on Orvieto and even causing Manfred to withdraw from the northern border of his kingdom and to return to Apulia, as he had done in 1262[170], 'in order to surrender to his usual delights' (*suis consuetis delitiis potiturus*) as the pope himself declared[171]. This is an important contemporary assessment, since it testifies to a weakness of character in Manfred, which explains his remarkable indolence in the recent past and in the months to come. He should have pressed on to Rome and Orvieto, but he preferred to abstain from a major military effort even now, obviously underestimating the grave danger ahead[172]. After an ill-conceived and premature attack on Rome itself by one of his captains in Lazio, Peter of Vico, had ended in defeat (March 1265) in Trastevere[173], Manfred definitively lost the chance of ever gaining control over that city. Their recent victory in Rome considerably consolidated the position of the Guelphs and Provencal troops in the city that was now ready to welcome Charles of Anjou rather than Manfred as her senator. The attack of the Tuscan Ghibellines from the north Urban IV was so afraid of after the battle of Vetralla never materialized. Urban could have stayed in Orvieto, but it was in Perugia that he died on 2 October 1264[174].

Clement IV elected pope

Urban IV had created no fewer than fourteen new cardinals during his pontificate, six of them from France. Two of the French cardinals were absent on a foreign mission at the time of Urban's demise: Cardinal Simon de Brion was papal legate in France and Cardinal Guy Foucois was in France as well, from where he was trying to broker a peace in the civil war between the king of England and his barons[175], but there was still one of the French cardinals created by Innocent IV, Cardinal Eudes

---

169 On Doria see *supra* p. 437.
170 See *supra* p. 448.
171 Martène, *Thesaurus* 2, col. 83.
172 See also *infra* p. 458.
173 On the attack on Rome see Saba Malaspina 2,13-14, MGH *SS* 35, 145-147.
174 *Annales Sancrucenses* (1234-1266), MGH *SS* 9, 646: '*Eodem anno Urbanus papa quartus in Perusio 6. Nonas Octobris obiit*'. According to the chronicles of Orvieto (*Annales Urbevetani*) ad ann. 1264, MGH 19, 270, the pope died 'on his way' (*in via*) to Perugia, where he was buried.
175 On this civil war see *supra* p. 450, fnt. 153. Cardinal Foucois was denied admission to England and was still in France when Urban IV died: Tholomaeus of Lucca, *Historia ecclesiastica nova* 22, 27, ed. Muratori 11, Milan 1727, col. 1155: '*venit in Franciam usque ad transitum maris in Angliam; sed transire non potuit, quia non fuit permissus*'.

de Châteauroux[176], alive in 1264 to form a strong French alliance in the conclave deciding the papal succession. The Perugia conclave of 1264 was attended by some twenty cardinals, making for a decisive majority of about fourteen votes to elect a new pope. Two very influential Italian cardinals, Giancaetano Orsini and Riccardo Annibaldi, were known supporters of the choice for Charles of Anjou as king of Sicily and consequently may have suggested a French cardinal to succeed Urban IV in order to ensure the continuing support of the king of France and to expedite the ongoing negotiations with Charles of Anjou. There may have been other cardinals less enthusiastic about this, such as Cardinal Ottaviano Ubaldini, who had the reputation of being a Ghibelline cardinal, but the college elected a French prelate, Cardinal Guy Foucois, as successor to Urban IV. Since the cardinal was still in France at the time, his election was kept secret until his arrival in Perugia. Cardinal Foucois had to travel through Lombardy in disguise, due to the strong Ghibelline presence there, and only arrived at Perugia in 1265, where his election was publicly announced on 5 February 1265. The new pope chose the name of Clement, fourth of that name[177].

Clement IV was a hard man, disillusioned by his long experience in secular and ecclesiastical politics. He knew Charles of Anjou personally and must have had no illusions about that man. Nonetheless, it was Clement IV who finally reached a definitive agreement with the count on the Sicilian succession. On 26 February 1265 he issued a bull containing the conditions of the grant of the kingdom of Sicily to Charles of Anjou[178]. The covenant between the Church and Charles of Anjou

---

176 See *supra* p. 320, fnt. 83.

177 For biographical details see Tholomaeus of Lucca, *Historia ecclesiastica nova* 22, 29-30, ed. Muratori 11, Milan 1727, col. 1156-1157. Guy Foucois was an extraordinary man. He had entered the Church only late in life, after the demise of the mother of his children. He was from the Languedoc where he had practiced as a lawyer in the service of the counts of Toulouse, like his father Pierre before him. Later he entered the service of the king of France, becoming one of the closest legal advisors of Louis IX. After joining the Church in 1246, he was elected bishop of Le Puy and, later, archbishop of Narbonne, while still serving in the royal administration at the same time. He was created cardinal-bishop of Sabina by Urban IV in 1261.

178 The bull '*Cum iam dudum*' is published in J.C. Lünig, *Codex Italiae Diplomaticus* II, Frankfurt/Leipzig 1726, no 43, col. 945-966, and in Saint Priest, *Histoire de la conquête de Naples par Charles d'Anjou* II, Paris 1849, App. C (332-364). On the very same day the pope officially restated that Prince Edmond of England never had been seized of the kingdom of Sicily, due to his failure to meet the conditions imposed on him, and that consequently the pope was at liberty to dispose of the Sicilian fee as it pleased him: Lünig, *Codex Italiae Diplomaticus* II, Frankfurt/Leipzig 1726, no 42, col. 941-946. The conditions of the grant of Sicily are repeated in the papal confirmation of 4 November 1265 of the investiture of Charles with that kingdom printed in MGH *Epp. saec. xiii* 3, no 646, 643-653 and in Gius. del Giudice, *Codice diplomatico del regno di Carlo I. e II. d'Angiò*, Naples 1863, no IV, 12-27 (with a different numbering).

held 35 articles, meticulously elaborating on the three main objectives of papal policy regarding the kingdom of Sicily: the establishment of the complete freedom of the Sicilian Church, implying that Charles was to lose the last of the special ecclesiastical privileges of the kings of Sicily still enjoyed by Frederick II[179], to wit the right of approval (*assensus*) of episcopal and other clerical elections in Sicily[180]; the kingdom of Sicily was to be held from the Holy Roman Church as a hereditary fief in the male and female line, subject to an elaborate set of specific rules of succession aimed at supporting the all-overriding interest of the papacy, the complete exclusion of a possible union of the kingdom of Sicily with the German Empire, the kingdom of Italy, or any other territorial interest on the Italian peninsula but for the traditional Sicilian posses-sions on the peninsula south of the Papal State, Apulia, Campania, and Calabria[181]. Consequently, the election of Charles of Anjou as senator for life of Rome was a serious embarrassment. This was why Charles was to swear an additional solemn oath that he would not accept that office for life but for a limited period only, not exceeding three years[182].

---

179 On the traditional ecclesiastical privileges of the kings of Sicily see *supra* p. 101, 188 and 227.

180 Lünig, *Codex Italiae Diplomaticus* II, col.961 (Art. 21); Saint Priest, *Histoire* 356 (Art. 21); MGH *Epp. saec. xiii* 3, no 646, 651 (Art. 18) and Del Giudice, *Codice diplomatico*, no IV, 23 (Art. 15): '*Omnes insuper ecclesiae tam cathedrales quam aliae regulares et saeculares, nec non et omnes praelati et clerici, et omnes personae ecclesiasticae saeculares et religiosae, et quaecumque religionis loca cum omnibus bonis suis in electionibus, postulationibus, nominationibus, provi-sionibus et omnibus aliis plena libertate gaudebunt, nec ante electionem sive in electione vel post, assensus vel consilium aliquatenus requiretur*'.

181 See the summary of papal policy in the bull '*Cum iam dudum*' in Lünig, *Codex Italiae Diplomaticus* II, col.961 (Art. 19); Saint Priest, *Histoire* 355 (Art. 19); MGH *Epp. saec. xiii* 3, no 646, 647 (Art. 8) and Del Giudice, *Codice diplomatico*, no IV, 18 (Art. 5): 'since it is truly the policy of the Roman Church that the kingdom of Sicily and the aforementioned territory are never united to the Empire so that there will never be an emperor who is king of Sicily at the same time. But what we say about the union of that kingdom and territories with the Empire, we explicitly intend to apply to the union of that kingdom and territory with the Roman or German kingdom, and with Lombardy and Tuscany as well' (*cum prorsus intention-is sit Romanae Ecclesiae, ut Regnum et terra praedicta nullo umquam tempore Imperio uniantur, ut scilicet unus Romanorum Imperator et Siciliae rex existat. Quod autem circa unionem ipsorum Regni et terrae cum Imperio dicimus, hoc ipsum circa unionem eorundem Regni et terrae cum regno Romano, aut Regno Teotoniae, seu cum Lombardia vel Tusciae intelligimus, et volumus esse dictum*).

182 Lünig, *Codex Italiae Diplomaticus* II, col. 964 (Art. 35): 'The arrangement in the matter of the senatorship is as follows: The noble Lord Charles, count of Anjou and Provence, must promise under oath that he will do his best in good conscience not to swear to the Romans to rule the city for life, also that he will resign the senatorship after a term of three years, to be reckoned from the day on which the kingdom of Sicily is granted to him, or when he has conquered all of that kingdom, or the major part of it, to which the lesser part is unable to resist, or when, which God forbids, it has been clearly established that he is unable to conquer it' (*Ordinatio vero super senatus articulo hæc est: Nobilis vir Carolus, Andegaviæ ac Provinciæ comes, præstito juramento promittat, quod dabit operam bona fide, ut Romanis juret non regere*

The conditions were finally accepted by Charles at Aix-en-Provence late in April 1265. He had promised to leave the Provence for Italy within three months after that[183], but Charles already left Marseille for Rome on 14 May next with a fleet of some twenty galleys, carrying a limited number of knights (without horses) only since the main army, with the cavalry, was to reach Rome by land[184]. It was a hazardous undertaking because a great Sicilian fleet was out at sea waiting for an opportunity to intercept the Provencal fleet. Bad weather saved Charles, as it had once saved Innocent IV[185]. On 21 May he arrived at Ostia unaccosted and was welcomed at the palace of St Peter by four cardinals sent by the pope for the purpose[186].

Clement IV was not particularly impressed by Charles' appearance at Rome: '*the noble man Charles, the senator of the City and the count of Anjou and Provence, has come to town without money and horses*', he wrote to Cardinal Simon de Brion in France[187], urging his legate to collect the French tithes destined to finance Charles' crusade against Manfred, since King Louis IX himself, a lukewarm supporter of the papal Sicilian policy at best, was disinclined to subsidize the adventure of his brother who was in deep financial trouble. The pope was rather desperate about Charles' prospects, since it was uncertain whether his

Charles of Anjou in Rome

---

urbem ad vitam. Item, quod finito triennio a die quo fiet ei regni Siciliæ concessio, computando, vel si infra triennium ipsum totum prædictum regnum vel majorem ejus partem, cui minor non possit resistere, acquisierit, vel si forte, quod absit, illud acquirere non poterit, et hoc liquido constiterit, senatum omnino dimittet). The article continues with the obligation of Charles to reestablish papal control over the city after resigning his senatorial office: '*dabit operam bona fide, ut idem senatus ad dispositionem et ordinationem Romanae Ecclesiae revertatur, cives scilicet Romanos ad hoc, sicut melius et honestius poterit, inducendo*'.

183   Lünig, *Codex Italiae Diplomaticus* II, col. 963 (Art. 32): '*infra tres menses immediatae sequentes sit in terris conterminis Regno Sicilie*'.

184   *Annales Ianuenses* (Lanfranci Pignolli *e.a.*) ad ann. 1265, MGH *SS* 18, 252: '*In ipso anno die ascensionis Domini in mane fecit transitum per mare Ianue domnus Karolus, filius Ludovici quondam regis Francie et comes Provincie, cum galeis 27 et cum allis lignis minutis usque in 13, eundo Romam, cum per summum apostolicum eidem fuisset regnum Sicilie attributum, transducens secum usque in quantitatem militum quingentorum et ballistariorum mille*'. See also *Annales Placentini Gibellini* ad ann. 1265, MGH *SS* 18, 514: '*De mense Madii comes Provincie vocatus ab Urbano papa rex Sicilie, cum comitiva sua militum absque equis cum 22 galeis per mare intravit Romam ... multi alli per terram per Lombardiam a Capinaci retro iverunt ad pedes et ad equos*'.

185   See *supra* p. 322. For the details of the voyage of Charles of Anjou to Rome and his escape from the Sicilian fleet see Saba Malaspina 2,17, MGH *SS* 35, 151-152.

186   Clement IV to his legate in the duchy of Spoleto and the Marche of Ancona, Cardinal Simone Paltineri, in Martène, *Thesaurus* 2, col. 134 (20 May 1265). The Cardinals Riccardo and Annibale Annibaldi, Orsini, and Savelli, Romans all of them, had been ordered some days before to go to Rome as quickly as possible to receive Charles: letter of Clement IV to these cardinals in Martène, *Thesaurus* 2, col. 130.

187   Martène, *Thesaurus* 2, col. 138: '*Nobilem virum Carolum Senatorem Urbis, Andegaviae ac Provinciae comitem ad Urbem venisse noveris pecunia carentem et equis*'.

army would ever be able to reach Rome over land and, even if it did, how that army was to be sustained financially[188]. Manfred seems to have believed at the time that Charles' army would never reach Rome and that he would be able to easily deal with it even if it did[189], which may explain why he was waiting for events to develop rather than striking at Rome and Charles of Anjou proactively as the pope expected him to do any time. Manfred's negligent inactivity allowed Charles of Anjou to close a series of treaties with Guelph cities and war-lords in Lombardy and the Romagna to support the progress of his army from the Provence through the Italian kingdom. In August and September 1265 he concluded treaties at Rome with Obizo II d'Este and Ludovico Sambonifacio from Verona, two powerful Guelph war-lords, and with representatives of the cities of Mantua and Ferrara, as well as with Genoa, Parma, Piacenza, and Bologna[190]. He had already concluded similar treaties with Milan, Novara, Como, and other Lombard cities on 23 January 1265 and with the margrave of Montferrat on 14 May

---

188   Martène, *Thesaurus* 2, col. 219 (from a letter of Clement IV to Charles of Anjou (28 October 1265)): 'if, God forbid, your army does not arrive, we cannot clearly see from what you will live while awaiting its arrival, with what plan you are able to keep the town or with what force you can open a transit to the army once it has been checked in its progress; and even if it comes, which we hope, we consider it no less obscure how an army of that size can be sustained. We have been unable to secure a necessary loan for you with us and we have been turned down three times by your dear brothers in Christ, our sons the king of France and the count of Poitou, when we have asked three times for their support of you' (*si, quod absit, militia tua non venerit, unde vivas sub expectatione eiusdem, quo ingenio Urbem tenere valeas, qua potentia impeditum semel militiae transitum aperire, liquido non videmus; et si venerit, ut speratur, unde tantus exercitus valeat sustentari, non minus judicamus obscurum. Nos enim apud nos necessarium tibi mutuum invenire nequivimus et apud fratres tuos carissimos in Christo filios nostros inclytum regem Franciae et nobilem Pictavensem comitem ternam repulsam invenimus super tuo presidio precibus tertiis repetitis*). For the repeated papal requests of financial support for Charles to the king of France see the letter of Clement IV to Louis IX of 18 July 1265 in Martène, *Thesaurus* 2, col. 165-166, also in Del Giudice, *Codice diplomatico* no IX, 34-35. On 1 August 1265 the pope wrote to Charles of Anjou that the papal treasury was empty (*thesaurus apud nos nullus latet*), advising him urgently to ask his brothers, Louis IX and Alphonse of Poitiers, for financial support (Martène, *Thesaurus* 2, col. 173-175, also in Del Giudice, *Codice diplomatico* no X, 36-38). King Louis refused to comply: see yet another petition by the pope to the king from 17 November 1265, outlining the dire financial situation of Charles (Martène, *Thesaurus* 2, col. 241-243, also in Del Giudice, *Codice diplomatico* no XXVII, 74-77).
189   There is an undated letter in Martène, *Thesaurus* 2, col. 274-275 by Pope Clement IV to Manfred, one of the last the pope wrote to him, containing a reaction to a letter by Manfred. The contents of Manfred's letter may be inferred from the papal answer to it. Manfred seems to have predicted that Charles' chances of success against him were rather dim, due to the closure of all the means of access to the Sicilian kingdom over land and sea (*terrarum marisque conclusio*) and the might of the Sicilian army, Saracenes and excommunicates, opposing him (*Saracenorum et excommunicatorum multitudo*). Manfred's letter must have been written soon after he had heard that Charles of Anjou had arrived at Rome.
190   Del Giudice, *Codice diplomatico* no XI, 39-44 and no XIV, 47-48.

1264[191]. By the end of 1265 his diplomatic preparations were completed and his army was on the move through Lombardy and the Romagna[192], arriving at Rome early in January 1266, shortly after Charles had been crowned as king of Sicily[193].

Clement IV confirmed Charles' investiture with the kingdom of Sicily on 4 November 1265, almost six months after Charles' arrival in Rome. The pope did so in a pompous bull, emphasizing his *plenitudo potestatis* in secular affairs: '*Placed above the nations and kingdoms by him by whom kings rule and emperors command and who alone has power in the kingdom of men, we are sometimes even obliged to dispose of kingdoms, and especially those who belong to the Church of Rome, together with our brethren for the sake of peace and justice and to raise to their thrones men we have deemed worthy to govern over their subjects*'[194]. Charles had expressed his wish to be crowned as king of Sicily at Rome by the pope himself, but Clement refused to leave Perugia, indicating that not Rome, but Palermo, was the proper place to crown the king of Sicily[195]. In the end Charles was indeed enointed and crowned as king of Sicily at St Peter's in Rome on 6 January 1266, but not by Clement himself but by five cardinals acting as his representatives[196].

---

191   Del Giudice, *Codice diplomatico* no XI, 41, fnt. 1.
192   The army of Charles of Anjou had reached Lombardy in November 1265 (*Annales Ianuenses* ad ann. 1265, MGH *SS* 18, 252). Nominally, it was commanded by a mere child, Charles' son-in-law Robert of Béthune ('The Lion of Flanders', 1249-1322), but in fact by Robert's guardian, Gilles de Trazegnies, called 'le Brun', who happened to be *connétable de France*, commander in chief of the army of France, as well (Guillaume de Nangis, *Gesta sancti Ludovici* ad ann. 1265, *Recueil* 20, 420).
193   Saba Malaspina 3,1, MGH *SS* 35, 158: '*Gallicorum post hec superveniens multitudo*', '*post hec*' (thereafter) referring to Charles's coronation.
194   MGH *Epp. saec. xiii* 3, no 646, 639: '*Constituti ab eo, per quem reges regnant et principes imperant et qui solus habet in regno hominum potestatem, super gentes et regna, necesse habemus interdum de regnis ipsis, et specialiter que Romane ecclesie iuris et proprietatis existent, cum fratribus nostris ad pacem et iusititiam populorum perpetua stabilitate disponere ac in eorum soliis ad regimen gentium subiectarum quos dignos credimus sublimare*'.
195   Letter of Clement IV to Charles of Anjou (20 December 1265) in Martène, *Thesaurus* 2, col. 251-253, also in Del Giudice, *Codice diplomatico* no IX, 78-80.
196   See the instruction of Clement IV (29 December 1265) to the Cardinals Raoul Graspermi, bishop of Albano, Anchero Pantaléon, priest of S. Prassede, Riccardo Annibaldi, deacon of S. Angelo in Pescheria, Goffredo de Allatri, deacon of S. Giorgio in Velabro, and Matteo Orsini, deacon of S. Maria in portico Octaviae in Del Giudice, *Codice diplomatico* no XXX, 81-83. For the unction and coronation itself see the deed of the cardinals just mentioned testifying to the execution of their commission in Del Giudice, *Codice diplomatico* no XXXIII, 87-89.

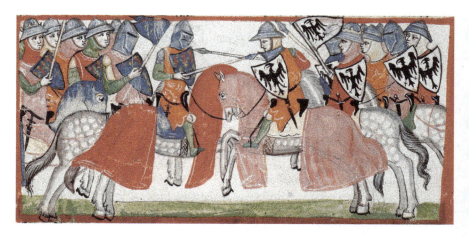

The Battle of Benevento
(Giovanni Villani, *Nuova Cronica*, Biblioteca Apostolica Vaticana, Ms Chigi L.VIII 296, *f.* 103 *rᵒ*)

Death of
Manfred

Charles of Anjou left Rome on 20 January 1266, shortly after the arrival of his army[197]. The new king of Sicily could not afford any delay: his financial situation was desperate[198] and there were now only the spoils of war to reward his largely mercenary army. The mercenaries were not the only men in his army expecting to be rewarded soon: there were also many exiled Guelphs from the cities in Tuscany, Florentines most of them, dependent on Charles and exiled Sicilian nobles who expected to be reinstated in the estates which they had lost and Charles had solemnly promised to restore[199]. He needed a quick victory to satisfy not only all of these men, but also the subjects of Manfred whom

197 Andreas Ungarus, *Descriptio victoriae* (written in 1272) 32, MGH *SS* 26, 569.
198 See also Andreas Ungarus, *Descriptio victoriae* 32, MGH *SS* 26, 569: '*in ipsa quoque Urbe milites Christi non modicam in hac parte pati penuriam sint coacti*'. According to Andreas, Manfred had induced the bankers of Rome to refuse a loan to Charles, causing 'the soldiers of Christ to suffer great deprivation'.
199 See the conditions of Charles' investiture (supra p. 455-456) in Lünig, *Codex Italiae Diplomaticus* II, col.962 (Art. 28); Saint Priest, *Histoire* 359 (Art. 28); MGH *Epp. saec. xiii* 3, no 652, 647 (Art. 23) and Del Giudice, *Codice diplomatico*, no IV, 24-25 (Art. 21): 'All exiles from the kingdom of Sicily and the aforementioned territory, of whatever estate they are, are to be returned to the kingdom and the aforementioned territory at the order of the Church. There shall be a full restitution to them of the property and rights due to them' (*Omnes exules regni Siciliae et terrae praedictae, cuiuscumque conditionis existant, ad mandatum Ecclesiae reducantur in regnum et praedictam terram. Ipsisque de bonis et juribus eis debitis restitutio plena fiet*). On these exiles and the restitution of their property see also Saba Malaspina 3,7, MGH *SS* 35, 166-167.

he had been able to bring over to his side[200]. Treason, indeed, paved the way for Charles of Anjou into the Sicilian kingdom. When he crossed the border of the *regno* at Ceprano, the bridge over the Garigliano was left undefended[201], allowing Charles to proceed quickly, taking the formidable fortress of Rocca d'Arce and the strongly defended town of San Germano (now Cassino)[202] as he was going along, on his way to Capua where Manfred had concentrated his forces[203]. This impressive display of military might by Charles of Anjou instigated many defections: no fewer than thirty-two castles in the area instantly surrendered to Charles[204], soon to be followed by some major cities in Campania, such as Gaeta and Naples[205].

The city of Capua was the gateway to the Sicilian *regno*. It had been heavily fortified by Frederick II, who had an impressive city gate constructed in the northern part of the city walls, where the via Latina coming from Rome enters the town, featuring a monumental statue of himself. Yet Manfred decided he could not risk to be besieged there by Charles of Anjou. The town had traditionally sided with Naples

---

200 Saba Malaspina (2,21, MGH *SS* 35, 157) indicates that some Sicilian nobles already had defected to Charles of Anjou prior to his invasion of the kingdom. On treason by Sicilian magnates at the start of Charles' campaign see also *Annales S. Iustinae Patavini* ad ann. 1266, MGH *SS* 19, 188: '*Eodem tempore quidam magnates Apulie, a principe recedentes, regi Carolo adheserunt*'.

201 Charles of Anjou crossed the bridge over the Garigliano at Ceprano unopposed, as is testified by contemporary sources (*Annales Placentini Gibellini* ad ann. 1265(1266), MGH *SS* 18, 515; *Annales Ianuenses* ad ann. 1266, MGH *SS* 18, 255). According to Villani, *Nuova Cronica* 8,5, ed. Porta I, Parma 1990, 413-414, it was due to treason by Count Riccardo of Caserta, Manfred's brother-in-law. This may have been the inspiration of Dante's famous lines in *Inferno* 28, 16-17: 'Ceperan là dove fu bugiardo ciascun pugliese' ('Ceperan', where all the Apulian band turned traitors' (transl. Dorothy Sayers)). The relation between Dante's *Comedia* and Villani's chronicle is uncertain though. They may both have used another source, now lost (not being the *Storia Fiorentina* by Ricordano Malispini, a fourteenth-century plagiarist). The story of Count Riccardo's treason itself is unlikely, since he defended San Germano against Charles of Anjou a few days later (see the next fnt).

202 According to the best informed authority at the time, Pope Clement IV himself, San Germano was defended by Count Riccardo of Caserta and Giordano d'Agliano (of Montaperti fame, see *supra* p. 438) and a considerable force of German mercenaries, Lombard and Tuscan Ghibellines, and Saracens from Lucera. Riccardo and Giordano escaped, but one of Manfred's close relatives, Manfredo Lancia, was taken prisoner there: letter of Clement IV to Cardinal Ottobuono Fieschi (25 March 1266) in Martène, *Thesaurus* 2, col. 301-302, also in Del Giudice, *Codice diplomatico* no XLIV, 122-128 (123).

203 On the progress of Charles of Anjou in the north of the *regno* see Saba Malaspina 3,3-5, MGH *SS* 35, 159-164 and Andreas Ungarus, *Descriptio victoriae* 32-36, MGH *SS* 26, 569-570.

204 Andreas Ungarus, *Descriptio victoriae* 36, MGH *SS* 26, 570.

205 For the early defection of Gaeta and Naples after the capture of San Germano see *Annales Placentini Gibellini* ad ann. 1265(1266), MGH *SS* 18, 515. See also *Annales Ianuenses* ad ann. 1266, MGH *SS* 18, 255: '*multe terre et loca ... ad mandata domni regis Karoli devenerunt*'.

in the pursuit of communal 'liberty'[206] and now that Naples (errone-
ously, as it turned out) expected to be granted that liberty by Charles
of Anjou[207], many citizens of Capua must also have believed so, which
is why Manfred decided to leave that unreliable town and to retreat
to Apulia to make his stand there, where he expected to be joined by
additional troops[208]. At the same time, Charles of Anjou, not daring
to risk a possibly protracted and costly siege of Capua, had left the via
Latina heading for the mountains north-east of Capua and the city of
Benevento. Manfred was heading the same way and on 25 February
1266 Charles of Anjou caught sight of Manfred's army, close to
Benevento. On the evening of the next day Charles wrote an urgent
letter to Pope Clement IV reporting on the great victory which he had
won that day[209]. Manfred's army had been utterly defeated. When
writing his letter to the pope, Charles was not yet certain about the
fate of Manfred[210], but two days later Manfred's body was identified
by Count Riccardo of Caserta, who had deserted his brother-in-law in
the battle[211], as had Manfred's other brother-in-law, Tomasso d'Aquino,

---

206 See *supra* p. 223 and 420.

207 For this see Saba Malaspina 3,7, MGH *SS* 35, 167: 'For they believed that after the
advent of King Charles the kingdom was ready for the wished for peace and the restoration
of complete freedom' (*Credebant enim, quod regnum iam esset votive tranquilitati paratum et
ex adventu regis Karoli libertati omnimode restitutum*). For the short-lived 'restoration' of the
freedom of the Sicilian cities by Innocent IV see *supra* p. 428.

208 Andreas Ungarus, *Descriptio victoriae* 40, MGH *SS* 26, 571 has a story that Manfred
even planned to burn and destroy Capua and to deport or even kill the inhabitants.

209 The letter of Charles of Anjou is published in Del Giudice, *Codice diplomatico* no XL,
110-113.

210 Del Giudice, *Codice diplomatico* no XL, 112: 'On Manfred, whether he has been slain
or captured in battle, or has fled, there is as yet no certain information. But the charger he
is said to have ridden, which we have captured, offers strong evidence about his fate' (*De
Manfredo autem utrum ceciderit in conflictu, vel captus fuerit, aut evaserit, certum adhuc aliquid
non habetur. Destrarius autem, cui insedisisse dicitur, et quem habemus, casus affert non modicum
argumentum*)

211 Del Giudice, *Codice diplomatico* no XLI, 114 (letter of Charles of Anjou to Clement IV,
1 March 1266): 'It so happens that on 28 February his naked body was found among the bodies of the slain. Since there must be no mistake in a matter like this, I have had it shown to our
vassal (!) Count Riccardo of Caserta and to the former Counts Giordano and Bartholomaeo
(d'Agliano) and their brothers as well as to others who have known him well and have had
dealings with him. They have recognized it and have confirmed that it was beyond any doubt
the aforementioned Manfred' (*Contingit, quod die Dominica 28 Mensis Februarii corpus eius
inventum est nudum inter cadavera peremptorum. Ne igitur error sibi locum in tanto negotio ven-
dicaret, Richardo comiti Casertano, fideli nostro, nec non Iordano et Barchino olim dictis comitibus et fratribus eorum aliisque etiam, qui eum familiariter noverunt, et tractaverunt, dum vivebat
ostendi feci. Qui recognoscentes ipsum praedictum esse olim Manfredum praeter omnem dubium
affirmabant*). Looting the bodies of slain combattants after a battle was the prerogative of the
foot soldiers of the victorious party, which is why the bodies of nobles were usually stripped.

the count of Acerra[212]. In a sudden and rather uncharacteristic fit of 'natural compassion' (*naturalis pietas*), Charles ordered the body of his slain adversary to be buried 'honourably, though not religiously' since Manfred was an excommunicate[213]. Charles had little compassion with Manfred's wife and children though. They were hunted down, captured, and incarcerated for the rest of their lives[214]. Thus Hohenstaufen rule in Sicily finally ended, little more than seventy years after Henry VI had been crowned king of Sicily in 1194[215].

Conradin

The political reaction to the death of Manfred was different in the Sicilian kingdom and the Italian kingdom. Until his demise, Manfred had been the uncontested absolute monarch in the Sicilian *regno* and consequently there were no political parties, no Ghibellines and Guelphs, in the *regno*: there were only subjects owing obedience to their lord. Accordingly, the death of Manfred created a power vacuum in the Sicilian *regno*. This is why Charles of Anjou, after exterminating Manfred, had established his authority in the Sicilian *regno* in one single battle without having to conquer the territory at large: after Benevento, there was no one left there to seriously challenge him. The Sicilian barons formerly loyal to Manfred and surviving the bat-

The Sicilian exiles and Italian Ghibellines turn to Conradin

---

212   For the treason of Riccardo di Caserta and Tomasso d'Aquino of Acerra see *Annales Placentini Gibellini* ad ann. 1265(1266), MGH *SS* 18, 515-516.

213   Del Giudice, *Codice diplomatico* no XLI, 114 (letter of Charles of Anjou to Clement IV, 1 March 1266): '*Ego itaque naturali pietate inductus corpus ipsum cum quadam honorificentia sepulturae, non tamen ecclesiasticae, tradi feci*'. On Manfred's funeral see Saba Malaspina 3,13, MGH *SS* 35, 177 and also *Annales Ianuenses* ad ann. 1266, MGH *SS* 18, 256 and G. Villani, *Nuova cronica* 8,9, ed. Porta I, Parma 1990, 424). According to Villani, Manfred was buried at the head of the bridge crossing the river Calore near Benevento. All soldiers laid a stone on his grave, thus forming an impressive burial mound. It displeased the vengeful clerics. At the order of the pope, Archbishop Bartolomeo Pignatelli of Cosenza had Manfred's body disinterred and had it put under somewhere at an unmarked site on the northern bank of the river Garigliano, *i.e.* outside the borders of the *regno*, a disgraceful act to be exposed forever by some famous lines in Dante's *Purgatorio* 3, 130-132.

214   On the capture of Manfred's wife and his children see the letter of Clement IV to Cardinal Ottobuono Fieschi (25 March 1266) in Martène, *Thesaurus* 2, col. 302, also in Del Giudice, *Codice diplomatico* no XLIV, 123-124: '*Uxor vero Manfredi cum liberis a Tranensibus infra castrum tenebatur inclusa, nec evadere poterat manus regis*'. Manfred had three sons with his second wife, the Byzantine Princess Helena Dukas: Enrico, Federico, and Azzolino. They were incarcerated for thirty years in Castel del Monte and later transferred to a dungeon in the Castel dell'Ovo in Naples, where they finally expired. Queen Helena had already died in Nocera castle in 1271. Her daughter Beatrice was the only child of Manfred to be released, in 1284, thanks to her brother-in-law Peter of Aragon who was married to Constance, a daughter of Manfred with his first wife Beatrice of Savoye (see *supra* p. 403): see *infra* p. 556, fnt. 254.

215   See *supra* p. 147.

tle of Benevento had no choice but to condescend to Charles. All of them tried and many of them failed. Most notably among the latter were Manfred's former chamberlain Count Manfredo Maletta; the Lancia brothers, close relatives of Manfred, Galvano and Federico; and Corrado and Marino Capece, who had fought at Manfred's side at Benevento and had only escaped execution thanks to the intervention of their relative Archbishop Bartolomeo Pignatelli. There was nowhere for them to go now but to far away Bavaria, to Conradin, where another member of Manfred's court, Peter of Prezza, already had arrived soon after Benevento[216]. The situation was different in the Italian kingdom where Manfred had been merely the head of a political party. His death deprived the Ghibelline party in the Italian kingdom of Sicilian support. The effects were soon to be felt in Tuscany and especially in Florence, where the Ghibellines had been in control ever since the battle of Montaperti (1260)[217]. Florentine Guelph exiles under Count Guido Guerra had fought Florentine Ghibellines in Manfred's army under their captain Pier Asino degli Uberti at Benevento[218]. The Guelphs had prevailed and now expected Charles of Anjou to assist them in ousting the Ghibellines from Florence and Tuscany at large. They were duly accommodated. Late in 1266 Guido Guerra was back in Tuscany with his victorious army of Guelph exiles, reinforced by a considerable French detachment. He was immediately elected *podestà* of Lucca, the first city to defect from the league of Tuscan Ghibelline cities[219]. The presence in Lucca of Count Guido with an army of victorious and vengeful Guelph exiles from Florence caused an immediate reaction in Florence

---

216   On all of these Sicilian exiles coming to Germany see Saba Malaspina 4,3, MGH *SS* 35, 181. Some of them were already in Germany by the end of August 1266, since on 18 September of that year the pope was aware of their presence there (the letter of Clement IV to the archbishop of Bremen, cited *infra* fnt 226). A month later (on 18 November) he writes that the Italian exiles with Conradin were 'predominantly from Sicily' (*precipue de regno predicto*): MGH *Epp. saec. XIII* 3, no 657, 666. On Peter of Prezza see a charter issued by Conradin in 1267 containing a grant to Peter and printed among the *pièces justificatives* in C. de Cherrier, *Histoire de la lutte des papes et des empereurs de la maison de Souabe* III (2nd ed.), Paris 1858, 516-517. It is said there (516) that Peter had left Sicily immediately after Benevento, leaving his wife and children behind, 'and came to us in Germany and has stayed there for a long time' (*ad nos in Theutoniam venit ... et diutius est moratus*).
217   See *supra* p. 438.
218   Pier Asino degli Uberti had been taken prisoner at Benevento. For his capture see the letter of Charles of Anjou to Clement IV reporting his victory at Benevento (Del Giudice, *Codice diplomatico* no XL, 112). He was deported subsequently to a prison in Provence, together with Giordano d'Agliano and others. After a failed attempt at escape Pier Asino and the other prisoners had their right hand and left foot hacked off. All were later executed: *Annales Placentini Gibellini* ad ann. 1267, MGH *SS* 18, 524.
219   *Gesta Lucanorum* ad ann. 1267, MGH *SS rer. Germ. N.S.* 8, 315: 'Fue podestà di Lucha lo conte Guido Guerra'. Lucca had been the last Tuscan city to yield to Ghibelline supremacy in Tuscany: see *supra* p. 438.

itself, where Manfred's vicar in Tuscany, Count Guido Novello, lost control. In a desperate effort at reconciliation, the Florentines elected *two podestì* in 1266, a Guelph and a Ghibelline from Bologna, both of them members of a religious order established to reconcile Guelphs and Ghibellines, but instead of reconciling with the Ghibellines, the Guelphs remaining in the city felt encouraged to burn and plunder the houses of Ghibelline nobles[220]. Many Tuscan Ghibellines, now hard pressed, decided in 1266 to turn to the last male representative of the house of Hohenstaufen alive, Conradin, to come to their rescue[221]. Just like the Sicilian exiles, they had to overcome some embarrassment in doing so, because in the recent past they had all been supporters of Manfred who had 'stolen' the Sicilian kingdom from the rightful heir of Conrad IV, Conradin, which is why in the more distant past, before Charles of Anjou had entered the Italian arena, the *Guelphs* of Italy had appealed to Conradin to come and rescue *them* from Manfred and his Ghibelline supporters[222]. The pope was informed of the Ghibelline contacts with Conradin at a very early stage[223]. Though initially unim-

---

220 According to Dante (*Inferno* 13, 103-109) Cattalano dei Malavolti and Loderingo degli Andalò were members of the order of the 'Cavallieri della Beata Maria Vergine Gloriosa', established in 1261 by Pope Urban IV to promote civil concord. The members tried to achieve that laudable objective by feasting and dining, which is why they were commonly known as the 'frati godenti' ('the merry brothers'). Being a religious order, the *frati* were under papal control and consequently served the cause of the Guelphs: see the letter of Pope Clement to Cattalano and Loderingo in Martène, *Thesaurus* 2, col. 321-322. Accordingly, Dante relegated the two Florentine *podestì* of 1266 to the eighth circle of hell, in the sixth bowge, where the hypocrites dwell.

221 Thomas Tuscus (*c.* 1212-*c.*1282), *Gesta imperatorum et pontificum, De Corradino*, MGH SS 22, 521: 'The custodians of the boy were solicited by the Tuscan Ghibellines, the chamberlain acting as intermediary, offering them a large sum of money to send the boy to Italy with an army' (*sollicitantur a Gibellinis Tuscie pueri conductores, comite hec camerario procurante, ut magna accepta pecunia puerum cum exercitu in Ytaliam ducant*). The 'chamberlain' was Manfred Maletta, who had been Manfred's chamberlain and was already in Germany at the time.

222 See *supra* p. 438, fnt. 100. The epithets 'Ghibelline' and 'Guelph' had long lost their original meaning, *i.e.* the supporters of Frederick II and the adherents of his Guelph opponent, Otto IV (see *supra* p. 184, fnt. 74). 'Guelphs' now primarily supported papal policy, above all else directed at the prevention of Sicilian political predominance on the Italian peninsula, whereas 'Ghibellines' opposed papal secular power on the peninsula. A famous Ghibelline warlord like Guido da Montefeltre was not necessarily a supporter of Conradin (see *infra* p. 473 and fnt. 251), but he was an enemy of papal Italian politics.

223 Letter of Clement IV to his legate in the Marche of Ancona, Cardinal Simon Paltineri (Martène, *Thesaurus* 2, col. 416, 16 October 1266): 'We have understood clearly what you have written about the state of the Marche and we do not attach much importance to the envoys whom they send to their idol, young Conradin, on whose condition we are very well informed. We have learned that he is so destitute that he is unable to provide for himself, let alone come to the aid of his supporters. It is really a remarkable and foolish madness that these stupid and miserable men from the Marche and others believe that our beloved son in Christ Charles, the glorious king of Sicily obviously in possession of the kingdom, a man

pressed, Clement soon decided to publicly denounce Conradin since rumour had reached him that, once again, efforts were being made in Germany to have that boy elected as king of the Romans. As his predecessors Alexander IV and Urban IV had done at previous occasions[224], Clement IV strongly dissuaded the German electors to elect Conradin: anyone who even contemplated doing so was threatened with instant excommunication. He reminded them that they had already elected *two* kings and that the process between the two contenders, Richard of Cornwall and Alfonso of Castile, was still pending in his court[225]. As a matter of course, Conradin, belonging as he did to a brood of enemies of the Church and being still a minor, was absolutely ineligible. The German princes were additionally informed that anyone who assisted Conradin in his attempts to overthrow Charles of Anjou in the kingdom of Sicily was also to be excommunicated by operation of law[226]. A few weeks later, on 18 November 1266, Clement IV informed the world at large that anyone assisting Conradin against Charles of Anjou was to be excommunicated as of right and that he was initiating inquisitory proceedings (*processus*) against Conradin himself[227]. By that time, many Sicilian exiles and Ghibellines from all over the Italian *regno* were already in Germany, urging Conradin to take on his Sicilian inheritance and to come to the rescue of the Ghibelline cause in the Italian *regno*[228].

---

who has deprived a clever and rich occupant of his kingdom as wel as his life within 21 days, could not easily resist one destitute and empoverished boy' (*Quae de statu scripsisti Marchiae pleno collegimus intellectu, nec magnam vim facimus in legatis, quos ad suum destinant idolum, adolescentem scilicet Corradinum, cuius statum ad plenum novimus, quem intelleximus eo usque prostratum, ut nec sibi consulere, nec suis cultoribus valeat subvenire. Haec est sane mira prorsus et stupenda vesania, ut stulti et miseri Marchiani vel alii suspicentur carissimum in Christo filium nostrum C(arolum), regem Siciliae illustrem regnum plenissime possidentem, uni puero nudo et pauperi facile non posse resistere, qui prudentem et divitem possessorem in xxi diebus regno simul et vita privavit*).

224   See for similar attempts *supra* p. 430 and 439.

225   See *supra* p. 435.

226   Letter of Clement IV to the archbishop of Bremen (18 September 1266) with orders to publish the contents in his diocese, in H. Sudendorff, *Registrum oder merkwürdige Urkunden für deutsche Geschichte* I, Jena 1849, no 61, 111-114(114): '*has nostras sententias totumque presentium tenorem in tuis Civitate diocesi et Provincia, convocato clero et populo, facias singulis mensibus, vel, si expedire videris, pluries publicari*'. The letter is also inserted in the papal bull of 18 November 1266 on which shortly in the text.

227   Bull of 18 November 1266 in O. Posse (ed.), *Analecta Vaticana*, Innsbruck 1878, no 16, 141-146, also in MGH *Epp. saec. xiii* no 657, 666-670.

228   See the letter of Clement IV to the archbishop of Bremen (18 September 1266) in H. Sudendorff, *Registrum* 112: 'As you see, that young man, too haughty for his age, already styles himself king of Sicily and is involved in treacherous dealings with some enemies of the Church from Lombardy, the Marche, Tuscany, Apulia, and even from Sicily' (*Sicque multum prepropere tumidus adolescens iam se scribit Regem Sicilie et cum aliquibus inimicis ecclesie, Lombardis, Marchianis et Tuscis, Apulis etiam Siculis fraudelentis se commerciis implicat*).

Conradin ('Chunrat der Junge')
(Univ. Heidelberg, Cod. Pal. germ. 848 (Cod. Manesse), f. 7 rᵒ (Wikimedia Commons))

Conradin

Conradin was only fourteen at the time and still a minor. His grandfather, Frederick II, was just seventeen when he had entered upon his stupendous career, but Conradin was not the man his grandfather had been. Frederick II was raised in Palermo in extraordinary and very challenging circumstances, making him a man before his time, a shrewd politician, and an experienced judge of human character, as well as a polymath and a polyglot, fluent in at least five languages. Conradin on the other hand had been raised in the dull provincial comfort of a Bavarian castle, well protected by his ducal guardian and his mother, both of them constantly reminding the little boy of his special status as king of (far-away) Jerusalem, heir to the throne of Sicily, and possible contender for the imperial crown – surreal claims, all of them. One of the first (and most important) lessons Frederick II must have learned as an adolescent will have been that courtiers advising a king on his interest usually have their own interests in mind. Conradin certainly never learned that lesson, which is why he was completely swayed by the Sicilian and Italian exiles now urging him to come to Italy to defend his Sicilian heritage against a ruthless usurper and assuring him of the support of his partisans and subjects in Italy and Sicily. Excited by all these men, the boy quickly made up his mind: he had to challenge the usurper Charles of Anjou and take possession of the heritage of his father and grandfather[229]. It seemed a rather unrealistic plan, but had his grandfather not achieved a similar miracle at an age not much older than he was now? There were certainly men in his immediate environment, men like his uncle Duke Louis of Bavaria, his tutor Bishop Eberhard of Konstanz, and his stepfather Count Meinhard of Tirol[230], who must have realized the enormous risks involved, but Conradin was also something of an embarrassment to them. They must have known there was no future for him in Germany as a royal pretender, certainly not after the recent damning intervention of Clement IV, while even his claim to the duchy of Swabia was titular at best and strongly (and probably even rightly) contested by King Richard of Cornwall[231]. What were they to do about the boy?

---

229 *Annales S. Iustinae Patavini* ad ann.1267, MGH 19, 189: '*Romanorum, Pisanorum, Senensium, Papiensium et Veronensium literis et nuntiis excitatus, ad recuperandum paternum regnum cepit cordis desiderium ardentissime applicare*'.

230 Conradin's mother had remarried in October 1259. Her new husband was a powerful Alpine lord, Meinhard, count of Görz and Tirol. Conradin was seven at the time. He did not accompany his mother to the court of his stepfather, but was first brought to the court of his uncle, Duke Louis, and later (from 1262) entrusted to the care of Bishop Eberhard of Waldburg, a very powerful territorial lord and his tutor until his departure for Italy.

231 Charter of Richard of Cornwall, issued at Hagenau on 20 November 1262 in Winkelmann, *Acta imperii inedita seculi XIII*, Tom. 2, Innsbruck 1885, no 83, 75-76: 'It has been brought to our royal attention by reliable information that Conradin, the son of the

It was probably due to the initiative of Conradin's guardian Duke Louis of Bavaria that a conference was called to convene at Augsburg in October 1266 to decide on the future of the young prince[232]. There is a charter, dated on 24 October 1266 and completed in Augsburg, in which Conradin bestows all his possessions, 'in Germany as well as in Italy' (*tam in partibus Germanicis quam Latinis*), to his two uncles, the Dukes Louis and Henry of Bavaria, in case he should die without leaving an heir[233]. The document reads as a farewell to his German kin and is confirmed by the seal of his tutor, Bishop Eberhard of Konstanz, because Conradin was still a minor. It is testified to by no fewer than forty witnesses, most probably attendants of the Augsburg meeting. Some of them, such as Margrave Frederick of Baden[234], later joined Conradin on the Italian expedition that must have been decided at this meeting. The Sicilians exiles and Italian Ghibellines staying with Conradin will also have been there to report on the chances of that expedition to succeed. They assured the German supporters of Conradin present that Charles of Anjou easily could be expelled from the Sicilian

The Augsburg conference

---

former King Conrad, who calls himself duke of Swabia, not satisfied with the offense that he vainly usurps for himself the title of someone else, now presumptuously stretches out his hand to the duchy of Swabia, a special and noble part of the Empire, that has been incorporated into the Empire long ago and rightfully devolved to its proper and legal status and not granted to Conradin by the generosity of ourselves or anyone of our predecessors' (*fideli relatione pervenit ad nostre serenitatis auditum, quod Conradinus, olim Conradi regis filius, qui se ducem Swevie nominat, ea non contentus iniuria, quod in vanum sibi gloriam alienam usurpat, quod ad speciale ac nobile membrum imperii, ducatum scilicet Svevie, iam diu incorporatum imperio et ad ius et proprietatem ipsius legitime devolutum nec ipsi C(onradino) seu nostra seu aliqua predecessorum nostrorum clare memorie liberalitate collatum, presumptuose manum extendit*). It was an insult at the time to refer to the son of King Conrad IV by the dimunitive 'Conradin', certainly so in an official charter as this one, since the boy was officially known as Conrad. Richard was not kindly disposed to Conradin after repeated attempts had been made to advance the boy as a possible challenger to Richard: see *supra* p. 430, 439 and 466.

232   See the Bavarian *continuatio* of the Saxon world chronicle (1216-1314), MGH *Dt. Chron.* 2, 327: 'Do hielt er einen hof ze Choburch; do chom hin sin oehaim herzog Ludweich von Bairen und ander herren vil; der hof was groz'. For Augsburg rather than 'Choburg' see Böhmer in RI V,1,2 n. 4808a. On this conference see also *Annales S. Iustinae Patavini* ad ann. 1267, MGH *SS* 19, 189: 'Then he <Conradin> called the German princes on whose friendship he relied for a conference and after much talk back and forth it was decided on the advice of most of them that he should depart for Italy without delay' (*Tunc principes Alemanie, de quorum amicitia confidebat, ad colloquium convocavit; et post multa hinc et inde proposita est tandem maiorum consilio diffinitum quod ipse sine mora deberet in Italiam proficisci*).

233   Published in *Monumenta Boica* 30.1, Munich 1834, no 813, 350-351; also in *Monumenta Wittelsbacensia* 1, Munich 1857, no. 90, 219-221.

234   Margrave Frederick styles himself in the document as 'duke of Austria', a title as illusive as Conradin's title as king of Sicily. The duchy of Austria was firmly in possession of King Ottokar II of Bohemia at the time. He was married to the Austrian heiress Margaret. Frederick of Baden was a son of the other Austrian heiress, Gertrud, who had married Margrave Hermann of Baden after having been married to King Ottokar's older brother Vladislav, who had died in 1247. On the Austrian heiresses see *supra* p. 369.

kingdom and that the Sicilians were eagerly expecting the advent of their saviour Conradin[235]. There were good reasons to believe that story, since Charles of Anjou had revealed his true nature right after the battle of Benevento by allowing his troops to plunder and massacre the citizens of Benevento, a city officially belonging to the papal domain and consequently under the protection of the pope[236]. Charles was making it plain very early on that he had come to Sicily as a conqueror rather than as a liberator. Once again, as in the days of Henry VI and Conrad IV[237], the Sicilians were confronted with an invasion by a foreign prince accompanied by foreign adventurers expecting to be rewarded with land and titles. Charles was, moreover, under an obligation to restore their former estates to all nobles exiled from the Sicilian kingdom in the past by Frederick II and Manfred[238], something he could only do by dispossessing the actual occupants. All of this amounted to a massive reallocation of real property in the kingdom, which was sure to ignite social unrest within the nearby future. Another cause of unrest were the heavy, arbitrary, and indiscriminate taxes Charles immediately started to raise[239]. But there was more, indicating a Sicilian rising in the near future: Charles conducted himself in ways unbecoming of a king by treating the Sicilians with utter contempt, allowing his French captains to rob them as they pleased without hearing the complaints of his Sicilian subjects since he was neither approachable, nor kindly dis-

---

235 Thomas Tuscus, *Gesta imperatorum et pontificum, De Corradino*, MGH SS 22, 521-522: '*quod faciliter Karolus pelleretur a regno, eo quod regnicolis esset universis exosus et Corradinus econtra ab omnibus concupitus*'.

236 For the massacre of Benevento see the angry letter of protest sent by Clement IV to Charles of Anjou (12 April 1266) in Del Giudice, *Codice diplomatico*, no 45, 129-133. The massacre was a blatant breach of Charles' promise to respect papal authority over Benevento, part of the conditions of the papal grant of Sicily (Del Giudice, *Codice diplomatico*, no IV, 20 (Art. 10)).

237 See *supra* p. 151 and 420.

238 See *supra* p. 460 and fnt. 199.

239 On the excessive direct taxation (*collecta*) of Charles see a letter of Clement IV to the papal legate in Sicily, Cardinal Raoul Grosparmi, in Martène, *Thesaurus* 2, col. 443-444 (5 February 1267), and to Charles himself (6 February 1267, Martène, col. 444-446(445)): 'We do not, after having seen your excuses, want to justify the taxes you raise which have exasperated many people, nor do we want to call good what is bad' (*super exactionibus quas facis in regno, quae multorum exasperant animos, excusationibus tuis inspectis, blandiri tibi nolumus, nec dicere malum bonum*). Charles was under heavy financial pressure at the time. Not counting his enormous private debts to the bankers financing his expedition, he was also liable to pay 50,000 pounds of silver to the pope after the defeat of Manfred, as he had promised in the conditions of the grant of Sicily (Del Giudice, *Codice diplomatico*, no IV, 19 (Art. 8)) and for which the pope was already pressing him. According to Saba Malaspina 4,2, MGH SS 35, 180, the Sicilians were already looking back regretfully at the reign of Manfred at the time. The historian reveals a rare psychological insight here by stating that an oppressive regime corrupts the minds of the subjects: '*provocantur regnicole duris et diris oppressi flagiciis et iam mente corrupta violantur interius*'.

posed to his subjects (*nec adibilis, nec affabilis, nec amabilis*), as a good king should always be[240]. Even more important than the prospect of an imminent rebellion in the kingdom was the fact that large parts of it were not yet under effective Angevin control, most notably the island of Sicily itself. It must have been at the Augsburg conference that it was decided that one of the Sicilian exiles present, Corrado Capece, was to be sent to Sicily forthwith to open a second front against Charles of Anjou there. He was appointed as Conradin's representative (*vicarius*) on the Sicilian island in advance[241]. At the same time, Conradin sent letters and messengers to the Italian kingdom announcing his imminent advent. It was a provocation causing the pope to initiate legal proceedings against Conradin and ordering his legate in Germany, Cardinal Guy de Bourgogne, to let it be known there too that anyone supporting Conradin, 'though still tender of age, yet prematurely malicious' (*aetatis adhuc tenerae, sed malitiae prematurae*), was to be

---

240   From a letter of Clement IV to Charles of Anjou written on 22 September 1266, lecturing Charles on the conduct of a good king and advising good rather than arbitrary governance (Martène, *Thesaurus* 2, col. 406-408(407); Del Giudice, *Codice diplomatico*, no LIII, 179-186(182)). The improper conduct of Charles of Anjou irritated the pope. In another letter to his legate in Sicily, Cardinal Raoul Grosparmi, also from 1266, he complains of the fact that Charles improperly delays his court hearings (*parlamenta*), to the detriment of his Sicilian subjects (Martène, *Thesaurus* 2, col. 356-357). See on these issues also an earlier letter, probably from July 1266, from Clement to Charles, in Martène, *Thesaurus* 2, col. 368-370. These letters are important because they are written by someone who knew Charles very well. When he was still known to the world as Guy Foucois, the pope had been one of the closest advisors of an exemplary king, Charles' brother Louis IX. Accessibility of the king as the provider of peace and justice was essential to royal representation at the time, as Pope Clement knew from the example of his former master, King Louis IX. Guy Foucois will have been present when Louis administered justice and heard complaints from his subjects informally under an oak in the bois de Vincennes. For this famous scene see Louis' biographer Joinville, *Histoire de Saint Louis*, 1, cap. 12, 59, ed. Wailly, Paris 1883, 34-35. Knowing this and reading the letters just referred to, there can be little doubt that the writer despised Charles and that he at heart considered him unqualified for royal office, a conviction most probably shared by Louis IX himself as well (see *supra* p. 441).

241   Saba Malaspina 4,3, MGH *SS* 35, 182-183: 'After a seal had been forged provided with the title of king of Sicily, Conradin sent letters and messengers all over Italy, announcing his imminent arrival. Corrado Capece asked to be provided with letters for the captaincy and vicariate of Sicily, with the seal of Conradin, styling himself king of Sicily, attached, saying that he wanted to prepare the way for his lord and announce his imminent arrival as his precursor as soon as possible. And so, having obtained the permission of his superior, he came to Pisa' (*Conflato igitur et sculpto sigillo sub regis Sycilie titulo, Corradinus per Ytaliam litteras spargit et nuncios et suum adventum celerem fore pronunciat. Corradus autem Capicius de generali capitania et vicariatu Sycilie fabricatas sub ipsius Corradini sigillo litteras, in quibus se regem Sycilie confingebat, studuit obtinere, dicens, quod ad parandas domino suo vias et eius in regnum citum predicandum adventum volebat ut precursor sublato more dispendio properare. Sicque obtenta superioris licentia Pisas usque pervenit*). Malaspina must be referring to events happening soon after the Augsburg conference, since Pope Clement IV reacted on 18 November 1266 with his announcement to open inquisitory proceedings against Conradin (see *supra* p. 466).

Developments
in Rome
and Tuscany

excommunicated if that boy defied the papal instruction to stay away from Italy[242].

Meanwhile, Charles of Anjou acted in ways increasingly disturbing to the pope. The Ghibelline cause was in decline in Tuscany after Count Guido Guerra and his army of Guelph exiles, French knights, and men from Lucca had marched on Florence and expelled all the Ghibellines from that city on Easter 1267[243], but the Florentine Guelphs subsequently decided to follow the example of the Roman Guelphs by electing Charles of Anjou as *podestà* for six years[244]. Charles had resigned the office of 'senator' of Rome in May 1267, as he was bound to do by his promise to the pope, but contrary to that promise he did not actively engage in the restoration of papal control over Rome after his resignation[245]. Consequently, the Romans were at liberty to elect two senators irrespective of papal aspirations. Pope Clement was furious, calling the new senators 'thieves and robbers'[246]. The senators soon resigned though, after presiding over the election of a new *capitano del populo*, Angelo Capocci, a nephew of Cardinal Capocci, who was authorized by the people to find yet another European prince to govern the city as her senator. Capocci chose a Spaniard, prince Enrico of Castile, a brother of King Alfonso (June 1267)[247]. Enrico had been exiled from Castile by his older brother Alfonso, the elected king of the Romans[248], and subsequently made a fortune in Tunisia, serving there as a warlord in the service of the emir of Tunis, Muhammad al-Mustansir, who hired Christian mercenaries to fight the Berbers of present-day Morocco and Algeria. Enrico, a medieval venture capitalist and an adventurer, had

---

242 Letter of Clement IV to Cardinal Guy de Bourgogne of 17 December 1266 in O. Posse (ed.), *Analecta Vaticana*, Innsbruck 1878, no 17, 146-147. The quote is from the papal bull of 18 November 1266, referred to *supra* p. 466 that was to be publicized in Germany as well.

243 Tholomaeus of Lucca, *Annales Lucenses* ad ann. 1267, MGH *SS rer. Germ. N.S.* 8, 155-156: 'On the day of the Resurrection of Our Lord Count Guido Guerra, who was *podestà* of Lucca went to Florence with a French army and some men from Lucca and expelled all the Ghibellines from there' (*in die resurrectionis Domini comes Guido Guerra existens Luce potestas venit cum militia Gallicana et aliquibus Lucanis Florentiam et expulit inde omnes Ghibellinos*).

244 Tholomaeus of Lucca, *Annales Lucenses* ad ann. 1267, MGH *SS rer. Germ. N.S.* 8, 156: 'and King Charles was then made *podestà* of Florence for a term of six years' (*et tunc fuit factus dominus rex Karolus potestas Florentie ad VI annos*).

245 For these promises see *supra* p. 456 and fnt. 182 Clement IV was bitterly disappointed by the lack of endorsement of the restoration of papal control over Rome by Charles of Anjou: see his letter to some cardinals in Martène, *Thesaurus* 2, col. 324-325.

246 Martène, *Thesaurus* 2, col. 353: 'See how Rome, restored to her freedom, completely ignores the law. Two senators were elected, fulminating like thieves and robbers at home and abroad' (*Ecce Roma suae reddita libertati in sua conversa iam viscera nescit legem. Duo facti sunt senatores, praedones et fures intus et extra libere debachantur*).

247 For these Roman developments see Saba Malaspina 4,5, MGH *SS* 35, 184-185.

248 See *supra* p. 433-434.

heavily invested financially in the Sicilian enterprise of that other frustrated younger son, Charles of Anjou[249], but soon found out that he
had a bad debt on his hands. Consequently, he was on bad terms with
Charles and turned Ghibelline, making the new Roman senator an
obvious ally of Conradin[250]. In August 1267 Enrico's Roman *vicarius*,
the famous Ghibelline warlord Guido di Montefeltre from Urbino in
the Marche was with Conradin in German Augsburg to conclude a
treaty of alliance between his master and Conradin[251].

Accepting the office of *podestà* of Florence was an additional breach
of the commitments of Charles of Anjou to the pope since he had also
promised to abstain from accepting any political power on the Italian
peninsula outside the borders of the Sicilian kingdom[252]. Even more
disturbing to the pope was that Charles decided to enter the Tuscan
war zone personally instead of consolidating his hold on the Sicilian
kingdom as the pope urged him to do. Clement IV tried to save face
by appointing Charles as 'Peacemaker General' (*paciarius generalis*) in
Tuscany[253], but Charles was waging war in Tuscany rather than making
peace: to him 'peace' consisted in the subjection of the last Ghibelline
cities left there, Siena and Pisa as well as the town of Poggibonsi, where

---

249 Charles of Anjou and Enrico of Castile were cousins: Charles' mother, Blanche of
Castile, was a sister of Enrico's father, King Ferdinand III of Castile. Enrico was also related
to Conradin, since his mother Elisabeth of Hohenstaufen, a daughter of Philip of Swabia, was
a niece of Conradin's grandfather Frederick II.

250 On Prince Enrico of Castile and his involvement in Italian affairs (he aspired to become
king of Sardinia) see Saba Malaspina 4,4, MGH *SS* 35, 183-184. According to Malaspina,
Enrico and his brother Frederico, who had also been exiled by King Alfonso, had gone native
in Tunisia, 'hardly Christians anymore but rather resembling the Saracenes in their lifestyle
and conduct' (*fere christianae religionis obliti a Sarracenis ipsis vita parum et moribus differebant*
(183)).

251 There is a charter in the Vatican Archive, dated on August 1267, testifying to Guido's
presence in Augsburg, published by J. von Pflugk-Harttung in his *Iter italicum*, Stuttgart
1883, 688-689. Conradin grants extensive fees in Campania to Guido in return for Guido's
important services to the grantor.

252 For this commitment see *supra* p. 456.

253 Letter of Clement IV to the Florentines (10 April 1267) in Martène, *Thesaurus* 2, col.
456-457. Tuscany was part of the Italian *regno* and consequently belonged to the Empire,
but 'as long as the succession to the imperial throne is vacant' (*dum vacat imperium* (456)), as
it was after the election of two competing contenders, Richard of Cornwall and Alfonso of
Castile, the pope was entitled (according to canon law) to act as emperor *ad interim* (see for
this doctrine *supra* p. 335) and consequently was entitled to grant offices in the Empire but
initially preferred a rather fanciful title, '*paciarius*'. Charles of Anjou, however, styled himself
as *vicarius* in Tuscany, an official imperial title. For this see a letter by Clement IV to Charles
of Anjou from 17 December 1267 (Martène, *Thesaurus* 2, col. 548): '*tu vicarium te dicis et
Tusciae paciarium esse*'. For the meaning of the curious title *paciarius* see the official charter
issued by Pope Clement IV in Lünig, *Codex Italiae Diplomaticus* I, Frankfurt/Leipzig 1725,
no XV, col. 1073: '*paciarius seu pacis servator*'. In the end, however, Clement IV did appoint
Charles of Anjou as imperial *vicarius* in Tuscany: see *infra* p. 483.

many Ghibelline exiles from the other Tuscan cities had found refuge. For good measure, the pope excommunicated the citizens of Poggibonsi on 14 April 1267 because they had received partisans of and messengers from Conradin[254] who was summoned at the same time to appear before the pope himself not later than 29 June next (the feast day of Peter and Paul) since he had also blatantly disregarded the papal warnings of 18 November of the previous year[255].

Conradin
in Verona

In September 1267 a manifesto was published in Conradin's name announcing to all German princes that he intended to take on Charles of Anjou and recover his Sicilian heritage[256]. It was a public repudiation of the papal summons of 14 April 1267 and the bull of 18 November 1266, widely published in Germany[257] and discouraging all German princes from supporting Conradin in his Sicilian adventure. Conradin, or rather his Sicilian ghost-writer Peter of Prezza, recalled the recent turbulent history of the Sicilian kingdom: how his father had appointed the pope as guardian of his only son in his will and how that papal ward had been mistreated and betrayed by four succeeding popes and his uncle Manfred; how Pope Clement IV had not only ignored the title of Conradin by granting that kingdom to an 'undue possessor' (*indebitus possessor*), but had offended the honour of the Empire as well by appointing Charles of Anjou as imperial viceroy in all of Italy[258].

---

254 Bull of 14 April 1267 in O. Posse (ed.), *Analecta Vaticana*, Innsbruck 1878, no 18, 147-150(149): '*qui spretis predictis nostris inhibitionibus et denuntiationibus eiusdem Conradini fautores et nuntios receperunt*'. As we know from the letter of the pope to the Florentines (*supra* fnt. 253), Clement IV knew by then that one of the Sicilian exiles who had fled to Germany was back in Italy and even in Tuscany. This was Corrado Capece, the designated *vicarius* of Sicily (see *supra* p. 471, fnt 241), who was heading for Pisa to raise a fleet there to assist him in his Sicilian enterprise.

255 Bull of 14 April 1267 in O. Posse (ed.), *Analecta Vaticana*, Innsbruck 1878, no 18, 147-150, for the most part reproducing the previous bull of 18 November 1266. Pope Clement explicitly provided (150) that his summons of Conradin was to be published by having a copy of it attached to the door of Viterbo Cathedral 'so that Conradin and others, who are involved in this procedure, cannot excuse themselves later that it has not been brought to their attention or that they did not know about it' (*ita quod idem Conradinus et alii, quos processus ipse contingit, nullam postea possint excusationem pretendere, quod ad eos talis processus non pervenerit vel quod ignorarint eundem*). Obviously, the legal problems with the summons of Frederick II (*supra* p. 385-386) were still on the papal mind. Clement, an experienced lawyer, did *not* summon Conradin 'in a public sermon' (*in predicatione publica*) as Innocent IV had done with Frederick II.

256 Martène, *Thesaurus* 3, col. 20-23.

257 See *supra* p. 466.

258 Martène, *Thesaurus* 3, col. 23: '*Carolum per universam Italiam Romani vicarium imperii statuit*'. This was not entirely correct, but Clement IV did violate the rights of the Empire by appointing Charles of Anjou as 'peacemaker general' in Tuscany: see *supra* fnt. 253. Of course, the papal doctrine on the right of the pope as 'emperor *ad interim*' during a vacancy was never recognized in the Empire itself. Conradin was not alone, however, in interpreting the

Now that 'countless of our faithful subjects' (*innumeri nostri fideles*) in the kingdom had risen to support him, Conradin had finally taken up arms to vindicate his rights and to recover the heritage to which he was entitled. As a matter of course, Conradin was duly excommunicated on 18 November 1267, exactly a year after the papal caution of 1266[259]. By that time, Conradin was already in Lombardy.

Before leaving Germany, Conradin severed his ties with that kingdom: he sold or mortgaged much of what was left of the once substantial Hohenstaufen domains in Germany to finance his Sicilian adventure[260]. After taking leave of his mother, who seems to have been the only relative dissuading Conradin of his Sicilian adventure, he was on his way on 8 September 1267[261], accompanied by his uncle, Duke Louis of Bavaria, his stepfather Count Meinhard of Tirol, and many of the nobles who had attended the Augsburg conference, such as Margrave Frederick of Baden, with whom Conradin soon developed a close friendship[262]. It seems to have been quite an impressive army that reached Verona on 21 October 1267, where it was welcomed by the local strongman, the *capitano del populo* Lonardino della Scala, nicknamed 'the Mastiff' (*Mastino*)[263]. It was there, at Verona, that Conradin received encourag-

---

appointment of Charles of Anjou as 'peacemaker general' in Tuscany as really amounting to his nomination as imperial *vicarius*. See the *Annales S. Iustinae Patavini* ad ann. 1267, MGH SS 19, 189: '*rex Carolus ... venit Viterbium ad reverendum papam Clementem, et ibidem est ab eo vicarius imperii constitutus*'.

259 The official papal sentence of excommunication is published in O. Posse (ed.), *Analecta Vaticana*, Innsbruck 1878, no 19, 150-155.

260 Conradin's father, Conrad IV, had already sold or mortgaged much of the Hohenstaufen domains in Germany to finance his Sicilian enterprise: see *supra* p. 418. For some details of Conradin's transactions see *infra* p. 478.

261 *Notae Weingartenses* (1200-1300) ad ann. 1267, MGH SS 24, 830: '*circa nativitatem beate Marie cum sua expeditione procinctum movit*'.

262 For Conradin's farewell visit to his mother and her reservations about his adventure see Villani, *Nuova cronica* 8, 23, ed. Porta I, Parma 1990, 557. For Conradin's companions at his departure for Lombardy see *Annales Placentini Gibellini* ad ann. 1267, MGH SS 18, 523. It is interesting to note that Count Rudolph of Habsburg is also mentioned among his companions at the time (*Annales Mediolanenses* (1230-1402) cap. 40, ad ann. 1268, in Muratori 16, Milan 1730, col. 670): '*fuerunt cum eo Dux Austriae et Rodulphus Comes de Ausbourg, qui postea fuit Rex Romanorum*'. The 'duke of Austria' was, of course, Frederick of Baden: see *supra* p. 469, fnt. 234.

263 *Annales Placentini Gibellini* ad ann. 1267, MGH SS 18, 523: '*Die Veneris, 21. mensis Octobris, rex Conradus intravit Veronam cum maxima quantitate principum et militum ... fertur enim habuisse ibi 12 milia milites*'. On Mastino della Scala see *Annales Veronenses* ad ann. 1262 and 1263, MGH 19, 16: '*domnus Mastinus de la Scala factus fuit et creatus capitaneus totius populi civitatis Veronae de communi voluntate et consilio populi civitatis eiusdem ... ab anno praedicto <1263> usque ad annum 1277 regnavit et rexit idem domnus Mastinus de la Scala in civitate Veronae*'. Mastino had ousted the Guelph Sambonifacios from Verona in 1263. They were never to return: '*comites Sancti Bonifacii numquam in civitate Veronae penitus redierunt*'. Mastino della Scala's rise to power marks the beginning of a new phase in the constitutional history of

ing news from the Sicilian kingdom. Corrado Capece, his designated representative (*vicarius*) in Sicily[264], had succeeded in taking over control of the island from the local representative of Charles of Anjou, the Provencal knight Fulco de Puy-Richard[265]. Not long after this news had reached Conradin, the Lucera Muslims in Apulia revolted against Angevin rule[266]. They had been spared by Charles of Anjou up till then, but were under no illusion about their fate when Charles' position in the Sicilian kingdom was sufficiently secured[267] and as soon as they heard that Conradin had entered Italy, they raised the standard of revolt against the French[268]. The Sicilian kingdom was on fire, but Charles of Anjou was still in Tuscany, laying siege to Poggibonsi[269]. All he did was to send one of his captains, Guillaume l'Etendard, to Lombardy with only 400 Provencal knights to look after his interests there as his

---

many cities in the Italian *regno* at this time. The regime of *podesti* appointed for a certain term (*supra* p. 229) was replaced by a government of hereditary 'lords', a *signoria*, such as the Este family in Ferrara and the Della Scala's in Verona, who ruled that city for almost a century.

264   See *supra* p. 471.

265   The Sicilian expedition of Corrado Capece is an outstanding military achievement. He sailed from Pisa, where he was in April 1267 (see *supra* p. 471, fnt. 241), to Tunis, where he raised an army among the Christian mercenaries. He was assisted there by Prince Frederico of Castile, the brother of the Roman senator Enrico (see *supra* p. 473, fnt 250) and with the financial support of the Emir Al-Mustansir they succeeded in taking over Sicily in September 1267. On the whole affair see Saba Malaspina 4,9-12, MGH *SS* 35, 190-196 and Bartolomaeo de Neocastro (*c.* 1240-after 1293), *Historia Sicula* cap.VIII, *RIS*² 13.3, 7.

266   According to the Campanian *Annales Cavenses* ad ann. 1267, MGH *SS* 3, the Lucera Muslims revolted later, on 2 February 1268. Other Italian chronicles, however, indicate that they revolted 'about the same time' (*eodem tempore*) as the invasion of Sicily by Corrado Capece.

267   The Lucera Muslims had surrendered to Charles of Anjou after the battle of Benevento, but were forced to destroy the walls of their city. They had been guaranteed that they were not to be compelled to renounce their religion (Andreas Ungarus, *Descriptio victoriae* 71, MGH *SS* 26, 580), but had been ordered to surrender their weapons and horses (*Chronicon Parmense, RIS*² 9.9, 24). The Muslims cannot have implemented these conditions, since they were able to hold out for a considerable time against Charles of Anjou: see *infra* p. 497.

268   *Annales S. Iustinae Patavini* ad ann. 1267, MGH *SS* 19, 190: 'As soon as the rumour spread all over Italy that Conradin had arrived, the Saracenes living in Lucera, incited by that news, started a revolt against the French since they could hardly bear the rule of the French' (*Fama itaque de adventu Corradini per Italiam discurrente, Sarazeni in Nuceria habitantes, rumore huiusmodi confortati, quia graviter Francorum dominium tolerabant, ceperunt contra Francigenas rebellare*). For the timing about the same time as the Sicilian invasion see *Annales Placentini Gibellini* ad ann. 1267, MGH *SS* 18, 525: '*similiter*'.

269   *Annales S. Iustinae Patavini* ad ann. 1267, MGH *SS* 19, 190: 'But the king <Charles of Anjou> was vigorously fighting the rebels in Tuscany at the time' (*Eo vero tempore rex in Tuscia rebelles fortiter impugnabat*). *Annales Placentini Gibellini* ad ann. 1267, MGH *SS* 18, 524: 'At the same time Count Charles of Provence besieged the town of Poggibonsi in Tuscany with the Ghibellines from Tuscany, lingering there from the middle of July to 30 November' (*Eodem tempore comes Karolus Provincie castrum Podiibonizi in Tuscia ossedebat cum parte Guelphorum de Tuscia, moram ibi faciendo a medio Iulii usque ad festum sacti Andree*).

vicarius[270], yet another encroachment on the rights of the Empire and a confirmation of Conradin's claim that Charles of Anjou was acting as if he were 'imperial vicar in all of Italy' (*vicarius imperii Romani per universam Italiam*). In view of all these developments, the logical thing for Conradin to do would have been to proceed with his army from Verona to Tuscany, Rome, and the Sicilian *regno* as quickly as possible to retain the momentum and to join with the Lucera Muslims, but he did not do so. Instead, he remained stuck in Verona for no less than three months, from September 1267 to January 1268. There are many explanations, though hardly any excuses, for this delay. Charles of Anjou had many allies in the Italian kingdom: he had concluded treaties with Genoa, Mantua, Ferrara, Parma, and Bologna, as well as with Milan, Novara, Piacenza, Como, and other Lombard cities before entering upon his Sicilian adventure[271], while many other cities in the kingdom were dominated by the Guelph party. An attempt by Conradin to bring over one of the Guelph Lombard cities, Brescia, to the Ghibelline cause had ended in a miserable failure. Practically the only Lombard cities to adhere to the Ghibelline cause at the time were Verona and Pavia, making a further progress of Conradin's army through largely hostile territory hazardous, though not impossible, as later developments were to demonstrate[272]. Conradin's main problem, however, was that he had run out of money. By December 1267 he had lingered in Verona for three months, feeding his mainly inactive and consequently restless soldiers, and now depended on his Bavarian uncle for further financial support. By the end of December, shortly before Christmas, Duke Louis and the count of Tirol, both of them still with Conradin in Verona, decided the cause of Conradin was hopeless and strongly urged the boy to give up his adventure and return to Germany with them[273]. At this crucial juncture, an ambassador from Pavia arrived in Verona on Boxing Day 1267. He had left Pavia for Verona on Christmas Eve in great haste to prevent Conradin from leaving Lombardy since a rumour that he was about to do so on short notice had reached the Pavians. The ambassador, a lawyer named Detesalvo Botto, was authorized by the *podestà* of Pavia to guarantee safe passage to Conradin and his army through Lombardy to Ghibelline Pisa where, as the Sicilian and Ghibelline exiles with Conradin were assuring him, a 'very great

---

270   *Annales Placentini Gibellini* ad ann. 1267, MGH *SS* 18, 524: '*Eodem tempore ... erat Guillelmus Standardus vicarius istius comitis Karuli in Lombardia cum 400 militibus Provincialibus*'.
271   On Charles' many allies in the Italian kingdom see *supra* p. 458.
272   See *infra* p. 479.
273   *Annales Placentini Gibellini* ad ann. 1267, MGH *SS* 18, 524: '*dux Bayguerie, comes de Tirali volebant regem in Alamaniam reducere, summa vi operam dantes ut reverteretur cum tota sua gente*'.

treasure' (*maximus thesaurus*) was to be handed over to him[274]. This decided the matter. Conradin was now determined to proceed with his adventure in spite of the advice of his uncle and stepfather. Since he still needed more money to cover the expenses of his expedition to Pisa, he asked for another loan from his uncle. On 27 December the duke lent his nephew 1500 pounds of silver, for which Conradin mortgaged some of the real property he had not yet mortgaged before 'to his beloved uncle' (*avunculo nostro carissimo*), who was by now his major creditor as well as the main beneficiary on his demise[275]. His stepfather added another 500 pounds for good measure and received some castles as collateral[276]. This still proved insufficient, since on 10 January 1268 Conradin borrowed yet another 3000 pounds from his uncle, now mortgaging his rights over the city of Augsburg and an important castle not far from that city[277]. Having thus despoiled their relative, no doubt at a bargain, of practically everything he owned, Duke Louis and Count Meinhard finally took their leave of Conradin, taking their troops with them back to Germany[278].

Conradin
in Pavia

Conradin stayed behind in Verona with a substantially reduced army of about 3000 knights, for the most part Germans, his friend Frederick

---

274   For the whole story see *Annales Placentini Gibellini* ad ann. 1267, MGH *SS* 18, 524: '*Domnus Detesalvus Bottus … fidelis semper imperii civis Papie, tractatum habens cum domno Ianono de Beccaria potestate populi Papie et aliis sapientibus Papie … in vigilia nativitatis Domini … equitavit Veronam ad regem Conradum. Qui ab ipso rege et a principibus eius alacriter fuit receptus. Et habito tractatu et colloquio cum rege et principibus, in quo promisit regi se daturum ei securum transitum usque ad civitatem Pisis, ubi desiderabat esse super omnia, cum in Verona essent nuncii et magnates Apulie promittentes regi maximum thesaurum in Pisis se daturos*'.
275   See the deed printed in *Monumenta Wittelsbacensia* 1, Munich 1857, no 92, 223-224. For an earlier substantial loan and mortgages to Duke Louis see *Mon. Wittelsbac.* 1, no 91, 221-222 (24 October 1266, while still in Augsburg). For the arrangement on what little was left of the Hohenstaufen estates in Germany after the demise of Conradin without an heir see *supra* p. 469.
276   The deed to this effect, dated on the same day as the loan from the duke of Bavaria, is in Saint Priest, *Histoire de la conquête de Naples par Charles d'Anjou* III, Paris 1847, 381-382. It turns out that Duke Louis was also a beneficiary of this contract, since he was granted the right to redeem the castles.
277   *Mon. Wittelsbac.* 1, no 93, 224-226.
278   The *Annales S. Iustinae Patavini* ad ann. 1267, MGH *SS* 19, 189 have the following rather damning, but all in all quite realistic, assessment of Conradin's stay in Verona: 'And so he stayed in Verona for three months, achieving nothing, since he neither conferred benefits on his friends, nor inflicted harm on his enemies. In that space of time a considerable part of the army went home, after selling horses and weapons for want of money. The duke of Bavaria and the count of Tirol likewise returned to their realms, leaving him on his own' (*Mansit itaque Verone tribus mensibus, nichil viriliter agens, quia nec commodum amicis contulit nec damnum intulit inimicis. In predicto igitur spacio temporis, pro defectu pecunie venditis equis et armis, magna pars exercitus ad propria remeavit. Similiter dux Bavarie ac comes de Tiraulo, ipso relicto, ad sedes proprias sunt reversi*).

of Baden most notably among them, Sicilian exiles and Tuscan Ghibellines[279]. It was not even remotely enough to defeat the forces of Charles of Anjou[280], but Conradin hoped for reinforcements in Pisa and, especially, in Rome, where his ally, Prince Enrico of Castile, the Roman senator, was actively engaged on behalf of Conradin (and in his own interest) in making the city of Rome a Ghibelline stronghold: the leading Guelphs of the city – the Orsini brothers, Napoleone and Matteo, Giovanni Caetani, Giovanni Savelli, and many others – were arrested and the churches and monasteries of Rome were despoiled of the contents of their treasuries[281]. At about the same time, on 18 October 1267, Prince Enrico welcomed Galvano Lancia in Rome. Conradin's emissary entered the city proudly flying the Hohenstaufen banner and was accommodated in the Lateran Palace, a deliberate insult to the pope[282]. Galvano was in Rome to finalize the treaty between Prince Enrico and Conradin already prepared in Augsburg in August[283]. It is clear from this that Rome was to be the rallying point for the invasion of the Sicilian kingdom, as it had been for Charles of Anjou in 1266, but Conradin was still in Lombardy at the time. On 17 January 1268 Conradin and what was left of his once impressive army finally left Verona, on their way to Pavia. Surprisingly, there was little or no resistance to his progress and consequently he reached Pavia unharmed and unopposed three days later[284]. He was met there by ambassadors from

---

279   *Annales Placentini Gibellini* ad ann. 1267, MGH *SS* 18, 524: '*cum quantitate militum suorum circa 3000 de gente Theutonica, Apulie, Tuscie et aliarum ... et erat in sua comitiva dux Austrie*'. For Frederick of Baden as 'duke of Austria' see *supra* p. 469, fnt. 234.
280   For this see the comment of Saba Malaspina, 4,8, MGH *SS* 35, 189: 'the German company following him was insufficient, even if tripled in size' (*comitiva Theutonicorum, qui sequebatur eundum, non posset eciam triplicata sufficere*).
281   Saba Malaspina, 4,6, MGH *SS* 35, 186-188. As a matter of course, Prince Enrico was instantly excommunicated for this. It is interesting to learn from Malaspina's account that many contemporary Romans still adhered to the ancient Roman custom to deposit their money in a temple for safekeeping. The code of Gregory IX, the *Liber extra*, contains a special section (X 3,16) on deposit.
282   For the details of Galvano Lancia's stay in Rome in October 1267 see the angry letter of Clement IV from 21 October 1267 in *Liber censuum* 2, 15-16. The letter is interesting since it gives details on the conditions under which Galvano Lancia had been spared after Benevento (sse *supra* p. 464). The pope ordered Galvano to be cited before an ecclesiastical court for breach of these conditions, and, of course for his outrageous act of sacrilege for staying in the Lateran Palace, according to the pope 'a place even righteous men are hardly worthy to enter' (*ad que ingredienda viri etiam justi vix digni sunt habiti*).
283   See *supra* p. 473.
284   For Conradin's progress to Pavia 'without anyone standing is his way' (*nemine sibi obviante*) see *Annales Placentini Gibellini* ad ann. 1267, MGH *SS* 18, 524. See also an angry letter by Clement IV stating that the Lombards 'should be filled with shame for not having put any obstacle in the way of that damned Conradin on his way from Verona to Pavia' (*Lombardos puduerat Corradino perditionis filio de Verona venienti Paviam nullum obstaculum praestitisse*) in Martène, *Thesaurus* 2, col. 597.

Pisa relieving him of at least a part of his financial concerns by putting 17,000 ounces of gold at his disposal, whereas the Pavians themselves granted an additional sum of 12,000 pounds of their own currency. Even more welcome to Conradin himself may have been the arrival at Pavia of Ubertino Landi, a former companion of the Ghibelline warlord Uberto Pallavicini, Manfred's *vicarius* in Lombardy[285], and an experienced warrior. Landi was from Piacenza, now under Guelph control, and brought seventy battlehardened knights with him. They all swore fealty to Conradin, who rewarded Landi with the important county of Venafro in the Molise region, a county in the Sicilian kingdom once already granted to Landi by Manfred[286].

At Pavia, Conradin once more wasted precious time, lingering there for another three months. Charles of Anjou was still in Tuscany at the time. The Tuscan Ghibelline stronghold of Poggibonsi had finally surrendered to Charles on 30 November 1267 after a protracted siege and on very favourable terms to the Ghibellines: all of them were free to go 'unharmed and with all their belongings' (*salvis personis et rebus*) provided they swore an oath never again to raise arms against Charles of Anjou[287], an oath they certainly would not keep, as Charles must have realized. The siege of Poggibonsi amounted to defeat rather than victory for Charles of Anjou since he was after the Ghibellines themselves rather than the town which they had defended. With Poggibonsi gone, there were only two Ghibelline strongholds left in Tuscany: Siena and Pisa. The latter city was, as Charles correctly surmised, the greater threat. He intended to block Conradin's access to Rome through Tuscany completely and since Pisa could be accessed by land as well as by sea, he was seeking an alliance with Genoa to isolate that city. The alliance failed[288] and consequently the siege of Pisa failed as well. By this time (the end of March 1268), Pope Clement IV had become quite desperate[289]: the kingdom of Sicily was in open revolt against Angevin

---

285   On Pallavicini see *supra* p. 437. The once mighty warlord had recently lost his hold over Lombardy and was now an old man, living in retirement in his castle Cusaliggio, where he died in May 1269 after making his peace with the Church.

286   For all of this see *Annales Placentini Gibellini* ad ann. 1268, MGH *SS* 18, 525.

287   Tholomaeus of Lucca, *Annales Lucenses* ad ann. 1267, MGH *SS rer. Germ. N.S.* 8, 157: '*qui erant in castro reddiderunt se in manibus regis salvis personis et rebus et iuraverunt numquam contra regem venire seu arma assumere*'.

288   See on these failed negotiations between Charles of Anjou and Genoa *Annales Ianuenses* (Nic. Guercii *e.a.*), ad ann. 1268, MGH *SS* 18, 262.

289   On 7 February 1268 Clement had written yet another letter to Charles of Anjou criticizing Charles' strategy (Martène, *Thesaurus* 2, col. 574): 'There are those who think that you are better off in Tuscany, between your kingdom and the Lombards, so that you can easily turn to any of these directions as the situation requires. We, however, are even now convinced, as we have written to you many times, that you are of more use in your own kingdom' (*Sunt qui putant quod melius sis in Tuscia, inter regnum tuum medius et Lombardos, ut ad partem al-*

rule, on the island as well as on the Italian peninsula itself, but Charles of Anjou, 'the man who would be king', continued to engage in Tuscan affairs while in Rome the Ghibelline party was in complete control, preparing the imminent advent of Conradin and the invasion of the Sicilian kingdom. But, to the great relief of the pope[290], Conradin, still in Pavia, had been entrapped in Lombard affairs, assisting Ubertino Landi in an unsuccessful attempt to regain control over Piacenza[291], rather than proceed as quickly as possible to Tuscany where Charles of Anjou was effectively blocking the overland route to Rome. At the end of March 1268 Charles, though unable to isolate Pisa, had indeed effectively blocked the overland route from Pavia to Pisa by taking possession of all the castles and towns along the coastal road in the extreme north of Tuscany[292]. This is why, when he finally decided to march on Pisa on 22 March 1268, Conradin was unable to take that road and was forced to bypass it. The Pavians were able to secure a passage through the rugged mountains of the coastal Apenines, the territory of a befriended nobleman, Count Manfredo dell Carreto, and so Conradin and his army were able to reach the Ligurian coast and the

---

terutram possis facile te convertere, si necessitas idem requirat. Nobis vero visum est hactenus, sicut pluries tibi scripsimus, quod in regno tuo esses utilius). By the end of March he exploded (letter to Charles of Anjou of 28 March in *Ann. eccl.*, Tom. 22, Paris 1870, ad ann. 1268 §3, 219): 'We really do not know why we are writing to you, being a king who seems to hold his own kingdom in contempt. It is continually ravaged and, leaderless as it is, exposed to Saracenes and evil Christians and, having been bled by your own thugs, it is now being torn to pieces by others. What one kind of locusts has left, the other kind consumes. It will never lack destroyers as long as it misses a protector' (*Cur tibi scribamus ut regi, qui regnum videris contemnere, non videmus. Laceratum quidem continue tamquam acephalum, Saracenis et perfidis Christianis expositum, et a tuis primitus exhaustum furibus, diripitur nunc ab aliis, et locustae residuum bruchus comedit: nec in eo deerunt vastatores, quamdiu caruerit defensore).* The pope added a clear warning: 'You really must not believe that, if you lose it, the Church will once again not spare trouble and expenses to conquer it a second time. You may return to your counties and, contented with just the title of a king, await the outcome of the affair' (*Sane si illud amittis, non credas, quod Ecclesia labores repetat et expensas pro eo denuo acquirendo, sed ad tuos redire poteris comitatus, et regali contentus nomine, rerum exitum exspectare).* The contempt is, once again, obvious. For the papal criticism of the Tuscan policy of Charles of Anjou see also a letter by Clement IV to his legate Cardinal Simon de Brion (Martène, *Thesaurus novus anecdotorum* Tom. 2, Paris 1717, col. 562-563(563) (14 January 1268)): 'The king, though recalled by us so that he may present himself in the kingdom and especially in Sicily, which he has lost for the most part, is so busy setting the Pisan territory aflame that, while plundering their land, he seems to have forgotten the kingdom itself completely' (*Rex ... licet a nobis revocatus, ut damnis occurreret regni et potissime in Sicilia, cuius partem magnam amisit, in tantum in Pisanos exarsit, quod eorum fines depopulans, regnum proprium videtur penitus oblivioni dedisse).*
290   Conradin's lack of resolve at the time surprised his contemporaries. 'Conradin is asleep in Pavia' (*Corradinus Papiae somniat*) wrote Clement IV on 16 March 1268 (Martène, 2, col. 581).
291   For this see *Annales Placentini Gibellini* ad ann. 1268, MGH *SS* 18, 525 (8 February).
292   *Annales Placentini Gibellini* ad ann. 1268, MGH *SS* 18, 525.

little port of Vado, where ten Pisan galleys were waiting for them. It was not enough to transport the entire army to Pisa and so it was decided that Conradin should embark with a few hundred knights, while the main army, under the command of Frederick of Baden, was to return to Pavia and march from there to Pisa along an alternative route, bypassing the Angevin strongholds in northern Tuscany. Conradin and the troops that were to accompany him took to sea on 29 March, reaching Pisa only a week later, on 7 April 1268, due to very bad weather forcing the fleet to take shelter in Portofino for some days[293].

Clement IV
wields the
spiritual sword

When Conradin arrived at Pisa, Charles of Anjou arrived at Viterbo to meet the pope[294]. Clement IV decided to provide his Angevine protagonist with the ultimate ecclesiastical weapon. Conradin, 'that little sprout of a cursed brood' (*damnati stirpis surculus*), was excommunicated once again and deprived of the only kingdom undisputedly his, the kingdom of Jerusalem. But the pope did not stop at this: Conradin's partisans were excommunicated at the same time[295]. The list of excommunicated people and places reads as a register of Conradin's most prominent supporters: Galvano and Federico Lancia, Manfredo Maletta, and John di Manerio were among the Sicilian exiles to be excommunicated; Duke Louis of Bavaria, the count of Tirol and Frederick of Baden among the Germans; Corrado da Pisa, Corrado Trincia, Guido Novello[296], and Corrado di Antiochia[297] among the Italians; the cities of Verona and Pavia in Lombardy, Pisa and Siena, Grosseto and San Miniato in Tuscany, Fermo in the Marche and Citta di Castello in Umbria were all laid under interdict and the citizens excommunicated as well. The pope added Enrico of Castile, the Roman senator, Guido de Montefeltro and all their officials in a separate bull of excommunication on the

---

293 For Conradin's passage to Vado, the split up of the army and the subsequent passage to Pisa see *Annales Placentini Gibellini* ad ann. 1268, MGH *SS* 18, 526 and *Annales Ianuenses* (Nic. Guercii *e.a.*), ad ann. 1268, MGH *SS* 18, 262. It took Conradin and his army almost a week to cover the 150 km. (90 miles) from Pavia to Vado. Vado is about 50 km. (33 miles) *east* of Genoa. Conradin had been unable to use that port, since the Genoese preferred neutrality in this conflict. They did, however, send ambassadors to Conradin at Portofino.
294 On 12 April 1268 Clement IV wrote to Cardinal Grosparmi, his legate in the Sicilian kingdom, that Charles of Anjou had arrived at Viterbo at the same day as Conradin had arrived at Pisa: Martène, *Thesaurus* 2, col. 584-585; also in Del Giudice, *Codice diplomatico* II.1, Naples 1869, no 43, 144-147. It implies that the pope knew within a week that Conradin had arrived at Pisa.
295 The papal bull '*Dudum ad apostolicae*' is in *Ann. eccl.*, Tom. 22, Paris 1870, ad ann. 1268 § 4-16, 219-222.
296 Guido Novello had been Manfred's *vicarius* in Tuscany (see *supra* p. 465). He now sided with Conradin.
297 Like Conradin, Corrado di Antiochia was a grandson of Frederick II. His father was Frederick's bastard Frederico di Antiochia, who had died in or about 1256.

very same day[298]. At the same time, the pope released Charles of Anjou of one of the solemn oaths Charles had sworn before being invested with the kingdom of Sicily: his promise to lay down the senatorship of Rome after he had conquered the Sicilian *regno*[299]. If the excommunicated Roman senator Enrico of Castile did not repent before Easter next, which he was not likely to do, Charles would be appointed senator of Rome for the term of no less than ten years[300]. Shortly later, on 17 April, the pope also appointed Charles of Anjou as imperial *vicarius generalis* in Tuscany, emphasizing that he, the pope, was entitled to do so since he was acting as emperor *ad interim* 'whenever the imperial title is in doubt' (*fluctuantis imperii*)[301]. It is clear from all this that by now the pope had indeed been sucked into the abyss of the political Charybdis that was Charles of Anjou, a danger already recognized by his predecessor Urban IV[302]. In exterminating one monster, the house of Hohenstaufen, the papal *curia* had created another, Charles of Anjou, whom it was now forced to endow with powers outside the Sicilian kingdom which it had vehemently denied to Manfred and had once insisted that Charles of Anjou should never have.

Meanwhile, in Pisa, the bulk of Conradin's army finally arrived on 2 May 1268. Thanks to the help of a local lord friendly to Conradin's cause, Count Alberto Malaspina, Frederick of Baden had found a way through the Apenines, bypassing the strongholds Charles of Anjou held there, and had been able to reach the coastal road 'without any resistance' (*sine aliqua contraditione*), even taking the coastal town of Massa on his way to Pisa[303]. Conradin was now ready to proceed to Rome, but

Conradin in Rome

---

298   A part of the papal bull '*Visceribus matris ecclesiae*' is in *Ann. eccl.*, Tom. 22, Paris 1870, ad ann. 1268 § 21, 223-224. It is here (223) that Conradin is referred to as '*damnati stirpis surculus*'.

299   See *supra* p. 452 and 456.

300   The papal bull '*Ut pacificum Urbs*' is in Del Giudice, *Codice diplomatico* II.1, Naples 1869, no 42, 142-143.

301   Martène, *Thesaurus* 2, col. 587-588; also in Del Giudice, *Codice diplomatico* II.1, Naples 1869, no 28, 118-119. The pope initially had appointed Charles of Anjou as 'peacemaker general' (*paciarius generalis*) in Tuscany: see *supra* p. 473. The date of Charles' appointment as imperial vicar in Martène and Del Giudice (15 February (*XV Kal. Martii*)) is a clerical error and should be read as 17 April (*XV Kal. Ma(d)ii*): see Posse, *Analecta Vaticana*, Innsbruck 1878, 48 (no 602), giving the correct date in the official Vatican *Regesta*.

302   See *supra* p. 452.

303   For the advent of Frederick of Baden with the army on 2 May see *Breve chronicon Pisanum* (1101-1268) ad ann. 1268, *RIS²* 6.2, 115. For the progress of Frederick of Baden with the army from Pavia to Pisa see *Annales Placentini Gibellini* ad ann. 1268, MGH *SS* 18, 527. Of course, Pope Clement, once again (see *supra* p. 479, fnt. 284), bitterly complained about the negligence of the Lombards to let Frederick and his army escape Lombardy and join forces with Conradin in Pisa, having already allowed Conradin himself to reach Pisa unopposed (Martène, *Thesaurus* 2, col. 597 (15 May 1268)): 'we cannot stand their shameful behaviour' (*eorum verecundiam aegre ferimus*). The reason of the Lomdards' indecisiveness at

was, yet again, distracted, this time by the Pisans who wanted him to assist them in taking their revenge on Lucca, their old enemy recently having joined Charles of Anjou in ravaging the Pisan countryside. It was during the campaign against Lucca that messengers arrived from Rome, urging Conradin to come to Rome 'as quickly as possible' (*sine mora*). Accordingly, Conradin and his army finally left Pisa on 15 June, after staying there for two months[304]. The first stop was at the staunchly loyal city of Siena, where Conradin was warmly welcomed, receiving a generous subsidy of 60,000 pounds of their currency. It allowed Conradin to pay the soldiers of his now considerably enhanced army their wages for three months ahead[305]. It greatly boosted their enthusiasm, which explains their victory over an Angevin army, commanded by the French knight Jean de Braiselve, who was left behind in Tuscany by Charles of Anjou as his representative. De Braiselve was captured and emprisoned in Siena. He was a prestigious prisoner since Charles of Anjou had appointed him marshall of the Sicilian kingdom[306]. It looks as if young Conradin, clearly incited by the recent victory over a French force, highly overrated his prospects at this juncture. At Siena he promised to grant the city 'full autonomy' (*omnis iurisdictio*) over its territory '*once we have attained the height of the imperial dignity, to which we rightly aspire, following the footsteps of our forefathers*'[307]. He seems really to have believed at the time that, after reconquering his Sicilian kingdom, he could reunite that kingdom with the Empire as his grandfather once had done. It was an illusion, inspired by his misguided education as an imperial aspirant, but it encouraged him to continue his adventure, now leading him to the gates of the very city where emperors were traditionally crowned.

From Siena Conradin turned to Grosseto in the Maremme and from there along the via Cassia to Rome, leading him right past the walls of

---

this time seems to have been that practically all Lombard cities, the Guelph 'controlled' cities not excluded, were internally divided with the Guelph and the Ghibelline party in balance so that decisive *action* (rather than an uncommitted declaration of loyalty) on behalf of one of the contenders (Conradin or Charles of Anjou) would have resulted in civil war. Verona was an exception because Mastino della Scala firmly ruled that city (see *supra* p. 475) and was appointed *podestà* of Pavia in 1268.

304   For this episode see *Annales Placentini Gibellini* ad ann. 1268, MGH *SS* 18, 527 and for the date of Conradin's departure (*17 kal. Iulii, die S[i] Viti* (=15 June)) *Breve chronicon Pisanum* ad ann. 1268, *RIS*[2] 6.2, 115.

305   *Annales Placentini Gibellini* ad ann. 1268, MGH *SS* 18, 527.

306   The *Annales Placentini Gibellini* ad ann. 1268, MGH *SS* 18, 527 have a letter by Conradin jubilantly announcing his victory 'to his loyal subjects' (*fidelibus suis*) in Lombardy.

307   From a charter issued by Conradin at Siena on 7 July 1268 (published in Bern. Malavolti, *Dell'Historia di Siena scritta* II.2, Venice 1599, *ff.* 36, vo-37, vo (37, ro)): '*cum ad Imperialis dignitatis culmen, ad quod progenitorum nostrorum imitantes vestigia, non immerito aspiramus, scandere nos Deo auctore contigerit*'.

Viterbo, from where Pope Clement IV grudgingly observed the progress of 'the little sprout' he was incapable of stopping[308]. It is reported by a contemporary that the pope, watching Conradin pass by the walls of Viterbo, must have said that *'one should have pity with the boy who is seduced to be led to the slaughter'*[309]. There was no sign of impending doom, however, when Conradin finally reached Rome on 24 July 1268[310]. To the contrary, the Roman senator Enrico of Castile had seen to it that Conradin received a welcome worthy of a Roman emperor. There is a vivid contemporary account of his reception at Rome by the Guelph historian Saba Malaspina, who was a native Roman and may well have witnessed the occasion[311]. He resentfully concedes that Charles of Anjou had not received a similar glorious welcome on his advent in the city, three years earlier[312]. It is reported that the common people of Rome, 'imperialistically minded by nature' (*naturaliter imperialis*)[313], even hailed Conradin as emperor when he was triumphantly led to the Capitol[314]. It really must have turned the head of the boy, now sixteen years of age. He was living a dream of empire and great achievements to come, as everyone around him must have assured him. Here he was, in the capital of the world (*caput mundi*), surrounded by cheering masses, accompanied by a host of knights in shining armour, certain of victory. On a bright sunny day like this, anything seems possible to a boy of his age, except of course defeat, humiliation, and, ultimately, death.

Charles of Anjou was in Apulia when he was informed of Conradin's arrival in Rome. He had taken his leave of the pope at Viterbo late in April 1268[315], hastening to suppress the revolt of the Lucera Muslims

Defeat

---

308 Clement IV in a letter to the citizens of Perugia (Martène, *Thesaurus* 2, col. 609 (13 June 1268)): 'Conradin is about to pass by close to us. We do not have an army big enough to oppose his progress though' (*Conradinus ... iuxta nos transitum est facturus. Licet ad eius impediendum transitum nequeamus habere militiam numerosam*).

309 Tholomaeus of Lucca, *Historia ecclesiastica nova* 22, 36, ed. Muratori 11, Milan 1727, col. 1160: '*Tradunt autem, quod cum Clemens Papa de suo palatio videret per planitiem dictarum terrarium gentem Conradini transire, sic ipsum dixisse, quod dolendum erat de tali puero, qui sic seductus ducebatur ad victimam*'.

310 *Annales Placentini Gibellini* ad ann. 1268, MGH *SS* 18, 528: '*die 24. mensis Iulii intravit Romam*'.

311 Saba Malaspina, 4,13-14, MGH *SS* 35, 197-199.

312 Saba Malaspina, 4,13, MGH *SS* 35, 198: '*Nec fuit aliqua illius pompositatis et glorie comparatio, quando Romani regem Karolum venientem universaliter exceperunt*'. See *supra* p. 457.

313 Saba Malaspina, 4,13, MGH *SS* 35, 197.

314 Thomas Tuscus, *Gesta imperatorum et pontificum*, MGH *SS* 22, 522: '*eique Romani laudes imperatorias acclamaverunt*'.

315 Thanks to the meticulous research of the Napolitan archivist Camillo Minieri-Riccio (1813-1882), who reconstructed the itinerary of Charles of Anjou from the royal Sicilian

first before confronting Conradin as Clement IV had advised him all along. As from 20 May Lucera was under siege, but it proved a hard nut to crack. The town was surrounded by a ring of wooden towers, but the Muslims were able to destroy them all, routing Charles' troops with great slaughter in the process. But Charles did not give in, prolonging his siege of Lucera until 15 June, when he finally retreated to nearby Foggia. It is reported that about 2000 men in Charles' army lost their lives in these fights[316]. In Foggia Charles must have received the news of Conradin's advent in Rome. It was now clear that the battle for the future of the Sicilian kingdom was to be fought in that kingdom itself and it must also have been clear to Charles of Anjou that Conradin's best plan would be to join with the still undefeated Muslims of Lucera as quickly as possible. Consequently, he decided to intercept Conradin's army at a place as far away as possible from Lucera to avoid having the Muslims close on his rear. By the beginning of August his army was on the move from Foggia, joining the road along the coast of the Adriatic Sea, the via Appia Traiana, heading north.

Conradin left Rome on 18 August 1268[317]. His army had now been reinforced with Ghibellines from all over the Italian *regno* and Rome and with the additional troops of the Roman senator, don Enrico of Castile. He had about 6000 knights with him[318]. Conradin's war council, no doubt controlled by the German ministerial, Conrad Kroff, 'the commander of all the Germans in Italy' (*Theotonicorum in Ytalia morantium mareschalcus*)[319] and a veteran of the battle of Montaperti, decided to march into the Sicilian kingdom along the via Valeria rather than the via Latina, as Charles of Anjou had done, since the bridge over the Garigliano at Ceprano was now heavily defended, while at

---

archives (*Itinerario di Carlo I. di Angiò*, Naples 1872), we are well informed on the whereabouts of Charles of Anjou during the entire length of his Sicilian reign.

316 *Annales Placentini Gibellini* ad ann. 1268, MGH *SS* 18, 527-528: '*Eodem tempore Karolus erat in ossidione Nucerie, in qua civitate magnates de regno in defensione erant; et factis castellis ligneis a Karulo, intrinseci cavam facientes ipsa castella combuxerunt, et prelio incepto gentes Karuli in fugam converterunt. Reperitur in his partibus cecidisse de gente Karuli duo milia milites*'. See on the siege of Lucera also *Annales S. Iustinae Patavini* ad ann. 1268, MGH *SS* 19, 190.

317 Tholomaeus of Lucca, *Annales Lucenses* ad ann. 1262, MGH *SS rer. Germ. N.S.* 8, 161: '*Die autem XVIII. Augusti, eodem anno, exivit <Conradinus> de Roma versus Apuliam*'.

318 Medieval sources are notoriously unreliable as far as the number of combattants in a battle are concerned. The most reliable source on the strength of Conradin's army, the *Annales Placentini Gibellini*, states that he entered Rome with 5000 knights, or rather 5000 mounted men (*milites*): *Annales Placentini Gibellini* ad ann. 1268, MGH *SS* 18, 528. It also states that Prince Enrico of Castile had 300 mounted men with him. After adding the contribution of the Roman Ghibellines and some late arrivals from Lombardy, Tuscany, and the Sicilian kingdom, this amounts to an army of 6000 mounted men at most.

319 Conradin in his letter quoted in *Annales Placentini Gibellini* ad ann. 1268, MGH *SS* 18, 527.

the same time allowing for a quicker access to Apulia and the Lucera Muslims[320]. It was precisely what Charles of Anjou expected his enemy to do. By the end of August Charles was in Avezzano, a town near Lake Fucino, now completely drained but in the Middle Ages still one of the biggest lakes in Italy. West of Avezzano is an extensive plain, the Palentine plain (*campus Palentinus*). It was there that Charles of Anjou was waiting for his enemy to come out of the mountains to the north-west of that plain. Conradin arrived on the eve of 23 August, surprised to find Charles of Anjou and his army prepared to meet him there. On the next day there was a great battle on the plain near the present little town of Scurcola Marsicana, known in antiquity as Alba[321]. Conradin's army, though superior in numbers and initially successful, was completely routed by Charles of Anjou in the end[322]. On the evening of that fateful day, Charles wrote a letter informing Pope Clement IV of his great victory, as he had done after the battle of Benevento[323]: '*I bring to you, most Gentle Father, the joy long expected by all the faithful of the world, humbly sacrificing it as sweet incense to the Holy Roman Church, my mother, begging you, father, to rise and join in the meal of game your son is offering as his debt to the Almighty. We have killed so many enemies that the carnage inflicted on the other enemies of the Church at the field near Benevento seems rather modest in comparison*'[324].

---

320   For these considerations see *Annales Placentini Gibellini* ad ann. 1268, MGH *SS* 18, 528.

321   It is common knowledge that the battle was not fought near Tagliacozzo, but since both Villani (*Nuova Cronica* 8,26-27, ed. Porta I, Parma 1990, 451-458) and Dante (*Inferno* 28, 17) located the battle near that town, some 10 km. from the actual site of the battle, it has become usual to ascribe the famous battle to that town, in spite of the fact that Charles of Anjou had an abbey, dedicated to S. Maria della Vittoria, built near Scurcola to commemorate his great victory there. Charles' deed to that effect is in Del Giudice, *Codice diplomatico* II.1, Naples 1869, Appendix no III, 335-341, explicitly naming Scurcola. The present church of S. Maria della Vittoria in Scurcola was only built in the 16th century. The abbey is a ruin.

322   On the battle of Tagliacozzo/Scurcola see Saba Malaspina, 4,16-19, MGH *SS* 35, 202-209; *Annales Placentini Gibellini* ad ann. 1268, MGH *SS* 18, 528; Villani, *Nuova Cronica* 8,26-27, ed. Porta I, Parma 1990, 451-458; Primat of S. Denys († *c.* 1277) (Jean de Vignay), *Chronicon* ch. 19-21, *Recueil* 23, 30-36 and especially the letter written by Charles of Anjou to Clement IV on the evening after the battle in Martène, *Thesaurus* 2, col. 624-625, also in Del Giudice, *Codice diplomatico* II.1, Naples 1869, no LVII, 185-190. The precise progress of the battle and the reason (or reasons) of Conradin's final defeat have been the subject of an intense scholarly debate among military historians, two German generals among them, without a definitive conclusion.

323   See *supra* p. 462.

324   Martène, *Thesaurus* 2, col. 624 and 625; Del Giudice, *Codice diplomatico* II.1, Naples 1869, no LVII, 186 and 190: '*Expectatam diutius a cunctis fidelibus orbis terre letitiam vobis, Clementissime Pater, et Sacrosanctae Romane Ecclesie matri mee tamquam suavitatis incensum humiliter offerens, supplico ut surgens pater et comedens de venatione filii sui exsolvat gratias debitas Altissimo... Facta est itaque hostium tanta strages, quod illa que in agro Beneventano de aliis Ecclesie persecutoribus facta fuit huius respectu valde modica reputatur*'.

Humiliation

When writing his gruesome victorious letter to the pope, Charles of Anjou did not yet know for certain what had been the fate of Conradin and Prince Enrico of Castile[325]. As a matter of fact, Conradin had not personally engaged in the battle[326], as he was too young (and far too important), and consequently he was able to escape the scene of battle with some hundred knights fleeing the slaughter, Frederick of Baden and Galvano Lancia and his son among them. Prince Enrico of Castile was also able to escape the battlefield seeking refuge in a monastery, a very foolish choice since, as was to be expected, the abbot did his Christian duty by handing him over to Charles of Anjou who held him in prison for years[327]. Enrico was lucky, since, contrary to the military custom of the time[328], no prisoners were taken in or after this battle: it was a *bataille à outrance*. Every knight or soldier from Conradin's army still found alive after the battle was cruelly tortured and executed[329].

Conradin and his company of survivors headed for Rome as quickly as possible, where Prince Enrico's *vicarius*, Guido de Montefeltre, had been left behind to watch over the city. Guido was a vassal of Conradin[330] and Conradin may have been convinced that he could count on the loyalty of the man from Urbino. He was to be bitterly disappointed. On 28 August 1268 he was back in Rome[331], a city he

---

325   Martène, *Thesaurus* 2, col. 625; Del Giudice, *Codice diplomatico* II.1, Naples 1869, no LVII, 190: 'when writing this present letter, written immediately after the victory, there is no certainty about Conradin and Enrico, the senator, whether they have fallen in battle or have escaped' (*De Conradino autem et Henrico senatore urbis utrum in bello ceciderint an per fugam evaserint, nulla in confectione presentium, que statim post victoriam scripte fuerunt, haberi potuit certitudo*).

326   Thomas Tuscus, *Gesta imperatorum et pontificum*, MGH *SS* 22, 522: 'Corradinus qui non intraverat prelium'.

327   Saba Malaspina, 4,19, MGH *SS* 35, 209 and Thomas Tuscus, *Gesta imperatorum et pontificum*, MGH *SS* 22, 522.

328   For this see *supra* p. 244, fnt. 41.

329   For this see Saba Malaspina, 4,20, MGH *SS* 35, 209-210 and the letter of Charles of Anjou to the citizens of Padua, written on the day after the battle (Del Giudice, *Codice diplomatico* II.1, Naples 1869, no LVIII, 190-195(194)): 'Furthermore, Corrado of Antiochia and Thomas of Aquino and many others who have betrayed us have been taken prisoner, all of whom, except Corrado of Antiochia, have been sentenced to death because of the unspeakable crime of treason which they have committed against our majesty' (*capti sunt insuper Corradus de Antiochia et Thomas de Aquino et plures alii proditores nostri, qui excepto Corrado de Antiochia propter detestabilem proditionem, quam contra majestatem nostram commiserant, iam capitali sententia sunt damnati*). Corrado di Antiochia was the only exception because his wife held some important Guelphs captive in her castle at Saracinesco. Corrado was exchanged for these hostages and still lived to see Henry VII, Dante's 'alto Arrigo', crowned as Roman emperor in Rome on 29 June 1312. Since Corrado belonged to the illegitimate branch of the Hohenstaufen family (see *supra* p. 482, fnt. 297), he was not a danger to Charles' position.

330   See *supra* p. 473.

331   *Annales Placentini Gibellini* ad ann. 1268, MGH *SS* 18, 528: 'Rex Conradus ... cum quingintis militum qui ex prelio evaserunt ... intravit Romam die Martis, 28. mensis Augusti'.

had left less than a fortnight before, cheered on by the Romans. Now he returned as a defeated pretender, powerless and without friends[332]. Guido de Montefeltre, a heartless realist, considered Conradin's situation hopeless and denied Conradin access to the Capitol, indicating that he was now a *persona non grata* in Rome[333]. After the first Roman Guelphs returned from the battlefield announcing the impending advent of the victorious Charles of Anjou, Conradin's position in Rome was untenable[334]. He now made an unfortunate decision that sealed his fate. Instead of immediately heading north, to Tuscany and the still loyal town of Siena, he decided to take the via Valeria south again. His first stop was the isolated castle of Saracinesco, held by the wife of Corrado of Antiochia, some 50 kilometres (30 miles) east of Rome, where he went in hiding for a few days. It was there that what was still left of the company – Frederick of Baden, Galvano Lancia and his son Galeotto, some loyal Roman nobles, and a few German knights – decided to escape to the Tyrrhenian coast, most probably hoping to find a ship there to take them to the island of Sicily, still largely in the hands of Corrado Capece at the time[335]. They did indeed succeed in reaching the coast near Astura in Lazio, but there their luck ended[336].

The port of Astura and the surrounding territory belonged to a Roman noble, Giovanni Frangipani. The family was traditionally Ghibelline, but old loyalties were of little account under the present circumstances. The cause of the house of Hohenstaufen had definitively collapsed on the Palentine plain near Scurcola and the Frangipani's had to accommodate to new political realities, as did the other Roman families (and the pope): Charles of Anjou was, once again, elected senator for life by the people of Rome and this time Clement IV did not object[337]. Consequently, as soon as Frangipani received notice, early in September[338], of the presence of Conradin in his domain, he had

---

332   Saba Malaspina, 4,21, MGH *SS* 35, 211: '*Corradino, cui nullus post devictum a Gallicis bellum remansit amicus*'.
333   Dante banned Guido of Montefeltre to the eighth circle of Hell, in the eighth bowge, where the counsellors of fraud abide (*Inferno* Canto 27). He did not do so for the scandalous act of disloyalty displayed by Guido at Rome in 1268, however. Dante may not have known about it. This act is not in Villani and may have been missing in their common source.
334   For Conradin's short stay at Rome between 28 and 31 August see *Annales Placentini Gibellini* ad ann. 1268, MGH *SS* 18, 528 and Saba Malaspina, 4,21, MGH *SS* 35, 211-212.
335   On Corrado Capece in Sicily see *supra* p. 476 and fnt. 265.
336   The best source for the episode after Conradin's departure from Rome until his capture at Astura is *Annales Placentini Gibellini* ad ann. 1268, MGH *SS* 18, 528.
337   Charles already styled himself '*alme urbis senator*' in a letter to Louis IX of 12 September 1268 (see *infra* fnt. 338).
338   Charles of Anjou informed his brother King Louis IX of the capture of Conradin in a letter of 12 September 1268 (Del Giudice, *Codice diplomatico* II.1, Naples 1869, no LXII,

the boy and his companions arrested[339]. They were handed over (for a fair price) to Angevine officials who happened to be nearby[340] and subsequently relayed to Charles of Anjou himself. On 12 September 1268 the captives were handed over to Charles in Genazzano, some 60 kilometres (35 miles) east of Rome. Galvano Lancia and his son Galeotto were instantly (and publicly) executed by decapitation and Conradin and Frederick of Baden were incarcerated in chains 'by feet and hands' (*per pedes et manus*)[341]. The two young men must have been really shocked by now, but their nightmare was only just beginning.

Charles of Anjou left Genazzano for Rome on 15 September to take on his senatorship. On his way there, he passed the old town of Palestrina where the Colonna family had a formidable castle. Charles left Conradin and Frederick of Baden in the custody of Giovanni Colonna[342] before entering the city of Rome on 16 September 1268. The Roman Ghibellines were completely intimidated by the appearance of the king of Sicily and his victorious army. They had controlled most of the major strongholds in the city, the Colosseum, the Tiber island, the Castel S. Angelo, and others, but they were all surrendered to the Roman Guelphs without any resistance. Charles of Anjou was now re-established as senator for life of the city, without any reference to the title of the pope[343]. He had achieved what no Sicilian king, not

---

198-200). The actual arrest cannot have happened long before that date, probably on 8 or 9 September.

339   On the capture of Conradin and his companions see *Annales Placentini Gibellini* ad ann. 1268, MGH *SS* 18, 528; Thomas Tuscus, *Gesta imperatorum et pontificum*, MGH *SS* 22, 522; Bartolomaeo de Neocastro cap. 9, *RIS*² 13.3, 8; Riccobaldo da Ferrara (1245/'46-after 1320) *Historia imperatorum* (ed. Muratori 9, Milan 1726, col. 137, and Saba Malaspina, 4,21-22, MGH *SS* 35, 211-212. Thomas Tuscus, Riccobaldo, and Saba Malaspina have a story that Conradin had already taken to sea, but was overtaken by a faster boat sent after him by Frangipani. It sounds like fiction, but is nevertheless taken for a fact by many later historians, including Villani, *Nuova cronica* 8,29, ed. Porta I, Parma 1990, 459.

340   According to Saba Malaspina (4,22, MGH *SS* 35, 212-213) the prisoners were handed over to the Angevin admiral Roberto de Lavena, who had narrowly escaped a strong Pisan fleet, sent to support Corrado Capece in Sicily, shortly before and was on his way north when he passed the coast near the port of Astura.

341   For the precise date see *Ann. Clerici Parisiensis* ad ann. 1267, MGH *SS* 26, 583 (*die Mercurii post nativitatem beate Marie virginis*). For further details *Annales Cavenses* ad ann. 1267, MGH *SS* 3, 195; *Annales Placentini Gibellini* ad ann. 1268, MGH *SS* 18, 528 and a letter by Charles of Anjou to the citizens of Lucca from September 1268 (without a precise date) in Del Giudice, *Codice diplomatico* II.1, Naples 1869, no LXX, 214-217(215) (*Galvanum Lancia eiusque filium iam in capitali pena condemnatos*).

342   *Annales Placentini Gibellini* ad ann. 1268, MGH *SS* 18, 528: '*postea ducti sunt in Prinistinum in fortia Johannis de Columpna*'.

343   *Ann. Clerici Parisiensis* ad ann. 1267, MGH *SS* 26, 583: 'When news of the battle reached the city of Rome, the party of the Church and the king, thrown out of the city by the said Enrico who had plundered their land and possessions with all his might, returned to the

even Frederick II, had ever been able to accomplish: complete and permanent control over the city of Rome and its territory. He was now king of Sicily, senator for life of Rome, and 'imperial' vicar in Tuscany, where Ghibelline influence was now rapidly withering away, as it did in Lombardy. He had become the strongest force on the Italian peninsula, in clear defiance of the official papal policy never to allow a king of Sicily to rule over any other territory on the Italian peninsula[344]. The new monster created by the pope and his *curia* was triumphantly emerging and it was more terrifying than Manfred ever had been.

Charles of Anjou did not stay in Rome for long. After installing one of his leading courtiers, Jacopo Gantelmi[345], as his vicar in the city, he left on 2 October, returning to the Sicilian kingdom to quench the rebellion there. On his way back, he stopped at Palestrina to fetch Conradin and the other prisoners, taking them with him to the Sicilian *regno* where their fate was to be decided. They were subjected to the ultimate humiliation of being dragged along in chains all the way to Naples, so that everyone along the road could witness their capture[346].

---

city and coming back to their homes, without any resistance, they went to the Capitol and the Castel S. Angelo and other fortresses in the city and having driven their adversaries from there, they once more unanimously elected king Charles as senator and handed over the Capitol and the other fortresses of the city to the custody of the king, who, harmoniously elected by all, entered the city of Rome with great joy on 16 September accompanied by some cardinals' (*Auditis autem in urbe Rom. rumoribus de conflictu, pars ecclesie regisque, quam dictus Henricus de Urbe eiecerat quorumque predia et bona quelibet pro viribus devastaret, revertentes ad Urbem, ad propria, nullo invento contrario, remearunt, et ad Capitholeum accedentes et castrum S. Angeli et ad alias Urbis fortileccias, amotis ex ipsis adversariis et eiectis, prefatum regem Karolum denuo in senatorem unanimiter elegentes, dictum Capitholeum cum aliis Urbis fortilectiis ipsius custodie submiserunt; qui concorditer electus ab omnibus, dominica post exaltationem sancta Crucis subsequentis nonnullis cardinalibus cum eo existentibus, urbem Romanam cum gaudio est ingressus*). It is reported that Guido de Montefeltre sold possession of the Capitol for 4000 pounds: *Annales Placentini Gibellini* ad ann. 1268, MGH *SS* 18, 528.

344   For the official restatement of that policy see *supra* p. 456.
345   Jacobo Gantelmi had been Charles' vicar in Rome before: see *supra* p. 452.
346   *Annales Cavenses* ad ann. 1267, MGH *SS* 3, 195: '*ut ipsos sic captivos videret omnis homo*'. There were rumours at the time that Conradin had escaped, causing Charles of Anjou to write letters vehemently denying that rumour: see his letter to the Luccans, cited above in fnt. 341.

The Execution of Conradin
(Giovanni Villani, *Nuova Cronica*, Biblioteca Apostolica Vaticana, Ms Chigi L.VIII 296,
f. 112 *vᵒ*)

Death

There can be no doubt whatsoever that Charles of Anjou was not going to let Conradin live, not even in lifelong imprisonment, as he had done with Manfred's children[347]. Conradin represented an even stronger claim to the crown of Sicily than Manfred's offspring and had tried to overthrow Charles by force of arms. There was no way Conradin could get away with this with impunity. In terms of Sicilian law, the case against Conradin was unambiguous: here was an instance of *laesio maiestatis* if ever there was one. Galvano Lancia and his son, Sicilian subjects, had already been executed for that crime (without a trial) at Gevazzano and so had all the prisoners taken alive after the battle on the Palentine plain[348]. Charles of Anjou could have done so with Conradin as well *if* he had captured him on the battlefield. Conradin was an unrepentant excommunicate, as well as a public enemy at the time, and unrepentant excommunicates could be killed with impunity according to canon law as well as imperial law[349]. Conradin had, how-

---

347   On the fate of the children of Manfred see *supra* p. 463 and fnt. 214.
348   See *supra* p. 488.
349   On this issue see *supra* p. 391.

ever, received absolution by now[350], but it did not exculpate him from the crime he had committed. He had tried to deprive a legally invested and consecrated king of his domain by force of arms and was consequently guilty of the crime of *lèse majesté*. In a case like his, where the crime was evidenced by notoriety, the rules of 'due process' did not apply according to canon law[351] *and*, in a case of *lèse majesté*, according to the great code of Frederick II[352]. Consequently, there never was a 'trial' of Conradin and his companions in Naples. There was just a royal order, sentencing Conradin and the other prisoners to death by decapitation[353]. It was a mild sentence since, according to the letter of Sicilian law, rebels were to be treated as heretics and were to be burnt at the stake[354].

On 29 October, only ten days after Charles' arrival at Naples, Conradin and his friend Frederick of Baden were playing at chess in their cell[355] when they were visited by the 'Grand Constable', the chief officer of the Sicilian crown, Jean de Bricaudy, Sire de Nangey, informing them that they were to be executed on that very same day.

---

350   According to Saba Malaspina 4,22, MGH *SS* 35, 213. The Bollandist *Acta Sanctorum* (Tom. IX, Paris/Rome 1865, 189 C (20 March)) record a tradition attributing Conradin's absolution to the initiative of the blessed Ambrose of Siena (1220-1286), who allegedly received permission from Clement IV to administer absolution to the penitent Conradin, probably at Palestrina.

351   On this issue see *supra* p. 362.

352   *LA* 1,53,2 and see the commentary on this provision by Andreas de Isernia (*c.* 1220-*c.*1316) in *Constitutiones regni Siciliarum*, Naples 1771, *ad* 1,53,2 (p. 213): '*in crimine laesae maiestatis non servatur solemnitas iuris*'.

353   There still is some controversy over the matter of the 'trial' of Conradin in Naples, caused by some remarks by Saba Malaspina (4,23, MGH *SS* 35, 214), *not* present in Naples at the time, according to whom Charles abstained from passing sentence himself, but left it to a specially appointed 'court' consisting of four representatives (*boni viri*) selected among the magistrates from cities in the Campania and the duchy of Capua instead 'so that what was about to happen to Conradin would not look like his own judgement, but rather that of the people from the country' (*ut non suum, quod acturus erat de Conradino, iudicium videretur, sed pocius hominum de contrata*). Saba is the *only* contemporary source mentioning a special 'court'. Bartolomaeo de Neocastro (cap. 9, *RIS²* 13,3, 8) merely states that Charles ordered 'the magnates of the realm' (*primates regni*) to *witness* the execution. The learned notary from Ferrara Riccobaldo has some interesting observations in his *Historia imperatorum* (ed. Muratori, 9, Milan 1726, col. 137-138). According to him, Charles sought legal advice on the question whether Conradin could be sentenced to death and that the professor of civil law (*praestantissimus legum doctor*) Guido de Suzaria († before 1292) advised against it. This may be true, since we know that Guido, who read Roman law in Bologna in 1266, was invited by Charles of Anjou as one of his legal counsellors in 1267. Guido de Suzaria had been *podestà* in several cities of the Italian kingdom and may have been invited to join Charles' team of legal counsellors on account of both his administrative experience and his legal expertise. It is incumbent on a legal counsel to answer questions like the one at hand, but Charles did not heed the advice of master Guido and sentenced Conradin to death anyway.

354   *LA* 1,1.

355   Riccobaldo, *Historia imperatorum*, ed. Muratori 9, Milan 1726, col. 138.

Conradin and Friedrich were given the opportunity to make their last will and testament. Conradin merely confirmed the grant of what was left of his estate in Germany and Italy to his Bavarian uncles which he had already made in Augsburg, now almost exactly two years ago[356]. Having done that and having made their peace with God[357], they were escorted to a scaffold built on a market square near the sea, the present (and rather depressing) Piazza del Mercato, on the spot where the Church of S. Croce now stands. Conradin was composed till the end, even pardoning the executioner as custom prescribed. The last thoughts of the boy, still only sixteen, were with his mother and the grief which the news of his death would cause her[358]. Exactly a month later, on

---

356   See *supra* p. 469. Conradin's testament has survived. It is in Del Giudice, *Codice diplomatico* II.1, Naples 1869, Appendix II, no I, 333: '*Conradus, natus olim domini Conradi, filii quondam divi F. illustris rom. imperatoris, sanus mente et corpore addens testamento dudum ab eo condito, iterato, concessit dominis Ludowico et H. ducibus Bavarie avunculis suis, omnia bona juxta tenorem privilegii, que alias eisdem ducibus se asserit concessisse*'. There are a few additional legacies of small amounts of money to some German monasteries '*pro remedio anime sue*'. The document also contains the last will of Frederick of Baden.
357   *Chronicon Minoritae Erphordensis, Cont. I* ad ann. 1268, MGH *SS rer. Germ.* 24, 677-678: '*Prius tamen cuidam fratri de ordine Minorum pluries confessi sunt, et audita missa, sacrum sacramentum dominici corporis acceperunt*'.
358   Riccobaldo of Ferrara reports Conradin's last words: 'Oh mother! What grievous news you will receive about me' (*Ah genetrix! Quam profundi maeroris nuncium ex me suscipies*). The execution of Conradin, Frederick of Baden, and their companions is reported in many contemporary sources, but mostly rather succinctly. See, for example, the *Annales Placentini Gibellini* ad ann. 1268, MGH *SS* 18, 528: '<*Karolus*> *predicto rege Conrado et duci Austrie et comiti Gerardo de Pisis fecit in publico capita detruncari ... die Lune tercio exeunte Octobris*'. The most vivid and trustworthy accounts are in Riccobaldo da Ferrara, *Historia imperatorum*, ed. Muratori 9, Milan 1726, col. 138, who had it, as he emphasizes, from an eyewitness, and Saba Malaspina 4,23, MGH *SS* 35, 214-215. The report by Bartholomaeo de Neocastro (cap. 9 and 10, *RIS²* 13.3, 8-9) is largely, if not entirely, fictitious. The remains of Conradin were not given a proper Christian burial, despite his absolution. According to Riccobaldo he was interred close by, on the beach, 'in the manner of bodies surrendered by the sea' (*more cadaverum pelago eiectorum*) and according to Saba Malaspina the place was marked by a heap of stones, which is not unlikely since a similar grave was initially given to Manfred by Charles of Anjou (see *supra* p. 463). Saba adds that it was said by some that 'the friars of the place' (*fratres illius loci*) secretly exhumed the body of Conradin and sent it 'to his lamentable mother' (*matri miserabili*). This is almost true, but for the fact that Conradin's body was not returned to his mother but laid to rest in the nearby Church of S. Maria del Carmine, on a little square adjacent to the Piazza del Mercato. According to Riccobaldo, Charles' successor, Charles II (1254-1285-1309), had a church built over the grave of Conradin and his companions. This is the church Charles of Anjou himself allowed to be built by the Carmelite friars near the site of Conradin's grave, dedicated, as Charles explicitly stated, to the care of the souls of his father and mother rather than Conradin. The grant to the friars of Saint Mary of Mount Carmel of the land adjacent to the site of Conradin's execution, dated in July 1270, is in Del Giudice, *Codice diplomatico* II.1, Naples 1869, Appendix II, no II, 334-335. These were 'the friars of the place' indicated by Saba and this is the church, finished under the reign of Charles II, where the Carmelite friars have laid Conradin to rest. In the nineteenth century, King Maximilian of Bavaria ordered a statue of Conradin to be erected in the church. It was a late

29 November 1268, Clement IV died at Viterbo. He expired knowing that he finally had accomplished the ultimate objective of papal policy ever since the days of Gregory IX: the union of the Sicilian kingdom and the German Empire had been broken once and for all and the 'cursed breed' (*damnata stirps*) of Hohenstaufen seemed to have been finally and completely exterminated.

---

tribute to Conradin by a member of the house of Wittelsbach, the sole German beneficiary of Conradin's demise.

King Manfred
(*De arte venandi cum avibus*, Biblioteca Apostolica Vaticana, ms. Pal. lat. 1071, *f.* 1, *v*°)

6

Aftermath

The Grand Design of Charles of Anjou

The demise of Clement IV initiated the longest papal vacancy (*sedis vacantia*) in the history of the Catholic Church. The cardinals in Viterbo were bickering over the succession for more than two years. The controversy was not just personal, but highly political. There was now a pronounced French-Angevine fraction within the *curia* and an equally distinct 'Italian' party that was well aware of the grave danger to the freedom of Italy the papal policy had created over the last decade succeeding the demise of Frederick II. In the meantime, Charles of Anjou consolidated his power in the Sicilian kingdom. The Lucera muslims finally surrendered late in August 1269 after a prolonged siege. All Christians found alive in the town were massacred, but the Muslims, surprisingly, were not[1]. While Charles continued winding up all centres of resistance on the peninsula with stupendous cruelty, systematically terrorizing his subjects into submission[2], his marshall Guillaume

Charles of
Anjou represses
all resistance
in the Sicilian
kingdom

---

1 *Annales Placentini Gibellini* ad ann. 1269, MGH *SS* 18, 536: 'At the same time, in the month of September, the people of Lucera surrendered to the force and mercy of the king because their provisions had run out as a consequence of the long siege by Charles, the aforementioned king of Sicily. The Christians he found there were crucified for various crimes' (*Eodem tempore de mense Septembris illi de Noceria propter longam obsidicionem quam Karolus dictus rex Sicilie eis fecit deficientibus sibi victualibus, se tradiderunt in forcia et virtute dicti regis ... christianos <quos> ibi invenit variis penis cruciavit*). See also Saba Malaspina 4,27, MGH *SS* 35, 225-226. The Muslims of Lucera were allowed a respite, until the community was finally extinguished in 1300 by the son and successor of Charles of Anjou, Charles II. All Muslims were rounded up and sold as slaves and that was the end of the last Muslim settlement on the Italian peninsula.
2 Terror was the favourite political instrument of Charles of Anjou. He needed executions and the ensuing forfeitures of the estates of as many Sicilian nobles as possible to meet the demands and expectations of his own nobles and the former Sicilian exiles: see *supra* p. 460. Pope Clement IV was shocked by the extent of it and seriously criticized Charles in what must have been one of his last letters (*Ann. eccl.*, Tom. 22, Paris 1870, ad ann. 1268 §36, 228-229). The opponents of Angevine rule on the peninsula made their last stand in the little town of

l'Etendard was dispatched to the island of Sicily to quench the rebellion there[3]. The island was still largely in the hands of Corrado Capece and Prince Federico of Castile, who had been joined there recently by Federico Lancia, Galvano's brother[4]. L'Etendard followed the example of ruthless brutality set by his royal master, shocking even the contemporary and philo-Angevine historian Saba Malaspina. The marshall was *'a bloodthirsty man, crueller than cruelty itself, a man who despised every form of kindness or compassion*'[5]. He bolstered this reputation after the siege of the rebellious town of Augusta (Agosta) on the eastern coast of Sicily, halfway between Catania and Syracuse. The town was taken, not by storm but by treason from within, yet the entire population, men, women, and children, was cruelly massacred, including the traitors[6]. Next the marshall proceeded to the siege of the castle of Centuripe, west of the Etna, where Corrado Capece had taken refuge. Corrado and the other two Conradine captains, Federico Lancia and Prince Federico of Castile, had fallen apart by that time, which proved fatal to their cause. Prince Federico fell back on Agrigento, from where he arranged a free passage to Tunis, and Federico Lancia succeeded in escaping the fate of his brother Galvano by eluding the Angevine forces and still held out in a castle in Calabria for some time before he found refuge in Tunis as well[7]. Corrado Capece, now alone in a

---

Gallipoli, in the province of Lecce. The town was besieged by land and by sea from July 1268 till October 1269. The city was destroyed and the citizens, mostly schismatic Greeks, were dispersed. The 'traitors' (*proditores*) captured in the town were hanged, all 33 of them: Saba Malaspina 4,27, MGH *SS* 35, 216-217 mentions only 23 victims, but this must be a clerical error. We have a detailed list of their confiscated personal property in the account (*apodixa*) by the Angevin commander at Gallipoli (Del Giudice, *Codice diplomatico* II.1, Naples 1869, Appendix I, no XXIII, 311-322) according to which one of them had a copy of the *Codex Iustinianus*, and copies of two of the three parts of Justinian's *Digest*, the *Digestum Vetus* and *Novum*, with him (318). The books must have belonged to master Tomasso Gentili, who is listed among the 'traitors' executed in Gallipoli. He had been a justice in the Supreme Court (*magna curia*) of the Sicilian kingdom.

3   Saba Malaspina 4,25, MGH *SS* 35, 219: '*Destinat regalis providencia capitaneum in Siciliam quondam Guillelmus dictum Standardum cum electa comitiva equitum Gallicarum*'. For Guillaume l'Etendard see also *supra* p. 476. His appointment as vicar of Sicily occurred late in August 1269, after the fall of Lucera.

4   On Corrado Capece and Prince Federico in Sicily see *supra* p. 476, fnt. 265. Federico Lancia had been sent to the island by Conradin with a Pisan fleet to conquer Messina, the only Sicilian town still under Angevine control at the time.

5   Saba Malaspina 4,25, MGH *SS* 35, 219: '*Hic enim Guillelmus vir erat sanguinis ... omni crudelitate crudelior et tocius pietatis et misericordie vilipensor*'.

6   The story of the siege and the massacre of Augusta is in Saba Malaspina 4,25, MGH *SS* 35, 219-221, which is confirmed by *Annales Ianuenses* (Nic. Guercii *e.a.*), ad ann. 1269, MGH *SS* 18, 265.

7   On the departure of Prince Federico of Castile and his further fate see Saba Malaspina 4,26, MGH *SS* 35, 223-224, and *Annales Ianuenses* (Nic. Guercii *e.a.*), ad ann. 1269, MGH *SS* 18, 265. On Federico Lancia see Saba Malaspina 4,27, MGH *SS* 35, 226 and *infra* fnt. 11.

fortress besieged from all sides by a superior Angevine force and sensing his troops' discontent, decided that the time had come for him to admit defeat and save his men by surrendering himself to the marshall. L'Etendard had him blinded on the spot and hanged him on a prominent place on the seashore for all the world to witness the fate of the enemies of King Charles[8]. By the summer of 1270 the island of Sicily was 'pacified', but not for long. Charles of Anjou was never to be crowned king of Sicily in Palermo.

Charles of Anjou hated the island of Sicily, probably because it had resisted him from the start of his reign. He broke with the Hauteville tradition by making Naples rather than Palermo the capital of his kingdom and rarely visited the island. His longest stay there was in support of the second crusade of his royal brother, King Louis IX, who had landed in Tunis in the summer of 1270. Charles was on bad terms with the the emir of Tunis, Al-Mustansir[9], since the emir had supported Corrado Capece in his attempt at conquering Sicily on behalf of Conradin[10] and now hosted Prince Federico of Castile and Federico Lancia[11]. Charles' brother, on the other hand, hoped to convert Al-Mustansir to Christianity[12]. This is why the great fleet Louis had gathered at Aigues-Mortes to carry him and his fellow-crusaders to the Holy Land was diverted to Tunis rather than to proceed to Palestine (or even Egypt) directly. As a matter of course, Al-Mustansir was unwilling to convert to Christianity, certainly not with an army on his shores, and resisted the invasion of his emirate. Louis' second crusade ended in disaster, as had his first crusade[13], only this time with even more serious consequences to himself. The king fell ill, as did most other crusaders, and died, as did countless other crusaders, in his tent before the walls of

Charles of Anjou in Tunis

---

8   For the fate of Corrado Capece see Saba Malaspina 4,26, MGH SS 35, 222-223 and *Annales Placentini Gibellini* ad ann. 1270, MGH SS 18, 547.
9   On Al-Mustansir see *supra* p. 476., fnt. 265.
10   See *supra* p. 471.
11   According to the chronicle of Primat cap. 55 (*Recueil* 23, 81) Frederico of Castile and Federico Lancia were both in Tunis in 1270. The Latin Chronicle of Primat is lost, but partly survives in a French translation by Jean de Vignay (*c.* 1282-*c.* 1350), another monk from St Denys.
12   For the motives of King Louis see Guillaume de Nangis, *Gesta Sancti Ludovici* ad ann. 1270 (*Recueil* 20, 446-448). There were, of course, other less exalted motives as well, prevalent among the companions of Louis. Guillaume de Nangis mentions greed (the wealth of the emirate), the ease with which it could be conquered, but also the strategical consideration that by invading Tunis the pressure on the Holy Land would be reduced since it would force the mighty Mamluk Sultan of Egypt Baibars (*c.* 1229-1260-1277) to send troops to Tunis.
13   See *supra* p. 410.

Tunis on 25 August 1270[14]. It was the end of the 'Eighth Crusade', just another waste of lives and money as so many other crusades. Charles of Anjou, who arrived on the scene from Sicily only hours after the demise of his brother[15], was now the undisputed commander of the army[16] and used the opportunity to his advantage. After leading two successful engagements with the army of Al-Mustansir, he was in a position to negotiate a truce with the emir on very favourable conditions to himself, making him the main beneficiary of his brother's last crusade[17]: all the former supporters of Conradin still in Tunis were to be expelled, never to return to the emirate; the emir was to pay a huge indemnity (210,000 ounces of gold) to the leaders of the crusade and, in addition, to Charles of Anjou personally 'the tribute usually paid to the emperor' which the emir had not paid for the last five years. The emir further promised to pay an annual tribute of double that amount to Charles from now on[18].

---

14   For the demise, probably from dysentery, of Louis IX see Guillaume de Nangis, *Gesta Sancti Ludovici* ad ann. 1270 (*Recueil* 20, 460-462). The heir to the throne, Philip, also fell ill, but survived. Louis' youngest son was not so lucky. He was named 'Tristan' because he was born in disaster (see *supra* p. 410, fnt. 92) and now expired in another tragedy. Louis' biographer Jean de Joinville was not present at Tunis to witness his master's demise.

15   Primat (Jean de Vignay) cap. 39, *Recueil* 23, 57.

16   The heir to the throne of France, Philip III (1245-1270-1285), known to posterity as Philip the Bold, was still unwell at the time (Primat, *l.c.*(58)): 'monseigneur Philippe ... qui n'estoit encore pas commencié à garir'. Louis' other brother, Alphonse, who had also joined him on this crusade, fell ill as well: he died in 1270 in Genoa, on his way back to France. His demise without heirs caused the entire Toulousan heritage to revert to the king of France (see *supra* p. 206, fnt. 33), making Philip III an even richer king than his father had been.

17   There is a difference of opinion among scholars over the question whether or not Charles of Anjou was responsible for his brother's decision to sidetrack his crusade to Tunis before proceeding to the Holy Land or Egypt. I have no doubt he was. Louis started planning his second crusade at about the same time as his brother Charles was getting involved in Sicilian affairs (*supra* p. 445). Consequently, Louis may have selected Sicily as the gathering point of the crusading forces, as it had indeed been in the Third Crusade, when the kings of France, England, and Sicily had planned to meet there before setting out to the Holy Land (*supra* p. 141). But in 1269, when Louis was completing his preparations, Sicily was still not safe in Angevine hands. The Emir of Tunis had facilitated the invasion of Sicily by Corrado Capece and Prince Federico of Castile (*supra* p. 476, fnt. 265) and Charles wanted this backdoor (Tunis) to his Sicilian kingdom securely closed to other potential intruders before entering on his grander scheme, on which more shortly.

18   The Treaty of Tunis (21 November 1270) survives in the French national archives in a contemporary Arab version. It is printed (in a modern French translation by Silvestre de Sacy) in L. de Mas Latrie, *Traités de paix et de commerce et documents divers concernant les relations des Chrétiens avec les Arabes de l'Afrique septentrionale au moyen age,* Paris 1866, no V, 93-96. There is a short résumé in Primat cap. 55, *Recueil* 23, 81, explicitly mentioning Prince Federico of Castile and Federico Lancia as enemies to be expelled from Tunis forever. Primat must have seen the original French text of the treaty, now lost. The 'emperor' to whom a tribute was due by the emir of Tunis was of course Frederick II. The emir obviously had ceased paying it after Charles of Anjou was invested with the Sicilian kingdom.

The Emperor Michael VIII Palaeologus
(George Pachymeres, *Historia*,
Bayerische Staatsbibliothek, Cod.graec.
442, *f.* 173 vº (Wikimedia Commons))

Having secured a truce with the emir of Tunis for fifteen years, Charles of Anjou, now finally in undisputed possession of his Sicilian kingdom, was in a position to realize his Mediterranean grand strategy. He wanted to conquer what was left of the Byzantine Empire, especially, of course, Constantinople, now in possession of the schismatic Byzantine Emperor Michael VIII Palaeologus (1223-1261-1282)[19]. It was a plan he had contemplated for some time. In 1267 he had concluded a treaty with the nominal Latin Emperor Baldwin II while with the pope at Viterbo. Baldwin[20], a miserable wandering exile ever since his ignominious flight from Constantinople in 1261, was in no position to strike a deal with Charles of Anjou at arm's length, the less so since he had been seriously compromised at the court of France, and certainly so with Charles of Anjou personally, by the exposure of his friendly correspondence with Manfred[21]. In return for Charles' support for the reconquest of the Latin Empire, Baldwin agreed to marry his son and heir Philip to Charles' daughter Beatrice, with the added stipulation that, if the marriage should prove childless, the imperial title should devolve on Charles of Anjou and his heirs as kings of Sicily[22]. He further agreed to

Michael VIII, Charles of Anjou and Gregory X

---

19   See *supra* p. 448, fnt. 143.
20   On the Latin Emperor Baldwin II see *supra* p. 370, 447 and 448.
21   See *supra* p. 448.
22   The full text of the Treaty of Viterbo (27 Mai 1267) is printed in Buchon, *Recherches*, 33-37. For the stipulation see 35: '*si vos et Philippum … absque justo et legitimo herede de proprio corpore (quod absit!) mori contingat, memoratum imperium cum omnibus honoribus, dignitatibus, demaniis, feudis, jurisdictionibus, juribus et pertinentiis suis ad nos nostrosque in regno Sicilie heredes plenarie devolvatur*'.

grant to Charles full sovereignty over the principality of Achaea, comprising the entire Peloponnese. It was held from Baldwin by William of Villehardouin (1211-1246-1278), prince of Achaia, and it was the most important part of the ill-fated Latin Empire not yet fully reconquered by the Byzantine emperor[23]. After thus securing a legal title to the best part of what was left of the Latin Empire and a truce with the emir of Tunis, Charles was ready to strike, but was prevented from doing so by the diplomacy of the Byzantine Emperor Michael VIII.

Michael VIII was in desperate need of allies against the threat of Charles of Anjou, who had already procured an important alliance with the powerful King Stephen V of Hungary and Croatia by arranging a double marriage of his son and heir Charles with a daughter of the Hungarian king and a marriage of his daughter Elizabeth with Ladislaus, the son and heir of the Hungarian king, in 1270[24]. Simultaneously, Charles established friendly relations with the kings of Serbia and Bulgaria, traditional enemies of the Byzantine Empire, thus completely isolating Michael VIII on the Balkan peninsula. The Byzantine emperor was without friends and had to rely on his resourcefulness only. Michael VIII lived up to that challenge. His first initiative to stop Charles of Anjou from invading his empire was a diplomatic mission to Louis IX, whose reputation as a man of peace had also reached the shores of the Bosporus. The Byzantine ambassadors found Louis IX dying in Tunis[25]. With King Louis gone, Michael realized that there was only one authority in Western Europe able to stop Charles of Anjou and that this was the pope. He also realized that there was only one offer that was to secure papal support for his cause and that was the end of the schism between the Catholic and Orthodox Church by the submission of the Orthodox Church to the pope's authority. Fortunately

---

23   From the Treaty of Viterbo (Buchon, *Recherches* 32): '*nobis nostrisque in regno praedicto heredibus .... ceditis, datis, conceditis et donatis ex nunc feudum praedicti principatus Achaie et Moree ac totam terram quam tenet quocumque titulo seu tenere debet a vobis et ipso imperio Guillelmus de Villa-Harduini, princeps Achaie et Moree*'. According to feudal law, the vassal, Guillaume de Vilhardouin, had to consent to the transfer of the *dominium directum* of the fee he was holding from Baldwin. It was given at Viterbo on the authority of the prince of Achaia by the chancellor of the principality, Leonardo de Verulis, who was a witness to the treaty (Buchon, *Recherches* 37). I will not bother the reader with further details of the Treaty of Viterbo. It will suffice to state that Baldwin was only to keep the city of Constantinople and four islands in the Aegean, Lesbos, Samos, Kos, and Chios, for himself.

24   This double marriage had just as important consequences for European history as the double marriage of Prince Juan of Castile with the Habsburg Princess Margaret and of the Habsburg Prince Philip with Princess Juana of Castile procured by their father, the Emperor Maximilian I, in 1495. The latter double marriage resulted in Habsburg rule over Spain and the Roman Empire and the former in Angevine rule in Hungary and Naples.

25   On this Byzantine mission to Louis IX see the Byzantine historian George Pachymeres (1242-1310), *De Michaele Palaeologo* 5,9, ed. Bekker, Bonn 1835, 361-364.

for Michael, the new Pope Gregory X (1271-1276), finally elected in Viterbo on 1 September 1271[26], was an Italian standing aloof from the 'Angevine' and 'Italian' factions within the *curia*[27]. The pope preferred a policy of neutrality in order to achieve the primary objective of his pontificate: a new crusade to the Holy Land[28]. One of his first official acts after his consecration on 27 March 1272 was the announcement of a general council for the sake of the liberation of the Holy Land to be convened on 1 May 1274[29]. Consequently, Gregory X regarded any other major military operation as an unwelcome distraction, certainly so when aimed at the Byzantine Empire, still a power of some consequence in the Near East and a possible ally rather than an enemy. This is why the pope reopened negotiations with Michael VIII about a possible union of the Churches[30]. While still in Palestine, he had already

---

26   This is the conclave that was forced to come to a decision by the *podestà* of Viterbo by taking down the roof over the papal palace 'to allow the Holy Spirit to reach the cardinals', as one of them observed (Cardinal John of Toledo, an Englishman, in Bernard Guy (*c.* 1261-1331), *Vita Gregorii papae X* in Muratori 3, 597): '*discooperiamus hanc domum, quia Spiritus Sanctus non potest ad nos per tot coopercula pertransire*'.

27   Teobaldo Visconti, as he was known before his election, was from Piacenza where he was born in or around 1210. The new pope was extremely well connected, which is why he must have been elected. He was not a cardinal and had not even been ordained as a priest at his election, but he had travelled far and wide in the service of his mentor, none other than Cardinal Giacomo da Pecorara, who was also from Piacenza (on Cardinal Giacomo see *supra* p. 284), and of Cardinal Ottobuono Fieschi after the demise of Giacomo. At the time of his election, he was nominal arch-deacon of Liège but was in Palestine, in the company of his friend, Prince Edward of England, the future King Edward I. Visconti was also well acquainted with King Louis IX, whom he met during his stay in Paris. For the details of his election see *Annales Placentini Gibellini* ad ann. 1271, MGH SS 18, 554. For his relation with Louis IX and Edward I see the anonymous *Vita Gregorii Papae X* in Muratori 3, 600-601. Gregory X was a great admirer of Louis IX and as soon as he had been elected he ordered the Dominican friar Geoffroy of Beaulieu († *c.* 1274), the confessor of Louis IX, to write a biography in view of the impending beatification of the king. Gregory's letter to Geoffroy of Beaulieu is in *Ann. eccl.*, Tom. 22, Paris 1870, ad ann. 1272 § 59, 297. Geoffroy's hagiography of Louis IX is in *Recueil* 20, 3-27.

28   Immediately after his arrival at Viterbo and even before his consecration, Visconti wrote to the new king of France, Philip the Bold, urging the king to follow the example of his father and to lead a new expedition to the Holy Land. The letter is in *Ann. eccl.*, Tom. 22, Paris 1870, ad ann. 1272 § 5, 270. As is clear from this letter, his stay in Palestine (see previous fnt.) had made a deep impression on Visconti.

29   See Gregory's letter (*Salvator noster*) to the French clergy and to the king of France of 31 March 1272 in Giraud, *Les registres de Grégoire X*, Paris 1892, no 160, 53-55 and no 161, 55-56. The same letter was also sent to the king of England: Rymer, I.2, 121-122.

30   There had been previous negotiations on a possible union of the Churches with Clement IV in 1267. The initiative of Michael VIII was, however, rather rudely rejected by Clement IV who demanded that the emperor, the orthodox clergy, and the laity of the Byzantine Empire should submit to the authority of the pope and Catholic doctrine first before being readmitted to the community of the faithful. Michael's suggestion to convene a general council to settle all doctrinal differences was rejected as well: there were to be no compromises on doctrine, since Catholic doctrine was beyond any dispute. The letter of Clement IV to the Emperor

indicated to Michael VIII that he was willing to negotiate with the emperor and his clergy on the issue[31]. Michael VIII did not hesitate to embrace this initiative and accepted the invitation of the pope to send his emissaries and representatives of the orthodox clergy to a general council to confirm the reunion of the Churches at a venue yet to be decided. The idea to convene a general council for that purpose, first advanced by Michael VIII, only to be rejected by Clement IV[32], was now embraced by Gregory X because he wanted that council to propagate a new crusade to the Holy Land, as Innocent III once had done in the famous Fourth Lateran Council[33]. The pope subsequently informed Charles of Anjou about his invitation to Michael VIII, urging Charles to grant a safeguard to the imperial emissaries from Constantinople[34]. The papal initiative was a serious setback for Charles and the Latin Emperor Baldwin II since the pope obviously recognized Michael VIII as the legitimate ruler of the Byzantine Empire, implicitly accepting the collapse of the Latin Empire as a *fait accompli*. Charles must have been furious, but the Byzantine Empire was under papal protection for the time being, that is as long as negotiations about a possible reunion of the Churches were pending. He must have realized that the offer to reconcile the Latin 'Catholic' Church and the Greek 'Orthodox' Church was a deception of the Byzantine emperor to prevent him from attacking the Greeks and re-installing a Latin emperor in Constantinople, which, of course, it was[35]. Relations between the Roman pope, Gregory

---

Michael (4 March 1267) is in *Ann. eccl.*, Tom. 22, Paris 1870, ad an. 1267 §§ 72-79, 214-217. The main stumbling block standing in the way of reunion was, of course, the '*filioque*' clause in the Catholic Creed (elaborately explicated by the pope in his letter), which is certainly unorthodox since it is *not* in the original Nicene Creed adhered to by the Byzantine Orthodox Church, but inserted in Western Christianity nevertheless. On this issue see Clement IV § 75 (215): '*Credimus etiam Spiritum Sanctum, plenum et perfectum, verumque Deum, ex Patre* et Filio *procedentem*' (emphasis added). On the papal rejection of the idea of Michael VIII to call a general council see § 79 (216): 'We do not in any way consider a council to discuss or define anything of the kind, since it would be absolutely unfitting and consequently not allowed since it is unsuitable to cast doubt on the purity of the faith explained above' (*nos tamen nullo modo proponimus Concilium ad discussionem, seu diffinitionem huiusmodi ... quia prorsus indecens foret: immo non licet, nec expedit in dubium revocari praemissam veri fidei puritatem*).
31   On this initiative of Gregory X see the Byzantine historian George Pachymeres, *De Michaele Palaeologo* 5,11, ed. Bekker, Bonn 1835, 369-370.
32   See *supra* fnt 30.
33   See *supra* p. 210.
34   The invitation (dated on 24 Octobre 1272) to Michael VIII to attend the council and the request to Charles of Anjou to grant a safeguard to Michael's envoys (dated on 7 November 1272) are in Giraud, *Les registres de Grégoire X*, Paris 1892, no 194, 67-73 and no 198, 75.
35   For this assessment see George Pachymeres, *De Michaele Palaeologo* 5,11, ed. Bekker, Bonn 1835, 370: 'It was obvious that the ruler <Michael> sought peace out of fear for Charles since, if that would not have been so, an idea like that would never have entered his mind' (Δῆλον ἦν ὡς ὁ μὲν κρατῶν κατὰ δειλίαν τὴν πρὸς τὸν Κάρουλον τὴν εἰρήνην ἐζήτει, ὡς, αὐτῆς γε μὴ οὔσης μηδ᾽ εἰς νοῦν φέρειν ἐκείνην πώποτε). Michael VIII had to keep up

X, and the Roman senator, Charles of Anjou, must have been very strained by this time, which explains why the pope soon left Rome. He had been consecrated there and had been residing in his Lateran Palace since March 1272, but he already left for Orvieto in June of that very same year[36]. It also explains why the great council Gregory was planning was not to convene in Rome, but in Lyon, as far away as possible from Charles of Anjou's sphere of influence[37]. Invitations were sent to all the ecclesiastical and secular princes of Western Christianity. Consequently, all the great princes from Germany were also invited, the king of Bohemia, the dukes of Saxonia, Brunswick, and Brabant, the margraves of Brandenburg and Meißen, as well as the archbishops of Mainz, Cologne, and Trier[38]. Only the German 'king of the Romans', nominally the emperor to be, was missing since there was no king of the Romans. Richard of Cornwall had died in 1272 and the claim of his old rival Alfonso of Castile, contending that he was now the only elected king of the Romans qualified to be crowned as emperor, was rather strongly rebuffed by Gregory X, thus paving the way for a new German king to be elected by the German electors, subject, of course, to papal approval[39].

---

appearances nevertheless, forcing the Orthodox clergy to go along with his game and propagate the union of the Churches. The patriarch of Constantinople, Joseph Galesiotes, refused to comply and resigned (1275). Michael VIII replaced him by appointing Joannes Bekkos, a supporter of the union.

36   *Annales Urbevetani* ad ann 1272, MGH *SS* 19, 270: '*die dominica, quinta exeunte mense Iunii, domnus Gregorius papa X. intravit Urbemveterem*'. For Gregory's arrival in Rome see *Annales Placentini Gibellini* ad ann. 1271, MGH *SS* 18, 554: '*die dominico 13. Mensis Marcii cum tota curia intravit Romam*'.

37   In his announcement of the general council (31 March 1272): see *supra* p. 503, fnt. 29) Gregory had not indicated a specific place for the council to convene, merely stating 'that for the moment we keep that place a secret for a reason' (*in loco quem … ad praesens subticeamus ex causa*). It was only on 13 April 1273 that Lyon was designated as the venue of the council since that place would be more easily accessible for the princes on the far side of the Alps who were expected to participate: see Gregory's letter to the French clergy in *Ann. eccl.*, Tom. 22, Paris 1870, ad ann. 1273 §§ 1-3, 300-301 and to the king of France in Mansi 24, col. 58 (Giraud, *Les registres de Grégoire X*, Paris 1892, no 307 and 308, 118 does not have the full text of these letters).

38   Of course, no invitation was sent to Duke Louis of Bavaria since he was still an excommunicate at the time: see *infra* p. 508.

39   See Gregory's letter to Alfonso of 16 September 1272 in Giraud, *Les registres de Grégoire X*, Paris 1892, no 192, 65-67. It appears from this letter that Alfonso's lawyers had requested explicitly that the pope was to issue an injunction, forbidding the German electors to proceed with the election of a new king of the Romans after the demise of Richard of Cornwall. The request was denied as were all the other claims of Alfonso. It was a sad day for the lawyers counseling Alfonso since the papal decree effectively put an end to the law suit that had been pending in the papal *curia* for fifteen years (see *supra* p. 435).

The Holy Roman Empire

John of Procida
in Germany

While Michael VIII was successfully frustrating the aggressive policy of Charles of Anjou by diplomatic means, some Sicilian exiles who had been able to escape the wrath of Charles of Anjou after the battle on the Palentine plain ('Tagliacozzo') found refuge in safely Ghibelline Lombard cities, such as Pavia, and some left the Italian peninsula for Germany, where the last male descendants of Frederick II were known to be living at the court of the margrave of Meißen, Henry the Illustrious ('der Erlauchte'), a loyal supporter of the house of Hohenstaufen and heir to the Thuringia estate of Heinrich Raspe[40]. The eldest son and heir of Margrave Henry, Albrecht, was married to Margaret, a daughter of Frederick II with his third wife, Elisabeth of England. The sons of this marriage, grandchildren of the great Frederick II, were the last male heirs to the Hohenstaufen heritage[41]. In 1269 Peter of Prezza, once prominent in Manfred's and Conradin's court, but now living as an exile in Lombardy and earning a living there as a teacher in the beautiful art of writing an elegant letter (*ars dictaminis*), addressed a pompous 'Encouragement' (*Adhortatio*) to Henry the Illustrious inciting that prince to take on the cause of one of his grandsons, 'the third Frederick' (*Fredericus tertius*), and to encourage that boy (only twelve years old at the time) to acknowledge his Hohenstaufen heritage and to take revenge on Charles of Anjou for the murder of Conradin[42]. The Meißen princes were even visited by a very special Sicilian exile, John of Procida (*c.* 1210-*c.* 1298), once the personal physician of Frederick II, a witness to the last will of that emperor[43], a diplomat in the service of Manfred, and now living in exile plotting against Angevine rule in Sicily[44]. The illustrious Henry, his son Albrecht and his wife Margaret,

---

40   See *supra* p. 318.
41   The last surviving son of Frederick II, Enzio, had died on 22 March 1272 in his commodious prison in Bologna: *Annales Placentini Gibellini* ad ann. 1272, MGH *SS* 18, 556, mentioning that he had been buried '*cum maximo honore*'. The citizens of Bologna had grown very fond of their famous prisoner; his tomb is in the Church of S. Domenico in Bologna.
42   On Peter of Prezza see *supra* p. 464 and 474. The *Adhortatio ad Heinricum* is published (with an Italian translation) in Giuseppe del Re, *Cronisti e scrittori sincroni Napoletani* II, Naples 1868, 683-700.
43   See *supra* p. 417.
44   The presence of John of Procida in Meißen is mentioned in a letter of another Sicilian exile, Enrico da Isernia, living in Prague at the time, to his friend John (published by A. Busson, 'Friedrich der Freidige etc.' in *Historische Aufsätze G. Waitz gewidmet*, Hannover 1886, 332), writing that he met him there. John had sided with Conradin and had fled the Sicilian *regno* after the debacle on the Palentine plain. He must have been with Conradin when that unfortunate young man returned to Rome after the battle, but he did not join him on his fateful journey back into the Sicilian *regno*, hiding somewhere in the neighbourhood of Rome instead. Charles of Anjou ordered his immediate arrest, while in Rome himself, on

and young Friedrich himself must have been greatly honoured by all the sudden attention from abroad and even sent letters to the Lombard Ghibelline warlord Ubertino Landi[45] announcing the imminent arrival of the new pretender to the Sicilian crown, styling himself as 'Frederick III, by the grace of God king of Jerusalem and Sicily, duke of Swabia' (*Fredericus tertius Dei gratia Ierusalem et Sicilie rex, dux Suevie*)[46], elusive titles that were even more exaggerated than Conradin's titles, since the latter had never styled himself as a successor to the German crown in the same way as the young Meißen prince did by styling himself as 'the *third* Frederick' (*Fredericus tertius*). If the Meißen princes ever seriously contemplated 'Friedrich the Third' as a possible contender in the election for a new king of the Romans after the demise of Richard of Cornwall, they were soon to be disappointed. After the repeated failed attempts to raise Conradin to the German throne as an alternative to Richard of Cornwall[47], it was simply inconceivable that someone as close to the house of Hohenstaufen as Friedrich of Meißen, who even ventured to present himself to the world as *Fredericus tertius*, should ever be raised to the German throne. The pope would never allow that to happen. Gregory X might be a milder man than his predecessor had been, but he had confirmed explicitly all sentences of excommunication passed by Clement IV against all former supporters of Conradin, including Duke Louis of Bavaria, right at the beginning of his pontificate[48], demonstrating that he meant to continue the anti-Hohenstaufen policy of his predecessor. Accordingly, Friedrich of Meißen was never to be king of the Germans and Roman emperor[49]. But who was?

---

22 September 1268 (Del Giudice, *Codice diplomatico* II.1, Naples 1869, no LXV, 204-206), but John escaped, probably directly to Lombardy from where he went to Germany. On him see also *infra* p. 534 and fnt. 165 there.

45   On Landi see *supra* p. 480-481. If he was with Conradin in the battle on the Palentine plain, he had succeeded in escaping the slaughter after Conradin's defeat there and had returned to Lombardy.

46   See the letters of Friedrich of Meißen inserted in *Annales Placentini Gibellini* ad ann. 1269, MGH *SS* 18, 536 and 539.

47   See *supra* p. 430, 439 and 466.

48   See the decrees of Gregory X in Giraud, *Les registres de Grégoire X*, Paris 1892, no 162-166, 56-58, all dated on 21 April 1272.

49   This assessment is confirmed by a letter of some Genoese envoys with the Roman *curia*, sent to Genoa on 7 February 1273. They report to have had a conversation with someone (no name is mentioned) high in the *curia* (*amicus, qui est de maioribus curie*) who had assured them that 'the pope and the Roman Church want an emperor to be elected, but they do not want that Friedrich of Staufen or someone excommunicated becomes emperor' (*domnus papa et ecclesia Romana volunt, quod imperator eligatur et fiat, verumtamen non vult, quod Fredericus de Stuffa vel excommunicatus aliquis sit imperator*). The letter was first published by H. Breslau, 'Zur Vorgeschichte der Wahl Rudolphs of Habsburg' in *MIÖG* 15 (1894) 60-61(60). 'Friederich of Staufen' (*Fredericus de Stuffa*) cannot be anyone other than Friedrich of Meißen. 'Someone excommunicated' (*excommunicatus aliquis*) can only be Duke Louis of Bavaria.

Rudolph of
Habsburg
elected king of
the Romans

On 5 May 1273 the pope suddenly lifted the excommunication of Duke Louis of Bavaria by ordering the archbishop of Trier, Henry of Finstingen, to absolve Louis[50]. The archbishop was with Gregory to receive his *pallium* from the hands of the pope and, being one of the electors, will have informed Gregory about the electoral process going on in Germany at the time. As it happens, Louis of Bavaria was one of the contenders and had just formed an alliance with the powerful archbishop of Mainz, Werner of Epstein, the imperial arch-chancellor and 'warden of the realm' (*custos regni*) during an interregnum[51]. There was, however, another prominent contender, the king of Bohemia, Ottokar II (*c.* 1233-1253-1278). After he had succeeded to the Austrian duchy and its annexes (Styria, Carinthia, and Carniola) by his marriage to the Austrian heiress Margaret of Austria in 1252[52], Ottokar was by far the most powerful prince in Germany, ruling over a veritable empire of his own, stretching from the Sudetes in the north to the Adriatic sea in the south. The pope was rumoured to favour him at the time[53], but none of the other German princes wanted him: he simply was too powerful and had to be outmanoeuvred.

By the end of June 1273 Archbishop Henry of Trier was back in Germany, carrying the papal decree absolving Duke Louis of Bavaria, which he duly published on 13 July 1273[54]. He then joined a voting agreement concluded on 11 September by three other electors, the archbishops of Mainz and Cologne and Duke Louis of Bavaria, who was an elector as Count Palatine at the Rhine, making the majority of the electoral board. It was agreed that once three of them consented to a particular candidate, the fourth was bound to comply with their choice[55]. The mastermind behind it all, the archbishop of Mainz, had closed a deal previously (on 1 September) with Duke Louis that he would support Louis, but that, if the Bavarian failed to win over enough support, they would both support one out of two nobles: either Prince Siegfried of Anhalt or Count Rudolph of Habsburg[56]. It soon transpired that Duke Louis, though absolved, might still not be accept-

---

50   The papal decree is published in *Acta Academiae Theodoro-Palatinae* VI (1789) 324-325.
51   See the covenant between Louis and Werner of Epstein, signed on 17 January 1273, in MGH *Const.* 3, no 2, 8-9.
52   On the Austrian heiress see *supra* p. 369.
53   This may be inferred from the information supplied to the Genoese envoys (see *supra* fnt. 49) by an ambassador of the Bohemian crown they had met, a Lombard exile now living in Bohemia, who told them (*MIÖG* 15 (1894) 60): 'that it would not displease the church when the king of Bohemia was to be elected king of the Romans by the princes of Germany' (*quod non displicebat ecclesie, quod rex Boemie per principes Alemanie eligeretur in regem Romanorum*).
54   *Acta Academiae Theodoro-Palatinae* VI (1789) 325.
55   The contract is in MGH *Const.* 3, no 6, 11-12.
56   The agreement with Duke Louis is in MGH *Const.* 3, no 5, 11.

able to the pope who insisted that the German princes, meaning the seven electors, should reach a decision on the succession forthwith and that he would provide for a successor himself if they failed to do so in time[57], as he was entitled to do according to canon law[58]. This was not an empty threat, since the electors must also have been informed about the papal disposition to favour Ottokar of Bohemia[59]. Pressure on the electors had been coming from another side as well. On 5 February some of the cities formerly participating in the League of the Rhine now repeated the demands once made by that League in 1256 after the demise of William of Holland: they would never accept a contested election as a result of the electoral deliberations as had happened in 1257[60]. In September 1273 the archbishop of Mainz called a conference of the electors to convene in Frankfurt on 29 September. Though called on short notice, all electors appeared in person or represented by their plenipotentiaries, as the king of Bohemia did. On 1 October the final vote was called and Rudolph of Habsburg (1218-1273-1291) was elected king of the Romans[61]. Rudolph I was not one of the great 'princes of the realm' ('Reichsfürsten'), but neither was he the obscure and penniless little count King Ottokar claimed he was[62]. Quite the contrary: the

---

57   Ellenhard, *Chronicon* (1257-1304) ad ann. 1273, MGH *SS* 17, 122: '*<Gregorius papa decimus> precepit principibus Alemanie, electoribus dumtaxat, ut de Romanorum rege, sicut sua ab antiqua et approbata consuetudine intererat, providerent infra tempus eis ad hoc a domno papa Gregorio statutum; alias ipse de consensu cardinalium Romani imperii providere vellet desolationi*'.
58   See *supra* p. 335.
59   Archbishop Henry of Trier had recently been at the papal court and must have heard the same rumours there as had the Genoese ambassadors (*supra* fnt. 49). He may also have heard there that there were negotiations going on between Charles of Anjou and the Angevine Cardinals Ottobuono Fieschi and Simon de Brion about a possible bid for the German crown by King Philip III of France: for these negotiations see the documents, including a memorandum by Charles of Anjou himself, published by J.-J. Champollion-Figeac, *Documents inédits tirés des collections manuscrites de la Bibliothèque Royale* I, Paris 1841, no XXVIII, 652-656.
60   The demands of 1256 (see *supra* p. 431.) were repeated *verbatim* in the document issued by the cities in 1273: MGH *Const.* 3, no 3, 9-10.
61   See the continuation (1252-1275) of the Saxon world chronicle, MGH *Dt. Chron.* 2, 284-287(285-286): 'The bishop of Mainz, the imperial chancellor, invited the princes having the first vote in the realm, to come to court in Frankfurt on St Michael's day; and all the princes came ... On St Remigius' day the princes unanimously elected him <Rudolph of Habsburg>' (*Der bischof von Menze, des riches kenzeler, der leite den fursten, die di ersten kore habin in dem riche, einen hof zu Frankenforte zu sente Michahelis tage; dar quamen die fursten alle ... In sente Remigius tage koren die fursten in eintrechtliclichin*). The election was not unanimous though. See Ellenhard, *Chronicon* ad ann. 1273, MGH *SS* 17, 122: 'all the princes elected the lord Rudolph as king of the Romans, with the sole exception of the king of Bohemia, who refused to consent to his election as king' (*omnes principes ... elegerunt ipsum dominum Rudolphfum in regem Romanorum, excepto solo rege Bohemie qui absens erat, qui in eum tamquam regem noluit consentire*).
62   Ottokar to Pope Gregory X, protesting against the election of 'some unsuitable count, burdened by extreme poverty' (*quidam comes minus ydoneus ... penuriose gravatus sarcina paupertatis*) in MGH *Const.* 3, no 16, 19-20.

Emperor Frederick II had been his godfather[63], he had been a loyal supporter of the house of Hohenstaufen[64], and he owned extensive estates in the Elsass and the north-west of present Switzerland, from whence his family originated. Rudolph was crowned and consecrated king of the Romans at Aachen on 24 October 1273[65], cementing powerful alliances on the very same day by the marriage of his daughters Mathilde and Agnes to Duke Louis of Bavaria and Duke Albrecht of Saxony respectively[66]. In December Rudolph announced his election to Pope Gregory and the cardinals, sending his chancellor, Deacon Otto of the Church of St. Guido at Speyer, to deliver the message, humbly expressing his sincere hope the pope would look favourably on his cause and the empire[67].

The Second Council of Lyon

The Second Council of Lyon, starting its proceedings on 7 May 1274, had the same objective as the great Fourth Lateran Council: the liberation of the Holy Land. All other matters to be brought to the attention of the Council, such as Church Reform and the matter of the union of the Churches, were subordinate to that purpose, as was the matter of the Empire. In view of the coming Council, Gregory X had requested advice from some leading prelates. One of them was Humbert de Romanis (*c.* 1200-1277), the acting grand master of the Dominican order, who submitted an impressive memorandum on all the issues to be discussed by the Council. It is a remarkable document, if only because it reveals how problematic, if not divisive, the whole crusading idea had become by that time. It is most interesting on the issue of the future of the Empire, since his memorandum contains a special chapter 'On reform of the Empire' (*De corrigendis circa imperium*) as a

---

63 Matthias of Neuenburg (*c.* 1295-† 1364-1370), *Chronica* cap.2, MGH *SS rer. Germ. NS* 4, 9: '*<Fridericus imperator> qui et ipsum Rudolphum de sacro fonte levavit*'.
64 Count Rudolph of Habsburg had accompanied Conradin to Verona in 1268: see *supra* p. 475, fnt. 262.
65 Ellenhard, *Chronicon* ad ann. 1274, MGH *SS* 17, 123: '*9. Kalend. Novembris, id est primo mense sue electionis, Ruodolfus rex Aquisgrani coronatus est, et per archiepiscopum Coloniensem in regem est inunctus*'.
66 *Hermanni Altahensis Annales* (continuatio) ad ann. 1273, MGH 17, 408: '*Ipse etiam rex, adhuc existens in palacio Aquensi, ad quod iam pridem intronizatus a principibus fuerat, duas filias suas, unam domino Lodowico comiti palatino Reni, alteram duci Saxonie, matrimonialiter copulavit*'.
67 See the letter to Pope Gregory in MGH *Const.* 3, no 21, 23-24(24): 'we humbly invoke the most pious clemency of Your Holiness that you condescend with your usual benevolence to assist us in our cause with your favourable blessings' (*piissimam sanctitatis vestre clemenciam humili precum instancia deprecamur, quatenus nobis in assumpto negocio de benignitate consueta favorabiliter aspirantes auxiliatricibus hostiis adiuvare dignemini causam nostram*).

part of the issue of Church Reform[68]. Master Humbert saw no future for the Empire in its present form, associated, that is, with the German kingdom: 'the Empire has been reduced to nothing' (*imperium quasi ad nihilum est redactum*). This rather pessimistic assessment is correct as far as the old Italian kingdom was concerned: the German king and emperor had indeed lost all control over the ancient *regnum italicum* after the demise of Frederick II and even before his time the union of that Italian kingdom with the German kingdom had caused more harm than good according to master Humbert[69]. Consequently, he proposed to sever the constitutional ties between the Italian kingdom and Germany by turning the German kingdom into a hereditary monarchy, confined to the borders of the German kingdom itself, while the Italian kingdom should henceforth be ruled by one or two hereditary monarchs of its own 'under certain laws and statutes' (*sub certis legibus et statutis*)[70], concluding that 'there is much more urgently demanding to find some way to appropriately deal with this matter, if ever it can be found'[71]. These were really revolutionary ideas, since they implied that the king of the Germans ceased to be the obvious imperial nominee. But, as master Humbert himself realized, there probably was no way out of the imperial conundrum. He was right, since the Council dealt with 'the matter of the empire' (*negotium super imperio*) as the Fourth Lateran Council had already done[72]. There were two pretenders, Alfonso of Castile and Rudolph of Habsburg, and one of them had to

---

68 An extensive extract from master Humbert's memorandum (the so-called *Opus tripartitum*) is published in Mansi 24, col. 109-136. The matter of the Empire is discussed in Part Three, chap. XI (col. 132).

69 Mansi 24, col. 132: 'the Empire has been reduced to nothing, and much evil has been perpetrated under the rule of those, whatever their number, who have been elected or promoted to be emperor; peace and harmony have been disturbed and little good has come of it' (*imperium quasi ad nihilum est redactum, et a pluribus, quotquot fuerunt, electi ad imperium seu promoti, plura mala sub eorum dominio secuta sunt, et pax unita turbata, et strages hominum factae, et pauca bona secuta*).

70 Mansi 24, col. 132: 'In as far as the vacant Empire is concerned, it seems to me that the king of Germany should be hereditary rather than electoral and that he should henceforward be content with that kingdom and he would be much more respected and Justice in the German kingdom would be served much better. Further, that one or two kings should be provided for in Italy under certain laws and statutes' (*Circa imperium vacans videretur ... quod rex Teutoniae fieret non per electionem, sed per successionem, et esset deinceps contentus regno illo, et magis timeretur et magis Justitia in regno Teutoniae servaretur. Item , quod in Italia provideretur de rege uno vel duobus, sub certis legibus et statutis*). I should add that to master Humbert, as to all of his contemporaries, 'Italy' proper meant the Italian *regno*, excluding the Sicilian kingdom.

71 Mansi 24, col. 132: '*et alia multa sunt, quae realiter persuadent, ut quaeratur modus aliquis conveniens ad providendum circa hoc, si valeat inveniri*'.

72 See *supra* p. 207-209.

be selected since it was taken for granted that a Roman emperor should command the crusading army.

Frustrated at being thwarted in his own imperial ambitions, King Ottokar of Bohemia appealed to the pope, now contending that Alfonso of Castile was still the legitimate king of the Romans. At the same time, Alfonso continued pressing the pope to annul the election of Rudolph. By the time the Second Council of Lyon had started, Gregory X finally had enough of Alfonso's constant complaints. The German electors had made their choice, unequivocally preferring Rudolph of Habsburg over the Bohemian king and the Castilian royal pretender, and the two kings had to learn to live with that reality. In June 1274 Gregory informed the king of Castile that he had to give up his imperial ambitions and resign to the legitimate election, coronation, and consecration of Rudolph of Habsburg, sending his chaplain master Fredulus to explain to Alfonso in detail why he could not support him[73]. Gregory X wanted peace in Europe to realize his overriding objective: a crusade to the Holy Land to reclaim the places where Christ had lived and suffered. Deacon Otto, Rudolph's envoy with the papal court at Lyon, had full powers of attorney to negotiate the conditions subject to which the pope and his cardinals agreed to consent to the election of Rudolph and his subsequent coronation in Rome. As a matter of course, the *Liber iurium* of the Catholic Church as established and authenticated in the First Council of Lyon[74] had to be complied with, meaning that Rudolph was to swear to all the concessions formerly made to the Church by Frederick II and Otto IV. There was an additional condition in the document of the final agreement completed at Lyon on 6 June 1274: Rudolph was to recognize Charles of Anjou explicitly as king of

---

73   Letter from Gregory X to Alfonso of Castile in *Ann. eccl.*, Tom. 22, Paris 1870, ad ann. 1274 §§ 45-46, 337-338, to be read with the papal instruction to master Fredulus (§ 48, 338): 'we want you to explain to him on which various grounds we must not and cannot further delay the appointment of an emperor; and that we cannot support him in obtaining the imperial crown or the Empire since justice and the force of the facts prevent us from doing so, especially so since another has received the crown of the German kingdom at Aachen, fully according to the customs of the realm, and is in peaceful possession of the kingdom itself with the support of all who have a vote in the imperial election and of all the other princes of the kingdom and others as well, except one' (*volumus quod ei … exponas qualiter ex causis variis imperialis provisionem culminis … nec debemus noc possumus ulterius prorogare; quodque, justitia et facti qualitate vetantibus, sibi ad imperiale diadema, vel idem imperium obtinendum favere nequimus: praesertim alio, juxta eiusdem imperii consuetudines hactenus observatas, apud Aquasgranas regni Alamaniae coronam adepto, et regnum ipsum cum favore omnium vocem in electione imperatoris habentium, uno dumtaxat excepto, caeterorumque regni eiusdem principum magnatum, et aliorum pacifice obtinente*). See also Gregory's letter to Alfonso of 19 December 1274 (*Ann. eccl.*, Tom. 22, Paris 1870, ad ann. 1274 §§ 50-52) repeating these arguments.
74   On this important document see *supra* p. 361.

Sicily and as a vassal of the Roman Church, thus securing the definitive separation of the German Empire and the Sicilian kingdom[75]. As soon as his special envoy had returned to Germany to report to his master, King Rudolph sent a message to the pope assuring Gregory that he submitted himself and the Empire to the command of the pope and authorizing the arrangement Deacon Otto had agreed to[76]. The Empire and the papacy finally seemed to come to terms.

But for the ageing King James of Aragon (1208-1213-1276), none of the other European monarchs invited to the council actually personally attended. It must have been a disappointment to Gregory X, who nevertheless must have regarded his great council as a resounding success. Michael VIII had sent a personal representative and a delegation of the Orthodox clergy to Lyon to conclude the union of the Churches which was celebrated with great pomp. In spite of the fact that he had been educated by one of the medieval masters of political intrigue, Cardinal Giacomo da Pecorara, Gregory X was a rather naive man, trusting the assurances of the Byzantine emperor and his clergy present at Lyon, clearly unaware of the very strong anti-Catholic sentiment among the

---

75 MGH *Const.* 3, no 49, 42-44(44): 'And also that the same King Rudolph shall not by himself or by any other offend the vassals of the Roman Church and especially the magnificent Prince Charles, the illustrious king of Sicily, and his heirs, nor shall he offer counsel, help, and support, publicly or secretly, to anyone wanting to attack the same, or shall he invade the kingdom of Sicily, which the said king holds in fee from the same Roman Church, nor shall he occupy or invade any part of it by himself, nor shall he bring about that it is occupied or invaded by anyone else, nor shall he publicly or secretly offer counsel, help, and support to anyone trying to invade or occupy' (*Item quod idem rex Rudolpus per se vel per alium non offendet vasallos ecclesie et specialiter magnificum principem dominum Carolum regem Sicilie illustrem seu heredes ipsius, nec volentibus ipsum offendere prestabit consilium, auxilium aut favorem publice vel occulte, nec regnum Sicilie, quod idem rex ab eadem Romana tenet ecclesia, vel aliquam eius partem occupabit aut invadet per se vel per alium aut occupari vel invadi procurabit, nec invadere aut occupare temptantibus prestabit auxilium, consilium aut favorem publicum vel occultum*). The final document was read in the presence of the pope and his cardinals and the German prelates present at the council. It was also read in a German translation for the benefit of the German nobles present, such as Markgrave Friedrich of Nüremberg, a special confidant of Rudolph I also present at the council. For the official confirmation of these promises see *infra* p. 514.
76 MGH *Const.* 3, no 62, 53-54: 'See how we submit ourselves and our children as well as the empire that has been entrusted to us to your pious direction. But we thankfully acknowledge the display of benevolent favour and favourable benevolence you have graciously shown to the justice of our cause as our loyal subject <Deacon Otto>, who has just recently returned to us from the feet of your holiness, has told us and we will invariably observe the agreement that has been concluded in the presence of your holiness' (*ecce quod nostram et liberorum nostrorum personas necnon et creditum nobis imperium vestre pie disposicioni submittimus .... Ceterum super illius benevoli favoris et benevolencie favorabilis exhibicione, quam cause nostre iusticie graciose pretenditis, iuxta quod fidelis noster t(alis) nuper de vestre beatutudinis pedibis ad nos rediens ennaravit ... grata recipientes et placita necnon invariabiliter observantes, que per dilectos fideles nostros t(alem et t(alem) in beatitudinis vestre presencia sunt tractata*). Reading a letter like this, one misses the sublime irony of the letters of Frederick II to successive popes. There is no irony here, just hypocritical submissiveness.

Byzantines (and modern Greeks) caused by the fall and subsequent sack of Constantinople in 1204[77]. As Innocent III had already foreseen at the time[78], a genuine reunion of the Churches was completely unacceptable to the Byzantines after that shocking event, one of the saddest and most consequential incidents in European history. As a matter of course, the union celebrated at Lyon was not to last for long[79] but it did for the time being, serving the political purpose of Michael VIII. The other objective of the Second Council of Lyon, a new crusade to the Holy Land, was financially secured by the fiscal initiatives endorsed by the Council and the only matter to be decided now was the nomination of the commander in chief of the new crusade, none other than the newly elected king of the Romans, Rudolph of Habsburg.

Gregory X at Beaucaire

The Second Council of Lyon closed on 17 July 1274. On the previous day, its only long-lasting contribution to canon law, the decree '*Ubi periculum*', was passed despite the resistance of many cardinals. It was inspired by the long *sedis vacantia* following the demise of Clement IV and contains the regulation of the papal conclave still in force with only minor changes[80]. Significantly, the pope did not return to Italy after the Council, but remained in Lyon. He was still there on 26 September 1274 when he finally wrote a letter to Rudolph of Habsburg officially confirming Rudolph's election, more than three months after Rudolph had agreed to the conditions for his coronation[81]. It is a clear sign that there

---

77   Gregory had been warned by 'many men of high rank and status' (*quamplures magnae condicionis et status*), cardinals sympathetic to Charles of Anjou no doubt, that Michael VIII was insincere but he urged the Byzantine emperor in 1273 to proceed with the union nevertheless: 'may the voices of those slanderers be silenced who are only too glad to say that your majesty does not pursue this highly salutary business with the appropriate sincerity' (*obstruantur ora inique loquentium, qui celsitudinem tuam libenter forte notarent, quasi non in sinceritate debita hoc tam salubre negotium prosequaris*). Gregory X to Michael VIII on 21 November 1273 in Giraud, *Les registres de Grégoire X*, Paris 1892, no 315, 123.
78   See *supra* p. 168.
79   See *infra* p. 531.
80   '*Ubi periculum*' has been inserted in the code of Boniface VIII, the *Liber sextus*: VI° 1,6,3. It stipulated that after the demise of a pope, the cardinals present in the city where the pope had died should wait there for ten days for the arrival of their brethren absent at the time. After that period all the cardinals then present were to be confined to a hall in the palace where the pope had died, each of them with only one servant, with no entry or exit allowed to anyone and with only one opening to allow food and drink to be passed to them. If they had not reached a decision after thus being secluded for a period of three days, their food rations were to be restricted to one meal a day for a period of five days, after which they were to be provided with bread, water, and wine only. During the conclave no cardinal was allowed to communicate with the outside world on pain of excommunication.
81   From the official letter of confirmation in MGH *Const.* 3, no 66, 56: 'Although we have, not without a reason, delayed to communicate your royal nomination to you until now, we do, after having recently deliberated with our brethren, nominate you as king of the Romans on their advice. The reasons for this useful delay, or rather the well considered acceleration

was still resistance inside and outside the papal *curia* against the election of Rudolph, but Gregory had been able to impose his will, sending a letter proclaiming his 'nomination' of Rudolph to all the German secular and ecclesiastical princes on the same day[82]. Meanwhile, Alfonso of Castile, still not resigning his claim to the empire, was raising the stakes in Lombardy, where he could count on the support of many Ghibelline cities hostile to Charles of Anjou. In as far as the Lombard Ghibellines were concerned, Alfonso rather than Rudolph was king of the Romans and of Italy. In addition to this, Alfonso had secured an alliance with a powerful North Italian warlord, marquess William VII of Montferrat, who had married Alfonso's daughter Beatrice in 1271. The marquess was now a sworn enemy of Charles of Anjou, after having supported him before[83]. In a situation like this, political logic prescribes to bring about an alliance between Rudolph of Habsburg and Charles of Anjou, which is precisely what the pope was aiming at. In November 1274 the papal notary Berardo of Naples wrote to king Rudolph about a possible alliance with king Charles brokered by the pope[84]. The alliance, to be sealed by a marriage between one of Rudolph's daughters and Charles' grandson Charles Martel, was postponed for the time being though[85],

---

of this matter for the benefit of peace in the world and in the Empire itself, as we do hope, will be disclosed to you by our beloved son the Bishop-Elect <Henry> of Trento and friar Henry of the Minorites, envoys of Your Highness, not only for the sake of the truth, but also as an incitement to be careful' (*Licet itaque non sine causa distulerimus hactenus regiam tibi denominationem ascribere, cum fratribus tamen nostris nuper deliberatione praehabita, te regem Romanorum de ipsorum consilio nominamus. Causas autem salubris dilationis, immo potius consulte accelerationis huiusmodi ad totius orbis et ad ipsius maxime profuture pacem imperii, ut speramus, dilectus filius ... Tridentinus electus et frater Henricus de ordine Minorum, tue celsitudinis nuntii, non solum ad veritatis expressionem, set ad exhortationis sollicitationem aperient*). Friar Henry of Isny was a special confidant of Rudolph I, later to become archbishop of Mainz and chancellor of the Empire under Rudolph I.

82   Theiner, *Codex diplomaticus domini temporalis S. Sedis* I, Rome 1861, no 333, 187. King Ottokar of Bohemia and his ally, Duke Henry of Bavaria, received separate letters, urging them to comply with the election and nomination of Rudolph of Habsburg and to consider 'not what you want, but what is the proper thing for you to want' (*non quid velles, sed quid velle te decet*): A. Boczek, *Codex diplomaticus Moraviae* IV, Olomouc 1845, no 96 and 97, 133-135.

83   See *supra* p. 458.

84   Redlich/Starzer, *Eine Wiener Briefsammlung zur Geschichte des deutschen Reiches und der österreichischen Länder in der zweiten Hälfte des XIII. Jahrhunderts*, Vienna 1894, no 36, 38-39(38): 'Your Majesty must know that the envoy, sent by our lord the pope to the magnificent Prince Charles, the illustrious king of Sicily, about the initiation of negotiations between you and the same, has recently returned with others, ready to implement all of it together with the others' (*noverit vestra magnificencia, quod nuntius, quem dominus noster summus pontifex ad magnificum principem dominum Ch(arolum) regem Sicilie illustrem super tractatu inter vos et ipsum inchoato miserat, cum aliis nuper rediit aratus una cum illis ad omnia consumanda*).

85   See *infra* p. 526.

since Charles of Anjou demanded the transfer of the entire Piémont as a price for the alliance. It was unacceptable to Rudolph[86].

In December 1274 a force of 800 Castilian knights arrived at Ghibelline Pavia, where a league was formed swearing allegiance to Alfonso as king of the Romans. The new Ghibelline league consisted of the cities of Pavia, Novara, Asti, Genoa, Verona, and Mantua[87]. The pope warned Rudolph of the mounting danger in Lombardy, advising him to send a strong army to Lombardy to quench the rebels there[88], something Rudolph was completely incapable of doing: he did not have the financial resources to mount a Lombard campaign and had another opponent in the German Empire itself to deal with, King Ottokar of Bohemia[89]. Consequently, Gregory X finally decided to solve the

---

86 See the highly interesting letter to King Rudolph by Cardinal Uberto di Cocconato, in Redlich/Starzer, *Eine Wiener briefsammlung* no 38, 41-43. Cardinal Uberto was a very shrewd politician sympathetic to Rudolph's cause, if only because he disliked the politics of Charles of Anjou in Lombardy. Like some other cardinals, and probably Gregory X himself as well, he strongly believed that Charles of Anjou had become too powerful. Charles was never meant to extend his political influence all over the Italian peninsula. It was Cardinal Uberto who dissuaded Rudolph from concluding an alliance with Charles of Anjou on Charles' terms, informing him that the pope would not mind since Gregory himself had opposed the terms suggested by Charles.

87 *Annales Placentini Gibellini* ad ann. 1274, MGH *SS* 18, 560: '*De mense Novembris nono intrante dicto mense 800 milites Spagnoli guaraniti de bonis equis et armis applicuerunt Ianuam, et de mense Decembris venerunt Papiam, ubi honorifice a Papiensibus recepti sunt. De mense Ianuarii Papienses comuniter iuraverunt fidelitatem domno regi Castele tamquam regi Romanorum, et de eodem mense Novarienses iuraverunt similiter fidelitatem isto domno regi, et Astenses similter et Ianuenses, et ambaxatores Verone et Mantue*'. The recent arrival of the Castilian knights is also mentioned in Cardinal Cocconato's letter to King Rudolph (previous fnt.)

88 Gregory X to Rudolph (15 February 1275) in Theiner, *Codex diplomaticus domini temporalis S. Sedis* I, Rome 1861, no 338 (second letter), 190: 'We want you to know that your opponent, earnestly striving after your high office and honour, does not sleep in those parts <meaning Lombardy>, nor does he doze. Therefore, we urgently advice and encourage Your Royal Highness to prepare a strong and reliable army without delay that must be in those parts not later than by the end of May next with a good and experienced commander, not only to withstand the hostile enterprises, but to completely suppress them with the help of God' (*Scire te volumus, quod tui adversator culminis et honoris emulus non dormit in illis partibus <scl. Lombardiae>, nec dormitat ... ideoque serenitatem Regiam monemus attentius et hortamur ... quatenus omni mora et occasione postpositis, competentem militiam strenuam et expertam ... sic studeas preparare, quod saltem circa finem instantis Maii cum bono Capitaneo et probato sit in partibus supradictis non solum adversis obstatura conatibus, sed illis, deo auspice, repressis omnino*).

89 King Rudolph had convened a diet at Nürnberg on 19 November 1274. The statutes passed on that day (MGH *Const.* 3, no 72, 59-61) testify to Rudolph's determination to restore the rule of law in the Empire on the basis of the legislation passed at the famous diet of Mainz under Frederick II (see *supra* p. 277). The most important statutes passed at the Nürnberg diet were about the procedure to be followed in the lawsuit against King Ottokar of Bohemia for not having done homage to his Lord for the fiefs he held from the crown. In order to avoid the impression that the king was acting as judge in his own case, it was decided that the first prince of the realm, the Count Palatine on the Rhine (Duke Louis of Bavaria), should preside

problem of Alfonso of Castile himself. Alfonso had requested a personal meeting with the pope time and again, but Gregory had always succeeded in keeping him off. Late in March 1275, however, the pope agreed to a meeting with Alfonso at Beaucaire in Southern Languedoc[90], at the same time informing king Rudolph that he would meet personally with him later, at a date yet to be transmitted to the king[91].

The negotiations at Beaucaire were highly secretive[92]: no transcripts of the proceedings survive and probably never existed. Nevertheless, rumours about what had transpired there circulated widely. The papal correspondence during the protracted[93] conference reveals that Alfonso, after hearing from the pope himself that he would never be crowned

---

over all trials between the king and princes of the realm concerning real property allegedly belonging to the crown. The Nürnberg diet marked the beginning of the fall of King Ottokar: see *infra* p. 522, fnt. 108.

90   Gregory X to King Alfonso from Orange in Giraud, *Les registres de Grégoire X*, Paris 1892, no 710, 305: 'By the present letter we bring to your royal attention that we and our brethren intend to leave for Tarascon in the week after Easter and that we shall send a messenger to your royal presence who will let you know when you have to come to Beaucaire' (*ad Excellentie regalis notitiam presentium tenore deferimus quod ad veniendum Taraconem, infra octavas instantis festi Resurrectionis Dominice, nos et fratres nostri proponimus, Deo preduce, iter arripere, ad presentiam regiam nuncium premissuri, per quem, quando Bellicadrum venire debeas, tibi certius innotescet*). The pope sent an invitation to Alfonso's brother Manuel as well (Giraud, *Registres* etc., no 711, 305), obviously to help him to persuade his royal brother. Later, in a letter to King Philip III of France (Giraud, no 876, 352), Gregory conceded that he had agreed to meet Alfonso 'on his <Alfonso's> repeated insistence' (*ad multiplicatam ipsius instantiam*).

91   Gregory X to King Rudolph from Orange in Giraud, *Les registres de Grégoire X*, Paris 1892, no 708, 304: 'We are on the road and already close to the place where our beloved son in Christ, the illustrious king of Castile and Leon must meet us. Where and when you have to meet with us, we cannot yet tell you by the bearer of the present letter, but as soon as the negotiations with the same king have been satisfactorily concluded, with the help of God, we shall let Your Royal Highness know by letter and by messenger' (*in itinere constituti et vicini iam loco in quo ... carissimus in Christo filius noster rex Castelle et Legionis illustris, eidem loco similiter iam propinquus, nostram debet adire presentiam, ubi et quando nobis occurere debeas, per latorem presentium tibi non potuimus respondere; sed tractatu cum eodem rege, auctore Domino, feliciter consumato, id celsitudini regie premettendis propterea littteris et nuntio curabimus intimare*). Representatives of the pope and the king had already agreed in the city of Basel earlier in 1274 on a personal meeting between the pope and Rudolph: *Annales S̄ Rudberti Salisburgenses* (1200-1400) ad ann. 1275, MGH *SS* 9, 801: '*sicut decretum fuerat in Basilea*'.

92   *Annales Ianuenses* (Oberti Stanconi *e.a.*) ad ann. 1275, MGH *SS* 18, 282: 'Having dissolved the council and having granted everyone leave to depart, the said Pope Gregory, hearing about the arrival of the king of Castile, went to Beaucaire, where the king of Castile had come. And he had an encounter there with the said king of Castile, having many secret conversations with him' (*Dictus vero papa Gregorius audiens de adventu regis Castelle, separato et licentiato concilio, versus Bellicardum ubi rex Castelle venerat, suos direxit gressus, ibique cum dicto rege Castelle convenit, cum ipso ineundo plura secreta colloquia*).

93   Gregory X stayed at Beaucaire from 14 May until 4 September 1275, thus considerably delaying his conference with Rudolph I. The pope excused himself for this postponement, reassuring Rudolph that the delay 'would be of use to the world and to his <Rudolph's> undis-

emperor of the Romans, let out all his frustrations about what he perceived as humiliations. If he was not to be emperor of the Romans, he claimed the German duchy of Swabia for himself as heir to Philip of Swabia, his grandfather, nevertheless; the pope requested King Rudolph to have a careful look into this matter[94]. Alfonso claimed that the king of France was frustrating his claims to the little kingdom of Navarre[95]; the pope instructed his legate in France, Cardinal Simon de Brion, to bring the affair to the attention of the French court 'to get this divisive matter out of the way' (*ad tollendam dissentionis materiam*)[96]. Alfonso had a conflict with Charles of Anjou; the pope wrote to Charles, suggesting the king of France as a mediator to restore friendship between him and King Alfonso[97]. Gregory did his best to oblige Alfonso, but he was firm in his determination to make that king give up his imperial ambitions and seems to have succeeded by granting Alfonso the right to levy tithes on all clerical revenues in Castile and Leon for a term of six years[98]. He was now ready to meet with king Rudolph to formally conclude the negotiations about Rudolph's imperial coronation and to fix a date for that ceremony.

---

turbed status' (*moram quam speramus futuram mundo utilem et eius pacifico statui profuturam*) (Theiner, *Codex diplomaticus domini temporalis S. Sedis* I, Rome 1861, no 340, 192).

94   Letter of Gregory to King Rudolph (Beaucaire, 27 June 1275) in Gerbert, *Codex epistolaris Rudolphi I*, St Blasien 1776, no XI, 73-75(74-75): 'We beg Your Highness in the name of God and request that you may direct your mind in such a way that it becomes obvious for all that you are ready and willing with all your heart to satisfy the legitimate demands of the same king and to abstain from injustice to princes and that it is not your fault that a prolonged and unbroken peace between you and the same king is not established' (*Serenitatem Regiam rogamus in Domino et hortamur, quatenus in hoc, ad satisfaciendum justis desideriis eiusdem Regis, animum tuum sic habilites, sic coaptes, quod omnibus patenter appareat, te toto corde, omni promptitudine, ac intentione paratum, ab iniuriis Principum abstinere, nec tibi possit imputari, quo minus inter te et Regem eundum pax servetur perpetua et teneatur illibata*). Naturally, Rudolph denied that Alfonso had any legitimate claim to the duchy, since it now belonged to the crown: see Rudolph's answer to the papal request in Gerbert, *Codex epistolaris* no XII, 76-77.

95   King Henry I of Navarre, also count of Champagne, had died in 1274, leaving his daughter Joanna as heir to his kingdom. Joanna was only one year old at the time. Her mother, Blanche of Artois, placed herself and her daughter under the protection of the king of France, her cousin. It was agreed in 1275 that Joan of Navarre was to marry one of the sons of King Philip III of France. In 1285 she did indeed marry King Philip IV, thus adding Navarre and the important county of Champagne to the French royal domain.

96   Letter of Gregory to Simon de Brion (Beaucaire, 1 July 1275) in Giraud, *Les registres de Grégoire X*, Paris 1892, no 720, 308.

97   Letter of Gregory to Charles of Anjou in Giraud, *Les registres de Grégoire X*, Paris 1892, no 721, 308-309.

98   Gregory X to the bishop of Sevilla (13 September 1275, from Valence): 'You must know, my brother, that in order to secure peace in the world in the matter of the Empire, we have postponed very important matters, have done very hard work, and have not been able to avoid serious nuisances, but thanks to the mercy of the Almighty we have achieved that after our beloved son in Christ Alfonso, the illustrious king of Castile and Leon, has complied with our

King Rudolph of Habsburg
(Tombstone in Speyer Cathedral, Wikimedia Commons)

———

wish in that matter' (*Ob dandum super negotio Imperii pacificum orbi statum novit tua fraterni-*
tas nos grandia postposuisse negotia, multos subtinuisse labores, et gravia tedia non vitasse: quod de
omnipotentis misericordia fuisse supponebamus obtentum, postquam Carissimus in Christo filius
noster Alphonsus rex Castelle ac Legionis illustris super eodem negotio nostris beneplacitis acquiev-
it) (Theiner, *Codex diplomaticus domini temporalis S. Sedis* I, Rome 1861, no 342, second letter,
192). On the grant of the tithes see the papal decree of 14 October 1275 in Giraud, *Les registres*
de Grégoire X, Paris 1892, no 649, 281. It had already been suggested as the price to be paid
to Alfonso for his imperial resignation in Gregory's letter of instruction to his chaplain master
Fredulus (see *supra* p. 512): *Ann. eccl.*, Tom. 22, Paris 1870, § 49, 338. The pope was very angry
to learn later that Alfonso continued to style himself in his letters and charters as 'king of the
Romans' nevertheless and instructed the bishop of Sevilla to direct the king to refrain from
that, since otherwise the pope would not hesitate to discipline Alfonso 'with measures appropriate to the nature of the fact' (*remediis, que facti qualitas exiget* (193)), hinting at excommunication. The Genoese observers in Beaucaire also heard that Alfonso had finally complied with
the papal wishes in the matter of the Empire, but the Genoese chronicler doubted it since he
knew that Alfonso continued to style himself as 'king of the Romans' nevertheless (*Annales*
Ianuenses (Oberti Stanconi *e.a.*) ad ann. 1275, MGH *SS* 18, 282): '*Ferebatur verumtamen*
comuniter inter omnes, iam dictum regem concorditer a summo pontifice discessisse, et quod idem
rex Romano abrenuntiavit imperio. Utrum tamen talis fuerit falsa vel vera relatio ignoratur. Nam
idem rex semper postea et usque ad haec tempora in privilegiis et litteris que de sua manabant
curia, rex Romanorum se scribi faciebat'.

The Lausanne
conference

It is with the meeting of Rudolph I with Pope Gregory X that our dealings with the German Empire must finally come to an end since it was King Rudolph who definitively settled the geopolitical issue central to our history. The pope and the king of the Romans met at Lausanne in October 1275[99]. In two charters drawn up at Lausanne on 20 and 21 October 1275[100], Rudolph confirmed the great privileges Frederick II had granted to Pope Innocent III and Honorius III at Eger in 1213 and at Hagenau in 1219[101], now conclusively driving a territorial wedge between the kingdom of Sicily and the Lombard kingdom of Italy right through the middle of the Italian peninsula, effectively restoring the ancient Exarchate of Ravenna, now with Rome rather than Ravenna as the capital. It is the charter of foundation of the Papal State[102]. In the second charter, Rudolph additionally confirmed his promise[103] to recognize Charles of Anjou as king of Sicily and as a vassal of the Roman Church, thus securing the definitive separation of the German Empire and the Sicilian kingdom[104]. Rudolph, though originally a Hohenstaufen partisan, was a German territorial lord first and foremost and consequently had little interest in Italian affairs other than his imperial coronation. He conceded to the papal Italian demands only to strengthen his position in Germany and to have a free hand in his conflict there with King Ottokar of Bohemia[105]. After this satisfactory conclusion of their conference, Pope Gregory informed all the secular and ecclesiastical princes of the empire about the resignation of Alfonso of Castile and urged them, now that the matter of

---

99 *Annales Basileenses* ad ann. 1275, MGH *SS* 17, 198: '*Pridie Nonas Octobris Gregorius papa venit Lausannam. Rex Rudolphus venit ad eum festo Lucae cum regina et pene cum suis liberis universis*'.
100 MGH *Const.* 3, no 89, 80-81 and 90, 81-83.
101 See *supra* p. 194, 215 and 354.
102 See *infra* p. 523 and fnt. 115.
103 See *supra* p. 512-513.
104 MGH *Const.* 3, no 90, 83: 'We shall not by ourselves or by any other offend the vassals of the Roman Church and especially the magnificent Prince Charles, the illustrious king of Sicily, and his heirs, nor shall we offer counsel, help, and support, publicly or secretly, to anyone wanting to attack the same, or shall we invade the kingdom of Sicily, which the said king holds in fee from the same Roman Church, nor shall we occupy or invade any part of it by ourselves, nor shall we bring about that it is occupied or invaded by anyone else, nor shall we publicly or secretly offer counsel, help and support to anyone trying to invade or occupy it' (*Nec offendemus per nos vel per alium vasallos ecclesie ipsius et specialiter magnificum principem dominum Carolum regem Sicilie illustrem seu heredes ipsius, nec volentibus ipsum offendere prestabimus auxilium, consilium vel favorem publice vel occulte, nec regnum Sicilie, quod idem rex ab eadem Romana tenet ecclesia, vel aliquam eius partem occupabimus aut invademus per nos vel per alium aut occupari vel invadi procurabimus, nec invadere aut occupare temptantibus prestabimus publicum vel occultum auxilium, consilium aut favorem*).
105 This is Dante's analysis. The poet did not forgive Rudolph's betrayal, as he saw it: see *Purgatorio* 6, 97-114 and 7, 91-103.

the succession to the throne of the Empire finally had been settled, to remain loyal to King Rudolph and to accompany him on his upcoming journey to Rome to be consecrated and coronated as emperor of the Romans[106]. It was agreed at Lausanne that Rudolph should be in Rome on 2 February 1276, but Rudolph was never to be crowned and consecrated as emperor, nor was the grand design of the pope, a new crusade to the Holy Land, ever to be realized[107]. The crusading days were definitively over and the first king of the Romans to be crowned as Roman emperor in Rome after Frederick II was not Rudolph of Habsburg but Henry VII of the house of Luxemburg (c. 1273-1308-1312-1313), Dante's 'alto Arrigo', the last king of the Romans to undertake a serious effort to restore effective imperial control over the Italian peninsula, only to end, much to the chagrin of Dante, with his untimely demise on 24 August 1313. After this short episode, the political idea of restoring the 'ancient glory' (antiqua magnificentia) of the medieval Roman Empire, Dante's dream, was definitively an anachronism as well.

---

106   From Gregory's letter to all the secular and ecclesiastical princes of Germany (Lausanne, 15 October 1275) in Theiner, *Codex diplomaticus domini temporalis S. Sedis* I, Rome 1861, no 344, 193: 'The king of Castile and Leon, yielding to our admonitions and persuasions, has complied with our wishes concerning the affair of the Empire. Therefore, always loyal in your devotion to the same king of the Romans and faithfully pursuing his honour and interests, set off on the journey to accompany him for his coronation' (*Rex Castelle et Legionis paternis monitis et persuasionibus se coaptans, nostris super eodem imperii negotio beneplacitis acquievit. Propter quod ... persistentes in ipsius Regis Romanorum devotione constantes, ac eius honorem et commoda fideliter ac sollicite prosequentes ... sic vos accingite ad iter ... ad prosecutionem dicte sue coronationis*).
107   Pope Gregory X died shortly after the Lausanne conference, on 10 January 1276, in Arezzo. The ensuing conclave, for the first time gathering under the strict rules of the Lyon II Council, unanimously elected Cardinal Pierre Tarantaise on the first day. He chose the name Innocent V and died on 22 June next, to be succeeded by Hadrian V (Ottobuono Fieschi, a nephew of Innocent IV), who died on 18 August next. His early demise was a bitter disappointment for Guillaume Durant. He had dedicated his famous *Speculum* to Cardinal Ottobuone Fieschi hoping for advancement but his ambitions for the cardinalate 'were buried with the pope' (*spes ad cardinalatum fuit cum ipso papa sepulta*) as his commentator Joannnes Andreae observes (*Speculum*, Prooemium, ed. Basel 1574, 2, in the right margin). Hadrian V was succeeded by Johannes XXI (Petrus Hispanus, from Portugal), who expired on 20 May 1277. Due to the relaxation of the rules of '*Ubi periculum*' by Johannes XXI, his successor Nicholas III (Giovanni Gaetano Orsini, a Roman nobleman) was only elected on 25 November 1277. It was Innocent V who ordered King Rudolph not to come to Italy and to break off his journey if he was already on his way (Theiner, *Codex diplomaticus domini temporalis S. Sedis* I, Rome 1861, no 350, 197): '*expediat, et nostre propterea voluntatis existat, quod iter ad veniendum in Italiam non assumas, et si forsitan assumpsisti, nequaquam ulterius prosequaris assumptum*'. Shortly before this insulting letter, the pope had confirmed Charles of Anjou as senator of Rome and vicar of Tuscany (Theiner, *Codex diplomaticus* no 349, 197). It is clear from this from which way the wind in the papal *curia* was blowing at the time.

Rudolph of Habsburg succeeded in taking over the Austrian duchy with its annexes from King Ottokar II of Bohemia in 1276[108], establishing Habsburg rule there for centuries to come, from 1440 onwards as *de facto* hereditary Roman emperors until the Empire was finally abolished in 1806 and for little more than a century longer as emperors of Austria. However, when Rudolph's descendant Charles V triumphantly entered the city of Palermo as king of Sicily in 1535, to be hailed there for the first time as ruler over an empire reaching 'from the rising to the setting sun' (*a solis ortu ad occasum*), he did *not* do so as heir to the German imperial tradition, but as heir to the throne of Aragon to which the island belonged ever since his distant ancestor King Peter III of Aragon (*c.* 1239-1276-1285) had wrested Sicily from Charles of Anjou.

The Kingdom of Sicily

Nicholas III,
Rudolph I
and Charles
of Anjou

Charles of Anjou had been appointed senator of Rome in 1268 by Pope Clement IV for a term of ten years[109]. His tenure ended in 1278 and was not extended by Pope Nicholas III (1277-1280). The new pope, the fourth successor to the throne of St Peter after the demise of Gregory X in 1276, was a Roman nobleman, born as Giovanni Gaetano Orsini, and a Roman patriot detesting foreign control over his city. He advised Charles that his tenure was terminated as from 16 September 1278 and that he was to hand over the city to the control of the pope[110], at the same time sending two other native Romans, the Cardinals Latino Orsini and Giacomo Colonna, from Viterbo to Rome to oversee an orderly transfer of power[111]. On 18 July 1278 the pope issued a constitution providing for the future government of the city of Rome never again to fall into the hands of one senator for a period longer than a year and never again to fall into the hands of a foreign prince save by

---

108   King Ottokar II had been banned in May 1275 on the diet of Augsburg for failing to comply with the decision of the Nürnberg diet (see *supra* p. 516, fnt. 89) to hand over the Austrian duchy and its annexes to the crown. King Rudolph then invaded Austria and layed siege to Vienna, where Ottokar resided. Ottokar was forced to surrender and signed a peace treaty with Rudolph, assigning the Austrian duchy and its annexes to Rudolph (26 November 1276, MGH, *Const.* 3, no 114, 105-108). After this crushing defeat, Ottokar II tried to regain his lost Austrian possessions in 1278, but was defeated and killed in the battle of Dürnkrut (26 August 1278). His son Wenceslaz II (1271-1278-1305) was allowed to succeed his father as king of Bohemia. As a matter of course, he was to marry a Habsburg princess.
109   See *supra* p. 483.
110   Letter of Nicholas III to Charles of Anjou (Rome, 25 May 1278) in *Ann. eccl.*, Tom. 22, Paris 1870, ad ann. 1278 § 70-71, 442.
111   See their letters of instruction in Theiner, *Codex diplomaticus domini temporalis S. Sedis* I, Rome 1861, no 370, 215-216.

special permission of the pope[112]. The constitution was issued while Charles of Anjou was in Rome to negotiate with Nicholas[113]. The pope was negotiating with Rudolph of Habsburg at the same time[114], resulting in the final renunciation by Rudolph of all the residual imperial claims to the Romagna on 14 February 1279, duly confirmed by the princes of the Empire, as the pope had demanded, thus finally establishing the borders of the Papal State for centuries to come[115]. To console Rudolph with he loss of the 'garden of the Empire' (the Romagna), the pope had convinced Charles of Anjou to resign as 'imperial' vicar of Tuscany in September 1278[116]. By removing the German king from the

---

112 See the papal charter in Theiner, *Codex diplomaticus domini temporalis S. Sedis* I, Rome 1861, no 371, 216-218(217): '*sancimus, ut quandocunque et quotienscumque Senatoris electio ... imminebit, nullus Imperator, seu Rex, Princeps, Marchio, Dux, Comes aut Baro ... ad eiusdem Urbis regimen seu officium nominetur, eligatur, seu alias etiam assumatur absque licentia sedis apostolice speciali*'.

113 Minieri-Riccio, *Itinerario di Carlo I. di Angiò*, Naples 1872, 13. Charles stayed in Rome for an entire month.

114 There were problems about the extent of the territorial grants conceded by Rudolph to Pope Gregory X at Lausanne from the start, concentrating on the Romagna. According to the pope the entire Romagna was included in the Lausanne settlement, whereas Rudolph believed the Romagna to be excluded. He had even appointed Count Henry of Fürstenberg as *rector* of the Romagna, 'the garden of the Empire' (*hortus imperii*), in December 1275 (charter of Rudolph I in MGH *Const.* 3, no 100, 90). After the demise of Gregory X the Angevine faction in the *curia* contested this, insisting that Rudolph should renounce his claim to the Romagna in favour of the Holy See. This is the reason why Pope Innocent V prohibited Rudolph I from entering Italy before the matter of the Romagna was duly settled (see *supra* fnt. 107). To support the papal claim to the Romagna the extended text (*not* included in the 'Transumpta' of Lyon) of the ancient *Hludowicianum* was exhumed from the Vatican archives. On the *Hludowicianum* see *supra* p. 58-61. The problems were aggravated by the fact that Charles of Anjou had been confirmed in his position as vicar of Tuscany by Innocent V (see *supra* fnt. 107) in defiance of the legitimate claims of the Empire to that province.

115 See the documents in MGH *Const.* 3, nos. 197-199, 185-186 and nos. 221-223, 204-211. After demanding and receiving official confirmation of all the territorial grants contained in the Lausanne settlement as well as the Romagna in 1278, Pope Nicholas III sent word to the cities of the Romagna that they had to submit to papal secular authority forthwith. The bull '*Levantes in circuitu*' is in Theiner, *Codex diplomaticus domini temporalis S. Sedis* I, Rome 1861, no 365, 212-213. The pope was unable to establish effective control over all of these territories though, since the redoubtable Ghibelline warlord Guido de Montefeltre was opposing papal rule in the Romagna. The great lawyer Guillaume Durant was appointed by Pope Martin IV as commander of the papal army in the Romagna, largely consisting of Angevine troopers, Dante's 'bloody hordes from France' (*Inferno* 27, 44), to fight Guido. Later, the exile to Avignon (1309-1377) and the Great Western Schism (1378-1414) prevented the establishment of sustained control. The real architect of the Papal State is Cesare Borgia.

116 Charles' vicar in Tuscany, Raymondo de Poncellis, was instructed to hand over the castles he occupied in Tuscany in the name of Charles of Anjou to Cardinal Latino Orsini. See the letters to Cardinal Orsini and Charles' vicar, both dated on 16 September 1278, in Theiner, *Codex diplomaticus domini temporalis S. Sedis* I, Rome 1861, no 372 and 373, 218 (Gay, *Les registres de Nicolas III (1277-1280)*, Paris 1898, no 303 and 304, 113, does not have the text of these letters).

Romagna and the king of Sicily from Rome and Tuscany at the same time, Nicholas III emerges as the shrewd politician and true 'Italian' patriot he was, surely undeserving of the place in hell assigned to him by Dante[117]. The next initiative of the pope was to balance Angevine and imperial power in Italy by brokering an alliance between Charles of Anjou and Rudolph of Habsburg, now a powerful German potentate after his victory over king Ottokar of Bohemia[118].

The English intermezzo

There had been negotiations about a possible alliance between Charles of Anjou and King Rudolph in 1274 under the auspices of Pope Gregory X but they had come to nothing due to the exorbitant territorial demands of Charles of Anjou[119]. Since then, King Rudolph had opened negotiations with Edward I of England about a possible Anglo-German alliance to be confirmed by the marriage of Rudolph's favourite son Hartmann with Joan of Acre, a daughter of Edward. It is apparent from the correspondence between the German and English kings about this matter that Rudolph planned to designate Hartmann as his successor to the German throne and the Empire rather than his elder son Albrecht. He also promised the king of England that Hartmann was to be endowed with the kingdom of Burgundy, or the kingdom of Arles (*regnum Arelatense*) as it was known at the time, as soon as he, Rudolph, had been elevated to the imperial dignity[120]. The ancient Burgundian kingdom was situated in the south-west of the Empire but, though a constituent part of the German Empire ever since 1033[121], practically no German king, but for Frederick I 'Barbarossa' (who was married to a Burgundian heiress), had been able to exercise effective control over that kingdom. Powerful local counts dominated the largely Alpine region, the counts of Savoye and Provence most notably among them. Consequently, the overlordship of the German king there was purely nominal, as everyone was aware of at the time[122]. Rudolph I certainly knew since his own estates in the west of what is now Switzerland bordered on that kingdom. Creating a restored Burgundian kingdom

---

117 *Inferno* 19, 46 *ff.*

118 See *supra* p. 522, fnt. 108.

119 See *supra* p. 516.

120 Anglo-German negotiations about an alliance and the marriage of Hartmann and Joan of Acre started in 1277 and are well documented: see MGH, *Const.* 3, no 158-179, 151-165. Rudolph's promise to elevate his son as king of Arles is in no 165, 155 (25 April 1278).

121 The last king of Burgundy, Rudolph III, had died childless in 1032. During his lifetime he had granted his kingdom to the German King Henry II, who died in 1027. His successor Conrad II was the first German king of Burgundy. Since then, the Empire consisted of three kingdoms: Germany, Italy, and Burgundy.

122 Grandmaster Humbert's assessment that 'the Empire is reduced to nothing' (see *supra* p. 511) was true for at least two of its constituent kingdoms: Italy and Burgundy. See also *infra* p. 528, fnt. 139.

therefore amounted to an offensive act against the counts of Savoie and Provence, certainly so when actively supported by the king of England, who was, as duke of Aquitaine, still a major force in southern France at the time. The primary target of the projected Anglo-German alliance was Charles of Anjou[123], the count of Provence.

Margaret de Provence, the queen dowager of France, was a very headstrong woman and hated Charles of Anjou. She had even made her son Philip, now the king of France, swear a solemn oath to her never to make an alliance with that wicked man[124]. The queen dowager of France was a force to be reckoned with at the court of her son, as her mother-in-law, Blanche of Castile, once had been at the court of her husband, King Louis IX. She never forgave Charles for depriving her of her Provencal heritage and after the demise of Charles' wife, her sister Beatrice, in 1269 she renewed her claim to the Provence for herself and her sister, Queen Eleanor of England, King Edward's mother[125]. As she wrote to her dear English royal nephew (*nepoti nostro karissimo*), she had contacted King Rudolph on the Provencal issue and had even done homage to Rudolph for the Provence. She now requested Edward to assist her (and his mother) in retrieving what she considered to be hers[126]. The king of England responded by assuring Margaret that he was glad to be of service to his 'dear aunt' (*chiere Taunt*)[127]. A strong anti-Angevine alliance was about to be formed with the Empire at its core. It was not what Nicholas III wanted.

The negotiations about the Anglo-German royal wedding were success-fully concluded on 4 May 1278, but the marriage never materialized. Not only because Rudolph's son Hartmann conveniently drowned (20 December 1281) before the marriage was consummated, but primarily

Nicholas III plans to reform the Roman Empire

---

123 Significantly, part of the negotiations between Rudolph I and Edward I consisted of Edward's role as mediator between King Rudolph and the incumbent count of Savoye, Philip I. See MGH, *Const. 3*, no 171, 159 (3 May 1278). Since his election, Rudolph insisted on the recovery of crown land occupied by the ancestors of Philip of Savoy.

124 See *supra* p. 442.

125 On the title of Margaret to the Provence see *supra* p. 396.

126 Significantly, Margaret did *not* ask her son, King Philip III of France, for support. The king of France had fallen under the spell of his uncle, Charles of Anjou, a development Margaret had foreseen long ago: see *supra* p. 442.

127 For the letters of Margaret to Edward I see J.-J. Champollion-Figeac, *Lettres de Rois, Reines et autres personnages des cours de France et d'Angleterre* I, Paris 1839, 252 and 265. For Edward's positive reply see Rymer, I.2, 188 (20 September 1280). Margaret was also actively engaged in restoring good relations between her uncle Count Philip I of Savoy and King Rudolph. See her letter to King Edward in Rymer, I.2, 155. On the conflict between Philip of Savoy and King Rudolph see *supra* p. 525, fnt. 123. It was essential to establlish good relations between the count of Savoy and king Rudolph to ensure the neutrality of the former in a war with Charles of Anjou.

because the new pope, Nicholas III, wanted peace between Charles of Anjou and King Rudolph. He had been negotiating with Rudolph I since May 1278 about the affair of the Romagna, but also on a possible alliance between Charles of Anjou and Rudolph I, to be confirmed by another royal wedding, this time between Rudolph's daughter Clemencia and Charles' grandson Charles Martel. On 5 September 1278, only four months after the conclusion of the English wedding contract, Rudolph overcame his initial reservations about Charles of Anjou[128] and wrote to Nicholas III authorizing the pope to conclude a peace treaty with Charles of Anjou and sending two German plenipotentiaries to assist the pope in the affair on his behalf, brother Conrad, a trusted Minorite friar, and Rudolph's chief chancellor Gottfried.[129] It was from this moment on that the German fiancé, Hartmann of Habsburg, began dragging his feet, postponing his English marriage until his untimely demise finally released him from his vow[130].

Nicholas III had succeeded in convincing Charles of Anjou to resign as 'imperial' vicar of Tuscany in September 1278[131], but he had to offer Charles something in return for the loss of Tuscany. He now used the powers of attorney donated to him by Rudolph I to realize a plan inspired both by the details of the recent Anglo-German alliance with which he must have been familiar and by the memorandum which Grandmaster Humbert de Romanis had prepared for the Council of Lyon II[132]. He must have convinced Charles of Anjou that his position as count of Provence was under serious threat, while emphasizing at the same time that the only authority to grant a legally secure title to the Provence was Rudolph I, the titular king of Burgundy. Accordingly, he suggested that Charles was to do homage to Rudolph for his imperial fiefs, the Provence and Forcalquier in the Haute-Provence. This bitter pill was to be softened by the prospect of having Charles' grandson, Charles Martel[133], the intended husband of Clemencia of Habsburg,

---

128 The pope had to reassure Rudolph of Habsburg about Charles' reliability. Rudolph thanked the pope in a letter from 1279 for information about Charles 'which has given us good confidence that, whatever popular opinion may be and whatever private information may suggest about the illustrious king of Sicily, we do not have to be overly distrustful' (*data nobis nichilominus bona spei fiducia, quod de inclyto rege Sycilie quitquid vulgaris opinio predicet, quitquid private suggestio swadeat, nulla nobis meticulosa suspicio sit habenda*) (H. Baerwald (ed.), *Das Baumgartenberger Formelbuch*, Vienna 1866, no 69, 281).

129 Rudolph's letter granting powers of attorney to the pope is in MGH *Const.* 3, no 210, 194.

130 Kind Edward I was not amused by Hartmann's procrastination. See his letters to Hartmann and King Rudolph in MGH *Const.* 3, no 173, 160 and no 176, 162.

131 See *supra* p. 524.

132 See *supra* p. 511.

133 Charles Martel (1271-1295) was the eldest son of of the prince of Salerno, the eldest son and heir-apparent of Charles of Anjou, also called Charles (1254-1309), who was to succeed his father as king of Naples in 1285.

raised to the dignity of king of Burgundy and consequently considerably expanding Angevine power in the region, but it was a dignity only the king of the Romans was entitled to confer. It was the price Rudolph of Habsburg had to pay for his imperial coronation, but since the imperial crown was Rudolph's main ambition it was a price he was prepared to pay. The establishment of a new Burgundian kingdom independent of the Empire was part of a much more ambitious plan of Nicholas III for the reformation, or rather the dismemberment, of the Roman Empire. The German kingdom was to become a separate hereditary monarchy to be reserved for Rudolph I and his heirs[134], while the Italian peninsula was to be divided into three kingdoms: Lombardy, Tuscany, and, of course, the kingdom of Sicily, exactly as Grandmaster Humbert de Romanis had proposed[135].

In the first week of June 1279 the terms of the treaty between Charles of Anjou and King Rudolph were completed in Rome by the German plenipotentiaries (friar Conrad and Chancellor Gottfried),

---

134   The suggestion to turn the kingdom of Germany into a *hereditary* monarchy means a break with the traditional papal policy of emphasizing the *electoral* character of that monarchy (see *supra* p. 149 and 155, fnt. 36). Essential elements of the papal doctrine concerning the Empire, especially the decretal 'Venerabilem', depended on that (see *supra* p. 334). It may have been what many German kings, certainly including Rudolph I, aspired at, but it was *not* in accordance with traditional papal policy. If it was suggested at this occasion, it may have been to win over Rudolph I to the plans of the pope concerning the alliance of Rudolph I and Charles of Anjou. There is another explanation, however, which may be even closer to the plans of Nicholas III. If the traditional ties between the German kingdom and the Roman Empire were to be severed once and for all, the pope was free to elect any other prince as emperor of the Romans. It was a plan in accordance with prevailing doctrines of canon law, emphasizing the role of the pope as 'emperor *ad interim*' during an imperial vacancy (see *supra* p. 335) as well as the right of the pope to transfer imperial power as it suited him (see *supra* p. 336). If that is what Nicholas III really had in mind, it was a plan that would have completely changed European politics.

135   On this plan see also Tholomaeus of Lucca, *Historia ecclesiastica nova* 23,34, Muratori, 11, col. 1183: 'In the same year <1279> Rudolph gave his daughter in marriage to Charles Martel. As history books tell us, Nicholas III negotiated with the said Rudolph about revolutionary changes in the Empire about the same time, to divide the Empire in four parts: a German kingdom, that was to be reserved for the descendants of Rudolph; a Viennese kingdom, to be given as a dowry to the daughter of the said Rudolph, the wife of Charles Martel. In Italy, however, except the kingdom of Sicily, two kingdoms were to be created, one in Lombardy and another in Tuscany, but it was not yet specified to whom they were to be allotted' (*Eodem anno Rodulphus suam filiam in uxorem Carolo Martello tradidit. Quo etiam tempore, ut tradunt Historiae, Nicolaus III cum Rodulpho jam dicto tractat super novitatibus faciendis in Imperio, ut totum Imperium in quattuor dividatur partes, videlicet in Regnum Alamanniae, quod debebat posteris Rodulhi perpetuari; in Regnum Viennense, quod dabatur in dotem uxori Caroli Martelli filiae dicti Rodulphi. De Italia vero praeter Regnum Siciliae duo Regna fiebant; unum in Lombardia, aliud vero in Tuscia; sed quibus darentur, nondum erat expressum*). I should add that Tholomaeus of Lucca, as he is known in historiography (his real name was Bartolomeo Fiadóni), was a Dominican with excellent contacts in the *curia*. He was a pupil and the confessor of Saint Thomas Aquinas and stayed at the papal court in Avignon for quite some time later in his life.

representatives of Charles of Anjou, and the pope and his cardinals. They were transmitted to Germany by a special papal envoy, Paolo dei Conti di Segni, bishop of Tripoli, who was also instructed to inform King Rudolph about the details of the projected marriage between his daughter Clemencia and Charles' grandson[136]. He was accompanied by envoys of the crown of Sicily. As the pope emphasized, the terms of the draft were composed 'with great care' (*cum multa deliberatione*)[137] and he was right: the treaty contained a detailed mutual non-aggression pact; a carefully arranged procedure about Charles' infeudation with the Provence and the county of Forcalquier, allowing Charles to do homage to Rudolph by proxy rather than having to do so personally; it also stipulated a marriage between Rudolph's daughter and Charles' grandson, adding that the dowry was to be specified by the pope later[138]. What the pope had in mind as a dowry was the kingdom of Burgundy[139], but that kingdom was never to be resuscitated, nor was

---

136 MGH *Const.* 3, no. 238, 230-231 (7 June 1279). Gay, *Les registres de Nicolas III*, Paris 1898, no. 774 and 775, 357-358 does not have the text of the instruction. See also Saba Malaspina 6,13, MGH *SS* 35, 267-268: '*Interea pro contrahenda parentela inter regem Karolum et regem Alamanie ... dominus Nicolaus destinat in Theotoniam Tripolitanum episcopum, ut eius studio filia regis Alamanie predicti Karolo primigenito Karoli principis Salernitani nondum puberi possit coniugio copulari et cum eodem episcopo in regnum traduci*'.

137 For the articles of the treaty see MGH *Const.* 3, no. 237, 225-230.

138 MGH *Const.* 3, no 237 (Art. 21 and 22), 229: '*Item quod fiat matrimonium olim tractatum per dominum Gregorium, quod illa filia regis Alamaniae, de qua tractatum fuit et que debet dari primogenito principis, mittatur ad regem Sicilie, sicut et quando videbitur domino pape. Item de dote sit in beneplacito Romani pontificis*'. The treaty also dealt with a very delicate issue: the claim of Margaret de Provence. The lawyers advising the high contracting parties about this must have been pleased with the intricacies they concocted in getting around her claim. She was, indeed, enfeoffed by Rudolph in the past, but only insofar as she had any title to the Provence, a contingent future interest at best. Consequently, the enfeoffment of Charles did not prejudice her right. See Art. 5 of the draft (MGH *Const.* 3, no 237, 226) and Rudolph's letter to Pope Nicholas III on the issue (MGH *Const.* 3, no 239, 231-232(232)): 'But we remember quite well that we have conceded, conferred, and promised to the queen of France nothing more than whatever interest she said to have *at law* in the counties of Provence and Fourcalquier' (*Nos quidem clare meminimus, quod domine regine nichil aliud concessimus, contulimus aut promissimus, quam quod sibi in comitatibus Provincie et Folkekerie de iure dicebat competere*) (emphasis added). If, however, she claimed to have a right to immediate possession, she was advised to seek redress in a court of law, being the court of the king of Germany: see Rudolph's letter to Margaret of 28 March 1280 (MGH *Const.* 3, no 247, 240-241). Margaret must have been furious.

139 For this see also the letter of authorization (*Willebrief*) issued by the duke of Saxony, consenting to the grant of the 'kingdom of Vienne also known as the kingdom of Arles' (*regnum Viennense quod et Arelatensis nomine nuncupatur*) by King Rudolph to the grandson of Charles of Anjou (MGH *Const.* 3, no 258, 253). The document also states that the ancient kingdom of Burgundy had been 'neglected for two hundred years and even more by a long, even a very long, lack of oversight so that there is hardly any memory left of the rights and boundaries of that kingdom' (*per vacacionem diutinam immo longissimam ducentorum annorum et amplius sit distractum in tantum quod ipsius regni iurium et limitum memoria vix*

the reformation of the Empire as envisaged by Pope Nicholas ever to be realized[140].

Contemporary Statue of Charles of Anjou as Senator of Rome (Arnolfo di Cambio (1232-1302/1310), Capitoline Museum, Rome (Wikimedia Commons))

The terms of the Roman draft agreement were approved by King Rudolph in a number of separate charters, issued on 27, 28, and 30 March 1280[141], to be sent to Rome. On 10 May 1280 Charles of Anjou assented to the terms of the agreement for his part, also to be conveyed to Rome where all of these documents were to be held in

Martin IV and Charles of Anjou

---

existat), confirming the impression that the region was only nominally a part of the Empire at the time (see *supra* p. 524).

140   Tholomaeus of Lucca, *Historia ecclesiastica nova* 23,34, ed. Muratori 11, col. 1183, referring to the plans of Nicholas III to reform the Empire (*supra* fnt 135): 'But while these things were considered, all considerations were brought to an end by the demise of the pope, who died the next year' (*Dum autem haec attentantur, et attentatio et cogitatio evanescit et collatio per mortem Papae qui moritur in anno sequenti*).

141   MGH *Const.* 3, no 244-249, 237-243.

escrow pending the final completion of the agreement[142]. But Nicholas III was not to preside over the solemn ceremony celebrating the completion of his stunning diplomatic achievement. He suddenly died on 22 August 1280 in his summer residence Castro Suriano near Viterbo[143]. The subsequent conclave was a turbulent affair since the Franco-Angevine and the 'Italian' faction in the *curia* held each other in balance. Consequently, the conclave lasted for months[144] until the local Viterban *podestà* finally decided to force a breakthrough, as had happened in 1271[145]. Riccardo Annibaldi had recently been elected as *podestà* of Viterbo, replacing Orso Orsini, a relative of Pope Nicholas. The new *podesta* ordered his officials to break into the conclave and arrest two cardinals, Matteo and Giordano Orsini, a nephew and a brother of Nicholas III, opposed to the election of a philo-Angevine pope. Having been relieved of the presence of the Orsini cardinals, the intimidated conclave was quick to elect a thoroughly Angevine new pope on 22 February 1281, none other than the onetime chancellor of France and long-time papal legate at the court of France, Simon de Brion, who chose to be called Martin, fourth of that name[146]. Though it is much to the credit of the new pope that he left Viterbo for Orvieto immediately after his election, disgusted as he was by the incidents coinciding with his election, he was an instrument of Angevine pol-

---

142   MGH *Const.* 3, no 250, 243-245. An agreement creating mutual obligations was not completed by one comprehensive document (as the Roman draft was), but by two (or more) separate charters containing the individual promises of the contracting parties. The formal exchange of these charters marked the completion of the agreement. In this case a solemn exchange was to be performed in the presence of the pope: see *infra* p. 532, fnt. 151.

143   *Annales Placentini Gibellini* ad ann. 1280, MGH SS 18, 572: '*Die Iovis 22. Mensis Augusti domnus Nicholaus papa tertius in castro Serariani ab hac luce transmigravit*'. The chronicle adds that the demise of the pope caused many cities in the Romagna to rebel against papal (Guelph) oppression. For the sudden demise of Nicholas III see also Saba Malaspina 7,8, MGH SS 35, 275 and Tholomaeus of Lucca, *Annales Lucenses* ad ann. 1280, MGH SS rer. Germ. N.S. 8, 192.

144   The relaxation of the rules of '*Ubi periculum*' by Johannes XXI was still in force at the time: see *supra* p. 521, fnt. 197.

145   See *supra* p. 503, fnt. 26. For the details of what follows see the rather overwrought report of Saba Malaspina 7,8-10, MGH SS 35, 275-279. See also Tholomaeus of Lucca, *Historia ecclesiastica nova* 24,1, ed. Muratori 11, col. 1185 and his *Annales Lucenses* ad ann. 1280, MGH SS rer. Germ. N.S. 8, 193-194 and the sentence against Viterbo of Pope Honorius IV, who was present at the occasion when he was still Giacomo Savelli, cardinal-deacon of the S. Maria in Cosmedin, in *Ann. eccl.*, Tom. 22, Paris 1870, ad ann. 1281 §2 (482-483) and ad ann. 1285 §70 (571), citing from the same papal decree of 4 September 1285. Prou, *Les registres d'Honorius IV*, Paris 1888, no 485, 343 does not have the text of this papal decision. G. Villani, *Nuova cronica* 8,58, ed. Porta I, Parma 1990, 505, reports that it was believed at the time ('si disse') that Charles of Anjou had orchestrated the incident, which is most probably correct.

146   On Simon de Brion see *supra* p. 439, 450, 453, 454 and 518. The cardinal had recently been recalled from France by pope Nicholas III and consequently participated in the conclave electing him.

icy nevertheless. Among his first official acts was the reinstallation of Charles of Anjou as senator of Rome, thus undoing one of the keystones of the policy of Nicholas III to keep that monster at bay[147]. Another was the creation of seven new cardinals, four of them from France[148], thus securing a strong Angevine faction of six cardinals in the *curia*, now consisting of nineteen cardinals. What the new pope did *not* do, however, was the cancellation of the projected Angevine-Habsburg alliance so carefully prepared by his predecessors Gregory X and Nicholas III. Early in April 1281, shortly after the election of Martin IV, Charles of Anjou was at Orvieto to meet with the new pope[149]. Charles needed the neutrality of the Empire in the impending war with Michael VIII and the Byzantine Empire, now finally to be facilitated by Pope Martin IV. After Gregory X and especially Nicholas III had successfully frustrated his aggression against the Byzantine Empire, Martin IV gave in to his wish: the Byzantine Emperor Michael VIII was duly and solemnly excommunicated on 18 November 1281 on the square facing the Cathedral of Orvieto (*in platea maioris ecclesie*) with Charles of Anjou himself present at the occasion[150]. By that time, Princess Clemencia of

---

147 See Theiner, *Codex diplomaticus domini temporalis S. Sedis* I, Rome 1861, no 395, 248-251 (29 April 1281). The charter contains the *senatus consultum* appointing the pope as senator for life and the papal nomination of Charles of Anjou as his delegate during his lifetime. As in the former nominations of Charles as senator of Rome after his coronation as king of Sicily, it was explicitly provided that by accepting that office Charles was not acting in contravention of his original promise to the pope *not* to accept any office outside the Sicilian kingdom (251): see *supra* p. 360 and 374.

148 Tholomaeus of Lucca, *Historia ecclesiastica nova* 24,3, ed. Muratori 11, col. 1186: '*Hic autem papa eodem anno primo sui pontificates post suam coronationem sex cardinales instituit circa festum Pentecostes, hoc est anno Domini mcclxxxi. Videlicet Dominum Hugonem Anglicum tituli Sancti Laurentii in Lucina; Dominum Gervasium tituli Sancti Martini in Montibus; Dominum Gaufridum Burgundum tituli sanctae Susannae, et Dominum Joannem Coletta tituli sanctae Caecilae, et Dominum comitem Mediolanensem tituli SS Marcellini et Petri in Presbyteros cardinales; Dominum Benedictum Gajetani tituli S. Nicolai in carcere Tulliano in Diaconum cardinalem*'. Gervais Jeancolet de Clinchamp, Geoffroy de Bar, and Jean Cholet were French prelates. Tholomaeo forgot to mention another 'French' prelate elevated to the cardinalate, Bernard de Languissel, the acting archbishop of Arles (!). His elevation to the cardinalate and the see of Porto and Sa Rufina is confirmed by a letter of Martin IV to Bernard in Martène-Durand, *Veterum scriptorum et monumentorum … amplissima collectio* Tomus II, Paris 1724, col. 1283-1284. Benedetto Caetani was an experienced lawyer, archchancellor (*protonotarius*) of the Church, and later to become pope as Boniface VIII, on whom more later, p. 566-575.

149 Minieri-Riccio, *Itinerario di Carlo I. di Angiò*, Naples 1872, 17. Charles was in Orvieto with the pope from 3 April 1281 until 20 January 1282, suggesting that papal policy during this time was coordinated with Charles of Anjou, or rather that Angevine policy was implemented by the pope. The prolonged presence of Charles and his French retinue in the town gave rise to tensions between the locals and the French. There was a serious riot (*tumultus magnus*) against the French in the streets of Orvieto in 1281: Martinus Oppaviensis (often referred to as Martinus Polonus), *Chronicon* (continuatio pont. rom.) ad ann. 1281, MGH *SS* 22, 477.

150 Tholomaeus of Lucca, *Historia ecclesiastica nova* 24,3, in Muratori 11, col. 1186: '*At the insistence of King Charles*, this pope let it be known by his solemn envoys to Palaeologus, the

Habsburg was already married to Charles' grandson Charles Martel and the Habsburg-Angevine treaty solemnly completed under the supervision of Martin IV himself[151]. Charles of Anjou was now at long last in a position to realize his dream of a Mediterranean empire. While still with the pope at Orvieto, he concluded an alliance with the incumbent doge of Venice, another scion of the Dandolo family, to conquer the Byzantine Empire together. It was agreed that the fleet of Venetian war galleys and Sicilian transporters were to meet at Brindisi in the second half of the month of April 1282[152]. The Byzantine Empire seemed doomed, but the wheel of fortune now finally turned against Charles of Anjou.

John of Procida in Aragon

The rapprochement between Rudolph I and Charles of Anjou was a serious setback for the Sicilian exiles still hoping to find support for their cause in the Empire. John of Procida, however, must already have realized after his visit to Meißen[153] that Prince 'Friedrich the Third' was not the serious contender for the Sicilian throne he was looking for[154]. He must have recognized there was now only one serious contestant

---

prince of Constantinople, who had promised to return to the obedience of the Roman Church with his subjects in the Council of Lyon, that he was excommunicated, alleging that he had not kept his promise. This was an act bringing scandal and ruin to the said King Charles and much harm to the Church itself' (*Hic pontifex in primo anno sui Pontificatus* ad instantiam regis Caroli *Palaeologum Principem Constantinopolitanum, qui ad oboedientiam Ecclesie Romanae cum suis fidelibus redire promiserat in Concilio Lugdunensi, per nuntios suos solemnes ... denuntiari fecit excommunicatum, allegans, quod non servavit promissum. Quod quidem factum fuit dicto Regi Carolo causa scandali et ruinae ... nec non et ipsi Ecclesiae plurimum fuit damnosum*) (emphasis added). The text of the papal sentence of excommunication passed on that day is in *Hermanni Altahensis Annales* (continuatio) ad ann. 1274, MGH 17, 409. For the presence of Charles of Anjou see *supra* fnt. 149.

151   Clemencia and Rudolf's special plenipotentiaries, Bishop Joannes of Gurk and the royal Chancellor Rudolf, left for Italy shortly after 6 January 1281. The envoys reported to their master on 5 March 1281, informing Rudolf that they had safely surrendered Clemencia to the custody of the Sicilian envoys at Bologna on 2 March of that year and that a new pope had been created: MGH *Const.* 3, no 254, 247-248. The treaty was completed at Orvieto 'in the presence of the pope' (*coram sanctissimo patre et domino Martino*) by the German plenipotentiaries and Charles of Anjou personally (*in persona propria*) and duly recorded on 24 May 1281 (MGH *Const.* 3, no 256, 248-251).

152   *Fontes Rerum Austriacarum* II, *Diplomata et acta* XIV,3 (*Urkunden zur älteren Handels- und Staatsgeschichte der Republik Venedig*), no 373, 287-295 (3 July 1281). It was agreed that Charles was to provide an army of 8000 knights and the transport vessels, while the Venetians supplied the war galleys, forty of them. The treaty was concluded between the Venetian Republic, Charles of Anjou, and his son-in-law Philip of Courtenay, now titular emperor of the Latin Empire after the demise of his father Baldwin II, who had died in Naples in 1273.

153   See *supra* p. 506.

154   The Lombard Ghibellines were disappointed with 'Friedrich the Third' as well. 'He did not come, since there was a disagreement among the princes' (*orta discordia inter principes, non venit*) is the last the *Annales Placentini Gibellini* (ad ann. 1269, MGH *SS* 18, 540) have to say about him.

left who was willing and capable to really challenge Charles of Anjou: Manfred's daughter Constance of Hohenstaufen, married to Crown prince Peter of Aragon. It was a marriage Pope Urban IV had desperately tried to prevent, but King James of Aragon did not heed the papal objections and the marriage was celebrated in Montpellier on 13 June 1262 nevertheless[155]. As was customary, the Sicilian princess had a retinue of Sicilians following her to Aragon. Most prominent among her attendants was her foster-mother Bella d'Amico. Bella's son, Roger of Lauria, foster-brother to Constance, had been raised at the court of Aragon[156] as were two Lancia brothers, Corrado and Manfredo, the sons of Federico Lancia, Manfred's uncle[157]. Especially the presence of the Lancia brothers at the court of the king of Aragon was a constant reminder of the cruelty of Charles of Anjou, the murderer of their uncle Galvano and their nephew Galeotto[158]. But Constance did not need to be reminded since she and her husband, the infant Peter, were determined to avenge Manfred and to recover his Sicilian heritage from the Angevine usurper[159]. Peter succeeded his father in 1276 as Peter III and was bound to do homage to the pope since the kingdom of Aragon was a papal fief, like Sicily. His grandfather and namesake Peter II had even been crowned at Rome by Pope Innocent III[160], but Peter ignored this, a first sign that he was prepared to flout the authority of the pope[161].

---

155   See *supra* p. 444.

156   Saba Malaspina 10,23, MGH *SS* 35, 365 has Roger stating that 'I was raised in Aragon and have been brought up in accordance with the customs of the Catalans, but yet I am a born subject of the kingdom <of Sicily>' (*Ego ... in Aragonia fueram educatus et Catalanorum moribus enutritus, sum tamen regnicola natione*).

157   On Federico Lancia see *supra* p. 498 and 499. On Sicilian exiles in the court of Peter of Aragon see also Saba Malaspina 7,3, MGH *SS* 35, 270.

158   See *supra* p. 490.

159   Contemporary sources emphasize that it was due to Constance's insistence that Peter of Aragon decided to conquer the Sicilian kingdom. See Saba Malaspina 8,3, MGH *SS* 35, 271; Bartolomaeo de Neocastro cap. 16, *RIS²* 13.3, 13; Tholomaeus of Lucca, *Historia ecclesiastica nova* 24,5, ed. Muratori 11, col. 1187; Guillaume de Nangis, *Gesta Philippi Tertii* ad ann. 1280, *Recueil* 20, 516, and the Catalan historian Ramon Muntaner (1265-1336), *Crònica* cap. 37 (I used the French translation, published by Buchon, 248). There were, of course, sound political reasons as well. The Angevine kingdom of Sicily was effectively blocking Catalonian trade from Barcelona with the Eastern Mediterranean, especially since the emir of Tunis was forced into an alliance with Charles of Anjou (see *supra* p. 500). The purely personal motive of revenge must not be underestimated though. An unavenged murder brought disgrace on the surviving relatives of the victim: see, for example, Dante, *Inferno* 29, 22-36.

160   See *supra* p. 163.

161   Peter III was crowned on 16 November 1276 as king of Aragon at Zaragoza by the bishop of that city, in Valencia as king of Valencia, and installed in Barcelona as lord of Catalonia and as count of that great city: Muntaner, *Crònica* cap. 29 (Buchon, 241-242). Muntaner reports how King James' kingdom was divided between his two sons Peter and James who became king of Mallorca and lord of Roussillon, Perpignan, Cerdagne, and Montpellier. On

John of Procida had been prominent in the court of King Manfred[162] and Queen Constance must have known him well. It may have been at her suggestion that Giovanni was granted an estate in the kingdom of Aragon by her husband on 26 June 1275 as a token of thanks for services rendered in the past to Peter's father in law, King Manfred[163]. It is the first sign of John's presence at the court of Aragon, where his great qualities were soon recognized and duly rewarded: on 19 February 1277 King Peter granted the barony of Lutxen in the kingdom of Valencia to John on account of unspecified 'laudable and useful services' (*grata et idonea servitia*) rendered to King Peter by 'our dear friend' (*dilectus familiaris noster*)[164]. Little or nothing is known about the whereabouts and travels of John of Procida between his departure from Germany around 1270 and 1275. Popular legend has him travelling around the Mediterranean, from Sicily to Rome, Constantinople, and Aragon and back again, always scheming and plotting to overthrow Angevine rule in Sicily[165]. In reality, however, John may have been of service to King Peter in affairs closer to Aragon. Peter had to deal with a difficult and unpredictable neighbour, his brother-in-law King Alfonso of Castile, first before entering on his Sicilian adventure.

Alfonso of Castile overplayed his hand all his life[166]. He had aspired to be crowned emperor of the Romans only to be finally thwarted by

---

the subordination of the kingdom of Mallorca to the overlordhip of the king of Aragon see *infra* p. 537.

162   Salimbene, *Cronica* ad ann. 1266, MGH *SS* 32, 472: '*Johannes de Procida, potens et magnus in curia Manfredi*'. Manfred had granted the rich barony of Caiano, not far from Salerno, to John. Before it was granted to John, the barony had belonged to Guillelmo di Caiano, who had participated in the 1246 conspiracy (see *supra* p. 393) and consequently was expropriated. It was restored to his son Roberto in 1269 as we know from the record of the restitution inquest organized by Charles of Anjou: HB VI.2, 918.

163   See the Italian summary of the grant in Carini 2, 190: 'Perciò noi, attesi i grati servigi resi da voi, Giovanni da Procida, al nostro suocero, Re Manfredi, di felice memoria, vi accordiamo *etc.*'.

164   Carini 2, 3. The full text of the two charters on the barony of Lutxen are published in Saint Priest, *Histoire de la conquête de Naples par Charles d'Anjou* IV, Paris 1849, 197-200.

165   This is the tenor of the story in Sicilian dialect about John of Procida and the Sicilian rising of 1282, *Lu Rebellamentu di Sichilia*, edited by E. Sicardi in *Due chronache del vespro in volgare Siciliano del secolo XIII*, RIS² 34.1, now also available with an English translation by Louis Mendola, *Sicily's Rebellion against Charles of Anjou*, New York 2015. The book, composed in the 14th century, reads like the fiction it is, probably intended for public reading to an illiterate Sicilian audience since an educated public must have realized that the absurd dialogues between John of Procida, Pope Nicholas III, and the Emperor Michael VIII are completely unrealistic. The historical elements it contains are almost certainly derived from Villani's *Nuova cronica*.

166   Alfonso, who was married to Violante of Aragon, a sister of Peter III, has earned the sobriquet 'the Wise' because of his great learning, but his life and deeds justify the assessment that great learning does not necessarily amount to wisdom. It is a widespread delusion among academics.

Pope Gregory X[167]. Nevertheless, he kept on supporting and financing the Ghibelline cause in Italy via his son-in-law William of Montferrat, who was married to his daughter Beatrice. He was waging war with the king of France, Philip III, over the mountain kingdom of Navarre in 1276[168], a war he could ill afford, since the Moors were ravaging his country in the south, while his own house was divided against itself after the untimely demise of his eldest son and heir Fernando de la Cerda in 1275[169]. Peter of Aragon was deeply involved in this Castilian family feud, if only because his sister Violante, married to Alfonso of Castile, sought his protection. The problem was that Peter could not take the risk of a conflict with Castile if he wanted to proceed with his Sicilian plans. He had to have his back protected and therefore sought some kind of arrangement with the king of Castile securing at least the neutrality of that capricious man. Another problem was the subordination of his brother James, the king of Mallorca. The last, but certainly not the least, of Peter's problems was money. In all of these concerns the helpful hand of a skilful diplomat, which is what John of Procida most certainly was, was more than welcome. Peter of Aragon was able to solve all of the problems, one by one, within a relatively short time.

The Castilian problem was largely solved by the good connections Peter succeeded in establishing with Alfonso's son and self-proclaimed heir Sancho and Alfonso's son in law, the marquess of Montferrat. Peter's upcoming Sicilian enterprise was essentially a Ghibelline undertaking, aimed as it was at the restoration of Manfred's policy, and the marquess of Montferrat was the leader of the Ghibelline cause in Lombardy. The marquess may have been largely dependent of his Castilian father-in-law Alfonso for financial support and Castilian soldiers, mercenaries most of them, but all goods, money, and men from Castile had to be shipped to Lombardy through the great port of Barcelona. No wonder, therefore, that Montferrat established good relations with Peter

Overcoming
obstacles

---

167 See *supra* p. 514-518.
168 On this see *supra* p. 518.
169 It was a typical medieval conflict between the children (or rather the eldest son) of a father predeceasing his own father on the one hand and his surviving brother, their uncle, on the other. In this case between Fernando's two sons by his wife Blanche de France, a sister of King Philip III, and their uncle Sancho, now Alfonso's surviving eldest son who contended to be heir to the throne on the ancient principle of agnatic succession, excluding succession by representation. The result was a bitter family feud, with Alfonso preferring his surviving son Sancho and his wife Violante taking the side of her grandchildren rather than her son Sancho. The ancient Visigothic customs of Castile favoured Sancho, but Guillaume de Nangis (*Gesta Philippi Tertii* ad ann. 1274-1275, *Recueil* 20, 496-498) reports that, according to the pre-nuptial contract between Louis IX, Blanche's father, and Alfonso of Castile, it was agreed that Blanche's eldest son was to succeed Alfonso in case his son Fernando predeceased his father. The story is confirmed by Muntaner, *Cronica* cap. 40 (Buchon, 251).

of Aragon. By 1280 they were allies and must have decided on the opening of a separate anti-Angevine front in Lombardy coinciding with Peter's attack on Sicily[170]. What significantly helped to expedite an arrangement with the king of Castile himself was the fact that Peter of Aragon had been able, thanks to his sister Violante, to lay his hands on the two Castilian infants, the children of Blanche de France and the late don Fernando, Alfonso's eldest son, thus solving the Castilian family feud by the process of abduction rather than murder, which is what the Castilian infant Sancho must have had in mind[171]. On

---

170 William of Montferrat was the most powerful 'Lord' (*Signore*) in the Italian kingdom at the time. He had been appointed *capitano di guerra* for an extended period by a great number of Lombard cities: Milan, Pavia, Vercelli, Novara, Asti, Alba, Alessandria, Tortona, Turin, Como, Lodi, Verona, Mantua, and Genoa. In March 1279 the marquess even organized a Ghibelline parliament attended by all the cities under his control at Milan: *Annales Placentini Gibellini* ad ann. 1278, MGH *SS* 18, 571. On 28 October 1280 Peter of Aragon sent a letter to all of these cities, assuring them of his great friendship with the marquess and urging them to continue to support the marquess 'since you must know that no doubt the day will come soon on which you and all his subjects and friends may rejoice and all his enemies will bewail their utter destruction' (*quoniam indubitanter sciatis in proximo adveniet dies illa quod vos et alii fideles et amici ipsius merito poteritis congaudere et eiusdem adversarii ultimo exterminio contristari*): Carini 2, 41. In 1281 the Genoese sent two galleys to Barcelona to bring the marquess to Genoa from Castile. Shortly before in the same year the marquess 'had sent a great number of soldiers provided to him by his father-in-law the king of Castile in Genoese ships' (*magnam quantitatem militum misit in navibus Ianue, quos rex Castelle eius socer consignavit eidem*): *Annales Ianuenses* (Jacobus Aurea) ad ann. 1281, MGH *SS* 18, 292. There is a very important letter from King Peter (and written by John of Procida) to the king of Castile, his son Sancho, and Alfonso's influential brother Manuel (see *supra* p. 517, fnt. 90) dated on 18 January 1281 in Carini 2, 45-46. It confirms that King Peter had received the letters of credence of the marquess of Montferrat, Count Guido Novello, Corrado di Antiochia (a grandson of Frederick II, *supra* p. 482, fnt. 297), Guido de Montefeltre, 'and other counts and magnates from Italy and the kingdom of Sicily' (*et aliorum Comitum et magnatum Italie et Regni Sicilie*) sent to Peter by a special messenger from Castile. Peter then proceeds that he will not comment in writing on their mission but will send the messenger (Francisco Trogisio) back to Castile with an oral message to be delivered to the addressees 'especially on the subject of the repossession of the kingdom of Sicily, to which you have been so kind as to voluntarily offer your assistance by way of our dear squire Andrea di Procida' (*super Capitulo illo precipuo scilicet super recuperacione Regni Sicilie ad quod vestrum auxilium gratuita voluntate nobis per dilectum scutiferum nostrum Andream de Procida liberaliter obtulistis*). Andrea di Procida was a brother of John, often acting as his messenger. One cannot but agree with the editor (Carini 46) that the letter is conclusive evidence of the existence of a widespread anti-Angevine conspiracy preceding the Sicilian Vespers.

171 Assassination was an accepted element in the political process at the court of Castile. The wise Alfonso had his own brother Fadrique murdered in 1277. On the kidnapping of the sons of Fernando de la Cerda by King Peter and his motives for doing so see Muntaner, *Crònica* cap. 40 (Buchon, 251-252). Especially the consideration that King Peter had it in his power to set up a contender for the throne of Castile at any time when the future King Sancho acted against the interests of Aragon, sounds genuine. See also Bernat Desclot cap. 76, (Buchon, 624-625). Of course, the abduction of the sons of Fernando de la Cerda caused an outcry among European royalty, especially in the court of France. King Philip III of France insisted that the children of his sister were to be handed over to his custody, but Peter refused: he

27 March 1281 Alfonso and Peter finally concluded a treaty of mutual assistance against all enemies, Muslims or Christians[172]. The Treaty of Campiello[173], as it is called, between Castile and Aragon was agreed to by Peter of Aragon for himself, but also for his brother, King James I of Mallorca. James, who had inherited not only the island of Mallorca from his father, but also important lordships in the Languedoc, such as Perpignan, Montpellier, and Roussillon, aspired to full independence from the crown of Aragon but it was not what his older and much more powerful brother wanted. Peter succeeded to bully his brother into submission and on 20 January 1279 James agreed at Perpignan to a treaty with his brother, turning his kingdom into a fief held from the crown of Aragon and making himself a vassal of his brother, obliged to assist him against all enemies of the crown of Aragon[174]. It was not a happy union[175], but it sufficed for the moment.

The king of France, Philip III, was anxiously following developments in Castile and Aragon and had separate but equally inconclusive conferences with Alfonso of Castile and Peter of Aragon on the issue of Navarre and the matter of the Castilian succession in which

---

was not going to give the king of France the advantage over the king of Castile he had gained for himself. The pope was also concerned, supporting the request of the king of France, but Peter refused his urgings as well, emphasizing that he was merely acting in the interest of the children: see his letter to Pope Martin IV in Carini 2, 43 (6 December 1281). Young Prince Alfonso de la Cerda and his brother Fernando, ten and five years old at the time, were kept under close guard in Xàtiva Castle near Valencia for more than ten years. Their mother, Blanche de France, had been allowed to leave Castile and to return to France, where that unfortunate woman was locked up in a cloister for the rest of her living days.

172   On the treaty see Bernat Desclot cap. 76 (Buchon, 624). The text of the treaty (in Castilian) is in *Memorial Histórico Español* Tom. II, Madrid 1851, no 182, 33-37, showing that the marquess of Montferrat was also present at the occasion. In a secret document (in Latin this time) the high contracting parties released each other from the duty of assistance in the case of war with the Muslims of Spain (*Memorial* II no 184, 39-40). The reason seems to be that these wars were now turning into wars of conquest rather than defense and neither party wanted the other involved as a matter of law in their territorial acquisitions. On the next day, a very secret treaty was concluded between Peter of Aragon and Alfonso's son Sancho wherein the latter ceded all the interests he had in the kingdom of Navarre to Peter and promised to aid Peter in the conquest of that kingdom (*Memorial* II no 186, 41-42). It was a treaty directed against France and, if implemented, it meant war with France. It was coming soon enough: see *infra* p. 553-557.

173   *Memorial* II no 184, 40: 'this charter is completed in a place called Campiello, between Tarazona and Agreda' (*Facta carta in loco qui dicitur Campiello, sito inter Tirasonam et Agredam*).

174   The text of the Treaty of Perpignan is in Lecoy de la Marche, *Les relations politiques de la France avec le royaume de Majorque* Tom. I, Paris 1892, no 27, 446-449. The obligation of military assistance is in the following clause (447-448): '*Promittimus tamen nos et et nostri, et adhuc de presenti nos et successores nostros obligamus, quod juvemus, valeamus et deffendamus vos et successores vestros cum toto posse nostro contra cunctos homines de mundo*'.

175   See *infra* p. 555.

he claimed to have a special interest as protector of the sons of his sister Blanche and especially in the fate of her eldest son Alfonso de la Cerda. His conference with Peter of Aragon and his brother James in Toulouse was attended by an interesting third party, none other than Prince Charles of Salerno, the eldest son and heir of Charles of Anjou sent to the Provence as his regent by his father[176]. The main issue to be discussed there was, of course, the fate of the two sons of Philip's sister Blanche but Peter of Aragon had no intention of handing the boys over to their uncle Philip[177]. After this indecisive meeting with the king of France, Peter of Aragon returned to the Iberian peninsula to meet with Alfonso of Castile at Campiello where they completed their treaty of mutual assistance, thereby securing a Spanish alliance against a possible military reaction of France to his Sicilian expedition.

The Aragonese-Byzantine alliance

We do not know to what extent John of Procida was actively involved in all of these developments, but it is certain that he was instrumental in contributing to the solution of the financial problems of Peter of Aragon. Naturally, Peter was aware of the fact that Alfonso of Castile had been granted the privilege to levy tithes on clerical revenues in his Castilian kingdom by the pope[178] and Peter had requested that same privilege in his own kingdom, but Pope Nicholas III was less accommodating than his predecessors and denied his request[179]. It was now that John of Procida was able to facilitate an agreement between King Peter and the Byzantine Emperor Michael VIII. After his public

---

176   The prince of Salerno had left the Sicilian kingdom for the Provence in August 1279 (see Charles' letter of 21 August 1279 in Minieri-Riccio, *Il regno di Carlo I d'Angiò dal 2 gennaio 1273 al 31 dicembre 1283*, Florence 1875, 1279, 21. Aug. (p. 18)). He had also been acting as a mediator in the fruitless negotiations between the king of France and Alfonso of Castile shortly before the Toulouse conference: see on these negotiations Guillaume de Nangis, *Gesta Philippi Tertii* ad ann. 1279, *Recueil* 20, 512-515.

177   On the Toulouse conference in 1280 see Guillaume de Nangis, *Gesta Philippi Tertii* ad ann. 1280, *Recueil* 20, 514-515; Bernat Desclot cap. 76 (Buchon, 624) and Muntaner, *Crònica* cap. 38 (Buchon, 249-250). According to the two Catalan chronicles, the main issue discussed in Toulouse was a conflict between the king of France and King James of Mallorca about Montpellier, but the matter of the De la Cerda boys must have had priority for King Philip, since he had discussed their fate shortly before with King Alfonso. The king of France and the king of Aragon were *in pari delicto* since Peter of Aragon was not the only one holding a child as hostage. So did the king of France with the heir of the kingdom of Navarre, Joan of Navarre, then just six years old. See *supra* p. 518, fnt. 95.

178   See *supra* p. 518.

179   According to a papal instruction of 1 december 1278 (Gay, *Les registres de Nicolas III*, Paris 1898, no 199, 65-67) addressed to the collector of the tithes in the kingdom of Aragon, King Peter had already received a part of the tithes for his military campaign against Spanish Muslims. The collector was sternly rebuked for having allowed this to happen without papal approval, indicating that the pope was not inclined to give in to the repeated requests of the king of Aragon to assign the tithes to him.

excommunication by Pope Martin IV in 1281[180], Michael VIII desperately needed allies and it turned out that he could count on at least one friendly Italian state, the city of Genoa. Ever since Michael VIII had reconquered Constantinople, the Genoese entertained good relations with that city and were prominently present there. When Charles of Anjou invited the Genoese in 1281 to join the Venetian-Angevine alliance in the conquest of the Byzantine Empire, Genoa rejected that offer and immediately informed the emperor in Constantinople of the impending danger[181]. One of the Genoese envoys carrying this message to Constantinople was Benedetto Zacharia, who had been sent to Constantinople before as an ambassador of the republic[182]. He was accompanied by a representative of John of Procida, most probably John's brother Andrea, whom we have already met as a go-between for his brother[183]. It was during this mission to Constantinople that an alliance was forged between Michael VIII and Peter of Aragon[184].

---

180   See *supra* p. 531.

181   *Annales Ianuenses* (Jacobus Aurea) ad ann. 1281, MGH *SS* 18, 293: 'The said king <Charles of Anjou> invited the city of Genoa by his messengers to join in the conquest of the Greeks he was presently planning if they wanted to and to send him support and a reinforcement of galleys. But the Genoese replied that they were elsewhere engaged and consequently were unable and unwilling to participate. Immediately thereafter a galley was equipped by the city of Genoa and sent to the emperor, informing him of all that has just been said. The emperor was very pleased to hear all this from the city' (*Invitavit etiam dictus rex commune Ianue per suos nuntios, quod si volebant habere partem in conquisto quod super Grecos ad presens facere intendebat, quod eidem darent succursum et auxilium galearum. Ianuenses vero responderunt, quod aliis factis occupati errant, et propter hoc hiis intendere non poterant nec volebant. Unde in continenti per commune Ianue fuit armata galea una in Ianua per comune, et missa ad dictum imperatorem, significando eidem omnia supradicta. Dictus autem imperator gratum hoc a comuni valde accepit*).

182   For Benedetto Zacharia's earlier mission to Constantinople see *Annales Ianuenses* ad ann. 1264, MGH *SS* 18, 249.

183   See *supra* p. 536, fnt. 170. Popular legend (see *supra* p. 534, fnt. 165) has John of Procida travelling to Constantinople himself, but this is impossible since we know from the surviving Catalan documents from the period bearing his name that he was fully occupied in Aragon itself at the time. The Aragonese ambassy to Constantinople must have been his initiative nonetheless: see *infra* fnt. 184.

184   Tholomaeus of Lucca, *Historia ecclesiastica nova* 24,3 and 4, ed. Muratori, 11, col. 1186-1187: 'To begin with, mediators between Palaeologus and the king of Aragon were called for ... These were the mediators: one of them was Benedetto Zacharía from Genoa with some other men from Genoa who were in the country of Palaeologus. Another was John of Procida. And they, but above all John, were the mediators between one of the greatest princes of the world and the abovementioned king of Aragon to take away the kingdom from King Charles, a treaty I have seen myself' (*Primo namque assumuntur mediatores inter Palaeologum et Regem Aragonum ... Hi autem fuerunt mediatores; unus fuit Dominus Benedictus Zacharias de Janua cum quibusdam aliis Januensibus, qui Domini erant in terra Palaeologi. Alius autem fuit Dominus Joannes de Procida. Et hi, praecipue autem Dominus Joannes, mediatores fuerunt inter unum de majoribus Principibus Mundi, et Regem Aragonum supradictum, de auferendo Regnum Regi Caroli: quem tractatum ego vidi*). Tholomaeus of Lucca repeats this story in one

The Byzantine emperor might not have been in a position to send an army, which he needed himself, but he was able to advance money, of which he had enough. Having secured safe borders with Castile and ample financial support from Constantinople thanks to the diplomacy of John of Procida, Peter of Aragon was now ready to proceed with his Sicilian expedition

Early in 1282 it was clear that the king of Aragon was preparing for war. Troops were gathering and war galleys and transport ships were equipped in Barcelona for all the world to see and wonder where they were headed but King Peter kept his true intentions a well-guarded secret. When Pope Martin inquired for what reason he was mustering an army and a fleet, the king is reported to have answered that he would cut his own tongue if it ever ventured to express his intentions[185]. The king of France received an equally evasive answer to the same question[186]. King Peter was biding his time, waiting for Charles of Anjou and his army to leave the Sicilian kingdom for the Balkan peninsula to attack the Byzantine Empire but then, suddenly, something transpired that took him (and Charles of Anjou) completely by surprise: the island of Sicily rose in revolt against Charles of Anjou.

The Sicilian
Vespers

The Sicilian rising of 1282 is part and parcel of Italian national mythology, interpreting it as a spontaneous popular revolt against foreign oppression and excluding any idea that it was part of an interna-

---

of the versions of his *Annales Lucenses* (ad ann. 1282, MGH *SS rer. Germ. N.S.* 8, 197). In this version 'one of the greatest princes of the world' was referred to as 'another great prince, whose name is not known' (*alius magnus inter principes, cuius nomen ignotum*). There is much speculation about the identity of this prince, the third party involved in the alliance, whose name Tholomaeus refuses to mention. Popular legend (see *supra* p. 534, fnt. 165) had no doubt: it was Pope Nicholas III. Some modern scholars have suggested the king of England. King Edward is indeed mentioned as an ally and supporter of Peter in the *Annales Placentini Gibellini* ad ann. 1282, MGH *SS* 18, 574, but popular legend may have been right: Nicholas was no friend of Charles of Anjou and he had great plans for the dismemberment of the German Empire (see *supra* p. 527). He may have had great plans for the breakdown of the kingdom of Sicily as well, but there is no trace of it in his official correspondence, which is, of course, not sufficient proof that he was not involved since it was a very secret affair, as Tholomaeus of Lucca must have realized: mentioning the king of England would not have been an embarrassment to him, but mentioning the name of the pope as an accomplice in this delicate matter must certainly have been so to that pious Dominican friar who saw the document concerned with his own eyes. Important as this treaty is, nothing is known of its actual content but it must have been primarily about financial support from Constantinople for King Peter and the Sicilian opposition against Charles of Anjou.

185   Tholomaeus of Lucca, *Historia ecclesiastica nova* 24, 4, ed. Muratori 11, col. 1187: '*tradunt Historiae, Papam Martinum scripsisse eidem Regi Aragonum ad suggestionem Regis Caroli, quod volebat scire ad quid faceret istum apparatum. Cui praedictus rex sic dicitur respondisse, quod illud, quod faciebat, sic erat privatum apud ipsum, quod si lingua sua hoc manifestaret, amputeret ipsam*'.
186   Muntaner, *Crònica* cap. 47 (Buchon, 256).

tional conspiracy initiated by foreign powers, the Byzantine Empire, the kingdom of Aragon, and the Ghibelline alliance in Lombardy, to undermine and possibly even to eliminate Charles of Anjou as a political force dominating the Italian peninsula. That conspiracy, however, was a reality[187], but the interests of the parties to it did not align. The strategy of Peter of Aragon was to attack the Sicilian kingdom only *after* Charles of Anjou had sent his troops into the Byzantine Empire, whereas the Byzantine emperor wanted Charles of Anjou to be prevented from doing so by distracting him with an attack on his own kingdom by Peter of Aragon. The king of Aragon seems to have been outwitted by Michael VIII, who forced Peter's hand by inciting a rebellion on Sicily *before* Charles of Anjou had transported the bulk of his troops to the other side of the Adriatic. It was a brilliant move, testifying to the efficacy of the ancient tradition of the only *real* Roman Empire, the Byzantine Empire, exercising 'soft power' to deal with 'Barbarians', be they Huns, Goths, Turks, 'Francs'[188] or whatever, rather than brute force. Byzantine gold was the most effective weapon of that diplomacy and it will have done its work on Sicily as well. Since secrecy is an essential element of this diplomacy, it leaves little or no traces in official documents, but when- and wherever Byzantine interests were at stake, as in Sicily at the time, its presence should be taken for granted.

On Easter Monday 1282 (30 March in that year), just after evening prayers, the faithful walked out of the Church of the Holy Spirit just outside the Palermo city walls to participate in an Easter party customarily celebrated there. Some French soldiers were on patrol among the festive crowd to see if the ban on carrying arms was properly respected[189]. It seems that on this occasion some of the soldiers behaved improperly towards the women present there, causing offense among the Panormitans and quickly turning into a brawl. What began as a mere scuffle, soon escalated into a serious riot. A hidden knife is easily drawn on Sicily, especially when the honour of a woman is at stake, and after first blood was drawn there was a general outcry 'let's kill all the French' (*Moranu li Franchiski!*)[190]. And so it was done. The riot spread

---

187 See *supra* p. 536, fnt. 170.

188 'Francs' (Φράγγοι) is the collective term in Byzantine sources for all Latin Christians, whether they were from 'France' or not.

189 For the ban on carrying arms in the Sicilian kingdom see *supra* p. 224. For the instruction to the French soldiers on patrol see Bartolomaeo de Neocastro cap. 14, *RIS²* 13.3, 11.

190 Bartolomaeo de Neocastro cap. 14, *RIS²* 13.3, 12 (*Moriantur Gallici, moriantur*), also in Saba Malaspina 8,4-5, MGH *SS* 35, 288-289 and Villani, *Nuova Cronica* 8,61, ed. Porta I, Parma 1990, 510. Since the Palermitans did not speak Latin, I used the text of the tale of the Sicilian Vespers in medieval Sicilian dialect (*Lu Rebellamentu di Sichilia*), edited by E. Sicardi in *Due chronache del vespro in volgare Siciliano del secolo XIII*, cap. 24, *RIS²* 34.1, 19. On this text see *supra* p. 534, fnt. 165. See also Muntaner, *Crònica* cap. 43 (Buchon, 253-254) and

to the city itself, taking the local Angevine governor completely by surprise, and resulted in a massacre of every Frenchman the bloodthirsty crowd could lay their hands on, not even sparing clerics, women, and children. It is said that three or even four thousand people were slaughtered on that terrible day, not in Palermo alone but all over Sicily[191].

Riots rarely turn into a revolution. They only do so when the indiscriminate violence of the mindless mob is converted into a deliberate political direction by intelligent men with a plan of action. And this is what happened on Sicily in 1282. There were Sicilian nobles in contact with the court of Aragon, the Lombard Ghibellines, and the Byzantine emperor, men like Palmiero Abate, Gualtieri di Caltagirone, and Alaimo di Lentini[192]. After the killing spree in Palermo and other Sicilian towns (but for Messina, the seat of the governor of the island, Herbert d'Orléans) was over, leaving the Sicilian populace conclusively and fatefully compromised, order instantly was restored by the local nobles implicated in the anti-Angevine conspiracy. What was to be done now since it was obvious that Charles of Anjou would retaliate with brute force?

It is a clear sign of a premeditated revolt that the Sicilians quickly organized themselves along suspiciously familiar (Lombard) lines: within a few days after the Vespers, they elected *capitanei* governing the cities and concluded alliances among themselves, a Sicilian League, first of all between Palermo and nearby Corleone, a city with a population consisting largely of Ghibelline Lombard immigrants settled in Corleone by Frederick II in 1237[193]. They held a joint parliament in

---

Bernat Desclot cap. 81 (Buchon, 628-629). Other more or less contemporaneous accounts of the Sicilian Vespers are in *Annales Ianuenses* (Jacobus Aurea) ad ann. 1282, MGH *SS* 18, 294; Guillaume de Nangis, *Gesta Philippi Tertii* ad ann. 1282, *Recueil* 20, 516-517 and in *Anonymi Chronicon Siculum* (*c.* 1343) cap. 38 (Gregorio, *Biblioteca* 1, 301-302).

191   Saba Malaspina 8,5, MGH *SS* 35, 289: '*Irruunt in Gallicos … et quos capere possunt interficiunt universos*'. An estimated number of victims is in Villani, *Nuova Cronica* 8,61, ed. Porta I, Parma 1990, 511 and *Lu Rebellamentu di Sichilia*, ed. Sicardi 20.

192   These three Sicilian nobles are mentioned by Villani, *Nuova Cronica* 8,57, ed. Porta I, Parma 1990, 503. Thanks to the meticulous research of Helene Wieruszowski (*Politics and Culture in Medieval Spain*, Rome 1971, 223-278) we now know they (and many others) were indeed in contact with Peter of Aragon. She has published a letter from 2 May 1281 by King Peter addressed to no fewer than seventeen Sicilians, all of them mentioned by name (Palmiero Abate and Gualtieri di Caltagirone among them), no doubt the core of the Sicilian conspiracy, stating that he sends them two messengers (also Sicilians) 'recommended to be trusted by you like ourselves in the affair for which they are coming to these parts' (*super negociis, pro quibus ad partes ipsas incedunt, eos recomendatos habentes credere velitis ut nobis*) (Wieruszowski, 264).

193   Nicolas Specialis, *Historia Sicula* cap. 4, in Gregorio, *Biblioteca* 1, 302: '*Tunc Siculi Capitaneos sibi preficiunt, eorumque dominatum Communitatem appellant, Romanos in hac parte sequentes, qui, post ejectam Tarquinii regis superbiam, sibi annales consules prefecerunt*'. For the election of *capitanei* all over the island see Saba Malaspina 8,9, MGH *SS* 35, 293-

Palermo on 3 April to decide how to proceed. The decision taken there illustrates that the political objectives of the participants in the Sicilian conspiracy did not coincide: all of them – Peter of Aragon, Michael VIII, William of Montferrat, and the Sicilian barons – conspired to overthrow a common enemy, Charles of Anjou, but the Sicilians did so primarily because they were thoroughly dissatisfied by Charles' tyrannical regime and not necessarily to invite yet another foreign prince to their island. They were Sicilian patriots first of all and consequently did *not* invite Peter of Aragon to come to the rescue, but addressed their constitutional overlord instead, none other than the pope, possibly hoping the pope would involve himself directly in the government of Sicily as Innocent IV had done in 1254, when he had placed the Sicilians under his special protection and restored their 'liberties and privileges, and laudable customs and usages'[194]. Nicholas III or Gregory X, even Clement IV[195], might have seized this opportunity to rein in Charles of Anjou but not so Martin IV. He did not excommunicate the Sicilians forthwith but he did order them to submit to Charles of Anjou, their rightful king, immediately[196] and if they failed to do so, the cities and

---

294. For the early alliance of Palermo and Corleone see Saba Malaspina 8,6-8, MGH *SS* 35, 289-292 and for the settlement of Ghibelline Lombards in Corleone see the grant to the Lombard knight Odo de Camerana, *dilectus fidelis noster*, by Frederick II in HB 5.1, 128-131. Ruggero de Mastrangelo was elected *capitaneus* of Palermo (Saba Malaspina 8,5, MGH *SS* 35, 288; Bartolomaeo de Neocastro cap. 14, *RIS²* 13.3, 12) and the people of Corleone elected Bonifacio de Camerana as their '*rector*' in 1282 (Saba Malaspina 8,6, MGH *SS* 35, 290). He may have been a son of Odo. I take it for granted that the Lombards in Corleone were in contact with the Ghibelline alliance in Lombardy led by William of Montferrat (see *supra* p. 536 and fnt. 170).

194   See supra p. 428. Nicolas Specialis, *Historia Sicula* cap. 3 (R. Gregorio, *Biblioteca* 1, 300-301) reports a fruitless Sicilian ambassy to the pope complaining about Charles of Anjou immediately prior to the rising. For the provisional decision to rise against Charles of Anjou under the banner of the pope see Saba Malaspina 8,7, MGH *SS* 35, 291. After Messina had also joined the rebellion another conference was held at Messina early in May 1282 (Saba Malaspina 8,10, MGH *SS* 35, 296-297). Bartolomaeo de Neocastro (cap. 21, *RIS²* 13.3, 16) reports that, by then, the men from Palermo had already contacted Peter of Aragon. The disagreement among the Sicilian rebels explains why some of them (like Gualtieri di Caltagirone) later even turned against Peter of Aragon. See also *infra* p. 353 and fnt. 237.

195   Clement IV was highly critical of the government of Charles of Anjou from the very start: see *supra* p. 471 and fnt. 240. He may have been a Frenchman, but, knowing Charles of Anjou from personal experience better than any of his cardinals, he might have regarded the Sicilian rising as the logical outcome of Charles' style of government.

196   The papal bull reacting to the Sicilian Vespers is in *Hermanni Altahensis Annales* (continuatio) ad ann. 1282, MGH 17, 412-414. It contains a concise history of Sicily from the days of the deposition of Frederick II by the council of Lyon I to the excesses of the Sicilian Vespers. In as far as the Panormitans and the other cities on Sicily are concerned, it provides as follows (413-414): 'But since the city of Palermo and some other towns and villages in those parts are said to have revolted against the said King Charles, who holds that kingdom from the Church, we have decided not to apply the rigour of the law against them but rather preferring to exercise the leniency of the clemency we always follow in our actions, desiring and wanting

townships on the island were to be placed under interdict[197]. Cardinal Gerardo Bianchi from Parma was sent to the island as special papal legate to convey this message to the rebels[198]. It seems that by now the pope and the *curia* were also informed about the existence of a widespread conspiracy against Angevine rule in Sicily since the best part of the papal bull of 7 May 1282 was not directed against the Sicilians but addressed to all foreign potentates, '*strictly forbidding them to molest, attack, or disturb, by themselves or by others, us, the Church, and the above-mentioned king of Sicily, who holds that kingdom from the Church, in the aforementioned kingdom or any part of it by occupying or invading that kingdom or by causing that kingdom or any part of it to be occupied or invaded*'[199]. It was a clear warning to Peter of Aragon, who must have been perceived as the chief instigator of the rebellion by then.

Peter of Aragon
comes to Sicily

When the Sicilians drove the French from the island of Sicily in April 1282, Peter of Aragon was still in Catalonia. It was only some days

---

them with fatherly love to correct the error they have fallen victim to, we do strongly order the counties, cities, and communities of the said towns and villages to submit to our command and to the authority of the Church and the said king without any delay or objection. We also strongly order the said counties not to invite or receive the abovementioned molesters, disturbers of the peace, thieves, and housebreakers into their cities, towns, and villages, giving them advice, counsel, or relief and not to submit in any way to their command or to the authority of anyone among them and not to publicly or secretly give advice, counsel, or relief to anyone among them acting against us, the Church, or the abovementioned king' (*Ceterum quia predicta civitas Panormitana et nonnula castra seu ville illarum parcium contra prefatum regem Karolum, qui regnum ipsum ab eadem tenet ecclesia, rebellionis spiritum assumpsisse dicuntur, nos circa illa nolentes in hoc iuris rigorem observare, set uti pocius mansuetudinis lenitate, quam in actibus nostris libenter amplectimur, intendentes ac volentes eadem ab huiusmodi erroris inicio paternis studiis revocare, comitatibus, civitatibus et universitatibus castrorum ac villarum predictarum districte precipimus, ut sublato cuiuslibet difficultatis et dilacionis obiectu, ad nostra mandata et ecclesie ac regis predicti redire procurent, eisdem comitatibus districte precipimus, ne predictos molestatores, turbatores, occupatores seu eciam invasores, aut dantes eisdem in predictis consilium, auxilium vel favorem, in civitatem, castra et villas sei districtus eorum quovis modo recipient vel receptent, nec ipsorum vel alicuius eorum dominio vel regimini quomodolibet se submittant, neque ipsis vel eorum alicui contra nos et eandem ecclesiam ac regem predictum in ea inpendant in predictis consilium, auxilium vel favorem publicum vel occultum*).
197 *Hermanni Altahensis Annales* (continuatio) ad ann. 1282, MGH 17, 413: 'The cities and alliances who dare to contravene our abovementioned orders by deceit, fraud, malice, dishonesty, or tricks, we want to subject to the ecclesiastical censure of the interdict, which we do pronounce as from now' (*Civitates quoque et communitates quaslibet, que contra moniciones et precepta nostra predicta quocumque dolo, fraude, ingenio, arte vel machinatione venire presumpserint, ecclesiastice sentencie interdicti, quam ex nunc in illos proferimus, volumus subiacere*).
198 Saba Malaspina 8,11, MGH *SS* 35, 298.
199 *Hermanni Altahensis Annales* (continuatio) ad ann. 1282, MGH 17, 413: '*ne in predicto regno vel eius parte nos et eandem ecclesiam et prefatum Sicilie regem, qui predictum regnum ab eadem tenet ecclesia, per se vel per alium aut alios molestent seu impetant aut perturbent, occupando vel invandendo hostiliter, seu occupari vel invadi hostiliter faciendo regnum ipsum vel aliquam partem eius*'.

after 3 June 1282, more than two months after the Sicilian rising, that his fleet left Catalonia, *not* for Sicily but for 'Ifriqiya', the medieval Arab designation of what is now known as the Maghrib. He planned to interfere in a civil war going on there[200] and to establish a secure bridgehead to the island of Sicily at the same time, but the campaign was officially presented as a crusade against the infidel. On 28 June Peter of Aragon and his armada reached the port of Alcol, halfway between Tunis and Algiers[201]. It was from there that Peter sent envoys to the pope requesting permission, yet again, to levy tithes on clerical revenues in his kingdom to finance his holy endeavour. On their way to Italy, the royal emissaries made a detour to Palermo where they contacted the rebels there. As was to be expected, their mission to the pope was unsuccessful, but they were able to inform King Peter on their return to Alcol that all Angevine troops on Sicily had either been massacred or had fled the island[202].

Peter of Aragon encountered unexpected resistance at Alcol. The local insurgent who had invited him to the Maghrib in the first place already had been defeated and slain by troops of the emir of Tunis, thus depriving Peter of local support for his 'African' campaign and even forcing him, unexpectedly, to fight the locals. He was now fighting the 'infidel' indeed, but it was not the war he intended to be engaged in. He was waiting for the Sicilians to provide him with an excuse for the invasion of Sicily since he had *not* disclosed his real intentions

---

200 The Tunisian Emir Al-Mustansir (on him see *supra* p. 472, 499 and 500) had died in 1277, leaving his emirate to his son Yahya, who was forced to abdicate and subsequently murdered in 1279 by his uncle Abu Ishaq Ibrahim, a brother of Al-Mustansir. The governor of the town of Constantine, Ibn al-Wazir, rebelled against Abu Ishaq Ibrahim in 1282, inviting Peter of Aragon to support him. For the (rather confusing) details see Muntaner, *Crònica* cap. 30-31 and 44 (Buchon, 242-244 and 254-255) and Bernat Desclot cap. 77-79 (Buchon, 626-627). Peter was still in the Catalonian port of Fangos with his fleet on 3 June, when he made his last will and testament there. It is in Carini 2, 240-241.

201 *Annales Ianuenses* (Jacobus Aurea) ad ann. 1282, MGH *SS* 18, 293: *'Applicuit autem cum dicto exercitu in Ancolo in vigilia beati Petri'.* The 'day before St Peter's day' is 28 June. Peter had made a stopover in the port of Mahon on Menorca before proceeding to the Barbary Coast.

202 Peter's ambassy to the pope is mentioned in a letter to King Edward I from 19 July 1282 in Rymer, I.2, 206: *'misimus Nuncium nostrum ad summum pontificem, ut nobis, super eodem negotio, subsidium largeretur. Quem idem nuncium dictus summus pontifex, audita supplicatione nostra, timens an Regem Siciliae accederet, sine responsione aliqua relegavit'.* On this mission to the pope see also Muntaner, *Crònica* cap. 52 (Buchon, 260-261); Bernat Desclot cap. 85-86 (Buchon, 631-632); Saba Malaspina, 9,10-11, MGH *SS* 35, 318-320; *Annales Ianuenses* (Jacobus Aurea) ad ann. 1282, MGH *SS* 18, 293, and Guillaume de Nangis, *Gesta Philippi Tertii*, in *Recueil* 20, 516-518. The story of the detour to Palermo is in *Anonymi Chronicon Siculum* cap. 40 (Gregorio, *Biblioteca* 2, 148-149). It is important that the envoys to the pope had already returned to the king at Alcol before 16 July since Saba Malaspina wrongly places this ambassy much later, early in August 1282, after the siege of Messina had begun and the Sicilians had already invited Peter to come to their rescue (see *infra* p. 547).

to his Aragonese and Catalan barons who might object to an unexpected change of the war theatre[203]. Fighting fellow-Christians rather than infidels for the conquest of a kingdom subject to the pope himself might not be a project in which they were all willing to be involved. This is why the king made a public demonstration of his reluctance when he received an ambassador from the city of Palermo arriving in Alcol early in July 1282 offering him the crown of Sicily. Peter seems to have known, furthermore, that not all Sicilians, especially the men from Messina who had recently joined the revolt, were willing to invite a foreign prince to their island[204]. He did not have to wait long for an invitation backed by all Sicilians, including the men from Messina.

Charles of Anjou besieges Messina

Charles of Anjou was in Naples when news about the Sicilian rising reached him but he waited for almost a month before taking decisive action[205]. He was about to join the Venetian fleet expected at Brindisi in the second half of April[206] and to embark on his campaign to conquer the Byzantine Empire. Charles was not to abandon that great enterprise lightly, but he was forced to do so after news about the defection of the city of Messina, the last Angevine stronghold on the island of Sicily, had reached him. It was only after that event that he did redirect his troops destined to conquer the Byzantine Empire to Calabria instead for the recovery of Sicily. The Byzantine emperor had now fully achieved his objective but the Sicilians were about to pay the price, facing the wrath of the mighty Charles of Anjou. On 6 July Charles of Anjou himself joined his army at Catona, a town on the Calabrian mainland facing Messina across the strait, determined to regain control over the island and to eradicate the rebels there[207]. His first objective

---

203 The Aragonese and Catalan barons must have wondered what the three special ambassadors from the Byzantine Emperor Michael VIII were about. On their presence with Peter of Aragon in Catalonia and on the expedition to the Barbary Coast see Peter's letter to Michael VIII (20 September 1282) in Carini, *Documenti* no 4, 4-5.

204 According to Bartholomaeo de Neocastro cap. 21, *RIS²* 13.3, 16), the Panormitan Nicolas Coppola had left Sicily on 27 April 1282 as a messenger of the people of Palermo to officially invite Peter of Aragon to come to Sicily. He had been heading for Catalonia first, but after finding out on Menorca that the king already had left for the Barbary Coast, he changed his course in that direction and met the king at Alcol shortly after Peter's arrival there. For Peter's show of reluctance see Bartholomaeo de Neocastro cap. 23, *RIS²* 13.3, 17-18). On the mission of Coppola see also *Anonymi Chronicon Siculum* cap. 40 (Gregorio, *Biblioteca* 2, 149).

205 Bartholomaeo de Neocastro cap. 31, *RIS²* 13.3, 22: '*transactis fere diebus triginta*'.

206 See *supra* p. 532.

207 Minieri-Riccio, *Itinerario di Carlo I. di Angiò*, Naples 1872, 17. Charles intinerary illustrates his reluctance to abandon his Byzantine campaign. He stayed at Naples during April and May and left for Calabria only on 13 June.

was, of course, Messina. The siege of Messina[208] started in earnest on 25 July after a last failed attempt by the papal legate Cardinal Gerardo Bianchi from Parma to persuade the citizens of Messina to submit to Charles of Anjou. Charles threw his whole expeditionary force against the city but it proved very hard, once again, to conquer a fortified city defended by a determined and unified citizenry before the invention of cannonry. A siege was always a hazardous and time-consuming enterprise and so it was this time. By the end of August 1282 time was running out on Charles of Anjou.

Alaimo da Lentini was elected *capitano* of Messina soon after the first hostile encounters with Charles' expeditionary force[209]. He was one of the original Sicilian conspirators behind the bloody Easter rising of 30 March and will certainly have been in contact with Peter of Aragon or his agents on the island by now[210]. Like other Sicilian nobles, he was a patriot first of all and may initially not have been favourable to the idea of installing yet another foreign prince as king of Sicily, but the intransigence of the pope forced him and the city of Messina into the camp of the supporters of the cause of Peter of Aragon and his wife Constance[211]. He must have realized that without foreign aid the chances of withstanding the Angevine onslaught were very dim in the end. Accordingly, he finally (and possibly reluctantly) joined the initiative of the Panormitans to invite Peter of Aragon. Peter was, indeed, the only hope of instant support, having an army and a fleet nearby at Alcol. In August 1282 new ambassadors from Sicily approached Peter of Aragon in Alcol inviting him to come to the rescue of the Sicilians

---

208   This is not the place to rewrite the history of the siege of Messina so heroically defended by the citizens against overwhelming force. The main contemporary sources are Saba Malaspina 9, 4-6, MGH *SS* 35, 312-315, and Bartholomaeo de Neocastro cap. 41-43 and 50, *RIS²* 13.3, 27-29.

209   Bartholomaeo de Neocastro cap. 37, *RIS²* 13.3, 25.

210   Alaimo's name is conspicuously absent in the list of Sicilian contacts mentioned by Peter of Aragon in his letter from 2 May 1281 (see *supra* p. 542, fnt. 192). Nevertheless Villani and popular legend has him among the three main conspirators. Alaimo was indeed among the Sicilian nobles greatly rewarded by Peter of Aragon directly after he gained control of Sicily. He was appointed Chief Justice of the Sicilian Kingdom (*magister iusticiarius totius regni Siciliae*) for life by Peter III on 22 October 1282 (see Peter's charter in Carini, *Documenti* no 178, 162-163). Alaimo is said to have had a terrible wife, Machalda of Scaletta, a very ambitious woman: she tried to seduce Peter of Aragon as soon as the king arrived in Messina (Bartholomaeo de Neocastro cap. 50, *RIS²* 13.3, 39).

211   For this assessment see Bartholomaeo de Neocastro cap. 41, *RIS²* 13.3, 27, where Alaimo is reported as having snatched the keys of Messina back from the hands of the papal legate when he learned that the only thing the legate had on offer was unconditional submission to Charles of Anjou, saying that 'it is better for all of us to die in battle than to be advised to return to our hated enemies' (*Melius est, quod omnes in proelio moriamur, quam ad invisos hostes redeamus admoniti*).

and assuring him of the support of all Sicilians[212]. This time, Peter of Aragon did not hesitate. His barons were now inclined to support his Sicilian expedition, horrified by the extensive report on the tyrannical misgovernment of Charles of Anjou produced by the Sicilian ambassadors at Alcol[213]. On 30 or 31 August 1282 Peter of Aragon and his army landed at the port of Trapani, on the western extremity of Sicily[214].

Charles of Anjou loses Sicily

On 4 September 1282 Peter of Aragon entered Palermo, travelling overland from Trapani[215]. It was from there that he sent two ambassadors, Pedro de Queralt and Rodrigo Ximenes de Luna, to Charles of Anjou on 13 September. They carried a letter from Peter to Charles informing the latter that he had come to Sicily vindicating the right of his wife and sons to the kingdom of Sicily at the express request of the Sicilians who had complained to him about Charles' misgovernment inviting him to come to their rescue[216]. Peter had ordered the Sicilian cities to send

---

212   According to Muntaner (*Crònica* cap. 54 and 57, Buchon, 262-263 and 264-265), there were two Sicilian missions to Peter of Aragon at Alcol asking him to come to Sicily. A first mission by Nicolas Coppola from Palermo, arriving at Alcol early in July, shortly after Peter had landed there (see *supra* p. 546, fnt. 204). It is the ambassy referred to in a letter from Peter III to Edward I informing the king of England about his decision to invade Sicily, dated on 19 July 1282 from Alcol, in Rymer, I.2, 206: 'And when we were resisting the enemies of the faith, as was our plan if it would have pleased the pope, envoys of some towns and cities of the kingdom of Sicily approached us beseeching us to come to that kingdom since all Sicilians unanimously called upon us to be their Lord' (*Cumque nos resisteremus inimicis fidei, ut nostrum erat propositum si dicto summo Pontifici complaceret, venerunt ad nos nuncii quorundam locorum et civitatum Regni Siciliae, exponentes nobis et supplicantes quod ad Regnum ipsum accederemus, quia omnes Siculi unanimes et concordes nos in eorum Dominum invocabant*). A second mission, repeating the invitation, but this time also supported by the citizens of Messina, occurred early in August 1282, after Charles of Anjou had started the siege of Messina. This is the Sicilian ambassy referred to by Bernat Desclot cap. 88 (Buchon, 632-634); Bartholomaeo de Neocastro cap. 44, *RIS²* 13.3, 29, and Saba Malaspina 9,6-7, MGH *SS* 35, 315-316.
213   According to Bernat Desclot cap. 88 (Buchon, 633), the Sicilians produced a document, listing all crimes and offences committed by Charles of Anjou and his officials against the people of Sicily. It was read at Alcol by 'a man learned in the law' (*hom savi en lley*). As we know from Bartholomaeo de Neocastro (cap. 44, *RIS²* 13.3, 29) there was indeed a law professor (*iuris civilis professor*) among the envoys from Messina, Franciscus Longobardus. He may well have composed the indictment against Charles of Anjou read at Alcol.
214   Bartholomaeo de Neocastro cap. 45, *RIS²* 13.3, 30: '*Penultimo Augusti ... applicat in Trapanum*'. *Annales Ianuenses* (Jacobus Aurea) ad ann. 1282, MGH *SS* 18, 294: '*Trapenam perrexit, ibique applicuit die ultima Augusti*'.
215   According to Peter himself in the summons directed at the cities of Sicily to send two representatives each of them to do homage to him as king of Sicily, dated on 10 September, in Carini, *Documenti* no 10, 9-10. He already styles himself in this summons as 'king of Sicily'.
216   Peter's letter has survived. It is printed in Wieruszowski, *Politics and Culture in Medieval Spain*, Rome 1971, 307: 'When we came to Barbary to fight the Saracenes, we sent our envoys to the Roman *curia* with some requests that were not granted to us and so we came to Sicily, having heard the Sicilians complain that you oppress and attack them like an enemy which is why they have implored our help. And since we do not want to let them down and cannot

their troops for the relief of Messina to Randazzo, north of the Etna, to be joined there by his own army[217]. When he arrived at the appointed rendezvous, Charles of Anjou had already raised the siege of Messina on 26 September 1282 and had retreated to Reggio on the mainland[218]. Peter of Aragon triumphantly entered Messina on 2 October 1283[219]. He had conquered the island of Sicily without a single battle.

Charles of Anjou will not have realized it at the time, but he had lost Sicily for the house of Anjou once and for all[220]. It is for this reason that it is here that our dealings with the Sicilian kingdom must also come to an end. The great kingdom created by Roger II of Hauteville and Pope Innocent II in 1139[221] had ceased to exist. What was left of

---

do so on account of our wife and sons to whom it is well known that the kingdom of Sicily rightfully belongs by inheritance, we demand that you desist from these injustices and molestations' (*Cum venisemus* [sic] *ad partes Barbarie ad impugnandum Saracenos, misimus nuncios nostros ad Romanam curiam cum quibusdam nostris peticionibus, qua non potuimus optinere, et propterea in Siciliam venimus audientes Siculos querulantes, quod vos gravati eos et hostiliter impugnatis, unde nostrum auxilium implorarunt. Et quia nolumus eis difficere nec possumus propter uxorem nostram et filios nostros, ad quos regnum Sicilie hereditatis iure dignoscitur pertinere, vos rogamus quatenus ab huiusmodi iniuriis et molestiis desistatis*). For the resemblance of this letter to Peter's earlier letter to King Edward I see *supra* fnt. 202 and 212. Saba Malaspina must have seen this letter since he gives a fairly good (but rather verbose) summary of it in 9,12, MGH *SS* 35, 322. The credentials for Peter's two envoys to Charles are in Carini, *Documenti* no 2, 3.
217 Carini, *Documenti* no 10, 9-10. The foot-soldiers in Peter's army mainly consisted of so-called 'Almogavars', savage mercenary frontiersmen from the Iberian peninsula. They were available for hire in the fourteenth century as the notorious 'Catalan Company'. The historian Ramon Muntaner was one of the commanders. Their descendants formed the nucleus of the indomitable 'Tercios' in the armies of Charles V.
218 The date of the end of the siege of Messina reported in the *Annales Ianuenses* (Jacobus Aurea) ad ann. 1282, MGH *SS* 18, 294, is confirmed by the itinerary of Charles of Anjou, Minieri-Riccio, *Itinerario di Carlo I. di Angiò*, Naples 1872, 18.
219 *Annales Ianuenses* (Jacobus Aurea) ad ann. 1282, MGH *SS* 18, 294: '*ipse autem rex Petrus intravit civitatem Messane die secunda Octobris*'.
220 Why did Charles of Anjou decide to retreat to the mainland without offering battle to Peter of Aragon? It seems a typical question raised by hindsight since we now know that Charles lost the island of Sicily for good, but it might not have looked that way at the time. Nevertheless, the question was already raised by contemporary historians: see Muntaner, *Crònica* cap. 66 (Buchon, 269). Our main sources, Saba Malaspina (9,15-16, MGH *SS* 35, 323-326) and Bartholomaeo de Neocastro (cap. 46, *RIS²* 13.3, 30-32), report that Charles and his advisors seriously deliberated on the strategy to be followed after the arrival of Peter of Aragon and his imminent advent on the battle scene near Messina. Charles of Anjou may have been a very cruel man, but, unlike so many cruel men, he was not a coward. He had been laying in siege before Messsina for three months now; he ran the risk of being besieged himself by a fresh force coming to the relief of the city; his army was in danger of being cut off from the mainland by the approaching Catalan fleet. It just seemed sound tactics to temporarily retreat to the safety of the mainland and to return later with a new expeditionary army, reinforced by troops from France already on their way (see Guillaume de Nangis, *Gesta Philippi Tertii* ad ann. 1282, *Recueil* 20, 522). Muntaner, an experienced military commander himself (see *supra* fnt. 217), agreed.
221 See *supra* p. 35.

it were two separate 'Sicilian' kingdoms, both of them destined to fall under foreign influence: the island kingdom of Sicily, 'Trinacria' as it was to be called[222], under Aragonese domination and the mainland kingdom of Naples under the influence of France. After Ferdinand II of Aragon (1452-1479-1516), grandfather to Charles V, conquered the mainland kingdom in 1504 and his grandson Charles V inherited his grandfather's great Mediterranean empire in 1516, the kingdom of Sicily was under Spanish rule and administrated by Spanish viceroys residing in Naples. In the end, the strategy of the papacy to invite a foreign prince to Italy to ward off the danger of encirclement of the Papal State by the king of Sicily[223] turned out worse than just counter-productive. It resulted in turning the entire Italian peninsula into a battlefield for the two major powers of early-modern Europe, Spain and France, to the great detriment of Italy and the Italians as Pope Clement VII (1523-1534) was to witness with his own eyes when he watched the terrible sack of Rome of 1527 from the (relative) safety of the Castel Sant'Angelo. Three years later, at Bologna rather than Rome, he was to be the last pope to consecrate and crown a Roman emperor, Charles V, who was to be the last prince to wear the crown of Sicily as well as the imperial crown.

Trial by Battle

Karl Marx famously wrote that history does, indeed, repeat itself, but 'first as tragedy and a second time as farce'[224]. The tragedy of the house of Hohenstaufen did, indeed, have a farcical sequel. The farce was preceded by an introductory comedy. Charles of Anjou challenged Peter of Aragon to decide the Sicilian affair by an ordeal: trial by battle[225]. It was completely out of tune with contemporary legal standards.

---

222   On 31 August 1302, King Frederick III (!) of Sicily, a son of Peter III of Aragon (on him see *infra* p. 576), concluded a peace treaty with Robert of Anjou, a grandson of Charles of Anjou, at Caltabellotta on Sicily, definitively dividing the Sicilian kingdom in two parts: a continental kingdom and the island of Sicily. Since it was too painful that the island king was to style himself as 'king of Sicily', it was agreed that he was to be 'king of Trinacria' instead, being the name of a mythological 'three cornered' island near Scylla and Charybdis, mentioned in Vergil's *Aeneid*.
223   For this strategy see *supra* p. 450.
224   *Der 18te Brumaire des Louis Napoleon*, in Marx-Engels, *Gesamtausgabe* Abt. I, vol. 11, Berlin 1985, 96: 'das eine Mal als große Tragödie, das andere Mal als lumpige Farce'.
225   For the following see Saba Malaspina 9, 24-25 and 10, 6-9, MGH *SS* 35, 333-335 and 348-351; Desclot cap. 104 (Buchon, 648-652); Muntaner, *Crònica* cap. 72-73 and 87-91 (Buchon, 275-277 and 292-300) and Bartholomaeo de Neocastro, cap. 68, *RIS²* 13.3, 51-52. The 'duel' between Peter of Aragon and Charles of Anjou caused a sensation at the time and was consequently widely publicized. See, for example, *Annales Ianuenses* (Jacobus Aurea) ad ann. 1283, MGH *SS* 18, 299 and *Annales Placentini Gibellini* ad ann. 1283, MGH *SS* 18, 575-576.

Trial by battle had been proscribed by canon law long ago[226]. Frederick II had banned it in the kingdom of Sicily[227] and so had Louis IX in his royal domain[228]. No wonder, therefore, that Pope Martin IV forbade Charles of Anjou to proceed with that 'ill-advised plan' (*inconsulte actum*)[229]. It was to no avail since, unfortunately, Peter of Aragon had accepted the challenge. Because there was a considerable difference of age between the contenders – Charles of Anjou was fifty-five at the time and Peter of Aragon was forty-two – it was agreed that each party was to be assisted by one hundred knights. King Edward I of England had provided a suitable neutral venue for the ordeal, a site near the city of Bordeaux in his French domain of Gascony. It was a very embarrassing affair for all the parties concerned since neither party seriously contemplated to decide the future of Sicily by the uncertain outcome of a single battle. Consequently, the matter had to be called off, but in a way that allowed either party to save face[230]. As luck had it, a date had been set for the battle (1 June 1283)[231], but not the time, allowing Peter of Aragon to arrive early in the morning finding no one to meet him in battle there. He left the place, claiming victory, as did Charles of Anjou, who arrived later on in the day also finding no one to oppose him[232]. After this charade was over, a more deadly farce was to develop.

Peter of Aragon had been excommunicated by operation of law on entering the kingdom of Sicily in defiance of the papal bull of 7 May 1282 strictly forbidding all foreign potentates, 'to molest, attack, or

Peter of Aragon excommunicated and deposed

---

226 *Decretum* C. 2, q. 4, cap. 22 (Nicholas I) and X. 3,50,9 (Innocent III).
227 *LA* 2, 32 and 33.
228 P. Violet, *Les Établissements de Saint Louis* 1, Paris 1881, 487-488.
229 See Pope Martin's letter to Charles of Anjou in Lünig, *Codex Italiae Diplomaticus* II, Frankfurt/Leipzig 1726, no 57, col. 1013.
230 Pope Martin IV had also sent a letter to the king of England to prevent the ordeal of Bordeaux. It is in Rymer, I.2, 219-220. See *infra* fnt. 231.
231 The deed (dated on 30 December 1282) containing the very detailed covenant of Charles of Anjou and Peter of Aragon to meet each other in battle at Bordeaux has survived. It is in Carini, *Documenti* App. no 7 and 8, 681-688 and 689-696. As was usual, it was made up in twofold, one copy for each of the contracting parties: see *supra* p. 530 and fnt. 142. Since king Edward I acted as mediator in this matter, both copies are also in Rymer, I.2, 213-215.
232 It must have been Edward I who devised a means to prevent the ordeal. Edward I and Peter of Aragon were on good terms at the time, as their correspondence illustrates. They had even arranged a marriage between Peter's son and heir Alfonso and Edward's daughter Eleanor. Edward's seneschal at Bordeaux was Jean de Grailly, one of the many Savoyards coming to England in the retinue of Queen Eleanor, King Edward's mother (see *supra* p. 363). De Grailly was a confidant of Edward I and the king often employed him on delicate diplomatic missions as this one certainly was. According to all our sources (*supra* fnt. 225), De Grailly advised Peter of Aragon, who had arrived in the neighbourhood of Bordeaux incognito on the eve of the ordeal, to leave the region as quickly as possible since he could not guarantee his personal safety. After having entered the lists first on the morning of 1 June, Peter, heeding the advice, immediately absconded.

disturb' the kingdom of Sicily on pain of instant excommunication[233]. Consequently, Martin IV pronounced on 18 November 1282 that the king of Aragon would forfeit his kingdom, a papal fief, if he had not repented by submitting himself to the will of the pope and left the island of Sicily by 2 February next[234]. Peter did not comply. To the contrary: in April 1283 his wife Constance, Manfred's heir, came to Sicily from Catalonia with her sons and John of Procida[235]. She received a warm welcome at Palermo, where she was hailed as queen of Sicily. Constance, a native Sicilian, was to take over control of the island while her husband went abroad for his 'duel' with Charles of Anjou. When Peter arrived at Bordeaux on the eve of 1 June 1283, the pope had already formally deprived him of his kingdom and announced that all good Catholics were allowed to take possession of it, subject, of course, to his title as overlord of the kingdom of Aragon[236]. Like Frederick II after his deposition in 1245, Peter of Aragon was now an outlaw, which is why he had been travelling to Bordeaux incognito. Back in Aragon, Peter had to prepare for a French invasion of his kingdom, leaving the

---

233 See *supra* p. 544.

234 The full text of Martin IV's bull is in Olivier-Martin, *Les registres de Martin IV*, Paris 1901, no 276, 107-114. It is a tediously long-winded document, full of repetitions and citations from his previous bull of 7 May 1282 (*supra* p. 544), including an amended concise history of Sicily from the deposition of Frederick II onwards. The excommunication of the Byzantine Emperor Michael VIII was confirmed on the same day (*Les registres de Martin IV*, Paris 1901, no 278, 115-116). Michael did not care: he had achieved all his objectives. Another person to be censured on that day was, interestingly, Corrado of Antioch, a grandson of Frederick II (see *supra* p. 482). He was among the Italians conspiring with Peter of Aragon (see *supra* p. 536) and harrassing the north of the Sicilian kingdom from his stronghold Saracinesco: Saba Malaspina 10,28, ed. Koller/Nitschke, MGH *SS* 35, 370-371. For his censure see *Les registres de Martin IV*, Paris 1901, no 277, 114-115.

235 Saba Malaspina 10,3, MGH *SS* 35, 345: '*uxor dicti Petri, filia quondam Manfredi, cum duobus suis filiis magistro Johanne de Procita comitata Panormum venerat*'; Bartholomaeo de Neocastro, cap. 62, *RIS²* 13.3, 48: '*sancto die Veneris vicesimo secundo eiusdem post orta sidera regina cum prole conspicua Messanam applicuit*'. See further Muntaner, cap.96 and 97 (Buchon, 305-306); Desclot cap. 103 (Buchon, 648) and *Anonymi Chronicon Siculum* cap. 42 (Gregorio, *Biblioteca* 2, 157).

236 The bull of 21 March 1283 is in *Les registres de Martin IV*, Paris 1901, no 310, 129-131: 'And therefore, exposing the kingdom of Aragon and the other territories of that king with the consent of our brethren, it follows that we deprive King Peter by way of sentence, as justice requires, of that kingdom and those territories and of his royal title, and, having deprived him of that, we release that kingdom and those territories to Catholics to take possession of it and someone will be put in charge of it, subject to the title of Rome, as the Apostolic See will deem to provide' (*Et ideo regnum Aragoniae, ceterasque terras regis ipsius, de fratrum nostrorum consilio exponentes, ut sequitur, ipsum Petrum regem Aragonum eisdem regno et terris, regioque honore, sententialiter, justitia exigente, privamus: et privantes, exponimus eadem regnum et terras occupanda catholicis, de quibus, et prout sedes apostolica duxerit providendum, in dictis regno et terries eiusdem, Romano ut praemittitur jure salvo*).

Sicilian affair to his wife, his son James, and John of Procida, now Chancellor of the Sicilian kingdom[237].

Like his predecessor Clement IV, Pope Martin IV had found another French prince, even another Charles, to serve as substitute for a king who had become a nuisance. This was Charles of Valois (1270-1325), a younger son of King Philip III, who was to replace Peter of Aragon. On 27 August 1283 the pope instructed Cardinal Jean Cholet, who was in France at the time[238], to close the negotiations with the court of France on the succession to the throne of Aragon on the terms dictated by the pope[239]. Unlike his father, who had only reluctantly supported the cause of his brother Charles of Anjou[240], Philip III was eager to cooperate and accepted the crown of Aragon on behalf of his son Charles of Valois, only thirteen years old at the time. As Philip's mother had anticipated long ago[241], her impressionable son was now completely under the spell of his imposing uncle Charles of Anjou, who was with him at the time. Margaret de Provence, the old queen dowager, must have been furious, but there was nothing she could do since the papal legate in France, Cardinal Cholet, was preaching a crusade against Aragon and her son and many French nobles were taking the cross to wage holy war on Peter of Aragon[242]. She may not have been the only one having

The Aragonese crusade

---

237 The letter of appointment, dated on 4 May 1283 in Trapani, just before Peter's departure from Sicily, is in Carini, *Documenti* no 722, 640. It is important to emphasize that John of Procida was from the mainland of the Sicilian kingdom and consequently *not* a native Sicilian which accounts for the mounting unrest among the native Sicilian nobility, about to break out into open rebellion against the new regime. On this mutiny and its suppression see Bartholomaeo de Neocastro cap. 64-65 and 75, *RIS²* 13.3, 49-50 and 55. Prominent among the rebels was Gualtieri di Caltagirone, one of the original anti-Angevine Sicilian conspirators (see *supra* p. 542). He was tried by his former co-conspirator, now Chief Justice of Sicily, Alaimo di Lentini, and sentenced to death by decapitation on 22 May 1283.

238 Cardinal Cholet had been dispatched to France as papal legate on 9 April 1283 'on urgent business' (*pro urgentibus negotiis*): *Les registres de Martin IV*, Paris 1913, no 450, 185-186. The 'urgent business' was, of course, the preparation of a crusade against Aragon. The cardinal was travelling to France in the company of Charles of Anjou, who was on his way to meet Peter of Aragon at Bordeaux (Guillaume de Nangis, *Gesta Philippi Tertii* ad ann. 1282, *Recueil* 20, 522).

239 The full text of the instruction of Cardinal Cholet is in Rymer, I.2, 223-225. The reason why it survives in English archives is due to the fact that Cholet was also instructed by the pope to prevent the king of England to facilitate the Bordeaux ordeal (see *supra* p. 551, fnt. 230). After the demise of Louis IX of France, Edward I of England was the leading European monarch and much in demand as a mediator. There is a report of the negotiations between the court of France and Cardinal Cholet, compiled by the cardinal himself, in Rymer, I.2, 229-230.

240 See *supra* p. 441.

241 See *supra* p. 442.

242 Guillaume de Nangis, *Gesta Philippi Tertii* ad ann. 1283, *Recueil* 20, 524: 'Around Christmas of the same year, Philip, the king of France, accepted the kingdom of Aragon of-

reservations. It is reported that none other than the heir to the throne of France, Philip, warned that defeating his uncle Peter might not be as easy as Cardinal Cholet contended[243]. If he did so, he was right.

Peter III realized that his monarchy, even his life, was at stake in the coming war with France. His subjects, especially the magnates (*ricos hombres*) among them, were well aware of that too. They had been taken by surprise when the 'crusade' to the Barbary Coast had suddenly turned into a war of conquest of another country against another Christian king[244]. Now that they were requested to support their king again in yet another war directly resulting from that unadvertised Sicilian enterprise, there was a high price to pay for their continuing loyalty. On 3 October 1283 Peter held a parliament (*cortes*) at Zaragoza consisting of the three estates of the kingdom, clergy, nobility, and representatives of the cities. It was only after he (reluctantly) had given in to the constitutional demands of the estates, confirming the freedom of Aragon by swearing to uphold the good 'customs, usages, freedoms, and privileges' (*fueros, costumbres, usos, franquezas, libertades, y privilegios*) in his famous 'Privilegio General', that the king was able to rally the nations of his realm behind him[245].

---

fered to him by the Church on behalf of his son Charles. And he was granted the right to levy tithes on clerical revenues for his expedition to conquer the said kingdom of Aragon. Cardinal Jean Cholet of the Roman *curia* was also preaching a crusade to attack the convicted Peter of Aragon. And then, after the king of France took the cross, many nobles and commoners also took the cross for this expedition' (*Eodem anno posterius annotato Philippus rex Franciae circa natale Domini ... regnum Aragoniae oblatum sibi pro filio suo Karolo ab ecclesia tunc recepit. Et concessa fuit sibi ecclesiarum decima, ad expeditionem dicti regni Aragoniae conquirendi. Praedicavit etiam cardinalis Romanae curiae dominus Johannes Coleti de cruce ut irent homines super Petrum Arragoniae condemnatum. Et tunc rege Franciae cruce signato, multi tam nobiles quam ignobiles ad huius expeditionem itineris consimiliter crucis signaculum assumpserunt*).

243   Desclot cap. 136 (Buchon, 680-681). After the untimely demise of his older brother Louis in 1276, Prince Philip was the heir-apparent to the throne of France. He was the second son born to his father from his marriage with Isabella of Aragon, a sister of Peter; Charles of Valois, born in 1270, was the youngest. Isabella died in 1271 and Philip III remarried with Maria of Brabant in 1274. Philip's relation with his stepmother was not good and the young heir to the throne of France may have taken to his grandmother Margaret. There were others close to the king opposed to the expedition as well. The abbot of St Denys, Matthew of Vendôme, requested king Edward of England to interfere and prevent the war: see the letter of Edward I to the abbot in Rymer, I.2, 227-228. Matthew of Vendôme had been regent of France in 1270, when Louis IX was on crusade, and he was the chief advisor of Philip III.

244   For this see *supra* p. 546.

245   The story of the concession of the 'Privilegio General' is in Jeronimo Zurita (1512-1580), *Los cinco libros primeros de la primera parte de los Anales de la Corona de Aragón* Lib. 4, cap. 38, ed. Zaragoza 1562, f. 184 v. - 186 v. The *Anales* of the humanist Zurita, who preferred to use contemporary official documents rather than chronicles, still are a major source for the medieval history of Aragon. Muntaner and Desclot were not interested in constitutional affairs. Zurita was.

In the early summer of 1285, King Philip III had gathered his crusading army and proceeded to the Aragonese border. Philip had secured an alliance with Peter's brother James, the king of Mallorca, who did not want to miss the opportunity to take revenge on his brother for bullying him into submission[246]. Accordingly, the king of France had decided to invade Aragon via the Roussillon, belonging to King James[247]. He opted for a combined strategy, linking his army to a fleet following the army along the Mediterranean coast for reinforcements and to prevent a sudden attack from the sea on his left flank. After a festive reception of the king of France by the king of Mallorca at Perpignan, the capital of Roussillon, the first obstacle to the progress of the French army this side of the Pyrenees was the city of Elne, less than 10 miles south of Perpignan. The town had closed the gates to the king of France and was punished accordingly. It was taken by storm, plundered, and pillaged, while al the people inside, men, women, and children, were massacred (end of May 1285)[248], leaving the impression of another Albigensian crusade on the men from Aragon and Catalonia and strengthening rather than weakening their resolve to resist the invaders from France[249].

The death of kings

While still in Messina in April 1283, Peter III had appointed Roger of Lauria, foster brother of his wife Constance[250], as admiral of the Catalan fleet[251]. It was a happy choice since Roger turned out to become the greatest naval commander in medieval history. The fleet had not accompanied King Peter back to Catalonia, but stayed in Italian waters for the time being, harassing the coasts of the Campania and Calabria and conquering the island of Malta in the process (June 1283). On the first days of June 1284 the admiral and his fleet were blockading the bay of Naples, trying to lure the fleet of the regent whom Charles of Anjou had installed there during his absence in France, his son Charles of Salerno, out into the open. Neither the prince of Salerno, nor his military commanders had any experience in naval warfare, but they

---

246   See *supra* p. 537. For the treason of King James of Mallorca see Guillaume de Nangis, *Gesta Philippi Tertii* ad ann. 1285, *Recueil* 20, 528-529; Desclot cap. 134 (Buchon, 673) and Muntaner, cap. 119 (Buchon, 332).

247   See *supra* p. 533, fnt. 161.

248   Guillaume de Nangis, *Gesta Philippi Tertii* ad ann. 1285, *Recueil* 20, 530-531; Desclot cap. 141 (Buchon, 690-692) and Muntaner, cap. 121 (Buchon, 334-335).

249   The memory of the horrors of the Albigensian crusade must still have been very much alive in Aragon and Catalonia at the time.The king of Aragon had been closely involved in the Albigensian affair, supporting Raymond VI of Toulouse against the French crusaders led by Simon of Montfort. Peter's grandfather, Peter II, had fallen in action in the battle of Muret in 1213: see *supra* p. 207, fnt. 35.

250   See *supra* p. 533.

251   The letter of appointment, dated on 20 April 1283 in Messina, is in Carini, *Documenti* no 690, 617-618.

decided to attack the Catalan fleet nevertheless, despite an express order of Charles of Anjou not to engage in any major battle during his absence and against the advise of the papal legate, Cardinal Gerardo Bianchi from Parma, who was in Naples at the time[252]. The result was catastrophic: the fleet from Naples was completely routed and Charles of Salerno himself as well as many Angevine nobles were taken to Messina as prisoners of war[253]. The heir to the throne of Angevine Sicily was now in secure Aragonese captivity, a priceless asset in coming negotiations[254], provided that Peter of Aragon survived the crusade unleashed against him. Roger of Lauria was to see to it that Peter did.

Philip III and his French crusading army had managed to circumvent the passes over the Pyrenees blocked by Peter's army and entered the plain around the city of Gerona on 27 June 1285. The siege of that city lasted all summer and by the time it finally surrendered, on 7 September, Philip had lost the war. His army was heavily dependent on supplies from his fleet, but Gerona was some 20 miles from the coast and the supply lines were constantly harassed by Peter's formidable Almogavar guerrilleros while the French fleet was under constant pressure from a naval force commanded by the Catalan merchants and privateers Ramon Marquet and Béranger Mayol. It was the first time in European military history that naval supremacy proved decisive in a major military conflict. Late in August 1285 Peter's admiral Roger of Lauria arrived near the Catalan coast with his fleet and in the night of 3 to 4 September he fell on the combined French fleet near the Formigues islands, close to Palamós, like a hawk on a rabbit. The French fleet,

---

252 According to Tholomaeus of Lucca, *Historia ecclesiastica nova* 24,9, ed. Muratori 11, col. 1189, the papal legate was so angry at the decision of the prince-regent that he ordered a notary to record his protest.

253 On the battle in the bay of Naples see Desclot cap. 121-127 (Buchon, 664-667); Saba Malaspina 10,13-15, MGH *SS* 35, 354-359; Guillaume de Nangis, *Gesta Philippi Tertii* ad ann. 1283, *Recueil* 20, 526-527, and Bartholomaeo de Neocastro, cap. 76-77, *RIS²* 13.3, 55-58. Immediately after the battle, a message from the victorious admiral was conveyed to Mary of Hungary, the wife of Charles of Salerno, summoning her to surrender the Princess Beatrix, Manfred's daughter (see *supra* p. 463, fnt. 214) forthwith, threatening to decapitate her husband if she failed to comply. Beatrix was released accordingly, after almost twenty years of incarceration, and was reunited with her half-sister Constance at Messina: Saba Malaspina 10,16, MGH *SS* 35, 359-360. The sensational naval victory of Roger of Lauria was reported by many contemporary sources: see, for example, *Annales Placentini Gibellini* ad ann. 1284, MGH *SS* 18, 578 and *Annales Ianuenses* (Jacobus Aurea) ad ann. 1284, MGH *SS* 18, 310.

254 The prince of Salerno was released from captivity only in 1288, three years after his father Charles of Anjou had died, thanks to the mediation of King Edward I of England. He had to leave three of his sons behind in Catalonia as hostages. The boys were only released in 1295, after a (temporary) peace agreement was brokered by Pope Boniface VIII in Anagni. It was at this occasion that the pope 'restored' the kingdom of Aragon to Peter's son James II (1291-1327). See on this treaty also *infra* p. 576, fnt. 76.

King Philip's lifeline, was completely routed[255] and the king is said to have been so shocked by the news of this irreparable loss that he fell seriously ill[256]. The fall of Gerona, three days later, was worse than a Pyrrhic victory since the French crusading army was about to disintegrate: the men were starving, sick, or dying, the king among them. Retreat was the only ignominious option, making the Aragonese crusade one of the greatest disasters in French military history. Philip III did not make it back into his kingdom alive. He died in Perpignan on 5 October 1285. Peter of Aragon had survived the crusade unleashed against him and his dynasty was saved, but he was not to enjoy the benefits of his triumph for long.

At the end of 1285 all the key actors in the aftermath to the extermination of the house of Hohenstaufen had expired: Michael VIII Palaeologus had already passed on in December 1282; Alfonso of Castile had died in 1284[257]; Charles of Anjou[258], Pope Martin IV[259], Philip III of France, and Peter of Aragon all died in 1285[260]. In France a young king ascended the throne, Philip IV (1268-1285-1314), *le roi de fer*. Like Frederick II, he was that rare phenomenon on a royal throne in medieval Europe: an adolescent of extraordinary intelligence, grown up to be a man before his time. He had watched and learned while his guileless father had allowed himself to be used as an instrument of papal and Angevine policies that were not in France's direct interest. The young king was determined not to repeat that mistake.

---

255   For the exploits of Marquet and Mayol see Desclot cap. 158 (Buchon, 714-715) and Muntaner cap. 130, (Buchon, 345-348). For the naval battle near the Formigues islands see Desclot cap. 166 (Buchon, 723-727) and Muntaner cap. 135-136 (Buchon, 353-355).

256   Desclot cap. 167 (Buchon, 727): 'When the king of France had heard and understood what has just been told, that his fleet had been lost and destroyed, he took to his bed for grief and despair' (Quant lo rey de Franca hac oyt e entes, segon que d'amunt es dit, que la sua armada era desbaratada e destroida, per dolor e fellonia gitas all llit).

257   Death must have come as a relief to Alfonso since he had practically been deposed by his son Sancho in 1282. He complained to Pope Martin, but only received a consoling response from that pontiff advising him 'to confide in God': Martène-Durand, *Veterum scriptorum et monumentorum ... amplissima collectio* Tom. II, Paris 1724, col. 1291-1292.

258   Charles of Anjou died on 7 January 1285. He had provided in his last will (details in Léonard, *Les Angevins de Naples*, 159-160) that his nephew Robert II of Artois, a son of his deceased brother Robert (see *supra* p. 410), was to act as regent of the kingdom during the absence of his son and heir Charles of Salerno.

259   Martin IV died on 28 March 1285 in Perugia; he was succeeded by Cardinal Giacomo Savelli, a native Roman who chose the name Honorius, fourth of that name (1285-1287).

260   Peter III survived Philip III for just a few weeks: he died in November 1285. He was succeeded as king of Aragon and Valencia and count of Barcelona by his eldest son Alfonso III (1285-1291). His younger son James was to succeed to the crown of Sicily: see *infra* p. 576.

Epilogue

The Comfort of Liberty

Having reached the end of this story, there remains one question to be answered: What does it mean? Is it all just 'sound and fury, signifying nothing'[1] or is there more to it?

Medieval Totalitarianism

The struggle between the Hohenstaufen princes and the papacy was more than a geopolitical conflict since it was also a struggle between two competing but equally totalitarian regimes. The Sicilian policy of Frederick II after his return from Germany in 1220 was dominated by his wish to restore royal power in his Sicilian kingdom as it had been in 'the good old days of King William II'[2], meaning royal power as it had been explained to him by the people instructing him in his early days on the constitution of the kingdom, Bishop Walter of Pagliara most prominent among them. They must have informed the young prince that the king of Sicily was head of the Sicilian Church ever since the days of his great-grandfather Roger I, because the king of Sicily *and his heirs* had been granted legatine powers by Pope Urban II in the Treaty of Salerno (5 July 1098)[3]. After the demise of 'good King William', succeeding popes had encroached successfully upon these powers, until they had practically all been suppressed by Pope Innocent III in his concordat with Frederick's mother Constance[4]. Frederick never accepted this. He wanted to re-establish complete control over the Sicilian Church after 1220. His second excommunication and his conviction on charges of 'contempt of keys' (*contemptus clavium*) at Lyon in 1245 were inspired by these attempts to bring back the Church of Sicily under royal control and establish 'absolute sovereignty' (*plenitudo potestatis*) over the state *and* the Church, just like the Greek emperors of the Byzantine Empire exercised as a matter of course. In a letter to the Byzantine Emperor Joannes Vatatzes Frederick II emphasized that 'the abuse of

---

1 Shakespeare, *Macbeth* Act 5, scene 5.
2 See *supra* p. 221.
3 See *supra* p. 101, fnt. 2.
4 See *supra* p. 188.

a destructive freedom' (*pestifere libertatis abusus*) by popes conspiring against kings and princes was a phenomenon typical of the West of Europe. '*Happy, therefore, are the rulers of the Orient who do not have to fear the schemes of popes*'[5]. This is as close as Frederick II ever came to a public denunciation of the doctrine of 'liberty of the Church' (*libertas ecclesiae*), the central theme of ecclesiastical policy (and canon law) in the West ever since the days of Gregory VII[6]. As far as Frederick was concerned, the Church was to be an institution of the state, rather than an organization independent of, let alone superior to, the state[7]. 'Freedom of the Church', meaning immunity from state control, was as repugnant to him as the 'elusive liberty' (*vaga libertas*) claimed by the Lombard cities[8]. Frederick II was not an enemy of 'freedom', an elusive concept indeed, but his notion of 'freedom' was defined along the lines of Roman law. It was obedience to the law that made men free[9] and he himself was, as he had so eloquently contended in his code, the father and the son as well as the master and the servant of the law[10], making Frederick's Sicilian kingdom a totalitarian state, based on the central tenet of late Roman public law that 'what pleases the emperor, has force of law' on the one hand and the divine origin of royal authority on the other[11]. Consequently, any resistance to the king amounted to an act

---

5   HB 6.2, 684-686(685-686) (end of 1248): '*pestifere libertatis abusum ambiunt … Hec autem tantum apud Occidentalem plagam et in Europa nostra potissime committuntur. O felix Asia, o felices orientalium potestates que … adinventiones pontificum non verentur*'.

6   See *supra* p. 30.

7   In the early history of the Church, shortly after Constantine had issued his toleration edict, this was a proposition shared by contemporary Christian authorities who still needed the authority of the state, the Roman emperor (Constantine), to eliminate dissenters. See Optatus (4th century), an African bishop, *De schismate Donatistorum* 3,3, ed. Ziwsa, *CSEL* 26, Vienna 1893, 74: 'the state is not within the Church, but the Church is part of the state, that is of the Roman Empire' (*non enim respublica est in ecclesia, sed ecclesia in republica, id est in imperio Romano*).

8   See *supra* p. 273.

9   For this see Cicero, *Pro Cluentio* 53, 146: 'The magistrates are the servants of the law, the judges are the interpreters of the law, and therefore we are all the slaves of the law, so that we may be free' (*Legum ministri magistratus, legum interpretes iudices, legum denique idcirco omnes servi sumus, ut liberi esse possimus*).

10   See *supra* p. 257.

11   Frederick had summarized his position in one of his public reactions to the sentence of deposition of the council of Lyon, a sentence he considered to be 'presumptuous and pretentious, since a Roman emperor, the imperial lord and master of majesty, is convicted of *lèse majesté*, thus ridiculously subjecting a man to the law who is, by his majesty, above all law, a man who cannot be disciplined with secular punishment by any man but only by God, since he has no secular superior' (MGH *Const.* 2, no 262, 365: '*Apparet nichilominus animosa nimis et ampullosa non minus ex ipsius inflicte pene severitate sententia, per quam imperator Romanus, imperialis rector et dominus maiestatis, lese maiestatis dicitur crimine condempnatus, per quam ridiculose subicitur legi qui legibus omnibus imperialiter est solutus, de quo temporales pene sumende, cum temporalem hominem superiorem non habeat, non sunt in homine, sed in Deo*').

of heresy *ex hypothesi*. 'True' freedom, therefore, consisted of complete submission to the will of the monarch, God's gift to mankind as the sole guarantor of peace and justice (*pax et justitia*)[12]. It was the kind of 'freedom' that jeopardized the 'public freedom' (*publica libertas*) of the subjects of the Sicilian tyrant, as Gregory IX had asserted so forcefully[13], thus making the pope the protagonist of the 'public freedom' of all Italians, if not of all Christian mankind. It was incumbent on the Church to resist all claims by secular authorities to absolute sovereignty over their subjects, if only to retain the Church's totalitarian hold over their subjects. Frederick II was deposed at Lyon for reducing his Sicilian subjects to 'a quasi-servile condition' (*sub servili quasi conditione*)[14] and as soon as the emperor had been deposed, Innocent IV congratulated the Sicilians that they had been delivered from the oppression of 'another Nero' (*alter Nero*) and were now about to enjoy 'the comfort of liberty' (*solatia libertatis*)[15]. Innocent IV was a lawyer and a scion of the proud city of Genoa and consequently he knew what the essence of 'public freedom' was to the Italian cities: their autonomy, their 'freedoms, privileges, and laudable customs and usages' (*libertates et immunitates, usus et laudabiles consuetudines*). It was the first thing he 'restored' to the cities of South Italy during the short spell in which he had effective control there[16]. Frederick II had conceded no autonomy to the cities of his Sicilian kingdom[17], whereas it was during his reign as king of Italy that the rebel cities of the Lombard League defied their monarch by codifying their local law, Milan in 1215, Genoa in 1229, and Bologna in 1245.[18] It was a development strongly supported by

---

12 Of course, this is not the concept of freedom Cicero would have subscribed to, since according to him (*De re publica* 1,39) 'the state is the affair of the people' (*res publica res populi*) based on consensus on the law (*iuris consensus*) as established by the people in its public assemblies. Although Cicero's treatise *De re publica* was lost in the Middle Ages, his famous definition of the state as a partnership (*communio*) of free citizens partaking in the legislative and electoral process was well-known in the Middle Ages since it was cited by St Augustine in *De civitate dei* 2,21.

13 See *supra* p. 260.

14 See *supra* p. 378 and for a similar accusation against Manfred p. 446.

15 MGH *Epp. saec. xiii* 2, no 168, 127.

16 See *supra* p. 428.

17 See *supra* p. 223.

18 The Milanese code of local law still presented itself as *Liber* consuetudinum *Mediolani*, that is 'The Book of Milanese *Customs*'. It was modelled on Justinian's *Institutes*, even adding a *Prooemium* from which we learn that it was compiled at the initiative of Brunazio Porcha, *podestà* of Milan in 1215, who ordered the *podestà* succeeding him to 'collect all customs henceforward to obtain in this city in one volume, so that no customs are to be cited from another source but the ones inserted in that volume' (*ut universae Consuetudines, quae in hac Civitate de coetero servarentur ... in unum redigeret ... ut non aliunde Consuetudines inducerentur nisi quae in illo volumine fuissent inventae* (Fr. Berlan (ed.), *Liber consuetudinum Mediolani anni MCCXVI*, Milan 1868, 3)). The later codification of Bologna already has the rubric 'These are

the teachers of civil law, prominently among them the learned *doctor* Hugolinus de Presbyteris ('Ugolino', † *c.* 1233), a citizen of Bologna and an important man in his native town[19].

The early medieval teachers of Roman law, such as Irnerius and Placentinus, supported the imperial legislative doctrine still adhered to by Frederick II: legislative authority rested with the emperor exclusively after the people of Rome had transferred their legislative authority to the emperor by the 'royal law' (*lex regia*) passed on his accession (Inst. 1,2,6; D. 1,4,1 pr.)[20]. This contention became politically untenable in Bologna after that city had joined the Lombard League and became the centre of anti-imperial policy in the Romagna[21]. Ugolino completely demolished the constitutional basis of the imperial theory as advanced by Irnerius, Placentinus, and others. What the *lex regia* had been about was *not* a transfer of legislative powers in a *proprietary* sense, as in the transfer of title to goods or land[22], but a *contractual* delegation of legislative authority by the people to the emperor as its representative (*quasi procuratorem ad hoc*)[23]. By stressing the contractual nature of the

---

the *by-laws* of the people of Bologna' (*Haec sunt* statuta *populi Bononie* (L. Frati (ed.), *Statuti di Bologna dall'anno 1245 all'anno 1267*, Bologna 1869, 5)). The first by-laws of Genoa were composed by the famous civilian (and teacher of Innocent IV) Jacobus Balduinus, who was 'podestà' of Genoa in 1229: *Annales Ianuenses* (Bartolomo scriba) ad ann. 1229, MGH *SS* 18, 173.

19   On Hugolinus see *supra* p. 177, fnt. 46.

20   Gloss of Irnerius on D. 1,3,32, cited by Carolus de Tocco († *c.* 1207) in his gloss 'Deest' on *Lombarda* 2,41(42) (*De consuetudine*),1), ed. Venice 1537, *f.* 181 vo and identified by Savigny in Ms. Par. Lat. 4451 (*Geschichte* 4,459): 'This text speaks according to its own time, when the people still had the authority to issue laws and consequently a statute became obsolete by custom with the tacit approval of all. But since that authority has been transferred to the emperor today, a contrary custom of the people is null and void' (*Loquitur haec lex secundum sua tempora, quibus populus habebat potestatem condendi leges, ideo tacito consensu omnium per consuetudinem abrogabatur. Sed quia hodie potestas translata est in imperatorem, nihil faceret desuetudo populi*). Placentinus, cited by Accursius in the Gl. 'Aut rationem' on C. 8,52(53),2: '*loquitur secundum sua tempora, secundum quae consuetudo erat populi et lex populi et sic una poterat aliam tollere. At hodie principis est facere legem et sic consuetudine populi tolli non debet*'.

21   One of Irnerius' successors, Martinus Gosia († *c.* 1166), who won the favour of Frederick I 'Barbarossa' on the Parliament of Roncaglia in 1158 (see *supra* p. 106), still adhered to Irnerius' imperial doctrine: see the Gl. 'Aut rationem' ad C. 8,52(53),2. He and his family were confirmed Ghibellines and his descendants were consequently banished from Bologna in 1274 (Savigny *Geschichte* 4,133-134).

22   This interpretation is still mentioned in the Accursian gloss, Gl. 'Contulerit' ad Inst. 1,2,6: '"They have transferred", meaning that they have handed over in such a way that the people do not have that right at all' (*Contulerit, id est transtulerit, sic ut ipse populus modo non habeat hoc ius*).

23   Hugolinus, *Distinctio* 148 (*Dissensiones dominorum*, ed. Hänel, Leipzig 1835, 585): 'They certainly have not handed it over so that it did not remain with them, but they have constituted him as their representative for the purpose' (*certe non transtulit sic, ut non remaneret apud eum, sed constituit eum quasi procuratorem ad hoc*). The so-called *Dissensiones dominorum* is a composition of a number of collections dealing with questions of law, mostly related to a

famous *lex regia* a new dimension was added to the ongoing debate
about the relationship between a prince and his subjects: the former
was the representative of the latter, implying that the authority to act in
the name of the people could be withdrawn unilaterally. Similar ideas
had been expressed more than a century earlier on purely philosophical
grounds by a German monk called Manegold of Lautenbach[24], but they
were now connected to very concrete questions of law and the very concrete institutions and rules of Roman law like the contract of agency
(*mandatum*), not only implying that the authority to legislate on behalf
of the people could be withdrawn unilaterally, but also that the authority to legislate still remained with the people itself, since a mandate had
(and has) no 'privative effect', as the civilians say, meaning that it did
not exclude the power of the principal (the citizenry) to still do himself
what he had authorized his agent (the king) to do for him. Accordingly,
the Italian communities were entitled to legislate for themselves, albeit
only within the limits of the jurisdiction of their city, despite the *lex
regia*. It was not a theory developed by a solitary monk and committed
to parchment in the isolated privacy of his cell, but it was widely circulated and publicly instilled in thousands of students in Bologna and in
the other cities of the Italian kingdom where law schools flourished[25].
This was the liberty Frederick II suppressed in his Sicilian kingdom

specific provision in Justinian's *Corpus Iuris* controversial among the early *doctores*. The collections vary in date, from the middle of the twelfth century to the collection attributed to
Ugolino, compiled around 1216.

24   Manegold of Lautenbach († after 1103), *Liber ad Gebehardum* cap. 47, MGH *Ldl* 1, 391-
392: 'Since no one can appoint himself as king or emperor, the people raise one person above
themselves, for the sole purpose that he may direct and rule the people in accordance with
the principles of just governance, rendering to everyone his own, rewarding the righteous, and
punishing the wicked people, in short, doing justice to all. But if he is in breach of the contract on the basis of which he has been elected and suddenly begins to unsettle and confound
all he was appointed to uphold, then he rightly has absolved the people from their duty of
obedience, since he was first in breach of the trust that obliges both parties to loyalty towards
each other' (*Cum enim nullus se imperatorem vel regem creare possit, ad hoc unum aliquem super
se populus exaltat, ut iusti ratione imperii se gubernet et regat, cuique sua distribuat, pios foveat,
inpios perimat, omnibus videlicet iusticiam impendat. At vero si quando pactum, quo eligitur,
infringit, ad ea disturbanda et confundenda, quae corrigere constitutus est, eruperit, iuste rationis
consideratione populum subiectionis debito absolvit, quippe cum fidem prior ipse deseruerit, quae
alterutrum altero fidelitate colligavit*).

25   According to Odofredus († 1265), a professor of civil law in Bologna, there were around
10,000 (*x milia*) students in Bologna at the time (in his commentary on Barbarossa's Authentica
'Habita', *Lectura in primam partem Codicis*, ed. Lyon 1552, *f.* 204 ro, l. col). Even if we accept
this to be a clerical error, there must have been thousands of students 'from all over the world'
(*de omnibus partibus mundi* (Odofredus)) in Bologna at the time indeed, since Odofredus also
reports that the lectures of his predecessor Azo were so popular that his students suggested to
him to give his lectures from the pulpit built into the outer wall of the Church of S. Stefano
(it is still there) so that they could gather on the square of S. Stefano to hear him (*Lectura in
primam partem Infortiati*, ad D. 27,1,6, ed. Lyon 1552, *f.* 52, ro, r. col).

and it was this 'elusive liberty' (*vaga libertas*) he wanted to crush in his Italian kingdom as well, as he had made abundantly clear when he banned the cities of the Lombard League in 1226, explicitly stating that '*they may not enact legislation and we have quashed what they have enacted in the past and what they will have made in the future shall be regarded as null and void as of right*'[26].

While Frederick's totalitarian monarchy was threatening the 'public freedom' of Lombardy and the rest of the Italian kingdom, he was threatening the freedom *and* the unity of the Church at the same time[27]. It was on account of the *libertas ecclesiae* that Innocent III had suppressed the ecclesiastical privileges of the crown of Sicily[28], but Frederick continued to exercise undue influence over the episcopates of his kingdom, bullying recalcitrant bishops into submission and driving others into exile. His conviction for the crime of 'contempt of the keys' (*contemptus clavium*) was the consequence of this policy: he had forced the Sicilian clergy to ignore his excommunication and consequently the authority of the pope. The emperor continued to hear masses and participated in the Eucharist in his Sicilian dominion as if nothing had happened. Despite Frederick's repeated affirmations that he accepted the spiritual *plenitudo potestatis* of the pope, his conduct in his own kingdom betrayed otherwise. Even worse, from the perspective of the pope, was that a committee of clerics, installed by Frederick after his deposition at Lyon, boldly had ventured to contend, after due interrogation and examination of the emperor (*interrogatus et examinatus*), that he was *not* a heretic[29]. Here was a group of impudent clerics presumptuously acting as a board of appeal in clear defiance of the definitive sentence of the pope. If the emperor, or any other prince, could escape the consequences of a papal sentence in this way, the spiritual authority of the pope *and* the unity of the Church were fatally compromised, clearing the way for independent churches under the supervision of secular authorities. It was a prospect ('Erastianism', as it was to be called

---

26   MGH, *Const.* 2, no 107, 139: '*quod statuta non fatiant et facta cassavimus, et quod, si de cetero fecerint, ipso iure inania et irrita censeantur*'. On the ban of the cities of the Lombard League in 1226 see *supra* p. 231.
27   For Manfred's hold on the Sicilian Church see *supra* p. 437.
28   See *supra* p. 188.
29   For this incident see the encyclical letter of Innocent IV, dated on 23 May 1246, MGH *Epp. saec. xiii* 2, no 187, 141-143. The committee consisted of Frederick's old friend Archbishop Berardo of Palermo, the bishop of Pavia, three abbots, and two Dominican friars. Naturally, Innocent contended that they all deserved to be excommunicated since they had aided and abetted the unrepentant excommunicate Frederick, the former emperor. As a matter of fact, Archbishop Berardo had already been excommunicated, which is the reason he and the other members of the committee were not received by the pope personally when they came to Lyon to submit their findings.

later) too awful to contemplate. No wonder therefore that the pope brushed aside the findings of Frederick's committee as presumptuous, completely irrelevant and null and void[30].

As inauspicious as the obvious inefficacy of papal censure in the Sicilian kingdom was to papal authority, so was the awe-inspiring efficiency of Frederick's bureaucracy, the primary instrument of the emperor to maintain the people of his Sicilian kingdom in 'a quasi-servile condition'. Innocent IV was too much of an administrative law-yer to ignore this and consequently he must have realized that it was one of the reasons why the repeated excommunications of Frederick II hardly affected the administration of the Sicilian kingdom. The spiritual sword of excommunication, whenever drawn against a prince, presupposed a feudal state, since the ultimate sanction consisted of the loosening of the ties of loyalty (*fides*) a vassal owed to his lord: he was released of his duty to assist his lord with 'aid and counsel' (*aux-ilium et consilium*), as was still expressed in the sanction of Frederick's deposition. But Frederick's Sicilian kingdom was not a feudal state. Frederick's barons owed their allegiance to the king not because they were his vassals, but because they were his subjects. True, feudal law applied in the Sicilian kingdom as well, but only as a part of *private* law, in the law of real property. As a matter of *public* law, however, it had lost all significance, if it ever had any, since the Sicilian kingdom was firmly rooted in Byzantine and Arab traditions of administration. The pros-pect of having this totalitarian Sicilian Leviathan expanded all over the Italian peninsula and the resulting encirclement of Rome and the papal state by an omnipotent 'Oriental' despot forced the pope to resist the union of the Sicilian kingdom and the kingdom of Italy at all costs. As soon as the Roman papacy had finally succeeded in definitively break-ing the dynastic ties between the kingdom of Sicily and the kingdom of Italy as well as the German Roman Empire by exterminating the Hohenstaufen race in the name of 'public liberty', it did not hesitate to advance its own claim to absolute ecclesiastical as well as secular authority (*plenitudo potestatis*) over all Christendom, thus confirming Frederick's warning, repeated over and over again, that papal presump-tion would not stop with him since it was aimed at the submission of all secular princes to the sovereignty of the pope supported by absurd, even outrageous, doctrines of canon law demonstrating the boundless capacity of humankind to believe utter nonsense. If successful, papal policy would have resulted in the establishment of hierocratic rule all over Europe, thus replacing one tyranny by another, as has happened in

---

30 MGH *Epp. saec. xiii* 2, no 187, 142: '*manifeste comperimus, quod huiusmodi examina-tionem fuerat per magne presumptionis audaciam, cum iidem examinatores nullam super hoc potestatem habuerint*'.

Iran in our own time, where Khomeini's ayatollahs deposed a despotic monarch only to replace that tyrant by an even more oppressive regime of clerics. It may safely be said that Europe was spared the repressive dominance of a 'restored' Roman Empire by the stubborn refusal of succeeding popes, Gregory IX most prominent among them, to acquiesce in the union of the Sicilian kingdom and the German empire. It may even be justly contended that medieval Italy was spared the autocratic rule of a 'reformed' Roman *Augustus* thanks to the pope's efforts, but it is thanks to the king of France that Europe was spared the totalitarian hierocracy of the Roman pontiff and his clerics.

Medieval Corporate Government

Half a century after the demise of Frederick II, another pope, Boniface VIII (Benedetto Gaetani, 1294-1303), tried to deal with another prince, King Philip IV 'Le Bel' of France (1268-1285-1314), in the same way as his predecessor Innocent IV had dealt with Frederick II at Lyon. The pope and the king of France were at loggerheads ever since Philip IV had started taxing the clerics in his kingdom without permission of the pope. The king of France was struggling with two rebellious vassals at the time, the count of Flanders and the king of England, and he desperately needed money to meet their challenge. Boniface VIII overreacted (as he always did) by issuing a decree (*Clericis laicos*) forbidding all secular authorities to raise taxes from the clergy 'without the authority of the pope' (*Sedis Apostolicae auctoritate seu licentia non obtenta*) and excommunicating by operation of law all secular authorities who did so[31]. The king reacted by prohibiting the export of money and bullion to Italy, depriving the pope of his revenues from France and thus forcing the pontiff to give in, first by trying (in vain) to convince

---

31 Digard, *Les registres de Boniface VIII*, Paris 1884, no 1567 (24 February 1296), col. 584-585: '*imperatores, reges seu principes, duces, comites vel barones, potestates, capitanei, officiales vel rectores, quocunque nomine censeantur, civitatum, castrorum seu quorumcunque locorum constitutorum ubilibet et quivis alius cujuscunque preminentie, conditionis et status, qui talia imposuerunt, exegerint vel receperint aut apud edes sacras deposita ecclesiarum vel ecclesiasticarum personarum ubilibet arestaverint, sasiverint seu occupare presumpserint, vel arestari, sasiri aut ocupari mandaverint aut occupata, sasita seu arestata receperint, necnon omnes qui scienter in predictis dederint auxilium, consilium vel favorem, publice vel oculte, eo ipso sententiam excommunicationis incurrant*'. Boniface VIII inserted this decretal in his codification of canon law, an appendix to the *Liber extra* and consequently called *Liber sextus* (VI), promulgated in 1304: VI° 3,23,3. It was repealed by Clement V at the council of Vienne in 1311 at the insistence of Philip IV (Clem. 3,17, cap. un.). See the Gl. 'Quoniam' (Johannes Andreae) ad locum: '*Et Rex Franciae qui fuit passiva causa constitutionis, fuit activa causa revocationis*'.

Philip that he had misinterpreted '*Clericis laicos*'[32] and finally by conceding that the king of France was entitled to tax the clergy in a state of emergency 'even without the permission of the pope' (*inconsulto etiam Romano pontifice*)[33]. It was a sign of weakness, as was the canonization of Louis IX, 'Saint Louis', shortly later, on 11 August 1297[34], to please and appease the anything but saintly Philip IV[35]. Peace was restored accordingly, but not for long.

In 1295 Pope Boniface VIII had created a new episcopal see in Pamiers, in southern Languedoc, naming Bernard Saisset, the abbot of the nearby monastery of St Antonin with excellent connections in the papal *curia*, as the first bishop. Bernard, a first-class troublemaker, held a grudge against Philip IV and tried to incite the most important vassal and ally of the king of France in the region, Count Roger-Bernard III of Foix, to rebel against the king. The count of Foix was a man whose loyalty the king could ill afford to lose since the count was instrumental in keeping the English at bay in the south-west of France[36]. The hold of the king of France over the Languedoc was still precarious, since the excesses of the Albigensian crusade were still not forgotten there and many nobles in the region, the ancestors of the count of Foix among them, had sided in the past with the counts of Toulouse against the crusaders backed by the king of France[37]. Consequently, the danger of the nobility of the Languedoc siding with the king of England in nearby

---

32   See the bull '*Ineffabilis amoris*' (20 September 1296) in Digard, *Les registres de Boniface VIII*, Paris 1884, no 1633, col. 614-620(618).

33   See the bull '*Etsi de statu*' (31 July 1297) in Digard, *Les registres de Boniface VIII*, Paris 1884, no 2354, col. 941-943(942).

34   For the full text of the papal sermon '*Rex pacificus magnificatus*' at the canonization of Louis IX on 11 August 1297 see Duchesne, *Historiae Francorum Scriptores* V, Paris 1649, 485-486. For the bull '*Gloria, laus et honor*', announcing the canonization of St Louis to the world, issued on the same day, Duchesne 486-491.

35   Boniface VIII could ill afford an all-out conflict with the king of France at the time because of considerable problems in his own Papal State. He was waging war on the mighty Roman Colonna clan in 1297. The pope even proclaimed a crusade against the Colonna's. It was only in October 1298 that Boniface was able to suppress that clan after taking their stronghold Palestrina and utterly destroying that ancient city (*Praeneste*) and its monuments. The Colonna's, two cardinals among them, went into exile: see *infra* p. 573.

36   England and France were at war in Guyenne since 1295. The count of Foix was one of the commanders of the French army. A peace between the two parties was brokered by Boniface VIII (as a private mediator, not in his papal capacity) in 1299. One of the terms of the peace treaty was a marriage between the eldest son of Edward I, also called Edward, and a daughter of Philip IV, Isabelle. It was a marriage of enormous importance since the son of Edward II and Isabella of France, Edward III, was the only male descendant of Philip IV alive when the Capet direct male line of succession became extinct in 1328 with the death of Philip's son Charles IV. He was succeeded by his nephew Philip VI, a son of Charles of Valois (see *supra* p. 553), but the succession was contested by Edward III. It was the cause of the Hundred Years' War.

37   See *supra* p. 201-203.

Guyenne rather than with the king of France was always present. The activities of the Dominicans in the region were making matters even worse, due to their relentless (and merciless) persecution of possible surviving Cathar heretics, causing fear and unrest among the population. It was the count of Foix himself who informed Philip IV of the situation and Philip reacted vigorously. He sent two royal 'investigators' (*enquêteurs*) to the region who arrested Bishop Bernard, seized his personal belongings and his correspondence, and sent him off to Paris to stand trial there for high treason. At the same time, Philip's commissioners frustrated the inquisitorial activities of the Dominicans by not executing the heretics delivered over to them for execution and sometimes even releasing the prisoners in the custody of the Dominicans. It was a twofold intrusion of clerical prerogative: the king had subjected a cleric, Bernard Saisset, to secular jurisdiction and he had interfered with the spiritual jurisdiction of the pope by obstructing the salutary activities of the Dominican Order in the Languedoc. Boniface VIII, overreacting yet again, now decided that the time had come to overthrow Philip IV.

On 5 December 1301 Boniface summoned the French high clergy, archbishops, bishops, and the abbots of the great monasteries, as well as the professors of theology and of canon and civil law in the kingdom of France to join him in Rome on the first of November next in order to sit in judgment over Philip[38]. Boniface, an eminent canon lawyer like Innocent IV, had learned from the misgivings about the Lyon trial, especially about the question whether Frederick II had been summoned properly[39]. Consequently, he did send a proper summons, the bull *Asculta fili* ('Listen my son')[40], to Philip, leaving no doubt about the fact that Philip IV was to be subjected to an official inquisition[41]. The king was notified that the pope intended to consult with the French clergy in Rome 'about the crimes committed by you and your men' (*de tuis et tuorum excessibus*) in order '*to correct that and your administration, and to see what we can do for the peace and welfare, and the good and proper*

---

38 See the summonses in Digard, *Les registres de Boniface VIII*, Paris 1871, no 4426-4429, col. 335-338.
39 See *supra* p. 385
40 Digard, *Les registres de Boniface VIII*, Paris 1884, no 4424, col. 328-335. The text of the letter was later re-edited in the Register of Boniface VIII under Pope Clement V at the order of Philip IV, erasing large sections offensive to the king of France, emphasized by italics in the Digard edition.
41 See the reference to the 'public notifications of infamy' (*clamosa insinuatio*) that had to precede an official inquisition (see *supra* p. 383) in *Asculta fili*: Digard, *Les registres de Boniface VIII*, no 4424, col. 331.

government of that kingdom[42]. If the king believed it was in his interest to attend, he was welcome to do so himself, or by his representatives, if not, the pope announced he would proceed in Philip's absence anyway[43]. The king reacted in a way that must have come as a complete surprise to the pope and the *curia*. Frederick II had countered the attempt of Gregory IX to have him stand trial in a general council by simply arresting the prelates on their way to that council and he had tried to obstruct his trial at Lyon by his usual methods of prevarication, but Philip's reaction was far more subtle, conceiving something Frederick II never would have contemplated. He introduced a novelty in French history by summoning a national parliament, consisting of representatives of all three estates – clergy, nobility, and the cities – from all over the kingdom, to convene in Paris on 8 April 1302, in the Notre Dame, to advise him on *'many difficult matters of extreme importance to us, our status and freedom, as well as to our kingdom, the churches, the clerics, the nobility, the laity, and each and every inhabitant of the kingdom'*[44]. The king was rallying the French nation behind him and he did so with great success, not in the least by circulating a 'fake' version of the papal summons sent to Philip IV, the 'bull' *'Scire te volumus'*, composed by his crafty Chancellor Pierre Flote (†1302), the prototypical representative of a new kind of minister assisting the king, laymen rather than clerics, steeped in the doctrines of Roman private and public law. Some of them, like Pierre de Belleperche (†1308) and Guillaume Nogaret (†1313), both of them chancellors of the realm under Philip IV, had even taught Roman law before entering on a career in the royal bureaucracy. In this document the pope was alleged to have addressed the king of France bluntly with the following words: 'We want you to know that you are subject to us in spiritual as well as in temporal affairs' (*Scire te volumus, quod in spiritualibus et temporalibus nobis subes*)[45]. It caused

---

42 Digard, *Les registres de Boniface VIII*, Paris 1884, no 4424, col.332: *'que ad premissorum emendationem tuamque directionem, quietem atque salutem, ac bonum et prosperum regimen ipsius regni videbimus expedire'.*

43 Digard, *Les registres de Boniface VIII*, Paris 1884, no 4424, col.332-333: 'If you think your interests are at stake, you may attend the proceedings, either personally or by loyal men informed and well instructed about your wishes in whom you can have full confidence, if not, we shall proceed in this affair and related matters as well as in others as divine grace has inspired us and in a way that is expedient, while the divine presence makes up for your and their absence' (*Si tuam itaque rem agi putaveris, eodem tempore per te vel fideles viros et providos, tue conscios voluntatis, ac diligenter instructos, de quibus plene valeas habere fiduciam, his poteris interesse, alioquin tuam vel ipsorum absentiam divina replente presentia, in premissis et ea contingentibus ac aliis, prout superna nobis ministravit gratia et expedire videbitur, procedemus*).

44 Picot, 1 (15 February 1302): *'Super pluribus arduis negotiis, nos, statum, libertatem nostros, ac regni nostri, nec non ecclesiarum, ecclesiasticarum, nobilium, secularum personarum, ac universorum et singulorum incolarum regni eiusdem, non mediocriter tangentibus'.*

45 The document is in Dupuy, 'Preuves' 44.

an outrage among the French nobility, traditionally wary of ecclesiastical presumptions[46]. They sent an angry letter (in French) to the cardinals in Rome protesting against the impudence of the pope to claim temporal ascendancy over the king of France and demanding that the cardinals, having a responsibility of their own in the governance of the Church, should put a stop to this unholy papal policy forthwith since it threatened the unity of Christendom[47]. The French clergy addressed the pope himself, urging him to cancel the council he had summoned to sit in judgment over the king of France[48].

Boniface VIII reacted furiously. On 18 November 1302 he issued a bull containing a last and comprehensive summary of the doctrine of papal *plenitudo potestatis* 'to be remembered forever' (*ad perpetuam rei memoriam*), the infamous bull *Unam sanctam*[49]. The infamy of *Unam sanctam* is not so much due to its content as to the timing. More than a century had passed since Innocent III had pronounced that doctrine for the first time in his Saint Silvester's day sermon of 1198[50] and there is nothing in *Unam sanctam* Innocent would not have subscribed to, but times had changed. What had been accepted a century before[51]

---

46   See *supra* p. 344 and 388.
47   Picot, no 6, 12-16 (10 April 1302).
48   Picot, no 5, 5-11 (10 April 1302).
49   Digard, *Les registres de Boniface VIII*, Tom. 3, Paris 1921, no 5382, col. 888-890. '*Unam sanctam*' was inserted into the so-called *Extravagantes communes* (1,8,1), a private collection of decretals composed around the end of the 15th century by the French canonist Jean Chappuis († after 1531) for his edition of the '*Corpus Iuris Canonici*', a collection of sources of canon law containing Gratian's *Decretum*, the *Liber Extra* (1234), the *Liber Sextus* (1298), a private collection of decretals of Pope Clement V (*Clementinae*), a private collection of decretals issued by Pope John XXII (*Extravagantes Joannis XXII*) and the *Extravagantes 'communes'*, meaning generally accepted decretals issued after 1298 not to be found in the other collections. The designation '*Corpus Iuris Canonici*' became 'canonized' after Pope Gregory XIII authorized a Roman edition of this collection in 1582. The 1582 Roman edition also has the *apparatus glossarum*.
50   See *supra* p. 332.
51   In June 1206, Philip of Swabia wrote a letter to pope Innocent III justifying his election as king of the Romans in opposition to Otto IV and completely submitting to the *plenitudo potestatis* of that pontiff (MGH *Const.* 2, no 10, 10 and 13): 'It is written, and we believe it can be proved on the authority of many quotations from both testaments, that the power over all men and the rights of kingdoms are in the hands of the mediator between God and men ... Since we piously believe that our Lord Jezus Christ has confided the keys to the kingdom of heaven and has transferred the right to bind and untie to the holy apostle Peter, we know and publicly declare that you, who have succeeded in his place with absolute sovereignty, are not to be judged and that a judgment over you is reserved to God alone, whose judgment and examination we do not seek to usurp for ourselves' (*Scriptum est et multiplici utriusque testamenti auctoritate posse probari credimus, quoniam in manu mediatoris Dei et hominum sunt omnium potestates et iura regnorum ... Cum enim nos pie credamus ... Dominum nostrum Jesum Christum beato Petro apostolo claves regni celorum contulisse et tradidisse ius ligandi atque solven-*

(except, of course, by Frederick II), had become arguable, if not even offensive, by now, certainly so in France where a learned Dominican theologian called Jean Quidort, also known as John of Paris (†1306), had recently published a treatise 'On Royal and Papal Power' (*De potestate regia et papali*) eloquently and forcefully rejecting the doctrine of papal ascendancy over royal authority in temporal affairs[52].

Boniface VIII, predictably, based his invective on the doctrine of the two swords: *'We learn from the Gospels that there are two swords in his power, the spiritual and the temporal. Surely, who denies that the temporal sword belongs to Peter has not heeded the word of the Lord. Consequently, both are in the power of the Church, the spiritual and temporal sword, but the latter is to be exercised on behalf of the Church, the former by the Church. The former by the hand of a priest, the latter on the authority and on sufferance of a priest. Accordingly, one sword has to be subservient to the other and the secular authority has to be obedient to the spiritual power'*[53]. It was the doctrine of the two swords as explained to Pope Eugenius III by his mentor St. Bernard more than two centuries earlier[54]. Boniface VIII proceeds to emphasize that the spiritual power is entitled to sit in judgment over the temporal power while it cannot be judged itself by any human authority: *'Because according to the revealed truth the spiritual power has to appoint the temporal power and to judge it whenever it does wrong. The truth about this concerning the Church and the ecclesiastical power is confirmed by the prophecy of Jeremiah "See, I have this day set thee over the nations and over the kingdoms"* <Jeremiah 1:10> *and the rest that follows. Consequently, whenever the temporal power turns*

---

di, scimus et protestamur, quod vos, qui in locum suum cum plenitudine potestatis successistis ... non estis iudicandus, sed iudicium vestrum soli Deo reservatur; cuius iudicium et examen ... nobis non querimus usurpare).

52   The modern text-critical edition (with a German translation) is F. Bleienstein, *Johannes Quidort von Paris, Über königliche und päpstliche Gewalt*, Stuttgart 1969; there is an English translation by J.A. Watt, *John of Paris on Royal and Papal Power*, Toronto 1971. The treatise of John of Paris circulated widely in Europe in the fourteenth century. I found it mentioned more than once (with obvious approval) by the learned Italian jurist Albericus de Rosate (*c.* 1290-1360) in his *In primam Codicis partem commentaria*, ad C. 1,1,1 no 19, ed. Venice 1586, f. 8 ro, r. col.: *'et in ipso libello alia pulchra de potestate imperatoris et Papae tractat'*. See for other references to John of Paris *In secundam Codicis partem commentaria*, ad C. 7,37,3, ed. Venice 1585, f. 106 vo – 109 ro. Albericus was an early admirer of Dante: Dante's *Monarchia* is also approvingly referred to by Albericus, in his commentary on C. 1,1,1 no 20, ed. Venice 1586, f. 8 ro, r. col.

53   *Extravagantes communes* 1,8,1 (post alia): *'In hac eiusque potestate duos gladios, spiritualem videlicet et temporalem Evangelicis dictis instruimur ... Certe qui in potestate Petri temporalem gladium negat, male verbum attendit Domini. Uterque ergo est in potestate Ecclesiae, spiritualis scilicet gladius et materialis. Sed is quidem pro Ecclesia, ille vero ab Ecclesia exercendus. Ille sacerdotis, is manu regum et militum, sed ad nutum et patientiam sacerdotis. Oportet autem gladium esse sub gladio et temporalem auctoritatem spirituali subiici potestati'*.

54   See *supra* p. 81.

away from what is good, it shall be judged by the spiritual power, but when a minor ecclesiastic deviates, he shall be judged by his superior. If, however, it concerns the highest authority, it shall not be judged by any man ... Accordingly, whosoever resists this power ordained by the Lord, challenges Divine order[55]. The pope concluded his diatribe with the following exhortation: '*Furthermore, we do declare, say, and pronounce that it is necessary for the salvation of all mankind to submit to the Roman pontiff*'[56].

On 12 March 1303 the king called an assembly in the garden of the Louvre that was to be addressed by his counsellor Guillaume Nogaret, 'the esteemed professor of Roman law' (*legum professor venerabilis*). The conference was attended by his other counsellors, his brothers Charles of Valois and Louis d'Evreux and the leading French secular clerics. Nogaret, who was from the Languedoc and whose parents had been executed for heresy during the Albigensian crusade[57], suggested the plan once advanced by Frederick II[58]: a general council of the Church to sit in judgment over the man who called himself Boniface, a usurper, a heretic, and a notorious simonist[59]. He urged the king to arrest that 'shameless man' (*flagitiosus*) to prevent him from escaping his trial and to provide for an interim caretaker to administer the Church until the council had decided over the fate of the pope[60]. No one present at this

---

55 *Extravagantes communes* 1,8,1 (post alia): '*Nam veritate testante, spiritualis potestas terrenam potestatem instituere habet, et judicare, si bona non fuerit. Sic de ecclesia, et ecclesiastica potestate, verificatur vaticinium Jeremie "Ecce constitui te hodie, super gentes et regna" et cetera que sequuntur. Ergo si deviat terrena potestas, judicabitur a potestate spirituali, sed si deviat spiritualis minor, a suo superiore. Si vero supprema a solo Deo, non ab homine poterit judicari ... Quicumque igitur huic potestati a Deo sic ordinate resistit, Deo ordinationi resistit*'.

56 *Extravagantes communes* 1,8,1 (post alia): '*Porro subesse Romano Pontifici omni humanae creaturae declaramus, dicimus et pronuntiamus omnino esse de necessitate salutis*'.

57 It was common knowledge at the time that Nogaret's parents had been executed as Cathar heretics. See the appeal filed on 14 April 1313 by Count Louis de Nevers (1272-1322) with the papal court against the king of France (in T. van Limburg-Stirum, *Codex diplomaticus Flandriae* 2, Bruges 1889, no 290, 217-227(223)): '*De dicto Guillelmo de Longharet notorium est ... patrem<que> ipsius Guillelmi et quosdam suos predecessores carnales, ut dicitur, dampnatos de heresi, merito igne crematos fuisse*'.

58 See *supra* p. 294.

59 It is reported that the king had the papal bull *Asculta fili* publicly burned after this event: Dupuy, 'Preuves' 59. The official record of Nogaret's accusation of Boniface VIII and his call for a general council to sit in judgment over the pope is in Picot, no 13, 28-34. For Nogaret as the prime initiator of the plan, see the continuation of the chronicle of Guillaume de Nangis ad ann. 1303 (*Recueil* 20, 588). The other Roman lawyer involved, Pierre Flote, also from the Languedoc, chancellor of France since 1298, had recently fallen near Courtray in the Battle of the Golden Spurs (11 July 1302).

60 Picot, no 13, 32-33: 'I beg and urge you to provide for a caretaker for the Roman Church itself, *while the person of that profligate is put into custody,* who can dispense with things that come up until a decision has been reached on a pope for the Church of God, in order to

occasion but for the king and Nogaret himself knew that the king had already decided to arrest the pope and bring him to trial[61]. A month later, in an assembly held on 13 and 14 June 1303, Nogaret's close co-operator Guillaume de Plaisians (†1314), another Roman lawyer from the Languedoc in the royal household, joined his mentor in a comprehensive indictment against Boniface, the more shocking details of which were doubtlessly supplied by the Cardinal Giacomo Colonna, then living in exile with the court of France[62]. It was on this occasion that the king publicly adopted the plan of his lawyers: a general council of the Church was to sit in judgment over Boniface VIII[63]. The

---

avoid any occasion of a schism and to prevent that the just-mentioned profligate obstructs or delays his trial' (*supplico et requiro ... ut de vicario ipsi Romane ecclesie*, persona dicti flagiciosi posita in custodia, *providear, qui administrare valeat que incombent, quousque de pontifice sit Ecclesie Dei provisum, ad omnem occasionem scismatis prorsus tollendam, et ut dictus flagiciosus persecucionem huiusmodi non impediat vel retardet*) (emphasis added).

61   On 7 March 1303, five days before the assembly in the Louvre, King Philip had provided Nogaret and three others with a letter of attorney, authorizing them to deal with anyone in the (unspecified) places they were sent to on behalf and in the name of the king. One of the royal delegates was an influential Florentine banker, Musciatto Franzesi (called Mouchet in France), who advised Philip in financial affairs. Philip's letter of attorney (in Dupuy, 'Preuves' 175) provided his delegates with unlimited credit in Italy. The contemporary Florentine chronist Giovanni Villani (†1348), who was working in the Florentine banking firm Peruzzi at the time, informs us that Nogaret and Musciatto Franzesi contacted that firm in Florence to raise all the money they needed: *Cronica nuova* 9, 63, ed. Porta 2, Parma 1991, 116.

62   The record of the indictment by Guillaume de Plaisians is in Picot, no 14, 34-53. On the two Colonna cardinals and their feud with Boniface VIII see *supra* p. 567, fnt. 35. One of the most serious charges brought against Boniface VIII was, of course, his dubious role in the resignation and subsequent demise of his predecessor Pope Celestine V (1294). Celestine (Peter of Morone) had been a hermit, living in the mountains near L'Aquila, before he was unexpectedly elected as successor to Pope Nicholas IV, who had died in 1292. After a *sedis vacantia* of almost two years, caused by rivalry between the Colonna and Orsini factions in the *curia*, the cardinals (for once) decided to elect a truly saintly man. It was a terrible mistake since the hermit, being a holy man, was completely unqualified for office. He resigned on 13 December 1294, the only pope before Benedict XVI to do so (Dante's '*gran rifiuto*' (*Inferno* 3, 60)). It was generally believed at the time that Cardinal Benedetto Gaetani had been instrumental in convincing Celestine to resign. After he had been elected as his successor, Gaetani, now Boniface VIII, had his predecessor arrested and imprisoned in a castle, where that unfortunate man expired on 22 May 1296.

63   The decision of Philip is in Picot, no 14, 47-49. There is an official reaction by Boniface VIII to Philip's call for a general council of the Church to sit in judgment over him. It is the bull '*Nuper ad audientiam nostram*' of 15 August 1303 (Digard, *Les registres de Boniface VIII*, Tom. 3, Paris 1921, no 5383, col. 890-894). As was to be expected, the pope completely rejected the idea: 'Will the standing of the Church not founder and the authority of the Roman pontiffs not become worthless if this road is open and widely available to kings and princes and other potentates? Whenever a Roman pontiff wants to initiate correctional proceedings and wants to resort to force, he will immediately be called a heretic or a notorious scandalizing criminal to escape correction and consequently the supreme power will be utterly confounded. We will not have this pernicious precedent stand in the schools of our time, let this insanity be far from us' (*Nonne Ecclesiae nutabit status et Romanorum Pontificum vilescet auctoritas,*

king immediately sent royal commissioners to all parts of his kingdom to inform the local estates, clergy, nobility, and the cities, of his decision and to ask for their support, again successfully rallying the nation behind him[64]. By that time, Nogaret was already on his way to Italy to arrest the pope.

Nogaret went to Florence first to raise enough money with the bankers there to buy all the military support he needed. From there he and his companions proceeded further into Tuscany, to the castle of Staggia where they stayed for some time to organize their raid on Boniface VIII[65]. Boniface was staying in his hometown Anagni at the time, unaware of what was coming at him. Nogaret and his company associated with a local strongman from Ferentino, some 7 miles south of Anagni, Rinaldo de Suppino, a 'mortal enemy' (*capitalis inimicus*) of the pope[66]. They were joined by another mortal enemy of Boniface VIII, Giacomo Colonna, appropriately nicknamed 'Sciarra' ('The Brawler'), and his mercenaries, all paid for by Nogaret. On Saturday 7 September 1303, Nogaret made his strike: he entered Anagni by surprise and was able to arrest the pope in his palace. Sciarra Colonna wanted to kill the pope outright, but Nogaret needed the pontiff alive to stand trial and so Boniface VIII was incarcerated in one of the dungeons of his own palace, where he spent 'a bad night' (*mala nox*)[67]. True as it may be that the pope was liberated subsequently by the efforts of the citizens of Anagni, the Anagni incident was a turning point, only comparable to the humiliation of the Emperor Henry IV at Canossa in 1077[68]. Boniface VIII was now (literally) a broken man and did not survive his misfortune for long: he died in Rome on 11 October 1303 to be succeeded, after the short intermezzo of Benedict XI (1303-1304), by

---

si talis regibus et principibus aliisque potentibus aperiatur via aditusque pandatur? Confestim enim Romanus Pontifex ... cum circa alicuius principis vel potentis volet correctionem intendere et mittere manus ad fortia, dicetur hereticus vel notorie et in scandalum criminosus, ut sic fugiatur correctio et supprema potestas penitus confudatur. Absit a secta nostrorum temporum hoc perniciosum exemplum, absit a nobis tanta vecordia). This and many other passages in this bull were later erased from the official record of Boniface's correspondence at the insistence of Clement V. They have been carefully reconstructed by Digard for his edition of the Register of Boniface VIII: see col. 890, fnt. 3.

64   See the extensive list of 'adhesions' in Picot.

65   *Cronica nuova* 9, 63, ed. Porta 2, Parma 1991, 116. Villani reports that Staggia Castle belonged to Musciato Franzesi. The impressive castle is still standing on the outskirts of the little village of Staggia in Siena province and is still locally known as the 'castello dei Franzesi'.

66   From a contemporary letter by a papal courtier (*curtesanus*) to his friends in England relating the events of Anagni, most probably an eyewitness. I used the edition in MGH *SS* 28, 621-626(622). Rinaldo closed a deal with Nogaret who guaranteed that Rinaldo and his followers would be compensated for all their eventual damages: Dupuy, 'Preuves' 175-176.

67   MGH *SS* 28, 623: '*papa habuit malam noctem*'.

68   See *supra* p. 333, fnt. 23.

a pope from France, Clement V (1305-1314), who moved the papal see from Rome to Avignon, where it remained for almost a century, firmly under the control of the king of France. There were to be no more unwelcome exercises of papal *plenitudo potestatis* to the detriment of the king of France coming from that quarter.

The conflict between Boniface VIII and Philip IV has been related in some detail since the ignominious end of the papacy of Boniface VIII marks the beginning of the end of papal aspirations to absolute sovereignty over all secular powers in Europe. The king of France was definitively emancipating secular authorities from the 'abuse of a destructive freedom' (*pestiferae libertatis abusus* (Frederick II)[69]) by the Church of Rome. His actions also terminated the established doctrine of canon law, explicitly referred to by Boniface VIII in *Unam sanctam*, that the pope could not be judged by anyone but God, a doctrine frustrating secular powers ever since the days of Charlemagne[70]. There had always been *one* exception to that rule in Gratian's *Decretum*: a pope *could* be deposed for heresy and since the concept of heresy was open to extensive construction it might even include personal conduct of the pope scandalizing the reputation of the Church[71]. It was unclear, however, who was authorized to sit in judgment over a pope who scandalized the Church[72]. By adopting the idea that a general council of the Church could sit in judgment of the pope, as Frederick II had once suggested[73], Philip IV concluded the work begun by Frederick II[74] but he did not do so by establishing an alternative absolute monarchy of his own as Frederick II had had in mind for Italy. Philip IV could never have

---

69 See *supra* p. 55.

70 See *supra* p. 340, fnt. 67.

71 D. 40, cap. 6 ('Si papa').

72 John of Paris, *De potestate regia et papali* cap. 22, ed. Bleienstein 193: '*Sed quis iudicabit eum haereticum?*'. In cap. 13, ed. Bleienstein 138, John argues that in this case the emperor might indirectly (*indirecte*) depose the pope 'because the emperor can prevent all and every single person to obey and serve him as pope by confiscation or corporeal punishment' (*quia posset imperator sub hypotheca rerum vel poena corporum inhibere omnibus et singulis ut nullus ei oboediret vel serviret ut papae*).

73 See *supra* p. 294. John of Paris, cap. 22, ed. Bleienstein 192, believed a general council could only decide 'on the status of the pope, that is, whether he is pope or not' (*de statu quidem papae, an scilicet sit papa vel non*). It seems strange that the tribulations of Frederick II are never mentioned by John of Paris, by Philip le Bel, or by any of his lawyers, but one ought to bear in mind that Frederick II was a convicted heretic and that his descendants in Aragon only recently had been excommunicated for trying to recover his Sicilian kingdom from the Angevine relatives of Philip. Consequently, any positive reference to Frederick II would have weakened rather than strengthened the case Philip le Bel was making.

74 Philip IV also (unintentionally) gave rise to the idea that a general council was the highest authority in the Church, an idea that was to gain more and more momentum in coming years and is known as 'Conciliarism'.

achieved his triumph over papal presumptions without the support of the estates representing the French nation. His case was not unique since his uncle Peter III of Aragon had also depended on the support of the estates of his realm to prevail over the crusading army sent by the pope to divest him of his kingdom. In both instances the policy of the king was legitimized by the consent of his subjects as represented by the estates of the realm. It was a policy repeated by King Frederick III (or rather II)[75] of 'Trinacria' (Sicily).

Frederick's brother James had become king of Aragon in 1291, after the demise of their older brother Alfonso III, who had succeeded their father Peter III as king of Aragon. James II had been king of Sicily since the demise of Peter III in 1285 and after he became king of Aragon as well, he left the island in the custody of his younger brother Frederick as his regent. James wanted peace with France and, above all, the lifting of his excommunication. The treaty of Anagni (20 June 1295), brokered by Boniface VIII, secured all that, at the price, however, of James' resignation of Sicily to Charles II of Naples, who had succeeded his father Charles of Anjou in 1285[76]. The Sicilians and James' younger brother Frederick, the governor of Sicily, refused to accept that treaty and consequently Frederick was elected king of Sicily by a Sicilian 'parliament' (*generale colloquium*) convened at Catania on 15 January 1296[77]. Frederick III was crowned king of Sicily on 25 March 1296 in Palermo and a few days later he promulgated a collection of 35 statutes (*capitula*), including his assurance to convene a parliament (*curia generalis*) once a year on the first day of November[78]. Frederick's great-

---

75 Frederick was the second king of Sicily called Frederick. The first was, of course, the Emperor Frederick II. This is why the Aragonese King Frederick of Sicily styled himself as the *third* Frederick, a reference to his imperial Hohenstaufen roots.

76 On the treaty of Anagni see Nicolas Specialis, *Historia Sicula* 2, 20 (Gregorio, *Biblioteca* 1, 347-348): 'papal authority released King James from the bond of his excommunication. He ceded the right he had to the kingdom of Sicily to King Charles' (*Jacobum regem ab excommunicationis vinculo pontificalis absolvit auctoritas ... jus quod habebat in regno Sicilie, Karolo regi cessit*). See also *Anonymi Chronicon Siculum* cap. 51 (Gregorio, *Biblioteca* 2, 162): '*Et ex praedicto tractatu dictae pacis idem rex Jacobus ... deseruit Siculos, Regnum et dominium dicti Regni et insulae Siciliae, quod tenebat et ipsam insulam dimisit et cessit Romanae Ecclesiae*'. On this treaty see also *supra*, p. 556, fnt. 254.

77 Nicolas Specialis, *Historia Sicula* 2, cap. 23 (Gregorio, *Biblioteca* 1, 351): 'And so a parliament was held in the Cathedral of Catania where all the Catalans, the men from Aragon, and all the magnates, and the representatives of the cities of Sicily assembled. The magnates and all the people agreed unanimously on the coronation of Frederick and they withdrew after setting a date for the coming coronation ceremony' (*Itaque convenientibus in unum Catalanis, Aragonibus, cunctisque magnatibus et Syndicis Siculorum, in Cathaniensi ecclesia generale colloquium celebratur ... de coronatione Friderici magnates et plebs omnis pari voto conveniunt et ad futuram solemnitatem coronationis huius die constituta discedunt*).

78 Cap. 3, *De generali curia semel in anno facienda* (in *Capitula Regni Siciliae quae ad hodiernum diem lata sunt*, Tom. 1, Palermo 1741, 48): 'We provide that once a year, on the feast day

grandfather, the Emperor Frederick II, the man whose name he was so proud to bear, never would have consented to anything like this, but Sicily had, by now, ceased to be the totalitarian state it had been under the reign of that monarch. Instead, it had finally become a 'normal' feudal state entering the western European mainstream of corporate government by the king and the estates of his kingdom, as had the English monarchy after Simon of Montfort (a son of the Albigensian crusader) had added ordinary knights ('commoners') as representatives of the cities and counties of the kingdom to the council of the English lords ecclesiastical and temporal in 1265. It was certainly not 'parliamentary government' as we now know it, nor was it a government by the king and the elected representatives of his people, far from that, but it was a government by the king cooperating with the three corporate entities representing the nation and, as such, it was the fertile breeding ground from which all of these modern institutions have matured. For centuries to come, *power* still rested undoubtedly with the king but his *authority* depended on his adherence to the good customs, privileges, and liberties of the corporations within his kingdom and the support of the estates of his realm, substantiating the fundamental contractual nature of western medieval royal government. *None* of the western European kings and princes of the 'Ancien Régime' ever exercised 'absolute sovereignty' (*plenitudo potestatis*) over his subjects, not even the ones who believed they did.

---

of All Saints, a general assembly shall be held in Sicily, where we demand to be present with us: the counts, the barons, the rightful and sufficiently instructed representatives of all cities, and others who are qualified and beneficial to us, to attend to the exaltation of our Majesty and the island and the prosperity and happiness of all, especially the Sicilians' (*Providimus, anno quolibet, in festo scilicet omnium Sanctorum, in Siciliae partibus generalem curiam celebrari; in qua nobis adesse statuimus, Comites, Barones et universitatum quarumlibet syndicos idoneos, et sufficientes, instructos, et alios ad hoc opportunos et utiles ad providendum nobiscum, procurandum, et exaltandum nostrae Maiestatis, ipsius insulae et omnium, specialiter Siculorum, statum salutiferum et felicem*). Of course, the king had to confirm all liberties, privileges, and laudable customs and usages of his realm: Cap. 2, *De confirmatione privilegiorum et legum* (*Capitula Regni Siciliae*, 47-48).

Select Bibliography

*

I. Original Sources

1. Collections of Sources and Sources Cited in Abbreviations

Amari, M., *Biblioteca Arabo-Sicula*, two volumes, Turin and Rome 1880-1881 (Italian translations of Arabian sources)

Ann. eccl. - Baronius/Raynaldus, *Annales ecclesiastici*, ed. Theiner, Aug., 37 volumes, Paris 1864-1883

Baerwald, H., *Das Baumgartenberger Formelbuch*, Vienna 1866

Berlan, Fr., *Liber consuetudinum Mediolani anni MCCXVI*, Milan 1868

Böhmer, J.F., *Acta imperii selecta*, Innsbruck 1870

Bouquet - *Recueil des historiens des gaules et de la France*, Première édition, 22 volumes, Paris 1738-1786

Bourel de la Roncière, C.G.M. *e.a.*, *Les registres d'Alexandre IV*, 4 volumes, Paris 1902-1959

Buchon - Buchon, J.A.C., *Chroniques étrangères relatives aux expéditions françaises pendant le xiiie siècle*, Paris 1841

Buchon, *Recherches* - Buchon, J.A.C., *Recherches et matériaux pour servir à une histoire de la domination française en Orient* I, Paris 1811

C. - *Codex Justinianus*, ed. Krüger, P., *editio stereotypa*, 11th ed., Berlin 1954

Capasso, Bart., *Historia diplomatica Regni Siciliae inde ab anno 1250 ad annum 1266*, Naples 1874

Carini - Carini, Isidoro, *Gli Archivi e le Biblioteche di Spagna in rapporto alla storia d'Italia in generale e di Sicilia in particolare* 2 volumes, Palermo 1884

Carini, *Documenti* - *Documenti per servire alla Storia di Sicilia* V, Palermo 1882

Caspar, E., *Das Register Gregors VII.*, in MGH *Epp. sel.* 2.1-2.2

Champollion-Figeac, J.-J., *Documents inédits tirés des collections manuscrites de la Bibliothèque Royale*, 4 parts in 5 volumes, Paris 1841-1874

Chronache e Statuti della Città di Viterbo, ed. Ciampi, Ign., in *Documenti di Storia Italiana* V, Florence 1872

Clem. - *Clementinae*, ed. Friedberg, E., Leipzig 1881 .

Corpus Iuris Canonici – *Corpus Iuris Canonici*, edition ordered by pope Gregory XIII, Rome 1582, an online version (with glosses) is available in the UCLA Library, Digital collections

CSEL - *Corpus Scriptorum Ecclesiasticorum Latinorum*, Vienna 1866 –

D. - *Digesta imperatoris Justniani*, ed. Mommsen, Th., *editio stereotypa*, 16th ed., Berlin 1954

DA - Deutsches Archiv für Erforschung des Mittelalters

Del Giudice, Gius., *Codice diplomatico del regno di Carlo I. e II. d'Angiò*, 3 volumes, Naples 1863-1902

Del Re, Gius., *Cronisti e scrittori sincroni Napoletani* 2 volumes, Naples 1845-1868

Delisle, L., *Catalogue des actes de Philippe-Auguste*, Paris 1856

Denifle, H., *Chartularium universitatis parisiensis* I, Paris 1889

Digard, G. e.a., *Les registres de Boniface VIII*, 4 volumes, Paris 1884-1939

Duchesne, Andr. and Franc., *Historiae Francorum scriptores*, 5 volumes, Paris 1636-1649

Dupuy - Dupuy, P., *Histoire du differend d'entre le pape Boniface VIII. et Philippe le Bel, roy de France*, Paris 1655

ERPG - Thiel, A., *Epistulae Romanorum Pontificum Genuinae* 1, Brunsberg 1868

Frati, L., *Statuti di Bologna dall'anno 1245 all'anno 1267*, Bologna 1869

Gabrieli, F., *Die Kreuzzüge aus arabischer Sicht*, Zürich 1973 (Arabian sources in German translation, from the Italian original (*Storici arabi delle crociate*, Turin 1957))

García y García, A., *Constitutiones concilii quarti Lateranensis*, Rome 1981

Gay, J.M.M., *Les registres de Nicolas III*, Paris 1898-1938

Giraud, J., *Les registres de Grégoire X*, 3 volumes, Paris 1892-1906
   – *Les registres d'Urbain IV*, 4 volumes, Paris 1901-1956

Gregorio, *Biblioteca* - Gregorio, *Biblioteca scriptorum qui res in Sicilia gestas sub Aragonum imperio retulere* 2 volumes, Palermo 1791-1792

Hänel, G.F., *Dissensiones dominorum*, Leipzig 1835

HB - Huillard-Bréholles, J.L.A., *Historia diplomatica Friderici secundi*, 6 volumes, Paris 1852-1861

HZ - Historische Zeitschrift

Inst. - *Institutiones Justiniani imperatoris*, ed. P. Krüger, *editio stereotypa*, 16th ed., Berlin 1954

Jaffé, *Bibl.* - Jaffé, Ph., *Bibliotheca rerum germanicarum* 6 volumes, Berlin 1864-1873 (repr. Aalen 1964)

Kempf - F. Kempf S.J., *Registrum Innocentii III papae super negotio Romani imperii*, Rome 1947

LA - Liber augustalis, ed. Stürner, MGH *Const.* 2, Suppl.

LF - Libri feudorum. Since medieval lawyers did not enjoy the privilege of using the text-critical edition published by K. Lehmann, *Das langobardische Lehnrecht*, Göttingen 1896 (repr. Aalen 1971, with Lehmann's *Consuetudines feudorum*, Göttingen 1892), I prefer the text as published in the Volumen part of the *Corpus Iuris Civilis*, preferably the edition Geneva 1625.

Liber censuum - Fabre, P. and Duchesne, L., *Le Liber Censuum de l'église romaine*, 3 volumes, Paris 1889, 1905, 1952

Liber pontificalis - Duchesne, L., *Le Liber Pontificalis*, 3 volumes, Paris 1886-1892, 1957

Lünig, J.C., *Codex Italiae Diplomaticus*, 2 volumes, Frankfurt/Leipzig 1725-1726

Mansi - *Sacrorum conciliorum nova et amplissima collectio*, ed. Mansi, Giov. Dom., 30 volumes, Venice 1759-1792 (available online at http://mansi.fscire.it/opere)

Martène, *Thesaurus* - Martène, E and Durand, U., *Thesaurus novus anecdotorum* 5 volumes, Paris 1717

Martène-Durand, *Veterum scriptorum et monumentorum ... amplissima collectio* 9 volumes, Paris 1724-1733

MGH - *Monumenta Germaniae Historica*, available online at www.mgh.de

Auct. Ant.	Auctores antiquissimi
Briefe d. spät. MA	Briefe des späteren Mittelalters
Capit.	Capitularia regum Francorum
Const.	Constitutiones et acta publica imperatorum et regum
DD	Diplomata
Epp.	Epistolae
Epp. sel.	Epistolae selectae
Epp. saec. xiii	Epistolae saeculi xiii e regestis Pontificum Romanorum selectae
Fontes iuris	Fontes iuris Germanici antiquae
LdL	Libelli de lite imperatorum et pontificum
LL	Leges
LL nat. Germ.	Leges nationum Germanicarum
Poetae	
SS	Scriptores
SS rer. Merov.	Scriptores rerum Merovingicarum
SS rer. Germ.	Scriptores rerum Germanicarum
SS rer. Germ. NS	Scriptores rerum Germanicarum Nova Series

Michaud, J.F., *Bibiliothèque des Croisades*, 4 volumes, Paris 1829

Migne *PL* - Migne, J.P., *Patrologiae Cursus Completus, Series Latina*, 221 volumes, including indices, Paris 1844-1864

MIÖG - Mitteilungen des Instituts für Österreichische Geschichtsforschung

Muratori - *Rerum Italicarum scriptores*, ed. Muratori, L.A., 25 volumes, Milan 1723-1751 (available online at www.centrostudimuratoriani.it)

Nov. - *Novellae*, ed. Schoell, R. and Kroll, W., 6th ed., Berlin 1954

Olivier-Martin, F.J.M., *Les registres de Martin IV*, Paris 1901-1935

Picot - Picot, G., *Documents relatifs aux États Généraux et Assemblées réunis sous Philippe le Bel*, Paris 1901

Posse, O., *Analecta Vaticana*, Innsbruck 1878

Prou, M., *Les registres d'Honorius IV*, Paris 1886-1888

Recueil - *Recueil des historiens des gaules et de la France*, Nouvelle édition, 24 volumes, Paris 1869-1904

Redlich, O., *Eine Wiener Briefsammlung zur Geschichte des deutschen Reiches und der österreichischen Länder in der zweiten Hältfte des XIII. Jahrhunderts*, Vienna 1894

RIS2 - *Rerum Italicarum Scriptores*, second series (1900-1975) (available online at www.centrostudimuratoriani.it)

Rymer - Rymer, Th., *Foedera, conventiones, literae et cuiuscunque generis acta publica inter reges Angliae et alios quosvis imperatores, reges, pontifices, principes vel communitates* 3d ed., Vol. I, part 1-4 (1066-1311), The Hague 1745

Savigny, *Geschichte* - Savigny, F.C. von, *Geschichte des römischen Rechts im Mittelalter*, 2d ed., Heidelberg 1834-1851 (repr. Bad Homburg 1961), 7 volumes (repr. Darmstadt 1956)

Schmale-Ott, I., *Quellen zum Investiturstreit* 2, Darmstadt 1984

Sudendorff, H., *Registrum oder merkwürdige Urkunden für deutsche Geschichte* I, Jena 1849

Theiner, Aug., *Codex diplomaticus dominii temporalis S. Sedis*, 3 volumes, Rome 1861-1862

Vignati - Vignati, Cesare, *Storia diplomatica della lega Lombarda con xxvi documenti inediti*, Milan 1867

VI. – Decretals of Bonifacius VIII, a.k.a *Liber Sextus*, ed. Friedberg, E., Leipzig 1881

Violet, P., *Les Établissements de Saint Louis* 1, Paris 1881

Winkelmann, Ed., *Acta imperii inedita seculi xiii et xiv*, 2 volumes, Insbruck 1880 and 1885

Wolff, G., *Vier griechische Briefe des Kaisers Friedrichs des zweiten*, Berlin 1855

X. – *Decreta Gregorii IX P.M.* ('*Liber extra*'), ed. Friedberg, E., Leipzig 1881

2. Individual Sources

Adalbert, *Continuatio Reginonis*, ed. Kurze MGH *SS rer. Germ.* 50

Alberich of Troisfontaines, *Chronica*, ed. Scheffer-Boichorst, MGH *SS* 23, 631-950

Albert Behaim, *Epistolae*, edd. Frenz, T. and Herde, P., MGH *Briefe d. spät. MA* 1

Amatus of Monte Cassino, *Ystoire de li Normant*, ed. Delarc, O.J.M., Rouen 1892

Ambrosiaster, *Liber quaestionum*, ed. Souter, *CSEL* 50

Andreas Ungarus, *Descriptio victoriae*, ed. Waitz, MGH *SS* 26, 559-580

Annales Alamannici, ed. Pertz, MGH *SS* 1, 22-60

Annales Altahenses maiores, ed. Giesebrecht, MGH *SS rer. Germ.* 4

Annales Aquenses, ed. Waitz, MGH *SS* 24, 33-39

Annales Basileenses, ed. Jaffé, MGH *SS* 17, 193-202

Annales Bertiniani (Prudentius of Troyes), ed. Waitz, MGH *SS rem. Germ.* 5

Annales Cameracenses (Lambertus Waterlos), ed. Pertz MGH *SS* 16, 509-554

Annales Casinenses, ed. Pertz, MGH *SS* 19, 303-320

Annales Cavenses, ed. Pertz MGH *SS* 3, 185-197

Annales Ceccanenses (a.k.a *Annales Fossae novae*), ed. Pertz, MGH *SS* 19, 275-302

Annales Clerici Parisiensis, ed. Waitz MGH *SS* 26, 581-583

Annales Corbeienses, ed. Pertz, MGH *SS* 3, 1-18

Annales Erphordenses, ed Pertz, MGH *SS* 16, 26-40

Annales Erphordenses fratrum praedicatorum, ed. Holder-Egger MGH *SS rer. Germ.* 42, 72-116

Annales Fossae novae, see *Annales Ceccanenses*

Annales Fuldenses, ed. Kurze, MGH *SS rem. Germ.* 7

Annales Ianuenses (Caffaro di Caschifellone *e.a.*), ed. Pertz, MGH SS 18, 1-356

Annales Laurissenses minores, ed. Pertz, MGH, *SS* 1, 112-123

Annales Laureshamenses, ed. Pertz, MGH *SS* 1, 22-39

Annales Marbacenses, ed. Bloch, MGH *SS rer. Germ.* 9

Annales Mediolanenses maiores, ed. Pertz, MGH *SS* 18, 357-382

Annales Mediolanenses ab anno mccxxx usque ad ann. mccccii, Muratori 16, 635-840

Annales Mettenses priores, ed. Simson, MGH *SS rer. Germ.* 10

Annales Palidenses, ed. Pertz MGH *SS* 16, 48-98

Annales Pisani (Bernardus Marango), ed. Gentile, *RIS2* 6.2, Bologna 1930-1936

Annales Placentini Gibellini, ed. Pertz, MGH *SS* 18, 457-581

Annales Placentini Guelfi, ed. Pertz. MGH *SS* 18, 411-457

Annales regni Francorum, ed. Pertz/Kurze, MGH, *SS rer. Germ.* 6

Annales Romani, ed. Pertz, MGH *SS* 5, 468-480

Annales Sancrucenses, ed. Wattenbach MGH *SS* 9, 637-646

Annales Sanctae Justinae Patavinae, ed. Jaffé, MGH *SS* 19, 148-193

Annales Sancti Disibodi, ed. Waitz, MGH *SS* 17, 4-30

Annales Sancti Georgii in Silva Nigra, ed. Pertz MGH *SS* 17, 295-298

Annales Sancti Gereonis Coloniensis (1191-1202), ed. Pertz, MGH *SS* 16, 733-734

Annales Sancti Jacobi (*Reineri Annales*), ed. L. Bethmann, MGH *SS* 16, 640

Annales Sancti Panthaleonis Coloniensis maximi, ed. Pertz, MGH *SS* 17, 723-847

Annales Sancti Rudberti Salisburgenses, ed. Wattenbach MGH *SS* 9, 758-810

Annales Sangallenses maiores, ed. Von Arx, MGH *SS* 1, 73-85

Annales Scheftlarienses maiores, ed. Jaffé MGH *SS* 17, 334-350

Annales Senenses, ed. Pertz MGH *SS* 19, 225-235

Annales Siculi, ed. Pertz, MGH *SS* 19, 494-500

Annales Stadenses, ed. Lappenberg, MGH *SS* 16, 271-379

Annales Urbevetani, ed. Pertz MGH *SS* 19, 269-273

Annales Veronenses (Parisius de Cereta), ed. Pertz, MGH *SS* 19, 2-18

Annales Weingartenses Welfici, ed. Pertz, MGH *SS* 17, 308-311

Annales Wormatienses, ed. Bethmann, MGH *SS* 17, 34-73

Annalista Saxo, ed. Waitz, MGH *SS* 6, 542-777

Anonymi Chronicon Siculum, in Gregorio, *Biblioteca* 2, 107-267

Anonymus Gallus*, Gesta ducum sive principum Polonorum*, ed. Szlachtowski/Koepke, MGH *SS* 9, 418-478

Anonymus Valesianus, pars posterior, ed. Mommsen, MGH *Auct. Ant.* 9

Anselm of Gembloux, *Continuatio Sigeberti*, ed. Bethmann, MGH *SS* 6, 375-385

Arnold of Lübeck, *Chronica slavorum*, ed. Lappenberg, MGH *SS* 21, 101-250

Arnulf, *Gesta archiepiscoporum Mediolanensium*, ed. Bethmann/Wattenbach, MGH *SS* 8, 1-31

Astronomus, *Vita Hludowici imperatoris*, ed. Tremp, MGH *SS rer. Germ.* 64

Balderic, *Gesta Alberonis archiepiscopi Trevirensis*, ed. Waitz MGH *SS* 8, 234-260

Bartolomaeo de Neocastro, *Historia Sicula*, ed. G. Paladino, *RIS2* 13,3, Bologna 1921/22

Behaim, see Albert B.

Benedict of Peterborough see *Gesta regis Henrici secundi*

Benedicti Sancti Andreae monachi *Chronicon*, ed. Pertz, MGH *SS* 3, 695-722

Bernard Guy, *Vita Gregorii papae X* in Muratori 3.1, Milan 1723, 597-598

Bernardus Marango: see *Annales Pisani*

Bernat Desclot, *Cronica del Rey En Pere e dels seus antecessors passats*, in Buchon 565-736

Bonizo, *Liber ad amicum*, ed. Dümmler, MGH *Ldl* 1, 568-620

Breve chronicon de rebus siculis, ed. Stürner, MGH *SS rer. Germ.* 77

Breve chronicon Pisanum, ed. Gentile, *RIS2* 6.2, 107-116

Bruno, *De bello Saxonico*, ed. Pertz, MGH *SS* 5, 327-384

Burchard of Ursberg, *Chronicon*, ed. Holder-Egger, MGH *SS rer. Germ.* 16

Caesarius of Heisterbach, *Dialogus miraculorum*, ed. J. Strange, Cologne 1851
   – *Vita Engelberti*, ed. Böhmer, *Fontes rerum germanicarum* 2, Stuttgart 1845

Casus monasterii Petrishusensis, ed. A. and L. Weiland, MGH *SS* 20, 621-683

Casus Sancti Galli, ed. Von Arx, MGH *SS* 2, 59-183

Chronica de Mailros, ed. J. Stevenson, Edinburgh 1835

Chronica monasterii Casinensis, ed. Wattenbach, MGH *SS* 7, 551-844

Chronica regia coloniensis, ed. Waitz MGH *SS rer. Germ.* 18

Chronica Sancti Petri Erfordensis moderna see *Chronicon Sampetrinum*

Chronicon Estense, edd. Bertoni, G. and Vicini, E.P., *RIS2* 15.3, Città di Castello 1908

Chronicon Minoritae Erphordensis, ed. Holder Egger, MGH *SS rer. Germ.* 24, 486-671

Chronicon Moisiaccense, ed. Pertz, MGH *SS* 1, 280-313

Chronicon Mutinense, ed. Casini, *RIS2* 15.4, Bologna (*s.a.*)

Chronicon Novaliciense, ed Bethmann, MGH *SS rer. Germ.* 21

Chronicon Parmense, ed. Bonazzi, G., *RIS2* 9.9, Città di Castello 1902

Chronicon Paschale, ed. Dindorf, 2 volumes, Bonn 1832

Chronicon Sampetrinum, ed. Holder-Egger, MGH *SS rer. Germ.* 42, 117-369

Chronicon Siculum, see Anonymi CS

Chronicon Suessanum, ed. Pellicia, *Raccolta di varie croniche … appartenenti alla storia del regno di Napoli*, Tome 1, Naples 1780

Clausula de unctione Pippini regis, ed. Wattenbach MGH, *SS* 15.1, 1

Corpus Chronicorum Bononiensium ad ann 1175, ed. A. Sorbelli, *RIS2* 18.2, Città di Castello 1938

Cronica Floridi Horti, ed. Jansen and Janse, Hilversum 1991

Diplovatatius (Tomasso Diplovatacio), *De claris iuris consultis, Pars posterior*, ed. Kantorowicz/Schulz, Bologna 1968

Durant, Guillaume, *Speculum iuris,* ed. Basel 1574, two volumes

Eike of Repgow, *Sachsenspiegel*, ed. Eckhard, MGH *Fontes iuris N.S.* 1

Einhard, *Vita Karoli magni*, ed. Pertz, MGH, *SS* 2, 426-463

Ellenhard, *Chronicon*, ed Jaffé MGH *SS* 17, 118-141

Estoire d'Eracles, in *Recueil des Historiens des Croisades, Historiens Occidentaux* 2, Paris 1859

Falco Beneventanus, *Chronicon Beneventanum*, ed. D'Angelo, Florence 1998

Ferretus Vicentinus (Ferreto dei Ferreti), *Historia rerum in Italia gestarum*, ed. Cipolla, *Le opere di Ferreto de'Ferreti* I, Rome 1908

Fiamma, Galvano, *Historia Mediolanensis*, Muratori 11, col. 531-740

Fragmenta memorialis potestatum Mutinae, ed. Casini, G., *RIS2* 15.4, 185-192

Fredegar ('Pseudo'), *Chronica*, ed. Krusch, MGH *SS rer. Merov.* 2

Gaufredus Malaterra, *De rebus gestis Rogerii, Calabriae et Siciliae comitis et Roberti Guiscardi ducis fratris eius*, ed. Pontieri, E., *RIS2* 5.1, Bologna 1928

Geoffrey of Viterbo, *Gesta Heinrici VI.*, ed. Waitz, MGH *SS* 22, 334-338

George Pachymeres, *De Michaele Palaeologo*, ed. Bekker, Bonn 1835

Gerhoch of Reichersberg, *De investigatione Antichristi*, ed. Sackur, MGH *Ldl* 3, 304-395

Gesta ducum sive principum Polonorum, ed. Szlachtowski and Koepke, MGH *SS* 9, 418-478

Gesta Federici I imperatoris in Lombardia, ed. Holder-Egger, MGH *SS rer. Germ.* 27

Gesta Federici I. imp. in expeditione sacra, ed. Holder-Egger MGH SS rer. Germ. 27

Gesta Florentinorum, ed. Schmeidler, MGH SS rer. Germ. N.S. 8, 243-277

Gesta Lucanorum, ed. Schmeidler MGH *SS rer. Germ. N.S.* 8

Gesta regis Henrici secundi, ed. Stubbs, 2 volumes, London 1867

Gildas, *De excidio Britanniae*, ed. Giles, J.A., *History of the Ancient Britons* II, Oxford 1844, 224-300

Gislebert of Mons, *Chronicon Hanoniense*, ed. Vanderkindere, Brussels 1904

Gratianus, *Decretum (Concordantia discordantium canonum)*, ed. Friedberg, Leipzig 1879 (repr. Graz 1959)

Gregory of Tours, *Libri Historiarum*, MGH *SS rer. Merov.* 1.1

Guillaume de Nangis, *Chronicon*, in *Recueil* 20, 544-582
 – *Gesta sancti Ludovici*, in *Recueil* 20, 309-462
 – *Gesta Philippi Tertii*, in *Recueil* 20, 466-539

Guillaume de Puylaurens (Guillelmus de Podio Laurentii), ed. Duvernoy, Paris 1976

Guillaume de Saint-Pathus, *Vie de Saint Louis*, ed. Delaborde, Paris 1899

Guillelmus Armoricus (Guillaume le Breton), *De gestis Philippi Augusti*, in *Recueil* 17, 62-116

Helmhold of Bosau, *Cronica slavorum*, ed. Schmeidler, MGH *SS rer. Germ.* 32

Henricus de Segusia (a.k.a. 'Hostiensis'), *Lectura super quinque libris Decretalium*, ed. Strassburg 1512

Hermanni Altahensis, *Annales*, ed. Jaffé, MGH *SS* 17, 381-407

Historia ducum veneticorum, ed. Simonsfeld, MGH *SS* 14, 72-89.

Historia Welforum, ed. Weiland, MGH *SS* 21, 454-471

Hugues de Poitiers, *Historia Viceliacensis* monasterii, in *Recueil* 12, 317-344

Innocentii IIII. PM *Commentaria in V. libros Decretalium*, ed. Venice 1570

Jean de Joinville, *Histoire de Saint Louis*, ed. Wailly, N. de, Paris 1883

Joannes Saresberiensis (John of Salisbury), *Opera omnia*, 5 volumes, ed. Giles, J.A., Oxford 1848

Johannes de Beke, *Croniken van den Stichte van Utrecht ende van Hollant*, ed. Bruch, H., The Hague 1982

John of Paris (Jean Quidort), *De potestate regia et papali*, ed. Bleienstein, F., *Johannes Quidort von Paris, Über königliche und päpstliche Gewalt*, Stuttgart 1969

Julianus Toletanus, *Historia Wambae regis*, ed. Levison, MGH, *SS rer. Mer.* 5, 500-535

Lamberti Hersfeldensis Annales, ed. Hesse, MGH *SS* 5, 134-263

Landulphus de sancto Paulo, *Historia Mediolanensis*, ed. Bethmann/Jaffé, MGH *SS* 20, 17-49

Liber censuum ecclesiae Romanae, ed. Fabre, P. and Duchesne, L., 3 volumes, Rome 1889-1952

Liber de unitate ecclesiae conservanda, ed. Schwenkenbecher, MGH *Ldl* 2, 173-284

Liber diurnus, ed. De Rozière, Eug., Paris 1869

Liber iurium reipublicae Genuensis I, Turin 1854

Liudprand of Cremona, *Historia Ottonis*, ed. Becker, MGH, *SS rer. Germ.* 41

Magnus of Reichersberg, *Chronica*, ed. Wattenbach, MGH 17, 439-534

Manegold of Lautenbach, *Liber ad Gebehardum*, ed. Franke, MGH *Ldl* 1, 300-430

Melis Stoke, *Rijmkroniek van Holland* 4370-4385, ed. J.W.J. Burgers, The Hague 2004

Matthew Paris, *Chronica maiora*, ed. Luard, H.R., 7 volumes (including Index and Glossary), London 1872-1880

Matthias of Neuenburg, *Chronica*, ed. Hofmeister, MGH *SS rer. Germ. NS* 4

Muntaner, *see* Ramon M.

'Nicolaus de Jamsilla', *Historia de rebus gestis Friderici II imperatoris eiusque filiorum Conradi et Manfredi*, in Muratori 8, Milan 1726, col. 489-616

Nicolaus de Carbio (Niccolo da Calvi) *Vita Innocentii IV*, ed. Pagnotti, F. in *Archivio della R. Società Romana di Storia Patria* 21, Rome 1898, 76-120

Nicolas Specialis, *Historia Sicula*, in Gregorio, *Biblioteca* 1, 283-508

Nithard, *Historiarum libri IIII*, ed. Pertz/Müller, MGH *SS rem. Germ.* 44

Notae Weingartenses, ed. Waitz MGH *SS* 24, 830-833

Oliver of Cologne, *Historia Damiatina*, ed. Hoogeweg, Tübingen 1894

Otto of St. Blasius, *Chronica*, ed. Hofmeister, MGH *SS Rer. germ.* 47

Ottonis episc. freisingensis Chronica, ed. Hofmeister, MGH *SS Rer. germ.* 45

Ottonis episc. freisingensis et Rahewini Gesta Friderici, ed. Waitz/De Simson, MGH *SS rer. Germ.* 46

Otto Morena, Acerbus Morena and Continuator, *Historia*, ed. Güterbock MGH *SS rer. Germ. N.S.* 7

Pachymeres, see George P.

Paulus Diaconus, *Historia Lombardorum*, ed. Bethmann and Waitz, MGH *SS rer. Germ.* 48

Peter of Eboli, *Liber ad honorem Augusti*, ed. Siragusa, G.B., Rome 1906

Peter of Vaux-de-Cernay, *Hystoria Albigensis*, ed. Guébin, P. and Lyon E., 3 volumes, Paris 1926-1939

Pietro Cantinelli, *Chronicon*, ed. Torraca, Fr., *RIS2* 28.2

Primat of S. Denys (transl. Jean de Vignay), *Recueil* 23, 1-105

Ralph of Coggeshall, *Chronicon anglicanum*, ed. Stevenson, J., London 1875

Radulph de Diceto (Ralph of Diss), *Imagines historiarum*, ed. Stubbs, 2 volumes, London 1876

Ramon Muntaner, *Cronica*, in Buchon, 217-564 (French translation)

Regino of Prüm, *Chronicon*, ed. Kurze, MGH *SS rer. Germ.* 50

Reineri annales, see *Annales Sancti Jacobi*

Relatio de concilio Lugdunensi, MGH *Const.* 2 no 401, 513-516

Riccobaldo da Ferrara, *Historia imperatorum*, Muratori 9, Milan 1726, 291-420

Richer of Soissons, *Gesta Senoniensis ecclesiae*, ed. Waitz, MGH *SS* 25, 249-345

Robertus de Monte (Robert of Torigni), *Cronica*, ed. Bethmann, MGH *SS* 6, 475-535

Roger of Hoveden, *Chronica*, ed. Stubbs, W., 4 volumes, London 1868-1871

Roger of Wendover, *Flores Historiarum*, ed. Coxe, H., 5 volumes (including Appendix), Londen 1841-1844

Rolandinus Patavinus, *Chronica*, ed. Pertz, MGH *SS* 19, 32-147

Romoald of Salerno, *Chronicon*, ed. Arndt, MGH *SS* 19, 387-461

Ryccardus de S. Germano, *Chronica*, ed. Garufi, C.A. *RIS2* 7.2, Bologna 1936-1938

Saba Malaspina, *Cronica*, ed. Koller/Nitschke, MGH *SS* 35

Salimbene de Adam, *Cronica*, ed. Holder-Egger, MGH *SS* 32

Saxo Grammaticus, *Gesta Danorum*, ed. Holder, Strassburg 1886

Sigebert of Gembloux, *Chronica*, ed. Bethmann, MGH *SS* 6, 300-374, with continuations (375-474)

Suger, *Vita Ludovici Grossi regis*, in *Oeuvres complètes de Suger*, ed. A. Lecoy de la Marche, Paris 1867

Thegan, *Gesta Hludowici imperatoris*, ed. Tremp, MGH *SS rer. Germ.* 64

Theophanes Confessor, *Chronographia*, ed. Classen, Bonn 1839

Thierry de Vaucouleurs, 'Vita metrica Urbani IV', Muratori 3.2, Milan 1734, col. 405-420

Thietmar of Merseburg, *Chronicon*, ed. Holtzmann, MGH *SS rer. Germ. N.S.* 9

Tholomaeus of Lucca, *Annales Lucenses*, ed. Schmeidler, MGH *SS rer. Germ. N.S.* 8
– *Historia ecclesiastica nova*, in Muratori 11, Milan 1727, col. 753-1242

Thomas Tuscus, *Gesta imperatorum et pontificum*, ed. Ehrenfeuchter, MGH *SS* 22, 483-528

Thomas Wykes, *Chronicon*, ed. Luard, London 1869

Tolosanus, *Chronicon Faventinum*, ed. Rossini, *RIS2* 28,1, Bologna 1936-1939

Villani, Giov., *Nuova Cronica*, ed. Porta, three volumes, Parma 1990-1991

Vincent of Prague, *Annales*, ed. Wattenbach, MGH *SS* 17, 658-683

Walter Map, *De nugis curialium*, ed. Montague Rhodes, James, Oxford 1914

Widukind of Corvey, *Rerum Gestarum Saxonicarum*, ed. Lohmann-Hirsch, MGH, *SS rer. Germ.* 60

William of Tyre, *Historia belli sacri*, Migne *PL* 201, 209-891

Wipo, *Gesta Chuonradi II imperatoris*, ed. Bresslau, MGH *SS rer. Germ.* 61

II. Modern works

1. General

Abulafia, D. (ed.), *The New Cambridge Medieval History V, c. 1198 – c. 1300,* Cambridge 1999

Böhmer, J.F., *Regesta imperii,* new editions, Insbruck 1889 -, available online at www. regesta-imperii.de

Dizionario Biografico degli Italiani, Istituto della Enciclopedia Italiana, Rome 1960 - (excellent and well documented biographies, available online at www.treccani. it/biografico)

Dunphy, G. (ed.), *The Encyclopedia of the Medieval Chronicle* 2 volumes, Leiden 2010

Jaffé/Loewenfeld/Kaltenbrunner/Ewald, *Regesta pontificum romanorum ab condita ecclesia ad annum post Christum natum 1198,* 2 volumes, Leipzig 1885-1888

Lexikon des Mittelalters, 9 volumes, Stuttgart 1999

Luscombe, D. and Riley-Smith, J. (edd.), *The New Cambridge Medieval History IV, c.1024-c.1198,* Cambridge 2015

Potthast, A., *Regesta Pontificum Romanorum inde ab a. 1198 ad a. 1304,* 2 volumes, Berlin 1874-1875

2. Specific

Abulafia, D., *Frederick II, a Medieval Emperor,* London 1988

Acconcia Longo, A., 'L'assedio e la distruzione de Gallipoli, 1268-1269' in *Archivio Storico Italiano,* 146 (1988), 3-22

Affeldt, W., 'Untersuchungen zur Königserhebung Pippins', in *Frühmittelalterliche Studien* 14 (1980) 95-187

Affò, Ireneo, *Storia della città di Parma* III, Parma 1793

Aquilecchia, Giov., 'Dante and the Florentine Chroniclers', *Bulletin of the John Rylands Library* 48 (1965) 30-55

Amari, M., *La Guerra del Vespro Siciliano,* 9th ed., 3 volumes, Milan 1886

Arnold, B., *Princes and territories in medieval Germany,* Cambridge 1991

Aurell, M., *The Plantagenet Empire, 1154-1224,* Harlow 2007

Baaken, G., 'Unio regni ad imperium', in *Quellen und Forschungen aus italienischen Archiven und Bibliotheken* 52 (1972) 219-297

   – *Ius imperii ad regnum,* Cologne/Weimar/Vienna 1993

   – 'Die Verhandlungen von Cluny (1245) und der Kampf Innozenz IV. gegen Friedrich II.', in *DA* 50 (1994) 531-579

   – *Imperium und Papsttum, zur Geschichte des 12. und 13. Jahrhunderts,* Cologne 1997 (collected essays)

Battelli, G., 'I Transunti di Lione' in *MIÖG* 62 (1954) 348-364

Berger, E., *Saint Louis et Innocent IV,* Paris 1893

Bergmann, A., *König Manfred von Sizilien,* Heidelberg 1909

Berman, H. J., *Law and Revolution, The Formation of the Western Legal Tradition,* Cambridge, Mass. 1983

Bernhardi, W., *Lothar von Supplinburg*, Leipzig 1879
  – *Konrad III*, 2 volumes, Leipzig 1883
Bloch, Marc, *Feudal Society*, 2 volumes, Henley-on-Thames 1965
Borst, A., 'Der Streit um das weltliche und das geistliche Schwert', in idem, *Barbaren, Ketzer und Artisten, Welten des Mittelalters*, Munich/Zürich 1988, 99-122
Boshof, E. (ed.), *Rudolf von Habsburg. Eine Königsherrschaft zwischen Tradition und Wandel*, Cologne 1993
  – *Die Geschichte des Christentums, Mittelalter*, 3 volumes, Freiburg i.B. 1991/2007
Boutaric, Edg., *La France sous Philippe le Bel*, Paris 1861
Bresslau, H., 'Zur Vorgeschichte der Wahl Rudolfs von Habsburg', *MIÖG* 15 (1984) 59-67
Brundage, J.A., *Medieval Canon Law*, New York 1995
Bryce, J., *The Holy Roman Empire*, ed. New York 1961
Busson, A., *Die Doppelwahl des Jahres 1257 und das römische Königthum Alfons X. von Castilien*, Münster 1866
  – 'Friedrich der Freidige als Prätendent der sicilischen Krone und Johann von Procida' in *Historische Aufsätze dem Andenken G. Waitz gewidmet*, Hannover 1886, 324-336.
Büttner, H., 'Aus den Anfängen des abenländischen Staatsgedankens. Die Königserhebung Pippins', in *Historisches Jahrbuch der Görresgesellschaft* 71 (1952) 77-90
Calasso, F., *Medio Evo del Diritto I, Le Fonti*, Milan 1954
Canagna, A., 'Genova nel Medioevo, una città turrita', in Pessa, Loredana (ed.), *Genova nel Medioevo*, Genoa 2016, 46-53
Capitani, Ov. (ed.), *Bologna nel Medioevo*, Bologna 2007 (essays by various scholars)
Carlyle, R.W., *A History of Medieval Political Theory in the West*, 6 volumes, Edinburgh/London 1970
Cartellieri, O., *Peter von Aragon und die sizilianische Vesper*, Heidelberg 1904
  – *Philipp II. August, König von Frankreich*, 4 volumes, Leipzig 1899-1922 (repr. Aalen 1984)
Caspar, E., *Pippin und die römische Kirche*, Berlin 1914
Cherrier, C.J. de, *Histoire de la lutte des papes et des empereurs de la maison de Souabe* (2d ed.), 3 volumes, Paris 1858
Classen, P., *Karl der Grosse, das Papsttum und Byzanz: die Begründung des karolingischen Kaisertums*, Sigmaringen 1985
Cleve, T.C. van, *The Emperor Frederick II of Hohenstaufen*, Oxford 1972
Coing, H. (ed.), *Handbuch der Quellen und Literatur der Neueren europäischen Privatrechtsgeschichte I, Mittelalter (1100-1500)*, Munich 1973
Cowdrey, H.E.J., 'Pope Gregory VII and the Anglo-Norman Kingdom', in G.B. Borini (ed.), *Studi Gregoriani* 9, Rome 1972, 79-114
Csendes, P., *Heinrich VI*, Darmstadt 1993
Colorni, Vit., *Die drei verschollenen Gesetze des Reichstages bei Roncaglia*, Aalen 1969 (Germ. transl. of the Italian original (1967))

Dagron, G., *Emperor and Priest*, Cambridge 2003

Davidsohn, R., *Geschichte von Florenz*, 10 volumes, Berlin 1896-1927

Del Giudice, G., *Il giudizio e la condanna di Corradino*, Naples 1876

Didier, N., 'Henri de Suse, évêque de Sisteron' (1244-1250)' in *Revue historique de droit français et étranger* 30 (1953) 244-270

Digard, G., *Philippe le Bel et le Saint-Siège de 1285 à 1304*, Liège/Paris, 1936

Dilcher, H., *Die Sizilische Gesetzgebung Kaiser Friedrichs II.*, Cologne/Vienna 1975
  – *Die Entstehung der lombardischen Stadtkommune*, Aalen 1967

Duby, G., *Les trois orders ou l'imaginaire du féodalisme*, Paris 1978
  – *Le Dimanche de Bouvines, 27 juillet 1214*, Paris 1973

Dunbabin, Jean, *Charles I of Anjou*, London 1998
  – *The French in the Kingdom of Sicily, 1266-1305*, Cambridge 2011
  – *France in the Making, 843 – 1180*, Oxford 1985

Engelmann, W., *Die Wiedergeburt der Rechtskultur in Italien durch die wissenschaftliche Lehre*, Leipzig 1938

Ennslin, W., 'Auctoritas und Potestas', in *Historisches Jahrbuch der Görresgesellschaft* 74 (1955) 661-668

Fasoli, G., *La Lega Lombarda*, in Schmale, F.J. (ed.), *Probleme des 12. Jahrhunderts*: Reichenau-Vorträge 1965-1967. Vorträge und Forschungen, Konstanz/Lindau 1967, 143-160

Favier, J., *Philippe le Bel*, Paris 1978
  – 'Les légistes et le gouvernement de Philippe le Bel', in *Journal des savants* 1969, 92-108

Feine, H., *Kirchliche Rechtsgeschichte I, Die Katholische Kirche*, 2d ed. Weimar 1954

Ficker, J., *Forschungen zur Reichs- und Rechtsgeschichte Italiens*, 4 volumes, Innsbruck 1868-1874
  – *Vom Reichsfürstenstande* 2 volumes, Insbruck 1861-1923

Folz, A., *Kaiser Friedrich II. und Papst Innozenz IV.; ihr Kampf in den Jahren 1244 und 1245*, Strasssburg 1905

Fournier, P., *Le Royaume d'Arles et de Vienne (1138-1378)*, Paris 1891

Freed, John B., *Frederick Barbarossa, the Prince and the Myth*, New Haven, Conn. 2016

Fried, J., *Donation of Constantine and Constitutum Constantini*, Berlin 2007
  – *Karl der Grosse, Gewalt und Glaube, eine Biographie*, Munich 2013
  – *Die Entstehung des Juristenstandes im 12. Jahrhundert*, Cologne/Vienna 1974

Friedl, C., Herde, P. e.a. (edd.), *Manfred – König von Sizilien (1258-1266)*, Göppingen 2015

Fuhrmann, H., 'Konstantinische Schenkung und Silvesterlegende in neuer Sicht', in *DA* 1959, 523-540.
  – 'Konstantinische Schenkung und abendländisches Kaisertum', in *DA* 22 (1966) 63-178

Ganshof, F.L., *Qu'est-ce que la féodalité?*, Brussels 1957

Gasquet, Am., *De l'autorité impériale en matière religieuse a Byzance*, Paris 1879

Geanakoplos, D., 'Michael VIII Palaeologus and the Union of Lyons 1274' in *The Harvard Theological Review* 46 (1953) 79-89

Görich, K, *Friedrich Barbarossa, eine Biographie*, Munich 2011

Goez, E., *Geschichte Italiens im Mittelalter*, Darmstadt 2010

Goez, W, *Translatio Imperii. Ein Beitrag zur Geschichte des Geschichtsdenkens und der politischen Theorien im Mittelalter und in der frühen Neuzeit*, Tübingen 1958
– 'Die Entstehung der italienischen Kommunen im frühen Mittelalter', in *Sb. der phil.-hist. Klasse der Bayer. Ak. d. Wissensch.*, 1944/46, Munich 1946
– 'Über die Mathildischen Schenkungen an die römische Kirche', in *Frühmittelalterliche Studien* 31 (1997) 158-196

Gregorovius, F., *Geschichte der Stadt Rom im Mittelalter*, 8 volumes, Stuttgart 1869-1872

Güterbock, F., *Der Prozess Heinrichs des Löwen*, Berlin 1909

Hageneder, O, 'Das päpstliche Recht der Fürstenabsetzung: seine kanonistische Grundlegung', in *Archivum Historiae Pontificiae* 1 (1963) 53-95

Hahn, A., 'Das Hludowicianum, Die Urkunde Ludwigs d. Fr. für die römische Kirche', in *Archiv für Diplomatik* 21 (1975) 15-135

Hampe, K., *Papst Innozenz IV und die sizilische Verschwörung von 1246*, Heidelberg, 1923
– *Geschichte Konradins von Hohenstaufen*, Innsbruck 1894
– *Urban IV und Manfred*, Heidelberg 1905
– 'Über die Flugschriften zum Lyoner Konzil von 1245', in *Historische Vierteljahrschrift* 11 (1908) 297-313

Hartmann, W. and Pennington, K. (edd.), *The History of Medieval Canon Law in the Classical Period, 1140-1234*, Washington D.C. 2008
– *The History of Courts and Procedure in Medieval Canon Law*, Washington D.C. 2016

Haskins, C.H., *The Renaissance of the Twelfth Century*, Cambridge M./London

Haverkamp, A., *Aufbruch und Gestaltung, Deutschland 1056-1273*, 2d ed., Munich 1993
– *Herrschaftsformen der Frühstaufer*, 2 volumes, Stuttgart 1970-1971

Hechberger, W. and Schuller, F. (edd.), *Staufer & Welfen*, Regensburg 2009

Heers, J., *Le clan familial au Moyen Age*, Paris 1974

Hefele, C.J. (and Knöpfler, A.), *Conciliengeschichte, nach den Quellen bearbeitet*, Vol. 5 and 6, Freiburg i.B. 1886 and 1890

Hegel, C., *Geschichte der Städteverfassung von Italien seit der Zeit der römischen Herrschaft bis zum Ausgang des zwölften Jahrhunderts*, 2 volumes, Leipzig 1847

Heinemeyer, W., 'Beneficium-non feudum sed bonum factum, der Streit auf dem Reichstag zu Besançon 1157', *Archiv für Diplomatik* 15 (1969) 155-236
– 'König und Reichsfürsten in der späten Salier- und frühen Stauferzeit' in *Blätter für deutsche Landesgeschichte* 122 (1986) 1-39

Heinisch, K.J., *Kaiser Friedrich II. in Briefen und Berichten seiner Zeit*, Darmstadt 19668

Herbers, K., *Geschichte des Papsttums im Mittelalter*, Darmstadt 2012

Herde, P., *Karl I. von Anjou*, Stuttgart 1979
- 'Die Schlacht bei Tagliacozzo' in *Zeitschrift für Bayerische Landesgeschichte* 25 (1962) 679-744
- 'Ein Pamphlet der päpstlichen Kurie gegen Kaiser Friedrich II. von 1245/46 ('Eger cui lenia')', in *DA* 23 (1967) 468-538
Hessel, *Geschichte der Stadt Bologna von 1116 bis 1280*, Berlin 1910 (repr. Vaduz 1965)
Hinschius, P., *System des katholischen Kirchenrechts* 6 volumes, Berlin 1869-1897 (old, but *very* useful)
Hintze, O., 'Typologie der ständischen Verfassungen des Abendlandes', *Historische Zeitschrift* 141 (1930) 229-248
Höfler, C., *Albert von Beham*, Stuttgart 1847
Holstein, H., *Lyon II*, in Wolter, H. and Holstein, H., *Lyon I/Lyon II*, Mainz 1972, 141-257.
Holzmann, R., *Wilhelm von Nogaret*, Freiburg i.B. 1898
Hove, A. van, *Prolegomena ad codicem iuris canonici*, Malines/Rome 1945
Huillard-Bréholles, A., *Vie et correspondence de Pierre de la Vigne*, Paris 1865
Jordan, E., *Les origines de la domination angevine en Italie*, Paris 1909
Kämpf, H. (ed.), *Herrschaft und Staat im Mittelalter*, Wege der Forschung II, Darmstadt 1960
Kantorowicz, E., *Kaiser Friedrich der Zweite*, Berlin 1928, to be read with the 'Ergänzungsband', Düsseldorf/Munich 1963
- *The King's Two Bodies, a Study in Medieval Political Theology*, Princeton 1957
Karajan, T.G. von, *Zur Geschichte des Concils von Lyon 1245*, Vienna 1850
Kehr, P., 'Der vertrag von Anagni im Jahre 1176', in *Neues Archiv der Gesellschaft für ältere deutsche Geschichtskunde* 13 (1888) 75-118
- 'Die sogenannte karolinische Schenkung von 774', in *HZ* 70 (1893) 385-441
Kempf, Fr., 'Die Absetzung Friedrichs II. im Lichte der Kanonistik', in J. Fleckenstein (ed.), *Probleme um Friedrich II.*, Sigmaringen 1974, 345-360
Kéry, L., 'Das Kirchenrecht als Instrument päpstlichen Führungsanspruchs', in: B. Schneidmüller, St. Weinfurter *e.a.* (Hgg.), *Die Päpste I, Amt und Herrschaft in Antike, Mittelalter und Renaissance*, Regensburg 2016
Knabe, L., *Die gelasianische Zweigewaltentheorie bis zum Ende des Investiturstreits*, Berlin 1936 (repr. Vaduz 1965)
Köpke R. and Dümler, E., *Kaiser Otto der Grosse (936–973)*, Leipzig 1876 (repr. Darmstadt 1962)
Kuttner, S. and García y García, Ant., 'A new eyewitness account of the fourth Lateran council', *Traditio* 20 (1964)
Lange, H., *Römisches Recht im Mittelalter I, die Glossatoren*, Munich 1997
Lange, H and Kriechbaum, M., *Römisches Recht im Mittelalter II, die Kommentatoren*, Munich 2007
Langlois, C.-V., *Le règne de Philippe III le Hardi*, Paris 1887
Lecler, J., 'L'argument des deux glaives dans les controverses politiques du moyen age: ses origines et son développement' in *Recherches de science religieuse* 21 (1931) 299-339; 22 (1932) 151-177 and 280-303

Lecoy de la Marche, A., *Les relations politiques de la France avec le royaume de Majorque*, 2 volumes, Paris 1892

Le Goff, J., *Saint Louis*, Paris 1996

Léonard, Emile G., *Les Angevins de Naples*, Paris 1954

Leupen, P., *Keizer in zijn eigen rijk*, Amsterdam 1998

Levison, W., 'Konstantinische Schenkung und Silvesterlegende', in *Miscellanea Fr. Ehrle* II, Rome 1924, 159-247

– 'Die mittelalterliche Lehre von den beiden Schwertern' in *DA* 9 (1952) 14-42

Lewis, A.W., 'Anticipatory Association of the Heir in Early Capetian France', in *American Historical Review* 83 (1978) 906-927

Lot, P. and Fawtier, R., *Histoire des Institutions Françaises au Moyen Age*, 3 volumes, Paris 1957-1962

Loud, Gr., 'Norman Sicily in the Twelfth Century', in Luscombe, D. and Riley-Smith, J. (edd.), *The New Cambridge Medieval History IV, c.1024-c.1198*, 442-474

Lunt, W.E., 'The Sources of the First Council of Lyon, 1245', in *The English Historical Review* 33 (1918) 72-77

Maassen, F., *Geschichte der Quellen und Literatur des canonischen Rechts im Abendlande bis zum Ausgange des Mittelalters* I, Gratz 1870

Maffei, D., *La donazione di Costantino nei giuristi medievali*, Milan 1964

Mas Latrie, L. de, *Traités de paix et de commerce et documents divers concernant les rélations des Chrétiens avec les Arabes de l'Afrique septentrionale au moyen age*, Paris 1866

Melloni, A, *Innocenzo IV. La concezione e l'esperienza della cristianità come 'regimen unius personae'*, Genoa 1990

Meyer, W., *Ludwig IX. von Frankreich und Innozenz IV. in den Jahren 1244-1247*, Marburg 1915

Meyer von Knonau, G., *Jahrbücher des Deutschen Reiches unter Heinrich IV. und Heinrich V.*, 7 volumes, Leipzig 1890-1909

Minieri-Riccio, Cam., *Itinerario di Carlo I. di Angiò*, Naples 1872

Mitteis, H., *Lehnrecht und Staatsgewalt*, Weimar 1933 (repr. Darmstadt 1974)

– *Der Staat des hohen Mittelalters*, Weimar 1940 (repr. Darmstadt 1980)

Mohler, L., *Die Kardinäle Jakob und Peter Colonna, ein Beitrag zur Geschichte des Zeitalters Bonifaz' VIII.*, Paderborn 1914

Moore, J. (ed.), *Pope Innocent III and his World*, London/New York 2016

Moynihan, J.M., *Papal Immunity and Liability in the Writings of the Medieval Canonists*, Rome 1961

München, Nic., *Das kanonische Gerichtsverfahren und Strafrecht*, 2 volumes, Cologne/Neuß 1874 (old, but still *very* useful)

Noble, T.F.X., *The Republic of St. Peter, the Birth of the Papal State, 680-825*, Philadelphia 1984

Norwich, J. J., *The Normans in Sicily*, Harmondsworth 1992

Ohlig, M., *Studien zum Beamtentum Friedrichs II. in Reichsitalien von 1237-1250*, Kleinheubach 1936

Opll, F., *Friedrich Barbarossa*, Darmstadt 2009

Ostrogorsky, G., *Geschichte des byzantinischen Staates*, Munich 1963

Otto, H., *Die Beziehungen Rudolfs von Habsburg zu Papst Gregor X.*, Insbruck 1895

Overmann, A., *Gräfin Mathilde von Tuscien*, Innsbruck 1895 (repr. Frankfurt a.M. 1965)

Pegues, F.J., *The Lawyers of the Last Capetians*, Princeton 1962

Pennington, K., *The Prince and the Law*, Berkeley/Los Angeles 1993

Powell, J.M., *The Liber Augustalis or Constitutions of Melfi*, Syracuse, N.Y. 1971 (transl. and introd.)

Previté-Orton, C.W., 'The Italian cities till *c.* 1200', in *The Cambridge Medieval History* V, New York 1926, 208-241

Puttkamer, G. von, *Papst Innocenz IV. Versuch einer Gesamtcharakteristik aus seiner Wirkung*, Münster 1930.

Raccagni, Gianluca, *The Lombard League (1164–1225)*, Oxford 2010

Redlich, O., *Rudolf von Habsburg. Das deutsche Reich nach dem Untergang des alten Kaisertums*, Innsbruck 1903 (repr. Aalen 1965)

Reynolds, S., *Fiefs and Vassals*, Oxford 1994

Riché, P., *Abbon de Fleury*, Turnhout 2004

   – *Gerbert d'Aurillac, le pape de l'an mil*, Paris 2006

Roberg, B., 'Zur Überlieferung und Interpretation der Hauptquelle des Lugdunense I von 1245', in *Annuarium Historiae Conciliorum* 22 (1990) 31-67

Rodenberg, C., *Innozenz IV. und das Königreich Sicilien, 1245-1254*, Halle 1892

Ropp, G. von der, *Erzbischof Werner von Mainz*, Göttingen 1872

Roth, K., *Genealogie des Staates, Prämissen des neuzeitlichen politischen Denkens*, 2d ed., Berlin 2011

Rübesamen, A., *Landgraf Heinrich Raspe von Thüringen, der Gegenkönig Friedrichs II.*, Halle 1885

Runciman, S., *A History of the Crusades*, 3 volumes, Harmondsworth 1965

   – *The Sicilian Vespers, A History of the Mediterrenean World in the later Thirteenth Century*, Cambridge 1958

Saint Priest, Alexis de, *Histoire de la conquête de Naples par Charles d'Anjou*, 4 volumes, Paris 1849

Sarti, M. and Fattorini, M., *De claris archigymnasii Bononiensis professoribus* 2 volumes, Bologna 1888-1896

Savioli, L., *Annali Bolognesi*, 3 parts in 6 volumes, Bassano 1784-1795

Schieffer, R., 'Graf Heinrich II. von Diez', in H. Keller (ed.), *Italia et Germania*, Tübingen 2001

Schirrmacher, F., *Die letzten Hohenstaufen*, Göttingen 1871

Schneidmüller B. and Weinfurter S. (edd.), *Die deutschen Herrscher des Mittelalters*, Munich 2003

Scholz, R. *Die Publizistik zur Zeit Philipps des Schönen und Bonifaz VIII.*, Stuttgart 1903 (repr. Amsterdam 1969)

Scholz, S, 'Die Pippinische Schenkung, neue Lösungsansätze für ein altes Problem', *HZ* 307 (2018), 635-654

Schönherr, F., *Die Lehre vom Reichsfürstenstande des Mittelalters*, Leipzig 1914

Schramm, P.E., *Kaiser, Könige und Päpste*, 4 volumes, Stuttgart 1968-1971 (collected essays)

– *Kaiser, Rom und Renovatio*, 2 volumes, Berlin 1929

Schulte, J.F. von, *Geschichte der Quellen und Literatur des canonischen Rechts*, 2 volumes, Stuttgart 1875-1880 (repr. Graz 1956)

Smith, Th. (ed.), *Authority and Power in the Medieval Church, c. 1000-c. 1500*, Turnhout 2020

Spagnesi, E., *Wernerius Bononiensis iudex; la figura storica d'Irnerio*, Florence 1970

Steinen, W. von den, *Das Kaisertum Friedrichs des Zweiten nach den Anschauungen seiner Staatsbriefe*, Berlin/Leipzig 1922

Stelzer, W., 'Zum Scholarenprivileg Friedrich Barbarossas (Authentica 'Habita')', *DA* 34 (1978) 123

Sternfeld, *Karl von Anjou als Graf der Provence (1245-1265)*, Berlin 1888

– *Ludwigs des Heiligen Kreuzzug nach Tunis und die Politik Karls I. von Sizilien*, Berlin 1896

– 'Das Konklave von 1280 und die Wahl Martins IV. (1281)' in *MIÖG* 31 (1910) 1-53

Stickler, A.M., *Historia iuris canonici latini I, Historia fontium*, Turin 1950

– 'Der Schwerterbegriff bei Huguccio', in *Ephemerides iuris canonici* 3 (1947) 201-242

Strayer, J., *The Reign of Philip the Fair*, Princeton 1980

– 'The Crusade against Aragon', in *Speculum* 28 (1953) 102-113

– *On the Medieval Origins of the Modern State*, Princeton 1970

Struve, T., *Die Entwicklung der organologischen Staatsauffassung im Mittelalter*, Stuttgart 1978

Stürner, W., *Friedrich II.*, Darmstadt 2009

Sumption, J., *The Albigensian crusade*, London 1978

Tierney, B., *Religion, Law and the Growth of Constitutional Thought*, Cambridge 1982

Toeche, T., *Kaiser Heinrich VI*, Leipzig 1867

Tramontana, S., *La monarchia normanna e sveva*, Turin 1986

Ullmann, W., *The Growth of Papal Government in the Middle Ages: A Study in the Ideological Relation of Clerical to Lay Power*, London 1962

– 'Some Reflections on the Opposition of Frederick II to the Papacy', in *Archivio Storico Pugliese* 13 (1960) 16-39

– *Law and Politics in the Middle Ages*, Cambridge 1976

– *The Medieval Idea of Law*, London 1946

– *Medieval Papalism: the Political Theories of the Medieval Canonists*, London 1949

Ullrich, H.U., *Konradin von Hohenstaufen*, Munich 2004

Verdier, F., *Origine et influence des juristes*, Nîmes 1896

Vian, G.M., *La donazione di Costantino*, Bologna 2004

Watt, J.A., 'Medieval Deposition Theory, a neglected *consultatio* from the First Council of Lyons', in G.J. Cuming (ed.), *Studies in Church History* Vol. 2, Cambridge 1965, 197-214
- 'The Theory of Papal Monarchy in the 13th Century. The Contribution of the Canonists', in *Traditio* 20 (1964) 179-317
Weigand, R., 'Magister Rolandus und Papst Alexander III, *Archiv für katholisches Kirchenrecht* 149 (1980) 3-44
Werner, M. (ed.), *Heinrich Raspe, Landgraf von Thüringen und römischer König (1227-1247)*, Frankfurt a.M. 2003
Whalen, B.E., *The Two Powers*, Philadelphia 2019
Wickham, C., *Early Medieval Italy*, London 1981
- *Medieval Rome*, Oxford 2015
- *Medieval Europe*, New Haven/London 2016
Wieruszowski, H., *Politics and Culture in Medieval Spain*, Rome 1971 (collected essays)
- *Vom Imperium zum nationalen Königtum*, Munich/Berlin 1933
Wilson, P.H., *The Holy Roman Empire*, Penguin Books 2016
Wolf, G. (ed.), *Stupor mundi*, Darmstadt 1966 (essays by various scholars)
Wollasch, J., *Cluny, Licht der Welt*, Düsseldorf/Zürich 1996
Wolter, H., *Lyon I*, in Wolter, H. and Holstein, H., *Lyon I/Lyon II*, Mainz 1972, 1-137
Zimmermann, H., *Die päpstliche Legation in der ersten Hälfte des 13. Jahrhunderts*, Paderborn 1913
Zisterer, A., *Gregor X. und Rudolf von Habsburg*, Freiburg i.B. 1891

Index of People and Places

*

Simplified Genealogical Trees

(names of emperors are set in **bold** script and names of popes in ***bold italic*** script)

The Carolingian Dynasty and the Division of the Carolingian Empire

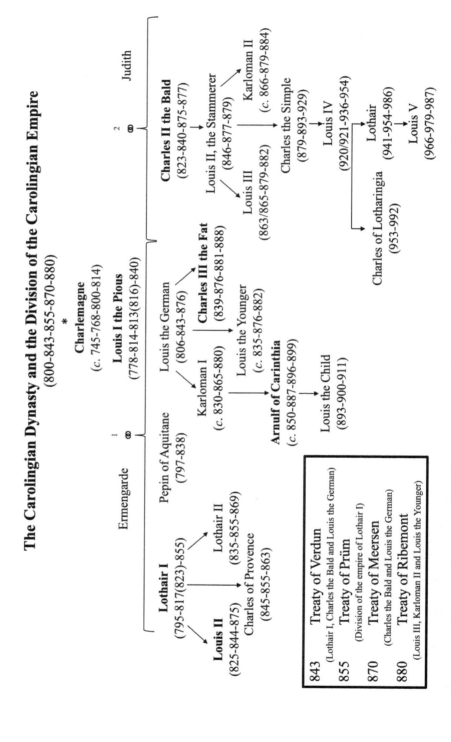

843   Treaty of Verdun
(Lothair I, Charles the Bald and Louis the German)

855   Treaty of Prüm
(Division of the empire of Lothair I)

870   Treaty of Meersen
(Charles the Bald and Louis the German)

880   Treaty of Ribemont
(Louis III, Karloman II and Louis the Younger)

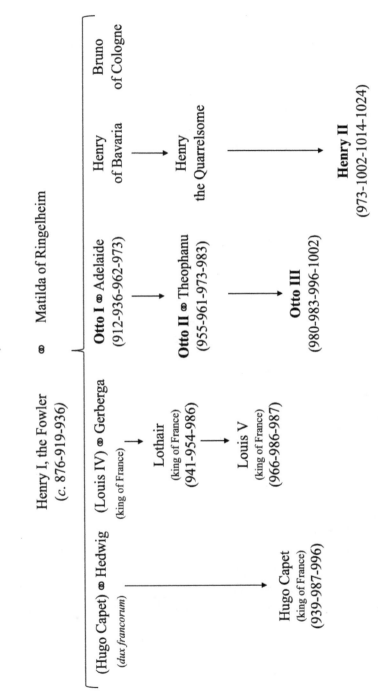

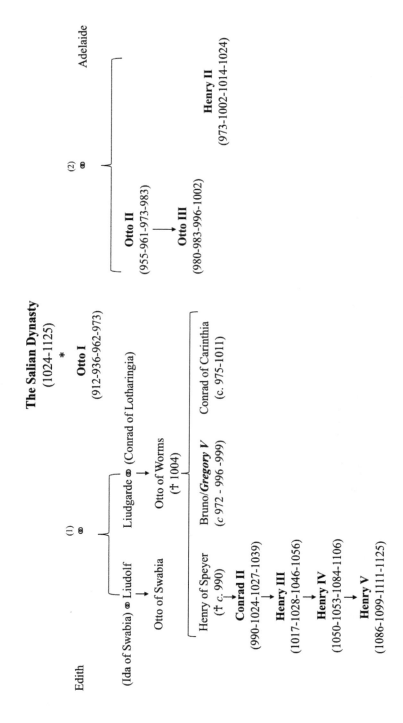

The Salian Dynasty
(1024-1125)

*

Otto I
(912-936-962-973)

Edith

(Ida of Swabia) ⊕ Liudolf

Otto of Swabia

(1) ⊕

Liudgarde ⊕ (Conrad of Lotharingia)

Otto of Worms
(† 1004)

Bruno/*Gregory V*
(c 972 - 996 -999)

Conrad of Carinthia
(c. 975-1011)

Henry of Speyer
(† c. 990)

Conrad II
(990-1024-1027-1039)

Henry III
(1017-1028-1046-1056)

Henry IV
(1050-1053-1084-1106)

Henry V
(1086-1099-1111-1125)

(2) ⊕

Adelaide

Otto II
(955-961-973-983)

Otto III
(980-983-996-1002)

Henry II
(973-1002-1014-1024)

The Hohenstaufen Dynasty and the House of Austria

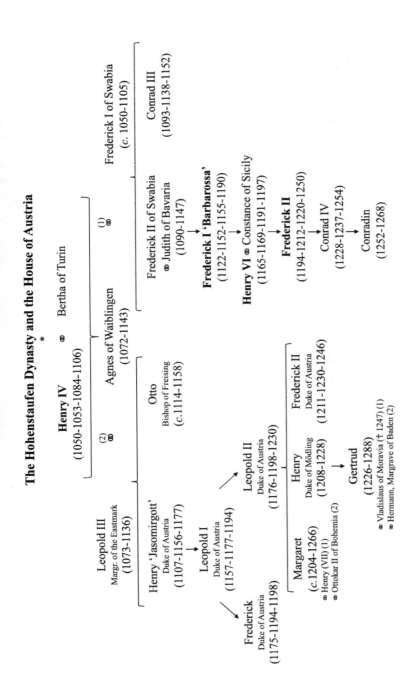

The Hauteville Dynasty
(1000-1198)

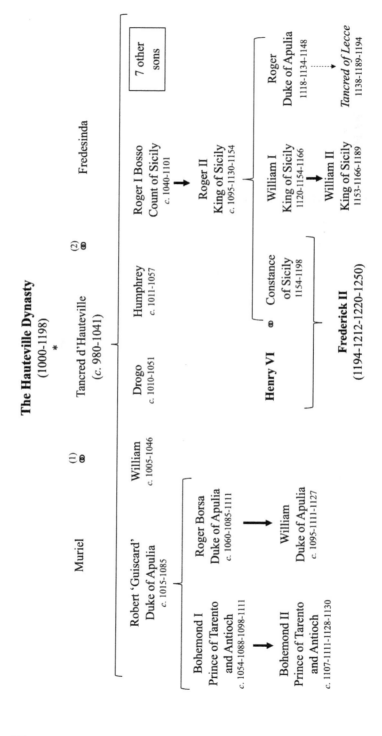

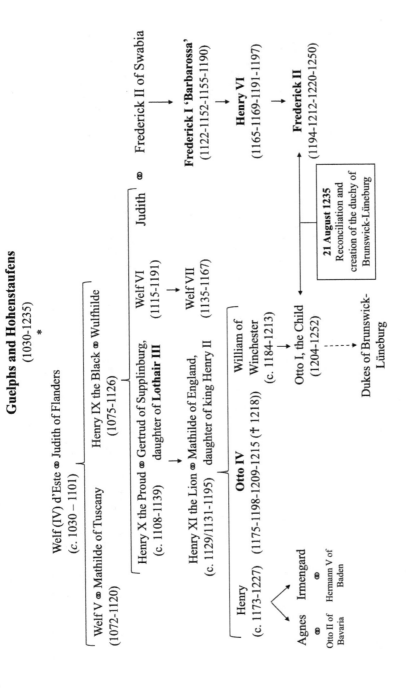

Guelphs and Hohenstaufens
(1030-1235)

*

Welf (IV) d'Este ⚭ Judith of Flanders
(c. 1030 – 1101)

Welf V ⚭ Mathilde of Tuscany
(1072-1120)

Henry IX the Black ⚭ Wulfhilde
(1075-1126)

Henry X the Proud ⚭ Gertrud of Supplinburg,
(c. 1108-1139)   daughter of **Lothair III**

Welf VI
(1115-1191)

Judith ⚭ Frederick II of Swabia

Henry XI the Lion ⚭ Mathilde of England,
(c. 1129/1131-1195)   daughter of king Henry II

Welf VII
(1135-1167)

Frederick I 'Barbarossa'
(1122-1152-1155-1190)

William of
Winchester
(c. 1184-1213)

Henry   Irmengard
(c. 1173-1227)   ⚭   Hermann V of
                      Baden

Agnes
⚭
Otto II of
Bavaria

Otto IV
(1175-1198-1209-1215 (✝ 1218))

Otto I, the Child
(1204-1252)

Dukes of Brunswick-
Lüneburg

Henry VI
(1165-1169-1191-1197)

Frederick II
(1194-1212-1220-1250)

21 August 1235
Reconciliation and
creation of the duchy of
Brunswick-Lüneburg

Descendants of Frederick II

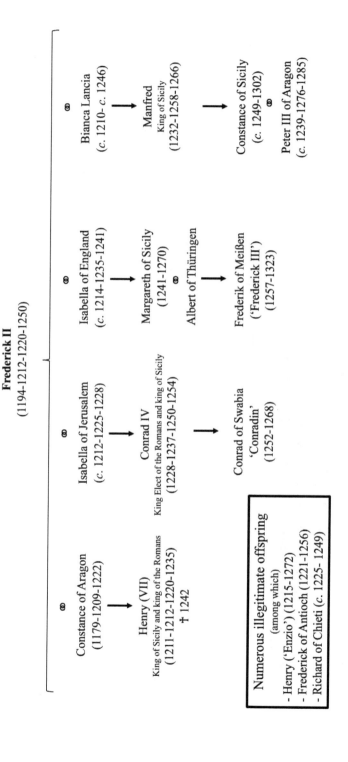

Frederick II
(1194-1212-1220-1250)
*

∞
Constance of Aragon
(1179-1209-1222)
→
Henry (VII)
King of Sicily and king of the Romans
(1211-1212-1220-1235)
† 1242

∞
Isabella of Jerusalem
(c. 1212-1225-1228)
→
Conrad IV
King Elect of the Romans and king of Sicily
(1228-1237-1250-1254)
→
Conrad of Swabia
'Conradin'
(1252-1268)

∞
Isabella of England
(c. 1214-1235-1241)
→
Margareth of Sicily
(1241-1270)
∞
Albert of Thüringen
→
Frederik of Meißen
('Frederick III')
(1257-1323)

∞
Bianca Lancia
(c. 1210- c. 1246)
→
Manfred
King of Sicily
(1232-1258-1266)
→
Constance of Sicily
(c. 1249-1302)
∞
Peter III of Aragon
(c. 1239-1276-1285)

Numerous illegitimate offspring
(among which)
- Henry ('Enzio') (1215-1272)
- Frederick of Antioch (1221-1256)
- Richard of Chieti (c. 1225- 1249)

The French Capetian Dynasty
(987-1328)

*

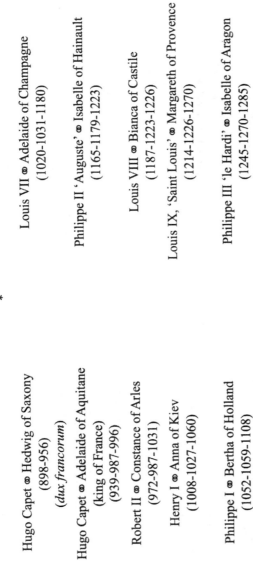
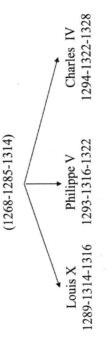

Hugo Capet ⚭ Hedwig of Saxony
(898-956)
(*dux francorum*)

Hugo Capet ⚭ Adelaide of Aquitane
(king of France)
(939-987-996)

Robert II ⚭ Constance of Arles
(972-987-1031)

Henry I ⚭ Anna of Kiev
(1008-1027-1060)

Philippe I ⚭ Bertha of Holland
(1052-1059-1108)

Louis VI ⚭ Adelaide of Maurienne
(1081-1108-1137)

Louis VII ⚭ Adelaide of Champagne
(1020-1031-1180)

Philippe II 'Auguste' ⚭ Isabelle of Hainault
(1165-1179-1223)

Louis VIII ⚭ Bianca of Castile
(1187-1223-1226)

Louis IX, 'Saint Louis' ⚭ Margareth of Provence
(1214-1226-1270)

Philippe III 'le Hardi' ⚭ Isabelle of Aragon
(1245-1270-1285)

Philippe IV 'le Bel' ⚭ Joanna of Navarre
(1268-1285-1314)

Louis X
1289-1314-1316

Philippe V
1293-1316-1322

Charles IV
1294-1322-1328

The Houses of Aragon and Hohenstaufen

*

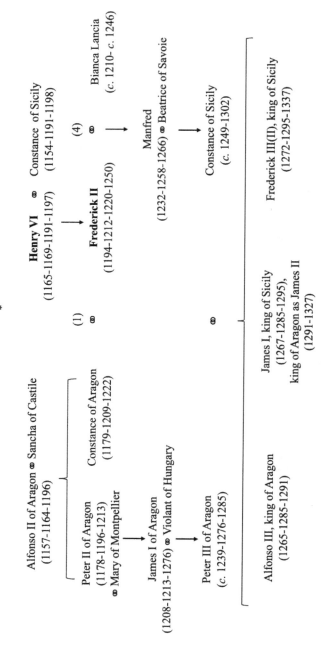

The Angevine Dynasty
between 1266 and 1382

*

Louis VIII ⚭ Bianca of Castile
(1187-1223-1226)

Charles*, count of Anjou and king of Sicily ⚭ Beatrice of Provence
(1227-1266-1285)

Charles II, King of Naples ⚭ Mary of Hungary
(1254-1285-1309)

Charles Martel (titular king of Hungary) ⚭ Clemencia of Habsburg
(1271-1295)

Robert I, king of Naples ⚭ Yolande of Aragon
(1276-1309-1343)

Charles I, king of Hungary
(1288-1308-1342)

Charles, duke of Calabria ⚭ Mary of Valois
(1298-1328)

Andrew, duke of Calabria
(1327-1345)

⚭

Joanna I, queen of Naples
(1325-1343-1382)

Louis I, king of Hungary
(1326-1342-1382)

* Charles of Anjou was a posthumous son of Louis VIII

623

Maps

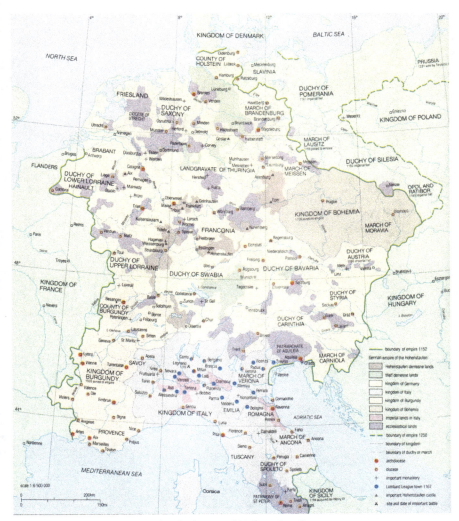

The Holy Roman Empire under the house of Hohen-Staufen

The Norman states of southern Italy

The development of the papal state

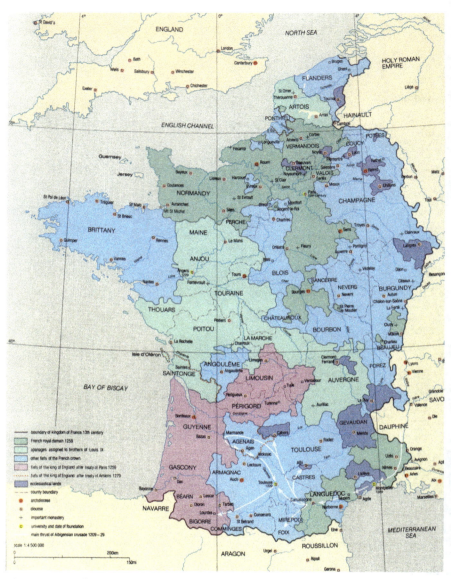

The kingdom of France under Louis IX

List of Illustrations

Maps
Source: Atlas of Medieval Europe, Donald Matthew, Andromeda Oxford Limited 1989, 1991